KU-484-865

MY NAME IS BARBRA

MY NAME IS BARBRA

BARBRA STREISAND

CENTURY

1 3 5 7 9 10 8 6 4 2

Century
20 Vauxhall Bridge Road
London SW1V 2SA

Century is part of the Penguin Random House group of companies
whose addresses can be found at global.penguinrandomhouse.com

First published in the US by Viking in 2023
First published in the UK by Century in 2023

www.penguin.co.uk

A CIP catalogue record for this book is available from the British Library

ISBN: 9781529136890

Cover design by Barbra Streisand
Book design by Claire Vaccaro
Photo archivist: Kim Skalecki

Image and text credits may be found on pages 971–76
Frontispiece by Steve Schapiro, compliments of The Steve Schapiro Estate

Printed and bound in Great Britain by Clays Ltd, Elcograf S.p.A.

The authorised representative in the EEA is Penguin Random House Ireland,
Morrison Chambers, 32 Nassau Street, Dublin D02 YH68

www.greenpenguin.co.uk

Penguin Random House is committed to a sustainable future for our business, our readers and our planet. This book is made from Forest Stewardship Council® certified paper.

This book is dedicated to the father I never knew . . .

and the mother I did.

Contents

Chapter Photo Captions

CHAPTER 1 . *My mother, Diana Streisand, and me at about two years old.*

CHAPTER 2 . *Me trying to be flirtatious as the office vamp in* Desk Set *when I was fifteen.*

CHAPTER 3 . *The headshot I sent out when I was sixteen. Most actors smile. Not me.*

CHAPTER 4 . *In the spotlight for the first time at the Bon Soir.*

CHAPTER 5 . *Me as Miss Marmelstein. I had to fight to do it in my secretarial chair.*

CHAPTER 6 . *Signing my first Columbia Records contract as Goddard Lieberson, Marty Erlichman, and Dave Kapralik look on.*

CHAPTER 7 . *Recording* The Barbra Streisand Album, *with Peter Matz conducting.*

CHAPTER 8 . *The Playbill for* Funny Girl, *with me and Sydney Chaplin.*

CHAPTER 9 . *The cover of the* People *album, shot at dawn on a Chicago beach.*

CHAPTER 10 . *On the set of my first TV special,* My Name Is Barbra.

CHAPTER 11 . *Michel Legrand and I instantly clicked working on* Je m'appelle Barbra.

CHAPTER 12 . *Me singing to a bemused elephant on* Color Me Barbra.

CHAPTER 13 . *I wore a Fortuny-style gown in* A Happening in Central Park. *(I still have it.)*

CHAPTER 14 . *Discussing a scene with William Wyler on the set of* Funny Girl.

CHAPTER 15 . *I was so elated to win the Oscar for* Funny Girl.

CHAPTER 16 . *Comparing profiles with Anthony Newley at his birthday party in 1965.*

CHAPTER 17 . *My beloved son, Jason, on location with me for* Hello, Dolly!

Chapter 18 . *I fell in love with Marlon Brando when I was thirteen.*

Chapter 19 . *All dressed up with Cecil Beaton on the set of* On a Clear Day You Can See Forever.

Chapter 20 . *All un-dressed up with George Segal on the set of* The Owl and the Pussycat.

Chapter 21 . *Prime Minister Pierre Trudeau and me on our way to a gala in Ottawa.*

Chapter 22 . *Hanging out with Ryan O'Neal and Peter Bogdanovich on the set of* What's Up, Doc?

Chapter 23 . *Talking politics with Bella Abzug at the fundraiser I threw for her.*

Chapter 24 . *I had to have Robert Redford as Hubbell in* The Way We Were.

Chapter 25 . *Singing with musicians from around the world in* Barbra Streisand . . . and Other Musical Instruments.

Chapter 26 . *I thought Henry (short for Henrietta) in* For Pete's Sake *should have a short, boyish haircut.*

Chapter 27 . *With director Herb Ross on the set of* Funny Lady.

Chapter 28 . *In the recording studio for my 1975 album,* Lazy Afternoon.

Chapter 29 . *I loved the photo by Francesco Scavullo on the cover of the* Classical Barbra *album.*

Chapter 30 . *A moment of fun with Kris Kristofferson during* A Star Is Born.

Chapter 31 . *Me and my first dog, Sadie. I didn't know I was a dog person until I met her.*

Chapter 32 . *Shooting* The Main Event *poster with Ryan O'Neal. He liked to tease me.*

Chapter 33 . *With the sensational Donna Summer.*

Chapter 34 . *Listening to the* Guilty *album with Barry Gibb (far right) and the team.*

Chapter 35 . *Recording the music for* Yentl *with Michel Legrand and the Bergmans.*

Chapter 36 . *Directing* Yentl *was challenging, and exhilarating.*

Chapter 37 . *At the Golden Globes, after winning Best Director and Best Picture for* Yentl.

Chapter 38 . *In the studio with Stephen Sondheim, recording* The Broadway Album. *He was one of a kind.*

Chapter 39 . *On stage at the* One Voice *concert, in my Malibu backyard.*

Chapter 40 . *With Larry Kramer, who wrote* The Normal Heart.

Chapter 41 . *Sharing a laugh with cinematographer Andrzej Bartkowiak and director Martin Ritt on* Nuts.

Chapter 42 . *Don Johnson and me on the day we recorded our duet, "Till I Loved You."*

Chapter 43 . *I absolutely adored Pat Conroy, the author of* The Prince of Tides.

Chapter 44 . *Directing* The Prince of Tides.

Chapter 45 . *With my leading man Nick Nolte in* The Prince of Tides.

Chapter 46 . *My teenage idol, Johnny Mathis, and me in the recording studio. How thrilling.*

Chapter 47 . *Fulfilling my promise to sing "Evergreen" for President Clinton at the 1993 Inaugural Gala.*

Chapter 48 . *Backstage at the MGM Grand with Marvin Hamlisch and the Bergmans on New Year's Eve, 1993.*

Chapter 49 . *With my mother, Diana Streisand Kind.*

Chapter 50 . *With Virginia Clinton, my "Southern mom."*

Chapter 51 . *Holding my two Emmys for producing and starring in* Barbra: The Concert.

Chapter 52 . *Speaking at Harvard's John F. Kennedy School of Government. I was terrified.*

Chapter 53 . *Celebrating with Jeff Bridges and Lauren Bacall at the wrap party for* The Mirror Has Two Faces.

Chapter 54 . *This is one of my favorite pictures of me and Jim, with his hair grown out!*

Chapter 55 . *I dressed for the rain at my* Timeless *concert in Australia.*

Chapter 56 . *With the world-renowned Dr. Noel Bairey Merz, director of the Barbra Streisand Women's Heart Center.*

Chapter 57 . *One of the high points of my life was singing with Jason on the* Back to Brooklyn *tour.*

Chapter 58 . *My sweet, precious Sammie never missed a rehearsal.*

Chapter 59 . *Backstage after a concert with my brilliant friend Madeleine Albright, U.S. Secretary of State.*

Epilogue *Jim and me with our beautiful granddaughter Westlyn Reign Brolin.*

MY NAME IS BARBRA

Prologue

An "amiable anteater"?

That's how I was described at nineteen in one of my first reviews as a professional actress. I was in *I Can Get It for You Wholesale*, playing a lovelorn secretary, and I could see the comparison . . . sort of.

Over the next year, I was also called "a sour persimmon," "a furious hamster," "a myopic gazelle," and "a seasick ferret."

Yikes. Was I really that odd-looking?

Only a year later, when I was in my second Broadway show, *Funny Girl*, my face was exactly the same, but now I was being compared to "an ancient oracle," "Nefertiti," and "a Babylonian queen." I must say I loved *those* descriptions. Apparently I also had a "Pharaonic profile and scarab eyes." I think that was supposed to be a compliment, though I have to admit one of those eyes does look cross-eyed at times . . . and it seems like the Pharaoh also had a big schnoz. People kept telling me, "Get it fixed." (I bet no one said that to *him*.)

Sometimes it felt like my nose got more press than I did. In the cover story in *Time* magazine, the writer said, "This nose is a shrine." (Sounds good!) Then he went on, "The face it divides is long and sad, and the look in repose is the essence of hound." (Not so good.)

So which is it? Am I a Babylonian queen or a basset hound?

Probably both (depending on the angle).

I wish I could say none of this affected me, but it did. Even after all these years, I'm still hurt by the insults and can't quite believe the praise. I guess when you become famous, you become public property. You're an object to be examined, photographed, analyzed, dissected . . . and half the time I don't recognize the person they portray. I've never gotten used to it, and I try to avoid reading anything about myself.

But sometimes I'll just pick up a magazine in the dentist's office, for example. (I happen to like going to the dentist, because I love how my teeth feel after they're cleaned. It's also an hour of peace with no phone calls.) Once when I was waiting, I saw a story about Neil Diamond, who was a grade ahead of me at Erasmus Hall High School in Brooklyn. Actually it was about his brother, who'd invented some crazy bathtub that had a stereo system and all sorts of electronic gadgets (perfect . . . for getting electrocuted). And it's not cheap . . . fourteen thousand dollars! I'm thinking, *Who would ever buy such a thing?* And then I read that I'm one of his customers! I didn't even know my friend Neil had a brother, and now I'm being used to sell his bathtub?!

That's irritating, but other stories cut deep. One night, my dear friend Andrzej Bartkowiak, a brilliant cinematographer who did two films and a documentary with me, came over for dinner. (Actually, he was cooking, because I'm a hazard in the kitchen. I can burn water.)

Andrzej had been to see his friend earlier (a medical doctor, by the way) and happened to mention that he was having dinner with me. The doctor said, "I hear she's a bitch."

"What?" said Andrzej. "What are you talking about?"

"She's impossible to work with."

"That's ridiculous. Have you ever worked with her?"

"No."

"Well, I have . . . three times . . . and she's wonderful to work with. In fact, she's a very nice person."

"No, she isn't. She's a bitch. *I read it in a magazine!*"

That's the power of the printed word.

And there was no hope of changing this man's mind. He chose to believe some writer who had never met me, rather than the person who really knows me. That upsets me deeply. Why couldn't he accept the truth?

For forty years, publishers have been asking me to write my autobiography. But I kept turning them down, because I prefer to live in the present rather than dwell on the past. And the fact is, I'm scared that after six decades of people making up stories about me, I'm going to tell the truth, and nobody is going to believe it.

Recently, my husband, Jim, and I were driving home from a movie and stopped at the supermarket because I suddenly had a craving for coffee ice cream. We walked into the market holding hands, and a man came up behind us and said, in a loud voice, "I'm so happy to see you back together!"

Back together? When were we apart? Did my husband move out and I somehow failed to notice?

You see, I like facts. I have great respect for facts, and the idea of just making something up really bothers me.

So I finally said yes to writing this book, after dancing around the idea for ages. I actually wrote the first chapter back in the 1990s, in longhand with an erasable pen . . . and then lost it. Now I wish I knew how to type, because once I started again it took another ten years, since I still have other commitments, like making records, and besides, I get really bored with myself. I'm trying to recall things that happened a long time ago. (Thank God for the journals I've kept, which have been invaluable.) And then sometimes I realize that I haven't been remembering the full story and have to dig deeper, no matter where it leads . . .

I wanted to be an actress ever since I was a child . . . maybe from the moment I was taken to my first movie, and stood up on the seat so I could see the screen. Still, it's amazing that my dream came true, and I'm very grateful to all the people who helped me along the way.

They say that success changes a person, but I think it actually makes you more of who you really are.

Frankly, I think I'm rather ordinary. I just happened to be born with a good voice, and then I guess there was something about my looks, my personality, whatever talent I had that intrigued people (or annoyed them). I know I ask a lot of questions. I have a lot of opinions, and I say what I think . . . and sometimes that gets me into a lot of trouble.

I'm not a very social person. I don't like to get dressed up and go out. I'd rather stay home with my husband and my dogs. Sometimes we'll invite family and friends over for dinner and a movie, or to play games like Rummikub, backgammon, or hearts. (I also play every night on my phone in the dark before I go to sleep, to clear my head of all the stress of the day.) I love painting with my son, Jason (he's much better than I am) . . . I can spend hours taking photographs in my garden . . . and because I don't go out much, I forget who I am to the outside world.

Which reminds me of something. Recently I was going to the dentist (to get my teeth cleaned again), and while I was waiting for the elevator, I noticed this woman staring at me. So I moved away, but she didn't stop. I thought, *Why is she still staring? Did I spill something on myself?*

And then I realized, Oh yeah . . . I'm what's her name.

I think it's time to dispel the myths about that creature.

And that's why I'm writing this book . . . because I feel an obligation to the people who are truly interested in my work, and the process behind the work, and perhaps the person behind the process.

So, here goes . . .

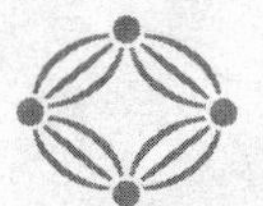

ONE

Pulaski Street

There's one thing that's very hard for me to deal with, and that's lying. Maybe that's because I was lied to as a child.

One day when I was eight years old, my mother came to visit me at a Jewish summer camp in the Catskills where she had sent me for a few weeks. I didn't like that camp. They had lousy potatoes (probably from a can) that tasted fake. I'd subtly slide them off my plate and throw them under the table, all the way down to the other end so no one would know I was the culprit. The only thing to look forward to was Friday night, when you could get a great piece of kosher cake . . . yellow cake with dark chocolate icing that I've been searching for ever since . . .

I was a very forceful child. I held on to my mother as soon as she arrived and refused to let her go until she reluctantly agreed to take me home with her. Quickly, I packed up my clothes and shoved whatever didn't fit . . . like my American Indian robe and the art projects I had made . . . into a cardboard box I found. Then we walked together to a car . . . and there was a man I'd never seen before sitting behind the wheel. I don't remember him saying one word to me during the whole trip back. Guess he was angry that it wasn't only him and my mom going home.

My mother didn't tell me that this man, Louis Kind, was going to be my new stepfather and that she was pregnant with my sister.

Lying by omission counts as lying too.

We didn't go to the only home I knew . . . my grandparents' apartment on Pulaski Street in Williamsburg. Instead, we pulled up to a tall brick building (one of many that all looked alike) on Newkirk Avenue in Flatbush, part of a big public housing project called the Vanderveer Estates (a very fancy name for a not-so-fancy place). We had apartment 4G, and I remember being very impressed that there was an elevator. I thought we were rich now. The rent was $105 a month, much higher than the $40 on Pulaski Street.

Louis Kind didn't sleep there that first night. I slept in the bed with my mother as usual and woke up the next morning with clicks in my ears when I swallowed.

I don't know to this day if it was a new extra awareness of my inner body or a physiological thing. But I do know that I was shocked by the abrupt change in our circumstances. Who was this man? Decades later, I finally asked my mother why she hadn't sat me down and explained that she was planning to marry him and she was going to have a baby.

"Well, you never asked," she said.

"But Mom, I was only eight!"

I never knew my father. There are no photographs of him holding me as a baby. That was very disappointing. I always wondered, How could that be? Why didn't my mother ever take a picture of the two of us?

And when I was older and asked her why she had never talked to me about my father, she said, "I didn't want you to miss him."

I never understood my mother's logic.

My father, Emanuel Streisand, was a very special man . . . a Phi Beta Kappa graduate of City College in New York, an athlete, and a teacher who devoted his life to education. He developed an innovative curriculum teaching English to juvenile offenders at the Elmira Reformatory, where he was assistant superintendent of schools. He later taught English at a vocational high school in Brooklyn while simultaneously working toward his PhD, taking courses at Cornell University, Hunter College, and then Teachers College at Columbia University. He was brought up in an Orthodox Jewish home, and you're not supposed to ride in any vehicle after sundown on Friday. The Sabbath is a day of rest. So if he had stayed late at Teachers College on Friday night, he would walk home all the way from West 120th Street to Brooklyn.

My father loved kids. To earn extra money during the summer of 1943, he took a job as head counselor at a camp in the Catskills. One morning in August, he was showing an inspector around in the hot sun when he developed a terrible headache. (He had a history of migraines.) That night he had a seizure. My mother and a friend tried to hold him still (little did they know that would hurt rather than help). The next morning an ambulance took him to a small local hospital, where a doctor gave him a shot of morphine, and he stopped breathing.

My mother always told me and my brother, Sheldon, that he died of a cerebral hemorrhage, and for many years we thought that could be a congenital defect. No one connected the headaches and seizures to a previous car accident, in which he had hit his head. They didn't have MRIs back then to determine what was going on inside the brain. Much later, I tracked down a copy of his death certificate, which said he died of respiratory failure, probably brought on by the morphine, which I also learned should not have been administered under the circumstances.

My father was only thirty-five years old. Suddenly Diana Rosen Streisand was a widow at thirty-four, with two small children . . . Shelly was nine, and I was fifteen months. Years later, my mother told me that for months after my father died, I would still climb up on the window ledge to wait for him to come home. In some ways, I'm still waiting.

With my father gone, my mother couldn't afford to stay in our apartment, and we moved in with her parents. My grandpa Louis Rosen and my grandmother Esther had a small one-bedroom apartment that now had to accommodate five people. They slept in what must have originally been the living room. We had the bedroom, where I shared the bed with my mother, and Shelly slept on a fold-out cot next to us. There was a small, cold kitchen that I was hardly ever in, but I do remember the smell of cinnamon cookies my grandmother baked for Hanukkah once a year. So we all basically lived in the dining room, which was furnished with a rectangular mahogany table, a credenza against one wall, a secretary on the other, and an old-fashioned wooden radio. We had no TV. We would sit and watch the radio.

I used to crawl under the dining table and play. It felt safe there. And I liked to turn the metal crank that made the leaves come apart. My earliest memory is of looking up from under that table . . . I must have been about three years old . . . and listening to a conversation between my mother and her sister. I realized that my mother was talking about one thing while her sister was talking about another. I could feel the miscommunication, but I didn't have the language to tell them.

I think that was the first time I realized how easy it is for people to misunderstand each other.

I liked being an observer . . . out of sight but still able to watch what was going on. I would often scoot under the table when one of my mother's suitors came to pick her up for a date. I never wanted her to go out. I was terrified she would never come back. I saw one guy named Saul kiss her and I thought he was hurting her, even though she was laughing. I remember the color of his teeth . . . brownish. To this day, it's the first thing I notice about a man, and it's one of the reasons I married Jim Brolin. He has great teeth.

I thought most men were weird . . . except my grandfather. When I was about five, he would take me to an Orthodox *shul* (Yiddish for synagogue), and I would sit next to him with the other men, while the women sat elsewhere. I could follow the Hebrew because I went to a yeshiva, where they taught us how to read the words, but I didn't know what they meant. You read Hebrew from right to left (this is probably why I can write backward), and it still feels comfortable, sometimes, reading magazines from back to front (which makes it seem as if I'm reading faster). I felt like a big girl, sitting beside the men. (Maybe that's why it was so easy, all those years later, to imagine myself as Yentl.)

I loved my grandpa, even though he once washed my mouth out with red Lifebuoy soap when I said a bad word. But I knew he loved me. I would sit on his lap and cut the hairs out of his ears. That's *real* intimacy.

His affection saved me. My view of men was that they either abandoned you or were mean to you. My stepfather was rude to my mother. My brother picked me up from school, but we were too far apart in age for him to want a little sister tagging along. My uncle Harry scared me. He used to take out his false teeth and make noises like a monster. My grandfather gave me a taste of what a good man could be.

I was not an easy child. I didn't want to eat (which is hard to believe). My mother was always trying to force food on me. She gave me tonics and cod-liver oil because she was convinced I was sickly. Plus, I was basically bald until the age of two. But I had lots of energy. Once I managed to climb up on a dresser and get hold of my grandfather's razor and nearly cut off my bottom lip trying to shave as I had watched him do. My grandmother had asthma and couldn't chase after me. She called me *fabrent*, which means "on fire" in Yiddish. So Tobey Borookow, a neighbor in the same building, took care of me after school while my mother was working.

I adored Tobey. She was the neighborhood "knitting lady." We would sit together, and she would tell me all the gossip while I held up my hands so she could wind strands of wool around them, making her skeins. I didn't have a doll, but I would fill a hot-water bottle as a substitute and pretend. Tobey knitted a little pink wool sweater and hat for it . . . maybe that's why I love the color pink . . . and I swear it felt more like a real baby than some cold doll.

Even now, when I see children with their dolls and little stoves and things, I want to play with them too.

I love the color burgundy . . . probably because Tobey also made me a burgundy sweater with wooden buttons. It was the only thing that set me apart from the other kids at the first camp I was sent to, the summer I had just turned seven. It was a health camp for kids, and I was anemic, so the fresh air was supposed to be good for me. But I was used to the hot, steamy air in Brooklyn, with everybody leaning out their windows because there was no air-conditioning. The country air was so fresh it hurt my lungs (and with all those trees, I actually developed an allergy, which later turned into asthma).

I hated that health camp. The first thing they did was dump me into a disinfectant bath and comb through my hair for lice. Then they handed me a starched blue linen uniform, with scratchy bloomers (probably why I dislike the color royal blue to this day). I was so homesick, and the tears would well up every afternoon when we were put down for a nap. (I never took naps after I turned three!) When one kid noticed and started to make fun of me, I insisted, "I'm not crying. I just have a loose tear duct."

I was much happier and healthier as soon as I got back to Brooklyn (I could breathe again!). I remember sitting on my bed in my grandmother's apartment, wearing my same old red-plaid shirt. But I felt different. Was I the same skinny marink who had left only a couple of weeks ago? My mother was happy that I had gained a pound or two. I used to like to look at my reflection in hubcaps, because they made me appear fatter.

The neighborhood was teeming with kids. We played in the streets, running back to the curb when a car came along. One of our favorite games was skelly. You flicked your bottle cap into numbered squares drawn in chalk on the asphalt, and then you hopped on one foot to pick it up. (It's a Jewish version of hopscotch.)

I got good marks at the Yeshiva of Brooklyn in everything except conduct, in which I inevitably got a D. I was so impatient and I never learned manners.

When the teacher asked a question, I'd shoot up my hand, and if she didn't call on me, I'd blurt out the answer anyway. It must have been around Hanukkah when one teacher told us that we shouldn't say the word "Christmas" or cross our fingers. Something about that just didn't make sense to me, and as soon as she walked out of the room, I kept repeating "Christmas! Christmas! Christmas!" And prayed to God that He wouldn't strike me dead.

I had two best friends. One was Joanne Micelli, a Catholic girl who went to St. John's Academy. I found the Catholics fascinating . . . the nuns, the priests, the outfits. When I saw a priest, I'd say, "Hello, Father," like Joanne did. I thought she was so lucky to have a real father, as well as a man named "Father" who seemed to love her too. And I was very impressed with the beauty of her church. The yeshiva was dinky in comparison.

My other best friend was Roslyn Arenstein, who was an atheist like her parents. We three girls used to sit on her fire escape (we'd drape an old army blanket over the railing to make a tent) and have very serious philosophical discussions. One day I said, "Look, Roz, I'm going to prove to you that there is a God." A man was walking down the street, and I said, "See that man? I'm going to pray that he steps off the curb." I prayed hard, with all my might, and sure enough he stepped off the curb and crossed the street. I had two thoughts at that moment. One: *Whew, that was lucky!* And two: *There is a God, and I just got Him to do what I wanted by praying.*

I guess that's when I began to believe in the power of the will.

I've always had a very strong will. When I came down with chicken pox, my mother put me in bed, since I had a fever, but I didn't stay there. I just put on my bright green hat and coat and climbed out the window to go and play with the other kids (luckily we were on the first floor) until my mother dragged me back inside.

I often told my mother what to do. I remember one time when she and her date (he was a butcher) were going to an Eddie Cantor movie and decided to take me along. I must have been about six. Since I was known as the girl on the block with no father, I did not want to be seen leaving the building with a strange man. So I told her, "I'm not going with you unless he goes down to the corner first and waits for us there." I still can recall looking up when we left to see if any of the neighbors were at their windows. And sure enough, there was Myrna, a big girl who used to bully me, watching us. I thought, *Oh no. I'll bet she's putting me together with that guy. I hope not!* God forbid, because she would tell everyone.

I was also known as the girl on the block with a good voice. I used to like to sing in the lobby of our building. The ceilings were high, so there was a nice echo, and I loved to run my hand down the cold brass banister. Sometimes I'd sit on the stoop with the other girls, and we'd harmonize to songs from the *Hit Parade*. My mother had a beautiful voice, operatic, and her father, I was told, used to sing in shul when the cantor was ill.

Tobey had a son named Irving. Since he was a boy and he was my friend, I called him my boyfriend, even though he once hit me over the head with his plastic gun. We played together every afternoon while Tobey looked after me. They had a tiny television with a big magnifying glass in front of the screen, and we loved to watch Laurel and Hardy. But when Irving heard his father come in the front door, he would turn to me and say, "My father's here. You have to go home now."

That hurt my feelings, and must have set me back years.

Mr. Borookow's name was Abe, and I can still to this day remember his particular smell. It sure wasn't aftershave.

I wonder if people who have fathers know how lucky they are. My brother had the benefit of a father's love and concern for the first nine years of his life . . . someone who took him to museums, bookstores, parades. Our father read books to him and bought him a radio. He introduced Shelly to drawing and painting, which became an important part of his life.

As a child, you really need someone to love you in order to give you a sense of self-worth . . . that you are seen and taken seriously . . . that your feelings count.

Now I suddenly had a stepfather who seemed to resent my brother and me. Lou Kind already had three kids that he didn't live with, and I doubt he wanted more. Once he appeared on the scene, everything was different. In our new apartment, I slept on a daybed in the hallway. My brother had the little bedroom. And my mother was in the big bedroom with this strange man.

The next thing I knew I had a baby sister, Roslyn. When I found out that babies take nine months to appear, I counted back nine months from my sister's birth and tried to get my mother to acknowledge what she had done on that date. I had heard about sex (an older girl filled me in, standing in the stairwell at school), but I couldn't quite believe it. And my mother did not take this opportunity to enlighten me.

I loved my little sister from the first moment I saw her. She was so beautiful . . . blond curly hair, green eyes. I would stare at her for hours, fascinated by her every move, every twitch of an eye. A living doll!

I hated my stepfather. I didn't like the way he mistreated my mother. And he never spoke to me. I remember riding in his Pontiac with the slanted back and watching him light a cigarette . . . Pall Mall. I liked the smell of the first strike of his match. Then he would exhale a perfect stream of smoke.

One day we took Roz Arenstein for a ride. We were both sitting in the back and I was talking, as usual. My stepfather turned around abruptly and said to me, "Why can't you be like your friend—quiet!"

Not long after that, my mother happened to mention that Lou was color-blind. So the next time we got in the car, I was worried . . . afraid that he couldn't tell the difference between the red and green lights. So I would announce the colors, trying to be subtle. "What a pretty RED light that is!"

No wonder he hated me.

Lou never asked me how I was or how school was going. He didn't see me. He wasn't interested in me. I could never get his approval or his affection, no matter what I did. One day I decided to try to make him like me. When he came home from his used-car lot, I called him "Dad" instead of Lou, which stuck in my throat. I had his slippers waiting for him, and when he sat down to watch his wrestling matches on TV, I crawled on my belly under his line of sight so as not to block his view. But it didn't work. He didn't treat me any better.

I think that's when I unconsciously decided that I would never lower myself for any man.

The other big transition in my life was a new school. After three years at the Yeshiva of Brooklyn, I was now going to start fourth grade at a public school, P.S. 89. The only time I had ever been in a public school was when the yeshiva put on some sort of program and rented the auditorium at P.S. 25, because the yeshiva didn't have a stage. That's where that first picture was taken of me singing, with my eyes closed, head back . . . nothing much has changed.

I remember being so scared that the nurse at P.S. 89, who gave every child a quick physical, could somehow "see" the clicks in my ears, and I wouldn't be allowed to go to school. I felt like an alien.

I was already different . . . odd . . . too skinny . . . and my mom would buy clothes for me three sizes too big, which didn't help. She bought my dresses in the Junior department, and then she'd sew three big hems and let one out each year. So I would be walking around in the same clothes forever.

In a way, I was like a wild child, a kind of animal, because I had no knowledge of social graces. I remember my friend Maxine Edelstein, who lived on the same floor. Every night at 6:00 p.m. her entire family would sit down at the table and have dinner. Once they invited me to stay, and there was such a warm feeling in that room. My family rarely had a meal together. I didn't know about napkins on your lap. I used to sit with one knee up on the chair. Or I would eat standing up over a pot in the tiny, narrow kitchen. When my brother got home, he'd do the same thing.

I had so little discipline. There was no routine and no rules. My mother never said you have to be home at 6:00 p.m. or whenever. I remember stealing a few of my stepfather's cigarettes and smoking in front of the mirror, pretending I was doing a Pall Mall commercial. I was sneaking up to the roof to smoke when I was ten and gave it up by the time I was twelve. I actually had to teach my mother how to smoke. I told her, "You look funny. Hold the cigarette like this."

Somehow I persuaded my mother to let me go to Miss March's dancing school, which was nearby, because I wanted to be a ballerina. I bought pink satin toe shoes and sewed pink satin ribbons on them. Every day after school, I put them on and walked around the apartment. I paid for those shoes myself with the money I earned showing people to their seats in Choy's Chinese restaurant. I also filled takeout orders. "*Si pic qvot*" . . . small spare ribs. "*Som teu*" . . . three egg rolls. I loved the musicality of the Chinese language. Said with a different tone, a word meant something else.

Muriel Choy became my second surrogate mother, Tobey being the first.

I loved Muriel. I could ask her any question, and she would explain things to me . . . things my mother never mentioned, like sex and cooking. I can still taste her delicious *lap cheong* (Chinese sausage), Chinese cabbage, and steamed chicken, and I still look for those fat, dry egg rolls that they served in the restaurant and that hardly anyone makes anymore. (A few years ago we finally found a place in Los Angeles that sells them. Jim and I sometimes eat three at a time.)

I also used to babysit for Muriel's children when she was working with her husband at the restaurant. One night when I was eleven, I was coming down from their apartment and rang my doorbell for what seemed like ten to fifteen minutes. No one answered, although I knew my mother and Lou were home. I went back up to Muriel's and got the spare key I kept there. I opened our front door, walked through the living room, and then opened their bedroom door. The two of them were physically intertwined, and it was as if I were invisible. I backed out, kind of in shock, and the incident was never mentioned.

After that, I vowed never to be invisible again.

There are moments in childhood that are so important to who you are going to become. They mold your life forever.

I couldn't rely on my mother. I remember one particular episode, when I was about seven. She was taking me to the movies for a treat, and we were walking down the street and she was smiling to herself . . . she would smile a lot to herself. Suddenly she stopped.

I said, "Mom, what's the matter?"

She said, "We're not going. I changed my mind."

I was so disappointed, and to this day I desperately want people to keep their word. It is so important to do something you say you're going to do. It's one of the Four Agreements in the book of the same name by Don Miguel Ruiz: "Be impeccable with your word."

I couldn't confide in my mother, even about my ear noises. After the first night when I told her about the clicks, she gave me a hot-water bottle to sleep on and never asked about them again. But they didn't go away, and one morning when I was in the sixth grade I woke up with something new. All these sounds . . . "pings" and "pongs," like musical fireworks . . . were going off in my head. That was really scary. Then the pings settled into a high-pitched ringing. I was so afraid that I didn't tell anyone. I tied a scarf around my head, hoping to shut the noises out, but it actually seemed to push them farther in. Nothing helped.

I never went to a doctor then. Years later I found out that this ringing in the ears is called tinnitus, and it has something to do with the connection between the inner ear and the brain. Various doctors have examined me over the years, but they can't do anything because there is apparently nothing to fix. Tinnitus is a condition without a known cause or a cure. It's a mystery.

Some guru once told me, "This is very special. You're on another level, a whole other plane, and you're hearing the sound of the universe."

"I don't think so," I said.

When people tell me, "I'm just like you," I'm tempted to respond, "Do you have a constant ringing in your ears?" It's enough to drive you crazy. And it used to make me very grumpy, but now I've learned to live with it. That's probably one reason why I need to keep busy all the time. I have to take my mind off it, to try to distract myself from the ringing.

I long for silence.

The ear noises were this terrible secret that I held inside and tried to manage on my own. I didn't expect any help from my mother anymore.

One day when I was twelve my brother's fiancée, Ellen, came to our apartment to meet the family . . . one of the few times we ever had a guest. Rozzie wanted ice cream after dinner and Lou gave Shelly some money and told him to buy enough for everyone. Then he looked at me and said, "But don't get any for *her*."

And then he said something that hurt my feelings. I couldn't remember the words, so years later I asked Ellen, and she said, "It was incredibly cruel. He called you ugly."

I must have blocked that out. I do remember that he made me feel awful, while my mother said nothing and just kept clearing the table. I went into the little bedroom (which I inherited after Shelly moved out), lay down on the single bed, and I remember having an out-of-body experience, where I was up on the ceiling looking down at myself lying there . . . numb.

I thought, *Why does he want to hurt me? Am I so unlovable?*

I lived a lot in my own head. After I read a booklet about the nine symptoms of cancer, I decided I had every one of them. But I never discussed my worries with my mother. When I got a chest cold, all she said was, "It's your fault. You went out without your sweater." Then she'd slather me with a mustard plaster (hot water mixed with Colman's Mustard Powder in between two torn pieces of sheet). When I had a sore throat, she'd wrap a thick sock around me like a collar and fasten it with a safety pin. "What if the pin opens?" I asked. "Then I'd really have a sore throat!"

My mother took care of me to the best of her ability, but she wasn't sympathetic like mothers in the movies. I remember being petrified when I woke up after a tonsillectomy when I was six . . . and she wasn't there. The last thing I had seen was this big rubber thing coming down over my face, delivering ether. I felt as if I were falling into a black hole. Circles were spiraling in my mind, accompanied by a strange droning sound like a drill. I fell asleep to the muffled voice of the doctor.

When I opened my eyes, I wondered, Was I still in this world? I was alone in the room. My mother wasn't there like she had promised. It turned out that she was walking around the block, probably nervous herself. She didn't understand how important it was for her to be physically present at moments like this.

So I kept everything inside, especially my fears. Once when I was about nine, I had this heaviness in my chest, and it wouldn't go away. One of the buildings in the project had a doctor's office on the ground floor, and I finally built up my courage . . . it took about a week . . . to ring the bell. And he wasn't in. But guess what? The simple fact that I dared to go see a doctor on my own took away my symptoms. In other words, the heaviness just disappeared.

That was my first psychosomatic illness.

Internalizing all these emotions can't have been healthy. And I was not naturally happy with life. I remember thinking, *This can't be it.*

Around the same time, I remember a gang of girls forming a circle around me in front of our apartment house. They were making fun of me. Was it something I was wearing? (I did have that scarf around my head.) What did I do to make them angry?

I escaped, crying, and ran upstairs to get Shelly to defend me. He refused to come down, saying, "Fight your own battles." I was sure my father would have helped me, but now I realized nobody was going to protect me. In hindsight, I guess that's when I began to build up a wall, my own shield, around myself.

Years later I realized that when my father died, I didn't lose only him. My mother left me emotionally as well. I can't blame her for that. She was suddenly a widow with two kids to support. I asked her once, when I was an adult, why she never hugged me or showed me any affection or said words like "I love you."

"I didn't have time," she replied. "And my parents never said those words to me, but I knew they loved me." She just assumed I knew how she felt. But I didn't.

Another one of the Four Agreements in Ruiz's book is "Never assume."

TWO

Why Couldn't I Play the Part?

I was fourteen when I took my first independent steps into Manhattan, landing on Fiftieth Street and Broadway from the IRT. My friend Anita Sussman and I were going to see a Broadway show . . . another first for me. Manhattan was a whole new world. When we climbed up the subway steps into the sunshine, I couldn't believe how open and wide everything seemed compared to Newkirk and Nostrand, the narrow streets surrounding the projects. And there were so many cars. You couldn't play skelly in Manhattan. You'd get run over.

Marquees were everywhere, displaying the names of various shows. The possibilities seemed endless.

We had tickets for *The Diary of Anne Frank*. Our seats were in the back of the balcony at the Cort Theatre, and I remember they cost $1.89. (Or was it $1.98?) The actors were far away, but we could see the whole sweep of the stage. I've realized, in retrospect, that there's something to be said for the bird's-eye view. Now that I can afford the expensive seats, I'm not sure they're really better. If you're too close, you can see the makeup, the sweat. It destroys the illusion.

I was mesmerized by the play. I remember thinking to myself, *Anne is fourteen; I'm fourteen. She's Jewish; I'm Jewish. Why couldn't I play the part?* I felt I could do it just as well as Susan Strasberg . . . especially since Anne had difficulties with her mother. She was convinced her mother didn't understand her. I could definitely relate to that.

From then on Anita and I would go to see Broadway plays practically every Saturday. I wanted to see serious dramas. I wasn't particularly interested in musicals. We saw Paul Muni in *Inherit the Wind*. I still love that play. It's about creationism versus evolution, religion versus science. Thank God reason and truth won out. Eva Le Gallienne and Irene Worth in *Mary Stuart* were also thrilling to watch. Here were two powerful actresses, both playing heads of state. I loved that.

I wanted to be a serious actress too.

When I think back, I did my first acting job when I was about nine. One day I said something my mother didn't like, and she slapped me across the ear. I thought, *I'm going to pay her back for that . . . give her a little aggravation.* So the next time she spoke to me, I pretended not to hear her. I acted like a little deaf girl, and it worked. She believed me and said, "Barbara! Answer me!" and I just kept saying, "What? What? Did you say something?" I completely scared her.

Most of the acting I saw was on TV. By that time we had our own set. (That was the one good thing about Lou Kind. He bought a Zenith television.) I would park myself in front of the screen and watch Milton Berle and Ed Sullivan. I also liked game shows where the host asked a question and you had to guess the answer, like *The $64,000 Question*. My favorite cousin Lowell and I used to play together and we invented a show of our own, which we called *Crack the Safe*.

First, we'd open the telephone book and randomly pick a name. Then I would call that person up, pretending to be the announcer on a radio quiz show, and ask, "Do you listen to our program *Crack the Safe* on WNIT?" (I'd make up the call letters.) People were excited to get a phone call from a radio program and usually said, "Oh yes! I listen all the time!" Then I'd explain the rules of the game. If they could identify five songs, they would win a cash prize. Lowell's job was picking out a 45 rpm and putting it on the turntable, while I held the receiver close by. "Do you recognize that tune?" If they answered correctly, we'd go on to the next song. "But first," I'd tell them, "we have to take a break for a commercial from our sponsor . . . Fab laundry detergent. Do you use Fab?"

"Yes!" they always said. "Fab is my favorite!" One lady was so enthusiastic she added, "It's bubbling away in the machine right now! As a matter of fact, it's overflowing on my floor." At this point, I'd usually have to shush Lowell, who'd be giggling in the background. We couldn't believe how gullible people were. Then I'd completely change my voice and act out all the parts of the commercial.

Other kids might have stopped there, but not us. If the person managed to guess all five songs, we'd take down his or her address. Then Lowell and I would go to McCrory's, the local five-and-dime, buy some fake money, enclose it in an envelope, and drop it in the mail.

I loved the five-and-dime. There were so many items that were not very expensive . . . combs, bobby pins, lipsticks. But I also had another method of getting what I needed, which I'm not too proud of. Sometimes I would steal things.

This was not as simple as random shoplifting. I was a very logical girl and I had my own system. It was all based on something I had noticed . . . people often discarded their receipts on the floor. I would look for them and pick them up. Most things were a dollar then, and the tax was three cents. So I would take an item that cost $1.03, something small like a lipstick or a compact that was relatively easy to slip into my bag. Then I'd head straight to the refund window . . . my heart beating fast . . . where I'd turn in the item with the receipt, collect the cash, and then use the money to buy something I really wanted.

I don't want you to think that this was fun. I was always nervous. It was a strange combination of excitement and fear. But the refunds were a good way to supplement the money I made as a cashier at the Chinese restaurant . . . I was paid a dollar an hour for working there, and fifty cents an hour for babysitting. Every bit came in handy, because as soon as I started earning money my mother said I had to buy my own clothes.

I remember one particular outfit that I loved . . . a skirt and top made of cotton printed with tiny pink-and-white checks, with lace trim. Then I bought shoes to match, low-cut pink flats that showed a bit of my toes. But then I also liked the more masculine, sporty look of the plaid shirt I wore at camp, with pants.

One day, I picked up a pair of Bermuda shorts at A&S (that's Abraham & Straus, Brooklyn's best department store). They were a classic blue-and-green plaid. I had just pulled them on in the dressing room to see if they were the right size, and then it occurred to me . . . I could let my skirt fall back down and just walk out, still wearing the shorts.

It was so easy. I must have brought in a couple of other things to try on, and I handed those back to the salesperson, thinking, *Oh my God, she doesn't know I still have the shorts on.* Nobody could see them under my skirt . . . or could they? I felt my heart pounding.

I can't remember whether it was on that same day that I took a pair of yellow socks. (I was getting carried away by my talent.) I already had a paper bag because I had bought something else, and as I was going down a crowded escalator, I just dropped the socks into it. Then I stopped to look at something on the first floor that caught my eye. Suddenly I heard a woman say, "I saw you put those socks in your bag."

Did I hear right? Or was this my guilty conscience? I quickly moved to the next counter, but she followed me. I was so petrified that I couldn't look up. I never saw her face. Deliberately I set the bag down and walked out of the store. And that was the end of my criminal career. I never stole anything again. I liked testing boundaries but I couldn't stand the humiliation and shame that I felt at that moment. Imagine what it would be like if I were ever truly caught and dragged into a manager's office!

Now if I go to a hotel and I like a little doodad such as a tiny dish that holds mustard or something, I always ask if I can buy it.

Lou Kind moved out when I was thirteen, which meant I never had to watch another wrestling match. I was happy he left. (I couldn't tell whether my mother was happy or sad about it because she never discussed it.) I hated the condescension in his voice when he spoke to her. Without him, the atmosphere inside the apartment became a lot calmer. My best memory of that time is lying on my bed, reading movie magazines and eating Breyer's coffee ice cream. It came in a square box, divided into sections like Neapolitan, except it was coffee on each side with a slab of cherry vanilla in the middle . . . with whole pieces of cherry. I would eat that first and save my favorite flavor, coffee, for last. I wanted that to be the taste that lingered in my mouth. (I used to eat a pint of coffee ice cream whenever I could and still stay skinny as a rail. Why couldn't that be true now?)

Shelly and Ellen got married, and for their honeymoon they were going to Europe on the SS *Constitution.* Some of the family came to see them off. I was dazzled by the huge ship and the thought of crossing the ocean to see the world. People on board were drinking champagne and laughing and talking in a beautiful, wood-paneled room. Meanwhile, I was practically ill, wanting so desperately to go with them. My mother said, "Shelly, give her five dollars." But my brother ignored her. (Years later, when I reminded him of this, he sent me a five-dollar bill, framed.) I couldn't believe that he was sailing away and I had to go back to our gloomy apartment.

The movies were my escape. Right next to my high school, Erasmus Hall on Flatbush Avenue, was the Astor Theatre. It showed foreign films by directors like Akira Kurosawa and Jules Dassin, and though their names meant nothing to me at the time, I loved their work in *Rashomon* and *Never on Sunday.* I didn't mind the subtitles, or the fact that the films were all in black and white. I think that was the beginning of my love for monochromatic images.

Although I was also seduced by the bright, saturated colors at the Loew's Kings, where they showed big Hollywood musicals in Technicolor. I remember Howard Keel and Kathryn Grayson in *Kiss Me Kate.* I thought she was beautiful, with her high, vibrating voice.

The Loew's Kings was one of those extravagant movie palaces with red-velvet seats, an exotic painted and gilded ceiling, and Mello-Rolls . . . the best ice cream cones . . . flat on top with the ice cream packed inside, all the way down to the bottom of the cone. I've never seen anything like it before or since. Very practical. Fewer drips. And the candy! My usual was two packages of peanut M&M's and a box of Good & Plenty, with soft black licorice inside the hard pink or white cylindrical shells. It was like eating jewelry.

That's where I saw Marlon Brando for the first time in *Guys and Dolls.* My friend Barbara Sankel had already shown me a photograph of him. I thought, *Eh, he's okay.* And then I watched him on-screen and fell in love. I thought, *Oh my God, who* is *this creature? What a face! Those eyes . . . those lips . . . those teeth!* I wanted to be in the movies just to kiss Marlon Brando!

Guys and Dolls was the only movie that I ever sat through twice in one afternoon. I had come in halfway through some other film. In those days, they had double features, but I rarely watched both movies from beginning to end. I didn't realize that theaters had schedules and you were supposed to come in when a movie started. I would just walk in whenever I felt like it, and then stay after the second feature to see the beginning of the first.

I can't even remember what the other film that day was because *Guys and Dolls* blew everything else out of my head. I was riveted to the screen. After it ended, I had to sit through the whole other movie, bursting with impatience (another two Mello-Rolls helped). I was so entranced with Marlon Brando that I couldn't wait to see him again.

I liked love stories, like *Anna Karenina* with Greta Garbo. I used to imagine myself as the heroine, living another life. When I saw *The King and I,* I wanted to be Anna, the devoted teacher, not Deborah Kerr. I wanted to wear those hoop skirts and live in Siam.

Later, I realized that in the stories I loved the most, the characters don't end up together . . . which is interesting, since we all think we want a happy ending. And yet it's the tragedy, the loss, the missed opportunity that really resonates and stays in our minds and hearts forever. *Anna Karenina* ends sadly . . . which allowed me to cry. I never cried easily. But in a movie theater I could let my tears flow.

Anna Karenina was also the first classic novel I ever read. I went straight from Nancy Drew to Tolstoy. I was completely taken with Anna, dying for love. After all, isn't passion what we all want in our lives?

I loved the world of make-believe. It was so much more vivid and alive than anything I was experiencing. Walking out of the dark theater into the harsh light of reality left me so depressed. I was hit with the smell of the street . . . the garbage . . . the dirt. My mother didn't want me to go to the movies because she said I was always grouchy for a couple of days afterward.

I didn't like reality. I was a misfit in high school, never completely comfortable in those halls even though I got high marks and was a member of the Arista Society, which required an above-90 average. I always cared about my grades. I was a diligent pupil who turned in each homework assignment on time and in excruciating detail. I still have a paper I wrote as a freshman, entitled "My Thirteen Years" . . . complete with a "13" made out of construction paper on the cover, a table of contents, and family photographs. Here's an excerpt to give you an idea of the contents:

"An exciting moment in my life took place in the auditorium of Public School 89 on June 24, 1955 at 9:15 a.m. It was my graduation. I remember feeling very funny walking across the platform to receive my diploma. I could hear the click of my heels, and I thought my slip was showing. I remember feeling strange when I was walking down the steps to my seat. I felt as if all eyes were upon me." (It was not a feeling I enjoyed, then or now. This is why to this day I hate attending awards shows or being on the red carpet.)

"I liked my teachers, but somehow I was glad to leave." (Yes, that's still me. When I'm done with something, I'm *done*.) "This past summer I went to the beach about three times a week. Nothing out of the ordinary occurred."

Not the most promising material, I know . . . but I already had my plans for the future. "Ever since I can remember I've been interested in dramatics. Once in a while I take out my poetry books and my *Theatre Arts* magazines and act out the plays. I've recently heard of the American Academy of Dramatic Arts, in which they include vocal lessons in their course. I am going to look into the matter further." I go on to declare, "Now that I am an Erasmian I hope to be able to participate and contribute to any extracurricular activities" and "I will try to perform all of my duties to the utmost of my ability. That ends the story of my life. All I can say is I will try to get the full benefit out of what I can, and I will try to make my life as pleasant as possible, for myself, and for those with whom I come in contact."

Not a bad goal . . . I was definitely earnest, as you can see. But I didn't look like the other honor students I hung around with. They wore brown oxford shoes with laces and thick glasses. I had streaked hair, which I did myself. I would take a piece of cotton, soak it in hydrogen peroxide straight from the bottle, and bleach strands of my hair. Then, when I got tired of that look, I bought Noreen henna rinse at Woolworth's and tried to get rid of the bleached part. What I didn't know was that inside each capsule were tiny little crystals in different colors, so chunks of hair turned red, green, and blue. I looked like a London punk rocker . . . way ahead of that time . . . although it was a complete accident.

I also liked to play around with makeup. I used to take my mother's dark purple lipstick and mix it with zinc oxide (which I used to treat blemishes) to make an unusual magenta color. Borrowing her lipstick was nothing new. When I was two, she caught me just as I was about to fall off her dresser, where I had been happily smearing lipstick all over my face. My brother had a talent for art, and I used his blue watercolor pencils to make eye shadow. I may have overdone it at times. When I received the Spanish medal for having the highest mark in the class (99), the teacher, Mrs. Thomas (pronounced Toma*th* with that Castilian li*thp*), handed it to me and said, "You don't have to wear blue on your eyes to get an award."

Bobby Fischer, the chess prodigy, was also a student at Erasmus. I can still see him sitting alone in the cafeteria, wearing a brown leather cap with earmuffs and thick brown corduroy pants. And he was laughing to himself. That's what intrigued me. He looked like some sort of deranged pilot from a 1940s movie. One day I got up the courage to go over and say hello, but he wasn't very friendly. He was more interested in the *Mad* magazine he was reading. That was the last time I approached him. He was another loner, like me.

After Irving Borookow (I broke up with him when I was seven), I never even had a date all through high school, except once with a boy who was Spanish . . . tall and quite good-looking. I don't remember his name but I remember his face, and what I was wearing . . . a navy-blue dress with a white collar and cuffs. I might have talked too much, since he never asked me out again.

And that was it for youthful romance. Once, Ira Trachtenberg, a shy blond boy who also lived in the projects, wanted to take me to Manhattan to see *A Star Is Born* with Judy Garland. But I was afraid he'd get beaten up, and then how would I get home to Brooklyn?

Besides, I liked Joey Bauman better. He was a tough guy. He could protect me. I have a great picture of the two of us. I'm sitting on his bike, and I don't look too bad. Kind of cute, as opposed to my lousy graduation picture from middle school, with the worst 1950s hairstyle.

My best friend as a teenager was Barbara Sulman, who also lived in the projects. Years later, when I was shooting *The Prince of Tides* in New York, she left a note in my trailer on the street. I was so happy to hear from her and called to invite her back to visit. She looked exactly the same as she did at thirteen, only taller. We used to tell each other our dreams. I wanted to be a famous actress, and she wanted to be a secretary and have two kids and a husband. Both of us got our wish.

Barbara and I used to go to Brighton Beach together, Bay 2, spread out a towel, and lie in the sun. We'd slather ourselves in baby oil, with a few drops of iodine in the bottle to make our tans even darker. When I got home, I couldn't wait to pull off my bathing suit, still gritty with sand, and take a shower. Then I could look at the contrast between the white, unexposed skin and the skin that was in the sun to see how tan I was. It was almost a competition. We would meet after our showers to compare our tans.

I did a lot of things on my own. I was always very independent. That probably happens when you have a parent who works. You learn how to fend for yourself.

I didn't cook but I liked to bake . . . I was always looking to replicate that yellow cake I loved at the Bais Yaakov summer camp . . . Fischer's cupcakes came the closest. And then I had other favorites. Ebinger's, the German bakery around the corner from our building, had the best chocolate blackout cake. Schenley's, the Jewish bakery, was where I'd go to buy a Charlotte Russe for a treat, just because it looked so pretty with that cherry on top. And then there was the Jewish "appetizing" store, Besterman's, for sour green tomatoes, lox and bagels, and smoked butterfish, a flat little fish with shiny gold skin that tasted great. On the corner was a drugstore called Cookie's, with round seats that twirled at the lunch counter. And then catty-corner to Cookie's was a little Italian candy store where you could get licorice in red and green and brown, as well as black. They served Cokes straight from the soda fountain spigot and made great egg creams too. I don't know why they're called egg creams. There's no egg in them, only milk, Fox's U-Bet chocolate syrup, and seltzer. My mother always tried to give me malteds to fatten me up, but I never liked them. Too thick.

Because she was busy with my little sister, I went to many other places alone, like the dentist . . . Dr. Norman Greystone, across the street. He told me I had fifteen cavities, and I was convinced he was trying to make money by drilling holes in my teeth . . . although I'll admit I did eat a lot of sweets.

I was fourteen when he pointed to my canines (the ones that are pointy) and explained that they were still my baby teeth. Most kids lose those by the time they're ten or eleven, but mine hadn't fallen out, so he wanted to pull four teeth, two on either side, to make room for my adult teeth to grow in. I was horrified. "No way," I said. I didn't want to have huge holes on each side of my mouth. I told him I'd allow him to pull out one tooth on each side, hoping Mother Nature would take care of the rest. (I don't remember even asking my mother if I could do this. I had made up my mind.)

And then Dr. Greystone sent me to an orthodontist because he saw that one front tooth was starting to grow in behind the baby tooth, so I needed braces. Great. I was already insecure about my looks, and the last thing I needed was braces. When the orthodontist told me he wanted to put all these wires on my teeth, I said, "I'm sorry, but you'll have to somehow put them behind my teeth, so they don't show." Apparently he could hide the wires on the top teeth but not the bottom, so I told him to forget about those. That's why my bottom teeth are still crooked.

By the way, it took two years for the new teeth to come down. This is why people thought I was so serious. I never smiled for that entire time. It was too embarrassing. And laughing was out of the question. Maybe it would have been faster if I had let Dr. Greystone do what he wanted. But I was thinking ahead. How could I go onstage with braces and two large gaps in my mouth?

You see, I had big plans. That same year I pretended to be older so I could get into the summer apprentice program at Malden Bridge Playhouse in upstate New York. (By the time I went, I had turned fifteen, which I thought was grown-up enough.)

I used to read a paper called *Show Business* that was sold on newsstands in Manhattan, and that must have been where I learned about Malden Bridge. I can still see the guy who ran it, John Hale. He was a tall, thin string bean who looked like John Waters. I'm not even sure I had to audition, and the competition wasn't stiff, because if you had $150, you got in. It's funny when I think of it now. You actually had to pay for the privilege of doing all the dirty work in the theater. In any event, I didn't have $150, and neither did my mother. When I asked if I could go, she said no. To her it must have sounded as if I wanted to join the circus, and she was appalled. But I was determined. I reminded her that my grandfather had left me $500 when he died, and I said, "I want some of it to go to summer stock."

My mother and I did not have the typical mother-daughter relationship. I always had a certain power over her. Or maybe I was so relentless that I wore her down.

She gave me the money.

Things were looking up! I went to Malden Bridge with my best friend from Erasmus, Susan Dworkowitz, who also wanted to be an actress (and had already picked her stage name, Susan Lanell). She was a tiny girl who used to put white pancake makeup on her face. With her red lipstick and black hair in a pixie cut, she looked like a little porcelain doll. Imagine her next to me, with my homemade magenta lipstick and blue eye shadow. The two of us must have been quite a pair.

The playhouse had something like a ten-week season, and the first play opened in June, but we apprentices didn't get to go onstage until July. The play was *Teahouse of the August Moon*, and we both had walk-on parts. Susan seemed perfectly cast. I wasn't, but that didn't bother me. I was so excited to finally be onstage . . . a professional stage with a real theater company! Susan and I had bought Max Factor theatrical makeup kits, and I still remember the thrill of opening up each cylindrical stick and breathing in the smell of the greasepaint.

I was worried about the gaps in my teeth, so I used to take Aspergum, which was lighter than regular gum and closer to the color of my teeth, and mold it into the shape of a tooth and stick it in my spaces. You can guess what happened next. More than once, right in the middle of a performance, one of my Aspergum teeth fell out, and I had to quickly swallow it.

My favorite time was when we knocked down the set at the end of each week, to repaint the flats for the next show. As we all worked into the wee hours of the morning, delicious Campbell's tomato soup and grilled cheese sandwiches would appear. Nothing better! I think I also discovered peanut butter and jelly, on soft white bread, while I was there. I was used to bologna and Velveeta cheese.

In the fifth play, I got a part with actual lines . . . Elsa in *Desk Set*. I was perched on a desk and had to play this flirtatious character. I didn't know how to be flirtatious. When you grow up without a father, I don't think you relate quite as easily to men. You don't develop your femininity in response to his masculinity. What do little girls do to get attention from their daddy? They cuddle up to him when they want a new toy or a new dress. They kiss him and say, "I love you." They learn how to manipulate. I had no idea how to manipulate men or even react to them, since I had had no relationship with my stepfather. Instinctively, I must have used a part of myself that I didn't even know existed to play this role.

So I was completely surprised when I read my first review in the local newspaper: "Barbara Streisand turns in a fine performance as the office vamp—Down boys!"

Wow. "Down boys!" Was he kidding? Did this reviewer really think I was sexy? I was so amazed . . . and proud. It was the first time anyone had ever referred to me as attractive in any way.

At the end of the season, the apprentices got to put on their own show as a reward for spending most of the summer backstage, unseen. The play was *Picnic*, and I was cast as Millie, the heroine's kid sister. I had seen the movie starring William Holden and Kim Novak, with Susan Strasberg as Millie. (There she was again.) And I got another good review: "As the homely sister, Barbara Streisand is transformed from a tomboy to a pretty girl, aware of her powers, in a wholly believable transition."

That critic was prescient. "Homely" to "pretty" . . . that basically describes the template for my whole career.

And that was it. My path was set. What a glorious summer! I could hardly bear to go back to high school. I decided to double up on my math and science courses so I could graduate six months early and get started! But in order to do that, I needed permission. The principal, Mrs. Cameron, called my mother in for a conference to ask why I wasn't applying to college with a 93 average. My mother wasn't convinced that college was so important. Her highest ambition for me was to learn how to type so I could work as a secretary in the school system and get paid vacations. (That's why I grew my nails so long . . . so I'd never have to type.)

In English class that year, the books I chose to report on were by Stanislavsky. I read *My Life in Art*, his autobiography, and *An Actor Prepares*, the first book of a trilogy that explained his theories about acting, and continued with *Building a Character* and then *Creating a Role*. I wrote a paper on Shakespeare's sonnets. I remember taking the subway all the way up to the Heckscher Theatre on Fifth Avenue and 104th Street to see George C. Scott in *Richard III* on a very cold and snowy night. I loved Shakespeare.

So had my father, as I discovered when I finally got to look through his books. After he died, my mother had tied them all up and put them down in the basement at Pulaski Street. Years later I retrieved them, and now they're my treasures . . . all the plays of Shakespeare and works by Charles Dickens and Mark Twain. You can see where I scribbled, as a child, in some of the copies. He must have been reading them while I was close by. I still have his copy of Charles and Mary Lamb's *Tales from Shakespeare* on my bedside table. It's a charming book, summarizing the stories for children. Who knows? Maybe he had bought it to read to me.

Erasmus did not offer acting classes, but I did hear about a Radio Club that met somewhere outside of school. I auditioned with a speech from George Bernard Shaw's *Saint Joan*. It's the scene where she's in front of the tribunal, pleading for her life, and she talks about the voices she hears in her head. I had learned from reading Stanislavsky that you should always try to find something in yourself that relates to a character in order to play it successfully. I certainly heard things in *my* head, so I could be completely truthful when I said Joan's lines. Acting is believing . . . that was the title of another book I read back then. It was one of my favorites.

There was another line from the play that caught my eye. It comes when Joan is weary from all the tribunal's questions and in despair because they refuse to believe her answers. She says, "It is an old saying that he who tells too much truth is sure to be hanged."

That hit me like a revelation, and I've never forgotten it. I've always believed in telling the truth, but it's gotten me into trouble over the years.

I remember steaming open the letter from the club, addressed to my mother, to find out if I had gotten in. And I had. But I can't recall if I actually ended up going. I always enjoyed the challenge of getting into something like that, but once I was accepted, I often lost interest. Maybe I went once, and the reality didn't live up to my fantasy . . . or maybe it was too far away.

I was also accepted into the Choral Club at Erasmus. I thought Mr. DePietto, the head of the music department, was very handsome, but he didn't pay any attention to me. Nobody in high school was particularly impressed with my voice, and neither was I. My mother, on the other hand, thought she had a very good voice . . . and she really did. She would sing at the drop of a hat, at bar mitzvahs and other family gatherings. But she never did anything with her talent. When she was seventeen, she and a girlfriend signed up to sing in the Metropolitan Opera Chorus, but they only went to one rehearsal, got home late, "and worried our parents," as she told a reporter decades later. "So both of us girls gave it up and put it out of our minds."

Even though she had dropped her own musical ambitions, did she retain some for me? . . . because she took me into the city to audition for MGM when I was nine. How did that come about? Were they looking for young talent and just put an ad in the paper? Was it my mother's idea, or did I have to persuade her? I'm not sure. I do remember telling everyone on the playground, as I was doing my tricks on the slide, that I was going to MGM . . . I loved the lion that roared at the beginning of all their movies . . . and that I would probably be famous soon. Little did I know that an audition was not the same as getting a job. When my mother and I arrived, we were greeted by Dudley Wilkinson, a distinguished white-haired man who was the head of talent. He shook my hand, and then I was shown into a glass booth . . . very strange, because I couldn't hear anything from outside, except when they spoke to me through a loudspeaker. I sang "Have You Heard?" by my favorite singer back then, Joni James. I doubt I had any accompaniment. And I don't think I ever heard from them again.

When I was twelve, I also auditioned for a TV show called *Startime Kids*. I think they actually wanted me for that one, but before I could be on the show, I had to attend their classes. I may have gone a few times, but the classes were early on Saturday morning, and it was too much of a schlep for me and my mom to get there. She didn't want me to continue, and I don't think I was that unhappy to stop.

We went up to the Catskills for a week the summer I was thirteen, where my mother met a piano player who told her about a studio where you could make your own record. She was thrilled by the idea and decided to do it. And I thought, *Great, I'll make a record too.*

My mother and I picked out our songs and went to the Nola Studios on December 29, 1955, to record them. My mother sang "One Kiss" in a light operetta style. Quite beautiful . . . better than Jeanette MacDonald, I thought. But she could hardly get a chorus in edgewise because the piano player kept launching into endless, elaborate refrains. I was just a teenager and what did I know . . . it just felt wrong. As soon as he started that with me, I said, "No, no, can you just play a shorter interlude?"

I sang two songs that day. One was "Zing! Went the Strings of My Heart" and the other was "You'll Never Know," a song I really liked, with music by Harry Warren and lyrics by Mack Gordon . . . a serious song. I was not all that comfortable with up-tempo pieces. The piano player and I had figured out where he was going to play, and where I was going to sing. But then, on the last few notes, something came out of my mouth that completely surprised me. Instead of singing the melody as it was written and as we had planned, very simply: "You'll never know what you don't . . . know . . . now . . ." I sang three totally different notes. Higher, with a jazzier rhythm, and with an odd minor note at the end.

I thought, *Holy mackerel! Where did that come from? Is this what they call inspiration?* I didn't know that a musician might call it improvisation . . . and it means riffing on the melody. It was only years later, when I was sitting in acting class, that I realized that this kind of thing is exactly what we were all trying to achieve . . . to be completely in the moment . . . without preconceptions . . . so that we could react with pure spontaneity.

I started going to acting classes in Manhattan when I was fourteen. My first teacher was William Hickey, who was a member of the Herbert Berghof Studio in Greenwich Village, founded by Berghof and his wife, Uta Hagen. I must have read about it in *Show Business*. But I didn't stay with Hickey long. Frankly, I couldn't understand what he was talking about half the time. I remember doing a scene for him from *The Glass Menagerie*. I thought I did a decent job with Laura, especially her limp . . . I seemed to gravitate to characters with a flaw. Then he asked my partner and me to do it again. But before we got very far, he stopped me and asked, "Don't you remember your blocking?"

"What's blocking?" I had never heard the term before. After he explained that each actor was supposed to repeat his movements, I said, "You mean you have to move in exactly the same way, to the same spots? Why?"

I questioned everything. I must have been very annoying to have around.

I went back to *Show Business*, and that's probably where I saw an ad for the Cherry Lane Theatre. So I just went there one day and asked if I could work for nothing and learn. At the time they were doing a production of Sean O'Casey's

Purple Dust that had already been running for quite a while. Anita Miller was playing the part of Avril, and I would watch her intently as I worked backstage several evenings after school and on weekends.

On the first résumé I ever wrote, when I was sixteen, I called myself the assistant stage manager, but that was an exaggeration. I did manage to learn a lot about lighting and sound while I was there, but I had no real title. I also claimed that I was the understudy for Avril, which is partly true. I did learn the part, but nobody had asked me to. I loved speaking with an Irish accent. I'd come into the theater and greet the stagehands, "Top o' the mornin' to you, boys!"

Again, annoying to be around.

Anita and I became good friends. We would talk about acting, and she knew that I was looking for another class. Her husband, Allan Miller, happened to be a teacher, so she told him about me. Apparently he wasn't interested in encouraging a fifteen-year-old to go into the theater. He thought I was too young and that the business was too hard, but that didn't stop me.

One night Anita invited me to have dinner at their apartment. She was a great cook, and made delicious peas with sugar and breadcrumbs . . . I can still taste them. As we were eating, I told Allan how much I wanted to be an actress, and he agreed to take me on. Years later he explained that what he found himself responding to, almost against his will, was my aching desire. I was "so raw, so primitive, so open" that he capitulated. He offered to let me come to his classes in exchange for babysitting their young son, Gregory, who was a sweetheart. I basically fell in love with the whole family.

Meeting Anita and Allan was the beginning of my real education. Their apartment was filled with books. I was particularly interested in contemporary plays, and on their shelves I found works by Tennessee Williams, Arthur Miller, and Lillian Hellman. Allan had a brother, and one night when we were babysitting together he pulled out a record and put it on the player. It was Vivaldi's *The Four Seasons*, and I thought, *My God, what's that?* I had never been exposed to anything like it. I wanted to hear more classical music. I listened to Stravinsky's Violin Concerto, still one of my favorites . . . Respighi's *Pines of Rome* . . . Stravinsky's *The Rite of Spring*. With most music, after I've listened to it once I don't need to hear it again, but these are pieces I never get tired of . . . along with Ralph Vaughan Williams's *The Lark Ascending* and Maria Callas singing Puccini's arias. I bought the records for myself when I found them on sale.

I was like a sponge at this time, drinking everything in.

Meanwhile, I was attending as many of Allan's classes as I could. I thought they were far more interesting than anything that was going on in high school. More and more, it seemed as if my real life was taking place elsewhere . . . at the Cherry Lane Theatre and in acting class and at home with the Millers. They were like my surrogate parents. I only went back to Brooklyn to sleep, change clothes, and go to school. Sometimes on weekends I would go home with Anita after the show and sleep over on their couch.

Acting class was where I felt creative. I remember one particular exercise, when Allan told us to pick an inanimate object and give it life. I chose to be a chocolate chip. First I imagined I was put into a hunk of dough along with my fellow chips, being kneaded and shaped into a cookie . . . pushed around. Then I was placed inside a hot oven. Oh, the agony of it! I began to melt. That was painful. Then suddenly I was taken out into the cold air and, for a moment, I was relieved . . . the cool air soothed my hot body. But I didn't realize I would quickly become stiff and solid . . . misshapen . . . paralyzed. I couldn't move. Here I was, stuck on a tray with other cookies, waiting to be eaten . . . Aaargh!!!!

I think it was one of my best pieces of work.

The first significant scene I did was from Tennessee Williams's *The Rose Tattoo.* I was playing a young girl who is intensely attracted to a boy but is so sexually inexperienced that she doesn't know quite what to do.

Frankly, I was just as inexperienced as the character, and I had no idea how to approach the scene. At first I thought I would pretend that I was on fire and he was ice, but that image turned out to be too painful. It hurt when I touched him, and that wasn't the effect I wanted.

Allan advised me to pick an intention . . . to decide what I was trying to do in the scene. I decided that my character wanted to touch him and wanted him to touch her. But being a virgin, I didn't think she would approach him in an overtly sexual manner. Instead, she would try to explore his body in more innocent ways to get that feeling of contact.

My partner and I began the scene. I think I may have tried to entwine my fingers with his. At one point I found myself standing on his feet . . . like a little girl dancing with her dad. At another moment I pretended I was blind, and while he was talking I was touching his face . . . his eyes, his nose, his cheeks . . . just exploring what it felt like to touch a man's skin . . . the stubble of his beard. I didn't have a boyfriend, and it was all foreign to me.

I remember closing my eyes so I could concentrate on touch alone . . . to make the feelings more intense. It was completely awkward, but I felt it was right for this girl. I had no idea what I was going to do next, and neither did my partner. I think I even jumped on his back at one point. By the end of the scene, he was red as a beet.

I was very surprised when the class started applauding.

Allan told me it was one of the sexiest scenes he had ever watched. And I wasn't even trying to be sexy!

I had no qualms about taking on the most daunting roles. I even tackled Medea. I did her monologue from an adaptation by Jean Anouilh: "Why was I born maimed? Why have you made me a girl? Why these breasts, this weakness, this open wound in the middle of myself?" I was fifteen, and she was a married woman with two children, but I totally related to her. She was exploring what it means to be a woman. I think I did a pretty good job, considering.

One guy who saw that asked me to do a scene with him for his Actors Studio audition. You have to understand that the Actors Studio was the equivalent of Mount Olympus for actors, and Lee Strasberg was its resident god. I was excited to do the audition. We prepared a scene from *Dino*, a television play by Reginald Rose. My classmate didn't get in, but I got a letter saying that they were impressed with my work and asking me to come back and audition on my own. I could hardly believe it. That letter became one of my most prized possessions. I asked Anita to audition with me, and we decided to do a scene from N. Richard Nash's *The Young and Fair.* I was so nervous that I cried through the whole thing. It was over the top, out of control.

Weeks later I got a letter telling me I was not accepted but encouraging me to try again, when I was older. I think their policy was not to take anyone under the age of eighteen.

So, they didn't want me enough to make an exception?

Okay. Maybe I didn't want *them.* But the Actors Studio stayed in my mind, precisely because I hadn't succeeded. It remained a challenge, and I was still intrigued by the thought of working with the famous Strasberg, the father of Susan. (There she was again!)

I used to write letters to Lee Strasberg as I rode back and forth on the subway to Brooklyn. I wanted to share my observations on acting. I had noticed something. There was a guy in Allan's class who wasn't particularly talented and had no charisma whatsoever. But when he did a simple relaxation exercise where you just sit in a chair, and without much movement test different parts of your body for tension, he suddenly became interesting. A tiny twitch of the eyebrow . . . a flick of a finger . . . an intake of breath all seemed fascinating. The simple mystery of being human and not doing much else kept me glued to him.

That exercise showed me the power of simplicity. I wrote to Strasberg that I'd discovered "the something in nothing." People who were self-indulgent and loved to vomit out their feelings were missing the point of what the Method was all about.

I also wrote Strasberg that when you have the privilege of being up on a stage, raised above the audience, you owe them something more . . . something truthful. It seemed to me that truth has an energy that touches people.

In one letter I actually wrote, "I hear you're a starfucker" (probably referring to his relationship with Marilyn Monroe). Can you imagine? Years later, when I did a scene for him at the Actors Studio in Los Angeles, I read some of these letters out loud to him. (I didn't mention that one.) I had never actually mailed any of them. But it was still extremely satisfying to write to someone I respected and articulate my own thoughts.

The summer after my junior year, Anita and Allan were invited to do a play at the Clinton Playhouse up in Connecticut, and they asked me if I wanted to go with them. While they were both acting, I would babysit. That sounded better than being stuck in Brooklyn. Even though I didn't get to be onstage, I hung around the theater and became friends with the actors. Along with Allan, the other leading man in *A Hatful of Rain* was a young actor who was doing summer stock for the first time. His name was Warren Beatty, and he asked me to cue him on his lines. If that was a come-on, I missed it entirely. He also played the piano. I was impressed. We used to eat together occasionally and talk about life. He was twenty-one, tall with movie-star looks, and women were already falling at his feet. I was sixteen.

Warren has told the story of how we met and says that he did in fact make a pass at me, but I turned him down. (Trust me, that didn't faze him. He quickly went on to someone else.) My mother had totally terrified me about sex. She made it sound as if kissing was dangerous until you were married. I wasn't even supposed to hold hands . . . she told me you could get a disease!

In any event, Warren and I became friends for life. He had star quality then and he still has it now. And every time we get together we reminisce about those days.

Back at school in September, I had just four more months to get through before I could get my diploma. But I had one last obstacle to overcome. At Erasmus you couldn't graduate until you had passed a swimming test. And that was a real nightmare for me because I was afraid of the water. I think it started when I was seven . . . I had tried to swim at that health camp and wound up underwater. A nice older girl, Marie, had to rescue me. Then, one Sunday when the Borookows took me with them to the Brooklyn Botanic Garden, I was walking along the edge of the pond and I fell in. The water wasn't deep, but I panicked. Tobey was very comforting. She wrapped me up in her coat and we went home in their car . . . a fabulous black car with a flat top, like the one in *It Happened One Night.* And she let me walk around in her red leather high heels while my clothes dried out.

It was actually my mother who instilled this fear in me. She never went into the water, but just stood at the edge and let it lap around her feet. Like handholding, it was dangerous, according to her. She told me, "Don't go into the water because you'll drown." Even when I went into the shallow water at Brighton Beach, I clutched on to my inner tube for dear life.

So here I was at sixteen, sitting for what seemed like forever on the slippery edge of the Erasmus pool . . . the whole place reeking of chlorine. Where had all those good grades gotten me? I still had to get across this damn pool.

I decided that I was going to swim, even if it killed me. I think I closed my eyes and sort of fell into the water . . . and somehow splashed and paddled my way across.

I graduated from Erasmus Hall on January 26, 1959. I had been looking forward to this day for so long, but when it came, it was anticlimactic. I was more thrilled to be cast in what I considered my first professional production in Manhattan, a play called *Driftwood* (after I had spotted the casting call in

Show Business). It wasn't exactly Broadway, more like off-off-off-Broadway . . . actually in the playwright's loft, with a few folding chairs for seats, and you had to climb up five rickety flights of stairs to get there. And it wasn't all that professional, come to think of it, since no one got paid. But it was a real part. I was finally done with high school . . . and on my way.

THREE

This Night Could Change My Life

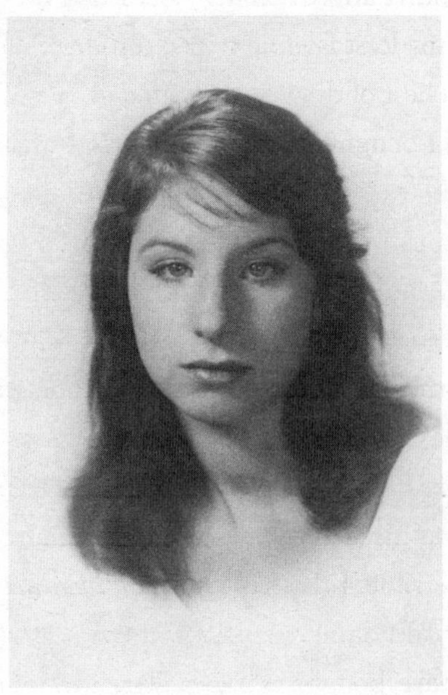

Clearly *Driftwood* was not going to be my path to stardom. I played the leader of a gang of thieves . . . a woman named Lorna, with a mysterious past. (How mysterious could I have been at sixteen?) I remember eating an egg salad sandwich before the first performance and promptly throwing it up because I was so nervous. Joan Molinsky, who later changed her name to Joan Rivers, was also in the cast. I thought she was funny . . . although the play wasn't a comedy . . . and so lucky to be from a wealthy family on Long Island. Not only did she have a father, but he was also a doctor! Wow!

The play didn't last long, but I was undaunted. I had already found a real job in the want ads and that meant I could commit to an apartment in Manhattan with my pal Susan Dworkowitz, aka Lanell.

It was a tiny third-floor walk-up at 339 West Forty-Eighth Street between Eighth and Ninth avenues that cost $100 a month ($50 each), but to me it was heaven. Actually, its only asset was the fact that it was right next to my acting class at Curt Conway's Theatre Studio, where Allan taught. That meant I could save on the subway fare!

For the first time in my life, I had something to decorate. I went down to one of those cheap carpet stores on lower Fifth Avenue and bought a fake Persian rug for $39.95. We couldn't afford a couch. All I had brought were two round-backed chairs in one of my least favorite colors, turquoise, taken from my mother's apartment, and an old chest of drawers we found at one of the local thrift shops on Ninth Avenue. And I bought a fish tank. I thought fish were great, and they were something to look at . . . to watch them move . . . like a fire, since I had no fireplace.

I also had no art. In the antiques shops on Second Avenue, I found gilded frames for almost nothing. They might have a few chips and scratches, but I thought that added to their beauty. I hung them up on the walls, just framing empty space.

My job was at Michael Press, a printing company just a few blocks away from my new apartment. I was hired as a file clerk, stuffing and licking envelopes . . . God, that glue tasted terrible. I thought, *Why am I putting this into my mouth?* So I took a glass of water and dampened the flap with a wet finger. Now that I think of it, I should have bought a brush. The guy who invented that little sponge-bottle thing must have made a fortune. It made so much sense.

I also answered the telephone when the switchboard operator went to lunch. I would try all these different voices, pretending to be French, Italian, and British, just to entertain myself. And who knew when I might need to play a character with an accent?

My life was simple then. I made fifty-five dollars a week, forty-five after taxes, and as soon as I got paid I'd cash the check at Seamen's Bank for Savings (they gave you a gift when you opened an account, so our drinking glasses said "Seamen's Bank for Savings"). That was my first and most important bank account. I always knew the balance down to the penny and was so proud when I managed to save anything.

I'd take my forty-five dollars home and divvy it up into different envelopes marked "Rent," "Gas and Electricity," "Phone," "Laundry," "Subway," and "Food" (that got the biggest chunk). I loved to eat at the Automat. I'd put in my five cents and open the little glass door and pull out a sandwich, a piece of pie, maybe a bowl of soup. Their sweet potatoes were great, but then I got sick on their sliced lamb and didn't eat lamb for years. I also liked going to the deli. Not the Jewish delis. They gave you too much meat. I couldn't get my mouth around those sandwiches. I would go to the Gentile ones and order my favorite . . . a roast pork sandwich with mayonnaise on soft white bread. Delicious.

Everything was an adventure, even doing the laundry. When I lived in the projects, the washing machines were in a deserted, creepy basement with pipes running all over the place, and I was afraid to go down there. Now Susan and I stuffed our dirty clothes in pillowcases and schlepped them over to the laundromat between Ninth and Tenth avenues.

I loved the feeling of clean sheets but I never could figure out how to make a bed. Even in camp, when they showed us how to make hospital corners, I had trouble remembering how to do it. Susan didn't care one way or the other, so neither one of us ever made the bed properly. Interesting how it's the simplest things that bother you. I have a vivid memory of standing in the doorway of the bedroom, looking at the rumpled sheets, and thinking, *I have to become famous just so I can get somebody else to make my bed.*

I was reading a book around that time that left a deep impression on me, *The Quintessence of Ibsenism* by George Bernard Shaw. I thought it was going to be about Ibsen's plays, but it was more of a philosophical look at the concepts behind them and how they're expressed in different personality types. For years I've said there was a line in it that really spoke to me: "Thought transcends matter."

But recently when I ordered a copy of the book and looked through it again, page by page, I couldn't find that line. How could that be? I had to search out other editions just to make sure, but it wasn't in any of them.

Then where did I read it?

Or did I just make it up, out of my own mind?

Well, wherever it came from, it's an amazing concept. Because if thought can transcend matter, that meant if I could think something, want something, maybe I could make it happen. I knew that the mind was very powerful, even as a child. Look how I made that man cross the street! (Sort of.)

Imagine that . . . Just a thought, very quiet, could change things. Maybe imagination could create reality. Maybe I could imagine being an actress, and actually become one. Even though my mother kept saying, "Don't get your hopes up."

I knew I didn't look like those other girls in the movies. I'm not sure if she actually told me, "You're not pretty enough to be a movie star." But I knew that was what she meant. My mother was very pretty, with a nice little nose and blue eyes. She fit the picture. I didn't.

But I held on to that idea: "Thought transcends matter."

I would hurry home from work to go to acting class, or meet another student to rehearse a scene in the evening. Allan was teaching four different classes, and he says I showed up for all of them. But I was also curious about other teachers. I wanted to make sure I wasn't missing anything. At one point I signed up for classes with Eli Rill, who was also part of the Actors Studio. But since I didn't want to hurt Allan's feelings, I made up another name . . . Angelina Scarangella. I picked it out of the phone book. I thought it sounded so beautiful, and I used it for years, whenever I wanted to be incognito. At Mount Sinai Hospital, where I gave birth to my son, Jason, I was listed as Angelina Scarangella. And to this day, whenever I do a concert tour, the name on my dressing-room door is Angelina Scarangella. (Now that I've told you, I guess I'll have to come up with something else.)

I tried a few classes with Rill, but I didn't really relate to him. I was more comfortable with Allan, who had me working on a scene from Christopher Fry's *A Phoenix Too Frequent.* I was a servant girl in ancient Rome, stuck in a tomb with my mistress, because we were both renouncing the world so we could join her dead husband (don't ask). And then a handsome soldier shows up. I was supposed to be pining for this guy, but I wasn't particularly attracted to the actor. So, remembering that you should always be real and honest, I put a piece of chocolate cake in the wings. I could look over his shoulder and see the cake and at least be attracted to that!

Cis Corman was playing my mistress, and this was the beginning of our lifelong friendship. She told me she had already noticed me because I wore a rust-and-brown plaid coat (bought at Loehmann's, the discount clothing store) and would stand in the back of the class, eating cottage cheese out of the container.

I was definitely not the most social creature. But she liked how I questioned everything. I really wanted to understand. And if I didn't, I kept asking. I was still blurting things out, just as I did when I was six years old at the yeshiva.

I used to go over to Cis's apartment to rehearse. That's how we became buddies. She was thirty-two years old, twice my age, with a doctor for a husband . . . the ultimate goal (according to my mother). Dr. Harvey Corman was a distinguished psychiatrist, and they had four children, the oldest not much younger than me. So Cis was at a completely different stage of life. Now that I think back, I realize I often had these kinds of intense relationships with older women. I suppose it's obvious. I was looking for a mother. But I also think we just recognized something in each other. Cis was very alive, eager to go places and do things. She was always available to me, and that was amazing. Sometimes we'd talk three times a day.

I'd call and say, "Guess what just happened?"

She'd laugh at my stories, and then I'd laugh at myself, and we'd both crack up all over again. We were perfect for each other . . . even though her friends wondered what she was doing with a person half her age.

Cis and Harvey became another set of surrogate parents. They lived in one of those great old rambling apartments on the Upper West Side, with ten rooms. I loved to hang out in their kitchen. The refrigerator was always full and everything in there was so neat and orderly, unlike my mother's. All the food looked so tempting . . . smoked salmon, potato salad, and sliced fruit, fresh and ready to eat under Saran Wrap. And they always had ice cream.

The scene we were working on in Allan's class was going to be part of a showcase . . . an opportunity for all the students to invite guests to come see them perform. Harvey was very supportive, and of course he was there, full of compliments for both of us after the show. He was so considerate of his wife and genuinely interested in me . . . such a change from Lou Kind.

I looked around for my mother. Actually, I was kind of embarrassed to perform in front of her. She was so against me being an actress that it made me feel weird to know she was in the audience watching me. I dreaded what she might say. And sure enough, she didn't disappoint me.

"Mom, what did you think?"

She frowned and said, "Your arms are too skinny."

That was it. She had nothing to say about the performance. She didn't congratulate me or comment on my acting. It was as if she hadn't even seen me perform. What did I have to do to get her attention and approval?

No wonder I wanted to become an actress. It was a way to escape myself and live in someone else's world.

Dustin Hoffman was also studying acting at the Theatre Studio and working as the janitor there, in exchange for classes. He was kind of cute, in a funny-looking way, and he was seeing a friend of mine from acting class, Elaine Sobel. She wore glasses but was very pretty, like a girl in a 1950s movie who takes off her glasses and lets down her hair and voilà! When Dustin got a part in an off-Broadway play years later, that was big news . . . the janitor from Curt Conway got an acting job!

In those days, I spent a lot of time at the Forty-Second Street library. I wanted to look up all the plays that great actresses like Sarah Bernhardt and Eleonora Duse had done. I read *L'Aiglon,* which is the story of Napoleon's son and was written by Edmond Rostand for Bernhardt. She was fifty-six years old at the time and had no qualms about playing a twenty-year-old boy. She took on Hamlet as well, and played the fourteen-year-old Juliet at the age of seventy-four. The woman was fearless. She was also brilliant in more conventional romantic roles, such as Marguerite in *La Dame aux Camélias* by Dumas fils, which Duse played as well. Years later, when I was sitting in on some of Lee Strasberg's classes, I saw films of them both. Duse was so stunningly simple compared to Bernhardt, whose style was more florid. It almost felt like overacting to me. But I still related to Sarah, because she was Jewish . . . well, half Jewish. And how about the fact that her initials are the same as mine, only backward?

I've talked to so many people who say their parents took them to the theater and gave them great books to read, to fire up all those synapses in the brain. And I felt envious. I know my father would have done that for me. I needed to catch up, and that gave me the initiative to see and do as much as I could in this incredible city, with all its cultural riches. I had this deep thirst for knowledge, and I was like an open vessel, waiting to be filled.

Susan and I had a great time exploring New York. I remember going to see José Greco dance the flamenco and Ravi Shankar play the sitar. We dreamed about going off on a freighter together to see the world. You could do that back then, and it didn't cost much.

Susan was going to acting classes as well, and one night Allan and Anita were going to see her in a showcase, while I babysat. I was convinced they'd think she was brilliant and then start to like her more than me. Would they let me go and take her in? Then I'd be abandoned again. So I was very nervous . . . like a defendant on trial, waiting for the verdict.

Finally they returned, and I practically pounced on them at the door.

"How was the play?"

"Okay," said Allan.

"What did you think of Susan?"

"She was okay."

I wanted more details. Turns out they thought she was fine, but they weren't raving about her performance. And I was relieved, and a bit ashamed at my relief, because I wanted Susan to be good. I just didn't want her to be better than me.

Someone had told me that if you posed for the students at the Institute of Photography they gave you free headshots. So I did it. And the people at Michael Press printed out 8 x 10 glossies for me. Then, after I had worked there for about nine months, I was let go. I remember starting to cry when they told me, and they quickly assured me that it was not because of my work. The company was downsizing. Then somebody explained how to sign up for unemployment, and I cheered up. It was incredible. I got almost as much money as I had taken home while I was working, and I didn't even have to work! Except I had to stand in line every week to get my check and tell them about all the jobs I had tried for and of course I had to make some up, because I was not trying to get another job as a file clerk. I wanted to be an actress.

Eventually I got caught. I had told them that I went over to CBS to apply for a job, which was the truth . . . but it was for a part in some TV show rather than a secretarial job. And they checked up on it and I was found out. My punishment was that I would have to stand in line each week, as if I were going to get my check. But they were not going to give me any money for five weeks. They cut off the payments. I thought, *Forget this. I can't waste my time. I've got to find some other way to make money.*

I picked up a few stray jobs, like ushering in the theater. I only did it a few times . . . once on New Year's Eve, because of course I didn't have a date. But at least I got to see the show and I got paid $4.15 an hour. You had to wear a black dress and put on this huge white collar, and I would hide my face because I was pretty sure I would be famous some day and didn't want anybody remembering that I had shown them to their seats.

I also modeled for several drawing classes at the Art Students League. None of that nude stuff. I was too shy for that. But I was happy to sit there for a few hours fully dressed and get paid for it. The guy who hired me said my face was "interesting." I didn't know I had an interesting face. What did that mean? Odd? Different? Beautiful? Intriguing? It sounded good. It seemed positive. Although when you don't know what to say about something, you usually call it "interesting."

At least it wasn't derogatory.

Once an older man asked if I could come model for him in his apartment. I thought, *Uh-oh.* (My mother had trained me well.) Then I thought, *I might as well give it a try.* But when he opened the door, I suddenly changed my mind. I was scared to be alone with him, so I turned around and went home. That was the end of my modeling career.

And I wasn't getting any work as an actress. I was told that you have to make the rounds, which meant that you spent the whole day going from one casting agent's office to another, knocking on doors and asking if they had a job. I didn't know how to sell myself. What was I supposed to say? "You better sign me up. I'm terrific!"

They wouldn't even let me read. How could they tell anything about your talent if they wouldn't even let you read? I couldn't beg these people for a job. It was so degrading. My pride was more important to me. I thought, *If this is what it's like, maybe I should be a hat designer . . . or a manicurist.* I told everyone who turned me away, "You know, I'm not coming back here again. You'll be sorry!"

I remember going to David Susskind's office for a walk-on part as a beatnik in one of his television shows. The character's name was April, and I was born in April, so I thought, *Well, that's a good sign. Maybe I'll get the part.* I was wearing black tights and a trench coat, which was how I normally dressed, so I already looked like a beatnik. The casting director was a woman named Faye Lee. She looked up from her papers and said, "I need to see your work."

"My work?" I didn't understand the logic of that. "Why do you need to see my work? This is a walk-on. I have no lines. Just look at me. Either I look right for the part or I don't."

"I still need to see your work."

"But how can you see my work if I can't get work because people like you won't hire me until they see my work?"

She stared at me as if I had just poured a glass of water on the floor, and showed me to the door.

Put it this way, I lasted two days making rounds.

So I decided to try to get into Lee Strasberg's private classes. (Forget the fact that I had already tried the Actors Studio. Why not go straight to the top?) Usually you have to write a letter and wait about six months to a year for an interview. But I was impatient. Who has time to wait a year? I've always been one for instant gratification, which probably has something to do with my father. Subconsciously, I'm thinking about how his life was cut short, and that I have to get it all in . . . fast.

I called Strasberg's office and his secretary answered. I happened to be reading a book of plays by Tennessee Williams so I had those cadences in my head. All of a sudden, in my telephone-operator mode, I started speaking with a Southern accent. I gave her this whole shpiel about how I wanted to be an actress but my parents were going to force me to come home if I didn't get into Mr. Strasberg's class. When she asked me where home was, I glanced down at the book and said, "Uh . . . uh . . . Tennessee." She bought it . . . I couldn't believe it! . . . and set up an appointment for me to see Mr. Strasberg the next day.

I remember exactly what I wore . . . an olive-green dress with an Empire waist that I had bought in a thrift shop, and olive-green Pappagallo shoes with a little bow in front and a curved heel. I loved them . . . very eighteenth century. I always felt I should have lived in another era.

I managed to be on time (not my strong suit) and was ushered into his office . . . a beautiful, book-lined room, dark, with creaky wooden floors. Here I was, finally face-to-face with Lee Strasberg . . . the most famous acting teacher on the planet.

He was someone who had probably always looked old, even when he was young, and he spoke very quietly. He had an odd vocal tic . . . he kept doing this nasal snort as he talked, which was a little distracting. He reminded me of my uncle Irving.

I sat down, and he asked me, "Who are your favorite actors?"

I knew exactly what he wanted me to say, and what any other eager young actor would say to curry favor with the master. The right answers were Kim Stanley and Marlon Brando. But something got into me . . . I always had a mischievous streak.

"Rita Hayworth and Gregory Peck."

I was hoping he'd understand that I ultimately wanted to be in the movies (not realizing he wasn't a mind reader).

He was silent. We stared at each other. Then he said, "So you want to study with me?"

I told him the truth.

"Well, I know you're the best. You basically invented the Method, along with Stanislavsky, and I want to be a great actress, so why wouldn't I come to you, the master? But here's the thing. I really don't have the money to take your classes. I already have a scholarship at another acting school with Allan Miller, who studied with you and teaches your Method. And I'm actually quite happy there."

That was an interesting moment for me. I wasn't intimidated at all. I realized I actually didn't *need* anything from him. It was just that I had so much respect for his knowledge. I've always wanted to learn.

"So I guess I really just wanted to meet you and talk to you about life . . . and music . . . and art."

He looked at me as if I were nuts. Needless to say, I didn't get in.

I thought about it afterward. Didn't he find me interesting?

Guess not.

I saw a notice about a play called *The Insect Comedy* and went to the audition at the Jan Hus Playhouse, part of a community center at a church on East Seventy-Fourth Street. The play was written by two Czech brothers, Josef and Karel Čapek, back in 1921, and it was this weird, surreal piece about insects acting like humans, and of course you were supposed to draw all kinds of parallels. I played a butterfly in the first act and a moth in the second. Terry Leong did the costumes, and he took a sketch I drew of a blouse with long, wide sleeves, like a butterfly's wings, and made it out of lavender silk for me.

And that's where I met Barry Dennen, who was also in the cast (and spelling his name Barré at the time). I was drawn to him. He was smart. He spoke

French. He was twenty-two years old and quite knowledgeable about all sorts of things. He even knew how to cook, which was a huge plus for me. He lived in a studio apartment on West Ninth Street in Greenwich Village in a building with a canopy and a doorman, so I was impressed. To a girl from the projects, this was the Ritz!

Barry had a vast collection of old records from the 1930s and '40s, and he played all this great music for me . . . Lee Wiley singing "I've Got Five Dollars," Ruth Etting singing "Love Me or Leave Me," Helen Morgan singing "Why Was I Born?"

Barry came into my life at exactly the right time, with exactly the right music. Now, how unlikely is that?

I was about to go off in a new direction, even though I didn't know it quite yet.

I really responded to these songs, in a way that I never did to the latest hits on the radio. I wanted to know more about them, so I looked them up and found out they all came from Broadway shows. Maybe that's why I liked them . . . because they were sung by a character and came out of a story. The song was not just a song. The play gave it more context and meaning.

I remember listening to Lee Wiley sing "Stormy Weather" and thinking, *Who wrote that song?* It's so dramatic. I found out it was Harold Arlen, and when I looked him up I realized he had composed all these songs I had heard at the movies and loved, like "Somewhere Over the Rainbow" from *The Wizard of Oz* and "The Man That Got Away" from *A Star Is Born*.

I thought, *This man is a genius.* His music seemed to capture all the angst I felt inside. It had real emotional substance because, as I again discovered, so much of it was also written for Broadway shows.

I wanted to go to the source, so I tracked down cast albums from those shows . . . like Arlen's 1954 *House of Flowers*, based on a short story by Truman Capote. Here was this Jewish composer, the son of a cantor, writing the most extraordinary musical set in Haiti. Arlen and his fellow songwriters, George and Ira Gershwin, knew how to find those minor notes that touch the heart and seem to come from deep within, out of pain and sadness . . . like the dark, haunting melodies that were the essence of Hebraic music, gospel, and the blues.

I always related to music like that, and there was one particular song on that album that really touched me . . . "A Sleepin' Bee." I liked it because it was a song you could act. It told a story. Emotionally, you could go from A to B to C, and that intrigued me.

And it's not as if I was getting much of a chance to act onstage. *The Insect Comedy* lasted only three nights. (I guess no one wanted to see a play about two beetles debating capitalism.) After it closed, I couldn't find another acting job. I must have read in *Show Business* that they were looking for a girl to play the part of Liesl in the touring company of *The Sound of Music*. So I sent a picture and résumé to Eddie Blum, who was the head of casting for Rodgers and Hammerstein. Months later, when I had already forgotten about it, I got a call from Blum.

"I want to meet the girl who had the nerve to send out such a terrible picture," he said. Looking back on it now, I have to admit he was right. I was wearing a plain white cotton dress that used to belong to Anita and staring straight ahead . . . no smile . . . no personality. I didn't know that you were supposed to smile. I had fallen out of the habit . . . for two years I had been keeping my mouth shut so that people wouldn't see the gaps in my teeth.

I was always told, "You're so serious." And it's true. I usually kept to myself and just did my work. I didn't have much fun. I didn't know *how* to have fun. My family never had fun . . . we didn't go on outings . . . we never went anywhere.

I stood in front of Eddie and sang "A Sleepin' Bee" for him. Obviously I didn't fit the part of a young, blond Austrian girl. I suppose I looked too Jewish, which hadn't occurred to me. But Eddie was impressed, I guess, because he told me I was a really good singer and that I needed a really good pianist, and he found one for me . . . Peter Daniels, who was wonderful. (He, too, came into my life just when I needed him.) We worked together for many years after that.

Meanwhile, Susan did set off on that freighter. I chickened out at the last moment. I think part of me wanted to go with her and see the world, and the other part wanted to stay put. It felt as if things were beginning to happen for me . . . nothing so concrete as an actual job . . . but the thought that Eddie Blum was interested in me was enough to keep me afloat.

And then something went wrong on Susan's freighter after a few days out at sea, and it had to turn around and come back to port. I thought, *Whoa, it's lucky I didn't go*. I was upset for her . . . she ran out of money and had to move back home. But I admired her initiative . . . she was an adventurer.

I advertised for another roommate, but the girl who moved in came onto me, which scared the hell out of me. I moved out in a hurry, leaving her my fish tank and all my furniture, and my mother's silverware, which she wasn't happy about.

I went back to Brooklyn, where my mother and Rozzie were living in the same project but in another building. I had my own room with a closet, which was a big improvement over our former apartment, and a Victrola. (I know it's called a record player, but it will always be a Victrola to me. I still say "icebox" instead of "refrigerator" sometimes.) Over and over again, I would play these jazz records . . . Ornette Coleman, Stan Getz, Miles Davis . . . that I found in a Greenwich Village record store, along with records by Ma Rainey and Bessie Smith. In the supermarket they had albums on sale for $1.98, and that's where I bought Billie Holiday's *Lady in Satin* and Johnny Mathis's *Good Night, Dear Lord.* He was my favorite male singer, ever since I saw him on *The Ed Sullivan Show* when I was fifteen. He was mesmerizing, with those dark, soulful eyes and that tremulous, expressive voice. I remember thinking, *Oh my God. Isn't he the greatest?* And he could hold notes forever . . . that must have inspired me subconsciously.

I was discovering more and more classical music. I would stand there and conduct Tchaikovsky's *Romeo and Juliet* in front of the bathroom mirror, with tears streaming down my face. The story was so romantic, and the music was so beautiful. The orchestra would come to a crescendo, and suddenly I'd hear a clanking noise. Was that the radiator or a new sound in my ears? (My ear noises hadn't stopped.)

I didn't stay long in my mother's apartment. I liked my independence, and moving back home felt like a step backward. Besides, it was too inconvenient to commute to acting classes back and forth from Brooklyn. I had nowhere to go in the middle of the day.

Then Barry invited me to stay with him. There were two daybeds on either side of his studio, and I took one of them.

Let me set the record straight. Barry and I were never lovers. We were close friends. I thought he was probably gay, but then he told me he had a son, so I figured he was bisexual. At moments, there might have been some sort of sexual tension between us. But it was all very confusing. I was still so inexperienced that I didn't know what was going on. Was it Barry, or would that feeling have happened with anybody? Maybe it was just my own hormones acting up. Anyway, to explain why we were living together, we told people we were cousins.

Barry was one of the first men to pay attention to me. I didn't think much of myself, although I knew I had a decent voice and some talent as an actress. I thought I was good as Joan of Arc, really good as Medea, and brilliant as a chocolate chip. Allan made me feel I could act, and Eddie Blum told me I could sing. I had never taken singing all that seriously, but I needed a job. And nobody was interested in a teenage Medea.

Barry liked my voice, too, and he had a professional Ampex tape recorder. We made a tape of me singing "A Sleepin' Bee" and "A Taste of Honey," with him accompanying me on his guitar, and mailed it off to some important agent, who promptly lost it and sent me back an empty tape months later with a note: "Sorry. Here's a replacement."

It was Barry who told me about a club across the street called the Lion, where they had a talent contest every week. (The prize was fifty dollars, but it was the free dinner that really tempted me.) I was sitting with Cis and Harvey in their kitchen when I told them that I was going to enter this contest.

Cis asked, "What are you going to do there?"

"I'm going to sing."

"Barbara," she said, "I've known you for two years and I've never even heard you hum."

"Well," I said almost defensively, "I *can* sing."

"Okay, sing a song for us."

"I can't. I'd be too embarrassed."

"Please, just sing anything."

"Okay, but I can't look at you."

So I turned to face the wall and sang "A Sleepin' Bee." When I turned around, they both had tears running down their cheeks. I was shocked and very pleased.

Cis, Harvey, and Barry all came with me to the Lion on the night of the contest in June 1960. I was so naïve . . . I didn't even realize it was a gay bar until I noticed that Cis and I were the only women in the whole place. I told Burke McHugh, the manager of the club, that I was born in Smyrna, Turkey, because I thought that sounded interesting. I didn't want people to typecast me and have a preconceived notion of who I was just because I was born in Brooklyn.

So he introduced me as Barbara Streisand from Smyrna but he didn't pronounce Smyrna properly. He said, "Smerna." So I spoke up (just like in the yeshiva, again): "No, *Smearrrrrna*, with a rolled *r*."

I remember standing beside the piano player. (I hadn't discovered stools yet. But in fact there was no room for a stool . . . there wasn't even a stage.) I could see the audience, who were sitting at little tables and eating dinner so close I could have picked up a fork and grabbed a bite. That was a little disconcerting.

I was singing "A Sleepin' Bee" for the first time in front of all these people (even a small crowd was intimidating).

I closed my eyes (probably to shut out all those strangers looking at me) and began the song very quietly. But then, on the last line, "When my one true love, I has found," I found myself going for the octave on the word "love" . . . holding the high note and then taking a moment to really feel the emotion . . . before I finished the rest of the song.

For a minute the whole room was silent. Then everyone burst into applause.

I was startled, but it felt good. The audience was shouting for more, so I began the only other song I had prepared, "When Sunny Gets Blue," which I first heard on a Johnny Mathis album. And the applause at the end wouldn't stop.

I won the contest, which meant I was invited to compete again the next week, and also perform for the crowd a couple of nights a week. And I could have all the London broil I could eat . . . my favorite from their menu.

So I had to learn more songs, and rehearsed at the home of a piano player named Peter Howard. He was a funny little guy with thick glasses and no sense of humor. And he had a little dog named Gus, who would come into the room, look at me, then stand erect on his two hind legs and pant. I thought, *Well, at least* he's *attracted to me.*

And then I kept winning. For the second contest, I remember singing "Lullaby of Birdland" in honor of my uncle Larry, who loved that song and had sadly died of a heart attack at forty-four. He and his wife, Muriel, were always kind to me. She was very pretty, with beautiful white teeth and long red nails. Those nails made quite an impression on me as a child, and I think that's what made me want them too.

That night I was wearing my mother's Japanese silk pajama top that my uncle Harry had brought home for her from World War II. I wore it backward, with the buttons in back, so it looked more like a blouse.

Then I did something I'd never done in my life, before or since. Suddenly I found myself walking through the tables as I was singing. I don't know what got into me (I guess I was happy). It was one of those moments, like in the recording studio when I was thirteen . . . an inspiration that came out of nowhere . . . totally unplanned and unconscious. And then I never sang that song again!

My limited repertoire also included "Long Ago and Far Away" by Jerome Kern, with lyrics by Ira Gershwin, and "I've Got Five Dollars" (thank you, Lee) by Richard Rodgers, with lyrics by Lorenz Hart. I never sang those again, either, after the Lion. (Maybe I should take another look at them.)

Burke thought I was really good and arranged an audition for me at the Bon Soir, a more sophisticated supper club over on Eighth Street. I thought, *Boy, if I'm going to do this for real and sing every night, maybe I better learn some technique so I won't get hoarse.* Someone suggested a vocal coach. She was an exotic older woman named Joyce, probably in her fifties. That seemed positively ancient to me then. She looked like someone out of an old photograph album, and she taught out of her dark, musty, cluttered apartment on West Fifty-Fourth Street, surrounded by fringed pillows and Persian carpets (the real ones). It was the kind of place where you would expect to see cats.

I walked in and got straight to the point. "So, what's this singing thing you teach?"

She stared (and probably dropped any idea she might have had of going into an esoteric discussion about the mechanics of singing) and just asked me to sing something for her. I had only gotten through the first line, "When a bee lies sleeping," when she stopped me.

"No no no no no. Your pronunciation is all wrong. The vowels must be shorter in order to make a proper tone." She started talking about the roof of the mouth and how you get a better sound when the mouth forms an oval and you drop your jaw. (Huh?) "When a *beh* lies sleeping," she sang.

"But the word is *bee*."

"Dear, this is singing, not talking."

"Why can't I sing like I speak? When I say the word 'bee,' my mouth widens naturally, and now you're telling me I have to make an oval shape?"

"That's right! Put your lips together like this and say *beh*."

"But that looks funny. And it sounds funny. No one says *beh*. The word is BEE!"

That was my first and last singing lesson. What she was suggesting felt all wrong to me. I knew I had to do it my way . . . what came naturally to me.

Anyway, I was an actress first, not a singer.

Right before I auditioned at the Bon Soir, I have a vivid memory of walking down the street and thinking, *This night could change my life.* It was like a premonition. I was wearing a simple black dress with one of my favorite thrift-shop finds . . . an antique black Persian vest embroidered with silver thread.

The Bon Soir was a typical Greenwich Village nightclub . . . small, dark, and you had to walk down a flight of stairs to get in. In fact, it was so dark that the waiters carried little flashlights. The Three Flames, a jazz trio led by Tiger Haynes on guitar, was the resident band. And Larry Storch was the headliner that night. After his show, Jimmy Daniels, the emcee, announced that they had a little surprise, and I came out onto the stage . . . a *real* stage, because this was a real nightclub.

It was the first time I felt a spotlight on my face, and it was warm and comforting. And thanks to my new friend, the light, I didn't have to see the faces of the audience, because suddenly everything was black out there. I could concentrate on what I was doing as an actress with the song I had chosen . . . putting myself in the place of this young girl looking for love. I tuned out the sound of glasses clinking and started to sing, "When a bee lies sleepin' in the palm of your hand . . ."

It was easy to relate to that girl. She's met someone she might want to belong to, and when he seems to want her, she's happy. But she's still wondering if he's what he appears to be. When I hit that high note on "my one true lo-OOOVE" near the end and held it, I could hear some people clapping. And when I finished, the applause went on and on.

Whoa! That was exhilarating. I had to take a few bows, which was kind of awkward. I think I put my palms together and dipped my head, like some sort of Tibetan monk. I never really knew how to bow or what to do during the applause. I still don't. Applause makes me self-conscious. So I usually go right into the next number. I think I sang two more songs . . . I can't remember what they were . . . but I'll never forget what happened afterward. I stepped off the stage, and Larry Storch grabbed me by the arm and said, "Kid, you're gonna be a star!" Like in the movies! I was stunned. Was this really happening to me?

Then Tiger Haynes's girlfriend, a very short woman named Bea, came over to me and said, "Little girl, you got dollar signs written all over you."

Suddenly a new world opened up. I was eighteen years old and I had a contract to sing at the Bon Soir. I was hired for a two-week engagement, at $125 a week ($108 after taxes), beginning in September.

It felt so odd. I had never even been in a nightclub until I sang in one. What was I doing here? I was supposed to be onstage, playing Juliet. But I needed a job and I couldn't get one as an actress. So I might as well sing . . .

But September was a couple of months away, and now that my run at the Lion was over I needed to work. My brother, Shelly, got me a temporary job at the Ben Sackheim advertising agency, where he worked. I know he was trying to help, but I could tell he was embarrassed by me. I still dressed like a beatnik, and he made me walk in front of him on the street. I often had runs in my stockings, and he told me to change them. But I couldn't see them if they were in the back, so they didn't bother me.

So there I was, back in an office, answering the switchboard again. I put on my best secretarial voice. "Good morning. Ben Sackheim Agency." And then I'd try to connect whoever it was to the right person. But sometimes I got flummoxed with too many calls and would connect an ad man who wanted lunch to a client instead of the deli, and he'd end up asking the Chrysler rep for a pastrami sandwich.

This was the summer I met Bob Schulenberg, an old friend of Barry's who had recently moved to New York from Los Angeles. He was an artist who walked around with a sketch pad, and whenever we were together, he would draw me and made me look pretty good, so I thought he was talented. We got on immediately.

I had already been told by several people that I should get a nose job and cap my teeth. I thought, *Isn't my talent enough?* A nose job would hurt and be expensive. Besides, how could I trust anyone to do exactly what I wanted and no more? I liked the bump on my nose, but should I consider a minor adjustment . . . just straighten it slightly at the bottom and take a tiny bit off the tip?

No. It was too much of a risk. And who knew what it might do to my voice? Once a doctor told me I had a deviated septum . . . maybe that's why I sound the way I do. Besides, I liked long noses . . . the Italian actress Silvana Mangano had one, and everyone seemed to think she was beautiful.

Bob had no problem with my nose and thought my face was very interesting, just like the man at the Art Students League. He saw me with the eye of an artist, and I learned something from the way he drew me. I could see the shadows he made under my cheekbones and in the crease above the eye with his drawing pencils. I thought, *Let me try that with makeup.* So I used my eye pencils, eye shadow, and foundation to create the same effect.

One night, he glued on false lashes to define my eyes and make them look larger. Frankly, I thought they actually hid my eyes. Besides, they were uncomfortable, and I could never get them on properly. Instead, I drew black eyeliner past the outside corner of each eye, to elongate them . . . like the faces on the Egyptian mummies I had seen at the Metropolitan Museum of Art. (The Egyptian collection was my favorite part. I used to feel at home there, like I belonged. Is there such a thing as reincarnation?)

Just as I was more comfortable with music from another era, I felt the same way about clothes. My whole wardrobe was straight out of the thrift shops. I couldn't believe the beautiful clothes you could find there . . . velvet dresses from the 1920s (silk velvet, which has a totally different feeling from the velvet they use now, which is partially synthetic) . . . an elegant turn-of-the-century coat made of Battenberg lace . . . a printed taffeta bed jacket. The quality and craftsmanship were so much better than anything I had ever seen in Abraham & Straus. And everything was so inexpensive! They also had a pair of wonderful Edwardian shoes with beads embroidered onto the leather. (Can you imagine?)

Someone must have loved all these things, because they had been so well cared for. They stood the test of time. I never thought twice about wearing them, even though they were secondhand. I figured that the people who owned them were wealthy, so therefore their hand-me-downs were clean. Going to the thrift shops was like a treasure hunt, and I still have most of my finds today. They're like old friends from the past.

In August I was liberated from the switchboard when I got an acting job, and I think everyone at the ad agency was relieved when I left (my brother most of all). Lonny Chapman, who taught at my acting school, asked if I wanted to be in a summer-stock production of *The Boy Friend*, although I found out later it was only because another girl had dropped out. Even so, I happily went up to the Cecilwood Theatre in Fishkill, New York. It was my first musical, and I played Hortense . . . pronounced "Or-tahnse" . . . the French maid, so all that fooling around with accents came in handy. And whenever I wasn't onstage, I was planning my show for the Bon Soir.

Harold Arlen's *House of Flowers* had given me a good start, but I wanted to explore all sorts of possibilities. So I listened to as many Broadway cast albums as I could find. I gravitated to those songs because they had a story behind the lyric that I could hang on to as an actress. And if I thought of each song as a miniature three-act play with a beginning, a middle, and an end, singing suddenly became more interesting to me. I could use all the techniques I had learned in acting class . . . concentration . . . personal identification with the words . . . using a sense memory to bring up an emotion.

I was searching for songs that spoke to me, and I needed to see the sheet music to look at the lyrics. Someone told me that publishers give sheet music for free to professional singers, but I knew they wouldn't recognize my name. So I asked my mother to call and pretend she was Vaughn Monroe's secretary (he was popular at the time). She'd say, "Mr. Monroe is thinking about singing such-and-such song," and lo and behold, they sent the sheet music right over!

It was the perfect illustration of something Goethe said, which I've always loved: "At the moment of commitment, the entire universe conspires to assist you." And I had committed to giving this singing thing a try.

The Bon Soir was part of the nightclub circuit, and the entertainment was the draw. That meant there'd be a notice in the papers, maybe a sign outside. That's when I started thinking about my name.

I never really liked the name Barbara. When I was a kid, playing secretaries with a friend, I called myself Sydney. I liked men's names . . . Sydney Streisand . . . that had a nice alliteration. Samantha was my other favorite name (I eventually used it for my dear dog).

And then there was the question of Streisand. Various people, like casting agents, were always suggesting I change it. They wanted something simpler . . . Barbara Strand or Sands . . . but that felt phony. Plus, how would my old friends know it was me, once I became famous?

Then it occurred to me that I could just take out that middle *a* in Barbara. Now I'd be Barbra . . . that was different and unique. I liked the way it looked too . . . and down deep I would still be the same Barbara Joan Streisand, if you see what I mean.

Because I couldn't change Streisand, even though everybody has always mispronounced it. They say "Stryzand" or "Stryzin," but why are they saying a *z* if there's no *z* there? You'd think people would see "sand" and pronounce it with a soft *s*, like sand on the beach . . . but they don't. Maybe I should have changed the spelling to "Strysand" with a *y*, but I didn't like the look of that. So I just figured I'd keep it as it always was.

On opening night at the Bon Soir, September 9, 1960, I was third on the bill, after the Three Flames and a comedy act by two guys named Tony and Eddie. Phyllis Diller was the headliner, so she would be the last to perform. Peter Daniels was playing for me by now, and I think my first song was Fats Waller's "Keepin' Out of Mischief Now" . . . a mischievous song, witty and provocative. I switched tempos when I felt like it and played with the melody. And the band would chime in: "Oh, yeah!" It was fun to sing.

I remember exactly what I wore that first night . . . another one of my thrift-shop treasures . . . a high-necked, long-sleeved top from the turn of the century. The black-velvet bodice was boned, so it had a beautiful shape . . . and it laced up in the back. How smart! You could tie it as tight as you liked or loosen it, depending on what you ate for dinner. And it was embroidered with the most beautiful cut-steel beads that would glint in the spotlight (later I noticed more than a few had fallen on the floor). Who knew that one day I'd be wearing clothes from the same period in *Hello, Dolly!* But to me, at this moment, it wasn't a costume. It was a work of art, and I wanted to share it with the audience. I had my friend Terry Leong make me a short black-velvet skirt to go with it. So I was juxtaposing the contemporary with the antique, to give it a modern twist. Then, to finish off the look, I wore a pair of antique ivory satin shoes with a square black buckle in front, made of more cut-steel beads in the shape of a butterfly.

My set list that night also included "A Sleepin' Bee," "I Want to Be Bad," "When Sunny Gets Blue," "Lover, Come Back to Me," and "Nobody's Heart Belongs to Me." I tried to put them together in a way that flowed musically, lyrically, and emotionally. I was always conscious of not wanting to bore the audience, not to mention myself. I wanted the evening to have rhythm and pace, so I might move from a quiet, pensive ballad to a more up-tempo piece. And since I had picked songs that fed me as an actress, I could sense the audience being pulled along with me. It was a new and heady feeling, to realize I could change their mood along with mine.

I'd been trying to figure out what I could do that would be unexpected. And then it came to me. In a sophisticated club like this, wouldn't it be fun to sing a children's song? Something completely offbeat and silly.

Barry suggested "Who's Afraid of the Big Bad Wolf?" I looked at the words, which I had never paid any attention to before, and thought, *I can do something with this.* The wolf was after three poor little pigs, and my heart went out to them. I happen to love pigs. They've got those funny flat noses, and they're very smart. (I collect all sorts of little pig tchotchkes. Too many.)

I launched into the song that night with all the tra-la-las and huffs and puffs, and when I was finished, the audience roared with laughter. I walked off the stage while they were still clapping and went into the narrow dressing room (more like a closet) I shared with Phyllis Diller, who told me that every hair on her body stood up as soon as I hit my first notes.

When I took off my antique shoes (too precious to wear on the street), I was shocked. Even though they were fifty years old, they had been practically pristine when I put them on. But now the leather inside was burned almost black, just from the heat of my body. (I kept them anyway even though I could never wear them again.)

The show was over.

I was starving. Bob and Barry took me to the Pam Pam, our usual spot. It was open twenty-four hours a day, and they served the best baked potato, very well done so it was crispy on the outside and soft inside, just the way I like it. And they had a great medium-rare hamburger. The guys were in a mood to celebrate, but I immediately asked them for notes. I wanted to know what I could do to improve my performance.

On the second night, I wore a gorgeous Victorian combing jacket, made of fine white cotton trimmed with ribbon and lace. It was the kind of thing Victorian ladies would put on over a nightgown or a dress while they were brushing their hair, to protect their clothes. The original ribbon was frayed, so I had threaded a new pink satin ribbon through the lace to match a pair of pink satin shoes from the 1920s. They had the most charming buckles, with a bit of the pink satin gathered up inside them like a rose. My mother was in the audience that night, and after the show she asked me why I was singing in my underwear.

Her comment on my performance this time was, "Your voice isn't strong enough. You should drink a guggle-muggle." That was a horrible concoction she used to make for me with warm chocolate milk and a raw egg, to fatten me up.

Luckily, the reviews didn't agree with her.

> *"A startlingly young, stylish and vibrant-voiced gamin named Barbra Streisand is one of the pleasures of a club called the Bon Soir."*
>
> —*The New York Times*

> *"The Bon Soir has swung into the new nightclub season with the find of the year. She is Barbra Streisand, a Brooklynite whose voice and poise belie her scant eighteen years."*
>
> —*New York World-Telegram*

> *"She's never had a singing lesson in her life, doesn't know how to walk, dress, or take a bow, but she projects well enough to close her act with a straight rendition of 'Who's Afraid of the Big Bad Wolf' and bring down the house."*
>
> —Dorothy Kilgallen

That was great, but the good stuff went right by me, and I focused on the bad. In fact, I didn't even remember any of those compliments from the critics until recently, when I looked in an old scrapbook my mother kept. (It's coming in very handy now.) At the time, all I registered was that some of the reviewers mentioned my vintage clothes as if they were a gimmick.

What? I thought those clothes were beautiful, and frankly, they were all I could afford. But I didn't want them to be distracting. Phyllis Diller was so sweet about it and said I needed a proper evening dress to sing in. She took me shopping and bought me an expensive cocktail dress. But I didn't know who I was in an outfit like that. It felt wrong on me.

How could I tell her? She had been so kind, and I was worried about hurting her feelings. But if I wasn't going to wear it, she'd certainly notice, so I had to explain. I asked her if she'd mind if I returned the dress and used the money to buy fabric and have something made. She understood completely. What a relief!

Meanwhile, my two-week booking was extended again and again until it turned into eleven weeks. I was enjoying myself. Peter Daniels knew just how to follow me on the piano. Tiger Haynes and Averill Pollard (who played bass) still laughed at my jokes, and I loved how they called me "Baby." By now I had begun to improvise, chatting with the audience between songs, and they were laughing too. I was using reality . . . letting the audience in on what I was thinking and feeling. This was a discovery. After years of being told I was "too serious," I finally thought, *Oh, maybe I* am *funny. Great. I can use this too.*

One night, I came on to do my first song and forgot that I still had gum in my mouth. So I stuck it on the microphone stand, and it got a big laugh. Then sometimes I would repeat that, when I felt like being funny.

I wasn't scared to sing in front of people anymore. It was only later, when I became more successful, that I got more and more frightened. I had nothing to lose when I was young.

FOUR

The Bon Soir

I was starting to develop a following. I heard that people were apparently coming to the Bon Soir just to see me. Frankly, I found this hard to believe, but the club was full every night. The only reason I left in November was that another singer, Felicia Sanders, had already been booked. Tiger Haynes told me that she had sung with the big bands back in the 1940s, and when she did a certain song, a tear would run down her cheek on exactly the same note every night. *Wow*, I thought, *how does she do that?*

Why would you want to?

It was so different from the way I worked. I'm not the kind of performer who can cry on cue. First of all, I never knew where or even *if* the emotion was going to come in any particular song. Each night I tried to sing it as if I were singing it for the first time. I phrased it differently or hit different notes, depending on my mood.

It's amazing how much notice I got singing in this little club. There was even a mention in *Variety*: "Cameo-faced chantoosie Barbra Streisand . . . has a warm and sharp set of pipes." "Cameo-faced" . . . I think that was a compliment. And I acquired an agent, Irvin Arthur. He worked with Joe Glaser's agency, the Associated Booking Corporation. Joe had represented Billie Holiday and Louis Armstrong, so that sounded good to me. Now Irvin would be my agent for clubs. I liked Irvin. He had had polio as a child and walked with a cane.

Irvin recommended me to Ted Rozar, who came in to see me one night and introduced himself backstage as "the only Gentile manager in the business." That got my attention . . . at least he had a sense of humor. He took me out for dinner to a fancy restaurant with red-velvet chairs and white tablecloths. That was new. My idea of a restaurant was one of those Irish places on Eighth Avenue with dark leather booths and good corned beef and cabbage. Or I'd go to the Greek place for egg-and-lemon soup and spanakopita.

Those red-velvet chairs sealed the deal for me. I thought, *I might as well sign with him . . . at least he'll pay for some of my meals.*

So now I had two professionals working for me, and what did they come up with?

Nothing. Absolutely nothing. For months. It was disturbing to be out of a job again. I couldn't believe I had no other offers.

Finally Irvin got me a booking at the Caucus Club in Detroit, opening on March 2. I packed my bags as if I were going off into the wilderness . . . who knew if they had a decent drugstore in Detroit? And I got on the train. I had never been anywhere, except the Catskills and my great-aunt Gussie's place in Connecticut for a few days when I was about five. I have a picture of me with the two dogs on the property . . . Jeff and Snuffy. People didn't have dogs where I came from, in those small Brooklyn apartments.

And now I was going to a strange city all by myself, where I would be living in a hotel! It was thrilling, even though the Hotel Wolverine in downtown Detroit wasn't exactly luxurious. But I had my own bed and my own bathroom and my own closet and my own dresser. I'd never had a dresser before . . . not to mention a bathroom that I didn't have to share with other people.

The Caucus Club was supposed to be Detroit's equivalent of New York's '21' Club . . . where I had never been, so I had no idea if it was true (it wasn't), and it was more of a restaurant than a nightclub. Everything was à la carte, and a hamburger cost $2.20, which I thought was ridiculously high. The room where I sang wasn't really designed for entertaining. There was a column in the middle, and I would sit on a stool in front of the piano and lean one way for one song . . . and then on the next song lean the other way, so each side of the room got to see me.

My wardrobe may not have been quite up to local standards. I owned three dresses, which made life simple. It didn't take much time to figure out what to wear. (Kind of like now, where I basically wear the same loose black top and pants every day.) One of them was a long woolen knit, like a tube, that I would roll up from the bottom or down from the top, to make it look a little different from night to night, or even song to song.

But my major problem was the piano player. There was no money to bring Peter Daniels with me from New York, so I had to work with the club's regular pianist. This guy looked at me strangely. We had no rapport, and he was surprised that I knew so few songs. But since I was expected to do several shows a night and I don't like to bore myself, I needed a few more. So once again I turned to my favorite composer, Harold Arlen, and found "Right as the Rain" and "I Had Myself a True Love." Then we added "Lorelei," by the Gershwins. But it was like pulling teeth to get him to come up with an interesting arrangement. He wasn't inventive, like Peter.

Peter and I just understood each other musically, and he could play chords that spoke to my soul and resonated deep within me. I've always gravitated toward music with an edge . . . notes next to each other that don't normally go together, so you get a rub. It's the kind of dissonance you hear in Bartók's Violin Concerto no. 1 (which I also bought at the supermarket) and Mahler's Symphony no. 10, another of my favorites.

But this guy's chords were conventional . . . ordinary . . . dull. Maybe he had had too pleasant a childhood. There was no angst in the way he played. The depth was missing. He didn't hear what I was hearing, and I couldn't explain it to him since I couldn't read music . . . and still can't. I don't know how to describe a chord in musical terms. I just hear the notes in my head. I can't name them. But that didn't matter to Peter. He'd play various combinations until we found the right one.

I'd say, "That's it! That's the chord, but it's missing one note."

And then I'd sing that note.

And when he put it into the chord, I'd say, "That's it! That's what I hear."

And then I'd ask, "What is that note?" And he'd explain, "It's an E with a flatted fifth. You always seem to want to hear the ninth or the eleventh . . . the odd note . . . instead of the typical notes in a conventional chord."

Whatever. I still don't understand it. Luckily, Peter did.

The piano player in Detroit also didn't want to play the charts that Peter had written. Either his ego was too big . . . or too small. Probably he didn't know a good thing when he heard it. The one nice thing he did was put me into a cat food commercial (an experience I used for Esther Hoffman when we made *A Star Is Born*). I still get a check every year for about fourteen dollars (at least I'll never go hungry again).

In those days I was always late. I'd dash into the club three minutes before I had to be on, drop my coat, and run onstage. But once I was on, I could think very, very clearly. I felt calmer onstage than in real life. Onstage, I was in control. When I'm performing, I'm not rushed. I could take my time, and the audience just had to adjust to my pace.

Les Gruber, the owner of the club, had told me that it would be nice if I sat down and talked to the customers. He wanted me to be friendly, even though schmoozing with strangers wasn't my thing. I had never done that at the Lion or the Bon Soir. If someone wanted to talk to me, they had to come backstage. But there was no backstage at the Caucus Club. I'm not even sure there was a dressing room.

It's funny, me spending all this time in a nightclub, because it's not somewhere I would normally be. I don't drink and I wasn't very sociable. If some man offered to buy me a drink, I would say, "I'd prefer a baked potato," and that often put an end to the conversation. Still, I managed to make many good friends there, like Bernie Moray, who ran Robinson's Furniture Company, and Dick Sloan, who owned a chain of movie theaters. It seemed a lot of business was transacted over plates of Dover sole at the club, and these guys were regulars. They were older . . . well, in their late thirties, which seemed old to me. Bernie was married and so was Dick, I think. They just happened to be kind and supportive, along with another couple, Bobby and Marilyn Sosnick. Those four were like family to me, and the Sosnicks invited me to their house for dinner many times. Between sets, I also hung out with Neil Wolfe, who played piano in the cocktail lounge. He was a very sweet guy with thick, wavy hair who was madly in love with a blond girl who looked like Kim Novak, and he talked about her constantly. He was really nice to me, and we became fast friends.

I also met a very elegant lady named Doris Fisher, who wore beautiful clothes and had a splendid apartment. But what impressed me most was that she had written the song "Put the Blame on Mame," sung by Rita Hayworth in the movie *Gilda*.

Once I had my songs down, I had a lot of free time. I can't recall much about Detroit's cultural sites, but I do remember the racetrack. I would bet two dollars . . . just picking a horse by instinct. I knew nothing about horses, but I often won! So I'd get six dollars for the two dollars. At least I was making a profit! You could also rent a horse in the park on Belle Isle, and that's where I learned how to ride. Put it this way . . . I learned how to sit on a horse while it walked around slowly, occasionally nibbling a few leaves off a tree. It was nice to be a bit closer to the sky.

I was just settling into Detroit when I had to leave unexpectedly. Ted Rozar also had Orson Bean as a client, and Orson was going to be guest-hosting *The Jack Paar Show* and agreed to have me on. That's how I made my first television appearance on April 5, 1961. It was also my first plane ride . . . I had to fly from Detroit to New York because there was no time to take the train. And I was terrified because of my ear noises. Would my eardrums pop? Would blood pour out? Would I be deaf for the rest of my life?

I took the chance and survived that flight. Actually I enjoyed it, because the coach section had terrific food on those little plastic trays. (I've always liked miniatures.)

I was clothed for my appearance by the Robinson Furniture Company, as I announced on the show. Bernie had given me a tour of the showroom, where I noticed a couch upholstered in some lovely burgundy damask and said, "This would make a great dress." So he gave me some of the fabric. (Actually, it was the same color as the drapes in my dining room now, also made out of burgundy damask. Some things never change.) I mailed Bernie's fabric to New York, along with a sketch, and Terry Leong made it for me. He already had my measurements. And I bought a beautiful pair of satin shoes from this fabulous store called Fiorentina and had them dyed to match. They cost forty dollars . . . a huge splurge for me.

On the night before the show, I slept at my brother's house on Long Island because he asked me to. His wife, Ellen, was about to give birth, and he wanted me to come with him to the hospital the next morning, where she was scheduled to have a C-section. But everything got too hectic, and I couldn't sit beside him and wait for my niece, Erica, to be born because I had to pick up my shoes and get to the studio for a rehearsal.

When I walked into the store, who should be sitting in a chair trying on some shoes but that Faye woman, the casting agent who had shown me the door when I went to audition for a TV walk-on.

"What are *you* doing here?" she asked when she noticed me, clearly surprised to see me in this exclusive shop.

"Well, I'm on *The Jack Paar Show* tonight and I'm picking up my shoes. What are *you* doing here?"

It was an extremely satisfying moment.

I don't even think I was nervous that night. I was just singing my song, "A Sleepin' Bee," which I'd already done a hundred times before. And I felt wonderful in my upholstery-fabric dress and those elegant Fiorentina shoes. I was five foot five and weighed 110 pounds . . . still very skinny. I used to take a couple of scarves and stuff one on each side of my underwear to fill out my hips. Not in back. I already had a big tush. Then I changed into a simple black sheath for my second number, "When the Sun Comes Out." The audience was still applauding when Orson waved me over to join him and the other guests.

I was overjoyed that night . . . genuinely excited . . . and that's the truth. Phyllis Diller was also on the show, and that made me feel very comfortable. Bernie and Dick had sent flowers to my dressing room, and I got to thank them on air. I knew they were watching. It was thrilling. I sat down, gushing about all the cameras and the lights because I was completely fascinated by them . . . so this is how they put on a TV show. I was sitting under the hot lights, but my hands were cold, as I said to Orson, and Phyllis gave me her gloves to warm them.

When I flew back to Detroit, Les Gruber gave me a bonus because he was so pleased at the free publicity for his restaurant on national TV. And he extended my run.

After eight weeks in Detroit, I took the train to St. Louis, where I was booked into the Crystal Palace, a nightclub owned by Jay Landesman, who was willing to take a chance on young talent. His wife, Fran, was a lyricist, and she showed me one of her songs, "Spring Can Really Hang You Up the Most." Of course spring to me means allergies. But this song had a haunting melody and a lovely lyric, and it became part of my repertoire. I liked the Landesmans and their nightclub, which was the fanciest I had ever been in . . . stained-glass windows, antique chandeliers, red-velvet upholstery. They put me up in an apartment right above the club with beautiful old wood, marble sinks, and a tiled fireplace. I never wanted to leave.

I was the opening act for the Smothers Brothers and another comedian, Marc London. I used to stand in the back after I had sung my songs and watch Dick and Tommy work. I thought Tommy was very funny, acting like a six-year-old to his straight-man older brother. I really identified with that kind of innocence. The child was still so much a part of me. I found myself attracted to his talent . . . he knew how to get the laughs . . . and he was sort of cute in a WASPy way with that close-cropped blond hair and pale skin.

I was experimenting with a new, contemporary song . . . "Soon It's Gonna Rain" from *The Fantasticks*, another show I had tried out for and didn't get. It was an offbeat musical, and the character who sang the song was sixteen. At the time I thought, *I'm sixteen and I'm offbeat. Why didn't I get that job?*

I remember seeing it at the Sullivan Street Playhouse and being impressed with the simple, sparse set . . . a wooden platform, a quarter moon painted on a circle of cardboard that reversed to become the sun. All the focus was on the story. And the accompaniment to the songs was just a harp and a piano . . . what a wonderful combination. (Many years later the producer, Lore Noto, told me, "I can't believe we didn't hire you.")

In the show, "Soon It's Gonna Rain" was a simple, innocent song sung by two young people who are falling in love and looking forward to the rain so they can go inside and be together. But I interpreted it in very personal terms. I identified with that girl. In the beginning, she's shy . . . tentative . . . but when the rain comes, I chose to have the music build . . . the drums roll . . . as her emotions build. It's her sexual awakening. Then, instead of ending where the song ends, I went back to the beginning and sang the first two lines with new knowledge and a feeling of joy and pride, as if she's at last become a woman. And the song ends on a high note . . . like a release. She got her wish and experienced love or sex, whatever you want to believe.

When I try to describe it, the process sounds so analytical, but it's really more intuitive. I was just in touch with my feelings and tapping into the part of me that related to the lyrics of the song.

Sometimes it seemed very strange to be standing in a nightclub singing all these songs about love when I knew so little about it.

In May I went back to New York and back to the Bon Soir, where they wanted me again for a month's engagement. This time I was opening for the comedian Phil Leeds, and Renée Taylor was the headliner. I thought she was very funny. One night she lost a cap from a tooth . . . it flew right out onto the stage. That made me laugh, which was not very nice of me.

But that's the kind of thing that gets me, when for a moment a person's dignity is undone . . . there's a crack in the façade, and you see straight to the vulnerability we all share. We're all pretending to be so civilized, so in control, but we're not.

Otherwise, it's not easy to make me laugh. I don't think most things are funny. My husband will tell a joke and everybody around the table laughs, except me. I'll say, "What's funny about that?" And sit there, trying to analyze it. Then, when something in a TV show or a movie is genuinely funny, I'll say, flatly, "That's funny."

I take comedy very seriously.

One night I had just finished my set and was heading for the dressing room . . . if you can call it that, since there was barely any room to get dressed, or undressed. I was sharing it with Renée. She was getting ready to go on and I had just closed the door behind me when I heard a knock. It was a man, and I stepped outside to talk to him. He immediately began to compliment me, saying, "I got chills as soon as you started singing."

"I'm not a singer, really," I told him. "I'm an actress, and I'm only doing this because no one will hire me to act."

"If you're as good an actress as you are a singer, then there's no stopping you. I just saw you do comedy, drama. You made me laugh, you made me cry. I think you have a big career ahead of you . . . records, television, theater, movies."

"I've always wanted to be a movie star," I admitted.

"Well, Barbra, I have the feeling you're going to win every award in this business, first time out of the box . . . the Grammy, the Emmy, the Tony, the Oscar."

How amazing . . . it was as if this man I had just met was validating all my dreams.

He asked if I had anyone to represent me, and when I said that I already had a manager, he didn't push it. Instead he was very sweet and polite. He simply handed me his business card and said that if I ever needed anything, any help in any way, to please give him a call.

That's how I met Marty Erlichman, who had come to the club to see his friend Phil Leeds. But as soon as he heard me sing he forgot about Phil and came straight backstage to find me. He ended up missing Phil's act entirely.

I felt comfortable with Marty from that first moment. He was like a guy from my old neighborhood . . . dark hair, glasses, kind face, a bit chubby. Turns out he grew up near me in Brooklyn. We spoke the same language.

It felt good to be back in New York, except for one small inconvenience . . . I had no apartment, since I was no longer living with Barry. It started to go wrong when he went home to California to see his parents. On the night he was scheduled to return, I had bought all his favorite things at the deli and set out a feast to surprise him. But he didn't show up. I was worried. Had his plane crashed? And then he didn't appear the next night . . . or the next . . . and no phone call.

Eventually, after about a week, he nonchalantly walked in the door. I was furious. Turns out he had just decided to stay longer but couldn't be bothered to call and let me know. Apparently his parents weren't aware that I was sharing his apartment, and he didn't want the number to show up on their bill. Come on . . . was he that intimidated by his parents? Couldn't he have found some way to get in touch with me? His story didn't make sense.

And then I came home early one night, and ran into a strange guy with a towel wrapped around his waist coming out of the bathroom. That was a shock, and I remember thinking, *Oh my God, I shouldn't be here.* Barry had never brought anyone home before . . . how could he, with me living there? Of course he was gay, and he had a whole other life that didn't include me. Somehow I had thought that since we got along so well, we could just continue with our roommate arrangement. But now I realized I was in the way.

I turned around and walked out the door. I called my friend Elaine Sobel from the street and went straight to her apartment.

I was upset, which in hindsight seems unfair, since I had no claim on Barry.

We weren't romantically involved . . . we had never even kissed. Still, I guess I felt rejected. Maybe it took me back to that moment as a child, watching Laurel and Hardy with my friend Irving, when suddenly his father walked in and I had to leave.

I wanted a relationship like the ones I saw in the movies, built on mutual love and respect and kindness. And I realized I was not helping myself by living with someone who could not really be a partner. I wanted more.

Barry and I remained friends, but later, after he refused to return some tapes of me singing, I just put him out of my life. I can do that with people who disappoint me. It's not one of my finest qualities. I can build a wall and shut them out.

But at this point, he was one of the few men I knew, and I didn't understand any of them. Eddie Blum, the casting director for Rodgers and Hammerstein, was someone I considered a friend. I'll always be grateful to him for encouraging me. Once he invited me up to his country house for a weekend, and I met his petite blond wife and his daughter. It was fun to sit beside him and drive his Caterpillar tractor through the fields. Lee J. Cobb was his neighbor, and that impressed me . . . I had been a big admirer of his talent ever since I had seen him in *On the Waterfront*. I really liked Eddie, until he came to see me in Detroit and made a pass at me. What? He was old enough to be my father!

One last thing about Barry. I'll always be grateful to him for believing in me when I was a teenager. But in 1997, he wrote a book about me and made up this crazy love affair between us (maybe he thought he needed to spice up our friendship to sell more copies). I was so hurt I couldn't even read it.

It's odd, to say the least, to hear about various men who claim to have been my first lover . . . especially when I have no idea who they are. Listen, I know I've forgotten a few things, but this isn't one of them!

It wasn't Barry, and it certainly wasn't some guy in my acting class who apparently talks about our nonexistent romance in several of the unauthorized biographies that have been written about me. I've never read these books because I can't stand the lies. But some people I know have read them, and things get back to me, like what this guy said. And I was dumbfounded. I can't even imagine who he might be. I don't remember his name, so I called Allan Miller, who was teaching the class, and he doesn't remember him either! Trust me, I wish there had been some handsome, talented student who was interested in me . . . and who interested *me*.

The idea that someone could make up a story about a romance with me . . . well, it's disgusting. It feels like such a profound invasion of my life. And then the story gets perpetuated in book after book, because the people who write them just keep recycling the same made-up junk.

Here's the truth. I was eighteen when I had my first love affair . . . although to call it a love affair seems like a stretch of the imagination. This man and I had a few interesting evenings together. On a night with a full moon, he handed me a cigarette, and I took a puff and went weak in the knees. I thought it was him. Turns out it was marijuana, which I had never smoked before (and rarely after). One thing led to another . . . I'm not going to go into details. Use your imagination.

The next day when we ran into each other he just said "Hi" and kept going, as if nothing had ever happened between us. So that was that. Not exactly *From Here to Eternity*. Once again, I felt unseen.

God, I hated him for not being kinder. But it started my wheels spinning. Some nights I felt like a cat in heat . . . my body ached for him . . . feelings I had never experienced before. At least it gave me some more material to work with when I did *The Jack Paar Show* for the second time, on May 22. Orson Bean was guest-hosting again and invited me back. When I sang about wanting someone, for the first time I actually understood it.

After the taping, I stood in Cis's kitchen and dialed my aunt Anna's number on the wall phone. The show was airing in a few hours and I wanted to make sure she watched it. There's a song in *Yentl* that begins with the line: "There are moments you remember all your life," and this was one of them. Someone answered the phone and I was told that my beloved aunt had died, in my uncle Harry's arms. She had come home from the hospital after a routine hysterectomy and developed an embolism.

It felt like every time I went on TV, something happened to the people I loved. The first time, my niece Erica was born. And now, my favorite aunt was gone. I was heartbroken. She was the mother of two boys, Lowell and Harvey, and she was always eager for me to visit. I think she appreciated having a girl around. She loved me, and I loved her. We spent a lot of time together. I enjoyed sleeping over at her apartment on Eastern Parkway. Sometimes we would push the furniture aside and Lowell and I would dance to Tito Puente records. Harvey would dance with my mother. I love that Latin music . . . the samba and the mambo. Lowell and I practiced together and danced for the family at his bar mitzvah. He and his father were into baseball, and Harvey was into decorating. He would pick out fabrics for his mom. When I was six or seven, I called him a girl. He didn't speak to me for two years.

What did I know? But I was clearly picking up on something. Later Harvey came out as gay, but people didn't acknowledge feelings like that back then. I just thought it was neat that he could explain the difference between linen and velvet.

I'm not the most positive person to begin with. It's always easy for me to look on the dark side of things, and with my grief over Aunt Anna's death I began to feel frustrated with my life. It felt like I was biding my time at the Bon Soir until somebody would hire me to act. But then I'd tell myself things weren't so bad. I was earning a living. And every night was the equivalent of acting in a show. Sometimes I would stand onstage and do a relaxation exercise, like we did in class, starting with my toes and moving up to my arms and my fingers . . . directing my mind to each part of my body, sensing it and relaxing each part, one by one. I'm sure the audience had no idea what was going on.

Week to week I kept honing my performance. I was told that nobody opened with a ballad, which of course made me want to do it even more. I could close my eyes and go into my own space, moving inward rather than outward.

When I watched other performers, some of them seemed odd to me. They were so eager to please the audience, telling them how great they were, saying things like, "I only feel alive when I'm onstage." Really? They seemed so needy . . . reaching out and asking the audience to love them. It made me squirm.

Even though deep down, I might have been more needy than they were.

I just didn't believe you should show it. That didn't feel right to me. It was undignified. I didn't want to have to ask to be loved. That was too embarrassing. For me, the secret is not to reach out. That's futile. Instead you have to reach in. And I discovered that the more I turned inward the more the audience was drawn to me.

That's the power of thought. It not only transcends matter, it also communicates . . . if it's truthful. In other words, you can't fake emotion. Everything has to come from a place of truth, deep within yourself. And then other people will respond and identify with you.

Sometimes, if I wasn't feeling anything, I just had to accept that. And then I would be still, and concentrate. When I first sang "Cry Me a River," I used one of the exercises we did in class . . . evoking an emotional memory by recreating someone's face. I would think of that young man in the moonlight, handing me a cigarette. And it made me angry but from a real place. Eventually I could go straight to those emotions as soon as I began the song. My response to the music became almost Pavlovian.

Meanwhile, I still had no place of my own to sleep. Elaine offered me her couch, but Dustin Hoffman was still courting her and I didn't want to impose on them. For a while I took a room at the Hotel Earle, because it was conveniently around the corner from the Bon Soir. All the furniture was sprayed with speckled paint so you didn't notice the dirt. I remember Stanley Beck came up to my room one time. We first met in summer stock at Malden Bridge, where he directed me in *Picnic*. He was the leading man of the company, and the leading lady was Emily Cobb. (Years later I was happy to get her a small part in *The Way We Were*, handing out antiwar leaflets at a table across from the Plaza.)

Stanley and I reconnected when I went to see Jean Genet's *The Balcony* at Circle in the Square downtown, and there he was, onstage. He was a very masculine guy, kind of good-looking, and we had a few casual dates. But I was so nervous when he came to my room that I had to ask him to leave. I said I felt sick, because I wasn't ready to be physical with him. You see, I do remember the men in my life, because they were so few and far between when I was young!

A week after my Bon Soir engagement ended, I appeared as a guest on a local TV show, *PM East*, thanks to the producer, Mert Koplin, who had seen me at the club. Mert was a warm, lovely man, unlike the host, Mike Wallace, who was kind of cold and distant. He definitely did not have the typical TV host's genial personality. In fact, Mike was mean . . . which worked for him later when he was hammering questions at interview subjects on *60 Minutes*. But it was a real stretch when he tried to be charming and draw out a guest on *PM East*.

I was the one who pulled him aside before the show and said, "Listen, I don't just sing. I can talk." I showed him my key ring and said, "Why don't you ask me about all my keys?" So when I sat down with him, he said, "I have here your worldly possessions" and held up my wallet and my key ring.

"Where'd you get them?" I replied, playing along with the bit.

"And ten keys. What are all these keys to, Barbra? What do they open? You have ten pads here in New York?"

"No, not ten. I have six."

Well, six may have been a slight exaggeration, but I did have a regular circuit of places where I could camp out on the folding aluminum cot I bought for $12.95 at Whelan's Drug Store and carried around with me. My cousin Harvey had an apartment on West Eighteenth Street, which I could use during the week, since he was only there on weekends. Then on Fridays I would move to Peter Daniels's rehearsal studio on Eighth Avenue, which was empty except for a piano. But it was spooky to come in there late at night. The building was deserted and more than a bit grim.

Mike tried to make a joke of it. "So you sort of sleep all around town?"

I sleep around town but I don't sleep *around*, I explained. "You have to make the distinction."

In fact, one of the keys belonged to Don Softness, *PM East*'s press agent, who also became mine. When he heard that I had no apartment, he offered me the keys to his office, where there was a comfortable couch I could curl up on. The only condition was that I had to be out by 8:30 a.m., before his employees arrived. Little did I know that he would appear early one morning and make a pass at me. Even though I thought he was attractive, with short-cropped gray hair, I gave him back his key.

Meanwhile, I was looking for a job again. In acting class I had bonded with Rick Edelstein when we did a scene together from *The Petrified Forest*. I liked Rick. He seemed more mature than the other guys, because he was already married with four children. At night he worked as a waiter at the Village Vanguard, a well-known jazz club, and he took me there to audition for the owner, Max Gordon. Miles Davis happened to be playing there at the time, and Rick arranged for his guys to back me up. But Max Gordon didn't get me.

Just as I was running out of money, I got a job in Canada, at the Town N' Country restaurant up in Winnipeg. I don't think the Canadian audiences got me either. Especially when I would do songs they had never heard of, like "Come to the Supermarket in Old Peking."

After that, I was booked for a return engagement at the Caucus Club. That was great, but they only wanted to pay me $150 a week (same as before), and I had gotten $175 at the Bon Soir. I thought they should match that and throw in some food as well. After all, it was a restaurant. But Ted Rozar couldn't get Les Gruber to budge. I was already annoyed with Ted, and now he couldn't get me a raise.

That's when I pulled out the card I had saved from Marty Erlichman and called him. Marty said, "I'll take care of it," and immediately got on a plane to Detroit. He negotiated a new deal with Les Gruber, and suddenly I was making $200 a week, and dinners were included. I was impressed. I only found out later that even Marty couldn't get them to raise my salary, so he threw in the extra $50 a week out of his own pocket. And it's not as if he had money to burn. Marty's office at the time was a phone booth on Fifty-Third Street and a roll of dimes.

Nevertheless he stayed in Detroit, watching over me. Ted had never done that. I could see that Marty offered a whole new level of commitment. Suddenly I had a protector for the first time in my life. I wanted Marty to be my manager, which meant that somehow I had to get out of my contract with Ted.

Frankly, I don't think Ted was all that upset at the thought of losing me. But it's very human . . . you may not be interested in something, but as soon as someone else wants it, you want it too. Marty asked him what it would take to buy me out of my contract, and Ted threw out a figure . . . five thousand dollars. Meanwhile, I had stored some boxes of antique clothing in his office, and he was holding them hostage until this was settled.

While we were in Detroit, Marty became friendly with Bobby Sosnick, who was still coming to the club almost every night. They used to sit together and drink martinis. When Bobby found out that we were trying to pay off Ted and that Marty was working out of a phone booth, he handed Marty a check for ten thousand dollars, telling him to spend five thousand on me and five thousand to open up an office. He considered it an investment in my career.

Now all this was very interesting to me. How many people get to find out exactly what their price is on the open market?

I have to say, I was the tiniest bit disappointed when Marty managed to bargain Ted down from $5,000 to $1,250 and then to $750. Really? Was that all I was worth?

I think Marty and I got a bargain.

At least it meant Marty didn't need Bobby's check after all, which was good, because he didn't want to sell a piece of me, and I didn't want that either. Although there was one small problem. Marty didn't have the $750. I had forgotten this until Marty told the story at a birthday party I gave for him in 2014.

I asked, "Where did you get the money?"

He said, "Someone loaned it to me."

"Who?"

"It was you!"

Remember, I had been saving money since I opened that bank account when I was sixteen.

So, I retrieved my cartons of clothes, and that was the end of my relationship with Ted, although I was still working with Irvin Arthur. One day I went to his office, and he told me that Enrico Banducci, the owner of the hungry i club in San Francisco, was sitting in the next room, but he couldn't convince Enrico to hire me.

I decided I had to change his mind. But it's not in my nature to barge in somewhere and sell myself. The only way I could do it was if I pretended to be a whole other character. I marched in and told Enrico that he was going to be very sorry if he didn't hire me. "You'll be begging me for a contract, because I'm going to be a big star. And you could have had me early on." I did this whole number, totally scared to death. I think I even sat in his lap, which is totally unlike me . . . must have been a moment of inspiration. And I got the job! I was really proud of myself for convincing him.

Meanwhile, I was still auditioning for acting jobs. When I was singing at the Lion, I had met an agent named Jeff Hunter, who was one of the very first people to support me. He thought I had talent and was particularly impressed with what I did with my hands when I sang. Years later, he told me, "No one has ever used them as well as you do." He promised to look out for me, and if anything came up that he thought I was right for, he'd let me know. And he followed through . . . he sent me to audition for an off-Broadway production, *Another Evening with Harry Stoones*. It was written by a young guy named Jeff Harris and it was a comedy revue, with blackout sketches and some songs, which Jeff also wrote. There were eight of us in the cast, including Diana Sands, who had starred in *A Raisin in the Sun* on Broadway, and Dom DeLuise, who was just starting out. I was listed last in the program.

The whole experience was lots of fun. I got to play different characters and sing several songs . . . one was about the perils of New Jersey. I sang it in a black 1940s dress, with 1940s platform shoes. Then there was a droll comic song called "Value," in which I got to explain why I'm in love with a guy named Harold Mengert.

Who was it that said, "Satire is what closes on Saturday night"? (I just looked it up. It was George S. Kaufman.) Well, we proved him right. We opened and closed on Saturday night, October 21, 1961, after weeks of rehearsal, nine previews, and one performance.

But Jeff Hunter came to that opening night and was impressed. He sent me out to audition for another production that definitely changed my life. I will always be grateful, and indebted, to him.

I Can Get It for You Wholesale was a major Broadway show, written by Jerome Weidman, with music and lyrics by Harold Rome. Arthur Laurents, who wrote the book for *West Side Story* and *Gypsy*, was directing. The producer was David Merrick. They were all Broadway royalty, and I thought there wasn't much of a chance that they'd want to hire me.

That's my negativity, which I inherited from my mother. She always told me, "Don't count on anything good, because then God will snatch it away." And I probably used that negativity to protect myself.

I came in to audition in November. Since the play took place in the 1930s, I was wearing my 1930s coat, to put me in a period mood. It's made of karakul, the smooth honey-colored fleece of a lamb, trimmed around the collar and the hem with matching fox fur (this was before PETA). I bought it in a thrift shop for ten dollars and thought it was the most beautiful thing I had ever seen. What made it so special was that the inside was just as lovely as the outside . . . the lining was embroidered with colorful baskets of flowers, done in chenille threads, with a little pocket made of ruched silk. Somebody had to really care in order to go to all that effort for something hardly anyone would see. I loved that idea, and I still have that coat. (The lining fabric has fallen apart, but the chenille flowers are still intact.)

Someone announced my name, and I stepped out onto the bare stage at the St. James Theatre, still wearing my coat, so everybody else could appreciate it. But of course whoever was announcing my name mispronounced it, so I had to correct it. As I was explaining this, I was setting down my shopping bag. I always carried some food . . . unsalted pretzels, Oreos (but I have to remove that white guck in the middle), almonds . . . because you never know when you'll want a snack. I think that idea came from my mother. Maybe it's part of the collective unconscious of European Jews, because what if a pogrom came and you had to get across the border fast? You have to have a little something to eat until you get to the next country.

I shaded my eyes and looked out into the dark theater, but I couldn't make out any faces. "Hello! Is anyone out there? What would you like me to do?"

A voice replied. "Can you sing?"

I thought to myself, *If I couldn't sing, would I be standing here?* But I said, "I think I can sing. People tell me I can sing. What would you like to hear?"

Nobody answered quickly enough, so I said, "Do you want something fast or slow?" I was like the guy behind the counter in the deli. Order your sandwich, already! Pastrami or corned beef?

Someone said, "Anything you like."

"Well, this is a comedy, right?" I said. "So I'll do a comedy song."

I pulled my sheet music out of my shopping bag and headed over to the piano, not noticing that the pages, which were all attached and folded up like an accordion, were unfurling behind me into a long, twenty-foot tail. Actually, I was only pretending not to notice because I had done it deliberately. I knew I could be funny, and I thought I should show them. I heard some snickers from the audience, so it seemed to be working.

I told the accompanist, "Play the one on top," and launched into "Value":

Call me a boob, call me a schlemiel.
Call me a brain with a missing wheel.
Call me what you will, but nonetheless I'm still in love with Harold Mengert
And it's not because he has a car. Arnie Fleischer has a car.
But a car is just a car . . .

The man who was talking to me . . . who turned out to be Arthur Laurents . . . was laughing, and then he asked, "Do you have a ballad?"

"Oh yeah, I have several." I turned back to the accompanist and asked him to play "Have I Stayed Too Long at the Fair?" It was a song from another obscure show, and I loved it because it was about yearning, about wanting somebody to care, and I completely related to that.

Jerome Weidman was there that day, and later he described what happened next in a magazine article. I wish I could write so poetically. All I can say is I stood on that stage and went into my own inner world, forgetting anyone else was there.

> *"Softly, in a voice as true as a plumb line and pure as the soap that floats, with the quiet authority of someone who had seen the inevitable, as simply and directly and movingly as Homer telling about the death of Hector, she told the haunting story of a girl who had stayed 'too long at the fair.' It was a song, of course, and a good one. But emerging through the voice and personality of this strange child, it became more than that. We were hearing music and words, but we were experiencing what one gets only from great art: a moment of revealed truth."*
>
> —Jerome Weidman

There was silence after I finished the song. Then they asked me to sing another, and another.

I could hear them talking among themselves, and then Arthur stood up and asked if I could come back in a few hours.

"Why do I have to come back?" I asked. "You didn't like what you just heard?"

I think Arthur laughed and explained that David Merrick would be there later, and they wanted him to hear me.

"No. I can't come back," I told him. "I have to go to the hairdresser."

I could practically hear their shock. I was well aware that nobody would ever say no to a request to come back for another audition. And I was aware that what I had just said was funny. But it was also the truth.

"I'm opening tonight at the Blue Angel and I have to get my hair done. Hey, all of you should come!"

"Can't you come back after your appointment?" Arthur asked.

I called out to Marty, who was sitting in the back of the theater, "Marty, do I have time?"

I can just imagine him holding his head in his hands. "Yes!" he said vehemently. "Yes, you have time!"

The Blue Angel was a supper club on East Fifty-Second Street that was a step up from the Bon Soir, because it was uptown. Marty had persuaded Max Gordon, who was one of the owners, to take another look at me, and this time he hired me.

So I went to the hairdresser, and when I got back to the theater and walked onstage, I asked, "So what do you think?"

They were taken aback, assuming I was talking about my audition.

"No, my hair!" I said. "It's different. Do you like it?"

I don't think they knew what to make of me.

I sang my songs again for the group, which now included Merrick. It seemed to be going well, but I wasn't sure. There was clearly some sort of consultation going on down there in the seats. It was only years later that the stage manager, Bob Schear, told me that Merrick called him over as soon as I finished the first song and said, "Don't let her go. In fact, lock the door."

I had come in for the part of the ingénue, but now they asked if I would be willing to play the part of the lovelorn secretary, Miss Marmelstein. Arthur said they had been planning to cast the role with an older woman, but now they were rethinking it.

"Sure," I said. "Why not? After all, I'm an actress."

They gave me the music to her song and asked if I could come back the following week and sing it for them. On my way out Bob Schear stopped me to make sure he had my address and phone number.

"My address? Well, during the week I'm usually at West Eighteenth Street but then on weekends I sleep in this rehearsal studio on Eighth Avenue."

He looked confused. "Don't you have an apartment?"

"No, but I'm looking for one. I read the ads in *The New York Times* every night and I can't find an apartment that I can afford."

"I can ask my landlord," he told me. "I think there's an empty apartment in my building."

It was a tenement building at 1155 Third Avenue, near Sixty-Seventh Street, and Bob's landlord was Oscar Karp, who couldn't have been more appropriately named because he also owned the seafood restaurant, Oscar's Salt of the Sea, on the ground floor. Bob went home and talked to him that night, and it was only after Bob promised to guarantee the rent that Oscar agreed to show me the apartment. It was a third-floor walk-up, and as soon as you started up the narrow, bare-bones staircase, there was the smell of fish.

It was as if I couldn't escape that odor. My father's parents owned a fish store, and I still remember the sight and the smell of all those dead fish, packed in ice on slanted metal trays. My grandparents lived over the store, but we rarely visited, because they never liked my mother and blamed her for my father's death. (That wasn't fair.)

To this day I can only eat fish that doesn't smell.

The apartment was a railroad flat, with four little rooms in a line and a bathtub in the kitchen, and the rent was sixty dollars a month. As soon as I saw it, I said, "I'll take it." So I, too, would be living over fish. But at least food was close by, and I became good friends with Oscar.

Things were looking up. I had an apartment on the East Side of Manhattan, where I had always wanted to live . . . and that meant I was not going back to Brooklyn . . . and I had a callback for a Broadway show.

I learned Miss Marmelstein's song. When I came back to do it for Arthur and the group, I said, "I'd like to sit in a chair, if that's okay." I wanted to sing the number sitting down for two reasons: one, because I was nervous and didn't want to stand, and two, because I thought it would be funny if the secretary did her song in a secretarial chair, the kind on casters, so she could roll around the stage, pushing herself with her feet. I just saw it that way in my head.

Just before I started to sing, I remembered I had gum in my mouth and stuck it under the chair. The song seemed to go well. Everyone laughed, and Arthur said, "Thank you. We'll be in touch," or something like that.

Later I found out that Arthur had gone over to the chair after I left and tilted it, to see if the gum was still there. I guess he wanted to know if the moment had been spontaneous . . . had I really been chewing gum? Or was it just a funny bit of business that I had worked out before I got there?

Arthur says there was no gum.

Listen, I wouldn't have left my gum on their chair, spoiling their property. That's not nice. The truth is, I pulled it off before I got up and started to chew it again. There was still some flavor left in it.

FIVE

Miss Marmelstein

Before I left that audition, I remember standing on the stage and announcing, "I just got a new phone. So somebody please call me!" And I told them my number. I didn't have any furniture in the apartment yet, but I had gotten a phone installed, and I was so eager for somebody . . . anybody . . . to call me.

And somebody did. That night the phone rang, and a voice on the other end said, "I'm Elliott Gould. I was there this afternoon and I thought you were brilliant."

And then he hung up.

I had no idea who he was.

Then I found out I got the part . . . my first part in a real Broadway show.

Now, a normal nineteen-year-old would probably have been surprised and delighted, but you know by now that I was not exactly normal. I just thought it was *bashert,* as they say in Yiddish, which means "meant to be." It felt as if I were simply fulfilling the vision that I had as a child. This was my destiny . . . and I was ready to get on with it!

I don't think I was even nervous on the first day of rehearsals, which started at the beginning of January 1962, at the old Ziegfeld Roof studio, on top of the New Amsterdam Theatre. That first day is a theatrical ritual. The whole cast is assembled around a table. Everyone is introduced . . . the set designer shows a model of the set . . . the costume designer shows a few sketches. I watched and listened. They were all adults. I was still a teenager. And I was painfully shy in any sort of large group. I didn't know how to approach people or start a conversation. I was completely lacking in social skills.

We began to read the script out loud. I looked at the tall young man with dark, curly hair playing the lead . . . so that was Elliott Gould . . . the voice on the phone. He had a sweet smile and warm brown eyes. The girl playing the ingénue (the part I had initially been sent in for) was Marilyn Cooper. She was cute and petite, with the tiniest nose, and everyone called her Coopie. Her character was the romantic interest for Elliott's character, but they made an unlikely pair. When they stood next to each other, she barely came up to his chest.

Eventually we took a break, and everyone went off to have a smoke or headed to the pay phone to make calls. Elliott was smoking a thin cigar and he came over and offered me one. I had never smoked a cigar before, but I took it. Actually it was more like a brown cigarette, and the smell was rather nice. They came in a tin and were called Schimmelpennincks (all you have to do is say the name out loud and you'll know why I laughed). It was such a sweet, funny way to approach me. I instantly liked him, and we began to talk.

Before we knew it, the break was over and we headed back to the table with the rest of the cast to continue reading the script. My part wasn't that big . . . my lines were few and far between . . . so I had plenty of time to work on my bio. The press agent had asked us to put something together for the *Playbill* and I got a little creative with mine: "Barbra Streisand is nineteen, was born in Madagascar and reared in Rangoon, educated at Erasmus Hall High School in Brooklyn, and appeared off-Broadway in a one-nighter called *Another Evening with Harry Stoones.*"

I was just trying to make it more interesting, because frankly, I never thought I was all that interesting on my own. And I figured, if a Jewish girl from Brooklyn is playing a Jewish secretary named Yetta Tessye Marmelstein, what's the big deal? It wasn't exactly a stretch. Wouldn't it be more intriguing if there were some mystery about me . . . if I came from some exotic foreign land? And I liked the alliteration . . . "reared in Rangoon." (I think I changed it the following month and said I was born in Aruba and went to the Yeshiva of Brooklyn. I thought that was even funnier.)

By this time, I had sat in a lot of theaters and avidly read the actors' bios, and they all seemed to belong to the Actors Studio.

My last line was: "She is not a member of the Actors Studio."

I thought that was funny too . . . and perhaps I was still a little hurt at not having been accepted, even though I was technically too young. I'm sure one of the motivating factors in my success was to prove all those people wrong. They'd be sorry when I was famous!

In any event, the *Playbill* people didn't get the joke. Eventually they made me change it.

Compared to me, with my slim bio, Elliott was a pro. He had been performing since he was a kid, doing a song-and-dance act in a top hat and tails up at a hotel in the Catskills when he was ten, and playing the Palace at thirteen, as part of a vaudeville act. His mother pushed him into show business . . . totally the opposite of mine . . . and he wanted to please her. But he had never before had a principal role. He was a chorus boy in another Broadway show, *Irma La Douce*, when he auditioned for *Wholesale.*

This was Elliott's big break . . . and mine.

Unlike him, I had never looked for jobs in the chorus. Frankly, I don't think it even occurred to me. Working my way up slowly didn't figure into my plan. I was too impatient. I like instant gratification. And I always knew it was all or nothing for me . . . I had to go right to the top or into another profession. I wanted a part with substance. Otherwise it wasn't worth my time.

I was scared, too, because when I was fifteen, I used to picture my life as if it were projected on a television screen. And when I looked into the future and imagined myself at nineteen, the screen went black. What did that mean? Was I going to die before I turned twenty?

So I thought I was lucky to still be here, and I was determined to make the most of it.

Rehearsals did not go brilliantly for me. It was not that I had any problems playing the part. I had worked in an office and even sat at a switchboard. I knew this girl. She wasn't me, but she was somebody I recognized . . . who didn't have a boyfriend . . . was never asked out on a date . . . always overlooked. Technically I was too young for the role, because she was supposed to be a spinster, and after all, I was only nineteen. But that didn't bother me.

The only issues I had were with Arthur Laurents. We started to work on the beginning of the play. Miss Marmelstein is in the office of her boss, whose dressmaking business is jeopardized because some of the garment workers are striking. We would do the scene, and Arthur would see a gesture he liked and say, "Lock it."

"Lock it?" I replied. "What does that mean?"

"Do it just like that every time."

I had no idea what he was talking about. "Like what?"

"Just the way you did the scene now," he explained. "I like how you pointed your foot."

"My foot?" I had already forgotten what I'd done.

"Yes. I like the way you pointed your foot. Do it the same way."

Huh? How could I replicate it when I couldn't even remember what I did?

And then he would get angry with me, yelling, "What is the matter with you? You have no discipline! You never do it the same way twice!"

Well, of course not. I was taught to be in the moment . . . to listen and react . . . that was what seemed right to me. One night I might feel like leaning back in my chair, or looking up at a different point, or saying a word with a slightly different inflection. And what did it matter, as long as I said the words as written? I was searching. I was experimenting. You need a certain amount of freedom to create.

As long as I'm in character and being truthful, it usually works. I believe that if I'm truly feeling something, the audience is going to feel it too. What comes from the heart goes to the heart.

Arthur had a different attitude. For every scene, he wanted a series of set poses . . . you do this, and then you do that. He kept trying to "correct" me, and it just went in one ear and out the other because it wasn't the way I worked. The tension between us came to a head over my one solo in the show, "Miss Marmelstein." The poor, put-upon secretary has finally had enough. Everybody throws work at her, but nobody pays any real attention to her. In fact, they don't even know her first name. And no one has ever given her a nickname. I could relate to that. I never had one either.

So she sings:

Oh, why is it always "Miss Marmelstein"?
Nobody calls me, "Hey, baby doll!" or "Honey dear" or "Sweetie pie"

When we first started to rehearse the number, I assumed I would be performing it in my chair. After all, I had done it that way at the audition, and everyone seemed to like it. In fact, I thought that's why I got the job. (Never assume.)

I thought my idea made perfect sense. I was simply taking my cue, as an actress, from the situation. Wouldn't it be funny to push myself around in the chair with my feet while I sang the song?

"Oh no no no no no," said Arthur. "Forget all that. Now we're going to stage it." Obviously he thought they could come up with something better.

That was what Herb Ross was being paid to do. He was the choreographer, and he proceeded to stage my big moment with people walking back and forth behind me. Very distracting. And he had me walking and singing at the same time.

I said, "This feels wrong to me. Who is she talking to? If there are all these other people onstage, does she do one line to one person and then the next to another?"

It was so confusing. I didn't get it. I kept telling Arthur that it didn't work. One day, when I was sitting on the floor after doing the scene for the umpteenth time, he really lit into me in front of the whole cast. It was embarrassing. I put my head down, hiding my face with my hair.

I had two personalities, in a way . . . one was the street kid who was not going to take any shit from anybody, and the other was the little girl who was very vulnerable and easily hurt.

Jerome Weidman came over to comfort me. He had noticed my hands moving in my lap and thought I was so upset that I was trembling.

But I wasn't trembling at all. In fact, I was busy drawing a floor plan of my new apartment.

"See," I showed him. "I guess this is where you'd put the couch. But I don't have a couch. Do you think there's even room for a couch?"

Clearly Arthur and I didn't always see eye to eye, but I had already gotten one good thing out of the production . . . my railroad flat. And I loved it, even though I'll admit it had a few flaws. For example, the front door opened straight onto the bathtub, which was in the kitchen. Actually, it's a little optimistic to call it a kitchen. It didn't even have a proper sink (it was about the size of two ice cube trays).

If I wanted to wash the dishes, I had to do it in the same tub where I took a bath . . . and did my handwashing. I would kneel beside it with my newly clean bras hanging above and dripping down on me. I swear that's why I have a bad back today, from always leaning over that tub. I got a piece of wood that I put on top when I wasn't using it, so it could double as a counter. But the height was all wrong . . . if I wanted to chop vegetables, I had to sit on the floor.

The living room was small and the bedroom was even smaller, so narrow that I could barely fit in a single bed. And once you opened the door, there was no space for a bedside table. An interior window looked into the kitchen, and I thought that was odd, but charming. I could put lace curtains on it! The only real window in the bedroom looked out on a brick wall. (This is why I dreamed of having an apartment with a view someday.)

The bathroom . . . well, it's hard to even call it a bathroom, because there was only a toilet, with no sink, no shower, and no cabinets. The space was so tight that it felt claustrophobic. I had to do something in there to provide some distraction, so I cut out interesting newspaper articles and glued them on the wall to make my own version of wallpaper, then brushed some varnish over them.

All right, so the apartment wasn't ideal, but the important thing was that it was mine, all mine. And at least I could always pick up an order of fried clams at Oscar's and eat them upstairs.

Immediately, I began to decorate. I bought a ten-dollar print of Rembrandt's *A Woman Bathing in a Stream*. She was lifting her creamy white shift above her knees and stepping into the water. The colors were monochromatic . . . many shades of brown with a splash of Rembrandt red . . . and since the picture was a bit smaller than my antique frame, I used black electrical tape to create a matte around it. I hung it on the living-room wall, with my other antique frames. But those I left empty, once again. And then I had some old family photos, oval-shaped and made of tin. I loved the soft sepia tones. One was of my great-grandfather (all three are now hanging in my den). And in one of my rounds through the thrift shops, I found an old hat rack, so I could display all my vintage hats.

I'll never forget the moment I walked into the National Gallery in London many years later and saw "my Rembrandt" hanging there! Oh my God, this was the real thing! I remember the vibrancy of the paint . . . how it glistened. I thought my cheap print was beautiful, but this was jaw-dropping.

Another reason I was so eager to take the apartment was that it was around the corner from where *PM East* was taped. Mert Koplin kept asking me back to sing a few songs and talk with Mike Wallace. I think they liked me because they never knew what was going to come out of my mouth. Once I talked about the perils of drinking milk because I had read an article in *Prevention* magazine that explained how a mother cow pushes her calf away as soon as he grows teeth. So why are we drinking milk after we develop teeth? It made perfect sense to me, and I wanted to share this information with the world.

This is probably where I got the reputation for being "a kook."

The more outrageous I was, the more they liked it. (Actually, some of the things I said about health were accurate, considering what we know today.)

On one show the topic was success, and I was the unknown among all these famous people, like Anthony Quinn, Mickey Rooney, Rod Serling, and David Susskind, who were all working together on the movie *Requiem for a Heavyweight*. I sang "Ding Dong! The Witch Is Dead" and then came over to join the discussion. I could sense that Susskind, who had a refined, almost scholarly demeanor, had absolutely no idea what to make of me. I was excited and giggly and I turned to this famous producer, whom any young actress would want to please, and said exactly what I was thinking: "I scare you, don't I?"

Susskind couldn't let that go unchallenged. "No, you don't, really. I'll tell you what you do for me. You make me want to invent a language because I know the word 'out,' but you're after 'out.'"

And my gleeful response was, "I'm so out I'm in!"

Then Mike Wallace steered the conversation back to success, and after some more talk, I sang "Bewitched, Bothered and Bewildered." When I rejoined the group, Susskind complimented me. (I guess I finally chose a song he liked.) "You sing beautifully," he said. "This girl is going to be a big star. She is loaded with talent. She projects, she's got a poignancy and a power and an emotion that she gets across to an audience. But she sings the remotest, most esoteric songs . . . and I think a lot of the audience says, 'What?' 'Who?'"

I disagreed. "No, no. They don't, though."

And when the conversation turned to how difficult it is to make it in show business, I confronted Susskind again.

"You wouldn't see me when I went up to Talent Associates." (That was his production company.)

"Because I don't see actors or actresses," he explained.

"None of your people would even let me read or anything. That's why I decided to give up the theater rather than going through that kind of thing."

I was still smarting from the way Faye Lee, his casting agent, had treated me that day in his office. And now I'm arguing with him on TV. I was speaking up for every frustrated actor!

On another show I told Mert to have Mike ask me about Zen Buddhism. I was very into Zen Buddhism, until I lost the book. I had been reading Alan Watts's *Spirit of Zen*, and one line had jumped out at me: "With our eyes on the horizon we do not see what lies at our feet."

That was a profound lesson for me. I wondered what else I was missing . . .

Usually I played along with Mike for the camera, but something in his attitude rubbed me the wrong way that day. I was singing at the Blue Angel when we taped that particular show, and when he mentioned that my engagement had been extended he added "and she owes it all to Zen Buddhism."

I could tell he wanted me to go on and on about "enlightenment" and how I was a Zen Buddhist, which I wasn't, just so he could make fun of me. That was to be expected, but I drew the line at making fun of any religion.

When I got quiet, he pushed. "But you wanted to talk about it. So you go ahead and talk."

I stared at him. "I used to like you." (There was laughter from the crew in the studio.)

"No, this is the truth," I said. "I really like what he does. A lot of people don't." (The laughter got louder.) "I like the fact that you are provoking. But don't provoke me!" (Another laugh.)

I was fresh. I was talking back to the host of the show, and everyone seemed to like it. I guess people thought I was funny. I don't know. I didn't realize I was breaking the rules. Mike didn't intimidate me. I never really felt intimidated by anyone.

Back to *Wholesale.* I was getting to know the cast. I remember liking Lillian Roth, who played Elliott's mother. She had a beautiful smile, with dimples, and was warm, like Phyllis Diller. And Roth had a fascinating past . . . a career as a singer, an actress, then a struggle with alcoholism . . . a story she told in her autobiography, *I'll Cry Tomorrow*, which was made into a movie I saw, with Susan Hayward.

Sheree North and I shared a dressing room. She played the showgirl who tempts Elliott's character and I grew fond of her.

But initially it was only Elliott who was my pal. As we got to know each other better, we discovered that we both liked games. So when we were done for the day, he'd take me to play Pokerino and Fascination at the penny arcades along Forty-Second Street, right outside the New Amsterdam. Then we'd eat Chinese food for dinner. These weren't really dates . . . they were just convenient, and neither of us had anything else to do. Anyway, I could barely function on dates . . . I never knew what to say or do . . . and the few I had had up to then were uncomfortable.

Besides, I wasn't particularly attracted to Elliott, until one day when I happened to see the back of his neck . . . and that did it. I'm not sure why. It was just a bit of exposed flesh, and I wanted to touch it. Suddenly he became more than a friend. He was a man with a man's body, and something changed in me.

Isn't it interesting how someone can unexpectedly become more attractive? It was as if I were seeing him through new eyes . . . he was already tall and dark, and now he became handsome. I wanted to run my fingers through his thick, curly hair.

I never went for the Tab Hunter types . . . blond and blue-eyed. Those kinds of guys were too pretty for me. I preferred a face like my father's . . . masculine, with soulful eyes, a good mouth. Brando's mouth was superb. I thought Elliott was a cross between Humphrey Bogart and Jean-Paul Belmondo, with one of those Schimmelpennincks dangling from his lips. He told me I was a cross between Sophia Loren and Y. A. Tittle. I didn't have a clue as to who Y. A. Tittle was . . . still don't.

Elliott had a great sense of humor. Once I was talking to him about the Dalai Lama . . . Elliott told me he had never heard of him before . . . and the next day I got a package of corned beef, pastrami, pickles, and coleslaw with a note, "From the Deli Lama."

Listen, if you can make me laugh, you're halfway home.

I was nineteen years old, and he was twenty-three, but we were still two innocents, really, and I think we recognized that in each other. It was probably part of what attracted me to him.

And then one night we went to see a Japanese horror film about this giant moth that wreaks havoc on Tokyo in the course of rescuing its two miniature human handmaidens. (Plot was not its strong point.) I can't sit through today's horror films . . . they're way too violent . . . but I was fascinated by movies like *Them!*, *The Blob*, and *The Day the Earth Stood Still* when I was a girl. I loved being scared silly back then. My favorite ride at the amusement park was always the Haunted House.

When the movie was over we stepped out of the theater, and it was snowing. It was so beautiful . . . the streets transformed by the newly fallen snow, the city suddenly quiet and muffled. We walked over to Rockefeller Center, and I was looking down at the skating rink when Elliott suddenly bent over and picked up some snow, to make a snowball. I ran, and he started to chase me, and we had a snowball fight at 2:00 a.m. Then he called a truce, came over to me, and delicately washed my face with snow. And he kissed me, very lightly. It was so romantic, like something out of a movie.

Later that night he told me he thought I was exquisite . . . the first time any man had ever said anything like that to me.

He was the leading man in the show, and he hadn't gone after Marilyn, the cute girl, or Sheree, the sexy girl. He fell in love with me.

It was great that we had found each other, because no one else was particularly entranced with us. In fact, we were both on the verge of being fired. Elliott was "a sweater" (not the kind you wear). He actually sweated so profusely that beads of perspiration flew off him when he danced. And I remained "undisciplined."

I was still struggling with Miss Marmelstein's song. I kept saying over and over again, "This doesn't feel organic. It's not true. It feels awkward to me."

Herb tried every which way to stage the thing, but he and Arthur could not make it work.

I begged, "Let me do it as I did it at the audition! You liked it then. It seemed true to the character and the piece. She's a secretary, sitting in her chair and complaining about her situation to the audience." When you've got a line like "Do you know what I mean?" that's a clue. She's taking them into her confidence, and I could see myself in the chair, rolling down to the footlights to get closer, with my feet paddling like a duck.

I was going with my gut, which is what I've relied on all my life. And if I was given a direction that didn't feel right, I would say so.

Apparently most young women, given their first part in a Broadway show, do not challenge the director. They feel lucky enough just to be there.

That was not me. I was very independent. I think it was due to the way I was raised, which on some level was terrible and on another level probably contributed to my success. My mother had hardly any control over me, so I never learned to defer to authority. I was used to doing my own thing . . . whether it was going outside to play or going into New York alone on the subway . . . whatever.

At that time the usual procedure for a show headed to Broadway was to preview it first in another city or two so any problems could be fixed out of town. We were scheduled to play for two weeks in Philadelphia and then three weeks in Boston.

At the dress rehearsal before we opened in Philadelphia, the "Miss Marmelstein" number still wasn't working. I had tried my best to do it Arthur's way, because I always believe in serving the director's vision. But I've never been good at faking. It had to be real for me in some way. And it wasn't.

I was getting desperate. I didn't know what to do. I thought, *I've got to call Marty. Are the nightclubs still asking for me?*

I sincerely felt I might be better off walking out. But I'm not a quitter.

I decided to approach Arthur one last time, thinking, *Maybe he'll fire me . . .* but I didn't care.

I told him, "The number's not working. *Please* let me try it in my chair."

By now he had become completely frustrated with me. And he finally snapped, "Okay! Okay! Do it in your goddamn chair!!!"

On opening night I did it my way, and thank God the song stopped the show.

I was thrilled, but there was another thought in the back of my head . . . *Oh no. Arthur's not going to like this. He's going to be really pissed off that I was right.*

Arthur said nothing to me after the performance. He didn't come to my dressing room and offer something complimentary like "Great. It finally worked" or

"Well done." I suppose in some corner of my mind I was hoping against hope that he would . . .

The next morning the cast assembled for notes. It's the usual drill. After a show, the director will tell you what worked and what didn't, give you ideas on how to improve your performance.

Instinctively I was bracing myself. Still, I was not prepared for what Arthur did that morning, in front of everyone. He bawled me out, and he was not just angry. He was in a rage. Jerome Weidman was there and he described this moment in a magazine article: "As the director's words went hurling toward her like so many venom-tipped darts, the rest of the cast seemed to cringe away, as though afraid to be splashed by criticism so savage and so total that it might be permanently disfiguring even to those who happened to be in the neighborhood."

Or as I'd put it, Arthur was shouting. Some of the things he said were so painful that I've blocked them out.

I ran off the stage crying.

I couldn't believe it. I had stopped the show. That was my crime . . . even though I was praised for it in the reviews. The local critics were not all that taken with the production . . . the reviews were mixed, at best . . . but they had singled me out: "Barbra Streisand brings down the house" and "She stops the show in its tracks."

Meanwhile, David Merrick doubled my salary from $175 to $350 a week, and my picture, in the chair, went up outside the theater.

After Philadelphia we moved on to Boston, where Arthur kept reworking various scenes. My part in another song, "What Are They Doing to Us Now?," had been expanded, so I was now leading the chorus of employees desperately clutching the office furniture as it's being repossessed out from under them.

But Arthur left my solo alone. And every night it stopped the show. God, he must have really hated that.

When we got to New York, I invited Bob Schulenberg and Barry Dennen to come to the friends and family preview. Bob remembers it better than I do:

"The audience started screaming after 'Miss Marmelstein.' When we went back to her dressing room after the show, Barbra said, 'Don't do that.'

"'Do what?'

"'Scream "bravo."'

"'Barbra, that was the whole theater screaming. Not just me.' She didn't comprehend it. Then we went across the street to Sardi's for a drink, and as she walked in, people applauded. So the word was out."

I was happy to get such a response, but Arthur was not going to give in quite so easily.

I will never forget what he did to me on opening night, March 22, at the Shubert Theatre in New York. I must have come in through the lobby, because I remember standing in the back of the house and looking down at the stage. Suddenly Arthur was standing next to me. I can still see his face. He had a jawline like a snake . . . square and wide at the bottom. And like a snake, he was about to strike. He said viciously, "You're never going to make it, you know. Never! You're too undisciplined!"

A good director wouldn't talk to an actor that way. You wouldn't try to destroy them right before opening night. It was as if he wanted me to fail, even to the detriment of his own production! Whether he knew it or not, he was trying to ruin my confidence and make me so upset that the scene wouldn't work that night. Then maybe we'd have to go back to his and Herb's staging.

And there may have been a whole other layer to our conflict. I think Arthur had a little crush on Elliott. Perhaps Arthur blamed me for his unrequited feelings and was punishing me out of jealousy. Who knows?

Arthur was a complicated man. But I knew what was going on. And I think I also knew, *That's the way it's going to be for me. I will do that to people. I will make them angry.*

My mother and my brother came to the show on opening night and then joined me afterward at the party at Sardi's, where everyone was waiting for the reviews. The only reason I can tell you what they said is because my mother saved them. (Thank goodness for her, because I saved nothing.) Walter Kerr in the *Herald Tribune* mentioned "a sloe-eyed creature with folding ankles named Barbra Streisand (yes, Barbra is spelled right, and Barbra is great)." Howard Taubman in *The New York Times* called Elliott "a likeable newcomer," and said I was "the evening's find." But other reviews were not as kind to Elliott, and I could feel his pain and therefore I felt injured too.

So I couldn't really celebrate. It was the first time I experienced that feeling of guilt. I did not want to get better reviews than he did. After all, Elliott was the star of the show, and I was eager for him to be acknowledged. He was very good in a difficult role. Couldn't they see that?

My heart skipped a beat. I thought, *Oh no. Don't do this to me now. Don't let me overshadow the guy in my life.* I wanted him to keep loving me . . . not resent me.

Years later, Elliott told me about a moment deep into rehearsals when he was standing in the wings, watching the Miss Marmelstein number, and he found himself thinking, *I really want to give her support. Her career is more important than mine.*

What a generous reaction!

My fears were unwarranted, because he was genuinely happy for my success. Suddenly reporters wanted to interview me, and I complied, because usually it involved going out for a meal. I was so naïve that I just told them whatever came into my head. When I was interviewed for a Talk of the Town piece in *The New Yorker*, I bluntly asked, "What do you want to know?" and went on to declare, "I was bald until I was two. I think I'm some sort of Martian. I exist on my willpower, being Taurus. My birthday was April 24th. I hate the name Barbara. I dropped the second 'a,' and I think I'll gradually cut the whole thing down to B. That will save exertion in handwriting."

Clearly I wasn't concerned with what impression I might be making. There was absolutely no filter. It was just such a novelty to finally have someone listening to me. I told the reporter about my father . . . and my mother, who never liked to leave Brooklyn. "She's there now. She did come to the opening night of *Wholesale*, but I don't think she understood what I was trying to do in it. Why should she? The things that interest her about me are whether I'm eating enough and whether I am warmly enough dressed. She's a very simple, nonintellectual, nontheatrical person who lives and breathes."

With Elliott, I had found someone who really got me. On opening night in Philadelphia, I had given him a flower with a note: "To my clandestine lover." Elliott remembers his reaction: "I had never heard the word 'clandestine' before. It sounded like a pirate movie."

By the time we opened in New York, we were spending most of our time together. Elliott is six foot three, and I can't believe the two of us slept together in my narrow twin bed. As he told me years later when we were reminiscing, "Now that's intimacy. I've never slept better in my life."

We were like Hansel and Gretel . . . two children alone in the woods who had found each other. It felt as if we were playing house in that tiny apartment. I loved decorating, but cooking was not one of my strong points. My idea of a homemade meal was to open a can of corn, dump it into a pot, add milk and heat, and that became corn soup. I'd also add corn to Aunt Jemima's pancake mix and fry it in Crisco, to make corn fritters.

And my absolute favorite meal was TV dinners, but they had to be Swanson's. They made the best fried chicken, which came with mashed potatoes and mixed vegetables . . . corn, carrots, green beans, and peas . . . in a neat little tin tray, which was great because there were no dishes to wash in the tub! That fried chicken was the height of culinary goodness, as far as I was concerned. I would make three of them for the two of us sometimes, because the portions were small . . . and for dessert, we'd have a slab of Sara Lee chocolate cake. (I didn't like the tiny square of apple cobbler that came with the TV dinner . . . too sweet.) Before serving the cake (which also came out of the freezer bin), I had a particular technique. I would put it under the broiler until the icing fizzled and you could see little bubbles in it. And it got darker and slightly crystallized, which made it taste even more chocolatey. I thought it was the closest thing to a homemade cake. When I was singing at the Caucus Club in Detroit, I met Nathan Cummings, the owner of Sara Lee. That was a thrill. He was a celebrity to me.

At one point Elliott and I invited David Merrick and his associate, Jack Schlissel, who always made me laugh, over for dinner. Elliott could make very good roasted potatoes, so he did those, along with a leg of lamb, and I made my sweet peas with sugar and breadcrumbs, as Anita Miller had taught me. We didn't have a dining table, so we improvised and ate on top of my antique sewing machine. (It was the old-fashioned kind, that came as part of a table. You lifted a piece of wood in the middle and the sewing machine emerged.) Don't ask me how we fit four place settings on it.

At the beginning of April I was nominated for a Tony Award for Best Performance by a Featured Actress in a Musical. (It should have been shared with the chair.) The next morning I was on the *Today* show, which was a challenge, since I had to get up so early and sing before I was barely awake. I was a person from the theater . . . I ate dinner after the show and rarely went to bed before 3:00 or 4:00 a.m. And then I'd get up at noon. (That's still my preferred schedule.)

So I'm not at my finest at eight in the morning. I managed to sing "Much More" and "Right as the Rain," and then the host, John Chancellor, invited me over to talk. I guess he was trying to be sunny and warm, because he asked if I was made of "sugar and spice and everything nice."

Now really, how are you supposed to answer that? I just said, "No."

The poor man tried to recover. "What, then? Songs?"

"Flesh and bones."

I was always so literal.

And I have absolutely no memory of the Tony Awards. Elliott says we attended, and he was probably more upset than I was when I lost to Phyllis Newman in *Subways Are for Sleeping*. (Forty-seven years later I invited her to my *One Night Only* concert at the Village Vanguard, so no hard feelings!) In those days the Tonys were given out at a dinner at the Waldorf-Astoria. No television cameras, so I can't even tell you what I wore. And now my assistant tells me I actually did win the New York Drama Critics poll. Are you kidding me? That's a very nice thing. Was there a ceremony? Did I go? I have no memory of that either.

In fact, I was thrilled by all the recognition I was getting, but you'd never know it from some of my responses. I recently listened to a radio interview I did at the time. The reporter starts off by congratulating me on my reviews and the Tony nomination, then says, "It's all coming pretty fast for you. How does it feel?"

Obviously he expected me to be enthusiastic and animated, gushing about how exciting it was.

Instead, here's what I answered, in a rather flat voice: "It doesn't feel like anything."

He tries to give me a cue: "You mean you can't feel a thing right now?"

But do I pick up on it and give him what he wants? *Nooooo.* I answer him honestly. "Well, it's just factual, you know. I can't do things I want to do at night because I have to be at the theater every night."

"Already she's complaining!"

You can see why I rubbed some people the wrong way. I didn't play the game. I'm not sure I even knew that there *was* a game. I didn't know how to be charming. If I did, I wouldn't have told the truth. I would have made something up. As Joan of Arc says in Shaw's play, "He who tells too much truth is sure to be hanged."

I didn't realize that I was hanging myself.

And yet I was so excited just a year before when I was on TV with Orson Bean for the first time. What had happened in the interim? Was I shell-shocked? Did I not believe in my success? And I was so serious. The last thing I said before the reporter cut me off was: "I feel like I have a lot to do and not much time to do it in."

The truth is, I was already bored with the show after only a few weeks. There were no other scenes to learn, no other ideas to try. I was ready to go on to another role. And I didn't have any qualms about telling people as much, including reporters.

After dealing with Arthur and all the constrictions that came with doing a Broadway show, I had a whole new appreciation for singing in nightclubs . . . where I was free to direct and star in my own show, exactly how I envisioned it.

That's why I said yes to another run at the Bon Soir in May. After the curtain call on Broadway each night, I would tear off my costume and rush out to hail a cab to take me downtown.

On that stage I was completely in charge. Now that I was making some money, I could have walked into Bergdorf Goodman and bought a cocktail dress or an elegant gown, something more like what other singers wore on TV. (Around this time, I did buy my first fur coat, sold to me as "Zorina," aka "Alaskan sable," but in reality . . . skunk. I couldn't wear it in the rain, because if it got wet it smelled like skunk.)

But the whole point about clothes for the Bon Soir was that I didn't want to look like other singers. I was envisioning something entirely different . . . a man's black-and-white herringbone tweed vest with a white chiffon blouse, loosely tied with a bow at the neck. The matching skirt, long to the floor, would have a slit up the side, lined in red, so you just caught a glimpse against the tweed. It was an outfit that was both masculine and feminine at the same time . . . I've always loved that dichotomy. (And I'm still wearing similar vests and skirts. I haven't changed my style in all these years.)

I'd sketch something out and then go shopping for men's fabrics with Terry Leong. When Terry decided to move to Europe, he introduced me to Tony Antine, another talented dressmaker. They made it easy for me to design my own clothes. We would have fittings at my apartment, and then they could stitch it up on my sewing machine, which operated not by electricity but by pushing a pedal. (I still have it, and it works brilliantly.)

I knew my clothes were unconventional, but I didn't feel right in conventional dresses.

I had stopped wearing antique clothes onstage when I realized that reporters were reviewing the clothes, as well as me. I didn't want anyone to think of them as a gimmick. Most people who hit on something distinctive will typically stay with it. But that's the odd thing about me. As soon as anything was successful, I moved on.

The same thing happened when I first saw myself on TV. I noticed I was making a gesture while I was singing that I wasn't even aware of . . . my thumb and middle finger touched like a Buddhist statue or a yogi. I didn't do yoga. Where did that come from? Did I see it somewhere? (Maybe I was a Balinese dancer in a past life.)

Even though the gesture was instinctive, it looked suspiciously like a mannerism to me. And I didn't want to be mannered, so I consciously stopped doing it. I didn't want to be accused of being affected. I could imagine people imitating it, and I didn't want to be imitated.

As I was refining my look, I was also refining "the act" . . . although I don't like that word. That suggests something phony. And I was trying to be authentic onstage.

The band would play some music to introduce me as I walked out, and sometimes I'd let that music play for a long time while I just stood there silently. It quieted the audience down and gave those who were eating and drinking a chance to look up and notice me. And then I'd go into the song "Much More" from *The Fantasticks.* It has such a good lyric, one that would let the audience get to know me:

I'd like to do the things I've dreamed about, but never done before
Perhaps I'm bad or wild or mad, with lots of grief in store
But I want much more than keeping house . . .
Much more! Much more! Much more!

It was as if it were written for me.

I liked to open with a ballad because I felt up-tempo songs were not important, and I think the first moments onstage are very important. Sometimes I'd do two ballads in a row . . . stay in the mood. An innocent song, like "Right as the Rain," was perfect for me, because I could be the young girl falling in love. And "Nobody's Heart Belongs to Me" by Rodgers and Hart . . . what a great song to do, because the lyric says one thing while the character is feeling another. So I could pretend I was okay without a lover . . . "Heigh-ho, who cares?" Actually she does care, but she's not going to show you until the very end of the song, when her true feelings (and mine) come out.

Certain songs just seem to talk to each other. When I started to combine "Like a Straw in the Wind" with "Anyplace I Hang My Hat Is Home" (both by Harold Arlen), I thought, *This is like writing a little play.* I love it when a character starts out one way and completely changes by the end, and this medley allowed me to bring out the drama and run the full gamut of emotions. It's quiet and kind of languid at the beginning, where she's drifting "like a straw in the wind," and then builds up to a cry . . . "my man is gone" . . . and we hear her pain. But then her emotions keep shifting, sometimes from one bar to another, and so does the rhythm as she goes from insisting that she likes being unattached . . . "free and easy" . . . to sadness, anger, and finally defiance, as the same words take on a whole new meaning.

And then I'd change the mood. I didn't want to be labeled . . . categorized . . . pinned down. As soon as the audience was thinking, *Oh, she sings ballads* . . . I'd do something totally unexpected. Suddenly I'd burst out with "You better not shout, you better not cry. You better not pout, I'm telling you why" . . . and then switch to a deadpan "Santa Claus is dead."

That got their attention . . . and a big laugh.

I still remember the thrill of finding a book of sheet music with five songs that Leonard Bernstein had written for kids. One of the pieces was called "My Name Is Barbara." Can you believe it? I was amazed that such a thing existed. I couldn't afford special material, so it was like a gift. Now that's *bashert.*

Once again, "at the moment of commitment, the universe conspires to assist you."

Another of Bernstein's songs began with the words "I hate music, but I love to sing!" Sometimes I walked out onstage and opened with that. Immediately people shut up . . . wondering what in the world I was doing. It was perfect for me because I could totally identify with it. These songs were written for children to sing . . . "My mother said that babies come in bottles" . . . and I could act that child. I could *be* that child because deep down in my inner core I was still a child. That part of me is still very much alive.

In one evening, I could be a dozen different people . . . a whole repertory company, in a sense. The songs I chose were all like little plays, except without any other actors. Now I kind of liked singing in those clubs. I sang about eight songs, so I was on for about forty-five minutes. I thought it was perfect.

SIX

Those Cockamamie Songs

Memory is fickle. There are moments that are indelibly engraved in my mind . . . I can still see the other person's face and I know exactly where we were standing . . . and others that have become a little more misty and watercolored over the years.

Jule Styne was my darling prince . . . a brilliant songwriter who would be pivotal to my career . . . and yet I can't remember exactly when we met. I'm told he saw me in *Wholesale*, but I think we actually met at the Bon Soir, on one of those nights when I was doing the midnight show after the curtain came down on Broadway. Marty was aware that Jule was writing the music for a new show, based on the life of the vaudeville comedienne Fanny Brice. That was a name that meant nothing to me at that point.

But Marty knew who she was and thought it might be a part for me. That's why, when I appeared on *PM East* on April 24, 1962, my twentieth birthday, he had arranged for me to be presented with not only a cake, but also the "annual Fanny Brice Award" . . . which hadn't existed until that moment. It was something that he and Don Softness had dreamed up. And Mert Koplin was happy to go along. I'll always be grateful to Mert, who was one of my earliest advocates. Whenever there was a guest on the show . . . some famous actor or producer who might help my career . . . he would make sure I was invited.

And this award was all part of their attempt to get me noticed by the producer of the Fanny Brice show, Ray Stark. Working every angle he could think of, Marty called Jeff Hunter to get Jule's number and invited him down to the Bon Soir.

Jule came, he saw, and he was so excited that even I couldn't help but respond. Here was this small man with a huge talent, heaping so many adjectives on me . . . "great" . . . "sublime" . . . "thrilling" . . . that it was dizzying. I knew who he was . . . the composer of *Gentlemen Prefer Blondes*, *Gypsy*, and *Bells Are Ringing* . . . a man who had written more hit songs than I could count . . . but he didn't attempt to impress me with his own credentials, as I had noticed most people were quick to do. Instead Jule just wanted to talk about me. He was curious and funny and delightful. I liked him immediately.

And he must have liked what he heard because he came back night after night and brought all sorts of people along with him. He was like a convert to a new religion, trying to persuade other people to join. In fact, it's thanks to Jule that I met two of my dearest friends, Marilyn and Alan Bergman, who became part of my family. They're the husband-and-wife team who had written the lyrics to "Nice 'n' Easy," sung by Frank Sinatra, and would go on to write the lyrics to many great songs for me, like "The Way We Were" and "Papa, Can You Hear Me?"

They had been working with Jule on a show he was producing and directing and had just spent the whole day auditioning singers when he said, "Come on. I'm going to take you downtown to hear a fantastic girl singer." As Marilyn tells the story, that was the last thing she and Alan wanted to do. "Jule," she protested, "we've been listening to girls sing all day!"

"Not like this," he said.

"He was right," Marilyn recalls. "As soon as Barbra started to sing, I realized Jule was not exaggerating."

Alan adds, "As soon as Barbra started to sing, Marilyn started to cry."

"Barbra came out on a very small stage . . . Peter Daniels was playing the piano for her . . . and I think her first song was 'My Name Is Barbara.' And I will never forget 'A Sleepin' Bee,'" says Marilyn. "I was swept away by her talent."

"You knew instantly that she was an original," says Alan. "And it's more than just the voice. In order to be a great singer, you need three things . . . the head, the heart, and the throat . . . the intelligence from the head, the feeling from the heart, and the chops to sing from the throat. And Barbra has the whole package."

I remember sitting in the tiny dressing room that night after the show when I heard a knock at the door. Marilyn's lovely wide-open face peeked in first, and then she and Alan came in. She looked at me and said, "Do you know how wonderful you are?"

I thought, *Huh?* I had no idea how to respond. I was probably even a little suspicious. My first reaction when people gave me a compliment was to shrink away, thinking, *What do you want from me?*

Years later Marilyn told me that as soon as she said it, she thought, *What a stupid question.* And then she answered it silently, to herself, *Of course she does. She must.* Because she felt nobody could be that talented and not know exactly what she was doing.

The next time I saw Marilyn and Alan was at Jule's apartment. It was one of those elegant Park Avenue places . . . except that the only furniture was a piano, a card table, and some chairs. I think I had more furniture in my little railroad flat than the Stynes did. And they lived on Park Avenue, no less!

The explanation was simple . . . I heard that Jule was a compulsive gambler, and he must have gambled away all the furniture (not an unusual occurrence, according to the Bergmans). It was a Saturday afternoon, and I had come by between the matinee and evening performances of *Wholesale* to hear a few scenes and some of the score from a new musical he was developing. I think it was called *Carte Blanche*, about a credit-card business, and he thought it might be something for me. I didn't have much time, and I was already thinking about the Chinese dinner I was probably going to miss.

Jule's wife, a pretty redheaded Englishwoman named Margaret (whom everyone called Maggie), was not only lovely. She was also intuitive, and she read my mind.

"Barbra, can I make you a sandwich? I'll bet you're hungry."

Hungry? In those days, I was always hungry. Matter of fact, I still am.

"Do you have any chicken?" I asked.

Maggie disappeared into the kitchen and came out with a chicken sandwich on white bread, with mayonnaise. It was delicious.

Marilyn still has an image of me sitting there "in a long black coat with high black boots and a black Russian fur hat. Barbra was eating her sandwich, and I couldn't take my eyes off her long red fingernails against the white bread."

Now this just proves how tricky memory can be. My nails were short while I was in *Wholesale* . . . after all, I was playing a frumpy secretary. But I don't want to contradict Marilyn, and I'm sure she saw those red fingernails at *some* point.

I do know that I didn't think much of what I heard of Jule's musical that afternoon. The writers were there, and I didn't want to hurt their feelings. So I just said, "I don't think I'm right for this, but you know what? It would be perfect for Carol Burnett!"

I found out later that these guys actually wrote for the television show she was on at the time, hosted by Garry Moore. Point is, I think they actually wrote it with her in mind. I'll bet she turned it down, and that's why they came to me.

But I wasn't interested either. And then I went on to describe the kind of show I would like to do, if and when I got the opportunity.

"First of all, it would be dramatic, not a musical comedy per se but a serious story, with music. And the character would have to have dimension and range. Maybe the script would start when she's younger and then follow her as she grows into an adult, with a love story along the way."

Little did I know that I was describing my next part.

Isn't it interesting? If you believe, which I did, that thought transcends matter . . . or put it this way, that imagination can create reality . . . it makes you wonder.

It turns out that Ray's Fanny Brice project was going through its own difficult process of development. And if I were more of a mystic, I'd say Ray was waiting for me to grow up so I would be able to play Fanny.

The facts are that Ray had been trying to develop this project for more than ten years. He was married to Fanny's daughter, Frances, and in some ways the whole thing was a gift to his wife . . . he would commemorate her mother's career and her marriage to Fran's father, an attractive yet morally challenged gambler named Nick Arnstein. Initially Ray had planned to do it as a movie, and I heard he'd commissioned several screenplays by writers like Ben Hecht, among others. Finally, in 1960, he turned to Isobel Lennart, a successful screenwriter who had written *The Sundowners*, with Robert Mitchum and Deborah Kerr herding sheep in Australia, and *Love Me or Leave Me*, with Doris Day as singer Ruth Etting and James Cagney as her gangster husband. (Ray might have seen in them a parallel to Fanny and Nick.)

Isobel managed to produce a screenplay Ray liked, called *My Man*. Then, when Ray changed his mind (he probably couldn't get it financed) and decided to aim for Broadway instead and do it with music, she suddenly found herself writing the book for a musical. Writing for the stage is different from writing for the screen, and Isobel was the first to admit that she was learning on the job.

In the summer of 1962, when I first got involved, the script was not in good shape, and Isobel was reworking it with the help of the brilliant Jerome Robbins, who had conceived, choreographed, and directed *West Side Story*. Ray had hired Jerry to direct because he thought Jerry was the best, and he desperately needed some creative input. Ray knew he had no show without a script, and he was still searching for a leading lady. Jerry was pushing for Anne Bancroft, who was by then an established star and had already won a Tony (and would soon win an Oscar) for her role in *The Miracle Worker*.

I was a mere blip on their radar, just another name on a long list . . . which I've seen, in a letter from Ray to David Merrick that's in Jerry's archives. On it are Eydie Gormé, Mimi Hines, Carol Burnett, Anne Bancroft, Mary Martin, Tammy Grimes, Zohra Lampert, Judy Holliday, Suzanne Pleshette, Kaye Stevens, Paula Prentiss, Mitzi Gaynor, Chita Rivera, Lee Becker, and me. (I had to look up Lee Becker. She was a dancer and actress who had been featured by Jerry in *The King and I* and *West Side Story*.) Clearly I was the least famous person in that group.

Nobody was advocating for me until Jule saw me at the Bon Soir and became my most fervent supporter. He was the one who brought Ray to the club. Then Ray came back with David Merrick, whom he had asked to be his partner in producing the Fanny Brice story, since he had never done a musical on Broadway. I'm told that Ray immediately responded to me, although his wife, Fran, did not . . . she didn't think I was an appropriate choice to play her mother.

Apparently she was envisioning someone older, more elegant and refined . . . although half the appeal of the real Fanny Brice, at least to me once I learned something about her, was her unpretentiousness. She was born on the Lower East Side of New York, where her parents ran a saloon, and she never attempted to hide her origins.

Fran, on the other hand, was very grand. According to Maggie Styne, her first reaction on seeing me was, "That girl play my mother? I wouldn't hire her as my maid!"

And Jerry was not particularly interested in me either, because he felt they should go with a proven actress, someone who could sail right over the weaknesses in the script. (He had never seen me onstage, or anywhere else, at this point.) But Ray, as I only learned much later, had reservations about Anne Bancroft.

And so did Jule. He was writing songs that required a singer with range, and he wasn't sure Bancroft could handle them. And as he acknowledged after he had heard me sing, "In my head, I was really writing for Barbra." Maggie later told me that when he first saw me at the club, he clutched her and said, "This girl has to be Fanny Brice!" And then she added, "I'll never forget it. He practically broke my arm."

Now all he had to do was convince the rest of the team.

It was Jerry Robbins whose opinion would count the most, and he was proving to be elusive. Jule had tried to bring him to the Blue Angel, where I was appearing for a month, beginning in mid-July, but apparently Jerry refused to accompany him, complaining that Jule was "too enthusiastic." He wanted to go on his own. But he still hadn't managed to get there by the beginning of August. Meanwhile, Isobel Lennart, who lived in Los Angeles and couldn't come to New York, asked her friend Doris Vidor, daughter of Harry Warner (one of the Warner Brothers) and widow of director Charles Vidor, to go to the Blue Angel and see what I was like. After Doris gave her report, Isobel asked her to tell Jerry as well.

I only saw Doris's note to him recently (it's also in Jerry's archives). She wrote, "I have rarely seen anyone so talented but it was the personality and what she stirred in me that impressed me so. There is a sadness and a deep emotional impact that this girl projects to the audience that is very unique. It seemed to me that she *was* the young Fannie Brice as you want her to appear."

This is one of the unexpected benefits of writing a book. I had mixed feelings initially, because I don't like to live in the past. I've been there . . . done that . . . and moved on. But if I'm going to recreate those days, I want to be accurate, and that forced me to do some research and look up some things . . . and how wonderful to find something like this.

I didn't know Doris Vidor, and she didn't know me, and yet somehow she had peered into my soul. I wish I had known about her note at the time. I would have liked to have had the opportunity to thank her.

And maybe her note did the trick, because Jerry did come down to see me, and we finally met. Afterward, on August 9, he sent Isobel a telegram that said: JUST HAD LONG EXHAUSTING TALK WITH BARBARA AND I FOUND HER VERY TALENTED VERY CUCKY VERY AMBITIOUS VERY RIVETING VERY VOLATILE VERY UNPREDICTABLE STOP WILL BE READING HER MONDAY. (In those days, you called Western Union to send a telegram and told them what you wanted to say over the phone, and someone misspelled my name, as well as "kooky.")

I was equally riveted by Jerry. I found *him* to be incredibly talented and utterly fascinating.

Jerry had started out as a dancer, and he had a dancer's body, with that panther-like finesse. He was charismatic . . . enigmatic . . . and sexy. He exuded charm. And I thought he had great taste. I knew he had codirected one of the first shows I ever saw on Broadway, *The Pajama Game*, as well as choreographing *On the Town*, *The King and I*, and *Peter Pan*, which he also directed. And then he helped create, and directed, the glorious *West Side Story* and *Gypsy*. So he already had a stellar place in theater history. I admired him immensely and I really wanted to impress him.

Ray sent me a rough draft of the second act . . . Isobel was in the midst of revising the script, working closely with Jerry, and it was still in flux. I don't remember that first audition . . . I only know the date it occurred from that telegram in Jerry's archives. But Jule has said he was there and that I was wearing my black boots and my Cossack hat. Apparently Jerry worked with me on the scene, but when I read it for everyone, I didn't do it exactly as he had planned. As Jule tells the story, Jerry called up to me onstage and said, "You're supposed to cry, Barbra."

And I said, "Mr. Robbins, I'm sorry. But I can't cry with these words."

And Jule says Isobel was there, and that she jumped up and said, "I don't blame you, Miss Streisand. They're terrible words. And they're mine." Well, that sounds like Isobel. She was very honest and direct.

I think Jule is actually describing one of my later auditions, when Isobel had flown in and I read a scene for the group. I do remember telling Jerry I couldn't cry, because as soon as the words flew out of mouth, I thought, *Oh no. What the hell did I just say?*

I thought I had lost the part right there.

And I'll never forget Jerry's reaction. Instead of getting annoyed with me for not crying, he understood. He knew the script needed more work and he liked the fact that I wasn't going to fake it and pretend to have an emotion I couldn't feel. He thought that was honest and real . . . and if I had that kind of instinct for the truth, he saw the potential in me. After all, he wanted an actress to work with, not just a singer.

But the final decision was still up in the air. Much later, I found out that Anne Bancroft had dropped out once she heard the score, announcing, "I want no part of this. I can't sing these songs." Apparently Carol Burnett said, "I'd love to do it, but what you need is a Jewish girl." Eydie Gormé was seriously considered, but she wanted them to hire her husband, Steve Lawrence, to play Nick Arnstein, and nobody was thrilled with that idea.

But all I knew at the time was that they weren't rushing to hire me.

Jule, my faithful knight, the one who was willing to battle even Fran Stark for me, was doing everything he could. When I appeared on *The Tonight Show* on August 21, the guest host, Groucho Marx, announced that he had had dinner with Jule "on the coast last week and he said you'd be just great for that show he's doing . . . what's the name of it?"

"The Fanny Brice story."

"He said, 'It's between her and the girl who works with Garry Moore.'"

"Carol Burnett."

"And the Bancroft girl. Well, that's pretty big-league company. If they're considering you against those two others, I would say that you have arrived."

But it didn't seem that way to me, so I made a joke, telling him that "I go to department stores and they still don't wait on me."

In truth, it felt like nothing much had changed, even though my picture was up on the wall outside a Broadway theater. And saying the same words and doing the same thing every night was becoming harder and harder.

I felt stuck.

I was grateful for *Wholesale.* I needed the money, and it was nice to be on the same stage as Elliott every night. But I always worried that the show was about to close. It wasn't doing that well . . . they were keeping it going on twofers . . . and I didn't want to be associated with a flop!

If *Funny Girl* wasn't happening, I needed something else.

Marty was already on to the next thing. His major focus was on getting me a recording contract. He had already approached Goddard Lieberson, the president of Columbia Records and a legendary figure in the industry. A composer himself and a connoisseur of the arts, Goddard was an elegant man . . . married to Vera Zorina, a famous Balanchine ballerina . . . and he had given Columbia a new sheen of prestige. He produced many of their great classical records . . . which I was buying at the time, so I had noticed his name. But his tastes also ranged to Broadway musicals, where he championed the concept of the original cast album and produced some of the best, including *South Pacific*, *The Sound of Music*, and *My Fair Lady*.

He was also the producer of the original cast album for *I Can Get It for You Wholesale* and came into the studio to supervise while we were recording it.

He and I had already met when Marty brought me in to audition for him. I was very impressed. I thought he was sophisticated and smart. But Goddard thought my voice was "too Broadway" for middle America . . . that I was too specialized a taste and wouldn't get the kind of airplay you needed to break through, now that rock and roll was all the rage. He didn't think there was an audience for a girl who sang ballads . . . and obscure ones at that.

It also probably didn't help that one of his associates, John Hammond, was dead set against me. Hammond had recorded Count Basie and Billie Holiday, and when he first heard me he wasn't sure if I was black or white. Apparently he didn't want any competition for Aretha Franklin, whom he had just signed to the label . . . or at least that's what Marty heard through the grapevine.

So Marty was surprised to get a message on his answering service that Goddard wanted to see him. Marty got excited, assuming Goddard had changed his mind about me. But it turned out that what he actually wanted was for me to sing on an album he was planning to commemorate the twenty-fifth anniversary of the show *Pins and Needles*, with music and lyrics by Harold Rome, who had done the same for *Wholesale.*

Of course I said yes. I needed the money. I think I got two hundred dollars, no percentage.

The show reminded me of *Wholesale. Pins and Needles* was a satirical revue, originally produced in 1937 by the International Ladies' Garment Workers Union to entertain its members, and it was performed by the people who cut the fabric and operated the sewing machines. It was easy to see the beginnings of themes that Rome developed later. Elliott loved the songs. They weren't my taste, but I could play around with "Doing the Reactionary" and "Nobody Makes a Pass at Me," which was kind of a "Miss Marmelstein" number. It was easy.

So now I had been featured on two albums for Columbia, but Goddard still wasn't willing to sign me. I didn't save reviews, but thank God for my mother's scrapbook, which has a *New York Times* review of the *Wholesale* cast album by John S. Wilson, who wrote, "The musical version of Jerome Weidman's *I Can Get It for You Wholesale* is not apt to be remembered for Harold Rome's music and lyrics, but it must inevitably go down in the books as the Broadway debut of Barbra Streisand. Miss Streisand has such a vivid and pungent style of delivery that she rises out of the laboring ordinariness of her surroundings on this disk like a dazzling beacon."

It was nice of him to be so complimentary, but believe me, every time I got a good review, I felt bad for Elliott. I wanted him to get the same kind of attention. By this time, I had seen Judy Garland in *A Star Is Born* and I thought, *Jesus, I don't want to have a life like that . . . where the woman becomes more famous than the man and he dies.*

But all my good reviews still hadn't translated into a recording contract.

So Marty was determined to get me more exposure. At the end of May, I made a guest appearance on *The Garry Moore Show*, because Jeff Hunter invited the producer to see me in *Wholesale* and he liked me.

I had fun doing that show. For the opening number I rode out on a golf cart with Robert Goulet, who was starring as Lancelot in *Camelot* on Broadway. I sang "When the Sun Comes Out," and then I did another song for the first time . . . "Happy Days Are Here Again" . . . and it instantly became a signature for me.

That kind of cheery, upbeat song would not have been my usual choice, and here's how it happened. There was a segment on the show called "That Wonderful Year," and that night they were celebrating 1929. Not the most wonderful year, frankly, because that's when the stock market crashed and the Great Depression began.

Ken Welch, the musical director, showed me a list of possible songs, and one of them was "Happy Days Are Here Again," which Franklin D. Roosevelt had used as his campaign song. We tried it, and I said, "I can't sing it like that. It's too fast. What if we slowed it down and made it more of a ballad?"

I was always doing things like that, switching the tempo and reimagining a song. Then Ken and his wife, Mitzie, came up with a great concept . . . I was a rich woman who had lost everything in the crash and I walk into a bar to have a drink . . . but I have no money to pay for it. Suddenly I had a character to play, and I immediately responded to that. I was already thinking, *What else could I do to tell you more about this woman?* So I swanned into the bar like a model on a runway, clasping my mink stole around my chest with one hand, and paused for the waiter to pull a chair out for me. Then I ran a finger across the chair seat, checking for dust.

Meanwhile, this wonderful music was playing . . . a short succession of notes that starts the song. It's called a musical figure, and it was written by Ken and Irwin Kostal, who was the conductor on the show and did a fantastic orchestration. And Ken and Mitzie wrote a terrific verse. I sang to the waiter, "Will a four-carat earring buy a glass of champagne?" And I take off my earring and hand it to him. "Champagne, got to celebrate! 'Cause my last million dollars just went right down the drain . . . I'm broke, I'm poor, I'm back where I started. And Joe, I'm sure I've never felt so lighthearted." I toss back the whole glass in one gulp, and then I ask for another . . . and hand him my other earring. As I drink glass after glass, more jewelry comes off until I finally give him my mink stole, in exchange for the bottle. The song took on a completely different tone . . . more dark and ironic. And the audience loved it.

The TV appearances were meant to introduce me to a whole new audience, because Marty was determined to prove that my appeal could reach beyond the Greenwich Village clubs. When I did my two-week run at the Bon Soir at the end of May, this time I was the headliner. My salary had jumped from $175 to $1,250 a week, as Marty just reminded me, adding, "And you got that even though you were only doing one show a night, because you were also starring in *Wholesale*."

And the reviews were really, really good, as he also reminded me.

Leonard Harris wrote in the *New York World-Telegram & Sun*:

> *When Barbra Streisand appeared at the Bon Soir several months ago, one timorous nightclub reporter said she "might be" the best young singer around. With Barbra again at the Bon Soir, the time for courage and correction has arrived.*
>
> *All the hedging words are hereby deleted. The star of "I Can Get It for You Wholesale" is the best—no maybes, no "young" or "old" or other qualifiers needed. She's 20; by the time she's 30 she will have rewritten the record book.*
>
> *Her voice has sweetness, range, color and variety. Pick the best singer of any style, and Barbra can challenge her on her home ground. And Barbra's own style—elfin, humorous, but packing a real punch—is original and unforgettable.*

You can bet Marty made sure Goddard was aware of that notice.

And when I went back to the Blue Angel for a month of more midnight shows in July, guess who showed up on the final night, without a reservation? Goddard Lieberson, and Marty saw to it that he got a seat. After the show Goddard called Marty and told him, "I've changed my mind" and offered me a contract.

Thank God I had something new to occupy me. On October 1, I signed my contract with Columbia Records and two weeks later I was in the studio, recording my first single . . . "Happy Days Are Here Again," with "When the Sun Comes Out" on the B-side. I remember that studio because it was in an old Presbyterian church on East Thirtieth Street . . . one huge room with a one-hundred-foot ceiling . . . and the acoustics were fabulous. Someone told me that Leonard Bernstein, Vladimir Horowitz, and Miles Davis all loved to record there, and I could see why. That space made any music sound magnificent. It was even better than my lobby, where I liked to sing when I was five!

My dear, devoted Marty . . . who always thought about what was best for me, rather than what would make him the most commission . . . had negotiated an unprecedented contract for a first-timer. In exchange for less money up front, I got creative control, which was more important to me than anything else. I was just a small person . . . a *pishica*, as they say in Yiddish . . . but I was adamant about this. It meant I got to choose the songs I sang, and if I didn't like the way an album turned out, I could can it. The concept . . . and the responsibility . . . were all mine.

For the first album, I think somebody at Columbia suggested that I do it live at the Bon Soir . . . certainly cheaper than going into a studio with a full orchestra, which may have been the attraction for them. I was back at the club for a monthlong engagement, beginning in mid-October, and I thought it was a great idea because I wanted to capture the flavor of a live performance, with a real audience. These were my people . . . the men and women who frequented that club had discovered me, in a sense, and they were very loyal. They liked me and they liked my material. They didn't think my songs were too esoteric . . . or "too Broadway."

Neither did David Kapralik, the A&R man at Columbia who really pushed Goddard to sign me. On the first night we were scheduled to record, Dave came down to the club to introduce me, and even he, my big supporter, managed to mispronounce my name. I very softly corrected him, then went right into "My Name Is Barbara" to open the show and had barely started the next number, "Much More," when there was another problem . . . the microphone suddenly stopped working. Mike Berniker, who was producing the album, said, "Uh, we have a fuse that went."

I said, "You're kidding!"

Here we were, all set to record with all this professional equipment, and something as basic as a fuse blows out. So we had to stop before we even got started! Luckily the engineer was able to patch something together, and I could continue the set.

It felt good to be in such familiar surroundings. My old pals were playing for me . . . Tiger Haynes on guitar and Averill Pollard on bass, who had both accompanied me the very first night I auditioned for the Bon Soir and were so kind to me, always. John Cressi was on drums and, of course, Peter Daniels was at the piano. And we did all my old songs . . . "A Sleepin' Bee" and "Cry Me a River" and "Keepin' Out of Mischief Now."

But when we listened to the tapes, it was clear that the sound quality wasn't good enough because of the poor acoustics at the club. The sessions had to be scrapped.

Meanwhile, my first single had come out . . . but hardly anyone was aware of it. Columbia didn't promote it and they didn't press a lot of copies, so even if someone did happen to hear it on the radio and wanted to buy it, it wasn't in the stores. Marty was furious. He knew it never even had a chance. He was pushing Columbia to release another single right away, and a music publisher had approached him with a song . . . "My Coloring Book," by John Kander and Fred Ebb. I wasn't keen on the lyrics or the melody, which I thought were just okay. But Marty felt that in order to get more attention from the disc jockeys, I needed to do something more contemporary. He believed in this song, and I believed in Marty, so I recorded it, with "Lover, Come Back to Me" on the B-side.

Frankly, I was more interested in the album, and as long as I could do exactly what I wanted on that, I wasn't too concerned about the single.

Unfortunately, the publisher who brought "My Coloring Book" to Marty had neglected to mention that two other singers, Kitty Kallen and Sandy Stewart, were also recording it . . . and all of our versions came out at the same time. "I got suckered," says Marty. "You learn. But it didn't hurt Barbra because she got the airplay and it established her in that market."

I sang it on *The Ed Sullivan Show* on December 16, and Ed Sullivan couldn't pronounce my name either. During rehearsals, I kept hearing him say, "Here's a young Columbia recording star, a very great talent . . . Barbra Streis-land." It was driving me crazy, and I wanted to make sure he didn't get it wrong on the broadcast. So just before I went on, I whispered to him one last time from behind the curtain, "STREI-*SAND*! STREI-*SAND*! Like sand on the beach," and he started to laugh right in the middle of the introduction . . . "She's breaking me up over here" . . . but at least he got my name right, for once.

Even now, after six decades in show business, people are still mispronouncing my name.

Does anybody say Oprah WINE-fry? *No.* Judy Gar-LAND. *No.*

Someone recently showed me that when you ask your iPhone a question about me, even Siri says my name wrong.

So I called Tim Cook at Apple. And was told they're going to fix it. And they did.

Back to Ed Sullivan.

I came out and wrung every bit of emotion out of both songs from my second single . . . and that appearance undoubtedly helped, because sales of the record spiked afterward. Marty was pleased, but I was a little worried. I never thought of myself as someone who could appeal to the masses. In fact, I was actually thinking maybe I was getting too popular.

I was always an odd duck. And I wanted to make it on my own terms. I didn't want to change and pretend to be someone else.

Marty reassured me. He said I didn't have to.

In fact, that's why I went with Marty in the first place, when I originally met him at the Bon Soir. He wasn't like other people in the business, who were always telling me to "change the nose, change the clothes, and stop singing those cockamamie songs."

I loved those cockamamie songs, each and every one of them. And now I was going to record them, for posterity.

And I'd have a lot more time, because *I Can Get It for You Wholesale* closed on December 8, after running for nine months.

Finally, I was free.

Free to focus on my album . . . and nobody, but nobody, was going to tell me what to sing.

SEVEN

It All Comes Together

As soon as I knew I was going to record an album, I wanted to find out who did the arrangements for Harold Arlen, because that was the person I wanted to hire to do the same for me.

I always said Harold Arlen was my favorite composer, and when Arlen himself appeared at the club to see me, you can imagine how thrilled I was. In walks this dapper man with a little mustache like my father's. Arlen was another Jewish composer, like George Gershwin, who felt the pain of the oppressed and could put all that angst . . . and also the joy of love . . . into his soulful music. We talked for a bit, squeezed into my dressing room, and he gave me his phone number. Arlen was so kind that I felt comfortable enough to call him up one day to tell him I was doing an album and ask who he would recommend.

When he said "Peter Matz," the name sounded vaguely familiar, and then I remembered where I had seen it . . . on the cover of an album called *The Music of Harold Arlen*. That was all I needed to know. So Marty arranged an appointment, and the three of us met at a restaurant. I remember walking in and seeing this nice-looking guy with dark curly hair and a warm smile. He wore glasses and looked intelligent. I liked him right away.

Peter was thirty-four years old. Married, with a child. And far more worldly than me . . . he had traveled, living in Paris for two years after college, before moving to New York. He'd worked with Marlene Dietrich and Noël Coward on their nightclub acts. And he'd been nominated for a Tony the previous year, like me, as the conductor and musical director of the Richard Rodgers musical *No Strings*.

I thought he was sophisticated, charming, and very attractive in that Jewish intellectual way. His seriousness was combined with a dry sense of humor, which was very appealing to me. He liked to read, and we often talked about books.

In January I was at his apartment on West End Avenue almost every day, so we could go over each song I planned to do. Peter would sit at the piano and play for me as I sang. And I'd tell him what I heard in my head, because his job was to take these songs, which I was used to doing with just a piano, guitar, and bass, and expand them by writing parts for other instruments in the orchestra.

What I particularly loved about Peter is that he really listened to the lyrics as well as the music and tried to tease out every nuance, just as I did. We were on the same wavelength. He understood emotion. And he was so sensitive to my voice . . . he knew how to show it off and he could build on the drama of a lyric. I thought his arrangements were unusual, and yet they always had a certain sound . . . there was something in the way he wrote for horns and flutes, and in the way he handled the strings . . . that was very distinctive to him.

We recorded the whole album in just three days at the end of January . . . which I can't believe. Nowadays it can take a year sometimes to choose the songs, work out the arrangements, write the orchestrations, record the album, and then edit and mix it. But the process was much simpler back in 1963.

Although Peter and I had talked them through, I only heard his arrangements for the first time at the recording studio. (Nowadays my arranger can demo the orchestration with a synthesizer so we can make any changes together before we get to the costly sessions with the musicians.)

We'd do three or four songs a day, beginning at the top and going through to the end . . . unless someone made a major mistake, in which case we'd have to start over.

But you couldn't do that too often. There was simply no time and no money. Imagine the intensity when you've got a whole studio full of people concentrating on the same page of sheet music. The adrenaline kicks in, and it feels amazing. I thrived on that sense of excitement . . . and danger, because it could go wrong at any moment.

Then we'd simply pick the best take to put on the album . . . even though I might be flat on one note or someone might have played a wrong chord at some point. Too bad. That was it. We didn't fix it in those days!

Back then there were only three tracks . . . one for the vocals and two for the orchestra. And I don't think you could edit a track once it was laid down.

Now a recording can have over a hundred tracks, and every note can be manipulated. Mixing a record is like putting together a giant jigsaw puzzle. You can take bits and pieces from different takes and add or subtract instruments . . . fine-tune the sound . . . even change a syllable.

Does it help, having so many choices . . . an almost infinite number of combinations and possibilities?

I wonder sometimes.

And I still go back to one take, one performance usually . . . because that's where the feeling is the most complete . . . and I may just fix a note or two.

I thought I should listen to that first album again before I wrote this. Frankly, I had to force myself. I never listen to my records or watch my movies once they're finished. (Even my friends know better than to play my albums around me.) I suppose there are people who enjoy watching their own work . . . like

Gloria Swanson in *Sunset Boulevard*, or Ronald Reagan in real life, who supposedly liked to watch his old films . . . but that's definitely not me. Been there, done that . . . and I'm afraid I'd want to make changes.

Columbia had given us a small budget, which meant we couldn't afford a full orchestra. Maybe thirty pieces, if that. Today, I might have seventy or eighty pieces. It seems counterintuitive, but the larger the orchestra, the quieter and more intense the sound can be . . . because you get more depth to the notes from all those instruments.

That's the kind of orchestra I heard in all those movie musicals and that's what I was imagining, but instead Peter had to scramble, putting together various combos of musicians for each session . . . so it could seem a little thin in comparison.

The first song is "Cry Me a River," and it basically sounds the same as it did at the Bon Soir. Peter Daniels did that original arrangement with me . . . I remember wanting to sing it starting with the bass only . . . and Peter Matz always said that he owed a lot of what he did on this album to Peter Daniels.

I liked this song, because the lyric is so interesting to dramatize:

You drove me, nearly drove me out of my head
While you never shed a tear . . .

Told me love was too plebeian
Told me you were through with me
And now you say you love me . . .

When Julie London sang it originally, her voice was soft and sultry, and she stayed in tempo all the way through. But I had a different interpretation. This girl is angry at being jilted . . . it nearly drove her mad. And if I'm going to express those feelings, I couldn't stay in tempo. In real life, we often change rhythms as we speak. And since I was approaching the song like telling a story, it was more dramatic that way . . . You told me *what?!* And then, after betraying me, you have the nerve to come back?? Well, I'm going to make you prove that you love me.

It's passionate and bitter, and then the mood shifts and goes upbeat with "My

Honey's Loving Arms." That song just swings along and is much more fun. Hear those squeaks that punctuate the opening bars? That's Peter Matz. It's a very particular sound.

I follow the melody in "I'll Tell the Man in the Street," but in "A Taste of Honey" the instruments have to follow me. I wanted it to feel more ad-libbed, as if I were speaking rather than singing. And I heard it as very pure, basically just my voice and a guitar, as I had done it with Barry on his guitar.

I was trying to vary the musicality. And I doubt I was conscious of this at the time, but it works like a good audition. See, I can be angry, then cute, then sweet, then plaintive. Peter was so attuned to the actress in me and the drama of each song, which made it fun to work together.

And he was so clever. If, for example, I couldn't make a high note, I'd ask him the same thing I asked Peter Daniels: "Isn't there a way of going down in the key, to make it sound like you're going up?" It just made sense to me, mathematically. And both Peters could do it. Even today, when I'm working on an album with Bill Ross, my brilliant arranger and conductor, all I have to do is start to suggest it and he knows exactly what I mean. I still think of it as a trick, but to accomplished musicians like these guys, it's easy.

There's one song on the album I'm afraid to listen to . . . "Happy Days Are Here Again." My concept was that the whole world was collapsing (I had been terrified by the recent Cuban Missile Crisis), but I wasn't happy with the ending. I'm *geshreying* (yelling, in Yiddish), getting so emotional that it's embarrassing. And I wanted the music to crash at the end, like a Mahler symphony . . . with beautiful *and* tragic chords! Not just unpleasant ones. But I couldn't explain it well enough to Peter, I guess, and I didn't want to criticize his arrangement.

Besides, there was no time. I remember the pressure I felt in the studio to work quickly. The budget for the whole album was only eighteen thousand dollars, and even in the 1960s, that was extremely tight. Frankly, I still feel the same kind of pressure when I'm recording today (only the dollars are bigger).

A couple of years later, I sang "Happy Days" on my first TV special and had Peter do a different arrangement for the ending. That's the version that's on the *Greatest Hits* album and that's what I would sing in my concerts . . . although I'm still changing it. Even after all these years, I never got it exactly right.

The last song is "A Sleepin' Bee." That's actually the only song by Harold Arlen on this album, so I was thrilled when he agreed to write the notes for the back cover. One of my greatest memories is going to Harold's Central Park West apartment and sitting down with him at the piano, where he played his songs and we sang together.

Harold's notes on my album were beautifully written. He starts by asking, "Did you ever hear Helen Morgan sing? Were you ever at the theater when Fanny Brice clowned in her classic comedic way?" (Well, that was prophetic.) And then he goes on to say, "Have you ever seen a painting by Modigliani?"

Wow. That choice was kind of uncanny, because if I had to pick my favorite painter, it would probably be Modigliani. But then I also love Vincent van Gogh, Egon Schiele, Edward Hopper, Gustav Klimt, and Edvard Munch. (Luckily this is not a contest, like the Oscars, so I don't have to pick just one.)

Back to "A Sleepin' Bee." There were certain things about the arrangement I didn't like, but I never told Peter. I think I had a bit of a crush on him by then and didn't want to hurt his feelings. Besides, there was no time to fix it, and we couldn't leave it out. This was the song that started my career, and you can hear that girl yearning for love.

At this point, I was yearning for everything.

But I don't think I sang "A Sleepin' Bee" much after recording it for this album. First, because of the arrangement. And second, I guess I had outgrown that innocent young girl, gingerly holding a bee in her hand. I was moving on.

Once the sessions were done and the best takes were chosen, there was still the question of a title. The people at Columbia Records had their own suggestions. Most of them were completely forgettable. But there is one that is etched into my memory . . . *Sweet and Saucy Streisand.* You can probably imagine my reaction to that.

I remember looking around the room at these guys and saying, "Why don't we just call it *The Barbra Streisand Album*? That's what it is. And that's what people are going to ask for if they saw me on some TV show and walk into a store."

The photo on the cover was taken at the Bon Soir by Columbia's staff photographer, on one of the nights we were recording the show for the live album that never was. I'm wearing the herringbone tweed outfit with the white chiffon blouse.

The photo seemed all right to me, but nothing special. Then the designer, John Berg, showed me a few different typefaces, and I picked one, which I'm now told is DeVinne Italic. It was strong and simple, and yet it still had a certain delicacy. (There's that dichotomy I love again.) I ended up using it on many albums.

And I put "Arranged and Conducted by Peter Matz" on the cover. I didn't have to do that, but I liked Peter and he had made the whole thing very easy. I was grateful.

The Barbra Streisand Album was released on February 25, 1963, just four weeks after we recorded it. Boy, that's quick. (I should have asked them to release it on the twenty-fourth, my lucky number.) And the reviews were very good, I'm told, although I have no memory of them. But I do remember a letter that I got from Arthur Laurents soon afterward. He wrote:

Dear Barbra,

You may get momentarily angry when you read this letter but re-read it and think of why I took time out to write you: because I think you have an extraordinary talent and because I have a personal fondness for you. (And the fondness is despite, I must confess, the elements in you that come out of your being frightened, young and ambitious.)

This has all been prompted by listening to your album—which epitomizes everything that has been happening to you since your success in WHOLESALE. *To be blunt, the album is bad and the fault is primarily yours. You have fallen into the trap that most young performers fall into—but you have plunged in defiant, know-it-all head first.*

One of the aims of any artist in any field is to be simple—and that is one of the most difficult goals to achieve. Your album is an absolute mess of mannerisms, decorations, whipped cream on the frosting on the icing on the over-elaborate cake which, actually, is made of the very finest ingredients. The ingredients are your voice, your ability to sing, your instinct as a fledgling actress, your sensitivity as a person.

When I first heard you sing Cry Me a River, *I first realized what the song was about. On the album, the song is the over-dramatic scream of an hysterical woman.*

Then he goes on to criticize every song, in three typewritten pages.

And you know what? I agreed with him, and told him so in a letter. I rarely have anything good to say about my own work. I've always been my own harshest critic.

I found Arthur's letter in my files but I didn't keep a copy of my reply, and it's only thanks to Stephen Sondheim that I have one now. His archivist happened to be going through Arthur's papers at the Library of Congress and came across it and thought I would be interested, so he sent it to me. Here's how I responded:

> *Dear Arthur,*
>
> *Your letter did not make me angry at all—I am the first to say I hate the album—I froze up in front of the mike—the pressure of having to do it in three hours and not go over the budget, musicians that had to leave—musical segments that couldn't be resolved, conceptions that were not worked out well enough between me and the arranger—all led to a horrible album—and because of my self-destructive, lazy nature I just said the hell with it. Instead of relaxing I tightened up and tried to compensate for lacks and what came out was a hysterical void.*

It appears from my response that I was not only completely willing to accept Arthur's criticism but even to expand on it. It was as if I'd internalized his harsh words and added more of my own. As I wrote, "Knowing me, you should know I crave criticism."

A psychologist might be able to explain why I was so ready to dismiss an album that actually meant so much to me, especially since I already knew that Arthur could be cruel and manipulative.

At least I wasn't about to concede to every one of my supposed transgressions. Arthur accused me of imitating Lena Horne, and that really rankled me. Horne had this great sexy body, wrapped it in gorgeous gowns, and sang in her unique style. It had nothing to do with me. So I defended myself. I hadn't even seen her yet . . . and besides, I had too much ego to copy anyone. It would never even occur to me. I always had my own way of doing things, for better or worse.

That's the truth.

It's interesting how he goes on to put himself in the position of the authority:

> ***It is your first album. Learn from it. It is peculiarly difficult for you, unfortunately, to learn from experience, to admit you need help, to take it. You indulge in great chatter about being an artist and I suspect the only person you trust is yourself. Barbra, you simply do not know enough to rely only on yourself at this stage. (And as a human being, you* must *believe other people can be trusted; otherwise, life will be very thin indeed.)***

Actually, I've always hesitated to call myself an "artist" . . . to me, that's Modigliani or Rembrandt . . . and frankly, I'm not sure a true artist really listens all that much to other people anyway.

I did have a problem trusting other people. Arthur's right about that, but the whole subtext of his letter was that he was the true teacher, the guru, the only one I should trust to help me mend my ways. As he wrote, "Unfortunately, no performer in the world has or ever has had perfect taste. That is why directors are needed."

I think he was trying to reassert himself in my life now that I'd had more success. But as I wrote, "Your letter was . . . vicious . . . I think you really wanted to hurt me—not help me."

Perhaps he was still smarting from our conflict over "Miss Marmelstein." And the fact that I was right may explain some of his anger.

Still, I found something positive to say, because I did think he wrote good dialogue that made for strong characters. "You're a great writer—I wish you would write something for me." (And eventually he did, with *The Way We Were* . . . but I'll tell you that story later.)

So I wasn't crushed by Arthur's criticism. But I was unreasonably hard on a record that went on to win Album of the Year and Best Female Vocal Performance at the next Grammy Awards. (I don't remember any congratulatory note from Arthur.)

It's funny . . . you'd think I'd remember my first Grammys. But the only reason I have any recollection at all is because Quincy Jones, who became a dear friend, also won his first Grammy that night, and years later he sent me a picture of the two of us, with other winners. I don't know why I didn't pay more attention to awards. Maybe I just didn't know how to react to them . . .

So, this was an exciting time, and yet a lot of it is just a blur to me now.

> *"She is 20 years old, she has a three-octave promiscuity of range, she packs more personal dynamic power than anybody I can recall since Libby Holman or Helen Morgan . . . She is the hottest thing to hit the entertainment field since Lena Horne erupted, and she will be around 50 years from now if good songs are still written to be sung by good singers."*
>
> —Robert Ruark, reviewing Barbra at the Blue Angel in January 1963

In order to build interest in the album, Marty began putting together a tour. And then Elliott and I were both asked to be in a production of *On the Town* in London, and I was torn. Elliott had always been able to come with me wherever I was performing, but now he decided to take this job. I was happy for him, yet not sure it was right for me. It would have been the worst possible time for me to be out of the country, right after my album was released.

But if I turned it down, we'd be separated for months . . . maybe even longer if the show was a hit . . . and neither of us was sure how that would affect our relationship.

Elliott and I had a dinner with Marty at Sardi's, and it got a little tense when the subject of whether or not I was going to London came up.

Elliott looked at me and asked, "What's more important? Me or this recording thing?" And I said, "You are," and told him I'd go with him.

That was exactly what he wanted to hear. He needed to know that I cared more about him than my career. And now that I had given him the answer he hoped for, he had no intention of holding me to it. He said, "That's very sweet of you. But you're not going to come to London. You're going to stay here and do your tour."

It started out in February at a nightclub called the Frolic in Revere Beach, outside Boston. (Marty told me it was run by gangsters, and I remember thinking, *That's good. If there's any problem, they can protect me!*) Who would have guessed that by the end of the tour I would be selling out the 6,700-seat Shrine Auditorium in Los Angeles?

Nineteen sixty-three was the year that everything came together for me.

After the Frolic, I was booked at the Chateau in Cleveland. While I was singing there at night, I was also doing *The Mike Douglas Show* during the day. Mike was such a sweetheart. He had me on for a whole week and did everything he could to promote me and the album. I think I sang every song on it, in between acting as his cohost. I helped interview other guests, did comedy sketches, and even taught Mike how to play skelly like a Brooklyn kid.

Back in New York I did *The Tonight Show* again. Johnny Carson was also very supportive, and said, "I've been reading so many good things about you . . . Nice picture and a write-up in *Time* magazine."

"Terrific," I replied.

"I suppose pretty soon when you get to be a big star, we'll never see you again."

You can probably guess what he expected me to say . . . something like, Oh no, I love being on your show!

And what did I do? I said, "No, never," half kidding and half telling the truth.

He quickly made a joke out of it. "She probably means it too!"

And I did, in a way. After 1963, I never went on Johnny Carson again (although that was more of a coincidence than a deliberate choice). The fact is, I wasn't really comfortable on live TV, especially those kinds of shows where you basically dropped in for five minutes. It was hard to perform with musicians I didn't know. It made me too nervous.

Before he left for rehearsals, Elliott did come with me to Miami, where I was performing at the Eden Roc Hotel. And while we were there, he gave me a ring, and I bought one for him too. Elliott felt anxious about leaving me. "I don't want you to stray," he told me. "I want to confirm our relationship. We're marrying one another spiritually."

And then I went on a radio show, and the host spotted the ring on my left hand and asked if Elliott and I had gotten married. I didn't know what to say, and I wasn't experienced enough to deflect the question. Elliott and I *were* wearing these wedding rings and we were living together, which wasn't as acceptable then as it is now. I just wanted to put an end to the questions, so I said, "Yes. We got married," and that became the big news.

It seemed so silly to me. What difference did it make to anyone else? I thought it was our own private business, and now it had become public. I didn't like being scrutinized.

Elliott flew off to London, and I flew off in the opposite direction, to San Francisco, to play the hungry i club. Remember I had forced myself to make a pitch to the owner, Enrico Banducci, when I was just starting out? Well, this was the first opportunity I had to fulfill that commitment. I was on the bill with Woody Allen, but we barely met. We were both such loners that we never said anything to each other. He would read in his dressing room, and I would read in mine.

I think it was on this trip that someone asked me, "How do you hold a note so long?"

After a moment of thought, I said, "Because I want to."

It's a matter of will . . . I wanted to hold the note, so I did. But then I started thinking about it and wondering, *How* did *I hold a note?* And what had been an unconscious, effortless thing suddenly became conscious . . . and I couldn't do it anymore.

This really spooked me. For the first time in my life, I was having vocal problems. I missed a few high notes. I came down with laryngitis in the midst of doing two shows a night. So I went to see a vocal coach, Judy Davis.

She asked me to sing, while she watched closely.

I was very nervous . . . Had I damaged my voice? Was it lost forever? But she immediately reassured me. "What you are doing when you sing is utterly correct. It's fine. It's natural. And I couldn't teach you how to do it any better. But what I can show you is the physiology of what happens when you sing, so you understand it better."

That was interesting. She took out a chart and explained various things about vocal projection. I was so relieved that there was nothing wrong with me. She told me to relax and just continue as I was, and I will always be grateful to her.

And as I was leaving her office, I realized something. I had imagined a problem where there was none, and now that I was aware of that, I could take it away. It reminded me all over again of the power of the mind. I think the real reason I lost my voice was because I felt guilty about not being in England with Elliott.

The next time I opened my mouth to sing, my voice was back.

As soon as I had a break, I went to London to visit him. Elliott splurged on a room for us at the Savoy Hotel . . . it was a tiny room at the top, formerly used by servants, but it was charming. And Joe Layton, who was directing *On the Town*, let him out of rehearsals for a day or two. Elliott was playing a sailor, and he remembers what Joe said to the other two actors who were playing his buddies when Elliott came back: "See how happy Elliott is? That's how I want you to look."

When the show moved to Oxford for previews, I came along. I remember the hotel had these very high, soft beds. While Elliott was in rehearsals with Joe, I hung out with Joe's wife, Evelyn. We would often go shopping during the day. In a great little five-and-ten, I found the most beautiful pale lipsticks. (I don't like dark colors, because my mouth is too big, and I don't want to draw attention to it.) I wore them for years in all my movies.

When I came back to America, I flew to California to tape *The Dinah Shore Show*. That really impressed my mom, who loved Dinah Shore. These guest shots (I had also done *The Ed Sullivan Show* again) were working . . . the album was climbing the charts . . . and word of mouth from my sold-out run at the hungry i probably helped.

For the last two weeks of May, I was back in New York as the opening act for Benny Goodman and his jazz band at Basin Street East. (After the first performance, Goodman decided not to follow me and went on first.) Truman Capote, Cecil Beaton, and Tennessee Williams were in the audience on various nights. That was serendipitous, since Truman Capote wrote the book and cowrote the lyrics for *House of Flowers*, the show that gave me my first song, "A Sleepin' Bee." Cecil Beaton and I would later work together on *On a Clear Day You Can See Forever*. And Tennessee Williams seemed to know me, although I'm not sure we ever met. (I think I would have remembered that!) And yet he wrote one of the most insightful things about me:

> *I am not here to analyze Miss Streisand . . . but I recognize the shy, discarded child who had a story to tell, but no idea how it could be done. I acted scenes with my sister and my mother, and soon words were my salvation, friends {with whom} I could spend time safe and sure of my standing. I think that Barbra Streisand is, first and foremost, an actress, a wonderful actress, who found that fate and*

a giddy God had endowed her with an instrument that even she does not fully understand.

And then she could be heard and seen and loved.

She tells stories with the turn of that head, those feline eyes, those hands that end in nails lethal and self-protective: You will listen, she says, and you will learn and you will love, but you will not get close.

There are limits.

Not to the talent, but to the relationship between this artist and her audience.

We might want to understand her, ask her how she does things, and that would limit and define her and—put her right back in that cage from which she has escaped.

The great artists are always in flight.

God, how did he intuit all that? I would have loved to spend time with him and talk about many things. I could have told him the story of how I was reading one of his plays when I called Lee Strasberg's office. I bet he would have laughed.

The management at Basin Street East was kind enough to let me out for one night so I could sing for President John F. Kennedy at the annual White House Correspondents' Dinner. Someone told me that he had seen me on *The Dinah Shore Show* and asked for me personally. You must know by now that I can be remarkably blasé about a lot of things, but this was exciting, even for me. Marty and Peter Daniels came along, and Peter conducted the orchestra as I sang three songs, ending with "Happy Days Are Here Again." With JFK as our president, I felt those words were actually true and I sang it joyously.

Since I loved clothes from the Napoleonic period, I designed an Empire-style gown with a scoop neck and short sleeves. It was made of soft gray wool with a row of buttons down the front, getting larger in size toward the bottom. The gray wool parted in the center of the gown, so you could see the cream sheath underneath.

After the dinner everyone who had performed lined up to meet the president. The protocol people were very clear . . . this was a quick meet and greet. We were not to detain him by asking for anything as plebeian as an autograph.

When JFK got to me, he told me that I had a beautiful voice and asked, "How long have you been singing?"

I said, "About as long as you've been president."

He laughed, and then I did exactly what we were told not to do. I asked him if he would sign a card from the dinner for my mother. When he handed it back to me, I told him, "You're a doll." That's a real Brooklyn expression . . . and I guess some people were a little surprised to hear me saying it to the president. Frankly, it just slipped out.

And he *was* a doll. He glowed. There was an aura around his head. He was like a rock star . . . I heard girls screaming outside, I swear.

I tucked the card into my cleavage, and then somehow managed to lose it before I got home. I couldn't believe it! But I still have that gown, hanging in my collection of antique clothes. (By now it's an antique too.)

I recorded my second album over three days in June, and added a song Peter Matz had written for me, "Gotta Move," which we had already done during a February session. It had a lot of energy, and he saw something in me that he used for the lyric:

Gotta move, gotta get out, gotta leave this place
Gotta find some place, some other place, some brand new place
Some place where each face that I see won't be staring back at me
Telling me what to be and how to be it!

(By the way, that recording was featured in a Super Bowl commercial for Bud Light beer in 2022. Not my usual demographic . . . but I'll take it!)

This album also featured five Harold Arlen songs, which I loved because they were all character driven and soulful. I started with "Any Place I Hang My Hat Is Home," then went on to "Right as the Rain," "Down with Love," "When the Sun Comes Out," and "Like a Straw in the Wind." For the finale, I used the medley of "Like a Straw in the Wind" and "Anyplace I Hang My Hat Is Home." I liked juxtaposing those two philosophical statements . . . I move anywhere, yet I'm at home anywhere.

And what did I call this album? You should be able to guess: *The Second Barbra Streisand Album.* When I look at the cover photo now, I think, *Ugh. It's terrible . . . taken from the wrong angle.* (I didn't know better then.) The only thing that looked good was my hair! (Fred Glaser in Chicago gave me that haircut.)

But the notes on the back . . . written by my dear Jule Styne . . . still make me feel wonderful: "Barbra is the first girl I have ever heard who is a great actress in each song . . . At its beginning, she establishes her character; next, she creates a conflict (making all the lyrics mean so much more than they seem to), then she reaches a tremendous conclusion—so that, even after hearing only one song, lasting only a few minutes, one is completely overwhelmed."

Jumping ahead for a moment, my third album was called *The Third Album* . . . the last of my numbered albums. (I was getting bored with that pattern.) Most of it was recorded in 1963, even though it wasn't released until February 1964, and most of the songs were my old standbys . . . show tunes. But I was working with a new arranger, Ray Ellis, on "Melancholy Baby," "Taking a Chance on Love," "As Time Goes By," and "It Had to Be You." I had gotten Ray's name from my favorite Billie Holiday album, *Lady in Satin*. I figured he must be good if she chose him. And sure enough, Ray was terrific, and we continued to work together for years. Like Peter Matz, he had his own distinctive sound, and he was very fond of flutes.

The cover photo was taken by Roddy McDowell on the set of *The Judy Garland Show*. (So I wouldn't have to do another photo shoot.) Somehow I thought it would be intriguing to use it small, in the upper right corner. Looking at it now, I wonder why. Maybe I just wanted something different from the close-ups on the previous two albums.

Sammy Cahn, who wrote the lyrics to so many great songs like "Come Fly with Me," "High Hopes," and "Three Coins in the Fountain," had seen me at the Riviera Hotel and wrote the liner notes:

"In defiance of all the rules, she went into her opening number . . . a ballad instead of the traditional up-tempo opener . . . I was just getting over the shock of it when I noticed, to my amazement, that everyone had stopped eating. Even more amazing, the waiters had stopped serving . . . I have only known one or two people in all of show business who had this power with an audience. I never waited to see who closed the show, but rushed backstage and fell in love!"

I used to fondly call Sammy "my dentist," because he looked like one! Sammy was not only a great lyricist, but a very sweet and funny man.

In between all these recording sessions and club dates, the auditions for *Funny Girl* were still going on. Jerry Robbins had asked me to come back three or four times (Marty says there were seven auditions, but I only remember four), and there was still no decision. I was starting to feel frustrated. What was taking them so long? I asked Marty to find out. He called Jeff Hunter, who told him, "Look, that's the process." Marty asked if he should call David Merrick. Jeff said, "I wouldn't upset that apple cart." But by now Marty was friendly with Merrick, who told him, "Call Jerry." So Marty did.

Jerry was frank. He told Marty, "I knew Barbra could do the first act . . . the young girl . . . as soon as I heard her sing. But in the second, she's a married woman with a kid. I'm not sure she can make the transition."

I was barely twenty-one years old. The character of Fanny Brice goes from nineteen to thirty-six in the course of the play. Jerry was looking for a certain kind of maturity in those later scenes, and he told Marty he wanted to see me again the next day.

How could I become more mature overnight? I had no idea, so I called Allan Miller, my old acting teacher.

I think Allan laughed when I first told him what I needed, but he was willing to give it a try. When he came to my apartment to work with me, we started thinking about what maturity means . . . listing words like "responsible" and "secure." But that was a little abstract for me.

Then we talked about various public figures who could be called "mature." But that was another dead end . . . I don't like to imitate anybody.

As we were talking, Allan's eyes landed on a picture hanging near our heads . . . my Rembrandt print of a young woman bathing.

He suddenly asked, "What about her? Does she seem mature?"

"Kind of." But I couldn't describe why.

Allan prompted me, "What's she doing?"

"She's dipping her feet in the stream and lifting her skirt so it doesn't get wet."

"Yes. Is she splashing, or laughing, or playing around?"

"No, she's just dipping her feet."

"Exactly. She's only doing what's necessary."

Now I knew where he was going with this. "Oh, I see!" And I made some sort of gesture with my hands.

Allan asked, "Did you have to wave your hands around in order to tell me you understood?"

"No," I said, shaking my head.

"Did you need to shake your head?"

"No," I said.

"There," he said. "That's it. Now you sound very mature to me."

I understood the point he was making. It was about simplification . . . about doing only what's required, and nothing more. It was about the absence of movement. When you're older, you're not hopping around from foot to foot, like a restless teenager. You're more contained.

I could do that. And it worked. I got through that audition.

And then we heard back. They wanted me to come in one last time, for one last look, and do one final monologue for them. And they promised this would be it.

Of course I was nervous. So of course I was late.

Jerry was not happy. "We've been waiting almost an hour for you. This better be good."

Not the best start. I apologized and made some excuse, but I also knew that it was completely my fault. He had every right to be angry.

But I couldn't let it throw me. I may have tried to be cavalier . . . or at least not desperate about whether or not I got the part. But at that moment, when it seemed that I might have lost it for no good reason, I suddenly knew how much I wanted it.

I stood very still. I closed my eyes for a moment and tried to empty my head of all these rushing thoughts . . . anxiety and fear. I concentrated on the scene . . . my intentions . . . and let the words carry me to the emotions.

I was in the moment.

When I finished, Jerry jumped up and hugged me. He said, "That was great. As far as I'm concerned, you're Fanny Brice."

I was incredibly happy . . . quite thrilled . . . and kind of stunned.

The official announcement that I would be starring in *Funny Girl* didn't come until the end of July, but they weren't ready to start rehearsals for a while because they were still writing the show. And that suited me just fine, because I still had all these club dates to fulfill.

I spent the last three weeks of June in Chicago, where I was singing at Mister Kelly's. My first album was up to number 14 on *Billboard*'s chart. Joan Baez and I were alternating as the bestselling female vocalist.

In July I was the opening act for Liberace at the Riviera Hotel in Las Vegas.

He'd seen me at the Bon Soir, and then we both happened to appear on the same *Ed Sullivan Show*. Lee was a sweet man who wanted to do whatever he could for me, so he offered me this gig. But this was a whole new crowd for me. His fans were not naturally my fans, and I don't think they knew what to make of me. For the first few nights they barely paid any attention to me. They were just waiting for him.

Lee felt bad for me, and he decided to do something about it. "Listen," he said, "here's what we're gonna do. I'll go out and open the show, do about ten minutes, and then I'll introduce you as my discovery. Give it the old schmaltz!"

It worked like a charm. I came out and did the exact same show, but this time by the end of it, people were on their feet, applauding wildly. My mood turned around. I could actually enjoy myself. The comedian Dick Shawn was working nearby, and we'd meet up after our shows and go for long drives into the desert, where the stars were much brighter, away from the city lights. He kept up a running stream of jokes as he drove, and I don't think I've ever laughed so much.

I was feeling great. My first album had climbed to number 8. But Elliott was not doing so well. *On the Town* was struggling, and it closed much sooner than expected. He flew back to New York and then came to see me in Las Vegas. Something happened when he arrived. I think we had a fight . . . I must have told him that I had been spending time with Dick Shawn, and he got jealous.

I told him I wasn't attracted to Dick. (He had a very hairy chest, and it just didn't feel right to me.)

But I'm not sure that made Elliott feel any better. He could sense that while he was away, I'd kept one foot in and one foot out of the relationship . . . as if I were still looking around.

I was very honest with him. "I haven't known that many men. What if I need to sow my wild oats? What if I meet Marlon Brando and I want to be with him?"

Elliott looked at me and did a slow take: "Yeah, well, if I met Marlon Brando I'd want to be with him too."

I burst out laughing. Elliott had a very droll sense of humor, and it gets me every time. So when he went back to New York, I told him to start looking for a new apartment for the two of us. It was time to say goodbye to that bathtub in the kitchen.

Elliott turned out to be a wiz at finding real estate, and I soon got a stack of Polaroids in the mail of an apartment for rent that he liked. I wanted him to take pictures with a person in them so I could see the scale. He went back with our friend Ashley Feinstein, who had been Arthur Laurents's assistant on *Wholesale.* (I still have those Polaroids, with one or the other of them in each room.) After one look at the new photos, I said, "Take it."

It was a duplex penthouse in the Ardsley, an Art Deco building at 320 Central Park West, designed by the architect Emery Roth in 1929. It was elegant and spacious, with six rooms, two fireplaces, a curving staircase, and French doors that opened onto a huge terrace overlooking half the city. Lorenz Hart, who was the lyricist half of the famous Rodgers and Hart . . . they wrote "Blue Moon," "Bewitched, Bothered and Bewildered," and "My Funny Valentine," among many other great songs . . . had once lived there with his mother.

Quite a dramatic change from my railroad flat over the fish restaurant.

We moved in August, but I barely had time to arrange our meager bits of furniture before I had to fly back to Los Angeles to perform at the Cocoanut Grove, the famous nightclub in the Ambassador Hotel. There were fake palm trees scattered around the room . . . left over from Rudolph Valentino's movie *The Sheik*, apparently . . . and the whole place was crazy and exotic and fun. It was a big deal to play there. Marty said every agent in Hollywood was coming to check me out, because I had no representation at the moment, and they had brought their biggest stars along with them . . . Henry Fonda, Kirk Douglas, Jack Benny, Edward G. Robinson, Ray Milland, Jack Lemmon. I think Ray Stark also had something to do with the guest list on my opening night. After all, I was going to be starring in his show, and he wanted a starry reception.

Marilyn and Alan Bergman were there, and as they were heading to their table, they stopped to talk to Milton Berle and his wife, Ruth. "She was a piece of work," says Marilyn. "She looked at me and said, 'I can't believe we're all here to see some *fakakta* folk singer.'" (*Fakakta* is Yiddish for lousy.) I later became great friends with Milton. I can still do a card trick he taught me.

But his wife's attitude was probably shared by more than a few people in that room. So I was really nervous. There was no dressing room at the club . . . instead they gave me a suite on the first floor . . . and I was an hour late for my own show, touching up makeup, hair, and wearing a new outfit for the first time. I had designed a creamy-white satin middy blouse trimmed in black. I loved that look . . . like sailors used to wear, but in satin, so it was both masculine and feminine at the same time. And the blouse was loose enough to allow me to breathe comfortably when I sang. I envisioned it with a long black skirt, slit to above the knee. I drew it up and had it made at a costume company, in different color combinations, like burgundy and ivory.

When I finally walked out onstage, I stood still for a moment and just listened to the applause. I had to stop and absorb it. It was unbelievable, in a sense, and yet it was happening. All these big stars had come to see *me*. Even I had to admit it was dazzling, and said to the crowd, "I'm the kind of nut who read movie magazines till a couple of years ago, and here you all are, alive!" And then I added, "This is a strange room . . . so wide. If I had known you were going to be on both sides of me, I would have had my nose fixed."

That broke the ice, and the room erupted in laughter. Oh boy, now I could relax and sing. At the end of the show, they wouldn't stop applauding. Finally I said, "I don't know any more songs." That's when Tony Curtis shouted out from the audience, "Just start at the top and do it all over again!"

It was an incredible reception. I couldn't have asked for anything more. When I could finally get off the stage, I went to my suite to change for the after-party. Freddie Fields and David Begelman, who had just formed their own agency, Creative Management Associates, were already waiting to congratulate me. Marty always wondered how they had managed to get in before we did.

I put on a gown I had designed, made of gingham . . . tiny red-and-white checks . . . with long, puffy white chiffon sleeves trimmed in a band of the same gingham at the cuffs. To me, that was the height of elegance . . . to wear a long gown but have it made out of kitchen curtain material that only cost sixty-nine cents a yard.

Why spend a thousand dollars on a fancy beaded gown? I would rather buy simple gingham and spend what I saved on antique furniture for my new apartment. Besides, I've always loved gingham. But I'm sure some people in Hollywood thought I was wearing a tablecloth.

Marty escorted me to the party, and I was happy to see some familiar faces . . . Jule and Maggie Styne had flown out from New York to be there. Otherwise I hardly knew anybody . . . except for Ray Stark and the Bergmans. I've seen pictures of me that night with Natalie Wood and Robert Wagner. But I've also seen photos where I have my hands in front of my face, hiding from the camera. I think I was a little overwhelmed.

I remember meeting James Mason, with that deep, resonant voice I knew from *A Star Is Born*. When he took my hand in his, I noticed that his hands were rough (maybe he was an outdoorsman). I'm told Steve McQueen was there, but I don't recall meeting him. (How could I forget?)

Elliott wasn't there for my opening, but he did fly out so we could be together on his birthday, August 29. It was supposed to be a surprise, but then my mother called me. "Don't tell Elliott that I told you," she said, "but he's coming to see you." I was so mad at her. I asked her later, "Why would you spoil the surprise?"

And she said, "I was worried you would have a heart attack."

She was always trying to instill her fears in me, and I spent a lifetime (and a lot of money on therapy) trying to get out from under them.

The news that I was going to be starring in *Funny Girl* was the hook for more interviews, and for once I happily complied. Inevitably the subject came around to my "husband," and I had to talk about Elliott, digging myself deeper into the hole I had created. It was getting very awkward. What if somebody found out that we were not really married?

I loved Elliott. He was familiar to me . . . from Brooklyn, down-to-earth. But I still wasn't sure I was ready for marriage. After all, I was only twenty-one, and he was my first serious boyfriend. I didn't want this marriage thing to become such a big deal.

One day, I looked at him and said, "Let's just do it."

So on September 13, we got into Marty's rented car and drove to Carson City, Nevada, where you could get married very easily. Unlike New York, where you had to get a blood test (which frightened me because I hate needles) and wait three days. So I preferred Nevada. Very convenient.

(Decades later, when I was developing a movie about the photographer Margaret Bourke-White, I found out that she and the writer Erskine Caldwell had also gotten married in Carson City. I loved that coincidence.)

I was wearing my simple seersucker suit as we took our places in front of a justice of the peace, who had a slight speech impediment. Put it this way, "Dearly beloved" was very hard for him to say. Elliott and I looked at each other and started to giggle. I know it wasn't polite and I'm not proud of it, but we were in a nervous mood to begin with and we couldn't help it.

I apologized. "Sorry. Could you start from the top?"

I don't remember much else about the ceremony, except that when the justice asked me to promise to "love, honor, and obey," I asked if we could leave out the "obey" part.

Marty had come along for the ride, so he could be our witness. Did we at least celebrate with a meal in Carson City? Knowing me, I must have been hungry. And then we all drove right back to Lake Tahoe so I could do the Friday night show.

Then Elliott and I had a fight. Poor guy . . . he must have done something to bother me because I was pissed off and angry on our wedding night. I can't even remember what it was about, probably because it was only a symptom of something deeper that was troubling me. As Elliott says now, "I don't think you really wanted to get married."

Right. I had liked our private moment in Florida with that thin little ring . . . I had initially put it on to test what marriage might feel like . . . and now I was wondering, *What did I just do?*

We were bound together legally, and the bond suddenly felt too tight.

Elliott and I were so alike . . . two Jewish strays, in a way. I'm not sure two people who are so alike should marry each other. There was no mystery.

While I was singing at Harrah's, Liberace made sure I had a nice house. It was a wood cabin, surrounded by pine trees, right on the lake. It came with a boat, and I was out on the boat with Elliott one afternoon when the phone rang. Marty picked it up. It was Ray Stark, and he told Marty that he had just bought out David Merrick. He was no longer the coproducer of *Funny Girl*.

I was so busy with my albums and the tour that I hadn't had much chance to think about *Funny Girl*. I knew they were still working on the show . . . Jule had played me some new songs while he was in California . . . and I still hadn't seen a final script. But I didn't learn about the real turmoil till much later. Apparently Ray was balking at the changes that Jerry thought were essential to fixing the script. So Jerry quit, and his lawyer sent Ray a letter forbidding him to use any of the ideas that Jerry had contributed to the show. Ray's attorney wrote back stating that Ray was unaware of any ideas that Jerry had contributed to the show. So Jerry drew up a detailed list, and it was clear that his fingerprints were all over the script. Would they now have to start all over? Merrick probably wanted to get out while the going was good and focus on his own show, *Hello, Dolly!*

Of course Ray put Merrick's departure in the most positive terms, as if it wouldn't change anything at all. But when Marty hung up the phone, he started thinking. Something was nagging at the back of his brain. Wasn't the contract I had signed with David Merrick?

He called the lawyer in New York and asked her to look it up. And sure enough, Marty's memory was right. So then he asked her another question. If David Merrick was out, was that contract still valid?

The answer was no. You can't transfer a personal service contract.

For a few months now Marty had been telling Ray that he was underpaying me. I already had one bestselling album, and now the second was out, and it was climbing the charts even faster than the first. "Barbra was on her way to becoming a big star," Marty recalls. "And there was some question whether it even made sense to do *Funny Girl* at all, when she could make thousands of dollars more a week in clubs."

But I was an actress, not a singer, and I wanted to go back to the theater. It was important to me to do this play. Marty ended up renegotiating my contract. He understood the economics of Broadway and behaved very reasonably, even though Ray balked all the way. He screamed and hollered and threatened to replace me. Marty stood his ground. I couldn't remember what my salary was, so I had to call Marty. He told me he negotiated it up from two thousand dollars a week to twenty-five hundred. At that time an extra five hundred dollars was a lot. And he did manage to get my commitment to the show down from twenty months to eighteen.

I didn't care about the money. I was just excited to be doing something I loved.

After I finished my stint at Harrah's, I had a few days before I had to be back in Los Angeles, so Elliott and I decided to go on a honeymoon. We took off from Lake Tahoe in a car Elliott had borrowed. He didn't have a license . . . and it soon became very apparent that he really didn't know how to drive. The car would jerk forward and backward as he attempted to switch gears. I was getting sick to my stomach. And then to top it all off, as we headed toward Big Sur, the fog rolled in off the ocean. We could barely see six inches in front of us. Elliott sat hunched over the wheel, trying to peer into the gloom. I was terrified.

For some reason he had thought it would be a great idea to take me to Esalen, the original New Age retreat. Of course we got lost, and when we finally arrived, it was very late, and the whole place looked deserted. Finally someone showed up and checked us in and then picked up a flashlight to lead us down a dirt path through the trees. The air did not smell like pine. In fact, it stank. I asked, "What is that smell?" and our guide said, "Oh, that's sulfur from the hot springs. Everyone comes to bathe in the water. It's very healing."

Clothing was optional.

Yuck!

I gritted my teeth and tried not to walk into any of the rocks that loomed up out of the darkness. Branches brushed my face. The cabin, we saw when the guide opened the door and turned on the light, was all bare wood and bare floors. I felt as if I had suddenly been transported back to that camp I hadn't liked when I was eight. The bed was basically a futon, so thin that there wasn't even the slightest bounce when I sat down.

I looked around the room. No TV?

"That's it," I told Elliott. "I can't be without a TV." (Sounds like my dialogue from *The Owl and the Pussycat.*)

And we were starving, but there was no such thing as room service in this place. How could they even call themselves a hotel? I was used to the Catskills, where you could get a pastrami sandwich at any hour of the day or night. Jewish hotels are all about food.

We got back into the car and drove to the nearest motel . . . with blinking lights outside lighting up the letters "TV." We stopped at a diner along the way, picked up cheeseburgers and French fries, and ate in front of the set.

That was it for the honeymoon.

Besides, with everything that was happening, real life was beginning to seem more like a fantasy. That first taste of Hollywood was seductive. Elliott and I frolicked in the pool at the Beverly Hills Hotel while Bob Willoughby photographed us for *Glamour* magazine. Danny Thomas and his wife, Rose Marie, couldn't have been nicer and invited us over to dinner. That was like being welcomed into his family.

And then there was the more regal side of the town, like going to a dinner party at the home of Bill and Edie Goetz. He was one of the original partners in what became 20th Century Fox, and she was the daughter of one of the founders of MGM, Louis B. Mayer. I had never seen a home like this, with paintings by Monet, Degas, Cézanne, Picasso, and Modigliani hanging on the walls. There was a self-portrait by Vincent van Gogh that particularly fascinated me, because it was unfinished. (Later, I think the whole thing was determined to be a fake.) But this was the first time I realized that some people could actually buy a great painting and have it in their home. That was amazing to me.

And I discovered something else, as I met more and more celebrities (there was quite a parade through my suite during my stint at the Cocoanut Grove). And guess what? They turned out to be human after all. This one was short, that one was going bald, this one drank a little too much. It was kind of funny . . . and enlightening . . . and comforting.

I liked California from the first time I arrived, and I knew someday I'd live there. What's not to like? The sky was blue, the breeze was warm, and you could pick oranges off the trees. I wanted Marty to rent a convertible, and we drove down Sunset Boulevard, but I didn't have much time for sightseeing. I was too busy working. I sang with Bob Hope and Dean Martin on an NBC special. And at the beginning of October, I taped a guest spot on *The Judy Garland Show*. That was the appearance that meant the most to me, and to Marty. When Freddie Fields and David Begelman were camped out in my suite at the Ambassador Hotel, trying to persuade Marty that they should represent me, he said, "Deliver me the Garland show and you got her." The next day Marty had the contract in his hand. Freddie and David also represented Judy . . . and now they represented me.

There was an extraordinary group of people behind that program. Norman Jewison, who went on to direct many fine films, was the executive producer, and Gary Smith was the production designer (who later worked with me on some of my own TV specials). Mort Lindsey was the musical director (who later conducted for me as well). Mel Tormé provided special musical material. And then, of course, there was Judy . . . legendary . . . soulful . . . divine.

A few years earlier, I had been walking down the street in Manhattan when I saw a sign that said Judy Garland was taping a show. I walked in and joined the audience. That's where I saw her perform live, and she was magnificent. Now I would be singing with her.

I used to give credit to Mel Tormé for our duet. But in his autobiography he explained that it was actually Judy's idea to combine "Happy Days Are Here Again" and "Get Happy." Mel described how he walked into her dressing room when she was playing my song. She lifted the needle off the record and moved it back to the beginning, saying, "Listen." And then she started singing her song, in counterpoint.

I'll never forget singing that duet. We sat next to each other (me in my white middy blouse), and I noticed she was shaking. She grabbed my arm, as if to steady herself, and then clasped my hand and held on to it tightly. She never let go of me until the end of the song. I couldn't believe it. I thought, *This is Judy Garland! Why is she frightened?*

My heart went out to her.

She was only forty-one years old, and I was twenty-one. Now, many years later, I understand. Somehow you become more scared as you get older. And the more successful you are, the more the pressure increases . . . there seem to be more people out there just waiting for you to fail. Judy liked to drink Liebfraumilch, a kind of sweet white German wine, and she offered me some. I don't like the taste of wine, so I didn't join her. And I didn't need anything to take the edge off, because I wasn't nervous. I was simply delighted to be singing with her.

There was a segment where Judy introduced her guests, called "Be My Guest," and done to a tune Mel wrote . . . with special material that he also wrote for each guest. When she brought me out, I sang, "Well, if I really am your guest, I have a small request."

She replied, "Anything you wanna do."

"Anything?"

"Anything!"

And I said, "Can I replace you?"

That was scripted dialogue, written by Mel or one of the writers and given to me to say because they thought it would get a laugh. And somehow, over the years, this has been twisted into a totally different story . . . that I came out onstage and really meant that!

Ridiculous.

People were looking for some sort of rivalry between us. And when they couldn't find anything, they made it up. I found Judy to be completely generous. We sang a medley of songs, taking turns, and she wasn't just focused on herself. She watched me and responded to me. She would reach out and brush back a strand of my hair, like a mother. And Judy's own daughter, Liza Minnelli, says that her mother's first reaction on hearing me sing was to say, "I'm never going to open my mouth again." She was like that, very self-deprecating. And deeply vulnerable.

Unlike the next guest. In one of those "spontaneous" TV moments, Judy was complimenting me on the way I could belt (I never thought of myself as a belter) when suddenly an inimitable voice rang out, and then the camera turned to Ethel Merman, spot-lit in her seat in the audience and belting out a song. She came up onstage to say hello and lead "the new belter," me, and her fellow belter, Judy, in a spirited rendition of "There's No Business Like Show Business." I gamely joined in (wearing my burgundy middy blouse now) and tried to look enthusiastic, even though I barely knew the words. But it didn't matter, because you couldn't hear me, or Judy, anyway. Ethel completely drowned us out.

When I saw the show later and watched that number, I thought I looked as awkward and embarrassed as I felt. I could never relate to lyrics like "There's no business like show business."

We taped the show on a Friday night, October 4. Bill Paley, the founder of CBS, and James Aubrey, its president, were in the audience as well. They liked what they saw so much that they wanted to get it on the air right away. No matter that there was already another show in the can and scheduled to run. They had ours edited on Saturday so it could be broadcast on Sunday, October 6.

To my surprise I was nominated for an Emmy for Outstanding Performance in a Variety or Musical Program or Series, and so was Judy (actually, all the nominees, except me, were stars of their own weekly shows). We both lost to Danny Kaye.

Judy and I became friends. We spoke on the phone, and she came to one of the rare parties I gave at my New York apartment (four in thirty-five years). I think she arrived late. And I remember her saying something I never quite understood: "Don't let them do to you what they did to me." I should have asked her what she meant, but I didn't want to appear too nosy.

Six years after we did that show, she was dead at the age of forty-seven.

What a tragedy . . . and such a loss. She was an extraordinary talent. As Marty said after I did her show, "There's no more reason to be a guest on any of these cockamamie television shows. You just couldn't top that."

The day after I taped with Judy, I appeared at the Hollywood Bowl with Sammy Davis, Jr., and the Dave Brubeck Quartet. This was a huge step up from all those little nightclubs, and even the room I had played in Las Vegas. That night the Bowl held 17,500 people.

It's an amazing place to perform, because you're outside, under the stars, in a big amphitheater dating back to the 1920s . . . where everyone you can think of has appeared. The audience can order dinner brought to their seats or come with a picnic supper and listen to the music.

Right in front of the stage was a huge semicircular reflecting pool. There was a walkway around the rim, and most performers liked to casually stroll around the pool at some point during their set, so they could get closer to the audience.

Not me. I was afraid I'd fall in . . . like I fell into the pond at the Brooklyn Botanic Garden when I was five. (Decades later I sang there with my son on a very cold night in November . . . I had to sing in my coat . . . and Jason strolled around what used to be the pool, but I was still too scared to do it.)

"I had never heard of her. Neither had the audience. She was trembling like a leaf backstage before she went on. Then she walked out and killed that crowd. Sammy Davis, Jr., followed her, and he presented every bit of his showmanship . . . but it wasn't easy, after Streisand."

—Dave Brubeck on the Hollywood Bowl concert

I was stunned by the reception. To hear that many people applauding was extraordinary. It made me feel I was leaving Los Angeles on a high note.

Back in New York, *Funny Girl* rehearsals were scheduled to start . . . but then there was another postponement. I didn't mind having more of a break.

Marty saw it slightly differently, because it gave him the opportunity to schedule some more tour dates and capitalize on the momentum from my albums. And he had gotten a call from the White House . . . the president and First Lady were inviting me to come and sing for them on December 5. Wow, that sounded great.

Meanwhile, I had all these rooms to fill in our new apartment and was completely consumed with decorating.

One of the first pieces I bought was a burled walnut captain's desk for eighty dollars from Renée Taylor's West Side antiques store. It had a secret compartment, which fascinated me, and I kept it in the entrance hall. I found an old enameled dental cabinet with lots of little drawers, and thought they would be perfect for my ribbons, vintage shoe buckles, and antique sewing items.

The focal point of the bedroom was a huge Jacobean bed from the 1700s, beautifully carved, with a canopy. I hung it with olive-green damask, so I could feel like Shakespeare's Desdemona (*before* the smothering). On East Fifty-Seventh Street I discovered Lillian Nassau's beautiful store filled with Art Nouveau furniture . . . like a superb cabinet by Émile Gallé . . . and Tiffany lamps.

Then, in some of the same shops that sold period furniture, there was period jewelry. I loved antique jewelry . . . just like antique clothing, the quality and the craftsmanship were at a whole other level from any contemporary piece. I had discovered a dealer named Larry Ford, who had a shop in the Diamond District. An antique seed-pearl-and-diamond bracelet in his display case caught my eye. I tried it on, and it fit perfectly. It was exquisite, but it was so much money . . . $750 . . . which would be nothing today for a piece like this. Still, I hesitated . . . and as I was thinking, I realized something. This piece was probably designed to be a choker originally. I had an idea of how it could be made back into a choker, so it could be worn both ways. I sketched out a white-gold extension and asked Larry if he could make it for me. When he said yes, I decided to treat myself . . . this would be my first piece of serious antique jewelry. And after all, it was like getting a bracelet *and* a choker, so I could justify the price!

One day in late November, I was back at his shop to pick it up when we heard on the radio that President Kennedy had been shot. Larry and I looked at each other in disbelief. And all normal activity across the city, and the country, suddenly ceased. Stunned, like everyone else, I just wanted to go home. I hailed a taxi and got in, and as we were driving through Central Park I stared out the window, numb. We passed a man sitting on a bench . . . wait a minute, was that Elliott? I quickly told the driver to stop, handed him some cash, and got out.

It *was* Elliott, and as soon as he saw me running toward him he got up to meet me. Neither of us could believe that we had somehow found each other at this moment. We hugged, holding on tightly. And then we sat down and commiserated . . . we were both deeply, unimaginably sad, and like many other people, probably in a state of shock. We had no energy to move.

Still, somehow, the show had to go on. So at the end of the month I began the last leg of my tour, which Marty put together on such short notice that there wasn't time to promote it. Even so, the first date in Chicago had sold out, and Marty was able to squeeze in a second. Then it was on to five more cities, and finally, the Shrine Auditorium in Los Angeles.

The little clubs I had loved so much were now a thing of the past. I was operating on a whole new scale, singing to an audience of thousands. It was not the kind of intimacy I was used to . . . but I think what made it possible for me to segue seamlessly into these huge auditoriums was that I treated them exactly the same. I did the same show. I spoke extemporaneously. The only thing that got bigger was the orchestra, and thank God I had Peter Daniels to conduct for me, because he made me feel safe. These were my first one-woman concerts.

Both of my albums were now in *Billboard*'s Top Ten. The second album got all the way to number 2. Do you know who kept me from reaching number 1? The Singing Nun: "*Domi-nique-nique-nique s'en allait tout simplement.*" People just couldn't get that catchy refrain out of their heads. I never did dislodge her . . . and then in February the Beatles landed in America and overtook us both. Their sound was sensational, so I had no complaints.

Even I had to admit that 1963 had been an extraordinary year. I had been making $125 a week, and now I was being offered incredible sums to sing for a week . . . $8,000, $10,000, $15,000. It was all like play money to me. I couldn't even comprehend it.

And then at the end of December I was named Entertainer of the Year by the editors of *Cue* magazine. It was my first cover story, and my first award (the Grammys weren't given out until May 1964). And it came with a dinner where they presented it, which at this stage of my life was actually an incentive.

But by then I was very busy, because rehearsals for *Funny Girl* had finally started.

EIGHT

Funny Girl *on Broadway*

I had described the kind of project I wanted to do in Jule Styne's apartment, and here it was . . . the role people say I was born to play. I liked that the script was a serious look at Fanny Brice's life, not merely a recreation of her comedy routines. She could make people laugh with her Baby Snooks character, where she wore a little girl's smock and talked in a little girl's voice, and then make them cry with her signature torch song, "My Man." I hadn't had a part like this before, with real emotional range. And what really got me was the love story and how the music grew out of that.

I looked at some photographs and listened to one of her records, but I knew early on that I didn't want to just imitate her. I had to understand her from the inside out. I was interested in her brain, her heart . . . who she was as a person. I needed to find ways to identify with her.

Obviously, we were both Jewish, born in New York City . . . she was raised on the Lower East Side . . . so there would be a similar cadence in our speech. I'd already noticed that if I spoke in the Brooklyn accent I had heard growing up, with that distinctive Jewish delivery, people would often laugh. I remember thinking, *Why? I wasn't trying to be funny.* And I was a little worried because I didn't relate to her style of comedy . . . that broad Jewish humor.

And then something happened that relieved all my concerns. I was handed a manuscript that instantly unlocked her for me. It was a transcript of a series of conversations she had had with Goddard Lieberson, who was interviewing her for a book that was never published. Talk about serendipity . . . we had Goddard in common. (Again, "At the moment of commitment, the universe conspires to assist you.") This was like a gift from God (and Goddard's nickname was "God," by the way). He gave it to me to read . . . I think it was about a hundred pages long . . . and it was very revealing about her on an intimate level, which is what interested me as an actress.

I always want to find a connection to the person I'm playing, and then I try to go as deep into it as I can. What qualities of the character are also present in me? Some people try to escape themselves when they act, but I think I actually get closer to myself . . . discover and bring out more of myself in the process. I'm not a character actor, really, or at least not the kind of actor who leaves herself totally behind. You have to be really clever to do that, and I'm not that clever.

For me, it's about, *How can I serve the character? What do I think and feel or have experienced that I can use?* We all have so many selves. You can call on different aspects of your own psyche.

Once I read Fanny's own words, I realized that she and I were so alike it was almost scary. We both had Jewish mothers who were concerned about food and marrying us off . . . not necessarily in that order. We both had the kind of confidence that barrels right over obstacles, combined with serious doubts about our looks.

We both appreciated beauty and wanted to surround ourselves with it. Art, furniture, jewelry, fur coats . . . it was like we were making up for our humble beginnings. She loved great clothes, and we even liked the same colors . . . off-white, black . . . colors that weren't too distracting. And we both loved interior decorating. She collected Chippendale furniture, and I remember when I first saw it on the set (when we did the movie) it looked so peculiar to me. I thought, *What does she see in that? It's so dark and stuffy.* I was into French furniture at the time and didn't appreciate it, although I certainly did later on. In fact, I have similar pieces in my living room now.

Fanny and I were also drawn to the same kind of men . . . good-looking . . . and sometimes a bit of a bad boy, even though I think we both knew instinctively that getting involved with them would never work out. But reason, when it comes to love, simply does not apply.

I felt she was a kindred spirit, and I thought that if I could tap into the essence of her . . . pull out the parts where we were alike and be true to that, I would be true to her.

Of course, some of the more inconvenient truths were fictionalized for Broadway. Fanny fell in love with Nick Arnstein, a professional charmer who earned his living by gambling, among other things . . . and some of those things happened to be against the law. When he got into trouble, she remained unfailingly loyal to him, even though he wasn't so loyal to her. But who wants to hear that in a love story? It's not exactly Romeo and Juliet.

So the facts were sanitized, to make Nick more sympathetic. He had to be less of a con man and more of a tragic figure, if you want the story to break hearts. Fran Stark's image of her parents had to be respected. They were sacred figures in her mind, and she could only bear so much reality.

Meanwhile, my dear Jule Styne was working on the songs, with Bob Merrill doing the lyrics after Stephen Sondheim passed on the project. Ray had initially been considering Mary Martin for the lead, and Jule later told me that Steve had objected, saying that they had to get a Jewish girl. "And if she's not Jewish, she at least has to have a nose!" I asked Steve about this a few years ago, while we were discussing songs for my *Encore* album. He laughed and said the quote sounded vaguely familiar, and added, "But the real reason I turned it down, even though I loved working with Jule . . . we had just done *Gypsy* together . . . was that I had made a vow to myself, once and for all, that in my next show I had to do the music as well as the lyrics."

I understand, but to think I could have worked with Stephen Sondheim back then and felt that spark of recognition, like I had instantly felt with Jule and Jerry . . .

Instead, Bob Merrill was a cold fish. When I first heard the song "People," I looked at the lyrics and I had a question for him.

"Isn't it people who *don't* need people who are the luckiest people in the world?" (I was half kidding.)

"No," he said bluntly, and that was the extent of that discussion.

Jule, on the other hand, was a mensch, and I adored him. He was warm and supportive and loving. I felt he saw me and understood me and appreciated me. He wanted to give me music that would show off my voice. If he saw a conflict brewing between Bob and me, he would sashay in and defuse it with humor. He was delightfully impish . . . there was always a laugh around Jule. And he had one quirk, which I'll illustrate with this exchange.

Say I said something like, "Jule, I can't make up my mind. Do you like the green dress for this number or the blue dress?"

"I like the blue dress."

Then I'd say, "But on the other hand, the green is a lighter color and might go better with the set."

"Oh yeah, green. Definitely the green!"

See what I mean? Maybe he just wanted to make me happy. He was a complicated man who had his own demons, but he never imposed them on his collaborators. I loved working with him. He made me laugh . . . which isn't easy . . . and his music could make you cry.

And the rehearsal pianist was another mensch . . . a nineteen-year-old sweetheart named Marvin Hamlisch. In addition to playing the piano, he got coffee for people, and since I didn't drink coffee, he was assigned to bring me a chocolate doughnut. Instead of just one he always brought me two . . . and so our musical love affair began.

Marvin was like a kid from my block. He spoke with the same kind of rhythm as I did . . . fast-talking . . . fast-thinking . . . New Yawk–style. We would compare notes on food. He knew which deli had the best smoked whitefish. And years later, when I was obsessed with quenelles, he was one of the few people who even knew what they were and could recommend a restaurant that served them.

Marvin was a warm presence in what can be a cold, merciless profession. And he was brilliantly talented. That was clear even then.

I loved the rehearsal process. I loved working through a scene, and it didn't faze me if we got a completely new version from Isobel the next day. She was a smart, thoughtful woman who was a pleasure to deal with. If I had a problem with a line, all I had to say to her was, "This doesn't feel right." And she'd rewrite it. Unlike Bob, she listened carefully and was happy to accommodate me or anyone else who had a suggestion. Looking back, I wish I had had more finesse in asking for a line change. But I didn't know any better. I just said what I thought.

I have a feeling that Isobel never felt conventionally pretty, and perhaps that's why she could write this character so well. But we never talked about it. She and I didn't socialize. We were just two serious ladies, trying to get it right. I never really knew how she felt about me until I read a tribute she wrote when I was roasted by the Friars Club in 1969:

> *It was my first show, so I was expecting trouble—from everyone but Barbra. A twenty-year-old kid, in her first starring part? Why, she'd be so happy to have it, so grateful, so overawed—there wouldn't be a peep out of her that wasn't thank you!*
>
> *And here she was—pointing one of those mile-long fingers at a page in the libretto and saying "I liked your first version of this scene much better."*
>
> *Stalling while I thought up something devastating to say back, I glanced at the page. A minute later I put back the earlier version. Meekly. The twenty-year-old kid was right . . .*
>
> *Get a new scene to her at two in the morning, and she'll perform it perfectly the next night. I know. I did it for thirty nights in a row.*
>
> *And then there's the greatest of all writer gambits: "You don't like that line? Fine! Write one yourself!"*
>
> *I hate admitting publicly that I'm a coward but I never—not once—dared say that to Barbra. I was too afraid that she could, that she would, and that it might—might, mind you—be a better line than mine.*

I wish I had gotten to know her better. That was a missed opportunity.

Just as Ray had gone through various writers, he had also gone through various directors. I was heartbroken that Jerry Robbins was no longer involved, because I had such respect for him.

Ray hired Bob Fosse next, and we had a couple of good meetings in New

York. But he lasted only a month before he decided that he couldn't deal with Ray either. Too bad, because I really liked Bob too. I still remembered his choreography from *The Pajama Game*, which I saw when I was fourteen. And I could tell, just by looking and talking to him, that he was extremely talented. He had that mystery about him as well. It's a kind of charisma. You could see it in his eyes, his body movements, even in the way he dressed. He wore an open shirt, with khakis. Casual and effortlessly stylish, just like Jerry.

Garson Kanin, the third director Ray hired, was more formal. He always wore a tie. And that was kind of indicative of his mind-set. He was more rigid and contained. He looked as if he were from another era, and I found him very distant. I wish I had known then that he had directed *The Diary of Anne Frank*, the first play I ever saw on Broadway . . . I might have liked him better.

I knew I wasn't the most experienced person in this rehearsal room. I had only worked with a couple of professional directors. Still, I felt something was definitely wrong with this picture. Wasn't a director supposed to talk to his leading lady? Garson just sat there in the fifth row with his wife, Ruth Gordon, and whispered back and forth with her. They were an odd couple. He was fifty-one . . . slight, thin, not a powerful physical presence. She was sixty-seven, and if you saw her from the back, you might think she was a younger woman because she was in good shape. But as soon as she turned around, you saw her true age. That was kind of refreshing. She could have tried to mask her wrinkles, but she didn't.

You wouldn't think of these two as a natural pair, but they were devoted to each other. And I'll always be grateful to Ruth for introducing me to my beloved Gracie Davidson, who used to be her dresser, as well as Margaret Sullavan's, and became mine.

Gracie was quiet at first. She didn't say much, and that was very restful. But once we got to know each other, she would tell me stories. She lived up in Harlem, and I loved her tales of the Cotton Club. One day she said, "By the way, Adele Moon, who used to be Fanny Brice's dresser, lives in my building."

I couldn't believe it. I thought that was amazing. And here we were in the same theater, the Winter Garden, where Fanny Brice had made her last appearance with the Ziegfeld Follies in 1933. I wanted to meet Adele, but Gracie said she was ninety-two years old and didn't want to talk about Fanny.

Gracie was like a mom. She was with me for seventeen years and lived in my house, until she had a stroke. She was there for the birth of my son. She came with us to Hollywood. We would drive together to and from the studio every day, and she'd call me Barney Oldfield (he was an old-time race-car driver) because I would speed . . . no doubt because I was late. Gracie had a daughter, Dorothy, who was about my age, and we related to each other as if we were sisters. Gracie knew how to make me laugh, and she would laugh, too, until tears rolled down her cheeks.

Back to Garson. I wish Ruth had whispered a few tips about how to talk to actors into his ear. She had starred in Chekhov's *The Three Sisters* on Broadway the year I was born, and I had a feeling she might actually have more insight into the actor's process than her husband. I'd try something new in a scene and look to Garson for a reaction. Nothing . . . no comment. Occasionally he would nod his head and smile. But he didn't offer any useful suggestions like Jerry had during my auditions . . . or point me in a new direction . . . or have me improvise. Ray told me that Garson liked what I was doing, which is why he left me alone. I suppose he thought I was good. But I didn't think I was good enough. And I knew I could be better.

Then suddenly, when Garson did see something he really liked, he'd say, "Freeze it." Oh no. Is that the same as "Lock it?" I'll bet it is. Now I had two guys, Arthur Laurents and Garson, who didn't understand the way I worked.

Once again I tried to explain. "I can't do it exactly the same way every time."

To freeze something is to kill it, in my opinion.

I didn't understand the logic. If a performance could be fresh every evening, why wouldn't a director want that? Of course you have to create a basic framework . . . you know that certain things work and the lines and the staging remain the same . . . but within that structure it seemed to me that you could still be open. Just because I might move at a slightly different moment, that shouldn't mean I was condemned to turn into a pillar of salt.

I tried to persuade Garson, to no avail.

Then he would get annoyed, and that might prompt him to finally get out of his seat and come up onstage and actually speak to me. Once he gripped my wrist so hard that it hurt. As he was pressing down on my pulse, he spoke in a very low voice so that I couldn't understand anything he was saying. It just didn't make sense to me, maybe because he was stopping the flow of blood to my brain.

I would've rather he yelled at me. I knew he was angry, and yet he spoke in this controlled voice. I was used to people yelling in my neighborhood, which was full of Jews and Italians. He was like a Jew who didn't want to be Jewish. He seemed to be trying to contain his emotions, which I was definitely not used to.

It was as if we spoke two different languages. His was incomprehensible to me and I'm sure mine was equally foreign to him. The tools I relied on . . . like using sense memories to trigger an emotion, or improvisation to find something new in a scene . . . were not part of Garson's vocabulary.

I felt as if I were flying blind. I had heard more constructive criticism and delved deeper into a scene in acting class. And here we were, professionals on Broadway!

You can't see yourself onstage. I desperately needed some feedback. So I called Allan Miller and asked him to come to a run-through, right before Christmas. I trusted him and wanted some perspective. Afterward, we went to a Chinese restaurant and talked for two hours, and he gave me his notes. It was like old times. This was how the process was supposed to work. Here was that exchange of ideas that I found so exhilarating. This was exactly what I had been missing.

When I got home I called Marty and asked him to work out some sort of financial arrangement with Allan, so he could come to rehearsal every day. Since I was concerned that Garson would be offended if he knew what Allan was doing, we made up a story. Allan was my cousin from Philadelphia who had come for a visit, and this was the only way he could spend time with me. I did tell Ray the truth. He said, "Do what you have to do. Just don't let Garson find out."

As Allan watched the rehearsals, he also had some suggestions for Sydney Chaplin, who'd been cast as Nick Arnstein. Great! Maybe that would give our scenes more energy. When I told Sydney who Allan really was and invited him to come to my apartment on Sunday afternoon so we could both work with him, he was all for it.

Sydney was tall, dark, and handsome, with graying temples and often a cigarette holder in his mouth. And he had perfect teeth. (You know I like good teeth.) He also had the kind of sophistication I associated with European men . . . not that I knew any, at this point, except from the movies. And he was a professional charmer, which made him perfect for the role of Nick.

I was kind of fascinated with him. He was Hollywood royalty . . . his father was the great Charlie Chaplin, one of the few comedians who could make me laugh . . . and Sydney was also the only person I'd met who had a valet. (He had just come into his inheritance.) And he was very attentive . . . I could feel his attraction to me, which was kind of nice.

I still remember exactly where Sydney was standing, in front of the paneled folding doors to my French living room, on that Sunday we met with Allan. I loved those doors, and usually kept them open so you could see the fireplace as soon as you walked into the foyer. (I always had a fire burning in the cold months.) But on this afternoon, I closed them to create a backdrop for Sydney and me. We started with our first scene, where Fanny meets Nick, and Allan encouraged us to improvise.

When Nick comes backstage and knocks on the dressing-room door at Keeney's, I thought it would be funny if I was down on the floor, on my hands and knees, so that the first thing I'd see would be his beautiful patent leather shoes, and then my eyes would run up his tuxedo trousers to his white ruffled shirt, and finally to his face. "Gorgeous!"

I was thinking visually, as if I were directing this scene in a movie and the camera represented my point of view, so that the audience would see Nick Arnstein for the first time through Fanny's eyes. As it gradually pans up to his face, it's a more dynamic reveal. And when Fanny realizes she's still down on the floor, she feels like an idiot and tries to mask it by quickly pretending to be a dog. I barked, "Arf arf!" and Allan and Sydney both laughed.

So did Garson, when I showed him, and he kept that bit in the show. (I still think it would have worked beautifully in the movie, but Willy Wyler didn't go for it. And I deferred to his judgment.)

With Allan, Sydney and I took a totally different approach to the material. We tried all kinds of things. It was fun, and very freeing. Suddenly it felt as if there were all sorts of possibilities in this play.

Back at rehearsals, when we broke for lunch, Sydney would come over to me and ask, "Do you want to get a bite to eat?" I would say, "Sure," because that meant we could continue where we left off and talk about the script. Sydney was very responsive. He was interested in my ideas about the play and ready to put them into action. It helped to know that he was feeling the same frustrations with Garson. We were comrades-in-arms.

In January the whole company moved to Boston for several weeks of previews. My lunches with Sydney evolved into dinners. And our conversations naturally veered into other subjects. Sydney was well traveled, worldly. He had played tennis with Greta Garbo and turned the sheet music pages while Albert Einstein played the violin.

Little by little we became friends, and then the friendship morphed into something more.

When you're playing a character who falls in love with another character onstage or on-screen, you have to find all the ways you could really love that person. And in that process, sometimes the two people actually do fall in love, for a while at least . . . or maybe I should say, fall in attraction. It's not real love, in most cases. For actors and actresses, it's an occupational hazard. A part of you becomes the character, and you act as that character would. You become vulnerable to the person playing opposite you . . . sometimes.

And I was definitely vulnerable. Elliott and I were having problems. It's funny . . . like Nick Arnstein, he loved to gamble. But in real life it wasn't funny at all. I had no experience with this sort of thing. I didn't know how to help him. The show was absorbing all my time and attention. It was my first starring role, and I was completely wrapped up in it . . . and growing closer to Sydney.

After all, acting is believing. I started to believe I was falling for Sydney . . . because he was falling for me.

When you're on the road, it's as if you're in another world. You're living out of a hotel room, so everything is slightly unreal to begin with. And then at the same time it feels hyperreal, as if everything you do . . . think . . . feel . . . revolves around the play. You're not with your significant other, so at this moment you're more involved with the character than the actual life you've left behind. You and the character are becoming one . . . melding together.

Treacherous territory.

Allan came to Boston as well, because the show was still a work in progress, and I needed his eye. By now he was sitting up in the balcony, so no one would notice that he was still there. And we put him up in a different hotel from the one where Garson, Ruth, and I were staying.

I happened to be in the lobby one day when Ruth was picking up a large package that had just arrived for them. She explained that they traveled with their own sheets and pillowcases and sent them, along with their clothes, to their housekeeper in New York to be laundered and then mailed back.

They *what?*

The Kanins were the original germophobes. They didn't trust the hotel laundry and preferred having their things washed in their own water by hands they knew using soap they liked. My reaction was, *Holy mackerel!* I was very impressed. Still, I thought that was a little nuts!

I'll never forget opening night in Boston. There was a huge snowstorm. Roads were blocked. Flights were canceled. Elliott managed to make the trip, but my new agent, David Begelman, was stranded and missed the show. Sue Mengers, who was Elliott's agent, also had a client in the cast . . . Kay Medford, the lovely lady who played my mother and was so dear to me. She always had her dog with her, and he looked like Sandy, the dog in the Little Orphan Annie cartoons. He was her faithful companion. It was a delight to watch Kay take a small part and make it memorable. The way she could milk a laugh out of the most ordinary line was a wonder.

Sue couldn't get to Boston either. Maybe she and David were lucky. The show went on and on and on for four hours . . . the curtain didn't come down until after midnight. And it probably didn't help the suspension of disbelief when the microphone that was taped between my breasts started picking up police calls, loud enough for some people in the audience to hear.

Frankly, that was the least of the show's problems. The reviews were mixed, but all of them seemed to agree on one thing . . . that the second act was a huge letdown. And it was becoming more evident every day that Garson didn't know how to fix it. The atmosphere was tense. And it was in the midst of all this pressure that Garson climbed up to the balcony one afternoon during a rehearsal and discovered Allan with his pad and pencil.

Garson was furious. He rushed down and cornered Marty in the lobby.

"How dare you bring in an acting coach? I'm the director here!"

When Marty tells the story, he describes how he couldn't stop watching a little vein in Garson's forehead that got bigger and bigger as Garson got madder and madder. Marty actually took a step backward, afraid it was going to burst.

One reason why I've had Marty in my life for almost sixty years is that he's exceptionally wise, and knows how to pick his battles in order to get what he wants. Instead of escalating the situation, he let Garson vent, and when Garson was finally able to walk away, Marty began to wonder. How had Garson found out? Allan had been extremely careful to arrive before Garson came to the theater and to leave only after Garson did . . . which was relatively easy, because Garson was a creature of habit. He came and went like clockwork and rarely left his seat on the floor. So what was he doing up in the balcony?

Allan assumed he had come up to check on the sound . . . but Garson had never done that before.

Then Ray came up to Marty and said, "I hear you and Garson had words. What happened? Did he quit?"

The penny dropped.

Obviously the show was in trouble. Ray must already have been talking to Jerry Robbins to try to persuade him to come back and fix it. So he would now have to pay two directors, unless Garson miraculously quit.

Had Ray tipped Garson off about Allan?

If so, it didn't work. Neither man got his wish. Garson did not quit, and Allan remained in the balcony, with Ray's permission. And Garson just had to turn a blind eye to his presence.

In the first week of February, we moved to Philadelphia for more previews. The show still needed work, and Ray decided he could wait no longer. On February 19, Garson abruptly left the production, and Jerry reappeared.

I was ecstatic. Finally I had a director I trusted and a man I enjoyed working with. Jerry had a brilliant theatrical mind. He thought in pictures and he understood every aspect of a production. He could expound on a character's motivation or pinpoint the wrong gel on a particular light. And he knew how to tell a story. He was able to recognize the truth when he saw it or felt it in an actor's performance, and if it wasn't there yet, he could help you achieve it. I was told that when he agreed to come back, he said, "Streisand has gotten so good, I want the rest of the show to live up to what she's doing."

"A tug-of-war goes on in all departments.

"The kook's looks are ravishing. Her beauty astounds, composed of impossibly unconventional features. Her movements are wildly bizarre and completely elegant. Her body is full of gawky angles and sensuous curves. It scrunches,

elongates and turns on in spotlights. Her El Greco hands have studied Siamese dancing and observed the antennae of insects . . .

"Her cool is as strong as her passion. The child is also the woman. The first you want to protect; the second, keep. She comes on with defiant independence, yet communicates an urgent need for both admiration and approval. She laughs at sexiness. She is sexy. She tests you with childish stubbornness, impetuosity and conceit, concedes you are right without admission, and balances all with her generous artistry and grace . . .

"At rehearsals, she often arrives late, haphazardly dressed in no-nonsense clothes, her hair shoved up under a cap. She accepts the twelve pages of new material to go in that evening's performance and pores over them while schnorring part of your sandwich and someone else's Coke. She reads, and like an instantaneous translator she calculates how all the myriad changes will affect the emotional and physical patterns, blocking, costumes, exits and entrances, etc. When she finishes reading, her reactions are immediate and violent—loving or hating them—and she will not change her mind. Not that day. During the rehearsal, in her untidy, exploratory, meteoric fashion, she goes way out, never afraid to let herself go anywhere or try anything. Nor can she be pinned down. And in the few hours' rehearsals, she has probed into and examined what she must do, *but what will* happen *onstage is being studied behind her eyes and in her nerves. That night onstage, in place of the messy, grubby girl, a sorceress sails through every change without hesitation, leaving wallowing fellow players in her wake."*

—Jerome Robbins

Can you imagine what it was like to have this man's eyes focused on you? For practically the first time in my life . . . and certainly for the first time by a Broadway director . . . I felt *seen*.

The opening in New York, which had already been postponed once, was postponed again, and then again, to give Jerry more time. He took the show apart and put it back together in a quicker, sharper, more inventive way. And everyone was working at fever pitch to implement his changes.

God, working with Jerry was so stimulating! This is why I love the process . . . even more than the result. I had to really *think*. It was like putting on a new show every day. Each performance was an adrenaline rush. Some people were overwhelmed and exhausted. I thrived on it. Peter Daniels, who was the assistant conductor, always said I worked best under "battle conditions." And Sydney was courting me, as Nick was courting Fanny, so that added a whole new level of excitement to our scenes.

I felt as if I were using every fiber of my being. I was looking at every scene with fresh eyes, now that I had Jerry for a partner. He understood the way I worked. He had been one of the very first members of the Actors Studio, which was founded by his friends from the Group Theatre, Robert Lewis, Elia Kazan, and Cheryl Crawford. So we spoke the same language. I could talk about sense memory and some of the other techniques that were part of the Method, and he knew what I meant.

Jerry liked my improvisation with the "Arf arf" when Fanny first meets Nick, and he had a good idea. He suggested that Nick bark back at her. That would have been funny. We must have tried it, and for some reason, it didn't work. Maybe it was too inelegant for Nick (and Sydney).

I love people who have ideas. When Jerry spoke, you listened. He was magnetic, and he had the kind of innate knowledge, taste, and integrity that's very rare.

Jerry took a cool, calm look at the show and grasped something essential. "The story is Fanny's," he said. The audience was totally invested in her, and every time the focus moved to Nick, that connection was broken. People shifted in their seats. Programs rustled. All of the excitement we had built up, culminating in that rousing "Don't Rain on My Parade" at the end of the first act, completely dissipated in the second. Part of that was just the nature of the story, which turned depressing as Nick and Fanny's marriage fell apart. But all the effort to keep that relationship going came from Fanny. She embodied the momentum, and that meant the focus had to stay on her, in Jerry's opinion.

He began to make surgical cuts, getting rid of some songs and scenes for subsidiary characters in order to streamline the show. That I could understand. But I also noticed he was eliminating a lot of Sydney's scenes, including his solo songs. I thought, *Oh shoot.* Those were practically my only opportunity to be offstage for a moment and catch my breath. I was truly sorry to see them go, and even more worried about how Sydney would feel about it. There was one song in particular that I missed, a lullaby called "Sleep Now, Baby Bunting" that Nick sang to our daughter. It was such an interesting moment for Sydney to play, because it revealed his inner conflict . . . his love for his daughter but also his resentment of Fanny, who's raking in money onstage while he's losing it on horses and in gambling casinos.

Jerry had very clear ideas about the dynamic between Fanny and Nick . . . after all, he had worked with Isobel for months as they developed the script. As he told us, "This is the story of a strong woman who, in order to feel like a woman, picks an elegant, loving, but weak man. And her own strength corrupts and kills his love and manliness."

The things that initially attract them to each other are the exact same things that break them apart. As Jerry explained it to us, "Nick is attracted to Fanny because she is all the things he isn't . . . He's a man whose whole life is an act, but he doesn't admit it. He's not willing to do the work that's needed to achieve his goals. Fanny, on the other hand, knows all about hard work and she's very realistic. So Nick thinks that if someone this honest and real believes in him, then there must be something worthwhile in him."

This was the kind of character analysis we had never gotten from Garson.

You never know just what insight is going to illuminate the character for you. One day we were talking about why Fanny stays with Nick, and Jerry said, "She's so grateful for his love that she refuses to look honestly at his situation. He's a man afraid of what he is inside and wants to be beloved for how he seems. She's a woman who's afraid of how she is outside and wants to be beloved for what she is inside."

I wasn't so sure about that. Every woman wants to be admired for both, I think. But the point is, with Jerry, we had something meaningful to discuss.

Finally, I was getting notes from my director after each show. And they were very specific:

"On floor sooner in Keeney dressing room before first meeting with Nick" . . .

"Too rough—Sadie—Your attitude should be more elegant—like a showgirl" . . .

"Smell roses." What a lovely idea.

"Look at chaise longer before 'Are you planning to make advances?'"

Jerry was a master at choreographing comedy. The song in that seduction scene, "You Are Woman, I Am Man," was originally sung only by Nick. But it wasn't going over that well and Jerry had an idea. He went to Jule and Bob and asked them to write a countermelody with lyrics that told you what Fanny is thinking. We put it in the next day and the audience roared.

I noticed during rehearsals, as Isobel made all the changes Jerry asked for, that she was starting to write to my speech rhythms. And as everyone got to know me, my personality and the character began to converge. Jerry was quick to play that up. He thought it worked to the show's advantage.

"'I'm not bossy'—then laugh—you know that you are."

Jerry and I worked the same way . . . we looked for the truth in everything. And that applied whether we were doing comedy or drama. It actually didn't make any difference. It still had to be the truth. And he understood that I had my own way of getting there. He never tried to box me in.

Just as I wanted to be in the moment for a scene, I needed the same kind of freedom for each song. Obviously the words and the music didn't fundamentally change. But sometimes I might vary the phrasing a bit, depending on my mood. So I needed a conductor who could follow me. He had to sense where I was . . . what I was feeling that night . . . and be in the moment with me.

That did not describe Lehman Engel, the conductor for *I Can Get It for You Wholesale*. One night, when I had no doubt played around with the timing and perhaps improvised a few notes on "Miss Marmelstein," he knocked on my dressing-room door after the performance.

"Barbra, darling. Can I ask you something?"

"Go ahead," I said, as I proceeded to take off my makeup.

"Do you know how many people are in that orchestra out there?"

"Hmmm . . . about twenty-five?"

"And do you know what they've been doing all their lives?"

"What?"

"Waiting to play for you."

This was making no sense. "Lehman, what are you talking about?"

"How can they play for you if I don't know what you're going to do?"

I stopped midswipe and turned to look at him. "Can I ask you a question?"

"Sure."

"What are you doing while I'm acting up there?"

"I'm watching you."

"Yeah, you can watch me more than I can watch you! So I guess you'll just have to follow me because I can't follow you . . . unless you want to sing the song and I'll conduct the orchestra."

He and I never really developed much of a relationship.

Thank God for Milton Rosenstock, who had been the conductor on Jule's *Gypsy*, among other great shows, and was now doing the same job on *Funny Girl*. He was like a father to me . . . a kind, lovely man with his beautiful gray mustache and beard. He would come back to my dressing room every night just to relax a bit and rehash the show before we both went home.

He might say something like, "How about that moment at the end of 'Don't Rain on My Parade!' You really speeded it up."

"Yeah. What did you think?"

"I think it played great. Didn't you feel the excitement?"

I got my first taste of what a great conductor could be like in Milt, and I want to thank him. He was a great musical partner. Peter Daniels was the first . . . Marvin Hamlisch was another . . . and today Bill Ross is my favorite conductor, because he practically breathes with me.

After two months on the road, we finally came home to the Winter Garden Theatre in March for three final weeks of previews. Jerry was still changing things, down to the very last minute. On opening night, March 26, just before the curtain went up, Sydney and I were still rehearsing a new version of the final scene . . . we had already learned forty-one others, which had all been discarded. The just-typed lines had been handed to us only an hour before. When we played the scene that night, it was the first time we had done it in front of an audience. (The forty-second version stayed . . . another one of my lucky numbers.)

And then the applause started even before the curtain came down. There was a standing ovation and supposedly twenty-three curtain calls. I doubt there were actually twenty-three . . . that sounds like an exaggeration . . . but it's all a blur. All I could think of was that this thing we had worked so hard on . . . the story, these songs, the show, this performance . . . was now finished. So that was it . . . opening night was over. I'm not sure if I felt happy. I think I was numb.

I headed for my dressing room. I had to get changed for the party that Ray was hosting at the Rainbow Room, but people kept coming in to congratulate me. There were hugs and kisses from Jerry, Jule, Milt, Isobel, and Ray . . . Marty . . . Elliott. Sydney had found me in private before I went on and presented me with a pair of emerald-and-diamond earrings from Cartier. I was shocked that he would give me such an extravagant gift. Now I was thinking, *Holy shit. How do I show my husband these earrings?* What would he think? He'd ask me questions I didn't want to answer.

And soon I'd have to stand there smiling next to Elliott while Sydney stood next to his pretty French wife, Noelle, who was as sweet as her name. What had I gotten myself into? And I thought, *I'm not that good an actress . . . better we stay far apart.*

Meanwhile, the line of people outside the door was growing longer . . . I'm told Goddard Lieberson was there. I know I have a picture taken with Ethel Merman in my dressing room that night. But I can't even remember all the faces. Everyone was saying the most wonderful things, but that wasn't what I was eager to hear. I turned to Elliott and asked him to go see if he could find Allan and Anita . . . because I wanted to know if Allan had any notes for me. Was there anything he didn't like in my performance tonight . . . anything he thought I could do better?

Finally the well-wishers were gone, off to the party, and I slipped on a black-velvet dress, by Don Loper, bought off the rack at his Beverly Hills store. The straps and the bodice were trimmed in black satin, and it had an unusual neckline. Instead of scooping down over the breasts it went up, to a slight peak in the middle. I thought it looked very simple and sculptural, like something out of a John Singer Sargent painting . . . my own variation on *Madame X*. And it was constructed so beautifully inside, with a boned bodice. It made me look very thin. This is so typical of me . . . I remember more about the dress than the party.

It was already in full swing when Elliott and I finally arrived at Rockefeller

Center and stepped off the elevator on the sixty-fifth floor to make our way through the crowd and into the ballroom. I clutched his arm, because flashbulbs were going off in my eyes and I was blinded by the glare of television lights and cameras. Reporters were sticking microphones in my face. People were pawing me, grabbing at my velvet cape from the 1930s. (I had admired it at the costume company and asked if they would sell it to me, but they said they couldn't. So I was doubly surprised, and pleased, when Ray presented it to me.)

All of a sudden the reality of success, fame, whatever you want to call it, hit me. And I didn't like it.

I recently listened to a radio interview I did that night with a very nice guy named Fred Robbins. I can still see his face, very sweet . . . his nose swung a bit to one side . . . and he asked me excitedly, "What does this mean to you, this opening night, Barbra?"

Here's where you would expect me to be just as excited as he was, but instead I'm quiet and subdued . . . kind of exhausted. I was relieved that all the preparation was over, but I was suddenly faced with another fact, which I had somehow glossed over in the midst of all the turmoil of getting ready for opening night. Now I would have to be onstage doing the same thing *every* night for eighteen months. It was like a prison sentence to me.

I was facing the reality . . . the letdown. No more scenes to learn? No changes?

This is probably why I didn't sound so thrilled when I told him, "I don't know. It's not that kind of a thing where I've sort of been waiting for this moment all my life, strangely enough . . . it's a night . . ." Wonderful on one hand, but on the other, "It's one of many things that I want to do."

"Was tonight's performance any different, any more exciting than any of the others?"

"No . . . less."

"Why?"

"Because opening night audiences are very sophisticated and they come there judging, you know, and when anybody comes to judge, it stilts everything . . . so the whole thing is very pressured. I hate opening nights. They're just horrible."

Here I go again, telling this poor guy who just wants some happy talk what I'm really thinking. Even Ray Stark, in that same interview, mentions that the audience was "colder" than what we were used to. Thank God for Jule, who steps up to the microphone and actually sounds excited. "We've written some songs and we heard them really sung tonight by Barbra Streisand . . . this girl is unique, honest . . . no fake . . . honest. She's one of the greatest singers of my time and I've heard 'em all!"

I didn't see half the people who were there that night. But I do remember Jason Robards and Lauren Bacall, who were so lovely and enthusiastic and well dressed. Little did I know I'd eventually work with him on one of my television specials and direct her in a performance that was nominated for an Academy Award.

"I was just stunned by this tremendous performance. I don't know, I felt, what am I doing there? A twenty-one-year-old girl like this has got all that talent and class."
—Jason Robards

"I absolutely saw the best thing I ever saw in my life in that girl. She can act, she can sing, she has an electric personality, which is what makes a star."
—Lauren Bacall

I've seen pictures of Bette Davis and Angela Lansbury, and now I'm wondering why I didn't meet them. That would have been a thrill. Then Marty told me Bette Davis was the guest on *What's My Line?* a few days later and said: "I've fallen madly in love this week with Barbra Streisand. I think she's the most wonderful thing I've ever seen . . . I just sat with my mouth open in awe."

I wish I had had a chance to talk to her. I loved her movies. But I was keeping my head down and trying to escape being interviewed . . . unlike my mother, who of course was there and eagerly awaiting her turn in front of the microphone.

"Well, Mama Streisand, what do you think about this whole thing?"

"Well, I'm terribly elated."

"Where does the spark come from?"

"Actually, her singing would come from her mother and her acting ability would also stem from her mother. Her intelligence, however, stems from her dear father, who was a PhD and a most spectacular teacher who had helped many pupils on the road to gain self-respect since he once worked at the Elmira Reformatory as an assistant principal."

At least Mom was enjoying herself.

Sometimes I can be a little tone-deaf. When Fred Robbins asked if I ever thought anything like this would happen in my "wildest dreams," I said, "Of course."

Now I see how that could come across as arrogant, but I was simply being honest. I always sensed that I would be famous. Somehow I just knew it . . . ever since I stood in that doorway and stared at my unmade bed. I had a vision, and sometimes I think I willed it all into coming true. I had wanted to be an actress since I was a young girl, and I thought the time had come for the world to catch up to my dreams.

The demands started immediately . . . for interviews, for TV appearances. People were waiting outside the stage door every night, begging for autographs. The more rabid fans started to follow me. Once, on a rainy day, a kid put his coat down over a puddle in the street for me to walk on, as if I were some sort of princess. I was shocked. I told him to pick it up and not to do that again . . . for anyone.

I thought I had gotten a lot of attention after *Wholesale*, but it was nothing compared to this. A week after *Funny Girl* opened, I was on the cover of *Time* magazine. And then a few weeks later, I was on the cover of *Life*.

Publicity, in Ray's opinion, translated directly into ticket sales. So I did dozens of interviews, and the reporters had a field day. I still hadn't learned to think twice before I opened my mouth.

As I said to a reporter from *The New York Times*, "Well, here I am with a big show, and I'll probably get bored doing it after a while. Doing it again and again, the challenge wears off. Anyway it's nice while it lasts. I always knew I hadda be famous and rich—the best. I knew I couldn't live just being medium."

When I look at these articles today, I cringe. Did I really say that?

Maybe I was just joking . . . but I don't think so. When you can't hear my tone, the words sound so cocky on the page. And that's ironic, because that's not the way I felt.

In the midst of all the accolades, I had a premonition of what was in store.

I wasn't the underdog anymore, the kooky kid from Brooklyn they could root for. I was fair game.

It was a woman reporter who took some of the first shots at me, in that profile for *Life* magazine. Why are women so tough on other women? Is it jealousy? Anyway, this woman was snarky. She painted a portrait that I didn't recognize and put words in my mouth that I definitely did not say.

Suddenly my grace period was over.

Reporters were kind to me when I was the odd, skinny girl from Brooklyn, wearing thrift-shop clothes and singing in little clubs. Then there was *Wholesale* and my record albums and *Funny Girl*, and by then their narrative was set. I was their ugly duckling who had somehow turned into a swan. We all grew up on fairy tales. Who doesn't love a Cinderella story?

And then they couldn't resist chipping away at the fantasy they had created.

I was disillusioned with these interviews. Why waste my time when they didn't print what I said? Why wasn't the truth enough? But I learned very quickly that if you tried to correct a story, it only drew more attention to it. And I didn't want this kind of attention. I didn't like being looked at so closely. I felt as if I were pinned to a dissecting table, sliced open and studied.

This was not what I had dreamed of when I wanted to be famous.

You have to remember that negativity was my natural state. My mother's normal way of looking at things was negative, and I was her child. The world had disappointed her. Her first husband had died. Her second husband had walked out on her. And she no longer believed in dreams . . . not her own, and not mine.

On opening night of *Funny Girl*, when I looked for my mother in the audience, she wasn't there. Later, when I asked her why she wasn't in her seat, she said, "I was too nervous. I had to walk around."

So she missed my performance. My mother didn't see me . . . once again.

I grew up without her approval, with no support for my dreams. I don't remember her ever giving me a compliment. Once, when I asked her why, she said, "I didn't want you to get a swelled head." Again, she was from a different school of thought: "Never give your kids too much praise." So I wasn't used to compliments. No wonder I didn't trust the applause.

I didn't know how to respond. Say thank you, I guess. I was always slightly embarrassed. When I was singing in nightclubs, I would start the next number right away. It was as if I were afraid to acknowledge the applause. God forbid I should take it in. And I never wanted to risk waiting until it died down.

Now, in *Funny Girl*, people were clapping as soon as I walked onstage. It was actually disconcerting. I felt like saying, Wait, I haven't even done anything yet! And if you could get applause for nothing, then how much was it worth?

The reviews said I was great. But what's great? I didn't know. I hoped I was a good actress and I thought I could sing. But then the critics went on and on. Kim Skalecki, who started as my assistant in 1977 and now keeps my archives, just showed me the reviews again. No wonder I reacted the way I did.

> *"If New York were Paris, Broadway could temporarily consider renaming itself the Rue Streisand. Some stars merely brighten up a marquee; Barbra Streisand sets an entire theater ablaze . . . Her profile might have come from an ancient bas-relief found in the valley of the Nile, but her tongue is asphalt-coated in the speech patterns of Manhattan's Lower East Side . . . She can bring a song phrase to a growling halt, or let it drift lyrically like a ribbon of smoke. Her lyrics seem not to have been learned by rote, but branded on her heart . . . Actress, songstress, dancer, comedienne, mimic, clown—she is the theater's new girl for all seasons."*
>
> —*Time*

One reviewer wrote, "Magnificent, sublime, radiant, extraordinary, electric—what puny little adjectives to describe Barbra Streisand." That's very gratifying . . . for about a minute. But then my next thought was, *How the hell could I live up to that?* All these people were now coming to see this great performance. What were they expecting? How great did I have to be? What if I didn't radiate some night?

I didn't want to disappoint them.

I still have those feelings of doubt. At the core of my being are two fundamental qualities . . . a confidence in myself and also a deep insecurity. And the insecurity feeds the confidence and the confidence nurtures the insecurity. They work hand in hand. As Brugh Joy, a physician who became interested in healing not only the body but the mind, told me years later, "Each one balances the scale."

Funny Girl changed my life . . . and introduced me to the world. I was playing a young woman who was awkward and unattractive at the beginning of her career. That's the character, so that's what I conveyed onstage. And evidently it was such a successful portrayal that people confused the character with me. The title, the dialogue, and the very first song, "If a Girl Isn't Pretty," made such a point about Fanny being funny-looking (it was written before I was cast, by the way) so that's what the audience saw, and that's what they believed about me.

It was only the rare individual, like Isobel Lennart, who noticed any discrepancy. In that same Friars Club tribute, she wrote,

> *How would you like to write a libretto about a homely little girl, have what seemed to be a homely little girl engaged for the part—and then, the first time she has an audience—on opening night in Boston—have her turn beautiful in front of your eyes? And get more beautiful at every performance, so that—by opening night in New York—she's obviously one of the great beauties of all time?*

After Richard Burton and Elizabeth Taylor came to see the play, they took me to '21' for dinner. And I found myself in the ladies' room with Liz and Natalie Wood, two gorgeous movie stars, and they were asking *me* how *I* did my makeup! (I turned Natalie on to my lip gloss.)

Another dichotomy . . . the "homely little girl" was being featured in fashion magazines. In 1964 I appeared in three different issues of *Vogue*, photographed by Cecil Beaton, Bert Stern, and Irving Penn. This was a little intimidating . . . after all, Beaton was the official photographer to the Queen of England! Our paths had crossed once before in 1963 at Basin Street East. Then, when we both were in Los Angeles that fall, he asked if he could photograph me. I was nervous about the shoot, so I typically arrived late . . . so late that his assistants had already left. "What a pity," he said. "And now the light has changed." He had wanted to photograph me outdoors, but it had gotten too dark. Still, he managed to take some great shots inside . . . focusing on what he called my "Cleopatra profile," with a "bold flow from forehead to nose." He even loved the bump on my nose! His picture of me was in the March issue, to coincide with the opening of the show.

I was a star on Broadway, but I never thought of myself as a star. (I still don't.) I was just excited to be able to buy as many slices of honeydew melon as I wanted and eat only the ripe top parts. To me, that was the height of luxury. So it never occurred to me to ask for a car and driver, like other lead actors had. I took cabs to the theater . . . that's how I got to work. And sometimes . . . well, most of the time . . . I was a little late leaving my apartment. It was a flaw, I'll admit, but I also didn't want to be in my dressing room too long. I liked to be thrown onstage to deal with the reality of the moment.

So I'd be standing on the street, trying to hail a cab, and sometimes there'd be none in sight. I lived way uptown, at West Ninety-Second Street, and cabs up there could be few and far between. And it was a long way to the Winter Garden on West Fifty-First Street.

I would get frantic. I can remember walking down Central Park West with tears streaming down my face, desperate to get to the theater. Once I knocked on the window of a truck while it was stopped at a light . . . "Hey, could you please help me? I'm the star of a Broadway show and it can't go on unless I get there. Could you give me a lift to Fifty-First Street?" Another time I hitched a ride in a police car.

That's when I decided there was no choice . . . I had to get a car . . . so I bought a secondhand 1959 Bentley, which was less recognizable than a Rolls-Royce and yet it still had those beautiful lines . . . and I found a Tiffany glass vase to put in the back, to hold flowers.

For about two weeks I also had a chauffeur, but he didn't work out. Once I caught him washing out his socks in my sink. And frankly, I was always kind of embarrassed to ride in that car. I decided I would run the risk of being late and go back to taking cabs, just so I could be anonymous.

Lee Strasberg was in the audience one night and came backstage afterward. That was exciting. Here was the legend himself, the man to whom I had written all those letters on the subway about my thoughts on acting (which I never sent), the expert on the Method . . . and now he was complimenting me. I was so pleased, but I felt I had to confess something.

"Lee, you know, I'm always late. Sometimes I can't catch a cab and I barely make it onto the stage. So I don't do your preparation. I know an actor's supposed to prepare, but I don't do it. And I feel bad."

He looked at me and said, "That's your preparation . . . not to prepare."

I thought that was rather profound. And it was definitely true for me. In the first scene, Fanny walks out onto a bare stage, stops in the middle, and looks out at the empty theater. Of course it wasn't empty in reality . . . the audience was there . . . but it gave me a moment to kind of get my thoughts together. I could center myself. So that was the extent of my preparation, and it happened onstage.

I learned how to read the audience before the show even started. There were speakers in my dressing room . . . every theater has them, so an actor can follow the action onstage and know when his entrance is coming up . . . and when they're on they pick up any noise in the auditorium. So I could hear the rustling of the audience as they came in and assess their personality by the sounds of conversation as they were getting into their seats, and by how they responded to the overture.

Audiences are very different, you know. On a Tuesday or a Thursday night, you get the real theatergoers. They're quieter, more serious. I like people like that. On Friday and Saturday night, the atmosphere is boisterous. You have a lot of couples, full of dinner and drinks and out for a good time . . . they're looking for action and are often more focused on that than the play. On matinee days, Wednesdays and Saturdays, the women usually outnumber the men. There's a lot of chatter and the rustle of shopping bags. They're happy to be at the theater and eager to laugh.

The audiences who came to enjoy . . . the positive ones . . . were the people I worked hardest for. They were appreciative, so I felt the need to give back. If I sensed negative vibrations, I held back. Most actors would try to win them over. I didn't.

It's not as if I were a proven star, someone they had seen many times and already knew they liked. Most people might have heard about me or read about me, but they had never seen me in the flesh. And they tended to have one of two attitudes . . . "Show me, because you can't be as good as they say," or "I can't wait to see this. I hear you're so good."

And I could feel the difference.

Of course I, too, was different every night. If I was tired, I might not be able to do the show with the same level of energy. It's a difficult task, keeping a performance bright and spontaneous when you're doing it eight times a week. I loved the theater and I hated it, although that's a little strong. I loved it because I got to express so many feelings and be a different person. And yet it was frustrating because it was so intangible . . . fleeting. You have to constantly recreate the magic, night after night. And some nights it's harder than others.

And there was no point in trying to fake it. I'm sure some actors can, but I don't know how.

And does an audience know the difference?

Somehow, they just do. They can feel it. I've always had great admiration for the audience. Individually, they may not be the smartest person in the room . . . but collectively, they are brilliant. I used to say they were like a barometer, measuring the truth.

The relationship between an actor and the audience is fascinating, and it's like walking a tightrope. There are certain laws you cannot break. When an actor violates the fourth wall and breaks the delicate balance between fantasy and reality, the magic is gone. You need to be in the moment, listening, and thinking and dealing with whatever happens. I remember watching *On the Waterfront* and being so impressed with a scene between Marlon Brando and Eva Marie Saint. It's that moment when she drops her glove, and he picks it up and pulls it on over his own hand. Even as a teenager I found that gesture incredibly revealing. I could just feel the truth of it. I was sure it wasn't planned. Years later I asked Marlon about it. And just as I thought, it wasn't scripted. The glove dropped, and Brando just reacted to it as his character would and made something tender out of the moment.

One night in *Funny Girl*, a hanger fell that wasn't supposed to fall . . . and instantly you could feel the fourth wall crack. I could sense the audience wondering, Is that part of the play? What's the actress going to do? Is she going to pick it up?

And if you don't acknowledge the hanger, it's a problem. Because in real life, if a hanger drops, you'd pick it up. And if you lose sight of that reality . . . if you ignore the hanger and pretend it didn't drop . . . you remind the people watching that this is not real life but only a play. It breaks their fantasy. You can lose the audience in a second. And then it's hard to get them back.

I was getting more adept at working with an audience and finding the emotional truth in each scene every night. My father used to give gold stars to my brother, Shelly, when he did a good job on his schoolwork. He was gone, but I still wanted those gold stars.

And I got one, or at least the equivalent, in a letter from Henry Fonda. I was thrilled when he came to see me at the Cocoanut Grove, but this was even more meaningful. He wrote:

Dear Barbra,

I was unable to come back to see you the other night—but it's just as well—I would have embarrassed you.

I've known for a long time that you can sing up the well known storm—remember I'm your first fan—and it should come as no surprise to one who feels you can do no wrong that you can also act*—but Holy Cow! (to keep it in P.T.A. language) you were doing it with such beautiful* economy*, which is the operative word here, that I flipped all over again.*

I'd talk about specific scenes, but I don't want to make you self-conscious about them.

I'm terribly proud of you. I'm sending my children to watch you and learn.

You're beautiful. I love you.

I cherished that letter, and another from Frank Sinatra, who wrote, "If I hadn't been speechless last nite, I would have said you are magnificent and I love you."

Decades later, in 1993, Frank asked me to sing "I've Got a Crush on You" with him, for his *Duets* album. Afterward he sent me a gold Tiffany clock engraved with those words, followed by "Love, Frank," plus another note:

Singing with you was a dream come true. Thanks again.

Much love,

Francis Albert

I saw Frank later that year in Las Vegas, when I was preparing my show at the MGM Grand and he was performing nearby. After his show, he joined me and Marty for a late supper and we wound up going to see Don Rickles together. But what I remember most about Frank is another night much earlier in my career, when I ran into him at a party and he said, "Kid, if anybody ever bothers you, just call me. I'll take care of it."

Whoa! Here was someone who was ready to protect me. Luckily I never had occasion to call him.

Back to *Funny Girl.*

By now it seemed almost absurd that I had allowed myself to get involved with Sydney. Like many a man who's been told he's delightful too many times, he loved to hear himself talk, and he would tell the same stories over and over. I was getting bored. All we had in common was the show. His favorite haunt was Sardi's, where I always felt as if we were on display. I preferred diners. Once, when Elliott and I were coming home from a party, I had this sudden urge for rice pudding . . . without raisins. Some people like it with raisins. I don't, and rice pudding without raisins is harder to find. Every restaurant we looked into was closed, but Elliott managed to find a diner on Tenth Avenue that was open twenty-four hours, and they had great rice pudding.

Could you imagine Sydney Chaplin, with his Savile Row suits and his French ties, at a diner? Neither could I.

I didn't want to have secrets from my husband, and one day I told him what had happened. I needed him to help me get out of it . . . to tell me he loved me.

I think he understood and he forgave me, but he was hurt. And I didn't want to hurt him anymore.

I told Sydney that we couldn't go on like this . . . that I was in a marriage I wanted to keep.

Our flirtation was over, and everything seemed okay for a while. But I guess he wasn't used to a woman putting an end to things. It wounded his vanity and his pride. He was angry. And he knew exactly how to punish me.

One night onstage, in the middle of a scene, he started to mumble under his breath. At first I thought I was hearing things. After all, I do have noises in my ears.

Then I realized, *No, he's actually talking.* But what is he saying? Is he trying to improvise something new for the scene?

Wait a minute. Did I hear right? No, that couldn't be right. He couldn't possibly be saying these mean, hostile things . . . words like "shit" and "crap" and "damn." But he was. He was cursing me out. He'd taunt me, calling me a bitch, or worse . . . the most vicious names. While the audience assumed he was whispering sweet nothings in my ear, he would actually be jeering, "You really fucked up that scene."

I had never experienced anything like this. When I'm acting with someone,

I'm listening very closely to what they are saying, so it was hard not to react. I had to force myself to continue with the dialogue as written. But it was like playing to a wall that talked back, because Sydney wasn't actually interested in doing the scene. He was just going through the motions. He did everything he could to upset me. It was as if he wanted to annihilate me. If he couldn't avoid looking at me, he would look at my forehead, rather than into my eyes.

It was devastating, and I tried to handle it discreetly. I went to his dressing room to talk to him. "Please let it go. We're both married." But he didn't want to hear what I had to say.

It was becoming a nightmare. Now, every night at seven thirty as I prepared to go on, I felt sick to my stomach. It wasn't only the pressure of having to live up to the audience's expectations. Now I also had to deal with a new enemy . . . my costar.

Sydney made me physically ill. Sometimes I threw up. I went to a doctor who gave me opium drops . . . a bitter brown liquid to put on my tongue. That would enable me to get through the performance.

But my stomach still wobbled like jelly. Once the curtain went up, I was onstage for almost every minute of the show, and suddenly I was scared. What if I got really sick and had to run to the bathroom? Would I have to stop the show and say, "Pull the curtain down?" And then what? Would the stage manager come out and apologize?

This is what started my stage fright.

My face would get flushed. I thought, *Oh God, I'm going to faint.* For the first time in my life, I was frightened that I would forget my lines. Sydney's behavior threw me completely. I'd have to think, Where am I? What scene are we in? What am I playing? The men's bathroom was closer to the stage, and once or twice I actually had to run in there.

I was going through hell, and nobody else in the company knew it. I was too embarrassed.

I went to see Sydney in his dressing room again.

"Why are you doing this? Why can't you let this go so we can be friends?"

He was utterly cold. The guy who was so charming when we first met was no longer there. Instead he had become someone I didn't recognize. I never thought he could be so vindictive. Why couldn't he just leave me alone and be happy with his pretty French wife?

When the taunts didn't stop, I decided I had no choice. I went to the stage manager, Dick Evans. He called a meeting with Ray, Sydney, and me, and we all tried to reason with Sydney. I told him that if I had been doing anything wrong or offensive to him, just tell me, and I would try to correct it.

He had nothing to say, other than some feeble excuse . . . that there were "things he didn't like about the show, the staging, the writing, but it wasn't up to him to do anything about it."

Things calmed down for a while, but then he started up again. Dick was now sending him daily notes about his behavior. Sydney started to do things that interfered with the staging, refusing to take my arm as I passed the chaise and pull me down beside him at a particular point in the "You Are Woman, I Am Man" song, for example, so I was forced to walk past the chaise and then come back, without any motivation. When Dick reprimanded him again, his curt reply was: "Don't give me any notes." And he announced, "I'm tired of doing the show her way and now I'm going to do things my way." He refused to reinstate the bit of business, as requested.

Sydney's behavior, so destructive and unprofessional, drove me into analysis.

When I was eighteen, Cis's husband, Dr. Harvey Corman, had mentioned that Columbia University was doing a study and offering free therapy for those who qualified. I was intrigued by the idea and had gone up to meet the doctor in charge. And then I told him I really didn't think I needed therapy, hoping he still might find me interesting and take me anyway . . . just as I did with Lee Strasberg. But this doctor apparently had the same reaction as Lee. I didn't get in.

Now I really needed help, and Harvey recommended a colleague.

I was having panic attacks. I was petrified to go onstage every night. I wanted to quit, for reasons of health, but I'm not a quitter. In January I broke down in tears after a show when Sydney had been particularly nasty. Ray went in to talk to him, and Sydney shouted at Ray to get out of his dressing room.

Finally, in April 1965, Ray and the company brought him up on charges before Actors' Equity. Ray was definitely not averse to the possibility of getting rid of Sydney. He was paying him a lot of money for a part that had been substantially cut by Jerry.

But it didn't work. At his hearing Sydney completely charmed the panel, which was made up of men only. I guess you actually have to murder someone in order to be fired by Equity. That night I had had enough. While I was waiting in the wings to go on, I was steaming from all my bottled-up anger, and according to Dick's notes, I told Sydney to "Just shut up and follow the script." He didn't, and at the end of act 1, I told Dick that I was not going on for the second act.

It was him or me.

Poor Dick somehow persuaded me to continue, but that was it, as far as I was concerned. I felt like Ingrid Bergman in *Gaslight.* I was afraid that Sydney was actually going to drive me insane.

There was another meeting with Ray, and I remember Sydney standing onstage, shouting, "I don't need any of you! I'm Charlie Chaplin's son and I have five hundred thousand dollars in the bank." (Five hundred thousand dollars then was like $5 million or more today.)

And then he was gone. Johnny Desmond replaced Sydney Chaplin on July 1, 1965.

Looking back, I can't believe that this horrible thing happened and I had to endure it for over a year. But I refused to let him destroy me.

I've never worn those emerald-and-diamond earrings.

However appalling Sydney's behavior was, I have to admit he was better for the part. Johnny Desmond behaved as if he were in a nightclub. At his first performance, after I sang "People," he looked at the audience and started to clap, as if to say, "Give the little lady a hand." I stared at him, aghast, and as soon as we were offstage, I told him, "Please don't ever do that again. In the theater, there's what we call the fourth wall between the actor and the audience, and you never, ever break it. That's cheap and vulgar, and then the magic is gone."

It's so ironic. I was the star of a hit show, but every night I couldn't wait for it to be over. I had gotten my wish . . . I was famous, I suppose, because the newspapers and magazines seemed to track my every move. But the reporters still twisted my words or misinterpreted them to give the article a negative slant. I remember reading some of these articles and thinking, *This is terrible. It's just going to make people dislike me.* I was so pained by that.

That's when I started to withdraw. I had hired a new press agent, Lee Solters, and now I wanted him to keep me out of the papers. Even the complimentary articles, the ones that painted me as this huge success, made me squirm because they made my life sound so enviable.

I could never understand why people envied me. I wanted to plead, Please don't envy me. I get sick to my stomach every night. I walk out on the street and there are people following me. I don't know what they want. I'm not that great. I'm really not . . . so please don't build me up so high because I know you're just going to be let down.

I always thought that the only thing I had to give in exchange for my success was my talent . . . my work. I've never understood the other part of fame. It's like a bargain with the devil, almost. I mean, how much of your soul and your private life do you have to give up?

I will give my all, give everything I have in my creative work, but I will not give up my entire life. Yet being onstage every night left me little time for a life. I was this funny girl, in the public's eyes. But as I told *Life* magazine, "When I am not performing . . . I don't think I have that definite a personality."

I never thought I was that interesting, and certainly not at twenty-one.

I was a personality before I became a person.

NINE

People . . . People Who Need People

"People . . . people who need people . . ."

I sang it first when I was twenty-one, and fifty years later it's still the song that's most associated with me. But what most people don't know is that it was almost cut from *Funny Girl*.

As Jule Styne tells the story, Garson Kanin didn't like it. Barely two weeks into rehearsal, he called Jule and Bob over and said he wanted to discuss the song.

"I don't think it's right for the character," Garson explained. "She's just met this man. Why's she getting all philosophical?"

Jule was stunned. "I think it's the best song in the show," he replied.

He wasn't alone in that opinion. In fact, on December 20, 1963, after a long day at rehearsal, I was in the recording studio from midnight until 3:00 a.m. singing "People," because Ray wanted it released as a single to promote the show. Peter Daniels was playing the piano, and he recalls, "When 'People' was finished, no one spoke . . . There was nothing but silence. When it was played back, Jule Styne almost broke down and wept. It was a very emotional moment."

Jule told Garson, "It's going to be fucking number one on the *Hit Parade*!"

Bob said, "It has to be in the show . . . When you put a spotlight on Barbra and she sings this song, she'll bring the house down!"

Garson was unconvinced. He still thought it didn't work, though the problem wasn't the song but the way he had staged it, with too many cast members looking on and practically joining in. It wasn't until February that it got fixed, when Jerry Robbins took over during previews in Philadelphia and turned it back into a tender moment between just Fanny and Nick.

By that time the single had been out for a month, and the music was so familiar to the audience that they started applauding as soon as they heard it in the overture. And as Bob had predicted, when I sang it, it did stop the show. He and Jule even had to write an encore for it.

About a week after we opened in March, we recorded the cast album for Capitol Records, which had invested in the show. But in exchange for allowing me to appear on a rival label, Marty negotiated the right for me to record several songs from *Funny Girl* on my own album for Columbia.

"People" was a huge hit, and when I recorded a new album in July and August, it made sense to make it the title song. I should explain that the version on this album (and the single) is different from the way I sang it in the show. On Broadway (and on the cast album), it has the original introductory verse and a big horn fanfare at the end. But for the single, we dropped the introductory verse (the song was already longer than the normal three minutes), and Peter Matz did a different arrangement, with a softer, more reflective ending.

I had already used the songs I'd been performing in clubs and concerts on my first three albums, so I was now back to square one, looking for new material. I still loved discovering hidden gems from overlooked musicals. "Don't Like Goodbyes" is another song from *House of Flowers*. "How Does the Wine Taste?" came from a musical that closed in Philadelphia called *We Take the Town*, and

Irving Berlin's "Supper Time" came from one of his lesser-known musicals, *As Thousands Cheer.*

I always thought Jule wrote "Absent Minded Me" for this album, and it's true . . . he did write a new melody specifically for me, but the lyrics were recycled from an earlier song by Bob Merrill that I didn't even know existed until recently. I have to say I like Jule's version better. It's a sublime melody, and Bob's lyrics were witty:

I'm losing a key or missing a glove
Just like me to lose my love

And then I chose "Will He Like Me?" from the musical *She Loves Me* and "My Lord and Master" from *The King and I*, which was a show I loved.

When it came time to talk about the cover, the record company wanted another close-up of my face (the convention for almost every album back then). But that didn't seem very interesting, and frankly, I was looking for a way to avoid another photo shoot.

I've never enjoyed having my picture taken. It's too much fuss, and it takes too much time. That's when I remembered a shoot I'd done for a magazine a year before, when I was singing at Mister Kelly's in Chicago. I had agreed to meet the photographer, Don Bronstein, after my show, and he took some pictures out on the street in front of the club. By then it was very late, two or three in the morning, and he had this idea . . . wouldn't it be fun to go out to the beach and take some shots at sunrise?

I was game . . . after all, I was twenty-one years old, and staying up all night didn't faze me. I think we went to an all-night diner to eat while we waited, so that was an added enticement.

I remember he took some shots of me in various poses, and then I asked him to take one from the back, while I was just standing on the sand and looking out at the sun rising over the lake. It was a pale lemon disk in a softly colored sky shading from blue to violet to pink. I had never really watched a sunrise before. I was just quietly taking in the wonder of nature. And he caught an honest moment, which is what I always strive for in my work.

And that's the photo I brought in to the art director for the cover. He took one look and said, "You can't put a picture of your back on the cover. People want to see your face."

But I thought it was perfect because it had a certain mystery and captured the mood, in an understated way. The marketing department was appalled, and other executives at the label also vehemently disagreed with me. And that's when the "creative control" clause in my contract came in so handy, because I was able to get the cover I wanted!

I must admit it was a sweet victory when *People* won the Grammy for Best Album Cover. Peter Matz won for arranging, and I won for Best Female Vocal Performance. That was very gratifying, because I didn't know if the album would be a hit. It was an interesting time in music, especially for traditional singers, because rock and roll and Beatlemania were in full swing. In fact, my wonderful A&R man, Jay Landers (who's been with me for over thirty years), just told me that *People* replaced the Beatles' *A Hard Day's Night* soundtrack as the number 1 album in the country. They won their first Grammy that same year for Best New Artist, and *Funny Girl* won for Best Broadway Cast Album.

It's funny . . . even though the Beatles and I were the same age, somehow I gravitated toward music from an earlier era. I loved ballads, and Jule gave me "People" to sing and, as I wrote for a tribute celebrating his career, "it rang chords all over the world."

When I sang it onstage, it was a love song for a character who didn't have a partner in her life. The meaning changed as I got older and took on a broader point of view. But the essence of the song's underlying message remains the same. Even though the external world . . . fashion, politics, popular culture . . . is always changing, people don't really change that much internally. We all basically want the same things in life . . . love, family, community . . . the desire to connect. We all need each other. In other words, we're all "people who need people."

Even though I get bored singing the same old material over and over, I will never stop singing this song, and appreciating it, and loving the man who wrote it.

Thank you, Jule.

TEN

A Kid Again

My first TV special came at just the right moment. I had been saying the same lines and singing the same songs night and day for over a year in *Funny Girl*, and I jumped at the chance to do something new. Marty saw it as the next step in the career that we had always envisioned, and he made a deal with CBS to make TV specials exclusively for them, in a lucrative contract that could run as long as ten years. But what made this particular deal remarkable was that he negotiated the same key clause that he had fought for in my recording contract. Once again I would have creative control.

That was the only way anything like this could work for me.

I didn't relate to the typical variety show format, where the star introduced some guests, and they'd chat and maybe do a song or a sketch. I had done enough TV shows by now to know the routine, and I knew it wasn't right for me. I didn't see myself as a host. I didn't think I was charming enough. I had to do something different . . . something more comfortable for me.

Marty understood that and put me together with the most extraordinary team. Dwight Hemion would direct. Tom John would design the sets. Joe Layton, who had been a friend ever since he directed Elliott in *On the Town* in London, would stage the production numbers, although that barely describes his contribution. He basically codirected the show, while Dwight deftly handled the camerawork. Peter Matz would arrange and conduct. And I was determined to put this whole thing together without missing even one performance of *Funny Girl.*

Initially I didn't know what form the show should take, so we just started tossing ideas around. Everyone was creative. There was no ego. All of us were excited and hoping to make something new and fresh.

Gradually a concept emerged. I didn't want to do the conventional opening monologue. I didn't want to talk. I wanted to sing first . . . and I thought the song should be something unusual and original that would immediately intrigue the viewer. And as soon as I said that, the choice seemed obvious . . . the short song with the haunting melody by Leonard Bernstein, that I first sang at the Bon Soir . . . a song that seemed almost destined for me . . .

So, the program started with a screen that was completely black. You just heard my voice, singing "My mother said that babies come in bottles." And then a tiny picture of me as a six-year-old gradually got bigger and finally morphed into a close-up of me live, singing the last words of the song: "My Name Is Barbara." Just a face, against the black background . . . and these were the days when television was still black and white, so you had all that deep, rich contrast. The image was stark in its simplicity. I always liked the power of black and white, ever since my high school days watching foreign films.

And then I went straight into "Much More," the song from *The Fantasticks.*

Only when it was over did you see the title *My Name Is Barbra.* So it's four minutes into the show before you even know what you're watching. My thought was, *Why not establish a mood . . . entice the audience?* Isn't it more interesting to discover it slowly? (And pray the viewer doesn't switch channels!)

It seemed natural to think of the whole program as a little play . . . or a miniature movie . . . with three acts. That was familiar to me because it was also the way I approached my songs. And this would be a play about the push and pull I was feeling in my life . . . I was expected to be this adult woman, but inside I was still that little girl. It all felt a bit disorienting, like *Alice in Wonderland.*

So after a commercial, the first act began with me singing, "I'm late, I'm late, for a very important date," which was the White Rabbit's song in the Disney movie. Again, it introduces a mystery. What is this woman late for? Where is she going? It's not just a song, but also the beginning of a story. I run into room after room because I'm looking for something.

I'm wearing a gown that I designed and Bill Blass made for me . . . a long, Empire-waisted version of my middy blouse made in navy-blue chiffon, with a white collar and a red bow. I wanted the light chiffon so the dress would move with me and billow out in back as I ran up and down ramps and stairs and explored the different rooms, with small groups of musicians playing different instruments as I sang different songs.

And every song we chose had real meaning for me. "How Does the Wine Taste?" was a sensual song. I saw it as a metaphor for an innocent virgin wondering how sex feels . . .

I was only twenty-two, and still uncertain of my own sexual appeal.

But Dwight made me feel beautiful, and sexy. During rehearsal, he'd be watching the monitors and he'd say something like, "Turn your face two inches to the right." Then suddenly he'd be oohing and aahing, "Oh, God. Look at that close-up! Fantastic!"

I remember those close-ups. I was impressed with them myself. I could hardly believe that was the same face I saw in the mirror. Dwight was able to capture my face and show me something I had never seen before. I didn't know my own face very well at this point. I hadn't given much thought to what angles were best for me. It was only later, after I had seen myself many times on TV, that I realized the two sides of my face were very different . . . the left side is softer, more feminine. From the right, my features are more prominent. And that's why I've come to prefer the left. It was safer. But as I've also noticed over the years, there are certain angles on the right that are very good. The problem is, I can never pinpoint where they are. Is it from up high? Or down low? I don't know. In other words, it's hit or miss.

And yet Dwight kept hitting it right time after time. I don't know how he did it, but he did. I could trust him, and he was so supportive that I could just focus on my inner work. What a thrill . . . I was collaborating with people I loved and trusted . . . and that gave me the ability to be free and spontaneous. They were my team, and I knew I was safe and secure in their hands.

So even though it was a TV special, I could explore some deeper parts of myself. I always felt alone, ever since I was a kid. And since I still identify with the child in me, I thought, *Why not have another room filled with boys playing instruments?* When I walk in, I'm almost too large for the small room. I sit down and play "A Kid Again" on a toy piano (I loved that tinkling sound). There's a close-up of my fingers, and my simple, thin gold wedding band. When I sing "I wish I were a kid again," it isn't a happy song for me, and that knowledge gives the song a certain poignance.

Then a door flies open, and the curtains at the windows billow in the wind as I hear children's voices outside chanting, "Crazy Barbra, crazy Barbra." I needed something to draw me outside, and that image came from my childhood . . . it felt like what those girls were saying when they ganged up on me. And somehow I appear to get smaller and smaller as I approach the door. That was a trick of the set design, and we were all astonished when we saw it on film.

I turned to Tom and said, "That's brilliant. How did you do that?"

He explained that the room was built in forced perspective, which creates an optical illusion that made me look smaller as I walked away. Frankly, I still don't understand it.

And when I step through the door, I become a child again, dressed like a five-year-old in a middy blouse and skirt, white tights and Mary Janes. I'm running around on Tom's playground set, which was wonderfully surreal and quirky, like a child's drawing come to life. And when I climb up on a huge chair, I'm too small for it . . . like Alice after she drinks the potion.

Shooting this section was the most fun. After the curtain call on Broadway, I left the theater around 12:30 a.m., went straight to the TV studio, and stayed until 4:00 a.m. I thought we could make a sequence out of three songs, starting with "I'm Five" by Milton Schafer and ending with "Sweet Zoo" by Jeff Harris, who wrote *Another Evening with Harry Stoones.* And I wanted to do the whole thing in one take, with no cuts, so I could stay in that child's mind. But to do it in one take was a challenge, because the sequence was five minutes long. The camera had to follow me as I almost trip over some enormous crayons on the floor, mischievously splash my foot into a fake puddle of water, and then climb on a jungle gym. Joe and I had worked out the staging, with enough leeway so I could improvise a bit, and Dwight managed to capture it all. Peter's score was equally inventive, accenting the action with intriguing sounds. I would have liked to take off my makeup for this number, but there was no time, since I had to be an adult again in the next scene. I go back through the door, but now the boys are gone, and I'm alone, singing a beautiful song called "Where Is the Wonder?" It's about never wanting to lose the wonder of a child.

I run off singing "I'm late" again, and the mystery of what I'm late for is finally revealed in the next room, the one I was looking for all along. I walk in, and suddenly I'm in the midst of a full orchestra. The musicians have all come together to accompany me as I sing "People," to finish the first act.

After a commercial, the second act begins with me perched on a drum, wearing casual pants and a turtleneck, with a completely different hairdo . . . my own hair this time, which was much shorter than the wig I wore for the previous act. Instead of ignoring the fact that my hair has miraculously changed, I joke about being backstage "having a haircut." We're now at least twenty-two minutes into the show (not counting commercials), and this is the first time I've addressed the audience.

I hadn't noticed that until it was recently pointed out to me. It just felt normal, but I realize that what's normal to me is not necessarily normal for most people. I guess I just wanted to cut all the filler out. The only reason I used to talk so much in my later concerts is that I wanted a rest between songs. And of course I didn't have a script when I sang in nightclubs. I just improvised.

We hired Bob Emmett to write one brief comic monologue about a pearl button. That was a variation on something I used to do at the Bon Soir. I loved those stupid stories. We didn't have an audience in the studio, and I had to use my instinct to pause where I thought the laughs would be.

One of the writers we initially interviewed was Shelley Berman, who suggested something interesting . . . moving outside the studio to shoot on location. That really wasn't done on TV in those days, but Joe and I loved the idea. This would be the opposite of the first act . . . instead of becoming a child, now I'd transform into a sophisticated woman. So we used the song "Second Hand Rose" to lead into a shot of me arriving at the elegant department store Bergdorf Goodman in a horse-drawn carriage. We shot this in the middle of the night, when there was very little traffic on the street. And this is where Marty has his cameo . . . he's the top-hatted coachman helping me out of the carriage.

I used to browse through Bergdorf's when I couldn't even afford to buy a bottle of nail polish. That store represented the height of fashion, and now they had turned the whole place over to me. I must say, that was thrilling. As a teenager, I decided I had to get famous for various reasons, and one of them was to get waited on in department stores. Now stores let me come in after hours to shop. It's one of the perks of fame, and they even put out little treats to eat! Often I'll take my goddaughters or some very close friends along. (It's a far cry from the days when my height of sophistication was the A&S on Fulton Street.)

The concept for the music at Bergdorf's was intentionally ironic . . . to do a medley of Depression-era songs, like "I Got Plenty of Nothing," while I'm draped in furs, gallivanting through this temple of luxury. With my back to the camera, I let a blue fox coat seductively drop off my shoulders to reveal a backless gray dress I had designed. Then, in a complete shift of character, I'm a newsboy singing "Brother, Can You Spare a Dime?" in white mink knickers and a white mink cap.

Emeric Partos made all the furs for me, including that glorious sable coat I was flinging around, as if I were a matador, in "Nobody Knows You When You're Down and Out." I was supposed to stomp on it with my heels, and that worried me. I kept saying, "Are you sure I'm not going to hurt it?"

Emeric said, "That fur is stronger than you are."

As I leave the store, I'm wearing my version of something I'd seen in pictures . . . a formal riding outfit from the Edwardian period. I asked Emeric if he could make one for me in fur, and he chose white karakul (like my vintage coat). Halston, who wasn't famous yet, designed the tall white top hat, and I'm not sure who added a rhinestone-encrusted riding crop. It was all a wonderful fantasy, which ends with me back in the studio in my sweater, singing "The Best Things in Life Are Free."

And then in the third act, we're back to the simplicity of the beginning, with just me onstage, in a simple black gown. I had Bill Blass make it for me as well, from my sketch. I'm back to being Barbra . . . the girl and the woman. It's the resolution of the first two acts.

This was the only segment where we had a live audience. We showed them a tape of the first two acts of the show (just for their applause and laughter, which we added to the final tape), and then I came out onstage to sing live. These were songs I had done many times in clubs, like "When the Sun Comes Out" and "Lover Come Back to Me" . . . that was one I could have fun with, rhythmically. Sometimes I'd look at Peter in front of the orchestra, holding the baton, and he'd give me the most genuine smile that said, "Things are going well. This take is working!" And that made me feel good, and I'd smile back. We always had this connection, and spontaneous moments like that helped me react, because I could never put on a fake smile for the audience. I only smile when something's funny, and I smile at people I love.

I had asked Dwight if I could have some monitors in front of me so I could see each shot in real time. If I turned and caught a glimpse of Joe in the wings, beaming, I might stay there in profile a little longer if the angle was interesting. I was already thinking like a director . . . helping to compose the picture, looking for those good shots.

I told the audience, "There's a musical on Broadway now called *Funny Girl* . . . It's very good. I like it. In fact, I go there every night." And they burst out laughing. I did three of Jule Styne's songs from the show, and then I sang "My Man," which we didn't use on Broadway because the entire score had to be written by Jule. But it was the song most associated with Fanny Brice, and I think this was the first time I sang it in public. It's a fitting finale to the third act.

And then, almost like an encore, I did "Happy Days Are Here Again." But I wanted to underplay it . . . "throw it away," as they say . . . by putting the credits over it. It was an odd thing to do at the time, but something felt corny to me about saving my big song for the end. So it started very simply, and then I let the song build. (This is when I had Peter change the ending of the arrangement, which I never liked on my first album.) The lighting was also simple and dramatic, and Dwight did some great camerawork. On the very last line of the song, in time with the music . . . boom boom boom . . . multiple images of my face appeared, and then the two on the sides break away as he moved in for a close-up of the shot in the center.

I'm really proud of this show. It had style, shape, an emotional arc, drama, comedy . . . and I felt very fortunate to work with such talented men. Then, a week before the show was scheduled to air, Marty sent a tape over to CBS for the executives to preview. After he saw it, Michael Dann, the head of programming, told Marty that he had single-handedly destroyed my career. Dann wanted all sorts of changes, but because I had creative control, we didn't change a thing.

My Name Is Barbra was broadcast on Wednesday night, April 28, 1965. I was performing at the Winter Garden Theatre, of course, where we had just broken for intermission. The whole cast crammed into my dressing room to watch the first fifteen minutes of the show before we had to go back onstage.

After the curtain came down that night, I headed over to Bergdorf Goodman for a party celebrating the special, given by the owners of Bergdorf's, who lived in a penthouse apartment above the store. At one point I slipped away from the crowd and went into a bedroom, when I was told that Lee Solters was calling with the first reviews. He read me what the critic from UPI wrote: "Miss Barbra Streisand, 23, of Brooklyn, last night starred in her first television special, and the result was a pinnacle moment of American show business in any form, in any period. She is so great it is shocking."

I said, "Did he really write that?" I could feel my face flush. Lee continued to read: "She may well be the most supremely talented and complete popular entertainer that this country has ever produced." Oh my God. It felt like that moment when I first heard the *Funny Girl* reviews . . . could these people really be describing me? Because when I'm doing something, I never really know whether it's good or bad. And I'm always ready to believe the worst. So this kind of praise felt almost too good to be true.

Lee kept reading. At this point I was only processing bits and pieces of what he was saying: "A great comedienne" . . . "A great actress" . . . "Beautiful" . . . "Haunting" . . . "Girlish, ladylike, intense, hilarious" . . . "She touches you, to your toes. And then she knocks you out."

Wow. I could retire on this review. But here's the thing. It didn't satisfy me. In fact, I kept asking Lee, "Was there anything the critics *didn't* like?" I wanted to hear more specifics, not just superlatives.

In September the whole team reassembled at the Emmy Awards in New York. That was an exciting night. Garry Moore was the host, and I was already fond of him because he was one of the first people to put me on TV. And now here we were, up for six Emmys for outstanding program, direction, performer, music, choreography, and art direction. We won five, including my first Emmy for "individual achievement by an actor or performer." I was wearing the black dress from the show under a long black lace coat with sequins that sparkled in the light as I walked up to the podium. Garry handed me the Emmy, and I announced that I had a run in my stocking . . . "Of all nights!" . . . and told the audience that I loved "this television thing," because I had figured out that I would have to perform in *Funny Girl* for fifty-eight years to reach as many people as had watched the special in one night. And I quoted a fan letter that said, "Dear Miss Streisand . . . just a brief note to tell you how much I liked the show, and of all the people on it, I thought you were the best one."

My only disappointment was that Dwight didn't win in his category, which seemed outrageous to me, but the Directors Guild made up for it when they gave him their award for Outstanding Directorial Achievement in television. The show also won the prestigious Peabody Award for excellence, which was a huge thrill, and I also won a Grammy Award for Best Vocal Performance for the album, which came out shortly after the telecast.

I had suggested they use that same picture of me as a six-year-old, from the opening of the show, for the cover of the album. I did it for two reasons: one, I was too lazy to take another picture, and two, the album had children's songs on it, so why not use a picture of me as a child? It was taken by my brother, Shelly, who had just gotten a new camera, and I remember pulling a squashed magenta bow off a box of candy and sticking it on my dress, because I wanted to perk it up for the picture. I was so happy when that photo was nominated for Best Cover . . . Shelly's one and only Grammy nomination, along with the graphic designer from Columbia Records. Too bad they didn't win. Well, you can't have everything.

But I was still thrilled because I had never anticipated any of this wonderful acclaim in the first place. As I was doing the show, I knew it felt right to me. The concepts were good. My team was very good, and I thought I was pretty good . . . I just didn't know *how* good.

By the way, I don't think I'm the only one who was pleasantly surprised by the response. The executives at CBS must have been extremely relieved. And Michael Dann did call Marty after the broadcast to apologize and admit he was wrong!

My Name Is Barbra was shown again in October 1965, and that coincided with the release of another album, *My Name Is Barbra, Two . . .* But most of the songs had no connection to the special. I just liked them.

I first heard "She Touched Me" because Elliott sang it. He was doing a show on Broadway called *Drat! The Cat!*, and was busy with rehearsals while I was busy with the album. The show closed a week after it opened, which was a huge disappointment. But that song about the first spark of love was very moving. So I simply reversed the genders and recorded it as "*He* Touched Me," and the song was a hit.

Don Costa did the arrangement, and this album marks the beginning of our professional relationship. He was shy and quiet, but his work was amazing, and he used chords that were so unexpected. He was very inventive . . . I never quite knew what the orchestra was going to sound like when he was involved. Don didn't play the piano, and he used to come in with his guitar and pick out something to show me what he was thinking, but that didn't tell me much. So I was always pleasantly surprised when I heard the finished version.

Another song was given to me by David Shire, whom I got to know when he was the pianist in the pit during the second year of *Funny Girl.* One day at the theater, between the matinee and evening performances, he was showing me some songs he had written with his partner, Richard Maltby, Jr., and I liked one called "No More Songs for Me." The tone was somber, and I could always relate to that kind of music and lyric.

I told Don, "I hear this with mostly cellos," and he wrote a great arrangement. On the day we were scheduled to record it, we were doing other songs first and as usual we ran out of time. But I still had to record this last song. I said to Marty, "I don't care what it costs for overtime. I need to finish it!" (That's why my records often cost more than they're supposed to. I care about the song, not the money.)

We had started out with a large cello section, but by this point most of them had had to leave to go to other sessions. Only four remained, so I said, "Okay, I'll do it with the four cellos. And in the mix, we'll turn them up!" So that's what's on the record, and it sounds damn good, because Don's arrangement was so good.

He did a total of five songs on this album, including "The Shadow of Your Smile." I wanted something different from the version in the Elizabeth Taylor/Richard Burton movie *The Sandpiper*, so I suggested doing it as a bossa nova. And Don did a beautiful chart. He always found a way to give me more than I imagined.

The album distracted me . . . for a bit. And the special had been a very satisfying experience.

But I still had to be at the Winter Garden day after day, night after night.

ELEVEN

Je m'appelle Barbra

I desperately needed something else to focus on.

So when an executive at Columbia asked if I'd be interested in recording a few songs in French, for an EP to sell in the European market, I said yes.

I'd always loved the French language, but I'd never really studied it. I had taken a few lessons at one point, but the sound of the teacher's voice was so monotonous that it put me to sleep . . . literally. My eyelids would get so heavy that I'd have to say, "Can you wait for a few minutes?" And he did, while I dozed off right there on the couch.

So singing in French would be a challenge, but I figured I had a good ear. After all, I used to answer the phone at Michael Press in all those foreign accents. And I was pretty good at languages. Besides, I was eager to stretch myself.

Columbia suggested bringing in someone who knew the French repertoire.

I was still going to foreign films and had recently seen Jacques Demy's *The Umbrellas of Cherbourg*, in which all the dialogue was sung. I was taken with two songs that had wonderful melodies . . . "I Will Wait for You" and "Watch What Happens." The composer was Michel Legrand.

Well, it turned out that the Columbia executive happened to be managing Michel on the side. So Michel flew in from Paris and on the night he arrived he saw *Funny Girl*, and then we met backstage.

After a few minutes of conversation, I was completely charmed. Michel was so warm and engaging, with a shock of dark wavy hair, glasses, and a tie that he quickly loosened so we could get right to work. He sat down at the little upright piano in my dressing room and started to play.

That became our routine. Luckily he was a night owl like me! He would come to the theater after the show at midnight, when everyone else had gone home and we had the place to ourselves. He'd play a song for me, and if I liked it, I'd give it a try. He had all sorts of ideas, and better yet, he could make me laugh, which made it even more fun. Evidently he enjoyed our sessions as well. I'm going through old articles as I write this and I see he said, "When I finally emerged out into the street, I'd look at my watch and be shocked to find that it was 4 or 5 a.m. I hadn't felt the hours pass. It was a euphoric time."

One of the first pieces we looked at was "Autumn Leaves." I wasn't aware that it was originally a French song. All I knew was the English version, with lyrics by Johnny Mercer, which described how memories of a former lover always came back in autumn. So of course I wanted to see the French lyrics as well in case there was something there that might affect my interpretation. I need to analyze a lyric, just as I would analyze a script. Michel explained that the words were originally a poem by Jacques Prévert that had been set to music. And when he translated it for me, I realized there was a whole other layer to the song. Even the French title . . . "Les Feuilles Mortes" (Dead Leaves) . . . is darker. It was written just after World War II, and the images, like fallen leaves "picked up by the shovelful," suggested the death and destruction of war. Events beyond their control have separated these lovers. Their footprints on the sand are erased by the sea, and the memories they shared are blown away like leaves "into the cold night of oblivion."

The song was somber and very moving, and I didn't want to do it in the conventional way, with an orchestra. I heard it as a small, intimate sound, more like a string quartet, and suggested that to Michel. Then I said, "And what if it started with just one instrument, I don't know, maybe a cello?" Michel loved that idea but decided to use a viola, and brought in the virtuoso Emanuel Vardi, who played what turned into a beautifully complex introduction. I thought that would settle into a long legato sound, perhaps with two instruments that could build when I started singing. But instead the viola made a plucking sound, which is technically called pizzicato.

Once I began the familiar part of the song in English . . . "The falling leaves drift by the window" . . . the viola switched from pizzicato to arco, which is played with a bow. And then my favorite part is the bridge . . . "Since you went away" . . . where you hear the entire string quartet, with those long, sustained notes . . . until the viola reverted to that plucking sound again. Only for the last chord did the full quartet come back in.

After a few takes Michel thought we had it. As he later recalled to an interviewer, "She loved the song so much, she said to me, 'Let's do it again . . . just for the pleasure.' I loved her attitude."

What he didn't realize was that the only part of the orchestration I loved was singing with the legato strings, and especially the quartet. I had told him I didn't like the pizzicato section, but he laughed and gave me a hug, in his charming French way. He said, "Trust me, it's the right thing."

And I let it go, because I didn't want to hurt his feelings.

In retrospect, I should have said, "Michel, it doesn't sound right to me. I want to hear more of the quartet. Let them play to the end. Don't go back to that plucking sound." To me, it was like coitus interruptus . . . just before the climax, the quartet stopped.

Point is, it reminded me of a very important lesson (that I thought I had learned) . . . never ignore my first instincts. If the music doesn't sound like what I imagined . . . or better . . . all I need to say is, "It just doesn't feel right."

You really can't argue with that. Those are my feelings, and I'm the one singing the song. And it won't help to try to talk me into anything intellectually, because this is a visceral reaction that starts in the pit of my stomach, goes up to my brain, and ends up in my throat. And even if the result isn't perceived as successful by the rest of the world, it's right for *me.* Today, I try not to settle for anything less.

And here's another thing, and this is why I never listen to my records again unless I'm going to sing a song from one of them in a concert . . . I usually hear something else I would change. In this case, I wouldn't choose to do those two high notes at the end. I should have sung a lower note, darker, so the song would end with a bit more sadness. And one more thing . . . now I really wish I had sung the whole song in French!

The first recording sessions for the EP were also done after the show, starting at midnight. Michel told me that normally it would be suicidal to record someone after they had just spent two and a half hours singing onstage. But I felt the opposite . . . *Funny Girl* was my warm-up.

I was so excited about the project that in addition to the EP I was already envisioning a whole album of French songs for the American market.

When Columbia heard, they got nervous and told Marty he had to discourage me . . . it wouldn't sell . . . it was a crazy idea. But I didn't care whether it was commercial or not. Besides, I had already decided that I wasn't going to sing *every* song in French. Sometimes I would do only a few verses. I felt that even if people didn't understand every word, they could still respond to the melody and the emotions.

I ended up singing three songs by Michel on the album, including "La Valse des Lilas" ("Once Upon a Summertime"), which he had composed ten years earlier, when he was just twenty-two. That got me thinking. I was already twenty-three. There was no time to lose! Could I write a song? Maybe with lyrics in French?

So I did . . . I composed the melody, and Eddy Marnay, a lovely man who wrote lyrics for Michel, wrote the lyric for me. I told him how I picked out the tune with one finger on a piano, so that's how the song starts . . . "Avec un doigt sur un piano." And then I was thinking about having a first love: "J'avais dans mes mains, ton coeur et le mien." In essence, it means I held your heart and mine in my hand, and with my first love, I found my first song . . . "J'ai trouvé cette chanson."

The lyric simply describes how I wrote the song. It was the truth, which always works for me. And since it was the first melody I ever wrote, I thought we should just call it what it was . . . "Ma Première Chanson."

Michel and I continued to work on the album that would become *Je m'appelle Barbra* at intervals over the next year and a half. And when we did the final recording sessions, I was pregnant with Jason, so it was a labor of love in more ways than one.

I've joked that it was the least popular album I ever made, but now that I've looked at the statistics . . . number 5 on the Billboard Albums chart . . . it actually sold better than I thought.

Of course it also represents the beginning of an extraordinary musical partnership with Michel . . . and eventually the Bergmans . . . that culminated in *Yentl.*

TWELVE

Gotta Move

Funny Girl was still packing people in, but I couldn't wait to get out. I hung a big calendar on my dressing-room wall and crossed off each night. My contract was up in December, but Ray didn't want to let me go. And he was very clever. He knew there was no way I would sign up for more shows in New York, and that's when he came up with the idea of doing it in London. At first I said, "No. Absolutely not." But Ray kept pushing . . . it would be a short, limited run . . . and the more I thought about it, the more I didn't want anyone else to play it in London but me. I liked the idea of living there for a while too . . . think of all those quaint little shops, not to mention those lovely English teas with warm scones and tiny sandwiches.

My final performance in New York was on Saturday night, December 25 . . . Christmas 1965 . . . and what a great gift. There was light at the end of the tunnel! I had invited old friends like Bob Schear, the stage manager from *I Can Get It for You Wholesale*, to come to this show. He lugged in one of those old, bulky reel-to-reel tape recorders and hooked it up to the loudspeaker in my dressing room so I could have a recording of my closing night . . . just for me. And I wanted to make a copy for Jule, who was here again for me at the end just as he had been at the beginning, always supportive, and always ready with another joke or a new song up his sleeve.

Bob had arrived early to check out the sound, and he said there were people in the audience who had seen the show ten or fifteen times. And of course Marty was there, and Elliott in the front row, next to Cis.

Before the show began there was one of those announcements that all theatergoers dread, since it usually means the star you have come to see is out for some reason, and someone else is playing the role. A man's voice came on over the loudspeaker and said, "Ladies and gentlemen, in this evening's performance, the role of Fanny Brice will be played by . . . Barbra Streisand." The whole place burst into relieved laughter and applause. And then the overture began.

From the moment I walked onstage the audience was right there with me, hanging on every word and anticipating every song. It felt as if I were being carried along on waves of applause. And I was actually enjoying myself, knowing this was my last time onstage at the Winter Garden. Each scene went off smoothly, until I got to "People." I thought, *Oh good, only two more songs till intermission.* And then, in the middle of the song, just as I sang the words "With one person, one very special person, a feeling deep in your soul says you were half, now you're whole," suddenly I was overwhelmed with emotion. My voice broke. I couldn't even catch my breath, much less sing, because of the lump in my throat. I couldn't say the words. I was crying.

I don't cry easily, at least not in real life. I cry at the movies, when it's a love story that doesn't work out or something tragic about a child or a dog, but for me to start crying in the middle of a song onstage was horrifying . . . one of those moments when time stops and you just don't know what's going to happen next.

Nobody else did either. Everyone was holding their breath, wondering, Is she going to run off? Is she going to collapse? Should we pull the curtain down? Someone snapped a picture of Cis and Elliott at this moment, and they were crying, too, with those crumpled-up faces people make when they're *really* sobbing. I kept that picture for years, tucked away in my little captain's desk.

As I stood there, stunned, a rush of thoughts was racing through my head.

Why was I crying? Where did this emotion come from? Obviously from somewhere deep in my subconscious, because it totally surprised me. Here I was, counting the days until I could get out of this show. It had become a virtual prison to me, and yet I was all choked up. Memories came flooding back to me . . . all my auditions . . . the revolving door of directors . . . forty-two versions of the last scene . . . the debilitating conflicts with Sydney and Ray. And it suddenly hit me . . . in spite of all the struggles during the run, I realized how much this show truly meant to me.

Somehow I managed to finish the song. But I think the audience knew they had witnessed something very real. As soon as I sang the last line, "People who need people are the luckiest people in the world!" they burst into applause. They kept yelling "Brava! Brava!" like at the opera, and the applause didn't stop, it went on and on. Thank God, because it gave me a chance to recover enough to finish the rest of the act.

And it was so clear to me . . . what really got to people was the fact that I was trying to hold the emotion back. I kept telling myself, *You don't want to cry. You cannot cry . . .* as the tears were coming down. And that's what made the audience react so strongly and cry along with me.

Of course you can't hold an emotion back if you don't have it in the first place . . . that's a given. But what really interests me as an actress is the power of restraint.

By the end of the performance, I was drained . . . exhilarated and relieved almost in equal measure. And there was a sadness, because I knew in my heart that I would never be back on a Broadway stage again. The experience with Sydney had been so traumatizing that it spoiled that for me, forever.

Meanwhile, the audience leapt to their feet for a standing ovation and didn't sit down again as the cast came out for their curtain calls. When I finally appeared to take my bows, the applause reached a crescendo. I looked out at the audience and suddenly felt such gratitude toward all these people who were so appreciative. I could see the faces of friends and family who had always been there to support me. When I was presented with a huge bouquet of red roses, I did something I had seen at the ballet. The prima ballerina will always pull out one rose and give it to her partner, as a thank-you. So I pulled out one rose and tossed it to Elliott in the front row, but Cis reached out and intercepted it. (I'm not sure Elliott ever forgave her. In fact, fifty-six years later, he just sent me a birthday note and brought it up again.)

And then I handed the bouquet to the nearest cast member and began to speak:

> *It's a very difficult thing to be standing here now. I don't like speeches and I don't like to give speeches and I don't like to break the illusion of the play normally for the audience. But I found out onstage . . . I mean, tonight is very special for me.*
>
> *It's been a long time . . . two years . . . it's a big chunk of my life and it's been wonderful. I want to thank everybody connected with* Funny Girl *. . . the marvelous cast we have {and as I turned to look at them, my voice broke again}, Johnny Desmond and Kay Medford and Lee Allen, who's leaving tonight also, and everybody. If I start listing names, I know I'm going to leave people out.*
>
> *But I would like now to do something that will let me pay my respects . . . my final respects to the memory of the great lady who this play is about, and to the Winter Garden and to* Funny Girl.

And then I began to sing "My Man," the song that was Fanny's signature. It was my small way of saying thank you not only to her, but also to the audience. I wanted to return their love with a token of my own. And I was also singing it for Ray, who had always wanted it in the play. I sang the first line without any accompaniment, then the piano joined me, and then the orchestra kicked in. When I finished and bowed my head the house erupted into applause and cheers and another standing ovation. Then the orchestra went into the first chords of "Auld Lang Syne," and the cast linked arms and started to sing, and the audience joined in. We finished the song together, and people shouted "Hip, hip, hooray! Hip, hip, hooray!" Then the cast and I left the stage and the orchestra played "People" as the audience put on their coats and filed out.

And it was over.

I had gotten into the habit of giving notes, and this last night was no exception. I had noticed that the artificial flowers were a little dusty, so I pointed it out to the prop man. I wanted everything to be right for Mimi Hines, who was taking over my role on Monday.

Backstage, a tall, charismatic man was waiting for me with his arms held out . . . Jerry Robbins. I was so happy to see him again. After all, he was the one who had given me this part. Thank God he hired me, or my life might have been very different. I rushed into his arms and gave him a big, long hug.

Working with Jerry confirmed something I had always intuited. I needed and loved to work with strong people . . . people with passion and integrity and soulfulness and creativity. Jerry started out as a choreographer who went beyond the world of classical ballet and contributed so much to modern dance. And then he became a director and was equally gifted at that. Maybe subconsciously, looking at the trajectory of his career, I realized that when you have that kind of talent or vision, you can take a chance and explore other areas. The integrity of that vision will translate into other mediums.

And don't worry if you're scared. Everybody who's really good is scared. Use that fear to forge ahead and try something new. I certainly learned a lot from Jerry about how to tell a story . . . where to put the focus . . . and remembered it when I began to direct.

Jerry was different . . . a Jewish kid. I was different and Jewish as well. There are mystical things that bind people together, and I think our Jewish roots were one of those things. Jerry and I recognized each other . . . the pain of being different, and the huge need to express ourselves. There was a soul connection.

> *"She always surprises. Her performances astound, arouse, fulfill. When she sings, she is as honest and frighteningly direct with her feelings as if one time she was, is or will be in bed with you. The satisfaction she gives also leaves one with terrible and pleasurable hunger. For what will become of this woman? She is still unfinished. Where will she go and what will she do? With all her talent and radiance, glamour, uniqueness, passion and wit and spontaneity, she is still forming. There is more to come, things will change, something will happen. The next is not going to be like the last; she promises more and more surprises. Thus she adds the special mystery to her already*

extraordinary gifts and achieves the true sign of a star. She is one of those very rare and fascinating performers who spellbind and then irresistibly pull you on to find out what will happen in the next moment, the next act, the next play."

—Jerome Robbins

The last time I saw Jerry was at City Center in New York. I had bought tickets for *Afternoon of a Faun*, a famous piece he choreographed with two ballet dancers, in practice clothes, done on a spare and simple set . . . just a barre and a mirrored wall to represent a ballet studio. I'll always remember one particular moment. The Debussy music was growing big and full and exultant, and just when you would expect the dancers to rush into each other's arms, Jerry took the opposite tack. Instead of the movements becoming bigger, they became smaller, more intimate. And it was beyond beautiful.

Afterward I went backstage. I didn't even know if Jerry would be there that night, but he was. We stood on that empty stage, smiling at each other. He had such a sweet, genuine smile. It was so great to see him again, have a lovely talk, and give him another hug.

You can see in his work that he wasn't afraid to go deep into the inner self and explore all sorts of psychological complexities. He's one of my happiest memories from the stage production of *Funny Girl*. I loved Jerry, and I miss him. Like so many good men, he died too young.

Now that my New York run in the play was over, I would have a little break before we opened in London in April. But I didn't have time to enjoy it, because I had to go straight back to work on my second TV special. Once again I was collaborating with my wonderful team . . . Joe, Peter, Dwight, Tom, Bob, and Marty. Since the first special had been so successful, we decided to stick to the same three-act structure. I wanted to go outside the studio again, and this time the show would be broadcast in color. And what do I think of when I think of color? Paintings.

So I said, "Let's go to a museum."

I had always been very interested in art. When I was sixteen, I made my first purchase . . . that ten-dollar Rembrandt print. I used to wander around the New York galleries and imagine what it would be like to be rich enough to actually own one of their paintings. When I was seventeen, I saw an exhibit at the Galerie St. Etienne and fell in love with Gustav Klimt and Egon Schiele. I remember one painting . . . just a tiny baby's head at the top, while the bulk of the canvas was a colorful, kaleidoscopic blanket. I asked the price and was told it was $200,000, which was an unbelievably high amount to me. Today that painting hangs in the National Gallery in Washington, D.C., and is worth many millions.

At twenty-two, with money from my albums and *Funny Girl*, I made my first major art purchase at Richard Feigen's gallery . . . a small painting by Matisse. I loved his work. It was a woman, sitting in a chair, done in 1924. And I was born on the twenty-fourth, so that seemed auspicious, and the thought of owning anything by this artist was too tempting. But it was a lot of money to me . . . fifty-five thousand dollars . . . and I didn't really love this particular painting, so I was hesitant. Richard was very kind. He said that if I changed my mind within eighteen months, he would buy it back from me. That closed the deal.

I took it to Matisse's son Pierre, who confirmed its authenticity but agreed with me that it wasn't very special. That's when I realized that just because it's by a great artist doesn't mean it's a great painting.

And then I remember walking past Klaus Perls's gallery on Madison Avenue and stopping to stare at a nude by Amedeo Modigliani. Something about his work had always touched me . . . maybe it was his passion. I went in, asked about the price, and was told it was $70,000. But I had no money left . . . I had just bought the Matisse. (I should have returned the Matisse, which I ended up doing anyway, and immediately bought the Modigliani. I'm still haunted by that painting. Today it's hanging in the Metropolitan Museum of Art, and a similar Modigliani nude was recently sold at Christie's for $170.4 million.)

Anyway, I had this idea of doing the first act of the show in an art museum. I think we approached the Metropolitan Museum of Art and asked if we could film there, but they were open seven days a week, which made it difficult. The Philadelphia Museum of Art, though, was closed on Sunday, and the director there was more receptive. So we all drove down to Philadelphia to check it out. As soon as I saw that grand limestone staircase in the entrance hall, I said,

"This is incredible!" And then, as we walked through the galleries, I saw a painting called *The Concert Singer* by Thomas Eakins and thought, *How perfect.* I turned to my guys and asked, "What if I go into the painting? What if I *become* the painting?"

And that was the genesis of the first act.

I had found a song called "Draw Me a Circle," and that's how we started the special, with a drawing of a circle that gradually became a face. It looked like something a child would draw with crayons. Then the drawn eyes dissolved into a shot of my eyes and my face, and then my face dissolved back into the drawing, as paint splattered across it. It was colorful and whimsical and set the tone for the entire show.

I had been playing one character for so long . . . and now I wanted to play as many characters as possible. So that's what I did.

The first act opened with me walking through the museum, dressed like a Victorian parlor maid in a dark green velvet dress (which I had found at Filene's Basement) with a white apron. We imagined me as sort of a caretaker, dusting the statues and generally watching over the place as I walked through it alone at night. And then I would go into various rooms and "become" various paintings as I sang various songs.

Joe had timed everything out to the second, because the choreography had to get me to the right place at exactly the right moment. And we could only film during the hours the museum was closed . . . from 6:00 p.m. Saturday until the staff began to arrive on Monday morning. That meant we had only thirty-six hours to complete this extremely complicated sequence, with many setups and costume changes. That was already a big challenge.

And then disaster struck. Two of the three Marconi color cameras that CBS had sent down with us immediately went out. (This was the first time they had used the cameras on location.) And there was absolutely nothing we could do. There were no spare parts . . . the technology was too new. So Joe had to quickly restage every scene to shoot with only one camera.

We couldn't stop to sleep. I sang "One Kiss," wearing a pink gown like the woman in *The Concert Singer*, at 5:30 in the morning, and I remember being so tired that I could hardly hit the high notes. "One Kiss" was one of the songs my mother sang when we both went to Nola Studios to make our records when I was thirteen. I thought my mother would be pleased at my tribute to her.

(Instead, when she saw the show, she was angry, complaining, "You copied me! You stole my song!")

Next I transformed into Marie Antoinette, singing a funny version of "The Minute Waltz" in between eating petits fours and glancing out at the waiting guillotine. (I did manage to get an hour's nap while they set up the shot, but I couldn't risk disturbing that elaborate wig, so I lay down with my neck on a block of wood, like a Japanese geisha.) And then it was on to the modern art room . . .

I wanted to use Peter's song, "Gotta Move," because I thought it had just the right frenetic energy for those abstract paintings. Now I'm in my own short hair, wearing a kind of crazy op-art dress, and for a surreal touch, I stuck on colored rhinestones in the area right above my eyes, just under my eyebrows. I glued each of those suckers on myself, with Duo adhesive. (What was I thinking?)

But my favorite character in the sequence . . . and my favorite painting . . . is Modigliani's *Portrait of a Polish Woman.* (I loved that painting so much, I actually tried to buy it from the museum. But they didn't go for it.) A shot of me looking at the painting dissolves to a shot of me dressed like the woman, sitting at the same kind of table. Something about the way her eyes are looking down made me imagine she was hurt by her lover. So I sang "Non C'est Rien," a song about trying to cover up the pain.

Then I get up and walk out of the shot, and you see me back in the gallery looking at the painting . . . only this time I'm still wearing her dress and the painting is of the empty chair. In other words, the woman has exited the painting, which is kind of scary. That image came into my head, and I can't tell you why intellectually. I just visualized it and thought it would be interesting. Ah, the mystery.

And finally, since various people had compared my profile to Nefertiti's, I thought it would be fun to transform into her. I love that shot in the Egyptian room, where you see me reflected in the pool of water, and then the surface ripples and my face becomes hers. (Of course, those were the days when I could look at myself upside down. Now it would be horrifying.) This scene caused a bit of a problem for the museum. For years frustrated visitors have come up to the information desk, saying they're searching for the Egyptian room but can't find it. No wonder, because it doesn't exist. Tom built this set back in the studio in New York. And he did a brilliant job, right down to the last detail. I told him I wanted to end this section with that same little face from the opening of the special. So the camera pans up, and there it is, etched amid the hieroglyphics. We've come full circle . . . literally . . . and that's the end of the first act.

By the way, there's another circle I only discovered recently when I bought a painting by Modigliani called *Madame Hanka Zborowska.* As I was looking at it closely, I thought, *Why does she look familiar?* And then I found out that she's the same Polish woman in the painting at the museum! I had responded to her so deeply in 1966, and now somehow she came back to me . . . maybe it was *bashert.*

For the second act, I wanted to do something with animals, my other favorite thing, along with art. And I wanted Sadie to be part of it. Sadie was my beloved poodle, given to me by the cast of *Funny Girl* at a surprise party for my twenty-second birthday. There was a large box under the cake, and someone said, "Reach in." I felt something furry . . . a fur hat? Wait a minute, if this is a hat it's moving . . . and I pulled out this tiny puppy with a poodle haircut. I had never had a dog. I didn't even know I was a dog person until I met Sadie.

So my team came up with a circus theme, which meant I could interact with all sorts of animals. I sang "Funny Face" to a Shetland pony. I shook hands with a little baboon. And this was my favorite part . . . I did a soft-shoe with five little penguins to "Sam, You Made the Pants Too Long." Those penguins were so sweet. They actually jumped up on the beats. Unfortunately they didn't like the hot lights in the studio, and we had to keep stopping between takes to put them in a refrigerated crate to cool them down.

Joe thought it would be funny to have me walk into a cage with a tiger, only to nonchalantly walk past it and be more afraid of a kitten, who somehow manages to roar and scare me away (after a few bars of "What's New, Pussycat?"). Easy for Joe to say. Before we even did the first take, the tiger got loose, knocking everything over. Joe was willing to shelve the bit. I was terrified, but I thought, *What the hell?*, and did it anyway. Because if it works, the shot is worth it. And if you don't survive, well, it's all for the sake of art!

After that, I compare profiles with an anteater . . . "an amiable anteater" . . . as I sing, "We have so much in common, it's a phenomenon," a snippet of a song called "Small World," from *Gypsy.* I'm wearing a silver-sequined bodysuit by

Norman Norell that I also found at Filene's Basement, for eighty-nine dollars. No wonder it was discounted . . . I remember thinking, *Who's going to buy this thing?* But it was perfect for the show. We paired it with a pink ruffle around the neck and an orange chiffon top and pants. (This was before I decided I hated the color orange.)

Then the circus leaves town. I'm all alone singing "Have I Stayed Too Long at the Fair," but then Sadie flies into my arms. And now I'll never be alone because I have my beloved girl, always happy to see me, and I sing "Look at That Face" to her. That's a fabulous song, written by Tony Newley and Leslie Bricusse, and Tony was a new friend. I loved how Sadie would always lay her head on my shoulder, like a child, and that's how we finished the second act.

The third act was a live concert, just as in the first special. Because I wore black then, I wanted to wear an off-white dress now, and I had one (another bargain . . . a thirty-dollar Empire-style wool dress). My only jewelry was a pair of drop earrings, made of fake diamonds and pearls. I would wear those same earrings two years later, when I sang "My Man" in the final scene of the film of *Funny Girl*. And then I lost them. Years later, when I was on a small fishing boat in Cabo San Lucas, the captain said to me, "You know, my mother has your earrings. She was a furrier, and you left them in the pocket of a coat."

I was elated. I gave him my address and he promised to mail them back to me, but I never got them. I wish he had kept his promise. I still miss those earrings. They were hardly worth anything, but they had sentimental value to me.

David Shire was Peter's assistant on this show, and I liked a new song he and Richard Maltby, Jr., had written called "Starting Here, Starting Now." One day, when David was sitting at the piano and we were working on the arrangement, I asked if he could do a big build near the end on the word "now," leading into a key change at the top of the note that would go even higher. That's what I heard in my head. David tried it, and then he looked at me and said, "Wow. That has nothing to do with the way I originally conceived this song."

I said quietly, "Oh . . . you don't like it?"

"Like it? I *love* it. You just turned a run-of-the-mill number into an aria."

I was thrilled that *he* was thrilled.

"Now the song has real drama," he said.

And I used it at the end of the show, over the credits. The lyric suggested a new beginning, and I thought that would be interesting to add to the end. I like to leave on a high note, not only musically but also emotionally.

And that was it, my second special. Since *Color Me Barbra* had a similar structure to *My Name Is Barbra*, I thought of them as bookends. We taped it in January, and as soon as we were done, I got on a plane to Europe.

Both TV specials were sponsored by Chemstrand, which made nylon yarn for carpets. Who knew that they would merge with Monsanto and become this big chemical company? I thought they just made rugs!

The company was so pleased with the response to the first special and so excited about the second that they basically offered me a European vacation as a reward. We were already talking about a third, but I hadn't given much thought to what it could be . . . after all, you can't have *three* bookends. Maybe it would have something to do with fashion . . . anyway, the idea was that I'd go to the Paris collections and pick out clothes to wear on it.

Diana Vreeland, the editor of *Vogue*, had been very complimentary and saw something in me, when other people were making jokes like this: "My wife went to the hairdresser's and said, 'I want the Barbra Streisand look.' So he smacked her in the nose with the hairbrush."

Vreeland invited me to lunch at her apartment and that was fun, because her home was as stylish as she was. In her famous living room, the walls, curtains, and almost every piece of furniture were covered in a pure-red flowered fabric . . . she called it her "garden in hell." We ate in the dining alcove, where the walls and the banquettes were upholstered in equally bold stripes. I'd heard she was imperious, but I found her to be very warm, with a unique personality . . . funny and down-to-earth . . . that made her very attractive. She spoke of me as a fashion icon, long before anyone imagined I'd ever make the best-dressed list. When she heard I was going to Paris, she said, "Let's do it for *Vogue*! I'll send Richard Avedon to photograph you in the latest couture."

What a treat, to have four weeks to gallivant around Europe! I had visited England when Elliott was in his play, but neither of us had been to France or Italy. And the best thing was that I could invite Cis and Harvey to come along, and Chemstrand was paying for everything!

God, we had fun. We ate at the best restaurants and stayed at the best hotels. I remember walking into our suite at the Hotel Hassler in Rome and being astonished at its size . . . you could have tucked our whole New York apartment into it, twice. And it was fit for an emperor . . . decorated with elaborate moldings, silk draperies, and lovely Empire furniture. Cis and I each picked out a bedroom. They were also enormous . . . the beds were the size of a small boat. I felt as if I were Cinderella, having a sleepover at the palace.

And then we went back to the living room, where there was a beautiful mahogany dining table . . . so of course the first thing we wanted to do was eat. We called room service, and an elegant Italian waiter appeared and began to reel off a long list of specialties, each one sounding more exotic and delicious. When it was Elliott's turn to give his order, he said, "I'll have a pastrami sandwich, please."

I gasped at the look on the waiter's face. I guess he had never heard of pastrami.

And then Elliott said, "On rye."

We almost died laughing. In fact, I remember laughing so hard that my ribs hurt. I couldn't catch my breath. Every time Cis and I looked at each other, we started laughing again and couldn't stop. Finally, we had to retreat to opposite sides of the suite so we could recover while we waited for the food. Elliott and I practically crawled to our bedroom at one end of the hall, while Cis and Harvey went off to theirs, miles away at the other end of the suite.

One night in Paris we met Eddie Barclay, a French record producer who worked with Michel Legrand and Jacques Brel. I really liked Jacques Brel, who I thought was both a wonderful singer and a great songwriter. I had played his album *La Valse a Mille Temps* many times, and there was one song on it that I really responded to . . . "Ne Me Quitte Pas" . . . a plea to his lover not to leave him, which was so passionate and vulnerable. When Eddie mentioned that Brel was performing in Marseille, I decided we had to go. I didn't want to miss my chance to see him in person. Eddie said he'd tell Brel's manager that I loved that song and looked forward to hearing him sing it.

So we flew to Marseille, and since the city was famous for bouillabaisse . . . a fish stew originally made by the local fishermen (using the fish they couldn't sell, I think) . . . I wanted to taste some. I tried to order it for dinner at the hotel, but it was not on the menu that night. I was so disappointed, but it was too late to go anywhere else because we had to eat quickly and rush to the theater. I was wearing my beige fur coat with a matching fur hat. Cis liked it so much that I had both pieces copied in black-and-white fox for her. So we looked like these odd fur twins. As we took our seats, I heard this chorus of whispers, "Chapeau! Chapeau!" At first I thought they were complimenting us on our hats, but then I realized they wanted us to take them off so we didn't block their view.

Another disappointment . . . Brel didn't sing my favorite song of his. The night was not going well.

Then we went backstage after the show. Brel opened the door to his dressing room with a beer in one hand and a young woman in the other. I don't think he was thrilled to be interrupted, and he definitely did not appreciate our fur ensembles. He had a thing about the bourgeoisie, and I suppose we looked very bourgeois to him.

Sometimes it's best not to meet your idols.

I've never forgotten how disappointed I was when Brel wouldn't sing the song he was famous for, and that made me think. Back at the Bon Soir, when someone in the audience would call out, Sing this or that, I'd say, "I don't take requests" . . . almost like a joke. And then years later, when I was preparing my own concerts in Las Vegas, I dropped my old songs, eager to explore new material. But the fans loved those songs and wanted to hear their favorites, just as I had wanted to hear mine from Brel. And I realized that it's really not a nice thing to refuse. So even though I wasn't thrilled to sing "People" or "Happy Days" again and again, I did it . . . and tried to find something fresh in the song each time.

Back to Marseille. On the way back to the hotel, I spotted an ice cream stand, and we all got double-scoop cones, so I was full when we walked through the doors. The manager greeted us with a huge smile as he said, in a thick French accent, "Surprise, surprise! We've made bouillabaisse for you, Madame!"

Well, what could we do? That was exceptionally kind, so of course we had to go into the restaurant and eat it. How could I disappoint him? The stew tasted very garlicky after the ice cream. And something in it definitely didn't agree with me, because I started throwing up a few hours later. I barely made it onto the plane the next morning because I felt as if I were going to be sick again any minute. And then the flight was so bumpy that it made me even *more* nauseous. It was the first and only time I took out that bag they put in the seat in front of you. I thought, *Really? No way. No matter what happens, I'm not gonna throw up into this little paper bag.* So I held it in.

I was nauseous for the next ten days. I had to drag myself out of the hotel in Paris to attend the collections. I've seen photos of myself, wearing a jaguar suit and hat that I designed, sitting in the front row at Chanel and staring straight ahead. I was afraid that if I so much as moved, I might start to gag in the middle of the show. I can see now, looking at the picture, that Marlene Dietrich was sitting just four chairs away from me, but I had no idea at the time. The whole day is kind of a blur. I have a vague memory of meeting Coco Chanel, because I have the photo of the two of us smiling at each other, she with her strong, wonderful face. Normally I would have been very excited and full of questions, but I felt so miserable that I just wanted to lie down.

Every burp reminded me of that bouillabaisse.

I know I went to more shows. I felt awful as I was getting ready to go to Dior, which made me late. And when I walked in, I was embarrassed to find they had delayed the show for me. (The Duchess of Windsor was not pleased.)

But I did love the outfits. This was when I still enjoyed getting dressed up in designer clothes. I was very chic when I was twenty-three.

And I loved being photographed by Avedon. I had already worked with him once for *Harper's Bazaar*, where he shot me with a sleek geometric haircut and chunky black-and-white-striped bracelets stacked on one arm. The photos were in black and white as well . . . very stark and stylish. I used one later on the cover of *Je m'appelle Barbra*. Avedon was handsome, with tousled hair and big black glasses that magnified his piercing eyes. His studio was simple and spare, just like his aesthetic. He often preferred to photograph people against a sheet of white paper . . . no props, nothing to distract from his subject. And he knew exactly what angles would work for my face. I didn't have to say a thing. He didn't waste time fooling around with lights. If he was photographing me from the left, the hot light would be on the left. I remember he used a strobe, with a white umbrella reflector to diffuse the light.

At one of our sessions, I said, "I'd like to photograph *you*." And he let me, which was an intriguing turnaround. I think I even used his camera.

So imagine, I'm in Paris with Avedon, which was like a fantasy (he was the model for Fred Astaire's character in one of my favorite films, *Funny Face*, with Audrey Hepburn), and I've been dreaming about chocolate soufflé, foie gras, vichyssoise, and those delicious ham-and-cheese sandwiches on a baguette. But now the mere thought of food turned my stomach. I was losing weight by the day because I had no appetite. Nothing agreed with me . . . even the baked potatoes that Elliott brought to the studio. My skin was a pale shade of green. I could barely speak. No wonder I look a little grim in some of the photos.

Meanwhile, I didn't understand what the French hairdresser, Alexandre, was doing to my hair, and some of the clothes the stylist showed me were so far out . . .

After my thrift-shop days, I had become more proper in my taste. I wore pearls a lot when Elliott and I went out. I wanted to look elegant and understated. Now Alexandre . . . who was famous for styling the hair of Princess Grace, the Duchess of Windsor, and Elizabeth Taylor for *Cleopatra* . . . was piling hairpieces on my head and twisting them into these weird sculptural chignons. If I had felt like myself, I would have made more of an effort to change some of these looks because I really didn't like them. "You sure about this?" I asked him. "Because it feels odd, and I think it looks odd."

But I was too weak to argue. I kept thinking, *These people are the best in the business. They must know what they're doing.* And I didn't want to offend anyone.

The shot they ended up using on the *Vogue* cover made no sense to me. I'm smiling brightly, which is hard to do when your lips are tightly clamped around the stem of a daffodil. (Don't ask.)

This was not the cover I had imagined.

By the time *Color Me Barbra* aired on March 30, 1966, I was back in Europe . . . eating again and in rehearsals for the London production of *Funny Girl.* Lee Allen and Kay Medford had come over with me for the three-month run, but I had a new Nick . . . Michael Craig . . . and a whole new company that had to learn a show that Lee, Kay, and I could probably have done with our eyes closed. Nevertheless, we went over every scene. I was nervous about how the English would respond. After all, this was London, home of great theater and brilliant actors like Laurence Olivier and Judi Dench.

And I missed my Sadie terribly, who couldn't come with me because of the British law that any dog had to spend six months in quarantine before being admitted to the country. I would be home by then! Thank God I had tea and scones to console me, and I went down to the East End to get fish and chips, wrapped in newspaper. Most people were dismissive of English food, but I actually loved it. It was simple . . . roast beef and Yorkshire pudding with horseradish sauce. What could be better?

Thinking about what I was going to eat next was one way of relieving the stress. I was worried that there was no way I could live up to the hype. Tickets for the entire run had sold out before we even opened, on April 13, 1966. The night before was a benefit for one of Princess Margaret's charities, so she was there, and I felt the audience was oddly cold. Were they too busy watching *her* watching *me* to react normally?

I had met her that fall at a party in New York, where she told me she had all my albums. I was surprised and pleased. Now I really wished she could have seen the show with a more typical audience. Afterward the cast lined up onstage to greet her, and when she said something very complimentary, like "You were so wonderful," I told her, "You should be here on a night when you're not here."

Celebrities can be distracting for the audience. And there were several there on opening night . . . Peter Sellers, Britt Ekland, David Niven, John Huston, Tommy Steele, Rex Harrison, and Leslie Caron. There were six curtain calls . . . apparently a lot in England. Maybe they were just being polite.

Frankly, I was just glad it was over, and eager to get back to my dressing room where Marty, Elliott, Cis, and Gracie were all waiting. I was rushing to change out of my costume and get ready for the after-party when Cis held up a tiny pair of knitted baby booties and announced, "I'm going to be a grandmother."

Immediately I thought of her eldest son. "Did Jeff get some girl pregnant?"

"No, it's you!"

"What??!!!"

I had completely forgotten that I had taken a rabbit test with a friend of Cis's . . . the comedian Jonathan Miller's wife, Rachel, who was also a doctor. This test is how they used to determine if you were pregnant (but why was a rabbit involved?), and it took a week to get the results. Cis, Elliott, and Gracie all knew, but they deliberately waited to tell me until after the pressure of opening night.

I was so astonished. I went out with my friends to the party, but I spent the rest of the night in a daze. I remember Rex Harrison saying "Congratulations," and I said, "Thank you," but for an entirely different reason. I was thinking only about the baby.

The news was a shock. Elliott and I had lived together since I was nineteen, and now I was about to turn twenty-four. For years I had honestly thought there was something wrong with me, because I had never gotten pregnant. Having a baby seemed like something for other women, not for me. And then I remembered one night, right after I arrived in London for rehearsals. Elliott and I were in our suite at the Savoy Hotel, having an argument about something . . . I can't remember what. And that led to becoming physical, and then it's a matter of seduction and resistance and anger and passion . . . I don't know. And I stopped fighting and just went into my body . . . to feel, to forgive, to share, to be kind, to be vulnerable. And that's when it happened . . . I could feel the moment when I conceived.

How amazing. I was so happy! I finally felt normal for once! And then I thought, *Oh my God.* Marty had just set up a huge concert tour of twenty cities back in the States, to start as soon as I finished the London run. And then there was the third TV special. And most important, the movie of *Funny Girl*.

It all sounded like so much work, when all I wanted to do was stay home and veg . . . be pregnant . . . and read all about babies. This was a miracle! Everything else would have to wait.

Ray had finally signed the contract for me to do the film, but boy, did he put me through the wringer first. Everything with him was a power struggle. He refused to give me the part unless I agreed to give him the option for three additional movies. That seemed a little like blackmail. The last thing I wanted was to be in business with Ray for years. But when I balked, items would begin to appear in the gossip columns about other actresses being considered for the role. (Ray was very cozy with those columnists.)

"I don't believe he can take *Funny Girl* away from you," Marty told me.

I wasn't so sure. "You know Ray," I said. "He would cut off his nose to spite his face."

I remember sitting with my agent, David Begelman, in my burgundy den in New York and trying to decide what to do. He asked, "Are you prepared to lose it?"

I had to stop and think. "No. I'm not. I can *not* afford to lose *Funny Girl*."

Then, after a moment, I said, "David, doesn't a producer find material?"

"Yes."

"Well, that seems like the hardest part of the bargain. Ray's a well-known producer. Let *him* find good material for me."

Then I could justify this. I told Marty, "It's okay. I'll do three more movies with Ray. Make the deal."

And then there was the matter of salary. Marty said to Ray, "Just give her a dollar and ten percent of the gross." That was typical of Marty . . . he was always thinking of the long term, rather than short-term gains.

Ray wouldn't do it. Instead he paid me $200,000, and the salaries for the additional three pictures would be in roughly the same range. Marty didn't like that but he was forced to agree, although he did say, "If the picture works, we want a bonus."

Ray said, "Okay, I'll give you five percent of the net or two hundred thousand dollars."

And I'm going to jump ahead for a moment and tell you what happened. When *Funny Girl* came out, I chose the 5 percent. But Ray said, "No, I've decided to give you the two hundred thousand dollars."

So how about that? I could never trust him to keep his word.

Back to London and my unexpected pregnancy. I was already concerned about continuing in the play. I thought at least I'd better stop jumping on the couch in the seduction scene. And I had evening sickness instead of morning sickness every night before showtime. (I guess that's because of the time difference . . . it was morning in New York.) I wanted to leave in the worst way, but how could I do that? We had just opened. Besides, I'm not a quitter. I hadn't quit when Sydney Chaplin put me through hell, and I wasn't about to quit now.

Cis and I were discussing this on a shopping trip with her young daughter, Nina. We had just stepped onto one of those great red English double-decker buses when I suddenly noticed that Nina was left behind on the sidewalk. Instinctively I jumped off the moving bus, fell to the ground, and rolled. I didn't stop to think about being pregnant. Cis got off at the next stop and hurried back to find us.

I was so scared that I had hurt the baby, and we rushed to my gynecologist right away. (He also happened to be the queen's gynecologist, which I liked.) And he said something that was very reassuring: "If a fetus is meant to be, it will stay attached."

So that convinced me it was safe to finish the run. I started knitting backstage and was very enthusiastic about making a blanket for the baby. I made individual squares of burgundy, coral, brown, and red and then put them together in a patchwork pattern (I still have it).

I remember feeling that first flutter at four months . . . like a little butterfly was in there. I wanted to linger in the wonder of it all. In late June I went into the studio to record the first songs for a Christmas album. I was thinking that my baby would be born around Christmas, and that gave me an idea. I talked to Lan O'Kun (who had written those funny lyrics to "The Minute Waltz"), and he composed a song for me, "The Best Gift," which of course was about a child.

I decided I could handle four concerts out of the twenty, not more, which prompted the papers to add up all the money I would be losing by cutting the tour short and start writing about "the million-dollar baby." As if you could put a price on a child!

At the closing-night party in July, the rest of the cast drank champagne while I stuck to seltzer. And then I was on a plane back to America, where Elliott and Sadie met me at the airport. I did my four concerts and then happily went home to relax and eat and wait for my baby, with Sadie at my side. I bought various medical books so I could follow what was going on. I've always been fascinated by the way the body works. And to think there was a whole new human being growing inside me!

I loved being pregnant. It was the most creative time in my life. I booked sessions with a Lamaze coach, planning on natural childbirth because I wanted to avoid drugs. I didn't want to miss a moment of the birth experience. I had a record of a woman calmly doing her panting, as I was taught, through each contraction, and I played it over and over again, copying every pant. (I sounded just like a dog in heat.) At the end you hear the cry of the baby being born, which always made me cry too. I wanted my experience to be as serene as that record.

Well, record schmecord. The universe had other plans.

First of all, my baby was ten days late and in a breech position, which I found out a week before I was due. That made me nervous. So when my water broke, I was not exactly calm. In fact, my teeth started to chatter. Elliott drove me to Mount Sinai hospital, where I checked in under my old acting-class pseudonym . . . Angelina Scarangella.

In those days even with breech births, they put you through labor. (Not today . . . it's an automatic, preset Caesarean.) After eight hours of contractions, the baby still hadn't turned around. And those contractions were nothing like the record. It felt like I had a washing machine inside my stomach. My panting didn't help a bit. Also my contractions didn't come regularly. They were totally out of whack . . . coming after eight minutes, twenty, five, then fifteen. Nothing was ordinary about this birth. And I kept wondering, *Is there something wrong?* I was becoming more and more frightened, and my blood pressure was getting high. Finally the doctor decided to do a Caesarean. I was awake . . . they just gave me a spinal, which was so spooky as I started to lose all the feeling in my legs and was scared that it was never going to come back. They set up a curtain so I couldn't see myself being cut open . . . thank God, because that would have done me in.

My dream of a natural birth was gone. I felt like a total failure.

But then our son was born, so beautiful, strong, and alert . . . on December 29, 1966. As soon as I held him in my arms I was flooded with happiness, because he was healthy. I felt so grateful.

I marveled at his perfect tiny fingers and toes, looked into his eyes, and wondered, Who are you? We named him Jason Emanuel . . . Jason, just because we liked it, and Emanuel, after my father. But the nurses called him Flirt, because of the way his eyes would follow them around.

They kept us in the hospital for ten days, because they were monitoring my blood pressure. Elliott found a picture of a dog that looked like Sadie and hung it by my bed, since she wasn't allowed to visit. We spent New Year's Eve in my room, celebrating with Cis and Harvey, who brought champagne and balloons.

I actually didn't mind staying in the hospital. It was a place to rest and contemplate what had just happened, and try to comprehend the enormity of what it meant . . . to carry life and bring it into the world. Elliott was with me almost the entire time, and I had that first feeling of being a family. And now I finally felt like a woman, functioning with all the equipment that God gave me. I had experienced something transcendent.

I couldn't stop looking at Jason. I couldn't believe that Ell and I had made this little human. He was, and always has been, the best gift.

THIRTEEN

What if Nobody Shows Up?

In April 1967, three months after giving birth, I was back in the studio rehearsing for *The Belle of 14th Street.* A year had passed since *Color Me Barbra* had aired, and CBS was eager for another special. Marty and I had basically agreed to give them one a year because we thought one was enough . . . and would keep it "special." But my pregnancy meant everything had to be postponed, and now we were behind schedule. If we were going to catch up, I had to get two in the can before I began filming *Funny Girl*, because once that started, I couldn't do anything else. Ray had pushed the movie back for me as well, but I had committed to be in Hollywood in May to begin preproduction.

That left us about two months to make two specials.

First up was *The Belle of 14th Street.* It was Joe Layton's suggestion to recreate a vaudeville show, like you could have seen at one of the theaters on Fourteenth Street in New York at the turn of the century. I thought it was a great idea, because, again, I could play many different characters that were on the bill. It also meant I could have guest stars, but not in the usual way, with me as the host. Instead my guests could do their own acts as well. I was happy . . . I wouldn't have to be in every scene!

Frankly, I was enjoying being a mother and didn't have the time or the interest to devote to a TV show. I was glad to let Joe and Bob Emmett figure out the whole thing. (Dwight Hemion wasn't available this time around, so Joe was directing.)

We taped the show over four days at the end of April. I'm not even in the opening number . . . I gave that to my guest star, Jason Robards. A classical actor like Jason wouldn't normally be a guest on a show like this. He was famous for portraying Eugene O'Neill's tortured characters, which is about as far as you can get from musical comedy. But I've always wanted to do Shakespeare and I'd read that sometimes actors would perform excerpts in vaudeville. So I said to Joe, "Let's do some Shakespeare, and why don't we go after a real actor to play opposite me?"

It was funny . . . I was excited to do Shakespeare, and Jason was excited to sing! So here was this fabulous dramatic actor, doing a song and dance with six hefty ladies, inspired by an act of the time called the "Beef Trust Girls." (I had nothing to do with the numbers that didn't involve me.)

Bob condensed *The Tempest* into seven minutes (absurd, I know, but it was the closest I got to Shakespeare for years!). And it was a treat to work with Jason, who really got into the spirit of the thing . . . declaiming his lines with abandon. We both played various parts (after some quick changes backstage, which we showed, along with antics like Jason's character taking a swig from a liquor bottle).

The concept was that we were a husband-and-wife theatrical team who traveled around the country doing their act. I loved playing the wife character. I got to wear a big bouffant hairdo and speak in an even bigger Southern drawl . . . "I'd just like to throw y'all a big kiss!" And I got to use my German accent as the haughty opera star Madame Schmausen-Schmidt . . . it's hard not to laugh, just saying her name.

I have a feeling the vintage vaudeville routines left some people cold. But I didn't question Joe's choices or get immersed in the creative process this time. I was just glad to get it done.

I really shouldn't commit to something unless my heart is in it.

After *Belle*, for the next special I wanted to go back to basics with something very simple . . . just a concert. Marty came up with the idea of doing it live in Central Park.

Of course, nothing is ever simple, especially when you're giving a free concert outdoors in New York City in the summer.

A Happening in Central Park was scheduled for Saturday night, June 17, and I could only fly in for the weekend, because I was already in the midst of rehearsals for *Funny Girl* in Los Angeles. (Ray gave me one extra half day off so I could get there in time to have a dress rehearsal on Friday night.)

My plane didn't land till almost midnight. Marty picked me up, and we drove straight to Central Park. He had warned me that there could be lots of people there, gathered to watch, so I was prepared for that. But when we got to Sheep Meadow, where the stage was set up, there was no one around except our crew. *Oh my God*, I thought. *What if nobody shows up for the concert?* (Later we found out that the park closes at midnight, which explains why there was no crowd.)

I went into my trailer to change into my first gown so we could see how it looked under the lights. I had bought an original Fortuny dress in one of my favorite colors, burgundy, and liked it so much that I asked Irene Sharaff, who did the costumes for *Funny Girl* on Broadway, to copy it in pale pink for the concert. Mario Fortuny, who lived in Venice at the turn of the century, designed the most amazing clothes . . . they look like something one of those Greek maidens at the Acropolis might have worn. Each dress is basically a column of the most infinitesimally pleated silk, and it clings to the body in the most beautiful way, just suggesting the curves underneath. I also asked Irene if she could make a pleated pink chiffon cape to go on top . . . I thought it would billow in the wind, so if people sitting far back couldn't see my face, at least they could see the cape! (There were no large-screen monitors back then to project to the crowd what the TV camera was seeing.)

Robert Scheerer, the director, wanted to block out some camera moves and check out the lighting. I had to get accustomed to the stage, which was literally transparent. Tom John had made it out of clear plexiglass, which was a brilliant idea . . . it didn't interrupt the natural beauty of the park and seemed to float over the rock formations. It looked as if I were walking on air . . . I just had to be careful not to go a step too far and walk right off it.

We continued working until 3:30 in the morning, and then Marty dropped me off at home so I could sleep for a few hours before I had to be up again. It rained that night, and there was more rain in the forecast. This was not good news. Marty had managed to get rain insurance from Lloyd's of London, but as he pointed out, "It's not just the rain. What's even worse is the mud. How are people going to sit down?" There were no chairs for the audience . . . people were just expected to bring a blanket and perhaps a picnic and find a spot on the ground. But if Sheep Meadow was a sea of mud, it would really be a mess. So Marty had also tried to get mud insurance, but no one at Lloyd's could define "mud" or how much there would have to be in order to collect on a claim, so he gave up on that.

The weather was not our only challenge. Marty was worried about people being able to hear. This was two years before Woodstock and the era of big outdoor concerts. The typical sound systems weren't designed to cover a huge expanse like Sheep Meadow . . . ninety acres. So he hired Phil Ramone, a sound engineer who was known to be inventive. And Phil rigged up a system of twelve towers throughout the meadow, with new "long throw" speakers on top. When Phil and I were introduced at the rehearsal, he told me that he'd figured out how to combat the delay so that people in back, who were thousands of feet from the stage, would hear the music at the same time as the people in front. What he neglected to mention was that this had never been done before.

I woke up on Saturday and anxiously looked out the window . . . at least the rain had stopped. I headed to a studio to rehearse with the orchestra, then to the meadow for a sound check. But it was still so humid that the strings kept falling out of tune, and Mort Lindsey, who was conducting for me again, was concerned.

And then one of the trucks, in the process of delivering a spotlight, managed to cut through a bunch of cables running from the stage to the sound truck. This was a disaster that jeopardized Phil's whole system. He had to quickly find more engineers to come to the park and splice all the wires inside back together with soldering guns.

And here's another problem with a free outdoor concert . . . we had no idea how many people were going to show up. I thought I'd be lucky to get 25,000. We were told that 60,000 would be great. The largest crowd that had ever assembled in Sheep Meadow was 75,000, for Leonard Bernstein and the New York Philharmonic.

It turned out we didn't have to worry.

By 6:00 a.m. fans were already staking out their place on the grass. By 4:00 p.m. there were 60,000 people. And by 9:00 p.m., when the concert was scheduled to start, the meadow was packed with 135,000 people . . . with another 15,000 on the fringes . . . and more listeners leaning out their windows on Central Park West. (That made me feel right at home, because it reminded me of Brooklyn.) Parks Commissioner August Heckscher came out onstage and announced to the crowd that they were the largest audience for a performance in the park's history.

Elliott was there, of course . . . also Mayor John Lindsay, future congresswoman Bella Abzug, Calvin Klein, and Andy Warhol. The audience was spread out over the meadow (no mud, thank God). And suddenly it all came together. The humidity had gone down, the cables were back up, and the orchestra was ready.

But we couldn't begin right away because the sky was still too light, and we had to wait until it got darker before we started to film . . . which finally happened at 9:45, when Mort Lindsey raised his baton and the overture began.

Had we not waited we wouldn't have been able to get the opening shot that I had envisioned for the TV special, with a camera, mounted on a helicopter, moving through the city at night as I sing "The Nearness of You" in voice-over. First the camera is focused on the spire of the Empire State Building, all lit up. And then it travels over to Times Square and up Broadway and then over to Central Park, where it hovers over the one brightly lit patch in the midst of all the darkness . . . my stage. And then we cut to a shot of the crowd . . . unfortunately it would have cost a fortune to light up all ninety acres of Sheep Meadow, so you can't really see how huge it is. And finally it goes to a shot of me, finishing the song onstage. If it had been too light, the shot of me wouldn't have matched the night view of the park.

Actually, the shot I had imagined would have gone from the views of the city to the park and then zoomed right into my face, but the helicopter was not allowed to fly close enough for a zoom. And "The Nearness of You" was not actually the first song I sang (it was the second), but it seemed to fit the romantic, nocturnal mood of that opening montage much better than my first song, which was "Any Place I Hang My Hat Is Home." So we started the TV special with it. I think I did at least twenty-eight songs that night . . . I know I sang for two and a half hours. But the special was only an hour long, so we had to cut out half the songs, and then we switched others around, for pace.

After that opener, you see the footage of me actually coming out onstage for the first time. As the orchestra plays "Happy Days Are Here Again," I walk down the steps and lift my arms to spread my pink chiffon cape out like wings. When the audience gives me a standing ovation, I shrug and say, "I didn't do nothin' yet!"

It got a big laugh, and we were off. That remark wasn't written, by the way. In those days I didn't plan what I was going to say. I just went with whatever I felt in the moment.

That was a magical night. I did old standards, like Arlen's "Down with Love" . . . new songs, like "Love Is Like a Newborn Child" . . . dramatic songs, like "Cry Me a River" . . . and silly songs, like "Marty the Martian." And Mother Nature was on my side. In a song called "Natural Sounds," when I sang the line about "the rushing sound of wind in the trees," the wind actually came up out of nowhere and blew my hair, right on cue.

For the second act, I changed into a red Donald Brooks gown, thinking red would work well at night. I encouraged the crowd to sing along with me on the last verse of "Second Hand Rose" . . . they had joined in spontaneously during the sound check, and I thought that was fun. Unfortunately you can hardly hear them on the DVD, because we didn't have microphones in the audience. And then I thanked them all, this "lovely bunch of . . . people," and on that last word, I started singing "People," the last song of the show. And then I walked off the stage.

The applause wouldn't stop until I came back. I waited for several moments until the audience quieted down, and then I did something that I thought would be unexpected as an encore. On a hot summer night in the middle of June, I sang "Silent Night." It's such a beautiful song, about a mother and child . . . why save it only for Christmas?

And then I started to sing the song we had planned for the end, "Happy Days Are Here Again." But I couldn't see a red light on any of the cameras, and I panicked. I thought, *Oh my God, the cameras went dead!* (Just like for *Color Me Barbra.*) I could see one camera starting to move back along the track that Robert Scheerer had built for this particular moment, but its light wasn't on either. *Great,* I thought, *this is the finale of my show and it's not being filmed!* I think someone gestured to just keep going. So I thought, *Okay, nothing I can do. I'll just sing it for the people in the park.*

As I finished, the crowd surged toward the stage. I waved goodbye and vanished into the darkness. The concert was over, and we missed the rain by forty-five minutes.

The next day the *New York Times* reviewer remarked that I "seemed completely relaxed—'free and easy' as she sang in her first song." Little did he know . . .

In fact, I was unusually nervous. On Friday night, Marty was told that 260 of the 300 cops who had been assigned to the concert were going to be pulled away and reassigned to the Soviet premier, Aleksei Kosygin, who had just arrived in New York to address the United Nations. That was disconcerting. The Six-Day War between the Arabs and the Israelis had just ended, and tensions were high. Plus, it had recently been announced that Omar Sharif would be my costar in *Funny Girl,* and some people didn't like the idea of an Arab man romancing a Jewish woman.

I shouldn't have worried, because we didn't even need the police we did have. There were no problems with the crowd . . . everyone behaved very well . . . although I did read that they left a lot of litter behind, including a sterling silver wine bucket, a merry widow corset, and a dental plate. (How could you forget that?)

But something did happen that night that truly frightened me. I forgot the lines to one of the songs I knew best, "When the Sun Comes Out," and there were no teleprompters to rescue me back then. I went blank, and I was not charming or funny about it. It was my worst nightmare come true, and it was happening in front of 150,000 people. It really threw me . . . I felt an absolute lack of control . . . and it was terrifying.

I didn't perform in a live concert setting again for twenty-seven years.

After the show I was told that the cameras actually were on for "Happy Days," and that's why you can see me singing it on the DVD. But you know what I just found out? Robert Scheerer, years later, admitted that he deliberately turned off all the lights on the cameras "so she wouldn't know where I was . . .

I didn't want her to know where I was shooting {from}. I wanted to be able to cut where I wanted to cut, and not have her feeling that she had to look a certain way. It was too restrictive."

What??

That doesn't make any sense. I know what I'm doing, and I like to know where the camera is because then I can play with it. Did he really think he was going to get a better performance by tricking me like that?

I don't like being tricked. And I was so upset while I sang that song, and it was completely unnecessary.

This is why I like to be in control.

FOURTEEN

Funny Girl *in Hollywood*

Once again it was Elliott who found a place for us to live, this time while I'd be filming *Funny Girl.* The English country–style house came with a Hollywood pedigree. Garbo and Marlene Dietrich had both lived there, so that sounded good to me!

We had barely unpacked when Ray Stark called and said he was giving a big party to welcome me. He invited a few hundred people, and apparently they all said yes, because he reeled off the names of every movie star you could think of . . . John Wayne, Jimmy Stewart, Gregory Peck, Gary Cooper, Cary Grant, Merle Oberon, Jennifer Jones, Rosalind Russell . . .

I don't like big parties. They're not fun for me . . . I get shy. And I worried that all these amazing stars were going to be looking at me and thinking, *What's so special about her?*

The whole idea made me sick to my stomach. When it was time to get dressed, I was so nervous I actually threw up. I must have changed my clothes six times . . . Is this outfit good enough for Hollywood? What about my hair?

I went into a spiral of negativity, fueled by a combination of indecision and fear. Finally Elliott and Marty basically dragged me out of the house.

By now I was an hour and a half late to my own party. Ray and Fran were pissed. Marty tried to make excuses and explained that I was physically ill, but Ray didn't want to hear it. He just wanted to walk me around and introduce me to everyone right away. But I held back. These were faces I had only seen on-screen. What was I supposed to say to them? I had no talent for small talk. Even simple compliments like "I've always admired your work" or "I'm a big fan of yours" suddenly sounded hollow to me. In a desperate effort to stall, I asked Ray who was there, and he looked around and pointed out Steve McQueen, Natalie Wood, Ginger Rogers, Marlon Brando . . .

"Marlon Brando??" I couldn't believe this famous loner, who shunned most of the trappings of Hollywood, had come to a party for *me*. "I want to talk to him."

Brando was sitting at a table with a couple of other people, and I sat down there and never got up. He was the actor I most admired. I had met him before, once in New York and then again in London (more about that later), and felt an immediate connection. We picked up right where we left off.

Of course there were gossip columnists at the party . . . Ray made a point of cultivating them . . . and apparently I did not pay them the homage they felt they deserved, because they reported that I had barely bothered to show up and wrote about me as if I had deliberately insulted all of Hollywood.

To be honest, some people probably disliked me before I stepped off the plane, since without even a screen test I arrived with signed contracts for three major motion pictures . . . *Funny Girl*, *Hello, Dolly!*, and *On a Clear Day You Can See Forever*. But that first burst of publicity . . . those mean-spirited columns . . . certainly didn't help. Suddenly I had a reputation for being rude, when I was really just scared.

I didn't realize that it might be wise to try to do something to change it. Not that I would even know how . . . I had already learned that most reporters had some preconceived idea of me, and that's what they were going to write. It almost didn't matter what I actually said. They weren't really listening. And they weren't going to be positive, because it's much harder to make a positive piece interesting. It's the negative pieces that get all the attention.

Anyway, I didn't have time for interviews. I had work to do.

I was twenty-five years old and making my first movie.

I had told Ray that I wanted a serious director, someone who was known for directing dramas, not musicals. Most people think of a musical as a piece of froth, but *Funny Girl* was a serious, poignant story, even though it had musical numbers, and I was eager to work with someone who knew how to bring out the drama and give it more depth. I had been very impressed with Sidney Lumet's *Twelve Angry Men* and *The Pawnbroker*, so Ray hired him. I had already met Sidney socially and found him to be warm and friendly.

But then Sidney decided he didn't want to use Isobel Lennart to write the screenplay. That worried me. Why would he ignore the woman who had basically created the character? Who could possibly know the material better?

Yet Sidney was a great director, and I guess he wanted to develop his own version. So he hired another writer he was more comfortable with, and I thought, *So be it.*

He was very excited at the prospect of reimagining the story. One day he called me and said, "The script is done. You're going to be a very happy Jewish girl!"

That's always been the kiss of death for me. I'd rather people didn't tell me how much I'm going to like something. It just builds up my expectations. Better to just say, "Hope you like it," and leave it at that.

I still remember exactly where I was when I read the new script . . . curled up in my four-poster Jacobean bed. (I often work in bed. Might as well be comfortable.) From the very first pages my heart sank. Sidney had set the opening number, "If a Girl Isn't Pretty," in a park full of baby carriages and had the camera looking at all the cute babies . . . until it came to one not-so-cute baby, bawling . . . and that was Fanny.

Oh dear. I immediately felt overwhelmed by fatigue and thought, *I need a nap.*

When I woke up I read on. During "I'm the Greatest Star," he had the instruments in the orchestra pit start to magically play by themselves. It was enough to turn my stomach. I went back to sleep . . . as if it were a bad dream I'd somehow wake up from in the morning.

The next day I picked up the script again and read some more. There was a scene called "Learning Her Trade," with the young Fanny standing in the wings of a vaudeville house, studying Sophie Tucker and Eddie Cantor. This bothered me enough that I called him up to discuss it.

"Sidney, I think there's a problem here. People who are originals don't have to stand in the wings and study other performers."

He said, "My father was in vaudeville and he stood in the wings."

"But your father didn't become a star."

I think that was the point when I realized this was not going to work. Somehow he had merged Fanny's story with the story of his father.

I called Ray and said, "We need Isobel back. I think Sidney is way off track."

Sometimes the material just isn't right for a director . . . I don't think musicals were Sidney's forte . . . and he went on to make more great films, like *Dog Day Afternoon* and *Network*.

Meanwhile, I still wanted a fine, serious director, so Ray approached William Wyler, and when he agreed to do it, I was thrilled.

Can you imagine how lucky I felt? For my first film I was going to have the great William Wyler, the man who led more actors to Oscar-winning performances than any director before or since . . . Bette Davis in *Jezebel*, Greer Garson in *Mrs. Miniver*, Fredric March in *The Best Years of Our Lives*, Audrey Hepburn in *Roman Holiday*.

> *"I did* Funny Girl *strictly because Barbra was in it. I would never have done it otherwise."*
>
> —William Wyler

When I met Willy for the first time, he stared at my face, then put his hand gently on my chin and turned my head so he could examine my profile. It was like something out of a 1940s movie, when a young woman is discovered and her life changes. Willy was sixty-five when we started filming, which isn't so old nowadays, but to me he seemed ancient . . . an old master of the movies.

It was a match made in heaven. Willy and I had a wonderful relationship. Every morning I would stop by to discuss the day's scenes with him, bringing my folders of all the alternative versions, starting with Isobel's first draft of the screenplay, *My Man*, written in 1960, and continuing through all the variations of the stage play . . . the changes that were made in Boston, Philadelphia, and New York.

Willy would pick and choose what he liked. We collaborated from day one because he knew that I knew this character. I had played the part a thousand times, literally, before I made the movie. And Willy was totally open to my ideas, which must have startled some onlookers . . . a first-time movie actress who dared to have an opinion! But I've noticed that people who are inherently talented are never threatened by other people's ideas, because they're secure in their own. Sometimes Willy took one of my suggestions, and sometimes he didn't. Often he'd say, "Do it my way, and then we'll do it your way, and we'll see which is better." He always made me feel part of the process.

On July 11, the first day of shooting, we were in an abandoned railroad station, built in the 1880s, with a soaring ceiling, Romanesque brick arches, and wrought-iron gates. We were doing the scene where the Ziegfeld girls arrive in Baltimore. There's a moment when I step off the train, and I suddenly had an idea. I asked Willy, "What if we do a takeoff on Garbo's entrance in *Anna Karenina*?" It's a famous scene, where she's hidden behind a burst of smoke coming off the train wheels, and then it clears to reveal her beautiful face as she stands in the doorway of the train. I thought it would be funny to do the same shot, but this time it would reveal me, coughing and waving the smoke away.

That was a suggestion Willy didn't take, but he did let me do a modified version at the bottom of the train steps. When the photographer comes over and says, "How about a smile, Miss Brice?" I strike a few dramatic poses for him . . . and then I do the cough from the smoke. And I improvised a line, "So shoot the picture!" which I said with my teeth clenched in a smile, because he was taking so long. Then I kept talking like that with my teeth clenched as the girls walked by. It was a funny moment, and Willy kept it in the film.

Although I didn't realize it at the time, I was thinking like a director, envisioning the scene in my head and imagining what more we could do with it. And Willy encouraged me. He understood the way I worked, and my need to feel free enough to invent something new on the spur of the moment. He never tried to keep me down. (God, he was great!)

In fact, he was my best audience. Sometimes I'd do a scene and look over to see what he thought, and he would be crying or laughing . . . which unfortunately spoiled the soundtrack. I had never seen a director do that . . . he was right there in the moment with me and allowed himself to react, just like a real audience. It was wonderful. He was like an emotional mirror. And then sometimes he would smoke and cough, and the smoke would swirl in front of the lens and the cough would be picked up by the microphone. So the take was ruined. But so what? We just did it again. It was such a gift to have someone that responsive guiding me.

I think you can tell how a director feels toward the actor or actress he's working with when you look at a film. It shows in the performance. And I think Willy was proud of me. That's why my film debut came out as well as it did. He liked me and he wanted the audience to like me, so he presented me to them very lovingly.

The other gift I was given on this movie was Harry Stradling, who was born in 1901, one year before Willy. Harry was one of the great cinematographers, and it was a privilege to work with him. He had photographed all the big stars . . . Marlene Dietrich, Vivien Leigh, Katharine Hepburn, Ingrid Bergman, Rosalind Russell, Carole Lombard . . . and he managed to bring out the distinctive beauty of each actress. I loved those women. And I saw myself as a bit of a throwback to the 1940s, when heroines were smart and sassy and strong . . . they had to be, because their men went off to war. They wore tailored suits, held important jobs, kept the family going, and made the choices that drove the plot.

When I arrived in Hollywood, the studios were churning out beach party movies. It was the era of cute little blondes with turned-up noses, like Sandra Dee, and I definitely didn't fit that image. No one would have looked at me and thought, *That girl should be a movie star!* I have a strange face . . . very different from each side. Most movie stars are easy to photograph because they have symmetrical faces . . . big heads with attractive, regular features and big, expressive eyes. I have a small head, a crooked nose, my mouth is too big, and my eyes are too small.

Harry enjoyed the challenge. He really looked at me and studied the shape of my face. So we got to know each other when we were doing the makeup and lighting tests.

I was worried about those. What if I didn't look good enough on the big screen? Would they send me home?

I told myself that great photographers like Richard Avedon and Cecil Beaton had liked photographing me. And Dwight Hemion showed me how good I could look on my TV specials . . . but that was a much smaller screen.

When the makeup people came to analyze my face, I thought, *Great, they're the experts. Let's see what they can do.*

But when they were finished and I looked in the mirror, I didn't recognize myself. They had put rouge on my cheeks (I put it under my cheekbones) and used dark lipstick (instead of the paler shade I preferred). I said, "Thank you very much," but then I asked, "Would it be all right if we also did a test with just me making myself up?" The studio said, "Fine."

Guess which one Harry picked?

Mine. So I did my own makeup throughout the film, and I've continued to do it ever since.

Willy had never done a musical before (and he was partially deaf), so Ray hired Herb Ross, the accomplished choreographer I already knew from *I Can Get It for You Wholesale*, to do the musical sequences. I was sitting beside Herb, who supervised the tests, when I first saw my face up on the big screen. I was kind of shocked . . . I actually looked beautiful.

It was the first time in my life I had ever seen myself that way. I was glad the theater was dark, because it was embarrassing how pleased I was.

> *"On-screen she looked a miracle. How could anyone have known that her skin was going to have that brilliant reflective surface, that she was going to look radiant—that was just a wonderful plus."*
>
> —Herbert Ross

I was so relieved that I actually got worried again. This character is supposed to be unattractive, and I suddenly thought, *Maybe I look* too *good. Isn't that wrong for the part?* But that didn't seem to occur to anyone else.

It was Harry's vision of me up there. He loved that I was different and he wanted to show me off. As he said to a reporter from *Life* magazine, "I like the nose. No, you can't make Barbra look like Marilyn Monroe. But she does have a beautiful face—because she's got something in back of it."

And he sure knew how to light. At that time, they used hard light . . . the kind of light that hits you directly in the face. It makes your eyes bright . . . your teeth white . . . your skin shine. You can't do better than hard light if you want a glamorous look. And it's very much of that era. If you look at most movies today, you can't see the color of the eyes . . . that requires an eye light, and contemporary cinematographers often don't bother with it. Because my eyes were so deep-set, Harry even rigged up what he called a Streilight, named after me and held by the "best boy" (his key assistant), who followed me around as I moved. And then there was something called a cucoloris. That's a screen, cut out in random patterns so it creates a dappled effect . . . imagine standing in a forest, under a canopy of leaves. It fractures and softens the light.

If you look at that list of actresses Harry worked with, it's clear he liked women with opinions. Dietrich was known for her knowledge about lighting. But I'll bet nobody ever asked him as many questions as I did. I was fascinated with his lights and all the different effects he could achieve with them. Thank God he didn't seem to mind. In fact, I think he enjoyed talking to someone who was so interested in his craft. He was a wonderful teacher, kind and generous with his explanations.

We spent hours experimenting with half-light, overhead light, and just a hard, strong spotlight (which made me look best). I could feel the light . . . somehow I could sense when it was flattering and when it was not . . . and he knew that I could, so he listened to me. I got to know the camera as well, and could anticipate what angles would work for me. I could tell him, "It feels like the camera is too low." And he would look again, and if he agreed, he would say in his nasal voice, "Boys, raise the camera two inches." And if he didn't agree, he'd say, "No, it's fine. I think it's good where it is." And I deferred to him always, because I respected his expertise. I felt totally safe in his hands. So much so that I wanted him for every picture I made, and he did my first four films . . . until he could no longer work.

Of course, that's not what got printed in the press. As we were filming, the papers kept publishing all these stories about how Harry and I were not getting along, or how I was telling William Wyler how to direct. That's ridiculous. I don't know where they were coming from . . . or maybe I can guess. It could have been Ray. He wanted every bit of publicity he could get.

Willy tried to correct the rumors. He was quoted saying, "I kept hearing reports that Barbra quarreled with me on the picture, but there was never any evidence of it . . . With me she worked desperately hard on her part. She kept trying to improve herself . . . She was totally dedicated. She trusted me, and I trusted her."

It pains me to read that I was telling him, and Harry, what to do. It was the beginning of the diva myth that has followed me all my life. I was not giving orders. I was asking questions. That's how I learn.

But I guess some people had a hard time with a woman who had opinions, and word went out that I was taking over.

Right before we started filming, Elliott got cast in his first major movie, *The Night They Raided Minsky's*, directed by William Friedkin. He had to move back to New York to shoot, so suddenly I was out in Hollywood on my own. Jason stayed with me, and since I was working such long hours, our nanny brought him to the set every day. That way I could cuddle him between takes.

I was so happy for Elliott. And the truth is, I don't think either of us was too upset about the separation. Something had changed between us. Frankly, we'd been drifting apart for a couple years. So when he went to New York, I didn't miss him as much as I should have. I was too busy falling in love with film.

Making *Funny Girl* totally consumed me.

We shot all the musical sequences first. Herb handled those and Willy directed the dialogue scenes. And Willy seemed fine with that. He had no desire to deal with choreographing the dance numbers. And of course, Willy knew he was ultimately in charge. Nothing Herb did was going to go up on that screen without his approval.

I think we had twelve weeks to rehearse the musical sequences. What a luxury! That would never happen today. Herb's wife, Nora Kaye, was a former ballerina, and she gave a ballet class for the company every morning. I was right there at the barre, doing pliés along with the dancers. I was in heaven. Finally, I could live out my childhood fantasy and be a ballerina!

One of the new numbers written especially for the film was a parody of *Swan Lake* (on the set, we called it *Chicken Lake*). For a moment, it looks as if it could be the actual ballet. Herb had the corps de ballet doing the classic steps and was using a new kind of gyroscopic camera that gave him those great overhead shots.

And then Fanny makes her entrance. My headdress and tutu in that number were modeled after Anna Pavlova's, except I definitely had a few more tail feathers on my tush. And I was a Swan Queen who talked back . . . with a Brooklyn Jewish accent no less. When Prince Siegfried, who was played by a well-known dancer, Tommy Rall, pointed his crossbow at me, I scolded him, "Whattaya gonna do? Shoot the svans? Dese lovelies? My svans girls? What are ya, dumb?"

All the dancers are en pointe, except for me (I was game to try, but Ray didn't want me to risk a fall). And I had almost *too* much fun doing the comic bits. When I jump up and down, I'm holding my breasts. And when I call "Prince!" and he leaps across the stage toward me, I put my hands on my hips and say, "Was that necessary? You couldn't walk over here like a poysen?" Later in the ballet, when he lifts me, I go straight up to the ceiling, flapping my arms. And then I fly back and forth above the stage (that harness was *not* comfortable).

I think we spent a full week shooting this scene, and Willy ended up using less than four minutes. He cut out the part where the prince shoots me by mistake, instead of the villain. Then, bent over from the arrow in my stomach, I walk over to the prince, pull the arrow out, and stab him with it. I thought it was hilarious, but Willy apparently felt the sequence was too long. Looking at it now, I still miss that finish.

I don't think it was Willy's favorite number.

Sometimes Willy would drop by the set and take a look, but Marty says he was rarely there during the first few weeks of shooting, when we were doing the musical numbers. And then one afternoon Willy was watching dailies and noticed that someone had chalked in "H. Ross" on the clapper where it said "Director." That was it. Willy was on set from that day on, according to Marty.

I watched *Funny Girl*, for the first time in at least fifty years, in order to write this chapter. What's wonderful about movies is that they capture time. In the theater, a performance evaporates as soon as you do it. Nothing remains . . . only a memory, and only for the people who happened to be there.

But when the cameras started to roll, I remember feeling that I was playing this role for posterity. Every time we finished a scene, I would fold down the page in my script (just as Willy did), and think, *That's done. It's safe on film . . . forever.* It was very satisfying, and somehow reassuring that something would live on. I've always been obsessed with mortality, ever since my father died so young.

Now, when I watch the film, it's like a time capsule. Every scene takes me right back to the day we shot it.

First off, that opening sequence . . . what an entrance Willy gave me! You see a theater marquee for the Ziegfeld Follies, and then a woman in a leopard coat and hat . . . but only from the back. It's not until she stops in front of a gilded mirror in the wings of the theater that we see her face for the first time.

And I say the first words in the film . . . "Hello, gorgeous."

I smile, and then the smile crumbles. Suddenly you see fear, insecurity, loneliness. Fanny is worried that the man she loves is about to leave her.

But that's not Fanny in the mirror. That's me.

"Hello, gorgeous." It was so ironic . . . I was just the skinny marink from Brooklyn. I had come so far and fought so hard for this role. I was the star of this movie . . . I had achieved my dream . . . but at the same time, I was losing my husband. And I didn't know how to fix it, or if I even wanted to. And I had a nine-month-old baby. I felt so vulnerable. You can see it in my eyes.

After a moment, I turn away and walk onstage. I look out at the empty seats, then pick out a few notes from "People" on the piano, before slamming my hand down on the keys. That smashed chord was a mysterious sound, and Willy used it to cut to a wide shot from above, of this little person in a big theater. I slowly walk to center stage, hear imaginary applause, and then, with an imaginary machine gun, I shoot at the imaginary audience once, twice, ending with one last shot to the balcony.

Shooting the audience wasn't originally in the script. It came out of what I thought Fanny was feeling at the moment . . . that the audience and the obligations of her career had come between her and Nick.

We shot this interior at the old Pantages Theatre in downtown LA, which had once been a vaudeville house. I walk down to sit in one of the seats and put my hands together under my chin. (God, my nails were way too long. It's ridiculous.)

Then I lean my head back. I remember Harry lighting this shot. He was so excited. He and Willy couldn't wait to do close-ups. I can still hear Harry calling to his boys, "Okay, put on the seventy-five!" or "Put on the one hundred!" for the lenses he wanted.

But I'm an actress who doesn't particularly like close-ups. (I had acne as a teenager and didn't want people to see my pores.) I preferred what Harry used to call the "two Ts" shot, with the bottom of the frame just above the breast. I thought that was close enough.

I could spend hours discussing shots with Harry and Willy. It was an invaluable education in filmmaking. Willy even invited me to watch dailies with him, which was apparently a rare privilege, although I didn't realize it at the time. A lot of actors don't want to see them. But I was very objective about myself. It was "her" up there, never me. I was disconnected from that figure on the screen.

Maybe I would be a better actress if I was more focused on my part alone. But I was concerned about the whole movie. How does that scene pertain to the next one? Does that moment serve the story?

Willy was known to be a perfectionist (no wonder we got along). Apparently he had a nickname . . . "Forty-take Wyler" . . . but I don't remember doing anywhere near that many takes on any scene. I'd say we did an average of four to six. Laurence Olivier tells a famous story about working with Willy on *Wuthering Heights*. After each take, Willy would tell him to "Do it again." Finally, completely exasperated, Olivier said, "For God's sake, I did it standing up. I did it sitting down. I did it fast. I did it slow. I did it with a smile. I did it with a smirk. I did it scratching my ear. I did it with my back to the camera. How do you want me to do it?"

Willy just said, "Better."

He may not have been able to articulate exactly what he wanted . . . or maybe he just had no interest in analyzing a performance. His comments were usually simple: "Faster" . . . "Slower."

It was fascinating to me that this master filmmaker was a very modest man who spoke in simple words. He didn't come at a scene from an intellectual point of view . . . what mattered was whether he was moved or not.

We had fun with each other. I could tease him. "Come on, Willy. You can't hear what I'm saying, so how can you tell if it's good or not?"

He'd laugh, and say, "Yeah yeah yeah. We'll play it back louder in dailies."

He knew what he wanted, and this is what was most important to me . . . he knew the truth when he saw it . . . or felt it. If Willy thought a scene was right, I knew it was right. I didn't have to second-guess him, and that was a terrific feeling. I trusted him completely.

After that opening sequence, the film goes back in time, as Fanny thinks back to her beginnings in the theater. For the first two numbers ("If a Girl Isn't Pretty" and "I'm the Greatest Star"), I'm in a middy blouse and bloomers, and I think I got her body language right . . . she's gawky and awkward. Herb set up the shots, and then I sang the songs, lip-syncing to a prerecorded track. I had sung the entire score with an orchestra, conducted by the wonderful Walter Scharf, before we even started shooting.

I hate lip-syncing. I'm no good at it, because it doesn't allow you to be in the moment. Instead you have to try to sing a number exactly the way you did it months before, and the whole effort feels so artificial. But that's how musicals were done.

At least I got to do the roller-skating number, which had been cut early on for Broadway because they felt it was too dangerous to do every night. That's when Fanny meets Nick Arnstein for the first time. Look at Omar Sharif, in that beautiful ruffled shirt . . . he's charming . . . charismatic . . . with that flashing smile.

Choosing Omar to play Nick was not exactly obvious. I was impressed with him in *Lawrence of Arabia*. But he was an Arab born in Egypt, playing a Jew born in New Jersey . . . and that became a bit of a problem soon after he was cast, when the Six-Day War between Israel and Egypt broke out. Some people at the studio got nervous and wanted him replaced. But Willy, who was Jewish, stood his ground. He said that firing an actor just because he was Egyptian was not the American way, and "If Omar doesn't make the film, I don't make it either!"

Omar stayed in the picture, but that wasn't the end of the controversy. When a publicity still of the two of us rehearsing a number reached the Egyptian press, it sparked a movement to revoke his citizenship. One headline read: OMAR KISSES BARBRA, EGYPT ANGRY. My response was, "Egypt angry! You should hear what my aunt Anna said!" (That's a joke, by the way.) And when the movie came out, it was banned in Egypt, along with the rest of Omar's movies. All because the character he played was Jewish and he fell in love with a Jewish girl.

For Fanny, it was love at first sight. For me with Omar, not so much. When I first started rehearsing with him, I thought he was rude. He didn't cover his mouth when he coughed. And I wondered why the hairdressers had straightened his hair, plastering it down like a wet rug. Yuck.

Omar apparently had a similar reaction to me. As he told one reporter, "The first impression is that she's not very pretty. But after three days, I am honest, I found her physically beautiful, and I start lusting after this woman!"

I have no idea what I did to put him under my spell. Nothing much, I bet. But when someone responds to you, it brings out your femininity. And as he became more attracted to me, I became more attracted to him.

I was starting to feel my power as a woman.

I sensed it with Willy as well. When we were discussing a scene, he might beckon me to come closer. "What did you just say? Whisper it in my ear." That made everything I said to him feel very special, and I liked that intimacy. So when I wanted to tell him something, I would automatically whisper into his good ear. I could see he liked it, and that brought out something tender in me.

Willy was very courtly . . . a true gentleman. He would ask me to lunch, and if we had time, he'd take me to the Captain's Table, one of those old Hollywood restaurants with dark mahogany booths upholstered in red leather and waiters in jackets and ties who would toss your salad at the table. I enjoyed being with him, and of course peppered him with questions about his early films.

I read somewhere that Willy often had a kind of professional crush on his leading ladies. Which is great for the work, because if the director makes you feel appreciated, then you want to please him even more . . . and I'm sure Willy was well aware of that. In fact, he probably cultivated it, because that kind of chemistry transmits to the screen . . . it adds that little extra something to a performance. If you asked him about it, Willy would just grin mischievously and say, "How do you think all those women got all those Oscars?"

Bette Davis has said that Willy was the love of her life, but he was too discreet to discuss anything so personal, and his behavior was impeccable with me.

So much of me and Fanny had somehow merged. There's the moment when she's trying out for the Ziegfeld Follies and she dares to challenge the great Flo Ziegfeld. I came up with that bit where she rolls her sheet music into a telescope to peer up at him in the balcony. I'd tried it one night in the theater, and it got a laugh, so I kept it. I identified with Fanny when she tells Ziegfeld, "I can't sing words like 'I am the beautiful reflection of my love's affection' . . . It's embarrassing."

And I identified with Fanny even more when she defies him and stuffs a pillow under her bridal gown, turning his grand finale into a comic number. It's a huge success, and he's forced to relent (just like Arthur Laurents in *Wholesale*), even saying he'll choose an extra song for her.

But Fanny doesn't want him to choose her song. As she says, "One of the things I really feel definite about is choosing my own."

And that's exactly what I had specified in my recording contract. (Isobel always said she tailored the script to me.)

In the play, and now the movie, I had to make the transition from an awkward young girl into a mature woman, and it starts to happen after I sing "People." When Nick cups Fanny's chin in his hand and leans in for their first kiss, it was a very important moment, the most intimate in the film. When I saw it in dailies the next day, I felt it wasn't emphasized enough, and shared my concern with Willy. Even though I was still avoiding big close-ups, I thought the camera should be as near as possible . . . to see all the feelings registering on Fanny's face . . . fear, nervousness, anticipation. Suddenly she's experiencing emotions she's never felt before. She's aware of her body in a whole new way. Her face tells the story.

Willy agreed, so we did it over . . . it's the only close-up that big in the movie. And then Fanny turns back into a girl, for a moment, lightening the mood with a little soft-shoe shuffle as Nick drives off in his car (I'd first tried that little dance step on Broadway, and it worked).

The whole sequence is staged and directed beautifully. But as I'm looking at the movie again, there are a few things I'd change. Why is my hair so big? Of course, it was the 1960s, and bouffant hairdos were in style, but some of those wigs have enough hair for two people! And I notice the shift in the quality of the film every time Harry uses a filter for the close-ups, which was the style at the time. After the clear and sharp two-shot, the image blurs slightly in the glamour shot, and to me, it's a distraction. That's why I made sure to use the same filter for both the two-shots and the close-ups when I directed my own films.

But one thing I wouldn't change is the dress, with those little bobbles on the sleeves and green chiffon layered over pink silk. Irene Sharaff, the costume designer, was always layering two colors over each other in surprising ways, which creates a lovely shimmery effect. I think it's my favorite dress in the film. (I still have the original version, from the Broadway play, in my antique-clothes closet at home.) Irene was not a warm and fuzzy person. She always seemed aloof. But that didn't matter, because she was very, very good at what she did.

I was always excited to find new ways to do things in the movie. In the big seduction scene, where Nick invites Fanny to a private dinner, they sing "You Are Woman, I Am Man." Onstage, it's a duet, but when we were rehearsing the film, I asked if I could sing most of my part in voice-over. It makes sense . . . we're listening in on Fanny's thoughts as she's reacting to Nick's advances. It's funnier that way . . . and I figured it would be one less song to lip-sync! (I've always been drawn to voice-over and took full advantage of it years later, when I did *Yentl*.)

It was easy to flirt with Omar. By this point, he and I had gotten closer. When he asked me to have dinner with him one weekend, I went.

I was curious about his life in Europe. I found out he was a bridge champion, and from then on we often played cards on the set. You can tell a lot about a person when you play a game with them. Do they follow the rules or bend them to their advantage? Are they cutthroat about winning, or gracious? And when you're playing cards, it's nice to simply sit near someone and feel their presence. You don't have to talk unless you want to, and that was a relief.

Then there were more dinners . . . I remember driving up the Pacific Coast Highway to a seafood restaurant on the water. Omar and I would be in the back seat of his car, holding hands and talking, while up front his driver kept his eyes on the road.

So that's how we got to know each other, and it worked for the characters.

Probably the most iconic number in the film is "Don't Rain on My Parade," along with "People" and "My Man." And wouldn't you know . . . for that number, Irene put me in my least favorite color . . . orange.

It was a hot July day, and that outfit was made of wool crepe. As I ran through the train station again and again with my yellow roses and my suitcases for each take, I could feel the sweat trickling down the small of my back. And I was wearing a fur hat and carrying a fur muff! I thought I was going to faint. But looking at it now, I have to say it was worth all the discomfort. Herb staged the whole sequence brilliantly. I love the shot through the iron bars that divide one track from another, with me walking on one side and the camera following me on the other, so the bars flash by in front.

Beautiful.

Herb really knew how to use those old, glorious spaces. And the camera movements reflect the music, with just the right cuts in just the right places. It reinforces the rhythm.

And I see why Irene wanted me dressed in orange . . . so you can pick me out instantly in that shot of the moving train from a distance, with me sitting at the window. By the way, that's Cis Corman, holding my dog, Sadie, in the seat across from me. I knew I was going to be on that train for hours so I had my best friend and my little Sadie to keep me company. It looks like a pleasant ride, but it was sweltering inside that train car.

The audience has no idea what an actor, and the crew, go through to get even a simple shot. When I get out of the taxi and arrive at the pier . . . "Hey Mr. Arnstein, here I am!" . . . I stop short, and the music suddenly stops as well. I realize the boat has sailed. And then the music starts up again and builds in momentum as I run down the dock toward a tugboat. The next shot was taken by a fearless cameraman, hanging out the door of a helicopter as it flies in toward the tugboat, which is now sailing down the harbor. It's a long shot, and thanks to that orange outfit, you can make me out, standing at the prow. As the camera gets closer you can see that I'm holding my bouquet of yellow roses up in the air, echoing the Statue of Liberty holding her torch, right behind me. That's Herb again, taking full advantage of the setting.

The boat whistle blows, and now here's the climax:

Get ready for me, love, 'cause I'm a comer
I simply gotta march, my heart's a drummer
Nobody, no, nobody, is gonna rain on my parade!

In that tugboat sequence I had an earpiece in my right ear, to feed me the prerecorded track so I could lip-sync to my earlier performance. But there was one glitch. Something happened to the playback. It skipped a beat . . . maybe the boat hit a wave. If you listen carefully, you'll hear a brief stop . . . there's a tiny piece of the track missing. I hoped the sound people could put back that missing note. But they said they couldn't do anything about it . . . apparently it was something to do with the sync. I couldn't believe it . . . but I'm probably the only person who's bothered by it.

By the way, did you notice the number on the tugboat? I didn't, until I saw the dailies. It's "24." My lucky number.

I wish I could redo my arrival at Nick's stateroom on the ship, holding my wilted roses. The first time we rehearsed it, I just naturally giggled when the steward opened the door. I begged Willy to shoot it right away . . . just to get it on film . . . but that wasn't the way he worked. I think the holdup may have had something to do with the lighting, or some other technical problem he was trying to solve. But after a few more rehearsals, I wasn't laughing anymore, and I couldn't fake it. So the moment was gone.

It taught me something. The first time an actor tries something is often the best. So when I directed, I tried to film the actors as soon as the camera is there and the scene is on its feet.

There's one other moment in the second act that bothers me. One day Willy was in such pain from his bad back that he had to stay home, and Herb shot the scheduled scene instead. Nick and Fanny are married, and Fanny is talking to her friend Eddie. It's her first day back at work since having the baby.

I'm struggling to do sit-ups. (That didn't take much acting.) "Look at me. I'm breathing like a whale. The way that baby slowed me down, I ought to sue her! But she's so pretty, isn't she, Eddie?"

He responds fondly. "Frances? She's the cutest little thing I ever saw . . . alive . . . alert."

"But she's pretty?" I ask again, and I said it in a vulnerable way. It's very important to Fanny that her daughter is pretty, because she doesn't want her child to face the kind of rejection she did because of her unconventional looks.

Her old friend Eddie understands immediately and says, "Yes, Fan. She's pretty . . . very pretty."

It's a revealing moment, because Fanny is exposing all the pain she felt. When we watched the scene in dailies, I thought it worked well. But Willy decided he needed to shoot the whole scene over again.

Why? I wondered. He said he didn't like the way it turned out. And of course it was his prerogative to shoot it again. But I thought to myself, *Is it because Herb shot it?* Herb was a choreographer who wanted to direct, and he insisted that he get credit as director of the musical numbers. Did that stick in Willy's craw?

Every artist has to have a healthy ego in order to succeed. Perhaps Willy didn't want another director's touch on one of his scenes, and I completely understood that.

So we reshot the scene, and came to that line: "But she's pretty?"

Willy said, "I want you to be tougher . . . stronger."

I was taken aback and said, "But that's not what she's feeling. Fanny isn't just tough at this moment. She's also extremely vulnerable." The line almost made me cry. I thought the audience should see the hurt she had felt all her life because of snide remarks about her looks.

Willy didn't agree with me. And he seemed very adamant, so I did it his way. But it's the one moment I don't believe in the film because I think it's the wrong choice.

It's the only time I saw evidence of Willy's own vulnerability. But it's just a tiny flaw, amid so many other masterful moments.

Usually when Willy wanted something, it worked brilliantly. After Nick misses Fanny's opening night (the big *Swan Lake* number), Willy cuts directly to a close-up of Fanny sitting alone in her living room in the dark, her head tilted back on the sofa, smoking. I asked him and Harry, "Are you sure you want to do this? It isn't my good side." But they said yes, and I was surprised when they proved to be right. It was a very interesting shot and it showed me something about my own face. From certain angles, the wrong side works.

I like when I'm wrong. I learn something.

Willy's camerawork is amazing in this scene. After Nick finally stumbles home from his poker game, he tries to apologize to Fanny, reading reviews . . . flattering her . . . but she is silent. The whole time, Willy keeps the camera only on Nick, reinforcing the fact that he's on the spot. The audience only sees my face when Fanny stands up and furiously confronts him. (Irene was kind enough to let me wear my own burgundy Fortuny dress in this scene. It's sophisticated, and shows how far Fanny has come from those childish middy blouses.)

Then the scene ends on a different close-up of me . . . almost the reverse of how it began. We see the other side of my face now (the good side). I'm standing instead of sitting, and the light has been turned on. Fanny is no longer in the dark . . . she has realized something fundamental about her husband. Nick chose gambling over her. Something inside her has changed.

What a great way to let the camera help you tell the story. Willy never indulged in the kind of fancy camerawork that draws attention to itself. What makes him so good is that his first concern is always the story, and he lets it unfold naturally. He always has the camera in the right place and comes in for a close-up at the right time, so you're watching what he wants you to watch.

And Willy didn't bother with expository shots. When Nick gets out of jail and comes to Fanny's dressing room, we don't hear a knock at the door and have her open it. Instead, we first see Nick as Fanny sees him, unexpectedly reflected in her dressing table mirror . . . so both their faces are in the same shot. Willy always cut straight to the emotion.

Nick has come to tell Fanny that their marriage is over, but she understands almost instantly and saves him the trouble. It's only because she loves him that she can repress her own feelings and pretend to want the same thing.

On Broadway, after Nick leaves, I sang a reprise of "Don't Rain on My Parade," starting slowly at my dressing table and then building to a strong finale. It was a declaration that Fanny's life was going to go on. But for the film, Ray wanted to use one of Fanny's signature songs, "My Man," because it was famous, and now both of us were associated with the song. I had sung it on my first television special and recorded it on the accompanying album in 1965.

I discussed it with Harry and told him it would be great if I sang it on a bare stage that was all black, with me in a black dress. I liked the simplicity of that. All you would see is my face and my hands against the black. I had done something similar on TV and thought it was very effective. But Harry said, "No. Too stark." He wanted to put some lights on the side, so that's what he did . . . pretty magenta, blue, and purple lights on a few poles.

It was the last scene we shot, and when I came in to see dailies the next day, the screening room was full. Marty was there, along with all the executives from Columbia, and after the song was over, people actually applauded. They were congratulating Willy and predicting big box office and speculating about Oscars.

Meanwhile, I was sitting silently next to Willy. He turned to me and said, "Barbra, what do you think?"

I looked at him. "I think I could do it better."

A deathly silence fell over the room.

It was clear to me that I needed to do it live, instead of lip-syncing to a prerecorded track. It didn't feel truthful, because I was locked into the lip-sync and couldn't express what I was feeling in that moment. I knew I should be crying coming off the scene in the dressing room where Nick and I part. But I hadn't cried on the prerecord.

So I said, "Willy, the emotion isn't there. I'd like to do it over. And I'd like to do it live."

He stared at me . . . thought about it for a moment . . . and then said, "Okay, let's do it."

That wasn't as easy as it sounds. The movie had already wrapped. The crew had dispersed. But Willy made it happen. It may have taken a couple of days, but we got the people we needed back on the set. Walter Scharf played the piano for me, offstage. And Omar came, too, which was extremely kind of him. He was standing in the wings, out of the camera's range but where I could look at him if I wanted to, to trigger my emotions.

I told Willy that only the first part of the song, which was in close-up, had to be live. Then I could just be in the moment, and whenever the tears came, the vocal would match the picture. The last part, when I regain control of myself, was fine . . . and it was a long shot, so the lip-syncing wasn't so obvious.

I think we did ten takes of that opening, and you can hear the raw emotion in my voice. Each time, it hit me at a different place.

People still come up to me to tell me they cried when I sang that song. And what makes people cry? I think it's because Fanny is overwhelmed with emotion, and she's desperately trying to get control of herself and not break down. That's what grabs people's hearts and makes the moment so powerful and extraordinarily painful. It wouldn't be as moving if she just let loose and started sobbing. Like I discovered that closing night on Broadway . . . it's the restraint.

When you, as the character, are trying to hold it together even though you're falling apart inside, the audience is right there with you, rooting for you to make it through, to be okay.

Thank God Willy let me do it again. Who knows? That might have been what won me the Oscar.

As the song comes to an end, the camera moves back . . . I throw my arms out, tilt my head back, close my eyes, and the spotlight on me goes out. The screen is black, and the film is over.

. . .

Every day during the shoot, as Willy and I were watching dailies together, I'd think to myself, *Take 2 of this scene is best.* Or, *For that scene, I like the first two lines of take 1, and then the last part of take 4 is best.* And when Willy showed me the rough cut of the film, I thought, *My God, he chose exactly what I would have chosen, 95 percent of the time.* That's how much we were in sync.

I had been late getting to the studio more than a few times during the course of filming, and I felt very bad about that. It was a fault of mine . . . but I'm never late to a set anymore. So at the end of the shoot, I gave Willy an antique watch, engraved "To make up for lost time. Love, Barbra."

Willy in turn gave me a director's megaphone stamped "Barbra Streisand DGA" and engraved "To Barbra From Willy." I was so thrilled that he thought enough of my ideas to give me such an inspiring gift, encouraging me to direct. It was funny and prophetic and it's one of my most prized possessions.

And Harry wrote me a wonderful letter after we finished the film:

> *Let's try and find a story, not a musical. You should do something different.*
>
> *If we found something you liked, you could play the part and also direct. Isn't that something you would like to do? Just think . . . the first successful woman director in the business.*
>
> *The film could be made for well under a million. We would not need a studio, shoot the film on live locations and cut down the 40% the studio adds to a film.*
>
> *Barbra, this is something I have thought about for years and it takes someone like you to get the thing rolling.*
>
> *I am sure you know I am extremely fond and proud of you.*
>
> *Love and kisses, Harry*

I had always thought of Harry as this grandfatherly figure, but he was actually ahead of his time . . . anticipating the independent film movement. And like Willy, he always supported and encouraged me. I was honored that both men thought I should direct.

Filming *Funny Girl* was such a wonderful experience that I was dismayed when anyone said otherwise. Anne Francis, who played the feisty older showgirl, went on *The Tonight Show* and blamed me for the fact that her part was significantly cut. I thought, *What is she talking about?* I had no control over what was in or out of this movie. Willy was in charge. He and Robert Swink edited the film, and Willy ended up cutting her part, just as Jerome Robbins had ended up cutting the same part in the play. Decades later she confessed that her press agent had put her up to it and apologized in an open letter to me. But the damage was done.

If I *had* had more control over what was in the movie, I would have put back more of the *Swan Lake* sequence. Ray actually let me try to reedit it, though the film was already finished and prints had been made, so I doubt there was ever a question of going back into it. I think I just wanted to preserve the original number, to see it all put together, so at least it would exist somewhere. We had worked so hard on it . . . it took so much time to choreograph and rehearse and shoot . . . that I couldn't believe it would just end up on the editing room floor. How could you throw all that away? (My instinct has always been to hold on to the trims . . . the sections of film that were cut and discarded . . . in every movie I made. I thought they were valuable . . . to me, even if to no one else.)

So Ray arranged for an editor to work with me.

I was completely engrossed in the process. It was like putting a puzzle together, with one major difference . . . you could fit it together in many different ways. And I was dismayed to discover that some pieces were already missing. Nobody could find a certain section of the footage, which meant that I couldn't cut it exactly the way I would have liked.

Even in such a short sequence, I was faced with hard choices. I hated to lose the pas de deux (where the male and female leads dance together). It was funny, but that would have made it too long.

I did the best I could, and I still have the sequence. It was the first piece of film I ever edited. And I wrote Ray a letter of thanks, and added that if he was ever going to give me a present, what I wanted "is not a 30-karat diamond, but a 30-pound Moviola!" (That's the machine we used for editing.)

This was one of my happier times with Ray. Frankly, he and I were often at odds with each other. More than once, when we were doing the play, I had to tell him to get out of my dressing room. Fundamentally, I couldn't trust him.

But when Ray was sweet, he could be very sweet. After the movie he sent me a note saying he didn't think I was a "problem," but even if I was, it didn't matter because I sang "like a boid." And he ended with this:

> ***OK, Barbra—fix your own makeup—do your own hair—check the lighting—rewrite the screenplay—design the clothes—select the furniture—check the publicity—but, just keep singing!***

Okay, so maybe I was a little hands-on.

The film was scheduled to open in September, and Columbia Records was planning to release the soundtrack a month earlier, to build interest. They sent me the tracks as soon as they were finished, because I wanted to review them. I remember listening to "You Are Woman, I Am Man" and thinking, *Wait a minute, something's off. It sounds odd.* And then all of a sudden I realized what it was. I couldn't hear myself breathing. I called up the sound editor, and he proudly told me that they had "cleaned it up" and taken out all the breaths that naturally occur as you're singing.

I was shocked. No human being can sing without breathing.

I said, "Where are those breaths? In a garbage pail or something? Please find them and put them back in." And they did.

The premiere was in New York on September 18, 1968, at the Criterion Theatre in Times Square. Arnold Scaasi made me a peach-colored gown topped with a sheer layer of jeweled tulle, with a tulle cape to match. (The dress was an A-line shape, with no waist. I always gravitated to loose-fitting clothes, so I could eat those pastrami sandwiches.)

Being a guest at my own opening was a new experience for me. Usually all my friends are enjoying the show while I'm up onstage, working. This time I could sit back and watch, like everyone else, and not be worried about forgetting my lines or not hitting a note. The performance was already there, preserved on film forever.

I love film! It's the perfect medium for me. You do each scene, and then that's it. Done. People can be watching me act my heart out, singing and sweating . . . meanwhile I'm at home taking a lovely bath.

It was the first time I had seen the movie with an audience, and I was nervous. How would they react? After my first song, "I'm the Greatest Star," they started applauding. And then they kept applauding after almost every song. Ray was ecstatic. "Audiences never do that!" he told me and everyone else in sight. "Maybe they'll applaud at the end of a movie, but not all the way through it. This feels just like opening night on Broadway!"

After the film there was a big party in a tent in Times Square. Elliott and Cis and Harvey were there. And of course, as always, Marty was right beside me.

The premiere was a benefit for one of Mayor John Lindsay's youth programs. Lindsay was a Republican, but I liked his policies and even sang at a benefit to raise money for him a year later, when he was running for a second term.

He welcomed me back to New York and said, "Brooklyn has given us many great talents, and if there is one person who exemplifies that talent, it is Barbra Streisand . . . This is a great, great evening for all of us."

Then he said the movie was great, "and I have a feeling that it's never going to rain on your parade."

That was too much for me. Suddenly, in a dire tone, I interrupted, "Wait . . ."

He laughed, but there's my negativity coming out . . . or just that old Jewish superstition . . . don't tempt God by telling him how great things are going to be!

One premiere wasn't enough for Ray, who arranged three more. The next was in Los Angeles in October, and then in January we flew to London, for another hosted by Princess Margaret and benefiting one of her charities. Elliott was my escort in Los Angeles, but he didn't come with me to Europe. I took Cis instead.

I wore a dark green velvet gown, topped with a green velvet jacket trimmed with a sable collar and cuffs. I had asked Arnold Scaasi to make all the fur detachable . . . why waste it on just one dress? So I had him make three other outfits where it could snap on or off, for different looks.

I had a good time at that premiere in London. I had already met Princess Margaret, who was very friendly that night. And I liked her husband, Lord Snowden. He had acquired a title when he married her, but he did not seem entitled . . . he was very down-to-earth and easy to talk to.

David Frost was seated at my table (extremely witty and lots of fun, although he did spit when he spoke. You had to dodge it). On my other side was another very elegant man who looked vaguely familiar . . . and then he was introduced to me as Pierre Trudeau. Cis and I looked at each other and raised our eyebrows, because months earlier I had been complaining about how impossible it was to meet men. We were both lying on her bed, thumbing through *Life* magazine, and there was an article about Pierre Trudeau, the newly elected prime minister of Canada.

The writer described him like this: "Nothing about the next prime minister of Canada is ordinary. He wears what he likes, when he likes—and is apt to appear in the House of Commons wearing an ascot and sandals. He has a brown belt in judo, skin dives off Tahiti, and once slid down the banister in the House of Commons carrying an armful of important legislation."

Wow. I was intrigued by that dichotomy . . . the serious politician and the bohemian. Those two don't usually go together. "That's the kind of man I would like to date," I told Cis.

And suddenly here he was . . . my dinner partner. That was kind of extraordinary. How did he turn up here? Did I somehow manifest him?

Trudeau was very dapper, intelligent, intense . . . kind of a combination of Albert Einstein and Napoleon (only taller). And he was doing important work. I was dazzled.

Then he leaned over and asked me to dance. I suddenly felt shy . . . awkward . . . I could just imagine all the eyes in the room on the two of us. And I thought, *That will be the picture on the front page of the London* Times . . . and I didn't want more publicity. So I told him, "I don't dance in public."

He must have thought I was odd, or a little uptight. But he was very polite. He turned to Cis and gallantly asked her to dance. She happily accepted. And guess what picture was on the front page the next morning? Cis and Pierre dancing.

I just assumed that would be the end of my acquaintance with Pierre Trudeau. Too bad, because he was very interesting. Little did I know that he would reappear in my life only a few months later.

FIFTEEN

Hello, Gorgeous

The reason why I was even thinking about the prospect of dating . . . and why Elliott hadn't come with me to Europe . . . was because by this point we were apart more than we were together.

We had always had our disagreements. I remember a moment during the *Funny Girl* run on Broadway when we were going somewhere in the Bentley with his agent, Sue Mengers. Elliott was driving and somehow we got into an argument (I don't even remember over what), and he just stopped the car and got out in the middle of the street. I had to open my door, run around to the other side, and jump into the driver's seat to get the car moving again. It was scary, but Sue and I had to admit it was kind of funny as well.

I had been working constantly, and maybe I just chose to overlook the problems with Elliott. Even though my career happened to be taking off when his seemed to have stalled, I didn't sense that he was bothered by the fact that I was making more money than he was. But as Elliott has said elsewhere, he was actually very troubled by it. Maybe that's one reason he got involved with heavier gambling.

I'm not giving away any secret here . . . Elliott has been very open about his affinity for gambling in various interviews. I knew he was into sports, following baseball and football and basketball. But I didn't realize he was betting on these games. And when I found out, I thought it was for very little money, like when I used to go to the racetrack and bet two dollars on a horse.

But for Elliott, the gambling got a bit out of hand.

The parallels to Fanny Brice and Nicky Arnstein were not lost on me. And I didn't know how to deal with it any more than she did.

While Elliott was shooting in New York and I was shooting in Los Angeles, the rift between us just got wider. Even though we were technically together, we were already leading separate lives.

And that made me feel alone again. That's probably why I said yes when Omar kept asking me out to dinner. He was good company, and it was nice to feel the warmth of his attention. But it never went beyond that to anything more.

And then he kept writing to me after we wrapped and he left for Europe to make another movie. I actually forgot about those letters until I began writing this book and found them in a stash of personal mementos . . . probably because I didn't know quite how to react at the time. There are lines like: "The thing I want most in my life is to have you with me, to go everywhere together, to hold you in my arms, to put you to sleep and to wake you up. To kiss you, talk to you, love you with all my being . . . And all the time you're singing to me."

He had me until the line about my singing.

But all joking aside, I think he was still living in the fantasy world of the movie.

He went on: "I bought all your albums and I play them continually and pretend all the lyrics are addressed exclusively to me. Some nerve, huh? . . . Good night, my angel. I'll hug my pillow all night and dream of you. Your man, maybe?"

It was a little overwhelming. These were real love letters (unlike anything I'd ever received), and he kept trying to persuade me to join him in Paris for New Year's Eve. I thought, *What have I gotten myself into?*

Omar and I had a great time working together. He was a wonderful leading man, but this would be taking our friendship to a whole other level. I still had a husband, even though we were having difficulties, and a baby. I felt the whole notion of meeting in Paris was a fantasy. And I'd rather keep it a fantasy than test the reality. Our attraction to each other worked for the movie, but I couldn't see a future with him. I've always been able to visualize things, whether it was making a film or singing a particular song or designing a house. And if I couldn't visualize it, I couldn't do it.

The romance from the movie was over . . . at least for me.

Omar was very disappointed when I wrote back to him and told him I couldn't come. Recently I had the chance to meet his grandson, who said Omar told him: "Aside from your grandmother, Barbra is the only woman who ever captured my heart. If things had turned out differently, she could have been your bubbie!"

I don't know about that . . . but it's sweet.

To be honest, that episode with Sydney had scarred me for life. And I never wanted to venture there again.

By the time I was nominated for an Oscar as Best Actress for *Funny Girl*, Elliott and I had announced our separation. Still, I invited him to be my escort for the ceremony in April 1969, and he came over to my dressing room on the Paramount lot, where I was filming *On a Clear Day You Can See Forever*. It was easier to just stay there and get dressed, rather than going home, because the event started so early. Arnold Scaasi and my hairdresser, Fred Glaser, were there to help me.

I had two outfits laid out. The first was a long black Empire-style gown with a round neckline and long sleeves, made of sheer fabric over a solid black slip. Below the ribbon under the bust, the skirt fell in tiny pleats to the floor. I had paired it with a sheer organza cape with a hood, which I thought would make a beautiful entrance on the red carpet. It was very elegant, and I loved it.

The second outfit was a younger look. It was a pantsuit that Arnold had designed specifically for the Oscars, and it looked great in the sketch! It was made of black net studded all over with large rounded plastic sequins and accented with a white collar and cuffs (a look I've always liked). It worked really well with the chin-length wig I was already wearing from the day's shoot, which meant I could just keep the wig on . . . rather than have Fred go to the trouble of putting my hair up in a more elaborate hairdo to suit the gown.

I was torn between the two outfits, and then I thought to myself, *Gee, I might be fortunate enough to win another Oscar someday, and that's when I can be more elegant, but this time I should probably look more like the twenty-six-year-old girl I am.* And Elliott, Fred, and Arnold all preferred the pantsuit.

But really, the choice came down to the hair and was purely practical, because I was already a little late (as usual). So I went with the pantsuit and we quickly left for the Dorothy Chandler Pavilion.

I think I was more nervous about the event than the award. The one thing I was looking forward to was seeing Gregory Peck, who was the president of the Academy. I had been to the Golden Globes two months before, and I felt like such an outsider there . . . as if everyone else knew how to behave but I didn't. And then when I actually won, it all seemed even more strange and unreal. Thank God for Greg . . . he was a great friend of Willy's and had visited the *Funny Girl* set to watch us work. He greeted me as if we were old friends, and we posed for pictures (he received the Cecil B. DeMille Award that night). His big, warm hug made me feel like I was part of the Hollywood community for the first time.

Gregory Peck was a lovely man who believed in me early on. Before I knew him, his house was for sale, and I actually went over to look at it. I opened the door to his audio closet, which was filled with LPs, and was touched to see he had all my albums. (But whoever wrote the label on the shelf misspelled my first name, so I pulled out a pen and crossed out the extra *a*.)

I think the first time I spoke to him was at some Hollywood party, and I was scared to approach him because I admired him so much. Of all the male movie stars, I thought he was the most handsome, but also very underrated as an actor, because his work was so simple.

I couldn't miss this opportunity, and since I'm no good at small talk, I just asked him what I wanted to know: "Do you get annoyed when people talk more about your looks than your acting?"

If he was taken aback by the blunt question . . . after all, we didn't know each other . . . he didn't show it. Instead we stood there in the backyard, on the edge of a wooden platform that was covering a pool, and had a real conversation. He was very thoughtful, but basically his answer was yes.

It was the kind of discussion I like. And years later, our talks continued over dinners, when he and his lovely wife, Veronique, moved in right up the street from me on Carolwood Drive.

Back to the Oscars. *Funny Girl* was nominated for eight Academy Awards, including Best Picture. I was so happy that my pal Kay Medford was nominated for Best Supporting Actress and that my dear Harry Stradling was nominated for Best Cinematography, and Walter Scharf for Best Adaptation Score. And I was nominated for Best Actress.

I never thought I would win. I was so excited (and humbled) just to be nominated. And as I've always felt, why does it have to be a competition? Why not just give five awards for the best performances of the year? (Even the number five seems arbitrary . . . some years there might be four, others six.) I appreciated the wonderful reviews, and the movie was a hit . . . either the top-grossing film of the year, or the second highest, after *2001: A Space Odyssey.* (I guess it depends on how you calculate.) But I figured that all the negative stories in the gossip columns would turn voters against me. And as the night wore on and the movie proceeded to lose one award after another, I was getting even more pessimistic. After all, I was up against four of Hollywood's most extraordinary actresses . . . Patricia Neal, Joanne Woodward, Vanessa Redgrave, and Katharine Hepburn.

The ceremony must have lasted three hours. Best Actress was one of the last awards, and by the time Ingrid Bergman came to the podium, I was clutching Elliott's hand.

She announced the nominees and then opened the envelope and said, "The winner . . . it's a tie!" And then she stopped short, visibly surprised. "The winners are Katharine Hepburn in *The Lion in Winter*" . . . I thought, *Okay. She was wonderful* . . . and then she added, "and Barbra Streisand."

I was shocked. I couldn't believe it. I looked at Elliott, and he was smiling, so I wasn't dreaming. I had to quickly take out my gum and put it on the bottom of my seat, all the while frantically thinking, *What the hell am I going to say?* Anthony Harvey, who had directed *The Lion in Winter*, was sitting right behind me, and since he was accepting for Katharine Hepburn, he took my hand and we walked to the stage together. Thank God, because his grip is what saved me from falling when my heel caught on the hem of those pants and made me trip going up the steps. (Arnold, you made the pants too long!)

So I was kind of a mess, and after Ingrid Bergman handed me the Oscar, I almost dropped it. (Who knew it was so heavy?) I was glad Anthony spoke first, because that gave me a chance to catch my breath. And then it was my turn. I was still examining the famous gold statue that I was holding in my hands. It was absolutely beautiful, so I said to the statue, "Hello, gorgeous." I didn't plan on saying it, just as I hadn't planned on winning.

The audience erupted in laughter and applause, and then I started thanking everybody, saving the best for last . . . William Wyler. I knew how lucky I was to have Willy directing my first film. I was the fourteenth actor to win an Academy Award under his direction. He was sensitive and perceptive. He knew when a performance was right and he would not settle for anything less. I loved Willy, and will be eternally grateful to him. His legacy will live forever. He understood the mysteries of the human heart.

I concluded my speech by saying, "Somebody once . . . asked me if I was happy, and I said, 'Are you kidding? I'd be miserable if I was happy!' And I'd like to thank all the members of the Academy for making me really miserable! Thank you."

And then I walked offstage with Ingrid Bergman.

Phew! *That* was over.

The final award was Best Picture, and we lost that, too, to *Oliver!* (*Oliver!* And Stanley Kubrick's brilliant *2001: A Space Odyssey* wasn't even nominated!)

I was really disappointed that *Funny Girl* didn't win more awards. But the worst was yet to come. When I put on that black net pantsuit back in my dressing room on the lot, it had looked chic and fun, and everyone had approved. None of us realized that it would turn transparent under the lights. When I saw the footage on TV, I was horrified. It looked as if I had nothing on underneath. (It was actually lined in nude georgette.) I was so embarrassed. And I'm still horrified, thinking about it now. The outfit was more talked about than the fact that I had won the Academy Award.

When I called my mother the next day to ask what she thought of my Oscar, all she could say was, "What kind of dress was that to wear in public?" For once, she was right!

Katharine Hepburn was kinder. I still have the telegram I received from her:

Dear Barbra,

I think that you are really first rate and full of whatever it is and I am proud to share that perch with you for the next year. Incidentally I just hope that osmosis transfers a little of what you have to me.

With warm regards,
Kate Hepburn

I returned the gesture by sending her flowers, along with a note:

Dear Kate (I feel I should still call you Miss Hepburn),

How very nice of you to send me such a lovely wire. I, too, am most honored to share this with you. But there's one question I have to ask—

It's tough enough being in the same business with you—but do you have to start singing as well!!!! [Hepburn was about to star in the musical Coco *on Broadway.]*

With much admiration,
Barbra

Elliott says he was stoned that night (which I didn't know). He had begun to change when we were living apart. He had met a young woman who was part of a crowd that was "using" I don't know what. And they were living together in Greenwich Village by that time.

But my breakup with Elliott was never about other people. I was angry with him about a number of things, and more than a little frightened of the drugs. I wasn't a pot smoker, although I do remember one night in LA when we went out with Peter Sellers and Britt Ekland. I must have had a puff or two of what they were smoking, or else I just got a contact high, because we were giggling all through dinner. At one point we were making up all sorts of crazy flavors for ice cream. "What if they had steak ice cream!" I said. We all thought this was hysterically funny, so you can guess how far gone we were.

And in 1970, when I was performing in Las Vegas, I did a little routine about my nerves and how some people take pills, but I can hardly swallow aspirin, and anyway it's better not to rely on an emotional crutch. Then at the end, I'd pull out a fake joint and light it and talk funny, as if I were holding in the smoke. It got a big laugh. On New Year's Eve I actually lit a real joint that someone had given me and passed it around to the rhythm section. But I didn't like how pot made me feel . . . dizzy and woozy and out of control.

And I never smoked it again.

I'm basically too much of a realist to be attracted to drugs or alcohol (never liked the taste of it anyway). Life is fascinating enough.

But Elliott was taking it much further, or so I heard. It made me pull away from him even more.

We were so innocent when we met . . . like two kids against the rest of the world . . . two Jewish oddballs who found each other. And then we succumbed to convention and got married, at an age that now seems ridiculously young . . . I was twenty-one and he was twenty-five.

I hadn't really been ready for marriage in 1963, but I was very ready for a legal separation in 1969. I needed to be on my own and do the exploring I had never done. I wanted adventure. I wanted excitement.

SIXTEEN

Pandora's Box

And that leads me to Anthony Newley . . . dear Tony . . .

I had seen him on Broadway in *Stop the World—I Want to Get Off* at an Actors Fund benefit (while I was doing *Wholesale* in 1962), and thought, *My God, this guy is so talented.* He not only acted in it, but also wrote the book for the show *and* the music, with Leslie Bricusse . . . wonderful songs like "What Kind of Fool Am I?" I was so impressed.

One night after *Wholesale* closed, Marty took me to the Playboy Club to check it out. My former manager had committed me to sing there for several weeks, over the course of three years. As I said to Marty, "You've got to get me out of it. How the hell am I going to sing in this joint? There's no stage." And anyway, it would have felt as if I were going backward in my career.

Then I looked up and saw a man and a woman walking down the stairs into the club. He was very handsome, with dark wavy hair, and she looked ravishing in a red dress. He was talking. She was laughing. It's an image I've never forgotten.

I remember thinking, *Oh my God, what a beautiful couple!* And then I realized it was Tony Newley and Joan Collins, the actress he had married that year.

I didn't make any effort to talk to them . . . to me, they seemed untouchable. They were stars, and I was still just a supporting player.

But by the following year I was back on Broadway, a star myself in *Funny Girl*. Tony had returned, too, when *The Roar of the Greasepaint—The Smell of the Crowd* opened in 1965. And he sang another beautiful song that made an imprint on me, called "Who Can I Turn To?"

I was in awe of him. I loved his unusual face and his crooked smile . . . and he had that Cockney charm. When Tony was just sixteen, David Lean had cast him as the Artful Dodger in his film of Dickens's *Oliver Twist*, and he still looked exactly the same to me. I was very taken with that cheeky little boy in the movie, and twenty-some years later, he was still delightfully cheeky.

Tony and Joan and Elliott and I all became friends over time. They came to see me when I did a one-night concert in Forest Hills on my night off from *Funny Girl*. Elliott and I went to Tony's thirty-fourth birthday party at Danny's Hideaway, a New York steakhouse. I sang one of his songs, "Look at That Face," to my dear Sadie in *Color Me Barbra*. And then he and Joan moved to LA, and soon we were living there, too, so I could begin work on the film of *Funny Girl*.

Joan gave a party for Tony's thirty-sixth birthday at their house on Summit Drive. And I did something I never do. People were standing up and giving little speeches. So I got up and sang the first line of "People," but I changed the words to "Newley . . . people who need Newley . . . are the luckiest people in the world." All I sang was that one phrase, but the fact that I even had the desire to do it should have been a dead giveaway, at least to me . . .

Funnily enough, Elliott and I ended up renting that house, through an agency, when Tony and Joan went off to Malta to make a movie he was directing. I was busy with *Hello, Dolly!* And by the time they came back, we had moved into a house Elliott found on Carolwood. This was the time when our marriage was fracturing, and it turned out Tony and Joan were going through something similar. Coincidentally, both the Newleys and the Goulds announced their separations in 1969.

I had heard Tony liked younger women. He called himself a bad boy, and I suppose he was, in a way. And I've always had a weakness for bad boys (remember Joey Bauman, back on the playground). Tony had left school at fourteen and become an actor and a musician. So he and I had similar temperaments, with the added enticement that he was just different enough for me to be attracted to him.

With all his charisma and sexuality, Tony was a force that women gravitated to. That's the thing about men who are promiscuous . . . they're even more tempting because they present a challenge. You think, *Can I be the one to change him into a one-woman guy? Would he love me enough to do that?*

So Tony and I "opened Pandora's box, and released a torrent that will rend our worlds or bind us together forever," as he wrote in a book of poems he gave me.

It was a wonderful affair.

He wrote me the most marvelous letters, usually decorated with some sort of sketch or collage. He was so inventive.

> ***I write you a poem on parting for the second time:***
>
> ***I shall miss our nightly visits, daily talks***
>
> ***Your broken glasses, little squawks***
>
> ***Alice and the telephone***
>
> ***The lark ascending***
>
> ***Coming home.***

I had introduced him to "The Lark Ascending," a glorious piece of music by Ralph Vaughan Williams that we would play over and over again.

And then he added "P.S. On many more things I would like to dote. If you had any sense, you'd destroy this note."

That's Tony. He was smart, witty, and such a good writer. He could also be quite insightful: "I'll call you tonight and hope to hear that fabulous voice all honey and lemon telling me not to be bad. Barbra, the two people in one . . . the Diva and the child (will no one EVER see that)."

That got my attention. Like Jerry Robbins, he understood the child within me, and that's one of the reasons that I responded to him.

Tony loved to tease:

> ***Dear Diva, I've been the greatest fan of yours for a long time now. If the enclosed LP {he had sent me his latest album} is heated over an open flame it can be fashioned into the sweetest flower bowl. I worship you. TN***

That made me laugh, but I wasn't sure about that word "worship." It was lovely to hear but almost too much to believe.

And the fact is, it made me uncomfortable when a man went on about my voice. I couldn't help but wonder, *Is that all he loves, rather than the real me? Is he just a big fan?*

I think that's when I started to pull away again, like I had with Omar.

Here's another note from Tony:

> ***For Christ's sake, try and miss me.***

Tony was often traveling, and we really didn't know each other well enough for me to feel truly committed. And I guess I wasn't returning his calls fast enough.

Because the next note was:

> ***Darling B. Will you please cut down on the phone calls? Love, Tone***

This was a guy who knew how to woo women, and I must not have been quite as responsive as he would have liked at times . . . probably because I continued to be a bit wary, always holding back. I was afraid he would hurt me. But I was there on opening night when he did his nightclub act in the Empire Room at the Waldorf in October 1969, and the papers took note of it. It was hard to be anonymous, as I would have liked.

He would often sign his letters with "Love, Simon." I didn't know it then, but I later found out that was the name of his first child, with his second wife (Joan was his third, and she and I are still friends). The boy was born with severe defects and only lived six weeks. Now I understand why he chose to call himself by his son's name. He was still living with that pain.

Tony clearly had his demons, as most creative people do.

And he did hurt me. He did something that really upset me, and it changed the way I felt about him. I was angry and refused to talk to him. So that was the end of our relationship.

I loved that he loved the child in me, but he didn't take care of the woman in me.

Decades later, in 1992, he gave Sue Mengers (who was also his agent) a disc and said, "Would you please give this to Barbra for me." I didn't know what to expect. Was it a song he had written and wanted me to sing?

I'll never forget . . . I was sitting at my dressing table at Carolwood when I played it. The song was called "Too Much Woman," and here are the lyrics:

Can't seem to talk about you very well
Hard to find the colors for your smile
Although you haunt my conscience like a child
Hungry in the dark, the lark ascending
Why did we discard our happy ending?

I heard you on the radio today
All at once I'm falling back in time
That voice you stole from heaven
Though even God forgives you for the crime.

They played you on the radio today
I could swear you sang for me alone
What kind of fool would lose you?
The greatest love I've known.

How strange that we should meet again this way
Shaking hands as though we'd never met
I never really wanted to be free
I never really wanted to be free
But you were too much woman for me.

I was stunned . . . and taken aback . . . flooded with emotions that I had buried. I had to listen to it many times in order to process it.

I was so moved by that song and bowled over by the fact that he wrote it for me. It was like another love letter.

But I didn't call him after I heard it. I was flattered, and yet what was there to say?

"Why didn't you try harder to reach me years ago?"

Or . . . "Did you really love me that much?"

Here he was, a powerful man, and I was too much woman for him? Was he really that fragile?

Well, so was I.

It's the fragile part of me that people often overlook, or are afraid of. They just see the powerful.

When I put someone who's hurt me out of my life, I let go of them and don't look back. I've built up this mechanism to protect myself, I guess.

I must have told Sue to thank him for me. And that was that.

Tony died in 1999. There were moments over those last years when I thought of calling him to talk about our time together, but never did. And now he was gone. It was so sad. He was an extraordinary man . . . a wonderful actor, a great musician, a poet.

In 2016 I finally got to pay tribute to him in my own way. We found a video of Tony singing "Who Can I Turn To?" on TV and turned the song into a duet, so he and I could sing together. It's on my *Encore* album, and I did it live on my concert tour that year. Every night, as I sang along with him (the video was projected on a screen above the stage), I really listened to him and could totally relate to every word and feel his vulnerability:

And maybe tomorrow, I'll find what I'm after
I'll throw off my sorrow, beg, steal, or borrow my share of laughter.
With you I could learn to . . . with you on a new day . . .
But who can I turn to if you turn away?

All his passion and his pain are in that lyric. Memories overwhelmed me, and I could feel myself "falling back in time" when I sang that song. The past became present, for a moment, and I suddenly understood something very personal. Both Tony and I came from painful childhoods. We were always looking for love, and when things didn't go the way we wanted, we learned to build walls to protect ourselves, from the pain . . . the pain that never quite leaves you.

But I no longer want those walls around me.

Now, as I'm writing these words about Tony, my eyes well up. Maybe if I had reached out, I wouldn't have spent so many years alone . . .

I should have called him.

SEVENTEEN

Hello, Dolly!

When I was a kid, I had two crushes. The first and the most important was Marlon Brando. My second, smaller crush was Gene Kelly, especially in *Marjorie Morningstar.* There was something very endearing about his smile. I watched him fall in love with Natalie Wood on-screen and imagined what it would be like to have someone fall in love with me. But I was just a teenager, grateful to be in an air-conditioned movie theater eating Mello-Rolls and Good & Plenty. And that's the Cinderella story of my life . . . little did I know that I would get to meet Natalie Wood and become good friends with Marlon Brando and wind up being directed by Gene Kelly.

The movie Gene and I made together was *Hello, Dolly!*

I didn't want to do the film. I thought I was wrong for the part . . . too young, which seemed obvious. The character in the play is a middle-aged widow, and Carol Channing was in her midforties when she created the role on Broadway.

I think I was only twenty-four when Ernest Lehman first approached me about taking the part. He would be the movie's producer and the screenwriter (and had also written the screenplays for *West Side Story*, *The Sound of Music*, *North by Northwest*, and *Who's Afraid of Virginia Woolf?*), so I had a lot of respect for him. I just couldn't understand why he wanted *me*.

I tried to talk him out of it. I asked him why he wasn't hiring Carol Channing, and he told me that he had seen footage from *Thoroughly Modern Millie* and felt her personality was just too big for the screen. So even if I didn't take the role, there was no way he was going to hire her. Believe me, I wanted him to give it to Carol!

I told him that I thought the story would be more poignant if Dolly was an older woman, lonely after her husband's death and grasping at what could be her last chance to marry again. He listened politely and pointed out that a woman could become a widow at any age. He said he was sure I could be as poignant as anyone, and he knew I could bring out the comedy in the script. And he couldn't wait to hear me sing the score.

That was all very flattering, and even more persuasive because Ernie wasn't a flatterer. He was shy and quiet, which made me pay attention to what he said.

And he was prepared to wait over a year to make the movie, because I was already committed to *Funny Girl* . . . and being courted by the wonderful Howard Koch, the producer of *On a Clear Day You Can See Forever.* Marty was so proud. All of a sudden he was closing deals for three major motion pictures before I had even set foot on a sound stage. As he kept saying, "You're an international star before you've even shot one roll of film!"

I still had my doubts.

As soon as Gene Kelly was hired to direct *Dolly*, he flew to New York to have lunch with Marty and me. I suggested the Oak Room at the Plaza Hotel, because they had great vichyssoise, steak Diane, and chocolate soufflé. The first thing I said to Gene was, "I loved you in *Marjorie Morningstar.*"

I think he was pleased. Only ten years had passed since he appeared in that film, but he looked so different than he had on-screen . . . much older, with his hair graying at the temples. I was eager to talk about his concept for *Hello, Dolly!* and before we even ordered our food, I was peppering him with questions.

"How do you see this movie?" I thought it was such a slight, old-fashioned story and I was hoping he could approach it in a new way. "What's your vision?"

Gene studied the menu.

"What kind of style are you thinking of?"

He looked up and asked, "What do you mean?"

"Well," I said, "do you see it being filmed like a play . . . straight on, in static shots . . . or do you like the camera moving? And this is a period film, so do you imagine the colors as soft and muted, or do you see it as bright? I love foreign films, and they sometimes shoot scenes from unexpected angles or through objects, like a lace curtain, which could be interesting . . ."

He stared at me blankly. I should have known right then and there that communication was going to be a problem. And in retrospect, I probably scared the shit out of him.

Later I was told that Gene had cast Walter Matthau as Horace Vandergelder, the man Dolly wanted to marry.

What??? Walter was old enough to be my father!

That seemed peculiar . . . so I'm too young, and he's too old. What kind of a pairing is that? And I was surprised by other choices. You'd think the ingénues, at least, would have to go younger so they would provide some contrast to me. But no . . . the actors who were cast were about my age, and two were even older than me!

I thought, *I have to get out of this movie.* "Too late," said Marty. "The deal's already signed. You'll be sued."

Oh my God. So I decided to make the best of it.

Funny Girl wrapped in December 1967, and then I basically had one month at home before I had to go back to work in February to start rehearsing *Dolly*'s dance numbers, prerecording all the songs, and standing still for hours while they fitted my costumes. Sometimes I think those costumes are the best part of the film, and I especially liked the fact that I had only six of them. I hated fittings, even back then!

Irene Sharaff was the costume designer, and this was the third time we had worked together. She was a formidable woman, a bit cold, but with exquisite taste . . . very aristocratic with her hair pulled back into a tight bun, and lots of exotic bracelets and rings. I appreciated her skill, and she appreciated my instincts. She once gave me the most beautiful Balinese sculpture of a hand, carved in wood, and told me it was because she admired the way I used my hands.

I wanted Dolly to be a redhead, so I suggested colors I loved that would go with her hair . . . pink, burgundy, peach, green, and especially lavender. For the first scenes, Irene put me in a wonderful wine-colored jacket trimmed in beige lace, worn over a beige lace blouse and paired with a fabulous skirt that she made out of vintage paisley shawls, cut and stitched together. I thought that was genius. And the ensemble was topped off by the first of several amazing hats, this one crowned with feathers in autumnal colors.

For Dolly's trip to New York, she designed an elegant lavender dress, criss-crossed with ruched ribbon and dotted with tiny flowers (each one hand sewn onto the dress). I loved it. Stars today usually ask for their clothes from a movie and get them, but this was only my second film, and they didn't give them to me. When that dress came up for auction in 2011, I thought, *This is my chance.* I had to have it. I figured it would go for five thousand to ten thousand dollars, but then the bids kept shooting up and up. And I wanted it so badly that I found myself paying seventy-three thousand dollars. (Yikes!) It's now displayed in the antique clothes shop in the basement of my barn house. To me, it's a work of art, and I wanted to preserve it.

Then there was a negligee in softly pleated peach chiffon. It floated around me and just offered a glimpse of the corset underneath. Irene let me take the negligee home with me at the end of the shoot, and it's also hanging in my antique clothes shop. And there was a dress in soft dusty pink, and a creamy silk taffeta wedding gown. That taffeta was originally going to be just the underskirt . . . Irene was planning to cover it with elaborate lace. But when I tried it on to check the fit, I thought it looked so beautiful on its own . . . very simple and pure . . . that I convinced her to leave it as is and just add a bit of trim. And I loved the way she let the scalloped lace hang down from the brim of the hat.

I've saved the best costume . . . or the worst, if you're asking me . . . for last. That's the famous gown that Dolly wears at the climax of the film, when she steps slowly down the staircase at the Harmonia Gardens and is serenaded with the one song that most people remember from the show . . . "Hello, Dolly!"

It's the big moment, and the scarlet dress that Carol Channing wore onstage in that scene was also the one outfit that people remembered from the show. But I didn't want a scarlet dress. I never wear red. In my opinion red only looks good with brown or black hair. Besides, why would we want to duplicate the play? I was thinking of dark green velvet, but Irene was concerned that that might look too Christmasy in the scene, with its red-coated waiters and the red-carpeted stairs. And I saw her point. So she designed an elaborate gown in a warm, golden bronze, and had it completely embroidered in gold threads and encrusted with jewels.

It was enormously expensive . . . the most expensive dress ever made for a film, according to the press release. Apparently Irene had used real gold thread and real gemstones, which made it shimmer under the lights. But all that beading meant that it also weighed a ton . . . forty pounds, to be exact. It was so heavy that I could barely walk in that dress, much less dance.

And here's an anecdote that says everything you need to know about Irene. When we were rehearsing the number on the set, I wore a muslin version of the dress, since the real thing wasn't finished yet. And I was tripping over the train as I danced, and so were the professionals dancing with me. Michael Kidd, the choreographer, pulled Ernie aside and said, "The train's got to go."

Ernie was hesitant and said, "We better call Irene."

So Irene was summoned to the set. As Michael explained the problem, her expression didn't waver. All she said was, "Perhaps I'd better see what you're talking about."

So the music began again, and I proceeded to trip over the train again, and so did the other dancers.

"See what I mean?" said Michael. "You have to change the train."

"No, Michael," she said icily. "*You* have to change the choreography."

Ultimately, the train was shortened.

People kept telling me that the dress looked magnificent on film, but it was a nightmare to wear. After we finished shooting that scene, I never wanted to see it again.

Unfortunately, the dress was the least of my problems. I knew who Fanny Brice was, but I had no idea who Dolly Levi was. She was foreign to me, and I wanted help. I didn't relate to the story and I had to dig deep to find the parts of me that I could use for this character. Dolly was supposed to be a lovable matchmaker who had a scheme for every situation. She's extremely good at manipulating people. Well, that's not me. If I had had half her skill, maybe I could have figured out how to get out of the film. Or at least gotten what I needed from Gene Kelly.

He didn't seem to want to talk on a deeper level about character or motivation. I was on my own when it came to shaping my performance. And it's interesting now, in doing research for this book, to discover that he was regretful about it. As he said a few years later, "If only there had been more time, I'd have tried to help her work out a clear-cut characterization. But we had a tight schedule, and I left it up to her." (That makes me like him better now.)

I was disappointed when the reality of the man didn't live up to the fantasy I had from watching him on-screen. He would make scathing remarks to women on the set. One day he was so rude to a female dancer that I asked him privately, "Why were you so mean to her?" And he basically laughed it off and said, "Yeah, I was pretty tough on her, but that's okay. I used to yell like that at another dancer, and she became my wife."

Thank God I had the support of Gracie . . . my assistant and surrogate mother. And my darling Harry Stradling . . . I didn't have to worry about the camera if he was behind it. I knew I was safe. And as always, Jason was brought to the set every day so I could play with him whenever I had a break. I would pick him up while I was in costume and carry him around, under those big hats. (No wonder his first word was "hat." I was always wearing them, on set or in real life. One, because I like hats . . . all sorts, from caps to turbans. And two, they covered up my flattened hair after the wig came off.)

On the lot at 20th Century Fox, trailers were used as dressing rooms. When the incredible set decorator Walter Scott asked what kind of furnishings I wanted in mine, I said, "You know what I'd really love? Could you create something like Sarah Bernhardt's private railway car?" (It made sense, because the trailer was the same shape as a railway car.) Sarah traveled all over the United States in hers, when she did her American tours.

"Sure," Walter said. "What's your favorite color?"

"Dusty rose." I've always loved that color . . . it looks a bit antique . . . as if it had a past.

Well, Walter took my idea and ran with it. When I saw the trailer for the first time, I was dazzled. I swear, just walking in helped me get into character. Jason and Sadie and I could lounge on a brass daybed done in dusty-rose damask and cocooned with rose velvet draperies. The walls were upholstered in rose velvet and damask as well. I needed a dressing table since I do my own makeup, and I asked if he could build one with a sliding top, to hide all the stuff . . . an idea I still use to this day. He and the studio craftsmen really outdid themselves. I was ready to move in. (I should have bought that trailer at the MGM auction years later, but I thought, *Where am I going to keep it?*)

These same craftsmen also built the huge outdoor set that recreated New York City in 1890, centered on a street lined with buildings that stretched the entire length of the lot. It was amazing. They even had an elevated train chugging along up above, with horse-drawn trolleys down below. The whole thing covered fifteen acres and apparently cost $2 million to build (in 1967 dollars).

This is where we shot the big parade sequence, with thousands of extras, that ends the first act of the film. As she's watching the parade, Dolly spots Horace marching with his regiment and runs to talk to him. When she walks away, she finds herself in the midst of a marching band and joins them as she sings "Before the Parade Passes By."

Gene thought the scene should end with the camera coming in for a tight close-up on me. Meanwhile, I'm thinking, *Why would you want to end on a close-up of me, when you've got this fabulous set and a cast of thousands? So that's your climax, me holding one note, with my mouth open?* What's there to see besides my silver fillings, which I've never bothered to change?

So I made a suggestion. "What about shooting it the other way?" I said. "You know, start close and then end wide?" That way the audience would see the whole expanse of the parade, with all the marching bands and the banners and the spectators lining the street, while Dolly gets smaller and smaller in the distance. I mean, if you're going to spend a fortune on a set, why not show it off?

Gene didn't agree with me, so I talked to Ernie. He liked my suggestion and we ended up shooting it both ways. Even Gene admitted that my way was better when he saw the dailies. So that's what's in the film.

I had many questions. I always have questions about any film I'm doing, and Ernie was always receptive. Often it turned out that he was questioning the same things. I'd call him at night to ask him about lines in the next day's scene or discuss an idea for a shot. I don't know how I would have gotten through the movie without him.

He was a voice of reason in the midst of an atmosphere that was becoming stranger every day. I don't think I'm paranoid, but I felt as if Gene and Walter had an attitude toward me, and it was not positive . . . especially on Walter's part. In fact, he was overtly hostile, and I couldn't figure out why.

We had first met a few years before, and didn't hit it off then either. It was 1965, and I had gone to see a revival of *The Glass Menagerie*, starring my friend and neighbor Rosie Morgenstern (her stage name was Piper Laurie), who lived in my building at 320 Central Park West. She was playing Laura, the first role I ever did in acting class. Afterward I went backstage to congratulate her. I was sitting in her dressing room when the door opened and Walter Matthau poked his head in. He looked at me and said, "Oh, you must be Barbara Harris. Had your nose done, huh?"

I stared at him, dumbfounded. Barbara Harris? But she has a tiny nose. Was that a joke? If so, I didn't get it. (I still don't.)

Then three years later I found myself playing opposite him.

I'll never forget the day we were shooting the scene by the horse and buggy, on location in Garrison, New York. I had an idea for something that I thought would be funny . . . it was a bit of business, with Dolly popping up, hat first, out of nowhere beside the buggy when Horace didn't know she was there. So I asked Gene, "What do you think of this?" and tried it out. The crew started to laugh but then all of a sudden everyone went quiet, because Walter started screaming.

He closed his eyes and yelled, "Who the hell does she think she is? I've been in this business thirty years, and this is only her second movie . . . the first one hasn't even come out yet . . . and now she's *directing*? Why don't you shut up and let the *director* direct!"

And then he looked at me with pure venom and said, "You may be the singer in this picture, but I'm the *actor*! I have more talent in my farts than you have in your whole body!"

I was stunned. When I would offer an idea on *Funny Girl*, Willy Wyler either liked it or he didn't. And Omar would never lash out at me like Walter did. This hit me like a ton of bricks.

I had no defense. I had no words. I just stood there and was so humiliated that I ran off the set, crying. I'm not proud of that. I wish I could have answered him back. But I never want to be mean or malicious. That's not who I am. I want to be strong, not unkind.

Filming stopped for a while, until I composed myself. I don't remember Gene coming in to talk to me and I don't remember Walter ever apologizing.

It felt as if there were more to this outburst than I understood. Something was going on, but I wasn't sure what. The atmosphere on set was fraught . . . Gene was competitive with Michael Kidd about the choreography, Irene declared that she would never work with Ernie again, and Ernie was desperately trying to placate one person after another.

Put it this way, it was very hard to go to work every day.

One of the few scenes in the movie that I actually liked was the one in Harmonia Gardens, where Dolly sits down with Horace to have dinner and says, "You go your way" . . . and gestures with her right arm in one direction . . . "and I'll go my way" . . . and gestures with her left arm in the same direction. I thought that was funny. And the dialogue was very fast, which I love.

I had to keep eating as I talked. Walter had very few lines, but he kept flubbing them, so we had to do the scene over and over again. All that food was making me sick to my stomach, and Walter seemed to be enjoying my discomfort. The dumplings, made of egg whites, tasted terrible. The turkey got dry very quickly under the lights, and on my umpteenth bite, I started to choke. At that point I had had enough and said, "I can't do this." I didn't scream or raise my voice. I just got up and turned to Gene and told him, "I'll be back when he knows his lines."

I swear Walter was fumbling them on purpose, just to be mean, because he always knew his lines in every other scene. And why didn't Gene call him on it? That was his job. He shouldn't have left it up to me.

And guess what? There *was* something going on. A few days later, after things had calmed down, I went to Walter's dressing room and asked if I could speak to him. "I'm curious," I told him. "Why are you so hostile to me? What did I ever do to you?"

"Not to me," he replied, "but to a friend of mine."

I was mystified. "What are you talking about?"

"You hurt my friend."

"Walter, who's your friend? I don't understand."

"Well, every week Gene and I get together with a group of guys to play poker, and one of them is Sydney Chaplin. He's a good friend of ours, and you treated him badly."

"*I* treated *him* badly? Walter, that's not true."

And then I told him what really happened, figuring, What the hell? Clearly, he had already heard Sydney's version. Suddenly it all made sense. I was up against the boys' club.

I was told that at one point Walter went in to see Richard Zanuck, the head of the studio, to complain about me. Dick sat there and listened silently. Then he replied, "I'd like to help you, but the film isn't called *Hello, Walter!*"

Finally, my ordeal ended when we finished shooting in July 1968. Ernie gave me a wonderful gift . . . an original letter written by Sarah Bernhardt. It's one of my favorite things. I have it displayed in the foyer to my Art Nouveau room. Every time I look at it, I think of him.

Apart from that, I have very few good memories of the movie. It was fun singing with Louis Armstrong. We had the same booking agent for nightclubs, Joe Glaser, and I remember Joe telling me that every week he had to give Louis a thousand one-dollar bills to keep in his pocket, because that made Louis feel rich. I completely identified . . . kind of like me and my envelopes, divvying up my forty-five-dollar salary every week from my first job. Louis was a doll. And I adored working with Harry Stradling again. And I had a lovely relationship with Michael Kidd.

But I still thought the huge production numbers overwhelmed a flimsy story. So I'm always surprised when people come up to tell me how much they liked the movie. I'm glad *someone* had a good time.

The film was edited and ready for release by the end of 1968, but instead it sat on the shelf for a year . . . thanks to David Merrick, who produced the Broadway show. He had sold the rights to 20th Century Fox on condition that the movie wouldn't come out until the play had ended its run. And it was still running, after four years! Finally the studio paid Merrick off, and the movie opened on December 16, 1969. By that point I was on my fourth movie, *The Owl and the Pussycat*, which was filming in New York, so that's where they had the premiere.

It was one of the most terrifying experiences of my life. The sidewalks and streets outside the Rivoli Theatre on Broadway were a mob scene, with a thousand screaming fans. And as we pulled up in the limousine, they quickly surrounded us and peered in, pounding on the windows and banging on the doors. I felt trapped, like an animal in a cage. Photographers were trying to grab a shot through the windows, and flashbulbs were going off. More and more people pressed up against the car in the crush, and they began to rock it. It was like that scene with Marlon Brando in his car in *The Ugly American*. I began to panic.

And this went on for what seemed like forever, until the police were finally able to pull people off the car and clear a path through the crowd so we could get out and run to the theater. I was shaking so hard I could barely walk . . . and then a photographer lunged at me and would have knocked me down if it hadn't been for Marty, who blocked him. They got into a scuffle, and I saw the photographer swing his camera at Marty, and then someone pulled me away and rushed me inside. I was screaming, "Where's Marty? You've got to help Marty!" And then I saw him in the lobby. The camera had hit him above the eye, breaking his glasses, and there was blood trickling down his face.

I could still hear people yelling outside, and I thought, *This is crazy. It's inhuman. I never want to come to another premiere!*

This is when I really began to hate "stardom."

I can barely remember the rest of the evening. Nothing seemed to register after those moments of pure fear.

And it's funny. For all these years, I've thought that the critics didn't like me or the movie. But my archivist, Kim, just showed me the reviews, which were actually very kind. Vincent Canby had issues with the movie as a whole, but he called me "a National Treasure" in *The New York Times*. And Pauline Kael, whom I respected, went straight to the heart of the matter in *The New Yorker*:

> *In* Hello, Dolly! *Streisand has almost nothing to work with . . . The movie is full of that fake, mechanical exhilaration of big Broadway shows . . . She's not like the singers who are sometimes passable actresses if you don't push them beyond a small range. She opens up such abundance of emotion that it dissolves the coarseness of the role. There's no telling what she can't do. Almost unbelievably, she turns this star role back into a woman, so that the show seems to be about something. Barbra Streisand has a protean, volatile talent that calls for a new era in movie musicals.*

Sometimes I wish I could see myself through other people's eyes.

EIGHTEEN

Brando

First, he sent a message. Someone came up to me at a party and said, "Marlon Brando told me, 'If you ever see Barbra Streisand, tell that bitch she's great.'" I must have been nineteen or twenty years old. I wonder where he could have seen me? Maybe it was a TV show.

A year or two went by, and I was invited to sing at a benefit for SNCC, the Student Nonviolent Coordinating Committee, which was actively involved in registering Black voters in Mississippi, among other things. It was held on April 25, 1965 . . . a Sunday, my day off from *Funny Girl* . . . and I was a little starstruck to be part of the same program as Harry Belafonte, Sidney Poitier, Diahann Carroll, Sammy Davis, Jr., . . . and Marlon Brando.

I had admired Harry Belafonte in the movie *Carmen Jones* and seen Sidney Poitier on Broadway in *A Raisin in the Sun.* So I was very excited as I walked into the Grand Ballroom of the Hilton Hotel that night. Not only could I help an important cause, but I was also going to meet these two magnificent men who had such talent and intelligence. And they both had such dazzling smiles . . . not to mention those teeth!

But the pièce de résistance was Marlon Brando . . . the man who in my opinion was *the* most gorgeous, *the* most brilliant, *the* most talented human being on earth!

I had just turned twenty-three and was wearing a gray chiffon Donald Brooks gown, Empire-style, and almost backless except for two wide shoulder straps attached with big rhinestone buttons.

Before I went on I was standing in the wings to the left of the stage, trying to find Brando. Maybe I could get a glimpse of him before we were formally introduced.

Suddenly I felt someone kissing my back. Who would dare do that? I turned around and it was *him*. My idol.

I blurted out exactly what I was thinking. "You're destroying my fantasy."

He said softly, "You can't have a back like that and not have it kissed."

I think my heart stopped for a moment. What a line! It was like something out of a movie.

I wish I could have thought of an equally clever comeback, but I had never learned how to be seductive. And then I heard Sidney Poitier introduce me and I had to leave Brando there and go onstage. I had chosen a song called "Supper Time," a strong, poignant anthem sung by a woman about her husband who "ain't comin' home no more" because he had been lynched.

I was so nervous, knowing that he was watching me from the wings . . . Brando . . . the greatest actor of all time, as I had decided when I was thirteen. I started to sing, and then I heard a noise from backstage, and it completely threw me. I stopped, which is something I normally would never do. As a professional, you learn to just carry on. But I was so stunned by his presence that I wanted the song to be perfect, for him.

So I started again.

At least he was seeing my left profile . . . my better side.

About a year later, I was in rehearsal for *Funny Girl* in London when Warren Beatty invited me to a party at his girlfriend Leslie Caron's house. Elliott was in New York, so I took my dear Gracie with me. We walked into the living room and there, straight ahead, was a long couch facing in the opposite direction, so we could only see the backs of the people sitting on it. As Warren introduced me, their heads turned one by one. (This was very cinematic . . . good staging, if we had been making a film.)

"You know Leslie . . . Herb Sargent . . . James Coburn." And who was the next person? Marlon Brando!

As soon as Brando turned around, the first words out of my mouth were again exactly what I was thinking: "Did you get your teeth capped?"

Some opening line. Couldn't I have thought of something more charming? *Noooo . . .*

I had just seen *Bedtime Story*, and noticed his teeth looked different. I had always thought he had beautiful teeth, just crooked enough to make them interesting, with a little overlap in front.

He said, "As a matter of fact, yes, this one," and pointed to it.

Warren went on to introduce me to the rest of the guests, none of whom I remember. Except for Tarita, the Polynesian beauty who was Brando's third wife. She was at the far end of the couch.

Then, being very shy, I walked away and started a conversation with someone else, even though Brando was the only one I wanted to talk to. I'm thinking to myself, *How stupid! Why did I say that?* That was my big opportunity. Why hadn't I tried to engage him?

The truth is, I didn't know how.

That's when I felt someone take my hand, and a voice, the inimitable Marlon voice, said, "You look bored."

Again, what a line. Perfect. Was I in a movie? Maybe life could be like the movies, because this was really happening. Could he actually have been intrigued by what I said?

You see, you can never go that wrong with honesty. It may be blunt. It may make people move back a bit. But it brought Brando to me. He held on to my hand and led me into another room where we could talk alone.

Why did I feel as if I knew him? Why did it feel as if he knew me? Instinctively you sense when there's a connection . . . even before a word has been spoken. Somehow you recognize each other. Is it a vibration? Or something chemical, like pheromones? I can't explain it. It's almost mystical . . . metaphysical.

We spent four hours alone in that room, where he told me the story of his life . . . about his mother and father, who were both alcoholics. That's so typical of us. We skipped the small talk and went straight to the nitty-gritty.

His father thought acting was for sissies and didn't believe in him, just as my mother didn't have confidence in me. There was an air of disapproval. We both grew up with that feeling of not being seen. My father, who I was sure would have understood me, died. Marlon had a mother who was supportive, but she abandoned him in a sense by turning to drink.

That wound, that void, is a hole you can never fill.

By the way, I never spoke about any of this while Marlon was alive. I never revealed anything about my encounters with him. That's another thing we had in common. If anybody gossiped about us, we would stop being their friend.

I remember him telling me about a room he was once in with a woman, and how the sheer white curtains were softly billowing in the breeze as they made love. That's the kind of sense memory you can use as an actor . . . just think of those curtains, and all the feelings of that moment come back to you. He told me that he never really got along with Anna Magnani when they were making *The Fugitive Kind.* I couldn't believe it. I thought she was so extraordinary as an actress, and assumed he would adore her. Apparently she was attracted to him (and I could understand why), but he wasn't attracted to her.

About three hours into the conversation, he looked into my eyes and said, "I'd like to fuck you."

I was taken aback. "That sounds awful," I said.

After a moment of thought, he said, "Okay. Then I'd like to go to a museum with you."

"Now that's very romantic. I'd like that." He'd hit on a fantasy of mine . . . to walk through a museum with someone I was very attracted to and look at great art . . . exploring it together.

Then I remembered his wife in the other room. "What about Tarita? Why did you marry her?" Marlon and I didn't mince words.

He looked toward the other room and said, after thinking about it, "She's like a ripe piece of fruit."

The thing is, I knew exactly what he meant. She was luscious, but was that enough?

We talked about marriage . . . relationships. And then out of the blue he said something that shocked me.

"I don't think you're going to be with Elliott much longer."

I was taken aback. "I'm married to him. What do you mean?"

"He's not good-looking enough for you."

At first I was offended. I know most people wouldn't call Elliott gorgeous, but I certainly thought he was nice-looking. It was only years later that I realized how insightful Marlon's comment was. Did he know more about my search for beauty, at that point, than I did?

Was he searching for the same thing? Tarita was certainly beautiful and had already given him a son. I was beginning to think I couldn't have children. Little did I know I was already pregnant when I walked into that party.

The day my pregnancy was announced in the newspapers, Marlon tracked me down and called.

"So what are we going to name it?"

"I'm not sure. Any suggestions?"

"I like the name Christian." That was what he had named his son.

I asked, "What if it's a girl?"

"Christiana."

Then our lives went in different directions until one day in 1972 when I was living in Los Angeles, and so was he. The phone rang, and I picked it up and heard his voice.

"Come with me to the desert. We'll see the wildflowers and sleep under the stars."

Wow. Again, nothing so predictable as, "Hello. How are you?" which I never say either. I'm the same way with email. I often forget the niceties and go straight to the point.

I was thirty years old, newly divorced, with no special man in my life. He was forty-eight and divorced from Tarita.

I said, "I don't know you well enough to sleep over in the desert . . . but I'll go with you for the day."

Now, looking back, I can hardly believe my response. How stupid! Today I would be more adventurous, but I was too insecure sexually back then, still a nice Jewish girl from Brooklyn with my mother's admonitions echoing in my head. Free love was not my style. Besides, how do you brush your teeth in the desert? Do I sleep with my makeup on?

It could be too much reality.

But a day trip was fine, and I got dressed for the desert in navy-blue terry-cloth pants and a navy-blue T-shirt. Marlon picked me up in his jeep. I have no idea where he took me. It seemed as if we drove through the dry, crackling sagebrush for hours. When we got hungry, we stopped at some godforsaken little hamburger joint in the middle of nowhere, with a screen door that creaked as we walked in. The interior was just rough wood and faded paint tinged with the smoke of a thousand cigarettes. We sat at the counter, on those round stools that twirl. There was only one other customer in the place. I wonder if he was surprised to see Marlon Brando and Barbra Streisand walk in.

I was surprised myself. This was Marlon Brando sitting next to me!

Part of my brain was thinking, *Why does he want to be with me?*

And then I remembered, *Oh yeah. I'm what's her name. I've made movies, sold a lot of albums. So why* wouldn't *he want to be with me?*

There were always those two competing feelings. I sort of knew my own power and yet I didn't. I was operating from two entirely different ends of the scale . . . and not much in the middle.

The reasons for that are no doubt complex, and it would probably take another twenty years of therapy to figure them out. But who has the time or the interest? I don't find myself that fascinating. (That's why I eventually stopped therapy. I had learned enough.)

It's funny, I never thought of myself as a movie star even after winning an Oscar. Stars were people like Sophia Loren, whom I met when she came to see me in *Funny Girl* in London. She was so happy to hear I was pregnant and sent a sweet gift . . . blue baby booties . . . when Jason was born. She had been trying to have a baby for the longest time, and when she finally gave birth to a boy on Jason's birthday two years later, I sent her a gift and we joked about the coincidence. And Elizabeth Taylor, now that's a movie star! After I got to know Elizabeth, I realized she was one of the great broads, as down-to-earth as they come and hilariously raunchy.

But Brando, for me, had always retained a certain mystique. I don't remember ever telling him that I had idolized him since I was a teenager. And I still adored him, although he was a little chubbier, and his lips were thinner than they had been in *On the Waterfront*. One of his most intriguing features was his mouth, but lips shrink as you get older. His hair was thinner, but he still had that bump on his nose . . . another thing we had in common, although he had probably acquired his in a fight and mine was there from birth. My father, who was a very handsome man, had a bump. I had a bump. Marlon had a bump. Between the bump on his nose and his smile, he had me.

As we were driving home from the desert, he told me about working with Bernardo Bertolucci on *Last Tango in Paris*, and how he felt used because the story became so personal. He felt tricked into revealing his own history. I was puzzled at first. Isn't that what it's all about, in a way? Using your own experience to identify with the character?

But then I understood what he was saying. There's a point where it goes too deep. And for him, this was cutting too close to the core. There's a point, in other words, where you're exposing too much . . . especially if it's for someone else's movie. You have to keep something for yourself.

I didn't quite comprehend his anger, but I listened and tried to be sympathetic. I was just so happy that he felt comfortable enough to discuss it with me.

After that trip, we used to talk a lot. One day I was in the kitchen at Carolwood when he called and said, "Sing me a song."

"Sing you a song? What do you think I do, sing around the house? I don't even sing in the shower. That's like me asking you to recite a soliloquy from *Hamlet*."

And then, to my amazement, he proceeded to recite a soliloquy from *Hamlet*! I remember thinking, *Who's going to believe this? Marlon Brando doing Shakespeare in my kitchen!* I was holding the phone and wishing there was some way of capturing the moment. But this was the 1970s, and I didn't have a tape recorder handy, and God knows I didn't want to risk stopping him.

After my mouth closed and I could speak again, I told him how wonderful that had been, and asked, "How many soliloquies do you know?"

"Don't change the subject," he replied. "Now it's your turn."

So I had to sing him a song . . . but which one? I decided on Rodgers and Hart's "Nobody's Heart Belongs to Me." I sang it because it was short and yet it told a story . . . about a woman who is alone . . . no man in her life. But she insists she's fine with that, although she's really not. Thinking about it now, I was using the song to tell him what was going on in my life, even though that was unconscious.

When I was younger and alone, I would stay on the phone with Marlon for hours. He was very comfortable with women. Perhaps that had something to do with his beloved nanny. He told me that when he was four or five, he used to crawl into bed with this beautiful eighteen-year-old girl, part Danish and part Indonesian, and sleep beside her, both of them naked.

Brando was such a sensual man. After one two-and-a-half-hour conversation, as I wrote in my journal, "When we said goodbye, he said, 'I kiss you gently on your inner thigh and on your lips.'"

The language of the body was very natural to him.

As time passed and I was in new relationships, our phone calls got shorter. After a while I'd get restless and tell him, "I have to go now. Goodbye."

When I first started seeing Jon Peters, we went away together at Christmas to ski. But Jon got sick and needed to go home, so on New Year's Eve we were back in the bedroom at Carolwood when the phone rang. Jon picked it up and after listening for a minute said, "Sure, sure," and hung up.

"Who was it?" I asked.

"Some guy who said he was Marlon Brando."

If looks could kill. "Shmuck, that *was* Marlon Brando! He's my friend!"

Jon looked at me for a long moment and said, "Oh my God, that's right. Since you're Barbra Streisand, that *could* be Marlon Brando."

Marlon came over to the ranch once, when I was living with Jon. We didn't have anything as conventional as a couch in the living room. We had just put a mattress down in front of the fireplace and covered it with patchwork quilts and pillows made of antique fabrics. (What can I say? It was the '70s.) I remember Marlon trying to lie down among the pillows, and then he couldn't get up because he was too heavy. That's when I decided it was time to get a couch.

I don't think he liked Jon that much, although he related to the part of him that was Cherokee. Marlon was a vocal supporter of the rights of Native Americans. We would have long discussions about politics. Taking a stand on an issue could actually hurt an actor, especially back then. Brando didn't care. He considered politics the responsibility of every citizen. That was the way I felt too.

One night he called after watching *The Way We Were* on TV and said, "You're a wonderful actress." I was thrilled. "You should wear red lipstick," he told me, and I replied that it had been right for the character but not for me personally. And then in the next sentence he started criticizing the way I talked in real life. "Why do you keep saying the word 'like'?"

He was right . . . I had started using the word a little too much, the way teenagers from the Valley were doing, almost as a verbal tic.

"Stop it," he told me.

Then I would accuse him of being critical, like my mother. But when I heard others use the word so often I could hear how awful it sounded. Marlon was right. Either something is or it isn't. It's not "like." Like what? Why do you need the word? It's completely unnecessary. I stopped saying it.

Another time I was in my motor home heading to a film set when Marlon called and said he had just been watching *Funny Girl.*

"You were really good, but you run funny."

"What do you mean, 'funny'? Like pigeon-toed?"

"No, not pigeon-toed. You run like a girl."

"Well, how else am I *supposed* to run?"

Now that I've just watched it again he was right. I *do* run funny.

I never asked Marlon about acting because I thought, *Ugh, who wants to be asked about acting?* That's like someone asking me how I sing. How can I explain it? It's a gift, a talent. But one night in the mid-1980s when I was living with Richard Baskin, we were in bed when Marlon called. I could see it was going to be a long conversation, and I didn't want to annoy Richard, so I put Marlon on hold and went into the bathroom to continue the call. I was filming *Nuts* at the time, and there were problems . . . so I sat there and told him everything I was going through.

Somehow he started to talk about his process. By this point I was no longer so concerned about what he might think of me, so I asked him how he learned lines. He said that he never could remember them, so he would write them out on his hands or under a table or on the ceiling. I had always thought he made such interesting choices as an actor, staring downward, for example, when the audience was eager to see his face. He was rarely looking where you would expect. And now I knew why . . . he was looking at his lines! What a clever idea.

Then he told me how he abandoned that for an even better system. He wore a tiny earpiece through which his assistant would feed him each line, and then he'd repeat it.

"How can you act with someone talking in your ear?" I asked. "Doesn't it interfere with your rhythm, being in the moment?"

He said no. I couldn't imagine it, but he did it brilliantly.

For both of us, acting was not intellectual. He thought the mind was the enemy of the actor. Marlon's technique was instinctive, and so was mine. I couldn't identify with actors who had planned out how they were going to deliver each line, who knew exactly where the intonation would go, and what the key word in the sentence would be. I'm not saying that's wrong. It has worked for some very fine actors, including Laurence Olivier. I've heard he sculpted his performances like an artist chiseling marble. I remember sitting in a London theater watching him play Othello. I thought he was brilliant, but a man behind me was booing him. I was so angry that I turned around and said, "How dare you do that? He was wonderful!"

"No," the man replied, "I've seen it seven times and he was off tonight."

"Well, then don't ruin it for the rest of us."

How dare he think it should be exactly the same every night? To me, that would be boring. I like surprising myself. If I'm in the moment, things come out differently each time. It's fresher and more real to me . . . and, I hope, to the audience. I work from the inside out. Brando works from the inside out. Olivier works from the outside in. I don't care how somebody gets there, as long as I believe it in the end.

I loved to watch Brando, because he was always in the moment, and because it was real, it was slightly out of control . . . you see a life, a mind, thinking . . . you never knew what he was going to say or do next.

Brando is as compelling as any of the characters he plays. That's what makes a movie star. You have to have a strong enough personality that it pervades whatever you do.

In 1994, when I was putting together the filmed version of my Las Vegas concert, I wanted to show him what I had done with the song "I'll Know" from *Guys and Dolls* . . . I had substituted a picture of myself for Jean Simmons on the screen so I could become his leading lady for the duet.

That's the closest I ever came to acting with him. My dream had been to play the young Cleopatra to his Caesar in George Bernard Shaw's *Caesar and Cleopatra* (and if I couldn't get him, my second choice would have been Orson Welles). And then I wanted to play the grown-up Cleopatra to his Antony in Shakespeare's *Antony and Cleopatra*. I thought we could film both plays for television. Just imagine how brilliant he would have been in those roles.

I should have fought harder to make it happen.

Marlon sat in my white office and looked at the *Guys and Dolls* sequence. And then he wanted to see the whole concert! That made me feel great.

A few months later, I invited him over for dinner, and he was very late. Eventually, the phone rang, and it was Marlon, explaining that he had been stopped by the police for speeding.

"I had to tell them I was going to Barbra Streisand's house for dinner."

Well, I hope it got him out of a ticket.

When he finally arrived, he couldn't extract himself from his car. He had gained so much weight that he was stuck behind the steering wheel, and I had to grab hold of his arms and pull him out.

When I finally managed to get him inside the house, he said, "Let's not talk. Just look into my eyes."

He had collapsed onto the couch, and I was kneeling on the rug, with a coffee table between us, looking up at him. The silence didn't last very long . . . probably until I started to giggle. After dinner we went downstairs to watch a movie, although I'm not sure we ever got to it because we kept talking. He was rubbing my feet and telling me the story of making *On the Waterfront*, which happens to be my favorite movie of his. I was so curious about it. I wanted to know everything that happened the day they shot the taxicab scene. (At one point, there's a close-up of the cabdriver's face in the rearview mirror. You know who it was? Nehemiah Persoff, who played my father in *Yentl*. I always remembered that shot. That's one of the reasons I hired him.)

I was asking Marlon how that famous scene, with the "I could have been a contender" line, came to be. Had it all been in the script? And he told me it wasn't written the way it appears on-screen. In fact, he didn't believe that the older brother would threaten the younger, whom he obviously loved, quite so brutally. So he asked the director, Elia Kazan, if they could do one take where they improvised their own version. Kazan told them to go off by themselves and work on it, so they did.

When Rod Steiger pulls out the gun and points it at Brando, Brando was supposed to say, "Put down the gun." But instead he just pushed it away gently and looked at him, shaking his head and saying, "Charley . . . Charley . . . Oh, Charley."

What he was feeling was beyond words. He and Steiger were doing what felt right to them in the moment. And that's the take Kazan ultimately used in the movie.

Brando was proud to tell me that it had been his idea, and I completely understood. It's so human . . . even the greatest actor of our time wanted to be acknowledged for having made certain choices.

Good actors are often looking at the script in its entirety and may rewrite their lines. We're always working on our own dialogue, trying to make it more authentic and to get even closer to what we feel the character would say, and good directors are open to good suggestions. They'd be fools not to be.

Marlon told me he rewrote his part in *Apocalypse Now*, and he was lucky enough to be working with Francis Ford Coppola, a great director who allowed him to do it. Whatever Marlon did, it sure worked. He was brilliant in that role.

Unfortunately, the next time we spoke was after his daughter died. I could imagine how devastated he must have been and wrote him a note: "I was so sorry to hear about Cheyenne. I know how much you loved her. Sometimes certain people have a hard time here on earth and they need to go to other places. My sincere and best wishes for you."

He called to thank me, and we talked for a long time.

Neither of us trusted many people, and it's interesting how a lot of the people we trusted were the same . . . Quincy Jones, Mike Medavoy, Carol Matthau. Once for a dinner at Quincy's house, Marlon showed up wearing a burgundy sweatsuit with stripes down the side. By this point he was probably 280 pounds. He told me he was eating a quart of ice cream every night. I could relate . . . I love ice cream too. There's nothing like a big, fresh scoop of McConnell's Brazilian Coffee, packed into a crisp cone and handed to you at their store in Santa Barbara. The intensity of the flavor, made with real coffee beans . . . the smooth, rich texture . . . By the way, you can't get McConnell's ice cream at just any supermarket, and this particular flavor is even harder to find. So you can imagine all the reasons I suddenly invent to go to Santa Barbara. Jim and I will hop into the truck and drive up the coast. That store is like a vacation spot to me. I can't wait to get there, so sometimes we also have to stop at their store in Ventura along the way. But the last time we were there, they only had coffee ice cream with chocolate chips, which ruined it for me.

Sometimes in an emergency situation, I may call Dan Bifano, my rose expert who lives in Santa Barbara, and ask him to bring me a couple of pints when he comes down to check on my garden once a week. For my birthday one year he gave me a whole tub. I regret to admit it didn't last that long, and I paid for that indulgence on the treadmill for weeks.

Back to Quincy's house. As we were all sitting around the table, I brought up a recent article in which Marlon had talked about how much he disliked the movie business. I identified with him. I had been trying to get a film version of Larry Kramer's play *The Normal Heart* off the ground for over twenty years, and the struggle of selling it to a studio was so degrading.

In the piece Marlon said he hated acting.

"Come on," I said. "There must be a part of you that likes it, or did like it."

He said, "Acting is for girls."

I shouldn't have pressed it, but it was as if he were channeling his father, and that upset me. I don't know why I was so belligerent that night, egging him on.

"I do it for the money," he insisted.

"Really, Marlon?" I asked. "Weren't there times you enjoyed playing certain roles?"

I could see he was getting annoyed, but I didn't like his making light of his talent. It felt as if he had become stuck on the past and all that anger, when I wanted to talk about the present . . . to share new ideas.

The movie business is tough. Marlon had to audition for *The Godfather.* The studio didn't want him. They thought he was difficult, not right for the part, and they treated him like a has-been. So he turned on a video recorder, stuffed his cheeks with Kleenex, and taped himself as Don Corleone. He got the part.

The fact is, I don't always like being an actor either. I dislike getting made up, getting my hair done, being fussed over. I don't like costume fittings or learning lines or getting up at the crack of dawn. I've been in movies where I'm completely engaged, and others where I'm not. I think directing is the more challenging (and fulfilling) profession. Marlon directed one movie, *One-Eyed Jacks.* I never did find out why he never directed again. In his autobiography he says that a director has to get up too early in the morning. But I'm sure there were other reasons. Gosh, there was so much I didn't get to ask him.

Why do certain people gravitate to acting? So many actors seem to have had unhappy childhoods. Marlon could never get approval from his father. Success, when it came, didn't matter to him. He couldn't enjoy it. It was hard for him to accept the praise, just as it was for me. People who don't praise you feel more familiar, so they're the ones you believe. I don't remember the good reviews . . . only the bad. Marlon stopped giving interviews because he was tired of being misquoted, and so did I. And of course that only made it worse, because then the media decided we were arrogant. Reporters get offended when you refuse to see them, so they dislike you even more . . . and make up stories to fill their columns anyway. To be hounded by the press was horrible. That's why Marlon wanted to escape to that island near Tahiti. I understood it completely.

As Marlon got older, he started to mumble. It was almost as if he had a lisp, as if he could barely make the effort to speak. When he came to dinner for the last time at my house in Malibu, he was like an accident waiting to happen. He walked in with blood dripping down his leg, which he had somehow hurt in the car. John Travolta, who knew Marlon, was also a guest that night, and he did some hocus-pocus healing thing, as Jim and I watched. Marlon told John that he felt as if he had left his body for a moment and was looking down on himself from above . . . powerless, unable to move . . . the same sensation I had had in my bedroom after Lou Kind had been so cruel to me.

I had also invited Jim's son Josh to join us, because I knew how much he admired Brando. Kelly Preston suggested we take a snapshot of us all, which is something I wouldn't normally do because I don't like people taking pictures of me. But I'm glad I have it.

Now I'm reading Marlon's autobiography again and watching a documentary on his life, and I keep finding other parallels with him. He used to make up crazy stories about where he was born. I thought that was only my thing! (Remember my *Playbill* bio . . . reared in Rangoon.) And neither of us went back to the theater after our early successes. He had two long runs, in *I Remember Mama* and *A Streetcar Named Desire*, and after a few weeks he wanted out of the play, just as I had. He would often get to the theater at the very last minute, just as I had.

Neither of us really liked the attention that came with fame. Initially we wanted to be seen, but then people didn't see us anymore. They just saw the myths. They confused who we are with the parts we played. I didn't bargain for that kind of attention. It was superficial. They didn't know me, so how could they claim to love me? Besides, I didn't want love from everybody. I wanted it from my family and a mate.

Marlon died on July 1, 2004. The memorial service was at Mike Medavoy's house. Jack Nicholson, Warren Beatty and Annette Bening, Johnny Depp, and Michael Jackson were there, along with Marlon's family. Quincy Jones, Sean Penn, and Ed Begley, Jr., spoke. I hadn't known that Marlon was an inventor. Ed reminded us that Marlon had patented a tuning device for his conga drums. That same kind of curiosity and imagination carried over to his concern for the environment. Marlon wanted to turn his Tahitian island into a living laboratory to research and develop solar energy, biofuels, and aquafarming. In order to support that dream, he was in the process of designing an ecofriendly resort that would enable him to share the beauty of his paradise in a sustainable way. (For example, deep sea water would be the source of the cold for the air-conditioning system.)

Once again Marlon was ahead of his time in his commitment to preserve and protect our planet. That's a cause I've been supporting for decades as well.

I don't like to fly, but Mike Medavoy and his lovely wife, Irena, recently invited Jim and me to go to Tahiti with them and stay at the resort, which has now been built in Marlon's memory, along with a research center.

It's an extraordinary place . . . stunningly beautiful and utterly peaceful. I sat and looked out at the ocean and thought about Marlon, who wanted to escape the world . . . and yet tried to do so much for it as well.

He was a complicated, remarkable man, and I treasure our friendship. There was no one else like him.

One of my fondest memories is when he called me from London after seeing *The Way We Were* on TV (for the second time).

"In the last moment, you were so vulnerable that I fell in love with you all over again," he said. "We should have done more when we were younger, fucked a lot, had children. Go kiss yourself in the mirror for me."

NINETEEN

Daisy and Melinda

Wow, I thought, what a terrific role . . . two roles, actually.

On a Clear Day You Can See Forever starts when a contemporary New York girl, Daisy Gamble, attends a college class given by Dr. Marc Chabot, who's a psychiatrist as well as a professor. He's talking about hypnosis, and Daisy is so susceptible that she gets hypnotized accidentally. That gives her the idea of approaching him outside of class and asking if he could hypnotize her to quit smoking. It's her one bad habit, but as the doctor discovers, she also has some unusual gifts . . . she could find an object before he even knew he had lost it and predict when the phone was going to ring. And as an extra added attraction, she could make flowers grow.

When Dr. Chabot hypnotizes Daisy in his office, something extraordinary happens . . . she becomes an entirely different person and reveals a past life as

Melinda Winifred Waine Tentrees, an elegant courtesan in early-nineteenth-century England.

What fun! I could be both the kooky, self-deprecating girl (not exactly a stretch) and a sophisticated woman of the world (who spoke with a proper English accent). The two characters embodied the kind of dichotomy . . . insecure versus sure of myself . . . that I felt so often in my own personality.

And what an unusual subject for a musical . . . I was fascinated by extrasensory perception and I believe in reincarnation and the transmigration of souls, especially after an experience I had years after I did this movie. My friend Donna Karan and I went up to Deepak Chopra's institute in Massachusetts for a retreat, where you eat vegetarian food and get Ayurvedic treatments. (They pour oil over your head. She loved it. I hated it.) And you get special massages by two women, one at your head and the other at your feet. Their movements are supposed to be coordinated. They look at each other and then they move together, one taking your right arm and the other the left. That seemed funny to me, and I kept making jokes, saying things like, "Oops, girls. The beat is off. You're not together." So instead of relaxing and enjoying the experience, I had everyone giggling.

Next we were supposed to go into a room to meditate. Donna and I went in together and pretty soon I heard her snoring. Meanwhile, I'm trying to concentrate . . . the idea is to quiet the mind so you can go deeper into your consciousness. You're given a word to say to yourself, a mantra, and then you repeat that word if you need to as you let your thoughts just pass through your mind. You're looking for the gap . . . the silence in between the thoughts and the mantra. I remember when I first got my mantra. I was talking to my friend Sandy Gallin, who was a devoted meditator and told me over and over again how it's calmed him, and I said, "You know you're not supposed to reveal your mantra to anyone." And then of course I blurted mine out accidentally.

Meditating did not come naturally to me. You're supposed to do it for fifteen minutes twice a day, but I could hardly sit still for that long, and my mind was too busy, noticing things like one of my curtains was shorter than the other or deciding that it was time to clean out the bathroom drawers. But here at this retreat, there was really nothing else to do. And all of a sudden, the thoughts running through my mind became fewer and fewer . . . so less need to repeat the mantra . . . and I went into that deep silence . . . the nothingness . . . without a thought.

And in that silence an extraordinary thing happened. I could feel something inside me emerge, past the shell of myself, leaving my body behind. And I thought, *Oh my God, what is this?*

Is it part of me? What's me?

Was it my soul leaving my body? Whatever it was, it floated out into a dark universe. It was scary, and I wanted it to come back into my body. But it was also hopeful . . . the idea that a soul could float free. So who knows? Maybe it's true that the soul lives on after you die, and who can say where it goes? Does it ever migrate into another human being?

I don't pretend to know the answer. I'm just asking the question.

Have you ever met someone and immediately felt a connection to them on a very deep level? It's as if you already know them, without a word being spoken. Somehow you recognize each other. And if you talk and spend time together, it feels as if you're really seen. Is this what they mean by a soul mate?

Cis, my dear friend, was definitely a soul mate. I know we felt that way about each other. We had a connection that was undeniable.

There are certain people you just respond to, and it's almost mystical. When I was a teenager and read about Sarah Bernhardt, I couldn't believe the parallels between us. After her first performance, her mother told her, "Your arms are too skinny," just as my mother had done. And the more I read, the more resemblances I found. She, too, was hounded by the press and once said, "I am the most lied-about woman in the world." She, too, was politically active, and was criticized for it. She, too, didn't hesitate to speak up.

Could it be possible that something of her was reborn in me?

Well, nothing's impossible.

At the end of the retreat, Deepak gave us one of his books, and Donna and I drove back to New York. When I got to my apartment, I went out on the terrace outside my bedroom to look at the flowers that had been planted in the boxes while I was gone. I had ordered mums in pink and white, but these were rust and yellow! I called the plant place and said, "These flowers are the wrong color."

The man said, "Oh, the nursery didn't have pink and white so we got these."

I said, "Well, didn't it occur to anyone to ask me before you planted them?"

And then I thought, *What the hell.* It was such an ordeal just to get flowers and potting soil up to the 22nd floor. Besides, I didn't want to kill the poor things by throwing them out. So I simply closed my lace curtains so I didn't have to look at them. A couple of weeks later Cis peeked out through the curtains and said, "Oh, you changed the flowers."

I said, "What? I never changed them."

She said, "Well, they're pink and white now."

I couldn't believe it. How did rust turn to dusty rose and yellow to off-white . . . just what I wanted! I immediately called the plant place to see if they were a special kind of mum that changes color.

"No" was the answer.

Then I called Deepak and asked him, "What's going on? How did those flowers change color?"

He said, "Well, you clearly haven't read the book I gave you."

"No," I told him. "I haven't had a chance yet."

"Well, look at the chapter about desire."

So I looked at the book. And sure enough, it was about how desire can manifest change. Had the flowers changed color because I wanted them to? Maybe this was another example of that very quiet but very intense power of the will . . . the kind of will that I had felt rise up in me when I stood in the doorway of my bedroom as a teenager, wanting to be a famous actress who could afford to have someone else make my bed.

Maybe something of Daisy had rubbed off on me during the filming. She could make flowers grow, and I couldn't. But I could make them change colors!

So, the idea that a soul that once belonged to Melinda could come into Daisy made perfect sense to me. Both of them were attracted to the wrong men, in two different centuries, but the pattern was the same. And until you recognize and break the pattern, you're destined to repeat it. In other words, you keep being reborn until you learn the lesson and then the soul can rest.

Clearly Alan Jay Lerner had his own theories about all this. He wrote the screenplay for the film as well as the book and the lyrics for the original Broadway show. Alan was a complicated man with a frenetic personality. I remember he wore sunglasses indoors to protect his eyes from the light, and white cotton gloves to stop himself from biting his nails. I was eager to pick his brain and explore everything we could about ESP and reincarnation. Burton Lane, who wrote the music, seemed rather shy in contrast and didn't talk much.

And once again, just as with Ernest Lehman on *Hello, Dolly!*, I had a real friend in the producer, Howard Koch. Howard was the one who pursued me for the role, and after I agreed to take it, he wanted my approval before he hired a director and a costar. We both thought Vincente Minnelli, responsible for many classic musicals, would be a great choice to direct. Vincente's last two films had not done as well as expected, and he hadn't made a movie in five years, but that didn't matter to me. What was more important was that he had directed *Gigi*, which I loved, and I believed he would have just the right touch. And when I met this sweet man, I liked him immediately.

Casting the leading man was not quite so easy. Richard Harris, who had just played King Arthur in the movie version of Lerner and Loewe's *Camelot*, turned us down. There were rumors that Frank Sinatra and Gregory Peck also passed, but I'm not sure if that's true. Too bad, because I would have been thrilled to work with either of them. Louis Jourdan, who had starred in *Gigi* for Vincente, originally played the role of the doctor in the play but bowed out before the show came to Broadway. And that could have put the idea of a Frenchman into Howard's head, which led us to Yves Montand. I had seen him in French films like *The Wages of Fear* and was vaguely aware that Edith Piaf had taken him under her wing when he started out as a singer in the 1940s. So I was intrigued and couldn't wait to meet his wife, Simone Signoret, whom I loved in *Ship of Fools*. Rumor was that Yves and Marilyn Monroe had had an affair while they were shooting *Let's Make Love*. And since I was a great admirer of Marilyn's . . . her beauty and her vulnerability always appealed to me . . . that made him even more interesting.

Howard was also kind enough to ask my opinion about a costume designer. Since the two characters, Melinda and Daisy, were so different and were born almost two hundred years apart, I thought, *Why not have two designers, one for each period?*

I had already been collaborating with Arnold Scaasi on outfits for premieres and other special occasions, so I suggested he do Daisy's modern clothes. Luckily Howard was willing to take a chance on him, even though he had never designed costumes for a film. I would discuss ideas with Scaasi . . . he'd do a sketch or I'd do a sketch . . . and then we'd refine it, gradually building up this chic wardrobe that could have come straight from the pages of a fashion magazine. Of course it made no real sense. What college student actually dressed like this in 1969?

Well, maybe she was rich? We decided not to worry about it, and just think of it as another aspect of the fantasy. Daisy liked flowers, so that became a theme, and we took it to the nth degree in her bedroom, where her flowered nightie matched her flowered sheets. Another dress in a different flowered pattern matched an upholstered chair, the wallpaper, and the curtains. That was an idea that came straight out of my New York apartment, where I had done a similar thing in my den . . . making a dress out of the same paisley fabric that I used on a Victorian settee.

It must have been Vincente's idea to hire Cecil Beaton to design Melinda's wardrobe, since they had already worked together on *Gigi*, and that made me so happy, because I thought he was a genius. Just imagine, this was the great Cecil Beaton . . . the man who had dressed Leslie Caron in *Gigi* and Audrey Hepburn in *My Fair Lady* and won Oscars for both films. He had impeccable taste, and he was so interesting to talk to. He told me once that I had an "ancient" face, which sounded intriguing. I felt as if he had a vision of me that I could only glimpse. He gave me a new sense of myself. And he was very warm and loving.

Melinda lived during the height of the Regency period in England, so that meant Empire-style dresses, with a high bust and then a fall of fabric, straight to the floor. That style happens to be perfect for me. (I was born in the wrong era.) I have long legs and a short middle section, so a dress with a tight waist doesn't hit me in the right place.

Cecil and I were on the same wavelength. I was dazzled by his designs. He had an encyclopedic knowledge of the period, and then he would add some imaginative detail to a historically accurate gown, just to seduce the camera. I love detail, too, and we had a grand time seeing who could find just the right accessory to delight the other. I had a small collection of cameos, and brought them in to show him and said, "What if we strung them together to make a headpiece?" Cecil executed that notion brilliantly, and I wore it in the scene in the casino. (I still have it.)

At one point in the film, Dr. Chabot tells Melinda that he can no longer see

My parents, Emanuel and Diana Streisand.

I got my long legs from my father (also my short waist).

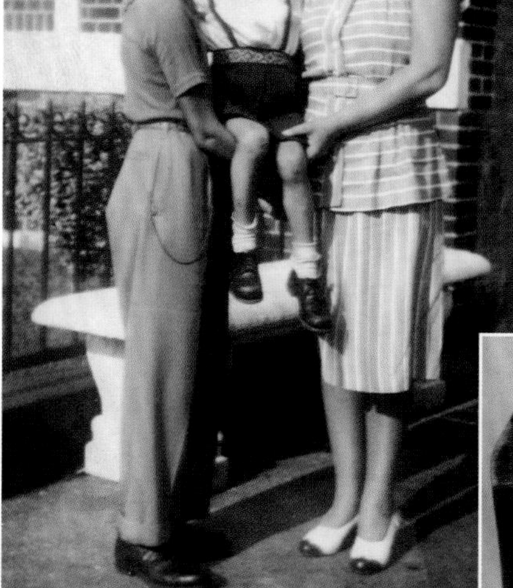

Four years old with my brother, Sheldon, and my mother.

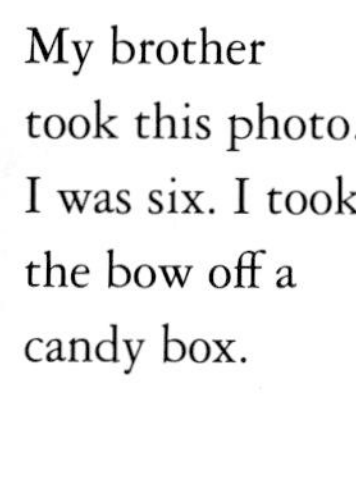

My brother took this photo. I was six. I took the bow off a candy box.

Shelly made the American Indian headdress for the Boy Scouts.

My first singing performance at seven.

My high school graduation photo from Erasmus Hall in Brooklyn.

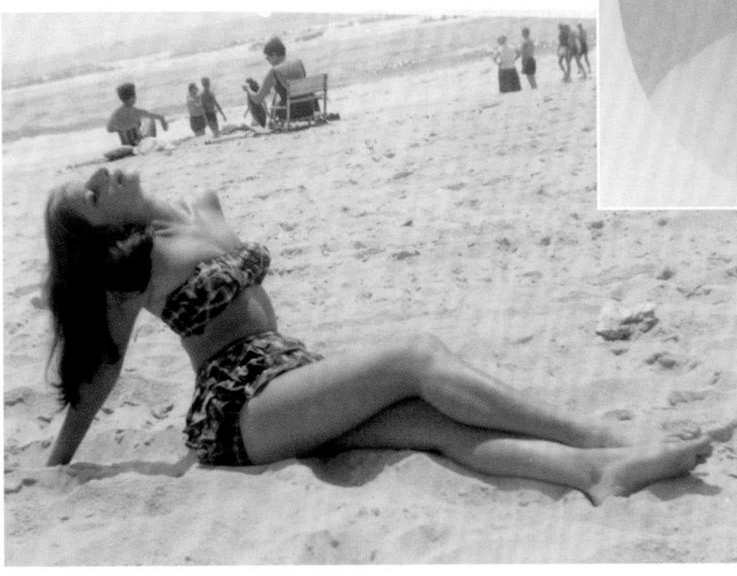

My favorite plaid bathing suit at fourteen.

1961: *Another Evening with Harry Stoones.*

1960: *The Boy Friend* at the Cecilwood Theatre—I was Hortense, the French maid.

An out-of-town gig.

1960: Bon Soir—sharing a dressing room with the wonderful Phyllis Diller.

1961: I bought this 1930s karakul fur coat for ten dollars. And wore it to my audition for *I Can Get It for You Wholesale.*

1964: My two Grammy wins for my first album, *The Barbra Streisand Album*—Album of the Year and Best Female Vocal.

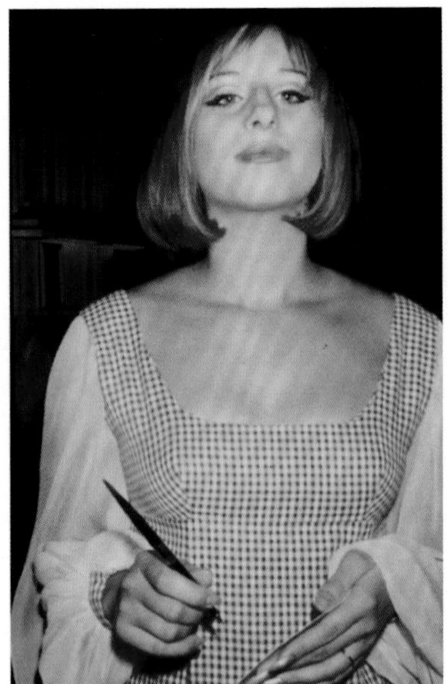

1963: My LA debut at the Cocoanut Grove—I was twenty-one. There were so many famous people coming to see me, I was the least-known person in the room. I made my gown out of a gingham tablecloth.

1964: In *Funny Girl* on Broadway at the Winter Garden Theatre.

Cis and Harvey Corman were my second family. I was sixteen years old when I met Cis in acting class—she became my best friend, a great casting director, and the president of my film company.

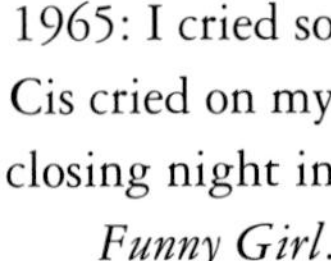

1965: I cried so Cis cried on my closing night in *Funny Girl*.

1964: *Funny Girl* rehearsal with Milton Rosenstock, the musical director.

1963: After our honeymoon at the Beverly Hills Hotel.

1965: The Broadway cast of *Funny Girl* gave me my sweet Sadie for my twenty-second birthday.

1966: Our first European vacation in Paris with the Cormans.

1964: *Funny Girl* team—Ray Stark, Isobel Lennart, Jule Styne, Jerome Robbins.

1965: My first TV special, *My Name Is Barbra.*

I played singing I'm five.

Marty and me.

1966: My second TV special, *Color Me Barbra,* was shot in color. We are watching playback with Joe Layton and Peter Matz.

1966: *Color Me Barbra*—My sketch design became the pink gown.

1966: *Color Me Barbra*—We *really* did have a small circus on set.

1967: *The Belle of 14th Street* TV special—I designed the coral gown with antique beaded net over it, to go with an antique jet beaded top I found at a thrift shop! —one of my favorites.

1967: *A Happening in Central Park*—150,000 people showed up—a magical night, even though I forgot some lyrics, which led to years of not performing live.

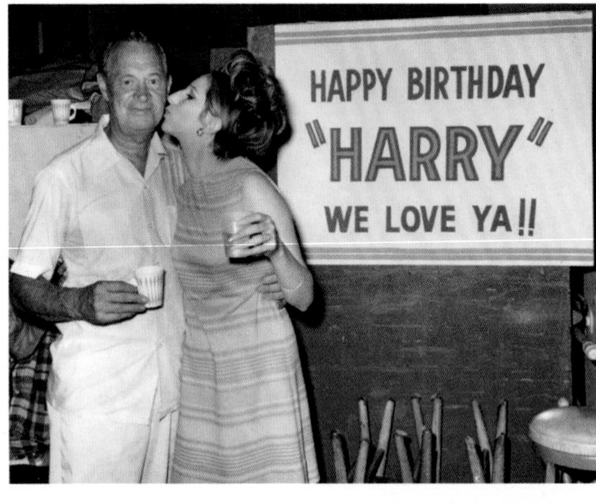

1967: The wonderful Harry Stradling was the cinematographer on my first four films—I loved him.

1967: I was lucky to have the great director William Wyler on my first film.

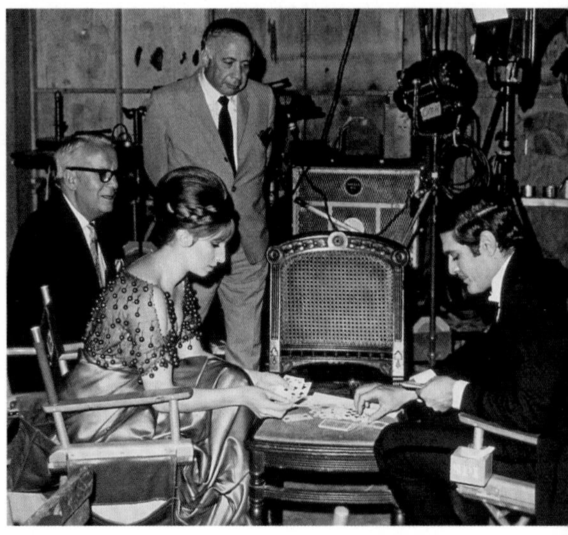

1967: On *Funny Girl* set with Omar Sharif—he was a master at cards.

1966: Elliott took this first photo of us as mother and son.

1968: The first word Jason ever said (after "mommy") was "Hat! Hat!"

1967: *Funny Girl* set—Jason always came to the set every day.

1969: First Artists—Paul Newman, Sidney Poitier, and I started our own production company to be able to make the films we wanted to make.

1969: In London, while filming *On a Clear Day You Can See Forever*—I was always interested in art, here starting my art collection with Egon Schiele and Gustav Klimt.

1969: The Friars Club tribute to me with Entertainer of the Year—I should have worn this for the Oscars!

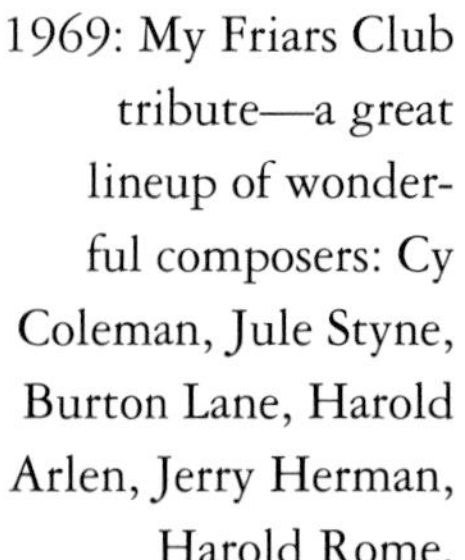

1969: My Friars Club tribute—a great lineup of wonderful composers: Cy Coleman, Jule Styne, Burton Lane, Harold Arlen, Jerry Herman, Harold Rome.

1969: I wanted my trailer to resemble Sarah Bernhardt's railroad car.

1970: *On a Clear Day*—My period costumes by Cecil Beaton were so very beautiful, it was like playing dress-up every day in the most gorgeous clothes.

1969: *Hello, Dolly!*—The gold dress by Irene Sharaff was made with pure 14-karat gold thread and Swarovski crystals—it was so heavy they had to make a removable train so I could dance in it

1969: *Funny Girl*—Winning my first Academy Award for Best Actress.

1970: Jason and me at the Royal Pavilion in Brighton, England.

1970: *The Owl and the Pussycat* with George Segal—we had a lot of fun and laughter on the set.

1971: Visiting Elliott on the set of Ingmar Bergman's film—Ingmar and I were hoping to work together.

1971: Elliott and me in New York watching Jason on the playground.

1973: *The Way We Were*—I only wanted Robert Redford to play Hubbell and was thrilled when he agreed.

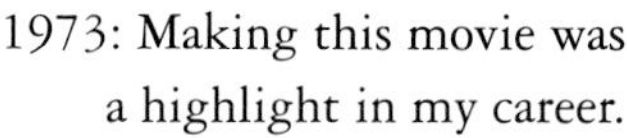

1973: Making this movie was a highlight in my career.

1972: *What's Up, Doc?* I didn't understand this screwball comedy but liked working with Peter Bogdanovich and Ryan O'Neal.

1979: Jon Peters and me.

1974: *For Pete's Sake*—Jason visiting the set.

1975: *Funny Lady*—Queen Elizabeth came to our London premiere, where I asked why only the women had to wear gloves to shake her hand.

1974: Prince Charles visiting me at Burbank Studios while I was recording songs for *Funny Lady.*

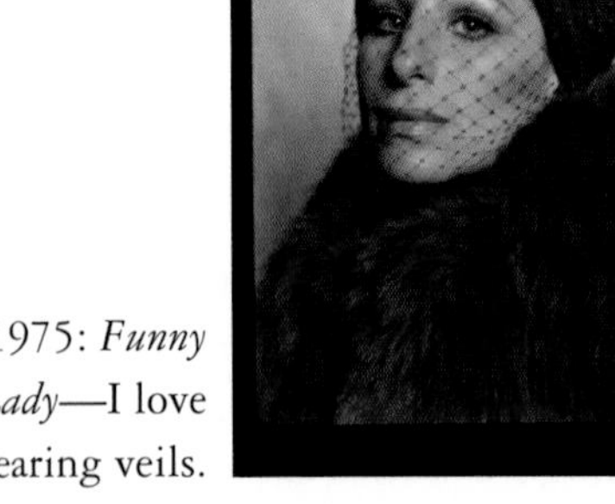

1975: *Funny Lady*—I love wearing veils.

1975: *Funny Lady*—a photo shoot with James Caan.

1977: *A Star Is Born*—I loved winning the Academy Award as the first woman to win for composing the music for "Evergeen."

1976: Learning to play the guitar for *A Star Is Born*. I had to cut my nails on one hand.

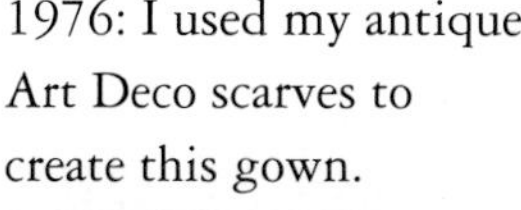

1976: I used my antique Art Deco scarves to create this gown.

1977: Willy Wyler came to our film premiere—it meant so much to me to have him there.

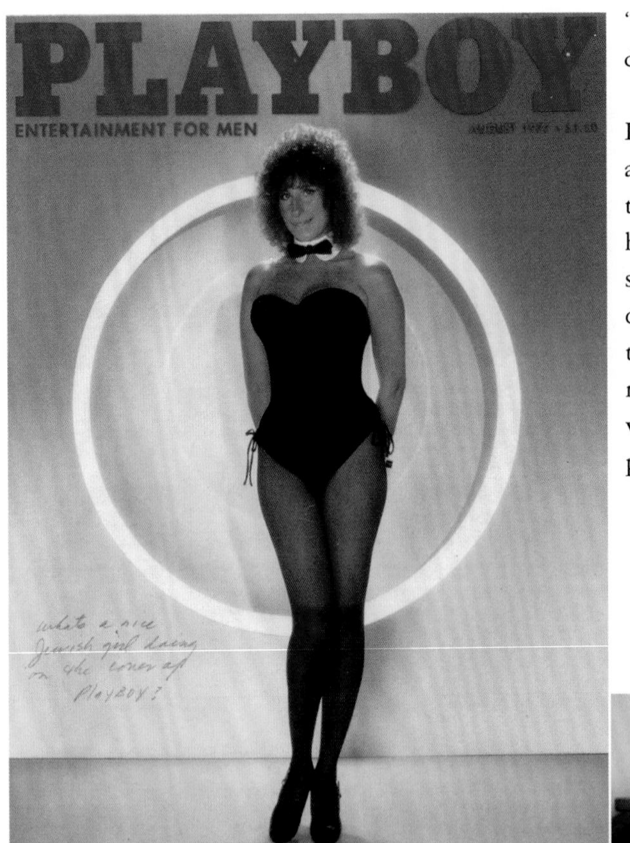

"What's a nice Jewish girl doing on the cover of *Playboy*?"

In 1977, I was asked to do an interview for *Playboy* (in those days the interviews were highly thought of). Then they said, "We want you on the cover too." I agreed to try on the Bunny outfit . . . which fit me, but not my feminist values. So I killed the photo . . . until now.

An antique velvet robe from my own wardrobe.

1979: Ryan O'Neal, my favorite boxing partner in *The Main Event*.

her. He's become obsessed with her and knows he must break it off. She says, "I shall miss you." It was a sad scene, and what came to my mind was a tiny painting I had on my shelf of Madame Recamier, a Frenchwoman from Melinda's era, lying on a divan and wearing an utterly simple white gown. I thought Melinda might wear something similar, so I showed it to Cecil.

He knew the image and loved the idea. And since I like monochromatic things, I said, "Instead of white, what would you think of making it in peach?"

He said, "Yes! In peach chiffon, exactly the color of your skin, to make it even more sensual."

"Great! You can't tell where the gown ends and I begin, in a sense."

Cecil actually improved on the painted version of the dress, and the set designer produced a divan so I could recreate Madame Recamier's pose.

I've never had as much fun working with a costume designer as I had with Cecil. And I've never felt so beautiful in any costumes as I did in his. He could transform everyday life into an exotic realm, and I was happy to follow him there.

"By any standards, Miss Streisand is extraordinary. The camera is never indifferent to her, in a good photographer's hands. Her face alone or her personality alone, could fascinate. Together, they also captivate . . . I've never to this day met anyone so young who had such an awareness and knowledge of herself. Of any actress I have ever worked with, I believe she had the widest range as a performer . . . Her face is a painting from several historical eras. Barbra as an Englishwoman, an Egyptian, or a Ming empress would be unforgettable."

—Cecil Beaton

For the last two months of 1968, I was immersed in preproduction, with all the songs to record, rehearsals, and costume fittings. In January 1969, right before we were to begin shooting, Paramount threw a "Reincarnation Ball" at the Beverly Hilton hotel to publicize the picture. Everyone was supposed to "come as the person you would like to have been in a previous life," and I came as the French writer Colette. (Marty was my escort, dressed as Louis Pasteur.) I loved her work . . . she was so earthy and intuitive . . . and I liked the fact that she had lived an unconventional life, on her own terms. I also loved her look . . . dark eyes, frizzy hair . . . so I had my hairdresser, Fred Glaser, curl my own short hair. I wore a Battenberg lace coat from 1900 that I found at an antiques show, and then I designed a sleeveless floor-length gown with more lace at the neck and the hem to match the coat.

I enjoyed making *Clear Day* . . . even though I don't smoke (gave it up when I was twelve), and I had to smoke all the way through it. It was fun playing two parts . . . as well as the Cockney girl that Melinda truly was. (So it was actually three parts!) Also I had my beloved Harry Stradling behind the camera, looking after me for the third time. And I adored Vincente. He was so kind, and we had a great rapport. If I had an idea for a scene, I didn't hesitate to tell him. And then I'd ask, "How do you see it?"

He'd tell me and I'd say, "Ooh, that's good."

And he'd say, "No, I like your idea better."

And I'd say, "No, no. I like *your* idea better."

And we'd end up laughing, because I usually preferred his ideas and he preferred mine.

I do remember walking onto the set of the doctor's office for the first time and thinking, *This is ridiculous.* No professor or psychiatrist would have had an office this big, with a double-height ceiling, a stately fireplace, enough furniture to fill a hotel lobby, and a spiral staircase up to the second level. Maybe the size made it easier to move the camera around, but it was unrealistic (just like my clothes for Daisy). You have to remember that this was conceived as a big musical, even though that era was ending.

And in the center of it all was Yves Montand. I could tell he was uncomfortable in the part, and that made me feel bad for him. Here was a man who was virile and strong when he was singing in French, wearing his trademark brown shirt and pants. He could fill concert halls. But when he stepped onto an American sound stage, he had to struggle to act in English. It was as if he wasn't the same person, and that made acting with him a bit strange.

Daisy was supposed to be attracted to him, and that was a challenge, because there was no chemistry between us. None.

Apparently some people used to say that I was very aware of the camera, as if that were a bad thing. Well, let me tell you, Yves was also aware of the camera. He was very concerned about how he looked, and he favored his left side. So did I, so you can imagine how well that worked when we were standing opposite each other.

And I confess I did something that I'm not particularly proud of, but it was impossible to resist. I played a little trick on him once in a scene. I improvised a line and said something like, "You know, I can do these things with flowers" and pointed to a plant on the windowsill. "See that plant over there?"

But he wouldn't look and risk exposing his right side.

Jack Nicholson was in the movie, too, although you'd hardly know it. He had already finished shooting *Easy Rider*, but it hadn't come out yet, so I had never heard of him. I thought he had a good face, nice teeth, and a very distinctive sound to his voice. We had a scene together up on the roof, where he's sitting cross-legged beside me. Vincente gave him very specific instructions about how to sit: "No, cross your leg over like that. Turn your body a little to the left." He kept rearranging Jack's body, and Jack was looking more uncomfortable by the minute. He must have felt as if he were being put into a straitjacket.

When I saw *Easy Rider*, I said, "Wait a minute. Is that the same guy from our movie?" I couldn't believe it. Jack Nicholson is such a great actor, but I don't think he had a chance to show it in *Clear Day.*

In April we flew to England to shoot on location at the Royal Pavilion in Brighton. I have a story about that plane ride, but first let me back up a bit and tell you about a dinner at Howard Koch's house. That's where Richard Baskin, who will reappear in my life, says we first met. I don't remember that moment, but he was just a college student then whose parents were good friends with Howard and his wife. Shirley Baskin, Richard's mother, had recently lost her husband (Burt Baskin, who cofounded Baskin-Robbins), so Howard invited her to come on the trip to England with us.

Shirley brought a box of brownies with her and passed them around on the plane. Oh my God, they were the greatest. They had walnuts in them! Now, I understand why people don't make brownies with walnuts anymore, because of nut allergies. But brownies without walnuts? What's the point? If I'm ever given plain ones, I get some walnuts and push a few into each brownie.

Well, for years Shirley told people that I had eaten the whole box of brownies on the plane, which is a complete exaggeration . . . although I admit I probably had more than two (maybe six . . . they were little!). A few years ago, I went to her art opening (she covers objects in beautiful lacquered postage stamps) and we laughed again about whether or not I ate the whole box. She was a lovely lady who lived to be 101.

Back to the movie and the Royal Pavilion, which was built by King George IV as an Oriental fantasy, complete with domes and minarets and Chinese wallpaper. We were the first movie ever allowed to film there, and I had never seen anything like it. I couldn't decide whether it was grotesque or beautiful, and then I realized it was both . . . grotesquely beautiful, like some of Gaudí's work. We shot the banquet scene in the actual banquet hall, and there was something very powerful about being in the real place. The atmosphere was palpable, and it was easy to become Melinda, sitting at this vast table with gold and silver place settings and seducing the attractive man sitting across from me.

Cecil outdid himself with my gown for this scene. It was an ivory column of crepe silk . . . embroidered with pearls, rhinestones, and silver thread . . . which parted in front to reveal a rhinestone-embroidered underskirt. The plunging neckline left little to the imagination. And to top off the dress, Cecil designed an amazing crepe silk turban that would be the envy of any Indian maharani . . . embroidered in rhinestones and dripping with pearls.

Cecil always gave me equal credit for the turban, because I wore them regularly. As he said, it was "both our ideas, really . . . to wrap the Streisand features in a glorious white turban, to further accent her strong features. At the same time, she was totally feminine, beguiling, shamelessly sexual."

People tell me it was a very erotic scene. While the song "Love with All the Trimmings" played in voice-over (thank God I didn't have to lip-sync), I caressed my cheek with a champagne glass and then let it slide slowly down to my décolleté, all the while holding the eyes of the man opposite me. The shot went back and forth between a close-up of me, him, me, him. And I think Harry put a special filter on the lens that made all the rhinestones sparkle.

I had another idea for the moment when Melinda and that character, Robert

Tentrees, kiss, and asked Vincente what he thought of going around us, from one profile to another, for a 180-degree shot, and he was receptive. Harry said, "Well, Jesus, that's tough to light on both sides . . . but let me try it."

He did, and it worked brilliantly.

Unfortunately, the actor playing the part of Tentrees, Melinda's second husband-to-be, wasn't the sort of man I could look at and swoon. And I saw fear in his eyes, which was a turnoff. So I felt no attraction to him and had to conjure up something else to fantasize about. (This time, it wasn't chocolate cake.)

Afterward Howard came up to me and asked, "Who were you thinking of?"

I said, "I'll never tell."

Listen, it's one thing to emote in front of a camera when you're actually attracted to your costar. It can get complex, deciding how much to show, but at least you can use the reality of what is. When there is no reality and you're completely uninterested in someone, it gets a little harder to express desire.

It helped that I was feeling positive about myself at the time. George Lazenby, who had just played James Bond in *On Her Majesty's Secret Service*, happened to show up on the set one day. He was virile, handsome, and charming, and he liked to flirt. That was fun. He would often ride up on his motorcycle and scoop me up for dinner at some country inn. But I was careful not to get too cozy. I was busy learning lines and taking care of my son. (Jason was with me, as always, and the costume department made him an outfit like the Queen's Guards wore, complete with a little bearskin hat.)

And I didn't want to repeat Melinda's mistake. She was drawn to the wrong man, who treated her badly and deserted her. And Daisy made the same mistake, trying to please a boyfriend who didn't appreciate her. And now she's drawn to Dr. Chabot, who by this time has fallen in love with the seductive, confident Melinda, and he disdains this little Daisy creature. When Daisy accidentally finds out that he's in love with her other self, she sings a song called "What Did I Have That I Don't Have?" I loved that song, with those smart lyrics:

I'm just a victim of time, obsolete in my prime
Out-of-date and outclassed, by my past!

There is no love story between Daisy and the doctor . . . although we find out at the end that in a future life, they will apparently get together. (If this sounds complicated . . . it is.) And when Melinda berates herself for falling in love with Tentrees, Dr. Chabot tries to comfort her, explaining, "A man must be strong enough for you to respect him but weak enough for you to love him."

That was my favorite line from the script, and it's so true. I love strength but it's the vulnerability in a man that goes straight to my heart.

While we were filming in England, there was no time to go antiquing or look in the art galleries, which was frustrating. I had fallen in love with Art Nouveau, and had a growing collection of Art Nouveau glass and furniture and wanted the paintings to go with them! I had already discovered Egon Schiele and Gustav Klimt when I was younger, and they led me to the Vienna Secession movement . . . the Austrian version of Art Nouveau. (Later, I furnished two offices in the Vienna Secession style, with furniture by the architect Josef Hoffmann.)

I didn't know anything about Klimt or Schiele when I first came across their work in a New York gallery. I just responded to it instinctively. They really spoke to me. I can't tell you exactly why or how. I just recognized something in their work. Maybe the fact that both my father's parents came from Austria had something to do with it. And with Schiele, if I had to pin it down, I think I was drawn to the sadness, and the sort of unfinished quality.

I must have asked the dealer in New York to tell me who might have some of their work in London, and the Marlborough Gallery had three pieces, which they kindly brought over to my hotel. One was a painting by Klimt called *Ria Munk on Her Deathbed*. She was only twenty-four years old, in love with a forty-year-old womanizing writer, and when he broke off their engagement, she shot herself. Her mother commissioned this deathbed portrait. She belonged to one of the most prominent Jewish families in Vienna, who were great patrons of Klimt. They recognized the beauty of his art when most of their countrymen dismissed it as depraved.

Marlborough had two watercolors by Schiele, a "Male Nude" and a "Nude with Mauve Stockings." I bought them both, for $8,000 each. And I bought the painting of Ria Munk for $17,500.

That should show you how early this was . . . long before most people were aware of them and way before their prices skyrocketed. Years later I ended up selling all three pieces at various times, for a nice profit . . . but nothing like the multiple millions they would be worth today. It's a good lesson . . . you should never sell art you love. I regret it to this day. It was a stupid decision, made impulsively in an effort to clear the decks and break the hold of possessions.

After London, we flew to New York for more location work and then to Los Angeles in May. The shoot went on longer than expected, which is not unusual, and my contract expired. I had no problem working the extra few days, but I did have one request. I had admired the clear leaded-glass Victorian panels that were used to create a gazebo at the entrance to the casino set, and I said to Howard, "I'll do it for nothing if you give me the glass panels."

"They're yours," he said. He was happy to get rid of them because he had no interest in storing them. I still remember the day the big wooden crates arrived at my house and I eagerly opened them up . . . only to discover that just a few of those panels were real. The rest were fakes, made by the studio, to fill in the gazebo. I hadn't noticed that. (Ah, the magic of movies.) By the way, the studio rented them back from me for five hundred dollars, to use in *The Great White Hope.* I put that money into my original savings account, at Seamen's Bank in New York, which I opened when I still had the third *a* in my name. And I still appreciate the value of five hundred dollars. To me, that's *real* money. I never felt like the salaries I made in the movies were real. (Maybe because I didn't see the checks. They went straight to my business manager.)

On this movie I did get to keep some of my wardrobe. I still have that elegant Madame Recamier dress and the fabulous ivory crepe gown (although the turban was unfortunately destroyed in a flood years later). I gave the rest to an auction to benefit my foundation. I had no more room in my closets.

I should have kept those exquisite costumes. And it's typical of me. I had a hard time seeing the value of those old costumes because I had a hard time seeing my own worth.

At the end of the film I wanted to give Vincente a special gift. I had noticed that he took only cream in his coffee, never sugar. So I found an antique silver coffee service, took away the sugar bowl, and had the pot engraved with the words "To Vincente, whom I adore . . . Love, Barbra," and on the creamer, "You're the cream in my coffee."

Vincente gave me a sketch of Sarah Bernhardt, beautifully framed, and told me that I was destined to play the legendary actress. That was a wonderful surprise. How did he know that I was fascinated with her?

When I was a teenager, researching her in the library, I saw a photograph of her playing Hamlet and thought, *What a great idea . . . a woman playing a man's part.* After all, men played women's parts during Shakespeare's time. I felt inspired and wanted to play all of Sarah's roles.

And you know what? Deep down, I still do.

TWENTY

How Many Singing Prostitutes Do You Know?

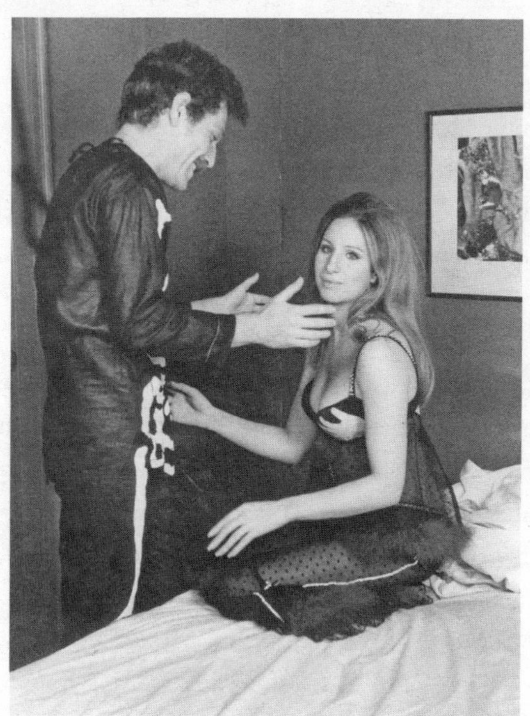

I liked the idea of doing *The Owl and the Pussycat* as soon as Ray Stark suggested it. I had seen the play in London with Alan Alda and Diana Sands, so I already knew the material. I thought it was hip and funny and different from anything I had done before. It was a romantic comedy . . . but with a little less romance and more realism. And the plot was a contemporary take on the old notion that opposites attract. Felix, a mild-mannered would-be writer who actually spends his days working in a bookstore, meets Doris, a brash would-be actress who supplements her meager income by turning tricks, but only part time . . . "I may be a prostitute, but I am *not* promiscuous!"

I've noticed something. If you look at movies from this period (*Klute*, *McCabe and Mrs. Miller*, *Cinderella Liberty*), you might think that the only professions available to a woman were housewife or hooker.

In any event it was a good part. I would finally be playing someone my own age! I could even use my own hair, instead of a wig. And I had an idea. Why not cast Sidney Poitier opposite me? That would preserve the interracial casting that had worked so well onstage. The author of the play, Bill Manhoff, hadn't specified the race of either character, so there was no dialogue that dealt with that issue. I thought that could give us a new opportunity for the movie, so I said, "Let's make it more socially relevant." And it might lead to some funny jokes. Maybe Sidney could belong to this elegant Black family, and when he takes me home for dinner, they're shocked and look down on this trashy white girl. It could have added a whole other layer.

But the studio didn't go for it.

So then I said, "How about Oskar Werner?" I thought he was wonderful in *Ship of Fools*. That would give us a Jewish girl and a German man, and we could play with those stereotypes and make fun of each other. Social commentary is always more palatable when it comes in the form of comedy.

The studio didn't think that was a good idea either.

But no great loss, because we were lucky enough to get the delightful and hilarious George Segal . . . I think he was suggested by his pal Buck Henry, who was writing the screenplay. Buck shifted the setting from San Francisco to New York and wrote fast, funny dialogue that captured the rhythms of the way New Yorkers talk. We didn't have to change a thing. My friend Herb Ross was the director. Once again I had requested that Harry Stradling be the cinematographer, so I felt I was in good hands. And it was great to be back in New York, where we shot the whole movie, beginning in the fall of 1969. I could come home every night to my own apartment.

The only problem I had was Ray, who announced to the newspapers that the character was being rewritten to make her a folk singer in her spare time.

I called him up and said, "Ray, I told you I'm not going to sing in this movie."

I had already done that in three films. I thought it was about time to prove to myself, and the industry, that I could carry a film with my acting alone.

I guess Ray wasn't sure that I could.

He was well aware of my feelings, but he kept feeding false information to the press, telling them I was going to sing four songs . . . just as he had lied earlier, to force me into signing his contract by saying he was going to give the role of Fanny to Anne Bancroft or Carol Burnett. I was furious with him all over again. When a reporter finally asked me if I was going to sing in the movie, my answer was blunt: "How many singing prostitutes do you know?"

Sometimes I wonder . . . did Ray enjoy riling me up? Did it give him some sort of perverse satisfaction to make me angry? I think it was a power struggle between the patriarchal producer and his rising star. Even after I had made my refusal abundantly clear, he still showed up with a song he had commissioned in hopes that I would sing it under the credits, or as background to some sort of montage.

That was the last straw. I said, "Ray, there is *no way* I'm going to sing in this movie!"

And when he tried to make me feel bad . . . as if I were hurting the film by wanting to play the character as originally written . . . I stood my ground and tried to ignore him.

Thank God everyone else associated with the film was more agreeable. I couldn't wait to get to work every morning because I was having such a good time. George and I instinctively had a great rapport, and it enabled us to be very free and spontaneous with each other. He was such a good actor, with a wide range . . . from serious drama in *Who's Afraid of Virginia Woolf?* to pure farce in *Where's Poppa?* And he played banjo in his own jazz band. We became instant friends. I vividly remember the peach pie his wife, Marion, made when I visited them one summer in the Hamptons. It was the best I've ever tasted, with fresh peaches and homemade whipped cream . . . not too sweet.

George and I made each other laugh a lot. It was fun to do some of those crazy scenes . . . like when he crouches behind an aquarium and pretends to be a TV for Doris, who couldn't go to sleep without one. (I'm not even going to attempt to explain. Just watch the DVD.) And I'm wearing that wild outfit . . . lounging pajamas made of black polka-dot net with a pink satin handprint on each breast and "Doris" written in pink satin across my butt. (By the way, that particular ensemble was not the costume designer's idea. It was Buck's. He actually wrote it into the script.)

Most of the film was shot on location . . . out on the streets, in a bar near

Times Square, at the Doubleday bookstore, in an Eighth Avenue thrift shop. So this was the real New York, rather than some sanitized Hollywood version. The city was not in great shape back in 1969. It was gritty and dirty, and that's what we showed. The set for Felix's apartment, with multiple locks on the door, teeny-tiny rooms, and a weird interior window, was reminiscent of my old railroad flat over Oscar's fish restaurant. I drew it for the art director because I was always interested in set design, and he used some of the elements. But Felix's apartment was nicer than mine had been . . . at least the tub wasn't in the kitchen! Still, it was basically decrepit.

And the same realism extended to the script, which was pretty risqué for the time. George had a full-frontal nude scene . . . well, not quite. A conveniently placed desk lamp acted as a fig leaf. After catching him naked, Doris was supposed to laugh, and keep on laughing.

Have you ever tried to laugh for a solid minute, without stopping? It's not easy.

I asked our prop guy, "Is there such a thing as a laugh record, with all different kinds of laughs?"

He said, "I'll see if I can find one."

I played it before every take, because it made me laugh when I heard it. Then I had to pretend to get the hiccups, from laughing so much . . . which was also more challenging than you'd think. It's actually hard on the body to keep hiccuping.

But that was a breeze compared to my anxiety about my own so-called nude scene.

When Herb first asked me if I'd do one, I said, "Absolutely not."

Then he asked, "What about topless?"

This was the era when filmmakers had begun pushing boundaries and seeing how far they could go with nudity, and I guess Herb decided our movie should be one of the first. He wanted me to take off my top and walk over to the bed, where George would be waiting for me. This was the moment when Felix and Doris wind up making love, after they each got evicted from their own apartments and rang the doorbell of Felix's friend . . . played by Robert Klein, a gifted comedian who would open for me later in Las Vegas. His girlfriend, by the way, was played by Marilyn Chambers (billed here as Evelyn Lang), who went on to star in the porn film *Behind the Green Door*. Maybe they should have asked *her* to do the nude scene!

Frankly, I was very uncomfortable with the whole idea, for two reasons. One, I'm shy. Two, What would my mother think?

But I'm an actress who always tries to serve the director's vision, and Herb was very persuasive. He *really* wanted me to do it.

Easy for him to say.

"I'll only do it on one condition," I told him. "That I have the right to kill it if I don't like it."

And he agreed.

The set was cleared, so the only people present were Herb, Harry, and George. George was already in position, lying on the bed, but I was so nervous that I kept discussing the scene with Herb . . . procrastinating, I'll admit. This went on for so long that George actually fell asleep.

I love men. He could take a nap while I was practically hyperventilating.

I told Herb, "I can't do it. Look at my arms. I have goose bumps!"

He just laughed. Nothing was going to change his mind.

"Oh, what the hell," I finally said. "Let's get it over with."

But just before the camera rolled, I took Herb and George aside and pulled them into a closet with me. I took off my top and said, "Here, look at my breasts." It was my un-dress rehearsal. I didn't want to be topless for the first time in front of the camera.

We all came out of the closet. Herb said "Action!" and I tossed off my top and walked across to the bed. "Cut. Print," Herb said. "That was beautiful, Barbra."

When Herb showed me the footage privately the next day, I closed my eyes at first. But then I forced myself to look.

And I killed it. I killed it because I thought it was too real. In other words, there's movie reality, and then there's real reality, and I felt it was too real for a comedy like this. I thought it was a distraction . . . "Oooh, Barbra is showing her breasts" . . . that would hurt the film and step on the humor of the next shot, when Felix burrows under the covers. If you show too much, it can make the audience uncomfortable.

Besides, a ticket to a movie back then only cost $3.50. As I told Herb in jest, "We'd have to charge much more if they're gonna see my breasts!"

He kept his word and gave me the footage.

Even without my topless scene, the film still got an R rating. Apparently I was the first female star to say the word "fuck" on-screen. Actually it was "Fuck off!" . . .

spoken to a bunch of guys catcalling Doris as she and Felix are walking down the steps at Lincoln Center. After she has the nerve to challenge them, they get out of their car and chase us into the parking garage, where we manage to lose them.

I think we did an alternate version with the words "Up yours!" for TV. But on the DVD, for some unknown reason, they chose to cut out the line entirely, so now the violent reaction from the men makes no sense. I had never watched the DVD, and only looked at it now to write this chapter. Too bad. I would have tried to get that line back in. I thought it was funny . . . and real!

We shot the last scene of the film in Sheep Meadow in Central Park, where I had given my free concert eighteen months earlier. It was an intense scene . . . Felix and Doris get into a fight and then forgive each other, and George and I both had to go through a spectrum of emotions. I was having a hard time crying as we did take after take. And the later it got, the more distracted I became, because I knew I had to get dressed up and appear at the *Hello, Dolly!* premiere in a few hours, and I wasn't looking forward to it.

I thought Buck did a wonderful job writing the moment when Doris and Felix finally reconcile. They pretend that they're meeting for the first time and start all over again, this time with no pretenses. And the final shot has them going off to look for an apartment together. "Who knows?" says Felix. "We might even find a place with a television set."

"{Streisand and Segal's} rapport has a beautiful, worked-out professionalism. Were Hepburn and Tracy this good together, even at their best, as in Pat and Mike*? Maybe, but they weren't* better. *Segal is a very unusual actor: he never does anything wrong. You never catch him out in a false gesture or doing things his character wouldn't do . . . Streisand, who is easily the best comedienne now working in American movies . . . has the instinct and the discipline to control her phenomenal vitality. She is like thousands of girls one sees in the subway, but more so; she is both the archetype and an original, and that's what makes a star."*

—PAULINE KAEL, *THE NEW YORKER*

Most of the reviews were really positive. And the public liked the movie as well. *The Owl and the Pussycat* was the tenth-highest-grossing film of the year. The only shadow over the whole experience happened three weeks before the end of the shoot, when my beloved Harry Stradling felt too ill to continue and had to leave. I was so worried about him, because he had already had a heart attack several years before we did *Funny Girl.* Harry flew home to Los Angeles, and Ray brought in Andrew Laszlo to take over (and I'm sure Harry told him exactly what to do, because he faithfully replicated Harry's style).

It felt odd to be working with someone else. Nobody could replace Harry. He was so much more than a cinematographer to me . . . he was a cherished friend and a mentor and a father figure. I was so blessed to have him behind the camera. I trusted him implicitly and I genuinely loved him.

Harry left in December, and on February 14 he had another heart attack and died, just hours after he was nominated for his fourteenth Oscar, for *Hello, Dolly!* He was only sixty-eight years old.

I was devastated. I can still hear his distinctive, nasal voice: "Boys, raise the camera two inches." I wish we had had the chance to do an independent film together, as he'd suggested. That would have been a wonderful experience.

At least I had something else to occupy my mind. On January 27, just a week after we finished filming, I was on my way to Canada to see Pierre Trudeau.

TWENTY-ONE

The Prime Minister

After our initial meeting at the *Funny Girl* premiere in London, Prime Minister Pierre Trudeau sent a lovely note to congratulate me on winning the Oscar. That was back in April 1969, and I sent him a note in return to thank him. We spoke a few times but couldn't manage to get together again, because I was busy shooting *Clear Day*. And he was busy running a country.

Then, when I was in New York that November filming *The Owl and the Pussycat*, he flew down to see me . . . and meet with U Thant, the secretary-general of the United Nations. I was very impressed. Pierre was deeply engaged in world affairs. He was operating at a whole different level than anyone else I knew, and that intrigued me.

He wanted to take me to dinner, wherever I would like to go.

Well, definitely not to some chic hot spot! I love to eat but I don't like being watched while I'm doing it. I was looking for something private, with just a few tables, and had read about Casa Brasil, a small, intimate restaurant in an Upper East Side brownstone where there was no printed menu and only two seatings each evening, so you had to reserve in advance. And you ate whatever the woman who owned it was serving that night. I remember an appetizer of hearts of palm, then roast duckling, and when she said there was tapioca for dessert, I was taken straight back to my childhood. I hate Jell-O, and couldn't eat junket (ugh!), but every so often my mother made tapioca, which I loved. But when this tapioca arrived, I was aghast. The normally pearly white beads were bright red, because they had been cooked in red wine. I prefer my tapioca the traditional way, straight from the box. And it should take only a minute to cook (it's not called Minute Tapioca for nothing!).

Any nervousness I may have felt quickly evaporated, because Pierre was so easy to talk to. We had a good time. Afterward in the car on the way to drop me off at my apartment, he took my hand, and my first thought was, *Oh my God!* All I could think was how my mother used to scare me, telling me not to hold hands with a boy . . . as if I might catch some infection. I was still so old-fashioned.

On another night I took Pierre to my favorite Chinese restaurant, a little dive on the corner of Bayard Street and the Bowery in Chinatown, where there were all kinds of strange things on the menu, like little birds with their heads still on. I always ordered the snails in black bean sauce . . . not those big French snails with lots of garlic (which are delicious, don't get me wrong). These were different . . . cooked in delicate Chinese spices and so tiny you had to use a toothpick to pry them out. Most of the customers were Chinese, and I loved that nobody recognized us . . . they were too busy eating!

Pierre loved the place as well. He was so elegant, yet totally unpretentious and perpetually curious . . . an adventurer who had backpacked through the

Middle East and Asia as a young man. And he had real charisma, generating so much excitement before and after his election that the Canadian press gave it a name . . . Trudeaumania.

Many women found him attractive, and so did I. He had a great smile and cheekbones that could have been carved in marble. And it was nice to be with a man who had his own light shining on him, so I could stay in the shadows a bit.

One night he came to my apartment, and I made dinner for him myself. I had taken cooking lessons with a Persian woman, but I only had time for a few, so my repertoire was limited. In fact, it consisted of exactly three dishes . . . moussaka, Persian rice, and chocolate soufflé (my favorite) . . . so that's what I served. He was very impressed. So was I! (This was the first, and probably the last, time I cooked a serious meal for somebody.)

It was easier to just stay home with Pierre, because whenever we went out, we risked being swarmed by paparazzi. He took it all in stride. Later on, when one reporter shouted, "How long have you known Barbra?" Pierre shouted back, "Not long enough!"

Once I was done filming *The Owl and the Pussycat*, I had more free time, and Pierre wanted me to come to Ottawa and accompany him to a gala celebrating the centennial of the province of Manitoba. I wasn't sure I was ready to share our relationship with the public, but he didn't have any such qualms. And before he went into politics, Pierre had been a lawyer and a law professor, so he knew how to make a very persuasive case for himself.

Still, I was hesitant. I remember standing in my kitchen with Elliott, who had come over to see Jason, and discussing it with him.

I said, "He's come to see me several times, so now it's my turn. But I don't know what to do. Should I go or not?"

Elliott said, "You should go."

And that basically confirmed what I was already thinking . . . it would be interesting to see this man on his own turf. But I was a little nervous about making the trip alone. I asked Pierre if I could bring a friend . . . kind of like a chaperone, because it felt as if I were going to be presented at court. He said, "Of course." So I flew to Ottawa with Cis by my side. We were invited to stay at the official residence, and as we drove up to the gate, I noticed the address . . .

24 Sussex Drive. *Oh my God*, I thought, *this is meant to be* . . . twenty-four, my lucky number.

Pierre had arranged for Cis to be escorted to the gala by one of his staff. We were all at the house, getting ready to leave, and I was the last one to emerge from my room. I remember the moment, because Cis described it often over the years: "When you appeared at the top of the stairs dressed all in white, from head to toe, you should have seen the look on his face. His eyes bulged, and his mouth dropped. You were like some fabulous snow queen, and he couldn't take his eyes off you as you walked down the steps."

That was a beautiful outfit . . . an Empire-style cream wool gown with a short jacket, trimmed on the collar and cuffs in cream-colored fur, with a matching fur hat and muff . . . sort of like Anna Karenina. Arnold Scaasi had made it for me, based on my sketch. I wanted a muff for two reasons: one, I always loved the way they looked in period films, and two, they gave you a place to put your hands and keep them warm. (It's cold in Canada!) I wore muffs a lot back then, and always asked Arnold to put a zipper in the lining so I could tuck in a lipstick, a tiny mirror, and a hankie . . . and then the muff could double as a purse.

Pierre looked very attractive in black tie, with his signature red rose pinned to his lapel. I felt a flutter of excitement.

When we arrived at the National Arts Centre, Pierre jumped out of the car almost before it had stopped and came around to the other side, just so he could personally open the door for me. From that moment on, it seemed as if all eyes were upon us.

I felt a little like Jackie Kennedy as I walked into the auditorium on the arm of this distinguished man, the leader of his country.

He was greeting people on all sides . . . everyone was eager to have a word with him . . . and when we eventually made our way to the royal box to take our seats, the whole audience stood up. It was thrilling, like something out of a fairy tale . . . he was the prince and I was the princess, for that night. Then the lights dimmed for a performance by the Royal Winnipeg Ballet, and he held my hand in the dark. (This time, I wasn't thinking about my mother!)

After the curtain calls, we were whisked backstage to congratulate the dancers. That was an unexpected role reversal for me. I was used to being the performer, waiting politely in a receiving line to be greeted by the VIPs. Now suddenly I was on the other side.

The next day I attended a session of Parliament and watched Pierre field questions as deftly as if he were batting back tennis balls. At one point a member of the opposition party announced, "I should like to ask a question of the prime minister—if he can take his eyes and mind off the visitors' gallery long enough to answer it." That provoked a burst of laughter from the room, and Pierre blushed. I blushed, too, and laughed at the same time. It was a heady moment and one I'll never forget.

I also remember a delicious lunch of oyster stew back at the official residence, with just the two of us. (He gave me all his oyster crackers, which made me like him even more.) And that night Pierre gave a dinner for me with about thirty guests. He wanted me to meet his friends and some local artists. When it got to be 10:00 p.m., I was kind of shocked when everyone got up to leave. Was it something I said? No, as I found out when I asked an aide. As a matter of course, guests were always given a departure time beforehand. Pierre had a tight schedule and he was very disciplined about keeping to it.

Later that night I mentioned to Pierre that I sometimes wished guests wouldn't stay quite so long, but I'd never have the nerve to tell them so up front. He laughed and said, "Sometimes protocol comes in handy. And anyway, I'd rather be with you." (Good answer!)

I was charmed when I saw that his bedtime snack was a glass of milk and a few Mallomars. He offered the cookies to me, and I took one, but I pulled off the chocolate-covered marshmallow top because I only wanted the graham cracker bottom.

Soon after that visit he asked me up again, for a weekend at his country house. This time I came by myself. We drove to his official retreat on Harrington Lake, and it felt as if we were leaving the rest of the world behind. It was a big, rambling cottage overlooking the water. He pointed out a little house on stilts he had built and said it was a sauna. He was eager to show it off, so after we unpacked I found myself walking through the snow with him to take a sauna. After I had been sitting there for a while, modestly wrapped in a towel, he said, "Now we have to go into the water."

What??? That was never going to happen. As you know, my swimming skills leave a lot to be desired. And this was a freezing-cold lake. I'm a wimp. I won't even put my toe in a pool unless it's warmer than 86 degrees.

"Come on!" he said. "Don't you want to try it?"

"No thank you."

So I sat on a bench, shivering in my fur coat, and watched Pierre dive naked into the icy lake. Oh my God! And then he topped it off by coming out and rolling around in the snow. Apparently going from extreme heat to extreme cold is good for your circulation and the whole cardiovascular system. (I'm not convinced.)

My mother would have been horrified. She barely allowed me to go out in the snow, because I'd catch a cold. And she had frightened me to death about swimming. So Pierre's willingness to leap right in was part of what made him so attractive to me. He was an outdoorsman. He had climbed mountains! And then, of course, there was his mind. Obviously, he was my superior intellectually, and I've always loved being with people who can teach me something.

Pierre was the head of the Liberal Party and ahead of his time. He reformed Canada's laws on abortion and legalized homosexuality, declaring, "the state has no place in the bedrooms of the nation." He was a globalist in the best sense of the word, a strategic thinker who understood that we're all connected. He was one of the first Western leaders to establish diplomatic relations with Communist China, stating, "We are not so much threatened by fascist or Communist ideologies or even nuclear bombs as by the fact that two-thirds of the world goes to bed hungry every night." He believed in multiculturalism and managed to defuse the French separatist movement in Quebec, reunifying the nation. And he strengthened the laws on gun control.

Pierre was a proud progressive, and I loved his politics and was in awe of his accomplishments. I remember one afternoon . . . I was lying with my head on his lap, while he was reading official papers and I was reading a script. I thought to myself, *This is bliss!*

My fantasy was I would move to Canada and *really* learn French, so I could speak to all those French Canadians. I would campaign for him and become totally involved in all his political causes. And I'd only do movies made in Canada because, after all, I would never dream of asking him to move to LA. His life was more important than mine. My work might give people some pleasure, but his work was important to the whole world!

I think another reason that I was drawn to him was because he was like my father, both an athlete and a scholar, which is so rare.

But he was also old enough to be my father. Pierre was fifty, and I was twenty-seven, and that felt a little odd to me. And when he began to get more serious, the fantasy bumped up against reality. I didn't know how to deal with someone who was at such a different stage in his life and clearly thinking it was time he got married. I was just coming out of a marriage and not ready to jump into another. I'm pretty sure he wanted a wife and children of his own. I already had a son, and I was reluctant to take him so far away from his father. Also, after I had had such a rough time giving birth to Jason, the doctors had warned me that it would be a risk to have another child.

Frankly, I was a bit scared of the intensity of this relationship.

And I was in the midst of a thriving career. Did I really want to step away from it now and devote myself to a man? I was torn, but deep down I knew that the answer was no. I was not willing to give up the work that challenged and sustained me, for anybody.

So I fled to Los Angeles, to put more distance between us. Thank God I had somewhere to live. I had bought the house I had been renting on Carolwood because I was basically too lazy to move my clothes. And maybe subconsciously I knew I'd wind up in LA eventually. When Marty and I first visited, it just felt right to me. And I was tired of walking with my head down, hunched over against the freezing wind during the New York winters. Even in my Central Park West apartment, the building turned off the heat at 10:00 p.m., so I was always cold. I had to buy portable electric heaters and move them from room to room. And the amount I had already paid to rent the Carolwood house went toward the purchase price, so that seemed like a good deal.

Back in my own world, the whole episode with Trudeau began to seem more and more like a dream.

I admired Pierre so much. He was someone I could completely respect . . . a statesman, a visionary, an iconoclast. He was a captivating combination of contradictions . . . an elegant man who was still enough of a free spirit to wear sandals to Parliament. No matter what he said or did, he was always articulate and graceful, always dignified. But for me, there was something missing. My brain was in love, but not my body.

I feel very privileged to have known him, and we stayed in touch for over thirty years. When he bought a historic Art Deco house in Montreal, built in 1930, he called me, because I was the one who had introduced him to the style. I had shared pictures of the Art Deco house I was building out in Malibu, and now he wanted to share his house with me. He was so proud of it and said, "I have the real thing! Come and see it." I never managed to get up to Montreal, but he came down to New York several times, where he escorted me to a United Jewish Appeal gala in my honor in 1983. And in 1994 I invited him to an Elie Wiesel Foundation dinner, where I was giving a speech to honor Hillary Clinton.

Pierre served as prime minister for over fifteen years, and in recognition of his efforts to stop the proliferation of nuclear weapons around the globe, he was awarded the Albert Einstein Peace Prize.

In 2000 I heard he was ill and wrote him a note telling him how much our relationship meant to me. When he died later that year, the world lost a great leader . . . and I lost a great friend.

Fast forward to 2003, when Jim was playing Ronald Reagan in a miniseries that was shooting in Montreal. Whoopi Goldberg kindly lent me her bus and her drivers so Renata Buser (my amazing personal assistant and my right hand since 1974), my three-month-old puppy, Samantha, and I could drive across the country to visit him. (Yes, I spent three days on a bus to get from Los Angeles to Montreal. That's how much I hate flying . . . and so does Whoopi.)

I always regretted not seeing Pierre's house sooner, and this was my chance to remedy that. A visit was arranged, and when Jim and I rang the bell, the front door was opened by a good-looking, dark-haired young man . . . This was the first time I met Pierre's eldest son, Justin. He showed us around, pointing out the details as his father would have done. Pierre spent years restoring the Maison Cormier to its original condition, and now it's a National Historic Site. Then we sat down and talked with Justin about his father. I felt sad and happy at the same time, because it was very moving to be there with his son.

Justin and I kept in touch. In March 2006, he and his wife, Sophie, whom he had married the year before, came to dinner at our house in Malibu. Sophie was an entertainment reporter, in town for the Oscars, and I thought she was delightful. What a lovely couple! Seven months later, when I was doing a concert tour with a stop in Montreal, I invited them both to come, and they sat in the front row. I told the audience that Sophie and Justin were there and took a moment to reminisce about his father.

And then when I went back to Montreal on another concert tour in 2012, they were again in the audience. By now they had two children, and when they came backstage after the show, they brought me a copy of *Maclean's* magazine with Justin on the cover. The article inside called him Canada's "most popular politician." I could see why. He's smart and charming, just like his father.

Three nights later, performing in Ottawa, I said, "Ottawa brings back a lot of memories," and talked about my trip there in 1970 to see Pierre Trudeau. And I told the audience how much I admired his son Justin: "He is so full of progressive ideas for the people and for this wonderful country, so who knows? He may be occupying Twenty-Four Sussex Drive himself in a few years!"

I felt so proud when Justin was elected prime minister of Canada in 2015. (Like all the nice Jewish boys back in Brooklyn, he went into his father's business!) Justin is a forward-thinking politician who wants to bring out the best in people. He has that quality that's so essential in a true leader . . . humility. He's kind, he's compassionate, and he cares more about the people than the corporations. Pierre would have been so proud of him.

TWENTY-TWO

A Screwball Comedy

In the spring of 1970, after doing four movies one right after the other, I really had no desire to go back to work. Even though I always had Jason with me on the set, he was now three years old and I just wanted to stay home with him and see what it felt like to have a normal life . . . to make pancakes for him, to play games, to sit outside and read to him and feel the sun on my face, rather than the glare of the spotlight.

There were certain public appearances I couldn't avoid, like the Oscars. It's a tradition that the winner of the Best Actress Award comes back the following year to present Best Actor, so in April I stood onstage and handed the gold statue to John Wayne. Then, days later, I was onstage in New York, where I was presented with an honorary Tony Award as Star of the Decade. This meant a lot to me, because it was given by the theater community, which had adopted me early on, so I felt very grateful.

But it was no wonder I was tired. I was juggling two careers . . . as an actress and a singer . . . and while I was making four movies I had also been recording five albums (and that doesn't include three soundtracks). Obviously, the more time I spent on films, the less time I had for my music.

In 1967, when I looked at the schedule for filming *Funny Girl*, it was clear that I would be occupied for at least seven months. So Marty and I decided to squeeze in some sessions for a new album in March, before I left to begin the picture. That album was *Simply Streisand*, and I have so little memory of it that I had to call Marty and ask him how it came about.

"That was my idea," he said. "I love those old standards."

So this one had classics like "My Funny Valentine" and "More Than You Know." I didn't usually record hits. My attitude was, let other people do that. I did want to sing "I'll Know" (from *Guys and Dolls*), but some of the other choices didn't interest me and my heart wasn't in it.

It took decades for this album to go Gold, meaning to sell five hundred thousand copies or more. That was unusual, as Marty reminded me, "because all of your first seven albums went Gold almost immediately." I broke that streak with *Simply Streisand*, which I did for Marty, and the album right before it, *Je m'appelle Barbra*, which I did for me.

Meanwhile, Goddard Lieberson had put Clive Davis in charge at Columbia Records, and Clive was pushing me to be more contemporary. Rock and roll dominated the airwaves, and I was the same age as these new artists, but as Clive saw it, I was stuck in a time warp, singing old songs. I could see he had a point. So in 1969, I switched gears and released *What About Today?* with music by singer-songwriters like Paul Simon, Jimmy Webb, and John Lennon and Paul McCartney . . . even though I wasn't sure what I could add to these songs.

On the back of the album, I wrote that it was "dedicated to the young people who push against indifference, shout down mediocrity, demand a better future, and who write and sing the songs of today."

But if the album was meant to appeal to those young people, you certainly couldn't tell from the cover . . . a Richard Avedon photo in which I looked more like Colette than a fellow rebel out on the streets, storming the ramparts. I already had that picture, and since it was good, I thought, *Use it.* Easier than doing another photo shoot. But if I was trying to be contemporary, I probably shouldn't have looked like a Parisian from the nineteenth century.

And the selection of songs conveyed a similarly mixed message. I had fun doing "With a Little Help from My Friends," in an almost jazzy version where I played with the rhythm, slowing it down and then speeding it up, improvising and talking back to the lyrics. That was modern, but then the next cut was Burt Bacharach and Hal David's "Alfie," the kind of gorgeous ballad I used to sing when I was just starting out.

As Marty told me after *What About Today?* was released, Clive felt the album didn't go far enough. He thought I still sounded like a Broadway singer because of the traditional arrangements. And he was right . . . though I didn't know there was anything wrong with being "a Broadway singer." (I guess they don't sell many records.)

Apparently Clive wasn't enthusiastic about my next venture either . . . an album I was already working on called *The Singer,* inspired by Kurt Weill and Bertolt Brecht. I had been intrigued by their particular brand of satirical political theater ever since I saw *The Seven Deadly Sins* at City Center in New York when I was sixteen. It was like nothing I had ever experienced . . . a "sung ballet" directed and choreographed by George Balanchine, with Weill's score, Brecht's libretto, and Lotte Lenya in the lead role of Anna. And then there was a ballerina playing her mirror image, as if the character were split in two. (You can see why I found that fascinating.) I wanted to do something with that same sense of mystery and depth, to explore that German Expressionist bitterness and angst.

Let's just say Clive did not share my excitement. In fact, he told Marty in no uncertain terms that I should drop that idea.

But there's a side note to this story. In September 1975, I received a letter from the great George Balanchine himself:

Dear Miss Streisand,

For sometime now my associate Lincoln Kirstein and I have wanted to revive my production of Kurt Weill's Seven Deadly Sins *. . . but always there is a* *problem with finding a singer who has projection, diction, range, looks and can act.*

I know your work and you are the only one who could do the role of "Anna." In truth, I would only consider reviving this work if you agreed to sing it.

Imagine how thrilling it was to read that!

So what did I do? I wrote back:

Dear Mr. Balanchine,

Thank you for your warm and wonderful letter. One of the most memorable performances I have ever seen was your production of Seven Deadly Sins *with Lotte Lenya . . .*

I find it an honor and a great compliment that you would consider me for your revival.

But unfortunately I had to turn him down, because I was already completely immersed in preproduction for *A Star Is Born*, which was going to start shooting in a few months.

This is typical of me. I get so obsessed with my current project that anything else feels like a distraction . . . and I lost this opportunity. I would have loved to work with Balanchine. I should have tried harder to make it happen.

But I have to be honest . . . there was a part of me that was relieved to be unavailable, because I also remember a feeling of insecurity. I wasn't at all sure that I could live up to what I had seen Lenya do. She was magnificent, she *was* that character, and frankly, I didn't think I could ever be as good.

Anyway, I guess the mere thought of me singing in the style of Weill and Brecht made Clive shudder. That was not his idea of "contemporary." He wanted to put me together with a hip young producer, Richard Perry, to see if we could come up with a hip new sound.

I thought, *Okay, let me try it.* I was open to suggestions . . . as long as he didn't try to turn me into something I was not. Just because something was popular didn't mean it was good for me! And I was always a bit leery of commercial success, even my own. It made me worry . . . was I losing my edge? I liked having a small, special following.

Still, I was willing to go in a new direction. I wanted to stretch myself. And I liked Richard from the moment we met. He was tall and lanky, with a mop of dark, curly hair and a big smile, which matched his big heart. For the first time I was working with a producer my own age . . . we were both twenty-eight and both born in Brooklyn. We became fast friends.

Richard had a knack for matching the right song to the right artist, and he had a clear idea of where he wanted to take me musically. At our first meeting he arrived laden with songs, and we listened to them together. Whatever hesitation I may have felt about our collaboration soon vanished and I thought, *This could be fun . . . and musically liberating.*

He brought me Joni Mitchell's "I Don't Know Where I Stand" and Harry Nilsson's "Maybe." And then one day he brought me Randy Newman. Randy sat down at the piano, and I remember thinking he was such an intriguing person, with a quirky charm. And his lyrics were as unusual as he was:

Maybe I'll write you a letter, maybe I'll give you a call.
Maybe I'll drop you a line when I'm feelin' better
Maybe I won't after all . . .

(Maybe that song should have been called "Maybe.")

It was actually called "Let Me Go," and Randy's own version had sort of a laid-back quality. But Richard and I felt that it would be interesting to try a more bluesy approach that reminded me of Bessie Smith.

And then there was Laura Nyro. Richard was an early fan, and we chose three of her songs, including "Stoney End." I remember singing it at the first recording session for the album, which, as Richard reminds me, started at 7:00 p.m. and finished at 5:30 in the morning. I'm a night person, and working long hours was nothing new to me. But Richard tells me it was the longest session in the history of the Los Angeles Musicians Union. Well, we did do five songs (half the album!) that night, and nobody complained (unheard-of, Richard says).

Actually, it's kind of ironic that "Stoney End" became the title of the album, because that song was not an easy fit for me. I had to put my head into a different space and I had no idea what it was about. The lyrics were baffling. What did "going down the stoney end" even mean? It seemed kind of grim, and yet the melody was up-tempo, so that was confusing.

And Richard wanted me to sing on the beat, which is always hard for me, because it doesn't allow me to phrase as freely as I usually do.

I said, "I can't do this! I have to sing it the way I feel it." That was one of those moments when I was ready to chuck the whole thing.

Richard refused to accept that. "I know you can do it," he kept saying. "Just try."

Easier said than done. It felt like he was holding my feet to the flames. But eventually, gritting my teeth, I found a way to do it so it would feel relatively natural to me.

Before "Stoney End" was released as a single, Richard and I made a bet about whether it would be a hit. He said yes, I said no. And then we happened to be driving down Sunset Boulevard together when the DJ on the radio announced that it was number 1 in Los Angeles. What a great way to lose!

Happily the album went on to become a big success as well, quickly going Gold. Clive and Columbia were thrilled. Richard and I worked together on a follow-up album, *Barbra Joan Streisand*, which included more songs by Laura Nyro, Carole King, John Lennon, and Burt Bacharach and Hal David . . . and it, too, went Gold.

That Gold was gratifying. And I had proved something to myself . . . I *could* change with the times.

But I didn't perform "Stoney End" again till many years later. Whenever I was planning a concert, my team would beg me to sing it . . . "The fans will go wild!" But I always backed away, because I never felt truly comfortable with that song. It really didn't register with me that it was important to sing my hits.

Finally, after much cajoling, I tried a snippet of it at the Hollywood Bowl in 2012. It was the last show of my *Back to Brooklyn* tour, and my team was right . . . the crowd *did* go wild.

More recently, an interesting thing happened when we were discussing songs for my Hyde Park concert, in 2019. For years everyone has been singing this version of the first verse:

I was born from love, and my poor mother worked the mines
I was raised on the good book Jesus, 'till I read between the lines.
Now I don't believe I want to see the morning . . .

I sang it, too, even though I never understood it. (What mines? What lines?) But now, Jay Landers discovered that Laura had also written an alternate version:

I was born from love, and I was raised on golden rules
'till the love of a winsome Johnny taught me love was made for fools
Now I don't believe I want to see the morning . . .

Ohhh, so she got her heart broken! Forty-nine years later, I could finally relate to the lyric.

Back to 1970. Actually, the success that really made me happy that year was not mine, but Elliott's. When I presented the Best Actor Award at the Oscars, Elliott was there as well. But not as my escort . . . this time he was invited in his own right, as one of the nominees for Best Supporting Actor for his role in *Bob & Carol & Ted & Alice.* I was thrilled for him. Finally, he had broken through, even though he was not the usual leading man, but something different . . . maybe not conventionally handsome, but endearing, with a wicked sense of humor.

After all, I wouldn't have married a schnook!

I was disappointed when he didn't win, but it hardly mattered because by then *M.A.S.H.* had been released, and it was another huge hit. In September he was on the cover of *Time* magazine with the banner headline: STAR FOR AN UPTIGHT AGE. That was a pivotal moment in his career. I loved that he was no longer living in the shadow of my success. He had his own.

It kept him so busy that he didn't see Jason as much as I would have liked. I wanted them to have a strong bond, and I always tried to make sure that Jason's image of his father was positive.

I was a little wary when Elliott asked me to invest a chunk of money in the production company he formed with Jack Brodsky, whom we knew as a publicist for Ray Stark. But I wanted to show my support, so I did it, thinking I'd never see a penny back. And guess what? They made one picture that was a hit . . . Woody Allen's *Everything You Always Wanted to Know About Sex.* So to this day I get checks. I think they're more than I get from *Funny Girl.*

This was a heady moment for Elliott. And in the midst of various offers, one stood out. Ingmar Bergman wanted him to be in his next movie, *The Touch*, with Bibi Andersson and Max von Sydow. It would be Bergman's first English-language film, and his first with an American actor. And he chose Elliott. Now that really impressed me.

I saw my first Bergman film, *The Seventh Seal*, at the Astor Theatre when I was in high school. I was mesmerized by it and still remember the man in the hood . . . what a powerful image . . . stark and mysterious. And then I saw *Wild Strawberries.* I remember the clock without hands and the coffin tumbling out onto the street. And then the hand reaching out . . .

It's as if these images bypass the conscious mind and go right into the subconscious. You can never forget them. Later I read that a lot of those visions came straight out of Bergman's dreams.

When Elliott invited me to come visit while he was shooting in Sweden, I had to go. Who could turn down a chance to meet Bergman?

And when I stepped off the plane, there he was! He had driven out to the airport with Elliott and Liv Ullmann to pick me up. And he scooped me up in his arms and gave me a big hug. It was so generous and kind, as if we were already friends. And that's indicative of the man. He had a wide embrace . . . for people and ideas and life.

I spent several days on the set watching him direct. At one point, I saw him kneel down at Elliott's feet . . . out of the frame of the shot . . . and literally talk to him as the camera was rolling to catch an emotional moment and get the reaction he wanted.

It was such a simple, intimate technique, and it worked so well. (Twelve years later, when I was directing my first film, *Yentl*, I used it with Amy Irving for the wedding-night scene.)

It was fascinating to be on Bergman's set, and it was bringing up all sorts of emotions in me. I wanted to work with Bergman myself, and I had a whole new respect for Elliott. But this moment together in Stockholm was complicated.

We had been separated for over a year. But now we were staying in the same hotel room, sleeping in the same bed. Why had Elliott invited me to come? He was probably proud to introduce Bergman to me, but was it also about us? I think we both were unsure about what was going to happen next. After all, we had a son we both adored. I had grown up without a father and I didn't want that for Jason.

It was that last moment of connection before you decide . . .

I was confused by all the contradictory feelings that were coursing through me. I remember going with Elliott to Max von Sydow's house for a dinner party, and it was very isolated and scary there at night. Suddenly I got an asthma attack and had to leave.

Amazing how the body works. Maybe I just knew deep inside that my marriage was over.

Then, when I was sitting on the plane to go back to New York and, as usual, feeling nervous about flying, there was a delay. The pilot announced that it was a mechanical issue and they needed a part. I watched through the window as a guy on a bicycle rode off to get it and thought, *This is not a good sign. Should I get off this plane and go on another?*

But what if that next plane was destined to crash? I better stay put.

And at that moment of commitment, once again the universe conspired to assist me. It so happened that the woman sitting next to me was a well-known psychiatrist, and we started a conversation. She made it possible for me to stay on that plane and not have an anxiety attack. I think we talked for the whole nine-hour flight . . . about relationships . . . letting go . . . my fear of being alone . . . and my feelings for Elliott.

Years later he told me he hadn't realized that this was his last chance with me.

In any event, neither of us chose to take it.

And while we're on the subject of Bergman, let me jump ahead because I've heard stories that I asked him to make a film version of *The Merry Widow*, when in fact the opposite was true. He asked me, in a letter he wrote on December 10, 1972.

Frankly, it never would have occurred to me to do *The Merry Widow*. I might have caught a glimpse of the old movie, with Jeanette MacDonald and Maurice Chevalier, but I never thought of it for me. The idea was his alone . . . he had directed the operetta in 1954 and had "always loved it," as he wrote to me. "The music is of highest quality . . . and the story is very clever . . . It has a wonderful flavor of Vienna and Paris at the turn of the century, and a lot of tenderness and humour."

He continued, "I will make the picture if Barbra Streisand agrees."

I wasn't at all sure about the subject matter . . . it sounded a little old-fashioned. But I would have done *anything* with him. We talked on the telephone. His whole approach was very generous. He referred to me as his collaborator.

Six months later he sent me a second letter, and said he was working on the screenplay and "it proceeds nicely." He thought it would be a good idea to meet when he was finished, so we could both have "the script in our hands, so we can discuss the facts of life and art." I couldn't wait!

A month later I got a third letter, updating me on his progress. He mentioned a dinner with Dino De Laurentiis, who was apparently willing to finance the film. Bergman told me he would be finished with the script in another four months and asked me to keep my schedule clear to shoot it, beginning in August 1974. And in the last paragraph, he wrote, "I'm often sleepless, and then I get out of my bed in to my study and sit down in my nice comfortable chair looking at the sea and the sunrise and listening to music. The night of July 14 there was a concert with Barbra Streisand for nearly an hour. I felt very happy and grateful."

I could picture him sitting there, and I was so touched that the music that made him happy was mine.

And then he sent me the first act of his screenplay. I thought it was brilliant . . . bawdy and delicious. The opening scene was in a tavern where the men were bending the women over chairs . . . very sexually free and open. After all these years I still remember that image. Once again the visuals were so strong.

I loved it, and I told him so.

Then he sent me the second act, and it was disappointing. Many things that had already been set up in the first act were basically repeated. The story didn't go anywhere. It just didn't feel right to me yet.

We talked on the phone, and I told him how I felt . . . that the second act needed work. I thought we would continue the discussion and fix the problems. I was eager to be directed by him. I trusted him instinctively. And I told him about something I had been working on . . . my idea to do a film based on a short story by Isaac Bashevis Singer, "Yentl, the Yeshiva Boy."

About a week after that conversation, I received a very thoughtful and lovely fourth letter from him, saying,

> *I really feel that your attitude is very generous when you say that you are ready to leave yourself in my hands. But dear Barbra, if you don't feel any real enthusiasm for the part, it is much better to be realistic and drop our cooperation this time.*
>
> *On the other hand, I have a suggestion. I am ready to discuss another project with you (why not the very interesting story you told me). I would like very much to work together with you in a picture of common vital interest and stimulating enthusiasm.*

I was heartbroken, because I didn't want him to drop *The Merry Widow.* All it needed was some tinkering in the second act, just like any other first draft. But I guess he didn't want to rewrite it. He probably thought it was fine and was just withdrawing politely. I tried to tell him not to give up so easily, but then the financing fell apart. And Bergman decided to put the project aside.

I'll always wonder what the film could have been, because he got such rich performances out of the actresses who were his muses . . . Ingrid Thulin . . . Bibi Andersson . . . Liv Ullmann. They revealed so much of themselves on-screen, and I'm sure that had something to do with his skill as a director . . . looking to go deeper.

Bergman understood the beauty of stillness. Over and over again, he managed to create so many quiet yet compelling moments. He had a profound sense of truth, and that's what I respond to on-screen.

It felt as if our paths crossed again at the 1984 Academy Awards, but only spiritually, because I didn't attend the ceremony, and neither did he. *Fanny and Alexander* was up for various awards and so was *Yentl*, which I had finally managed to make after fifteen years. That felt very humbling, and I was honored. It was my first film and one of his last.

I was always in awe of him, and still am. His impact is immense, and his influence is universal. Bergman had a unique vision and a distinctive style . . .

strong and simple, in mostly black and white . . . very minimalist. His imagination was vast, and the images he conjured up will live forever.

Back again to 1970 and the reality of my own personal life. I was depressed. My relationships were not going well. I wanted to find a teacher or a businessman, someone not in show business.

But one night at a dinner party at a friend's house, I met Ryan O'Neal. I think Sue Mengers had brought him—he was one of her clients—and he fancied me and asked her for my number. Ryan had just made *Love Story* with Ali McGraw, and he called and invited me to a screening. He was funny and charming and didn't take anything too seriously, including himself. Of course it didn't hurt that he was very pleasant to look at.

We started seeing each other, and it was kind of a new dynamic for me . . . easy and casual. I remember a moment early on when he told me, "I love you," and I said, "What do you mean? You don't know me."

Trust me to be so literal.

Meanwhile, he was very attentive. I was having fun with him. He brought some laughter into my life.

And then something happened that shattered my equilibrium. I got a call from John Calley, the head of production at Warner Bros., who was a lovely man and a good friend. He told me that Elliott, who was just a few days into shooting his new movie, *A Glimpse of Tiger*, had had some sort of breakdown. Apparently he had fought with the director, threatened his costar, and was now refusing to show up on set. So the studio pulled the plug on the movie.

What? I could barely comprehend this. Some people blamed Elliott's behavior on drugs. Years later he told me, "I didn't have a problem with drugs. I had a problem with reality."

Whatever the truth, this was a disaster. Not only was Elliott's reputation in tatters, but he was also on the hook for a lot of money if the studio decided to sue him. And nobody would want to work with him again. I was frantic, and I think that's when John Calley suggested that I take over the movie . . . they would rewrite Elliott's part for a woman. I told him to send me the script. I'd have done whatever it took to salvage the project and get Elliott out of this mess. After all, he was Jason's father.

Suddenly I was making a movie for Warner Bros., and John kindly asked me who I would want to direct. I had heard good things from Sue about this new guy named Peter Bogdanovich, who was also her client and had just made a film called *The Last Picture Show*. Peter was still putting on the finishing touches, and hardly anyone had seen it, but she arranged for John and me to go to the studio to watch it.

John had to leave in the middle (after whispering that it was great), and I sat there alone, entranced. Peter had done something that was unheard-of at the time. He had shot it in black and white, which suited the starkness of the Texas landscape and made each image stand out. By the end, I was crying.

Peter was waiting for me when I came out, and I told him how wonderful the film was. We kept talking as he walked me to my car, and we were still talking as I got in and sat down. "I'd love to do a picture with you," he told me, "but not *A Glimpse of Tiger*. I don't like the script."

"Why not?"

"It's soft, sentimental, and uninteresting. It's supposed to be a dark comedy, but I don't think it's funny."

"Actually, I just did a comedy," I told him. "I want to do a drama."

"I just did a drama," he answered. "*I* want to do a comedy."

And we both laughed at the irony of the situation.

Frankly, I wasn't all that taken with *A Glimpse of Tiger*, either, and I wouldn't mind dropping it for something else, because I was very interested in working with Peter. So I called John, and John called Peter and told him, "Okay, so let's say you're going to make a picture with Barbra Streisand. What would you do?"

And Peter said, "I'd do a screwball comedy. Daffy dame. Square guy. She screws up his life but then they get together at the end. Something like *Bringing Up Baby*."

John said, "Okay. Go ahead. Who would you get to write it?"

Peter had worked with Robert Benton and David Newman at *Esquire*, so he suggested them. And since they had written *Bonnie and Clyde*, John thought that was a great idea.

So that's how *What's Up, Doc?* began.

Meanwhile, I wasn't exactly sure what Peter was talking about, but I was game. And I had my own idea about who should play the guy . . . Ryan O'Neal . . . because I knew he could be funny in real life.

John was happy with that, because Ryan was hot . . . he had just been nominated as Best Actor for *Love Story*, which was on track to become the top-grossing film of the year. Who wouldn't want him in their movie?

Well . . . Peter. He told Sue that Ryan wasn't right for the role. And then she asked him if he had seen *Love Story*, and Peter said he had no intention of seeing it. Sue said, "I'll pay for you to go see it. It's playing in Westwood."

So Peter went, under duress, and then called Sue up and admitted Ryan was attractive, but said he didn't see even a glimmer of a hint that Ryan could play comedy.

"Have lunch with him," Sue said.

And that did the trick. Peter responded just as I had. He thought Ryan was very amusing, charming, and funny in a self-deprecating way. Peter warned Ryan that if he did this movie, he was going to make fun of him mercilessly . . . cut his hair and put him in a seersucker suit.

Ryan was all for it. He said he'd love to do it.

Peter asked if he had seen *Bringing Up Baby* or *The Awful Truth*. Ryan didn't know those movies, and I don't remember if I had seen them, so Peter showed them to us. I could appreciate the style of *Bringing Up Baby* . . . I liked the bickering relationship between Katharine Hepburn and Cary Grant, and I love fast dialogue. That's what I responded to in great Tracy-Hepburn movies like *Adam's Rib* and *Pat and Mike*. But I didn't think *Bringing Up Baby* was ha-ha funny, and neither did Ryan. Still, we both trusted Peter and were willing to take a chance.

The deal was made with Benton and Newman to write a new script, but they were due to start another picture in three weeks, so that's all the time they had. Peter was optimistic. As he tells the story, he said, "If Howard Hawks and Ben Hecht could write *Scarface* in eleven days, I guess we can do this in three weeks." Peter worked with the writers every day, and by the end they had a script, but it wasn't quite right. And Peter knew it. As he said, "Maybe Hawks and Hecht actually took a little longer . . . and we weren't Hawks and Hecht."

He did a quick polish himself and then had us read it out loud. I didn't really understand the story, which seemed to be about suitcases . . . one held Ryan's rocks, a second held my clothes, and a third held a socialite's jewels . . . but I liked the characters. Ryan and I said yes. And then Peter brought in Buck

Henry, who was my old pal from *The Owl and the Pussycat*, to punch up the laughs.

Buck is one of those people who's just instinctively funny, in spite of his very serious demeanor (which makes him more funny). He told Peter, "You're going to hate me, but I don't think it's complicated enough." So he added a fourth suitcase, this one holding top-secret papers, because the Pentagon Papers were front-page news at the time.

At one point Peter called Buck to see how he was doing with the rewrite, and Buck said, "Right now, not so good. I've lost one of the fucking suitcases and I don't know where I put it."

He wasn't the only one. I could never keep track of those suitcases either. Frankly, I couldn't follow the plot. I didn't know who was stealing what from whom and eventually I just gave up. I mean, what was the point of trying to make sense of it? This wasn't serious drama. It was a farce, and Peter knew exactly how he wanted us to play it.

As he told Ryan, "Think Cary Grant."

And when Ryan seemed unsure about what that actually meant, Peter called Cary Grant and arranged for Ryan to meet him. "Maybe he can give you a tip."

Ryan seemed a little dazed after the encounter, and I couldn't wait to hear what words of wisdom the great Cary Grant had offered.

"Well, he said get a tan, because then you won't have to spend as much time in the makeup chair."

"Is that all?"

"One more thing. 'Wear silk underpants.'"

Even with the pants, Ryan was feeling a little insecure about his comedic skills. He admitted he had no idea how to play this character. So Peter would literally act out each scene for him before we'd shoot. He'd do all the lines and make all the faces exactly the way he wanted Ryan to do them.

Peter was very funny, and when I told him so, he explained that he had started out as an actor when he was fifteen and studied with Stella Adler. So he was a performer at heart. You can get a glimpse of this in the trailer, which shows him lying across the piano and singing "As Time Goes By." He was standing in for me, which he liked to do, so the cameraman . . . the brilliant László Kovács . . . could figure out his moves.

I loved working with László, who was part of a new breed of cinematographers . . . he had shot *Easy Rider* and *Five Easy Pieces*. He really knew how to light, and he was also kind and caring. He had that twinkle in his eye . . . a joy for life. It's a wonderful feeling to trust your cameraman. You can concentrate on your own work and know that he's watching out for you.

The production designer was the very talented Polly Platt, Peter's ex-wife, who became my good friend. And the editor was the ingenious Verna Fields, who would become famous a few years later for editing *Jaws*, and who also became a dear friend. So Peter had assembled a great team, and it was a very congenial set.

When we first started shooting, I'd come in with ideas every morning, just like I had with Willy.

"Peter, what do you think if I walked into the hotel very confident, and then I tripped and fell on the floor?"

And he'd say, "Nope."

So that was the end of that. It was almost funny when he said "Nope." He was so completely sure of himself. Peter wasn't interested in having a discussion or reaching some sort of compromise. Physical comedy is very specific, and he knew what he wanted and already had it all blocked out in his head. So as far as he was concerned, it would be a waste of time to let us improvise.

I quickly realized that the best way to make this work was to shut up and do whatever he told me. I know . . . not like me at all. But I was trying to be a team player and this was Peter's game.

Frankly, I didn't think some of the jokes were funny, which worried me. I was starting to have doubts about the film, and that threw me off. I remember one moment when I wasn't sure what my character was feeling, and Peter said, "Try it this way" . . . and read the line. Now, you have to understand that for a professional actor, that's the one thing a director is not supposed to do.

I was surprised and said, "Peter, you're giving me a line reading?"

"I'm just giving you an indication of how it might be said," he replied.

That night I happened to mention the incident to Sue on the phone, but not in any negative way. I was just telling her about my day. But later Peter told me that she had called him and said, "Are you giving Barbra Streisand line readings?"

"Sue, this is the way I work. She doesn't have to do it exactly the same way."

"Well, she's not happy about it."

Actually, that wasn't true. I had never had a director give me a line reading, so I admit it was odd. But it didn't bother me. I'm not that fragile.

The fact is, I wasn't offended, but apparently Sue had taken it upon herself to be offended for me . . . and decided to reprimand Peter. Or maybe she was just being overprotective in her overbearing way. But this is the kind of thing that drives me crazy. It happens when an artist's representative starts to think they are the artist, and can speak for the artist, and have the same power as the artist. Agents get scripts and turn them down without even telling their client. Publicists make demands and ask for things that would never occur to the artist, and then it's the artist who gets the bad reputation.

I'm not even sure exactly how Sue became my agent. Before this, we had merely been friends. Initially, she was Elliott's agent, though by the time I was doing *Funny Girl* on Broadway, it was clear to both of us that Sue was using him in an effort to get close to me. But I wasn't in the market for a new agent. I already had the big guys David Begelman and Freddie Fields, so why would I switch from them to her?

And then she began to work for them at their agency, CMA, and gradually seemed to take over as my agent by default. (I only realized later that David and Freddie had set their sights on bigger things. Both eventually left to run studios.)

Sue was very entertaining and could turn anything into a great story . . . but I could never quite trust her. Sometimes at her house I would overhear her on the phone with a client: "Hi, darling. Yes, everything's going well. Don't worry. They thought you were marvelous." And then she'd hang up the phone and exclaim, "Bitch!" in a totally different tone.

I looked at her and asked, "Do you talk like that about me?"

"Oh no no no no no," she'd insist. But I wasn't so sure.

Sue was like a sniper. She could zero in on a person's weak points and eviscerate them in a sentence, but somehow people still found her charming . . . when her wicked wit wasn't aimed at them.

And she had absolutely no boundaries. I remember one summer in New York when Elliott and I rented a house in the country for a week or two so Jason could play on the beach. Cis and Harvey came to visit, and so did Sue, who would swim nude in the pool, in front of Harvey, whom she barely knew. And she was definitely not slim, but she didn't care. I was shocked, but also impressed that she was so free . . . unlike me. She was also openly frank about her escapades with men. One day the phone rang when she was at my house having lunch, and I picked it up. It was a crank call, some guy just breathing heavily, and I said, "Hold on a minute," then looked at Sue and said, "It's for you."

We laughed about that moment for years. Sue was good at making me laugh, and once I was on my own, I used to bring her to parties because I didn't want to go alone. She's always said that's how she met many of her clients.

She was the ultimate networker and a classic busybody. Her interference this time with Peter was relatively minor, and luckily it had no effect on my working relationship with him. He knew that I valued his input, and as the shoot went on there were other moments when I said, "I don't understand what you're going for. Just show me what you want. It's okay . . . give me a line reading."

It was sort of amusing. I could tell Peter was aching to play my part . . . not to mention all the other parts as well! And he was very funny when he did, so why not just go along with it? After all, he was the director and this was his vision . . . not mine. And I always try to serve the director's vision.

Peter likes to tell a story about the moment when we were filming the song "As Time Goes By" and he said, "You know that line 'On that you can rely'?"

I said, "Yeah."

"Can you emphasize '*can*'?" he asked.

"Now you're giving me line readings on a fucking *song*???"

We both laughed. And I tried it, and it worked.

Peter was so enthusiastic and bright. His mind moved fast and he was always pushing us to speed up the pace, which was easy for me, coming from Brooklyn where everyone talked fast. Ryan had a harder time, but he managed. There were scenes where everyone was talking so quickly and the dialogue overlapped and then there were all these funny bits of business that had to be timed exactly right. I loved that!

Oh my God, some of the stunts were scary. You think I wanted to cross a street with *two* speeding motorcyclists coming at me?

No. I'm a chicken. I just closed my eyes and prayed . . . and then walked as they each narrowly missed me only to crash into each other, as planned. (What I did for art!)

But the most terrifying thing was riding that bicycle up and down the hills of San Francisco, with Ryan perched in front of me. That was an incredible chase scene, with one gag after another . . . the ladder, the plate glass, the Chinese dragon, the cement . . . and then driving that VW bug down that zigzagging street and finally straight into San Francisco Bay.

It's a miracle that no one got hurt. Actually Ryan did injure himself in a scene in his hotel room, where he finds me in his bathtub. He was supposed to back away and trip, but when he landed he did something to his back and had to have surgery after we wrapped. (Classic . . . you survive a whole chase scene, then get hurt falling on a soft carpet!)

I remember that scene for another reason. Some gossip columnist wrote that I "demanded" a different tub. The truth was that the first tub was too shallow, and the bubble bath wouldn't hide my breasts, which I didn't want to show. So they had to get a deeper tub, a change that was for a purely practical reason.

Peter kept the atmosphere light and we all laughed a lot. And Peter was laughing the loudest, because he was having such fun directing. It was a very good cast . . . Madeline Kahn was hysterical, in her first movie . . . Austin Pendleton was terrific, Kenneth Mars was hilarious.

Was I funny? Did Ryan and I set off sparks? I wasn't so sure.

My romance with him had fizzled out before the shoot began. I think I was too serious for Ryan. He just wanted to have fun and didn't like it when I went into my intense mode. So we split, but remained on good terms. Still, it was awkward at times, having to fall in love with him for the camera, when all that was over. My friend Graham Nash came to my rescue. He lived in San Francisco and would visit me on the set and take me out to dinner. So that was a nice consolation.

I spent Christmas 1971 in Las Vegas, performing at the Hilton. I never liked all the forced festivity around the holidays, and at least this was something to do on New Year's Eve, especially since I was alone. I had told Elliott back in June that it was long past time to resolve our situation. He was still with the girl he had been living with in Greenwich Village, and now she was pregnant. So he flew to the Dominican Republic to get us a quick divorce.

A few weeks after I came home from Vegas, Peter screened the movie for me, Ryan, John, and a few others. There were some laughs, but no one was rolling in the aisles. And suddenly I got nervous. It was as if all my initial doubts about the film had been confirmed . . . maybe it wasn't just that I didn't get the jokes. Maybe the movie actually *wasn't* all that funny.

According to my contract, in addition to my salary I was due to receive 10 percent of the gross, going up to 15 percent at breakeven. But what if nobody came to see it? The tax rate at the time was 70 percent . . . I swear, it almost didn't make sense to work, because by the time they took out the tax, you were left with so little. My business manager was telling me that I didn't have that much money in the bank and advised me to sell my 10 percent of the movie back to Warner Bros.

It turned out to be the stupidest deal I ever made in my life.

When the movie opened at Radio City Music Hall in New York, it broke all the house records. If you stood on the street outside the theater, the laughter inside was so loud that you could hear it through the walls. *What's Up, Doc?* was a huge hit and became the third-highest-grossing film of the year, surpassed only by *The Godfather* and *The Poseidon Adventure.*

So the joke's on me.

TWENTY-THREE

A Woman's Place

It's wonderful to make people laugh, but after the crazy slapstick of *What's Up, Doc?*, I wanted to get back in touch with the real world.

And the real world was complicated. The 1960s had been tumultuous. After the shock and horror of John F. Kennedy's assassination, I just wanted to crawl under the covers. Instead, I agreed to sing at the Democratic National Convention in 1964 to support his successor, fellow Democrat Lyndon Johnson, and *Funny Girl* closed for one night on Broadway so I could perform at his inauguration in 1965. But there was no joy in it for me.

That April, after the peaceful protest marchers led by Martin Luther King, Jr., were brutally attacked in Selma, Alabama, I was proud to be part of *Broadway Answers Selma*, a one-night performance by an extraordinary lineup . . . Harry Belafonte, Sammy Davis, Jr., Martin Sheen, Sir John Gielgud, Ethel Merman, and the list goes on. These Broadway stars got together on their one night off to raise money for the Anti-Defamation League and the Southern Christian Leadership Conference. Three weeks later I was back onstage with Harry, Sammy, Sidney Poitier, Diahann Carroll, and Marlon Brando to raise more money for the Student Nonviolent Coordinating Committee, to enable them to continue their crucial work of getting Black people registered so they could exercise their legal right to vote.

In January 1968, in the midst of the Vietnam War, I was part of the *Broadway for Peace* concert at Lincoln Center, with Harry and Diahann, Paul Newman, Joanne Woodward, Carl Reiner, and many others. Leonard Bernstein played the piano for me as I sang his song "So Pretty," with poignant lyrics by Betty Comden and Adolph Green about a country:

Full of lovely temples painted gold, modern cities, jungles ages old
And the people are so pretty there, shining smiles, and shiny eyes and hair
Then I had to ask my teacher, why war was making all those people die?

I've always asked questions. And as I became more aware politically, I kept asking more. Nothing about the war made sense to me.

A few months later, I sang at a fundraiser for Eugene McCarthy, who was brave enough to challenge even his own party on the issue of the war. Once again Bernstein accompanied me. It was not exactly normal to have the great Leonard Bernstein as my pianist, but he was eager to participate in any way he could . . . all of us were so passionately against the war.

In 1970 I became a big supporter of Bella Abzug, who was running for Congress in New York. Bella was outspoken. She was brash. She didn't conform to the usual stereotype of a politician and I didn't conform to the usual stereotype of an actress, so I could identify with that. And Bella was a strong voice for the issues that mattered to me . . . women's rights, gay rights, civil rights, nuclear disarmament, protecting the environment, ending the war. She was a wife, a mother, and a highly accomplished lawyer who was willing to fight for what she believed in.

That's why they called her "Battling Bella." She wouldn't take no for an answer, and she refused to stay in her place. In fact, she even turned that to her advantage in her campaign slogan, which was "This woman's place is in the house . . . the House of Representatives." She wanted to break down barriers and make sure every woman . . . and every man . . . had equal opportunity to be all that they could be.

I wanted Bella to get elected because we desperately needed her voice in the rooms where decisions are made. Women are half the population, and it's still ridiculous how few of them are in Congress. It really feels as if it will be women who have to save the world because so many men have made such a mess of it.

So when Bella asked me to campaign for her, I said yes. I stood beside her on a flatbed truck, and we rode around her district. This was not easy, because campaigning does not come naturally to me. I don't like speaking in public. It makes me nervous, and I get tongue-tied. So giving a political speech to people on the street is my idea of a nightmare.

Bella, on the other hand, was born to perform and could talk to anyone. That was her great gift. And even more important, she knew how to listen. She was genuinely interested in other people. She'd laugh and joke and speak Yiddish to the Jewish men and women who gathered round our truck on the Lower East Side, curious to see what was going on. Here we were, two Jewish girls . . . Bella from the Bronx and Barbra from Brooklyn . . . who made good!

She would introduce me and hand me the microphone. I have no idea what I said, but I do remember stopping at Yonah Schimmel's for knishes. The blueberry cheese . . . Oh my God! I went back there recently, and it wasn't quite the same . . . but I guess it's hard, even for a knish, to live up to your memories.

I also hosted a fundraiser for her in a town house I briefly owned on the Upper East Side. I first fell in love with the original Art Deco grillwork on the front door and bought it after I was turned down by a Park Avenue co-op and a Fifth Avenue co-op because I was an actress. I guess they thought I was going to play loud music and give wild parties, which is not my style. (I think I had one big party in the thirty-five years I lived on Central Park West.)

Or was it because I was Jewish?

In any event the rejection hit the papers and prompted an investigation by the state attorney general into co-op board practices.

So I had this empty town house and it all happened very quickly . . . I just wrote out an invitation on my stationery and said: "There will be stars of stage, screen!—drinks—canapés—but *no* furniture!!"

Campaign volunteers pitched in to help me get the house in shape. I was down on my hands and knees scrubbing the floor, because the woman who formerly lived there was a hoarder who never cleaned it. And apparently when she was forced to leave, she shot her way out of the house. Yes, you read that right. That's what can happen when you're dealing with real estate in New York! The police told me that she was threatening people with a gun, and there was a bullet hole in the window. I saw it with my own eyes. (Lucky for me, she was so busy hoarding that she never updated the house, and all the beautiful Art Deco details from 1929 were still intact. And it even had a garage!)

Anyway, we cleaned it up, and I think we charged twenty-five dollars a head for the fundraiser. Then people kept asking Harry Belafonte and me for autographs, so we started selling those as well.

It was a lot of fun . . . Gloria Steinem was there, and William vanden Heuvel (who had been assistant to Robert Kennedy when he was attorney general). It was actually the only party I ever had in that house, because I ended up not moving into it. (I couldn't give up the views from my Central Park West apartment.)

On a Sunday night two days before the election, I was at Madison Square Garden, performing at *Broadway for Bella*, along with people like Lauren Bacall, Gwen Verdon, and Alan Alda.

I went on around 10:00 p.m. and closed the show with six songs, including "Happy Days." I had sung it for two presidents at that point . . . John F. Kennedy and Lyndon B. Johnson . . . and I wanted to sing it for Bella.

I still remember being so nervous for her on election night. I was in a cab on my way to campaign headquarters with Pete Hamill, a reporter who was covering the race for the *New York Post*, when we heard over the radio that Bella had lost. I was crushed. But by the time we got there more results had come in, and Bella had won! It was like a miracle! We were stunned and gloriously happy.

On her first day in Congress, she introduced a bill calling for the withdrawal of U.S. forces from Vietnam. Now that's chutzpah . . . in the best sense. And she said something once that has always stayed with me: "Women have been trained to speak softly and carry a lipstick. Those days are over."

Bella didn't go politely through the halls of Congress. She kicked the door open to make way for other women. And they followed her lead.

By 1971, the women's liberation movement was in full swing. Women were marching for equal pay and pushing Congress to pass the Equal Rights Amendment. (Bella was one of its sponsors.) And I was trying to act on those principles in my own life by taking more responsibility for my movie career. My agent, Freddie Fields, had an idea for his clients . . . me, Paul Newman, and Sidney Poitier. He thought we should form our own company, and he set up First Artists in 1969. The concept was that each of us could make whatever film we wanted, for a budget of $3 million to $6 million, and we'd have complete autonomy . . . in exchange for no money up front. If the film was a hit, we'd be paid handsomely on the back end. If the film was a dud, it was too bad for the artist . . . no pay . . . and we were also personally liable for any costs over the budget.

So it was a gamble, but I like taking risks. And it was definitely an extraordinary deal, but not unprecedented . . . Mary Pickford, Charlie Chaplin, Douglas Fairbanks, and D. W. Griffith had been acting on a similar impulse when they formed United Artists in 1919. Still, I have to give Freddie credit for being farsighted. (Later, Steve McQueen and Dustin Hoffman joined as well.) Then I took the next step by forming my own production company, Barwood Films. And I made Cis my partner, since she was my most trusted friend and gave great notes on scripts.

I was determined that my first film for Barwood and First Artists should be something meaningful, something that tackled contemporary social and political issues. So I chose *Up the Sandbox*. It's the story of Margaret Reynolds, a loving wife and mother. Her days are spent looking after two small children and barely keeping her household together, but in her fantasies she's leading other lives, like discussing politics with Fidel Castro. She's an intelligent woman who has been buried under diapers, taking care of everyone except herself. But now she can no longer suppress her own desires. She wants her own fulfilling career . . . and her family too.

It was a dilemma faced by so many women, including me. Like any other mother, I was struggling to find the right balance between my work and my child. I had made five movies in four years. The hours were long, and I didn't want to spend so much time apart from Jason. I was lucky to be able to afford a wonderful Scottish nanny named Babs (who'd survived World War II, so Hollywood didn't faze her), but I didn't want my son to be raised by other people.

There was a part of me that longed to stay home and just be with my child, but there was also another part of me that needed some form of expression . . . just like Margaret. She's deeply in love with her husband and children, but she'd also like to write, and possibly go back to school.

My question was, Why shouldn't it be possible for a woman to have a family *and* a career? Margaret wanted both. And so did I.

The project came to me through Irwin Winkler, who had given Freddie the novel by Anne Richardson Roiphe for me to read. Irwin was going to produce the movie with his partner, Robert Chartoff, and they hired a Pulitzer Prize–winning playwright, Paul Zindel, to write the screenplay. It was important to me that we got Margaret right, so I spent days going over the script with Paul when he came up to Las Vegas, where I was doing my show at the Hilton over Christmas and New Year's Eve. While I was busy singing at night, Paul was busy gambling, and he won twenty-five thousand dollars!

The director Irvin Kershner came up to work with us as well. I had seen a film he made called *Loving*, starring my friend George Segal, and was very impressed. Kersh had a great eye. He knew how to capture real life. And you can see that not only in the incredibly intimate performances he got out of each actor, but also in the sets. The apartment Margaret lives in is one of the most realistic New York apartments I've ever seen in movies . . . cluttered, quirky, a little cramped. Turns out Kersh had a friend with an apartment on Riverside Drive that he thought would be perfect for this family, so he took lots of photos and had the art department duplicate the layout and recreate it on the sound stage, down to the elevator. I really appreciated his sense of detail. And he was a lovely man who became my friend for life.

He saw that I was interested in where he put the camera, so when he was setting up a complicated shot, he'd say, "Barbra, come take a look." And then he had me sit on the camera dolly and he'd take me through the shot, with my stand-in, so I could see exactly what the camera would see.

If he wasn't sure about something, he wasn't afraid to admit it. He'd say, "Barbra, I'm kind of stuck. What do you think?" And I'd try to come up with an idea. We had a great rapport. As he said later on, "She truly was collaborating in many, many scenes because of the nature of the script." He felt it still needed work when we had to start shooting, so we were often making changes as we went along.

The whole thing feels offbeat and a little offhand . . . more improvisational . . . and more like a European art film than a Hollywood star vehicle. In this movie, I wanted to be a real person, not a glamour girl. And that's why I wanted the same cinematographer who shot *Loving* . . . the great Gordon Willis . . . because he made everything look so real.

Gordy (who also shot *The Godfather*, which came out as we began filming) was a shy, fascinating man. (Anybody who is truly gifted is fascinating to me.) He taught me a lot about light . . . and the beauty of turning it down. You don't see every actor's features in every minute of the film. Sometimes they're in shadow or otherwise obscured. He trusts the darkness, and he likes to take chances. You couldn't even see my eyes half the time, because he didn't believe in using an eye light. Gordy's style was very un-Hollywood, very un-theatrical. There are no glamour shots. In fact, there are hardly any close-ups. Instead, I was shot though doorways and panes of glass, just caught in a moment, and he did it magnificently. I look very natural . . . like you would see me in real life.

When we first started shooting, I told him, "You know, I prefer the left side of my face."

He thought I was crazy, and said, "Barbra, are you going to go through this whole film moving right to left? Aren't you ever going to go left to right?"

I laughed, and said, "Okay, okay. Photograph me any way you like."

Point is, I trusted him.

He didn't believe me about my face and was determined to prove that the right side was better, or at least as good. So I stopped thinking about camera angles and just put myself in his hands. And Gordy, with his genius, made me look damn good. He showed me a side of myself that I didn't know.

But the funniest thing is, at the end of the shoot he came up to me and said, "You know what? Your left side *is* better." I loved his honesty. So I never felt self-conscious asking for that again, because Gordy confirmed it.

Up the Sandbox opens with just the tinkling sound of a toy piano . . . I suggested that to Billy Goldenberg, who was doing the score, because I thought it'd be appropriate for a movie that dealt with children and motherhood.

I've always loved the first shot in the film . . . a baby being bathed, with my hand washing his bare tush . . . and then I wrap him in a towel and set him down on the floor to tend to his sister in the tub. That little girl was so free and reacted so naturally that what we improvised was often better than the written lines.

I related to Margaret because I felt that the character could have been me, if my father had lived and I had married another teacher like him and had some babies. And it tapped into my own relationship with my mother, who was always telling me I was doing things wrong, just like Margaret's mother in the script. And I was also questioning the role-playing that is so ingrained in us . . . how the man works and the woman stays home with the kids.

The central conflict of the film is interior, which made it difficult to dramatize. Margaret finds out she's pregnant again and is not sure how she feels about having a third child. She's torn between that primal urge to mother, and her desire for a fulfilling career of her own. And what was most interesting to me is that the movie didn't come down on either side. In fact, it was truly a women's lib picture because it was about a woman's right to choose which path was right for her, and that also meant she had the right to choose whether or not to have a baby.

This was quite a radical idea back then. When the movie was being written in 1971, abortion was allowed (with various restrictions) in only six states in the country and Washington, D.C. It wasn't until 1973, a year after the movie was released, that abortion was decriminalized nationwide with *Roe v. Wade.* (Now, as I'm writing this, the Supreme Court has shockingly taken away a woman's right to control her own body. The idea that we have to fight this battle all over again, after abortion has been legal for fifty years, is profoundly upsetting.)

Abortion is not the subject of this film. In fact, the word isn't even uttered until eleven minutes before the end. But Margaret is thinking about it even if she doesn't say it out loud. It's an option, if she so chooses . . . and that doesn't make her a bad person.

When Margaret finds out she's pregnant (from a doctor who asks more questions about Paul, her husband, than her), her first impulse is to share the news with Paul, played by David Selby (brought in by Cis, who did the casting). But when Margaret drops in on him at the university, she finds him having lunch with a female colleague. And she leaves without saying anything. As she's walking down the hall, she turns back to see the colleague coming out of his office and stops her to ask, boldly, if she's having an affair with her husband. The woman answers yes, but then reassures Margaret that Paul "loves you very much. He told me." And then the woman goes into her own office.

Margaret walks away, and then suddenly we see a repeat of the woman coming out of Paul's office. This is the first inkling that something odd is going on. This time Margaret is tempted to talk to her but she doesn't. She's too afraid. And that's when we realize that the whole conversation we just witnessed between them took place only in Margaret's mind . . . it's a fantasy.

I liked that. We didn't use any of the traditional techniques, like a blurred dissolve, to cue the audience in on the fact that this scene was only imagined. So it had mystery . . . did that really happen? And it established the style of the film, which glides back and forth between reality and fantasy.

The imagination is powerful. Fantasies can make for a rich inner life. They can lead you into new places. If I had never had a fantasy about being an actress, perhaps I wouldn't have become one.

Later, at a soda fountain with her kids, Margaret runs into her former professor of Latin American Studies, who still remembers a paper she wrote and reminds her that she was once a promising writer. He invites her to a press conference (or did he?) that Fidel Castro is giving, and in another fantasy, Margaret stands up and asks a provocative question. She speaks out, and says something I believe myself, even now:

"Our world is fragile, as you know. It is in great danger. It needs every drop of love and care or else it will die. Where are we going to find this loving care? In the military academies? In the councils of state? No! In its women. And if we must use power, let us speak about the power of mothers who can instill in their sons a true masculinity and thereby create a new breed of men who will not have to run around with toy weapons and uniforms to show their manhood. Men who will use their muscle to build and preserve rather than destroy. Men who will not be afraid to stand up for love instead of hate. No, we do not have to become more like you, sir. We only have to become more like ourselves."

Castro is intrigued, and invites her up to his hotel room, where he plies her with wine. Then we cut from her being chased around a hotel bed to two bodies in bed. But it's actually Margaret and her husband now, making love, and when she wakes up, she stares at the glass of wine on the bedside table.

In real life, sometimes an object, a color, a sound . . . or a glass of wine . . . can trigger a memory . . . or a fantasy. And people we've just seen in Margaret's real life reappear in her fantasy life in another guise. If you look closely, the Spanish-speaking waitress in the drugstore comes back as Castro's associate.

We shot these fantasies the way we thought they should be done, and like in a European film, we didn't explain everything. We were walking a fine line, leaving it to the audience to figure out, and unfortunately the transitions were so seamless that the audience probably couldn't tell where reality ended and the fantasy began. It was subtle, which I thought was great. But apparently most people didn't get it.

I didn't realize this until later. While we were shooting, I was completely immersed in my character. And the story felt especially personal to me because it was the first time that I took situations from my own life and put them in a film. I had gotten my mother an apartment in my building, and she used to appear at my door unexpectedly all the time, and I said the same thing to her that we had Margaret say to her mother: "I've told you sixteen million times not to come here without calling first." When Margaret refuses to take the chain off the door to let her in, her mother reaches in with a giant pair of pliers and cuts it. (That's the only part that didn't actually happen to me.)

I also told Kersh about a family reunion we had at my cousin Harvey's house, with all these relatives who hadn't seen one another in a long time. And some of them had never gotten along to begin with, so it was quite awkward. My brother, Shelly, is a person who always takes pictures wherever he goes. At that party, I couldn't even talk to him because he was always behind his camera, so I said, "Shelly, you're not really here. I guess you won't experience this until you develop the pictures."

That inspired the anniversary party scene and gave me the idea to shoot it like a home movie in 8mm, and cut back and forth to the 35mm used for the rest of the film. It was a wacky idea in a way . . . a movie within the movie . . . but Kersh and Gordy liked it. The first half of the scene was not even scripted. Every actor was given a few personality traits for their character before we started filming, and then we just improvised. My mom used to burst into song at the least encouragement, so we had a character singing loudly while everyone else ignored her. And a niece (like father, like daughter) keeps annoying Margaret by snapping pictures of her.

Halfway through the party, Margaret's mother takes it upon herself to announce that Margaret is pregnant. In a fantasy, Margaret stops her by pushing her mother's face into the cake. Bravo to the actress Jane Hoffman, who was willing to be pushed!

Every Friday night I'd bring in beer and sandwiches for the cast and crew to celebrate another week's worth of footage in the can. We had weekends off, and one Saturday I was at the LA Forum, singing in a concert organized by Warren Beatty to raise money for George McGovern's presidential campaign. It was April 15, 1972, and I thought the other performers were terrific . . . James Taylor, Carole King, Quincy Jones . . . and I was so afraid that I'd be booed off the stage, because my music wasn't as contemporary as theirs. So I wanted to go on first and get it over with. But Marty said, "No. You're the biggest star and you should close the show. And you're going to get more applause just by walking onstage than any of them will get walking off, and if I'm wrong about that, I'll represent you for the rest of my life for nothing."

Well, Marty wasn't wrong. And it was a great night. Warren had persuaded his pals . . . big stars like Jack Nicholson, Julie Christie, Burt Lancaster, Raquel Welch, James Earl Jones, Goldie Hawn, and Gene Hackman . . . to act as ushers, so the audience was excited before they even sat down. But I was so nervous that I had the lyrics to "Stoney End" (which I could never remember) written out in chalk on the floor of the stage. I had to confess to the audience to explain why I kept looking down. And they applauded. (Nothing like the truth!)

At the end of May I flew to Nairobi. For some crazy reason, we actually went to Africa to shoot the African fantasy we made up, where the women are in charge and the men churn the butter and look after the kids. (If it had been up to me, we could have driven thirty minutes and done it all in the Valley.)

Africa was a place of both beauty and terror for me. One morning I was late to the set because a giraffe was standing in the road and refused to move. What an amazing creature, backlit by the sun. That was glorious. But I didn't appreciate the monkeys scampering into our camp and stealing my stuff. And when you're trying to fall asleep at night, the last thing you want to hear is lions roaring.

After work, Gordy and Kersh would take me to a little restaurant on the river, where a big piece of meat was always hung on the opposite bank, to attract animals. That was the show . . . waiting for the animals to come and feed. It made me feel weird watching them eat, as if we were invading their privacy. But at least that way, they weren't interested in eating *us*.

One evening I was just going to slip out after dinner and walk back to my room when the guard stopped me and said, "You can't go without me." Thank God he was there, because on the way back the beam of his flashlight landed on a rhinoceros with his big horn, right in front of us. That was frightening.

I also picked up a parasite while I was there, so I was very uncomfortable and losing weight. But even worse was the intense heat. My support team (which by now included my dresser, Shirlee Strahm, and my hairstylist, Kaye Pownall, in addition to my dear Gracie) and I spent many hours stuck in a hot trailer on the set, with swarms of flies and no air-conditioning. In my worst moments I thought, *I'm going to get heatstroke and die like my father*, but those three women got me through it. (I first worked with Shirlee and Kaye on *Clear Day*, and we all really bonded. I did a total of eleven films with them.)

Africa did offer one unexpected pleasure . . . being with the Samburu people and singing with the children. And I made friends with one particular woman from the tribe. Even though we couldn't speak to each other, we still managed to communicate. She showed me how to make an outfit just by ripping pieces of fabric and holding them together with safety pins. She also made her own jewelry out of telephone wire and beads. To do her eye makeup, she broke off a twig from a tree and pulled a thread from her husband's skirt, to make a kind of Q-tip. Then she found a piece of soft blue rock, spit on it, and rubbed the twig in the color and applied it to her eyelids. I let her put some on my own eyes, which was a big deal for me, because I always do my own makeup!

Of course I brought Jason with me, as I did whenever I went on location. He loved Africa. He was five, and I knew the animals would be a big attraction, but he was also fascinated when I read him a book about the archaeologists Louis and Mary Leakey, and how they dug up fossils and discovered that Africa was the birthplace of early man. So I buried some chicken bones for him to find so he could have his own archaeological dig.

I think that's another reason why I responded so personally to *Up the Sandbox* . . . Margaret was trying so hard to be a good mother, and so was I. The movie asked a very important question: Why is the role of a mother so undervalued in our society? It's a very important job . . . molding the next generation. But some women who had no other profession than housewife thought less of themselves than they should . . . just like Margaret, who felt inadequate next to her husband's female colleagues. The whole point of the film was to empower women and remind them of their worth, no matter whether they chose to work inside or outside the home . . . or both.

In the final fantasy Margaret checks into an abortion clinic but leaves before the procedure, sailing out on her hospital bed straight into a playground full of children. (One of them was Jason, who's the kid pushing the roundabout and then jumping on.) Then she's flung out of bed and lands in a sandbox, with the playground suddenly empty around her . . . and we cut back to reality, as she wakes up in an empty apartment. Paul has taken the kids to the park, and next we see her waving to him and the children as they go spinning by on the carousel. Her husband asks, "How do you feel?" (She had fainted the night before.)

And she says, "I'm pregnant."

So Margaret has made her choice. She's going to have this baby. And that's the excitement and the thrill at the end, when she blithely goes off in the taxi, smiling beatifically as she waves good-bye to Paul, who's left standing with their two kids.

That smile says, I'm going to do it all. I'm going to do more than I've ever done before. I'm going to fulfill my potential.

Margaret loves her family but she has decided that her husband has to do more of the work, and now it's his turn to take care of the children, while she goes off to do her own thing . . . at least for the day, and hopefully many more.

I am so proud of this film . . . even though it was a total flop. I remember taking a friend to see it at a theater in Westwood right after it opened, and there were only four people there. I was so embarrassed. And it really shook me. It felt like audiences didn't want to see me as an ordinary housewife. They weren't interested in the unadorned me. This movie had no elaborate sets and no fancy costumes, and they clearly preferred the bigger Barbra, belting out a song or making jokes.

Would they only accept me in musicals or comedies? I knew I had a bigger range than that. (After all, I played Medea when I was fifteen!)

Around this time, Marty was approaching the networks with the idea that I would do various classics on TV, including *Romeo and Juliet.* And the universal response was, "Is she going to sing in it?"

Well, *noooo.* As Marty politely pointed out, that had already been done, brilliantly, in *West Side Story.* They lost interest. It was very discouraging.

People want to put you in a mold. They want you to play the same part over and over again because that's how they first saw you and liked you. But that can be stifling. And just as I was trying to grow as a person, I was also trying to grow as an actress.

It was painful. One of the things that kept me going was a note that I had gotten from Orson Welles. He was planning his own TV special and wanted me to be in *The Merchant of Venice.* He wrote:

> ***Dear Barbra Streisand,***
>
> ***Please, please, please!***
>
> ***I really promise you fun and I know it could be an authentic TV event.***

So at least *he* thought I could do more. Why didn't that happen? Who knows . . . but it definitely counts as another lost opportunity.

Part of the problem with *Up the Sandbox* was the ad campaign, which was very misleading. It portrayed the movie as a rollicking comedy, and people were expecting something like *What's Up, Doc?* So they were disappointed when they got this strange little . . . well, I don't know exactly what to call it. But it's certainly not a comedy, or I guess you could say it's a serious comedy. Actually it's a drama with a few laughs.

And the studio decided to release it at Christmas, which made no sense because it was *not* a holiday picture.

And it was hampered by an R rating, just because you happened to see the bare breasts of the African tribeswomen and Castro (you'll have to watch the movie for that story). I thought that was ridiculous. There is nothing dirty about breasts!

So the response to the film was muted, to say the least, and for all these years, I've thought of it as a kind of unappreciated child. I was almost afraid to look back at the reviews, but to my surprise they were good, and some were even wonderful.

> "Up the Sandbox *is something rather special: A smart, imaginative, unconventional comedy about middle-class married and domestic life that also is extraordinarily*

> *touching, truly* loving. *This is by several light years the most endearing and fundamentally joyous new movie the holiday season has to offer."*
>
> —GARY ARNOLD, *THE WASHINGTON POST*

> *"Barbra Streisand has never seemed so mysteriously, sensually fresh, so multi-radiant. As Margaret, wife of a Columbia instructor and mother of two, she's a complete reason for going to a movie, as Garbo was . . . If there is such a thing as total empathy, she has it."*
>
> —PAULINE KAEL, *THE NEW YORKER*

Rewatching the movie now, there are things I would do differently. I would fight harder to keep the moment where Margaret and her Black revolutionary boyfriend kiss. That was in a fantasy sequence where they're blowing up the Statue of Liberty. (In Margaret's mind it was a false symbol, since she felt there was no liberty for her, as a woman.) The studio made us cut the kiss but they kept the explosion, which says a lot about our world.

Even though this was my first film for my own company, I realize now that I was reluctant to assume my own power, which is kind of ironic considering that the movie is about a woman finally taking control of her own life. I notice that I didn't even take a producing credit . . . Marty is listed as the executive in charge for Barwood Films. That's so typical of me. I didn't pay attention to credits. All I cared about was making the film as good as it could be.

Peter Rainer, the film critic, recently told a friend of mine that he thought *Up the Sandbox* had been overlooked and was ripe for reevaluation. That would be interesting . . . I'd be curious to see how people would respond to it today, more than fifty years later.

I still think it's a good movie and I still believe in its message . . . and women are still struggling, in our society, to be all that they can be.

TWENTY-FOUR

The Way We Were

It was Ray Stark who initially asked Arthur Laurents to write something for me. Arthur told me that Ray was impressed with the huge success of *The Sound of Music* and *The Miracle Worker* and thought, Why not combine the two and have me teaching handicapped children in Brooklyn to sing? Arthur wasn't enthusiastic about that idea, to say the least, but he came over to discuss it with me. I liked it even less, but as we were talking, the subject turned to politics. Arthur knew I was politically active, and as I was ranting about the state of the world, suddenly he was reminded of a very smart girl he knew in college who came from a lower-middle-class family and was president of the Young Communist League. Her name was Fanny Price . . . funny coincidence, or was it a sign? He said, "She was intense, passionate, and Jewish, like you."

Arthur went home and wrote a treatment, and as soon as I read it, I thought, *Holy mackerel! This is fantastic.* I absolutely fell in love with the story. This girl, Katie Morosky, touched me profoundly. She was passionate about life and concerned about the world. I understood her completely. I knew why she fell in love with Hubbell Gardiner, the good-looking jock who was also a gifted writer. Arthur told me that Hubbell was a composite of several people he knew, including Peter Viertel, the Hollywood aristocrat who went hunting with Ernest Hemingway and wrote screenplays for John Huston.

I read somewhere that David Lean said if you had five great scenes in a script, it could make a great movie. Well, there were definitely five in *The Way We Were*, so I called Ray, very excited, and said, "I love it!"

And he said, "Oh, I'm glad you love it, but if you want to do it, we'll have to add another picture onto your contract."

"What? You mean just because I love it, you're not going to let me do it unless I give you an extra picture? That's not fair."

He didn't care.

I was so upset. Remember, he wouldn't let me do the film of *Funny Girl* unless I signed with him for an additional three pictures. I'd already done *The Owl and the Pussycat. Funny Lady* (the sequel to *Funny Girl*) . . . which I definitely wasn't thrilled about . . . was in the works. And I assumed *The Way We Were* would be the third and our deal would be over. My mistake. That lesson again: Never assume.

Once again Ray reneged on his word. He had arbitrarily decided that *The Way We Were* wouldn't count toward our contract. This made no sense, and to this day I'm confused about the terms of this contract. I called Marty to ask how this happened and he said, "That's the way Ray did business. He was a tough negotiator. He wanted to keep hanging on to you and those were the games he played. And he did it with everyone. He was not a well-liked man."

This was a blatant attempt on his part to squeeze one more film out of me.

Ray said, "Look, I'll pay you much more money for this if you do it outside the contract. I'll pay you what you got for *What's Up, Doc?*"

I didn't care how much money he was offering me. It wasn't a matter of money. It was a matter of principle. I did not want to be under contract to this man for one more minute than I had to. So I stood my ground.

I said, "As far as I'm concerned, *The Way We Were* counts toward my commitment. That's the contract we made. You can't blackmail me like this."

It wasn't a practical decision on my part, because it meant I would just get my original 1965 salary, instead of five times that (which is what I got for *What's Up, Doc?*, plus that big percentage of the profits that I stupidly sold back to the studio). But I didn't care, because I was one step closer to being free of Ray.

I've noticed that standing up for a principle can be costly. But at least I can be true to my own values.

I think Arthur was the one who suggested Sydney Pollack to direct. He told me that Sydney was an actor himself and had taught acting in New York at the Neighborhood Playhouse. I thought, *Great . . . he'll be sensitive to the actor's process.* I had seen his movies *The Slender Thread* and *They Shoot Horses, Don't They?*, which showed he could handle serious issues. So I encouraged Ray to hire him. And I liked Sydney from the moment we met, and felt comfortable enough to ask him to consider Harry Stradling, Jr., as cinematographer, because of my love for his father.

And I had a particular actor in mind for Hubbell . . . Robert Redford . . . who happened to be good friends with Sydney, so everything seemed to be falling into place.

Many people first noticed Bob in *Barefoot in the Park*, but that didn't make much of an impression on me. It was a light comedy and he was perfectly passable. It was only when I watched him in *This Property Is Condemned*, which Sydney directed, that I saw there was a lot going on behind those crystal-blue eyes.

I was drawn to him not because of his appearance . . . guys with blond hair and blue eyes were never my type. I did think he was very handsome . . . a wonderful jawline . . . great teeth. But what intrigued me most about Bob was his complexity. You never quite know what he's thinking, and that makes him fascinating to watch on-screen. Like the greatest movie stars, Bob understands the power of restraint. You're never going to get it all . . . and that's the mystery . . . that's what makes you want to keep looking at him.

Bob is that rare combination . . . an intellectual cowboy . . . a charismatic star who is also one of the finest actors of his generation. But like my husband, he's almost apologetic about his looks, and I liked that about him.

So I wanted Redford for Hubbell. But he turned it down.

Since Sydney and Bob were so close, my best hope was that Sydney could somehow persuade him. I have to give Sydney credit. He was as persistent as I was, because we both felt that only Redford would make the picture work. It's like playing tennis . . . I knew my own game would go up when I was opposite a strong player.

But Bob was concerned that the script was so focused on Katie that Hubbell's character was underdeveloped. (He was right.) Bob asked Sydney, "Who *is* this guy? He's just an object . . . He doesn't want anything. What does this guy *want*?" In Bob's opinion, he was "shallow and one-dimensional. Not very real." "A pin-up girl in reverse," as Sydney put it.

I wanted Bob to be happy, so I told Sydney, "Give him anything he wants. Write more scenes to strengthen his character. Make it equal." So Sydney hired two excellent writers, David Rayfiel and Alvin Sargent, to beef up Bob's part and go deeper, beneath that golden-boy exterior. And I told Ray to pay him whatever he wanted. "Take it from the salary you would have paid me!"

But Bob's answer was still no. I was heartbroken.

Ray was pressing us to move on and hire someone else. Apparently he thought any blond actor would do and Ryan O'Neal was next on his list. Sydney kept begging for another week to work on Redford. I told Ray to give it to him and kept praying. The negotiations went down to the wire. I was in the middle of filming *Up the Sandbox* in Africa, and one day I got a telegram from Sue Mengers that simply said: "Barbra Redford!" That's when I knew he'd finally said yes . . . and I was so thrilled! The courtship had been tough, but Bob's reluctance had a big influence on the script and ultimately resulted in a richer, more interesting character.

Hubbell and Katie were different . . . very different. He was the fair-haired, taciturn WASP with no particular political bent and she was the dark-haired, outspoken Jewish girl with strong antiwar opinions. The script was built on the idea that opposites attract. And that was true.

Bob and I were genuinely curious about each other, and I believe that's what comes across on the screen. Once he asked me about Brooklyn. What was it like growing up there? I guess he thought I was kind of exotic, but to me, he was the exotic one, growing up in sunny California. Did he surf? Fish? Swim in the ocean after eating?

I knew he did other daredevil things, like skiing. To come down a mountain on two thin blades, very fast . . . that's not one of the skills you acquire on the streets of Flatbush. But I would listen to him talk about where he had gone skiing over the weekend and his descriptions were so evocative . . . standing alone at the top of a mountain, surrounded by the beauty of the wilderness. It was a little scary but it sounded good, and I thought, *Gosh, could I ever do that?* He really inspired me to learn how to ski, not something I would normally do (you could break bones!).

Bob has always been kind of a loner, and that's part of his charm. I'm not big on casual socializing either. This was a story about two people who were aware of each other but moved in different circles, and I think Bob and I made an instinctive decision not to spend too much time together at the beginning. We wanted the discovery process to happen on-screen.

We shot the movie in sequence, for the most part, which is a great gift to an actor. Then, by the time Katie and Hubbell were comfortable with each other, so were we. At one point, when we were filming scenes on the beach in Malibu, Bob appeared on his motorcycle and asked me if I wanted to take a ride. Now, I'm not the kind of girl who always dreamed of racing down the road on a bike, hair flying in the wind. (You get knots!) I got on behind him and held on to his waist for dear life. But oddly enough, once we got moving, I wasn't scared at all. I felt perfectly safe with him.

I had no idea where we were going. I remember that we went through a tunnel and then rode up into a canyon I never knew existed, to this mysterious place dense with old oak trees. We crossed over a stream and the air smelled of wild fennel. It felt as if we were way out in the country, far from civilization, very private.

Little did I know that one year later I would be living there, in a house built like a contemporary barn. I never made the connection until long after I had moved in, when I was driving through the tunnel one day and suddenly realized that this was where Bob had taken me. I ended up keeping that property as a second home for over twenty years, until I gave it to the state of California to be used as an environmental center.

It was great fun to work with Bob. He and I had a real rapport and the audience could sense it. It's hard to explain why a certain combination of two actors works, but in one interview, Bob tried: "Barbra . . . her femininity brings out the masculinity in a man, and her masculinity brings out a man's femininity, vulnerability, romanticism, whatever you want to call it."

No wonder I liked him. He's very perceptive.

Before I began to write this chapter, I watched the movie again for the first time since 1998. That's when I got involved in a documentary about the making of the film . . . a special feature called *Looking Back* that was part of the twenty-fifth anniversary DVD.

Sydney, Arthur, and I were each interviewed, and I was surprised to hear Sydney say that Bob and I worked very differently . . . that I wanted to rehearse a scene over and over while Bob just wanted to do it. I don't remember it like that at all! I never like to rehearse too much. Often my best performance is the first take . . . it's the most spontaneous . . . the most original . . . and the last thing you want is to lose that spontaneity with too many rehearsals.

The audience can tell when an actor is truly thinking, feeling, reacting. It's impossible to fake an emotion when your face is in close-up on a screen twenty feet high. The camera sees right through to the truth. When you pay attention and really listen, that comes across . . . and in my opinion that's the secret of great acting. Bob and I are both listeners, and we had to listen closely because neither of us ever knew exactly what the other was going to do. We played off each other in a wonderful way, because we both believed in the importance of being in the moment.

You can see that in a scene near the beginning of the film, where Katie is walking home from a job and spots Hubbell sitting at a table outside the local hotel. She crosses the street to avoid him, but he sees her and calls her over.

Momentarily at a loss for conversation, she tells him, "Mrs. Simpson married the Duke of Windsor. It'll be in the papers tomorrow."

"How do you know that?" he asks. "The papers aren't even out yet."

"Oh, I work in the linotype room two nights a week."

"You never quit, do you?"

Katie has to juggle all these jobs in order to pay for school, but she doesn't feel like sharing that with him so she just shrugs her shoulders and says, "Well, thanks for getting me across the street."

It's only when she starts to walk away that he tells her his real news . . . that he's sold his first short story. Katie softens, genuinely thrilled for him. And then there's this lovely moment when he says, "Put your foot up here," because he's noticed her shoelace is untied. It was Alvin Sargent who added that bit to the scene, originally written by Arthur. And as Bob tied my shoe, he gave my foot a pat and held it a little longer than necessary. And that small gesture told you so much. You understood that there was something brewing . . . a connection between the two of them.

There's another gesture that's indelibly associated with the movie. The first time you see it is when Katie spots Hubbell, seven years after they graduated from college, asleep on his stool at the bar in El Morocco. He's a vision in his crisp white navy uniform, and he takes her breath away. Bob had this shock of hair that fell over his forehead, and as we did the scene, it seemed perfectly natural for me to brush it back from his eyes. It wasn't in the script . . . it was just something I felt like doing, in the moment.

It was so intimate coming from me, Barbra, and yet totally right for Katie too. It's probably something she's wanted to do since their days in college, but never dared. Now he's fast asleep on a bar stool, so what the hell?

When I saw the way people reacted to it in dailies . . . everybody loved it . . . I decided I should find a few more times in the story where I could repeat it. (Again, I'm always thinking of the piece as a whole.) It's a physical gesture that brings us closer together . . . and it might mean something later on. It works kind of like a memorable melody in a great score. All of a sudden the music comes in and you don't have to say anything. It's Pavlovian. The feeling is there automatically.

That seems to be the gesture that everyone remembers. In fact, Katie Couric even asked me to do it to her, when I appeared on her talk show decades later. It just shows you how a spontaneous gesture, derived from the truth of the moment, can really resonate.

By the way, that black-and-white dress I'm wearing in the El Morocco scene, with red Bakelite cherries at the neck, was something I bought in a shop in Los Angeles. And those are my own Bakelite bracelets. I never wear red lipstick in real life, but I wore it here because it was right for the period. I found several

1940s-style dresses at that shop and wore them in the movie, because I didn't particularly like the costume sketches I was shown. They didn't seem right for me or my character. Ray saved a lot of money on my wardrobe because of my ready-made finds.

As Katie touches Hubbell's hair, the music in the nightclub fades away, and we hear Marvin Hamlisch's beautiful love theme for the first time. The music cue starts with the sound of chimes (Marvin was inspired by the ones he heard coming from the clock tower at Union College in Schenectady, New York, where we filmed the campus scenes). Then, as I begin to hum the opening melody and sing the words, the credits appear . . . and those chimes provide a lovely transition as the film flashes back to Hubbell and Katie in college in 1937, where their story begins.

When a movie, especially a love story, has a great theme song, it adds an extra emotional dimension that lingers long after you've left the theater. The song "The Way We Were" is probably as famous as the movie itself. It proves how important music can be to a film . . . imagine *The Wizard of Oz* without "Over the Rainbow" or *Breakfast at Tiffany's* without "Moon River."

Ray gave me a list of potential composers that included Marvin, my old friend from *Funny Girl* on Broadway, and I said, "Yes, absolutely! Get him!" And it was logical to bring Marilyn and Alan in to do the lyric, because they were also good friends and Oscar-winning lyricists. I like working with people I know and trust, because then the process becomes so much more fun and you can speak in shorthand. That's when it gets exciting for me.

But the song that you know today is not quite the song I heard when Marvin first played it for me. That's always an important moment for both the composer and the singer . . . and a bit nerve-racking. You want to like it. You want it to be good. All I knew at that point was that it was going to be called "The Way We Were."

Marvin sat down at the piano in my living room and began to play a gentle, repeating chord, and then the melody came in. My ears perked up. I loved it. That first line of the melody was sensational. But then it went downhill, literally. The notes under the second line ("misty watercolor memories") were going down the scale, which felt too somber to me. And then I heard the bridge, which was beautiful, but the ending needed work.

It's hard to describe music in words. It's much easier to understand if you watch the documentary on the DVD, where Marvin plays the original melody and then the final song, so you can *hear* the changes I suggested.

As he explains, "We sat around and she would start to hum little things and slowly it became the big change." What he's referring to is the way the notes now go up . . . in an ascending sequence . . . instead of down, under "misty watercolor memories." I remember standing next to Marvin at the piano and singing it that way, which was how I heard it in my head.

I wish I knew where ideas come from . . . sparked by that impulse that says, It just doesn't feel right. It doesn't sound right. But I can't really analyze it because I did it instinctively.

And Marvin agreed with me and immediately incorporated it into the song. As he says very generously on the DVD, "She's really been very helpful in writing it." And this is what was wonderful about making music with Marvin. He was confident enough in his own talent to be open to change.

All songs go through an evolution. Marvin had gotten the most important part right . . . those first nine notes, which stay in your mind. And then I had another suggestion when it came to the last lines:

So it's the laughter, we will remember
Whenever we remember, the way we were . . .

Again, the original melody under "We will remember / Whenever we remember" was going down the scale but I instinctively sang it going up, and then I wanted the notes to go even higher. It just felt right to me, emotionally and musically, that the melody would soar at the end to capture the passion of this love affair and the emotional impact of its loss. (That's the actress in me, feeling the drama of the moment.)

And Marvin took that suggestion as well, so the song now builds to a climax on the highest notes, and then drops to low notes at the very end on the words "the way we were," becoming even more quiet and sad to express the realization that the relationship is over. And that's the way I sang it.

As for the lyric, a lot of it was right there from the beginning, like that poetic image "misty watercolor memories" and the superb last verse, with its insightful lines:

Mem'ries may be beautiful and yet,
What's too painful to remember, we simply choose to forget . . .

But even great lyricists like Marilyn and Alan make changes as a song evolves. For instance, there was an early version (with the old melody) that began with the line "Rain falls on a distant afternoon." That was intriguing, but other lines like "warm chestnut kisses" and "we gave the sunrise to one another" were just too mushy for me.

What's great about the Bergmans is that they kept working until they came back with a much better lyric. Except there was one more thing . . .

The first line was now "Daydreams light the corners of my mind." Daydreams . . . somehow that word just didn't seem right. It felt weak, too vague for the emotions the music was evoking in me. Besides, the movie is not about imaginary daydreams. It's about real memories. So I said, "Why not start with the word 'memories' as well? It's more powerful and it will tie the whole song together."

The Bergmans understood exactly what I was thinking. It made sense, because the first time you hear the song in the movie, Katie is remembering Hubbell, as the story flashes back in time. And it clearly worked . . . many people think the song is actually called "Memories."

So that's the way the four of us operated. It wasn't about ego. All that mattered was making the song as good as it could be. And the final music and lyric captured that sense of regret in such a heartfelt, universal way. I was hoping the song would push all the right emotional buttons for the audience . . . and it seemed to do just that.

Oh, and there was one last bit of improvisation . . . I found myself humming over the introductory bars. I do that often when I'm recording, to clear my voice and warm up. It usually gets cut from the track. But Sydney loved the hum and thought it was perfect for the title sequence, because he felt it eased the audience into the song . . . and the flashback . . . in a gentler, more organic way.

We started shooting in September 1972 at Union College. I was thirty years old, Bob was thirty-six, and we were supposed to be in our early twenties, but no one objected. If the story is strong and the actors are good, the audience suspends disbelief. For the first few weeks, that parasite I had contracted in Africa was still bothering me. I had a constant headache and found it hard to focus. Everything was hazy and surreal. Thank God for Kaye, who was doing my hair again, and would rub my head and feet every night to put me to sleep. I couldn't keep food down. It was awful. I was so skinny my legs looked like toothpicks. I weighed 115 pounds, which actually worked well for a college student. Gradually, I started to feel better and was able to eat again.

David Rayfiel had a house near the college and invited me to stay with him while we were shooting. But I said no, because I could sense his attraction to me and I didn't want to get involved. I can't deal with a new relationship and work at the same time. He was very attractive, six foot three with thick salt-and-pepper hair, a handsome face . . . a sweet man and a wonderful writer who sent me the most beautiful letters. But I backed away. Perhaps it was because he was too nice, and at that time I was not interested in people who were too fond of me. It was one of my problems . . . I was drawn to men I couldn't have.

Let me be clearer about that. I was still working out issues surrounding my stepfather . . . even though his name was Lou Kind, he was anything but. David, on the other hand, was really kind and thoughtful, so he didn't fit my familiar pattern. And he was totally available, so he didn't present enough of a challenge, I guess. Too bad . . . I adored David as a person (we remained friends for the rest of his life), and I didn't want to hurt him. I'll bet that was another reason why I was so queasy during that first month.

Back to the movie. I really identified with Katie, and it was interesting how many pieces from my own closet also worked for her. That's my vintage brown skirt and tortoiseshell necklace I'm wearing when Katie is giving a speech on campus promoting world peace. It was under threat in 1937 because of the Spanish Civil War. Katie is an idealist who is president of the Young Communist League (the YCL) at a time when many progressive thinkers were attracted by Communism's support of workers' rights and the utopian concept of a more equal society. Her skeptical classmates are heckling her. I often felt like an outcast growing up, so that seemed completely natural to me. And that's my own vintage dusty-rose sweater I have on in the library, where I'm sneaking looks at Hubbell in between studying. I liked that hairdo with all the curls, a wig styled by Kaye (who, by the way, also made the best salad dressing, using ground sunflower seeds way before they were popular).

Once again, in this movie I'm the unconventional-looking woman in love with the handsome prince . . . Hubbell . . . star athlete, the big man on campus. Everything comes so easily to him, even writing . . . compared to Katie, who agonizes over her short story and is so hard on herself (like I can be). When Hubbell's story gets chosen to be read aloud in class, she's so devastated that she tears up her own and throws it in the trash.

I needed to cry in that scene, but for some reason I couldn't. So Sydney just took me aside and put his arms around me and that was all I needed . . . I completely broke down.

It was so exciting to come to work every morning with actors and a director whom I respected. If you were stuck, Sydney could give you that little trigger. He spoke the actor's language . . . or, with that simple touch, no words were necessary.

When Katie runs into Hubbell at El Morocco, she hasn't seen him since he cut in on Frank McVeigh, her colleague from the YCL, to dance with her at their senior prom.

Now it's 1944, the world is at war . . . he's in the navy, she's working at a radio station. And Hubbell, who's had too much to drink, is in no shape to go anywhere by himself, so she has to bring him home with her. While she's making coffee, he falls asleep in her bed. Katie stares at him, quietly takes off her dress and her slip, and slides in to join him. She can't quite believe she's lying next to this man she's had a crush on for so long. Delicately, she touches his hair, and he moves closer, kissing her neck, and then begins to make love to her, automatically, because he's basically asleep.

You may think this is the kind of scene that comes naturally. You don't have to act. Just be in the moment . . .

But in fact it's always difficult for me. I'm a very private person, and it's hard to be intimate when other people are watching. It's awkward and scary, and in this case, my own emotions blended into Katie's. I'm thinking, *She doesn't want him to stop, but she's almost afraid to react.* Would that break the spell? And then she's experiencing all the usual doubts . . . Will she disappoint him? Will he disappoint her?

Because if he wakes up, then what?

All these emotions are playing across her face. But at the end, her fleeting smile dissolves when she says, "Hubbell . . . it's Katie. You did know it was Katie?" And a tear falls from her eye.

Hubbell doesn't remember a thing the next morning . . . or at least pretends not to. Bob is great in that scene. All he wants to do is get out of there gracefully. He doesn't even stay to eat the breakfast Katie has prepared for him. But when he comes back to town and calls to take her up on her offer of a place to sleep, Katie uses all her ration stamps to buy food for him. (Well, she's Jewish!)

She's coming home laden with groceries and catches him just as he's leaving, blurting out, "I've got steaks and baked potatoes and sour cream and chives and salad and fresh-baked pie. I would have made a pot roast. I make a terrific pot roast, but I didn't know whether you'd ever had pot roast or whether you liked pot roast. I mean, anyway there wasn't time because it should be made the day before . . . you've got to stay for supper, that's all there is to it!"

Redford says, "What kind of pie?" with the emphasis on "pie." I thought maybe the emphasis should be on "kind" . . . i.e., if it's the right *kind* of pie, he'll stay. I thought it would be funnier and more charming if Hubbell were more amused by her. And that prompted me to ask Bob, "Would you ever let me direct you?"

"Yeah, I would," he said, which really pleased me and represented a big leap of faith on his part, because I hadn't directed anything at this point.

Hubbell does stay for supper, just because Katie has guilted him into it. It's only when she pulls out his novel after the meal and tells him honestly what she thinks of it that he's truly intrigued.

Katie believes in him, but she's also unafraid to tell him where his book falls short, and that's the real beginning of their romance. People often fall in love with their teachers . . . mentors . . . someone who cares enough to push them to be their best.

There's a beautiful sequence where he's looking at her as if seeing her for the first time, they're touching each other, and then they make love in front of the fire. In Arthur's original script, Hubbell leans over her and says, "It'll be better this time."

So he *did* remember that they had made love that first night! But the line was cut. I'm not sure why. Perhaps Sydney thought it made Hubbell less likable . . . but to me it was so much more interesting if Hubbell acknowledged his earlier behavior, and subtly apologized for it.

I thought Sydney's staging of the breakup scene at the radio station was so smart, with Katie and Hubbell initially separated by the glass wall of the booth. Hubbell says, "Look, Katie—" and she interrupts him, "Oh, God. Please don't start a sentence with 'Look.' It's always bad news." He tells her their relationship isn't working, and she thinks she knows why. "I don't fit on Beekman Place. That's what's really wrong." She doesn't want Hubbell to see her cry so she turns her back on him for a moment, until she can compose herself. But he puts down her key and walks out.

In the next scene, Sydney had me calmly taking Hubbell's jacket out of the closet and neatly folding it into a suitcase. Then I carefully gather up his manuscript pages and close his typewriter case, tilting my head back to try to hold in the tears.

I remember that day very clearly. My first instinct as an actress (and as a woman) was that Katie would be angry. As I know from experience, when you're profoundly hurt, you often react with anger to cover up the pain. I would have liked to try having her grab his clothes out of the closet and throw them in the suitcase, pull his shaving cream out of the medicine cabinet and dump it in the wastebasket, rip his page out of the typewriter and slam the case shut.

But Sydney saw it differently. He wanted me to be sad and teary, so that's what I did. Looking at the scene again, Sydney's way definitely works, especially once it was underscored with Marvin's beautiful music. But I was also thinking of the film as a whole, and worried about having three scenes in a row with tears . . . since in the next scene, where Katie calls Hubbell on the phone, she can't stop crying. That's another reason why I felt some anger would have been a better lead-in to that scene.

I mentioned that there were five scenes that I loved in the treatment, and the telephone scene is one of them. And it was there right from the beginning, almost word for word.

I think it's one of Arthur's best pieces of writing. I didn't have to prepare before we shot it. I didn't want to discuss it. I didn't even want to rehearse it. I just wanted to do it. The words alone always moved me. You just say them and you cry.

An actor only has to rely on technique and use the Method when a scene is difficult to relate to. But when it's totally natural, you just let it be . . . let the emotions flow. You're the vessel for this character to speak through. It's as if the emotions well up from the subconscious. You react out of pure instinct.

Katie dials the phone, and the first thing she says when Hubbell answers is, "It's me." The tears started immediately. I put my hand over my face and ad-libbed something: "Hubbell . . . Wait a minute. Hold on a minute. Don't go away," while I pulled a handkerchief out of my pocket.

I must have asked them to give me a handkerchief, because I knew this scene was going to make me cry. I just didn't know where or when.

"Listen, Hubbell. This is kind of peculiar. I know that I don't have to apologize for what I said, because I know that you know . . . anyway the peculiar thing is, it's really a request, a favor. See, I can't sleep, Hubbell, and it would help me so much if you could, well, if I had someone to talk to. You know, if I had a best friend or something to talk about it with. Only you're my best friend. Isn't that dumb? It's so dumb!" (I heard my voice going up an octave.) "You're the best friend I've ever had."

I love that idea. He's her best friend, and she has nobody else she can talk to about him, except *him*. That felt so true.

"And it would help me so much if you could just come over and see me through tonight. Listen, Hubbell, I promise I won't touch you or beg you or embarrass you. But I've got to talk to my best friend about someone we both know."

We did two takes of the scene. On the first, I was oblivious to the camera. I wasn't in control of my voice or my tears, and I certainly wasn't paying any attention to the mechanics of the shot. But on the second, I remember thinking, *Why is the camera staying so far away during this long speech?*

I've always been able to feel the camera as it's moving in, and the closer it comes, the less I do . . . just instinctively. But that didn't happen here, so I just kept sobbing.

And now, all I can think is, *Why do I keep holding that handkerchief in front of my face?* I was probably self-conscious about my nose running.

This is painful to watch. I can't believe how long my hand is in front of my face. You can't see the eyes. You can hear the emotion but you can't see it.

Don't get me wrong. Sometimes that's great . . . but not here.

This is where I needed Sydney to say, "Barbra, I want you to try it without the handkerchief this time. Or pick it up but then put it down. I don't care if your nose runs!"

In his memoir, Arthur says, "How I wished I could have directed her in that phone call! There was no reason for her to hide her face; Barbra Streisand understood rejection. What she needed was help from someone who understood her."

Arthur blamed Sydney and said, "It was never reshot and—if done properly—it would have won her the Academy Award."

I didn't want to believe that.

But now that I'm looking at my performance here, I'm thinking, *It's not good enough.* I was so eager to do this scene that I couldn't help myself . . . all the emotion just overflowed. I should have put that handkerchief down . . . and I should have done less. To see Katie trying to control her emotions would have been more heartbreaking. Again, it's the restraint that moves you.

I wish I could do it over.

Sydney was an actor himself. He understood how important this moment could be. If only he had slowed me down, done a few more takes to give me the time to calm down a bit . . . asked me to try it a different way.

This is difficult to write about. I adored Sydney. I respected him as a director and loved him as a friend. We used to tell each other secrets. Mine went with him to the grave, and I would never tell his. And I trusted him to do what was best for the film. But I think he felt responsible for persuading Redford to do the movie even though I had the more showy part, and perhaps subconsciously he was trying to redress the balance by paying less attention to some of Katie's most important scenes. I just assumed Sydney would protect me as an actress. But maybe he was more protective of Redford. I never realized it until watching the movie now.

Arthur, in his own memoir, recounted what he said to Sydney: "You're going to build up Redford's part because . . . he's the blond goy you wish you were. The picture is Barbra's no matter what you do because the story is hers. Be careful you don't destroy it trying to give it to him."

Arthur could be very cruel, and I think he's too harsh on Sydney here. For me, the story became more compelling when Katie and Hubbell were more evenly matched. That's how we know they're meant for each other. And that's what makes it so moving when Hubbell does come to see her after the call, and she asks why they can't be together.

He says, "Because you push too hard. Every damn minute! There's no time ever to just relax and enjoy living."

He's right. Katie does push too hard, encouraging him to finish his book . . . but only because she believes in him so deeply. And that's what finally wins him over.

"Katie, you expect so much."

"Oh, but look what I've got."

In the next scene, they're on a sailboat, with the Malibu coastline in the background. Then we see Katie setting a bride-and-groom cake topper on a shelf in their beach house. So we know they're married and they've moved to LA, and it's all done without words, in a few shots. (Nice work, Sydney.)

Bob loved to tease me, just as Hubbell teases Katie. I think the most fun we had was shooting the party scene where everybody is dressed up as a Marx Brother. I was Harpo, Bob was Groucho . . . and the real Groucho Marx even stopped by the set to visit. (His costume was definitely the best.) When Katie's about to start a fight with the director who's making a movie of Hubbell's book, Bob clapped his hand over my mouth. Of all the ways in my life that people have tried to shut me up, that was by far the funniest.

But for me, the most interesting moments to play were when the story suddenly turned from light to serious on a dime. There's a scene where Katie is cooking, dreaming about moving to France so Hubbell can finish his novel there. He quickly changes the subject to ask about her job (she summarizes books for the movie studio). Katie describes a phony synopsis she wrote, just to entertain herself: "You see, there's this kibbutz of Chinese Jews living in a rice paddy . . . and she cooks Communist rice patties." They laugh, and then she says she's got another one for him. "Loudmouth Jewish girl from New York City comes to Malibu, California, and tells her gorgeous *goyishe* guy that she's pregnant."

Bob's reaction is perfect. Hubbell is speechless for a moment, and then comes over to embrace her . . . gently. He's so happy. The fact that they're going to have a baby brings them closer. On another evening at the director's house, we see them slow dancing all by themselves. (That's so much sexier to me than something more obvious, like a kiss.) And then the movie turns on a dime again, when the director finds a wire behind a Picasso painting, and all the guests are shocked to realize their conversation is being taped.

Arthur was dealing with a subject that few filmmakers were willing to touch . . . the way the government, afraid of Communism, focused on Hollywood in 1947 and summoned various directors, writers, actors, and producers to testify before the House Un-American Activities Committee. Most people, when they were questioned about supposed "subversives," named names. But the "Hollywood Ten" refused to answer, and for their integrity, they were blacklisted by the studios . . . which meant they could no longer work. Careers were cut short; lives were ruined.

Arthur was blacklisted himself, so this story was very personal to him. Unfortunately, a lot of that story didn't make the final cut.

Katie plans to travel to Washington in support of the Hollywood Ten, even though Hubbell doesn't want her to go. He's angry.

"Going to take the baby with you?"

"I thought I might."

Hubbell replies, "Well, nothing like an early education."

The dialogue often skirts around the real subject. The words are rarely on the nose. That's the best kind of writing.

Hubbell pours a drink and says, "We're kind of back where we started, aren't we?"

"That's not true, Hubbell," she replies.

Originally, there was more to Katie's speech. She went on to say, "In college, I stood under a maple tree selling Loyalist Spain. And you wouldn't let Jews into your fraternity house. Now you've married one, and she's going to have your baby. We live on the beach in Malibu, California, and that is not where we started."

It was a subtle indictment of prejudice and a confirmation of their own bond. But it was cut, and now the scene goes straight to Hubbell saying, "Okay. Now why don't we all stay home?"

"I can't," Katie says.

The rest of the sequence, where she explains why she can't sit back while their friends are in jeopardy, is also missing. Katie is a political animal. Hubbell is not. Politics . . . and the conflict it caused . . . is glossed over with that cut.

When Hubbell arrives at Union Station to meet Katie on her return, they're engulfed by the press. Reporters shout questions, and as Katie answers, she's attacked by an angry man who calls her a "Commie bitch." Hubbell rushes to protect her, punches the guy, and is hit himself as the police hold him back. (That scene was written by David to give Hubbell some backbone.) Then the two of them take shelter in an empty restaurant.

I thought the next part was brilliant. It explains Hubbell's point of view, and what he says is valid. Arthur wrote a version and then David and Alvin refined it, adding their own sensibilities. Hubbell is really taking her on about the Hollywood Ten, and for once, he's just as passionate as she is. And Redford is terrific in this scene.

"I'm telling you it's a waste . . . and that those men and their families are only going to get hurt and that nothing is going to change . . . nothing! And after jail, after five or six years of bad blood, when it's practical for some Fascist producer to hire some Communist writer to save his ass because his hit movie's in trouble, he'll do it. They'll both do it. They'll make movies. They'll have dinner. They'll play tennis. They'll make passes at each other's wives. Now what in the hell did anybody ever go to jail for? For what? A political spat?"

But Katie is ready to storm the barricades.

"Hubbell, you are telling me to close my eyes and to watch people being destroyed so that you can go on working, working in a town that doesn't have spine enough to stand up for anything but making a blessed buck!"

"I'm telling you that people, people are more important than any goddamn witch hunt. You and me . . . not causes . . . not principles."

"Hubbell, people *are* their principles."

The difference between Katie and Hubbell is distilled into those last three lines . . . and they were Arthur's.

At some point, there was talk of cutting "people *are* their principles," but I felt it said so much about Katie and objected so fiercely that the line stayed.

Arthur could telegraph a lifetime of emotion in a few words. Not that everything he wrote was perfect. When I heard about early versions of the story . . . where Hubbell has an affair with the director's wife, the director comes on to Katie, Katie comes on to a tennis pro . . . I thought all that was ridiculous. It diluted the central romance and made Hubbell very unappealing, which doesn't work in a love story because you need the audience to be rooting for both people.

But the essence of Arthur's story was amazing, and that's what I kept fighting for through all the many rewrites he did and the various fixes made by other writers. I was very touched that he had written this for me and I wanted to protect it.

Arthur was well aware of my efforts. As he wrote in his memoir, "She had been a wonderful pest, dredging up a scene here, a line there from my early versions, lugging them to the set and utzing Sydney to put them back. She knew Katie Morosky better than he did and fought like her for her."

The fact is, Sydney didn't like Arthur . . . that's why he brought in his own writers . . . and Arthur didn't like Sydney. So I ended up acting as the intermediary. I'd often call Sydney at night to talk about a scene, and read him some lines from an earlier version, hoping to reinstate some of Arthur's words. It's the same thing I did with Willy, when I showed him the various versions of *Funny Girl*.

Sometimes it worked and sometimes it didn't, because Sydney had his own vision. And I thought some of the choices he made in the edit were very good. He cut the scene where Katie sees Hubbell go off with his old college girlfriend, and instead lets the audience know that she knows much more subtly, in the projection room scene. After watching his not-so-good movie, everyone skips out except Katie and Hubbell. He mocks a comment from one of their friends, and when Katie defends her, he says, "Katie, the day you die you'll still be a nice Jewish girl."

"Are you still a nice Gentile boy?" she asks, taking the conversation in a whole new direction.

"I never was," he replies, and continues, "Katie, what's wrong with us has nothing to do with another girl. Oh, give up. Please."

"I can't. I hate what you did to your book." (That's more upsetting to her than a one-night stand, which disturbs her but would never break them up.) "I hate the picture. I hate those people. I hate the palm trees. I wish it would rain. Oh, I want . . . I want . . ."

"What?"

"I want us to love each other."

Arthur had written one more line to that scene. Hubbell says, "We do. That's the trouble, Katie. We do."

I have no idea why Sydney cut that line. Maybe he was trying to avoid complexities. Me, I look for them. It makes you want to see the movie over and over, to peel more of the layers back.

But now, to the most devastating loss. It never even occurred to me that Sydney would take out two major scenes . . . the crux of the film, in my opinion . . . two of the five great scenes that I loved in Arthur's treatment.

The first takes place after the scene in the projection room. It's another day, Katie is on her way home with groceries, and as she's driving through the UCLA campus, she sees a girl making a speech. A small crowd is gathering, and she pulls up and stops the car to listen. The girl is telling the students that they must support members of the faculty who refuse to take a loyalty oath. She says, "The witch-hunters have already begun to blacklist our teachers, to put informers in our classrooms, our laboratories."

I remember shooting this scene as though it were yesterday . . . a scene that I thought was the very definition of the title, *The Way We Were*. It's about looking back at your past and remembering the way you were. I didn't have to prepare for it, and I didn't need any rehearsal.

I liked the way Sydney had set up the camera to capture my reactions in one shot. What hit me first, as Katie, was how much this student reminded me of my younger self in college, speaking out about the Spanish Civil War. I'm smiling . . . my God, did I look like that? Did I sound like that? Were my clothes equally pathetic? But then the camera moves in gradually as my emotions turn. The girl is earnest and sincere, and she's getting heckled by the crowd, as Katie had been. I knew exactly what she was going through, and my eyes welled up with tears.

I'm thinking, *What has become of me?* Where is that girl I once was, with all that passion . . . trying to save the world . . . ready to fight injustice? And now I've sold my soul, spending my time writing synopses of stupid books and making up ridiculous plots about Chinese rice patties just to entertain myself. By the end of the push-in, I'm sobbing.

I did it in one take, because the situation was so right. I could already imagine the finished scene in the movie . . . Marvin's beautiful theme would start playing under the girl's voice, and the snide comments from the crowd. And Katie's reaction would have even more impact because it would happen in a single shot.

I couldn't wait to see the dailies, because I thought it had gone so well. Since

I didn't work the next day, they arranged a screening for me and I was sitting by myself when that scene came up. There was the picture, but there was no sound.

What happened?

It turned out that the sound man had asked Sydney, "Does she have any lines?" Sydney said no, so the guy went on to the next location. This meant I would have to loop the crying . . . to somehow recreate the emotion in a recording booth. Why didn't Sydney keep the sound man?

It probably was an honest mistake, but still . . . this was an important scene.

Much later, when Sydney came to my house to show me the rough cut of the movie before it went to preview, I was dumbfounded by the way this scene had been edited. It went from the shot of me driving up, to a small crowd gathering around this girl speaking, then cut to me smiling at her. Then it cut to a closer shot of the girl, then back to me crying.

You can't do that! Where's the transition? You need to use the whole take to see the shift of emotions on Katie's face. Sydney said the push-in was too long, but I timed it and it was just a few seconds.

Now it looked like two totally different takes, and the switch was not believable. He cut out the few frames in between . . . cut out how one emotion turned into another . . . and diminished the impact of what she was going through.

And then in the final film, Sydney ended up cutting out the scene entirely. I was stunned. Here was a moment that shook Katie to her very core. It made her stop and think about her past and reassess her future. This was her epiphany. It was such a crucial scene, and the whole sequence was less than a minute.

I was *so* disappointed.

I missed this scene so much because it worked not just emotionally, but also structurally. After their blowup in the projection room, I felt that Katie and Hubbell both needed time away from each other. Arthur had written the scene for Katie at UCLA, and Alvin and David added a good scene for Hubbell on a boat to balance that. He's with his best friend, J.J., and they're playing their favorite game, reminiscing about the past, and J.J. asks, "Best year?"

Hubbell answers, "Best year . . . nineteen forty-four . . . no, nineteen forty-five . . . forty-six." He's thinking back to the time when he and Katie were first together. It's a subtle way to indicate that he still loves her and it was so right, to have them both remembering the way they were.

Then in the next scene, Katie and Hubbell come together in their Malibu living room, about to eat dinner. This is the second scene that I couldn't believe was cut from the film.

Hubbell stands there fiddling with a corkscrew when he suddenly asks, "Who is Frank McVeigh?"

Katie is surprised. "Frank McVeigh? Old Frankie . . . we went to college with him . . . at least I did. We were in the YCL together. Why?"

"He informed on you."

"He what?" She sits down, stunned. "The little rat. It's so crazy. He was my date at the senior prom and you cut in for ten seconds. I guess it was obvious I liked you better than him. What could he tell them anyway? I mean I left the Party during the war, for God's sake."

Frankie (played by James Woods) had been jealous of Katie's attraction to Hubbell all those years ago, and now he finally got even. It's so human . . . it's often something petty that prompts people to do terrible things.

The next lines Arthur wrote were never filmed. Katie asks Hubbell what the committee could possibly accuse her of having done.

"They say you tried to get the studio to make a subversive film."

"I *what?*"

"You recommended a book which they claim was outright propaganda for Communist China."

And then she starts to laugh, because she realizes he's talking about her phony synopsis about the Chinese kibbutz and the Communist rice patties! (I tried to get those lines back in, but Sydney said no one would believe it . . . that it was too ridiculous.)

Arthur always said that the climax of the picture was when the love story and the political story came together . . . and this is the scene where it happened. In 1947, as far as the studio heads were concerned, Katie was subversive. And if Hubbell, who was employed by the studio, had a subversive wife, that was grounds to fire him.

Frankie's betrayal means that Katie will be called before the committee and expected to name names.

Katie says, "Hubbell, there is no justification for informing, none! And there's something very wrong with any country that makes for informers."

"Christ, is that what you think I want you to do?" he answers. What a great line. This is where we see Hubbell's strength of character and his love and support for Katie.

"I don't know . . . All I know is that if I don't name names, you can't get a job in this town!"

"Okay," he says. "Then I'll have to finish my book." So he's not going to ask her to compromise her values. He brings over their plates and says, "Let's eat."

Katie sits down on the sofa, stares off into the distance, and says, "It's amazing how decisions are forced on you, willy-nilly."

She looks at Hubbell. "You never did want to finish your book, did you?"

"I don't know. I guess I never really thought there was much point."

"And you never really wanted to go to France, did you?"

"No, I didn't. You wanted me to."

And now we see *her* strength of character, because she's willing to sacrifice what means the most to her . . . her marriage . . . in order to save him. She says, "If we got a divorce, you wouldn't have a subversive wife . . . and that would solve everything, wouldn't it?"

"No," Hubbell answers. "No, it wouldn't."

But Katie has already decided, and she knows it's the only decision . . . the proper decision . . . because she is not going to name names, and she does not want him to be punished for her beliefs. They have come to a crossroads, and she finds herself reminiscing. "Wouldn't it be lovely if we were old? We'd have survived all this. And everything would be easy and uncomplicated, the way it was when we were young."

"Katie, it was never uncomplicated."

"But it was lovely, wasn't it?"

"Yes. It was lovely," he says.

Which leads to that heartbreaking line, "Will you do me one favor, Hubbell? Will you stay with me till the baby's born?"

It's precisely because she loves him deeply that she makes the decision to let him go. And it's also about being true to herself. She can't stay in Hollywood. But she knows that Hubbell, to the contrary, belongs there. And there's a whole other layer to her decision as she suddenly confronts a truth about their relationship . . . she's been pushing him all these years to be something he doesn't want to be . . . to live somewhere he doesn't want to live . . . to write something he doesn't want to write.

She's been assuming that Hubbell shares her vision of him, but the reality is he's afraid he can't live up to it. As he said to her back in New York when they first broke up, "You expect so much." That's been a huge pressure on him, and she finally hears what he's been saying all along, and now she understands. So she releases him, and there's strength and love and generosity in her response, because it's incredibly painful to her.

Almost none of this is left in the film.

What we see instead is Hubbell setting down their plates on a table as the scene begins with Katie's line, "It's amazing how decisions are forced on you, willy-nilly."

What decision? The line makes no sense. We have no idea what she's talking about because the Frankie McVeigh scene has been cut . . . and it's the climax of the story. The fact that Katie has been informed on is the catalyst for everything that happens next. Without that scene and the UCLA scene, the plot is eviscerated and we've lost the essence of her character, as well as his . . . because Hubbell's lines show he was prepared to stand by her.

Without those two crucial scenes, there's nothing about her feeling that she has lost her sense of self in Hollywood . . . nothing about being informed on . . . nothing about what actually forced her decision. All of that is gone. So now you think they split up simply because he shtupped this other girl one time.

You can hear Sydney on the documentary, describing how they previewed the picture on a Friday night in San Francisco and saying it was a flop. Then he says that he took out "about five scenes, and they were all politics," and on Saturday night the picture was a hit. (By the way, Marty was there and he says the picture played great on both nights.)

I agreed with Sydney on three of those scenes. They involved subsidiary characters having political discussions that went on so long even I lost interest.

Yes, right, cut those extraneous scenes (about fifteen minutes) . . . no great loss . . . but don't cut the two scenes that were pivotal to the plot. Don't cut the crucial three and a half minutes that the whole film revolves around.

It was such a betrayal of Arthur's story. It destroyed the soul of Katie's character . . . and destroyed me.

I was so upset back in 1973 that I asked if I could have the deleted scenes, and I've kept those trims in my vault (along with outtakes from my recordings, TV specials, and certain films). Then in 1998, when we were doing the DVD for the twenty-fifth anniversary, I asked Sydney if I could show those deleted scenes in the documentary. He could easily have said no, but instead he very generously said, "Okay," because he understood how passionate I was about this movie. That was Sydney being a real friend.

In the documentary, both Arthur and I talk about how those cuts eliminated vital information. Sydney admits, "I don't say to this day that I'm right." The fact is, Ray Stark and the studio were pushing him to take out the politics because they thought it would bore people. As Sydney explained to one journalist, "While we were shooting we were rewriting. We were getting so much pressure. Columbia was going under at the time; they hadn't had a big hit in years, and the picture was going over budget. Bob didn't get along with Ray Stark, and neither did I. We didn't know how to mix the politics and the love story and make it work."

Ray was nervous. Arthur writes in his book that Ray told Sydney to make those cuts after the first San Francisco preview. So Sydney and Margaret Booth, Ray's favorite editor . . . a tough woman from another era . . . went up into the projection booth with a razor blade and cut the film hastily, in one chunk. And in my humble opinion, they threw out the baby with the bathwater. Perhaps no one had time to think about what that did to the picture as a whole. And since Sydney was under so much pressure to produce a hit, he capitulated . . . taking out the politics and taking less of a risk.

I took my pleas to Ray, which was useless. He didn't support me, and I was very disappointed in him. We were back to our old dynamic . . . always a power struggle. Ray really let me down.

I felt absolutely powerless. My mind just flashed back to that moment as a young girl, standing in my mother's bedroom doorway and being ignored. Once again, I felt unseen and unheard. I begged Sydney to put those two scenes back in. But he didn't.

This was the moment when I thought, *That's it.* I had always had creative control of my albums, my TV specials, and my concerts. Now I realized, *I have to be more in control of my films as well. I have to direct.*

Of course, it's hard to argue with success. The movie became a huge hit . . . and Columbia's second-highest-grossing film up till then (they told me the highest was

Funny Girl). I never knew that Sydney attributed much of that success to me until researching this chapter, when I read this quote from him: "You have to credit Barbra with going a long way to saving Columbia's bacon—putting it politely—single-handedly."

That touched my heart.

The Way We Were was nominated for six Academy Awards, but I thought there was something odd when I saw the list. No nomination for Best Picture. Sydney wasn't nominated as Best Director. Arthur wasn't nominated for his screenplay.

Maybe the reason the movie missed out on the big awards was because people sensed something was missing and didn't understand why Katie and Hubbell broke up. Several critics pointed out gaps in the storyline. Pauline Kael wrote, "The decisive change in the characters' lives which the story hinges on takes place suddenly and hardly makes sense." Roger Ebert said, "Inexplicably, the movie suddenly and implausibly has them fall out of love—and they split up without resolving anything, particularly the plot."

I was honored to be nominated for Best Actress, but I was very disappointed that Bob wasn't nominated for Best Actor for our movie, because he was amazing in it. (He did get nominated for *The Sting*.)

At least "The Way We Were" was up for Best Original Song, and the Academy asked me to sing it on the broadcast, but I was reluctant . . . my stage fright again. When I get nervous, my heart pounds and it affects my voice, which starts to shake and I lose control. It's a terrible feeling and I didn't want to go through that. So they asked Peggy Lee to do it, which was fine with me. (Besides, I wanted to be thought of as an actress first, not a singer.) But in retrospect, I wish I had been stronger and sung the song.

And now, in reliving this time in my life, I realize that my emotions were more conflicted than I could even admit to myself back then. And that's probably why I didn't want to go to the ceremony. I felt embarrassed that crucial parts of the performance were not even in the movie. I just couldn't bear the thought of sitting in that auditorium and having to smile for the cameras and pretend everything was great. So I hid backstage.

Frankly, I was relieved when they didn't call my name. The winner was Glenda Jackson for *A Touch of Class*, but she wasn't in the audience either (so at least I wasn't the only one).

The only people from our movie who went home with Oscars that night were Marvin for the score and the music for the song, and Alan and Marilyn for the lyrics. I was happy for them because they all truly deserved to win.

I know the song contributed enormously to the movie's success, yet Sydney told me that Redford didn't want me to sing at all. Bob confirmed this on *Oprah* in 2010, when he surprised me by showing up to reminisce about *The Way We Were.* Maybe he didn't realize how seamlessly Sydney and Marvin would integrate the song into the movie, to the extent that they're irrevocably linked to this day.

Like the film, the song was a huge hit. When Marty first heard it, he said, "I'm tone deaf, but if I can hum this melody after hearing it only once, then so can the rest of the world. It's going to be number one."

In addition to the Oscar, it won the Golden Globe Award for Best Original Song and the Grammy Award for Song of the Year.

And the way Marvin used the song in the last scene was particularly moving. The melody starts over the shots of Central Park through the seasons that signal the shift in time and place as Marvin's chords become more plaintive.

We had taken a hiatus before we came back to New York to shoot the final scene. Sydney and I flew back together on the plane, and it was time well spent, because I managed to convince him to put back more of Arthur's words.

The scene starts with a shot of the iconic Plaza Hotel. Then we see Katie walking toward it. She spots Hubbell at the entrance. He spots her, and does a double take (it's very hard to do a good double take, and Bob's was great). He smiles. She smiles, and crosses the street to talk to him. Music is playing beneath all this. They hug and kiss in a long shot. He's with another woman and introductions are made. We can't hear the dialogue but we can see how friendly they are through their body language.

Now the camera is closer. He asks her if she's still married (so clearly she's moved on too), and Katie asks him what he's doing in New York. He tells her that he's been writing a television show. Then the doorman says his taxi's ready. Katie says she's late, and invites him to come for a drink as she runs back across the street to pick up a stack of "Ban the Bomb" leaflets (she's back doing what she loves). Suddenly she hears Hubbell, alone this time, saying, "You never give up, do you?" I love that echo, from the scene in the projection room and from the scene earlier, tying her shoelace . . .

"Only when I'm absolutely forced to," Katie responds. "But I'm a very good loser."

"Better than I am." *Very* good line. It says everything . . . without saying it.

"Well, I've had more practice." Then she says, "Your girl is lovely, Hubbell. Why don't you bring her for a drink when you come?"

"I can't . . . I can't."

Katie, sensitive to him as always, says, "I know."

And that's when I reached out and brushed his hair off his forehead. And he clasps my hand as we come together in an embrace. We held on to each other for that extra minute or two, remembering the way we were, before we let each other go.

I knew from the moment I first did that gesture in the nightclub that it would really resonate at the very end of the movie. And when I touch his hair, the music starts again, underscoring the emotion and reminding you of everything that has happened since they met.

"How is she?" he asks. He hasn't seen their daughter since she was born. (I always imagined Katie would send him pictures of her on her birthday.)

"She is just beautiful. You would be so proud of her, Hubbell."

"I'm glad. Is he a good father?"

"Yes, very."

"Good."

He looks down and takes a leaflet. Then the music swells as they look at each other one last time. He says, "See ya, Katie," and walks across the street and out of her life again.

"See ya, Hubbell," she says softly.

That's another poignant echo, from their goodbye after that first night at her apartment. And then as the film cuts to a long shot, leaving Katie standing on the street and handing out her leaflets, you hear my voice singing the song over the credits. By now, the audience is usually sobbing. But at the first screening, people didn't cry . . . and when Marvin didn't hear that sobbing, he instantly knew why. He had scored the ending with a different melody, worried he might have overused the theme. "Big mistake," he said, and went into his own pocket (when the studio balked) to get the orchestra back to rerecord the ending with the familiar music. And I can't imagine the movie without it.

It's very gratifying to read that *The Way We Were* is now considered a classic.

The American Film Institute named it number 6 on their list of the 100 greatest love stories, putting it right up there with *Gone With the Wind* and *Casablanca.*

I, too, love *The Way We Were* and consider it a highlight of my career. I think it's one of Bob's best performances . . . and probably one of mine as well . . . and I'm thrilled whenever I see us listed as one of the screen's most romantic couples. We made something that will last a long time . . . much longer than most real marriages.

Sydney did an excellent job and made a wonderful film. I know the picture works, but not as brilliantly as it could have . . . not with those essential scenes missing. It's still a great love story, but why not have the underlying complexity and power of the political dimension as well as the emotional?

Writing this book brought back all those memories, so in the spring of 2021, I asked Marty to call Tom Rothman, the head of Sony (which owns Columbia), to find out if they had anything planned for the fiftieth anniversary in 2023.

When Marty told me they were going to reissue the original film on a new Blu-ray, I thought, *Oh my God, this may be my chance to finally restore those missing scenes, not only for me but for Katie, and also for all the people who love this film.* I *had* to persuade Tom to release an extended version as well.

I truly believe that if Sydney were alive today, he'd agree to put those two scenes back into the movie . . . because they're about much more than politics.

So I did something I've been aching to do since 1973. I still had all the trims saved, and I hired Mike Arick, the same editor who had worked with me on the first DVD, to sit beside me at my Avid editing machine and put them back into the film. I felt such a sense of purpose and responsibility . . . as if I were fulfilling a commitment to Arthur, and to Hubbell and Katie. I also wanted to retrieve some of her speech explaining why she had to go to Washington to support their friends, because it shows her political fearlessness. And it was important to me to put back that last, very revealing line at the end of the projection room scene, when Katie says, "I want us to love each other," and Hubbell responds, "We do. That's the trouble, Katie. We do."

I realize now why Sydney had to cut that line . . . it contradicted his premise that their relationship was over. As he said in the documentary, "This story reaches a point where you know these two people are finished, and it's at the end of the projection room [scene]."

I didn't agree, and that's not what Arthur wrote. Katie loves Hubbell and isn't the type to leave him over a one-night stand with an old girlfriend. And that line confirms that Hubbell still loves Katie. It was there from Arthur's first script, and one of the reasons I like it is because it's so true . . . love is complicated. I guess Sydney tried to simplify it because he couldn't have them both declaring their love at the moment they're supposedly "finished."

But I'm looking at this from the audience's perspective, too, and we're rooting for this couple to stay together. And the only reason they don't is because Katie has been informed on, and she decides to end the relationship in order to protect him. This is what brings the audience to tears. Imagine how excruciating it is to love someone and be forced to deny yourself that love.

There were other moments I would have included, like a scene where she's encouraging him to stay at the typewriter and keep writing, but I knew if I tried to restore too much, I risked losing the chance to restore anything at all. I could only add a few minutes. So I had to prioritize and focus on what was most important to the story. And the original footage fit right in, because it was supposed to be there. It was *bashert*.

A few weeks later I rushed the reedited version of the movie over to Tom Rothman, because we had a phone appointment that day. He hadn't had a chance to watch it when we spoke, but his first reaction was not promising. He basically said, "You can't change the movie. It has to be the way Sydney left it."

"I'm not trying to replace the original film," I told him. "It's a classic, and it will live forever. All I want is to give people the option of watching the extended version as well. Release both versions in one package."

I explained that for years after the movie's release, Sydney was still not sure about those cuts. But Tom wanted to hear that in Sydney's own words, so I followed up that call with an eight-page letter, citing production memos where Sydney says the UCLA scene is "very good." And the Frankie McVeigh scene was important because, as he wrote, "We must see the price that both this relationship and life in general costs these two people."

It was sad for me to see how Sydney continued to question his work on the movie. As he said in one interview, "I think it is a picture that is severely flawed. And it is saved, really, by the two performances." (I think he's being too modest.) As he said in another interview, "The pressure I was getting was just unbelievable . . . Truthfully, nobody had any faith in the picture."

Now, having directed a few films myself, I completely understand that pressure. Also, the blacklist went on into the early '60s, which was not that far away in 1973. Many people in Hollywood did not want to be reminded of their participation . . . or offend the Republicans in power in Washington. Richard Nixon was president, and he had been very active in the HUAC. As Sydney said in another interview, "There was resistance from the studio . . . As a result, we had to emasculate the picture . . . it did not successfully blend politics and love story to the extent it should have, or could have."

We sent Rothman the letter in mid-July, and then I waited, and waited . . .

As the summer wore on with no response, there was one person I really wanted to talk to . . . Robert Redford. I wanted to explain what I was doing and see how he felt about it.

So I called him up, and Bob was wonderful . . . open and thoughtful and engaging, as always. He said he would support me "absolutely," which meant so much to me. We talked for over an hour about everything, from working together on the film to politics and art.

When we were finally hanging up, he said, "I gotta go, Babs. I love you dearly, and I always will."

I said, "I love you too," and invited him and his wife, Sibylle, to come have dinner with Jim and me the next time they were in LA. I told him, "I love talking to you," and he said, "I love talking to *you*. I always do." It was a sweet reminder that the connection we had during that movie still exists.

Bob's vote of confidence made me even more determined to persuade Sony to let me put those pivotal scenes back where they belonged. In August, I sent Tom an email, gently nudging him by mentioning more reasons to support my case. He replied that it was a complicated situation and would take more time to resolve because he and many others were on vacation.

Okay . . . but I sent another email to thank him for his reply . . . and used the opportunity to make another pitch. In other words, I was relentless.

And thank God . . . Tom finally relented! In mid-September he called to tell me that the extended cut would be going into the new Blu-ray, as well as the original.

I was speechless for a moment. *Hallelujah!* After all, I had been hoping for this since 1973! And then in the midst of expressing my gratitude and telling him how much this means to me, I said, "Oh . . . *one more thing* . . . while we're at it, could you also do an iTunes release like we did for *A Star Is Born*, where both the original cut and my recut version (with added scenes) are available for the same price?"

There was silence at his end of the phone. But I quickly went on to say, "Young people don't even buy Blu-rays anymore. They stream everything, and that's a whole new audience for the film."

I was encouraged because he didn't say no right away, but as he reminded me, "Nor did I say yes." It wasn't until four months later that I was told he had approved the joint iTunes release.

I can't tell you how happy I am that people are now going to be able to see this film the way it was originally conceived. It's only taken fifty years, but my dream has finally come true!

As Hubbell said to Katie, "You never give up, do you?"

No . . . Katie never did, and neither do I.

TWENTY-FIVE

With a Little Help from My Friends

They say art imitates life, but sometimes it's the other way around. A few months after we finished filming *The Way We Were*, in the spring of 1973, I was asked if I'd be willing to do a fundraiser for Daniel Ellsberg, who was on trial for leaking the Pentagon Papers. He put his life on the line because he believed that if Congress, and the American people, could finally read the truth about the Vietnam War, they would put an end to it.

Well, I'm a stickler for the truth, I was against the war, and just like Katie, I felt it was important to support people who were willing to stand up for their principles.

Ellsberg had been on trial for four months, and was basically out of money. If he couldn't raise enough, fast, he'd have to cut short his defense. So the whole evening had to be put together very quickly. Stanley Sheinbaum, chairman of the ACLU, arranged for a tent to be put up in the producer Jennings Lang's backyard and invited two hundred people at $250 per couple. The idea was that I would take bids from the audience to sing a particular song. Now, I don't usually take requests, and I normally rehearse any sort of concert for weeks, so this was a huge departure for me. I didn't know what would happen from one moment to the next, which was exciting but also a little scary. Thank God I had Marvin Hamlisch beside me at the piano, with a big songbook so I could look at the lyrics if I needed to.

Peter Bogdanovich offered a thousand dollars if I would sing "You're the Top," as I had done over the credits for *What's Up, Doc?*. I said, "The picture did thirty-five million, Peter. You're only giving me a thousand dollars? Okay. There's only one caveat. For a thousand dollars, I ain't singing the verse!"

David Geffen was there with Joni Mitchell and asked me to sing her song "I Don't Know Where I Stand." I was a little nervous to sing it in front of her and said, "Forgive me, Joni" (only half in jest), but it was nice to be able to tell her, so publicly, "I love your music and I also love the way you sing." Someone asked for "With a Little Help from My Friends," and it was kind of a trip to sing it while three of the Beatles . . . George Harrison, Ringo Starr, and John Lennon (with Yoko Ono) . . . were in the audience. And the bids over the phone were a hoot. Carl Reiner called from, as he said, "the actual toilet of the Friars Club . . . and there's a bar mitzvah going on." We did a duet on "Twinkle, Twinkle, Little Star." Marty's wife, Miko, called from Japan and asked me to sing Marty's favorite song, "The Very Thought of You" . . . for 263,000 yen. And since the night of the benefit, April 7, 1973, happened to be Daniel Ellsberg's forty-second birthday, I was delighted to sing "Happy Birthday" to him.

We raised fifty thousand dollars, a big sum in those days. Recently, Dan came up to me at our mutual friend Lynda Resnick's house (she actually helped him copy the Pentagon Papers on her Xerox machine) and thanked me all over again.

He said it was our fifty thousand dollars that enabled them to continue the trial another two weeks . . . and those two weeks turned out to be crucial. That was just enough time for the news to break that Dan's psychiatrist's office had been burglarized and Nixon was behind it. The charges against Dan were dismissed on the grounds of government misconduct, and then the Watergate hearings began. And that was the beginning of the end for the president.

As we were talking, Dan said that he was one link in the chain of actions that forced Nixon out. Then he looked at me. "And you're part of that chain. What you did was essential."

All I can say is I'm proud to have helped in any way.

And I want to go back to *The Way We Were* for a moment, because suddenly that summer I found myself facing my own version of the blacklist, just like Katie. One of the revelations of the hearings was that Nixon was keeping an "Enemies List," and I was on it . . . along with people like Edward Kennedy, George McGovern, Shirley Chisholm, Bella Abzug, Eugene McCarthy, Paul Newman, and Gregory Peck.

That was chilling. What was Nixon planning to do to the people on that list? We'll never know, but frankly, any fear I felt was overwhelmed by a sense of solidarity with those who saw that weak, dishonest man for what he was, and spoke out to uphold the rule of law. And I was honored to be in such illustrious company.

That was the summer I was also working on *Barbra Streisand . . . and Other Musical Instruments*, my fifth TV special for CBS. It had been five years (and seven movies, *and* multiple albums) since *A Happening in Central Park*, because I didn't have time to do one before and besides, my attention was elsewhere. But Marty had assembled my old collaborators, Dwight Hemion and Joe Layton, so that made me feel comfortable, plus some new additions . . . Gary Smith, now producing with Dwight, whom I'd met on Judy Garland's show, along with Ken and Mitzie Welch to write musical material, just as they had done for me on Garry Moore's show. And then there was an extra added attraction . . . Since Dwight and Gary were currently working in London, a city I've always loved, we would shoot there.

Once again the show was basically all music, with very little talk. It began with just my voice, doing vocal exercises (ironic, since I never do them in real life). I'm tuning up alongside the members of the orchestra, and you think it's going to be a typical concert. But then all kinds of musicians start walking in . . . we had bagpipers from Ireland, guitar players from Spain, elephant horn players from Africa, even an organ grinder with a parrot. When my chair wobbles, a man playing a saw kindly slices an inch off the leg for me.

The idea was to showcase all these fabulous musicians with their instruments from around the world. And since I've always said how bored I get singing the same songs the same way, I wanted to really shake it up here.

So we took the song "I've Got Rhythm" and that turned into a medley that led me into one musical culture after another. Joe's staging was brilliant . . . an unexpected sound draws me over to an opening in the floor. I slide down a rope and suddenly I'm next to an Indian musician playing the sitar. And then different sounds bring me again and again to different cultures, where familiar songs like "People" are transformed. They might be accompanied by a Japanese koto . . . or Turkish tambourines . . . or Native American drums. I loved segueing from one country to another, transforming how I sang and even how I moved. But if you look closely, you'll notice that there's one constant . . . a simple, flowing dress. I had bought the original from Holly's Harp in LA, had it made in multiple colors, and then accessorized it differently for each scene.

Then I switch it up again, and now instead of musicians, I'm surrounded by futuristic synthesizers . . . which of course malfunction and explode. When the smoke clears, I'm much happier to find myself beside a piano, played by the great Ray Charles. I've always admired him as an artist . . . he's someone who sings from his soul . . . and he turned out to be a lovely person as well. (It doesn't hurt that he's also good-looking and very sensual.) Our duet on "Crying Time" was the high point of the show for me. We did it twelve times, and Ray never sang it the same way twice. He liked to be spontaneous, just like me.

And then came the most unusual part of the special. To illustrate our theme . . . that the world is made of music, and you may find it in unexpected places . . . we commissioned Ken and Mitzie to write the "Concerto for Voice and Appliances." The performers included electric juicers, a percolating coffeepot, a whistling teakettle, blenders, sewing machines, alarm clocks, telephones, doorbells, and a washing machine operated by Marty, looking extremely elegant in a tux for his cameo. And then all the musicians from various cultures (and the parrot) came back onstage as I sang, "Make your own kind of music, sing your own special song . . . it's a musical world!" for the grand finale . . . topped off by two slices of toast popping out of a toaster.

I had fun making these specials, because I had a great team and we could take chances. But now that I had fulfilled my contract with CBS, I was actually relieved . . . one less obligation.

It was difficult enough just keeping up with my recording contract. When I was immersed in a film and couldn't deliver an album exactly on schedule, I'd tell Marty, "I'm too busy." And he would deal with Columbia. As he used to say reassuringly, "What are they going to do? Sue you?"

They never did, and I've loved being with Columbia Records since the beginning of my career.

I didn't have time to even think about an album while we were shooting *The Way We Were*, and then I had to turn to the special. But once that was in the can, I went into the studio on September 12 to record my own version of the title song from the movie. The plan was to release it as a single, and that meant we needed a different arrangement. Marvin's was exactly right for the film, but it had to be a little more rhythmic and contemporary for the radio. So Marty Paich stepped in and made it more "pop." As he remembers, "I think it was four hours for the recording and four hours for the mixing, which goes to show if you have the right artist and the right orchestra, you can make a hit record in one night." Those were the good old days. I loved staying late and finishing it right then and there.

Two weeks later the single was out.

We worked fast, because Columbia wanted to use the single to generate more interest in the movie, which was opening three weeks later. And it did . . . "The Way We Were" became my first number 1 single (and eventually the top-selling single of the year).

I was also building a new album around it, and went back into the studio to record Paul Simon's "Something So Right," Stevie Wonder's "All in Love Is Fair," and Carole King's "Being at War with Each Other." This was in the midst of the Vietnam War, and I was feeling overwhelmed by the scenes of death and destruction on the nightly news. People were protesting in the streets and clashing with the police, but Carole's song took a different approach. It got its power from reminding us of something so simple . . . how we are all connected:

Everyone comes from one father, one mother
So why do we complicate our lives so much by
Being at war with each other?

Good question.

And there were three songs by Michel Legrand and the Bergmans . . . including the terrific "What Are You Doing the Rest of Your Life?" When they first played it for me, I instantly said, "I have to record that!"

I was planning to call the album *The Way We Were*, and that's when Ray Stark threatened to sue me.

It turns out he didn't want my album to have the same title as *his* album, which was simply the soundtrack from the movie. Ironically, both were on the Columbia label, so they weren't in competition with each other, and both were coming out in January 1974.

There was nothing unusual about my putting my own pop version of the song on *my* album, and most people know the difference between a soundtrack and a regular album. Frankly, I thought they would help each other. Maybe once people heard one version, they'd be curious about the other.

So what was Ray's problem?

One Columbia executive had an opinion: "Stark isn't getting a cut of your version. That's really what this is all about. But in order to avoid a lawsuit, we have to drop the title of the movie from the album."

I should explain what was on the original cover of my album. I've told you how I always try to avoid taking pictures, so I used one from a shoot I had done with Steve Schapiro for *Harper's Bazaar* over a year earlier. I like the combination of black and red, which you often see in 1940s jewelry, and since I was about to start shooting *The Way We Were,* I was in a period mood. I wore my own black jacket and a black turban with a sheer black scarf, because I didn't want to bother with a hairdresser. I quickly did my own makeup . . . red lipstick like the '40s, dark smoky eyes, and red nails. And then at the last moment, I said, "Wait, I just want to get one thing" . . . and added my red Bakelite ring from the '40s.

We shot it on my balcony at Carolwood. I just walked outside, put my hand on the stucco post to show the ring and the nail polish, and that was it.

I thought the title *The Way We Were* should go above my hand on the post, ideally in red letters with a black shadow.

I gave the shot to the art department at Columbia, and when they sent the finished cover back to me, I took one look and asked, "What happened here? Something's strange."

Well, it turned out that someone had taken off the bump on my nose! I guess they thought I'd be pleased, but I actually like that bump. That bump and I have been through a lot together. It's mine, and I said to the art director, "If I wanted a nose job, I would have gone to a doctor. Please put the bump back."

And then, thanks to Ray, the title got stripped off the cover. So the album basically had no name. At the last minute, Columbia stuck on a sticker that said "Featuring the hit single THE WAY WE WERE and ALL IN LOVE IS FAIR." But it ruined the design and it was in the wrong color . . . bright pink! It should have been red at least, with black letters.

I think in some dark psychological way, Ray enjoyed fighting with me. He was always an agitator. And if I analyzed it more deeply, I'd almost say he was in competition with me.

Which is ridiculous.

Actually, I don't think he wanted me to succeed at anything, without him.

TWENTY-SIX

What Was I Thinking?

When I look at the list of films I turned down during this period, I have to wonder, What was I thinking? But that's easy to say in hindsight.

The plot of *They Shoot Horses, Don't They?* focused on a desperate young woman, and how long she could last in this marathon dance competition. I thought, *Oh my God, I'd have to dance for hours every day!* (I told you I was lazy.) But I was also worried because my mother always said that my father died because he worked too hard. And in the back of my mind I had this fear that the same thing would happen to me. So I didn't want to push myself. I never even exercised until I was thirty. Anyway, the part went to Jane Fonda, and she was perfect for it.

I also turned down *Klute*, because I had already played a prostitute, and the wonderful director Alan J. Pakula was not yet attached. Jane got that one, too, and won an Oscar for it. A few years later I was offered *Julia*. I would have loved to play that part, but I was busy working on *A Star Is Born*. Sue Mengers said, "Don't worry about it. It will never get made." And Jane got that as well. I've said to her jokingly, "I'm responsible for your career!"

And I would have put everything else down to work with the brilliant director Fred Zinnemann, but he wasn't part of *Julia* when I was approached.

Same thing with *Alice Doesn't Live Here Anymore.* When I read that script, no director was involved, so I missed my chance to work with the extraordinary Martin Scorsese. I was also hesitant because I didn't think people would accept me as a lousy lounge singer. (Little did I know I would end up playing one ten years later, in a flop called *All Night Long*.)

I even turned down *Cabaret* because I didn't like the play. Again, if I had known Bob Fosse was going to direct it, I would have said yes. I loved working with him for the brief time he was involved with *Funny Girl.*

So what did I choose to do instead? A piece of fluff called *For Pete's Sake.* It might as well have been called *For Marty's Sake*, because I did it for him. Marty wanted to produce movies, and this would be his first credit. He put the whole project together. He asked Stanley Shapiro, who had written some very successful comedies for Doris Day and Rock Hudson, to do the script. Marty thought Peter Yates should direct, and I said okay. I asked for the wonderful cinematographer László Kovács, because we had worked so well together on *What's Up, Doc?* And I weighed in on the decision to cast Michael Sarrazin as my husband, but that's about it. I thought Michael had an interesting face, and he had an interesting girlfriend, the English actress Jacqueline Bisset, so I thought he'd probably be good to work with.

He'd be playing Pete, who's driving a cab to try to earn enough money to go back to school, when he gets a stock tip on pork belly futures. (What are pork bellies anyway? And why would people bet on them? I don't think they bet on chicken.)

I was playing the devoted wife, who borrows the money her husband needs to make the bet from a loan shark and then gets caught up in all these comically perilous escapades trying to pay it back (I know it sounds goofy, but it was supposed to be slapstick comedy). Initially my character's name was Beverly, but I felt that was too common. So I thought, *Why not give her a man's name?* And I changed it to Henry, short for Henrietta.

I was in the process of figuring out how she should wear her hair when I happened to go to a party at Carol Burnett's house. I spotted a woman with a very short, boyish haircut and thought, *Yes! That's the look!* It would be perfect for Henry, and a welcome change from the period styles I had just worn in *The Way We Were*.

So I went up to this woman and asked, "Who cut your hair?"

She said, "Jon Peters."

It was the summer of 1973, and I asked my assistant to call Jon Peters to see if he would be interested in doing a wig for the movie. I wanted a wig for two reasons: one, because I didn't want to cut off my own long, straight hair, and two, when we were filming I could sleep later while my movie hair was being done in the makeup trailer.

Jon was very interested because, as he confessed later, he'd been telling people for years that he cut my hair. He took credit, in other words, for a cut that was done by Fred Glaser in Chicago. But that's Jon . . . he had a lot of chutzpah.

And clearly he also had a rather tenuous relationship with the truth . . . but I didn't pay enough attention to that at the time.

A meeting was set up at my house on Carolwood, and Jon says I kept him waiting for forty-five minutes. That's probably true . . . I was always doing ten things at once. Finally my assistant rang up and told me, "He's leaving."

"Don't let him leave," I said. "I'll be right down."

Jon was already revving up his red Ferrari when my assistant led him back into the house. And when I came over to greet him, he was clearly pissed. I was in the midst of apologizing when he said, "Don't ever do that to me again."

That got my attention. Most people would be more ingratiating and make light of the delay. I took a closer look at him. Jon was not exactly dressed for a business meeting. He was wearing a shirt unbuttoned halfway down his chest, tight jeans, and a Native American necklace. I thought, *Who* is *this guy?*

I told him that I had seen his haircut on this very attractive woman. He knew exactly who I was talking about and managed to suggest that he knew her *very well* . . . more than just as a client . . . as if he were worried I might think he was gay.

Well, that cleared *that* up. In fact, I had read somewhere that he was married to Lesley Ann Warren, who had done *Drat! The Cat!* on Broadway with Elliott.

I told him, "Your wife is very talented."

"We're separated," he explained. "But that's very nice of you to compliment her."

I steered the conversation back to the haircut. I asked if he could make me a similar wig, and he was totally confident: "That's easy. I can do that." It was only later that I found out he had never done a wig before.

I said, "Let's go upstairs to my makeup room" . . . which might sound fancy, but it was simply a little alcove with clear leaded-glass windows, so it had great natural light. There was just enough room for a white-painted desk, topped by a makeup mirror with lights that the studio had given me . . . a chair . . . and a stereo, so I could listen to music I had to record. But the best thing about it was that I had instant access to food, because the alcove also held an old-fashioned dumbwaiter, with pulleys, original to the 1929 house. So if I wanted a cup of tea, nobody had to walk up the stairs.

I wanted to sit down in front of the mirror so Jon could look at my hair. As he followed me up the stairs, I sensed his eyes boring into me. I stopped at the top, turned around and asked, "What are you staring at?"

"You've got a great ass," he said.

Nobody had ever talked to me like that before (or let's say, not within a few moments of meeting me). Jon didn't seem the least bit intimidated, and I liked that. It felt different . . . kind of honest. He wasn't treating me like some unapproachable star. It was very disarming. (By the way, I remembered his line and wrote it into *A Star Is Born* for John Norman to say as Esther is leading him up the steps to her apartment for the first time.)

Jon had to come to my house several times, because we played around with various cuts on several cheap wigs before he cut the real one. And in the course of that we got to talking. He told me that his father was a Cherokee Indian who died suddenly when Jon was still a child, and his mother remarried a man who wasn't nice to her, or to Jon. Just like my stepfather, so we had that in common. We were two rebellious kids from dysfunctional families. And he, too, had taken a letter out of his name, which was originally John. Like me, he wanted to be unique.

Jon was also very direct, like me. He told me, "You're this sexy young chick. You've got great legs, great skin, great boobs. Why do you dress like someone twice your age?"

He had a point. But I was modest and it would never have occurred to me to show off my body (except as a character, like in *The Owl and the Pussycat*). His words were the spark that eventually prompted me to ditch the A-line dresses and fancy couture and dress more like my contemporaries.

One day I was wearing platform shoes. And as I walked into the room, I instinctively sensed that Jon was a little self-conscious about his height . . . about five foot nine. So I kicked off my shoes and said, "See, I'm not that tall."

I guess I wanted to make him feel comfortable.

Obviously he was, because he soon asked, "Would you ever go out with me?"

I said, "No, you're not my type. I like men who are older, more sophisticated. I see myself with a doctor or a lawyer."

At our next meeting Jon showed up with a pipe between his teeth and wearing a velvet smoking jacket over his T-shirt and jeans. As a final touch he had acquired horn-rimmed glasses. The red Ferrari he originally roared up in had disappeared, and he was now driving a more conservative four-door dark green Jaguar (which was not his, as I later found out; it belonged to his cousin Silvio).

I had to laugh. Jon didn't look like any lawyer I'd ever met, but he did get points for trying. He has a very strong personality, and when he wants something, he goes after it.

"Do you want to go get some lunch?" he asked.

"I don't do lunch," I said. "Stop coming on so strong."

But he wouldn't take no for an answer. Finally I told him, "Look, if I'm going to take time out from my work, I'd rather play tennis." I was really into tennis at the time.

He said, "I'll play tennis with you."

I could see this guy wasn't going to give up, so I said okay.

That was the first time I ever went outside my house with him . . . to drive to the court. Jon was strutting around like a pro, but it quickly became apparent that he had never played before. He had no idea how to keep score. But you know what? He still beat me.

On the way back to my house, he stopped to get gas. When it was time to pay, Jon turned to me and said, "I only have a hundred. Do you have a ten?"

I was a little startled, but I gave him the money.

He never paid me back.

In retrospect I should have paid more attention to that. But I was feeling very much alone . . . the odd woman out when everyone else seemed to have a partner. I was just coming out of a relationship with a handsome businessman who wrote me the sweetest poems. He was eager to please and would do wonderful things, like surprise me with tickets to Hawaii or take me skiing on weekends. But he was still in another relationship and I didn't see a future together. So I had to end it after a few months.

Yet he was so upset by the breakup that he went to San Francisco, where Lesley Ann Warren was doing a play, and told her that her ex was seeing me. I guess he was hoping that she would stop the affair, but Lesley couldn't care less. She just thought he was a bit crazed. And I was appalled, especially since this man wasn't free to be with me anyway.

This is one reason why I was in therapy . . . I kept choosing unavailable men, and I was trying to figure out why.

My familiar state of mind, growing up, was feeling alone. And there was something that scared me about relationships. My role models weren't so hot. My stepfather wasn't nice to my mother or me. So in an odd way, going for these elusive men was almost a safe choice, because the outcome was inevitable. I would once again be left alone . . . returned to that familiar state.

And that would bring up all those old feelings about not being worthy of being loved.

As Harvey Corman once asked me, "Why do you settle for crumbs?"

I learned over time, and with help, that if you want to change, you have to do the work on yourself. It was more than a decade later when Brugh Joy, a superb doctor and Jungian therapist, said something that struck a deep chord in me . . . "Only when you become really conscious of the pattern can you break it."

Put it this way . . . I was fed up with my own routine.

Jon, at least, was available. He was persistent. And he caught me at a time when I was emotionally vulnerable.

I wasn't attracted to him at first. I thought he was nice-looking, but that's about it. And then he gave me a picture of himself as a little boy and he had exactly the same face as my dear cousin Lowell, when he was the same age. That was kind of amazing. It felt like a sign. But our relationship progressed very slowly, because I was wary . . . there was something I really didn't like about Jon. He was too aggressive, too pushy. And then one day he brought his son, Christopher, with him to my house, and I did like the fact that he had a son, just a little younger than Jason.

It made me long for a family. And Jon and I were kind of in the same boat. I thought how wonderful it would be for my son to have a playmate, and a male figure to be around. I just wasn't sure that the male figure should be Jon.

In September I flew to New York to start filming *For Pete's Sake.* I was so disengaged from that movie that I barely remember making it. It's such a blank in my life that it's like a movie I've never seen before . . . only I'm in it!

I know I told Gene Callahan, the wonderful production designer (who also did *Funny Girl*), that I used to hang empty frames in my first apartments, and that's why Pete and Henry's apartment is decorated with empty frames, painted white and hanging on a brown wall. And I really liked the simple white furniture he chose for their living room. It was only later, when I began to collect American Arts and Crafts, that I realized this was Mission-style furniture and it was only painted white for the set.

And I know that in the scene where Pete's taking a bath, I thought it would be funny if he pulled me in with him, to show how playful they are with each other. This is a really solid, loving marriage, and that's why she would go to such desperate lengths for him, even meeting with the neighborhood madam (played against type by Molly Picon) to see if she could pay back the loan that way.

What can I say? As for the rest of the movie, all I remember are the dog and the bull. That very intimidating German shepherd that chases me down into a subway car and back out into the street was well trained, but I was still scared of him. (This was before I had a German shepherd of my own, my sweet Charity.) Every reaction from that dog was great. I was very impressed with him.

Henry gets involved with some cattle rustlers, and that's a real bull poking his head into the cab of the RV as I'm trying to drive. I was terrified of him, too, but then he licked my arm with his huge tongue and I had to laugh.

Of course the cattle escape, and Henry follows their trail of destruction into a shop that sells fine crystal. The owner is standing there in shock, and Henry can't believe that all the glass on display is still intact.

She says, "Nothing broke?"

"It's a miracle," he says.

"Phew. Knock on wood," she says, tapping the wall . . . and twenty crystal chandeliers fall from the ceiling and shatter on the floor.

Peter Yates did a great job on that gag. This is probably why Vincent Canby in *The New York Times* called the movie a "boisterously funny old-time farce."

Well, at least *he* liked it.

My wig fell into the water during the bath scene, so we flew Jon out to fix it, only to realize that he actually had no idea what to do with it. (Although whatever he did worked.)

During that brief visit, he asked, "How come you're not doing concerts?"

I said, "I don't know." I wasn't about to go into details about my stage fright and how it got even worse after I forgot the words to that song in Central Park.

"Concerts are a huge undertaking," I explained. "Who's going to put them together?"

And he said, "Me!"

I thought he was nuts, but he clearly thought he could do that too. There was no limit to his confidence.

Once we got back to Los Angeles, I tried to keep my distance from Jon, but he pursued me. He said I reminded him of a butterfly . . . beautiful, but always just out of reach. He noticed I liked antique jewelry, and one day he showed up on the set with an antique diamond-and-sapphire butterfly pin. Then a week later he gave me another butterfly, this time a vintage silver-and-turquoise Navajo pin.

And he kept surprising me.

When I first walked into his house in the Valley, I thought, *This guy has an eye.* You could see it in the details. When I admired the old wood, Jon told me it was actually new. As he explained, he had friends who were toymakers and could do anything. They had scraped the wood, stained it, and burnished it with a blowtorch, so it looked weathered and worn. He had also hung antique lace curtains on the windows. I thought, *Wow, this is interesting* . . . a mix of the rustic and the refined . . . the masculine and the feminine. It wasn't what I would have expected from this macho guy. I liked that he wasn't afraid to let his feminine side show.

Gradually his persistence wore me down. I decided to try to open up to this man and take a chance on a new relationship. Finally, months after we met, we went away to the desert for a weekend. We stayed in the Al Capone cottage at Two Bunch Palms, and I remember sitting on the bathroom floor with him late into the night and talking about our lives. Isn't it interesting . . . somehow it's easier to share very personal information in a small room.

We were complete opposites in many ways. Jon liked horses . . . his father had taught him to ride. I had only a brief acquaintance with horses, and it had not ended well. When I was just eighteen and singing at the Caucus Club in Detroit, I had taken a horseback ride . . . actually a horseback walk . . . through the park. Then, many years later, my friend Polly Platt, the production designer on *What's Up, Doc?*, invited me to go riding with her. And the horse I was on suddenly decided to go back to the barn. It just turned around and took off, galloping like in the movies. My hat flew off my head as I held on for dear life. I never wanted to get on a horse again. I even developed an allergy to them, I was so afraid (just one of my many fears).

But Jon didn't seem to be afraid of anything, not the sea or sharks or snakes.

Once, at a gas station, I got out of the car to stretch my legs while Jon was refilling the tank, and a man came up to me and asked, "Are you Barbra Streisand?"

I said, "No." (Sometimes I don't want to be her.)

But this guy wouldn't let up. He followed me around, saying, "You look like her."

"Well, I'm not her." I tried to get out of his way.

And then he said, with a sneer, "I don't like her anyway."

Suddenly Jon materialized at my side and laid into the guy for insulting me. Jon grabbed him by his necktie so hard that the guy's shirt ripped down the back. (Must have been a very expensive shirt. The guy sued Jon and settled for seven thousand dollars.)

I was upset. Why did Jon have to overreact like that and make a scene?

But deep down, I was pleased.

My brother would never come to my defense when I needed him. But Jon did.

I realize now why I was drawn to him. He was Joey Bauman from the playground all over again. He was the tough guy . . . the one who would protect me.

And he could be very understanding. The first time we all slept over at Jon's house, Jason forgot to bring his special blanket. He was upset and wanted to go home. Jon sat down beside him and said, "If you really need it, even in the middle of the night, just tell me and I will go over to your house and get it." And that promise was enough to reassure my son. He slept through the night, and never asked for that blanket again.

I was very impressed with Jon's emotional intelligence.

As we became closer, Jon and I decided to look for a house where we could all live together. And we loved the first house we were shown, out in Malibu. It was very private, at the end of a canyon backing up to the Santa Monica Mountains. I had this vision of my son growing up surrounded by nature . . . no more tour buses stopping out front with loudspeakers announcing my name . . . just the murmur of the creek and the rustle of leaves on the three-hundred-year-old oak trees.

We bought the ranch on Valentine's Day in 1974. (It wasn't really a ranch, but there were so many acres of land around us that it seemed like one.) The idea was that we would buy this house together, and I assumed that it would be in both our names.

Then Jon said, "I have to talk to you about this. I've been thinking, I would really like to own this house all by myself." I was more than a little shocked, but he explained, "When we're at Carolwood, I'm living in your house, and when we come out here, I want you to be living in *my* house." I wasn't too thrilled because I thought the whole point was that this would be *our* house. And I was even less thrilled when he said, looking sheepish, "But I have to owe you the money because I don't have it right now."

It turned out he didn't have the money to pay for even his half. He gave me his red Ferrari (worth nineteen thousand dollars at the time, and which I couldn't drive) toward the price and promised to pay me the rest over the next five years, "with no interest," as he said. (Jon was a shrewd negotiator even then. But I also blame my New York business manager, who told me to put the house in his name for tax reasons.)

Sometimes I wonder why I didn't leave Jon right then and there. When we met, Gracie was living with me at Carolwood. And when she found out Jon was a Gemini, I can still see her shaking her head and saying, "Uh-uh, uh-uh, those men . . . they have two personalities, and you can't trust them." She wasn't wrong.

I think the main reason I stayed with Jon was that he knew what to do on Sundays. I was at a loss on my own, because as soon as I went anywhere with Jason, we were surrounded by people. All I wanted for my son was a normal childhood. I wanted to take Jason to the park, but even a simple outing like that became an ordeal, because I'd be recognized and followed, and I didn't want that attention. Jason didn't like it either. He was picking up my vibes. When I took him to a screening of *Willy Wonka and the Chocolate Factory*, along with Marilyn Bergman and her daughter, Julie, we couldn't move without being ambushed by photographers. They were even waiting for us outside the bathroom. After the movie, when we tried to leave unobtrusively by going out the back way, they ran around to meet us. Jason stuck his tongue out at one photographer. How could I reprimand him? I felt the same way.

But having a man in my life made a big difference. Now I had someone to shield me and we could do things together. Jon had ideas about where to take the boys, and we'd pack them up and go to the zoo, or Disneyland, or play on the old-fashioned rides at the Santa Monica Pier. It was wonderful to enjoy the world through their eyes. One day Jon came home with a lion cub and put it inside the huge aviary that came with the house. The boys were ecstatic, until Christopher nearly got bitten. So we called Tippi Hedren and arranged to bring the cub to her animal preserve.

Jon bought a horse . . . a black-and-white Appaloosa with wild, crazy eyes. Perfect for Jon, who liked the challenge of riding him.

And this was a time when I felt the need to challenge myself as well. I was determined to overcome my fear of horses, so I took lessons with Jason at the Malibu Riding Club and learned how to ride and even jump horses. And guess what? My allergies went away.

One day I was riding at the club and about to go over a hurdle when I saw Jon coming toward me. I said, "Watch this!" I was trying to show off and make him proud of me.

There's an old proverb, "Pride goeth before a fall," and clearly it's true, because the horse jumped, and I fell off. Jason, who was having a lesson in the next ring, somehow fell off at the same time. And that was the end of our horseback riding. Neither of us wanted to get up on a horse again. My fear came right back, and so did my allergies (which just proves how much the mind controls the body).

Clearly, I wasn't cut out to be a cowgirl, but I did like decorating our house at the ranch. It was a contemporary barn-shaped structure, cheaply built with aluminum doors and inexpensive parquet floors. But I loved the fact that it was basically one big room . . . and Jason and I have both gone on to build barnlike houses, so something about the shape obviously imprinted itself on us. There was a tiny galley kitchen that wasn't conducive to cooking (although I did make my hoisin spare ribs in there), a small powder room, two bedrooms for the boys, each with a ladder to the top bunk for their friends, and a big bedroom and bath for Jon and me.

It was quite a project to take that bare space and transform it. Jon brought in his toymakers to burnish the wood on the walls, and they also made most of the furniture. It was so simple . . . we'd discuss the kind of cabinet we needed in the morning, and by the next day it was built. No waiting around for months for your order to come in.

This was my hippie period. Instead of a couch in front of the fireplace, we had a huge mattress on the floor, covered with patchwork quilts and piled with pillows. The toymakers built a waist-high, L-shaped wooden cabinet to keep it all in place. I was collecting Tiffany lamps and set them out along the top . . . I loved the way they looked against the rough, burnished wood.

All the tacky aluminum doors were remade in wood, with multiple panes of glass. I used the clear leaded glass that came from the *Clear Day* set to frame the front door. I always wanted a great piece of wood for a mantel on the stone fireplace, but Jon and I could never agree on what it should be. The ceilings were so high that we could bring in a couple of huge trees in pots to divide the space, and we added skylights to give them more sun. It was glorious to see the sun pour down through the green leaves, which dappled the light . . . so when you were inside the house, it still felt as if you were in the midst of nature.

I remember it being especially lovely during Hanukkah and on Christmas morning, when the kids woke us up around 6:00 a.m., and I made hot chocolate and bagels for them. They couldn't wait to open their presents. So many people sent gifts that we had a rule . . . they could open them all and play with everything all day but then they had to decide on a few toys to keep, and we gave the rest to children's hospitals.

Christopher lived with his mother, but Lesley was very generous and let him spend a lot of time with his father. She even let Christopher live with us for one year, when Jon and I took both kids out of their city schools and enrolled them in the local Malibu school so we could live in the country full time. The kids could ride their bikes down the country road, and I biked too.

One day Jon came home and said, in a worried tone, "I saw this girl on a bike and thought, Oh my God, I'm attracted to another woman. Then I drove past her and realized it was you!"

The canyon was magical. Jason and Christopher could go off on their own or with kids from the neighborhood, exploring the woods and following the creek up to where it became a waterfall. Once Jason found an arrowhead. He and Christopher whirled around on rope swings and slept under the stars when they felt like it. I gave Jason a little movie camera, and he would make scary films with his friends.

Malibu is also where I met Renata, my longtime personal assistant. She was working as the nanny for a couple who lived nearby. One day I noticed a cross-shaped mark on her arm and asked, "What's that?" She said a rattlesnake had bitten her, so she cut her arm with a knife and sucked out the venom herself. I knew right then and there that I wanted this woman in my life! And she's been with me ever since.

I loved having some free time. I took a Chinese cooking class from one neighbor and went to the Renaissance Faire with another, shepherding our assorted children. Life was all very normal. No one else was in show business. But that gradually changed. Don Henley of the Eagles and Mick Fleetwood of Fleetwood Mac bought property in the same canyon, although we never socialized . . . we all wanted our privacy. And in 1978 all three of us, unbelievably, won Grammy awards (I got two for "Evergreen"), and we called it Grammy Canyon.

But I'm getting ahead of my story. Back in 1974, when Jon and I had just started sharing a house and our children, he decided he wanted to share my work as well. I was about to do a new album, and he said, "Let me produce it."

I thought, *What? Are you crazy?*

He said, "I want to bring out your sexy side."

Well, once again he got my attention. I never thought of myself as "sexy" and certainly didn't choose songs with that in mind. Was I missing something?

And maybe Jon's idea was not so crazy. It kind of made sense. We were in a new relationship, and that way we could go together to recording sessions. But in the eyes of Hollywood, the relationship was suspect. They saw it solely in terms of status, and felt we didn't match up. I was a "star," and he was a hairdresser. But I don't believe in putting labels on people.

And Jon had a big decision to make . . . whether to sell his shops or expand the business by franchising his name. Before we met, Jon had envisioned himself as another Vidal Sassoon. He was planning to make a lot of money by manufacturing his own hair products and opening franchises around the world. But then he got to know me and decided my world was more fascinating than his. And he wanted to be part of it.

I already knew I could produce a record. So I thought, *Let him do it.* It will give him some stature, and I can always rescue him, if necessary . . . because Jon knew nothing about producing records. As he said to a reporter, "I walked into the recording studio and I saw the 24-track board and I thought it was a 747. I didn't have the faintest idea. And she ended up doing most of the work, you know, because, like, at two in the morning I was tired and I would go to sleep." (He could be funny when he told the truth.)

Jon was way out of his depth and later he admitted it. "My instincts were good, but my abilities weren't. Barbra literally had to bail me out."

I saved him then, and I've saved him several times since.

But I was taken aback when Jon still wanted all the credit as producer. And all the credit for designing the album cover, because he said it was his idea to put a fly on a stick of butter for the album we called *Butterfly.* (I wanted that psychedelic portrait on the back to be the cover.) And it was so important for his ego that I didn't fight him or make him feel bad by pointing out that he needed help on everything.

Jon didn't know who to hire for the recording sessions. So I made those decisions. I chose Tom Scott, who is an amazing saxophone player and stepped in to arrange seven songs when we needed him. The remaining three were arranged by the great Lee Holdridge, whom I knew from his work with Neil Diamond.

There was an Isaac Hayes song that Jon wanted me to do, called "Type Thang," which was definitely outside my repertoire. But I was game. We were at the studio, and I was in the middle of recording it, when he suddenly stopped the band.

I came out of the booth and asked, "What's going on?"

Jon said, "Look, you're not getting it. You have this great instrument but you're not really getting down, you know?"

You could have heard a pin drop in the studio.

But the thing is, he was probably right . . . and I knew it.

"Well, I'm not Janis Joplin. I don't sing that way."

But Jon wasn't listening to me. He had some idea in his head and he started to tell me how to do the song. He was making no sense, so I cut him off and said quietly, "Why don't you show me?"

"Okay," he said, motioned to the band to begin again, and proceeded to sing the song himself.

Now Jon can't sing a note, but I let him go on without interrupting him. And when it was over, I said, very seriously, "You know, Jon, it's interesting. I think you have a disconnect between your brain and your mouth."

There was a burst of applause and laughter from the musicians. I went back into the booth and finished the song, and tried to be as funky as I could. But it was never great and it didn't end up on the album, by the way.

Music was an area where Jon and I did not always agree.

But I have to give him credit . . . he did encourage me to stretch. I would normally not gravitate to a Bob Marley song like "Guava Jelly." And there it is, along with another song called "Grandma's Hands," by Bill Withers, that I loved . . . and it turns out it's one of my husband's favorites.

I always assumed *Butterfly* was a flop, but we looked it up and it did surprisingly well . . . rising to number 13 on the charts and going Gold in just seven weeks. I must have had a very dedicated audience.

TWENTY-SEVEN

Funny Lady

When Ray Stark approached me about a sequel to *Funny Girl*, I was not enthusiastic. First of all, as much as I loved that movie, I had already spent years playing Fanny Brice.

Ray's theory was, If it worked once, it will work again.

That wasn't my theory. I didn't want to do *Funny Lady*, but I had a contract that I had to fulfill.

I wasn't impressed with the original script, by Arnold Schulman. And I didn't feel the same instinctive connection to the older Fanny, but in order to make this work I knew I would have to find it. She had a tougher exterior by this point in her life and she didn't try to be liked, which I could understand. She called everybody "kid" because she couldn't remember anybody's name. She was raising her children alone without the man she loved, and that must have made her sad. Like most great comedians, she was quite serious in real life. I could relate to that . . . but I couldn't relate to the slapstick routines that came naturally to her. The broad comedy that was part of Fanny's act had never appealed to me. I would have to come out of my comfort zone to do those songs, and I worried that I was going backward.

But then Jay Presson Allen did a rewrite that brought out Fanny's emotional life and made the role more intriguing. Here was a woman who finally lets go of her fantasies about men. She grows up. And that enables her to be open to a man like Billy Rose . . . a theatrical impresario who was not conventionally attractive (in real life), but he was smart and successful. And she thought that was what she needed. Fanny was always refreshingly honest about her relationship with Billy. As she said in that oral history she did with Goddard Lieberson, "I was madly in love with Nicky Arnstein, but I was 'in like' with Billy Rose."

I knew exactly what she meant. She recognized something in him and she responded. Billy was funny and brash, kind of like Fanny herself . . . a guy who also has a tough exterior but is gentle inside (or at least that's how he's portrayed in the movie).

I could identify with that. After Elliott, who was similar to me in many ways, I was drawn to people who were different from me. But I've learned that the more you come to accept yourself, the more you can be drawn to people who are like yourself.

Put it this way, I was really doing my best to find reasons to play this part. And it certainly helped that my old friend Herb Ross would be directing. So I set aside my doubts.

John Kander and Fred Ebb wrote the music (they were hot after the success of *Cabaret*), and we were prerecording some of the songs at Columbia studios when I had a visitor. Prince Charles was on naval duty with his ship in San Diego and made a brief trip to Los Angeles. As he described it, he was asked who he wanted to meet and he said, "I'm sure they thought I'd say Raquel Welch, but I said Barbra Streisand. I wanted to meet the woman behind the voice."

The prince was utterly charming when he came to the studio, but frankly, it's hard to have a real conversation when you're surrounded by fifty photographers snapping pictures. I was drinking tea and offered him a sip . . . and the future king of England actually drank from my cup, which was apparently unprecedented. When the British press reported on this, they turned it into the equivalent of an international incident.

He liked the tea, by the way, and asked, "What's it called?"

"Constant Comment."

I couldn't think of anything else to say, and I'm so work oriented that I was feeling guilty about all those musicians who were waiting for me to get on with the session. So I'm afraid I wasn't as gracious as I should have been. The fact is, both Prince Charles and I are shy, but somehow we still managed to connect . . . because that proved to be the beginning of an unexpected friendship.

Funny Lady started shooting in April 1974.

I was impressed with Vilmos Zsigmond's work on *McCabe and Mrs. Miller*, so I suggested him as the cinematographer when none of my pals were available . . . László Kovács was doing *Shampoo*, and Gordy was busy with *The Godfather Part II*. Vilmos had done his research into what American vaudeville was like in the 1930s and wanted to give the footage a more realistic look. But when Ray and the Columbia executives saw the dailies, they weren't pleased, and I couldn't disagree. The look was too dark and gritty for a sequel to *Funny Girl*, and Vilmos was let go. I wish I had had the opportunity to work with him on a different type of movie.

Ray called the veteran cinematographer James Wong Howe, and he was on the set the next morning. Jimmy was seventy-four years old and came out of retirement to do the picture. I loved working with this wonderful man, whose career spanned the history of Hollywood. Cecil B. DeMille gave him his start in silent films, and Jimmy went on to make over a hundred movies and be nominated for sixteen Academy Awards. (He won two, for *The Rose Tattoo* and *Hud*.) Considered a master of black and white, he could also shoot the kind of vibrant color that we needed. And even though he hadn't filmed a musical since *Yankee Doodle Dandy* in 1942, he jumped right in and kept the cameras rolling, with no preparation.

I immediately bonded with him. I told him about growing up with Muriel Choy and how she was like a second mother to me, and how I took orders at her Chinese restaurant when I was twelve. Meanwhile, Jimmy was setting up my first close-up. I was used to Harry Stradling, who always put some diffusion on the lens for close-ups. That was the style of the time, especially for musicals, although I thought it was odd. Again, why have a softer look for a close-up and then take off the filter for a wide shot? It seemed a bit jarring to me, but I had accepted it as the way it was done.

So I asked Jimmy, "What kind of diffusion are you using?"

"None," he said.

"Really? Why not?"

Jimmy explained, "This is a beautiful lens. It must have cost five or six thousand dollars, and it has great resolution, so I'm not going to ruin it by putting a two-dollar-and-fifty-cent piece of glass in front of it. I'd rather get the effect with lights."

And he did, amazingly enough, and I learned something. When I saw the shot in dailies, I immediately told him, "That's incredible. I'm thrilled."

Jimmy was a sweetheart. When we weren't talking about lights, we were talking about Chinese food. One of my favorite things is *cha siu bao* . . . a steamed bun filled with Cantonese-style roast pork. When I was in Australia in 2000 doing the *Timeless* concert, they had a Chinese restaurant in the hotel and I had *cha siu bao* for breakfast, lunch, and dinner. (Why not?)

Jimmy knew about my obsession and won my heart by bringing me homemade *cha siu bao*. God, they were delicious. Someone told me a funny story . . . at some point Jimmy opened up a Chinese restaurant, and a photographer arrived to take some pictures. He didn't know who James Wong Howe was, other than the owner of the restaurant, and when Jimmy tried to give him some advice, the photographer said, "You take care of the noodles. I'll take care of the photographs."

Funny Lady is another movie I haven't seen since I made it. I had sort of dismissed it . . . probably because my initial reluctance to do it colored the whole experience . . . and now that I've watched it again, I'm pleasantly surprised.

I thought James Caan was very good. He's the first actor I worked with who talked as fast as I do, so that was fun. He was a lovely person, and much more attractive than the man he was portraying. I met the real Billy Rose once, and he was short and stocky. Jimmy was tall and slim. And I notice that he leans forward in the movie . . . what an interesting choice, because it suggested a shorter man and captured his nervous energy. And he made him a bit of a slob, constantly eating pistachios and leaving a trail of shells in his wake. When Fanny comes into his club and he sits down at her table, she tells him that he has cigarette ash on his lapel. By now she's become quite elegant, wearing expensive clothes and buying antique furniture, while he has no manners . . . he lights his own cigarette, but not hers.

Fanny and Billy have a combative relationship, arguing with each other and tossing insults around. They were equals in that department. Each gave as good as they got. That was easy to play, because I had a lot of practice with Jon . . . and Ray.

Jon, like Billy, was a little rough around the edges. But both men just plowed ahead and got things done. Years later, when Jon was building a house in Beverly Park, he was showing me the grounds and said, "There will be huge rocks over here and then there's a bridge over there." When I saw it finished, sure enough, there was the bridge and there were the rocks, but when I touched the rocks I realized they were fake. (Perfect metaphor.)

Jon laughed and said, "Well, I wanted to save money." (Sounds like Billy Rose.)

And then there was Ray . . . the fight in Fanny's dressing room, where she tells Billy to get out as she's putting on an Indian headdress and brandishing her tomahawk, was based on something that actually happened between Ray and me during *Funny Girl*'s Broadway run. At the end of a screaming match, I yelled, "Get out of my dressing room!" while Gracie stood by with her mouth hanging open.

Sometimes Ray pushed me too far. And sometimes Billy pushed Fanny too far. Jimmy's own personality worked for the character since he, too, liked to joke around. There's a scene in Fanny's dressing room where Billy slaps her on the butt, and she says, "What are you, crazy?" And then he impulsively grabs her for a kiss, and she yells, "Stop it!" Meanwhile, she's reaching for the closest thing at hand . . . a tin of talcum powder . . . and dumps it over his head. She laughs and apologizes, a bit scared of what he might do, and in the script, Billy picks up the tin and throws the rest of the powder in her face.

I said, "I don't think he should hit her in the face with the talcum powder. It's toxic, and it would be terribly unhealthy to get that in your lungs."

Jimmy said, "Sure. No problem. You're right."

He promised to pick up the tin as if he were going to hit me, but then stop at the last moment.

"You can't blink," he said. "Just trust me."

And then we shot the scene . . . and he threw the powder right in my face.

So much for trust.

Jimmy thought it was hilarious. He could hardly stand because he was laughing so hard. I was in shock. It was awful. The powder filled my eyes, my nose, my mouth, my lungs. For a moment, I couldn't even breathe. I tried to spit out as much of it as I could and shake it out of my eyes. I was gagging and I had to turn away from the camera briefly. I couldn't even speak. But I didn't break character and I played along with the joke, even managing to laugh as he turns me around to look at both of us, white with powder, in the mirror.

No matter how I felt, I was not going to stop the take and I was determined to give Herb everything he needed . . . because there was no way I was going to do that bit again.

Conflict is always interesting to play. A fight between two people can be cleansing, cathartic, and also stimulating. Jimmy and I used each argument to magnify the sexual tension between Fanny and Billy. She's starting to find him attractive, almost against her better judgment . . . kind of like what happened between Jon and me. And then Nick Arnstein reappears, to throw a wrench in Fanny's new life. He comes back to her dressing room after her show, and as the camera pans up from his shoes . . . echoing how I first saw him in *Funny Girl* onstage . . . for a moment she's smitten all over again.

I was glad to see Omar . . . and this time they didn't straighten his hair. It was thick and curly, and he looked handsome. But the spark was gone. Whatever was between us had ended for me after *Funny Girl*, and now he had moved on too. Who knows what would have happened if I had joined him in Paris? But I didn't.

Fanny is still hoping Nick might want to get back together, and Herb staged this scene perfectly, from her flustered pratfall into the closet to the moment when Nick puts his arm around her and she kisses his hand . . . and sees the wedding ring on his finger. He didn't even have the nerve to tell her.

Fanny is alone, hurt, and angry, and that leads into the song she sings in the deserted theater, "How Lucky Can You Get." Watching it now, I think it's also staged beautifully. And Jimmy Wong Howe lit it very dramatically . . . when Fanny walks out on the empty stage, there's just one bright light hanging down. And I'm wearing a black satin gown that was dramatic as well, with a plunging halter top and practically no back, except for a few strands of rhinestones. I love the fluid lines of that 1930s look, and Ray Aghayan and Bob Mackie designed one gorgeous outfit after another for me.

So, I liked the clothes . . . I liked the funny *and* serious relationship between Fanny and Billy . . . but I still don't get some of the musical numbers, like "Great Day." The set was over the top, the costumes for the chorus were ridiculous, and it went on way too long.

"Isn't This Better?" was more my style. It's the simplest song in the movie, and yet it has a complex idea behind it . . . the lyrics describe Fanny trying to justify her new marriage. She and Billy are in a train compartment, and even on their wedding night they get into an argument. (Hmmm . . . so did Elliott and I.)

Jimmy Caan and I worked well together, ad-libbing and talking over each other. The argument escalates into a fight, and he gets a nosebleed, and she forgets her anger and gently takes care of him. The atmosphere suddenly shifts, they kiss, and then we cut to a shot of Fanny in the dark, sitting up in bed and softly singing.

It was all done in one take, the way I like to work, and Jimmy Wong Howe outdid himself in this scene. The lighting is beautiful . . . all shadow and gleam . . . barely picking out Fanny's face. It's as quiet and serene as the song. That's a bold choice. He was able to achieve that darkness and depth and yet still maintain a certain glamour. And the camerawork is equally good. As I'm singing, the camera pulls out to reveal Billy, asleep in her lap, while her hand caresses his hair. And then the camera moves back in on her face. It's very gentle, and the light also changes subtly. Intermittent flashes from outside the window illuminate her face as the train speeds through the night.

I knew how it felt not to be fully committed to someone. And later there's a good scene when Billy is pleased to find she cares for him more than he (or she) thought. That was well written.

And I loved the moment when Fanny finally sees Nick for who he truly is . . . shallow and self-centered. She was so impressed as a girl when she noticed that he had seven toothbrushes, one for each day of the week. But she's not that girl anymore, and says, "All these years, I've been in love with nothing but a set of goddamn toothbrushes."

I was so pleased to finally get those toothbrushes in! It was such a telling detail, from one of Isobel Lennart's early drafts of *Funny Girl*. I had told Willy about it, but there was really no place to put it in that movie. It works perfectly here.

Fanny walks out of Nick's room, liberated at last. We shot this in the Beverly Hills Hotel . . . you can tell by the wallpaper with huge green palm leaves in the hall. And then we have the sequence with the car and the biplane, when she's trying to rush back to Billy and surprise him (I think Ray was trying to duplicate the "Don't Rain on My Parade" sequence in *Funny Girl*).

I've already told you I'm afraid of flying. So you can imagine how I felt about getting into that 1937 biplane, with a completely open cockpit for the pilot and another completely open seat behind him, for me. I was so scared that I thought I was going to have a heart attack before we even took off.

We shot it at Santa Monica Airport, and the plan was that we would just go up briefly and come right back down again. The pilot revved the engine, the plane sped up and soared into the air . . . but then we kept flying . . . and flying. What was going on? I couldn't talk to the pilot . . . there was too much noise with the engine and the wind up there to hear anything. The first thing I thought was, *I'm being kidnapped.* And then, as we kept going around in circles, I thought, *The radio's dead. We're never going to be able to land.*

Whatever possessed me to risk my life for a goddamn movie?

I'm told I was screaming by the time we finally touched down . . . only twenty minutes later, the assistant director said, but to me it felt like a lifetime. Apparently planes were backed up at the airport, which is why we couldn't land right away. But I didn't know that, and trust me, I was never so happy to be on solid ground.

And as I'm watching the movie now, I'm yelling at the screen, "Why don't you just call him!!!"

Of course, by the time she gets to Billy, it's too late, and the surprise is on her . . . she finds him in bed with his new girl.

It's heartbreaking . . . just when she finally realizes she no longer loves Nick and actually loves Billy, he has moved on. And she's left alone again, just as she was at the end of *Funny Girl*.

The movie wrapped in July, and as always I signed an album for everyone and found special gifts for key people and my team. Jimmy Caan, who liked to compete in rodeos, got a sterling silver cowboy belt buckle. I found a vintage movie camera for James Wong Howe and had a plaque made for it, engraved with the words "Thank you for your talents, generosity, and cha siu bao." *Funny Lady* was the last film he made.

And *Funny Lady* was my last film for Ray Stark. Finally, I had fulfilled my contract, and to mark the occasion, I gave him an antique mirror with this message written on it, in lipstick: "Paid in full," along with a plaque, engraved with the words "Even though I sometimes forget to say it, thank you, Ray. Love, Barbra."

What I meant was, I will always be grateful to him for *Funny Girl*, and he did produce *The Way We Were* for me, which was wonderful. But I couldn't forget how he took advantage of me and wasn't generous when both those movies were big hits.

I had told Jon how Ray had reneged on various deals, and had once handed me a hash brownie at one of his parties without telling me. Ray must have been a little high himself that evening, because he had the nerve to put his hand on my knee. I quickly brushed it off and left immediately, shaking. It disgusted me. My heart was racing so fast from the marijuana that I could hardly drive home. And it kept racing, which made me so scared that I called Marilyn and Alan Bergman, who came right over to spend the night and watch over me. I so loved them for that.

The next morning I went to the doctor, who said my heart rate was two hundred beats per minute. Thank God for the pill he gave me, which finally slowed it down. But I couldn't drive alone after that for a solid year. It was a horrible experience, and I guess Jon wanted to avenge me. When he met Ray for the first time, Jon just picked him up and dumped him down on a sofa. That was the wild man in him. You can bet Ray did *not* appreciate that.

Jon could act a little crazy, but he did have a kind of radar for power . . . who has it, and how to get it and use it.

One day we were driving down Sunset Boulevard, and there was a huge billboard for *Funny Lady* looming over the road, with my picture. I said, "Yuck. That doesn't look like me."

"You can make them change it," he said. That hadn't occurred to me. I just assumed it was too late to do anything about it once it was up. But I called Marty and told him to ask Ray to change it, and Ray did.

I have to give Ray credit . . . he knew how to promote his own shows. He got

Funny Lady off to a big start . . . not just with a premiere in Washington, D.C., but also a concert at the Kennedy Center that was shown live on ABC. I performed songs from the movie and did a duet with Jimmy Caan. The evening benefited the Special Olympics, founded by Eunice Kennedy Shriver, so lots of Kennedys were in the audience, along with President Ford. And I was touched when Muhammad Ali, a champion of the Special Olympics (as well as heavyweight champion of the world), and two of the children presented me with a medal to thank me for my support.

Then, after more openings in New York and Los Angeles, we flew to London for yet another premiere, in benefit of another charity, and this time it would be attended by another head of state . . . Queen Elizabeth II.

I'm always happy to be back in England. I love everything British . . . the stores, like Thomas Goode with such beautiful china and silver . . . the politeness . . . the taxicabs . . . the architecture. But I didn't like the feeling I got when I was standing in the receiving line waiting to meet the queen. I struggled with whether I should curtsy or not. After all, she wasn't *my* queen. And the idea of curtsying to anyone felt demeaning. It reminded me of all those old notions of actors as second-class citizens, who had to enter through the kitchen . . . the prince and the showgirl . . . and tapped into the obstinate part of me.

Then there were all these rules. According to protocol, you're not supposed to speak until the queen speaks to you. And women were required to wear gloves.

Huh? That seemed like something out of another era. And if women were required to wear gloves, why not men?

When Jon dared me to ask her, I said, "How much do you want to bet?"

He said, "A hundred."

And I thought, *Why not?* (This is probably why I got a D in conduct back at the yeshiva.)

When the queen and I were finally face-to-face, I did do a kind of curtsy, and she said something complimentary (which of course I've forgotten). And then I asked, "Why do women have to wear gloves to shake your hand, but not men?"

She looked a bit startled. I doubt she had ever thought about it. She said, "I'll have to think about that one. I suppose it's tradition." Then she smiled graciously and turned to her aide, who kind of whisked her away. The next day the picture of us meeting was on the front page of all the English papers, and some mentioned my shocking question.

I thought to myself, *Why did I do that?* The fact is, I was trying to puncture the formality, with all of us lined up as stiffly as soldiers, and make light of an awkward moment. Well, at least I won the bet.

After London we flew to Paris for another premiere. And the first thing I did when we got there, as always, was go to Les Halles, the giant food market with all these great, old-fashioned restaurants serving the freshest seafood, straight off the docks. I loved oysters, and we ordered a huge platter. They were delicious . . . but a few hours later I was on my knees in the bathroom at the Plaza Athenée, throwing up.

I could hardly move, much less get dressed and appear in public. Sue Mengers kept coming in and out and she was not exactly a fountain of sympathy.

"Barbra," she said. "Come on! Get dressed. We have to leave."

Then Ray barged into the suite and started yelling at me through the bathroom door. "Barbra, we have to go!"

Jon began yelling at Ray, "Can't you see she's sick!"

Ray was apoplectic. "I don't care how sick she is. We have to leave *now.* The president of France is going to be there!"

I could hear their voices and I desperately wanted to get up, but each time I tried, I was hit by a new wave of nausea. Jon was holding my forehead as I was heaving. Finally I just closed my eyes and sank down onto the cool tiled floor. I felt like crying, but I was too sick to sob. A doctor eventually arrived and gave me a powerful pill that put me to sleep, not only for the night, but also for the entire plane ride home.

So I ended up missing my own premiere . . . but so did the president, as it turned out. Apparently he had to deal with some last-minute business, so I didn't feel *quite* so bad.

TWENTY-EIGHT

Lazy Afternoon

Finally, after ten years, Ray no longer had any hold on me, and I felt as if I had been sprung from jail. It was such a relief not to have that commitment hanging over me. I was a free woman, and I could do the kinds of things I never had time for before.

My old friend Rick Edelstein was directing a scene from *Uncle Vanya* at the Actors Studio in Hollywood, and I went to see it. Sally Kirkland, whom I'd met when she had a small part in *The Way We Were*, was in it, and it made me remember how much I wanted to do Chekhov and Ibsen and Shakespeare when I was a girl.

Afterward we were all talking with Lee Strasberg, and he asked, "What part would you want to play?"

I said, "Juliet."

I had such a clear concept for her . . . I wanted to play her so badly . . . but I thought I'd never get to do it.

Strasberg said, "Why not? Pick a scene."

So I did. Sally and I rehearsed and then did it for Lee a few weeks later. I didn't even invite my friends to come because I was afraid I wouldn't be good enough. Yet somehow word got out, and there was a line around the block, and the place was packed to the rafters.

It was the scene where Juliet has sent her nurse to meet Romeo to find out if he's going to marry her. But the nurse takes too long, and Juliet gets impatient. Since she's not quite fourteen years old, I thought that like any girl that age, her emotions would be changing by the minute. She's excited and anxious, hopeful and unsure. I wore a long dress to feel more in the period and plopped down on my stomach on an antique settee, thinking Juliet would try to distract herself by reading some romantic poetry and eating candy.

Then finally, out of frustration, she jumps up and says the first lines: "The clock struck nine when I did send the nurse. / In half an hour she promised to return."

I thought Juliet needed something to let out her anger. So I put up a game board so she could throw darts at it (in lieu of at the nurse). Where is she? How dare she keep me waiting!

As soon as Sally entered, I grabbed her, desperate to hear Romeo's answer. When she started rambling instead, I began to throw pillows at her in exasperation. With her beloved nurse, Juliet doesn't have to be proper and well mannered, as she is with her parents at court. She can just be herself. The nurse has to laugh and gives in, telling her that Romeo has arranged their marriage for that very afternoon.

Unlike the usual reading of the play and the Juliets I've seen, who run off happily, I stopped abruptly, frozen . . . with Juliet's thoughts running through my head in a jumble of joy and trepidation . . . Oh my God. Is this really happening? Am I ready for marriage?

Or was she just a girl in love with love?

Until that moment, it was a romantic fantasy, but now the reality of what she's done hits her, and she's scared. So I couldn't move, and Sally actually had to push me out the door, which we hadn't planned, but being in the moment, that's what happened.

When Lee started to give us his critique, I was so tense, because this was a very different interpretation. My Juliet was not some idealized, angelic creature, but more like a typical teenager. She could be a spoiled brat. That felt more authentic to me.

And then Lee didn't have any criticism, which surprised me. Nothing like "You should have tried this or done that." I remember because I would have liked to know if there was anything I could do to make it better. But I've forgotten what he actually said. (Maybe it was so technical that I had no idea what he was talking about.)

It was only decades later, when Sally came backstage after a concert, that she reminded me of what actually happened. "I remember the moment exactly," she told me. "Lee said, 'Barbra, you've just done the best Juliet I've ever seen.'"

Did he really say that? Sally insisted, "It's true. I was there!"

But that was the extent of my Shakespearean career. Meanwhile, I was enjoying being at home. I finally had time to breathe.

And then another project sparked my interest.

My friend Rob Friedman from Warner Bros. had given me a new album he thought I might like, called *Widescreen.* It was by a guy named Rupert Holmes, who wrote his own songs, and there was something about them that spoke to me. Each one was like a little play, with lyrics that were quirky and smart, funny and delightful and sad (sometimes all at the same time). I found myself listening to the record again and again, which is very unusual for me. Normally I hear something once, and that's enough.

I thought I might record a couple of the songs on my next album, so I got Rupert's number in New York and called him. He was a bit stunned when he heard my voice.

> *"All I know is that it was as if someone flipped a switch, and suddenly my life was wired with electricity and I saw what it was like to have light everywhere. It was really nothing short of a miracle in my life."*
>
> —Rupert Holmes

We had a great conversation, and I liked him so much that I invited him to come to LA. I thought we could work together on new arrangements for the songs I wanted to do. Then, once he arrived, it wasn't very long before I asked if he'd like to work with me on the whole album.

I was going on instinct. We just hit it off, and it didn't bother me that he was basically unknown and had never done anything on this scale before. I knew it was a risk, but I like risks.

I already had certain songs in mind, like "Lazy Afternoon," which became the title of the album. I have to thank Francis Ford Coppola . . . he suggested that song to me over a sukiyaki dinner. It was from a nearly forgotten 1950s musical called *The Golden Apple*, and I loved it, because it was slow and sensual and really conjured up the dreamy feeling of a lazy afternoon, when you just stop for a moment and relax . . . which was exactly what was happening in my own life, since I had this wonderful chunk of time with no movies, no commitments. And then when Rupert and I were talking about how I heard this song, I got this image in my head of Alice, lazing on the riverbank before the White Rabbit appears, and I said to him, "What if the music also conveyed a sense that something magical and wondrous was happening?"

And he managed to capture exactly that mood in his arrangement.

After only a few weeks we were already communicating on the level of good friends. And it was uncanny how he could give voice to feelings I hadn't even articulated. One day he came in and said he had written something for me, and he sat down at the piano and played "My Father's Song." It was about the father that all of us have wanted or needed at some time or another . . . a father who says, "Wherever you are, I'm here by your side."

How did he know?

I was deeply touched.

On another day, we were sitting at the piano, working out keys for several arrangements, and I was getting bored. I said, "I think I'll write a song," and started humming the beginnings of a melody. And then Rupert began improvising chords, following me along. After a few false starts and several revisions, I had a complete tune! It's a fascinating process . . . when you really get into it, there's a certain inevitability to the notes.

We quickly put it down on tape, and then began to talk about ideas for the lyric. The first bar of the melody emphasized three notes, so that suggested three words, and since I had written the song almost incidentally, I thought "By the Way" would be a good title. And then I said, "What if you keep coming back to that phrase in the lyric? Since it has different meanings, it might be interesting to see how many ways you can use it."

The next day Rupert came back with a draft (I love people who work fast), and as we were going over it, I had another thought. "You know what would really be great . . . if we could end the song with the title too."

It was like a puzzle, and he brilliantly solved it:

By the way, did I hear you say, if some night I seem too lonely?
You would stay, oh and by the way
Have I told you yet that only recently, he moved out on me?
He was gone long before he really left, I knew it
"By the way," he began to say, "Love takes time, I'm in a hurry"

. . . oh, and by the way, I thought I mentioned you can stay
Leave the lights, you don't look a thing like he did
And it's time to play, it's another day
Why can't we make love fall by the way?

See what I mean about each song being like a little play? I could really get into this character, who was still hurting from a breakup and had just met someone new. There's another line about how her ex "took the towels we stole from some motel in Tennessee." Now that's pure Rupert . . . so specific and visual it's practically cinematic. We can imagine that they were so happy in that little motel room, and now he's robbed her of even that memory.

It was fun sitting next to Rupert at the piano and creating this piece . . . and it's kind of funny to think that a song that came out of a short attention span will last forever!

He was so easy to work with. Then, on the night before the first recording session, I could sense something was wrong. I said, "You're not nervous, are you?"

"I'm terrified out of my mind," he admitted.

"Why?"

"Because it's you singing my songs, my arrangements, with a huge orchestra," he explained. "I'm conducting. It's the most spectacular thing that's ever happened in my life. I just hope I'm up to the challenge."

The next day at the studio, I walked over to him as soon as I came in and handed him a little package, wrapped in tissue paper. Inside was a deck of Rupert Bear playing cards from England, where this bear was a beloved comic-strip character. On the tissue paper, I wrote, "Dear Rupert, don't be frightened. You're the best. Love and thanks, Barbra."

Apparently it did the trick, because the session went off without a hitch. I think the first song we did was "Widescreen," which was appropriate, since it was the song that initially convinced me that Rupert was channeling my own thoughts. He wrote about something I had felt as a thirteen-year-old, walking out of a movie theater on a summer afternoon into the hot, humid Brooklyn street and wishing I could just go back in and live inside those Technicolor dreams.

The lyric ended with these lines:

Oh widescreen, take the world away
Break me from the day
Make me be what's not for real
And make me feel like a star
Make me what you are

But I was not that girl anymore. And now, when I reflected on the reality of life versus the fantasy of movies, I chose life . . . even in all its heat and humidity.

So I asked Rupert if he could change those lines for me, and he came up with words that reflected a new kind of maturity:

No, widescreen, dreams are more than you
How can lies be true?
All we have is life and mind, and love we find with a friend
Oh, let the movie end

Perfect.

I could sing that because I believed it. And Rupert understood.

The cover shoot was just as easy as the recording sessions. I asked Steve Schapiro to come to the ranch. I wrapped a scarf around my head because I didn't want to fool with my hair, put on a pink vintage-looking top and skirt and pink lipstick, and lounged on the mattress that served as the main seating area in the barn. I was barefoot and relaxed. It was kind of a bohemian look, to create a romantic, lazy atmosphere. I think Steve and I were done in about twenty minutes, which is what can happen when you have a good photographer whom you trust.

I had a cohesive vision for the cover and the album. And with Rupert, it was fully realized. There was a consistency of tone, and apparently some critics recognized it when *Lazy Afternoon* was released in October 1975. In the *Los Angeles Times*, Robert Hilburn wrote that Rupert "has given Streisand her most authentic connection yet with contemporary pop influences."

I like that word "authentic."

The album wasn't a huge success, maybe because it didn't have the kind of hit single the disc jockeys liked, to drive sales. But I still love it . . . actually, it was the first time I wrote my own liner notes, because I was so eager to share something about each song. It was kind of an odd and dreamy album, and I still remember it fondly.

TWENTY-NINE

Classical Barbra

You could say it all started with Maria Callas . . .

After I found Billie Holiday's *Lady in Satin* album and Johnny Mathis's *Good Night, Dear Lord* on a supermarket rack when I was a teenager, my next big discovery in my midtwenties was Maria Callas. I bought an album of her singing Puccini arias and it's the one record I kept playing over and over through the years.

Usually I don't have the chance to listen to music. And I don't play it during my rare dinner parties because it's too distracting. I'd rather focus on the conversation.

When I'm swimming in the pool, I may put on one of those calming nature recordings, because the dogs love it . . . it lulls them to sleep . . . and it quiets my brain so I don't have to think.

For me, listening to music is work. When I make a record, I have to listen to it day and night for months . . . before I sing and after I sing . . . first the orchestrations, then all the different takes, and then all the versions of the mix on all the different sound systems . . . in my living room, on my phone, in the car. So the last thing I want to do when I finally stop and relax is put on more music. I'd rather play games on my phone to take my mind off the day's problems.

I gave away all my vinyl albums in the 1980s, but I did buy a CD of Callas singing Puccini, just to have it. I've never grown tired of her voice. Recently I saw a documentary on her, and for the first time I could watch her face as she sang. She truly was an actress. She was not merely singing the notes, she was feeling every emotion, and it seemed to come from some place deep within. And I thought, *Yes, that's what I must have been responding to all along.*

There was one aria on that album . . . "Senza Mamma" from the opera *Suor Angelica* . . . that stayed in my head. The melody was so beautiful and full of passion. And that became the catalyst for *Classical Barbra.* I knew I didn't have a glorious soprano voice. (My mother probably would have sounded great, but she wasn't really interested in opera. Her favorite number was "Sunrise, Sunset" from *Fiddler on the Roof* and she couldn't wait to get up and sing it at bar mitzvahs, while I hid.)

But I thought I might be able to sing the aria in my range. And then when I met Claus Ogerman, I realized he would be the perfect person to do it with me.

Claus was incredibly gifted . . . a multitalent who could compose a concerto, conduct a symphony orchestra, and arrange a number 1 single. He crossed effortlessly between genres . . . jazz, pop, rhythm and blues, classical. He had worked with everyone from Frank Sinatra to Lesley Gore, Antonio Carlos Jobim to Oscar Peterson. He did a beautiful job arranging a Carole King song on my *Stoney End* album, but we didn't really get to know each other until we worked together at the end of 1970 at the Riviera Hotel in Las Vegas, where he arranged and conducted for me.

By that time the idea of doing a classical album had been percolating in my head for a while. I always like to stretch myself. It would be scary, but also kind of stimulating . . . a complete departure from anything else I had ever done. I was considered a pop singer and was supposed to stay in that lane. Besides, I have no training in classical music (no training in any music, actually). But I hate being confined to one category.

And it was my friendship with Claus that finally brought this project to fruition. I needed an arranger who was intimately familiar with classical material, and that described him. He was born in Germany, so he knew the full repertoire of German lieder . . . all those achingly romantic songs by nineteenth-century composers like Franz Schubert and Robert Schumann, which were usually performed by a singer accompanied by just a piano. And Claus knew opera, so he could steer me to arias that were right for me.

Well, I wanted a challenge, and boy, did I get one. The process was difficult but very rewarding, because I enjoyed learning something new. The album eventually included a delicate Debussy piece sung in French, a folk lullaby in a French provincial dialect, Hugo Wolf's melancholy "Verschwiegene Liebe" in German (with Claus playing the piano for me), a Handel aria in Italian, and a wordless Gabriel Fauré piece in which I just hum . . . and even one song in Latin, from Carl Orff's *Carmina Burana*. The very last song, "I Loved You," was the only one in English. It was a poem by Alexander Pushkin, translated from Russian, and set to music written for me by Claus.

We recorded the album in 1973, but it wasn't released until 1976. It took so long because I kept thinking, *Maybe I could make it better . . .*

But then I got so busy with *A Star Is Born*, working on the script *and* the score, that everything else got pushed aside. Meanwhile, Columbia was begging me for another album, and since I had no time to make one, I reluctantly let go of this. And you can bet Columbia wasn't all that eager to release an album of me exploring this esoteric repertoire.

Singing lieder is such a disciplined art form, and the rhythms are very specific, which is not my natural style. I like to be free to phrase however I want. I also felt the album should have a level of vocal purity, which I wasn't sure I had achieved. I wanted to write "This is a work in progress" on the back, but

Columbia asked me not to, so I didn't. (I wish I had. Come to think of it, I should put it on this book, too . . .)

There was some talk about calling the album *Follow the Lieder*, which seemed kind of fun and unpretentious. But we didn't want to turn it into a joke, so we went with *Classical Barbra* . . . simple and direct. For the cover, I chose a photo from a shoot I had done with Francesco Scavullo for *Vogue* a year earlier. (See a pattern here?) Leonard Bernstein generously wrote a blurb for the back, and the album went out into the world.

And then the most remarkable thing happened. Glenn Gould, the brilliant, intense classical pianist, reviewed the record for *High Fidelity* magazine.

> *"I'm a Streisand freak and make no bones about it . . . For me, the Streisand voice is one of the natural wonders of the age, an instrument of infinite diversity and timbral resource . . . No phrase is left solely to its own devices . . . Much of the Affekt of intimacy—indeed, the sensation of eavesdropping on a private moment . . . is a direct result of our inability to anticipate her intentions."*
>
> —Glenn Gould

He mentioned the "courage" it took to step outside my niche. I'm not sure I'd call it courage . . . more like crazy . . . but I wasn't thinking in either of those terms. I was just entranced by the music. And I wasn't looking forward to the reviews, but this one appeared like an angelic annunciation.

It was an extraordinary vote of confidence. Gould suggested a few other classical pieces he'd like me to tackle and even volunteered to play for me. (Why didn't I take him up on that? Another missed opportunity.)

In a 1974 interview Gould did for *Rolling Stone*, he said, "At her best, Barbra Streisand is probably the greatest singing actress since Maria Callas." Most people don't mention that I'm an actress, who just happens to sing as well. And it strikes me as kind of uncanny that he would mention Callas, since it was hearing her sing that particular aria that inspired the album in the first place.

But the biggest thrill was something that I never expected . . . being nominated for a Grammy for Best Classical Vocal Soloist Performance. That was a huge surprise . . . a *wonderful* surprise. Of course I never thought I would win (I lost to Beverly Sills), but that didn't matter. Point is, I had made it into a whole new category of music, and the nomination was like a seal of approval.

Claus and I remained friends, and here's something I wasn't even aware of. It turns out that he did some of the orchestrations for Billie Holiday on *Lady in Satin* . . . the same album I pulled off that grocery store rack when I was a girl. Isn't that amazing? It was like completing a circle, something that felt *bashert.*

But other things are just not meant to be, I guess. In the 1990s I saw Zoe Caldwell give a dazzling performance as Maria Callas in Terrence McNally's play *Master Class.* It was so moving and realistic about the endless work that goes into being an artist, as well as the sacrifices that are made in the name of art. I really identified with this woman . . . her search for perfection, her loves, and her losses. Immediately, I inquired about the film rights, but was told they were owned by Faye Dunaway. Every few years I would check on the status and was told she still had them, but she's never managed to make the movie.

So I didn't get to do that film, but a few years ago, my friend Billy Friedkin directed a production of *Suor Angelica* for the Los Angeles Opera, and I finally got to see the story around my favorite aria, "Senza Mamma." I never did sing it back when we were making the album. I thought, *How could I ever be as good as Callas?* To me, it was like this sacred thing, and it was hers, forever.

THIRTY

A Star Is Born

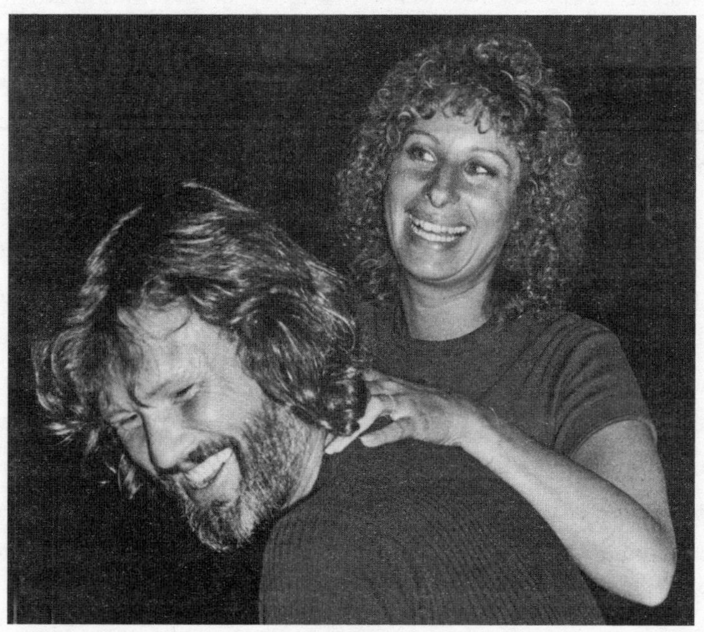

It was Jon who pulled the script out of a pile. He told Sue Mengers that he wanted to see everything that was sent to me, and he liked one by Joan Didion and John Gregory Dunne. It was a gritty, behind-the-scenes look at the world of rock and roll, and I had already dismissed it because I thought it was fundamentally cold. The love story between two singers seemed almost secondary. And even though it had no title, it was clearly a variation on *A Star Is Born* . . . the man's career is fading while the woman is about to become a huge success.

Jon said, "What a great story!"

I said, "Yeah, it's a great story and it's already been made two times."

He didn't realize that it was a new take on an old movie, because he had never heard of *A Star Is Born.*

The first version was released in 1937, with Janet Gaynor playing the aspiring actress, Esther Blodgett, and Fredric March as the troubled star, Norman Maine. Then it was remade in 1954 as a musical with Judy Garland and James Mason.

This was 1974, so the idea seemed to come around again every twenty years or so. It's one of those stories like *Romeo and Juliet* . . . it always works. I thought Judy Garland was extraordinary in it. Every emotion was so real, and the songs . . . many by the great Harold Arlen and Ira Gershwin . . . were fantastic! Why tamper with something that was already perfect?

I didn't want to do it, but I had a commitment to First Artists to deliver a film by a certain date. So I read it again.

As part of their research, the Dunnes had followed a rock band around (I heard it was Led Zeppelin) and wrote what was more like a documentary. Jon loved all the sordid details about life on the road, but what I responded to was the love story. It was the crux of the piece, in my opinion, and somehow it had gotten lost in the midst of too many scenes about managers, groupies, and motel rooms. The lead characters didn't even exchange a word until fifty-two pages in.

As I delved deeper and reread the script, I thought, *Maybe I could do something with this*. Bring out the love story . . . don't be afraid to call it *A Star Is Born* . . . and update the couple's relationship to reflect the times. It was the height of the women's liberation movement, and I realized I could say something about women through the character of Esther.

It's funny . . . I rarely thought about the women's movement when I was first moving forward as a woman. Was I paid less than a male performer? I don't think so. When I started making records, I couldn't even tell you what I got paid. I didn't care about the money. I just wanted creative control.

I was treated very well, but women in general were not so lucky. They were fighting for recognition, opportunity, and equal pay for equal work. Here was a chance to do a musical with what could be a powerful love story . . . and try to send a subtle message at the same time.

I'm all for women and women's rights, but people will just tune out if you're too abrasive. I didn't understand why feminists were burning their bras. What did bras have to do with it? (Maybe it was a symbol of constriction?) I hardly ever wore one anyway. Now I understand it in the context of revolution . . . sometimes you have to go to extremes in order to come back to the middle, a more balanced place.

You can trace the changing role of women if you look at the character of Esther in the 1930s and then the '50s as compared to the '70s. The women in the previous films were more passive. I wanted my character to not be afraid to say exactly what she thinks and challenge the men.

I was also interested in expressing something about the pressures of show business, which can drive performers to self-destruct. I thought the film could expose the truth about what it's like to be in the public eye. I knew about that from my own experience. The press, looking for drama, builds you up and then knocks you down. It's great to be admired by fans . . . until you start to feel pursued. I've had people follow me into the bathroom for an autograph.

And then I also wanted to explore the relationship between men and women . . . the excitement, the conflicts, the fun, the pain . . . the pain of loving, and losing. In the earlier versions, the lovers rarely spoke a harsh word to each other. She adored him, and he adored her. They never fought or disagreed.

Their kindness to each other was touching, but I also think those old Hollywood movies were responsible for a lot of disappointment. They made people yearn for a kind of romance that was very rare in real life, and if your own relationship wasn't like that, you thought something was wrong with it. I was living through ups and downs with Jon. Why not be honest about that? Use the truth.

Now I was getting excited about the story . . . it seemed full of possibilities . . . and I decided to commit to the project. I would produce it with Jon, since it was his idea to do it. I told myself that he wouldn't be constrained by all the previous versions, since he had never seen them. He could think outside the box.

And then, even though he was a novice with no experience, he didn't want to share the producer credit with me. That should have set off alarm bells, but I could see how desperately he wanted that stature. And I knew it would bring him more respect on the set. So I thought, *Okay, let him have it. I'll be executive producer.*

What I didn't know, and what no one told me, was that if the picture got any awards, only Jon, as the producer, would be entitled to receive them. I didn't realize that executive producers don't get awards, because I don't pay that much attention to credits, and I certainly wasn't thinking that far ahead. I just wanted to get this picture made.

And I wanted Sydney Pollack, someone I knew and respected, to direct. But after waiting months for him to decide, he turned us down.

Then Jon said, "I'll direct it myself!"

My first reaction was, Are you kidding?

But it did make me think. By this point I had made nine films, and here was this guy who had absolutely no experience, and yet he was convinced he could direct a movie.

Well, I thought that if *he* could direct, *I* could direct. But it was only a thought, and it didn't last long, because I wasn't convinced that I knew enough yet. And besides, I already had my hands full, trying to get a score for the film together quickly.

Marty just reminded me that he had a meeting with John Calley, the head of Warner Bros., and Marty said, "Can you believe Jon Peters wants to direct the movie?"

"As long as Barbra Streisand is in it," John said, "I don't care who directs it."

I wish I had had the confidence to just do it myself . . . it would have made the whole experience a lot easier.

We were still looking for a director when I approached Frank Pierson to do a rewrite. I had been impressed with his script for *Dog Day Afternoon*, and I hoped he could make the love story more prominent and still keep it real.

The Dunnes had changed the characters' names to Esther McQueen and John Norman Howard. His name was fine, but do I look like an Irish person? I'm proud to be Jewish, so I thought, *Why not make her Jewish?* Let's call her Esther Hoffman, instead of one of those innocuous names in movies like Brown or Jones. Everybody in Hollywood was so afraid to be Jewish.

I already had a cinematographer in mind. I had admired Robert Surtees's work in *The Last Picture Show* and *The Graduate*, so I met with him. I showed him photographs of people onstage . . . mostly frontlit . . . but sometimes backlit with colored lights. I wanted a theatrical feeling to surround Esther and John Norman, even in their private lives . . . to show that in some way, they could never escape the spotlight. Bob was superb. He appreciated the input and was thrilled to have some direction.

For the production designer I chose Polly Platt, who had done *The Last Picture Show* and *What's Up, Doc?*, where we had become friends. She did a brilliant job with the adobe house her crew built in the desert. I asked her to add skylights and high windows that sent shafts of light down on the characters (another variation on those constant spotlights).

I felt very confident in the team . . . and then Frank did something that shocked me. He blackmailed us.

After giving me a first draft that still hadn't captured the love story, he said, "By the way, I also want to direct this. And I'm not going to do another draft unless I get to direct it as well."

I didn't want him to direct . . . he had only directed one unsuccessful film and didn't know anything about musicals . . . but I was under tremendous pressure. We had to start shooting soon.

To try to stop myself from panicking, I took a deep breath. Maybe the situation was salvageable. Since I was the executive producer, and the deal at First Artists meant I had final cut, I knew I was ultimately in control. As long as we got the footage we needed, I would be able to shape it the way I wanted.

So I made a deal with Frank. "You can direct," I told him, "but you have to understand something. I'm personally responsible for this project . . . every penny of it. My company, Barwood Films, is making it for First Artists, and then I have to answer to the larger company, Warner Brothers. Any dollar we spend over the six-million-dollar budget comes out of my own pocket. So I'm going to be involved in every decision. You can have the credit, but we basically have to codirect."

He agreed.

I should have known it was not going to work as soon as I saw his house. It felt like a cold box . . . made of steel, glass, and concrete . . . and Frank was equally cold. We had problems with each other from the beginning. Looking back I realize it must have been difficult for him to accept a woman being in charge. In an effort to defuse the tension, I invited him to lunch at my house on Carolwood before we began shooting so we could talk about the best way to proceed.

I said, "I know we've had our disagreements, and I'm not your favorite person. But please, for the sake of the film, try to find *something* about me that you like. Otherwise it's going to hurt the movie."

I don't think Frank understood what I was saying. In fact, he completely missed the point.

"I love you," he said, "but I'm not the demonstrative type."

"I'm not asking for your love," I told him. That word sounded so hollow coming from him.

I was actually being very practical and objective . . . and giving him a clue into how to get the best performance out of an actor. I told him about working with Willy Wyler and Sydney Pollack, and how something wonderful happens when a director appreciates the stars of his film. The actors open up and trust. There's a relaxed feeling on the set.

But Frank and I never developed that kind of rapport. He had accepted his position up front as a collaborator and knew I was more than just an actress. But once we started shooting, he seemed to forget our agreement.

He was a director who didn't know where to put the camera. He would change his mind five times, driving the crew and the cameraman up the wall. After the first day of shooting, we were already a day behind.

We started with the scene where Kris Kristofferson, playing John Norman Howard, comes into a little club to unwind after his concert and sees Esther, who's singing there that night. He just wants to sit down and be left alone, but people rush over to take his picture. One guy asks him to get up and sing for his girlfriend, and gets belligerent when John Norman says no.

I put more of my own experience into this film than I had ever done before. And this scene in the club was based on things that have happened to me. I've noticed that normal boundaries . . . the kind of courtesy you'd extend to any stranger on the street . . . sometimes dissolve when people see "a star." They'll interrupt a conversation with my son to ask for an autograph or try to take a picture in a restaurant, when I'm in the middle of biting into a greasy spare rib.

Sometimes people will even ask me to sing, as if I were some sort of performing seal. They think it's easy, but it's not. I don't sing at home, I don't sing in the shower, and I don't sing at parties. So, to just stand up and sing something for a stranger? You might as well ask me to jump off a bridge. But if you don't comply with their request, some people can turn on you and get nasty, saying they're not going to buy your records anymore. In a way, they think they own you, because they paid for that album.

Let me be clear. I'm grateful to my fans. They have supported me for decades. But sometimes I just want to finish my spare rib.

John Norman ends up punching the guy, and the whole place breaks into a fight. Esther pulls him away, and they run out to his limo, just as the people following them start pounding on it. (That came straight out of the *Hello, Dolly!* premiere, which was still giving me nightmares.)

Kris knew this world from the inside too. The part of John Norman Howard seemed tailor-made for him. He almost didn't have to act. He was a musician, a songwriter, a poet . . . with an aching vulnerability that showed in his eyes.

God, he was attractive. I remember the first time we met, a few years before this project came along. Marty called and said, "Do you want to see this guy named Kris Kristofferson at the Troubadour? I hear he's good." So I went that night, and there he was onstage, so beautiful . . . with perfect white teeth . . . and barefoot. Incredibly sexy.

I thought, *Hmmm . . .*

We saw each other for a while after that . . . he and his Bull Durham cigarettes. He gave me hickeys on my neck. Thank God I had a two-piece bathing suit by Rudi Gernreich with a turtleneck top to hide them!

So I knew Kris and felt comfortable with him. There was one brief moment when Jon thought it would be brilliant to hire his idol, Elvis Presley, for the part. So Jon and I flew to Las Vegas, saw his show, and then went backstage to meet with Elvis and his manager, Colonel Parker. It took Elvis a while to appear, and when he finally walked in, he apologized. "Sorry to keep you waiting, but I have a problem. I've got this girl flying around in my plane right now" . . . he literally had her circling overhead . . . "and I can't decide whether I should let her down. What do you think?"

I said, "Why is she up there?"

"She kept talking and talking while I'm getting ready to go onstage and she was making me crazy."

"Let her down," I told him, "and tell her the truth. Explain that you need some quiet time to yourself before you perform. She'll understand that."

We talked about the film, and Elvis was interested. But obviously it didn't work out. Marty says that Colonel Parker asked for more money than we could afford. And Jon says the Colonel wanted to produce the film. I'm not sure about that. I do know that Elvis had gained a lot of weight and was no longer at the top of his game, although he was still drawing big audiences. Maybe the story was a little too close to his own life, and the Colonel talked him out of it.

When it fell through, Jon actually said, "Maybe I should play the part myself!"

He wasn't joking. He was ready to make his debut.

I said, "Jon, who the hell do you think you are? You're not a star. I hate to tell you, but you're only a legend in your own mind."

In any event, I had no regrets about Elvis. Kris was it.

Cast the right person, and you're already halfway there. For the part of Brian, John Norman's manager, I thought, *I'll ask Paul Mazursky*, who was a director and a writer. He had a natural authority, like the character. In other words, he didn't need much direction. I didn't have to make him feel strong and important. He already was.

I wanted new music for this film . . . nothing that had ever been heard before. And it was a wonderful opportunity. Since John Norman and Esther are both singer-songwriters, they could express themselves through their music as well.

Kris himself was a laid-back country music songwriter whose eloquent lyrics transcended the simplicity of the genre. (He had been a Rhodes Scholar at Oxford.) But for John Norman Howard's music, we needed something that was more aggressively rock and roll. And for Esther's music, it had to be something that I could identify with.

So I asked Rupert Holmes if he wanted to do the score, since we had developed such a great rapport working on *Lazy Afternoon*. I was delighted when he agreed. He was so thoughtful, asking all sorts of questions so he could find images that were personal to me and incorporate them into the lyrics. Rupert remembered that I was thinking of getting a beehive for the ranch and was fascinated by the fact that when it comes to bees, the female is in charge. He took that idea and turned it into the song "Queen Bee." I thought it was very clever. I mentioned that I had always wanted to play the cello and speak Portuguese and he worked that into the lyric for "Everything," which was about being bold enough, as a woman, to want more than just a husband.

I thought Esther was the kind of girl who would play the guitar, so I started to take guitar lessons. (I cut my nails on my left hand but kept them long on the right to pluck the strings.) I was so impressed with all these women songwriters . . . Joni Mitchell, Carole King, Laura Nyro . . . who could play the guitar or the piano and write their own music. When I was young, I wanted to play the piano.

My mother arranged for a few lessons, but I had to go to somebody else's house to practice, because we didn't have a piano of our own. It was very inconvenient, so I stopped. And anyway, if I couldn't play like Vladimir Horowitz instantly, I didn't want to play at all.

The guitar was much easier for me to handle. I could look at the symbols and pick out the chords. My guitar teacher said she also wrote music, and one day I asked her to play some for me. Suddenly I felt so inadequate. All I could do was sing other people's songs. I remember getting very emotional about it and retreating to the bathroom. When I started to cry, Jon was very sympathetic and encouraging. He said, "You can do it too! *You* could write songs!"

Actually I had written a couple of songs, but somehow that didn't seem to count in my mind.

Jon pushed me to challenge myself. And then Rupert, who had never written a score for a whole movie, became overwhelmed and flew home to New York. That came as a complete surprise. If he was frustrated, he never showed it to me. But we couldn't wait indefinitely, not knowing if or when he was coming back. We needed more songs, quickly, and I thought, *I've got to try.*

That's how I wrote "Evergreen."

I was hearing a melody in my head and then I had to find the chords that went with it on the guitar. To say I was unaccomplished would be an understatement. I drove Jason, Chris, and Jon absolutely crazy. I can still hear them pleading, "Could you stop playing that song!"

But I was searching for those elusive notes.

I think everyone was relieved when I finally got to the ending. In my mind I was hearing a specific range of chords changing under the last note as I held it . . . "evergreeeeen." But I couldn't find them. And then one day I just held the frets down at the bottom and then slid my fingers up each fret . . . and there they were. Wow! That was a discovery. I couldn't tell you what they were but I had my chords!

I remember sitting on the floor and playing the song over the phone for the Bergmans, who said, "That's nice."

But when I played it for Marty, he was very enthusiastic. "It's going to be number one on January twenty-second," he told me. I thought he was crazy, but he was right. (The movie was released in December 1976, and "Evergreen" was the number 1 single on January 15, 1977. He was only off by a week.)

After I finished the melody, I asked Kris to write the lyric. I liked the idea of the two leads in the movie writing a song together. But then he didn't produce anything, and I didn't want to push. (Years later, he finally gave me a copy of his lyric and explained that he had never sent it because he didn't think it was good enough.)

When I couldn't wait any longer, I went to Paul Williams, who'd done the lyrics for many popular songs. I sang my melody for him and asked, "Can you do anything with that?" He said, "It's beautiful. You've got your love theme."

I was thrilled that he liked it, but I still had so much trouble getting the words out of him. We eventually got to a version I liked . . . "easy chair" and "morning air" were great, but I wanted him to experiment a bit . . . try a few different images here and there. But he became belligerent. And then he stopped answering my calls.

We all knew he was drinking, which made working with him very difficult. All I could do was let go and accept the situation. And I'm so glad for both of us that what he did give me was damn good.

Many years later Paul apologized for putting me through that. He was going to AA and wanted to make amends, as part of the recovery process. And I very much appreciated that.

It's ironic. Finally I had my song, and I had taken guitar lessons for a year in order to be able to play it in the film. And then I ended up cutting out the scene.

It took place the morning after John Norman and Esther meet, when he comes back with a pizza for breakfast. He picks up some music she's been working on and asks her to play one of her songs for him.

Esther's reluctant, but he hands her the guitar. She says, kidding around, "If you laugh, I'll kill you." (That was an ad-lib.) And she's so nervous that she turns her back on him . . . just as I did when I sang for Cis and Harvey that first time. It's a very real moment, me struggling with the guitar and humming the melody of "Evergreen." When I finish, I turn around to see what he thinks . . . Esther really wants to impress him . . . but he's fast asleep on the couch, snoring. I loved that moment.

How could I have cut that out? I can be very hard on myself, and I'm more likely to cut my own scenes. When I'm in the editing room, I look at each moment very objectively, and in this case I was concerned about pace. I wanted to get right to the concert in the desert.

As they say, "Sometimes you have to kill your darlings."

Now, writing this book and looking at the film again after all these years, I'm not sure I was right. (And I just noticed I played a very interesting chord on the guitar that I forgot to use on the record! Oh well.)

There's a major difference between this film and most movie musicals. Usually you record the music in a studio and then play it back months later as you're shooting the scene. Some singers can easily replicate their vocal performance. Not me. And by now you know how much I hate lip-syncing.

So I said, "You know what? Let's do the music live."

I hired the wonderful Phil Ramone to figure out how to make that happen. He got us the two best mobile recording trucks to give us the equivalent of a sound stage at any location. It was so freeing, to have the energy of a live performance every time.

Frank wanted to use stock footage for the big concert scene. But Jon had a better idea.

"Why don't we put on a real concert? We can even charge admission and make some money from it!"

Brilliant! This was my world. I had performed in big arenas, but nothing quite so large as the Sun Devil Stadium in Tempe, Arizona, where we planned to shoot. Marty suggested we hire Bill Graham, a well-known concert promoter, and Bill lined up Peter Frampton, Santana, and several other acts to perform. The idea was to film the scenes we needed for the movie in between the real concert, and get the reactions of an actual audience, rather than trying to fake a crowd, as it's normally done, with strategically placed extras.

The problem was that everyone had to get there at dawn and be prepared to stay until dusk, in an open-air arena under the blazing sun. We weren't sure how many people would show up.

Seventy thousand people came. We put a camera in a helicopter for that spectacular shot where John Norman and Esther fly over the hill and suddenly see the packed stadium. We ended up setting a record for the largest concert in the state of Arizona. We paid the artists, covered our costs, and even donated twenty-five thousand dollars to the March of Dimes.

But when I saw what the crowd was like, I was petrified. They had clearly come for a rock concert, and I thought they would boo me off the stage if I went out there and sang "The Way We Were" and "People." I was afraid they'd think it was old-fashioned. And the setup was so different from my own concerts. I never had a large crew onstage with me. It was distracting. And then I was testing out new songs written specifically for the film, including "Evergreen." Plus, the band and I had barely had a chance to rehearse, which just added to my insecurity.

I decided the only thing to do was simply tell the audience the truth. I walked onstage and said I was going to sing a song I wrote that I had never performed before . . . and that I was very nervous.

Thank God their response was so positive.

And I was just warming up the crowd for Kris! He came out and did his number. We had various crew members with cameras out in the audience to pick up reactions and get that rough, handheld look I've always loved. I think we worked eighteen hours that day.

There are other concert scenes in the film, but those were shot in an auditorium and weren't quite as grueling. In the one that opens the movie, you see a Frisbee flying through the air, caught by the revolving spotlights, before you even know where you are. And then you hear thumping. The audience is getting impatient, waiting for John Norman Howard to appear, and they're stomping their feet.

I don't blame them. A performer shouldn't be late (I know, I know . . .). And then there's something that can happen with a rock and roll crowd . . . a moment when the mood can turn from merely restless to violent. And that's what we wanted to convey . . . how easy it is for people to turn on someone they've paid to see.

When Kris finally bounds onstage, just before things are about to veer out of control, you see him lit from behind, a dark silhouette against the blinding lights. We brought in Jules Fisher, a famous lighting designer I had met on Broadway, for all the onstage footage, so we could get exactly the kind of theatrical look I envisioned.

For the moment in another concert when John Norman unexpectedly pulls Esther out onstage, we needed something powerful for her to sing . . . something that could energize a crowd. I had been talking earlier to Paul Williams and Kenny Ascher, and asked, "Why is it always a man in the moon? Couldn't it be a woman? Why don't you write a song about that?" And that's how they came up with "The Woman in the Moon."

By the way, the convention was to shoot the wide shot first, then the medium, and finally the close-up. That didn't make sense to me. I knew the performance most likely to end up on-screen would be mostly medium shots or close-ups . . . so why wouldn't we shoot those first? My first take is often the best, and I didn't want to waste that performance (or blow my voice) on a wide shot.

So in this film we shot my initial performance in close-up, and had another camera going simultaneously to get the medium shot. Let's say we did three takes of the song. Then, right there on the spot, in the auditorium, I had to decide which take I liked best, because that would be the track they'd play for me to match when we shot it again in a wide shot, to include the audience.

God, it was exhilarating . . . all these split-second decisions.

But Frank and I continued to disagree, about this and other things. One time after I was a bit sharp with him I said, "I'm sorry. I have a little problem with tact. I don't know how to *schmeichel* you." (That's Yiddish for flatter you with smooth talk.) "I only know how to be direct."

"That's okay," he replied. "I agree with you and then behind your back I do what I want anyway."

So we had two different ways of working. Mine was more up-front. His was very sneaky. Passive-aggressive. Sometimes he'd decide a location wasn't quite right and go off to look for something else, without telling me, only to return to the original location. That wasted time and money.

One afternoon he just disappeared. It turned out he had gone off to see his analyst. As things got worse, I had to assume more control.

He never learned how to deal with actors. When I asked him one day what he thought about two different ways of playing a scene, he said, "I'm neutral."

"Frank, when you're directing, you can't be neutral. Because the actor has to have some feedback, some mirror, some response. Pick a way so the actor has something to try, even if it comes out wrong."

What I was attempting to tell him was that he had to communicate with the actors, use all their talents, make them feel free enough to improvise. Every extra is important! Every detail!

He put down my attention to detail. Whenever I got involved with the sets or the costumes, he seemed to regard it as, Oh God, how meddlesome.

Actually, I think he was uncomfortable with people. At lunch he sat alone.

He didn't try to talk to the actors and give them a sense of their characters, and a sense of their own importance in this film. He wasn't tuned in to any of the sensitivities that one has to have when you're dealing with an actor, who is exposing his mind, his being, his soul.

For instance, there's a famous scene that's in every *A Star Is Born.* In our version, John Norman is home alone and the phone keeps ringing, interrupting him as he's trying to write a song (and taping himself as he goes). No one is answering the phone, so he finally picks it up, and it's for Esther. He listens, and says, "No, this isn't her secretary . . . No, this isn't her answering service." Kris put down the receiver, and Frank said "Cut!" But he was too quick. He didn't allow Kris to complete the moment. All the hurt and pain he was feeling was right there on his face, and it was very moving to watch. But Frank missed it. That's when I tried to explain to him that there's nothing as cheap as film. He should keep the camera rolling a little bit longer to capture every nuance of emotion.

I come from the theater, where there are no cuts. So I like to shoot a scene or sing a song in one take, from beginning to end, rather than chopping it up into pieces. In the scene where Kris and I sing "Evergreen," I could see a way to do it in one take. I explained it to Frank and Bob, and that's how we did it.

It's a bit dangerous, shooting a scene in one take, but so exciting. What happens is everyone's on their toes . . . actors, director, camera people . . . because everyone's aware that one misstep can ruin the whole take. There are no other shots to cut to in the editing room . . . no coverage. So if something goes wrong, you have to start over.

On the first take, I was feeling good. I sang the opening bars of the song, and Kris joined in on the line "You and I will make each night a first." Then, after singing that one line, Kris bashfully turned away and stopped the scene. He was shy about singing with me.

I reassured him that I needed him in the song. This moment in the recording studio wasn't just about Esther, it was about the two of them together. For me, it was another love scene.

I told him, "Don't worry about making a mistake. There's no such thing as a mistake if you're in the moment. Whatever you do is fine. I'll deal with it."

So then we did take 2. First, you see a hand on a microphone . . . that determines the size of the shot (how close the camera is). Then Esther's face comes into the frame. She starts to hum. After a moment, another hand comes into the frame . . . you don't know whose it is . . . and the fingers intertwine with hers. Then the back of a head appears. You see this person lean down to gently kiss her hand.

By the way, that wasn't planned. I didn't want to plan this scene, or even rehearse it. I wanted to shoot it and see what happens. That's when it's really fun.

That little kiss on her hand is such an intimate gesture . . . and so in the moment. And my reaction is completely genuine. Being in the moment forces an actor to listen and respond because you don't know what's going to happen next. That's the kind of tension I love.

Now the camera begins to move . . . it's as if it's moving to the music . . . and as it comes around, we finally see a face. It's John Norman. He's listening intently . . . you can see how well these two people relate to each other. Kris gave a little shake of his head and laughed just as he was about to join in. But this time, when he started to turn away again, I pulled him back into the frame and held him there.

We laugh. I kiss him . . . because I was so grateful he didn't stop like he did in take 1!

He said something sweet to me under his breath . . . I can't remember what, but I know it wasn't part of the script. It made my heart skip.

We're in the moment. We're having a good time. The camera is revolving around us until it's over my shoulder and you just see Kris's face. Then it moves in the opposite direction and goes back to the two-shot again. He touches my hand. I touch his beard. I make fun of myself, clutching my throat as I hold the last long note . . . because I wasn't sure I could hold it! Remember, this was live.

Now the camera, still moving, is over his shoulder when he leans in and kisses me as the song ends. I'm smiling very broadly because I was genuinely happy!

Ironically, after all that, it was me who made the mistake . . . I forgot the words to my own song! On the line "I was always certain love would grow," I left out "always" . . . missed a beat . . . but it didn't matter.

It was the perfect take . . . spontaneous and real. The chemistry between us was palpable. You can't fake that kind of excitement. The camera picks up the truth. And it never could have happened if we were trying to lip-sync to a prerecorded vocal track.

I knew take 2 was it. I said, "Good, we've got it!"

Frank said, "I think we should do it again."

"Why?"

"It's the wrong size," he said. So, just to be polite, we did it again . . . and again. In the third take, the camera was too far away, and in the fourth take, it was too close.

Guess what's in the movie? Take 2. Why? Because that was the one. The truthful one, the natural one . . . and he didn't see it. He *couldn't* see it.

The fact is, Frank didn't know when he had gotten the performance.

Another time, I was singing a song, and the camera was on my profile. It was going very well. I could sense it. The energy was right. My voice was good. I'm in the middle of the song with my eyes closed, in my own world, connecting to the material . . . and he yells, "Cut!"

Astonished, I asked, "Why did you cut?"

"Your head went out of the frame."

"So what? It'll come back in."

He should have just told the camera operator to follow me. The one thing you don't do is stop a good performance. I had to take him aside and tell him privately, "Look, I know when a song is going well, and when it isn't, *I'll* stop."

Frank turned every day into a power struggle . . . determined to show everyone that he was in charge. I couldn't trust him not to step on a moment. Neither could Kris, and it got to the point where he came to me and asked if I could be on set for each of his scenes. I said, "Of course."

Kris was not formally trained as an actor, but he's smart and sensitive and he could say his lines as if he had just thought them up . . . and sometimes he had. He was free enough to improvise, and that made him a wonderful partner for me. He was brilliant in a demanding role, playing a burned-out rock star who has seen too many audiences. They keep crying out for more, more, and he gives too much of himself. Then, after the audiences are gone, he has nothing left.

I would try to encourage him when he was feeling insecure. I told him, "Don't worry about acting. Just *be*." He was so raw and natural, and I was very flattered that he wanted my direction. He'd say, "Tell me what you're thinking. What do you want me to do?" He put himself in my hands. He trusted me. I was very grateful for that.

One of the major flaws in the original script was that there was no love scene. It's always the toughest thing in a movie . . . How do you do a love scene that feels fresh? How do you make it special? I had hoped Frank could write one, but he never did. (I should have realized earlier that his talent was writing dialogue for men. Not romance.)

Before we started shooting, I spent months trying to figure out what the love scene should be. Meanwhile, I was meeting with Leon Russell to see if he wanted to write a song for the movie. We were sitting together at the piano in my house, tossing around ideas, when he got up to go to the bathroom. I started noodling around, playing something very simple I had written.

Leon came back in and asked what it was, and I told him it was a little classical melody that I had composed a few years before, when I was working on the album *Classical Barbra*.

He liked it and said it would make a good song. I didn't see how. Leon asked me to play it again so he could show me what he meant. As I played, he started to hum a countermelody, and it was so wonderful that it knocked me for a loop.

And that's how we wrote "Lost Inside of You."

After Leon left, I realized there it was . . . the scene I'd been waiting for . . . two people at the piano, connecting through their music. That moment between the two of us could get us into the love scene. *Of course* that's the way Esther and John Norman would come together, being intimate at the piano and then intimate with each other. It made perfect dramatic sense.

I had a tape recorder going during the session with Leon, and I transcribed what we had said, and that, with a few tweaks, became the dialogue in the film:

John Norman walks over and says, "Jesus, that's pretty. What is it?"

"Oh, just a little piece I wrote. I keep hoping it will be a sonata when it grows up."

"It'd make a hell of a song."

"I can't imagine that. It goes so high, nobody could ever sing it."

John Norman asks Esther to play it again, just as Leon did. And then he sings the countermelody just as Leon sang it to me.

Esther is stunned. She keeps looking at him in amazement, and hits a wrong note.

"I'm sorry. I'm sorry. Ooooh, that was *so good*! I got so lost in what you were doing that I forgot my own song."

By the way, that wasn't in the script. I was looking at Kris instead of the keys and hit a wrong note. But I didn't stop. I worked around it. Use the truth. It's what we look for, after all. Mistakes can be delicious.

It loosened us up, and then Kris started singing the line "When you came inside my life." He only got as far as "When you came" and then he cracked up, saying, "I gotta get past that word or you'll never forgive me." That made me really laugh, and I messed up my piano playing again. I never knew quite what was going to come out of Kris's mouth, and I loved reacting to what he gave me. So you got the spontaneity and excitement of two people discovering each other.

And that leads to their first kiss. He picks her up and carries her to some cushions by the fireplace. Esther is looking down at him as she lifts off her blouse, just as John Norman comes up into the frame to embrace her. (And shield my breasts. I like to leave something to the imagination!)

Then the frame goes to black. I envisioned this whole sequence where the camera goes from black to black as it keeps moving into a black Art Deco bathroom. The only light comes from the sparkle of umpteen candles stuck in beer cans arranged around a tub, where John Norman and Esther are bathing together.

The night before we were going to shoot that scene, I went to check out the set, and my face fell. I had asked for black tile with pink tile trim, and they had done just the opposite . . . pink tile with black tile trim . . . which wouldn't work for the dissolve.

The wonderful production design team stayed up all night, painting the pink tiles black and the black tiles pink, just so I could get what I needed.

Apparently Kris was planning to do the scene nude . . . I was wearing a little slip . . . but Jon insisted he put on some trunks. He was so jealous of Kris and possessive of me that it was becoming a problem. We had hired Jon's dear friend Uncle Rudy to play Mo, John Norman's driver, and I noticed he was keeping an eye on me to make sure I didn't stray . . . God forbid I should go into Kris's trailer or invite Kris into mine.

I didn't want to upset Jon, but all the stress he was causing was upsetting me. I don't remember if I finally had to ask him to stay off the set when we shot this scene, or if he decided on his own that he didn't want to be there.

The idea of putting makeup on Kris while we're in the tub came from something that had actually happened to Jon's cousin. He told us about it, and we thought it would show their sense of fun. When someone is truly masculine, they're not afraid of their feminine side. And it was all part of a theme . . . I was playing with masculine and feminine stereotypes throughout the movie.

I wanted Esther to wear men's clothes at times, and I deliberately put her in a Ralph Lauren suit for the scene where she tells John Norman that she wants to marry him. I liked the idea of the role reversal. Esther is really the driving force in this relationship. She sets the terms.

I was interested in being more sexually aggressive in this film . . . a different kind of character than I'd ever played. There's a moment in the love scene when Esther looks down at John Norman and undoes her belt. I was thinking of Clint Eastwood . . . you know how the guy always unbuckles his belt before having sex. That's why I wanted Esther to be on top. Why should a man always be the one doing the unbuckling?

Esther takes what she wants and is not ashamed to want . . . which I think is a big issue for many women. As she says in a lovely scene, which I stupidly cut out, "I want it all . . . you, music, cats, dogs, babies."

Many women feel the same way.

But John Norman is seriously depressed, and you can't save someone who doesn't want to be saved.

In the 1954 movie, Judy Garland is going into the kitchen to fix James Mason a sandwich when he calls her back for a moment, saying, "I just wanted to look at you again." Those are his last words to her before he walks into the ocean.

In our movie, John Norman gently wakes Esther early one morning to tell her where he's going, but he's really saying goodbye. He stares at her for one last moment, and Esther says, "What?"

"Just looking, babe."

She whispers, "I love you," and he does the same. Then he drives off, speeding faster and faster until he crashes his car, killing himself.

I had the idea that after John Norman's death, Esther would suddenly hear his voice in the house and think for a moment that he was somehow still alive. But it turns out to be a tape recording . . . the one he was making earlier as he was writing a song, when the phone interrupted him. The next part, where she's talking back to the tape and gets so angry at him for dying, was especially meaningful to me. It was a very personal thing I wanted to express. I'm still that person whose father died. As I grew up, I always felt as if I were missing something, and I was resentful. I wanted to be like all the other little girls whose daddies came home every evening.

My instinct was that Esther should cry. We did a few takes and as she's ripping up the tape, the camera moved in for a close-up. But no matter how hard I tried, the tears wouldn't come. You'd think this would be the simplest thing in the world . . . just use my father . . . but it didn't work. Eventually I got so angry at myself that I said, "Shit!" And that triggered the emotions. Using what I was really feeling opened up the spout. Why did John Norman have to die? Why did my father have to die? And it all came out.

In the final scene of the movie, Esther sings John Norman's last song, from that tape. So the movie opens and ends with a concert. Esther is appearing for the first time in public after her husband's death. As she walks to her place backstage, we see her from above, and her body casts a long shadow on the floor. That image was inspired by an Erté painting that I owned. It showed a little figure of a woman onstage with a huge shadow behind her, on the curtain. And it's true. When you're a performer, the shadow you cast is much bigger than you, the actual person. People blow you up and project all kinds of things onto you, which often have nothing to do with who you really are.

That shadow on the floor lasts for just a few seconds of film, and most people probably won't even notice it. But I do think the audience is very smart emotionally, and it leaves a subliminal impression.

Then the announcer says, "Ladies and gentlemen, Esther Hoffman Howard." That was our modern way of doing Judy Garland's "Mrs. Norman Maine" line . . . it's Esther's name plus his. She adds his name because she doesn't want people to forget him.

The curtain parts, and she steps forward, a dark silhouette against the lights. She starts very quietly, singing "With One More Look at You," the song he never got to play for her. She can hear him speaking to her through the music. He left her his feelings in the words. What a gift.

And then she segues into John Norman's signature song, "Watch Closely Now." It's slowed down at first, but then the tempo quickens until she's singing faster and faster . . . more like a rock star, more like him. He lives on in her.

We shot it in one continuous take, seven and a half minutes long, and the camera very slowly moves around her. Only the lights are constantly changing, to make it visually interesting.

When I sang the last note, the whole audience stood up applauding. I thought, *Great. We have it. Thank God that's done.* And then I went over to Jon and asked, "How was it?"

"I didn't cry."

I looked at him and said, "Fuck!" and walked away.

I went back to the hotel on my own. I watched the dailies with the crew. But I couldn't get Jon's comment out of my mind.

He should have had a bigger emotional reaction. It bothered me that he didn't cry.

And come to think of it, I didn't cry either. My technical side was in full gear for that shot. I had just run through the light changes with Jules and Bob . . . let's go to red here . . . pink here. Maybe I didn't really connect with the deeper feelings. And who knows? I probably wanted to get it over with . . . get it in the can . . . so I could play with it in the editing room.

I knew the set hadn't been taken down yet.

So I thought, *What the hell? I'll give it another try.*

I went in to Jon and announced, "We're going to do it again." But I told him he couldn't come watch. (I was still annoyed with him.)

So I did it once more, and that's the take that's in the movie. My eyes were tearing before I got to the end of the first song. The emotions were coming. Who knows from where? Of course, it's the material . . . losing someone you love, which triggers all kinds of memories, but it's also what's going on in your own head . . . me being upset with myself that I didn't get it the day before. The truth is, you don't know at that point whether it's the song or the story or something in you that you're connecting to, but somehow it all comes together and fills the emotional gap in a way that's right for the character.

By the time I went into the second song, his song, tears were rolling down my cheeks.

By the way, it's hard to sing when you're really crying. The vocal cords tighten and tense up. You can't hold a steady note. And then my nose started to run. I tried to wipe it quickly with one hand. And then, as the music gets faster and my head starts whipping back and forth, the drips were dripping. So I turned around for a second and wiped my nose again.

Nothing was going to stop me, or the show. Esther is rocking . . . getting high on the music and the memory of him.

I was moved by the story we were telling . . . Esther finally found someone to love . . . and he loved her back . . . and then he dies. That's pretty powerful.

When I finished the last notes of the song, Jon ran up to me. He had snuck in to watch . . . and this time he was crying. He was right. This time it was better.

After we edited the film, I was still working on this finale. We had a version in which I broke up the seven-minute take with some quick cuts, but I wasn't happy with it. I felt that the scene lost its tension as soon as we cut. I could just hear people in the movie theater thinking, *Okay, let's go now so we can be the first to get our car out of the garage.*

And then I didn't have time to try again and reedit the fast stuff before we had to fly to Phoenix for the preview. So I just put the one continuous take back in. At the very end, Esther has her head back and her eyes closed as the frame freezes. Then the credits roll while "Evergreen" plays over that last shot.

And the movie seemed to play very well. The preview audience fills out cards, giving the movie a grade, and we had something like 96 percent excellent, very good, and good. So I figured, *Leave it alone.*

Now, watching it again, I'm thinking, *Damn. I'm not sure I made the right choice.* Does it feel too long, with me singing it all in close-up? I know I got tired of looking at my head swinging back and forth.

I would make a very good critic . . . especially about myself.

Willy Wyler told me that he used to revisit his movies years after he made them . . . he'd take a print and recut it on a Moviola just for himself. At first I couldn't imagine why, but now I understand completely. It might be fun to reedit this someday. When Esther starts singing John Norman's song and it moves into rock and roll, the camera could move back. She becomes him, in a way, and I think we shot her from the same angles that we shot him in that first concert. You'd have to see the audience going crazy too. I remember I wanted to find better reaction shots . . . cut to people holding their breath . . . back to her close-up . . . then people with their mouths open in shock, when she starts singing his song . . . then a high shot as if John Norman were looking down at her.

But we didn't have all those shots. Somehow, in the rush of the day, some of the coverage I wanted slipped through the cracks.

I still like the concept of using those quick cuts. The whole thing might go faster. But would it have the same impact?

The fact is, I simply ran out of time. And then there was another last-minute crisis. We were looking at the latest cut when Laura Ziskin, who was Jon's assistant at the time (and went on to produce *Pretty Woman* and *Spider-Man*) said, "You know, you're missing the part where we see Esther Hoffman getting famous."

And I said, "You're absolutely right. What are we going to do? I can't go out and film it now." It was three days before the preview.

And then I thought, *Wait a minute.* Kris and I had done a real press conference at the Sun Devil stadium, which my friend Jeff Werner had filmed for a documentary about the making of the movie. Why not use that? No one will know it was really us, and not the characters.

I turned to Jeff, who is also a very talented editor, and said, "Could you edit the press conference footage to make it seem as if it were Esther being interviewed, instead of me? All we'd need is three and a half minutes."

And he did it, brilliantly.

Then my friend Verna Fields came by to play with me one Sunday in the editing room I had rigged up in an old tract house at the ranch, with black fabric pinned up over the windows. I showed her the sequence and said, "I think it works, but it's missing some excitement. I wish we had flashbulbs going off."

Verna said, "Just watch. I can do that."

To achieve the effect, I think she took some clear frames of film and edited them into the footage and all of a sudden . . . cut cut cut . . . I had my flashbulbs. I was thrilled. I can still see her standing at the Moviola, with lengths of film draped around her neck.

When the regular editor, Peter Zinner, came back to work on Monday and saw that sequence, he seemed annoyed.

Unfortunately Peter and I just didn't relate. Again and again I would ask, "Why don't we cut from this to that?," and he would say, "No. It won't work." And then I would have to push him. "Just try. I think it *will* work. And if it doesn't work, I need to see that with my own eyes so I understand why." Everything was a struggle.

I liked to have two teams of editors so I could keep working round the clock. One shift came in around 9:00 a.m. and stopped around 6:00 p.m. The next shift came in at 7:00 p.m. and stopped around 3:00 a.m. Helena, a wonderful

European woman who worked for me and Jon at the ranch house, fed everyone. Two women editors were part of the team, but I noticed that the guys were reluctant to let the girls do anything substantial. Women were fine to carry the film cans or change the reel, but other than that, the men were very territorial. Still, I could see that the women were equally competent when I gave them a sequence to cut. And when the house was threatened by a fire at one point, it was the women whose first thought was to save the film.

I can get completely entranced by the editing process. It's my favorite part of filmmaking, actually. It's fascinating, the way you can fine-tune an actor's performance. For example, there's that moment when Esther arrives at the crash site and kneels over John Norman's body, cradling his head, picking bits of brush out of his hair, wiping the blood off his cheek. I was imagining that he would be cold to the touch, so I said, "He needs a blanket. Could you please bring him a blanket." When the medics tell me I've got to move, I'm crying, "No, no, no, no, no, no." Paul Mazursky, playing John Norman's manager, has to pull me away as I'm pleading, "Be gentle with him, please. Don't hurt him."

An hour before, this man was alive, warm, beautiful . . . holding her . . . and now he's no longer there . . . inconceivable.

A lot of that scene was improvised. Actually, the only line Esther had in the script was "Be careful." We did two or three takes, and then in the editing room I listened closely. I was looking for the most heartfelt "nos" and I wanted the pain to build. So I might take each "no" from a different take.

I was so deeply immersed in the movie that I probably lost a lot of my objectivity by the end. I was facing a tight deadline. You see, Frank Pierson had already delivered his version of the movie, but the studio didn't like it. So I had my chance, as the producer, to do the next cut. But I had to work fast.

At first we were working with a temp dub (a preliminary soundtrack) that we did quickly, in three days. That's what we showed the studio initially, as part of my rough cut. Thank God they liked it.

But then you're thinking, now we've got to do it for real . . . this is for posterity . . . this is the music that's going to be heard all over the world. And you've got to get it right.

But what is right? Here's where my perfectionism comes in and drives me crazy. Because your ears start to play tricks on you. You're listening so hard that the piano, which sounded fine in the temp dub when you weren't really thinking about it, suddenly seems too soft. So the sound editors work on it . . . raise the piano . . . and play it back.

Wait a minute. Now it seems too loud.

I always had the temp dub running so I could refer back to it and listen to what we did originally . . . my first instinct. The problems for me seem to occur when I start second-guessing myself.

So we'd go back to that first impression to try to recreate the temp dub. This is how I spent seventeen weeks fine-tuning the sound, and I enjoyed every minute . . . or let's just say it was always productive . . . because I had a great team, led by Buzz Knudson, the head mixer (as well as Charity, my shy German shepherd, who would make herself comfortable at my feet). Buzz was a virtuoso at the mixing board and I adored him. He was one of those guys who's grumpy on the surface but a gentle sweetheart underneath, who would do anything for you.

And I should explain that what we were doing was unconventional. We had just started mixing at Todd-AO when a guy named Steve Katz, who worked with Ray Dolby, knocked on the door. He was selling a state-of-the-art way of transmitting sound with more channels and more fidelity. But what really got me was when he said it would surround the viewer with sound.

I said, "That's exactly what we need. In the very first scene of this movie, you're plunged into a rock concert. I want the audience to feel like they're right in the arena, with the music coming from all sides. I want it to be loud and exciting, so you feel it in your body . . . just like in real life."

It was a new, untested technology, but I like new ideas. So that's how *A Star Is Born* became the first film to have Dolby Stereo sound. (If you want to be technical, it was four-channel optical sound, Left, Center, Right, and Surround, on the 35mm prints.) We had already spent the $6 million budget on the film, and it would cost a million more to do this Dolby mix. Remember, the First Artists deal was that any overage came out of the artist's pocket. And I said, "I'll pay for it," because it was worth it to me. But when Warner Bros. saw the movie and heard the soundtrack, they liked it so much that they picked up the bill. That was very nice of them.

And then I wanted to make sure all our work didn't go to waste. So I'll jump ahead for a moment and share the letter I wrote, to go along with the film cans, when the movie came out:

You've just received, or will receive, a print of our film, A Star Is Born. *I understand that your theater is opening with it soon and wanted to share my good thoughts and wishes for a most successful run. Needless to say, I am very excited about the release of* A Star Is Born, *but at the same time, hold the fears of a mother "letting go."*

We have found that the film, for both picture and sound, is shown to its best advantage by using a few basic, but most important, guidelines. In setting your usual level of sound, please make sure that Reel 1 and Reel 2 are allowed to play as loud as possible. *They were intentionally mixed this way and provide exactly the right amount of energy for the film. If for any reason you must play them lower, it is imperative that the sound level be raised for Reel 3 and remain the same for the balance of the film. The color is also at its best at 14½ foot candle power.*

Thanking you in advance—and you should please take good care of my kid . . .

I guess I might be a little obsessive.

Back to the mixing. Since I was spending so much time on the sound stage at Todd-AO, I would have Renata bring Jason over to visit. He was almost ten years old, and one day he told me, "My dad says you're working too many long hours and not seeing me enough."

Whoa! That was a stab in my heart. And my guilt, always lurking, kicked right in. I was angry with Elliott for criticizing me in front of our son, rather than supporting me. But then I pushed that aside to focus on Jason.

Since I always tried to talk to him in adult terms, I looked at him and said, "You know, I hope that when you're older you get a chance to do something that you really love . . . that you have a passion for your work, like I do . . . and then I think you'll understand why I'm working so hard. It's like a mission, and when it's completed, I'll be home all day."

Then, in the midst of all this pressure, rushing to finish the dubbing and the editing, a friend slipped me a copy of an article that Frank was shopping around, about the making of the movie. Someone in his agent's office had read the piece and been so appalled that she had given my friend Joan Ashby a copy, thinking I should see it.

My heart stopped.

I couldn't believe what I was looking at, and I don't want to reread it now. I do know that Frank took great pleasure in ridiculing me and Jon, and our "$6 million home movie." He twisted the facts, and he made up stories, saying that he had to persuade me to put the moment with Leon Russell into the script, and that he had to convince me to hire Bob Surtees . . . when it was exactly the other way around.

I was furious and immediately called him up. "How could you lie like this?"

Was he delusional?

And he did something so deliberately cruel that it was unconscionable . . . he portrayed Kris as a drunk. The whole article was a huge betrayal. There are things that an actor shares with a director . . . personal, private things about himself, his family, or his friendships that pertain to the work and shouldn't be discussed in public. It's like the relationship with a priest, a doctor, or a lawyer. Frank was supposed to be a director, not a gossipmonger.

"I can't stop you from publishing this," I told him. "But please don't hurt the film, Frank. Give it a fair chance. Why are you trying to destroy the movie we've all worked so hard on?"

He said the article was purely private. Not for publication.

"Then why are you writing it?"

"For my own catharsis."

I said, "Then at least tell yourself the truth. The way it stands now, you're lying to yourself from the very beginning." If the movie was such a nightmare for him, why didn't he quit? I remember him telling me once, "You're making me look good."

But in the article, he told a different story . . . every anecdote was meant to paint him as the savior and Jon and me as fools. When I challenged him on it, he kept reiterating that the article was not for publication.

And I made the mistake of believing him.

I still didn't realize that I was dealing with a pathological liar. And as I've said, I cannot deal with people who lie.

This happened in early October, and a month later we were ready to preview the picture in Phoenix on Thursday night, November 11. In the spirit of reconciliation, I called Frank and asked, "Would you like to be there?" He accepted my invitation, and after he saw the movie he told me that I had done a great job. He was quoted in Army Archerd's column in *Variety* the next morning, saying, "I'm really happy about it! There are choices Barbra made that I wouldn't have made—but Barbra and I always basically agreed and I think she's a brilliant editor and she should get out on her own as a director." And that first audience loved the movie! I was exhilarated.

That didn't last long. Three days later, on Monday morning, Frank's article was published in a magazine, with my silhouette on the cover. I was horrified. It sent me straight to the doctor. My heart was beating so fast I thought I was having a heart attack.

I couldn't understand how anyone could be so destructive to the film as well as to himself. Maybe he felt as if he'd been swallowed up, lost in all the press attention that focused on me, Jon, and Kris. Perhaps, confronted with his own limitations on the set, his ego couldn't deal with it. And now he was trying to have it both ways. If the movie was a success, *he* did it. If it was a failure, *we* did it. Or perhaps he was merely bitter. Only his psychiatrist knows for sure.

All I know is that his behavior was unethical, unprofessional, and immoral.

No other article has ever touched off such a deep sense of injustice in me. And I was totally helpless, knowing that so many people would read it and believe it. I felt like that painting *The Scream* by Edvard Munch . . . a scream with no sound.

Of course, the press had a field day with Frank's piece. It put a black cloud over the movie before people even had a chance to see it. It opened on December 19, 1976, in Los Angeles and on December 25 in New York and the rest of the country . . . and got the worst reviews of my career. I was so upset that I didn't even want to go to New York for the premiere, but Jon and Kris convinced me that I had to go and hold my head up, and we all went together.

The New York critics were the most brutal. I heard that one critic was talking back to the screen when he saw it. I mean, he *hated* it. Roger Ebert loved it, but of course I only remember the negative. I couldn't believe what they chose to focus on. At the end of the film, in tiny letters in the credit crawl, going by very fast, it says: "Ms. Streisand's clothes from . . . her closet." That was the truth. I didn't have time to see sketches and have costume fittings, so I just went through my closet . . . I had a great collection of antique clothes I wore all the time . . . and picked out some things that I thought Esther would wear.

But I didn't have a dress that was right for the scene at the Grammys. That's when my eye was caught by some vintage Assuit shawls I had bought years ago, made of the thinnest bits of silver (like tinsel) on black tulle, so they had this slinky, snaky, shimmery effect. Just what I wanted . . . I took two and draped them around a dress form, on the bias, and designed a dress, gathered up on one side in the back so the fabric would fall from just the right height and puddle on the floor. Then I had a cloak made out of another shawl to go with it.

(It worked so well that I wore it to the real Grammys in 1977, to present the Record of the Year Award.)

I thought, *This is how Esther would dress . . . in a way that's very cool and elegant.* Remember, we were also trying to save money.

Well, from the reactions I got, you would have thought using one's own clothes was a crime.

I wish I could have brushed off the reviews. But I was devastated. And shocked, because I had heard such good things from the preview audiences and from professional people I respect. Miloš Forman called and told me he loved the picture.

I thought the film looked great on-screen. Bob Surtees had given it a luscious sheen . . . everything I envisioned and more. He wrote me a sweet letter soon after the movie came out, telling me that I deserved "most of the credit" because my ideas were "a constant inspiration" to him.

And Kris was so pleased with the movie and grateful to me that it prompted him to stop drinking (which I can say now because he's talked about it himself). But I was beginning to think, *Am I going crazy?* How can some people call the movie brilliant and others think it's a piece of trash?

Frank's article clearly affected the critical reception of the film. The review in the *Los Angeles Times* even quoted it. It felt as if some critics weren't even reviewing the movie. Instead, they were reviewing my relationship with Jon.

But guess what? The public evidently liked the film, because they bought tickets and it became the biggest movie of my career, and the second-highest-grossing film of the year. (*Rocky* was first.)

A Star Is Born was also my biggest payday, because I had a percentage of the gross as well as the profits, according to the terms of the First Artists deal.

My song "Evergreen" was at the top of the charts, and that certainly helped sell the movie. I was very excited when it won the Golden Globe Award for Best Original Song. The movie was nominated for five Golden Globe awards, and we won them all, including Best Actor, Best Actress, Best Motion Picture—Musical or Comedy, and Best Original Score.

I was so happy when Bob Surtees was nominated for an Oscar for Best Cinematography, Roger Kellaway was nominated for Best Adapted Score, and Buzz Knudson was nominated for Best Sound. (So I guess those seventeen weeks Buzz and I spent on the sound were worth it! We went on to do three more pictures together.)

And I can't express what a privilege it was to receive an Academy Award for Best Original Song . . . my melody and Paul's lyric. They told me that I was the first woman to be honored as a composer. Never in my wildest dreams did I ever imagine I would win an Oscar for writing music. It still remains very, very special to me.

And then "Evergreen" won three Grammy awards, for Best Arrangement, Best Female Pop Vocal Performance, and to top it all off, Song of the Year.

I'm still very proud every time I hear it on the radio.

Making *A Star Is Born* took three years of my life. It was physically and emotionally exhausting. I probably should have fired Frank, but I was afraid . . . afraid to start over with another person, afraid that I couldn't handle it alone, and afraid that I would be attacked for taking over.

What is so offensive about a woman taking control? Warren Beatty and Robert Redford, among others, were in control of their movies, and they don't get attacked for it. Redford was the producer and the star of *All the President's Men.* He was in the editing room, just like me. He supervised the dubbing, just like me.

And was it a huge mistake to hire my boyfriend to produce the movie? After I gave Jon his start on *A Star Is Born*, he went on to produce other films, like *Caddyshack*, which became a cult favorite. Jon was a street kid who had an instinct for what the audience wanted to see. He was talking about making films about comic book characters before anyone else saw their potential, and produced *Batman*, which made millions and started a franchise. He even ran a studio for a while with his partner, Peter Guber. So he had a vision . . . and so did I.

A Star Is Born came in on time and on budget. And it turned out to be the most successful film I've ever made.

So damn right I want to be in control.

I want to be responsible for everything I do in my life, good or bad. I have visions in my head . . . I hear music . . . I dream. And it's very rewarding to have them materialize, either on-screen or on a record.

I want to please the audience, and I've found that the best way to please an audience is to please myself.

Remember how I said it might be fun to go back into this movie someday and fix a couple of things that have always bothered me?

In 2018 I finally had the opportunity. Bradley Cooper had just made his version of *A Star Is Born*, and Netflix wanted to show my version as well. I said, "Great! But I'll do a special edition for you. I want to put back the scene of me playing 'Evergreen' on the guitar for the first time, and recut the ending."

I called Warner Bros. to ask them to get the relevant footage, which turned out to be more of a challenge than I expected. They told me it had been buried over forty years ago in a salt mine under Kansas City. That's where they keep their negatives, in a vault, so they don't disintegrate.

Day after day went by, and nothing arrived. I called Tony Rastatter, the very helpful supervising editor assigned to the search, and he said, "We're still looking." So all I had to work with was an old, dirty work print that I had kept in my own vault.

The more I looked at the original rough edit of Esther playing her song for John Norman, the more foolish it seemed to have taken it out. There's something so innocent about hearing me do it exactly the way I wrote it, humming the melody and accompanying myself badly on the guitar. And it conveys important information . . . it tells the audience that Esther writes her own songs. It's also the first moment of intimacy between the two characters. She's exposing her creative self to this new man, and he's becoming more intrigued with her. And it adds more emotional depth to the scene later on when they sing the finished song together in the recording studio, now with a lyric that's obviously about him. It cements their relationship and makes the love story even stronger.

Back in 1976 I had ignored all that and just thought, *Cut it out . . . less of me . . . keep the plot moving.*

Now, looking at the scene again, I also wanted to add more close-ups of Kris. I thought his reactions were very important. And I was grateful when Tony finally found a few more trims, so I had more of Kris to work with.

But there are always limitations. The reels from the last scene, where Esther sings the love song "With One More Look at You" and then segues into John Norman's signature rock song, "Watch Closely Now," didn't arrive until my very last day in the editing room, and I didn't get to watch four out of the seven reels they sent. In other words, I ran out of time again!

I had wanted the last song to feel more rock and roll, but the alternative cut that was done quickly back in 1976 didn't work. And now I finally figured out why. You can't just break up the long close-up of Esther with a bunch of wide shots at the end. When the close-up disappeared, you lost the emotional connection with her. So the secret was to constantly cut back to it. You practically have to be inside her brain, as well as watching her body dance more and more wildly as the music gets faster and faster.

I wasn't even aware I was moving that much when we shot that scene. But once I saw the footage, I thought, *Why not show it?*

As she's singing the lyric "watch closely now," I thought she could look up into the spotlight . . . as if the light is his energy and she's singing the song directly to him. She realizes he will always be part of her and that gives her strength.

But I didn't have the right shot, so Jim got on his laptop and found me some stock footage of a spotlight. Thank you, honey! I think it cost $170, and was well worth it.

I wanted to cut to the audience several times, but I only had one shot of the crowd. I'll bet one of those four reels I didn't get to see had others, but I was already almost two weeks late delivering it to Netflix, and I decided I could make it work with what I had.

Now the cuts start slowly and then they increase in speed and get wilder, until at the very end they come even quicker . . . cut cut cut cut . . . and then the frame freezes. The movie is over, and so was my editing session, at 2:00 a.m. . . . when Netflix practically ripped the film out of my hands.

Finally, after forty-two years, I think I made it better. But did I? I'm never quite sure.

And now I'm thinking, *Gee, maybe I should find a way to restore the missing footage from the* Swan Lake *ballet in* Funny Girl. And there are two scenes in *Yentl* . . . with the matchmaker, and when she's sewing Avigdor's jacket . . . that I had to cut simply because of time constraints. I'd love to put them back too.

Since I now know where all these old negatives are kept, maybe I'll go digging again!

THIRTY-ONE

Don't Believe What You Read

The soundtrack from *A Star Is Born* was number 1 for six weeks, and the Columbia executives were thrilled to tell me it had sold more than any other movie soundtrack up to that point (it eventually sold ten million copies worldwide, I'm told). And they were eager to capitalize on the album's phenomenal success. So a few months after the movie opened, I was back in the studio, working on another album, which became *Superman*. I already had a head start, since there were two songs that I loved but didn't make it into the movie because others happened to be a better fit.

One was "Answer Me," which began when I was sitting at the piano with Kenny Ascher, working on the arrangement for a totally different song. I said to him, "Wait a minute . . . I've got this melody in my head. If I hum it, can you write down the notes for me?" (This seems to be the way my mind works. Inspiration strikes when I'm supposed to be doing something else.)

It was kind of a complex melody, certainly not a pop song. I had no idea where it was coming from and couldn't predict where it was going. It just flowed out of me and kept surprising me as I was humming it! There are lots of strange intervals, so it might sound dissonant. But I've always been drawn to unconventional melodies. And Kenny was fabulous, following my lead.

We put the melody on a cassette, and then I talked to Paul Williams about the lyric. I said, "Maybe the song could start with those random thoughts that go through your head when you make love to someone for the first time, like wondering what it'll be like to wake up with this new person in the morning."

Paul liked the idea, and began the lyric like this:

Do you wake up very slowly? Does it take a while before you smile?
Are your dreams like premonitions? Have you lived them through?
Some people do . . .

And then the song unfolds, not following any traditional structure but more free-form, with a verse that then goes into another verse with a different melody:

I hope you'll answer me with patient eyes
No hurried words, foolish or wise
Answer me, answer me with soft silent touches
They'll tell me as much as I need to know

I don't know how to describe it. I guess you could call it an atonal tone poem.

"Answer me" was repeated throughout the song, and there's clearly a thread to my thinking because, just as with "By the Way," I asked Paul if he could end with the same phrase, just using it in a different way. And he wrote:

If we must part, should someone ask who's touched your heart
Perhaps you'll answer . . . me

It was lovely, but the words and the melody were a bit melancholy, which didn't quite work in the movie, especially since this was the beginning of a relationship, not the end. Meanwhile, I had that thrilling moment with Leon Russell at the piano that became "Lost Inside of You," and I knew instantly that it was a more meaningful way for the lovers to connect. So "Answer Me" fell by the wayside.

The other song we dropped was "Lullaby for Myself." I had asked Rupert Holmes to write something for Esther to sing early on that would reveal more about her . . . that she had lived with a man but now was alone and appreciating her independence. As always Rupert's lyric was grounded in realistic detail and had very smart lines like "And your aim becomes to please yourself and not to aim to please." It was great, but we ended up going with his other song that was even better for the movie, called "Everything."

I wanted more songs with a feminist slant for this new album. But I was in that postpartum phase . . . exhausted after pushing to finish the movie and still busy with publicity, so I didn't have time to look for them myself. That's where Charles Koppelman came in. We already knew each other, because Columbia had sent him over when they got nervous about Jon's progress on *Butterfly*. Charles was not a hands-on producer, but he had lots of contacts who fed him material. He brought in "My Heart Belongs to Me," which was a different take on old standards like "My Heart Belongs to Daddy," because this time the woman was *not* devoting herself to someone else, but taking ownership of her own heart. And what do you know? To my utter surprise, it became a hit single!

Charles put me in touch with talents like Billy Joel. Years later Billy told me that it was only after I sang his song "New York State of Mind" on this album that his mother finally considered him a success.

Charles also suggested I invite Neil Sedaka over to the ranch so I could hear some of his songs. Neil brought his wife, Leba, and she told me that she was initially afraid to come because she had read some gossip that I had birds flying around loose inside my house.

What? The reality was that I had two parakeets in a cage, just like plenty of other Brooklyn girls! I was so fed up with all these ridiculous stories, and instead of driving myself crazy by trying to respond, I decided to turn my feelings into a song. I already knew what the title would be: "Don't Believe What You Read." I thought it should have a rock and roll beat (not exactly my thing), so Charles gave my notes for the lyric to Ron Nagle, who had already written "Cabin Fever," the other rock song on the album.

For years, whenever I read something about myself that was completely untrue, my first impulse was to correct it. But Marty would talk me down and advise me to ignore it. I understood his logic . . . any complaint would just draw more attention to it. But lies make me mad, and it irked me that all this nonsense was in the public record. Some people thrive on publicity, but I hired a press agent to keep me *out* of the press. Yet nothing could stop the onslaught that came with *A Star Is Born.*

I was tired of turning the other cheek. So, in order to set the record straight, I agreed to do an interview with Lawrence Grobel, a writer from *Playboy* magazine who had been pursuing me. That may seem an odd choice, but *Playboy* was famous not only for their covers of half-clad, voluptuous women but also for their serious, in-depth interviews, and I thought, *What the hell. Maybe at least men will read it.*

I was planning to tell the whole truth about Frank Pierson's behavior and rebut every one of his destructive lies. So I was very angry when we started, but as the interviews continued for months, I realized that my anger was covering up a lot of hurt. And gradually I began to let go of it. I didn't want to give Frank any more space in my head. I also realized something else. In order to contradict all the cruel things he said about not only me and Jon, but also Kris, I would have to repeat them, and that was the last thing I wanted to do.

So I decided not to attack him the way he attacked me. And I'm much obliged to the executive editor, Barry Colson, who allowed me to go back into the text to reflect my changing attitude.

Of course, one of Grobel's first questions was about "the obsession you seem to have for taking control of whatever projects you are involved with."

Interesting, isn't it, that when a woman takes control of her own work it's considered an *obsession*?

I said, "First, let's clarify the word 'control,' because it has negative implications. Let's just say when I use the word 'control,' I mean artistic responsibility. If you mean that I am completely dedicated and care deeply about carrying out a total vision of a project . . . yes, that's true." I was trying to explain that I'm interested in all aspects of the work, down to the copy on the movie posters.

The one good thing about being interviewed is that it forces you to clarify your thoughts. But it can get very boring, to have to go on and on about yourself. When the writer started asking questions like "Do you have a lot of sexual fantasies?" I just decided to turn the tables and said, "Sure, don't you?"

He kept probing. "How innovative are you sexually?"

"*What?* Well . . . I do have some erotic art books!"

"How often are you the one to initiate sexual activities?"

"We're equal, honey, we're equal."

I mean, he was searching for more detail than even I wanted to know! And when he asked if I was once "romantically linked" with Warren Beatty, I said blithely, "One of my flings."

I was just tossing off a reply, playing the role of a jaded woman of the world. Actually, Warren and I go back a long way (back to summer stock) and there's some water under that bridge. Recently, we were on the phone talking politics and who knows what else when he said, "I remember why we broke up."

I said, "When were we together?"

Then I hung up and asked myself, *Did I sleep with Warren?* I kind of remember. I guess I did. Probably once.

My life was a little strange in 1977. Here I was, slammed by this negativity in the press, and yet my movie was a huge success. Women were even getting their hair permed like mine . . . I mean like Esther's! (My wonderful hairdresser, Soonie Paik, gave me that perm, and she's been with me ever since.)

People were ignoring the reviews. Some were even coming to see the film multiple times, which was a huge affirmation. I was so grateful . . . the first thing I wrote in the liner notes for *Superman* was "Thank you all for your tremendous support on *A Star Is Born*. You made all the hard work worth it!"

I was trying hard to enjoy this moment of success. It would have been easier if I was as confident and self-assured as the character I portrayed in the movie, but I'm not.

That's why the groundswell of support from the public meant so much to me. I was getting letters from women who said the movie inspired them to take more control of their own lives, to believe in themselves, and that was extremely encouraging.

In that spirit, I decided to wear a Superman T-shirt and little white shorts on the album's cover. It was the same outfit that Esther wore for a brief moment in the film.

That cover was a departure for me . . . actually the whole outfit was, because it was way more revealing than anything I would normally wear. But that T-shirt and shorts told you something essential about Esther's sense of self, her free spirit, and the way she embraced her own sexuality.

Now, on the album cover, it was me, Barbra, claiming my own strength and sexuality, or at least not being afraid of it anymore. And that was a big step for me, because I've always had such doubts about my looks. When I was a teenager, reading movie magazines and dreaming about being a movie star, I never really believed that was for me. I was thinking I'd be a theater actress, where the audience can't get so close.

I remember being kind of shocked when Warren Beatty once told me bluntly that "a movie star has to be fuckable."

Well, I was a movie star, so I guess some people thought of me that way.

Did I ever think I was sexy? No.

And now *Playboy* was saying that they wanted to put me on the cover of the issue with my interview. They told me that would be a first for the magazine, and I thought, *Well, no one will expect that.* So I said okay, as long as I had photo approval. At the shoot they handed me the Playboy Bunny costume . . . basically a skimpy black bathing suit with a push-up bra. Let's just say I had nothing like that in my closet. It was so different from my image and my own sense of self that it was almost disconcerting to put it on, but I have to admit it was also kind of fun, and quite flattering to my figure. But I didn't like the symbolism of the outfit. After all, I was a feminist and I didn't want to do anything that might be interpreted as a betrayal of the movement. And frankly, I thought, *Better not look* too *sexy, because then people might not take me seriously as a filmmaker.*

That's why I changed into the same white shorts I had worn on the *Superman* album, only this time they had replaced the *Superman* logo on the T-shirt with the *Playboy* logo.

It's interesting . . . as a teenager, you dream of being beautiful and seductive enough to attract men, but when the opportunity presented itself to me, I shied away from it. I had actually become scared of men coming after me, which wasn't irrational . . . at this point I was dealing with a stalker who one night broke into Kim's office adjacent to my house and took a shower. Another time he came back, stole my little convertible, and checked into the Beverly Hills Hotel, saying that he was my husband, the king of Israel, and that I was his queen. Luckily the manager called the police, and the FBI got involved. Then there was the day when Renata drove up to the house with Jason, who was twelve years old at the time, and as they walked toward the door, he spotted a man hiding under the car parked in the driveway. So they backed away and drove to our neighbor Gregory Peck's house to call the police.

Those are just a few of the incidents that frightened me. So the last thing I wanted was to be *too* provocative. That's why I ended up choosing the most conservative picture of me in the shorts, with not even a hint of breast or a glimpse of tush . . . which is ironic, considering this was *Playboy*. The only things I took off were my socks!

The Bunny suit photo would probably have sold more copies of the magazine, but I never allowed it to be published. At least I gave them a good cover line, which they used: "What's a nice Jewish girl like me doing on the cover of *Playboy*?"

Years later I gave my husband Jim a framed copy of that Bunny picture, but only for his closet. Nobody else has seen it. But now I'm putting it in this book because I'm proud that I had a good-enough body to carry off that outfit . . . the hair looks good, the chest looks good, and my legs looked great.

I weighed 119 pounds then and I'm not telling you how much I weigh today. Put it this way . . . it depends on how much ice cream I've eaten.

Back to the album. I had already scheduled that cover shoot when Charles called to say he wanted to play a song called "Superman" for me. I could hardly believe it. I had decided to wear that Superman T-shirt, and now here was a song with that title . . . it was like a gift from the universe. And even better, the song had a delicious twist. It was not about a man but a woman, empowered by love. I thought, *Perfect. I'll name the album* Superman.

And that photo seemed like a good image for the cover. After all the criticism and attacks, there I was, still standing.

Looking back, I realize I was also acting on one of my basic principles . . . but it would take a few more years before I could clearly articulate it. Women should be judged on the value of our work, not the length of our legs. We can be more than one thing . . . intelligent and sexy, strong and vulnerable, deep thinking *and* deep feeling. We shouldn't have to choose.

After *Superman*, the follow-up album was *Songbird*. Some people may have wondered why I had a dog on the cover instead of a bird, but I thought, *Why be that literal?* I didn't have a relationship with any particular bird, but I did have a fantastic relationship with my dog, Sadie. She was my first dog, and we were devoted to each other. She liked to be carried with her head close to my heart, or looking at the world over my shoulder.

Then, since the ranch was a great place for dogs, we somehow acquired five more, and their pictures are on the back cover, along with their puppies . . . just to leave no one out.

Jon thought of himself as a tough guy, and he wanted tough dogs, so he got himself a Doberman . . . Big Red, who sometimes took a nip out of visitors, just to show them who's boss. He also came home with a beautiful German shepherd. But to his chagrin and my delight, that German shepherd was so scared of people that she would just cower. Jon wanted to return her, but I identified with her fear. My heart went out to her . . . she must have been hurt in the past. I named her Charity, because she was so sweet. She was like my girlfriend. We went everywhere together, even to work, and I suppose she did protect me, in a way. People were instinctively afraid of her, not knowing that she was more afraid of them!

When I decided to go to New York for a few months, I couldn't leave her behind. Renata was going ahead to set up the apartment and said she'd take Charity, but then we remembered that she wouldn't listen to anybody but me. So I made a tape of my voice saying things like, "Charity, get in the car, honey" . . . "Now you can come out of the car" . . . "Go to sleep, sweetheart."

But during the two days before I arrived, Charity seemed depressed and wouldn't eat. Renata was worried. Then she had an idea . . . she put on one of my albums. Charity's ears perked up and she finished her food.

We also had another Doberman, Rocky, who lived at my Carolwood house, and he, too, had the gentlest soul . . . that's why you can never judge a dog by its breed. He was the most elegant creature, black and shiny, who always sat with his front paws crossed, like a statue of Anubis, the Egyptian god who took the form of a dog. That's Rocky, right down to the long ears (I never had his cut).

Once, when Cis and Harvey were staying at Carolwood, they drove in the gate, and Rocky dashed out. He was hit by a car, but luckily it was driven by a neighbor, who took him straight to the vet. He was a mess, with broken ribs, hips, and a punctured lung. When I came to see him, the vet told me he wasn't sure Rocky would make it, and if he did, he would need an operation in order to walk again. I didn't want to leave him alone so I took him home and nursed him myself, with Jason's help. His black coat turned white in patches from the trauma, but each day he got a little stronger, and after a month, he was running around again. It just shows that love can heal.

Oh, besides all the dog photos, there were also some songs on the album. "Tomorrow," from the musical *Annie*, was probably the best known, but it was not what ended up getting all the attention. The song that most people remember from that album is "You Don't Bring Me Flowers," which Neil Diamond composed with Marilyn and Alan's lyrics. He had already recorded his own version, and now I was doing mine.

And then something interesting happened.

A disc jockey in Louisville, Kentucky, was going through a divorce, and he was really moved by the lyrics. When he discovered that both our solo versions were in the same key, he had an idea. Why not splice them together and create a dialogue, as if you were listening to a man and a woman talk to each other about their relationship? He played his pieced-together tape on his radio station, and it got a huge response . . . record stores were getting thousands of requests for this duet that didn't actually exist.

So Neil and I went back into the studio and recorded it together (and as I quipped in a recent concert, "It's been good for florists ever since!").

The song hit number 1 on the charts and then was nominated for Record of the Year and Best Pop Vocal Performance by a Duo, Group, or Chorus . . . and we were asked to sing it live at the Grammys. I was reluctant, but decided that I had to do it for Marilyn and Alan.

When I came to rehearsal, the director had put three stools onstage: one for Neil, one for me, and one in the middle, topped with a bouquet of flowers. I took one look and said, "Do you mind if I make a suggestion? The line is 'You don't bring me flowers,' so let's not have a bouquet. And forget the stools. These people shouldn't be sitting close to each other. They're more separate now."

I'll never forget the look on his face. (This kind of incident may be why I'm called "difficult.") The director was dumbfounded, but I think he actually agreed with me.

The Grammy people had deliberately not told the press that Neil and I were going to perform (frankly, I wasn't sure myself whether I would actually have the nerve to show up). So I said to the director, "I'm so glad that you kept it secret, and you know what? I wouldn't even announce our names before we come out. That way, it will be an even bigger surprise for the audience. Just put two spotlights on either side of the stage and we'll step out into them, and then gradually walk toward each other as we sing."

I took Neil aside and said, "Let's work on this in my dressing room." When we were alone, I said, "Have you ever seen the movie *Brief Encounter*? The husband and wife sit in their living room and don't talk to each other. He's reading the newspaper, and she's sewing. That's us. Let's pretend that we've been married for twenty years, and the relationship is disintegrating."

Neil got it immediately. He's comfortable onstage, but I was literally shaking in the wings just before we went on. This was the first time I had ever sung at the Grammys, and I remember this moment so vividly. As I began to walk toward him, I could hear my voice wobbling. In my head, I was saying to myself, *Get control, girl!* And thank God I did, eventually.

The song was like a little play. The emotions came naturally out of the lyric and the staging . . . two people getting closer as they at long last tell each other the truth. I hadn't figured that out intellectually. I just felt intuitively that to do it as a normal duet, with the two of us standing next to each other, would not do justice to the story. I knew it would be more interesting if we were separate at the beginning, then there's a dramatic tension as we approach each other, and at the end, you understand the poignancy of this couple only coming together to say goodbye.

When Neil and I finally met in the center of the stage, I impulsively reached up and caressed his face. The audience went wild. Neil held on to my hand, and at the end of the song, he brought it to his lips and kissed it.

Nothing like that had happened in rehearsal. But we were free enough in the moment to react spontaneously.

The song stopped the show.

THIRTY-TWO

The Battle of the Sexes

I wanted to take a break from movies after *A Star Is Born* and just sit down and relax. But after a couple months of that, I got bored. I had to have a project. So I thought, *Now's the time to remodel that 1950s tract house at the ranch*, which I had used as an editing room. It was an L-shaped dump, stuccoed in dirt brown, with a flat roof, cheap sliding glass doors, and absolutely no redeeming features. I stared at this eyesore and thought, *What can I do with this? Is there any way to salvage it?*

It's not in my nature to tear something down. I would rather try to use what I was given. As I studied this house, I thought, *At least it has straight lines . . .*

a geometric shape . . . and that got me thinking about Art Deco. I had been collecting Art Deco objects for years, and had already designed an Art Deco screening room in the basement at Carolwood. If I could somehow turn this monstrosity into an Art Deco house, I'd have a reason to keep collecting!

That house, and the screening room, eventually became a showcase for an artist I discovered on a trip to Paris.

I was staying at a little hotel, and across the street was a bookstore, where a tall, slim volume in the window caught my eye. It had the most striking cover . . . a painting of a woman in 1920s clothes driving a green Bugatti, set against a black background with the words Tamara de Lempicka in gold letters across the top. I had never heard of her (and neither had most people back in the 1970s) but that cover turned out to be a self-portrait, and there was something about the sloe eyes, the red lips, the casual authority of her hand on the wheel that mesmerized me. Her style was such an original take on Art Deco, and during that period she had some success but had since been forgotten.

To find a woman painter to whom I responded so completely meant a lot to me. I wanted to see more of her work, and later at the Galerie du Luxembourg I saw her "Portrait of Ira P." . . . a woman in a white satin gown and a red shawl, holding a bouquet of calla lilies in her long, elegant hands (with red fingernails). I had to have it, and bought it for $67,000 (now her paintings are worth millions) and hung it in the screening room, which I had done in the same colors.

Eventually I would own five of her paintings, including "Adam and Eve," often considered her masterpiece. I hung it in the entrance hall of the Art Deco house . . . but that was a long way off at the moment (the house would end up taking five years to finish).

Meanwhile, Sydney Pollack and I were talking on the phone one day and he said, "Why aren't you working?"

I said, "Well, I'm designing a house. That's working."

"Yeah. But you're an actress. You should be acting."

"I've been reading scripts, but there's nothing great. Everything is just okay."

It was very frustrating. I had spent almost two years working on the script of *A Star Is Born* before we even started filming, and I wasn't eager to go through that process again. But as Sydney and I continued to talk, I remembered something François Truffaut told me when we met at my friend Mike Medavoy's house. We were talking about the difficulty of finding good material. And he said, "So every picture might not be great, but at the end of your career, you have a body of work . . . some good, some not so good, but you have to keep working. You can't wait for something perfect."

I thought, *Both of these men are brilliant directors, and they're right.* What was I doing? Waiting for Chekhov to come along?

It turned out that I didn't have a choice, because what finally made me go back to work was the pressure to fulfill my three-picture deal with First Artists. I owed them one last movie, and that's when we bought the rights to a script that became *The Main Event.* It wasn't the serious film I was hoping for, but it had a charm about it, and I could flex my comedic muscles. And since I was also the producer, with final cut, I would have some control.

It was the story of a sophisticated businesswoman who winds up managing a street-smart boxer after her business manager embezzles all her money, and here's why I decided to develop it further: It was about a woman in a man's world, which is a subject I know something about, and the woman was the boss. So that made for a clever take on the battle of the sexes . . . but underneath all the jokes, I saw an opportunity to say something meaningful about how the roles of men and women were changing. I'd been thinking about this for a while . . . along with sex discrimination, gender stereotypes, and the push for women's equality. I thought the story had potential, and I felt that, like all good comedies, it could resonate if it was also about something true.

From her first moment on-screen, my character, Hillary Kramer, is challenging gender stereotypes. She owns a perfume company, and for her latest perfume she's mixed two fragrances together. When she's told she can't do that, because one is for men and one is for women, she says, "Oh yes we can!"

And she knows exactly how to market it: "It's the only scent that a man can buy for a woman, a man can buy for another man, a woman can buy for a man, a woman can buy for another woman. Isn't that fantastic? Have I left anybody out?"

I loved that fast, zippy dialogue . . . kind of in the style of those 1940s screwball comedies . . . which of course made me think of *What's Up, Doc?* and Ryan O'Neal. He was my one and only choice to play the boxer, Eddie Scanlon. He was a great acting partner, funny, brilliant at pratfalls, and to top it all off, he already knew his way around a boxing ring, since he'd been boxing from the age of ten.

Casting is crucial to the success of a film. And I vividly remember how stressful the audition process can be, so I always try to put an actor at ease. For instance, when Patti d'Arbanville came in to read for the role of Ryan's girlfriend, I could tell she had to cough but didn't want to be rude. So I said, "Patti, it's okay to cough." And this delicate creature let out this huge honk.

I said, "You're hired."

Because I knew I could use it in the movie. You'd always hear that cough before you saw her and know she was about to appear.

So I liked the cast, and I loved the cinematographer, Mario Tosi. But I never developed much of a rapport with the director, Howard Zieff, who was oddly detached. He didn't get that involved with the script, while I was usually working with the writers, Gail Parent and Andrew Smith, trying to punch up the dialogue, often right up to the moment we filmed it.

More than halfway through the shoot, we still didn't have an ending. I spoke to my friends on the set and asked them to share any ideas with me. The first person who responded was the sound man, who gave me an interesting suggestion. When I mentioned this to Howard, he said, "The sound man? You want me to listen to the *sound man*?"

"Yeah," I said. "Why not?"

I've always felt you shouldn't be dismissive of anyone, because you never know where an idea is going to come from. Even my driver wrote up a four-page treatment, but I got nothing from Howard.

I guess he and I were not fated to connect.

And that reminds me of my other job on the film . . . keeping Jon Peters and Ryan O'Neal separate from each other.

Jon knew I had gone out with Ryan, and even though it was ancient history by now, he was still absurdly jealous. Ryan picked up on that, and whenever he saw Jon coming, he would do something intimate, like grabbing my butt or nuzzling my ear. He's very mischievous, and he took a special delight in tormenting Jon.

Once Jon became so incensed that he challenged Ryan to a fight. Men . . . they can be ridiculous. Jon was acting like a child.

Thank God we eventually came up with an ending, and the picture wrapped. But something was still bothering me, and it had to do with the love scene, which we had shot in a cabin up at Cedar Lake in the San Bernardino Mountains. Hillary and Eddie find themselves unexpectedly sharing a bed the night before Eddie's big fight. I thought it would be a nice reversal to have Hillary initiate the sex. And it was a funny scene, but it didn't culminate in anything more tangible than the fact that they slept together. I didn't think we had done enough to resolve their relationship.

And then I got it . . . what we were missing was a morning-after scene. Howard didn't agree with me, but I wrote it anyway with Gail and Andrew, and then Ryan and I went back to Cedar Lake with Mario and a small crew, and I directed it.

I wanted to show how different these two people were emotionally, and that led to the biggest role reversal. Usually, in movies, when a man and a woman sleep together, it's the woman who gets attached to the man, and then the cliché is that she wants to formalize the relationship and starts thinking of marriage. But in this case it's Eddie who gets attached to Hillary. And in the afterglow of their night together, he blithely suggests that they take all the money he plans to win in his big fight and open up a business together . . . "something like a car wash, or a diner . . . something that you can be a big part of too."

Hillary is taken aback, and says, "Really? I was kind of counting on going back into the perfume business someday."

"Nah, that's not for me."

"I know. It's for me."

"How can you do it if I don't want to do it?"

"Well, I could do it with the money you owe me."

"But wait a minute. We're together now. Why should I still owe you money?"

"'Cause that was the deal."

"But we made love last night, didn't we?"

"And that cost me forty-seven thousand three hundred and eleven dollars? Kid, I had no idea you had the meter running."

That got a big laugh when we previewed the movie. And then Eddie goes on to talk about how he's the man, so he should handle the money from now on, and says she's crazy if she thinks he's going to go around with somebody who makes more money than he does.

Hillary says that's ridiculous, and asks, "Who thinks that way anymore?"

"Everybody on my block."

This was a very real issue, which is why I wanted to bring it up. What happens to the power dynamic between a man and a woman when she's the major breadwinner?

Eddie has a very traditional concept of husbands and wives, and when Hillary says, "What? Are you asking me to get married?," he says, "Yes."

And she says, "Why? Are you pregnant?"

That got an even bigger laugh.

Then he complains that he feels "used," like "a one-night stand," and she reassures him by saying she still respects him in the morning.

I'm proud of that scene. We were taking all the conventional male-female responses and playing around with them. It made my point about women being equal to men in a nonthreatening way. And I was even more pleased when it turned out to be the most popular scene in the movie.

It was particularly interesting for me to explore what happens when a woman is the boss in the movies, because I was working out these issues in real life.

Jon kept asking me to marry him. And I kept putting him off. Just to placate him, I said, "If we're together for ten years, I'll marry you."

Clearly something was holding me back, but it's amazing how much you can overlook when you're so eager to have a family. When we bought the ranch out in Malibu, I saw it as the beginning of a new kind of life in this country environment.

But Jon and I were two very stubborn people, and our visions for the house didn't always coincide. He had some guys build what was supposed to be a bathtub out of stone, but it was impossible to take a bath in it because the stones were so rough that you couldn't sit down. When he set a tree stump next to a chair as a side table, I had to point out, "But it's slanted. You can't put anything on it. It'll slide off."

He won that fight, too, by saying, "It's my house."

I think one of the reasons Jon wanted to own that house was so he could have the last word. He needed to be the boss. I thought it might help if we talked to my analyst (Freudian, by the way, and a bit cold). The first question he asked Jon was, "So, what do you think of Barbra?"

Jon said, "You mean what do I *feel* about her."

And I thought, *Wow. Jon's right.* He was coming from a different place, not the mind but the heart. And I was impressed.

Then Jon suggested I see his therapist, which sounded interesting. I went there alone. The doctor seemed so warm and kind. After I sat down he said, "What problems are you having?"

I said, "Jon and I fight about a lot of things."

"Like what?"

"Business . . . finances. He always says, 'You don't trust me.' I think I have a problem with trust. I don't trust most people."

And he said, "Why should you? Trust has to be earned."

Suddenly I was so relieved. Tears filled my eyes. It's amazing how one sentence that is true and supportive can set you free.

I really liked that doctor and stayed with him for many years.

The fact is, I knew down deep that I could never commit to Jon.

I remember a moment on the set of *For Pete's Sake* when he was talking to Michael Sarrazin about stereos, and he said, "Sounds like you've got a terrible set. I'm going to get you a better one."

Weeks later, I asked him, "Did you ever buy that stereo for Michael?"

"Oh . . . no," he said. "But it doesn't matter."

"It does matter! When you promise to do something, you have to do it."

I could hardly believe it. I would feel so guilty if I didn't follow through on a promise. But Jon didn't.

He tends to ignore inconvenient facts, and his version of reality was often very different from mine. He always says we had this great love affair. I remember going skiing in Aspen early on with some friends, their kids, and our kids. Jon and I were arguing continually, and he said, "Aren't we having a great time?"

I said, "Jon, we're fighting every day. That is not my definition of a great time."

And then of course he got sick, as usual, and wanted to go home. That happened on so many vacations. He wasn't at ease outside his familiar territory.

I was getting restless in the relationship. There was a man I had met at the Bergmans' house. He was an extremely successful businessman who collected art, had houses in Europe and the United States, was politically engaged . . . and he liked backgammon. So did I, and we started to play together. (Jon didn't like games.)

You can find out a lot about a person by playing backgammon. And we had so much to talk about. He had innovative ideas, like suggesting that I should own my own movies. (My lawyer nixed that one.) I was impressed with his knowledge.

Point is, this man reminded me that there were other fish in the sea, and I was attracted to him. Not wanting to lie to Jon, I told him that I had met somebody who interested me and I needed to explore that relationship. I said I was planning to go away for a weekend and meet this man in New York. I told Jon I would be very discreet. I asked my friend Joanne Segel to accompany us to the theater and restaurants so I would not be seen alone with this man in public. I didn't want to embarrass Jon in any way.

He took it well. He seemed to understand. He didn't get angry. I think he was hiding his hurt, but he hid it very well, which made it okay for me to go. But I still felt uncomfortable. Joanne, this man, and I went to see *Sweeney Todd* on Broadway, and I was so nervous sitting there, thinking, *Should I be doing this at all? I hope nobody gets my picture with him.* I was so preoccupied that I couldn't enjoy the show. It was not until I went again with Jason that I thought, *My God, this is brilliant!* I didn't even appreciate the score the first time around. It just shows how your state of mind can completely skew your perceptions.

Of course, a mention of me and my mystery man in New York still made it into the gossip columns. Who could have tipped them off? I figured it was someone who talks to the press a lot, and I suspected Sue Mengers, but she denied it. And then years later she finally admitted that she was the culprit. She said, "I've always hated Jon."

I was hoping this new man would sweep me away into this other world that intrigued me. And because he was engrossed in his own business, he wouldn't try to share mine . . . unlike Jon. But it turned out he was *all* business. From the minute he woke up in the morning he was on the phone, trading currencies and making deals. (No wonder I usually end up with artistic types.)

I quickly realized that this relationship wasn't going anywhere, so I called Jon and said, "Come and get me."

He was on the next plane to New York. When he arrived, he said, "I'm going to take you shopping." And he bought me a Fendi fur coat . . . not a fancy Fendi fur. In fact, it was rather funny looking, made of pieces of fur sewn together with actual holes in between . . . kind of like a thrift shop coat. But I loved it because it was the same henna color as my hair.

Jon did give me some lovely gifts over the years . . . a ruby-and-diamond bracelet, a Cartier clock, and a motor home. This was when I was getting sick to my stomach all the time. I'd have to stop and pull into a gas station so I could use the restroom. But now I could travel back and forth to the studio in comfort, with my own bathroom. I loved that motor home and fixed it up in Art Deco colors . . . gray and dusty rose . . . and never had to pull over again.

But Jon could also be thoughtless, and sometimes quite mean. We would be driving in the car and I'd say, "Could you please close the window? I'm getting cold."

He'd say, "Get a blanket."

What kind of love is that? (My husband Jim would never say that. Instead he'd quickly close the window and turn on the heat.)

I was shocked sometimes by what came out of Jon's mouth. He said we had hundreds of acres when it was only twenty-four, which was plenty. And he told one reporter that he planted fifty thousand trees and moved forty million tons of rock, but that's typical of him . . . he always exaggerates.

The truth was never enough for him.

And he could be so volatile. His temper scared me.

At one point, after Jon made money from *A Star Is Born*, we bought a little ramshackle house together at the beach. And we were already arguing as we drove out to it one day, because Sue had just informed me that Jon was telling people that I wouldn't work without him.

I was furious. "How dare you say that? You know it's not true. It's a lie!"

Jon said, "Well, I want us to work together."

"But what makes you think I'm going to do all my movies with you?" I asked. "We're two separate people. We're not joined at the hip. Stop lying about me. I can't deal with lies!"

So he was already in fighting mode when we arrived at the house, and a truck was parked right in front of it, blocking the entrance. I thought we could still squeeze around it to get in the gate, but Jon was enraged. He kept honking the horn until finally this big, hulking guy appeared.

Jon said, "Move your fucking truck."

And the guy said, "I'll move it when I feel like it."

Well, that's all Jon needed to hear. He's only five foot nine, and yet he picked a fight with this guy who was at least six foot three. Jon headbutted him, but it backfired, because in a minute the guy had him in a headlock. I knew Jon would feel humiliated by that, in front of me, so I turned away for a moment. Then I heard a loud "Ouch!!!" and when I turned back around, Jon was on the ground with the guy on top of him. He must have had his hands around Jon's face, and I think Jon was biting him and then somehow the guy was biting Jon. So I bopped the guy over the head with my pocketbook.

As Jon said, "You saved me again. He bit my finger and it's practically down to the bone!"

Being with him was getting exhausting. I'd prefer to have all this drama in my movies, not in my life.

THIRTY-THREE

Enough Is Enough

The *Wet* album began with a Jacuzzi.

I was putting off going back into the recording studio because I was tired. I had just finished two projects . . . *The Main Event* and the Art Deco house, where I tiled some exterior walls in burgundy with touches of gray and black in a Deco design. And then the swimming pool, which had a Jacuzzi at one end, was tiled in black with touches of burgundy and gray. One afternoon I was in that Jacuzzi, surrounded by all this beautiful black tile that gleamed like patent leather when it was wet. I looked at it and thought, *This would make a great backdrop for an album cover*, very simple and sensual, just me in the water with wet hair. I asked Mario Casilli, who took the *Playboy* pictures, to shoot it

Jason's bar mitzvah with the Bergmans, our extended family.

Steve Ross was a great man and a dear friend.

Shelly, Judy, me, and Richard.

Richard Baskin and me in Sun Valley.

My cousins Harvey and Lowell.

My lifelong friend or "Cister" as we called her.

Yentl as Anshel.

Directing Mandy Patinkin and Amy Irving.

My film father, the lovely Nehemiah Persoff.

Yentl—directing my first film.

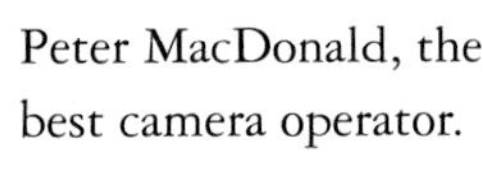

Peter MacDonald, the best camera operator.

I loved having lunch with the great Federico Fellini.

Franco Zeffirelli wanted me to do Shakespeare early on.

Javier Mendoza/Herald photographer

WHERE'S THE BABS? Barbra Streisand may not have attended the Oscars, but a group of about 100 of her fans made sure the Academy was made aware of their displeasure at the lack of any major nominations for "Yentl," which she wrote, produced, directed and starred in. In today's Q&A, some of them explain/See following page.

A *Yentl* protest at the Academy Awards.

Amos Oz—a great storyteller. I visited him in his kibbutz in Israel.

I asked Ray Aghayan to create a gown in the style of Gustav Klimt.

1984: Receiving the Scopus Award.

My friend cinematographer Andrzej Bartkowiak presenting me with the American Society of Cinematographers Board of Governors Award.

Working with Nick Nolte.

Directing Nick and Jason.

Loved these men on *The Prince of Tides*—Jeroen Krabbé, Jason Gould, Nick Nolte.

Looking through the lens to set up a shot.

My dear friend Peter Matz starting *The Broadway Album.*

My time with James Newton Howard, who wrote the score for *The Prince of Tides*.

Such an honor to work with Stephen Sondheim.

The Concert—so proud to win two Emmy Awards.

My favorite dance partner, Jeff Bridges.

The Mirror Has Two Faces—
a joyful time.

Discussing my vision with Andrzej Bartkowiak.

A family affair.

Two very special women, Virginia Clinton and my mother.

Working with Marvin Hamlisch was pure joy.

My goddaughter Caleigh.

Two amazing women—Coretta Scott King with me and Virginia.

with the water bubbling and the steam rising, and then we did another version in the wooden hot tub at the barn.

So now that I had the front and back covers, I had to fill in the album with songs.

I like following a theme. Since the concept was "wet," I wanted to call this the *Wet* album, and I thought all the songs should relate to water in some way. There's Harold Arlen's great torch song from the 1940s, "Come Rain or Come Shine." When I was eighteen, I had put it on a list of songs I wanted to sing, but even in my enthusiasm I realized a teenager singing a torch song might seem a bit ridiculous, so I never got around to it before. And then there were beautiful contemporary ballads like Michel Legrand's "After the Rain" and Lalo Schifrin's "On Rainy Afternoons" (both with lyrics by the Bergmans).

Ironically, the song that was the big breakout hit almost didn't make it onto the album. And the only reason it did was due to the persistence of the songwriters . . . and my son, Jason.

This was 1979, the height of the disco craze, and Paul Jabara and Bruce Roberts had already given me my first disco hit, "The Main Event/Fight" (probably what most people remember from that film). Now they had heard I was doing a new album and they had another song for me, "Enough Is Enough," but Charles Koppelman wasn't that fond of it. And the bigger problem was, as Bruce pointed out, "It was dry as a bone." So I asked if they could add some water, and they quickly came up with a new intro that began like this:

It's raining, it's pouring, my love life is boring me to tears . . .

So the title became "No More Tears (Enough Is Enough)."

Meanwhile, Paul had another idea. He thought it would be a real coup if he could put his friend Donna Summer . . . the Queen of Disco . . . together with me to sing it.

He wanted to bring Donna over to meet me, but somehow that request wasn't getting through, and finally he couldn't wait any longer and decided to call me directly. Jason happened to answer the phone, so Paul gave him the message. Jason, who was twelve at the time, was less than impressed by most celebrities, but when he heard the name Donna Summer, he got excited. She was his favorite singer, and he played her records all the time.

So Paul, Bruce, and Donna came out to my little beach house in Malibu. They played the song, and Jason loved it . . . so that was a great reason to do it . . . and he loved Donna. So did I. She was a doll, and I said yes.

Disco was Donna's domain and she was its fabulous star. I felt like a visitor in her world, because the music requires you to sing on the beat, and that's hard for me. So I had a question for her when we got to the studio.

"Is it all right if I sometimes go off the beat?"

She just looked at me and said, "You're *Barbra Streisand*, and *you're* asking *me* how to sing?"

Donna was completely down-to-earth, and we had so much fun doing that duet. There's a very high note in the song, at the end of the line "And we won't waste another tear." The word "tear" just builds and builds and goes on forever (about seventeen seconds, to be specific). We were rehearsing the song, sitting on stools, and when it came to that high note, we both just went for it. My head was back, my eyes were closed . . . it was a challenge, but I held that note. And then I opened my eyes and . . . Donna was gone!

She was lying on the floor. She had fallen off her stool.

I gasped and said, "Donna, are you all right?"

By this time everyone was gathered around her, and she was sitting up and waving them away, saying she was fine. And then she turned to me and explained, "I didn't breathe right. I guess I just ran out of air and passed out. But Barbra, when I came to, I couldn't believe it . . . you were still holding that note!"

And she started to laugh, and so did I.

Thank God she wasn't hurt.

And Francesco Scavullo took a good photo of the two of us for the cover of the single, which happily went to number 1 and has been played again and again on every dance floor ever since.

I remember the last time I saw Donna. It was at the house of our mutual friend David Foster (a brilliant musician we both worked with many times). She looked wonderful, and we reminisced and laughed some more. Soon after that I was so shocked to read that she was gone. That was hard for me to believe. She was too young and had so much more to give.

Donna had an amazing voice, and most of all, she was a lovely person . . . Jason was absolutely right about her.

THIRTY-FOUR

Guilty

In 1979 there was one project constantly on my mind . . . *Yentl* . . . and this was the year when I promised myself that I was going to do whatever it took to get it made. So when Charles started talking about yet another album even before *Wet* was finished, my reaction was, I don't have time.

I didn't want to look for songs. I didn't even want to hear them.

But Charles, who had his eye on the market, wanted to take advantage of discomania while it lasted. It had worked for "The Main Event/Fight" and then "No More Tears (Enough Is Enough)," so he thought, *Why not keep the party going and try for a third?*

I don't know whose idea it was to put me together with the Bee Gees . . . Charles and Jon had become friends and both claimed credit. But it couldn't have been too hard a sell, because I loved their music for *Saturday Night Fever.* So I said yes when Charles invited Jon, me, and the kids to a Bee Gees concert at Dodger Stadium. We sat in the midst of fifty-six thousand screaming fans, the show was very exciting, and afterward Charles made his pitch. He told me that Barry Gibb, one of the three brothers who made up the group, had just written and produced five of the current Top Ten Billboard singles . . . an unprecedented feat . . . and was looking to branch out and produce albums for other artists.

I was very impressed.

But I should explain something about the way I work. If you look at the majority of my albums, you'll notice the songs I chose were not exactly commercial. I never went into the studio thinking, *I've got to record a hit!* Of course, I was happy if a song went to number 1, but that was not my motivation. To this day I don't even remember which songs reached the top spot (I always have to call up Jay Landers and ask him).

So the world of Top Ten Billboard singles was not my world.

Still, I'm always open to new ideas and I like to challenge myself . . . so I called Barry.

He was very sweet. He told me he had been a big fan ever since he heard "People" in Australia, where he was living when it came out. I told him that I was a big fan of *his* music, and then asked if he would be interested in making an album with me.

There was silence on the line for a moment. And then Barry said, "I'm bowled over. Could you give me twenty-four hours to get up off the floor, before I give you an answer?"

It wasn't until years later that I found out he had actually been nervous and intimidated about taking the job. So he called Neil Diamond and asked what I was like to work with. "Just relax," Neil said. "She's fantastic to work with. Go for it." And Barry's wife told him she'd divorce him if he turned me down.

Charles and I first met with Barry at my Carolwood house, and Charles showed him some songs he had brought along. Barry considered them and then politely said he'd prefer to write his own material for me. I loved that idea. In fact, Barry was willing to do it all . . . produce, write, arrange, record, and even play on the tracks. All I'd have to do is sing!

Wow, I thought. *What a deal!* Barry's offer was like a gift, because it meant I could concentrate on *Yentl*, while he could concentrate on the album.

Perfect.

It was only about a month later that I got a call to come hear the new songs. I thought, *That was fast!* (and I was further impressed).

I was willing to get on a plane to see Barry, because it would also give me a chance to meet with Isaac Bashevis Singer again, who was in Miami at the time. He was the Polish-born author who wrote the short story that was the basis for *Yentl*, and he had recently won the Nobel Prize in Literature. Now that's a combination . . . Barry Gibb and I. B. Singer. That should give you a glimpse of what my life was like at this point . . . stimulating!

I sat in the studio and listened to demo tapes Barry had made of the new songs, with him singing my part in his unique falsetto. Some he had written alone, some with his brother Robin, and some with one of his partners, Albhy Galuten. I instantly responded to the melodies and the feel of the songs, but I was less certain about the lyrics. They were kind of abstract, with lots of intriguing, impressionistic images that were open to interpretation. (In other words, I didn't know what they meant.)

It was clear that my usual method of analyzing lyrics just as I would analyze a script, looking for subtext and nuances of meaning, was not going to work here. I was used to approaching each word literally, whereas Barry was writing figuratively. And his writing was nonlinear. There was no conventional narrative with a beginning, middle, and end, so there wasn't the kind of story line I was used to.

But I listened again and talked to Barry and made a decision. I decided to trust him, to just put myself in his hands and go with the flow.

Barry recorded all the tracks in Miami and then came out to Los Angeles to record my vocals. The whole process was incredibly streamlined. Barry just asked me to sing each song ten times and then he would take care of the rest.

Really? It seemed so simple.

I complied, but singing anything ten times gets kind of boring, so I had to find any excuse to take a break . . . like food. Whenever I'm intensely concentrating on something, I get hungry. I suppose a therapist would say it's an anxiety suppressant, but for me it's more basic. When I'm working, I need food! All I have to do is walk into a recording studio and I want to eat.

I'll usually have a table set out close to the musicians, laden with all kinds of treats . . . bagels, nova, cream cheese, peanut butter and jelly, prosciutto, honeydew melon, cheese, fruit, cookies, brownies (with walnuts!). Then there's another table for me and the engineers. And there's always dinner to look forward to (usually Chinese food, my favorite).

As Barry said to one reporter at the time, "She was a hard worker. She'd work from morning till late into the night . . . But we did have to lock her up when the food came, because she always wanted to eat. We had to keep her away from the food so she'd keep singing!"

Barry was determined to make it as easy for me as possible, knowing that I was eager to get back to my script. And he did. I did get involved with the mix, but not to the extent I usually do.

I do remember having reservations about one particular song, "Woman in Love." Not the melody, which I liked . . . it even sounded vaguely Hebraic, with its progression of minor chords. It was the lyric. And I started questioning it, forgetting my resolve to just go with the flow.

It begins like this:

Life is a moment in space, when the dream is gone it's a lonelier place . . .

Okay, so does that mean this couple broke up?

It continues:

I kiss the morning goodbye, but down inside you know we never know why . . .

Is she questioning why they're breaking up?

The road is narrow and long, when eyes meet eyes, and the feeling is strong
I turn away from the wall, I stumble and fall, but I give you it all . . .

Is she talking about meeting eyes with a new person, or is she remembering her past with this person? And what kind of wall? Is it figurative or emotional?

And then there's the chorus:

I am a woman in love, and I'd do anything to get you into my world and hold you within . . .

Anything?

This is the part I found really hard to sing. I suppose there are women who will "do anything" to get a man, but I just couldn't relate to that. And please don't misunderstand. I don't mean to put down anyone. But this made the woman sound like some sort of clever manipulator. Maybe I'm a little bit envious of that kind of woman, but it sure as hell isn't me. I wouldn't even know how to manipulate a man. Usually, I just build up my nerve and ask bluntly for what I want. (Although my husband says I do have my ways.)

Back to the lyric . . . I also questioned the next line:

It's a right I defend, over and over again . . .

What right? The right to use any means to get her man? And who is she defending against? Society?

It's interesting . . . if you're just listening to Barry's music and not paying particular attention to the words, the song sounds like an anthem of women's empowerment . . . it just wasn't the kind of empowerment I was working toward. So I was having a hard time identifying with this character.

And then I realized I was being too literal again. Everyone at Columbia was thrilled with the song. So I thought, *Fuck it. Forget the words. Just do it.*

A wise friend once told me, "Let go of your need to understand." It was a lesson, and I'm not that good at it even now, but I did manage to do it then . . . probably because I wanted to go back to writing *Yentl*!

Then at the last minute, when we were finished with the album, it dawned on me that we were missing a certain kind of song . . . something very uptempo, maybe a bossa nova . . .

Barry understood exactly what I meant, and he went off and came back with "Guilty," the only cut on the album written by all three Bee Gees. I really loved that one and said, "I think it should be the first song on the record and the title of the album. 'Guilty' is such a powerful word. It has all sorts of psychological implications, and people will respond to it." Besides, I knew a lot about guilt . . . I *am* Jewish!

That was my main contribution to the production process. Frankly, I was more involved with the cover than the album itself. The art director from Columbia had an idea . . . he wanted to photograph me with an angel on one shoulder and a devil on the other. That made no sense to me. Instead I asked him to hire Mario Casilli, the photographer who had done such a good job on my *Playboy* cover and the *Wet* album.

Mario came over to the recording studio where Barry and I were working to do some publicity stills, before we had a concept for the cover. I happened to be wearing a white blouse and white pants that day, and when I looked at the shots, I said, "That's it. We should both be wearing white, and let's shoot it against a simple white backdrop." I thought Barry was very handsome, and if we were both in white, against white, that would distill the photo to its simplest form. It would also create a monochromatic frame, the kind I always like.

An assistant ran out for a huge roll of white paper. Another went to Barry's hotel to pick up his white shirt and pants. And we shot the cover then and there, with no drama and no fuss.

I'm looking at it again . . . all that white had such purity and yet the album was called *Guilty*. That's an interesting dichotomy, but I wasn't thinking of that then. Often, I only figure out the reason why I do something later (sometimes years later, like now, as I'm writing this book).

I know I deliberately picked a shot where I had a guilty smile on my face . . . but just what are we guilty of? You'd have to listen to find out.

Before the album came out in September 1980, Columbia wanted to release a single to promote it. And guess what they chose? "Woman in Love" . . . the one song I was conflicted about. But the promo department was absolutely certain it would be a hit, and in the spirit of the whole project, I let them do it and hoped they were right.

And they were. It went to number 1, and then the album went to number 1. In fact, Jay tells me that *Guilty* went to number 1 all around the world and became my bestselling album of all time.

It also ended up being nominated for five Grammy awards, including Album of the Year. And "Woman in Love" was nominated for Song of the Year. (So what do I know?)

Barry and I won a Grammy that night for Best Pop Performance by a Duo or Group. I had asked him to wear white and so did I, to continue the concept from the cover. And I had written a few lines for us to say when we both walked out onstage.

"Barry, do you feel guilty?"

"No."

"I do."

"Why? Why would you feel like that?"

"I don't know. I feel like I'm cheating on Neil Diamond."

That got a big laugh, and Barry gave me a big kiss.

Years later, in 1986, we had a happy reunion when he generously consented to join me at my *One Voice* concert, where we both wore white again. We sang "Guilty" and "What Kind of Fool," our two duets from the album, and the response was tremendous. It was one of the highlights of the evening.

And Barry told me, "You changed my life."

That's because after we did that album, he suddenly had a whole new career as a record producer for people like Kenny Rogers, Diana Ross, and Michael Jackson.

In *Rolling Stone*, the critic Stephen Holden wrote that *Guilty* was "as beautifully crafted a piece of ear candy as I've heard in years." And in *The New York Times*, he declared that it "proves to be a sensational blending of talents . . . *Guilty* is just about perfect." Interviewed for *Billboard*, Barry talked about how well we worked together and said, "She's easily the finest female vocalist in the world."

I'd like to return the compliment. I've always looked back on the *Guilty* album as the easiest, most pleasant recording experience I've ever had. Barry just made the whole process a delight. He knew exactly how to showcase me as an artist, because he's a wonderful artist himself.

THIRTY-FIVE

Papa, Can You Hear Me?

In the winter of 1968, a package arrived at my New York apartment. Inside was a copy of a short story called "Yentl the Yeshiva Boy," by Isaac Bashevis Singer. I didn't know Singer's work and I didn't know the man who had sent it to me, a producer named Valentine Sherry . . . what an odd name, like something you'd see on a candy box. So I just glanced at his cover note and added it to the pile of scripts on my desk.

A few nights later I took it to bed with me . . . that's where I do most of my reading. I looked to see how long the story was . . . twenty-nine pages. I thought, *Great, I can get through this quickly.* And then I started reading, and my attention was caught by the first four words: "After her father's death." I felt my heart skip a beat. I identified with Yentl immediately. And by the time I turned the last page, I was completely captivated by this story of a young Jewish woman in nineteenth-century Poland whose "soul thirsted to study Torah" . . . which is like going to college and studying history, law, philosophy, and religion. So she disguised herself as a man in order to get the kind of education that was denied to women at that time. In the morning I called David Begelman, my agent, and said, "I've just found my next movie. It's called *Yentl the Yeshiva Boy*."

David was taken aback. I could practically feel him cringe at the other end of the line. He said, "Are you kidding me? We already turned that down for you. You've just played a Jewish girl and now you tell me that you want to play a Jewish boy?"

Now *I* was taken aback. "Wait a minute," I said. "You mean you turned something down without even discussing it with me? You can't do that!"

"Barbra, you're going to be a big star as soon as *Funny Girl* comes out. And you've got two more big movies on your plate. And now you're saying you want to do some *fakakta* short story? Don't waste your time."

I'm pretty sure David had dollar signs in his head, and he definitely wasn't interested in me doing some little art film. But there was something about this story that really spoke to me. So I called Valentine Sherry.

And that was the beginning of a saga that would engage me, frustrate me, challenge me, exhaust me, and exhilarate me . . . for the next fifteen years.

Sherry had already commissioned Singer to write a screenplay, which came in at 195 pages . . . way too long . . . and basically stretched out the story without taking into account that this was a different medium. The writing was fine. It just wasn't cinematic.

And Sherry had already hired a director, Ivan Passer. He was part of the Czech New Wave, along with Miloš Forman, and had made a wonderful film called *Intimate Lighting*, which was subtle and perceptive. So I was thrilled. Plus, I figured he'd have an innate understanding of Eastern Europe.

Passer began to rewrite Singer's screenplay, and in 1971 it was announced that I would be doing the film, now called *Masquerade*, for First Artists. But that turned out to be a little optimistic. There were still problems with the script. Sherry brought in another writer, Jerome Kass, who did a version, and then Passer worked with Kass on another draft. But I still had reservations, and it turned out that Passer had his own reservations . . . about me! He was concerned that I was too old for the part . . . and too famous. It was really Sherry who wanted me, and I was worried that Passer might feel I was being shoved down his throat.

When Sherry and I first met, I was twenty-five. Now I was twenty-nine, and although Yentl's age is never specified in the story, Passer assumed she was in her late teens. I wasn't focusing on her age . . . I was more interested in her dilemma . . . and if Singer thought my age was a problem, he never mentioned it to me when we met.

I went to see him at his New York apartment. I was excited and eager to talk to him, but he didn't seem very pleased to see me. He wasn't very welcoming and neither was his wife, who begrudgingly served tea, with some hard, dry Social Tea biscuits. I tried to get a smile out of him, but he was a bit of a sourpuss and kind of cold, emotionally. With his bald head and pale skin, he looked like an angry imp. I also visited him in Florida and invited him to my house when he was speaking at UCLA. Unfortunately we never managed to connect. I think he was miffed because his screenplay was being rewritten. He ended his involvement, and eventually Passer moved on to other projects as well.

I did too. I went on to make one movie after another, but I never lost sight of *Yentl*. Over the next few years I would regularly check in with Cis to see where we were on the script. By this time, I had bought the rights and I'd met with various writers. After seeing a Canadian movie called *Lies My Father Told Me*, about an Orthodox Jewish boy and his grandfather, I commissioned the man who wrote it, Ted Allan, to do a version, but he couldn't quite capture what I was after. And I also talked to Leah Napolin, who had adapted the short story into a play that ran on Broadway (since I owned the rights, the producers had to ask me for permission, which I granted), but our discussion never resulted in a screenplay.

And then I got so immersed in *A Star Is Born* that I couldn't even think about anything else for three years. By the time I turned back to *Yentl*, Valentine Sherry had passed away, and I still needed a script and a director. I had approached the French director Claude Berri, because I loved his movie *The Two of Us*, about an eight-year-old Jewish boy who hides his religion when he's taken in during World War II by an elderly Catholic couple.

This is the movie I chose when Steven Spielberg and I decided to show each other our favorite films (he picked Victor Fleming's *A Guy Named Joe*, with Spencer Tracy). I couldn't wait for Steven to see the moment when the old man, who's anti-Semitic, discovers that the boy he's come to love is actually Jewish. But guess what? There's no such scene in the movie. I had completely imagined it. The old man never learns the truth, but the boy learns something crucial about the basic ignorance behind most prejudice . . . and it must have saddened him that he couldn't share his secret with the man he dearly loved.

Anyway, it's a very simple and moving story, shot in black and white, and I was thinking of *Yentl* in the same way, almost as a kind of small, European film. I remember sitting in the bathtub at my house on Carolwood and having a long phone conversation with Claude in Paris . . . but he was busy with his own projects.

I had a wonderful meeting with Miloš Forman that turned out to be prophetic, although I didn't realize it at the time. After listening to me describe the story, he said, "Barbra, you obviously have a very clear vision of what this movie should be. Why don't you direct it yourself?"

I wasn't even considering that back then. But after producing *A Star Is Born*, I had more confidence in myself and thought, *Maybe it's time to think bigger.* Maybe I should take a risk . . .

It was October 1978. I was thirty-six years old. The window of opportunity was rapidly closing for me to do this role that had enthralled me for ten years.

I thought, *Life's too short.* It was now or never . . . put up or shut up. I didn't want to be an old lady, sitting in my rocking chair and muttering to myself, "I should have directed *Yentl*."

But I was scared.

Here I was, on location up at Cedar Lake in the San Bernardino Mountains, trying to do the best I could with *The Main Event.* Don't get me wrong. I enjoyed certain things about that movie. But making it wasn't easy, and then we got hit by a snowstorm, which meant more delays and more rewrites.

Jon and I were standing outside, in the cold, and suddenly all this pent-up emotion rose to the surface and I erupted.

"Why am I making this lightweight comedy? I'm not wasting my life on this kind of fluff. I've got do something I believe in . . . something I feel passionate about. I'm going to do *Yentl*!"

"No, you're not!" Jon said. "You know you're never going to make that movie! You've been talking about it for years. You can't play a *man*! It's ridiculous. We'll find something else to do together."

I stared at him. It was suddenly obvious . . . he didn't believe in *Yentl* either. I had read him the short story during the first weekend we spent together. What had he been thinking all these years as I worked on it? I had stupidly assumed he supported me.

Clearly not.

But if Jon thought his words were going to discourage me, he thought wrong. In fact, they were all I needed to hear.

"Just because you said that," I told him, "I'm going to make this movie *no matter what*! I'm going to make this movie over your dead body!" . . . or maybe it was "my dead body." All I know is it was one of our bodies, and I didn't care which!

I was so enraged.

When someone tells me I can't do something, it makes me even more determined to do it. That's just the way my mind works.

So, Jon thinks I can't play a man? Well, I'll show him. I dressed up in men's clothes one night and walked into the house when he wasn't expecting me. For a moment, Jon didn't recognize me, and I thought, *Uh-oh, I made a mistake.* What if he grabs his gun? Jon told me later he almost did. And he also admitted I had him. He realized that I just might be able to pull this off.

I met with various studio executives to pitch the movie.

"I have a short story by Isaac Bashevis Singer—"

"Who?"

"He was born in Poland and he writes these wonderful folk tales in Yiddish."

"Huh?"

"This is a story about a woman who dresses up as a man in order to study Talmud—"

"What?"

I might as well have stopped right there. But I kept going, hoping that my enthusiasm would spark some interest. Instead their eyes glazed over. They had no interest in making this movie. They didn't think anyone would come to see it. They thought the Singer story was way too obscure.

Let me tell you, it's not easy to get a movie green-lit. Twelve years later I was back pitching *The Prince of Tides* to another set of studio executives, and this time it was not some obscure short story but a bestselling book! So what was the response? "Well, the movie can never be as good as the book." Okay, one was too obscure, and now the other was too well-known! Go figure.

Obviously I knew *Yentl* was not exactly commercial. And there was the undeniable hurdle that I would spend most of the movie dressed as a man. The last actress who had tried that was Katharine Hepburn in *Sylvia Scarlett* back in 1936, and it didn't turn out too well.

So yes, *Yentl* was different, but I was determined to make them see its potential. To me it was a universal story about wanting something you can't have. Basically it was a love story, with a few twists!

Yentl was in love with learning, and then fell in love with a man who only loved her as a friend. She married the woman he loved to please him. But the woman fell in love with Yentl . . .

Well, it's complicated . . . and kind of Shakespearean. Cupid's arrows got very mixed up. Let's just say the movie was about all kinds of love.

And it was about a woman who defied expectations . . . a woman who wanted more than a conventional life of darning socks and cleaning house . . . a woman who wanted to fill her mind with ideas, not just what to make for dinner. And that felt very relevant to me, and the times.

That was not how the executives saw it. To them it was a movie about Jews, and even though some of them were Jewish themselves, perhaps they didn't want to see themselves on-screen. Maybe they were afraid the subject was too Jewish. Some of the moguls running studios, especially in Hollywood's early days, rarely married Jewish women. They were looking to assimilate.

I think Jews are still "the other," in some ways. For centuries they've been used as scapegoats . . . blamed over and over again for the ills of the world. I've always liked the essay Mark Twain wrote in 1899 for *Harper's Magazine*, "Concerning the Jews." Acting as an impartial observer, Twain (who wasn't Jewish) traced this history of prejudice and wondered if it was due to some flaw in the Jewish character. On the contrary, he came to the conclusion that "the Jew is a good and orderly citizen" and that the animosity actually had little to do with religion. In fact, he wrote, "I am persuaded that in Russia, Austria, and Germany nine-tenths of the hostility to the Jew comes from the average Christian's inability to compete successfully with the average Jew in business."

In an effort to restrict their success, one occupation after another had been closed to Jews over the centuries. In many countries they were prohibited from joining various guilds, so they couldn't pursue certain vocations. They were often not allowed to own property. All that was left to them was the ability to trade goods and manage money. So the Jews came to excel at commerce. They became merchants, shopkeepers, and bankers . . . professions where "the basis of successful business is honesty," according to Twain. But no matter what limits were placed on their activities, one thing remained constant . . . their respect for education.

Twain proposed that "ages of restriction to the one tool which the law was not able to take from him—his brain—have made that tool singularly competent." He cited a statistic that some Berliner had used to advocate for the expulsion of the Jews . . . that 85 percent of the most successful lawyers in Berlin were Jewish, and about the same percent of successful businesses in Germany were run by Jews. Then Twain said, "Isn't it an amazing confession? It was but another way of saying that in a population of 48,000,000, of whom only 500,000 were registered as Jews, eighty-five per cent of the brains and honesty of the whole was lodged in the Jews."

But that made them targets. People are afraid of "the other," and even more afraid of being identified as "the other."

When the studio executives refused to see beyond the Jewish context of *Yentl* to the larger theme of gender equality . . . this was about a woman who simply wanted the same opportunities as a man . . . their real concern was unspoken, but I could feel it. They did not want to draw attention to Jews and their world. As I wrote in my journal, Jews were apparently considered too "different, alien, especially now, and again, and it seems always . . ."

And as I write this now, nationalism, fascism, and anti-Semitism are on the rise, even in America. It's hard to believe that this could be happening yet again.

I've always been proud of my Jewish heritage. I never attempted to hide it when I became an actress. It's essential to who I am. And I wanted to make this movie about a smart Jewish woman who represented so many qualities I admire. So, she dresses up as a man . . . there are accounts in history of women who did the same. And people were always disguising themselves in fairy tales and getting away with it. I thought of *Yentl* as a realistic fairy tale.

Point is, it's not completely realistic, but it's also not a total fantasy either. It's both . . . and that's one of the reasons I liked it.

The less-than-enthusiastic response was very discouraging. And the fact that I also wanted to direct . . . I was an actress, as far as the men who ran the studios were concerned, and I should stay in my place. They thought I had a lot of nerve to believe that I could produce, direct, write, and star in a film. (My own thought about taking on all these roles was, *Great. Three fewer people to argue with.*) These men seemed to have this antiquated notion of an actress as some sort of frivolous creature who could not be fiscally responsible. I thought the Victorian era was over, but you wouldn't know it to listen to them.

I was rejected . . . and dejected . . . and then something happened that made me commit to the movie all over again.

My brother called me up one day and told me an incredible story. He had met a Jewish housewife on Long Island who happened to be a medium. She explained to him that a spirit had come to her when she was thirteen, just as it had come to her mother before her, and she could contact the dead.

"What???"

"Barbra, I can't even describe the experience I had. I talked to Daddy. We put our hands on a table, and it bumped its legs on the floor and spelled out Daddy's name. Then the table followed me around the room."

"Excuse me?"

Now, my brother is not into woo-woo at all. Shelly is a very meat-and-potatoes kind of guy. He doesn't read horoscopes or visit fortune-tellers. So this whole thing was completely out of character for him.

I listened to him and was dumbfounded. No way could I believe this. But I was very intrigued and I thought, *I've got to see this for myself.*

So when I was back in New York, I asked Shelly to arrange a session with this medium. Before we met with her, I decided that I wanted to visit my father's grave. Believe it or not, I had never been there. Not once did my mother bring it up or offer to take me. Or maybe I didn't want to go because I was subconsciously angry with my father for dying. I don't know.

I wasn't even sure exactly where his grave was. Shelly knew, and we drove to Mount Hebron Cemetery in Queens, where he led the way to the graves of my father's mother, Anna, and his father, Isaac. And then there was the grave of my father. The granite tombstone is inscribed with the words "Beloved husband, father and son" . . . "Esteemed teacher and scholar" . . . and marked with the Jewish star and the Phi Beta Kappa insignia.

I asked Shelly to take a photo of me standing next to his tombstone. It's the only picture I have of me with my father.

That evening the medium came over to Shelly's house in Great Neck. Ellen, my sister-in-law, didn't want anything to do with it and stayed in the kitchen, so it was just my brother, the medium, and me. I looked at her . . . she seemed like a nice Jewish lady, nothing out of the ordinary. We took our seats in my brother's brick-walled dining room . . . not at his big dining table. There was a triangular three-legged drop-leaf table where we could sit closer together, and when we put up the leaves it was about twenty-eight inches in diameter. First I looked underneath it, just to make sure the medium hadn't managed to attach any wires. Then we all put our hands on top of it.

The medium asked a question, "Is anyone here tonight?"

She had explained that one tap of the table leg meant yes, and two taps meant no. After a few moments, I felt one leg of the table move a bit, making a weak little sound.

The medium asked, "Who are you?" and was about to start going through the alphabet . . . apparently the table leg lifts when you get to the right letter, as it spells out a word. But she didn't have to go far, because it moved at *A*.

My voice was shaking as I asked, "Are you a woman?"

The leg weakly tapped once.

I said, "Are you my grandmother Anna?"

More forcefully the leg tapped yes. That's when I thought, *Ay yai yai, I don't like this.* I got scared and ran into the bathroom. As I was hiding in there, I heard a louder sound. The whole table was thumping.

I popped my head out. The medium was listing letters again, and the legs lifted on *M* . . . *A* . . . *N* . . .

Shelly said, "Manny?"

How did that table know my father's nickname? By now I had stepped back in the room and was gradually creeping closer. I heard the medium ask, "Do you have a message for anyone?"

And the table began to spell *B* . . . *A* . . .

The medium said, "Barbra?"

Then she asked, "What is the message to Barbra?"

The table was spelling *S* . . . *O* . . . *R* . . . *R* . . .

I think my brother was the first to guess the word: "Sorry?"

Oh my God. I couldn't believe it. If you had to think of one word that I was waiting to hear, all my life, from my father . . .

You couldn't make this up. If somehow the medium was putting words into my father's mouth, she would probably have had him say something more generic, like "I love you" or "I'm always with you." But instead he said, "Sorry."

It was staggering.

The lady asked, "Anything more?"

And then the leg started to pound again, and spelled out *S . . . I . . . N . . . G . . . P . . . R . . . O . . . U . . . D*. By now the legs were thumping so fast that I took my hands off the table. And my brother, who just had both hands resting lightly on it, wasn't holding it or pushing it as he followed it across the room. At one point a leg got caught on the threshold and he had to help it over. And then the table came back to where the medium and I were sitting. It moved back and forth between my brother and me, very slowly. And then it stopped.

Nobody said a word.

It was the scariest thing I've ever seen. I know it sounds unbelievable, but it's the fucking truth. And I never wanted to repeat the experience.

As soon as the medium left, I went upstairs to Shelly's bedroom. I was shaking. I sat down on his bed and called my best friends, Cis and Harvey. Harvey answered the phone, and I told him what just happened.

He said, "I don't believe it."

"But I just witnessed it!!"

"I don't believe in that stuff."

"What stuff?"

I felt helpless, as if nothing I could say would change his mind. I think my relationship with Harvey changed a little from that moment on. "Let me talk to Cis," I told him. When she, too, said, "Frankly, I find it hard to believe," I was disappointed. "Well," I told her, "I probably wouldn't have believed it either. But I'm here . . . I saw it with my own eyes . . . I heard it. That message was for me."

The fact is, I saw that table bang out those words and I felt the presence of my father telling me he was sorry he left me . . . and that had a profound effect. In some way it released me from the anger I had felt. And on my way home to Los Angeles on the plane, I began reading a paper my father had written, which Shelly had only given me now because I had never asked for it before.

Earlier I had read my father's master's thesis . . . a psychological analysis of the interactions between my mother and her three-year-old son, as she tried to get him to eat. Titled "The Case of Sheldon," it was keenly observed and almost like a play, reproducing their dialogue and ending each section with a summation of what she had done wrong and how her behavior was not conducive to the results she wanted. Very logical, so astute, and still relevant, even though it was written in 1938.

It made me really miss my father, which is probably why I never wanted to read this other paper until now. It was about how he used great writers like Shakespeare and Ibsen and brilliant poets like Byron and Keats to teach English to prisoners and juvenile delinquents. I felt so connected to him. I wanted to play Juliet and Hedda Gabler, and here he was, writing about these same plays that I used to read as a teenager in the Forty-Second Street library.

I did some of his sample tests, matching authors to their works. Imagine if I had grown up with a father like that. I would probably have gone to college . . . perhaps become a teacher, like him.

A week after my visit with Shelly, I opened a package of photos he had sent, and saw something that astonished me. It was the name on the tombstone next to my father's.

It wasn't Irving or Murray, the kind of name you'd expect to see in a Jewish cemetery. It was Anshel. Now that's not a common name. You don't meet many Anshels these days. In fact, the only time I had seen it was in Singer's short story, where it's the name of Yentl's dead uncle. (I changed it to her dead brother in the movie.) And when she disguises herself as a man, it's the name she adopts.

I was stunned. This was the sign I was looking for, telling me that I was meant to make this movie. Here I was, exploring all the ideas that could be part of *Yentl*, and discovering my father at the same time. He was in love with learning, too, just like Yentl. They were made of the same cloth. So was I.

His life was cut short, and in a sense, this was my chance to extend it. In order to play this part, I would have to put on the clothes of a man and become my father, in a way. He would live on in me, and in Yentl.

I now knew I would make this film.

But how? The major studios weren't interested. They wanted a Barbra Streisand movie, but to them that meant a musical, preferably, or at least a comedy. And this definitely didn't qualify.

Funny how things come full circle. I started singing in nightclubs because I couldn't get a job in the movies, and now it looked like the only way I could get this movie made was if I sang in it.

Of course that idea had already occurred to me. Over all the years I was pitching this story, every studio executive asked if I was going to sing, because in that case, they might be interested. At first I said no, because I wanted to prove myself as an actress, and later, even when Marilyn and Alan Bergman also suggested making it a musical, I was still less than enthusiastic. I was trying to be a director for the first time, and that was not how I saw this story. But now the message from my father . . . "Sing proud" . . . was echoing in my head.

I met with Eric Pleskow and my friend Mike Medavoy at Orion, an upstart studio that needed to ramp up a slate of films, fast . . . and they were more receptive to the story, and to me. When they asked if I was going to sing in it, I hesitated before I heard myself saying . . . "Yes."

It felt as if all the gods were pushing me in that direction, and at that point, in my mind, *Yentl* officially became a musical, or as I prefer to call it, a film with music. And when I explained that the script was still in process, Mike even encouraged me to write it myself. I had already worked on several drafts with other writers, but never thought of myself as qualified enough. Could I really write this?

I had to. I had no choice. I couldn't describe the movie I had in my head to yet another writer, who wouldn't capture my vision. I knew what I wanted, and the only way to get it was to put it down on paper myself. And Orion offered me a development deal.

I left that meeting totally energized, and as soon as I got home I called Marilyn and Alan and said, "Well, I guess we better start thinking about music!"

We began to discuss the possibilities. Once you had people opening their mouths to sing, it would automatically enhance the fairy-tale aspect of the story. But I didn't want to completely lose the realism. I certainly didn't see it as a conventional musical . . . that word seemed inappropriate for this material, which was too intimate and intense.

It was only when we let go of convention that we hit on something that made sense. The idea grew naturally out of the character. As soon as Yentl dressed in men's clothing and took on this whole other identity, she could no longer speak freely. She was hiding a secret. Her thoughts had to remain inside her head. So what if we had her express those thoughts in voice-over . . . not in speech, but in song?

The idea seemed obvious and felt completely right to all three of us. Only when Yentl was alone could she sing out loud (and at the end, when she feels liberated, on the boat to America). But otherwise, when she was with other people, the music would only be inside her mind . . . almost like a stream of consciousness in song.

This wasn't the first time I had used that technique. Remember when we were filming *Funny Girl*, I wanted to do my part in the "You Are Woman, I Am Man" duet in voice-over. Why would Fanny be singing her private thoughts out loud, when Nick Arnstein was right there, trying to seduce her? I was always trying to make things more realistic.

To have Yentl singing in voice-over felt true to me, in the same way.

But if we were faithful to that concept, it meant that none of the other characters could sing. I wasn't sure about that. How would people respond if the only person singing was me? I didn't want to be accused of being on some ego trip.

Marilyn and Alan told me to stop worrying. They were convinced that this was the perfect solution . . . a way to add music that grew organically out of the story and still retained its intimacy.

So there would be none of those generic movie moments when the happy villagers burst into song. Good, I thought, because I had no interest in doing a traditional musical with big production numbers, and I didn't want traditional Jewish music either. *Fiddler on the Roof* had already been there and done that. I wanted a score that felt more contemporary . . . music that couldn't be pinned down to a certain culture or period . . . music that people could relate to because it would feel timeless and universal.

Now, who would write the music? And the three of us just looked at one another and said, "Michel." Michel Legrand was our close friend, and he felt like part of the family.

So I had the lyricists and the composer. Now I just had to come up with the script.

I reread all the old versions and then set them aside. None of them matched the movie I saw in my head. I started writing an outline and as I was jotting down a quick description of each scene, I was thinking about Yentl's emotions. Where would it feel right for her to express them in song? How could I use that song to advance the plot? And then I gave the outline to the Bergmans and Michel and we worked out the details together.

In the first scenes I wanted to establish the fact that Yentl has no interest in traditional women's tasks. She would go to the market to buy a fish, but then she wouldn't bother to pick out a good one, like the other women. She lets the fishmonger do it for her because she's distracted by the bookseller's call and wants to look at what he's brought. When he tells her that she can't read the one she wants, she asks, "Why? Where is it written?"

And then we'd see her reading the book, while she's supposed to be preparing the Shabbat dinner . . . and burning the fish . . . while her father is giving a lesson. He asks his student a question, and Yentl can't resist blurting out the answer (just like me). After the young man leaves, I imagined her talking to her father about her frustration. She's no good at all these womanly tasks and would rather be reading.

In the story, Singer writes that her father said she had the soul of a man, because she was such an apt pupil.

Yentl asks, "So why was I born a woman?"

Her father answers, "Even Heaven makes mistakes."

It's a great line, but it wasn't my Yentl. I don't think heaven made a mistake in this case. Just because she was smart and wanted to study didn't mean she had the soul of a man. That struck me as a bit misogynistic . . . and I had been told Singer was a misogynist himself. And then some people have interpreted the story to mean that Yentl actually thinks of herself as a man, trapped in a woman's body. But for the story I wanted to tell, she never wanted to change genders . . . she just wanted to go to school! She's simply a woman who wanted an education . . . love . . . a full life.

In any event I thought this was the moment for a song that would express her longing and frustration, and Marilyn and Alan came up with the wonderful lyric to "Where Is It Written?" Yentl is questioning, Where is it written . . .

that I can't dare to have the chance to pick the fruit of every tree
Or have my share of every sweet-imagined possibility . . .

After she sets off on her own in her first journey as a man, I envisioned her alone in a forest, in the dark of night, in the throes of fear. She needs to talk to her father, so she should sing to him. And Michel composed the hauntingly beautiful "Papa, Can You Hear Me?" and the Bergmans wrote the perfect lyrics.

That was such a creative time . . . exciting, stimulating, gratifying. There were so many possibilities! It was as if every idea from one person sparked another idea from someone else. We could say anything, without second-guessing ourselves. It's wonderful to work that way . . . with no ego. It was a true collaboration. In one of our first meetings, I was so exhilarated that I said, "Can we stay in this room and never leave until it's over?"

One morning at the ranch, a friend was telling me about serving huevos rancheros to her husband for breakfast and I thought, *Boy, I wish someone would do that for me.* Wouldn't it be great to have a wife like that? (Since I don't cook.)

I told Marilyn and Alan about it, and they took the idea and wrote a clever set of lyrics for "No Wonder":

No wonder he loves her . . .
Before he even knows that he's hungry, she's already there with his plate
Before his glass is even empty, she's filling it up, God forbid he should wait!

We were all happy to be working together. Once Michel had a melody, the Bergmans would write a lyric, and then they would call me up and say, "Come over. We want you to listen to something." Michel would sit down at their piano and play it for me, and then I'd take the page of lyrics and sing it for the first time. And we would record it on my dinky little Sony tape recorder that always had the best sound. And Marilyn would always have the most delicious homemade cookies for me to munch on, with tea and dainty English sandwiches.

Then I'd go back to my house, and no matter how late it was, I'd be drawn to my desk to take another look at the script. Yentl wants to study the Talmud. How do you make that feel exciting on film? I wanted to know what kinds of concepts she would be grappling with, and quickly realized how little I knew about Judaism. My religious education had basically stopped at the age of nine, when I left the Yeshiva of Brooklyn and enrolled at P.S. 89.

Like Yentl . . . there was so much I wanted to learn.

I *love* doing research. I got totally immersed . . . watching documentaries . . . poring over book after book, examining pictures of Polish Jews from the period to see what kinds of clothes they wore and how their houses looked.

And I talked to various scholars. One was a young Orthodox rabbi from South Africa who presided over a little shul down on the Venice boardwalk. When I first met Daniel Lapin, he shook my hand. I was surprised. I thought a rabbi was not supposed to touch a woman's hand unless he was married to her, according to Orthodox law. So I asked him, "How come you did that?" And he said, "A more important component of the law is kindness. You should never embarrass someone or make them feel bad." I liked his attitude and I liked him. Daniel was also a mathematician who could be very metaphysical . . . and that combination of the concrete and the abstract always intrigues me. He told me that 4 (one of my favorite numbers) has a special symbolism that may derive from the four basic elements, the four seasons, the four points of the compass, the four sides of the square, the four corners of the world, the four questions, the four matriarchs, and the four promises God makes in the covenant. He also said that it's the most creative number in the universe. With four fours, he explained how you can make any number, starting with basic arithmetic and then moving on to more sophisticated calculations using square roots, exponents, and factorials.

I learned in yeshiva that every letter in the Hebrew language has a numerical value: Alef is 1, Bet is 2, and so on, until the number 10. (Then you start going up by tens.) And the numbers can relate to the meaning of a word.

For example, in Orthodox Jewish law the firstborn son is entitled to double the inheritance of any other child. Therefore the word for firstborn is made up of the letter that is number 10 and the letter that is number 20 (which is double the number 10).

Brilliant!

Jason began studying with Rabbi Lapin for his bar mitzvah, and I started meeting with him as well, to ask various questions that came up as I was working on the script. When I learned that the Jewish day school connected with the shul was about to close, I gave them a donation to keep it open, and they named it after my father, in thanks.

But one rabbi was never going to be enough for me. I always like to have different points of view. Marilyn and Alan recommended a rabbi named Laura Geller.

A female rabbi?

Terrific! That was just what I needed. Laura was a living, breathing version of Yentl . . . a contemporary pioneer as the first female rabbi on the West Coast. When we met, I thought she was astute and insightful, as well as gentle and soft-spoken. And she had a very inclusive attitude, which was typical of the rabbis I knew. They would never say, "I'm going to teach you." Instead they'd take a more humble approach and say, "Let's learn together." Laura and I talked about all sorts of issues. But since I needed to know what it was like to go to an all-male yeshiva, and she had never had that experience, she put me in touch with a friend of hers, Rabbi Chaim Seidler-Feller. He was charming, funny, and warm. But what really endeared him to me was that he had taken his wife's name and added it to his own when they married. He was a feminist *and* a rabbi . . . my kind of guy!

So now I had three rabbis to consult whenever I had a question: Rabbi Lapin, who was more conservative; Rabbi Geller, who was Reform; and Rabbi Seidler-Feller, who represented a Modern Orthodox approach.

Since I wanted to know exactly what yeshiva students do, I told them, "I'd like to learn some Talmud." Chaim thought we could start by reading some passages from the Torah . . . which corresponds to the first five books of the Bible . . . and discuss them, just as a yeshiva boy would do with his teacher. If you're very Orthodox, you probably believe that God dictated the Torah to Moses. Then various scholars have interpreted these books, and that became the Talmud. It's thousands of pages long, with many volumes organized around specific themes. The basic text, with commentaries, was completed in the sixth century, and then other scholars commented on the commentaries, so on one page you might find notes from the sixth and the twelfth and the fourteenth centuries, all interpreting the same passage! It's kind of fascinating, as if you're having a conversation across eras.

It reminds me of the way lawyers and scholars have been studying the Constitution of the United States and citing certain passages in various court cases. The questions raised are universal, but the answers are open to interpretation. For example, the Second Amendment says: "A well regulated militia, being necessary to the security of a free state, the right of the people to keep and bear arms, shall not be infringed." Today we're still debating what that sentence means. Does it refer just to an organized militia, or to private citizens, when it comes to walking around with guns?

When the Constitution was written, it took time to load a gun, which could fire only one shot at a time. Now we have assault weapons that can fire dozens of bullets in a few seconds. Should individuals be allowed to carry those?

But that's a whole other subject. Point is, it's still being argued. It's a debate that would interest a Talmudic scholar.

But the Talmud doesn't necessarily settle an issue, like a court of law. In fact, when discussing the different opinions of two rabbis, the Talmud often says both are right. Both are expressing the words of the living God and both are divinely inspired, even though they may contradict each other. The Talmud doesn't resolve the contradictions. It simply states them. And it's up to you to figure it out.

Of course, only men were permitted to study the Talmud in Yentl's time, so you can imagine how radical it was for her to be familiar with it. That's why she had to close the shutters when she and her father would read and discuss the text. It was not only a violation of the law. It was scandalous.

As Yentl says to her father, she envies the students who were "talking about life, the mysteries of the universe. And I'm learning how to tell a herring from a carp."

"Yentl," he answers, "for the thousandth time, men and women have different obligations."

"I know, but—"

"And don't ask why."

And then he relents and tells her, "Go on. Get the books."

So what started with me asking a few questions suddenly grew into a whole new fascination with the Talmud. I could trace the origins of various customs, like the rule of keeping two sets of dishes, one for meat and one for dairy, in an Orthodox household. The basis for that is actually very practical, because the juices of the meat carried bacteria, and it was more sanitary to keep the plates separate so as not to contaminate the other food.

A kosher butcher will slaughter an animal very quickly with a sharp knife, before it even realizes what is happening. And we now know that the adrenaline released by a frightened animal is bad for us to eat, so that was not only compassionate but also had a scientific basis.

Jews are not supposed to eat pork. And I'll bet that was practical, too, because pigs eat all kinds of garbage . . . and pork that's not cooked properly can give you trichinosis. But I happen to love pork, and when I was taking acting classes in Manhattan, I'd often go to the German deli and buy a pork sandwich with mayonnaise on white bread, to eat on the train. It was so *goyishe*! The yeshiva *bucher* (kid) in me always felt guilty. But when I was told about a certain commentary in the Talmud, it kind of relieved me. It said, "If a Jew is put in prison and forced to eat pork . . . Enjoy it!"

Now that's the kind of attitude I can relate to!

I studied with Chaim and Laura at my house, and sometimes we met in Marilyn and Alan's living room so they could be part of the discussion as well. I missed my chance to go to college, and I've often regretted it. This was my opportunity to indulge my love of learning, which is probably embedded in my DNA.

The writer Leo Rosten said something that has always stayed with me: "Knowledge, among Jews, came to compensate for worldly rewards. Insight, I think, became a substitute for weapons: one way to block the bully's wrath is to know him better than he knows himself."

It's so true. Jews were not taught to fight. Instead they were taught to be astute observers of human nature in order to outsmart their enemies . . . maybe that's why so many Jews became psychiatrists. And when the pogroms came and they were thrown out of their homes and their countries, knowledge was the one possession that could not be taken away.

I remember one moment in the study group that turned out to be pivotal for me. We were discussing Genesis, chapter 2, verse 21, where it says that God put Adam into a deep sleep and then took one of his ribs and made a woman out of it. But as Chaim explained, there is one commentary that says the Hebrew word usually translated as "rib" . . . *tzela* . . . may be more accurately translated as "side." In fact, that word occurs in only one other place in the five books of the Torah, and there it clearly means the side of a temple. I thought Rabbi Lapin, being Orthodox, would stick to the more traditional interpretation, but even he told me that the word probably meant "side."

But the King James Version of the Bible clearly says "rib."

Could the passage about Adam's rib have been mistranslated all these years?

That was mind-blowing. Look at what a difference one word can make! A rib seems such a small, insignificant part of a man . . . you could easily live without it. But if Eve was actually made out of Adam's side, that's a whole new concept. It instantly elevates her to be his equal. She's his other half.

That made so much more sense to me. I thought, *This is what Jewish scholars do* . . . they sit there and reinterpret the Torah. And they're still quibbling about it . . . "God-wrestling," they call it . . . even after centuries have gone by. I love that great Jewish tradition of questioning everything. The truth is arguable, even among the most learned. There's an old saying that goes "Ask two Jews, get three opinions."

I was fascinated with the question of rib versus side, and I wrote it into the film, as one of the Talmudic discussions between Yentl and Avigdor, who is a student she meets at an inn. He wants her to come study at his yeshiva, boasting that his rabbi is the best. But before she can get in, she has to be examined by the rabbi. When I wrote that scene, I remembered something that another rabbi I consulted said to me: "I know a good student by his questions . . . not his answers." I love that concept.

And that prompted this exchange: As Yentl is leaving the rabbi's study, he says, "He asks a lot of questions, this one."

Yentl apologizes. "Sorry. I've been told that before."

The rabbi says, "It's by their questions that we choose our students, not only by their answers. Your father taught you well, Anshel. Welcome to our yeshiva."

Then he assigns Avigdor to be her study partner, because he recognizes that she's very bright, and Avigdor is the best student at the yeshiva. Finally she has somebody to argue with who's on her level, like her father.

And I wrote a scene where she and Avigdor are walking by the river, past a flock of sheep, and debating that passage about Adam and Eve.

She says, "You're wrong, Avigdor. It's a mistranslation. The Hebrew word for rib never meant rib, it meant side."

He says, "Rib . . . side . . . what's the difference?"

"All the difference in the world! Since Adam was created both male and female—"

"Where is that written?"

"Genesis, chapter five, verse two. And if God took one side of Adam and not his rib and created woman, that means they're the same! We all are. Everybody is. Don't you see?"

"What I see is you've never been with a woman."

"What I mean is that they share masculine and feminine qualities since they come from the same source."

That was also news to me . . . that Adam was not gendered, or rather, he was two genders, both male and female originally. And the creation of Eve involved splitting him in two, into a man and a woman. Chaim explained that the concept probably has its origin in the myth of the androgyne, a creature who was both male and female and had two faces. I thought that was such a compelling idea . . . the divine androgyny of the soul . . . and it became fundamental to the script I was writing.

But Avigdor isn't buying Yentl's argument. And to illustrate that, I put two women . . . one of them breastfeeding a baby . . . into the scene.

Avigdor says, "Look, can you do that?"

"What?"

"Create life . . . give birth to sons? When you can do that, then tell me we're the same."

This is what drew me to Singer's story . . . the way Yentl is always asking questions, challenging the rules.

And who made those rules anyway? Men.

And some of those men have promoted a very selective version of the truth. One of the great revelations for me was the fact that the Talmud doesn't prohibit women from studying. It simply says that women are not *obliged* to study. So where is it written that women should not read certain books? Or must cut off their hair when they marry? Or refrain from singing?

Guess what? It's *not* written. God is fair. It's man who is not. And the chauvinists have selectively picked out whatever they could find in all the writings and interpreted it in such a way as to give themselves the authority to subjugate women. They wanted to keep women in their place, which, as far as they were concerned, meant the kitchen and the bedroom.

Yentl won't settle for that.

As I worked on the script, I was constantly jotting down notes to myself in my journal:

> *Yentl is about taking risks—venturing out—looking around to see more than a piece of sky* [*which became the title of the last song*].

> *Pursuit of a dream to study—Avigdor almost intrudes on it—by her falling in love with him—he's physical. She's not—he's sexual—she's not—yet! He's a scholar, like her father—complications!*

They meet at an inn—and part at an inn.

Yentl meets Avigdor's beloved, Hadass—Yentl is not the only woman in his life—she shares him—she's not too thrilled.

Swimming hole—feels sexual attraction—it's a new intrusion—physical passion.

There are so many details that you have to get right when you're doing a period film. I had big questions . . . is Yentl Hasidic? After visiting a Hasidic community in Brooklyn where they were even more unwelcoming than Singer . . . they would barely talk to me . . . I decided she wouldn't be. These people were ultraconservative, and I don't think that kind of fundamentalism is a good thing in any religion. It was a closed society . . . they didn't watch movies, they didn't listen to records, and they viewed any outsider with suspicion. I thought they would be warm and friendly, but instead they felt utterly foreign to me, and I'm sure I felt utterly foreign to them. They lived by a code of Jewish law that was far too rigid for the character I was creating.

So that was one big question answered. And I had little questions too . . . like what kind of fish would be for sale at the market? Would they wrap it in newspaper? And what would she use to carry it home . . . some kind of shopping bag?

The people at the YIVO Institute for Jewish Research were a huge help. They told me that the fish would probably be pike or carp. It would be wrapped in brown paper, not newspaper, because they were unlikely to have newspapers in a poor village. And she would carry it home in a basket.

I kept writing, and then I would reread my pages. I was worried . . . was the dialogue good enough? I needed a second opinion.

So I called Paddy Chayefsky, the brilliant author of *Marty*, *The Hospital*, and *Network*. I had sent him a note after I saw *Network*, telling him how much I admired his screenplay, and we became friends. Back in 1977, I asked him to read that early script written by Ivan Passer and Jerome Kass. Paddy was blunt and wrote back, "It's not a good script." He thought it should be more of a supernatural story, like *The Dybbuk*, and said, "Stop thinking of Yentl as a healthy, robust young woman who happens to want to be a Talmudic scholar. Either as a realistic or grotesque film, she is a pale, driven, haunted girl."

That was probably closer to Singer's conception of the character. In his story, Yentl laughs almost maniacally after she proposes to Hadass. She is planning to "exact vengeance for Avigdor . . . It was as if she had sealed a pact with Satan, the Evil One."

Rereading those lines now, I think, *Yikes.* I didn't like Singer's misogynistic streak. He clearly thought of Yentl as demonic. And I didn't agree with Paddy either. I didn't see her as a haunted girl, but as a normal, healthy woman, who wanted the same things from life that I did. And as for her marriage . . . well, people do crazy things for love. My Yentl marries Hadass only because she desperately wants to keep Avigdor close to her. There's no malice in it.

And on her wedding night in my script, Yentl uses her wits to get through a very sticky situation. She's hoping Hadass is scared, and tells her, "According to the Talmud, a woman has the right to refuse her husband." When that doesn't work, she says, "It's very clearly written that a woman cannot give herself to one man while she's still thinking of another," even as Hadass is telling her she isn't. Finally, Yentl manages to hold her off with humor and generous helpings of wine.

Singer's concept of the night was very different. He wrote, "Anshel had found a way to deflower the bride." And when Hadass's mother and her friends rush in the next morning to examine the sheets, he describes how happy they are to find traces of blood. That was way too clinical for me, and I didn't want the audience to go off on a tangent, speculating about how that could happen. Remember, I thought of this as a realistic fairy tale, and that violated the fairy-tale quality by going too far with the realism.

I can only be true to my own vision and not someone else's . . . even if it came from a great writer like Singer or Paddy.

That's why I was nervous when I called Paddy to ask if he would mind reading my first draft. "Just let me know if I'm going in the right direction."

I was afraid he would hate it, since my Yentl was nothing like his concept. I still remember exactly where I was when my assistant called to say Paddy had read the script and wanted to talk to me about it. I was sitting in Cis and Harvey's bedroom, and I immediately called him back. My hand was shaking as I held the phone.

He said, "I'm very impressed. This is good. I love the characters. I love the story. You're a writer."

I'll never forget that.

Thank God he liked it. I felt as if I had been blessed.

And then, just over a year later, I was sitting with Cis in the waiting room at Columbia-Presbyterian Hospital while Harvey was undergoing heart surgery. All of a sudden there was a flurry of activity. A gurney was being rushed into the operating room, and somebody said it was Paddy Chayefsky.

I felt awful . . . Harvey was coming out of surgery, and Paddy was going in. As it turned out, Harvey would live, and Paddy would die . . . way too young, only fifty-eight years old. The last time I spoke to him he was coughing, and I asked, "Are you all right?"

"Yeah," he said, "I have pleurisy."

He never mentioned that he had lung cancer.

I was also lucky enough to know Bo Goldman, who wrote the screenplay for *One Flew Over the Cuckoo's Nest*. After he read my first draft, he wrote back, "I love what you've done. It is alive, it lives, full of vitality, and most important, you've got the character of Yentl. The strange duality of her nature, the mercurial and the logical . . . just keep going."

These two men whom I so admired gave me the encouragement I needed.

It was a crucial decision to think of Yentl as a normal, healthy woman who was falling in love for the first time. I felt everyone could relate to that. And in our study sessions, I was discovering all these intriguing tidbits about the Jewish religion and sex.

For example, the Hebrew words for "man" and "woman" each have three letters. Two letters are the same in both words, and those letters spell "fire." I thought, how interesting. Fire could be interpreted as passion, and that's what a man and woman need to have between them in order to have a great marriage.

Then there is one remaining letter in the word for "man" that's different from the one remaining letter in the word for "woman," and if you put them together . . . they spell "God."

So that could mean that when a man and a woman come together in love, it's sacred. Or to say it another way, you need both passion and spirituality to make a more perfect union. We all want to have a soul connection with our mates . . . as well as physical passion.

When we read the Song of Solomon, I was moved by the beauty of the language and the lush descriptions . . . "Thy two breasts . . . Thy lips . . ." It's all about sex, and it's presented so openly and naturally. Clearly it's nothing to be ashamed of. As Chaim pointed out, you could even say it's the way in which we come closest to God's own act of creation.

What a healthy and loving attitude to sex! And that's how the Talmud treats it as well, with great respect. In fact, it's considered a blessing. On the Sabbath you're not supposed to work, cook, travel, or spend money . . . but you're supposed to make love!

Some rabbis discouraged the study of the more mystical texts of the Kabbalah until a man was over forty, married, and with children of his own, preferably. In other words, he had to be a mature, sexual human being. And Jewish law states that a husband must provide his wife with food, clothing, and sex. It's also very specific about her right to sexual satisfaction, which is surprising in a patriarchal society.

I was so amazed by one particular commentary, written hundreds of years ago by the scholar Nachmanides, that I had to work it into the film. It concerns how a husband should behave to his wife, so I had Avigdor whisper it to Yentl just after she's married Hadass:

> *Speak words which arouse her to love, desire, and passion . . . and words of reverence for God. Never force her. Her mood must be as yours. Win her with graciousness and seductiveness. Be patient until her passion is aroused. Begin with love, and when her mood is ready, let her desire be satisfied first. Her delight is what matters.*

Initially I thought, *How lovely and generous . . . he wants her to have an orgasm first!* And then I realized there was actually a very practical motive behind this advice. It would make it easier for her to get pregnant. Those little spermatozoa will have a smoother ride up to the egg! (So this Nachmanides really knew his biology.) Since the survival of the Jews was always being threatened, this kind of generosity would actually help propagate the race!

As fascinated as I was with all these ideas from the Talmud, I had to let many of them go and just focus on what I needed to tell the story. Likewise only a tiny bit of my research ended up in the film. Still, I had to understand the process of learning in a yeshiva . . . the way students argued a point . . . how they sway when they read. And I swear that knowledge comes through to the audience.

My script was in a constant state of flux. Lines would come out and go back in, only to be replaced by something else entirely. I never considered it done, because I always thought it could be better.

That's why I've always liked that Leonardo da Vinci quote. He said, "Art is never finished. Only abandoned."

After months of basically being locked in a room with the script, I had cabin fever. And that's when I got a call from Sue Mengers. She wanted me to take over Lisa Eichhorn's role in the film Sue's husband, Jean-Claude Tramont, was making, *All Night Long.* I had already read that script and turned it down, because I was focused on *Yentl* and had no particular urge to play a ditzy blond suburban housewife. But now Sue was practically begging me. She didn't want Jean-Claude's movie to fall apart. And she promised that she could get me a deal that was more lucrative than any actor, male or female, had ever had. (They must have *really* needed me.) I did like the idea of achieving that milestone for women. And I would be playing opposite Gene Hackman, whom I loved as an actor (I also thought he was sexy). Plus, this character was different than anything else I'd ever done. She had dreams of being a singer and a songwriter, but she had no talent.

I had passed on doing a similar role for Martin Scorsese, which I've always regretted, so this time I said yes. Frankly, I was desperate to take a break from writing every day, and thought I could look at my script with more objectivity when I came back. I also felt bad for Sue, who was trying to help her husband keep his job. I had always sensed that Jean-Claude resented all the attention she gave me, and in some way I suppose I was trying to make it up to him. Besides, it was only twenty-four days of work, so it wouldn't be too much of a commitment.

Now I needed to do some work on this character. How does she look, dress, sound? So I put on a blond wig, some tacky clothes, and the kind of costume jewelry I thought she might wear to check out the kind of place she might go to . . . a country-western bar in the Valley. As soon as I walked through the door, someone said, "Hi, Barbra!"

I thought, *Great. So much for that disguise, and now they'll think I dyed my hair and have lousy taste in clothes!*

I started filming in June 1980, and then in July the Screen Actors Guild went out on strike. Production was halted when we only had a few days left to shoot. Everyone was in limbo until the strike was settled.

This delay was not part of my plan, but I made the most of it and went back to work on *Yentl.* I had to decide where we would shoot, and Eastern Europe was the obvious choice. Jon had delegated a member of his staff, Rusty Lemorande, to work with me. So I sent him off on a recce (scouting trip) to check out Hungary, Poland, Yugoslavia, Czechoslovakia, and Romania. He was to meet with local production people and photograph possible locations. When he came back and showed me his slides, I got excited. There were streets in the old parts of Prague and Budapest that were exactly what I envisioned.

In September 1980 I made my own trip, first flying to Paris with Marilyn and Alan to work on the music with Michel, at his house in the countryside. Then I wanted to visit the locations that I had picked from the slides. Rusty, Cis, and I flew to Budapest, where there's an amazing Moorish-style synagogue . . . the largest in Europe, built in 1859. I met a wonderful rabbi who took me to his study, lined with shelves filled with beautiful old books, and that became the model for the rabbi's study where Yentl is examined to see if she will be admitted to the yeshiva.

But most of my favorite scouting shots had come from Czechoslovakia, and Prague was the city I really wanted to see. We decided to drive from Budapest. I like to play games on car trips to pass the time, and I taught Rusty the rules of Ghost, so he could play with Cis and me. It was the dead of night when we arrived at the border crossing. Two guards approached our car. After a brief discussion with the driver and a look into the car, they took our passports and vanished into their guard shack. And then we sat . . . and sat . . . a lot of time was passing, but we still weren't cleared to leave.

I was starting to get scared. After all, Hungary and Czechoslovakia were still Communist countries . . . there were soldiers with Kalashnikovs on the street corners. My imagination was suddenly working overtime. Could we be arrested?

Rusty eventually got out and made a trip to the shack to see if something could be done to help this process along.

Apparently not.

He returned, and said we'd just have to wait. Various people came out to peer at us, including a woman, at one point . . . but the gate stayed down and it wasn't opening.

Then we saw the guards approaching again. Was this it? Were we all going to be locked up?

No. They were just returning our passports. After another brief discussion with the driver and a long, last look into the car, we were finally free to go. As soon as we were through the checkpoint, I tapped the driver on the shoulder.

"What was that all about? Why did they stop us?"

It turns out that it wasn't much of a mystery after all. One of the guards had recognized me, and then of course he saw my name on my passport. When he went inside the office, he told everyone else. They all came out to get a look at me, and one guy apparently called up his wife and said, "You won't believe who's here . . . Barbra Streisandova! And if you want to see her, get in the car right now and come to the station!"

In Prague I wandered through the old city for hours with my interpreter, Mila Radova, who was wearing high heels as she walked over the cobblestones. I asked, "Isn't that uncomfortable?" She said, "No, I'm used to it." But I was concerned for her, and had a pair of shoes like I was wearing . . . wedgies with thick rubber soles . . . sent over from America. She loved those shoes, and from that moment, we were friends for life.

I loved Mila and I also had a visceral response to the place. It immediately felt right . . . and familiar. I would be walking down a narrow street and say to her, "This looks just like a photograph from one of my books. I think I've seen this street before. Let's walk around the corner . . ." And sure enough, we were suddenly in the heart of the Jewish quarter, with its old-fashioned storefronts. One of them became Peshe's bakery. It was perfect, with peeling green paint and a Jewish name carved in the stone above the door. I went back to Los Angeles totally encouraged.

My head was completely into *Yentl*, but then I had to switch gears when the actors' strike was settled at the end of October and pick up where we had left off on *All Night Long*. I wasn't looking forward to that. It already felt as if I had done that role a lifetime ago. Put it this way, it was a mistake to take this part. And I was very disappointed in Sue. I had a lot of problems with the script and had given the writer notes, which he seemed to agree with, but the rewrites Sue promised were never done.

Then one day in the midst of shooting, I suddenly felt this gush, worse than the heaviest period I'd ever had. I had been dealing with endometriosis and had to go to the hospital for a D and C. I vividly remember the nurse coming into my room to give me a pill or something, and she told me they'd be coming shortly to take me to the operating room. I was already getting woozy when they slid me onto a gurney and wheeled me into the elevator. I began to feel disembodied, as if I were watching myself from above. I wanted to get up and leave but I couldn't move. (It reminded me of the clinic scene in *Up the Sandbox.*)

Then the anesthesiologist explained he would be inserting a tube down my throat "through your vocal cords, but we'll be extra careful with you."

Great. Why did he have to tell me that? Now I was even more scared. Besides, I would hope they were extra careful with everyone! I was beginning to drift off, yet fighting to stay in control as he was going on and on about my concert in Central Park.

And then the next thing I knew was the tightness of a blood pressure cuff on my arm, and people were waking me up.

A couple of days later I was back on the set. That's when someone showed me an advance copy of the print ads for the film, and I was appalled. It was a cartoon drawing of me with my skirt hiked up, sliding down a fireman's pole, which completely misrepresented the film and made it seem like a slapstick comedy. (The same mistake had been made on *Up the Sandbox*, which had a drawing of me tied to a baby bottle.)

Besides, I only had a small part, but this made me look like the star.

I felt totally betrayed and told Sue, "This is misleading. I'm not the star of this movie, and I don't want first billing. It's Gene's story, and he's the star." They finally changed my billing, but they didn't change the drawing. This is why I've always wanted control, even over my image, but Sue neglected to put that in the contract.

It was very upsetting to think that I couldn't rely on her for basic oversight. But I had to face something even more fundamental, which I had overlooked for too long . . . I just couldn't trust her judgment. She hated *Yentl* and had been trying to talk me out of it for years. She would make snide remarks about it at dinner parties right in front of me. It was painful when Sue wouldn't support me. Once I had to tell her, "I can't talk to you because you sound like my mother. You're so critical and I don't need that from you. I do it on my own." So to hear her dismiss *Yentl* played into all my insecurities.

And even more disconcerting, she had developed a kind of symbiotic relationship with me, to the extent that she seemed to confuse herself with me and would speak for me, without my permission. And I was furious to find out that she had turned down projects without even showing me the scripts. (One of them was *Splash*. Years later on a plane, Brian Grazer, who produced it, told me I was his first choice for the female lead. But Sue told him the role didn't have enough lines. How ridiculous! I don't judge a part based on the number of lines!)

It was time for a serious conversation, so I called Sue. "You know," I told her, "you tried to talk me out of *Yentl*. Then you talked me into this movie. We just don't have the same taste in material. I think I need a different agent . . . but of course we'll still be friends."

There was silence for a moment, and then she said, "If I'm not your agent, I won't be your friend."

I was stunned. That was very hurtful. Was I just a meal ticket to her? I thought our relationship was primarily personal. She, too, had a critical mother . . . very negative . . . and we first bonded over that. And she had always made me laugh.

But this was different. This wasn't funny.

When I'm hurt, I withdraw. So I cut Sue out of my life. Stan Kamen at William Morris became my agent. He was kind and thoughtful, and we had a great business relationship. I think it makes sense to keep friendship and business separate. (Marty's been with me over sixty years, but we rarely socialize. I've never even been to his office.) And once Sue was gone, I noticed something. All those little leaks to the papers about my private life miraculously stopped.

Just to finish the story . . . Sue and I didn't speak for over two years. Then when *Yentl* opened, I received a telegram from her: "We just saw *Yentl*. It's brilliant." So I called her. She told me that she and Jean-Claude went with Ray Stark to the first matinee. "Ray and I thought it was amazing."

"What about Jean-Claude? What did he think?"

"He left in the middle."

"So he didn't like it."

And she said, "Actually, he was overwhelmed. He couldn't believe you made this movie."

After that phone call, Sue and I slowly started to talk again, but our relationship was never the same.

Back to getting *Yentl* off the ground. On November 19, 1980, we submitted our budget to Orion . . . we needed at least $13 million to make the movie. Just my luck . . . that was the day Vincent Canby's review of Michael Cimino's *Heaven's Gate* was printed in *The New York Times.* It was scathing, and the last line was the equivalent of a nail in Cimino's coffin: "*Heaven's Gate* is something quite rare in movies these days—an unqualified disaster."

The word of mouth on the film was already terrible. Cimino . . . and the studio, United Artists . . . had allowed the budget to balloon from $11.5 million to over $44 million, and he had delivered the film a year behind schedule. It was such a spectacular failure that it changed Hollywood. Every executive was suddenly focused on the bottom line.

I read the review and felt a pang of sympathy for Cimino, but I had no inkling yet that this was going to affect me. I was too busy getting ready to catch a plane back to Prague to scout more locations, and this time I brought my little Super 8 video camera with me. I wanted to get a feeling for how the film might look, so I put on a man's outfit from the turn of the century . . . a long black coat, black cap, and a white-collared shirt I had rented from Western Costume . . . and Rusty filmed me walking through those cobblestone streets. We had no special equipment, just natural light, and there was something so beautiful about that simple, eight-minute film . . . the shadowy archways and the pale stone walls . . . a dark silhouette against a frosted-glass door . . . and a dusty-pink stucco house that was perfect for Hadass's home. (I love that color.)

I showed the footage to a few people because I needed to know if I made a believable guy. The movie is a musical fable, so by definition you're already asking the audience to suspend disbelief, but was I asking too much?

The Bergmans were very reassuring. "Yes, we believe you're a guy," they told me. "Stop worrying!" And the studio agreed. I did think I looked like the people in my reference books. And I had already decided that Yentl should be twenty-eight, which made the age difference less of a stretch. (I was thirty-nine when we finally began filming, but thank God people have always told me I look young for my age.) An unmarried woman of twenty-eight would definitely have been considered a spinster in 1904, which is when I set the story because I like the number 4.

Now I think it was a mistake not to make her age clear at the beginning of the movie. But some critics were probably determined to attack me anyway, and they would have found something else if not my age.

Funny, I spent my early career playing parts that were too old for me, like Dolly Levi, and now this part was apparently too young. But Singer left her age ambiguous, and you could find men of all ages in a yeshiva. Yentl could have been one of them.

And besides, I never said I was making an exact version of Singer's story. I was using it as a vehicle to say something about women's rights in an unexpected context . . . a Jewish shtetl in Poland in 1904.

On that scouting trip, we went out into the countryside to look at little villages that might work for Yanev, where Yentl lived with her father . . . or Beshev, where she went to study at Avigdor's yeshiva.

Here are some of my notes from that trip, written in my journal on Thanksgiving Day, November 27, 1980:

> *Vbrno—good day—practically everyplace we went was right! The swimming hole for the boys.*
>
> *Chotetov—for Yanev—pretty good.*
>
> *Such pretty frost on leaves—like sugar coating!*
>
> *The prospective bride's house—perfect!—size of room—good light—the rest of the space good for filming—not too small—a toilet—and a great kitchen with homemade goodies—breaded and fried cauliflower—baked apples—little cakes, all kinds of preserved foods.*
>
> *The Zamosc Inn—charming—with straw hanging from the rafters.*

I remember walking up a little hill, and just as I got to the top, I was blinded for a moment by the setting sun. And there was the most enchanting scene:

> *A canal to put a ferry on!—and the knockout of the day to me—a stork's nest on top of a large tree.*

It was kind of weird and wonderful . . . a big, thick trunk with no top. There were no branches and leaves, just a bunch of twigs that the storks had piled on it. I thought it was amazing, and decided right then and there that we had to shoot here so I could incorporate the storks into the film.

> *We went to the American Embassy for Thanksgiving dinner, thinking they'd surely have a turkey (we saw a white one alive today)—Well, they had the same Czech hors d'oeuvres that I ate everyday—ham, salami, and more ham—dinner was ham sandwiches on white bread!*

Just before I was heading home, via London, on December 5, I wrote in my journal:

> *I can't believe the obstacles—yesterday talking to production people—now with the Soviets closing the border on East Germany—Czechoslovakia being 70 km from the Polish border may present a problem.*

Little did I know I was about to face an even bigger problem. Orion told me that they had decided I had to cut the budget from $13 million to $10 million. The debacle of *Heaven's Gate* had made everyone exceptionally cautious, and this was another period film with an ethnic subject . . . and I was a first-time director. That cut was daunting . . . almost a fourth of the budget, and I was already shaving costs down to the bone.

And then Jon made it all a moot point, because in his infinite wisdom he proceeded to insult Eric Pleskow. I had had a meeting with Eric and Mike on my own . . . not unusual, by the way, because Jon was often AWOL when it came to *Yentl* . . . and Jon got angry when he found out. He called Eric and said, "How dare you meet with Barbra without me?"

"Jon," Eric said, "Barbra is the star of this picture and the producer, the writer, and the director. I can meet with her anytime I like, with or without you."

And then Jon got very offensive . . . I think his exact words to Eric were "Fuck you."

I was furious with Jon. Frankly, I think he deliberately jinxed the deal with Orion because he wanted to move to Polygram, where he thought he could get a better deal for himself. There, he would be working with Peter Guber, who was a personal friend of his. And I guess that was more important to him than *Yentl*.

Polygram did pick up *Yentl*, but they didn't give it their full financial support. And I didn't feel fully supported by Jon either. Even though he and I were supposedly producing this together, he was barely involved in the film. He didn't join me on the scouting trips. I don't think he even read the script.

His behavior had already cost me one deal, and it was becoming more and more obvious to me that I had to end our working relationship. But that meant putting the film into jeopardy again.

I decided that I had no choice. Jon and I were drifting apart on many levels, and it was time to be independent. I knew I had to make this picture, and now that meant I'd have to be the sole producer as well. Jon didn't fight me. He probably knew, just as I did, that I really didn't need him.

So I started all over again on my own, pitching the project to other studios . . . showing my eight-minute video and playing a cassette tape of some of the songs. Here I was . . . according to various polls, a top box-office draw . . . recently named World Film Favorite at the Golden Globes for the fourth time . . . and I felt as if I were eighteen years old again, auditioning for a Broadway show. Warner Bros., which had grossed almost $200 million on my films (over $600 million in today's dollars), said no. Columbia, which had grossed even more, also passed. Paramount wasn't interested.

It kind of knocked me off my feet. They said I was a bankable star, but nobody would take any money out of the bank for me.

Ironically, it was at United Artists, the studio that had made *Heaven's Gate*, where we ultimately found a home. Steven Bach, the executive in charge of production, decided to take a chance on me. And what finally convinced him that I could direct was a tour of my Art Deco house, "all burgundy, rose, black, and gray, down to the teacups in the cupboard and the soaps in the bathrooms," as he wrote in his book, *Final Cut.* "Even the closets were hung with authentic Deco period clothes in burgundy, rose, black, and gray, and if nothing else demonstrated the visual sense she would exercise as a director, that house did."

But it was his colleague Norbert Auerbach who initially pushed for me. He was a lovely older gentleman, born in Vienna and raised in Prague. That was lucky, and it may have made him more receptive to the project. He came to my New York apartment, where I played him the songs. He loved them . . . he loved the story . . . he even suggested he could play my father!

On April 14, 1981, I wrote in my journal:

> *The Columbia space shuttle landed (safely) and we took off! Both two years late—United Artists made the deal!—may we be hopefully as successful!! Cis and I toasted with coffee ice cream and Frangelico.*

And then all of a sudden the rug was pulled out from under me *again.* I woke up one morning and found out that United Artists had been sold to MGM. Auerbach and Bach were out.

And guess who was running the new combined MGM/UA? David Begelman, my former agent . . . the man who never wanted me to do *Yentl* in the first place.

THIRTY-SIX

Directing Yentl

Was this a joke? I felt as if I were back where I started in 1968. David and I even laughed about it. He said, "Don't you ever give up?" I think he respected my tenacity and may have felt guilty that he didn't help during all the years I spent trying to get this picture made. Or else he just took pity on me.

I was not only able to keep the deal but I got to make it even better. Now MGM/UA would give me a $14.5 million budget, but in exchange I had to make several concessions.

I was paid nothing for writing the script. By now I had done three drafts but I never put my name on any of them because I didn't want people to be prejudiced against it before they even read it. I just called it "A Barwood Film." And since I'm constantly questioning my own work, I kept wondering if there were any improvements I could make. So when one studio executive suggested bringing in a more experienced writer to do a polish, I wasn't averse to it. I thought, *Fine. I'm so close to this script that it could be nice to get a new perspective. But I'm not changing anything unless I really like it!*

I had heard about Jack Rosenthal, a British writer who had done a teleplay called *Bar Mitzvah Boy* that was turned into a musical in London. (Jule Styne had composed the music, which seemed like a good sign.) So I had Jack take a crack at it. I didn't really like everything he did, but he added a few nice bits of dialogue, so I suggested we work together. (It's less lonely too.) I enjoyed those writing sessions. And even when we didn't agree, it was helpful because it forced me to clarify my own thinking.

I used to love staying at the Berkeley Hotel in Knightsbridge, because the bedroom had big glass doors into the living room, so you could see the fireplace from the bed at night. Jack and I spent many hours in that living room, where I looked forward to my daily sandwich of turkey on brown bread with sweet horseradish sauce or Branston Pickle . . . and then tea with scones and clotted cream and mashed fresh strawberries (way better than jam. And no raisins in the scones, please!).

I thought directors were supposed to do all this work on a script, and I was reluctant to call myself a writer, so I never asked for a writing credit. Instead, after the movie was shot, I turned in all sixteen scripts (three were mine alone) to the Writers Guild and left it to them to decide who should get the credit. They gave it to me and Jack, and I was thrilled to have my first writing credit.

Back to the deal. I got paid scale (the legal minimum) for directing, which was fine. After all, I was an unproven director.

But they also wanted me to take much less as an actress than I had made on my previous film. Frankly, I would have paid *them* to let me do this movie . . . but I didn't tell them that. And I also had to agree to return half my salary if we went over budget.

Okay. None of that really mattered to me.

But I did have to give up the one thing that was most important to me . . .

final cut. The studio would have the ultimate say . . . not me, as the director. Now *that* worried me, but I had to accept it, because it was the only way I could get this movie made. (As it turned out, I needn't have worried. Once I delivered the film, the studio never touched a frame.)

Now . . . finally! . . . I could focus on putting together a cast and a crew.

Initially, for Avigdor, I was thinking of Richard Gere. I wanted a face that was both masculine and feminine . . . playing again with the idea of androgyny . . . and he had a strong nose, a lovely head of hair, and a pretty mouth. He also radiated this potent sexuality. We met to talk about the role, and he was interested. But he didn't think it was a good idea for me to act *and* direct. He would do the film if I did one or the other, but not both.

So I had to look elsewhere. I wanted a strong, charismatic actor to play opposite me, because that had always worked well in the past, with Omar Sharif and Robert Redford. I met with Michael Ontkean and Harry Hamlin, who were both very good-looking, but neither felt quite right to me. I had seen Mandy Patinkin in *Evita* onstage and thought he was interesting, but there wasn't anything androgynous about him. Cis, who was doing the casting, brought him in anyway.

My way of auditioning actors is to talk to them first . . . just to get a sense of who they are as people. And then if I think they can play the part, I'll give them a scene to learn and ask them to come back and do it, while Rusty videotapes them. I've learned that some actors are very good at reading a scene but not so good at coming alive in front of a camera.

Not Mandy. I had given him the scene where Avigdor is telling Yentl that his marriage to Hadass is off, and he did something I'd never thought of. One minute he was laughing and the next minute he was crying. It was fascinating to watch. I love when an actor surprises me.

So there wasn't anything feminine about him, and he didn't have the face of a Hollywood heartthrob. He was basically a character actor. I hesitated and kept looking for months, and then I thought, *No. I want the talent more than the looks.* So we hired Mandy. I sent him the seven-volume *The Legends of the Jews* by Louis Ginzberg, which was like a crash course in the Talmud, and arranged for him to visit a yeshiva to observe the students. He had homework to do before he even stepped on the set.

For Hadass, at first I was thinking of Carol Kane. She had an antique face . . .

she looked like someone from another century . . . and then this unusual squeaky voice. I thought it had comic possibilities. But the studio wouldn't let me hire her. They said no. Absolutely not. You can't have three Jewish people as the leads.

I was shocked. What difference does that make? Did they expect me to vet actors according to their religion? And by the way, had nobody noticed that this was, after all, a movie *about* Jews?

In the end I decided not to argue, because Carol had already made such a strong impression in *Hester Street* that I thought it might be better to have a new face.

I had met Amy Irving when she was living with Steven Spielberg, and thought she had a lovely Pre-Raphaelite quality, with her pale skin and cascade of naturally curly auburn hair. We sent her a script, and then I heard from her agent that she had passed. She wasn't interested in playing another ingénue.

I saw Hadass as more complex than that, and invited Amy to come see me at my New York apartment so I could explain what I had in mind. I wanted to make her love the character as much as I did. She told me later that my passion for the film was so compelling that she couldn't say no. And Amy is an adventurer . . . she was ready to go with me on this journey. She's actually half Jewish (I deliberately didn't mention that to the studio), and she had just lost her father. That was kind of an unspoken tie between us, and I also think she liked the idea of supporting a fellow woman who wanted to direct. She was wonderful to work with and fully committed.

And now I needed to find my father.

Remember, it was those first four words . . . "After her father's death" . . . that had first captured my attention and deepened my response to this story. It was about a girl who had a great bond with her father and whose life was turned upside down after he died . . . just like mine.

My mother never talked about my father. It was only now, going through his papers, that I discovered more about him. He was on the debating team in college. He was in the chess club, the mathematics club, the drama club. He wanted to see California. One of his dreams was to become a writer.

Can you imagine? Was I meant to fulfill his dreams? I understood so much more about myself when I found out all these things about him. There were so many similarities between us. Even in his photographs, I could see the resemblance. I was built like my father. I looked like him, rather than my mother. I had his nose. I had his full lips. I had his eyes, set slightly close together.

Making this film was my way of exploring what having a father would have been like. And in writing dialogue and imagining scenes for Yentl's father, I got to create the father I never had.

Originally, Morris Carnovsky, one of the founders of the Group Theatre, was going to play the role. Then he had a heart attack. Fortunately he recovered and went on to live for another ten years, but it was impossible for him to do the movie.

Cis had seen Nehemiah Persoff in a one-man show he'd put together, based on the stories of Sholem Aleichem. I had always thought Nicky was a wonderful actor, ever since I saw him play the taxicab driver in *On the Waterfront.* And when we met, he had such warmth and kindness that I immediately felt he would be perfect as my father.

Since we would be shooting part of the film on location in Czechoslovakia, it made sense to have London as our base and do the movie with a British crew. I wanted Roy Walker as the production designer because I thought he had done a splendid job on another period film, *Barry Lyndon* (for which he won an Oscar) and *The Shining*, which had recently come out. I figured anyone who was good enough for Stanley Kubrick was good enough for me. Roy had already joined me on several scouting trips and was game for anything . . . he happily pretended to be my leading man while Rusty filmed us with the video camera.

Meanwhile, I kept going back to that footage we had shot in Prague, because there was something there . . . a look we had captured . . . that I wanted to make sure we preserved in the final film. It had to do with the place, of course . . . the evocative architecture . . . old stone buildings with one arch after another, sometimes spanning a street. For the shoot Roy even built an arch over a street that didn't have one. He just knew instinctively what I would want.

And the look of a film also has to do with something more intangible . . . color and light. That means the choice of a cinematographer is crucial, and the man I wanted was Vittorio Storaro, whose photography I fell in love with when I saw *The Conformist* in 1970.

I'll never forget one particular scene, which was in color, but the art direction (the set and the props) made it look as if it were black and white . . . gray wallpaper, stripes of shadow on the walls from the Venetian blinds, the actors' clothes in shades of black and white. The only burst of color came from a bouquet of yellow roses.

I love monochromatic frames . . . like those foreign films I used to see at the Astor Theatre next to Erasmus Hall High School. My little eight-minute film was basically in shades of black and white. The costume I wore was black and white, because that's what the yeshiva boys would wear every day. And then I could imagine just one other color in the frame . . . like the green of the grass in an outdoor shot.

Vittorio came to see me in Malibu, and I walked him through my Art Deco house. He was very impressed, and as soon as we finished the tour, he said he'd do *Yentl* with me. I was thrilled. It turned out that he's just as color oriented as I am. We both loved talking about the possibilities of color . . . how powerful color, or the absence of it, can be.

I told him that I had flown to Amsterdam to see the Rembrandts, because when I was thinking about how I wanted the film to look, his paintings came to mind. I was in London during one of our scouting trips, and I decided on the spur of the moment to take a little side trip . . . not realizing that there were more Rembrandts in the London museums. No matter. Amsterdam was lovely, and the paintings were worth the trip. I wanted to study them up close. There was that red . . . what I've always thought of as Rembrandt red. It's never pure red, but has more of a brown tone, so it's muted. It looks old. I've always been drawn to muted colors in paint. The only pure red I like is the color of Ruby Glow azaleas.

And I was curious about Rembrandt's blacks. How black were they? And it turns out that they're not actually black at all . . . or not black-black . . . they're more of a dark brown. And what about the faces . . . were the edges hard or soft? To me, they looked soft. No hard contrasts. And if I wanted to recreate that effect, it would determine what kind of lenses we would use, whether we wanted a high-density or a low-density filter, and the choice of film stock.

But most of all, I was looking at the light. In many of Rembrandt's paintings, you don't see the source of the light, but it illuminates the faces in the most beautiful way. Everything looks warm. I wanted my film to have the same luminescence as Rembrandt's paint. I wanted the faces of the students, who were searching for knowledge and truth, to be lit by an inner glow. I wanted to capture the light that comes from learning . . . the desire to connect to a higher source . . . because learning is literally enlightenment. And I wanted to use a lot of natural light. Vittorio was intrigued. He saw what I saw. He understood what I was aiming for. He could talk about light for hours, and so could I.

I wanted to hire him, but he would have cost $250,000 (a lot at that time) and a piece of the profits, which was practically unheard-of for a cinematographer. Those were his terms, and he also had to bring his five-man Italian crew along with him. But the studio wouldn't allow it. We just didn't have that kind of money in our budget. So I had to tell this exceptional artist that I couldn't afford him.

And then a few days later I woke up and thought, *I'm insane. I'm certifiably insane.* I had just given half a million dollars to set up a chair in my father's name for cardiovascular research at UCLA, but I couldn't give myself a $250,000 gift of Storaro? It made no sense.

But I have to confess . . . there was something else going on. I found myself attracted to Vittorio. He was smart and so talented and sexy in a very quiet way.

And then something happened to break the spell. I remember the moment. I was describing a shot I envisioned . . . the camera would start on Yentl, sitting behind a wooden railing in the upper balcony of the synagogue (the only place women were allowed) and then come down to her father, sitting with the men below. Vittorio said he saw the shot going the other way, from the father up to her in the balcony. And since this was my first film as a director, and he was a renowned cinematographer, I didn't quite have the confidence to disagree with him.

That was not a good sign, and definitely not the best basis for a working relationship. And I realized my crush on him would only make it worse. I might lose my power on the set or, let's say, relinquish it in an effort to please him.

That was a complication I truly couldn't afford.

If I was going to make this film, it needed to be my vision. And I didn't want to have to fight for it.

Years later Storaro told me that he always regretted not doing *Yentl.* By that time, I had more faith in myself and realized I would react quite differently if a similar conflict occurred.

And I'm still hoping to work with him. Wouldn't that be wonderful . . .

But as they say, one door closes and another opens. We found the gifted cinematographer David Watkin, who had done *Chariots of Fire.* I remember the first time he did a test shot of my face. He looked at the footage and said, "That's your nose?"

I love people who can make me laugh.

David was not intimidated by anyone. He was a master of his craft . . . he could give you the most beautiful light in the most simple way. And he was very modest about it. He never made a fuss, just quietly went about the set and did his job. And once it was lit, you could move anywhere on it and still be lit perfectly. I had never seen that before.

David did have one quirk. Sometimes he would disappear. We'd be looking all over for him until someone eventually came across him, fast asleep in some corner. It turned out he was narcoleptic, which I learned later. As soon as a scene was lit, he would fall asleep. He didn't feel he had to be available because he didn't believe in changing the light between takes. He was completely sure that he had gotten it right to begin with.

At one of our first meetings, I remember asking him about a certain scene in the script, and he looked at me and said bluntly, "I don't read the script. Peter does all the clever stuff."

I said, "You're joking."

"Peter" was Peter MacDonald, a brilliant camera operator who became the person I relied on most. The system in Britain is very different than it is in America. Here, the cinematographer does the lighting and works out the staging with the director. In England the job is basically split between two people . . . the cinematographer only does the lighting, while you and the camera operator stage the action. Thank God Peter read the script so I could discuss concepts with him!

He was very polite, very proper, very English, but underneath that cool exterior was the warmest heart, and I grew to love him. He was so amazing to work with, and every time he comes to America he visits me. I cherish my relationship with him.

All the elements that are part of preproduction were gradually falling into place. Roy had found a little village called Roztyly, about two and a half hours outside of Prague, which had just the kind of primitive beauty I envisioned for Yanev, the place where Yentl grew up. There were old wooden houses . . . and I saw just the one I wanted for Yentl and her father . . . and I was also taken with the graveyard, where the weathered tombstones were leaning over with age. I thought it was so touching that the villagers had built their cemetery on a hill, so the dead would have a beautiful view for eternity.

And then war broke out in Poland. Actually, the Solidarity movement had taken to the streets, and the government sent soldiers and tanks to quell the protests. But after having survived the studio negotiations, the fact that the fighting was only seventy kilometers from our location seemed like just another challenge.

While I was in Europe on one of these scouting trips, I called Willy Wyler. I told him, "I'm about to direct my first film, and I can't wait to sit down and talk to you about everything. Maybe you could give me some tips on what to do."

I could just imagine his mischievous smile when he said, "I'll tell you what *not* to do."

We were planning to get together as soon as I returned. And then when I got back to Los Angeles, I found out that he had died.

I was devastated. This was the man who had launched my film career, and I'll be forever grateful to him. There were so many things I wanted to tell him and ask him, and now I would never have the chance.

I called his wife, Talli, to give her my love and sympathy. And then she wrote me the most wonderful note, which said: "If you're on the set and you really don't know what to do, be very still and you might hear Willy whispering in your ear."

I used to carry that note with me everywhere. It made me feel as if Willy's spirit would always be with me, now that I was finally fulfilling his prophecy. Remember, he was the one who first told me I should direct.

And then Alan Parker, a friend who had directed *Midnight Express* and *Fame*, offered a more pragmatic piece of advice. He said, "If you can't decide how to shoot something, just tell them to build a track until you have time to figure it out." Which was sort of reassuring . . . although I never actually did that. I'd feel guilty if I asked the crew to work hard for nothing!

By January 1982 I was ensconced in a house in London's Chelsea neighborhood, deep into meetings with wardrobe, hair, and makeup people. Roy was constructing the interior sets at Lee International Studios, just outside the city, and the plan was to shoot there for about eight weeks, move to Czechoslovakia for about six weeks, and then finish up back in London.

But first we had to prerecord all the music. (No need to sing live on this film since almost all my songs would be voice-over.) We did this over two weeks in February, with Marilyn, Alan, Michel, and the orchestra at Olympic Studios, on the outskirts of London.

On *Funny Girl* we had three months to rehearse all the musical numbers. On *Yentl* I had nine days.

I remember walking onto the set for the first day of rehearsal. The whole crew was lined up to meet me. A tall, lanky man with a shy grin . . . Bill Keenan, one of the stagehands . . . shook my hand, and I noticed that his palm was sweaty. I asked, "Are you nervous?"

"A little," he said, with a thick Cockney accent.

"Well," I told him, "feel *my* hand. No one's more nervous than me."

Nervous? That hardly describes it. Many mornings, on my way to the studio, I had to ask the driver to stop somewhere so I could be sick to my stomach. I got to know every Wimpy's and McDonald's along the route (and then I'd buy a whipped-cream doughnut on my way out for later).

Once I got to the set I was so focused on the work that I felt fine. Luckily I had already blocked most of the musical numbers back at Carolwood. I had recruited Marilyn and Alan to play the tailors (wearing period caps) so I could work out the entrances and exits as Yentl is fitted for her wedding suit. And I corralled their daughter, Julie (and Renata as well), to play Hadass, so I could figure out her movements in the various dinner-table scenes. We videotaped all those run-throughs and then edited the footage so I could show Peter and David exactly what I had in mind, which made the actual shoot much easier. Everybody could see the whole scene and knew what they had to do.

The dinner scene where Hadass serves the food as the song "No Wonder" plays in voice-over was the most complex, because the song and the dialogue and the action and the camera movements all had to be coordinated. It required split-second choreography, because we were timing physical actions to the lyrics of the song . . . Mandy had to choke on the horseradish, and Amy had to pour water for him . . . spill the beets . . . pass the bread . . . at exactly the right moments. As Hadass and her mother hovered around the table, each of the other actors had various bits of business, and we needed to capture it all.

And then I needed one other element, because of course a conversation should also be going on in the background as we hear Yentl sing. So that was another layer that we had to choreograph, and all those layers are what made this particular scene so interesting to me.

I could even slip in a bit of Talmudic discussion. Steven Hill, who played Hadass's father, was a terrific actor who also happened to be an Orthodox Jew, and that's one of the reasons I hired him. He was strictly observant, which meant he couldn't work past sundown on Fridays, and we had to have kosher food for him. But I loved that. It was the reality of who he was. He could just "be" . . . which is a short way to describe what constitutes good acting for me. Steve knew this world intimately, and he also knew the Talmud. That gave him the kind of natural authority that I wanted for this role, and his voice already had the cadence of an erudite Jewish elder. Mandy had acquired some knowledge from the books I sent him, so I could tell them, "I want you two to have some sort of scholarly conversation at the table," and rely on them to improvise.

God, that scene was a challenge. I think it took up three of the nine days we allotted for rehearsals, because it was definitely the most complicated. And it all had to look effortless.

But that's the fun of directing. It was thrilling to shape it and refine it and watch it come together. I think that's why acting alone had become kind of boring to me. I always liked looking at the entire picture. I was concerned with the whole story. And now I felt like a painter with a fresh canvas, only this time I held the brush in my hand.

And it was my job to create an atmosphere of trust in which everyone could do their best work. I could see in the dinner scene that Mandy didn't like rehearsing. He would read a newspaper at the table and once he even dozed off. But Mandy's instincts, when he was actually paying attention, were good. At one point, when Avigdor was talking, he just lifted his arms and let Hadass put a napkin on his lap. He didn't even look at her. I thought that was wonderful . . . a perfect choice.

But there were so many moving parts in this scene, and I didn't want to burden my cast by forcing them to go through the motions again and again while we were experimenting with the camera. So I thought, *Let's do this with the crew.* I asked Beth Porter, my stand-in, to play Hadass. (In the film, she's the maid who's making eyes at Anshel over dinner.) Zelda Barron, the script supervisor, played her mother, and Steve Lanning, the first assistant director, played Avigdor.

That was fun. I told them they didn't have to act . . . just say the lines. They really got into it, and I think they enjoyed being on the other side of the camera for a change.

I couldn't have asked for a better crew. They were great, doing whatever they could to help me. The stage where we built the sets was vast, and I've always had a terrible sense of direction, so I used to get all turned around trying to find my dressing room. I came in one day to see that the stagehands had kindly marked the floor with a line of yellow tape (like the yellow brick road in *The Wizard of Oz*!) so I could make my way back and forth easily.

I was so grateful for their support . . . not once did I sense any negative attitude toward me as a woman in a position of power. There was no resentment or opposition. I think that had something to do with the fact that they had a queen as their monarch and Margaret Thatcher was the prime minister. So a woman directing a film was no big deal. And they had manners. The British are very polite.

We were scheduled to start shooting on April 14, and the night before, David Begelman called to tell me that a completion bond was being taken out with a 10 percent contingency, which is basically an insurance policy to protect the studio against any cost overruns. The premium for this bond would be $700,000, and it would be deducted from my budget. That was a real blow, but they gave me no choice. And then a few days later we had a confrontation about the boat. For the last scene in the film, when Yentl sets off for America, Roy had found a freighter docked in Liverpool that we could take out onto the Irish Sea. It was going to cost $15,000, and the studio refused to pay for it. They said, "Take the boat out of the movie."

But I had to have that boat. So I said, "I'll pay for it myself."

You'd think I would be thrilled to finally stand on a set and call out, "Action!" That's the image we all have in our heads of a director, and I did it a few times, but it gave me a funny feeling. It was almost too much power, in a way. Besides, in those first few seconds of playing a scene, I wanted to just be the actress, in the moment . . . not the director. So I gave that job to Steve Lanning. It was his first time as first assistant director on a major picture, and we had a good rapport . . . no ego, no competitiveness. I would look at him when I was ready and he would say, "Action!" But I was the only one who could say, "Cut."

When you're the director, you have to have the whole movie in your head before you even begin, because most films don't have the luxury of being shot in sequence, beginning on page 1 of the script. Instead, you're constantly jumping from one location to another and moving back and forth in time. And when you do a scene, you have to know where each character is emotionally so each new piece will fit right into the puzzle.

The first scene we shot was where Yentl and Avigdor have to share a room for a night, because his landlady has only one available. Yentl is trapped and tries to avoid getting into bed with him by sitting at a table across the room, pretending to study. He's trying to sleep and tells her to turn off the lamp and get to bed. As she's taking off her coat, she trips over his suitcase, and partially to distract him but also because she really wants to know, Yentl picks this moment to ask, "Who's Hadass?"

"The girl I'm engaged to."

As she catches a glimpse of herself in a mirror, she asks if Hadass is pretty. "No . . . beautiful," he says, and we see a twinge of sadness on Yentl's face. Avigdor exclaims, "Now will you get into bed!" Finally, she can postpone it no longer and quickly crawls in, but then moves so close to the edge that she practically falls off.

That was funny, and fun to do. The physical comedy was all improvised, and if Mandy didn't pick up on it, or either of us blew a line, I told the crew, "Don't cut. Just keep rolling."

That's because in my experience I'd noticed that if you stop to do another take, inevitably the hair or makeup people come in to touch you up or someone goes off to get a drink of water, and you lose the concentration. Then you have to wait for the camera to get back into position and slate it and start all over again. I'd rather make the adjustment right then and there . . . and just keep going.

I also like to shoot a complete scene, when I can. That's my theater background, where you get to play a scene from beginning to end, which makes for a more cohesive performance.

So then the challenge in film becomes, How can I do this scene in as few shots as possible?

And the most important consideration for me always is . . . How can I use the camera to serve the actor's performance, rather than the other way around?

I already knew a little about lenses simply from being an inquisitive actress. Most cinematographers like to use prime lenses, so that's how most classic films were shot. But in order to accommodate the movements of the actors and do those long takes without a cut, Peter explained that we'd have to use a zoom lens.

Then he went over to consult with David.

David said, "Tell me one film that used a zoom lens that was a success."

"*Cabaret*."

Without pausing, David replied, "Tell me *two* films using a zoom that were a success."

Clearly David preferred prime lenses, but we finally convinced him that the only way to do the kind of long, sustained shots I preferred was with a zoom . . . but always mixing it with camera moves, so it was never, ever an obvious zoom.

And by the way, the zoom itself softened the image a bit, which was right for the look of *Yentl* . . . a realistic fairy tale.

I would plan each shot, then I would explain what I wanted to Peter, and he would make it happen. For me, this is the most fascinating part of being a director. You're telling a story with the camera, which is very different from writing a novel. You need to tell it visually. And because I like to shoot a whole scene in one take, everyone has to be on the ball. One slight mistake, and you have to start all over again from the beginning.

As for the musical numbers, it was particularly important to me that they not be broken up with too many cuts. The music doesn't stop, so why should the shot? At least, that was the ideal.

The first song in the film . . . "Where Is It Written?" . . . begins after Yentl says good night to her father and closes his bedroom door. She stealthily walks over to the red-velvet case that holds his prayer shawl. And this is what's wonderful about making movies . . . I love details . . . I love specificity . . . and I could tell our terrific set decorator, Tessa Davies, that I wanted the velvet to be a specific shade of red. Not red-red or blue-red, but that dull, rusty red that I saw in Rembrandt's paintings. And she would find it! What a treat.

Yentl is longing to put on the prayer shawl, which she's not allowed to do as a woman, and as her fingers touch the case we hear the first notes of music . . . played on an old Eastern European instrument called a cimbalom, which Michel chose for its plaintive, haunting sound. Yentl takes out the shawl and holds it up behind her, so she's just a dark silhouette against the lamplight. I had described this sequence to Peter. I wanted the camera to be constantly moving in, and then it starts to move around her. It's over her shoulder, and then we see her reflected in the mirror as she begins to sing . . . then we see her in profile . . . then the camera moves in for a close-up . . . and it's all done in one take.

I always want things to flow. I want the camera to dance with the actors, because in a way they're partners and move together. That's why I made sure that Roy had the sets built so they could come apart easily. And in order to do that whole sequence without a cut, Peter had to have a wall pulled out so the camera could come around to see Yentl reflected in the mirror in front of her. And David had to be equally inventive with the lights, as the camera moves in for the close-up of Yentl cradling the shawl against her cheek.

Initially David said, "You can't do that. The lighting's no good for you there. The lamp is too bright. We'll have to cut and relight."

I said, "David, we *can't* cut. That will break the mood, and I really want to do the song in one take. What if we just put the lamp on a dimmer? Can you do that?"

He thought for a long moment and said, "Yes."

Point is, it was trickier than it sounds, but he made it work.

This sequence was important because it's also where I set up the musical concept for the whole film. At first we hear Yentl say a prayer while her back is toward us, and then she begins to sing. Initially her face and mouth are covered by the shawl but when she lifts her head, we see that she's singing out loud, because she's alone. Then she hears her father cough and moves toward his room. As she goes in, the song continues, but her mouth is no longer moving, and the sound quality subtly changes. When she comes out and closes the door behind her, she's singing out loud again as she picks up the dinner dishes and carries them into the kitchen. The song continues as we cut from Yentl cleaning up to Yentl in the synagogue, sitting with the other women up in the balcony. But now the song goes back into voice-over, because she's with other people. As the scene and the song end, we hear the women chattering as Yentl peers down at her father from behind the railings, and then we cut to chickens clucking behind the bars of their coop. I loved that transition.

It's very satisfying to work with people who like solving problems. David was so good with the dimmer that we used the idea again in the scene where Yentl comes looking for Avigdor . . . who's depressed because Hadass's father has called off the marriage. He's sitting by the window, lit by the setting sun, and the light gradually fades as they talk till it's almost dark. I liked that darkness. It suited the mood. You can barely see their faces.

Halfway through the scene I put a rumble of thunder in the background to set up the next scene . . . a dissolve to rain dripping from a roof, to suggest tears . . . as if the heavens were crying with Avigdor. The image helps tell the story, I think, just like that moment on a different rainy day when he and Yentl are so engrossed in conversation that they walk straight through a puddle. It says in an instant that she's found someone who's as interested in ideas and oblivious to the rest of the world as she is.

It's one of those telling details, and I'm a person who gets involved with every detail. Every object in Hadass's dining room was important to me . . . the crystal chandelier, the silver Art Nouveau pitcher, the chiming clock. They represented what I thought this family would own . . . a mix of Victorian and Art Nouveau furnishings that had evolved over the years. I wanted the bed linens and the lace curtains in Hadass's bedroom to have just the right feeling of age, and Tessa first tried dipping a sheet in coffee. That darkened it too much. I said, "Try tea, and just dunk it. Don't let it sit there too long." And then of course we had to decide which tea. Should it be PG Tips or Lipton? (Just kidding!)

Ten days after we started filming, I turned forty, and forty was obviously a big year for me. I think something happens when you hit that milestone. Remember, according to Jewish law, a man is not allowed to study the Kabbalah (the mystical side of the Torah) until he is forty. And in the Hebrew calendar, the year 1982 was 5742 . . . there's that number, 42, the year I was born.

I felt I was finally doing what I was meant to do, and using every ounce of my creativity. And everyone else was so creative. They made me feel that anything was possible. For the song "The Way He Makes Me Feel," I had a very specific vision, but I didn't know if it was doable, so I described the shot to Peter. As Yentl comes into her room, the camera pulls back to see her fall on the bed, and then it moves up over her head, and as she rolls over, it moves along with her to the foot of the bed. In other words, it's all one fluid motion.

"If it's too difficult," I told him, "I can change it and make it simpler."

And he said, "Absolutely not! We're going to give you exactly what you envision."

I thought that was extraordinary, and to this day I thank him for that gift.

That was how I saw the scene. That's what the music was telling me to do. Then the camera keeps moving, almost like another instrument in the orchestra, as we dissolve from one vignette to another in a continuous circle, as Yentl is preparing for bed.

First she's unwrapping the muslin that binds her breasts, and her outstretched hand dissolves into her hands in a basin, scooping up water to wash her face . . . and then we dissolve to her feet and move up her body as her nightshirt falls down and she touches her breasts . . . and then the camera comes full circle back to Yentl in bed. The sensuality of the sequence is enhanced by the fluidity of the camera and the music, and it ends when she blows out the candle and goes to sleep.

I was excited to come to work every morning, and the aroma of finnan haddie was enough to get my creative juices flowing. Two of the "sparks" (English slang for electricians) had to get up very early to drive in, and they would cook their breakfast at the studio, on a little burner on the floor. I would often sit down and share a bite with them. And I came to look forward to the English custom of breaking for tea around 4:00 p.m., and would often have Cornish pasties, scones, and sweets brought in for everyone.

Apparently the tabloid press was presenting a very different picture of my behavior. I don't know what they said, because I didn't read it, but everyone else did. Bill Keenan, the charming Cockney man who had reached out and shaken my hand that first morning, had the idea that the crew should respond. They sat down and composed a letter, which Zelda typed up, and I had no idea what they were doing until they showed it to me. They wrote: "Though undoubtedly a perfectionist, in her dealings with everyone—producers, camera, sound, electrical crews, props, wardrobe, makeup, hairdressers, stagehands, actors, stand-ins—she has shared jokes, chats, and pleasantries each and every day. She appears to have no temperament, her voice is scarcely heard on the set, her smile is seen constantly." And every single member of the crew and all the actors signed it. They sent it off to the London *Times* and all the other newspapers, but no one printed it.

Well, I never had to raise my voice, because people were finally listening. And when you have the power, it's lovely to give it away . . . and let others feel powerful too. I think the fact of being in charge made me feel humble, grateful, and more motherly than I've ever felt in my life. Being a director means getting the best out of everyone. So at different times, you have to be psychiatrist, architect, nurse, boss, sweetheart, friend . . .

Only one person disturbed my equilibrium.

There was a moment, a week or so into the shoot, when Mandy and I were doing a scene in the yeshiva. I think he had two or three lines, but he wouldn't look me in the eye. He just stared at my forehead. All of a sudden I felt as if I was back onstage with Sydney Chaplin. I thought, *Oh God. This can't be happening again.*

I took Mandy aside and asked, "What's wrong? You're not looking at me."

And he said, "Tough titty."

Huh? What had I done to provoke him?

I said, "I think you better come into my dressing room and talk to me."

As soon as I closed the door, I turned to him. "Mandy, you obviously have a lot going on inside . . . I can see that. Before every take you seem to have to get your energy up by kicking doors and cursing, which I don't really understand. I guess that's your way of working, and I don't want to interfere with that. But when you're screaming at people for a tissue or a line instead of just asking them nicely, it's very unnerving. Why are you so angry?"

His face crumpled and he said, "I thought we were going to have a more personal relationship."

"What?" I had no idea what he was talking about.

"I thought we were going to have an affair."

I looked at him as if he were crazy . . . 1) I would never have an affair with an actor I was directing, 2) he was married, and 3) I wasn't at all attracted to him.

But I couldn't tell him he was not exactly fascinating to me. I didn't want to hurt his feelings, so I simply said, "I don't operate that way."

Tears rolled down his cheeks.

And I suddenly realized what this was really about. I wasn't paying enough attention to him as a man . . . or at least not the kind of attention he wanted. And I thought back to a dinner I had had with Mandy and his wife, when I noticed that he practically fell asleep at the table when the subject moved off him.

I said, "Mandy, this kind of behavior can't continue. I'm prepared to replace you. We're only two weeks in. I can reshoot all your scenes if you can't be more professional. I've waited fifteen years to realize my dream and I will not let you destroy it."

I hoped I had gotten through to him. He promised me he would try.

I made a decision that I had to make this work, and I tried to be more understanding. Mandy was twenty-nine years old and a novice when it came to film. He couldn't sense when the camera was on him. I'd have to nudge him. And when he was off-camera, he had a tendency to skimp on his performance. (As for me, I think I give a better performance when the camera is *not* on me, because then I don't have to be conscious of it.) After doing her first scene with Mandy, Amy was upset and told me, "He never even looked at me. He's not giving me anything." I had to take him aside and explain, "You have to give her something to react to. You need to be in character. You have to be generous."

It was an ongoing struggle to get him to calm down and be still. He would always be moving around and gesturing with his hands. I'm sure he didn't like me constantly reminding him that all that movement dissipates his power.

I had learned something from watching all those films when I was a teenager. Look at the great movie stars, like Marlon Brando, Gregory Peck, Gary Cooper . . . they knew how to be still.

And I realized something else . . . you don't always need a close-up to sell an emotion. It's often more interesting if you can't quite see an actor's face straight on. Perhaps he's in profile, or he might even have his back to the camera. If there's real emotion inside, it reads even from the back.

It's true . . . sometimes less is more.

The secret is that you don't really need to "act." If you're really using that part of you that is the character, the audience acts *for* you, in a way. A truly great performance leaves space for the audience to imagine what you're feeling, so the actor and audience can experience those emotions together.

I tried to explain this to Mandy when we were shooting the scene at the inn, where Yentl first meets Avigdor. And since this is the moment when the audience is also meeting Mandy for the first time, I wanted to create a distinctive entrance for him. Avigdor is playing chess with another student, and we hear him before we see him. The camera is on his hand moving a chess piece and then it moves up to his face, and he says, "Your move." On the first take Mandy's eyes were darting around, and his hands were moving too much. I had to practically tie him down. I told him, "Try playing it like Gary Cooper."

I could tell he didn't know what I meant, so I said, "Don't move. Just look up and simply say the line."

I wanted Avigdor to be strong and masculine, with a certain maturity . . . to be the kind of man who would appeal to Yentl, and to the audience. Mandy was probably irritated. He must have felt as if I were putting him in a straitjacket. I realize now, in retrospect, that he wasn't used to being a leading man. And I was trying to make him into one.

I wasn't aware of everything that was going on in his head until years later, when he called to ask if I would write the notes for the back cover of an album he was about to release.

I said, "Mandy, you put me through hell. I can't write those notes for you. I'm sorry, but I just can't do it. Why did you give me such a hard time?"

"Well, I was scared."

"Really?" I guess people have different ways of reacting to fear. I was scared, too, but it made me quieter. I listened more intently.

But it was nice to hear the truth, finally. And I said, "I didn't know you were scared, because you hid it so well. And then you were so rude to everybody."

Some people seem to think that's how stars behave, but I've noticed that it's usually the other way around . . . the bigger the star, the smaller the attitude. They don't have to pretend to be important because they actually *are* important. Mandy certainly put on a good front of being confident, very full of himself. He never let me into his fear. I should have been able to see it. But I didn't. And perhaps that was my failing.

Anyway, what's important is what's on-screen, and ultimately Mandy was wonderful in *Yentl*. And I thought he was sensational in *Homeland*. He's certainly learned the power of simplicity . . . and restraint.

In contrast to Avigdor with his masculine energy, Hadass was the feminine aspect of the film. And to me, Amy became the doll I never had as a child. I could dress her up in lovely clothes, like lace blouses from the turn of the century, and put silk ribbons in her hair. I had her wear antique petticoats beneath her skirts, even though the audience would never see them. You move differently in period clothes, and you feel different when you have silk, lace, or fine cotton next to your skin, rather than some synthetic fabric. I thought it would help her get into character.

And I did everything I could to show off her beauty. I asked Roy to put an oval window in the door from the kitchen to the dining room in Hadass's house so the audience's first glimpse of her face would be framed, like a portrait on a cameo. Then I had him put a sconce on the wall so her glorious red hair would be backlit as she enters the room and stands there for a moment, carrying a platter with a perfectly cooked fish.

Storaro had told me about one of his tricks. He would use a reflector covered with gold foil to bathe an actress's face in warm light. And when Amy and I were doing a scene, I would hold one of these below her so she would literally glow.

As the shoot progressed, an interesting thing happened. I noticed that Amy began relating to me as if I were a guy. She'd take my hand as we were walking together or talking about a scene and my first reaction was, *Why is she holding my hand?* But then I thought, *Better let her. If it helps her to be in character, why not?* I didn't want to squash her fantasy. But when she wanted to rehearse the kissing scene, I basically said, No way. See you on the set.

I've told you about watching Ingmar Bergman crouch under the camera and talk an actor through a scene. It worked brilliantly with Amy in the wedding-night scene. She's watching her new husband change behind a screen, and I wanted her to go through a range of reactions . . . curiosity, anticipation, fear, excitement. She had no dialogue . . . everything had to show in her face . . . so I just positioned myself under the camera and said various things to help elicit those emotions.

Toward the end of June the whole company boarded a plane to Czechoslovakia for the second half of the shoot. As the pilot was revving up the engines and getting ready to taxi out, I called, "Stop the plane!" I had ordered scones with fresh strawberries and clotted cream as a treat for everyone, and the scones had arrived but not the cream. We had to wait a bit, but finally it was loaded on (and it was worth the wait). Once we were in the air, I walked down the aisles and served everyone. Peter laughed and said, "You must be the most expensive stewardess in history!"

It was not a great time in the history of Czechoslovakia. The Communists were in charge, and I was shocked to see how little there was to buy in the stores. And yet the people from the film commission were eager to give us anything we needed.

When we were casting in London and Czechoslovakia, I explained that I didn't want to portray Jewish people as I've seen done in some films . . . the stereotypical image with long noses. If you look at books or documentaries, you'll find that some Jews have long noses and some do not, just as in any culture. And I wanted real Jews to play members of the congregation in the synagogue because then they would know how to *daven* (to pray in the traditional way).

But it was also not a great time to be Jewish in Czechoslovakia. The government had shut down almost all the synagogues, and the community in Prague was very small. I think there was only one we could visit . . . a beautiful little place with old, crumbling plaster walls. Still, the film commissioners managed to find an assortment of Jewish men, so I could choose the faces I wanted. But the reality of the closed synagogues and the decimated community was sobering. I put a Jewish star on my cap in Czechoslovakia and wore it almost defiantly.

The rule was that the extras had to bring their own lunch, but because I was worried that they didn't have enough to eat, I made sure to share what we had provided for the crew. The main items in the local diet seemed to be potatoes, cabbage, bread, ham, and hot chocolate. (Right up my alley . . . basically carbs and sugar.)

I asked, "Where are the vegetables?"

They didn't seem to grow them. We had to import vegetables from England. I wanted my crew to be healthy.

There were no hotels near the little villages where we would be filming, and the commissioners helped us find places to stay. One woman moved out of her house so Renata and I could be close to the set. She would make the most delicious dish and leave it in the kitchen for me . . . little pockets of dough, kind of square like ravioli, but inside they were filled with apricot, and the whole thing was topped with a sauce made of rubbery cheese. I'm not making it sound good, but trust me, it really was delicious. We asked her for the recipe, and Renata tried to make it later, but it never tasted quite as good as hers.

Seeing a set for the first time is always a thrilling moment for me as a director, and Roy had outdone himself in recreating a turn-of-the-century Polish village. He built a synagogue from scratch, and houses and an open-air market. When I was looking through all the scouting shots, I had seen a photo of a village street in Hungary that had a trickle of water about eight inches wide running down the middle, and that image had stayed in my mind. I asked Roy if he could replicate it, and now here it was, flowing through the dirt and looking completely natural . . . which is not easy to do, by the way. It required a pump and pipes, and God knows what else, but he did it.

Roy was the one who told me, "You're like a female Kubrick."

That was a huge compliment, and I asked, "In what way?"

"It's how you draw each set, very specifically. You have the action all laid out in your head, so you know exactly where you want a doorway or a window and how big it should be. You've already done a lot of the work for me."

The first image in the film is a close-up of books being jostled in the back of a horse-drawn wagon as the bookseller makes his way toward the village. Books represent knowledge and the joy of learning, which will be a major theme. After we watch the wagon turn toward the village, the next image is a close-up of a feather floating down that little rivulet. Your eye follows the feather, and then a shoe comes into the frame and the camera pulls back to show a man stepping over the water on his way to the synagogue. And then we see Yentl's foot stepping over it on her way to the market.

This idea all started with that little rivulet . . . and the stream I saw on the scouting trip, beside the tree with the stork's nest. Wouldn't it be interesting if Yentl, as she sets off on her journey, crosses over different bodies of water, with each one getting wider and deeper as she goes? First the rivulet in Yanev, then the stream by the inn where she meets Avigdor, next a river on the way into Lublin, and finally the Atlantic Ocean as she heads to America.

When the idea first occurred to me, I know I wasn't thinking of the intellectual and subliminal and psychological implications of what it means to cross over water. I learned that much later, when I got interested in Jungian symbolism and read that water represents the subconscious. That's fascinating, because I operate from my subconscious a lot. I have very detailed dreams, which are so specific that I could make a movie from those images.

And water also represents the feminine, so it makes sense that it would be part of Yentl's journey, and that she would cross the biggest body of water to get to a place where she could be free to study as a woman.

But in the beginning I was simply going on instinct. It's almost visceral . . . just a feeling in the gut. It's not clearly thought out. I just saw these images in my head, and can you imagine how excited I was to see them come to life? Thank you, dear Roy.

Next to the tree with the stork's nest, he built an inn that looked like something out of a Rembrandt painting. Made with wooden beams and stucco walls in weathered sepia tones, it was basically a big barn with high ceilings, a loft, a roaring fireplace, and straw hanging from the rafters, as I had seen on that scouting trip. And then David had his famous Wendy light positioned outside the window to create a bright shaft of sunlight made palpable by the swirling smoke from the fire and the men's pipes. (Wendy was David's nickname. It's Cockney slang for a gay man, and David was proudly gay. When his invention became standard equipment, the light was named after him.) Typical of David, he had just appropriated something . . . an old Royal Air Force wartime searchlight . . . and turned it to his own purposes. He liked it because it was a strong one-source light and he would often use it to mimic moonlight on a nighttime shoot.

The Wendy light is also what he used, by the way, when I wanted to open a book and have the light from the pages illuminate Yentl's face. The beam hit the book and reflected onto me. David was the perfect choice for this movie because he knew how to do negative light . . . light that's reflected off some surface, like a wall or the ceiling, rather than hitting the subject directly. Many cinematographers will hang white sheets around the perimeter of a set to bounce the light back. David did something I had never seen before . . . he hung black velvet. He used it for the scene in the moonlit bedroom . . . the moment Yentl has been dreading, when Hadass demands her conjugal rights (as she's learned from the Talmud). They're both in silhouette as Hadass leans in to kiss Yentl, but I didn't want a perfectly flat black silhouette. Their faces are dark, but I wanted to see Amy's skin and my skin and hints of eyes and lips when they caught the glow.

That was a tricky shot. If the faces are flat black, they cannot convey emotion. But flat black was exactly what I wanted in another shot, when Yentl and Avigdor are seen in silhouette against the frosted glass of two dark wood doors. I wanted it to look like a similar moment in my little eight-minute film, which was shot with just natural light. So I asked David to turn off all his lights. He said, "Wait a minute. I have to have some light."

"Just try it," I said.

And David made it work. Even though you can't see their eyes you could still sense the tension between Avigdor and Yentl.

David was truly ingenious and could do amazing things photographically. Peter was a wizard with the camera as well. There were certain scenes I had always envisioned shot with a handheld camera . . . like the wedding sequence. I just turned Peter loose and let him do what he wanted, and he captured it all, from the exuberance of the dancing to the stolen glances between Yentl, looking longingly at Avigdor, and Avigdor looking longingly at Hadass.

So you have a vision . . . and then there's the reality.

On the day we were scheduled to shoot Yentl crossing the stream on her way to the inn, I was all set to go. Roy had built a primitive ferry . . . more like a raft with benches . . . and it was perfect, and everyone was in place. But I wanted the water to sparkle with sunlight and the weather would not cooperate. The sun stayed hidden behind clouds.

What do you do? Do you sit there and wait for the sun? How long can you afford to wait? How much is it going to cost? I either had to change my idea or find something else to shoot. Would it be feasible to switch gears and move to the inn? How long would that take?

When you're both the producer and the director, for every decision, you have to weigh the financial against the artistic. In a funny way, I enjoyed having to make those decisions.

I decided to move to the inn and shoot indoors.

On the following day we were back at the stream, but the sky was still not blue, and the water was not sparkling. I was crestfallen.

David tried to make me feel better. He said, "This light is beautiful . . . so soft and gray. It's actually prettier than the sun."

I knew he was trying to put a positive spin on the situation. But I said, "No, that's not what I see. This is a joyous moment for Yentl, and I want the water to be glistening."

Sometimes you can't get what you want, and you have to deal with the reality of what is and accept what the universe is presenting . . . but not this time. I had to have the sunlight. I could hear the music . . . it would be positive and uplifting, and I didn't want a gray day. So I did the only thing I could think of . . . I prayed. Using all my will, I prayed to God and my father. Please give me some highlights on the water!

My father was a religious man. And I was making this movie for him, to honor the tradition of scholarship he represented and to be the daughter he would want me to be. And I had a sense that he was protecting me all along. And as God is my witness, the clouds scattered and the sun came out and sparkled on the water.

As we were doing the shot of Yentl crossing the stream on the raft, I was looking up toward the inn, and suddenly I spotted a stork flying toward the nest. I shouted, "Oh my God, there's a stork coming back to the nest! Turn the camera around. Get the stork!" And Peter caught it.

That's what's great about being the director . . . you can change the shot.

I'm very grateful to those storks. When I first saw the nest on my scouting trip during the winter, it was empty. How nice of them to come back and be in residence while we were shooting. And we were lucky to get that shot when we did, because the next day the whole family disappeared. I guess the babies were grown, and it was time for them to fly away. I love things like that . . . you capture the moment and you can't repeat it. They were gone.

That image of a stork in the sky reappears several times in the film. I used it when Yentl is on the wagon heading to the yeshiva and again when she and Avigdor are on the road to Lublin. It was almost as if that stork was watching over her . . . and me.

One of the most personal scenes for me in the film was the one where Yentl is sitting under a tree in the backyard with her father. He's worried about her continuing the course she's on, studying late into the night and ignoring any opportunity to marry.

"Children are more important than the Talmud," he tells her. "Without children to pass it on to, the Talmud dies with old men when they die."

Yentl apologizes, and then he apologizes to her, saying, "You're a woman, but I didn't teach you how to be one."

Yentl can't bear for him to think that way. She's adamant that he has not made a mistake in teaching her what he knows. "Learning is my whole life," she says. "Please don't be sorry. I'm not."

"Too late to tell you to play with dolls, huh?"

And then I wanted him to look at Yentl and give her some kind of acknowledgment that he accepts her for who she is.

Nicky was wonderful, but he couldn't quite get the particular reaction I wanted. I tried to explain it to him, but that didn't work. And then, because I was acting with him in the scene, kneeling at his feet (with my back to the camera), I could talk and improvise with him. When he said, "What's to become of you, Yentl?" I said something to him that wasn't in the script . . . "I'll be fine, Papa, because I'm your daughter." And there it was . . . he smiled so lovingly as he shook his head and let out kind of a sigh, and then he cupped my face in his hands. It was exactly the reaction I wanted.

I was talking to my father, in a way, and Nicky related to me as if I were his own daughter. You can watch the two of us working on this scene in the Director's Reel on the DVD, and see the joy on my face when I knew we got it. I said "Beautiful!" to Nicky and then turned to Peter, snapping my fingers in triumph.

I got it because I was right there with him. It doesn't matter how you get a performance, as long as you get it. And I won't give up until I've got it.

Although I don't like to do a lot of takes. Usually two to four are enough for me, sometimes six or eight, because after that it's hard to maintain the spontaneity. That's why I like to film rehearsals, because the first time an actor does something is often the best . . . although there are some people who don't warm up until the tenth take. Point is, you have to accommodate each individual actor.

And in this scene, the universe conspired to assist me. The sun was setting, Nicky was facing in that direction, and the late-afternoon light was so beautiful. Usually a director will shoot the woman first . . . you want her to be fresh . . . but I always did my shots last. (I never wanted to appear self-serving.) But in this case, I think we did me first because I was waiting for the sun to go down a bit more so it would hit Nicky just right. And we caught the perfect moment. As he said his lines, his eyes were suddenly lit up by the last beam of golden light coming through the leaves of the tree. It was magical.

That scene was lit by God. David needed no artificial light.

Then the camera goes up the tree and catches the last flickers of light through the branches, as the shot dissolves to another canopy of leaves and comes down this tree in darkness . . . and we find ourselves at a graveyard. Yentl is kneeling to throw a handful of earth into a grave, and we know instantly that her father has died. When a man asks, "Who will say *Kaddish*?" she says, "I will" . . . to the shocked faces of the other mourners, because only a man is supposed to say the prayer for the dead. That's the kind of storytelling I like. It's all done with the camera.

Sometimes I'd look at a shot on the video monitor and say, "Ooh, that's good." And then I'd remember how my mother would spit three times over her shoulder, saying "Pooh, pooh, pooh!" to ward off the Evil Eye if, God forbid, she said anything complimentary. And I would think, *Better not say that.* God might take it away.

I found myself praying once more when we were about to shoot the scene where Yentl and Avigdor enter the city of Lublin. Prague was standing in for Lublin, and we planned a sequence with the two of them in a horse-drawn wagon, going across the Charles Bridge. It's a historic bridge, one of the most famous landmarks in Czechoslovakia, and it had never been closed to the public in more than five hundred years. But they closed it for us. We had about four hundred extras in period costumes and a crane in position. I was with Peter on the roof of a building very high up so I could supervise the dramatic overhead shot of Mandy and my stand-in coming through the archway onto the bridge.

And it was raining.

Yentl and Avigdor, dripping wet in an open wagon? That was not the image I had in mind. I thought, *This can't be happening.*

I prayed to God, and my father, with every bit of might I had in my being. And lo and behold, the clouds disappeared, the sun warmed the old stone, the light was dancing on the river . . . and I got my shot of Yentl joyously crossing another, much wider body of water.

At the end of August, we moved back to London. We were now shooting the final scenes, including the climax of the film . . . the moment of truth between Avigdor and Yentl, when she reveals that she's a woman. At first he thinks it's some kind of joke, but then she unbuttons her shirt to show him her breasts, and he is shocked, then scared, then furious. He calls her a monster, a devil . . . "You spit on the Torah!"

"I love the Torah!"

He's attacking her. "You married a woman! How could you do that?"

"It was your idea!"

I wanted them to be circling each other, around a table, so Peter set up two cameras going simultaneously, from opposite sides of the room. Mandy was out of control when we began. He was throwing things around, slamming his fists into the table and the wall. I was worried he was going to punch a hole right through the set. He was yelling so loud that it was hard to understand what he was saying, and then he'd lose track of where he was and shout, "Line! Line!"

I had to tell him, "Wait. Wait. It's too violent." Meanwhile, I was gesturing for the camera to move a little to keep Mandy in the shot. I suppose it would be confusing for some actors . . . to be acting with a person and having them direct you at the same time. But I didn't want to stop the cameras, or his momentum, even though he kept saying the wrong word . . . "Why didn't you tell me you were a man?" instead of "woman." I was already seeing the edited film in my head, and I knew I could put in the right line on the reverse shot (of my face and his back) if I had to. So when he made a mistake, I just told him to keep going because here's where his intensity really worked for the scene.

Avigdor is shaking her. "I want the answer . . . Why? Why?"

"I was afraid."

"Why?"

"I wanted to be near you."

"Why?"

"I didn't want to lose you."

"Why?"

"I loved you."

And then they drop to the floor, exhausted. She's sobbing, he's gasping for breath, and as they clutch each other his anger dissipates as he finally understands what he has been feeling all along. "I thought you didn't understand about love," he says. "My God, no wonder. All the times I looked at you and I touched you and I couldn't understand why. I thought there was something wrong with me . . . Yentl, I loved you too."

Slowly they lean in to kiss . . . and then he remembers Hadass, and the mood is broken.

That was not how I originally wrote the scene. In one version they continued kissing. And then we would have dissolved to the next morning, when they're lying in bed together, and he's running his hand down her neck to her bare breast and telling her how wonderful things are going to be now. (That's when I thought Richard Gere was going to play the part!)

Clearly that was my instinct . . . to have Yentl and Avigdor make love . . . but when it came to the crunch, I couldn't do it. By this point Mandy had been making my life miserable for months, and I just couldn't bear the thought of making love with him. I'm not that good an actress.

So I changed it. I rewrote the scene. And now that I look back on it, I wonder if I allowed my frustration with Mandy to overrule my instincts. Maybe I should have let Yentl . . . and the audience . . . have that moment.

The ending would have stayed the same. Everything would still fall apart in just a few minutes of discussion. Avigdor would say the same words he does now, that they'll get married and find a new yeshiva.

"For both of us?" Yentl asks.

And Avigdor makes a fatal mistake. He says, "You still want to study? . . . You don't need to anymore. I'll do the thinking. I'll take care of everything."

"No, I want to study with you, not darn your socks!"

"You're asking the impossible."

"Nothing's impossible." (I used that as the tagline on the posters.)

He's bewildered and says, "Don't you understand? I want you to be a real woman."

"I *am* a real woman."

"Then act like one! There's no gift from God that is more beautiful and more miraculous. You know everything without opening a single book. What more do you want?"

And Yentl, after a long beat, quietly answers, "More."

I guess this is one of my themes. Like Margaret in *Up the Sandbox* and Esther in *A Star Is Born*, Yentl wants *everything*. It's now clear to her that she has to leave. Avigdor is too steeped in tradition. He can't get past his innate prejudices. The following morning the two of them part.

In the next scene, we see Avigdor and Hadass together, reading a letter from Yentl. And that leads into the final sequence of the film.

On the day we shot it, I picked a little girl from the slew of extras to be reading a book (a future Yentl?) as the camera keeps moving over her head to reveal a boat filled with refugees. While we hear the opening of the song "A Piece of Sky" in voice-over, the camera continues across the crowd on the upper deck to find the back of a little figure alone at the stern below.

When I described this scene to Peter early on, I said, "Then I want the camera to go closer on her back and move around her in a half circle, over the water, until we see her face from the front . . . and it's Yentl, singing. And then I want the camera, without a cut, to follow her as she turns and makes her way across the deck, still singing this whole section of the song, until she goes inside. Is that even possible? I mean, how would you get the camera over the water?"

After a long moment, Peter said, "I think we could do it with a Louma crane, but it's never been used on a moving boat. Let me look into it."

I had never heard of it, but it turned out to be a remote-controlled camera on the extendable arm of a crane. Of course it took two days to rig a platform for it, cantilevered off the side of the boat, so it would never be seen in the shot. But it was exciting to use because it was so mobile. We could do it all in one continuous shot, just as I envisioned.

I felt so free . . . I could move when the music motivated me and walk wherever I wanted to through the ropes and luggage piled on the deck. We had the natural light of the sun, the playback functioned well, and it all worked beautifully, like a ballet. I was so happy.

We completed the whole first section of the song on the first day, and then it got cloudy. So we moved inside, where Peter had the Steadicam ready to shoot Yentl singing in voice-over as she walks through an interior passageway crowded with more refugees. That was easy. We got it in a couple of takes.

Then we moved to the upper deck to work on the most complicated part of the shoot, the last section of the song, which required a helicopter. And then nature really stopped cooperating. The weather turned very rough as a storm blew in. The boat started rocking so badly that in a short while, 150 out of 200 extras got seasick. Luckily I didn't because I was trying to squeeze in a rehearsal . . .

But then it became impossible to continue. The helicopter had to leave. The captain decided to turn the boat around and head back to Liverpool. In the midst of the turn, we were hit by a huge wave, and the boat suddenly tilted about 40 degrees. Equipment was sliding across the deck, and the crew was frantically grabbing bits and pieces to keep them from flying overboard. The Louma crane was chained to the platform but it was tilting, too, so the men were pushing like mad to keep it from toppling over into the sea. I looked up and saw one of our camera assistants bleeding from a gash above his eyes . . . he had been hurled against the side of the boat. I said, "Oh God, get the nurse!" . . . and was told she was seasick too! Luckily several of the extras were Jewish doctors, so they took care of those who were injured.

At that moment David Watkin suddenly emerged from the cabin, saw various people bandaged up, and said, "What happened here?" Peter told him, and he said, "Oh, that's why I fell out of my bunk." He had been asleep, as usual, and missed all the drama.

As we approached the harbor, things calmed down a bit. I went to the galley to get some hot tea for the crew, and as we were pulling into the port, I overheard them talking about going to the pub to have a few pints, which they definitely deserved!

Then early in the morning on the second day, we got another surprise, and not a good one. We received a report from the lab that the previous day's film was ruined . . . all the footage with the Louma crane of Yentl at the stern, lit by that gorgeous sun, was unusable because of condensation on the lens.

I couldn't believe it. Now we would have to redo that complicated sequence, and we were already under so much pressure to get everything else finished.

We decided to save the reshoot till the end of the day, with the setting sun, and started as we had planned with the Steadicam shot of Yentl coming up a dark staircase into the light. Then she strides through the passengers on the upper deck, still singing and no longer caring who hears her . . . "Papa, I've a voice now" . . . to end up at another railing, overlooking the wake of the boat and the past she's leaving behind.

I was having fun with the Louma crane, asking Peter to have it swoop in fast, like a bird, as I held the high note on "why settle *for*" and then swoop out on "just a piece of *sky*." It was such an ingenious tool.

And then for the finale of the song, I wanted the camera to pull back, as the boat recedes into the distance. For that, we needed the helicopter, which was hovering overhead, waiting for us. But it could only hover for twenty minutes at a time, and then it had to fly back to Liverpool to refuel, which took about forty-five minutes all together . . . eating up precious time. Meanwhile, the sea was getting choppy again. I was trying to keep my balance on the shifting deck and sing at the same time when there was another disaster . . . the playback machine went out, with the song on it! I had to ask my stand-in to get my boom box and crouch down below the camera so I could try to sing to a cassette tape (with no time-coded sync to the camera, which meant the scene might never work).

You know how much I hate lip-syncing, and now I had to do it to a track I could barely hear because of the noise of the helicopter right in front of me. The whole boat was rising and falling with each swell, pushing me closer to the whirling blades each time . . .

I was *really* terrified. Recently a helicopter on a movie set had crashed into the water, and three actors below were tragically killed.

But I had no choice. I *had* to get that shot! It was now or never, and *nothing* could have stopped me. So I just signaled to the assistant director, "Go!"

As the camera rolled and the music started, I closed my eyes and prayed to God and my father . . . and just sang.

The shot worked. I breathed a sigh of relief. I was still in one piece.

Then we had to wait for the helicopter to turn around and come all the way back to the boat, to do another take just in case.

And the day wasn't over yet. Now we quickly had to move down to the lower deck to redo the damaged shot and we didn't have much time before we lost the light. Miraculously, for that first moment at the railing, Yentl was lit by the last of the setting sun. But as she made her way back toward the cabin, the sun disappeared completely. I wanted to do one more take, but David said, "We can't shoot anymore. There's not enough light."

That's when Peter whispered in my ear, "Tell him to just shoot it anyway."

I said, "David, we don't have a choice. We have to shoot it right now."

"But it's too dark."

"Well, put up those white cardboard things" (otherwise known as bounce boards).

So the grips were crawling around on their knees so they wouldn't be seen, holding up the boards and moving along with me, as I headed toward the passageway.

And it worked. We got the shot . . . with no condensation this time!

This is what makes filmmaking exhilarating and terrifying at the same time. It was one obstacle after another, but we had to push through every problem and find a solution. It's the ending, after all!

Singer had a different ending to his story (his Yentl continues living as a man in Eastern Europe and presumably goes off to another yeshiva), but I envisioned something else. I wanted her to leave her old world behind and find a new world where women did have the opportunity to study and realize their potential. I thought that was a more positive way to end the story.

And there was no better place for Yentl to go other than the most progressive country and the most welcoming to refugees . . . America.

In some ways Yentl's struggle mirrored my own . . . she was trying to enter a man's world of education, and I was trying to make it in a man's world as a director.

And in the effort to be all that you can be, sometimes you wind up alone.

I wanted "more," just like Yentl. Before I moved to London to prepare and shoot the film, back at the beginning of January, Jon and I went skiing in New Hampshire with Cis and Harvey. That was basically our goodbye. We knew I was going to be away in Europe for at least a year.

But before I left, Jon wanted to cement our relationship. "I want to get married," he told me. "I want to buy a house together."

"I don't want to do that," I said.

I'm sure he was hurt, and that made him angry. "Well," he finally responded, "then I might have to find somebody else."

All I could say was, "Do what you have to do."

So I left for Europe and never really came back to Jon. When I turned forty soon after we began filming the movie in London, Kim and Jason flew over to help me celebrate and brought me the most wonderful present . . . a video they had made of all my friends, wishing me "Happy Birthday" and reminiscing about all the good times we had shared.

And they had not asked Jon to be in it, which made him furious. He came to London anyway, but was so mean to Jason that he almost spoiled the birthday for me.

Before I left for Europe, I put him in charge of turning a little house on the property into an editing room so I could work on the movie at home. I gave him a budget and told him that all I really needed was some editing tables, blinds on the windows, and a carpet on the floor to absorb sound.

And what did I find when I came home? Jon had spent $2 million and moved a mountain (literally) without telling me. He decided to push the mountain back and shift all that dirt around so he could put a Jacuzzi outside the bedroom on the second floor. (Like I would have time to use it?) That was completely unnecessary. He allowed a decorator to spend $400,000 on four rooms and a kitchen, in a house that no one was going to live in.

What I found out when I questioned the cost was that he had also built a road through the woods to a house he had previously bought on an adjoining property . . . and put it on my bill.

Of course Jon had moved the mountain without a permit and had no idea that he was destabilizing the land around it. During a rainstorm, the rest of the mountain came down on that house in a huge mudslide. Luckily it had a stone fireplace, because that was the only thing holding it up. But the basement flooded, which ruined all sorts of treasures, including that white Cecil Beaton turban from *On A Clear Day You Can See Forever* and costumes from my TV specials.

Jon never paid much attention to rules.

We broke up, and he moved out of the ranch. When he invited me to see the house he had found, I noticed a prescription bottle on the counter . . . with a woman's name on the label instead of his.

I asked who she was, and he said, "She's someone I've been seeing."

It's so interesting . . . suddenly I felt a pang for a moment, even though I had no desire to be with Jon myself. And I was grateful to him for not telling me about his new relationship while I was shooting. At least he didn't interfere with my work.

I threw myself into the editing process. What I love about making a movie is that it's never locked until that last moment, when you have to put the film in the can and send it to the theaters. Until then it's a living thing. We had an editing room set up near the stage at the studio in London so I could duck in between scenes and look at footage with my brilliant editor, Terry Rawlings. I like to edit as we go along, gradually shaping each scene. Terry followed us to Czechoslovakia. Then, after we wrapped at the end of September, he came with me to Los Angeles and we worked together in an editing room I set up in my office on Carolwood.

It's exciting . . . you have each actor's performance in your hands. I'm always looking for the sound of truth in the voice. You can hear it, and it's as satisfying as the right chord in music. Actually, a good film is like a great piece of music, with different movements and various tempos. I'm always very conscious of rhythm in film, and when I'm editing, I want to vary the rhythm. It's like staccato versus legato in music. You might have a scene that's fast, with quick cuts . . . and then you might move to something more languid, with long, sweeping camera movements.

I always think of Mahler's Symphony no. 10 or a ballet like *Swan Lake*, where the corps de ballet surges forward and back in a complex pattern of steps, and then they vanish, leaving only the two principal dancers onstage to perform a lyrical pas de deux. It works as a release, and a relief. After short, choppy, fast movements, you need to rest.

The pressure was enormous during the whole editing process. And the obstacle course hadn't ended . . . the executives at the head of United Artists changed four times after we signed the contract! David Begelman, my old agent, was long gone, and now Frank Yablans was in charge. We screened a rough cut for him, and thank God he liked it.

But then the completion bond company insisted that I finish quickly, even though the film wasn't scheduled for release for eight months. We were just a bit over budget . . . only 11 percent, not 100 percent, as one reporter claimed. And that was utterly normal for a picture shot on location. But the miserable bond company wanted it done. *Now.*

"Please," I kept telling them, "this isn't necessary. You'll ruin the movie, and I'm going to die from the pressure." But they didn't care. Somehow I still managed to do the work, and do it the way I wanted to. I had to, or else the bond company would have taken the movie away from me and given it to someone else to finish.

And then the rumors started. As soon as I got back to LA, gossip columnists were saying that the picture was in trouble. Why did they have to lie? It was as if some people were waiting for me to fail.

It got so bad that Frank Yablans had to issue a press release to rebut them. It said, in part: "I want to make it clear that Ms. Streisand is, has been, and will always be the credited producer and director of the film, retaining full artistic control. We at MGM/UA who have seen the rough cut are tremendously elated and proud to be associated with *Yentl.*" And he continued: "I've never dealt with a person more responsible in terms of cost than Barbra was on this film. Every dime ultimately ended up on the screen."

I can only make films about things that are very personal to me. In *Yentl* I created a father and I made him in the image of my own, even naming him Mendel, the Hebrew version of Emanuel. In many ways I think I've spent most of my life trying to regain what was lost . . . to attain the unattainable.

But one thing I learned from directing this movie was that I had to be my own father. I couldn't look for a man to save me. We make our own fate, and I was ready to take responsibility. And it gave me great pleasure to put that final chyron on the screen: "This film is dedicated to my father . . . and to all our fathers."

When I showed the finished film to my mother for the first time, in my screening room at Carolwood, her reaction wasn't "That's wonderful!" or "You did a great job." Instead she was angry, and she said, "Why are you dedicating it to your father? Why not to *me*? I'm alive."

As far as criticism goes, that was just the first shot.

THIRTY-SEVEN

Don't Change a Frame

On the day *Yentl* opened . . . November 18, 1983 . . . I was nervous. I went to the Village Theatre in Westwood at noon to make sure the sound was right and the picture was right, and said to myself, *That's all I can do.* Then I thought, *To hell with my diet!* I went and bought myself a ham-and-cheese croissant and then I needed something sweet, so I ran to the nearest candy store and bought all the chocolate-covered marzipan I could eat, sat there in the car, and stuffed myself. That's how scared I was that nobody would show up.

I knew I would be attacked, and that's why you don't see my name at the beginning of the movie (just like I didn't put it on my scripts). In fact, there are no credits at all until the end. I wanted the audience to get to know Yentl before they were reminded of me.

And even though the preferred directorial credit at the time was "A film by" . . . I thought, *No, don't do it.* The simpler "Directed by" was good enough for Willy Wyler, so I decided it was good enough for me. Besides, I was already worried that people would think I was doing too much. The press kept harping on the fact that I was the first woman to produce, direct, write, and star in a movie. When you list everything like that, it sounds like a lot, and I didn't want people to hate me for it.

The reality is sometimes it was scary doing all those jobs. In other words, I am not some supremely confident, fearless female. I read something once that really helped me: "Fear is the energy to do your best work."

I had invested so much of myself in this movie, and now all that was left was to let it go . . . send it out into the world and hope . . . pray . . . that the audience would like it.

I was prepared to be judged. I'm always eager for constructive criticism. I love reading a thoughtful, perceptive analysis of my work. But what I didn't expect were some reviews that seemed more about me than the film, and some of the most negative were from women. Maybe it's like female judges on marital cases . . . they're usually much tougher on other women.

I sat for an hour-long interview with Geraldo Rivera for *20/20* that aired the night before *Yentl* opened across the country (I did everything I could to support this movie), and after the program this young woman popped up on the local news who looked familiar. I thought, *Wait a minute. Isn't that one of Ray Stark's girlfriends?* (The week before she was hosting a cooking show. This week she's a film critic?) In any event, I can still hear her say, in a singsong voice, "I'll bet you're all wondering what I thought about *Yentl.* Well, I *liked* it, but I didn't *love* it."

So much for fifteen years of my life.

I doubt people paid much attention to her, but they do read *The New York Times*, and I was on pins and needles waiting for that review. Imagine how I felt when, in the first sentence, Janet Maslin accused me of wearing a "designer yarmulke."

What? That's ridiculous. All our costumes were either period pieces or copied from photographs of Eastern European Jews at that time. (Ingmar Bergman put a character in the same kind of yarmulke in *Fanny and Alexander*, and no one had a problem with it.) Maslin went on to disparage David Watkin's incredible cinematography. Apparently she has something against sunlight pouring through a window because, according to her, the scene with my father in the synagogue was overlit. And she ends her review by mocking the knitted hat I wore on the boat in the last scene. There was more focus on my hats than on the ideas I was trying to express!

I was shocked by this kind of trivial criticism. I had hoped people would see the movie as a celebration of women. I was standing up for something I've believed in all my life . . . gender equality. I wanted to empower each and every girl . . . woman . . . to be all that they could be. And I also felt the weight of responsibility as a woman director. If this movie was a flop, I was worried that other women would find it even harder to get their films made.

As part of the publicity rounds, I had also done an interview with Anna Quindlen, a writer I admired, for *The New York Times*. She told me she liked *Yentl* very much, and we discussed the ideas it raised. I watched for her article every Sunday, but there was nothing. When was it going to appear? Finally, I called to ask her, and she told me, "Next week, I think." But it never ran.

So guess what they printed instead? A piece by Isaac Bashevis Singer interviewing himself about *Yentl*. He may still have been smarting from the fact that we didn't use his script, and wrote, "I never imagined Yentl singing songs. The passion for learning and the passion for singing are not much related in my mind. There is almost no singing in my works."

"Almost?" I guess that was meant to be a joke.

I was touched when Walter Matthau's wife, Carol, sprang to my defense, pointing out that Eliza Doolittle wasn't a singer either. So does that mean that George Bernard Shaw's *Pygmalion* should never have been turned into *My Fair Lady*? In a letter to the editor of *The New York Times*, she wrote, "I was shocked to realize that Mr. Singer is a mean-spirited, ungenerous and cranky man. I am thrilled that Barbra Streisand lives dangerously and breaks ground."

I had never met Carol, but I called her up to thank her, and we became fast friends. She loved roses, too, and we had two good friends in common . . . David Rayfiel and Marlon Brando . . . so it felt as if our friendship was meant to be.

Carol's kindness meant a lot to me because I felt so battered. But now that I'm looking at the *Yentl* reviews again, I'm surprised to find a lot of them were actually complimentary.

"To put it succinctly and at once, Barbra Streisand's Yentl *is a triumph—a personal triumph for Streisand as producer, director, co-author and star, but also a triumphant piece of filmmaking . . . As director, she has elicited outstanding performances from her entire cast."*

—Arthur Knight, *The Hollywood Reporter*

"She has drawn a fascinating and loving portrait of a distant period and a culture . . . And she has made the noisy, argumentative, traditional Hebrew method of pursuing wisdom seem nothing less than passionately exciting. She has accomplished this with taste, sureness and a sly sense of fun."

—Sheila Benson, *Los Angeles Times*

"At one time or another, almost everyone has loved the wrong person for the right reason. That's the emotional ground that Yentl *covers, and it always has its heart in the right place."*

—Roger Ebert

As always, Pauline Kael's insights could be uncanny: "There is something genuinely heroic in the mixture of delicacy and strength that gives this movie its suppleness. Within the forty-one-year-old star-director are the perfectly preserved feelings of a shy, frightened girl of twelve."

How did she know? She saw straight through to the dichotomy at the core of my being. She also gave me one of the best compliments I have ever received: "And now that she has made her formal debut as a director, her work explains why she, notoriously, asks so many questions of writers and directors and everyone else: that's her method of learning. And it also explains why she has sometimes been unhappy with her directors: she really did know better."

It's a great gift to have a critic who can prompt you to look deeper into yourself. I always learned something from her reviews . . . even when we didn't agree. She objected to the ending, when Yentl goes off to America, and explained why: "Streisand wants to give the audience an educational and spiritual message. She wants Yentl to be—gulp—a role model. Where Streisand's instinct as an artist fails her is in her not recognizing that Yentl exists on a magical plane, and that the attempt to make her a relevant, contemporary heroine yanks her off it."

I don't think the two perspectives are necessarily contradictory . . . it's a realistic fairy tale, after all . . . and I wish she were still with us so we could argue that point together, like two scholars debating the Talmud.

Singer didn't like the ending either and said, "Weren't there enough yeshivas in Poland or in Lithuania where she could continue to study?"

No, there were not . . . unless Yentl continued to disguise herself as a man. The only place where she could be truthful about who she was and have the freedom to explore her full potential as a woman was America.

I may have forgotten the good reviews, but there is one article about *Yentl* that is seared into my memory. It was an interview I did with Dale Pollock for the *Los Angeles Times*, which was published a month before the movie opened. We talked about the saga of getting *Yentl* to the screen, and I told him what happened when Steven Spielberg asked if he could see the film.

Steven and I had been friends ever since he came to the premiere of *A Star Is Born* in Westwood. I think we bonded because we were two Jewish kids with chutzpah who knew what we wanted, and got it . . . even though we're both very shy when it's not about work. And we recognized that in each other.

Amazingly, Steven had sensed that kinship before we even met. He told me he watched me on *The Judy Garland Show* when he was sixteen and asked his mother, "Is she part of our family?"

Even though we rarely socialized, since we were both so busy, once a year we would sit next to each other at Evelyn and Mo Ostin's house on the second night of Passover, where the other guests included Sidney Poitier, Quincy Jones, and their wonderful families. Steven and I always had a lot to talk about, and because he, Quincy, and I also shared a close friendship with Steve Ross, the head of Warner Bros., we were part of another family circle. Even now, if Steven has something to ask me he will sign his note "little bro" and I'm his "big sis."

He was already an acclaimed director, and then I became a director, and what's funny about that is neither of us has any sense of direction! One night we were both invited to the same dinner, so Steven picked me up and we got completely lost. Then a few weeks later, he called me, very excited, and wanted to show me something that he just discovered. It was an early version of a GPS system, and I thought it was miraculous . . . just what we needed!

Steven was always ahead of the curve.

I had just gotten home from Europe and was still editing when he asked if he could see some of *Yentl* because he was very curious about Amy's performance, since she used to be his girlfriend (although they had broken up long before we started filming). I said, "Great. I can show you her scenes." He came over and we looked at the footage on the editing machine's small screen. I was nervous and unsure. Was it any good? And he said, "It's extraordinary. I can't wait to see the whole thing."

So I knew I did well by Amy at least!

Months later, when the film was basically finished, I followed through on his request and screened it for Steven and Freddie Fields at the theater on the MGM lot . . . just the three of us in a place that can hold 350. I sat in the back so Steven wouldn't feel me breathing down his neck, watching his every reaction.

As soon as the lights came up, he walked over to me, and the first thing he said was, "Don't change a frame!" Can you imagine how thrilled I was to hear that? It was like getting the seal of approval from one of the greatest directors in Hollywood. He said, "I wish I could be clever and tell you how to make your film better. But I can't!" Steven told me he was impressed on many levels. He kept going on about the beauty of the cinematography, the fluidity of the direction, and the wonderful performances. I was elated. And then he said, "I'd like you to direct a film for my company."

My first reaction was, Direct another film?

I had proved to myself that I could do it . . . but I wasn't sure if I wanted to do it again so soon.

Now, let me tell you how that story was printed in the paper. It said: "When

Steven Spielberg gave her some advice on editing" . . . What? The only advice he gave me was "Don't change a frame." And then the next words were taken completely out of context: "I got panicked . . . I shook. I thought *me*? Direct it?" They left out what he had just said.

I called Dale Pollock up and asked, "How could this have happened?" How could those two crucial lines . . . "Don't change a frame" and "I'd like you to direct a film for my company" . . . have been cut? Didn't anyone notice that the sentence made no sense without them?

Apparently not. Pollock said his editor told him that the article was too long, so the editor made some cuts, which Pollock didn't see until right before it went to press. He was very sorry.

Not sorrier than me. Because the damage was done. That little mistake skewed the story and gave certain people in the industry just the excuse they needed to believe that I, as a woman, must have had help from a man. And not only a man but perhaps the biggest director in town.

The fact is, Steven *never* read a script, *never* set foot on the sound stage, and I *never* once called him during the shoot.

But from the moment that article was published, he was associated with *Yentl*, and the story that he had advised me was planted in people's brains. When the movie opened in Europe, I was interviewed by the foreign press, and one reporter said, "I hear Steven Spielberg was your mentor."

I should have asked the *Los Angeles Times* for a correction, but I didn't even know that was possible, and Lee Solters, my publicist, never suggested it. Of course, hardly anyone notices a correction. Eventually the story got so big that Steven felt compelled to deny the gossip. In *People* magazine he said, "Everyone thinks I worked with her, but I didn't."

And he kept talking about *Yentl* to the press. He called it "the best directorial debut since *Citizen Kane*," and told one reporter, "I think she tried to put everyone ahead of her in her list of priorities. It's selfless directing . . . I have a feeling that all this comes from her experience not as an actress being directed and watching other directors work but from her autonomy as a musician and vocalist . . . If you listen to her songs, they're impeccable on every level. That's Barbra directing herself."

I should have fired my press agent and hired Steven! He was so generous in his praise. And he told me he fell in love with Amy all over again through the movie . . . and they got married. It was nice to think *Yentl* had something to do with that.

I wish I could have ignored the slights from the press, but it felt so personal . . . this need to diminish me. It's one thing to dislike my work. That's legitimate. But if they don't even believe that I *did* the work . . . or if they don't like my determination or my bluntness or the fact that I'm an actress too . . . that hurts. I'm vulnerable, just like anyone else. And I would never want to lose that vulnerability. It plays a huge part in my work.

But it can be very painful, and that's partly why I didn't direct another movie for eight years. I thought, *I can't do this. I don't know how to fight it.* I love the creative process . . . actually doing the work . . . but I don't like what you have to go through afterward in terms of publicity and promotion. I don't like the "show" part of show business. I didn't want to do it anymore, and that's the truth.

Plenty of male directors show their films to one another, and no one suggests it's because they need help. But when a woman shows her film, the assumption is that she must need rescuing. After all, how could she do this without male input?

Is it so threatening, so maddening that a woman dares to step outside the box, dares to have dreams?

And the people who object . . . what is being taken away from them? Why doesn't it make them feel that they should pursue their dreams too? Instead of thinking, We have to make her less, so that we feel like more.

One good thing about looking through my papers for this book is finding things I had forgotten about, like the letters I received from friends and colleagues after they had seen the movie.

> *"How proud I was of you last night—and how really touched and moved by what you've done! The picture is wonderful—and the* sheer size *of the accomplishment is awesome."*
>
> —Sydney Pollack

"Your picture is a masterpiece. Meryl Streep and I saw it at a screening and wept copiously. I was indescribably moved that Yentl's problem with the world was the same as your problem as a director in the world of movies. You both solved your problems with brilliance and heart and wisdom. You are a first-rate artist and I am your admirer."

—MIKE NICHOLS

"Dear Barbra, My admiration and respect to you for your determination to realize your dream. Yentl *is a great achievement for which you should be truly proud."*

—ELIZABETH TAYLOR

"Yentl *is magnificent. It is one of the best directed, best written and best acted films I've ever seen. I laughed and I cried and I was in awe of your accomplishment. Surely it's the 20th film you've directed, not your first . . . You can direct a picture of mine anytime. You are also the sexiest boy I ever saw."*

—NEIL SIMON

"Watching the movie, I was proud to be a woman, I was proud to be Jewish and I was proud to know you . . . bravo . . . this is a masterpiece."

—DIANE VON FÜRSTENBERG

And now the response from some studio executives was quite different from those I had faced initially. Michael Eisner, president of Paramount, wrote: "I wish you were not a motion picture star. I wish you were not a recording star. I wish you were not 'box office.' I wish pictures weren't made just because of your fame and talent. If you were solely a first time director, Paramount could afford to make an overall director's deal with you and we would have the benefit of someone who is enormously gifted and would make many great movies for us."

I wonder what would have happened if I had made such a deal.

The film made the Top Ten list in *Time* magazine and the National Board of Review. And then when the Golden Globe nominations were announced, *Yentl* was nominated for the big award . . . Best Motion Picture—Comedy or Musical. I felt like jumping up and down. And there was more. Mandy was nominated for Best Actor—Comedy or Musical, and I was nominated for Best Actress. Michel and the Bergmans were nominated for Best Original Score and Best Original Song, for "The Way He Makes Me Feel." And I was nominated as Best Director, along with Mike Nichols for *Silkwood*, Bruce Beresford for *Tender Mercies*, James L. Brooks for *Terms of Endearment*, Peter Yates for *The Dresser*, and Ingmar Bergman for *Fanny and Alexander*.

I never expected to be among them. So when the Directors Guild of America announced their nominations for Best Director and I wasn't included, I wasn't surprised.

The night *Yentl* opened, I remember going to a party where there happened to be quite a few directors. When I walked into the room with a friend, no one came up to me to chat. By the way, that's not unusual. I seem to elicit two reactions . . . either I'm swarmed, or people don't seem to notice me or pretend not to notice me. Of course it's different with people I know . . . they treat me like anyone else. But in a room full of strangers, I see everyone else talking animatedly and feel like the odd man out. When Jason was a teenager, I remember him telling me that he didn't like parties, because no one came up to him. So I told him what I had learned: "You can't count on people coming up to you. They don't come up to me either. I have to force myself to reach out, and you might have to do the same thing."

I stood there thinking, *Okay. Make an effort.* I saw Martha Coolidge and thought, *Great, a fellow woman director.* I walked toward her but she was involved in another conversation so I backed away.

Then I spotted Jack Nicholson, whom I knew from *Clear Day*. He had directed two movies, and I asked him whether he preferred to act or direct. Frankly, I can't remember his answer now . . . I think he said, "Act." But he didn't ask me about my experience. He just talked about himself.

Not one of the directors in the room asked me about *Yentl*. I got the distinct impression that they were not exactly happy that I had joined their club. In fact, I felt a chill. And I suppose it was even more complicated for the women. There were too few of us . . . only a handful in the DGA at that time, among many, many men. And I could imagine how they felt about making room for me. Women climbing up the ladder in many professions see very few spots at the top, and often feel compelled to protect their territory. What we should understand is that as more of us rise to the heights, the top of the ladder will grow.

As I was leaving the party, I saw a tall, dark, curly-haired man, who turned out to be Richard Baskin, leaning against the bar by the door. He stopped me and said, "I went to see *Yentl* today and loved it." You'll hear more about him later, because I ended up living with him for three and a half years, but that's another story.

On the night of the Golden Globes, I thought, *Too bad I don't drink.* (Again, that's not some puritanical impulse . . . I just don't like the taste. Although sometimes I'll have a glass of beer or a half shot of vodka in a lot of tonic.)

Everyone else in the room seemed to be enjoying themselves. Meanwhile, my stomach plunged as each of our categories came up. I was very disappointed when Michel and the Bergmans lost, because I thought they would definitely win.

But I never thought I had any chance of winning Best Director . . . and then Mark Rydell announced my name.

I clutched Marilyn's hand and made my way to the stage. I was wearing an antique choker and a black sequined skirt and top, which kept slipping off my shoulder, and I just said what came off the top of my head: "Gosh . . . I really did not expect this, believe me!" I was a little in shock, and I remember thinking, *Jim Brooks should have won.* I had to take a deep breath before I could continue. "Directing for me was a total experience. It calls on everything you've ever seen or felt or known or heard. It was really the highlight of my life . . . my professional life. This award is very meaningful to me."

I'm really bad at such moments. I see other people go up to accept awards, and they get so emotional . . . they laugh, they cry . . . and everyone loves that. I could never cry over an award. That's not who I am. So I'm always afraid that I won't have the emotions people expect. And I dread having to give a speech . . . the mere thought makes me tongue-tied.

Back in the pressroom they told me I was the first woman to win a Golden Globe for directing. I thought, *Wow! That's kind of amazing. I like firsts!*

But then I realized what that meant. How could they have ignored so many talented women? And that didn't change for decades. As I'm writing this, many wonderful movies in just the last few years have been directed by women . . . *Queen & Slim*, *Little Women*, *Mudbound*, *Wonder Woman*, *The Nightingale* . . . and they were all overlooked.

I had to return to my table because the evening wasn't over yet. Mandy and I both lost the acting awards . . . to Michael Caine and Julie Walters for *Educating Rita.* So I didn't have much hope when my old pal George Segal and Teri Garr were presenting the award for Best Motion Picture—Comedy or Musical. But then George opened the envelope and said, "*Yentl*," with a big smile.

Once again I made my way to the stage in a daze. There were so many people I wanted to thank, but I had to be brief and I knew I was going to leave somebody out, and I did . . . my dear Peter MacDonald, who was standing by my side every day during filming! He was the most important person on that set for me, and even now I'm mortified by the omission.

And then, last but not least, I said, "I would like to thank my father, who inspired me; my mother, who worried about me. She said, 'You're making a movie in Czechoslovakia?' These are all people who cared, and when people care, everything is possible."

(Little did I know that my future husband was also there that night . . . James Brolin was nominated as Best Television Actor—Drama Series for *Hotel.* He remembers that I walked by him at one point, and we locked eyes for a moment. That was all . . . but he never forgot it.)

Two weeks later the Academy Award nominations were announced. *Yentl* received five nominations . . . I was thrilled that Amy was nominated as Best Actress in a Supporting Role, and Roy Walker and his team were nominated for Art Direction, and Michel and the Bergmans were nominated for Original Song Score or Adaptation Score and for two original songs . . . "Papa, Can You Hear Me?" and "The Way He Makes Me Feel."

But *Yentl,* which had just won Best Picture at the Golden Globes, was ignored in that category, and I was passed over for directing.

I thought, *Well, they just didn't like the movie. It wasn't good enough.*

I was ready to believe that. Frankly, I never think what I do is good enough. I see my flaws more clearly than anyone else does and I'm usually the first person to point them out.

I tried to put a brave face on it. But the truth is, I was devastated. I came down with the flu and I rarely get sick, so that should tell you something.

It was easy to feel rejected. And I had to wonder . . . did they reject me because they didn't like the movie? Or is it because they didn't like me?

And then some people started saying it was because I was a woman. I didn't want to believe that. But now, looking back at clips from that time, it's clear that many people felt I had been discriminated against for just that reason. Gary Arnold, the critic for *The Washington Post*, had said in his review of the movie back in November that "it would constitute a Hollywood scandal if Streisand were denied an Oscar nomination for her direction of *Yentl*, which could also place her in the running for acting, producing, and screenwriting awards." I guess he was right, because now the press played up the controversy, and people took sides. Gregg Kilday wrote an article in the same paper headlined: THE SNUBBING OF STREISAND: DID THE ACADEMY JUDGE *YENTL* . . . OR HER? In another piece, he reiterated the lack of major nominations and observed, "It may not be polite to raise the issue, but the academy's shabby treatment of Streisand suggests two, deeply unpleasant facts: One, Hollywood isn't ready to applaud a strong-willed woman for directing, producing, writing and starring in a movie of her own. And, two, although many members of the academy are themselves Jewish, they do not look kindly on a fellow Jew who dares to raise the issue of Jewish identity in the midst of a popular entertainment."

It was an unusual experience . . . to have reporters like Gregg standing up for me. And he brought up an important point. Few movies were about Jewish subjects . . . *Gentleman's Agreement* was made in 1947 by very courageous people. Others would rather not risk any controversy. And it's understandable. Look at history and what has been done to the Jews, from being expelled from Spain in the fourteenth century to being exterminated in Germany in the twentieth. It's probably in our DNA by now . . . the instinct not to draw attention to ourselves.

Yentl broke that mold. And rereading these articles, I wanted to thank Lee Grant all over again . . . another actress who had also dared to direct. She told *People* magazine, "You want to know what I really feel? Screw 'em. So what? It's not the only game in town. What's important is that she keeps making films. She really kicked in the door for women with this one, not just opened it." And Bette Davis made a comment that I will always treasure: "Tell her it's only the best fruit the birds pick at." My wonderful cinematic father, Nehemiah Persoff, stood up for me in *People* magazine as well. He said, "We're still very primitive male chauvinists. If Warren Beatty had done this movie, they would have worshipped him again."

And the National Organization for Women jumped into the fray. After I was ignored by the DGA, the board of the California chapter passed a resolution stating: "We view this as another attempt to keep women in their place by not recognizing the quality and quantity of women's input into American society, and in this case because the film *Yentl* has feminist overtones, it is apparent that Miss Streisand is, too, being discriminated against because of her conviction and for being a woman." When I was asked about the DGA's dismissal on the night of the Golden Globes, I said, "Maybe in the next few years with more women directing, they'll get used to us."

But now, after being dismissed by the Academy as well, I didn't make a public statement. Frankly, I was sick of the whole situation.

Thank God I could leave it all behind. I don't usually enjoy publicity tours, but this time I was eager to head to Europe to help launch *Yentl* abroad.

In Paris, Michel joined the Bergmans and me for a press conference. That night, after the premiere, Pierre Cardin gave a party for us at Maxim's, which was the perfect choice because of its beautifully preserved Art Nouveau interiors. Taking a cue from the decor, I wore an Edwardian-style black dress with a high neck and a lace bodice decorated with intricate beading. I just looked through photos from that night. I'm sitting on a dark red velvet banquette with Jeanne Moreau and Charles Aznavour, and I'm the one eating the bread . . . so good, with fresh, room-temperature sweet butter. At a special ceremony, Jack Lang, the French minister of culture, presented me with La Croix d'Officier des Arts et des Lettres . . . given in recognition of an individual's contribution to the arts . . . which was a great honor.

Then it was on to Hamburg, where I answered questions from the German press and opened the film. We took a little side trip to the Black Forest and stayed at Brenners in Baden-Baden, one of those grand European spas that date back to the late 1800s. It was like something out of a novel by Thomas Mann.

In Rome I remembered why I hate being a "movie star." I just wanted to go shopping on the Via Condotti like everyone else, but the paparazzi were swarming like locusts. I tried to make a bargain with them. "If I let you take my picture, will you leave us alone?" They said "*sì*," but they wouldn't stop. They were incredibly aggressive, rushing right up to me. I was so frightened that I finally had to take refuge in a shoe store, where the staff quickly locked the door behind me to keep them out. And then guess who got arrested? My security guard, who was only trying to protect me by stopping one belligerent photographer who was shoving his camera in my face. We had to bail him out of jail, and the story was all over the papers the next day. They made it sound like a big drama, and of course they got it wrong. One photographer had a big dog that attacked the guard, but the papers said the guard attacked the dog!

Compared to that, the premiere wasn't so bad. I went to the theater earlier that day to do a sound check. It's still funny for me to hear another actress's voice coming out of my mouth . . . in Italy they dub every film into Italian. But they weren't allowed to touch my singing. I remember thinking, *Boy, this movie is just whizzing by* . . . and then the first song began. My voice was weirdly high-pitched, as if it were up a key, and the song was going much faster than I had recorded it. All of a sudden I realized what was wrong. They were speeding up the film. I got up from my seat and went back to the projection booth.

I said, "What are you doing? This isn't the right speed."

And the projectionist explained that it was better for the theater if the film was only two hours long . . . and *Yentl* was two hours and fourteen minutes . . . so he was just running it faster to get rid of those inconvenient fourteen minutes.

I went into producer mode and said, "I'm sorry, but you can't do that!"

Did they really think they could get that past me?

I was very touched by the warmth of the welcome from the Italian film community. Franco Zeffirelli gave me a wonderful party in his country house just outside Rome, where I got to catch up with Vittorio Storaro and his wife. (We picked right up talking about light and lenses again.)

I saw faces that I recognized from all those wonderful Italian films . . . everyone from Vittorio Gassman to Monica Vitti and Mariangela Melato. I adored those two women. We got along well because they were blunt and outspoken . . . if it weren't for their accents, you would have thought they came from Brooklyn! Mariangela was fabulous in Lina Wertmüller's deliciously provocative film

Swept Away. Her costar, a very shy Giancarlo Giannini, was also at the party. And meeting Giulietta Masina was a treat, because I've admired her since I first saw her in *La Strada* when I was a teenager. She was married to the great Federico Fellini, who invited me to a long, lovely lunch the next day at his favorite restaurant.

I sat there, completely entranced. Fellini had wavy grayish hair, glasses, and was dressed in a white shirt, a vest, and a coat and tie. He looked like any of the other prosperous businessmen at the adjoining tables. But there was something magnetic about him. He had the most penetrating gaze, as if he could see right through to the core of your being. Clearly he was the most famous man in the room, and yet he was totally unpretentious . . . very direct . . . very present. It felt completely natural to put my arms around him at the end of lunch and kiss him goodbye on the cheek. A good tight hug says so many things, without a word.

Lina Wertmüller was also incredibly kind. She gave me a dinner party and served the most wonderful square pasta with a delicious lemon and caper sauce . . . I can still taste it now.

In London, Princess Alexandra attended the premiere, which benefited one of the royal charities, the National Association for Mental Health.

And then we flew to Israel on El Al. That trip was harrowing. At first it felt as if the plane were struggling to get up in the air, and then once we were up, it kept shaking. I was trembling. There were Orthodox Jews who were kneeling and praying in the aisles. Was that normal, or did they know something we didn't? Were we about to crash? When we finally touched down in Tel Aviv, I couldn't wait to get off that plane, and even though it was after midnight, the runway was lined with photographers running to catch up to the plane. Oh no. Even here? I was too sick to my stomach to care . . . and just grateful to be alive.

I got all dressed up for the premiere and was surprised to see people in casual clothes, with many of the men in shirtsleeves. Well, it's a hot climate. I was nervous about how the Israelis would react but I needn't have worried. As the credits started to roll, the audience stood up and applauded for five minutes. Later, at the dinner, I was seated next to the U.S. ambassador to Israel, Samuel Lewis. That was fine with me, because I love talking politics . . . although I've noticed that some politicians would prefer to talk movies.

The following day there was a terrorist attack in a shopping area in Jerusalem, where we were headed next. One shooter was killed, and forty-eight people were wounded. That was sobering. I had Cis and Harvey, Marilyn and Alan, and Shelly and his wife, Judy, traveling with me, along with Kim and Renata. My friend Arnon Milchan, a very successful businessman born in Israel, had met us in Paris, and luckily he happened to have connections to Israeli intelligence, so he took charge of our security, and that made me feel safe.

So we left as planned, traveling in small vans with soldiers at our side. I've never seen people carrying quite so many weapons so openly . . . even more than in Czechoslovakia! And I was told that our security guards slept with hand grenades under their pillows. That was not exactly reassuring.

But I was not going to let my fear stop me, because I was going to Jerusalem to dedicate the Emanuel Streisand Building for Jewish Studies at the Hebrew University. This meant so much to me. I always wanted to tell my father how proud I was of him . . . proud to be his daughter and proud to bear his name. And this was my way of doing that.

Here was a place where women would be able to study the works of great Jewish scholars without having to disguise themselves as men. That was important to me. It was very moving to be on this campus, high on Mount Scopus, and look out at the Old City of Jerusalem on one side and the wilderness of Judea, the Jordan Valley, and the mountains of Moab on the other. As I said at the time, "You are keenly aware of the timelessness of the place and the timeless values the Hebrew University represents."

I'm tempted to enroll whenever I visit a university, but I guess that moment has passed for me. I think of myself as a perpetual student, always trying to learn. I feel as if I'll never know enough about anything . . . art, literature, history, the world. I will never have read enough books.

And I firmly believe that education is the key to peace.

After that ceremony, my obligations were done, and I was free to enjoy myself. Arnon hosted a dinner party for me, and Shimon Peres (who would become prime minister five months later) was one of the guests. Unlike most people, who will stare but hesitate to approach, he came right over to me and gave me a hug. We spent most of the evening talking together. I felt instantly comfortable with him, because he was just as I imagined my father to be . . . kind, empathetic, dignified . . . an educated man and a religious scholar. I couldn't believe that he knew so much about my music and my movies! He seemed to take the most heartfelt, personal pride in me as a Jewish girl who had made good.

Over the years I was privileged to spend more time with him. I'll never forget his response when I asked, "How can you help the Palestinian situation?"

He said, "By making their lives better."

He had a deep, compassionate soul.

Each day of that trip was packed. I met with the prime minister, Yitzhak Shamir, in his office. The mayor of Jerusalem, Teddy Kollek, gave us a tour of the Old City. We climbed up to the fortress of Masada and visited Yad Vashem . . . a memorial to victims of the Holocaust. When the big doors of the museum closed on our group, I felt a rush of terror. Suddenly I was transported back to the 1940s and the horrors of that time. I stared at those heartbreaking collections of hair, eyeglasses, and shoes, and thought, *Is there really a God? How could this have happened?*

I had that same feeling of panic when I visited Mauthausen, a concentration camp in Austria.

While we were recording the music for *Yentl* in London, I had invited the Bergmans to come with me one weekend to Vienna, to see the Bruegels in the Kunsthistorisches Museum. It was wonderful living in Europe . . . with just a few hours of travel, you could change cultures, currency, and language. But we had misjudged the time, and when we got to the museum, it was about to close. The guard said "*Achtung!*" (Attention!) as we entered and barred the way.

I tried to plead with him. "Oh no, no! We flew all the way here just to see the Bruegels!"

He was unmoved. "*Aus!*" (Out!)

I was so spoiled, because one of the perks of fame is that I've been allowed to visit many museums after hours. We went back to our hotel, and I went over to the manager and said, "Who's in charge in this country? I mean, do you have a king here or what? Somebody I could talk to?"

He said, "We have a burgermeister" (literally, the master of the town).

"Could I please speak to him?" I asked. "We've come all the way from London just to go to your museum, and it's going to be closed tomorrow, and we only have this one chance!"

He disappeared for a few minutes and then magically came back with an answer, from the burgermeister himself. "Ve vill ahr-range!"

And they very graciously let us come in the next day, when the museum was closed to the public. And a curator gave us a tour of the paintings. That was exhilarating.

But in the midst of so much beauty in Vienna (including delicious pastries), there was also darkness. On the way to Mauthausen, we stopped to see the Stadttempel, the oldest synagogue in Vienna and the only one to survive the Nazis. Terrorists had killed two people and wounded thirty at a bar mitzvah service five months before, so guards with rifles were standing outside.

And as we walked through Mauthausen, it was profoundly upsetting to look into the gas chamber and see the crematory ovens with their doors open . . . whitewashed, as if that could obliterate the smoke of death. You can never wash away that blackness. I had to leave because I had a panic attack. And as I looked up at the barbed wire on top of the chain-link fence on my way out, I thought to myself, *There but for the grace of God go I.*

While I was in Jerusalem I did an interview by satellite with David Hartman from *Good Morning America*, and of course he asked me about the lack of Oscar nominations for *Yentl*. By now all of that seemed very far away. I told him, "I feel that the media and people must be more positive than negative—in life, I think, in order for survival, for the planet's survival. So I would rather not theorize negatively about the reasons." I was tired of talking about it. I wanted to focus on the positive. I had made the movie . . . that was my real reward.

It was hard to believe that people in America could see me in real time, in Israel. And then we had to end the interview, because David said we were about to lose the satellite. I asked, "Where is it?" and he said, "Well, it's twenty-two thousand five hundred miles up if you really want to know." And I said, "Can you imagine? If only our hearts could expand as much as technology, we'd be in a very good place."

The last leg of the trip was going to be a tour of Egypt . . . a place I've been drawn to ever since I was a teenager and used to draw black eyeliner out beyond the corner of my eye, like Nefertiti. As we left Israel, I looked down from the plane and watched as the green land gradually got browner and drier as we flew toward Cairo. Cis and Harvey were with me, and our first stop was the Egyptian Museum. We wanted to see the mummies, but when we arrived, they weren't there. Apparently they were out on loan to another exhibition. Guess where? London. We were crushed.

Then we got back in the car to drive out to Giza to see the pyramids. That was a hair-raising ride, in the most unruly traffic I have ever seen. There were no stoplights at the intersections, and cars were zooming at us from all sides. I was terrified and had to keep closing my eyes. There was no escape. It was like being caught in a maze.

And then when we finally got to the pyramids, it was nothing like that image I had from the movies . . . stark, solitary pyramids surrounded by sand in the silence of the desert. Instead it was teeming with tourists and guys hawking trinkets and sodas and camel rides. In order to get inside a pyramid, you had to go through a dark, narrow tunnel, so small that I had to bend down. I was already feeling claustrophobic, and then someone behind me pinched my butt.

That was it. I had to get out. I had always felt that maybe I had lived in Egypt in another life . . . and now I was afraid that I had died here too. Everything suddenly seemed very scary. We scrapped the rest of the itinerary . . . I still regret missing Luxor . . . and left on a plane for London. I don't think we even stayed the night.

I got home just in time for the Oscars on April 9, but I couldn't bring myself to go. I had had enough of dressing up for premieres and red carpets by this point. And I really didn't feel like pretending, so I stayed home and watched it on TV. I was amazed to see protesters outside the Dorothy Chandler Pavilion. A women's group dedicated to equality in the film business had gathered in support of me. One sign said, "Oscar, can you hear me?" I was touched.

Out of our five nominations, only Michel, Marilyn, and Alan won for Best Original Song Score. Well, at least we got one.

Then an organization called Women in Film reached out to ask if I would accept an award. All of a sudden I felt included again . . . part of this industry. And by June 4, the date of the ceremony, I was ready to speak up. I was happy to accept their Crystal Award, given "to honor outstanding women who, through their endurance and the excellence of their work, have helped to expand the role of women within the entertainment industry."

I guess spending fifteen years trying to get one movie made definitely counts as endurance.

I had to give an acceptance speech, and I think they expected me to talk about the differences in how men and women are treated. And there was a lot to talk about . . . I had been so obsessed with *Yentl*, and it bothered me when people used that "obsession" with my work to put me down (it still does). It felt like men were allowed to be obsessed with work, but women were not allowed to be obsessed with work . . . only with a man.

And of course, there were all the movie executives who said that no one would be interested in seeing this movie outside of a small group in New York and Los Angeles. But as a matter of fact, the movie was more successful in Texas and Taiwan than it was in Brooklyn. So much for demographics!

The picture had found its audience all over the world, breaking records in unexpected places like Finland and Norway. By the date of this luncheon, it had already grossed more than four times its cost, and the soundtrack album was already triple Platinum. So that was immensely satisfying.

But as I was writing my speech, I realized that that wasn't what I wanted to focus on. I didn't want to just rail against the male-dominated power structure in Hollywood. Instead, I wanted to talk about an even more sensitive subject . . . women against women. I was still shocked that the harshest, most vitriolic, and most personal comments about the movie were made by women reviewers.

Why do we, as women, feel this need to compete with each other? Why are we so quick to tear each other down? Why are we so afraid of each other's success?

As I said in my speech, "It's as if we're still behaving like adolescent girls competing for a date with the football player, while he's out on the field learning tactics, strategy, and mutuality of interest. Men learn about teamwork, women don't. Men learn about power . . . how to get it, how to use it. Women don't."

When I finally became a director . . . when I got that power . . . I felt a deep calm. I no longer had to struggle to be heard. It wasn't about making people listen to me . . . it was about listening to everyone else. And I discovered that the most powerful thing you can do with power is to share it. The giving of power enhances your own.

I think sometimes women are trying so hard to be part of a man's world that in doing so, they take on the worst qualities of men.

I don't want to be more like a man. I'd rather be more like a woman.

I was grateful to be able to give that speech. It helped me articulate everything I was feeling. And I suppose, in a way, it was actually beneficial not to have been nominated, as it drew more attention to the problem of sexism.

You know, I actually called that woman on the local news who was so dismissive of the movie . . . since I knew her vaguely through Ray. And I asked her, "Why did you do that?"

Oddly enough, she didn't try to justify her remarks. In an unguarded moment, she simply told me the truth. "I was jealous. I always wanted to write screenplays and I never could."

Running head-on into all this bias was a life-changing moment for me. In Yentl's time, women were relegated to a certain role . . . to get married, cook, clean, have the children, take care of the man. When did that notion begin?

I have a theory about the caveman. Imagine what he must have felt, watching a woman give birth to a baby. All of a sudden this thing comes out of her body, kicking and screaming. Can you imagine the fear . . . the confusion . . . the sense of awe? Was she a witch or a demon or a goddess? Whatever she was, she was certainly powerful because only she had the ability to carry and feed another human being.

And maybe he thought, If she could create life, she could also destroy it . . . and some fear lodged in the male collective unconscious.

I bet from that moment on he decided that he had to keep her down on the farm . . . I mean, back in the cave. Somehow she had to be put in her proper place, which was subservient to him. But when he wanted her to focus on him, she was busy with the baby, who was sucking at her breast. That certainly made him jealous. The man felt left out. He wanted her affection. He needed her. And need often creates resentment.

I was so interested in this subject that in 1984 I endowed a chair at the University of Southern California to study intimacy and sexuality between men and women in a changing society. What happens when a woman acquires power? How does that affect her relationships with men? Do the dynamics of physical attraction change?

This isn't only a sociological question. It also has deep roots in religion.

Several faiths, including Jewish Orthodoxy, separate men and women in places of worship. I once asked a rabbi, "Why?" He said it's because women will distract men from prayer . . . from God.

In other words, Freud was right. Everything comes down to sex.

It's a complex issue. I feel for men . . . roles have changed so rapidly in a generation that it must be confusing. And now the #MeToo movement has forced us all to confront uncomfortable truths . . . and correct our behavior.

But for me, all these issues really became obvious with *Yentl.* That movie mobilized my commitment to women's equality. I became passionate about ensuring women get the same chances in life as men.

And that includes being allowed to direct a film.

THIRTY-EIGHT

The Broadway Album

After *Yentl* I was wiped out . . . burned out. I had been pushing so hard for so long to get that movie out into the world. But as soon as I had a few days to myself, I realized something. I had been so focused on my professional life that I had totally neglected my personal life.

Ever since Jon and I split up, I had been too busy to go out. It was only recently that I had started seeing someone new, but it was becoming clear that we were only destined to be friends.

And then the oddest thing happened. Remember Richard Baskin, the man I met at the party I went to on the night *Yentl* opened? Well, during the following week he kept reappearing, once at a political event at the Bergmans', where he came up to greet me, and my first reaction was, "Oh, you again." I didn't mean to be discouraging (and luckily Richard wasn't the type to be discouraged). I was just thinking it was kind of strange, since we'd lived in the same city for years and never met. (Although Richard did remind me later that we had met, briefly, fifteen years earlier when I was doing *Clear Day.*) And now we had run into each other twice in a matter of days. And then I saw him a third time at a screening of Courtney Ross's documentary about my friend Quincy Jones. Richard has told me the story of how he was already in the theater when I came in with another man and sat down four rows behind him. And he said to himself, *I'll turn around and look her in the eye, and if she smiles, I'll ask her out.*

Apparently I did smile, because he called Marilyn Bergman the next day and asked for my phone number. For our first date he took me to the Hamburger Hamlet on Sunset Strip, a restaurant that was as casual as it sounds. (They had good burgers and a drink that tasted like an amaretto malt.) Richard thought it would be quiet, and he was right.

I was comfortable with Richard from the start. He was a musician, and had composed music for Robert Altman's *Nashville*, so we connected on that level. And he was attractive . . . very tall, with a halo of dark curly hair, kind eyes, and a gentle manner. And then he did something very charming. He wrote a song for me . . . obviously to try to woo me . . . and it worked. Soon we were spending lots of time together and going skiing in Sun Valley, where he had a house.

I became so involved in this new relationship that I wasn't that interested in recording a new album, but I did owe one to Columbia. It was eventually called *Emotion*, and I barely remember it. All I can tell you is that it was fun writing a song with John Mellencamp . . . he did the music, and I did the lyrics for "A Step in the Right Direction" (which was exactly how I felt about Richard).

I had written another melody, and when I played it for Richard, he wanted to write the lyric. And that became "Here We Are at Last." I thought I was finally with someone who could be a real partner. The song proved we could work together, so I asked if he would like to collaborate on a music video for another song, "Emotion." I had this concept . . . a woman would be trying to arouse her sleeping husband, and when she can't, she starts fantasizing about other lovers. And since it's all a dream, why couldn't everything be color coordinated . . . all pink and black, then red and black, and back to pink and black. I thought that would be funny, visually. Then my outfits and my hair and makeup change color to match the sets. One moment was inspired by a favorite scene from *The Conformist* and was my homage to Bertolucci and Vittorio Storaro. A woman is sitting on top of a desk in a businessman's office when he pulls out a string of pearls to entice her. My yellow coat is the one note of color in the black-and-white frame.

We shot it in 1984 in London, which was way ahead of America fashion-wise. I'd see these incredible-looking kids with Mohawk hairdos and dazzling makeup on the streets and ask, "Do you want to be in my video?" I said the same thing to Mikhail Baryshnikov one night when he came over to the table in a Chinese restaurant where Richard and I were eating. Miraculously he said yes and played a role in one of my fantasies. As a child I wanted to be a ballet dancer, and who would be better than Misha to leap through a window, lift me up, and sweep me off my feet?

It was Richard's idea to ask Roger Daltrey, lead singer of the Who, to play my husband. He was a good sport (especially in the part where I hit him on the head with a book), and it was great to see him again in 2008, when we both received Kennedy Center Honors.

Making the "Emotion" video was a lark, but the album was a hodgepodge. I didn't relate to the material. And I told myself, *Never again.* Life's too short to spend time on something I don't believe in.

My next album was going to be different, and I already had an idea. I wanted to go back to my roots. And that meant Broadway, where I got my start as an actress and where each song was written for a particular character and the lyrics told the story. Some of the best songs ever written were conceived for Broadway musicals, which are now recognized as a uniquely American contribution to culture. This is the music I first heard as a teenager, watching the movie versions at the Loew's Kings in Brooklyn and then taking the subway to Manhattan to see them live onstage. This is the music I love.

So in 1985 I spent months listening to cast albums and making lists of songs that interested me, by legendary composers like Harold Arlen, the Gershwins, Jerome Kern, Cole Porter, Rodgers and Hart, Rodgers and Hammerstein, and Lerner and Loewe. And that's when I asked Peter Matz if he would like to produce the album with me. I thought it would appeal to him, even though Peter wasn't really a record producer. But he was part of that period in my life when I first sang these kinds of songs, and we had always worked well together. I sat beside him at my piano so we could experiment with arrangements . . . tempos and rhythms . . . and decide which songs were worth further investigation.

This project represented not only a reunion with the music I loved, but with Peter as well. It was ten years since I brought him in to work on *Funny Lady* (he arranged the music and conducted the orchestra). And before that he had conducted for me when I did two separate engagements at the International Hotel in Las Vegas . . . the first in the summer of 1969. I had just finished filming *Clear Day* and was nervous about performing live again. But I didn't want to disappoint Marty, who was so proud of the deal he had negotiated . . . as one of the hotel's executives told the press, it would make me "the highest-paid performer in nightclub history." And it also included stock in the hotel (that interested me more than the salary). Still, I was worried that Las Vegas, with its serious gamblers and tourists, wasn't really my crowd. And to make it even more stressful, the hotel was still a construction site. During one number on opening night, plaster dust mysteriously started to drift down from the ceiling. All I could do was try to turn it into a joke . . . "Look, it's snowing!"

From the moment I walked out onstage, I was thinking, *What am I doing here?*

So I was very grateful to see Peter's smiling face and feel his support. Ever since we met, I felt a bond between us. I loved his smarts, his seriousness, and his sensitivity. In fact, I had always been a little attracted to him and felt a reciprocal response, but he was married, and so was I, and neither of us ever acted on it. It was just there, subliminally. Then in Las Vegas, when I was on my own after my separation from Elliott and Peter's marriage was falling apart, something shifted.

One hot night at the house where I was staying, a few of us were in the pool . . . me, Cis, Peter, and Marty Farrell (who had written some jokes for the show). It was very beautiful and serene out there in the dark, under the stars . . . the flashing neon lights of the Strip seemed far away. We could have been anywhere in the world. Cis and Marty were quietly talking. I was holding on to the edge of the pool and bobbing around when all of a sudden, I felt someone swim up behind me . . . it was Peter, and he began to gently nuzzle my neck.

Never in our relationship had anything like that happened before.

And that was the beginning . . .

It's kind of funny. George Lazenby, then the world's latest heartthrob (as the most recent James Bond), flew all the way from England to see me, and I turned him down to be with Peter.

Friends like Phyllis Diller, Ernest Lehman, and the Bergmans also came to the show. Elvis Presley and his manager, Colonel Parker, sent me a lovely telegram that said: "Best wishes . . . We are greatly honored to have the International hotel folks think enough of Elvis to engage him to follow a great star like you."

Wow! Elvis had agreed to be the second person to play this room (two thousand seats, with an extra two hundred packed in) after my monthlong stint was up. On closing night he attended my show and came backstage afterward. He walked in with two bodyguards, and then gave the guys a look and gestured with his head (like in the movies), which clearly meant "Scram." So the two of us were alone in my dressing room. I was a bit nervous to meet him, so I started putting polish on my nails, because I didn't know what else to do. I'm not good at small talk, and I wasn't a big Elvis fan at the time (I came to really love him later). My shyness was paralyzing. I have no memory of our conversation. I barely looked up. But at the same level as my eyes was a huge silver belt buckle and his belly button, because his suit jacket was open to the waist and he had no shirt on, just his bare chest. His thick head of hair was dyed jet-black, and I thought, *Why would a young man dye his hair like that?* He was only thirty-four. Maybe he was prematurely gray?

Some people may find this hard to believe, but Elvis's presence barely registered with me . . . probably because I was too busy thinking about Peter.

That was a wonderful thing . . . to be friends for so many years and then have it turn sexual, so it went to a whole new level. It felt very natural. Still, love frightened me. It was so powerful.

Once I couldn't reach Peter and had a moment of panic. What if something had happened to him? Maybe he was hit by a car! I asked Harvey Corman to go look for him, and he found Peter in his hotel room, sound asleep.

Jason was with me in Las Vegas, as always. When it was time to return to LA, Peter rented a motor home, and we all rode back together, along with Peter's younger son, Jonas, who had joined him. The boys were about the same age, and we had so much fun on our little road trip that we prolonged it by stopping at Elliott's beach house in Malibu while he was away (with his permission, of course).

That was an idyllic time . . . playing in the sand with the boys and holding their hands while they splashed in the waves. For those few days we were our own little family. That was a dream come true. I remember taking a walk on the beach with our two sons as they collected sticks and stones and shells. At one point Peter and I just stopped and looked at each other, and I felt a shiver run up my body.

I was crazy about him.

After our interlude at the beach, Peter dropped Jason and me at Carolwood and checked into a hotel with his son . . . neither of us felt it would be right for him to stay at my home. But it was hard to be apart that first night. He came back and left Jonas with Jason and Babs, his wonderful Scottish nanny, so he could take me out for dinner. Nothing fancy . . . we went to Denny's for pancakes. I remember driving with him . . . the jacaranda trees lining the street had been in bloom, dripping with violet-blue flowers, when we started rehearsing for Las Vegas. But now all the flowers were gone.

When Peter flew home to New York, he wrote me wonderful letters, declaring his love and confessing that he had wanted to get involved with me for a long time, but had always pulled back. Now he was at work again on a TV show, *The Kraft Music Hall*, but was having difficulty concentrating. As he wrote, "Your face comes up in my head all the time . . . Sometimes it's more of a problem than I can handle. Over at the office there's a shelf full of recordings. I was there this afternoon trying to dupe and work and I looked up and you were staring at me from the cover of the *Je m'appelle Barbra* album. I had to cover you with Judy Garland for a few minutes until I got the arrangement finished."

No wonder I adored him.

In another letter, he wrote, "You are very much inside my mind so you should know my stomach is a mess. It has been since I left LA. Hard to believe it's exactly one week . . . along with your wonderful face the lovemaking comes back to my head all the time. It's never been so nice—an incredible mix of affection, preknowledge, exploration, tenderness, insanity, and love."

In looking through his letters I see a note I jotted down on the back of an envelope: "When I woke up the next day, I looked at my clock. It had stopped the night before at 1am." (I'm not surprised that my clock stopped, because part of my life stopped when he left to go back to New York.) "I miss you very much . . . I'm sure that anything you decide to do will be the right decision. I am with you always. B."

I know Peter was feeling very conflicted. In another letter he brought up the fact that "you have infinite ways to make a lot of money." But as he continued, "I make thirty-five hundred dollars a week on this show. It's a lot for my world but it's not a lot for yours. And I'm sure it would make trouble in our relationship."

That was actually a very good salary back then, although I wasn't thinking about finances. That issue didn't bother me, but it clearly bothered him.

And even more insurmountable was the reality of his marriage. I knew that he and his wife had been having problems long before we got involved, and he had put a lot of effort into working on them. Peter was such a good father, and ultimately he felt he couldn't just walk away from his kids.

I respected his decision . . . even though it was painful.

As he said in one letter, "All the consequences were there, clear as a high F-sharp."

So our affair ended, but we remained friends. He even came back to conduct for me again in Las Vegas in 1970, and then we hardly saw each other until *Funny Lady*, and now this album. Although there were moments, especially when the jacaranda trees were in bloom again, when I would be reminded of Peter and that singular summer.

Back to the album. When I approached Columbia with my idea of singing Broadway songs, Walter Yetnikoff and the other executives were apoplectic. "Are you kidding?" they said. "Nobody's interested in Broadway songs. It's old-fashioned. It's not commercial."

"Are you telling me a song like 'Somewhere' from *West Side Story* is not commercial?" I asked. "That doesn't make sense, because it was a big hit, and by the way, it's a ballad, like all these Broadway songs. And my biggest hits, like 'People' and 'The Way We Were,' are ballads. That's what I do best."

"We want you to do pop songs. Make another contemporary album."

"Great songs will always be contemporary!" I said.

I had been with Columbia for twenty-three years. I had made twenty-three albums (and ten soundtrack or compilation albums) for them. And now, after five number 1 albums and seven Grammy awards and millions of dollars in record sales, I basically had to sell myself again. It was actually kind of humiliating.

I was hearing the same sort of thing I'd heard all my life, ever since I was eighteen years old . . . "Why are you singing these cockamamie songs?" "It's not what's selling nowadays." "The whole idea is too risky."

In other words, no.

And this is why I'm so grateful to Marty Erlichman for making sure I had creative control and getting it written into my contract from the beginning. That meant I could make any album I wanted. But the record company informed me that they wouldn't give me my advance and wouldn't count the album toward fulfilling my contract unless it sold two and a half million copies, which they clearly thought it wouldn't.

Well, that was all the challenge I needed.

I was determined to make this album no matter what anyone said. And I thought, *Why not use the truth? Why not be honest about the opposition I was facing?* And it just so happened there was a song that dealt with this age-old conflict between art and business. It was called "Putting It Together," and it was from a musical called *Sunday in the Park with George*, written by the extraordinary composer and lyricist Stephen Sondheim.

Over those last few months, as I was sorting songs into piles, one name kept rising to the top, and it was Steve's. I knew he was brilliant because I had seen all his Broadway shows, but I had only sung two of his songs . . . a snippet of "Small World" from *Gypsy* on *Color Me Barbra*, and a version of an obscure song, "There Won't Be Trumpets" (which was cut from the show *Anyone Can Whistle*, directed by Arthur Laurents, by the way. And we ended up cutting it from the *Butterfly* album as well. It was only released in 1991 on *Just for the Record*). But now I kept circling back to Steve's work.

It's easy to see why. I like songs that have an emotional arc . . . a beginning, a middle, and an end . . . and Steve is so good at telling a story in song. He's the rare composer who is equally gifted at both words and music. It's a rich talent . . . rich in substance and wit. You can't help but be dazzled by the intricacy of the rhymes, the delicious double-entendres, and the clever plays on words.

I like how he always finds original ways to express himself. There's nothing flowery in his lyrics . . . no lazy rhymes like "moon" and "June." He deals with big emotions and also the most subtle feelings, often with a dash of irony that can suddenly change the mood from sunny to something darker and more poignant. He understands passion and can capture it in a lyric. His insight into human nature is profound. As an actress, I'm given so much to work with because there are so many layers to each song.

They're also interesting to sing because the rhythm is built into the phrasing. And as with the best melodies, it all seems inevitable. Everything just fits and feels right. And by the way, I'd like to thank him for putting the high notes on the vowels! Like the greatest songwriters, he knows how to write for singers.

I decided that the first song on the album should be "Putting It Together," because it was so relevant and true. I had to put this whole project together. And the song really illuminated the creative process. Steve had distilled all the struggle, anxiety, antagonism, and excitement experienced by any artist into that lyric. The only problem was that it was about the art world and a visual artist (George Seurat's grandson, who worked with lasers and light), rather than a recording artist.

But I had an idea, and I needed to talk to Steve.

Even though I had met him socially several times with Arthur Laurents, I didn't really know him personally. I had to get his number from Arthur in order to call him.

I told Steve how much I loved the song and explained how it resonated with me. "I'm going through the same thing with my record company, and I want to use your song to set up the whole album."

Then I took a deep breath and said, "So, is there any possible way . . . I know this is a lot to ask, but would you be willing to rework the lyric to make it about the recording industry?"

He thought for a moment (which seemed an eternity to me) and then said, "Sure. I'll try."

I was so excited I almost fell off my chair. You have to understand how remarkable that was. Most songwriters would simply refuse to change the lyrics to a finished song. But Steve believed, as I do, that art is a living process. It's not set in stone. And because it lives and breathes, it can change.

That phone call led to many more.

Steve told me that at first he thought it would be simple . . . that he could just change the line "I remember lasers are expensive" to "I remember vinyl is expensive." But then as he went through the song, he realized that all the references to the art world would have to shift to the music world. And that meant unraveling the rhymes and coming up with new ones. It was a much bigger job than he initially thought, but as he wrote in his own book, *Look, I Made a Hat*, "I felt beholden to someone who wanted to make the song so personal, and guilty about skimping on the obligation to make it as pertinent as possible."

For instance, I told him, "I can't believe that I'm still auditioning for this company after twenty-three years. Can you work that into the lyric?"

And he was so adept that he took my thought and turned it into these lines:

Even when you get some recognition, everything you do, you still audition

It was such fun working with Steve. In fact, it was one of the best collaborations I've ever had, because we're both New Yorkers. We talk fast and we think fast, so we were speaking in shorthand half the time. We didn't even have to finish a sentence because we already intuited what the other was going to say. It was exhilarating to be so in tune with someone. There were moments when I was screaming with joy over the phone.

We made a pact. If we disagreed about something, whoever felt more passionate about it would win. I think our only tiff (I can't call it an argument . . . it was more of a debate) was about these next lines:

A vision's just a vision if it's only in your head
If no one gets to see it, it's as good as dead

I thought he could change it to "if no one gets to hear it," but Steve objected. He said, "How can you hear a vision? You can only see it."

I said, "That's if you're thinking of a painting. But when I'm thinking about music, I can hear it in my head . . . meaning, I hear the record finished. It's a musical vision."

Now I can't even remember who won. I had to pull out the album and listen to the song. And I say "hear." So I must have convinced him, although in his book, the revised line is written as "If no one gets to share it." He solved it so we both won!

I even managed to persuade him to come to Los Angeles and stay with me so we could work more closely. I basically held him captive for several days. I remember a moment when we were out on the patio of my Art Deco house, sitting by the outdoor fireplace.

"Steve, the new lines are fantastic." (I began with the good news, and then gingerly continued.) "I know you've already changed so much and I hate to ask, but about the ending—"

"What?"

"I need a longer one . . . eight more rhymes."

I'll never forget the look on his face. He said, "Yesterday I gave you eight new rhymes!"

"I know, I know . . . but I think we need eight more. The song is so exciting . . . it's building to the climax. People will hear me practically gasping for breath. And just when you can't even imagine that there could be another rhyme, there is! They just keep coming and coming, one right after another! It would be incredible!"

He walked away, shaking his head in disbelief. I think he wanted to strangle me. But the next day he handed me eight more rhymes, and they were brilliant.

The work he did on this song was genius, and Steve was with us in the studio when I recorded it. Later, he told a reporter he was shy about asking me if he could attend.

Can you imagine? I was *thrilled* to have him there. I so respected his opinion.

It was an exciting day. Not only were we recording the song . . . my company, Barwood Films, was also filming a behind-the-scenes look at the process (for what became an HBO special called *"Putting It Together": The Making of the Broadway Album*). So the place was packed, with a camera crew and the soundmen and all the recording engineers, plus Peter, conducting the orchestra. (I was delighted to find out that some of the musicians had actually played for me when I was doing *Funny Girl* on Broadway.)

And, to make things even more complicated, I had come up with another idea. At the beginning of the song, I thought it would be interesting to hear some male voices dismiss the whole idea of the album, just as the Columbia executives had done. (My theory is that in some cases, the establishment wants to be the artist. They are secretly jealous of the artists and their power to create.)

So I wrote up a version of their conversation and asked three friends to come in and play the executives. Sydney Pollack was game . . . it was a nice turnaround to direct him after he had directed me in *The Way We Were*. Then there was David Geffen, who had his own record company, so that was basically typecasting. And Ken Sylk, a friend of Richard's, who was the only professional actor in the bunch. I planned to intercut our dialogue with the lines of the song, and of course I was rewriting at the last minute as we tried various things.

So there were a lot of moving parts, and naturally I wanted to do it live . . . in the moment and in a complete take. That would give each performance the kind of energy I love. It was very tricky because it had to be perfectly timed, with everyone saying their lines at just the right moment. And I had to switch back and forth between talking and singing. And the tempo of the song starts out slow but then gets very fast very quickly . . . boom boom boom. There are lots of words to say very rapidly, and there's no leeway. You have to do it exactly as written, or it all falls apart.

The guys were nervous about doing it all in one take, so I told them that we'd break it up into two segments . . . first the short part where they're telling me not to make the record, and then the bulk of the song, where I'm singing and they just come in at intervals. I tried to reassure them. "Listen, it's just a conversation between you and me. You've got the script, and if you make a mistake, don't stop. Just go on."

They still looked scared.

I said, "Relax. Just play with me. This will be fun!"

We went through the lines one more time, and I thought we were ready to do a take. The guys went into their booth, and I had one last talk with the cameramen to confirm that they knew what to do. I was so energized by the challenge. To me it was like the "No Wonder" scene at the dining table in *Yentl*, when the split-second choreography of action and dialogue had to fit into the song. It's something I guess I'm attracted to . . . I like doing three things at once.

Then I went into my booth, put on my headphones, and said, "Can somebody say take one?" Peter cued the orchestra, and we were off . . . like runners at the starting line. Amazingly we got through the first segment, and then everything paused for a moment. I went over to the guys to compliment them and make sure they were good to go on, and then I pinned up my hair and went back into my booth. Now the pressure was on me. This was the bulk of the song . . . about four minutes, but it felt like fifteen, because the song was so complex.

I looked at Peter and said, "I'm ready." The orchestra started up, and somehow I managed to do the whole thing in one take! I felt as if I had just run a marathon. And I was so happy that we got that performance on film and on tape. In the recording studio, just like on a film set, my first take is often the best.

But the guys forgot to come in on some lines.

I looked at them and said, "Vat happened, my darlinks?"

"We started listening to you singing!" David said.

We all laughed, and I walked out of the booth, so glad that I had managed to do the whole song in that first take. I could always fix the guys, but I couldn't easily replicate that first performance.

I went over to rehearse with them, and then Peter came over and said, "We're ready for take two."

I said, "Wait, before I do another take, I want to hear the one I just did."

And then something happened that had never happened before, or since. I was told it no longer existed. What?! Somehow my vocal track on that first take . . . the most alive, with the most energy, on pitch both vocally and emotionally . . . had been erased.

I think I lost my breath. I had to sit down. In my entire career no one had ever erased a vocal track without asking. You don't do that to *any* performer.

I was aghast. How could this have happened?

Back then we had only twenty-four tracks to work with (today, in the digital era, they're virtually unlimited), and apparently someone needed another track. To this day I don't know if it was Peter or Don Hahn, the engineer, who had decided to erase my first take, probably assuming that I'd be doing more.

Lesson #1: Never assume.

I wasn't even replaced on the vocal track by a real instrument. I was replaced by a synthesizer!

However it happened, Peter was in charge. And because I trusted him and had been so close to him, it hurt even more. It was as if he was erasing our love affair . . . at least it felt that way to me. I was devastated.

So the sound you hear on that song in the TV special was taken off a basic

2-track Nagra used by the video crew (to tape interviews, not music) . . . good enough for TV but not for the album. I had to do sixteen more takes in the studio that day (because I was so upset) and put the best pieces together . . . so the title of the song came true, in real life. And it was so hard to sing it over and over again, because I knew I'd had it on the first take.

I was so invested in this project. I still can't bear to think of that lost track.

The rest of the songs on the album meant just as much to me. We went through three different versions of Jerome Kern and Oscar Hammerstein II's "Can't Help Lovin' That Man" from *Show Boat* before we got it right. That movie made a big impression on me, sitting there at the Loew's Kings eating my Mello-Rolls. Peter's first arrangement, with a trumpet, was a little too jazzy. I remembered seeing Ava Gardner sing that song in the movie (I didn't know she had been dubbed) and wanted to hear it again. So I tracked down a copy of the LP, and it was a superb arrangement by Conrad Salinger, very simple with the most gorgeous harmonies on the strings. (Salinger did many of the great MGM musicals, like *Singin' in the Rain.*) It would have been difficult to improve on it, so I said, "Why don't we get permission to use that?"

Richard Baskin came up with the idea of adding a harmonica, and then suggested we get the great Stevie Wonder to play it. It would never even have occurred to me that he'd be interested, but Richard said, "Why don't you ask him?"

So I did, and he said, "Yes! Absolutely. What time and where?"

And he was terrific. He listened to the song a few times and then just started improvising. Each take was a little different but equally amazing, because they all came from his soul. He even played the first bars of "People" in his own little nod to *Funny Girl* at the very end of the song.

I've loved George Gershwin's *Porgy and Bess* ever since I saw the movie with Sidney Poitier and Dorothy Dandridge and was swept away by the score. So I decided to do a medley of two songs from it. Peter did an arrangement, and it had his particular sound . . . his distinct way of writing for horns and strings. He also was known for using various instruments to comment on a lyric, in a delightfully funny way. It's a bit like one of those old cartoons where whistles and drum rolls anticipate a pratfall. I'd call it a kind of musical filigree. He made the song charming.

While Peter's arrangement for the *Porgy and Bess* medley was good, it didn't have that rich, lush sound I wanted . . . to bring back the memory of what I felt watching that movie. And for that you need a big string section, because even though it may seem counterintuitive, the more violins you have, the softer the sound.

Once again we ended up going back to the movie. Alexander Courage, who worked alongside Conrad Salinger on *Show Boat* and *Porgy and Bess*, had gone on to do *My Fair Lady*, *Fiddler on the Roof* . . . and *Hello, Dolly!* So I felt comfortable calling him up, and he kindly agreed to do a new orchestration for me, based on what I had loved in the film.

Meanwhile, I was planning to sing "If I Loved You," from Rodgers and Hammerstein's *Carousel*. But I was worried about one note.

It's funny. When people ask me, "How do you hold a note?" my answer is, "Because I want to." But in this case I didn't know if I could even hit the note, because it was an E-flat, beyond my normal range. My high note has always been a D, and every arrangement was based on that. Still, I could hear this note in my head, so I called around to get a recommendation for a singing coach. Maybe there was some technique I could use to help me hit it.

When the teacher I found was sitting at my piano, I explained all this and said, "I don't think I can go that high. My voice sounds squeaky when I try."

Just to show him what I meant, I sang the passage that led up to the note and, by God, I hit it perfectly! And completely surprised myself.

I guess I really, really wanted to.

So that was that. No need for any lesson. I said, "Thank you very much" and began to usher him out.

"You know," he said as he was preparing to leave, "I teach the Streisand method."

"What's that? I don't have any method. I just sing instinctively."

He started to talk about breathing from the chest or the diaphragm . . . I didn't understand it then and I don't understand it now. Singing is just something that has always come naturally to me.

On the day we recorded "If I Loved You," I was completely immersed in that song. If you look at the lyric, you'll know why I liked it. There's so much to act. I played the scene in my head . . . She loves him. She doesn't know how he feels about her. And she's shy. She doesn't dare show him her true feelings, so she sings, "*If* I loved you." Then at the climax of the song, we hear all her passion on that high note (thank God I hit it again!), and after that she retreats into her shyness again for the last "*if* . . . I loved you."

I could see Peter while I was singing. It was one of his prettiest arrangements, and so many emotions were tumbling through my brain and my heart. I was wondering what he was thinking and feeling, because we hadn't talked about our relationship for years.

I sang the last lines:

Soon you'd leave me, off you would go in the mist of day
Never, never to know, how I loved you, if I loved you

I knew the truth behind that "if . . ."

Once you love someone, you'll always love them . . . somewhere in your heart.

Oscar Hammerstein, who wrote that perceptive lyric, was also a mentor to Stephen Sondheim, who clearly learned his lessons well. I ended up doing six songs by Steve on the album . . . eight if you count the two from *West Side Story*, where he wrote lyrics to Leonard Bernstein's music. That show is considered a classic now, but it was revolutionary when it opened in 1957 because it dealt with issues rarely seen on a Broadway stage, like gang violence and racial prejudice. It was gritty and dark, and I still remember the thrill I felt when I first saw it, watching the lead characters, Tony and Maria, fall in love.

How incredibly lucky that I eventually got to work with each of the men who created that show . . . Jerry Robbins, Arthur Laurents, Leonard Bernstein, and Stephen Sondheim.

Songs like "Something's Coming" pulsed with excitement, and Richard Baskin and Randy Waldman did a modern arrangement for me, with synthesizers. I listened to it and said, "Great. That's it."

The other Bernstein/Sondheim song on the album is "Somewhere," and what moved me now was how it related to a contemporary issue. Steve's lyric begins with the words:

There's a place for us, somewhere a place for us
Peace and quiet and open air, wait for us, somewhere

It's interesting how a song written in one era can take on a whole new meaning in another. In 1985 the death of Rock Hudson had raised public awareness of AIDS, and I was feeling overwhelmed with sympathy for the victims, while the government was turning its back and not providing enough research dollars. HIV-positive people, and those who loved them, were facing appalling discrimination. I kept thinking, *Where can we go? Where is this "somewhere"?* It wasn't in this country, and I didn't see it in other countries, so it might even have to be on another planet someday.

And that gave me an idea . . . the arrangement should have an otherworldly quality, with a kind of celestial sound. For that, we needed synthesizers again, and I thought the best person to do it would be David Foster. As the producer of the album, I was basically casting the right arranger for each song, just as I would cast each actor for a movie.

I spoke to David, and he got the idea immediately. Synthesizers were not what they are today, so it was a very complex process and it took him weeks to do the track. I worked with him to find just the right sounds, and then when he finally played it for me, I said, "It's a hair slow. Can you go back to the way it was on the demo? That was perfect."

But it had taken him so much time to complete this version that he said he couldn't do another, and I totally understood.

Is anything ever perfect? As you live, you learn that's very hard to achieve, if ever. It's the search for perfection, it's the pursuit of excellence that counts.

I'll bet when the Columbia executives looked at the lineup of songs, they were relieved to see that David Foster, a smart, hip Grammy-winning producer, was involved with "Somewhere." And they decided it should be the first single.

I also had a concept for a music video to go with the song. It would start way out in the cosmos, amid the stars. Then somehow the shot comes down to me in a theater, where I'm singing in front of an audience. At the end of the song, the camera twirls around me and then pulls back, showing an empty theater, and finally goes out into the universe again.

Billy Friedkin, the acclaimed director of *The French Connection*, was a friend. We had met when Elliott did his film *The Night They Raided Minsky's*, and I remember Billy bringing Jeanne Moreau out to the ranch when they were married during the 1970s. He and I had always wanted to work together, so I asked him if he would like to do this video with me. I explained my concept, and he realized it perfectly. He's so smart and thoughtful, which is why I asked him to be the interviewer on the TV special about the making of the album. He also introduced me to the gifted cinematographer Andrzej Bartkowiak (who was so lovely that I later hired him to do *Nuts* and *The Mirror Has Two Faces*). I wanted the visuals to have the same otherworldly quality as the music.

Billy figured out exactly how the camera would zoom down to Manhattan and into a theater, where I'm standing onstage, with a shadow behind me, like my Erté painting again. (In other words, the person is small but the shadow is huge, like in life!) As I sing, I wanted the camera to cut to faces in the audience from all over the world. Billy cast the right people. I was thinking about how we're basically all alike . . . we love our children and our families . . . and yet people are having a hard time getting along with one another. "Peace and quiet and open air" . . . such simple words, yet so elusive.

The single (and the video) were a success, and I gave all the proceeds from it to AMFAR (the American Foundation for AIDS Research) and PRO-Peace, an organization working to stop the spread of nuclear weapons. And Jay Landers tells me that many other singers have since used our celestial arrangement, even though it was never part of Bernstein's original. He says it's become the definitive version of the song.

But when we were about to release it, I didn't know what kind of response it would get. The person whose opinion mattered so much to me was Leonard Bernstein's, so I sent him a copy of the album. Here's the note I received in return:

> ***Dear Barbra,***
>
> ***I love your voice, your style, your guts, your arrangements*** **(Somewhere** ***is something else!) and I love you for sending me the album.*** **Putting It Together** ***is putting it mild.***
>
> ***Thank you.***
>
> ***Lenny***

That made me feel blessed.

Let me go back, for a moment, to that TV special on the making of *The Broadway Album*. I produced it and incorporated the "Somewhere" music video into it, and of course Billy got the credit for directing the video. But if you look at the rest of the credits, you'll see that no one is named as the director of the actual special.

This was only a year after I had been snubbed by the Academy on *Yentl*, so my logic was, if some people in the industry had a problem with me directing, I didn't want them to have a problem with this special. So I didn't put my name on it even though I directed it. I was afraid of more attacks and I shortchanged myself.

I'm not doing that anymore.

One last thing about the special. I wanted to replay the vocal to "Putting It Together" over the closing credits, and as we were editing, I suddenly had an idea for the perfect ending. So I wrote it out and called Sydney Pollack first to give him his line. We recorded it over the phone from the studio. Then I tracked down David Geffen, who happened to be in Hawaii, and rehearsed with him over the phone. Since he's not an actor, I had to give him a line reading (to get a little more drama).

So the very last words you hear on the special are Sydney saying a bit sheepishly, "Well, I guess we were wrong."

And David responds, "Wh-wh-what do you mean *we*? I had to *beg* her to make this album!"

And then you hear the last three notes from the orchestra, for a rousing finish.

I thought it was funny, and ironic as well, to have the head of the record company (the imaginary head, of course!) rewriting history and claiming credit for the idea he initially dismissed!

I can't end this chapter without telling you about one more Sondheim song . . . "Send in the Clowns" from *A Little Night Music*. I didn't know the musical well. I was just approaching this song as an actress, analyzing the lyrics as I would a script, and something about the emotional arc of the song seemed odd to me. So I called Steve and told him my problem.

I thought the line "Don't bother, they're here" was brilliant . . . such a dramatic moment. But it came in the middle of the song, and I wished it were at the end, since it felt like the climax of the piece.

So, being me, I asked, "Would you object to my changing the position of the line?"

At first he said something like, "Wait a minute. You can't do that." And then he said, "Let me call you back." And two hours later the phone rings and it's Steve, who says, "You're right."

What he realized, as he told me, was that it was a logical request. Onstage, that line actually did end the song . . . momentarily. Desiree, the aging actress who's singing, is still in love with the man she once rejected, who is now married to a much younger woman. Yet he has come back to her, and she thinks they might renew their relationship. But now he tells her, apologetically, that he's not ready to give up his fantasy of this young woman (who hasn't even slept with him yet!). He leaves the room, and Desiree resumes the song, with a new ruefulness in her voice.

But out of the context of the play, without that intervening scene (which was underscored by the music), there was "an emotional gap" between the two stanzas, as Steve put it.

So then I asked if he could write something to fill that gap and clarify what had just happened between these two people. I suggested he might use the music from the bridge because I thought it was exquisite and I wanted to return to it. And he deftly wrote a new lyric that told us more about their relationship:

What a surprise, who could foresee?
I'd come to feel about you what you felt about me
Why only now when I see that you've drifted away
What a surprise, what a cliché

And then I could end the song with that achingly sad line that used to be in the middle:

Isn't it rich? Isn't it queer?
Losing my timing this late in my career
And where are the clowns?
Quick, send in the clowns
Don't bother, they're here

Oh, the irony! The dynamic between these two characters has shifted, and now that Desiree has finally admitted her feelings, she feels foolish for hoping they could pick up where they left off . . . which makes her the biggest clown of all, as she at last understands.

Steve's new lines were perfect. Just the way I like things . . . simple and yet complex.

I was so impressed that he was willing to take a song he had written twelve years earlier, a song that had since become a standard, and examine it again. I thought it was incredible.

> *"Barbra Streisand has one of the two or three best voices in the world of singing songs. It's not just her voice but her intensity, her passion and control. She works the way Seurat worked on his painting, dot by dot, moment by moment, bar by bar and note by note . . . The only thing that surprised me was that she paid as much exquisite attention to detail in the orchestration as she did in her own singing . . . That's why it's so good. It's not just the gift, it's the willingness to take infinite pains."*
>
> —Stephen Sondheim

While I was mixing this album, I became intrigued with the technology behind recording, which I had never paid much attention to before.

I wasn't satisfied with the sound of the vinyl record. Why didn't it sound as good as the CD? Even though the engineers, who were far more experienced than I was, told me it was the same, my ear told me it wasn't. And in trying to figure out why, I began asking more questions.

It starts with the physical properties of a vinyl record. It's a round disc, incised with circular grooves, and the circles get smaller as they spiral in, and the grooves become narrower. The narrower the groove, the less sound it can actually hold.

So that would affect the decision about which song you put first, and which song you put last. I wanted to use "Somewhere" as the closing track, because it felt like the emotional climax of the album, but it was hard to get the full range of sound in those smaller grooves. The first master tape I heard had everything squeezed flat. The sound was compressed, and the song lost its build. So we had to go back in and beef up the equalization . . . in other words, rebalance the bass and treble and echo, so it would match what I heard in the recording studio.

And how does that translate to a cassette tape or a CD? I found out that each format has its own particular sound . . . and its own set of limitations. Vinyl is considered to be very full and warm, but you have to deal with that inner-groove distortion. Cassette tapes eliminated that problem but created another . . . a slight hiss. Then the invention of the CD brought a whole new clarity and accuracy to the sound. It's very crisp, but it can also sound brittle, unless you compensate for it in the mix. (This was more of a problem back in 1985, with early digital technology, than it is today.)

I'm told that some artists don't get that involved in mixing their own albums. But now that I understood more about the technology, I felt that we had to individually mix each song for each format. The CD alone took at least six weeks.

When I made my first albums, we basically picked the best take, and that's what's on the record . . . even if I went flat on one note. We didn't edit. And now, when we have the tools to make all sorts of fixes, I still try to keep the original performance intact as much as possible. Again, that approach goes back to my time in the theater and informs everything I do as a director, an actress, and a musician. I like to perform a whole scene, a complete song.

After I've been singing for hours in the studio, the fun is sitting down with the engineer at the board to start working on a rough mix right away.

Meanwhile, late that night or the next day, I'll listen to all the takes and fill out my comp sheets. These are an analysis of each performance. Each phrase of the lyric is typed out along the left margin, and then the number of each take across the top. When I like the way a phrase sounds in a specific take, I'll check it. There's a bit more to my shorthand . . . a slash indicates that part of the phrase is good, a question mark means it's a possibility. Then, after I've gone through all the takes, it's easy to see which got the most checkmarks.

Say it's take 2 and take 4. That's where I'd start. And by now I should have the engineer's rough mix, and I'll listen to that and compare notes. I might say, "What happened to take five, where I did that sigh?" And if I don't like a word or two, I'll look for a better version from another take to replace it. Then, if it still doesn't sound right to me, I'll go back into the booth and sing again.

Doing the mix is a process. It keeps getting refined along the way. And then the best part is when you do the final mix . . . that's the last chance I get to perform the song for posterity. And if I haven't gotten the full performance in a single take, I have to create it. And that means I get to reconduct the orchestra (metaphorically speaking). I might say to the engineer, "Let's raise the cellos on that high note" or "Where's that harp gliss I remember?" If I ask, "Can you bring it up here?" he might say, "I can't. It's attached to the violins" . . . which means the instruments were picked up by the same mic, and you can't change one without changing the other. That's when it gets frustrating.

I've been lucky to work with the best engineers, who are very sensitive to what I'm hearing. When I was a kid, even with my tinnitus, I was told I had supersonic hearing (kind of like my dogs). In the early days, I might ask an engineer, "Can you *utch* up the vocal just a hair?" And he would raise it one whole decibel, which is how they measure sound. And I'd say, "That's too much. Can you just give me two tenths of a decibel?" Some engineers would tell me, "You can't hear the difference unless you raise it at least half a decibel."

Well, *I* can hear the difference.

It was frustrating because they made me feel as if I were asking for the impossible. But when you have the right engineer, the impossible is possible because they hear it the way you do. And then working together is a pleasure.

By the way, it's the same with color.

When I was color-correcting the print of *Yentl*, I said, "Add the tiniest amount of red. It's just a little wisp of color . . . less than even a point on a whole stop." And once again they told me you can't see any change that small.

I understand. It's not that you can *see* the difference, but you can *feel* the difference.

I probably fuss too much, but I have to follow my own instincts. After all, this is the ultimate performance that will last forever. It's like capturing time. And I believe that it's worth any effort to try to get it right. And then I hope other people will like it as well.

When I was recording my *Encore* album, there was a moment when I was singing in front of a seventy-two-piece orchestra, and I stopped because I could hear an odd note in a particular transition within the song. I thought I might have been doing something wrong, and asked, "Do I have to get off a note or something before the next chord?"

Bill Ross, my wonderful arranger/conductor, was riffling through the score and said, "No, you shouldn't."

"But it sounded so weird when I hold the note."

Bill said, "It's just the major seventh of the note. It's nice. It should work really great."

But I wasn't convinced. I said, "Can I just hear that one bar then, please?"

So Bill told the musicians to play it again, but before they did, the concertmaster . . . Bruce Dukov, the first violinist . . . said, "Bill, you know what might be bothering her? We're right next to her and we're playing the B-natural—"

Bill took a closer look at the page and said, "Oh no. You shouldn't . . . Sorry about that. It was supposed to go to an A-sharp."

That one note was transcribed wrong.

Then Bill came over to me and put his arm around my shoulders and announced, with a big smile, "Never underestimate this woman's ears."

And the whole orchestra stamped their feet, and the string players tapped their bows on the music stands, in the musician's version of applause.

When we were mixing *The Broadway Album*, I spent months running back and forth among three different studios, each with different engineers, working on different songs till two in the morning. And Peter was missing all the fun. I had fought for him to produce it with me when Columbia wanted me to hire a more experienced producer. And I worried that I was being disloyal to Peter when we had to redo some of his arrangements. We ended up bringing in Jeremy Lubbock to work on "Send in the Clowns." I heard a strange, atonal countermelody in my head (kind of like Bartók) that would play along with my voice on the last part of the song. I couldn't tell him the exact notes to play because I don't read music . . . the only thing I could do was sing it to him. Jeremy wrote it for an oboe, and it was exactly what I imagined.

Making this album was intense . . . eight months of work . . . and I must have sung another half dozen songs in addition to those that made it onto the record.

And every time I saw Peter looking at his watch to see if it was time to go home, I felt disheartened. He was an important figure in my life. I will always love him, but this was the last time we would work together.

The final touch on the album was the cover. I wanted to take a photo on the empty stage of a Broadway theater, with those classic red-velvet seats in the background. I'm sitting in a secretary's chair, with a work light beside me and sheet music spilling on the floor, in a nod to my audition for *I Can Get It for You Wholesale.*

Even before the album was released, the advance sale was already up to eight hundred thousand. It went on to reach number 1 on the charts and became a huge success. (I've been told it has sold seven and a half million copies worldwide.) Point is, it definitely qualified for my contract.

Columbia was very pleased.

Meanwhile, Stephen Sondheim sent me a lovely note:

> ***Dear Barbra—***
>
> ***Now that it's all over, I just want to thank you again for the pleasure and the privilege of working with you, and for your hospitality too. I hope the album is a big hit, but even more I hope that you will be able to listen to it in a couple of years and not bang your head against the wall but listen to it with joy and pride (two well-known household detergents).***
>
> ***With love,***
>
> ***Steve***

And my faith in the audience was renewed. I'm convinced that if you do something for the right reasons, if you believe in a project and love the work and use the truth, people will respond.

Nothing works if you lie. No meaning will transmit, and the audience doesn't feel anything. As an actress, you could have perfect lighting, or as a singer, the best sound, but if there's no truth to the performance, you have nothing.

So technology isn't everything. A scene can be imperfectly shot, but if it has truth at its core . . . that's enough. Truth is universal. It hits home. It touches people's hearts and minds.

The songs on this album have both heart and soul. They're classics of the musical theater, and I'm very grateful that I had the opportunity to sing them. *I* had to live up to *them*.

The Broadway Album was nominated for a Grammy as Album of the Year, and I was nominated for Best Pop Vocal Performance, Female. I remember sitting in the audience on the night of the ceremony, February 24, 1987, and thinking, *Just look at the amazing women I'm up against:* Madonna, Tina Turner, Dionne Warwick, and Cyndi Lauper. And they all had big hits with contemporary music!

On the one hand, I felt sure one of them would win. But on the other, there was another thought at the back of my head . . .

When they announced my name, I walked up onstage, thanked the audience, and said, "It's especially gratifying to be honored for my work on *The Broadway Album* because it's a reaffirmation of the stature and quality of this timeless material. Singing the songs of Rodgers and Hammerstein, and Gershwin, Jerome Kern, Leonard Bernstein, Stephen Sondheim, was a reward in itself, believe me." Then I shared that second thought. "Actually, I have to be very honest with you. I did have a feeling that I *just* might win this award." The audience started to laugh and cheer, but I shook my head and said, "Wait. I'll tell you why. Because today is the twenty-fourth, and my lucky number has always been twenty-four . . . maybe because I was born on the twenty-fourth, I had my son when I was twenty-four, and it was twenty-four years ago that I took home my first Grammy in the same category. So, with your continued support and a little bit of luck, I might just see you again twenty-four years from tonight."

And twenty-four years later it just so happened that my album *Love Is the Answer* was nominated. It went to number 1 on the charts, but it didn't win that night. Still, it was lovely to be recognized.

And I've just realized that there's one more twenty-four . . . *The Broadway Album* was my twenty-fourth studio album. It just shows you that the universe works in mysterious ways . . .

THIRTY-NINE

One Voice

In April 1986 the fate of our world suddenly seemed more precarious. The first public indication that something had gone radically wrong came on Monday the twenty-eighth, when a technician in Sweden passing through a radiation detector at a nuclear power plant triggered an alarm. That set off a search for some sort of leak from the Swedish reactor, which turned up nothing. And then they realized that the source of the radioactive particles on the technician's shoes was actually the grass outside.

How did they get there? An analysis of the particles revealed components typical of Soviet reactors. The prevailing winds over the weekend had come from the southeast . . . could they have been carrying radioactivity from Russia? And it had rained in Sweden, which would have brought more particles down to the ground.

At first the Kremlin denied any knowledge or responsibility. But when Finland, Norway, and Denmark also reported exceptionally high levels of radiation, Russia was finally forced to admit that there had been an accident at their nuclear plant in Chernobyl, hundreds of miles away.

I was horrified when I learned the details. On Saturday, April 26, at around 1:30 a.m., an explosion in Chernobyl's reactor number 4 blew off the thousand-ton roof and sent a huge fireball into the sky. The reactor's core melted down and radiation was spewing everywhere. Yet the authorities waited until Sunday afternoon (thirty-six hours later) to inform people in the nearby towns and begin evacuating them. Meanwhile, the fire inside the reactor kept burning . . . they couldn't seem to put it out.

Estimates are that 50 million curies of radiation were released into the atmosphere, the equivalent of five hundred Hiroshima bombs. Trees, crops, animals . . . cars, shops, houses . . . everything was contaminated. A one-thousand-square-mile "exclusion zone" around the town would be uninhabitable for hundreds if not thousands of years.

The news was apocalyptic. I kept thinking, *How can we allow this kind of threat to our environment?* Because we're all connected. We all share this one planet . . . and suddenly I was reminded how fragile it was. Radioactive clouds were drifting around the globe, poisoning air, food, and water, and threatening everything alive. Something happened in Russia, and now we had to worry about eating cheese from France and apples from Oregon, because we were all downwind. It felt like a warning, this fire that couldn't be extinguished. Was this the beginning of the end of the world?

I was so frightened that I had to talk to someone, so I called Marilyn Bergman. We had commiserated about the state of the world many times. I would read about the nuclear arms race and get furious. What is it with these boys and their toys? Do they have missile envy?

The competition to see who could have the most weapons was infantile, and extremely dangerous. And then President Reagan decided he wanted to put lasers in space to shoot down incoming missiles, as part of his "Star Wars" fantasy. But as many scientists said (including Murph Goldberger from Caltech, who took the time to talk to me), even if only one or two got through, it would be enough to destroy the world.

How could we stop this madness?

I always felt intimidated by how much I didn't know. But simply on instinct, I thought, *This is crazy.* We should be buying books, not bombs. We should be filling grain silos, not missile silos. There were some fifty thousand nuclear weapons in the world at that point . . . weapons we could never use. It was as if technology had superseded common sense. The reality was overwhelming, and it left me feeling paralyzed and depressed. But Chernobyl shocked me right out of that.

I said to Marilyn, "What can we do? We have to do something!"

And Marilyn, ever practical, answered, "The only thing I know we can do is elect more people who share our views."

Ronald Reagan had won a second term in 1984, but the midterm elections were coming up in November. We could put a check on him if we could take back the Senate for the Democrats. (We already had the majority in the House.)

The Democratic candidates needed money.

"And you know how we could raise a lot of money?" Marilyn said. "If you gave a concert. People would pay a lot to hear you sing, especially if it was for a good cause."

I was hesitant at first. I hadn't given a real concert in almost twenty years, since 1967's *A Happening in Central Park*, when I forgot the words to that song and got spooked. Sure, I'd done a few weeks in Las Vegas, where I just picked the songs and sang them . . . I didn't plan a "show" . . . and I'd sung at various benefits. But I had no desire to get back up onstage. I didn't enjoy performing live anymore.

But as Marilyn said, "What's more frightening . . . singing live, or nuclear annihilation?"

Good point.

Marilyn was a founding member of the Hollywood Women's Political Committee, and I, too, had joined. So we were part of a group of very astute women, and together, we made a plan. We decided to focus our efforts on six senatorial candidates who also believed in protecting the planet . . . Alan Cranston in

California, Patrick Leahy in Vermont, Tom Daschle in South Dakota, Tim Wirth in Colorado, Bob Edgar in Pennsylvania, and whoever would win the Democratic primary in Maryland (which turned out to be Barbara Mikulski).

Then there were all the logistics to figure out. Where should the concert be held? We considered various venues, and then something occurred to me.

"You know what would make me feel more comfortable? Singing in my own backyard."

After all, what could be more appropriate than celebrating nature while we were in the midst of nature? (And that would eliminate the cost of renting a place, so all the money would go to the candidates.) We cleared a bit of space at the back of the ranch and constructed a simple wooden stage, with a half circle of chairs on tiers for five hundred people. I would be inviting guests to my home, which the committee felt would make the evening more special.

And I thought it better be special, because of the price they wanted to charge . . . five thousand dollars per couple. I thought that was too much.

"Nobody will come!"

But Marilyn said, "Just you wait. It will be a total sellout, and we'll have to turn people away."

It was Marilyn's idea to have me record the invitation, and this is what I said:

Hi, this is Barbra.

I could never imagine myself wanting to sing in public again, but then I could never imagine Star Wars, Contras, apartheid, and nuclear winters in my life. And yet they're in everybody's life . . .

Every time the Senate votes, our destinies are being shaped. With one vote, the courts have become less the voice of the Constitution and more the voice of extremists . . . With one vote, the MX missile was approved and the nuclear clock moved closer to midnight.

I feel I must sing again, to raise money so that we elect a Democratic majority in the Senate who will change all this. Let's send people to Washington who will solve problems, not create them. That's our message.

Join me on September 6 at my ranch, under the stars. I'd like you to come. We'll have dinner, watch the sunset, share the music, and send the message.

All the best, Barbra

Our HWPC members placed each cassette inside a pretty tin box and covered it with potpourri. Then they were hand delivered.

Marilyn was right. Everyone accepted, and I felt very supported by the Hollywood community, because so many turned out, including Quincy Jones (who brought Whitney Houston), Barry Diller, Jack Nicholson and Anjelica Huston, Sydney Pollack, Jane Fonda and Tom Hayden, Goldie Hawn and Kurt Russell, Whoopi Goldberg, Bette Midler, Henry Winkler, Sally Field, Bruce Willis, Chevy Chase, Penny Marshall and Rob Reiner, and Norman Lear. Steven Spielberg was in London but he sent a check for five thousand dollars, and so did Bruce Springsteen, even though he couldn't come either.

Thank God it didn't rain.

"It's going to be a once in a lifetime event for me to see her sing."

—Sally Field

"I've never seen her live, and a lot of people here haven't seen her live . . . It's a double treat."

—Bette Midler

"I have never heard her sing in public, but this is the night and I'm real excited."

—Whitney Houston

Drinks and dinner were served out on the tennis court, where Marilyn welcomed everyone and the extraordinary congresswoman Barbara Jordan introduced the candidates. Other political figures like Mayor Tom Bradley and Senator George Mitchell were also there to support the cause. Then the whole crowd walked over to the mini-"amphitheater," where Robin Williams did a brilliant monologue . . . he had generously agreed to be the opening act. He was so funny and sharp as always.

Meanwhile, I was scared stiff, as always. I had to keep reminding myself that these were my friends out there, but still I had made sure we wouldn't start until it was dark so I couldn't see them. I was sitting by myself in the guesthouse, trying to calm down, when Jack and Anjelica found me there. Jack is very laid back, with a dry sense of humor. He talks and laughs, and I never quite understand what he's talking about. Still, the two of them made me feel better.

The concert began with the opening bars of "Somewhere," played by just a few musicians to keep the costs down . . . supplemented by two big synthesizers. ("Eight guys and some big electric bill!" as I joked later.)

I sang the first lines of the song offstage, and then I was just a dark silhouette, backlit in a cloudy white haze, as I made my way through the band and finally stepped out into the light. The whole audience stood up and applauded, which certainly got things off to a good start.

After the song I confessed to the crowd, "I've spent more than a few sleepless nights wondering what I could possibly do that would be worth five thousand dollars. Then I figured out that I would be singing 3,924 notes. And that comes to a little over a dollar a note. And you know, some notes are longer and so they're worth about three dollars . . . some are shorter, fifty cents . . . but you know, it averages out."

People laughed, and we were off. I sang old songs, like "People," and new songs (for me), like "Over the Rainbow," which I introduced as a tribute to the woman who made it famous and was so kind to me.

Then with the opening chords of "Guilty," the mood got brighter and lighter. The audience heard Barry Gibb's voice before they saw him . . . then he came out of the shadows and joined me for the song. I was surprised by how much fun I was having. You can't help but move to that music. I think I forgot some word or missed a beat, but I did do some dipping and swaying. That's about as much dancing in public as I've ever done!

It was a magical night. Everything went off without a hitch . . . until the very last number, "America the Beautiful." (I wanted to remind people that Republicans do not own the flag.) I asked the audience to sing along, but I didn't realize they would stand up . . . and they blocked the teleprompter. (That was one of the reasons that initially convinced me to do the show . . . the fact that I didn't have to worry about forgetting the words.)

But now I couldn't see the teleprompter! I kept moving around, trying to find a spot where I could catch sight of it. Luckily we had filmed a dress rehearsal the night before, and we ended up using some of that footage in the televised version of the show.

We hadn't initially planned on filming the event. But in the midst of all the preparations, when it became clear that we were actually going to build a stage in my backyard, I said, "If we're going to go this far, why don't we film it for TV?"

So Marty approached HBO and made a deal. They would contribute to the cost of mounting the concert, as well as paying for onetime rights to broadcast it. But I was still so anxious about singing live that I had Marty add one condition . . . if I didn't like the way it turned out, the footage would be shelved.

Well, my old friend Dwight Hemion did a great job of directing it. He had eight cameramen around, taking interesting shots. Gary Smith produced it along with Dwight, and it was wonderful to work with them again, because I knew I was in good hands.

And it all worked!

We raised $1.5 million that night, which was the largest amount ever raised by a one-night live performance in the history of California (and more than Reagan collected at a competing fundraiser, with three times the number of guests).

And most important, five of our six candidates won. That turned the Senate over to the Democrats for the first time since 1980. It actually helped change the direction of the country.

Gloria Steinem came to interview me the day after the concert for the *Today* show, and I told her how I'd been dismayed for many years by what was going on in the world but felt too powerless to do anything, until Chernobyl shocked me into action. And I realized that performers are in a unique position. When we raise our voices, we can be heard.

I believe in the power of one voice (which is why that's the title of the special). And then Gloria asked me about power. I said, "I don't think being powerful is to be ruthless or to be unkind, or to yell and scream. I don't think that's powerful at all." There's a power in being gentle, as I learned when I directed *Yentl.*

And once again, I didn't want to grow old and regret not having taken the risk of standing up for what I believe.

I didn't want this effort to end here, so I donated all the proceeds from the HBO special, the album, and the video (and eventually the DVD) to create the Barbra Streisand Foundation and continue the good fight. I wanted to put my money where my mouth was and support not only nuclear disarmament and the environmental movement, but also other causes that were dear to my heart, like women's rights, civil rights, and fundamental human rights.

That was the beginning of a whole new commitment to speak out and become more involved in the wider world.

FORTY

Everyone's Right to Love

There are some love affairs you never quite get over. I fell in love with a play . . . pursued it, won it, lost it . . . and even when I was no longer formally involved with it, I was still trying to make it into a movie. It was an obsession that went on for more than twenty-five years.

I first saw Larry Kramer's *The Normal Heart* at the Las Palmas Theatre in Hollywood on January 8, 1986. It's a story set against the early years of the AIDS epidemic, when this new disease was ravaging the gay community. It was especially frightening because initially no one knew the cause or understood how it was transmitted. Young men were dying in droves, but the medical establishment and Ronald Reagan's government in Washington, D.C., looked the other way. Larry was at the forefront of the battle to force people to pay attention. The Gay Men's Health Crisis, an organization devoted to informing people about the threat and helping the victims, was founded in his living room. So the play is actually Larry's own story, a thinly fictionalized account of real people and real events, and Larry himself is the main character, Ned Weeks. Richard Dreyfuss played that part in Los Angeles and was terrific . . . so was Bruce Davison as Felix, Ned's lover . . . and Kathy Bates, who played Dr. Emma Brookner, based on an extraordinary woman, Dr. Linda Laubenstein. She was one of the first to sound the alarm and cowrote the initial paper identifying the disease. At one point, she was treating most of the New York patients.

By the end of the play . . . when Emma performs an impromptu marriage ceremony for Ned and the dying Felix, who's too weak to get up from his hospital bed . . . I was sobbing uncontrollably.

The Normal Heart is a fabulous play with a powerful theme . . . for me, it's about everyone's right to love . . . and I thought it could make a great movie. After seeing these characters, hearing their stories, and feeling their vulnerability, I hoped it might change some people's attitudes toward the gay community.

I immediately contacted Larry to acquire the rights. My lawyer talked to his agent, and after two months of negotiations, it was announced in March 1986 that I would be producing and directing the movie for Barwood Films, as well as playing the supporting role of the doctor. Obviously the subject matter was difficult, and I was told that the movie had a better chance of getting a green light from a studio if I was in it.

Why do I always go for projects that no one else thinks are commercial? They said it about *Yentl* and now they were saying it about this. But that didn't change my commitment. I'm drawn to stories about injustice. If something is unfair, like sexual discrimination, I'm compelled to do whatever I can to stop it.

Larry was already working on the screenplay even before I got involved, and now he sent me a lovely letter and wrote:

> ***You have become a muse of sorts—knowing you're there, you're interested, you have good feelings, the right feelings, for this play that has meant so much to me . . . I have enjoyed writing this more since I see you as Emma. The part has always been dear to me—and had there been time for it on the stage, there would have been more of her.***

If Larry was making the part bigger, thinking that would please me, he was mistaken. I was looking forward to directing other people and just playing a small role myself.

I thought Dustin Hoffman would be great as Ned, and he was interested, so we sent him a copy of the play and promised to send him Larry's screenplay as soon as we had it. I was interviewing production managers and hoped to start filming in September or October.

And then I read the finished screenplay and got this sinking feeling. The opening was dull . . . a scene with Ned and his brother, Ben, at the site where Ben is planning to build a country house . . . then we're in a locker room after a tennis game, with too much talk about being fat and body image . . . and by page 3 we're on Fire Island, famous for the beaches and parties that attract hundreds of gay men during the summer. Suntanned men were drinking, dancing, flirting, and jumping into the pool. It felt superficial. It seemed more about their lifestyle than their lives.

And there were many new scenes with Emma, including a subplot about an attraction between Emma and Ned. Why? I thought that was one romance too many, when I wanted the audience to be focused on the romance between Felix and Ned. It was clear to me that all her extraneous scenes had to go.

I adored Larry's play. I loved the great dialogue and the message . . . I never wanted to change any of that. But I wanted to make it more cinematic. Very few people were going to come to a movie theater to sit through a history of the gay rights movement. I wanted to make this story accessible to a wider audience. And I wanted people to get to know and love these men.

I invited Larry to come to my house in Los Angeles so we could work on it together. I explained that I thought we should set it up differently and introduce the main characters in a way that everyone could identify with, instead of making it all about their homosexuality right away. I wanted a kind of mystery . . . who are these people, and how are they connected? I didn't think the audience should even know who was gay or straight at the beginning of the film. They should just be people, without any labels.

We both felt that it was actually good for the movie to have a director who was heterosexual, because I would bring another point of view to the table. We kept talking till midnight each night he was here. I thought our sessions were creative and exciting.

Larry seemed excited as well, and flew off to see the London production of his play. And then in April, everything came to a standstill when Larry began objecting to some terms in the deal. That was disconcerting, because he had already agreed to it. Somehow we got past that, and he delivered a second draft. He had written a new beginning and made other changes, based on my input, but the script still had a long way to go. Larry went back to work, and then in August he decided that the deal was off. Our lawyers sent a letter to his lawyers explaining that we now legally held the rights, a position that was supported by none other than Larry's own agent, who confirmed that we had in fact made a deal.

At this point, several people advised me to drop the project, saying, how can you work with someone so unreliable?

In October I began filming *Nuts*, a movie that I had been developing long before I met Larry. But I couldn't let go of *The Normal Heart*. I called Larry, and he told me he had another offer. Really? Was all this turmoil just an attempt to sweeten the terms of *our* deal?

It wasn't until February 1987 that he finally committed (again).

Larry and I went back to working on the screenplay. As he said to the press, "She'll challenge you on every word. She'll act out the words. That fine-tuning—as a writer, you either love it or hate it. It's the way I work myself, especially on my novel, so I love it . . . She'll recall Draft Four when you've forgotten every previous draft."

I realized it must be hard for him to rethink his play . . . after all, Larry had already told the story in a certain way and now I was telling him that we needed to add certain scenes so the audience would feel more empathy for these characters. Like Ned, Larry was angry and he was passionate, and I thought he had every right to *be* angry, and I loved that passion. But I also wanted to see Ned's softer side. Some people had criticized the play as one tirade after another, and even though I didn't agree, I was aware that too much anger can be off-putting. If you're yelling too loud, people don't hear what you're saying.

Larry and I hit an impasse, and Cis, trying to help, approached other writers, including Michael Cristofer, Alan Bennett, David Seltzer, Alvin Sargent, John Sayles, William Goldman, and Darryl Ponicsan. Every single one of them passed.

Perhaps they didn't want to get involved with Larry, who had a reputation for being difficult. All I know is, no one wanted to touch this project. It may seem hard to believe now, but you have to remember that back then, attitudes were different. I remember being so surprised when a male friend of mine, an intelligent, liberal, sophisticated film producer, told me, "I don't want to see a movie about two gay guys." And Richard Dreyfuss mentioned that while he was doing the play, there would usually be someone in the audience who got up and left when Ned and Felix kissed.

Even I, a staunch liberal, remember watching the play for the first time and feeling a little uncomfortable with the character of Tommy, who was portrayed as a queen, with Southern-belle mannerisms. It struck me as a stereotype, and I didn't want people to be put off by it . . . because by the end of the play I adored Tommy. He was the most compassionate, considerate, and loving human being.

That was fantastic . . . to have my feelings completely reversed over the course of two hours . . . and I wanted the rest of the audience to experience that as well.

When Ned and Felix meet and go out on a date, I didn't want them to have sex immediately, as they did in the play, where one of the first things Felix says to Ned is "Just relax. You'll get laid." That was a big change for Larry, but again, I was trying to create a situation where everyone could relate. I wanted the audience to root for these two people to get together. I wanted this to be a love story, not a sex story.

But Larry didn't see it that way. He regarded his play, and the movie, as a gay manifesto. He was declaring, This is the way it is. We fuck first and talk later. That's the freedom we wanted and fought hard for, and even though this behavior was killing gay men, some of them did not want to give it up. Larry was trying to change this behavior, but he also wanted to show it, as an accurate reflection of these men's sexuality. He was ready to shock the heterosexual audience, and he didn't care if they were offended. But that attitude could leave him preaching to the choir. And it was not going to help the cause . . . or get this movie made.

Unfortunately, in his worldview, there was no discussion. You were either with him or against him. In 1988 he broke off our deal and spent several years trying to get someone else to make his movie . . . to no avail. Then in 1992, after seeing *The Prince of Tides*, he called Cis, told her he was very impressed, and asked if I was still interested in *The Normal Heart*.

Are you kidding? Of course I was. Columbia, where I had a first-look deal, optioned the rights for me.

In 1993 I was happy to lend my name to a staged reading of the play with the Roundabout Theatre Company in New York, to benefit ACT UP and Broadway Cares/Equity Fights AIDS. The cast, directed by Jerry Zaks, was stellar . . . it included Kevin Bacon, Eric Bogosian, Stockard Channing, Harry Hamlin, D. W. Moffett (who had played Felix in the original production at Joe Papp's Public Theater), Tony Roberts, and John Turturro. I introduced the play, and made a special point to thank Larry for spending so many years of his life demanding that people pay attention. He had been called a "loudmouth," "crazy," and an "outrageous pain in the ass," but what he was doing was brave and necessary.

Talking about this made me emotional. I said, "Homophobia is another disease that has to be cured." This is still my most fundamental belief . . . everyone deserves dignity and respect. We all need to open our hearts to love and compassion.

And that night I also told the audience that the movie "is now drawing close to becoming a reality."

But my relationship with Larry had by now become even more complicated. I was aware that he was going through a difficult time. He had been diagnosed as HIV-positive in 1988, and I understood that he felt an immense sense of urgency to get this movie made. He was desperate to get the word out before more people were infected with the virus.

I was just as eager to make the movie, but I couldn't make it without a script.

And that's where we came to another standstill, because Larry had reverted right back to the Fire Island opening and all the rest after we parted, and Columbia did not want to use that script.

Since we were getting nowhere, Larry finally agreed that I should get someone else to write it. He suggested the playwright Jon Robin Baitz, who was also gay. I had a good meeting with Baitz, who was very responsive, and then Larry managed to offend him so profoundly (harassing him with phone calls, questioning his commitment to the project) that he took another project instead.

I turned to another writer, Ramsey Fadiman. One of the reasons I picked him was that he wasn't well-known, and was open to helping me put my concept down on paper.

When I work on a script that I'm directing, I try to inhabit each character.

Ned is wary of Felix initially, because Felix is attractive, and Ned can't quite believe he'd be interested in him. I could relate to that. Even if a character is male and I'm female, I know that men have the same insecurities as women. And I figured most people in the audience would relate as well.

You know that feeling when you're *seen* by your partner, and cared for . . . it's a kind of comfort with each other that goes beyond sex. It's about love. How do you show that on film? I thought back to my own childhood and how I used to cut the hairs out of my grandfather's ears, so in my version, Felix gives Ned a haircut. That was like another kind of love scene to me.

And in the midst of this ordinary, casual moment, I chose to give them some serious dialogue. Felix tells Ned that he was married once, and has a son. It's an unexpected choice, to reveal important information this way, but that's what interests me as a writer and a director . . . scenes where more than one thing at a time is going on.

While I was working on my version of the script, Larry was moving ahead on his own parallel track and reworking his screenplay, which seemed to get longer with every rewrite. In an interview with *The Advocate*, he dismissed Ramsey as a "Hollywood hack," and in a letter to me and Gareth Wigan, the studio executive who was shepherding the project, he threatened to slap Columbia with a lawsuit unless they paid him immediately for his latest draft. This was not exactly the best move . . . why alienate the man who was trying to help us, not to mention the studio?

Ramsey and I kept working. It took several drafts before I had something that felt right to me. I thought my opening was very cinematic. The movie would start with an image of Ronald Reagan being sworn in as president, vowing to "preserve, protect, and defend the Constitution of the United States." Then the camera pulls back to reveal that we're watching this on television. A crumpled-up ball of paper hits the screen and falls to the floor, as we hear someone say, "Bullshit. It's all bullshit." The camera follows a dog as she picks up the ball of paper and returns it to the man who threw it, revealing Ned, who's typing furiously and simultaneously talking on the phone.

We then cut to a cork popping out of a champagne bottle, and a young secretary hands a glass to a handsome man, Bruce, watching the same scene on television with his colleagues at a bank. "We're in," says the guy standing next to him, who then turns his attention to the secretary's ass in her tight dress as she walks away. He nudges Bruce and says, "Wouldn't you like a piece of that?" Bruce smiles.

We cut to a street where Ned is walking his dog. He hears his name being called, turns around, and sees Craig, who's been jogging. Craig catches up to him and asks, out of breath, "How come you never returned my call?" Ned, who has never liked anyone who likes him, gives some lame excuse. And then Craig has a coughing fit as they're standing in front of an electronics store, where twenty-five TVs in the window are all tuned to Ronald and Nancy Reagan dancing at the inaugural ball.

We next cut to a door stenciled with NEW YORK CITY DEPARTMENT OF HEALTH as a man walks through and passes by our next character, Mickey, sitting at his desk and reading an article in *The New York Times* headlined: RARE CANCER SEEN IN 41 HOMOSEXUALS. And we hear Reagan speaking from a portable radio on a shelf.

So, in four quick scenes we've established the time frame and introduced four pivotal characters as they go about their lives. The audience has no idea if they're gay or straight. They just look like anyone else, and that was my point.

In the next scene, Ned comes into Dr. Brookner's office, because she has summoned him to help get the message out to the gay community. Then Craig is brought in by Mickey, because he's collapsed on the street. And then Bruce, the man who smiled in the bank, rushes in, and it turns out he's Craig's lover. It's only when these four men converge in Emma's office that we understand the connections between them and realize that they're all gay.

Larry, in contrast, still wanted the sexuality to be front and center. I understood that, but I didn't agree that we needed to show how they, as Larry put it, "fuck first." Several of his screenplays had scenes at the baths, where men go into little rooms and have anonymous sex with strangers. I said, "Larry, it's enough to talk about it, which we will. You don't have to show it."

Remember, this was a time when some people didn't care if gay people lived or died. I was trying to get that group to change their minds, and Larry's approach was probably not the best way to do it. But he delighted in pushing boundaries. He loved the hedonistic beach scenes on Fire Island. As he said in a letter, "The shots of ten, twenty, thirty thousand gay men walking along the ocean will make every gay man in the world want to see it and will scare the shit out of every born-again. But most importantly, Fire Island was what the 70s were all about in the gay world . . . all those gorgeous available men."

That's great if you only want gay men to come to the movie. I wanted this movie to appeal to the entire world.

I needed to hear how my script sounded, so we put together a reading in Los Angeles in April 1995 with a wonderful group of actors, including Tony Shalhoub, D. W. Moffett, and Stephen Spinella. The response was very enthusiastic. I felt excited again.

And it was my script that attracted two brilliant actors, Kenneth Branagh and Ralph Fiennes. I wanted Ken to play Ned and Ralph to play Felix, and both told me they wanted to do it. But unfortunately neither would be available for a year . . . Ken was committed to another movie, and Ralph was playing Hamlet onstage in London and then on Broadway.

Since we still didn't have a green light from the studio, I thought, *Okay. This is fate.* While we were waiting for the actors, I decided to make *The Mirror Has Two Faces*, which I had also been developing. That movie was fully financed and ready to go. And then I planned to start shooting *The Normal Heart* immediately afterward.

When Larry heard the news, he hit the roof. He fired off an incendiary letter to my agents at CAA, accusing them of sabotaging the project by refusing to make their clients available. Huh? He threatened to defame everyone at the agency by calling them out as homophobic to the press. And he declared, "Make no mistake, if this movie is not made, and made this summer, it is you and your agency that I shall blame."

For someone who was so ready to lay blame, he was definitely reluctant to take any responsibility himself.

It's ironic. In the play and in real life, Larry was kicked out of the organization he had founded because he was so hostile and obstreperous that he managed to alienate everybody, even his friends. And here he was again, antagonizing people he actually needed if he wanted to get this movie made.

And then he turned his fire on me. In April 1996 he told *Variety*, "This woman has had this play since 1986." (Not true, since he had reneged on our original deal and also took the project back for four years during that period.) He went on to question my commitment to the gay community, which was contradicted by the facts. While I was trying to push forward with *The Normal Heart*, my production company, Barwood Films, made the TV films *Serving in Silence: The Margarethe Cammermeyer Story*, which won three Emmys and brought home to millions of Americans the painful truth about the unconscionable treatment of gays in the military, and *What Makes a Family?*, about the unfair laws concerning gay adoption.

Larry was lashing out. He seemed to forget that I, too, had spent years of my life trying to get this movie made . . . without a cent of compensation, while Larry had been paid for each draft, and each time we renewed our option.

It's true that our option had expired at the beginning of the year, while I was in the midst of shooting *The Mirror Has Two Faces.* And he now demanded that if we wanted to renew it, we had to buy the rights not only to *The Normal Heart* but also to another play of his (which I couldn't see as a film) and commit to him as screenwriter. The price had also escalated.

All of these conditions were just making the project more untenable.

Larry had been talking to John Schlesinger about directing the movie before I got involved, so I said, "Why don't you ask him if he wants to direct it now?" John was a wonderful director, and he was gay. (Larry had changed his mind and now thought that was an advantage.) I said, "If you can't wait for me and you can raise the money now, get John to direct, and I'll just produce it." By the way, it was interesting to note that Schlesinger wanted $125,000 before he would even start to work. I was so naïve that I didn't realize most directors got paid for developing scripts.

And then Larry told me that he didn't need me to produce it.

I was deeply hurt, but I gave him what he asked for.

I issued my own statement, which said, "I'm painfully aware of the ticking clock. Therefore, I am now stepping aside and will no longer be involved with the project. I wish Larry only success in getting *The Normal Heart* made. I personally have a strong commitment to projects that reflect and further the needs of the gay community."

My son is gay, which made my commitment doubly strong. Jason really wanted me to make this movie, and I was looking forward to working with him on the film in some capacity. It meant so much to me and now it was gone.

I was polite in public. I never tried to embarrass Larry as he tried to embarrass me. In another interview for *The Advocate*, he even brought up my son's sexuality, which was not his business. Jason was open about it, but he's a very private person, and it should have been his choice when and where to discuss it in print.

I did send Larry a fax after I put out my statement and told him exactly what I thought. I vividly remember one of the lines: "You are so self-destructive."

So, once again, the rights reverted back to Larry, but nothing happened . . . again. And even though I had no contractual involvement, I couldn't let go. I still persisted in trying to get *The Normal Heart* made. I called Craig Zadan and Neil Meron, who had produced *Serving in Silence* and *What Makes a Family?* with me and Cis, and asked if they would be willing to help. I couldn't let this be the end. It just seemed such a shame that this story, this cause, was not getting the attention it deserved.

I was also still trying to interest various actors in the piece. I think it was in 1997, when I was on my way to a party given by the journalist Todd Purdum and his wife, Dee Dee Myers, President Clinton's former press secretary, that I ran into Ben Stiller on the path leading up to their house. I barely knew Ben, but I stopped him and said, "Did you ever think of being in a serious drama?" He was known more as a comic actor at this point. But I believe a good comedian will usually turn out to be a good dramatic actor. I could see Ned in him. So I said, "I have a great part for you in *The Normal Heart*."

Ben looked at me like "Are you crazy?" And he shrugged it off.

That's why it's kind of funny that, years later, in 2005, when Ben was doing a play directed by George Wolfe at the Public Theater, all of a sudden everybody else was thinking of him for the part. By that time, Ben and I had already worked together on *Meet the Fockers* the year before.

And then Craig and Neil called to say that Ben had such a great experience with George that he wanted *him* to direct it.

Another stab in the heart. Larry was thrilled about George. Once again he pushed me aside, but he still wanted me to play Emma and help get the movie green-lit. George had directed *Angels in America*, which I loved, and other hits onstage, but he had no track record when it came to movies. So I put my own feelings aside and thought, *Okay. I'll just play the part. I'll do anything I can to finally get this made!*

The problem was Larry's script, which he insisted we use. And by now it had ballooned to almost two hundred pages (way too long). As he explained in an email, "I am trying to write for you an epic script, like *A Man for All Seasons*, perhaps with an intermission, and with a part for Ben so encompassing and far-reaching that he will never ever have anything like this to play again."

And then he sent another email to everyone, threatening to pull the plug unless we started shooting immediately. That was just one link in a chain reaction. Craig warned that Larry was bombarding Ben with emails, and now Ben was thinking of backing out. Craig couldn't handle all of Larry's calls and stopped responding, which infuriated Larry. And George read Larry's latest script and then sat on it for six months, ignoring Larry's pleas to get back to him. We ended up waiting for George for two years . . . until the whole thing imploded.

We came so close. The movie could have been done, but once again Larry made it impossible.

Meanwhile, movies like *Philadelphia* and *Brokeback Mountain* had come out and gotten the kind of positive response I had been hoping for. Some people said the time was already past for *The Normal Heart*. It had been ahead of its time . . . especially in the play's last scene, with its simple acceptance of same-sex marriage . . . and now it was considered dated.

When it became clear that we couldn't raise the money to do it as a film, I thought, *All right, we'll do it on TV.* At least it would reach a wide audience. But even HBO would only pay Larry $250,000 for the screenplay, and he would not let it go for anything less than $1 million. No company was willing to take on the burden of that cost, and Larry refused to accept any revisions to his script.

This is where Larry and I had another major conflict. He had written a very explicit sex scene, with one man ejaculating on another man's stomach, and when I objected, he refused to modify it. He accused me of being repulsed by the idea of two men making love.

That wasn't true at all.

My objection had nothing to do with gender. I wouldn't be that graphic in a scene between a man and a woman either! It was about taste.

Even now, I couldn't give up on the project. I got a phone call from Craig, who said, "I just spoke to Larry's lawyer. He said that if you can get a cast together and present it to Larry . . . show him that you have all these people and they're ready to make the movie . . . maybe he'll let you do your version."

My screenplay was probably closer to the play than his, at this point. Larry had drifted further and further away from the original. In my version, the best scenes from his play were still intact, and I used as much of his dialogue as I could.

I knew it had to be a great cast if we were going to get financing. I gave Mark Ruffalo my script, and he loved it and agreed to play Ned. I sent it to Bradley Cooper, and he immediately said he'd play Felix. I was excited all over again.

I thought Julia Roberts would be wonderful as Emma . . . which meant I could skip the acting and just concentrate on directing. I discussed the part with her, and she seemed to love it.

So, I had this fantastic cast . . . Mark Ruffalo, Bradley Cooper, Julia Roberts . . . and then, oddly enough, suddenly no one could reach Julia and we couldn't get her agent to commit.

Then I received a letter from Larry, saying he'd got the money and asking me for the last time if I still wanted to direct the movie . . . but only with his screenplay as is.

I wrote him back and said, You know how much I love this project, but I cannot have my hands tied as a director. I have to be able to make certain changes to your screenplay, if necessary.

Julia was off in Europe, making *Eat Pray Love* with Ryan Murphy as her director. And the next thing I hear is that Ryan has written Larry a check for $1 million and will be directing the movie for HBO . . . with Julia Roberts and Mark Ruffalo. (Well, at least he didn't get Bradley Cooper. That would've sent me over the edge.)

And Larry continued to insult me in the press, demeaning all the work I had done. When he said things like I rewrote the script in order to make the woman doctor the star, I was appalled. He knew that wasn't true. He was rewriting history. And it was unfair to blame me for the movie not getting made. After all, he had had the rights for the past fifteen years and *he* couldn't get it made either . . . until 2014.

By that time many of the battles he was fighting had already been won. I'm thinking of milestones like laws mandating equal rights and benefits for same-sex couples, as well as new rules ensuring that LGBTQ+ people can serve openly in the military. And in a revolutionary change, same-sex marriage is legal in every state (at least for now). The culture has finally caught up to Larry's extraordinary play.

Twenty-seven years after I hoped to make it, I watched *The Normal Heart* when it was shown on TV. I was glad that a large audience would finally get to see this story . . . and anguished by what could have been.

I noticed that Ryan Murphy did make changes. Certain scenes in Larry's script were gone. So I called Ryan and asked, "How did you get that past Larry?"

He said, "Oh, I saw all that stuff. I just slowly took it out."

Now why didn't I think of that? I guess I just had to be honest with Larry. If I objected to something, I told him.

I disagreed with two big choices Ryan made. He started the film on Fire Island, and within the first few minutes, you saw four naked men having a mini-orgy underneath a tree. Who knows how many people turned it off after that scene? And Ryan chose to end his movie with a scene set at Yale, where Ned (and Larry) were so unhappy as students. Now Ned has come back for Gay Pride Week, something that would have been inconceivable decades earlier. He sits silently on the sidelines at a dance, watching the young people with tears in his eyes. Then there's a close-up of another Rolodex card with the name of a victim going into a drawer. And the screen goes black.

Where was that amazing speech that Larry wrote early on? I used it in my draft. My assistant went into the archives and pulled out my director's script from 1995 so I could look at it again.

The ending I envisioned also starts at Yale, where Ned is addressing students packed into a dining hall for a dance. A banner proclaims GAY PRIDE WEEK. "God," he says, "I remember standing here thirty years ago, wanting to kill myself because I thought I was the only gay man in the world. Now I stand here and look at all of you . . . smart, exceptional, young, openly gay men and women, living your lives honestly, bravely, with enormous integrity. You fill me with great pride."

Ned's speech continues in voice-over as we dissolve to a car driving uphill on a winding road. "We belong to a culture that includes Michelangelo, Leonardo da Vinci, Alexander the Great, Plato, Socrates, Aristotle, Proust, Byron, Walt Whitman, Colette, Henry James, Gertrude Stein, Tchaikovsky, Cole Porter, Montgomery Clift, Tennessee Williams, James Baldwin, Martina Navratilova, Virginia Woolf . . .

"Our faces are indelibly etched in time, and we stand here today as an essential and enduring part of the fabric of America and the world."

The camera then pulls back with a wide helicopter shot to reveal that the car has reached the top of a bluff overlooking the ocean on Cape Cod (today you could shoot this with a drone). Ned gets out and stands looking at the 180-degree view, with his dog running around at his feet. This is the land Felix left him. As the camera comes closer, Ned looks up at the sky and says, "Thank you, Felix . . . the light of my life. You were the man I loved more than anything. You always felt that you lacked courage. What you didn't know is that you possessed the rarest kind of courage . . . the courage to love and be loved."

So we've circled back to what I thought the movie was all about . . . everyone's right to love.

The camera begins to pull away as Ned shouts to the skies: "Felix, you told me to never lose my anger. Well, if you thought I was impossible before, just you wait. I will never, ever give up. I fucking promise you."

Finally the screen fades to black as the dog is howling, as if he's talking to Felix too.

It's funny. I'm looking at this script and cutting the dialogue, rethinking some shots, and wondering which lines in that last scene should be voice-over or not . . . as if I were going to make this movie tomorrow. And you know what? If I could, I would.

I'll always regret that I never got to make *The Normal Heart*. It's my loss.

But I'm glad Larry finally got it made. It's been very difficult for me to find a piece that I feel as passionate about. I would have been so proud to make that film.

This was a very hard chapter to write . . . very painful. I don't like reliving it. It will always break my heart.

FORTY-ONE

Nuts

By this time, Richard Baskin had moved in with me (along with his big golden retriever, Caleb). I'm not quite sure when we made that decision. Things with Richard were so easy, it just happened naturally. He still had his house . . . he just didn't live in it. He was kind, and after Jon, I needed that. I would wake up in the morning and find sweet little notes he'd left me. And he was smart, independent, and secure in himself.

One day he was playing tennis with his friend Terry Semel, the president of Warner Bros. In the course of their conversation, Richard mentioned he had heard that Debra Winger was dropping out of a movie Terry had in the works, called *Nuts.* Apparently her deal was falling apart . . . which Richard only knew because he was also friends with Debra and her ex-boyfriend, who had mentioned it to him in passing.

Richard told Terry, "If it's not going to work with Debra, you should think about Barbra."

"Really?" Terry asked. "Would Barbra do this?"

"I'm sure she would," Richard said.

I had told him that I had read Tom Topor's play and loved it. In fact, one newspaper columnist announced in 1981 that I was interested in that role, but I was completely engrossed in *Yentl* at that point, and apparently Mark Rydell, who was slated to direct, didn't want to wait for me.

Meanwhile, over the next few years, *Nuts* remained in limbo as various deals collapsed and the configuration shifted . . . the project moved from Universal to Warner Bros., where Terry picked it up. It was almost as if this movie was waiting for me . . . just like *Funny Girl.*

I've always been fascinated with the mystery of appearances . . . that's one of the reasons why I was so taken with *Yentl.* People may look a certain way from the outside but they can turn out to be very different inside. It's the old saying . . . never judge a book by its cover. Claudia Draper, the heroine of *Nuts,* had what appears to be a nice, middle-class upbringing, but she chooses to make her living as a call girl. When we first meet her, she's in a jail cell because she killed a client.

Claudia is a mess . . . she's wearing a rumpled coat over a hospital gown as she's led into a courtroom, where she speaks abruptly and acts a little crazy, physically attacking her attorney. In contrast, her mother and stepfather look very neat and act perfectly normal. You'd assume they're there to support her, but in fact they'd prefer to have her committed to a mental institution rather than stand trial and explain what happened (which is what Claudia wants to do).

So, is Claudia crazy? That's the question, but it turns out that the same question could be asked of several other people in that courtroom. Again . . . the mystery of appearances. What is crazy anyway? And what is normal?

I thought that concept was intriguing. Mark Rydell, whom I had met many times at Marilyn and Alan's, had been developing the script with various writers over the years. But when he showed it to me in 1985, I told him I thought it needed work.

He asked, "Who would you like to rewrite it?"

I said, "Alvin Sargent."

Alvin had done such a good job on the scenes he wrote for *The Way We Were* (and since then he'd won two Oscars for his screenplays of *Julia* and *Ordinary People*). I liked him as a person . . . he was sweet and gentle . . . and I loved his writing. So Mark sent it to him.

After a few weeks Mark called me up and said, "I wanna send the script to Darryl Ponicsan." Darryl had written the novel *Cinderella Liberty* and done the screenplay for the movie, which Mark had directed.

"What happened to Alvin?" I asked.

"We never heard back from him."

"Mark, it's not ethical to send the script to anyone else before you hear from Alvin. Just tell him you need a decision now."

And then I got another call a week or so later, this time from Hawaii, where Mark was on vacation. He said, "I'm going to send you a list of writers."

"Why? What happened to Alvin and Darryl?"

"Well, they're both out."

And then he proceeded to tell me what had occurred. Evidently the two writers were friends, and during a lunch together, Darryl asked Alvin, "What are you doing next?" Alvin said, "I think I'm doing *Nuts*." And Darryl said, "*I* was just offered *Nuts*!"

What a mess. Now we had lost two major talents for no good reason.

I called Alvin first, and he confirmed what had happened and added a detail that Mark had neglected to mention. Apparently after their lunch, he and Darryl immediately sent Mark a telegram, which read: "Dear Mark: From Hawaii, go straight to hell. Signed, Alvin and Darryl."

It was good to talk to Alvin. He was very frank about why he hadn't answered right away . . . he was going through a bout of writer's block at the moment. And that gave me an idea.

I called Darryl and told him the truth. "I asked for Alvin first because I had already worked with him, but I respect your writing too." Then I made him a proposal. "You and Alvin are both really good writers, with two different styles. You've got this tougher edge, and Alvin is more gentle. The two of you actually make this great combination . . . and you're friends . . . so how about writing this together?"

Darryl's first reaction was "No." He was clearly still very angry and said, "I don't want to work with Mark."

"Then do it for me," I told him. "Do it *with* me. You don't have to work with Mark at all. I'll work with you because I'd love it if the two of you could put down on paper what I have in my head."

And I told him a bit of what I was visualizing . . . that I wanted to use flashbacks to Claudia's childhood and examine the psychological roots of her behavior more fully. (There had been no flashbacks in the play.) I explained how the men she was forced to deal with . . . the incompetent male psychiatrist, the uptight prosecuting attorney, and her stepfather . . . really resonated with me. Claudia's complicated history with her stepfather reminded me of my own history with my stepfather.

I told Darryl, "I need both of you to explore this with me."

And to my delight, he said yes, and then Alvin said yes. That was so wonderful, and it proves honesty is the best policy!

And I had the most creative time I've ever had working with writers.

Terry and Warner Bros. gave us only one week to do the rewrite. I thought, *One week?!* It took me years to write *Yentl*!

But I felt we could do it, because it was so clear in my mind.

We plunged right in. Darryl, Alvin, and I sat around the dining-room table at Carolwood with the most recent script and the play, and we talked it through. Sometimes I had them work on different scenes . . . "Darryl, here's where your toughness is going to work" . . . "Alvin, here's where I need your tenderness." And sometimes they worked together. Or I might ask them to work separately on the same scene, to get two different takes on it. And then I would take the parts I liked best and put them together . . . or come up with a whole new idea, which we would then develop.

I wanted a free flow of ideas, and I didn't want anyone to censor himself, because you never can tell what's going to spark the next idea. When it's just about making the script the best it can be . . . when you can say whatever comes into your head . . . then everybody is free to fly and share their feelings in a place that's safe.

We never left that table. We worked, we laughed, we ate (Renata fed us three meals a day), and it was always fun. By the way, we didn't take time out to eat . . . everything was all on the table . . . food and pages (and food *on* the pages). And somehow we completed a script in seven days.

On Friday night, after the last page was typed and I had hugged Darryl and

Alvin goodbye I called Mark and said, "Well, we finished the script. Do you want me to messenger it over to you now?"

He said, "Oh no, no. I have a party to go to. I can't read it till Sunday."

That was kind of deflating. I had been feeling so good before I spoke to him, proud of the work we'd done, and I couldn't wait for him to read it. But I tried to hide my disappointment and called Terry, who was more enthusiastic.

On Sunday evening, when I still hadn't heard from Mark, I was getting anxious. When he finally called back that night, he asked how the script had turned out, and I said, "Well, I think it's quite good."

"How do the writers like it?"

"They like it a lot."

Then he told me, "Well, I can't read it until Monday."

Terry did read it over the weekend and called to tell me he loved it. We set up a meeting for Tuesday between Terry, me, and Mark to discuss the script. We sat in my office at Carolwood, where there was a big couch flanked by two easy chairs. I can still see Mark sprawled in one of those chairs, with his legs spread wide (his idea of a macho guy?) and holding ten pages of notes scribbled in big letters on yellow-lined paper. I sat in a corner of the couch, next to him, because I wanted him to feel we were a team. Terry was in the chair opposite Mark.

In hindsight, it's interesting that they chose to sit opposite each other and as far apart as possible because they were already at odds. Terry was ready to greenlight the movie, which Mark didn't appreciate because it turned out he didn't like our script. He preferred his own version. During the discussion Terry kept talking directly to me, and I tried to subtly signal him to look at Mark, so Mark would feel as if he was in charge, even though I didn't agree with his comments and said so.

Mark was attacking anything and everything. He actually complained that the script was typed "in the wrong format" . . . now that's clutching at straws. And he wanted more graphic sex. He kept saying, "Where's the lovemaking? She's a hooker, and we never see her doing it."

That just confirmed what I had already sensed. We saw this piece so differently.

Mark was already on shaky ground at Warner Bros. and he didn't seem to realize it. When he came in with a $19 million budget, even though Terry had only agreed to $16 million, I knew we were in trouble.

I called him and said, "Mark, please. Terry is going to fire you if you don't bring down the budget."

He didn't listen.

By this point I was begging Terry not to let him go. I could see that he was losing patience with Mark. "Dealing with this guy is like water torture," he told me.

I continued trying to protect Mark and the picture, and also my reputation . . . because I knew if he was fired, I was the one who'd get the blame. But you can't help people who won't help themselves. Mark wouldn't cooperate, and Terry fired him.

Now I had to find a new director.

If you're wondering why I didn't direct it myself, the Directors Guild had instituted a rule that a producer or actor on a film couldn't fire the director and then take over, after Clint Eastwood had done just that on one of his movies. I was functioning as both now, since Warner Bros. had asked me to be the producer, so directing this wasn't an option.

Someone at Warner suggested Martin Ritt. I had heard he was good with actors. He had directed Paul Newman, Patricia Neal, and Melvyn Douglas in *Hud* (both Neal and Douglas won Oscars). And Sally Field won an Oscar for *Norma Rae*, which Ritt also directed.

He read our script and liked it, which definitely made things easier. And then we met. Marty came in wearing a jumpsuit, which made him look kind of like a gas-station attendant, but he clearly loved them because he wore one every day . . . orange, blue, sometimes striped. And he was gruff and tough.

"I'd like to do this movie," he told me, "but I don't know if you can play the part."

I was completely taken aback. The character in this movie was a tough cookie. Didn't he know I came from Brooklyn?

I took a deep breath and very quietly said, "I'll show you, motherfucker, who can play this part!"

We stared at each other. Marty had a choice. If he wanted the job, he had to accept me as the actress and the producer.

I was so angry . . . but anger is often a way of covering up hurt. I thought I could do one of two things: Tell him to leave. Or use him.

Because I suddenly realized who this man reminded me of . . . my own stocky, sullen stepfather, Louis Kind, who never had any belief in me and never showed me any form of support. And I thought I could use that, as an actress, to help bring up my memories and emotions for the character.

I should have known our collaboration would be difficult. He wasn't Willy or Sydney. And I wasn't Sally Field. Don't take that the wrong way . . . I think Sally is a wonderful actress, but her persona is definitely sweeter than mine. Marty may have taken a more fatherly approach to her.

That was clearly not how he felt about me. Even though Marty told me he had seen *Yentl* and liked it, I don't think he was thrilled with the fact that I had just directed a film. He'd be working with a woman who had stepped onto his turf.

And here I was handing him a script that I had helped write, and he knew I would be in control as the producer, because I had final cut.

After I hired him, Shirley MacLaine asked, "How could you hire Marty Ritt? Don't you know he's a misogynist?" (I didn't.)

And so we began. I gave Marty free rein on casting. I've loved Karl Malden ever since I saw him in *On the Waterfront*, so it was a thrill to have him play my stepfather. Eli Wallach, whom Marty cast as the psychiatrist, Dr. Morrison, was a good friend of Cis and Harvey's, so I had met him many times over the years. And Leslie Nielsen played the creepy client on the date that goes so wrong (quite a departure from his hilarious turn in *Airplane*).

From the very beginning I really wanted Maureen Stapleton, who is such a gentle, vulnerable soul, to play Claudia's mother. One of my favorite people was David Rayfiel, and he had been married to Maureen for three years in the 1960s. (Isn't it interesting? When you like someone, they're usually connected to someone else you like.)

For the other leading role . . . Aaron Levinsky, the public defender appointed by the court to represent Claudia . . . Marty and I jointly decided to hire Richard Dreyfuss. I had recently seen him in *The Normal Heart* onstage and thought he was terrific. We were all set to make a deal . . . but then he accepted the lead in another film, *Tin Men*, and we had to start looking all over again. There was one brief moment when it seemed as if Dustin Hoffman and I might finally get to work together. But his demands were too much for the budget. And then

The gown I designed for my first concert in twenty-seven years.

My sketch brought to life by Donna Karan in stretch velvet (easy to breathe in!).

Women for Change National Organization for Women event.

The 44th president, Barack Obama, and me—lucky 4's.

Richard, Bill Clinton, and me at a fundraiser.

Speaking at Harvard about "The Artist as Citizen."

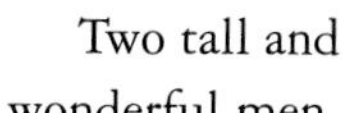

Two tall and wonderful men.

Introducing the Choy family to Jim.

Jim's hair when we first met: "Where's his great hair and beard?"

Our wedding day—Donna made the gown and Soonie did my hair. Renata took another great picture of me in my wedding gown in *People* magazine.

Family time with my son and sister.

Jim gave me my darling Sammie.

Jason—my pride and joy.

The Brolins—daughter-in-law Kathryn, Josh, me, and Jim at UCLA getting an environmental award.

Jim and Marty always by my side.

The Music, the Mem'ries, the Magic.

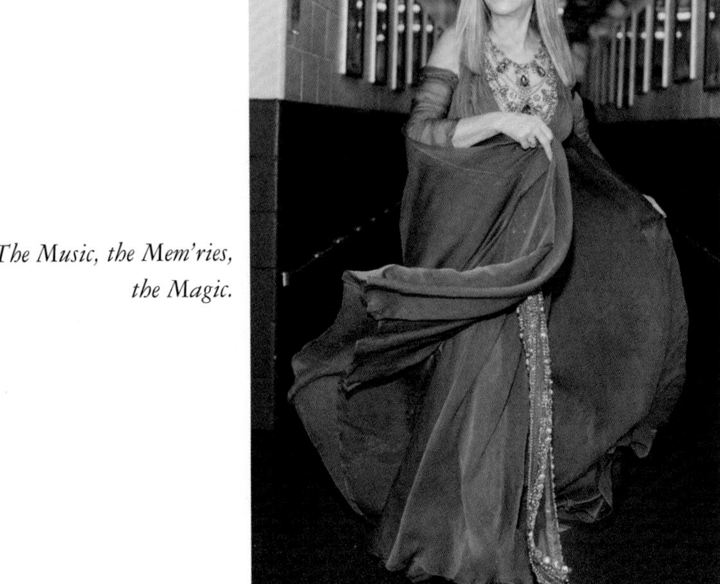

My precious Fanny, Scarlet, and Violet.

The sea of people at Hyde Park.

Renata, an extraordinary person who's been by my side for fifty years.

Stephan Weiss and his two wives: Donna was wife #1 and he called me wife #2.

Soul sisters made from the same cloth.

A magical night with Marlon, John, and Kelly.

Honored with the Chaplin Award presented by President Clinton.

All my women friends in the Senate.

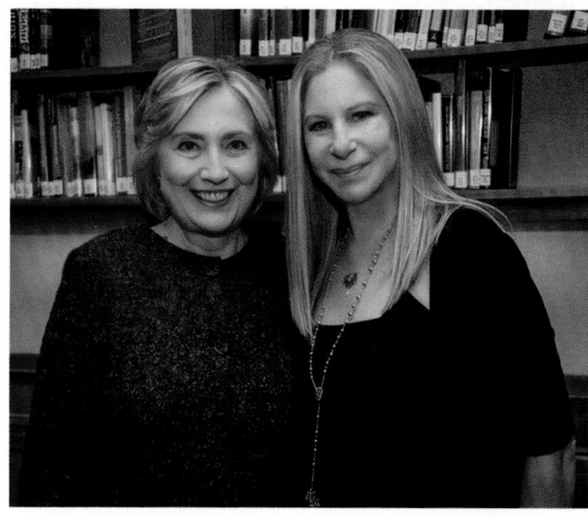

First Lady, Senator, Secretary of State, and the Woman Who Should Have Been President.

My darling grandchildren.

My daughter-in-law, Kathryn; her mother, Debbie; and the girls, Chapel and Westlyn. Three generations of women and the children who make life worth living!

My gorgeous, sexy, easygoing husband who has been by my side for over twenty-five years.

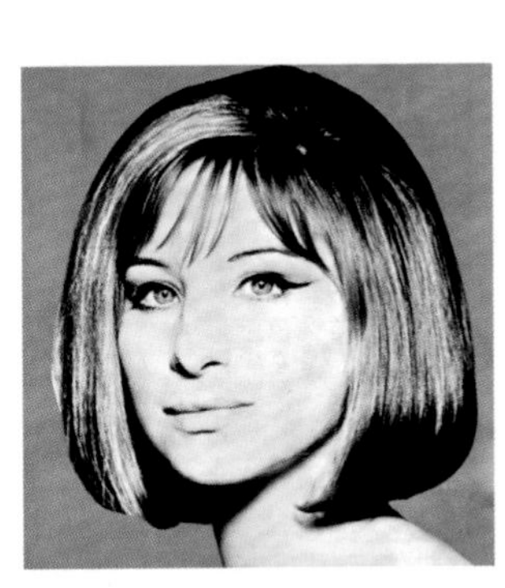

Barbra Streisand

44

Chopard
UCL

Goodman
ARMSTRONG

Some of my favorite album covers.

Richard came back into the picture when everyone agreed to postpone the start date to accommodate him.

That was a good decision. Richard is a wonderful actor who hardly needed any direction. He's a smart, disciplined person who's still free enough to be open to the moment. We worked well together (and I liked discussing politics with him too). He brought something very real and down-to-earth to the role. These are two people who get stuck with each other and aren't happy about it, but then they gradually come to appreciate each other because they're both kind of alike.

Waiting for Richard to be available also gave me more time to do research. I wanted to get inside Claudia's skin and try to understand what made her tick. I visited the Sybil Brand Institute (the county jail for women in downtown LA), and spoke to hookers. I went to see Madam Alex, who ran a high-priced brothel in Hollywood. (I think it was Jon Peters who told me about her.) I questioned her girls about how a session would normally proceed. I wanted a feeling for how they interacted with clients. What were these men like?

They told me that some men were afraid of women, and oddly enough, that meant they needed the woman to be the sexual aggressor. Many of their clients were impotent, among other problems. Frankly, these women sounded more like sex therapists discussing their work than call girls. And they had no shame about what they were doing. The general attitude was "I give them pleasure, and what's wrong with that?" I was intrigued to hear that the sex was actually not that important to a lot of men. It was really the company that they desired.

I visited Camarillo State Hospital for the mentally ill to interview doctors and patients. I remember noticing a young girl who was barefoot, sitting at a table and drawing very intently. There were two doctors escorting me, and I asked if she could come join us. That meant we needed another chair in the room. One of the doctors, who was wearing a cowboy belt with a big, ostentatious buckle, started to yell at the nurse, "Get another chair—now!" in a loud, thunderous voice . . . very angry. Why didn't he just pick up a chair himself? Or speak nicely? I swear to God, he seemed to have more issues than the patients.

That girl was very interesting. She liked to draw people as animals, and I asked, "What animal would I be?"

She studied me for a moment and said, "A llama."

And then as she was drawing me, she said, "When I get out of here, can I come visit you?"

I was caught off guard but instinctively I said, "No, you can't come visit me." I told her the truth. And then I was worried that I had done something that could be detrimental to her. But the other doctor reassured me. He said, "It's actually good you said that. Most people say 'Yes,' and that's not helpful for the patient."

At Bellevue Hospital in New York I talked to more doctors and observed more patients. I also went to the mental health facilities at UCLA. This is what I love about research . . . it's like taking a course in college. I was learning so much about people with borderline personalities and paranoid schizophrenia. I felt totally comfortable with them. (Don't jump to any conclusions.) It was their directness that appealed to me. They had no filter. They just said what they thought and completely ignored the rules of social etiquette.

That may have felt normal because it also describes me. I say what I'm thinking, and a lot of the time it's probably not appropriate. For instance, recently John Mayer surprised me by performing at my birthday party . . . we met when he did a duet on my *Partners* album, and I really liked him. I hadn't seen him in a couple of years, and the first thing I blurted out was, "How's your heart?"

I knew he was hurting over a relationship, and I just wanted to cut through all the small talk and get down to the nitty-gritty . . . something real. John was so struck by my directness that he mentioned it when he got up to sing, and said, "It made me want to make everyone else in the room disappear, so Barbra and I could just talk."

It's wonderful to have relationships with people who want to communicate on a deeper level. John responded, but some others don't. That kind of directness can make people uncomfortable. They pull back, change the subject, or walk away. I realize my bluntness can turn people off, but it's probably too late to change now. I'm impatient with small talk. I just don't want to waste any time.

Back to the patients. I could see a kind of gentleness and beauty in those who were mildly schizophrenic, who dreamed and fantasized and seemed to be exploring another world.

I think it's very hard to live in the real world sometimes.

As I once said to a therapist, "Sometimes I feel like I'm going a bit mad."

And he said, "We're all mad. You're mad. I'm mad. The only difference is I respect my madness."

That was very revealing. I thought, *Oh, it's okay.* It's not only me, but also people in all walks of life who feel this way, and maybe it's not such a terrible thing. It may even be part of the artist's experience to express it. That was very liberating. He stripped away half my anxiety with just those few words.

We began filming on September 30, 1986, in New York, and then we came back to Los Angeles to make the rest of the picture. I have a particularly vivid memory of our first day on the Warner Bros. lot, because I was so worried when I got home that night that I had to write about it in my journal. At the top of the page I wrote "Marty," and then listed ten things I "couldn't believe he didn't know."

These were very basic. Marty had the time sequence of the film mixed up. He was confused about where the scene we had just shot fit into the story.

It was the scene at the elegant hotel bar, where Claudia has arranged to meet Allen, played by Leslie Nielsen, so she can get a good look at him before she agrees to take him on as a customer. (She was picky, you know.) As she walks into the room, the men at the bar turn to look at her.

I also wanted to use that particular shot near the opening of the film. Claudia would flash back to that moment as she's led from a jail cell to the courtroom and has to walk by cells packed with men, leering at her and making crude comments. That would remind her of the men at the bar, who were thinking the same thing. And really, what was the difference? Only a layer of civility.

I thought that was an interesting juxtaposition, and kind of mysterious, because the audience wouldn't know yet what it referred to, because the rest of the scene comes later in the film.

I love mystery.

But Marty didn't get it. He asked, "How do you put those two pieces of film together?"

I said, "Well, you could do a shot of Claudia's face before you cut to the men at the bar, so we realize that this is what's going through her head. She sees the string of men in the cells, and that triggers the memory of the string of men at the bar."

"But you didn't say that in the script. You didn't write 'close-up on Claudia.'"

"Oh, I'm sorry we left that out. We just assumed you'd do it." (Never assume.)

Of course I didn't describe every little thing that was in my brain. Maybe I should have. I thought the point of the sequence was clear, and I was leaving it to him to decide how to film it. But then he wanted to put a woman at the bar, and I had to explain to him that he couldn't, because it would wreck the parallel structure . . . all men in the cells and all men at the bar.

Marty also didn't see that there was too much space between the men at the bar. And he didn't seem to mind that their acting wasn't good. He kept saying, "It's okay. Forget about it."

I can't forget about things like that. He let the AD position all the men facing the bar, which looked unrealistic. I had to give each man something to do. One could be smoking and facing the room, another could be reading a newspaper, and then the bartender should be taking orders in the background. By the way, Darryl Ponicsan is the first face you see at the bar (I love to use real people when I can), and the music that's playing is that melody I wrote, "Here We Are at Last."

Claudia sits down with Allen at a little round table, and Marty set up the shot over my shoulder to Leslie, using a 29mm lens. That's a very wide lens, and it made the back of my head look huge in the foreground, completely dwarfing Leslie, which was wrong psychologically. I thought we needed a longer lens for this intimate scene, and I asked our brilliant cinematographer, Andrzej Bartkowiak, and he agreed. So did Marty, after I explained it to him, and we switched to a 75mm lens.

Actually I had to explain a lot of things to Marty that day. I guess he wanted some guidance, because every morning he would come into my trailer with the pages we were about to film and ask, "How do you see this shot?" Although I noticed he was careful never to ask for my advice in front of the crew. I don't blame him. I'm sure he didn't want to appear as if he needed help.

But he kept saying to me, "I don't understand this. I've never made a movie with flashbacks." That was a problem, because flashbacks were integral to this script. I must have shared my concerns with Richard Dreyfuss, because I wrote in my journal, "Richard said, 'It's senility.'"

Marty was seventy-two (not that old!) and had had a heart attack, but that happened years earlier. He seemed physically fit now.

After that episode with the lens, I would call Andrzej every night to discuss the following day's scenes. And he pointed something out: "Marty never looks in the camera. He just sits in his chair. I think he's tired."

At the same time, I had to concentrate on Claudia. She's not a particularly likable character, but that's also what made her interesting. She's charged with first-degree manslaughter, and her original attorney, hired by her parents, insisted that she would have a better chance if she was found incompetent to stand trial rather than facing the murder charge in court. In other words, he was telling her to lie.

Claudia just wants to tell the truth. She believes she's innocent, and she has no intention of pretending to be something she's not in order to get some kind of deal. But no one wants to listen to her.

Again, it reminds me of that quote from George Bernard Shaw's *Saint Joan* that has always resonated with me: "He who tells too much truth is sure to be hanged." Joan of Arc said that at her trial, and that's one reason I identified with her as a teenager.

I'm a truth teller, and I've been crucified for it many times. I have opinions. I talk out of turn. I complain. Early on in my career, a reporter was following me around in Europe for an article, and I had to cut the interview short because I had a headache. I was simply telling her the truth. But her attitude was basically, You're rich and famous and you're not allowed to have a headache.

What she didn't understand was a headache is a headache. It hurts.

I'm always surprised by how many people can't handle the truth. They don't want to hear it. I like Claudia because she isn't afraid of the truth.

In her first conversation with Levinsky, who's been roped into taking her case after she's punched out the attorney hired by her parents, Claudia has to figure out fast whether he's there to help or to hurt her. She's aggressive and abrasive. She goes through a roller coaster of emotions . . . violent one moment and provocative the next, as she props her legs up on the table and disparages Dr. Morrison, the hospital psychiatrist. "He's a very weird guy. I flashed and he didn't even look. How about you, Levinsky? You weird too?"

"I must be okay. I'm looking."

Because she's a bit outrageous, I could use my "bad girl" side. And I wanted to appear a little crazy, so the audience would be confused. Maybe she *is* dangerous. After all, she killed a man.

A part like this is a gift to an actress, and I could identify with her anger. I think I'm still angry about many things, and I could use that anger and feel great in releasing it . . . just letting it out and not having to play nice.

It was fun to feel free. I could yell, I could cry, I could swear (which I do quite a lot in real life). I didn't have to worry about my hair, because the messier it looked, the better! I used the bare minimum of makeup. And I'm wearing a hospital gown for most of the picture, which was fine with me because I hate costume fittings! I had only three costume changes. Perfect. Less is more.

I also believe that when it comes to acting. In the scene where Claudia turns the tables on Dr. Morrison in his office, analyzing him, I thought Eli was a bit over the top. So I took Marty aside and whispered, "I think Eli is overdoing it. Wouldn't it be better if he were less agitated?"

I thought the quieter Eli was, the more menacing he would be.

Marty went over to talk to Eli, but when we did the scene again, nothing much had changed. So I went back to Marty and whispered again, "Tell him to think of Harvey Corman."

Marty said, "What? You mean the comedian?"

"No, no, no. Harvey Corman, his dear friend and mine. He's a psychiatrist who has a strong, quiet presence, and that's what Eli is missing. The words might be a little crazy, but his demeanor should be calm."

I had suggested that Eli wear a sweater and tie, and maybe smoke a pipe, like Harvey did. I wanted Eli to look authoritative, at ease with himself. And the performance got better.

I didn't want to betray the very serious situation by turning the doctor into a caricature. This is a realistic film about a difficult subject, and there's nothing pretty about it. The prison sets are gritty. The psychiatric ward is bleak. There's very little color. But since most of the movie takes place on one set . . . the courtroom . . . I wanted something that would engage the eye, and asked the art department to paint those faded classical murals on the walls, like something I had seen in my research. I loved those monochromatic sepia tones.

I didn't think we needed a lot of music in this movie, and that's why I was able to write the score myself. I only heard music in a few places, such as the scene where Levinsky goes to Claudia's apartment to pick out a dress for her to wear in court. As he's looking through her things, he learns more about her, and so does the audience. I wanted each prop to provide a clue to her persona, and

Anne McCulley, a wonderful set decorator, did a great job. You can see the child in Claudia by her possessions.

The music here is the closest it gets to a love theme, but this is not a love story. There's definitely a rapport that develops between the two characters. But it's not about some superficial sexual attraction. They come to respect each other and share a certain understanding. And if there is an undercurrent of sexual attraction, neither Claudia nor Levinsky chooses to act on it.

She is difficult, and just when he seems to be warming up to her (Levinsky brings her a pastrami sandwich!), Claudia lashes out again. It happens when he hands her a bag with her clothes. She didn't know he was going to her apartment, and she's furious that he didn't bother to ask. She pulls out a lacy black bra and panties that he packed and says, "What gives you the right to invade me? . . . I decide who sees my underwear."

Levinsky apologizes, but her use of the word "invade" is so telling. She sees his act almost as a physical violation. And then we cut to a flashback of Allen looking through her underwear, uninvited. He holds up a pair of panties and says, "I'd love to see you in these."

And that leads directly into the murder.

God, that was a nasty scene to shoot. I don't think we did a lot of takes. One would have been enough for me, frankly. When Leslie was pretending to strangle me, he got a little carried away and was actually choking me too hard. It really spooked me, and that's what you see on-screen. I played it scared because I was scared!

So one mystery is solved . . . we know she didn't attack her client in a fit of homicidal rage. He attacked her, and she killed him in self-defense. But Claudia is not on trial for murder here. This is simply a hearing to determine whether she is competent to stand trial. And it's still a mystery as to why her parents seem to be afraid of the facts and don't want her to testify in court.

And the other mystery is why Claudia so dislikes her parents. As the court is adjourning for a short recess, they come up to her and say, "We love you."

She looks at them with utter coldness and makes them repeat each word slowly. She's mocking them, and the audience is ready to turn on her for being so awful to her parents.

But for Claudia, it raises a basic question: What is love? People say "I love you" all the time, but then they don't act very loving. And the person who's hearing those words has a hard time responding, because it's very confusing. How can her parents say that and still behave the way they do?

There's a moment when Claudia's mother, Rose, is up on the stand, proclaiming her love for her daughter, and it triggers a flashback in Claudia's mind. She's a little girl sitting on her bed, crying, when her mother walks by her room with a drink in her hand. She just looks at her daughter, then closes the door on her.

That moment was profoundly upsetting to me. It hit me in a very vulnerable place, because it brought back memories from my own childhood. My mother never asked me how I was feeling. She never stood up for me when my stepfather belittled me. She never tried to stop him. She was willing to risk losing her daughter to keep her new husband.

I understand more about her behavior now, after years of therapy. I realize that it's hard for a woman who has already lost one husband to jeopardize her relationship with another. She would rather not hear or see or acknowledge his inappropriate behavior toward her child. And I realize that it's hard for a man to come into a new house with a new woman and take on her children too.

But that knowledge doesn't alleviate the pain.

The pivotal moment in the film comes when Levinsky realizes what's behind all of Claudia's behavior. It happens just when he's most frustrated. She's giving him no help, and he walks over to her and glances at the pad where she's been doodling. She's drawn her stepfather, her mother, and herself. But none of them has a mouth. He asks her, "What can't they talk about?"

She's angry and says, "Stop it!"

But he's just as angry and goes right back to questioning her stepfather. Levinsky starts out by saying that he must be a saint to love a frustrating woman like Claudia. He's very aggressive, needling Arthur that there must have been a time when he lost his temper. Rose jumps to her husband's defense and says, "Arthur would never do anything to hurt Claudia."

Claudia fires back at her. "How would you know, Momma?"

Levinsky looks at Claudia, whose head is bowed. Then he slowly turns to look at Rose, and suddenly he knows. He sees it. He solves the mystery. The realization happens without words . . . we just see it on his face . . . and Richard played that moment brilliantly.

He turns to Arthur and asks, "Did you make your stepdaughter your lover?"

His denials are futile, because we flash back to him embracing the young

Claudia, wrapped only in a towel, after her bath . . . then a quick cut to Claudia being pinned down on her bathroom floor by Allen. And in the courtroom, she breaks down, crying. "No, Daddy! . . . Don't let him touch me. Don't let him hurt me anymore."

I wanted to cry in this scene, and as you know, crying doesn't come easily to me. So I wrote something down on a piece of paper . . . something my own stepfather had said to me that hurt me terribly . . . and I used that to bring up those emotions.

I did a lot of research on the sexual abuse of children before we made this movie. The statistics at the time were staggering. I think it was one out of four girls, and one out of eight boys who had been abused . . . usually by a family member, or somebody who lived in the house, like a boyfriend or an uncle. And it happened even with fathers, and stepfathers. Clearly, it's a huge problem. The adult takes advantage of the innocence of the child. It gives him a sense of power over the powerless. And it creates lifelong damage to the victims. Many abused children become abusers themselves.

I was never abused sexually by my stepfather. The abuse I experienced was emotional. But I could identify with Claudia. Playing her was cathartic. I could finally exorcise the last vestiges of Lou Kind's hold over me.

I was doing *Funny Girl* on Broadway and hadn't seen him for years when my mother called and told me he was coming to the matinee. I had woken up that morning with a scratched cornea and couldn't keep that eye open. It was tearing uncontrollably. But there was no way I was going to let the understudy go on for me. So I called an eye doctor and had him meet me at the theater. He put a drop of Novocain or some anesthetic in my eye, to stop the tearing so I could give the performance. And after the curtain call I waited for my stepfather backstage.

But he never appeared. I never even knew what he thought of the show . . . or me.

The next day I was in my apartment when the doorman brought up a small package that Lou had dropped off. It was a tall jar filled with hard candies. They were pretty . . . various colors. That jar had been sitting on the edge of my tub since 1964. But after working on *Nuts* and reliving my history with Lou Kind, I looked at it differently. The candies were all stuck together by this point, kind of melting into one another.

Why was I saving this?

I stared at the jar for a long moment. And finally, after twenty-three years, I threw it away.

After the revelation about her stepfather, Claudia is more vulnerable than we've ever seen her. That night, Levinsky checks up on her in her prison cell, where she's lying in bed, drugged and barely responsive. "Maybe they're right," she says weakly. "Maybe I am crazy . . . I didn't tell him to stop . . . I just wanted him to love me, that's all."

It's that seed of guilt that has triggered her own behavior. During my research I learned that most of the women I talked to despised their fathers for invading them. But there were a few who actually said they enjoyed being touched by their fathers. "It felt good," one of them explained.

I was shocked, and yet I thought, *Yes, I can understand it* . . . perhaps in terms of the unconscious competitiveness between mothers and daughters. Or in Claudia's case, the hurt and anger toward her mother for turning her back on her.

At this point, Claudia is wondering if she *is* crazy . . . not in the way the psychiatrist says . . . but by allowing herself to be so self-destructive.

When we were preparing to record the music for this scene, I called Jeremy Lubbock, who did the arrangements. At two in the morning I began singing into the phone so he could hear the kind of chords I was imagining. We were doing a reprise of the main theme, but this time with more atonality. I wanted that soulful sound of the cello, with chords that rubbed. Jeremy was great at that.

On the night before we shot the last courtroom scene, where Claudia finally testifies, I went up to Marty and said, "I need you to protect me as an actress in this scene. When Claudia gets up on the stand, she's still feeling the effects of the drug. She should be a little foggy. So I don't want to know the lines too well. I want to have to search for the words. So this time could you please film me first?"

I knew if Marty shot the other actors first, I would be too familiar with the lines by the time the camera turned around on me, since I would have been saying them for hours.

But the next morning when I came in, I saw that Marty had the camera set up to film the men first.

I was shocked, and said, "Marty, this is the one time I asked you to help me, and you didn't."

He had some absurd excuse about how it would have cost more.

I told him, "I'm the producer and I'll worry about the cost. The point is we need to get my best performance here. This is the climax of the film . . . the scene where Claudia wins or loses her case."

He didn't say anything, so I had to make the decision. And thank God I was the producer. I said, "Please turn the set around."

And then the next day as we got deeper into the scene, Richard said, "I'd like to try something."

"Sure," Marty told him. "Go ahead."

After Richard did his thing, I raised my hand and said, "I'd like to try something too."

And Marty said, "No."

I said, "Excuse me?"

It was the most humiliating moment. I only wanted to work out the staging for my big speech with Andrzej, and have him try three different lenses. For only the second time in my life, I walked off a set because I was so upset. I had to hold my tongue . . . catch my breath. I didn't want to embarrass Marty or myself by losing control, or make the crew feel awkward. I remember thinking, *Shirley was right. He* is *a misogynist.*

What was Marty thinking? Why did he do it? Was it a show of power . . . "I'm the director and you're not."

I'll never know, but it was very disturbing.

It was painful to go through this movie without the support of the director. I don't remember one instance where he told me he liked what I was doing.

It's probably another reason why Claudia's big speech rang so true to me, when she's trying to explain herself to the judge. She says, "I know I'm supposed to be a good little girl . . . I know what you expect me to do. But I'm not just a picture in your heads . . . do you understand? I'm not just a daughter or a wife or a hooker or a patient or a defendant. Can't you get that? You think giving blowjobs for five hundred dollars is nuts . . . Well, I know women who marry men they despise so they can drive a Mercedes and spend summers in the Hamptons. I know women who crawl through shit for a fur coat. I know women who peddle their daughters to hang on to their husbands. So don't judge my blowjobs. They're sane. I knew what I was doing every goddamned minute and I'm responsible for it."

That's brutally honest.

Claudia became a prostitute so she could choose *when* she is sexual and with whom. She could name her price too. Claudia takes responsibility for who she is, and that's what I love about her. And she tells the truth, which is why she comes out of this with her dignity intact.

As she says at the climax of the film, looking at the psychiatrist and then the prosecuting attorney and then her mother, "Now he can sign a piece of paper saying I'm nuts, but it's only a piece of paper. And you can't make me nuts that way, no matter how many times you sign it, no matter how many times you say it . . . So just get it straight . . . I won't be nuts for you."

This speech felt so truthful to me that the tears just flowed . . . and this time I didn't need to look at any piece of paper.

Claudia is not going to let other people define her.

I've come to realize that I can't control what people say about me or write about me. I don't like to give interviews, because my words are often taken out of context. The only thing I can control is my work, and that's why I pay a lot of attention to it.

Marty never quite understood this film. He had been handed a finished script, and he would carry it around on set. But I had helped write that script. I knew every scene and why it was there.

After Marty completed his cut, I watched it and knew it wasn't the film I saw in my head. Warner Bros. didn't like it either. Marty's editing style, like his filmmaking, was very basic and workmanlike . . . the master shot, the two-shot. But that can get tedious, especially in what's basically a one-set courtroom drama. I envisioned something with more flow.

I could see visual associations that I wanted to bring out through the flashbacks. The image of water running into a bathtub recurs several times in the film. It was in the bathroom where Claudia was violated as a child, and her stepfather would turn on the faucet to mask the sound of something that shouldn't be happening. We also see her as a teenager and then an adult, locking herself in the bathroom, with the water running, to avoid her stepfather. And when her client turns on the faucet and says he wants to take a bath with her, it triggers those memories. When she says, "I don't do baths," he gets angry and starts slapping her around. I thought I could make those connections more visceral. I wanted to find more interesting transitions. So I went back into the editing room with the editor Marty had hired, who was not thrilled to be there with me. But he knew every frame of the film, and I needed to get it done, fast.

And I came up with a process, which was a crude precursor of what later became digital editing. If I liked a version of a scene, we'd play it back on the editing machine's screen, and I'd tape it with my little video camera. Then we could take the film apart and recut it using other ideas, and I'd tape that version too. We could do another, and another, and then I could go home and rewatch them all and decide which I liked best. It saved a lot of time, because we didn't have to send each version out to the lab to make dupes, and yet we were still protected. I had a video copy of every version, so we could always recreate the one I chose.

Marty's cut had ended on a freeze frame of Claudia, pushing open the courtroom door. I had another idea, based on something that I saw one day outside my house on Carolwood. There was a man wearing a bright Hawaiian shirt and singing loudly as he jauntily walked down the middle of the street . . . where he could get hit by a car! He seemed a bit crazy.

It gave me the ending of the film. I had Claudia come out of the courthouse onto the streets of New York and walk past an actor who I put in a Hawaiian shirt and had sing some made-up nonsense in this booming voice. She's walking around in a hospital gown, which makes her seem equally crazy. But we know she's not. She's a bit odd, she's unconventional, but she's not crazy.

Point is, you have to go deeper before you make judgments about people.

There's a moment in that last scene when a garment rack is wheeled by in front of her. And I suddenly had an inspiration. Being Claudia and being free, I thought it would be fun to swipe a red scarf off it and toss it around my neck. That seemed right for the moment, right for the character. She's still a "bad girl," in a way.

But wait a minute, that's too judgmental again . . . it's just like calling her crazy.

And when we deal in labels like that, we inevitably cheat ourselves. Claudia is unusual. She's a complex person, as we all are. Maybe she *is* a little nuts . . . but so are we.

The movie got great marks from the preview audiences, so Warner Bros. had high hopes and opened it on November 20, in time for the holidays. But this was not a Christmas movie. The subject was too dark. And to top it off, the stock market had just crashed a few weeks before, on October 19, the infamous Black Monday . . . the biggest percentage drop in history, at that point. I don't think a lot of people were in the mood to go out to the movies.

And the ad campaign was not exactly enticing . . . a close-up of Richard and me, with a very sour face. Yuck. That was my fault. I was trying to let audiences know that the film wasn't a comedy, but now I see the shot it should have been . . . me behind bars, sitting on the floor, and not looking so angry.

And I may have made a mistake as the producer. I wrote a letter to reviewers that said, "This is a psychological mystery . . . Please don't give away the ending." Maybe more people would have come if they knew what it was about.

We did get three Golden Globe nominations for Best Film—Drama, Best Actress, and Best Supporting Actor for Richard.

And we lost all three awards.

Ah, well. I'm still very proud of this movie. I think it has something important to say . . . and I always like it when justice wins out.

FORTY-TWO

No Regrets

In the midst of filming *Nuts* . . . when I was feeling incredibly pressured . . . I woke up one morning and said excitedly, "I've got the shot!"

Richard reached for a cigarette and then turned to me in bed, annoyed, and said, "Helloooo??? Good mooorning."

That was the moment when I knew our relationship wasn't going to last. I felt that he didn't understand my creative process, and I was hurt.

"Richard, if you were making a movie and you woke up with an idea, I'd say, 'Let me get a pencil and paper and write it down for you before you forget it.'"

So that was the beginning of the end.

Before I say anything more, I want you to know that I have many great memories of the three and a half years Richard and I were together. I love him dearly, he's the most loyal friend, and Jim and I consider him part of our family.

I also know that I was not easy to live with while I was working on *Nuts*. I was intense, consumed with the movie, and Richard was more laid back. He had fewer obligations and more free time. When he wanted to go skiing or take a trip, sometimes I couldn't get away. So he'd go off on his own.

He probably felt neglected. I admit it, I *am* obsessed when I'm in the midst of a project . . . to the exclusion of all else (except my son). My friends complain that they never see me, and that makes me feel guilty, and now I was feeling even more pressure because I didn't want to disappoint my lover.

Then, when I was finally able to take a break, Richard said, "I can't go away. I have work to do."

It felt as if he were paying me back. I got the message. He was exerting his own autonomy, making a point . . . *Now that you're free doesn't mean I am.*

He used to tell me, "You can't have things just when you want them."

I know that's true about me. Many times I need instant gratification, because I'm never quite sure that the person or the thing I crave won't just disappear.

It was easy to get involved with Richard because he was so sweet, and for the same reason it was easy to separate. He just moved back into his own house. (But his dog decided to stay with me.) There was no acrimony. We still cared for each other.

But once again, at the end of 1987, I was on my own.

Luckily my friends were there for me. Irvin Kershner came over for dinner, and he was full of stories about his latest adventures but also very engaged with the world. I loved our talks. Conversation always went to a deeper level with him.

And David Rayfiel wrote me one of his delightful notes, ending with "I love you—ya know." He always kept in touch, and we had a nice evening together. As I wrote in my journal, "He remembers everything I've ever said to him."

I also wrote, "Why is it that men I'm not attracted to find me so wonderful?"

And why did I push away the ones who were attracted to me?

I didn't want to continue this pattern. Every aspect of me wanted to change.

Was I doing something wrong? Most men seem to want someone who will focus on them, someone who's not a threat in any way. Was I too demanding? Too overpowering?

But that was just an image, not the reality.

If only someone would see that. Couldn't two people be loving equals? That didn't sound so impossible.

I knew I needed to find a better balance between my home life and my work life. After all, what's most important at the end of the day?

Personal relationships.

I wanted to share my life with someone. It was very lonely being me.

For Christmas I went to Aspen, and there, at a party, a man walked up to me. That was refreshing . . . if a guy makes the first move, he's already a step ahead.

And this guy was lean and tan, with an easy grin (and good teeth). His name was Don Johnson, and he was the heartthrob of the moment on the TV series *Miami Vice*. I have to admit, I'm very attracted to attractive men. (Okay, so I'm superficial!) It's almost like an aesthetic thing . . . like a piece of art. I collect!

We chatted for a bit, and then he took me by the arm and led me over to a more secluded spot, where we could talk more privately. I liked the fact that he took charge and basically scooped me up, as if we were the only two people in the room.

Then he sent flowers and called. At first, when he asked me out, I wondered what we could possibly talk about for an entire evening. But I was pleasantly surprised. I found he was very different from his "bad boy" reputation. He seemed caring and sensitive, sharing details about his difficult upbringing that he said he had never told anyone else. I thought, *Oh, he's not so tough after all.* He'd been misrepresented, just like me.

That was part of our initial bond.

And he could be very romantic. I remember walking into a restaurant to meet him, and as I sat down, he said, "I looked at you, and it made my heart sing."

Don had a lot of charm, and I wasn't the only one who responded. I remember going to a sushi restaurant with him, and a man came up and asked for his autograph, and a woman asked for mine. I loved the fact that he got as much attention as I did. For years I had always been apologizing to the men I was with . . . I didn't want them to feel overshadowed. But now, I could actually relax. Don was so different from me . . . he even liked all the attention from the press. As he said to one reporter, "I've been with thousands of women, but Streisand is supreme, unequaled in all the ways that count. I love her strengths, her direct approach to music, acting, people . . . She makes me laugh, and she makes me think."

In January Don had to be in New York and wanted me to join him. I hesitated at first but then I thought, *Why not?* I canceled my appointments and got on a plane, even though I hate flying, as you know. I'm an earth sign . . . Taurus . . . and we don't like to be suspended in midair. I was very nervous, and kept trying to distract myself with books and newspapers . . . anything I could think of. And then, as we were nearing New York and beginning the descent, my ears started to hurt. The stewardess stopped by my seat and said brightly, "This is exciting. It's the first time this pilot is going to be landing the plane!"

I stared at her, dumbfounded. I couldn't help but ask, "Are you kidding? Why would you tell me that? I'm a very nervous flier."

"Well, so you're both nervous! But you know what? He'll be fine!"

That was not helpful. For the next twenty minutes, I thought I was going to die. Unfortunately we had to circle the airport. It was bumpy, my ears were killing me, and I thought, *Here I am, looking forward to this romantic tryst, and this guy is going to crash the plane!*

After what seemed like an eternity, we finally landed. What a relief to be on solid ground. And I felt that little thrill in the pit of my stomach, seeing Don again. He took me to Atlantic City to see Mike Tyson fight. Normally a boxing match would not be at the top of my list, but Don loved all those boy things . . . watching football (which he tried to explain to me . . . hopeless), flying helicopters, racing boats. I remember the first time he took me out on his boat when I visited him in Florida. He wanted to show me how to drive it. I was scared at first, but suddenly I was going 70 miles per hour. And I liked it. It was exhilarating.

He loved to move fast, fly high, and play hard.

I never dated when I was an adolescent. So I guess you could say I was making up for lost time. And our connection certainly had that adolescent excitement. I felt like a high school girl, going out with the captain of the football team.

In February I had to attend the ShoWest convention in Las Vegas to accept the "Star of the Decade" Award. That was a lovely tribute, given by the National Association of Theater Owners. I admit I wasn't on time for the luncheon, but all was forgiven when I walked in hand in hand with Don. And then I stepped up to the microphone and said, "Sorry I was a little late, but I was auditioning for a part on *Miami Vice*." The crowd went wild.

(Actually I did do a walk-on on *Miami Vice*, uncredited and just for a lark.)

Being with Don was fun, pure fun. I was happy, and it showed. I can see it in photographs from that time. We were the "hot couple." And I noticed something. Of course Don was invariably described as handsome, but the press was saying positive things about my looks as well. It's interesting . . . for years, after *Funny Girl*, they kept referring to me as a "kook" or odd-looking. It's true I was different.

Eventually I grew into my face, I guess.

Or maybe it was something deeper. Now, when I had finally stopped worrying about whether I was attractive or not, when I had stopped putting myself down and saw myself in a better light, so did the magazines. They were actually using words like "beautiful" and "glamorous" to describe me. That was refreshing, and I thought, *Well, it must be a reflection of how I'm feeling.*

I think the world mirrors what we feel about ourselves. When a woman feels pretty, the world sees her as pretty.

Frankly, after a few months, I would have been happier with a little less attention when we went out in public. And looking back on our romance, I think our best times were actually when we were alone at Don's house in Aspen. And it was even better when Jesse, his six-year-old son, was there. Jason was grown and off on his own, going to film school at NYU, so it was wonderful to be around a child again, and Jesse was very special. I loved playing with him, watching him ride his bike, tucking him into bed, and making him feel "cozy" . . . that was the word we always used to say to each other. And his mom was Patti d'Arbanville, whom I loved working with on *The Main Event.*

I had become close to Don very quickly, so I was disappointed when he couldn't come to my birthday party in April. But he had a good reason. He was filming a movie in Calgary. Without him I was feeling lonely, and that's when Pierre Trudeau happened to call out of the blue. He invited me to go to Russia with him and said, "We'll hold hands in Gorky Park." That was sweet.

I should have gone to Moscow, but I went to Calgary instead. My sister, Rozzie, was singing up there, coincidentally, so I could see Don and support her as well.

That was a painful visit. I had the sense that Don didn't really want me there. He was making phone calls from the car as we were driving, talking to other people. And he didn't want to listen to a demo of our song.

That song had been my idea. I knew Don wanted to broaden his career . . . he had already recorded one album a couple of years earlier, at the height of his fame on *Miami Vice*. A single from it had gotten a lot of airplay, and he was hoping to build on that success. I wasn't even aware that he sang until he was coming over one day and said, "I'll bring my guitar so I can sing you love songs."

So it was only natural, when I was making a new album, to ask if he wanted to sing a song with me. It was called "Till I Loved You," and this was at the point in our relationship when I wanted to spend more time with him. So I thought, *Why not work together?* Recording a song was something I could offer, and I offered it to him.

The session in the studio seemed to go well. We were improvising at the end . . . having fun in the moment, and laughing. I had asked Phil Ramone to produce it, and we both liked the way it turned out.

Then somehow it all went wrong. Not the duet itself. It was Don's attitude afterward . . . singing with me apparently made him feel very insecure. And instead of talking about it honestly, he just became very cold, and mistrustful, and angry. I tried to be sympathetic. I certainly had no intention of ruining his career, but it turned out he was concerned about exactly that. It seemed like an overreaction to me, but clearly he was upset, and therefore so was I.

I wrote down my thoughts in my journal . . . that I couldn't care less if the single ever came out . . . that our relationship was more important than any record . . . and if he would just tell me what he was thinking, I would try to support him.

One thing I need in a relationship is honesty and communication . . . to be told how someone is feeling. But Don didn't want to talk about it, or anything that had to do with emotional issues. There was always some excuse to stop the conversation . . . a tennis game, a business meeting, a massage.

So I began to withdraw as well. I told him I had to work. (Sometimes I use work to distract me from myself.)

It was kind of ironic. The songs on the album, which I titled *Till I Loved You*, basically tracked the progression of a love affair, from the beginning to the end. And now ours seemed to be disintegrating as well.

He was redoing his house in Aspen, and I gave him a few hints about what a woman might like in her bathroom, like a little sink in the area where she'll be putting on her makeup. But I had a feeling that it wasn't me who would be using that sink. I remember asking him to come look at the house I now live in (years before I actually managed to buy it), but he was too busy.

Still, he wanted me to come to the opening of his film *Sweet Hearts Dance*, and I did. But even as he drew me back in, it felt as if he were simultaneously pushing me away.

His withholding took me straight back to childhood.

Don's silence was making me feel anxious. And I couldn't freely express my feelings without getting enormous anger back . . . not a safe place to be.

But wait a minute. Why shouldn't *I* have been angry?

As I've learned from therapy, if you repress, you repeat.

I've been trying for such a long time to change those patterns. I wanted a man who would give and receive . . . who wasn't afraid of honesty.

I was actually glad he was going back to Florida.

And then I called him in Miami one day, and Melanie Griffith answered the phone. They had been married briefly a dozen years earlier, and she often called when I was at Don's house. At that point she was in rehab, and Don had conquered his own drug habit and was trying to help. (By the way, I'm not revealing any secrets. Both of them have been very open about it.) I had no problem with him talking to her, but I did have a problem with him not having the courtesy to tell me the truth about their current relationship.

I can't be with a man who is not straight with me emotionally.

So that was it. The romance was over, and it was fun while it lasted. I have no regrets.

And now, thirty years later, I'll sometimes run into Don at a party given by mutual friends. We hug, and he always whispers in my ear, "I love you."

I don't say it back.

FORTY-THREE

I Fell in Love with a Book

"Last night I asked for a sign" . . . that's what I wrote in my journal on March 2, 1990. I was thinking of Brugh Joy, who was so attuned to the subconscious, as well as the conscious mind. He once said, "If you have to make a decision, ask for the answer in a dream." And this was a big decision. I needed to know whether I should direct a movie called *The Prince of Tides*, or build a house.

I had bought a piece of property on Summitridge Drive at the top of Beverly Hills, with a spectacular view of the whole city. I was going to build a Natchez-style house, two stories, with pillars and porches on the front and back. It would have had two parlors, one to the left and one to the right as you walked in, like in those great old Southern homes. Maybe a double staircase across a large foyer, framing that extraordinary view (when the smog wasn't blotting it out).

Outdoors, I had visions of Spanish moss dripping from the trees and swans skimming across a pond. (Okay, forget the swans. Turns out they can be vicious.) I had hired an architect and had plans drawn up.

Meanwhile, for the past year, I'd also been working on a script based on Pat Conroy's bestselling novel *The Prince of Tides.*

But now that project was on the verge of collapse. MGM/UA was having financial problems and had put the movie into turnaround. We were trying to negotiate a new deal at Columbia, but they wanted me to take a huge salary cut. (My fee for producing, directing, and acting was already less than they would've had to pay three separate people.) I thought that cut was too much, and if they had so little respect for my talents, I wasn't even sure we could work together.

That night, as I went to sleep, I was still torn between trying to make the movie happen . . . or building the house. So I asked for a sign, and turned out the lights.

What happened next was quite extraordinary. In the middle of the night, I suddenly heard a click that woke me up. I sat up and saw that the light over the painting above the fireplace had somehow clicked on. How could that be? I knew I had turned it off before I went to sleep. The painting was a portrait of a turn-of-the-century woman wearing a beautiful pink satin gown. The switch was right beside me. I turned it off again and fell back asleep.

And then a bit later it happened again. The light clicked on a second time.

Wait a minute. That's impossible. I reached over and turned it off again, but now I was completely mystified. What was going on?

In the morning it came to me that the light going on above the painting was the sign I'd been looking for. The woman was thinking about something, her chin resting on her hand . . . just as I was thinking about this movie . . . and the fact that the light was shining on her . . .

I thought, *That's it! Light up your art!*

Go to work . . . direct this movie. And when the light went on a second time . . . as if to say, "Girl, are you getting this message?" . . . it was reminding me to light up the *woman* in me . . . to be all the things a woman could be . . . gentle, strong, nurturing.

And in a few hours, I got a call that the studio had agreed to my terms (we compromised on the salary cut) and was ready to make the deal. By the way, the cochairman of Columbia Pictures happened to be Jon Peters. (Sometimes old boyfriends come in handy.)

So the picture was now a go, which just confirmed what I was already thinking. I've always been interested in how the mind works. And this is why I find dreams so fascinating, because they can reveal what's going on in your subconscious. And sometimes the meaning of a dream only becomes clear when you're ready to act on it. I had recently attended one of Brugh's conferences about dream interpretation with my dear friend Joanne Segel . . . my companion on so many spiritual odysseys . . . and her husband, Gil, where I dreamed that I was in the ocean, being tossed around by huge waves, while two male directors, Orson Welles and Warren Beatty, were swimming beside me.

It brought back all the angst I felt after *Yentl*, and Brugh and I talked about the dream's meaning. For me, it seemed to express my doubts. Would I get attacked again? Would these waves overwhelm me? Could I ever be as good as these guys?

Orson was a genius but he wasn't allowed to finish his last pictures and became an object of scorn in the press. Warren, on the other hand, was relatively unscathed. He had done a brilliant job on *Reds* . . . directing, acting, writing, producing . . . and nobody accused him of stepping outside his place or getting help from his friends when he showed them the movie.

When that happened to me, I got sick of the innuendo from the press. And I guess I retreated. Then Brugh asked me a simple question: "What is it in *you* that diminishes the woman in you?"

I thought, *Holy moly, he's right!* Of course . . . if I let myself feel diminished, then they will have won. I wouldn't have the courage to make another movie. Of course the waves *are* scary. "You might die in the water," as my mother used to say.

But I had to stop being afraid of going back in.

I first heard about *The Prince of Tides* from a music editor on *Nuts*. She had read the book and thought it was something I might be interested in directing. Don Johnson happened to be reading it as well. There were moments in the novel that reminded him of his own childhood, and he would stop to read those passages out loud to me. I was entranced with the lyrical quality of the prose and the depth of the insights.

So I had to read it myself, and I fell in love with it. I don't fall in love with that many books . . . the last one had been *Love in the Time of Cholera*, by Gabriel García Márquez . . . but I couldn't put *The Prince of Tides* down. And as soon as I finished all 567 pages, I was so excited that I went back to the beginning and started all over again. It was a sprawling story, with enough material for a thirteen-hour miniseries. How could I contain it within a two-hour movie? I didn't have a clue, but I wanted to try.

When I called my agent, Mike Ovitz, I found out that Robert Redford already had the rights and had commissioned several scripts. I didn't think any of them worked, but I knew there was a wonderful movie in there. They just hadn't found it yet.

Since I adored working with Bob on *The Way We Were*, I thought, *Why don't we do this together?* And we talked about costarring, but Bob wasn't sure if he wanted to make this movie. When it comes to saying yes or no, he's one of those guys who find it hard to commit.

Me too.

In other words, I understood his indecision. At this point I was still hoping to direct and star in *Skinny and Cat*, a movie about the photographer Margaret Bourke-White that I had been working on since 1984 . . . actually, Bob would have been great as her husband, Erskine Caldwell . . .

So I tend to go back and forth, because committing to one thing inevitably means closing off other options. But once I decide to do something, I want to get started immediately. I am congenitally incapable of waiting around for anybody. I think Bob graciously bowed to my enthusiasm and basically said, "Go ahead. It's all yours."

Then my great friend Steve Ross and his wife, Courtney, invited me to join them on a cruise through the Greek islands. It was the perfect opportunity to get away from my house and my office and the constantly ringing telephones. I wanted to clear my mind and, like a sculptor facing a block of marble, see if I could find the shape and contours of the movie in this huge, rich, beautiful, heartbreaking book.

On the boat I read it again and again . . . trying to absorb every detail, so the characters' memories almost became my own. I carried that book with me everywhere we went.

When you travel with Steve, everything is impeccably arranged. You don't have to worry about luggage or transportation or figure out an itinerary. In fact, you never even have to lift a finger because you are magically transported to the most interesting places. You eat at the most delicious restaurants, and the meals on board the boat are even more sublime (and quieter, which I prefer). Normally I'm the last one to leave the table because I'm tasting everyone's dessert and lingering over the conversation, but on this trip I couldn't wait to get back to my room and make notes on another chapter.

Steve had given me a beautiful room, bigger than my old apartment over Oscar's. It even had a desk on a platform looking out at the sea . . . as if it were saying, Come use me. Sit here and write.

I marked the moments in the story that stood out for me and underlined the images I liked . . . and jotted down other images that floated into my head. I was already visualizing certain scenes.

I've always been drawn to stories about transformation . . . about love and loss . . . and the hidden secrets that can destroy your life. I personally believe in the power of therapy to help bring those secrets into the light and open the door to healing. And that leads to the ultimate theme of forgiveness, of being able to accept and understand and finally embrace people with all their flaws . . . including yourself, with all your own.

In the first chapter of *The Prince of Tides*, the main character, Tom Wingo, finds out that his twin sister, Savannah, has tried to commit suicide for the third time. Savannah's psychiatrist, Dr. Susan Lowenstein, would like to talk to her family in order to learn more about her past, and their mother, Lila, is too busy to go . . . "We're giving a dinner party Saturday night and it's been planned for months" . . . so Tom flies to New York to try to help.

I had just gone to another one of Brugh's conferences, with many therapists and psychiatrists, about Jungian archetypes, art, and creativity, and all these ideas were tumbling together in my head. And suddenly everything seemed to relate to the book. Tom's quest is like the journey of the hero. He's the child of an abusive father and a loving but very complicated and somewhat manipulative mother. He's a man who has to stop denying the trauma of his past and finally confront the truth and let himself grieve. And then Savannah, who's also the victim of trauma . . . is her creativity a sort of madness, as Plato and Socrates used to debate? And what about the notion of twins . . . are Tom and Savannah some sort of variation on Apollo and Artemis from Greek mythology? They certainly were faced with more than their share of fates and furies.

I think all great stories contain elements of myth. And here I was, actually visiting the sites where so many of these myths took place. I would sit there on the sun-warmed stones and gaze at the ancient ruins. I was in that state where I just wanted to let everything seep into my pores . . . and see what thoughts came into my head.

On the island of Santorini we rode donkeys up to the top of one village, where there's typically a simple, domed church. I like going exploring, but this was scary. The path was right on the edge of a sheer cliff, with only a short wall between you and the sea hundreds of feet below. I felt sorry for the poor animals, trudging along in the blazing heat. And what if mine lurched all of a sudden? I'd be tossed over the cliff. (I walked down.)

Back on the boat, I could relax. Usually the bathroom just has a shower. But mine had a huge tub with another unexpected feature . . . a stereo system with speakers. I spent a lot of time lying back against the cool porcelain and listening to tapes from the conference.

The tapes, the dream analysis, the Jungian symbolism, the Greek myths . . . all of this falls into the category of research, even though most of it never winds up on-screen. But that research informed me, and therefore informed the film.

I wanted to explore everything. Why does Tom always make jokes when he's asked a serious question? Why was he unhappy in his marriage? What's his relationship with his sister? His father? And why is he so antagonistic toward his mother?

I'm fascinated by dysfunctional families. After all, I come from one.

By the end of the ten-day trip, having read the book four times, I knew the story I wanted to tell. I had the whole movie in my head.

I was never that interested in the subplot about the tiger, bought by the father and kept in a cage at his failing gas station in a misguided attempt to attract customers. I couldn't possibly cover all the twists and turns in all three siblings' lives over the course of thirty years. Instead I tried to go straight to the emotional heart of the novel . . . Tom's journey back into his past to help save his sister. In the course of that process a deep connection develops between Tom and Lowenstein, which changes everything for him. It acts as a catalyst that sets off a chain reaction that changes other relationships too. Once I had my through line, large chunks of the novel just fell by the wayside, and it became easier to see what belonged in the movie, and what did not.

I wanted to get the film I saw in my head down on paper, and after that trip I spent more than a year reworking the latest script I had inherited. It was by a writer named Becky Johnston, who based it on a screenplay that Pat Conroy had written before the book came out. I thought it made sense to work with her because she knew the material. At one point I even moved her into my Art Deco house for three weeks so we could continue day and night, writing new scenes and pulling the best lines of dialogue from the book. I was always pushing her to go back to Pat's words.

It reminded me of how I had to keep pushing Sydney Pollack to go back to Arthur Laurents's first script for *The Way We Were*. There's usually something valuable in the original material. Whenever a script is sent to me and it's labeled the second or third draft, I'll ask to see the first draft if I have any interest in it whatsoever. I want to see the writer's initial intention . . . before other people started commenting on it and asking for changes. Often the most interesting ideas get thrown out.

I had several problems with Becky's version of Pat's novel. I felt the focus was off, because she went into way too much detail about Savannah and her psychological struggles, when the true hero of the novel is Tom. We see events through his eyes, so he's the one we really care about. And just as I did with the original script of *A Star Is Born*, I wanted to bring out the love story, because it's his romance with Lowenstein that adds tension and drama . . . and leads to the final resolution.

But what I really couldn't comprehend is how Becky could ignore the crux of the story . . . a traumatic event in the past that profoundly affected all three children and their mother. The explosion of violence is shocking and terrible, but that scene and its aftermath is crucial to understanding these characters, because it's at the root of the family's emotional troubles.

And yet none of the previous scripts even mentioned it. Why not? Were the writers or the studio afraid of it? All I know is I couldn't conceive of making the movie without it.

Still, Becky was stubborn and didn't want to do it my way. She even threatened to take her name off the script. I said, "Fine." (She never did.) I finally had to tell her that this script was going to include a flashback to this terrible event that changed all their lives, and if she didn't want to type it for me, she could leave.

After that, we reached a détente. I would talk . . . I had to make every line real for the characters . . . she would type, and we argued constantly. Then she would hand me the revised scenes the next morning.

And then I began to doubt myself. In my journal, I wrote: "Feeling anxious . . . don't know quite why . . . How to get joy from the process? How not to be scared of disappointing myself."

Or disappointing Pat . . . or the public . . .

Sometimes I think half the obstacles in my path are of my own making.

In the middle of all this, Richard Baskin asked me to perform on a television special for Earth Day that he was producing. (As I said, we remained good friends.) I sang "One Day," which began as a melody written by Michel Legrand back in the late 1960s. As soon as I heard it, I asked the Bergmans if they could write a lyric . . . "but not another love song. Write something about the world." And they did. The song is a gentle plea for peace, and a vision of a greener planet. It was perfect for this show, which was directed by my old friend Dwight Hemion. And it gave me a break from the script. I realized that I didn't have to know all the answers at this point. I just had to trust that I would find them in the process.

I had already taken several trips to North and South Carolina to scout locations. And since I always have to be doing more than one thing at a time, I was also photographing various architectural details that I liked, in case I wanted to incorporate them into the house I was still thinking of building.

Now I went back to South Carolina, this time in a more optimistic frame of mind, and I found exactly what I wanted in the town where Pat Conroy grew up . . . Beaufort (called Colleton in the novel) . . . situated in the Lowcountry along the coast, between Savannah and Charleston. It was the second-oldest city in the state, founded in 1711, and it hadn't lost its antebellum charm. Shrimp boats, like the one Tom's father piloted, still cruised the waterways. It seemed so obvious that I wondered why we had ever looked anywhere else.

But one last piece of the puzzle was missing.

When I direct, I want to know everything about the characters. I wanted to know Tom. And how could I know Tom? By getting to know the man who created him. After all, this character came out of Pat Conroy's own experience, his life, his imagination.

I had been trying to get in touch with Pat for months to arrange a meeting, but he never responded. At first I was surprised. Then I just assumed he didn't want to be involved in the movie. And finally I got hurt.

But then fate, destiny, and my own intuition made me push even harder. I made one last attempt to track him down and found him at a hotel in Los Angeles. When I called his room and he picked up the phone, I was blunt, "This is Barbra Streisand. Why won't you return my phone calls?"

Pat was mortified. He explained that he thought the messages from me were a joke, left by a friend putting him on. He apologized profusely. And I invited him to meet me in New York and work with me on the script.

We spent two wonderful weeks together, totally immersed in the characters he had created.

Do you know how you just feel comfortable with some people immediately? That's how I felt with Pat. From the first moment we met, we started talking about the psyche . . . the importance of dreams . . . and the search for meaning. And he told me the most remarkable thing: "You know, I listen to music when I write. And I was playing your album *Songbird* while I was writing this book. So it feels very right to me that you should be directing this movie and playing Lowenstein."

That made me very happy.

I was intrigued by the idea of playing a psychiatrist because I have great respect for them and have learned a lot about myself through therapy. (Until I got bored with talking about myself and thought, *That's it. I've learned enough.*)

Who was it that said "The unexamined life is not worth living." (I just looked it up. It was Socrates.) But therapists are only human, and some whom I've met seem pretty confused.

I noticed that when I was interviewing therapists, trying to find someone I could relate to. One doctor I was thinking of going to actually sent me an angry letter when I didn't choose him, and said that I was making a big mistake. He sounded like a jilted lover. It was ridiculous. I thought *he* needed therapy. I certainly didn't need him to make me feel guilty . . . I can do that very well on my own.

I think some people become therapists because they have problems themselves and they're trying to find the answers . . . but it's often easier to solve other people's problems than your own. And that concept of the wounded healer really resonated with me.

I'm always looking for the truth . . . "the truth will set you free," as Jesus said in the Bible. (And that inspired the line I eventually used on the movie's poster: "A story about the memories that haunt us, and the truth that sets us free.")

What I love about Pat's writing is that he isn't afraid to expose himself in his work, and that makes him vulnerable. And I recognized that vulnerability. It's very familiar to me. In order to do my work as an actress and a singer, I have to expose myself emotionally.

Of course, Pat understood that. Years later, in an exquisite letter to me, he wrote:

> *When I tell people about you being the hardest working person I've ever encountered, I'm brought back to those magical days of the most glorious labor as I watched you struggle over putting that screenplay together with all the firestorms of creations burning in a fine light all around you. You put that same holy attention to choosing a song or buying the fringes for a lamp. It is that unquenchable passion which is the mark of your genius that sometimes exhausts you and leads you toward the margins of despair. The only bad thing I could find about you is that you reminded me so much of myself. By that, I mean my melancholy and deep insecurities and the wounds I carry into each day of my life as an artist.*
>
> *. . . I also witnessed how being the best offered so little comfort to you and how you (like me) shaped our ideas about ourselves with the hurtful materials of those who hated our work and refused to listen to those voices that loved us. Though I don't know what it means yet, the secret of art itself is contained somewhere in this illusion—but your genius could not be what it is without the suffering and the hateful put-downs and your overwhelming and successful desire to turn it into something colossal and long-lasting and surpassingly fine.*

His words took my breath away. God, he was perceptive. How extraordinary it is to be really *seen.* And I learned something by seeing myself through his eyes. Instead of dismissing my insecurities as a problem . . . something that I had to change . . . he showed me how to regard them as assets. He made me appreciate my own melancholy, by explaining how it could be transformed through art into something positive. I feel so humbled that a man of great talent . . . this genius . . . would take the time to analyze me so poetically.

When he came to New York, we started by reading the script out loud, Pat playing Tom and me playing Lowenstein. I wanted to hear how the words sounded in his voice to make sure Tom's lines had the right cadence and captured his lovely Southern lilt. Pat has described what that was like: "I was her costar for a couple of weeks. How many writers get to live a fantasy life like this? After we would read a scene, she'd say, 'You know, my lines sounded better to me.' I said, 'Well, here's the reason: You won an Academy Award and I'm just a guy. You're always going to sound better.'"

And I'm thinking, *Just a guy?* No, you're a brilliant novelist, a poet, and an incredible human being.

I had studied the version of the script that Pat had written years earlier and incorporated some of it into this latest draft. And now, reviewing the new script with him, I'd see places where I thought the dialogue I had could be better and asked if he could improve on it.

Pat would work on it overnight and hand me the new version in the morning. And sometimes I'd have to say, very gingerly, "Pat, this is beautiful. But nobody talks this way."

The kind of language that works on the page of a novel can sound way too flowery on-screen. The fact is, most people don't speak in poetry, and one of my jobs was to make the dialogue colloquial and relatable.

I was so concerned that I would offend him. After all, he was the bestselling author, not me. But Pat was very humble. There was never any resistance. He understood right away.

He was shocked that I knew the book so well. Even without it in front of me, I could say, "There's a fantastic description of Savannah's poetry on page five hundred and forty. Should we use any of it?" Or, "That passage about trying to save the whales that were stranded on the beach, did that really happen to you?" I had to understand every reference in the book, even if it wasn't in the screenplay.

I wanted to hear his stories . . . about his father, his mother, his family, his whole life. I was greedy for any detail that would help me flesh out the characters and understand the world of the movie. Obviously I'm not from the South, but Pat's wife at the time was Jewish and from Brooklyn, so I took that as a good omen. This collaboration was meant to be! I felt like Lowenstein to his Tom, trying to get to the essence of this man.

There was a dance called the shag that was mentioned in the book, and I had never heard of it.

He explained, "Well, that's how we used to dance in South Carolina when I was a kid."

I said, "Could you show me how to do it?"

Suddenly this rather shy, courtly Southern gentleman turned into this hip-shaking hoofer. Loose as a goose. Boy, he could really fling that tush around! We had such fun, dancing the shag right in the middle of my office. I don't think I was even doing the right steps, but it didn't matter, because Pat was *so* good. He took my hand and swung me in and out, and I just followed him. I was so impressed with his footwork!

When we sat back down, laughing, he pulled out a handkerchief, wiped his brow, and announced, "I have taught Barbra Streisand to shag. I can now die a happy man."

He was humble and generous and kind and warm and loving . . . a great hugger and a big man, so when he hugged you, it was a *big* hug. You felt totally enveloped.

He was a joy to work with. I was so honored that he entrusted his book to me. And he gave me a great gift . . . the opportunity to work with my son.

In the movie, Lowenstein has a son, Bernard, who's a brilliant violinist like his father. But he's been shut out of the football team at his prep school and would rather play football than the violin. Tom used to be a high school teacher and football coach before he lost his job, so Lowenstein enlists him to coach her son.

I had already hired a young man named Chris O'Donnell to play Bernard. He was nineteen years old, a good actor, and a good athlete.

I showed Pat his picture, and he said, "Barbra, that ain't the kid. He looks like a jock, and the whole point is that Bernard is not a natural athlete."

And then he noticed a photograph of my son, Jason, in a crystal frame on the piano and said, "*That's* Bernard."

In the book, Bernard is described this way: "He's an attractive boy who thinks he's ugly. He's very tall . . . he has enormous feet and black curly hair . . .

He had inherited his mother's long legs, her full lips, those dark expressive eyes, and a complexion as smooth as new fruit. Except for a constant scowl, he was an exceptionally handsome boy." I remembered the description, and I also remembered how much Bernard weighed: 140 pounds.

I called Jason up and asked, "How much do you weigh?"

"A hundred and forty pounds. Why?"

"You're hired," I said, and thought, *Oh my God. It was meant to be.*

Jason had read the part for me when I got some actors together so I could hear what the script sounded like, and he was wonderful. But I thought he might be too old, at twenty-three, to play a seventeen-year-old. And I was wary. Could he take direction from me? Could he separate the director from his mother? Should I risk hiring my kid? I knew we'd be setting ourselves up for a lot of criticism. Cis kept warning me, "You can't do this. You'll get bad-mouthed."

I said, "Well, I'll get bad-mouthed anyway, no matter what I do . . . so I might as well do what I believe in."

And Jason, who never asks me for anything, really wanted the role.

We paid Chris O'Donnell his fee and apologized, explaining that he wasn't quite what the author imagined.

Pat was right. Jason was Bernard, in so many ways. He understood Bernard's anger, his hurt, and his insecurity. And it was Pat's encouragement that led me to the right decision.

Pat was in New York with me on April 24, when I turned forty-eight. The doorbell kept ringing, and my assistant would open it and bring in yet another beautiful bouquet . . . from Jason and other dear friends . . . Richard Baskin . . . Don Johnson . . . Jon Peters. Pat was amazed. As he said, "I have many ex-girlfriends, and believe me, I do not get flowers from any of them on my birthday, or notes as lovely as these." He watched me lean over to inhale the scent of the latest arrival and said, "Frankly, I didn't think there were this many roses alive in New York City."

Pat gave me several books as a gift, including a copy of *The Prince of Tides*, inscribed on the title page to "Barbra Streisand, the Queen of Tides." And then a few days later, before he left to go home, he gave me a volume of poetry by James Dickey, one of his first writing teachers, and wrote this inside:

To Barbra Streisand,

I'd like to thank you for this extraordinary two weeks. You are many things, Barbra, but you're also a great teacher . . . one of the greatest to come into my life. I honor the great teachers and they live in my work and they dance invisibly in the margins of my prose. You've made me a better writer, you rescued my sweet book, and you've honored me by taking it with such great seriousness and love . . .

All praise and thanks and love,

Pat Conroy

April 30, 1990

When I read a letter like this, it reminds me how inadequate I feel as a writer. Look at that image: "they dance invisibly in the margins of my prose." You can see and feel what he's saying, not just read it. That is so brilliant. I could never come up with a sentence like that.

I can write scripts, and political articles, but to write a novel? With gorgeous language?

Forget about it.

I fell in love with his novel, and then I fell in love with the man. I will treasure these books, from my dear Pat, always.

So at long last, I had the script. But now I had to shoot it.

FORTY-FOUR

Directing The Prince of Tides

When I look back on the experience of making *The Prince of Tides*, I remember the heat and the humidity, which were relentless from the first day I arrived in Beaufort with the crew. For some unfathomable reason we were shooting during the hottest time of the year . . . June, July, and August . . . when it was 103 degrees outside and the humidity was 100 percent. My hair went limp. I brought all the wrong clothes. And the house I was renting was two hundred years old . . . beautiful architecture, with a porch, but what I didn't realize was how dark the rooms on the first floor would be because of the overhang.

And I'll never forget the moment when I was stepping into the bath and suddenly saw a huge water bug crawling out of the faucet.

I shrieked and ran out of the room, calling for Renata.

I hate bugs, but I was ready to endure the heat and everything else, because the landscape here was part of the story. The opening line of the book is "My wound is geography. It is also my anchorage, my port of call."

God, what an image. The word "wound" is so powerful, and Pat uses it over and over again in the book. For me, it was an echo of those lines I spoke as a fifteen-year-old Medea . . . "Why have you made me a girl? Why these breasts, this weakness, this open wound in the middle of myself?"

Tom, like Pat, grew up beside the salt marshes, where the Beaufort River meanders through tidal flats on its way to the sea, and he is indelibly connected to this place. Here, boundaries blur . . . land and water exchange places with each tide. Oyster shells are strewn along the mud, and heron, osprey, and egrets soar over the hip-high grasses.

I first saw the salt marshes when I flew over them in a plane and thought, *This is so beautiful.* It was late afternoon, and the golden light turned the water a gorgeous peach color. The contrast between the darker land and lighter water made strange shapes and shifting patterns as the sky was reflected in the water. The image was almost visceral. It reminded me of a map of the arteries and the energy coursing through a person's veins. I could already see the shots I would eventually use to open the film.

The camera glides over the salt marshes and then moves up a riverbank to a small white house, where you see Tom, Savannah, and Luke as children. Their childhood looks idyllic . . . racing after one another through the trees, playing with a puppy, following their mother to sit at the end of the dock and watch the sun set. To me they were like a flock of ducklings, and I gave the little girl a blanket to drag along behind her. It reminded me of my own baby blanket, made out of a dusty pink bouclé fabric that I would rub while I sucked my thumb to put myself to sleep.

Lila has pulled her children out of bed on a hot summer evening to show them one of the marvels of nature. As she points to the east and tells them to watch, the moon rises at exactly the same moment that the sun is setting in the west. Both sun and moon are visible at the same time, as day turns to night.

We had consulted the almanac to see when the moon would be full, compared times for moonrise and sunset, and figured out which date would give us our best chance to capture this phenomenon. Stephen Goldblatt, our cinematographer, had a special camera locked off, ready to swing from one to the other. And then when we were all set to shoot, the weather didn't cooperate. The sky was a mass of clouds. Neither sun nor moon was anywhere in sight.

I was in despair. Reality did not coincide with my vision.

But you can't fight the facts . . . and here, once again, I want to dispel the myth of the uncompromising artist. Life and art are often a series of compromises. When I'm directing and producing, I'm constantly weighing the financial against the artistic. Sure, the director in me might want to wait till the sun comes out, but the producer in me is warning that it will cost $100,000 to $150,000 a day.

I needed to find another way to convey what I was after. I had to accept what the universe was presenting and make it work. And in some cases, what appears to be a compromise might turn out to be even better.

I put the mother, with her arms wrapped around her children, on the dock, deciding to go with the emotion even if I didn't have my shot. And then I prayed, just as I had done eight years earlier on *Yentl* when we were shooting the wagon going across the Charles Bridge. (It seems as if I do a lot of praying on movie sets.)

And once again my prayers were answered. At the last minute, the setting sun broke through the clouds and bathed the family in a warm pink light. And that was all I needed. The moon never emerged, but I no longer needed it. I couldn't capture exactly what was in the book, but my prayers must have helped evoke something else that turned out to be just as beautiful.

And then, in the next scene, the idyllic image shatters. As their parents shout at each other, the children run out of the house to escape the fight and head for the dock and jump into the water with all their clothes on.

There's something so free and unconstrained about that. It reminded me of a moment when Jason was a child. He was playing in the pool at Carolwood, and when I walked over to see him, he said, "Mommy, come in the pool." And in a flash of utter abandon, I jumped in just as I was, wearing a skirt, a top, and shoes. I'll never forget the look on his face.

Then he giggled, and so did I.

In the novel, the children form a circle by clasping hands in the silent underwater world and only burst to the surface when they can no longer hold their breath.

I loved that image.

We shot the underwater sequence in a tank, because the real river would have been too dark and murky to see anything. And it took two weeks to get the color of the water right . . . sometimes it was too blue, too green, too light, too dark. And then I looked through the camera and said, "Wait! There's no plant life. It doesn't look natural." I had a picture in my head of long, thin grasses undulating in the water, but the prop people could only get fat ones. So we split each stalk up the middle.

I know. We were literally splitting hairs. But that's my attention to detail, which is either a blessing or a curse (probably both).

I had to hire children who were good swimmers, as well as being able to act. As they pop up to the surface, I wanted bright morning light, so we needed an arc light on the tank. And the camera was there to catch the ripples on the water . . . which dissolve into waves that roll onto another shore and reveal the grown-up Tom, playing with his own children in the late afternoon light of the present day. The camera moves fluidly along with the waves, as they carry the story into the next scene, without a cut. It's more organic that way.

I did a lot of thinking about the visuals in each scene, working out the most natural transition from one place to another.

The children were an integral part of the story . . . and I had to cast three sets of young Wingos, at different ages, and Tom's own kids. I love working with children, because they can be so free. They're not censoring themselves with any preconceived notions. And I spent a lot of time talking to them and doing a lot of improvisation, which we videotaped so I could make sure they didn't freeze in front of the camera. The girls who played Tom's daughters had to be very comfortable with Nick Nolte, who was playing Tom. I wanted them to crawl all over their daddy, like puppies.

Pat described Lila, Tom's mother, as very beautiful, and that was certainly true of Kate Nelligan, who originally came in to read for the part of Sallie, Tom's wife. I had seen her in Michael Weller's play *The Spoils of War*, and thought she was terrific, playing a seductive, ambitious woman who has a difficult relationship with her son. The similarities between that character and Lila made me quickly switch gears, and I had her read Lila's lines. Kate has an innate tension and force that worked brilliantly for this role. She's such a good actress that she didn't need much direction. I could say just a word or two to her, and she'd give me exactly what I wanted. Her instincts were wonderful. And she got the

Southern accent perfectly. When an actor doesn't have a good ear, you can hear the mistakes in tone, just as you can hear a wrong note in music.

Initially the casting agent suggested I hire two actresses . . . one for the young Lila and one to play her thirty years on. But that's never ideal. It's usually pretty clear that it's not the same woman. Luckily Kate was so gifted that she could play both ages, conveying a sense of maturity with her body movements and the help of some old-age makeup . . . which used to crumble when she ate lunch, so they'd have to redo it before we could shoot again (which took a couple of hours).

To play Sallie I was privileged to have Blythe Danner, who is so warm and lovely in real life that she just seemed to inhabit the role. Tom explains at one point that he fell in love with Sallie because she was so wonderfully normal . . . as opposed to his own complicated family. Coincidentally Blythe had also played the wife in *The Great Santini*, an earlier movie based on another Pat Conroy book, and she obviously had an affinity with Pat's heroines. I thought that gave her another level of experience and depth.

Melinda Dillon is an actress who's always interesting to watch. Her face is so open . . . she has a kind of delicate fragility that made her my first and only choice for the role of Savannah. I had followed her career, and told her, "You know who this character is. You don't have to act. Just be you."

Casting Tom Wingo was a challenge. I needed someone who would be believable as both a football coach and an English teacher . . . so he had to have a certain physicality as well as a literary sensibility. Toss in a kind of wounded quality and, absolutely crucial, he had to have sex appeal. I wanted women to swoon over him. It always seems to work for my films when I have a very strong, attractive male opposite me, and besides, it's more fun!

After Bob Redford passed, I approached Warren Beatty. He, too, turned it down. Early on, I met with Kevin Costner, who came to my house, took my hand, and talked to me about a western he was planning to do, which turned out to be *Dances with Wolves*. (I ended up presenting him with the Oscar for it, as Best Picture.) Richard Gere called and said he wanted to play Tom. Remember how he had told me he wouldn't be in *Yentl* because he didn't think it was possible for me to both act and direct successfully? Clearly, he had changed his mind. I would have loved to work with him, but I just didn't see him as Tom. I said, "Richard, you're not a guy from the South."

Nick Nolte, on the other hand, could pass more easily for a traditional Southerner. He had this cocky exterior, but I could still see a lot of pain in his eyes. And as we talked, I could sense he was at an interesting place in his life, where he was willing to explore deep feelings and allow himself to be vulnerable.

And he said he was eager to work with a woman director . . . that was refreshing.

Nick had gained forty pounds for his previous role and dyed his hair brown. I asked him to lose the weight, and we restyled his hair and took it back to a more appealing blond. Nick was an odd one. He would come to work wearing loose scrub pants, like a doctor, and carrying a plastic bag of his diet food . . . raw eggs and chicken.

I like to make use of the real-life idiosyncrasies of an actor, when I can. Nick was a chain-smoker. As soon as I said "Action," he'd light up a cigarette for one quick puff. So I thought, let me write this into the script . . . make him a guy who can't stop smoking. Then, when he's coaching Lowenstein's son, Bernard makes him throw away his cigarettes. But at the end of the movie, when Tom has a difficult decision to make, we see him smoking again.

At one point I noticed that Nick's face was looking a little red in the dailies. I heard he was going to tanning beds, thinking a tan would make him look more Southern. I pulled him aside and said, "You can't do that." His face couldn't be a different shade from one scene to the next. I wanted the hospital walls to be a warm gray for his monologue, when he's in the room with his comatose sister. And now I was going to have to make the walls more blue in post-production, just to take out some of the red in his face.

I needed to get to know Nick, to try to get into his psyche. I asked him to talk to me about his life. I asked about his relationship with his mother, his sister, his wives . . . so I could tap into those feelings to get something on-screen that felt real.

I wanted to be able to play Nick like an instrument . . . to hear the high and the low notes of human emotion. The voice can touch the heart, but only if it comes from the truth.

And in order to make that happen, I had to gain his trust, just like Lowenstein has to gain the trust of her patient's brother in order to help Savannah. Isn't it fascinating, when life imitates art?

On the first day of shooting, we did the flashback to the dinner scene, where

Henry Wingo spits out his food and shoves the plate across the table toward his wife, and then turns his anger on the ten-year-old Tom.

I love flashbacks. They show you exactly what happened, succinctly, rather than hearing about it secondhand. And to go from the present to the past and back to the present just seemed like the most natural way to tell the story cinematically. After all, it's the way we think . . . so you get a kind of stream of consciousness on-screen.

Since the flashbacks were some of the most difficult scenes emotionally, I wanted to do them first. And then the actors playing the characters in the present day could see the footage so they would have it in their heads, and be able to draw on the memories we had created.

What triggers this flashback for Tom is the simple act of making a meal. He's washing the shrimp he bought, and that brings back an altercation with his father. We cut from Tom and his shrimp to his father spitting out his Shrimp Newburg in disgust . . . "For Chrissakes, Lila, it's got wine in it!" He puts it on the floor for the dog . . . the puppy in the prologue is now full-grown . . . and announces, "Even the dog won't eat it!"

Tom comes to his mother's defense, saying, "I think it's good."

"Who asked you?" says his father, slapping him. And then he mocks him for being a sissy when Tom's eyes fill with tears. Lila says she'll warm up some hash for Henry and gets Tom and Savannah out of the way of his anger by asking them to help her in the kitchen. We go from the young Tom chopping an onion to the adult Tom dropping the pieces into the pan . . . from the young Tom adding pepper to the adult Tom doing the same thing.

When Lila opens a can of dog food and throws it in the pan, the children watch, open-mouthed. It's more interesting to tell the story through the kids' eyes. Then she serves it to her husband, who takes a bite and says, "Now *this* is food, Lila." And the dog smells something familiar and puts his paws up on the table, hoping for a bite.

I envisioned the first shot at the dining table to be on the plate of food being shoved down the long table straight to the mother, and described it to Stephen. He stared at me and said, "No. I can't do it. It's impossible."

I was taken aback. I was used to a more helpful attitude from my crew. I would never have heard the word "no" from Peter MacDonald, the brilliant English camera operator who made my life such a dream on *Yentl*. Nothing was impossible to him. His response was always, "If that's the way you see it, we'll give it to you."

Stephen was not so accommodating. After more discussion that went nowhere, I gave up on that shot, and settled for something close to it.

In the kitchen I had another shot all planned out. Lila would open the refrigerator door, take out some butter and rice, open the can of dog food and add it to the pan . . . all in one take.

Stephen said no to that as well.

I was getting frustrated. It probably didn't help my mood that there was no air-conditioning. We had built the interior of the house in a college gymnasium, and I couldn't find the production designer, Paul Sylbert, to ask if he could produce a few fans.

It was sweltering. I didn't want to take up any more time trying to persuade Stephen to shoot it my way. I just wanted to keep things moving.

After the first day of filming, we were already a day behind. (Oh no, was this going to be like *A Star Is Born* all over again?)

I called Peter in London for a reality check, and said, "You would have given me that shot with the plate. How come he couldn't do it?"

"Well, you would probably have to move the wall."

Point is, so what? You move the wall . . . a set is constructed so that it comes apart easily and gives you those options.

I was at a loss. Stephen was like an immovable object. I couldn't figure out how to communicate with him. And he wouldn't communicate with me. His camera operator, Ray De La Motte, was just as opaque. Usually a director will look at the camera operator after a shot, and he'll indicate thumbs-up or thumbs-down, to let you know whether he got it. Peter and I did that automatically.

Not Ray. It was very disconcerting. Neither he nor Stephen seemed to have any reaction to what I was doing. And I did not want to spend the time it would take to replay each take on the monitor . . . plus I didn't want everyone gathering around that thing. It breaks the momentum.

I made various attempts to have a private conversation with Stephen, hoping to establish some rapport. One night after we finished shooting, we finally had a talk. I asked him about his mother, since everybody is shaped by their mother . . . especially boys, in my opinion. Pat has a great passage about that in the book: "When my mother was sad or heartsore I would blame myself or feel I had done something unforgivable. A portion of guilt is standard issue for southern boys; our whole lives are convoluted, egregious apologies to our mothers because our fathers have made such flawed husbands."

And here I thought it was only Jewish boys who were burdened by guilt!

I asked Stephen, "Is your mother alive?"

"Yes."

"Is she a strong woman?"

"Yes."

"Does she work?"

"Yes."

"What does she do?"

"She's a psychiatrist."

I thought, *Oh no.* She's a working woman, she's a psychiatrist, and she told him what to do as a child. He's probably transferring his feelings about her to me. And frankly, his "no" sounded just like that of an eight-year-old rebelling against his mother.

Oh boy, I said to myself. *I'm cooked.*

When you're a woman and you're the authority figure in charge of a group of men, there can be a reaction.

Nick wasn't quite sure how to relate to me. Sometimes he was like a little boy pulling the pigtails of a girl he was attracted to. He would tease me, tickle me, try to get me to laugh. I was his director, but I was also the actress playing his lover. And in those moments when I became Lowenstein, the dynamic between us shifted. I guess it would be slightly confusing for anyone, as I constantly switched back and forth.

At times, Nick, too, could be like two separate people, sweet and kind when we were just talking together, and then back to swaggering around like some of the macho guys on the set.

When we were shooting the first Lowenstein scene, where Tom arrives in New York and goes straight to her office, we weren't done at the end of the day. I wanted to stay a few minutes late to get that last shot . . . a close-up of Nick while I'm questioning him. Tom's tired after his trip and worried about his sister. The city is not exactly welcoming, he's got a headache, and he's even more uncomfortable in this psychiatrist's office because he's not allowed to smoke. I wanted his exhaustion to show on his face when he says, "What do you want from me?"

Lowenstein answers, "I need you to be her memory."

Remembering is painful for him, and he replies, "I've spent my life trying to forget those missing details."

And then Tom makes a joke, asking, "You wouldn't have any morphine handy, would you?"

It made sense to do this scene now, when Nick himself was tired, because it worked for the character. Otherwise we would have to finish it in the morning (when he would be rested) and then take more time to turn the set around, to shoot me. (Again, I always filmed the other actor first, because their performance was more important to me than mine.)

I asked Thomas Reilly, the assistant director, if we could stay a little late, and he said, "I think the morning would be better." (Another unsupportive male.)

Stephen said, "No. I don't want to stay late." And Ray also objected.

And then Nick sided with them.

I was furious and embarrassed.

All I was asking for was another ten to fifteen minutes. There was so little left to shoot, but they didn't let me finish the day. (I learned a lesson: Don't ask . . . Tell!)

That night my phone rang at 10:00 p.m. It was Nick, and he said, "I'm sorry."

Happy that he called, I said, "I hope you understand that I only wanted the best for your performance."

He was very contrite. He said, "I should have supported you, but I was too embarrassed to go against the guys! I feel like a heel."

I accepted his apology, but I was still mad at the other three.

The next morning Nick had so much energy (maybe he was trying to make it up to me) that it took seventeen takes to get his performance back to where I believed him, as I had the night before. And then Tommy Saccio, my wonderful prop man, told me that Stephen and Ray and Thomas were over in a corner, muttering that I had called for so many takes just to spite them.

That's ridiculous, because I was also the producer, and who wants to waste money? Trust me, I don't enjoy doing seventeen takes of anything. And spending so much time on Nick cut *my* day short. But I wasn't going to let it go until I was satisfied with his performance.

When those guys told me they wanted to leave, I should have said, "Wait a minute. Are you telling me . . . the director and the producer . . . when to stop filming an actor's performance? We're shooting this now. And if you don't stay, you're fired."

But I didn't have the chutzpah. I didn't want to be disliked. I don't find it easy to fire people, and I made the mistake of catering to those men instead of doing what was best for the film.

I remember reading that some director fired fifteen people the first week of shooting. I would never do that. I was afraid to fire even one, because of the negative feedback I'd get . . . "Boy, she must be a ball-breaker."

My crew on *Yentl* would never have complained about those extra fifteen minutes. They would never have humiliated me like that. They didn't consider everything I said a challenge to their own masculinity. We were colleagues, working together . . . but that was England.

On this movie, I felt very alone.

At least I had Cis, whom I had made my executive producer on this. She and I took Paul Sylbert to her husband's office in a beautiful Upper West Side brownstone . . . with oak paneling, glass-fronted bookcases, tall windows, and a chandelier . . . so he could recreate it for Lowenstein. It's a masculine room . . . tough, in a way . . . which is probably what she had to be in order to achieve the level of success she has. And yet it's also elegant and understated, just like she is. I think a set should tell you a lot about a character, instantly.

And the way Tom reacts to it, when he comes for another appointment at the end of her day, tells us more about him. He's curious . . . thumbing through a book . . . and restless. He can't sit still. He keeps moving, turning a knob in the wood paneling to reveal a hidden door to a bathroom. Paul gave me such an argument about that door. I guess it was hard to make it so seamless that it looked like part of the paneling. It's very clever . . . I should have had Nick pause longer in front of it so you could really appreciate it.

I was playing decorator again, and I had chosen little Greek and Roman statues for Lowenstein to display on the mantel. Even though the statues weren't important to the scene, they were important to me. I realize that most people watching the movie won't even notice what they are, but I still think a detail like this can add another layer. To me they suggest the idea of what psychiatry is all about . . . examining the past and learning from it to move forward in the present. I'm not even sure if I thought about it intellectually at the time . . . I just imagined her having ancient Greek statues, and only now, looking at the movie again, do I realize their significance. (All those Greek myths and archetypes I was thinking about!) And even if the audience doesn't grasp the connection, they still get the feeling that those figures belong in Lowenstein's office.

Clothes reveal so much about a character as well. We put Nick in plaid shirts, khaki pants, and even suspenders in one scene . . . an homage to Pat Conroy, who liked to wear them. And I wanted Lowenstein to start out in tailored suits . . . dark colors . . . black, brown, and gray. There's nothing light about her, which mirrors her personality . . . she seems completely humorless in the beginning. Then, as she starts to soften up and respond to Tom on a more personal level, she begins to wear lighter colors . . . camel, pink, light blue, white . . . and softer clothes. Almost unconsciously, she's becoming more feminine.

After Tom has been in New York for a few weeks, he's planning to come home for a weekend, until he gets a phone call from Sallie. This is a small moment, but it's exactly the kind of small moment I like. It's about the truth. It's about real feelings. This was an emotional scene for Blythe, and I wanted her to have all the support she needed. So I had Nick in another room, actually talking to her over the phone. And I had her talking to Nick when we switched sets and shot his side of the conversation.

There was a storm the night we shot Blythe's side, and the noise was so loud that I added a line about it, because the audience would notice. Sallie tells Tom that she's not sure she wants to see him. "I didn't want to tell you this on the telephone. I wanted to tell you before you left. But the way you left . . . there wasn't any time."

She's crying, and he guesses what she is about to say.

"What's his name?"

I remember sitting in the editing room, carefully placing a breath here, a pause there. I've said that filmmaking is like painting a picture, and as you edit, you get to put on the final touches of paint. Every moment has to be truthful . . . you have to believe that there is life on the other end of that phone. If you listen carefully, you can hear her sighs.

She tells him the man's name, and after Tom blows up, making fun of the guy, he suddenly gets serious. When he asks her, "Are you really in love?" he sounds very vulnerable, almost like a child, asking about something so intangible that he's not even sure it exists.

After his brother's death, Tom tried to shut off his feelings . . . and in that process he also shut off his love for his wife . . . simply because he couldn't bear to feel anymore. He couldn't deal with the pain those emotions brought.

In a novel, you can get all that repressed emotion in the narration, but in a movie, if a character doesn't express it, you don't see it. So I decided to use voice-over again, like in *Yentl*. (And I used it throughout the movie whenever there was a passage of Pat's that didn't fit into the dialogue but that I couldn't bear to leave behind.)

Nick and Sallie hang up, and he goes to the desk and tries to put down on paper all the things he couldn't say out loud. We hear his voice reading the letter: "I wish the words 'I love you' weren't so difficult for me. I've missed you. I miss touching you. I don't know what keeps me at such a distance. I'm sorry I disappoint you, Sallie, but you're right to feel that way. How else could you react to half a man?"

And then we go back to the through line of the film . . . Tom's journey into his past. I wanted to flash back to one of the last times he was fully able to give and receive love . . . the moment when Lila cuddles the ten-year-old Tom, telling him, "I love you more than I love any of them" (meaning his siblings). Lila married an abusive man whom she doesn't love, and all that untapped passion has to find an outlet.

He says, "But, Mama!" He's confused, because he loves his siblings.

But she says, "I do. I can't help it. You're my favorite. That's gonna be our little secret."

Tom describes this moment to Lowenstein, and says, "It took me twenty years to tell Luke and Savannah about my secret. And when I did, they just fell on the floor, howling. You see, my mother took each of them into that room and told them exactly the same thing."

To Tom it's more evidence of Lila's duplicity . . . of how she cannot be trusted. And that attitude has affected all his relationships with women. Now he feels that his wife has betrayed him, and he lashes out at Lowenstein when she suggests that maybe he wasn't paying enough attention to Sallie . . . even though he has already admitted as much in the letter he wrote to her. Tom is still responding to things in the present as if they were the past, which is one definition of neurosis.

One's adult life is shaped by one's childhood. That's one of the themes of the book, and it explains why Savannah had suicidal tendencies, why Luke rebelled, and why Tom grew up to be cynical. The children were living out the roles that were assigned to them by their parents. Lila once called Savannah "the lunatic," Luke "the fanatic," and Tom "the failure." We may be programmed as children by our parents, but a therapist can help you realize that you don't have to stay in that role.

Some people have asked me why Lowenstein, the sensitive and dedicated therapist, seems so cold at the beginning of the film. Well, that's the way she was portrayed in the novel, and I wanted to be faithful to what Pat wrote. Besides, that gives me somewhere to go as an actress, so you can watch her gradually become warmer and more vulnerable.

The thaw begins when she and Tom meet unexpectedly at a party, and he apologizes for his outburst and asks her to dance. She reluctantly agrees, and then when she breaks away and says she has to leave, he insists on escorting her home.

I'm wearing my own white suit, long gold earrings, and a favorite gold necklace that I just happened to buy on my trip to Greece. It's by Lalaounis, a Greek jeweler who was inspired by ancient pieces. How appropriate for Lowenstein, although I wasn't thinking of her when I bought it. But when I reread that passage in the book, I thought it was kind of uncanny that I already owned just what Pat described her as wearing that night . . . a thick gold necklace, along with long gold earrings that dangled against her cheekbones.

Once again, the forces of truth and destiny . . .

Jason's first scene is after that party, when Lowenstein invites Tom into her apartment to meet Bernard. Bernard's behavior is so obnoxious toward both Tom and his mother that she has to apologize for him. (In just a few lines, Jason conveyed that whole character. I was staring at him, feeling so proud . . . then I remembered I was supposed to be embarrassed!)

Later I was criticized somewhere for portraying a psychiatrist whose own family relationships were dysfunctional . . . as if doctors weren't allowed to be human. But guess what? Sometimes therapists who are able to help other people may not always be able to help themselves. (They're trying to work it out too.)

And again, that's the character Pat wrote.

If she were perfect, she wouldn't be as interesting. It's the flaws that draw the audience . . . and Tom . . . to her. Lowenstein is someone who lives primarily in her mind, rather than her emotions. One of the reasons she fell in love with her husband initially is that he was a great violinist whose music moved her and took her to that other place . . . as she says, he has "that gift to make people feel." She admired him as an artist, although the man didn't turn out to be worthy of such admiration.

I thought Jeroen Krabbé, a Dutch actor, would be perfect as Herbert Woodruff, Lowenstein's husband. I had seen him in Dutch films by Paul Verhoeven, where he embodied both the arrogance and the charm of the character. Of course he couldn't play a note. All of the violin music was actually played by the world-renowned Pinchas Zukerman. I was lucky to get him to do the film, and so happy to be there in the studio when he recorded his pieces.

I love the way my fabulous editor, Don Zimmerman, juxtaposed classical music with the shots of Tom teaching Bernard how to play football. He timed the cuts to fit the music and it works brilliantly.

That whole montage is there to convey the passage of time . . . the football lessons are interspersed with a phone call to Tom's family and a session in Lowenstein's office . . . but it's also subtly hitting the theme of the film. Tom is an expert in this macho, masculine world, but at a loss in the world of feelings.

The session in Lowenstein's office opens with a shot of her legs, from Tom's point of view, as she paces back and forth. One woman writer criticized me for that, as if I had included it out of some sort of vanity.

Point is, Tom's attraction to Lowenstein is beginning to show. He's suddenly looking at her in a sexual way. How else could you telegraph that so quickly?

No matter what actress played Lowenstein, that's the way I would have told the story.

People tend to forget that Lowenstein and Tom were never doctor and patient. She's Savannah's doctor, not his. And by now they have become friends . . . equals. He's clearly comfortable with her, lying down on her leather couch very casually. As he gets up to leave, he mischievously tosses the football he's been fiddling around with to her. She catches it and throws it back . . . and the shot goes from the football moving through the air to Bernard catching it in the park . . . and we're back to a practice session.

I was definitely out of my league when it came to football. I don't know anything about the game (and neither did Jason). Thank God for Nick, who actually knew quite a lot about the sport and taught Jason some real moves. When

Tom and Bernard leave the park and walk to a bookstore, you can see the change in Bernard's body language . . . Jason learned to walk like a jock. As we were setting up that shot, I looked up, and there was Paul Newman, standing on the corner. He crossed Madison Avenue and came over to say hello. It was so great to see him. We had been partners in First Artists twenty years ago and now here we were, both directing . . . and acting. It felt as if that concept had nurtured us in many ways. Then we had to say goodbye so I could go back to work.

In the store Tom comes across a book that could only have been written by his sister, and yet the author is Renata Halpern . . . the same name he's found on bills in Savannah's desk. He realizes that his sister has a whole other identity, and the mood changes abruptly when he confronts Lowenstein about his discovery. He's furious that she hasn't told him about it. He's yelling, she's trying to respond rationally, and they're talking over each other, as people usually do in real life.

Directors always used to leave a space between each person's lines, to make it easier to cut, but that interferes with the way people naturally speak. It's artificial. It can ruin a performance. And when I'm filming one actor's close-up, I'll always have the off-camera actor miked as well, so the sounds of both voices will be real.

Tom is shaking her up . . . pushing Lowenstein out of her calm, professorial mode . . . and he makes her so angry that she throws a book at him, bloodying his nose. She's shocked and embarrassed.

At the restaurant where she takes him for a conciliatory dinner, she says, "I still can't believe I did that to you."

"Face it, Lowenstein. I bring out the animal in you."

That's the most overt acknowledgment of their changing relationship . . . in the guise of a joke, which is typical for Tom. In the book, Lowenstein is more flirtatious. She's the one who has a dream about him and tells him about it, but I thought that was too provocative. So I turned it around into his having a dream about her. He's the one who's doing the flirting.

And she's responding. Here's where we begin to see it reflected in her clothes. In her next scene, when she brings Tom and Bernard sandwiches in the park, her hair is looser, more curly. And she's wearing a soft pink sweater . . . the kind of color we've never seen her in before.

Tom takes Lowenstein back to Savannah's apartment to show her some home movies of him and his brother and sister as kids. The movies are a directorial device, a way of compressing a lot of background information into a few minutes of screen time. When you're dealing with a huge novel, obviously some of the narrative has to go. I can't tell every person's story, and this was my way of taking that big section on Luke and condensing it into just what the audience needs to know. Tom explains how Luke was the only one who wasn't afraid of that tiger . . . "he had a lot of courage" . . . and he tells her the story of how Luke died. It's obvious that Tom has always had great admiration for his brother, and as he stands in front of the projector, the flickering images play across his face. Lowenstein is looking at Tom, and it's as if the past is written all over him . . . and then his eyes blink in the white light as the film runs out.

We shot Nick saying his lines first. Again, when I'm directing, the other actor . . . not me . . . always has priority.

I was always the cover set, meaning if it rained and we couldn't shoot what we had planned, we would come inside to do Lowenstein's scenes. I had to be ready to move into acting mode at a moment's notice. But sometimes there was a short wait if I had to change my hair . . . make it straight or curly . . . to match what had already been shot of a particular scene. Cis overheard a few of the men on Goldblatt's camera crew making some snide remark . . . although they never said a word when we had to wait for Nick to change.

On the day we shot the home-movie sequence, Nick did his speech, and I thought he delivered it brilliantly. Now it was time for the camera to shoot me. As I'm saying my lines, I realized that Nick was not saying the same words that he had already said, in his close-ups. I told him, "Nick, you have to say the same words. You're still in the shot, and I won't be able to cut back and forth between us, unless you do."

Nick turned to the camera operator. "Ray, you don't see my mouth move, do you?"

And Ray said, "No, I don't."

I looked at the playback on the monitor, which was down by my feet, and confirmed that of course you could see his mouth move.

I went over to Ray and said, "I just checked the monitor. You see his mouth move. Why are you lying to him?"

He shrugged his shoulders and said, "The boys' club."

I doubt that this kind of thing happens to Martin Scorsese.

People often think that in order to be a successful director, you need to be controlling and demanding. But you don't get good performances out of an actor that way. If you really want to get the best out of people, you have to be gentle, kind, and caring. Nick would often come in depressed. I'd give him a hug and ask him what was going on. Sometimes, during the course of a day, he'd say, "Come here. Sit on my lap." I didn't always feel comfortable sitting on his lap, but if that was what *he* needed in order to feel safe and comfortable . . . then fine. I could do it. I was drawing on the most feminine aspects of myself.

As a director I want to nurture everyone and be open to any idea. At the first rehearsal, I'll always tell the actors to move wherever they like. I want to see their first instinct. I want to know what feels natural to them, even though I already know in my mind how I'd like the scene to play. They may have a better idea! The last thing you want to do is discourage an actor. You want people to feel free to explore.

The most difficult scene for Nick . . . his most emotional moment . . . is when Tom finally breaks down and tells Lowenstein the secret he's been hiding for so many years . . . the story of that traumatic event. I told Nick that he could choose the moment to do it . . . that we would wait until he felt ready.

It was getting toward the end of filming, and Nick still hadn't given the go-ahead. Ray was scheduled to leave before the shoot officially ended, and Stephen came up to me and said, "I want my camera operator for this scene."

"I'm sorry," I told him, "but I can't do this scene according to Ray's schedule. I told Nick that he could pick the day, and it's up to him."

So Ray left, and we brought in a wonderful camera operator, Dick Mingalone, who worked with Woody Allen. Dick was a gem . . . supportive, strong, with a good eye. I would explain to him what I had in mind, and he would frame the scene exactly as I wanted. After each take, I would look to him to see if we got it, and he would nod, or not. I had no need to check the monitor anymore because we were totally copacetic. I had the best three days of the shoot after Dick took over.

Before Nick did his big scene, he wanted to work with me on it over the weekend. I read the chapters from the book to him, so all the horrible details that were not going to be in the film would be in his brain. I showed him the flashback sequence, already edited. We had shot it with a handheld camera so it would have more of a wild, uneasy quality. The camera jerks and swerves to convey the sudden violence and terror. I wanted Nick to have those images in his head . . . to see it, hear it, feel it in every cell of his body, so he could draw on it emotionally.

It's the crux of the film . . . the unraveling of the mystery at the heart of the story . . . when he tells Lowenstein the story of that night.

"They broke into our house. Three men. Mama cried, 'Help us, Tom.' I wanted to, but I couldn't. One of them raped Savannah. One of them raped my mother. I guess that's not the answer to all of Savannah's problems . . . but I thought you should know."

Lowenstein is shocked by the information, but all her reaction is in her eyes. She remains deliberately calm. She hardly moves, almost as if she's dealing with a wounded creature that she doesn't want to scare away.

Quietly, she asks, "What were you doing while all this was going on?"

"I don't know."

"You don't know? Maybe you ran for help?"

Tom shakes his head.

"Why not?"

"I don't know. I don't know."

She senses that there's more to the story than what he's telling her, and she gently pushes him to confront it.

"You said before that three men came in. What happened to the third man?"

And then the camera goes to a close-up of Nick's face. I wanted to see into his eyes. It's the only huge close-up in the movie. He's like a deer caught in the headlights. His expression freezes. His eyes dart around.

"Tom . . . where was he?"

We're going back and forth from the flashback to Tom . . . and now he's shaking his head, as if it's impossible to believe or to say out loud what he needs to say to her.

"Tom, it's okay. Tell me about him."

And for the first time in his life, Tom finally tells someone the full story of his being violated by a man . . . *his* rape . . . as the horrific scene plays out on the screen. There's terror in the sound of his jeans being ripped . . . that's the kind of memory that stays with you on a sensory level.

And then Luke rushes in and kills two of the men with his shotgun, and Lila stabs the third.

Lila makes her children promise never to tell a soul, and Tom says, "I think the silence was worse than the rapes. Three days later Savannah tried to kill herself. She could keep quiet but she couldn't lie."

And then he attempts to make light of the whole sad story by breaking into a brief song-and-dance routine, singing "And that's what I like about the South!" as if he were Al Jolson.

The next moment is something that wasn't in the book but actually happened to me in real life. I used to see a therapist (a woman this time). And I was talking to her about an incident that had happened with Cis. We were in an antiques store, and I spotted a painting I liked. I showed it to Cis, and she suddenly wanted it as well. "You can buy anything you want," she told me. "Let me have this."

I was taken aback. It wasn't so much about the painting . . . which I ended up letting her buy . . . but about the fact that she seemed to have forgotten the part of me that was still that sixteen-year-old girl, Barbara Joan, who loved to go antiquing, as we did in the old days, when I had to think twice about spending ten dollars for some beautiful object that everyone else had overlooked. One of the reasons I loved Cis so much was because she had loved me when I was nobody.

We were very close, but now she seemed to see me through different eyes . . . as this wealthy woman who should give up this painting because I already had so much. She actually took it out of my hands. It was the first time I ever heard even a tiny bit of envy in her voice.

The therapist stopped me and asked, "How did that make you feel?"

I said, "Terrible." It plunged me right back into childhood, and a very dark, emotionally young place.

She said, "I don't hear it. Your voice doesn't connect with your heart."

I looked at her.

She explained, "You sound so detached. There's no connection between what you're saying and the emotions you must be experiencing."

And then she reached out and touched my hand.

Well, that simple act . . . that basic human touch . . . was so powerful. Freudian analysts never touched their patients. I was a bit stunned. It had an immediate effect on me . . . releasing all this feeling. I started to weep and couldn't stop. It was like a dam breaking. All the barriers I had put up came down.

She said, "I feel your pain," and then she took me in her arms and held me. I remember thinking, *Oh, this is what it must feel like to be held by your mother.*

I thought, *If it worked on me, it will probably work on Nick* . . . and it could be a powerful coda to his pivotal scene.

So I wrote it into the script.

After Tom makes his joke, Lowenstein is silent.

He says, "Say something, Lowenstein."

"How do you feel?" she asks.

"Well, I feel okay. I mean, I thought I'd be on the floor after telling you this but I feel surprisingly all right."

He flops down beside her, but the way his leg keeps jerking betrays his anxiety.

She sees right through him, and I had her say, "You've really learned how to cover your pain, haven't you? You've done that all your life. That thirteen-year-old boy is still in a lot of pain."

"Don't do this to me, Lowenstein. Don't do this to me."

She reaches out and touches his arm, then clasps his hand, saying, "I can feel your pain, Tom."

His face crumples.

She says, "Let yourself feel it. It takes courage to feel the pain, Tom. You can do it. You can handle it. Don't be afraid. It's okay."

And Nick breaks down, sobbing . . . and I held him in my arms, just as my therapist held me . . . rocking him, as you would a child.

Nick was absolutely brilliant in that scene. It required a very deep, intense, internal kind of acting . . . every emotion had to register on his face . . . and then he lets it all out and loses control completely.

I was so pleased when Billy, Nick's dresser, told me he had never seen Nick be so vulnerable.

I feel for men . . . even more after I had a son. I never understood why some people would tell a child, "Boys don't cry." What difference does being a boy make? If you're hurt, you should cry. But boys are taught that there's a certain standard of behavior that's considered masculine, and it doesn't include tears. So what do you do with all those emotions?

Tom is a man who's never looked back at his past . . . and he had to learn to come to grips with it. As a child, he was helpless to stop what happened that night, and for all these years he's had no outlet for the pain. It was an invasion of his body, his soul, his heart, his mind. And then years later, when Luke died, Tom was lost all over again. He hasn't really allowed himself to grieve for his brother, who he believed saved his life, or himself, or Savannah . . . and the childhood that ended for all three that night.

When Tom finally confronts the truth and allows himself to feel the pain, it's as if a weight has been lifted off his chest . . . he can breathe again . . . and it opens him up to other feelings. He can look at the women in his life with a fresh attitude. He can be more loving to others, now that he is able to accept and forgive himself.

That's the gift that pain gives you. It's a part of life and it can't be ignored. You need to accept the pain in order to feel the joy.

His sessions with Lowenstein in her office are done . . . she finally has the information she needs to treat Savannah . . . and only now does the romance between Tom and Lowenstein begin.

I couldn't sleep the night before we shot the first love scene.

We all know what to expect. Usually the couple is writhing around in bed, and you see close-ups of all these body parts. I was determined to do something different, but I couldn't think of what it could be.

Finally I said, "Let's have them kissing against a wall . . . backlit, so they're just silhouettes against the light . . . and we'll keep our clothes on." That was partly because I was shy but also because I thought it would be more original.

As a director, you want to design something that will be sexy and free. But as an actress, it's very uncomfortable for me to do this stuff in front of dozens of people. I don't get off on being an exhibitionist . . . maybe that's why I don't enjoy performing live.

I think Nick, on the other hand, was looking forward to it. I told you how he loved to tease me, and this would be the perfect opportunity. He's got the director in his arms, and she's supposed to lose control, according to the script.

Let me say right now that Nick is a good kisser . . . that was a nice surprise . . .

but then he would do something like put his hand up my dress, and I'd yell "Cut!"

He'd laugh and call me on it. "Why are you running away? Every time we've got a good thing going . . . just when it's starting to get hot . . . you say 'Cut!'"

Objectively I had to admit he was right.

It's difficult for me to separate the director from the actress in these kinds of scenes. Usually I can switch from one to the other seamlessly, but now, as the director, I had to watch myself do a love scene and I got embarrassed.

I had a hard time letting go.

Maybe that's where my limitations as an actress come in. Would I be a better actress if I was less in control?

Probably. But no use worrying about it now.

Anyway, whatever we got on film must have worked, because people keep telling me that Nick was so attractive in the movie. He hadn't done anything this romantic in a long time, and I was eager to bring out that aspect of him.

This is a film about love and compassion . . . and how it can transform people. Lowenstein's love changes Tom. His love changes her. Together their care and concern change Savannah. Tom's friendship with Lowenstein's son changes Bernard, Bernard's response changes Tom, and Bernard's new attitude changes his relationship with his mother.

We shot the scene where Tom and Bernard say goodbye in Grand Central Terminal . . . about as far as you can get from a controlled, private movie set. It was a workday, and we could only shoot from 10:00 a.m. to 3:00 p.m., in order to avoid rush hour. We had the use of one gate . . . Track 29 . . . a coincidence that I loved, because Jason was born on the twenty-ninth. But we couldn't close off the whole station, so we had to get what we needed in the midst of all this daily life. That was a challenge, because people were constantly walking through our shots. (You try telling New Yorkers to stop and wait.)

We had a Louma crane up on the balcony, because I wanted the camera to be able to pan in and out over a long distance, so you could really appreciate the soaring scale of the station. When Tom and Bernard first walk in, they blend in with the crowd . . . anonymous figures on a marble staircase beneath those huge windows, seven stories high. Then, when Tom asks Bernard to play the violin for him, I wanted the camera to gradually pan up and away so you get a bird's-eye view of this small figure in this vast space, playing this celestial music as sunlight pours in and commuters walk by, their shadows elongated on the marble floor.

When we chose the music . . . Fritz Kreisler's "Praeludium and Allegro" . . . I had no idea that Pinchas Zukerman, who was going to play it, considered it one of the hundred most difficult pieces. And Jason was starting from scratch. When he came to see me in South Carolina after his first few violin lessons and played "Twinkle, Twinkle, Little Star," I couldn't stop laughing. I must have hurt his feelings and I hated that, but it was just so awful! And I thought, *My God, what have I done to my son?*

But I knew down deep that he would pull it off. Jason worked on the piece for three months. He absolutely mastered the fingering and the body language and how he held the bow . . . so I could shoot him actually playing the violin. I was so impressed.

I couldn't show as much with Jeroen. He told me he would learn to play the violin, but that turned out to be a little optimistic. That's why you barely see his fingers when he performs at the dinner party and only see his reactions to the music on his face. And he's such a good actor that you believe he's really playing.

I saved the scenes where Lowenstein and Tom part for the end of the shoot. It just made sense emotionally . . . as actors, that's when you have the most amount of experience together . . . and it worked with the schedule. So the last scene we shot was the moment when Lowenstein comes out of the town house where she has her office and sees Tom standing across the street, smoking and pacing. All she has to do is look at his face and she knows instantly that he has decided to go back to his wife.

Bracing herself, she takes a long, slow walk across the street and says, "She called you."

He nods.

She touches his face and says, "Well, we knew this day would come, didn't we? But you're never quite . . . prepared for it."

He takes her in his arms, and she lets the papers she's holding fall to the ground. "Just hold me, please," he tells her. "I feel like I'm dying."

She's crying, he's crying, and the emotions of these adults are so deep, they resonate so far back, that what I heard in my head was the cry of a baby, which is why you hear a crying baby as a mother goes by, pushing her carriage.

Through tears, Lowenstein says, "One of the things I love about you is that you're the kind of guy who'll always go back to his family" . . . another great line from the book. Her arms are around him. We see her face over his shoulder, and she impulsively hits his back with her fists. "Ohhhhhh . . . I gotta find me a nice Jewish boy. You guys are killing me."

Looking at that shot now, I realize I made a mistake by not cutting my nails shorter. But when I first met Pat, he said, "I love your hands . . . your nails are just like Lowenstein." So I kept them the way they were (and believe me, it was hard to make time for manicures on location).

Making a film brings the cast, and the crew, closer together . . . if it goes well. And now it was almost over, and soon everyone would part. Just before we shot the last scene, Nick came into my dressing room, and we didn't have to say much to each other. There were no words. We just looked into each other's eyes and embraced, holding each other closely, with a deep appreciation and a kind of intimacy that's almost love.

Both of us were feeling so much pent-up emotion, and it worked for the scene, once we got in front of the camera. I knew how this moment felt because I had already experienced it in real life, with Peter Matz, who also went back to his family. And I could draw on another moment, when Jason was fifteen and traveling in Europe with some of his friends on an outreach program. We met up briefly in Rome, and as he was sitting beside me in the hotel room, he suddenly did something that he hadn't done in a decade . . . he put his head in my lap. I was stroking his hair, and he could probably sense how much I missed him. Maybe he was even feeling a little homesick. And I remember feeling an overwhelming love for him that was so big it scared me. What if he goes skiing in the Alps and runs into a tree? What if the train he's on crashes?

It was totally irrational . . . but very primal . . . like me crawling up to that windowsill when I was fifteen months old to watch for my father. But one day he didn't come home anymore.

Love is painful. I can still feel that loss . . . it hurts to love someone that much, because then you also have the fear of losing them.

But I could not end the movie with Lowenstein standing there in the street, sobbing, like a victim. I felt their relationship had to conclude on a note of acceptance, not just sadness.

And that's why Lowenstein and Tom meet for one last time in the Rainbow Room. They're sitting at a table when she says, despondent, "You just love her more. Admit it."

And Tom shakes his head, "No, Lowenstein. Just longer."

What a kind thing to say . . . another great Pat Conroy line, but it wasn't in the book. He actually improved on this moment when he wrote his screenplay, so of course I used it.

She smiles, takes his hand and kisses it . . . and then the camera pans to the dance floor, where we see they're the only couple left in the room, and they're dancing a slow dance together, like in Tom's dream. We shot this on location in the real Rainbow Room, very late at night, and only stopped when the sun came up.

I had at least three versions of the ending of the film . . . you know me, I'm the version queen. I like to have various options to play with in the editing room.

The scene at the table was longer initially . . . with more conversation . . . but I cut it down to the bare minimum. And then the Rainbow Room sequence concludes with a shot of the New York skyline . . . the skyscrapers sparkling with lights and surrounded by water . . . which dissolves into a shot of Beaufort across the water . . . which dissolves into a shot of Tom's wife and children playing on the beach.

So one body of water leads into another . . . just as in the beginning of the movie . . . and we go back to the water, as Tom returns home to the place he loves, and the family he loves.

On the day we shot that scene on the beach, I was warned that it was very overcast. But when I arrived on the set, I felt the clouds were a gift. The gray light was so soft on their faces as Tom and his wife and daughters embraced.

And the film ends as it began, with Tom speaking in voice-over, only this time his words are about Lowenstein: "Six weeks before, I was ready to leave my wife, my kids. I wanted out of everything. But she changed that. She changed me. For the first time, I felt like I had something to give back to the women in my life. They deserved that."

As we cut to various images from his daily life, he declares: "I am a teacher, a coach, and a well-loved man. And it is more than enough. In New York, I learned that I needed to love my mother and father in all their flawed, outrageous humanity. And in families, there are no crimes beyond forgiveness."

In the book, those last two lines appear in the prologue. But I thought, that's the lesson he learns, and I wanted to save it for the ending.

The last scene is Tom in his car, driving, as the voice-over continues: "And as I cross the bridge that'll take me home, I feel the words building inside me. I can't stop them or tell you why I say them. But as I reach the top of the bridge, these words come to me in a whisper. I say them as prayer . . . as regret . . . as praise. I say . . . Lowenstein . . . Lowenstein."

Then the music takes over, and the last image in the film is an echo of the first image in the film . . . it all comes full circle as we see the marshes, with the water gleaming in the late afternoon light.

It's not exactly a happy ending . . . but it's a true one.

FORTY-FIVE

Forgiveness

When I direct or produce a movie, it's an all-consuming process. I zero in on it to the exclusion of all else, and actually, that makes my life simpler . . . even with the constant demands of a movie set.

Everything else has to take a back seat . . . running an office, maintaining my property, paying the bills. (I don't even look at them while I'm shooting. I just delegate and hope for the best.)

Sometimes I think I should always live my life the way I do when I'm directing. I need that kind of very clear focus . . . otherwise I can get distracted by all the other claims on my time. In an odd way I find being on a movie set very calming. It centers me. And directing uses every fiber of my being. Everything I've ever learned, seen, felt, experienced goes into my vision of what the film should be.

And once I have the footage in the can, my favorite part begins . . . editing. Now I can eat whatever I want, since I don't have to be concerned about my weight. (By the way, the Sony lot even had an ice cream store. What more could you want?) I can play, picking the best take . . . the best reading of each line . . . to get the most out of each actor's performance. I loved editing *The Prince of Tides* with Don Zimmerman, who was very supportive. Once again I used my own video camera on a tripod to film each option before Don had to pull the film apart to try it a different way.

When we were in the thick of editing this movie, I remember thinking, *At least I don't have a husband to worry about.* I couldn't imagine what would happen if I were in a relationship. How would I balance the tunnel-vision part of me with the part that would want to devote some time to the partner in my life?

Luckily I'm now married to someone who understands when I have to concentrate on my work, just as I understand when he has to do the same thing. And Jim is very flexible. Sometimes he'll come along to the recording studio, just to keep me company. As long as he has his laptop, he can work anywhere. Not me. I can't do my work in the middle of someone else's creative process.

In the midst of editing I'm also thinking about scoring. Originally I had hired John Barry to do the music. I thought his scores for everything from the James Bond movies to *Out of Africa* and *Dances with Wolves* were brilliant, and I was eager to work with him. Since I like to shoot a film and edit it as I go along, I was able to show him a rough cut in November, soon after we finished filming. I was nervous as he watched it and very pleased when he said he loved it.

But it soon became clear that we had different ideas of what working together would mean. He wanted to go home to New York and do the whole score by himself, three thousand miles away, and then present me with a finished product. I wanted to be involved more closely, scene by scene, so we parted ways.

It was Marilyn and Alan Bergman who suggested that their friend James Newton Howard might be a good replacement. James was not yet the brilliantly successful composer he is today . . . although one movie he had scored, *Pretty Woman*, had recently come out and was a big hit. Marilyn and Alan arranged for us to meet at their house, over dinner, and I was very taken with

James. He reminded me of Peter Matz . . . someone who was smart, sensitive. He even wore glasses, like Peter. He seemed like a person you could trust . . .

I hired him.

The first step in scoring is a spotting session, where we watched the film several times as I pointed out places where I felt the music could go. Another evening after work we went to a restaurant, where James told me that he was happy all day, knowing he would see me. He was very sweet. Most men are not so open with their feelings. He said he felt an instant connection to me.

That was intriguing, but he was making me a little nervous. When he grabbed me at the end of the evening to kiss me goodbye I was so tense I broke into a sweat and pulled away.

It was nice to be pursued. I think we spoke on the phone almost every night before bed, telling each other about our pasts. He had just broken up with his girlfriend and was going through a difficult time. I thought it might be too soon to get involved . . . and he was a few years younger than me, which made me pause. But he was persistent. "I feel as if I'm in a dream with you," he told me. "I want to spend the rest of our lives together."

The rest of our lives together?

We barely knew each other. I told him, "Don't think so big. We're probably just an interim relationship."

It felt as if he were moving too fast, talking about the future. And it worried me that he was setting up all these expectations. I tried to put on the brakes and said, "Why don't we just date?"

But I have to admit, I loved all his passion and found it hard to resist. He would say the most beautiful things. I wish I could speak as poetically as that, but I can't. Those kinds of words don't come easily to me. I never heard them growing up, and they don't come naturally to me now.

Remember, my mother was not very expressive. You could never call her touchy-feely . . . more like stiff and wary. Cis was much warmer. She could make people feel good with a simple compliment, and I loved that quality in her. But it was awkward for me. I'm much better now, after learning from her and other wonderful women friends.

At first I thought James was sweet but a little funny-looking, and then he became really handsome to me. It just shows you how beauty is in the eye of the beholder (or is it in the heart?). He was also quiet and complex, and that always interests me. I was very attracted to the musician in him and felt he would compose beautiful music for the movie. After showing him the underwater footage, I dreamt that the two of us were underwater holding hands, like the children in the film. Clearly my defenses were breaking down.

One night at dinner I even gave him the last bite of my dessert . . . and it was a dessert I loved, molten chocolate cake with vanilla ice cream! I don't give away my dessert so easily. That's when I knew I was in trouble. (Before that moment, I'd only give my last bite to my son!)

We made plans to go away together at Christmas, and we had a great time, skiing in Deer Valley. James was very romantic, and he basically swept me off my feet. I remember another trip to San Francisco, where he filled the hotel suite with gardenias. He had this vision of love, and it had no limits . . . that's what kept me hooked.

And then reality would intrude. He was a complicated man, and he'd fall into these dark moods. He was also diagnosed with Epstein-Barr, which can result in chronic fatigue syndrome, and I'm sure that didn't help his frame of mind.

One minute he would be passionate and engaged and the next minute he would want to be alone. I wrote down a lot of what he said in my journal, trying to make sense of it. One night he told me, "I want to make you feel secure." That was perceptive. People who don't know me seem to be under the mistaken impression that I'm totally strong, but I'm many things . . . confident and tough when I'm fighting for something I believe in, but also very vulnerable when it comes to relationships.

I liked the fact that James saw beyond the image. I wanted to trust him, because it felt so good.

And then his mood would swing dramatically and he'd berate himself, saying things like, "I don't deserve your love." I don't know if he really believed that, or if it was just an excuse as he tried to find a nice way to let me down. He'd call me late at night, sounding very unhappy and confused. He told me that he still had feelings for his former girlfriend, even though he had fallen in love with me.

I could see that he was torn. He had broken up with this girl, and then declared he was in love with me, but he wanted children, and that was unlikely to happen with a woman my age (forty-eight at the time).

His former girlfriend was much younger. It did occur to me that if he loved me that much, couldn't we adopt a child?

I'd been thinking about adopting a little girl on my own, because I was so entranced with my goddaughter Caleigh. In one of those twists of fate, I became good friends with Christine Peters, the woman Jon was seeing when we parted. And when Christine decided to adopt a baby girl, she kindly let me borrow her often. I adored playing with Caleigh. But what finally stopped me from adopting on my own was the fact that the child would grow up without a father.

In any event, adopting didn't seem to be an option for James, which plugged right into my own insecurities. Would there ever be a person who'd love me so much that nothing else mattered?

The Duke of Windsor gave up his throne, for God's sake, for the woman he loved!

But I set those thoughts aside and tried to make James feel better. I told him that of course he'd think about this girl, since it's only natural to continue caring for the people we've loved. I knew he was fighting his own demons. Life wasn't easy for him.

And I probably wasn't easy for him . . . or let's say I'm not easy for most men. I have strong opinions. I can be stubborn. I get angry. And I've been in the public eye for a long time, which means people come up and ask for autographs. That's why I stay home most of the time.

And then there's money.

James told me at one point, "I can't afford what you can afford."

That can be a problem, and I'd heard it before. I don't think he understood that the fact that he made less made no difference to me. I told him, "I'd live within your means."

Maybe that's what really threw him . . . when I began to reciprocate his love. Some people prefer the chase . . . the romance . . . the fantasy.

At one point, he told me, "I'm overwhelmed with my love for you." Perhaps he was uncomfortable with his own feelings, and so he started to withdraw . . . withhold . . . pull away. He'd say, "I can't talk to you for a while."

Now I was completely confused. I'd cry.

"I don't want to keep hurting you," he said.

The constant push-pull was exhausting. At one point we had a session with a therapist. Oddly enough when I went to play back the tape from that meeting, it was blank. Interesting, don't you think? Was that a sign? What was it trying to tell me? I guess it meant that there was nothing more to be learned, beyond what I already knew deep down inside.

We were not going to be together. This was the reality. I had to accept it.

I decided I had to let go of James.

After we broke up, I remember riding in a car and being struck by this terrible despondency. And in the midst of all this, James was also writing the music for my movie. And you know what? I think in some way all the emotions we were going through actually helped the score. It was deeply felt.

I remember the day he called me and said he had the love theme. He came over to Carolwood and played it for me on the piano in my living room. As soon as he finished, I said, "That's it. That's Lowenstein's theme."

What a relief. I was very pleased. Emotionally, it fit the picture . . . beautiful, but a bit melancholy. Complex, and yet you could still hum it. It touched me.

Music is a magical thing. When it hits the right chords, you respond to it viscerally. I knew it would work perfectly behind the love scene in the hallway, and in many other places in the film. It expressed the relationship between Tom and Lowenstein, and ultimately the feelings that had developed between James and me. I think that made it even more poignant.

In May we began recording his music with a full orchestra on the famous MGM scoring stage. During the golden age of Hollywood, this was where so many great musicals and films were scored, like *The Wizard of Oz*, *Gone With the Wind*, *Singin' in the Rain*, *Gigi*, and *An American in Paris*. Everyone wants to use it, because the acoustics are so good. I recorded many of my recent albums and three of the soundtracks to my films on this stage, and I was so proud, and humbled, when they named it after me in 2004. At the ceremony, Howard Stringer, who was the chairman of the Sony Corporation (Sony had bought the MGM lot), was very complimentary, and now his brother, Rob, is the chairman of Sony Music Group, and he's a delight as well.

After our first day of scoring, James called me at about 11:00 p.m. in my car as I was heading home. I remember exactly what he said because I wrote it down in my journal: "I hated you today. You want to change my music. But even as I'm hating you, I love you so much."

God, that was a painful time . . . but pain can make for beautiful music.

As it turned out, I was able to separate my lover from my love for the music . . . to separate love and work. Even though it remained unspoken, we both knew that I had final say. If I felt a certain cue wasn't quite right, I would ask him for something different. I was not about to go against my artistic instincts . . . not for any man, and certainly not now, when I was trying to back away from him.

Endings are never easy. We were still connected to each other and we kept telling each other how we felt. There was all this leftover passion, and it was hard to disengage.

But we did turn out to be an interim relationship . . . even though at times I thought it might be something more . . . and he did go back to his younger girlfriend. He wanted children. And he got them, two in fact . . .

I don't regret a thing.

Our time together was deep, sexy, and romantic, and I'll always remember it because it's still there, in the great love theme he composed for my film.

And then Marilyn and Alan wrote lyrics for it. They entitled it "Places That Belong to You," and the studio wanted me to sing it at the end of the movie. I thought the song was beautiful, but I didn't think it belonged in the film. As I explained to the executives at Columbia, this is the story of Tom Wingo's journey, and the last thing you hear should be his words, not Lowenstein bursting into song about her own feelings. I felt it would be an abrupt jump that took the focus off the protagonist . . . the hero . . . and that's Tom.

Besides, the idea itself pushed various buttons for me. I thought, *Oh my God. Do I still have to sing for my supper? Isn't the film I've made enough on its own?*

I didn't want to include it.

Of course everybody tried to change my mind. Marilyn, Alan, and James naturally wanted me to sing their song. The studio thought having it in the movie would boost sales of the soundtrack. And everyone kept reminding me that it might even be nominated for an Academy Award, which is always good publicity for a movie.

I only agreed to record it. And in the editing room, I did try it every which way in the movie . . . at the top (definitely not), then over the end credits, which was the version we previewed in San Diego. Eighty-six percent of the audience voted to include the song.

But I couldn't do it. I had to go with my gut and not let myself be swayed by other people's opinions. I believed it would compromise the film. It seemed gratuitous and just plain wrong to have me singing at the end.

It was wonderful to have final cut, which meant that the studio couldn't force me to use it, just for commercial reasons. Although I did allow Columbia to include it on the soundtrack that was for sale in stores, along with my rendition of "For All We Know," the melody that Tom and Lowenstein dance to in the Rainbow Room . . . with the caveat that these were bonus tracks, *not* in the film.

I didn't show this movie to any of my friends before it was finished. I was afraid someone would once again claim I was looking for advice. One day as Don and I were color-correcting the print . . . and I have to say Stephen Goldblatt gave the film a beautiful look . . . he turned to me and said, "You've made a fucking good movie." Don is not the kind of editor who gives casual compliments, so I felt this warm rush of pride.

I was so close to it by then that it was hard for me to judge. Before we started filming, a studio executive told me the script was very good but that I should definitely take out the scene where Tom gets angry and throws Herbert's violin up in the air.

What? I thought that was one of the best scenes in the book . . . and the film.

And guess what? When we previewed it and asked the audience to tell us which scene was their favorite, most people picked the violin scene.

I don't enjoy previews. In fact, sitting there in the dark and watching the movie with an audience for the first time is agony to me. It's like being in a doctor's office and waiting to hear the results of a test. Is he going to find something awful? It feels like everything is on the line.

When 97 percent of the audience cards came back marked excellent or good . . . with twice as many excellents as goods . . . I was elated.

The studio was very happy . . . so happy that they decided that the film, which was scheduled for a September 1991 release, should be held until December, so they could make it their big Christmas movie.

My first reaction was, Oh no. I'm done with this thing and I just want to get it out! Now this was just going to prolong the suspense.

Making this film took three and a half years. I spent two years on the script alone, and then it kept changing during the filming. The process is so alive . . .

you might have a dream or see something in the course of daily life, and it becomes part of the fabric of the film.

I think directing and editing a film is truly my most creative time. It's the same fantastic feeling I had when I was pregnant. Every day things are changing, growing. It's the most miraculous experience.

One reason why I chose to pursue this as my life's work is because records and films, especially, preserve a moment in time. (In *Funny Girl*, I'm forever twenty-five.) And if our planet manages to survive, this medium will survive. If you make a good film, it will still exist long after you're gone. I find that very comforting.

And if it's about issues that you care deeply about . . . like *The Prince of Tides*, which is about forgiving and accepting and loving . . . it's very cathartic. Most of us have experienced some type of pain in our childhood. But if you keep on blaming your parents or whomever, you remain a victim.

Three weeks into the shoot, when I was filming in South Carolina, my sister called and said that our mother had to go into the hospital for a heart bypass operation. I was scared, and the news immediately put all my problems with the film into perspective. When I was faced with the potential loss of my mother, the movie became much easier to do, in a way. After all, it was only a movie . . . not as important as life itself . . . or my mother's life, specifically.

I stopped what I was doing. I had to talk to the doctors to find out every detail about the procedure. And my mother came through the operation beautifully. Thank God there were no complications. Like Tom in the story, I, too, needed to learn how to love my mother in all her "flawed, outrageous humanity." When the movie premiered in Los Angeles, I was grateful she could be there.

Apparently word of mouth after the film opened was great, because the box office kept going up, and we got a lot of good reviews.

"The Prince of Tides *marks Ms. Streisand's triumphantly good job of locating that story's salient elements and making them come alive on the screen.*"

—Janet Maslin, *The New York Times*

> *"Every frame of* The Prince of Tides *is marked with the intensity and care of a highly committed filmmaker who shows the same kind of heartfelt, unashamed emotional involvement with her characters that distinguished* [William] *Wyler's work."*
>
> —*Variety*

I was ecstatic to be mentioned in the same sentence as Willy. But there was one person whose opinion mattered more to me than anything else . . . and that was Pat Conroy. I had shown him the film as soon as it was finished, and here is the letter I received after it opened:

Dear Barbra,

A love letter. I'm writing this on Christmas day knowing the movie opens today. I hope it does well, but whether it does or not will not diminish my extraordinary gratitude to you for the passion and artistry you brought to the making of this . . . No one knows like I do what a cumbersome beast my novel was to turn into a film. I'd given up on the idea years ago. It required a grand vision, genius—it required a daughter of fire—and that's what you provided. You gave me my book back to me. Before you made this movie, I winced every time I heard the name of my book. It caused me pain and grief and regret. Now it's mine again and you gave it back to me. I keep telling people that you wrote the screenplay—I hope you don't mind that because it's the absolute truth and eventually Becky Johnston will return fire—but you wrote it and you did a great job and I'm proud to be part of what you accomplished.

Let me tell you this: I love the movie version of The Prince of Tides. ***I simply love it. The book has many flaws based on basic flaws of my character. But the movie sings and soars. Another thing. I loved the movie*** Yentl ***a lot better than I loved I. B. Singer's fucking story.***

Great love and praise,

Pat Conroy

I was struck by that phrase . . . "a daughter of fire." Remember how my grandma used to call me *fabrent*, which means "on fire" in Yiddish? How uncanny that Pat would choose that image.

I called Nick to make sure he had seen the reviews. The critics were going on and on about his work. *Variety* called it "the performance of a lifetime." I was so thrilled for him, and so proud.

When he heard my voice, he said, "I've had so many conversations with you in my head." He told me that he put on my tape of "For All We Know" and then had to take it off, because it reminded him of the Rainbow Room. He laughed, but I could hear the emotion behind his words and I was touched. And he told me how hard it was when he first came home . . . "I felt just like Tom Wingo."

I knew what he meant. There's a residual feeling when you come off a film that you know is good . . . you're missing that creative high and the people who shared it with you. It leaves an imprint on your life.

Years later I ran into Nick at a party. He sat down next to me and in a moment of unguarded truth said, "You know, I fell in love with you on that movie." That was a surprise. His words made me feel good, but I also understood what he meant. When you're doing a love story that works, you have to fall a little bit in love with your leading man or leading lady in order to feel those emotions. (Although it doesn't happen every time . . . I never felt any attraction to Yves Montand or David Selby or Walter Matthau, for instance.)

A similar thing can happen between a director and his star. I can see how Willy Wyler could have fallen a little bit in love with Bette Davis and Audrey Hepburn, because he was very warm with me. And think of Ingrid Bergman leaving her husband for Roberto Rossellini after he directed her in *Stromboli*. The bond that develops during a movie can be really strong. Willy was too old for me to think of him romantically, but I could relate to him as a father, someone to be trusted. And he knew that good work happens when actors trust their director and know that he wants to present them in the best possible light.

I used whatever male-female energy existed between Nick and me (we were such opposites) in order to get the performance I needed out of him. I had to make him feel like the man I wanted to see on-screen! I wanted every woman in the audience to fall in love with him . . . because that would make the film work.

I may be a pretty good actress, but I think I might be a better director!

I don't mean to toot my own horn, so let me say it another way. I'm a more *devoted* director. I want my actors to be the best they can be. And apparently my efforts to build Nick into a matinee idol worked, because after the movie came out, *People* magazine put him on their cover as "the sexiest man alive."

And Nick's agent, Jim Wiatt, called and told me that Nick said I was the best filmmaker he's ever worked with, and he can't wait to do it again.

In January I was sitting next to Nick at the Golden Globes when he won the award for Best Actor—Drama. He got up onstage and said, "I have to thank Barbra Streisand for wonderful direction." Those words meant so much to me. The film was also up for Best Film—Drama, and I was up for Best Director, but Nick was the only winner that night. Again, I felt proud and happy for him.

A week later I was nominated for the DGA Award . . . given by the Directors Guild of America for Outstanding Directorial Achievement in Feature Film. I was excited because this was an honor voted on by other directors, and that was very important to me. It meant they considered me a peer. And I was in stellar company . . . the other nominees were Jonathan Demme for *The Silence of the Lambs*, Barry Levinson for *Bugsy*, Ridley Scott for *Thelma and Louise*, and Oliver Stone for *JFK*.

It made me feel validated . . . but I also hate these contests, because they turn winners into losers, since only one of us gets to win. (It was Jonathan Demme, whose work was brilliant.)

In February I flew to London with Jason, Nick, and Marty for the London premiere . . . a benefit for Princess Diana's charity, the AIDS Crisis Trust. I was impressed with the way Diana visited hospitals and held the hands of AIDS patients. Her kind, open attitude did a lot to destigmatize the disease. And she was lovely to look at . . . tall, pretty, with a great figure. I liked her cropped hair, her blue eyes, and her longish nose. She was warm and friendly, and it was fun to sit next to her in the balcony of the theater at Leicester Square, watching the film. When it ended, people started to applaud. The lights came up. I was told that the princess has to stand up first . . . that was royal protocol . . . but instead Diana was smiling and clapping along with everyone else and she whispered to me, "You must stand up."

I said, "Really? You're supposed to stand up first. Are you sure it's all right?"

She said, "Absolutely!" and gave me a little push.

The zipper on my skirt had come down a bit as I was sitting, and she noticed and quickly started to zip it up for me as I got to my feet. Renata reached over to help from the row behind. I looked out at the crowd and said a few words: "The last time I was here was for *Yentl,* and you made it so special for me. Now, eight years later, you've done it again." People just wouldn't stop clapping. It was extraordinary.

When I finally sat down, Diana turned to me and asked, "Do you know how wonderful you are?"

I looked at her, and another moment from my life flashed before my eyes. Those were the same words that Marilyn Bergman had said to me at the Bon Soir, thirty years earlier.

I certainly didn't know it then. Did I know it now? I'm not sure . . . maybe a little.

I thought Diana was wonderful. I wonder if *she* knew how wonderful *she* was.

I was still in London the following day, when the Oscar nominations were announced. The film got seven nominations: Best Picture . . . Best Actor . . . Best Supporting Actress . . . Best Writing, Adapted Screenplay . . . Best Cinematography . . . Best Art Direction . . . Best Music, Original Score.

It was the first time Nick Nolte, Kate Nelligan, Pat Conroy, Becky Johnston, Stephen Goldblatt, and James Newton Howard had ever been nominated for an Oscar.

But . . . like with *Yentl* . . . I wasn't nominated for Best Director.

The list was the same as that for the DGA Award, except that John Singleton had the fifth slot for *Boyz n the Hood.* I knew John Singleton. He had asked me to sign for him to be a member of the DGA, which I was glad to do, and I thought he did a wonderful job on his movie.

Still, I couldn't help feeling left out.

So many thoughts go rushing through your head.

Okay. Maybe the Academy members just didn't like the movie enough. That's their prerogative.

But then they nominated it for Best Picture.

So what's going on here?

These awards are part popularity contest, and I've never put myself out there, winning friends and influencing people. I don't go to everyone else's openings, because I hate getting dressed up and wearing high heels. If I must go, I'll slip in the back door. I don't feel comfortable posing for pictures on the red carpet . . . I can't stand there with my hip out, showing off my dress and jewelry. (Besides, they always pick the wrong photos.) It's just my innate reserve, but some people probably take it personally. So why would they vote for me?

I've said that I became a director out of self-defense, and it's true. Nobody was offering me roles. I swear, people were frightened of me. I have this reputation for being difficult . . . another myth that's referred to over and over again in interviews, and the mere fact of repeating it gives it credibility.

What does being difficult actually mean?

Is it that I strive for excellence in everything I do?

I care deeply about every aspect of the film. I want the best performances from the actors, the best script, the best music. I want the audience to identify with the characters . . . to be moved.

Every good director has a vision. Every artist wants control. And as the commitment gets bigger, you have to exercise more control so the vision doesn't get diluted.

I love the way Stephen Sondheim said it in his lyrics for "Putting It Together":

Every moment makes a contribution, every little detail plays a part
Having just a vision's no solution, everything depends on execution
Putting it together, that's what counts!

I proved to myself that I could direct a movie with *Yentl*, and after that whole experience I wasn't sure I wanted to do it again. Many directors can go straight from one film to another. Not me. I'm too invested in each film emotionally. And here I was, going through the same thing with the nominations. And this time not being nominated hurt even more.

At first all the calls from friends and reporters made me feel very supported. And the fact of my snub brought the prejudice against women directors out into the open once again. It was shining a light on a real problem of sexism within the industry.

This was 1992, and only one female director had ever been nominated for an Academy Award . . . Lina Wertmüller for *Seven Beauties* in 1977.

And only two other women had been nominated for the DGA Award . . . Lina Wertmüller in 1977, and Randa Haines for *Children of a Lesser God* in 1987.

None of us won.

But I was just happy to have the Directors Guild medallion. It's gorgeous . . . made of silver . . . and it sits next to the one I have in gold, for winning the DGA Award for Directorial Achievement for my TV special *Barbra: The Concert* in 1995 (shared with my codirector, Dwight Hemion). I also have a plaque . . . I was nominated again in 2002 for *Timeless: Live in Concert* (shared with Don Mischer). They make a nice arrangement, all three of them.

I didn't attend the Oscars when *Yentl* got five nominations. But for *The Prince of Tides*, I thought, *This time I'm going . . . and I'm going with my son.* I wanted Cis to come along and bring her son too.

To my delight I really enjoyed myself that night. I was touched to see people holding banners outside, protesting again that I wasn't nominated as Best Director. I laughed when I heard Billy Crystal sing (to the tune of "Don't Rain on My Parade") "Seven nominations on the shelf. Did this film direct itself?" And then various stars, like the great Jessica Tandy, came out onstage and took the opportunity to comment on my exclusion. Liza Minnelli and Shirley MacLaine did a wonderful callout to me as "the director we'd most like to work with." I love when women have one another's backs. It was so kind and so supportive.

Frankly, I think that acknowledgment was even better than actually getting an award (I didn't have to speak!). And it had to suffice, because everyone from our group went home empty-handed that night.

But you know what? The seven nominations were really enough.

And a woman didn't win an Oscar for directing until 2010, when I presented the award to Kathryn Bigelow, for her wonderful film *The Hurt Locker.* That was an emotional moment. I was proud that the Academy thought I was the person who should hand it to her, if she won . . . as one woman director to another. So many other women had been overlooked over the years. That's why, when I opened the envelope, I ad-libbed, "Well, the time has come" . . . and happily announced her name.

And yet if I'm completely honest with myself, I did feel a little pang that it wasn't me.

It's funny . . . in *Yentl*, I was trying to say that a woman should be allowed to be all that she can be. And now in *The Prince of Tides*, it's a man who needs to know that he can be strong, but also gentle, nurturing to his children, and not afraid to cry in a woman's arms. In other words, I was promoting the idea that men should be all that they can be.

So, until the message gets across, I guess I'll keep making the same movie.

For years I felt guilty about my success. I didn't want people to envy me. Maybe that's why I would get sick to my stomach. But I'm tired of attacking myself.

And while making *The Prince of Tides*, I have to say that it gave me as much as I gave to it. I was forced to grow, to learn how to be a healthier, more accepting human being.

Just when I thought I could relax, because the movie had been so well received, another article was published in *The New York Times* . . . brief comments from nine psychiatrists, all male, who each analyze Dr. Lowenstein. The first one criticizes her for "indulging such clearly incestuous fantasies."

Incest? What is he talking about? Did I miss something?

Another doctor says, "The film is deeply reactionary: Lowenstein's professionalism is completely undermined—the first thing she does is serve Tom coffee." Give me a break. Where is it written that a doctor is not allowed to make a cup of coffee?

Another doctor declares, "Lowenstein commits the cardinal sin of psychiatry by sleeping with Tom Wingo." Another adds, "This movie perpetuates the stereotype of the therapist with a barren personal life who's 'cured' by falling in love with her patient."

That really got under my skin, and I wrote an article in response, "Physicians, Heal Thyselves," which was published in *Newsweek.* It was important to me to set the record straight. First, Tom Wingo was never Susan Lowenstein's patient, as these doctors would have known if they had been paying more attention to the film. He didn't solicit her help, and she didn't violate his trust. Second, even if they thought it was unethical for a doctor to get involved with her patient's brother, that's the story in Pat Conroy's book! They seemed to forget that the movie is a work of fiction, not a documentary . . . even though I tried to make it as real as possible and consulted with many doctors before I did the film, and not one of them questioned the plausibility of the plot. And third, why did *The*

New York Times article only quote male doctors? Couldn't they find at least one woman psychiatrist to comment?

Apparently not.

I have great respect for anyone who tries to help others. But doctors are human, and therefore imperfect, just like the rest of us. And as in any profession, some therapists are better than others.

In his book, Pat was dealing with universal themes, and those are the same kinds of themes that appeal to me.

This movie is about love, the love between brothers and sisters, husbands and wives, parents and children, men and women . . . and ultimately I think it's about learning to love oneself as well. Love enhances, it heals, it liberates, it transforms the soul.

The movie is about positive growth. People come to terms with the past and are able to move forward.

I wanted to make a film in which all the characters end up stronger, with a deeper understanding and appreciation for life itself, with all its complexities, joys, and sorrows.

On March 4, 2016, Pat Conroy died. Just writing those words brings tears to my eyes. He was only seventy years old . . . far too young, far too talented, and far too sweet and kind to leave us. When I heard the news, I was devastated. I lost a dear friend, and the world lost a great writer. He had so much more to give, and he was so generous with his time, his insights, and his emotions.

I wish I could call him up and hear his lilting Southern voice again . . . talk to him . . . complain to him . . . dance with him once more . . . and hug him for a long, long time.

I was so glad that I had recently taken the opportunity to tell him just how much he meant to me, in a letter I sent for his seventieth birthday. Here's how I ended it:

> *I once read an interview where you were quoted as saying that working with me was like working with the goddess Athena. That was extremely generous of you.*

If I'm Athena, you're my Apollo . . . the god of poetry, truth, and music. Your natural language is poetry . . . you write sentences that are like an incantation. You observe every nuance of human behavior and dig deep down to the truth . . . presenting it in all its glorious and stubborn complexity. And as far as music goes . . . let's just say you can come back and dance with me any time!

I'm sending you all my love and gratitude.

Barbra

FORTY-SIX

Just for the Record

I can't recall who was the first person to suggest that I write an autobiography, but I do remember how excited I was in 1984 when Jacqueline Kennedy Onassis, who was working as an editor for Doubleday, approached me. Everyone else had been easy to put off, for the simple reason that I was way too busy, and frankly, I thought at forty-two I was too young, with much more work still to come. But I had great respect for Jackie and felt the least I could do was listen to what she had to say. I cherished the memory of meeting President Kennedy at the White House Correspondents' Dinner, but I had never met her.

So I invited Jackie to come have tea with me. We sat in front of the big fireplace in my living room, where we were surrounded by floor-to-ceiling books (I knew she would like that room), and talked. She really did speak in that low, hushed, breathless voice that I first heard on TV. And there was that famous face, very pretty, with big, wide eyes that were almost too far apart. But what some might consider a flaw was in fact what made her even more beautiful . . . and more memorable, because it was unique to her.

I found her very engaging and surprisingly open for someone who had spent her life in the public eye. She projected a sincerity and almost an innocence that was unusual. And she was as curious about me as I was about her!

I saved the thank-you note she wrote me after our tea, which said in part:

> ***I think you have an extremely moving book inside you. Should you decide you want to bring it forth, it would be a wonderful experience to help you do so.***
>
> ***We are all inspired and sustained by other people's lives. We learn as much from each person's search as we do from the answers they find.***
>
> ***Your book would bring a lot to people, and I think doing it would be very enlightening for you.***

That was intriguing, but I was reluctant to commit to anything at that time. I was still very involved with *Yentl* . . . in March and April I was in Europe and Israel for more premieres, doing press conferences and TV appearances. Then I had to start work on the *Emotion* album. And besides all that, the thought of isolating myself in a room again to write, so soon after *Yentl*, wasn't appealing.

Still, the idea was in my head, and sometimes, late at night when I was alone, I used to think about how the book might begin, and jot down a few sentences . . .

Then life got in the way, and I was too busy living it to sit down and write about it.

Meanwhile, I had another idea for an album, which turned into an autobiography of sorts . . . a musical autobiography called *Just for the Record.* The plan was to pull together all this historical material that people would never get to hear otherwise, and it was one of those projects that just kept growing as I worked on it over the years. Eventually it got too big for one record and was finally released in September 1991 (three months before *The Prince of Tides*) as a boxed set of four CDs and a ninety-two-page booklet, where I shared some thoughts about each song. The first two CDs cover the 1960s, then there's one each for the '70s and the '80s.

This project was unlike anything else I'd ever done. It wasn't just a collection of recordings . . . it was a glimpse behind the scenes. Listening to those tracks was like stepping back in time. I could almost relive my life, hearing that young girl grow up and feeling all those emotions again, as memories of those moments came back to me.

I always knew that I wanted it to begin with that scratchy 78 rpm acetate disc of "You'll Never Know" that I made in 1955 when I was thirteen. And I thought it should end with that same song, only this time it would be a duet, with me singing along with my younger self and then finishing the song alone. In between would be all sorts of material, like tapes from my early TV appearances, including the duet I sang with Judy Garland on her variety show in 1963.

You have to remember that there was no YouTube back then, and no way to easily access these vintage shows. In fact it took years for us to track down all the various performances. And in many cases the news was disappointing. We found out that some programs had simply been erased, or taped over when they did another show. The only way to retrieve them was if some fan had happened to record the show off his TV, so Marty put out an announcement and asked people to share anything they had with us, which was clever. (That's Marty, who always had good ideas.)

I'm so grateful that my final performance of *Funny Girl* on Broadway was taped, so you can hear "I'm the Greatest Star" and "My Man" as I sang them that night. You can also listen to the one public performance I ever gave of the alternate version of "The Way We Were." Marvin and the Bergmans actually wrote two songs for the movie, because they finished the first one eight weeks before it was needed, and Alan decided they might as well try to top themselves. Both were good, and the only way to decide which to use was to put them both up against the movie. It was very clear. One worked. The other didn't. I dubbed the second song "The Way We Weren't."

Some of the tracks are very personal, like a tape recording of my mother singing "Second Hand Rose," which happened to be in the same key as my version from *My Name Is Barbra*, so it segues into that.

But one of the big highlights for me was excerpts from the night in 1969 when I was honored as Entertainer of the Year by the Friars Club. Seven of America's greatest composers . . . Harold Arlen, Jule Styne, Richard Rodgers, Harold Rome, Cy Coleman, Jerry Herman, and Burton Lane . . . each sat down at the piano and sang one of their songs, with special lyrics written for me (the great Sammy Cahn helped with those, I heard). Imagine how I felt, as a relative newcomer, watching these theatrical legends sing my praises!

Here are some snippets. To the tune of "Come Rain or Come Shine," Harold Arlen, whom I had revered ever since I was eighteen, sang:

I'm gonna love you like nobody's loved you
Come Ray or come Stark.
My Brooklyn princess who eats her cheese blintzes
Above Central Park.

To the tune of "Time After Time," Jule Styne sang:

Time after time, I tell myself that I'm
So lucky to be Jule Styne.

That brought down the house, and when everybody finally stopped laughing, Jule continued:

When things seemed so dark
I walked up to Ray Stark
And I said "Please meet a friend of mine."
Ms. Streisand sang and I played
He said, "She looks just like my maid" . . .
Which just goes to show
How much producers know . . .

And it finished with Richard Rodgers, who rewrote his own lyric to "The Sweetest Sounds," and spoke the new lines to the music:

The sweetest sounds she's ever made
Are still inside her head
The best reviews she's ever had
Are waiting to be read.
The notes that issue from her throat
Will still be lovely things

And the world will know its happiest times
When wondrous Barbra sings.

I had auditioned for Eddie Blum, the casting director for Rodgers and Hammerstein, when I was a teenager, but I had never met the illustrious Mr. Rodgers. And here he was singing about me!

Just for the Record also includes songs from projects that for one reason or another were abandoned . . . like two wonderful songs from an unfinished album that would trace the life cycle of a woman from birth to death. Michel Legrand had the original concept and wrote some beautiful melodies. Marilyn and Alan Bergman did the lyrics, which I loved. Then on the day in 1973 when we went into the studio to record the first songs, I had an idea. I asked if I could stand in the midst of the orchestra and sing. I felt it would be so inspiring to be surrounded by the musicians rather than off by myself in the vocal booth, behind glass.

It *was* thrilling, but it was an experiment that failed . . . as we found out when it was time to do the mix. It was almost impossible, because my mic had picked up not only my vocal, but also the sound of all the instruments around me. So if we wanted to raise the volume of the violins, my voice would get louder too. And if we tried to tone down the timpani, my voice would get too soft. Eventually we managed to get acceptable versions of a few songs. But I never could relate to the opening and closing songs about birth and death (they were too morbid), and Michel was reluctant to change the music. Meanwhile, we all became involved in other projects and never went back to the album.

And then came some unforgettable moments . . . like the satellite phone conversation I had with Golda Meir for *The Stars Salute Israel at 30* TV special in 1978. Because of the time difference and all the potential technical difficulties, we actually did the telephone call a few days before. I was sitting at the ranch while they had a camera at the former prime minister's home in Israel so they could show her on-screen while I recreated my side of the conversation onstage at the Dorothy Chandler Pavilion. Then, as a finale, I sang "Hatikvah," the Israeli national anthem, while the audience lit candles on both sides of the world . . . because there was an audience in Israel watching the concert via closed-circuit TV.

I was so honored to speak to this brilliant, beloved woman who was instrumental in the founding of the state of Israel. Sadly, only a few months later, she passed away.

I can still see her on-screen, completely unpretentious in her simple housedress, wearing no makeup . . . speaking humbly and smiling warmly, like the quintessential Jewish mother.

After almost ten years, it felt so freeing to finally release *Just for the Record.* I was feeling fulfilled in my work, having completed this and *The Prince of Tides.*

But now I had to promote the movie.

As part of the publicity campaign for *The Prince of Tides*, I agreed to be interviewed by Mike Wallace on *60 Minutes.*

That should tell you right there that I would do almost anything to help my movie. I knew Mike from when I was nineteen and used to go on his old talk show, *PM East*, and I was still wary of him, because he was never particularly nice to me. But *60 Minutes* was a very prestigious show. It would be great exposure for the film, so I let that override any personal concerns.

Of course the way the segment was presented to me was relatively innocuous. In Los Angeles I let down my guard, allowing his crew to follow me around while I worked with the editors to put the final touches on *The Prince of Tides.*

In New York we'd do one of those walks down memory lane, where I'd point out the apartment where I used to live, above Oscar's fish restaurant. And better yet, we'd actually get to go inside. I was curious to see it again, and it was just as small as I remembered, with the makeshift kitchen and a completely useless window in the bedroom, inches from a brick wall.

Then Mike and I sat down for the interview part in my apartment on Central Park West. Leaning back against the rose velvet–covered cushions on my Stickley sofa, I felt a wave of gratitude . . . coming from that railroad flat with a tub in the kitchen to a penthouse apartment with this big, comfortable office furnished with American Arts and Crafts furniture, and a view of the reservoir in Central Park instead of a brick wall.

As the crew was setting up, I asked a question about the lights and made a suggestion to the cameraman, because I knew by now where the light and the camera are best for me. I was just doing what I've done for so long that it's almost automatic, based on what I've picked up over the years from the best in the business, and after all, I had just directed my second movie.

Mike was clearly annoyed and got antagonistic immediately, making some snide remark that ended with could we just "start the interview, please."

It was very condescending, and I knew exactly what he was doing . . . trying to make me look "difficult" . . . which is why I specifically asked him to please not include these preliminaries in the final program (which of course he did anyway).

On camera, he said, "You would love to control this piece."

"Absolutely," I told him. "Are you kidding? Of course! I don't trust you."

There it was again . . . that old question of control. Of course I want to control my work, and how it's presented. If I were a male director, would he even ask the question?

And I went on to explain, "If I'm dealing with people who care about their work like I care about mine, they don't think I'm difficult because they have the same need for excellence. They're striving for the same thing. It's not *difficult.* As a matter of fact, it's fun" . . . to be specific, to care about every detail, to want the best.

But he couldn't hold that positive note. His shtick was to conduct an interview like a cross-examination. All he was interested in was the drama of negativity and conflict. He was like a lion, circling his prey, and he went straight for the jugular when he said, "You know something? I really didn't like you back thirty years ago."

Now, how was I supposed to respond to that? I said the first thing that came into my mind. "How come?"

Before answering, he said, "And I don't think you liked me either."

I told him the truth. "I thought you were mean. I thought you were very mean."

He said, "I didn't think that you paid much attention to me because you were totally self-absorbed back thirty years ago when we worked together."

Now that's interesting. So I wasn't paying enough attention to *him*?

"Wait, wait, wait," I said, "I resent this." You invited me as a guest on your show and asked me questions about myself, and when I answered them, you thought I was self-involved?

I truly didn't understand.

Maybe he didn't like the fact that I used to ask *him* questions as well . . . or go off on subjects that were intriguing to me, like nutrition. But that's why they kept inviting me back . . . because they thought I was an amusing guest.

And then Mike brought up psychoanalysis, and said, "I ask myself, what is it that she's trying to find out that takes twenty to thirty years?"

"I'm a slow learner."

I was trying to make a joke of it, but that was a low blow. And when Mike kept harping on it, I asked, "Why do you sound so accusatory? Are you against psychotherapy?" (Years later, it came out that he struggled against depression and had even tried to commit suicide. But for decades he said nothing about his own illness and therapy, fearing that it might hurt his career.)

Then Mike brought up the loss of my father in a disparaging tone, and said, "He remains almost desperately important to you, doesn't he?"

Getting a bit emotional, I said, "Yeah, I would have liked to have a father."

He said, "Well, you had a stepfather."

Yes, I had a stepfather, who couldn't hold a candle to my father in terms of education, character, or kindness. Mike refused to believe me when I told him that the man never talked to me, and in that moment he actually reminded me of my stepfather . . . mean. I tried to explain how Lou Kind's behavior made me feel as a child . . . how unseen I felt, how uninteresting I must be. I said, "I just thought that I was awful. I must be so awful."

And then all these memories flooded back, and I just broke down. I started to cry. I couldn't help it. I gestured for the camera to stop. I couldn't continue talking until I composed myself.

And then Mike went in for the kill. He showed me some film of him asking my mother whether she was proud of me, and she said, "Well, who wouldn't be?"

She was very defensive, I noticed. She couldn't say, "Yes, I am proud of her."

And then he looked at me and said, "You know what your mother told me about her relationship with you?"

"What?" I asked, afraid to hear the answer and still holding my wet tissue in my hand.

"She says you haven't got time to be close to anyone."

Well, that was extremely hurtful. It wasn't her words so much as her attitude.

I thought I had transcended the issues with my mother, but this moment brought all that pain back again.

I turned to Mike and said, "You like this . . . that forty million people have to see me do this" . . . break down on national TV.

Somehow I managed to pull the interview back to the film and said, "Here's the truth . . . I wanted to make a very strong point in the movie about grieving, about crying . . . In order to feel joy, you have to be able to feel the pain. I just don't want to have to do it in front of forty million people! It's a kind of private issue, you know."

When the program aired, I was shocked to see how Mike had slanted the story. Rather than focusing on *The Prince of Tides*, the segment seemed more like a therapy session with me. I didn't mind that he used the part where I cried . . . that was the truth . . . but I was dismayed that he left in the one part I had asked him to take out, and in the narration, said mockingly, "Watch *director* Streisand take over."

How demeaning. Women with strong opinions were not exactly hailed at the time (or even now, for that matter), and here he was putting me down and perpetuating the stereotype that it was somehow wrong for a woman to be in control . . . or direct a movie.

I called Mike and told him that I didn't like what he did. I understood his technique and couldn't blame him for trying to be provocative, but his attitude was so dismissive and disdainful.

I said, "Now I know why I never liked you thirty years ago."

And then my jaw dropped when I saw the following week's show. After Mike read some letters from viewers who were offended by his behavior, he announced, "But we also heard from Barbra . . . and she said she loved it."

What? Now I was really furious, because I had said no such thing. He flat-out lied. And being lied to is something I can't forgive.

I called Mike again and said, "How dare you lie? You used me when I was nineteen and now you're using me again, thirty years later!"

I was stunned by his overt hostility. It was only after I did the show that I read an article that mentioned how his parents had shortened their family name from Wallechinsky, and Mike also spoke of his strong Jewish mother, whom he seemed to dislike. Was Mike taking his feelings for her and unconsciously transferring them to me? (Fifteen years later, after being prompted by Lesley Stahl, he did say, "Barbra, I do apologize. I have nothing in the world but respect and admiration for you.")

The whole episode gave me the willies, and I couldn't shake that clip of my mother. It reminded me of something I had seen as a teenager. Edward R. Murrow was interviewing Marlon Brando, who had just won an Academy Award for *On the Waterfront*, and asked Brando's father if he was proud of his son. And his father said, "Well, as an actor, not too proud" . . . that's the part that hit me in the stomach. I felt bad for Marlon as I saw him cringe, and I remember thinking, *Oh my God. His father is just like my mother, so critical.*

And looking back, it's probably another reason why Marlon and I connected so deeply. We could identify with each other's pain.

I've often wondered why we're instinctively drawn to certain people. As Oscar Hammerstein put it so succinctly in a lyric:

Some enchanted evening, you may see a stranger
You may see a stranger across a crowded room
And somehow you know . . .

How do we know? It could be pheromones, or maybe it truly is an electrical current between two individuals. I've read that neurons spark in the brain and stimulate emotions that go out into the universe as brain waves. That makes sense. According to Einstein, everything is energy. I don't pretend to understand this, but I was curious enough to look it up and came across something intriguing. In quantum physics two particles can become inexplicably and inextricably connected, so that whatever happens to one instantly affects the other, even if they're miles apart. It's called "entanglement." And that basically describes love, doesn't it?

I felt that kind of attraction to Brando, and it's happened a few other times in my life . . . a strong connection to certain men. Brando was much older than I was, but in one case, the man was much younger . . . so you never can tell.

In fact, this particular connection was something I never would have predicted.

It began when Steve Wynn, the Las Vegas casino owner, told me he had a friend who "admired" me . . . Andre Agassi.

"Who?"

Since I don't follow sports, I hadn't heard of him. Steve explained that he was a tennis champion and was going to be playing at Wimbledon, so I said, "Oh, wish him well from me."

Then Andre called. He had just seen *The Prince of Tides* and wanted to tell me how much he liked the movie. We ended up talking for two hours.

I did manage to get a look at him on TV when he played at Wimbledon during that summer of 1992, and thought, *He's at the top of his game.* He was also nice-looking, and had good teeth! When he won I sent him a congratulatory telegram. And then there were more phone calls and, eventually, meetings. I liked talking to Andre . . . he was smart, and even more appealing to me, he was emotionally wise beyond his years.

It was a completely unexpected relationship, and it was fun. He sent me six dozen pink and yellow roses after one dinner. He came out to the ranch. I remember playing tennis with him as my partner in doubles (don't laugh), and I was trying so hard that I tore my meniscus. I actually heard it pop, but I didn't want to stop, even to ice it, because I didn't want to look like a wimp.

In September I went with some friends to the U.S. Open in New York to watch him play. When a reporter interviewed me about Andre, I told him what I honestly thought: "He's an extraordinary human being. He plays like a Zen master."

I meant that he was completely focused, and that quote was picked up everywhere, probably because people could sense it was true. When Andre played, he was very in the moment, with that deep animal groan as he hit the ball.

The press was all over us in London the following summer, when I watched Andre compete at Wimbledon. Donna Karan, her husband, Stephan Weiss, and Renata were with me, and there was also another game going on . . . avoiding the tabloid photographers. When Andre joined us for dinner, his driver actually hid him in the trunk of the car (it was funny at the time).

I think my friendship with Andre was just one instance of a whole new receptiveness on my part. I was happy after making *The Prince of Tides*, and I guess a little of its message rubbed off on me. I felt more open to other people, more ready to go out into the world.

When the Women in Film organization asked me to accept the Dorothy Arzner Directors Award (named after the first woman member of the Directors

Guild), I said yes, even though I knew it would mean giving a speech. To be honored as a director was so meaningful to me that I told myself to get past my fear of speaking in public.

They say courage is feeling the fear but doing it anyway.

While I was working on my speech, I kept thinking about the irony of receiving an award named after this pioneering director, when the situation for women in Hollywood hadn't really improved since her time. In fact, it was worse. The kind of gender discrimination I initially faced with *Yentl* was still the rule, not only in my profession but in every aspect of life, and I was sick and tired of it.

The Clarence Thomas hearings were a catalyst for me, as they were for many women. How could these male senators refuse to reopen the hearings when Professor Anita Hill's information first came to light? It was only after seven Democratic congresswomen marched to the Capitol and demanded a delay in the confirmation vote that Hill was allowed to testify. And then the men closed ranks, dismissing her accusations and denying the reality of sexual harassment. And adding insult to injury, they defamed her instead of focusing on the true culprit, Clarence Thomas. It was an appalling spectacle.

So I took my frustration and put it into the speech I gave in June 1992. It was important to me, and I wanted to be absolutely clear and direct. I felt as if I were speaking to all the women in the business who were feeling shortchanged:

Language gives us an insight into the way women are viewed in a male-dominated society . . .

A man is commanding—a woman is demanding.

A man is forceful—a woman is pushy.

A man is uncompromising—a woman is a ball-breaker.

A man is a perfectionist—a woman's a pain in the ass.

He's assertive—she's aggressive.

He strategizes—she manipulates.

He shows leadership—she's controlling.

He's committed—she's obsessed.

He's persevering—she's relentless.

He sticks to his guns—she's stubborn.

If a man wants to get it right, he's looked up to and respected. If a woman wants to get it right, she's difficult and impossible.

If he acts, produces, and directs, he's called multitalented. If she does the same thing, she's called vain and egotistical.

There was more to the speech (which you can find on my website). Point is, there was such a feeling of solidarity in the room. It made me feel bolder. In November I stood up for another cause I fervently supported . . . the fight against AIDS. It was a great honor to receive the Commitment to Life Award from the AIDS Project LA, and especially nice to have my old friend Warren Beatty present it to me. He started off by talking about how we met, when I was sixteen and babysitting for my acting teacher and his wife, and Warren was twenty-one and acting in a play with them in summer stock. He went on to extol my accomplishments over the years and then said, "Nothing's really changed . . . the courage, the honesty, the energy, the generosity . . . and the woman does have a real gift for babysitting!" . . . which got a big laugh.

I walked out from the wings, we shared a hug, and then it was my turn to speak. I was still so angry at the way the government had failed the victims of AIDS. I said, "The malignant neglect of the past twelve years has led to the breakdown of our country's immune system: environmentally, culturally, politically, spiritually, and physically. I keep asking myself, Why was our immune system not stronger? Why did we not have better resistance to that deadly virus of hatred?"

I also sang live that night. I had to, because I realized my own fears about performing live were petty, compared to the need to raise money to fight this disease. Singing was another thing I could do, in addition to contributing dollars to the cause. And luckily, I wasn't singing alone . . . the great Johnny Mathis stepped out from the wings and joined me in a medley of two songs from *West Side Story.*

The audience didn't know it yet, but that duet was actually from my latest album.

In addition to everything else that was going on during this period, I was working on a new project, *Back to Broadway.*

Ever since the success of *The Broadway Album*, I had wanted to do a sequel (and this time the record company was *a lot* more enthusiastic about the idea).

I thought it would be fun to work with Rupert Holmes again. Since I last saw him, he had written his own Broadway musical, *The Mystery of Edwin Drood*, and it wasn't until 1988 that our schedules coincided long enough to record half a dozen songs. But they needed more work, and then I got so deeply involved with *The Prince of Tides* that I had to set the project aside.

In 1992 I picked it up again and turned to David Foster to help me produce. By this time I had a whole new collection of songs I wanted to try.

I had considered "One Hand, One Heart" from *West Side Story* for my first Broadway album but finally decided the song was too short. Still, it was so simple and beautiful, and I suddenly thought, *Why not combine it with "I Have a Love" . . . start and end with that . . . so it would feel like a more complete piece?* It was almost as if the medley was meant to be. Even the lyrics worked well together.

That's when I thought, *I wonder if we could get Johnny Mathis to sing it with me?* Remember, Johnny was my favorite male singer, ever since I first saw him on *The Ed Sullivan Show* when I was fifteen.

Imagine what a thrill it was to sing with him! It felt as if I were fulfilling a childhood dream, and it brought back a rush of memories . . . sitting in that cramped living room, watching him on our little Zenith TV, and wanting desperately to be *somebody*, like him.

I never stopped being starstruck by him. Decades later I practically had to pinch myself when Donna Karan threw a birthday party for me at a little restaurant in Malibu, and Johnny turned up as a surprise guest . . . and sang for me! It's so lovely when you meet someone you've admired from afar, and they turn out to be exactly who you hoped they'd be . . . a real gentleman.

Somehow Andrew Lloyd Webber, who wrote the music for *The Phantom of the Opera*, heard that I was doing a new album and wanted me to consider a new song from his upcoming musical, *Sunset Boulevard.* He called Marty, and Marty put him through to me at the studio. I remember Andrew describing this song, "With One Look," as the standout number, the one that people would leave the show humming. I asked him to play it for me over the phone, but he said that wouldn't do the song justice. He insisted that the only way I could fully appreciate the melody and the lyric was if I came to London so he could play it for me in person.

Well, since I don't like to fly, we sent my new A&R man, Jay Landers, and he came back with two demos . . . "With One Look" and another song from the show, "As If I Never Said Goodbye." I liked the second song even better than the first, and decided to record both of them. They had strong melodies, and the lyrics gave me something to act. Andrew's show was a musical version of Billy Wilder's brilliant film *Sunset Boulevard*, with Gloria Swanson as Norma Desmond, the silent movie star who has outlived her fame. In the musical version, Norma sings "As If I Never Said Goodbye" at the moment when she returns to the sound stages at Paramount, thinking she'll be asked to make a comeback. Only later do we find out that all they really wanted was to borrow her antique car. I found that very poignant.

These new songs were complemented by more Broadway classics, like "Some Enchanted Evening" from *South Pacific*. "I can just hear you singing it," Jay said. "It's perfect for your voice."

Well, all *I* could hear was Ezio Pinza singing it on the original cast album in his amazing operatic voice, but that wasn't my style.

And then I thought, *I'd really like to work with Johnny Mandel*. I had just heard a new album that he produced and arranged for a fabulous singer, Shirley Horn. It was called *Here's to Life,* and oh my God, that woman was an inspiration! I just fell in love with her voice, her piano playing, and Johnny's fantastic charts with those long, sustained string chords.

I told Johnny and David that I didn't want to do "Some Enchanted Evening" the way it had always been done. I was thinking, *If I ever go back to performing in concert again, it's a great lyric for an opening song. So as an actress, how would I imagine it? How do I hear it?*

For me, it was like that moment when I walked into Leslie Caron's house in London and looked around the living room, feeling very timid and alone. She had a lot of interesting guests, but would there be someone I could connect with? And there he was . . . Marlon Brando, of all people.

I wanted to capture that kind of wondrous anticipation, when you're hoping for something extraordinary to happen, in the song. And the way I heard it in my head meant changing the form a bit. I told Johnny and David, "I want to be more tentative at the beginning." I wanted to stop after each phrase, like:

"Some enchanted evening" . . . stop. And then the music should answer me.

"You may see a stranger" . . . stop. And then the music echoes me again.

I said, "I need space, so you feel that hesitancy and yearning. I can't jump in with the next phrase right away."

As we went through the song, I had another thought. "I want to hear something incredible in the middle, just after the bridge . . . a big, swelling emotional transition. It's that moment when two people come together without any words, and it should be electric. I want sparks to fly. I want it to be a musical whirlwind, right before I go into the last verse . . . only this time let's do it with a key change."

I wanted my voice to soar to the heavens . . . and just hoped I could hit those high notes!

Because I was unsure if I could, I asked Johnny to do the arrangement in three different keys . . . that way at least one should work.

By the way, when something is too high for me, my old trick is to ask the arranger to do a "mischievous" key change. What I mean is that it's a hidden key change, where the chords modulate down, yet it sounds as if they're going up. You need an accomplished musician to do this.

Johnny and David are so talented that they understood, and they went off and recorded a demo that just floored me. For that climax they did such an amazing thing . . . I can't explain it technically. But if you put the record on, you can hear it . . . right after "wise men never try." It's thrilling, this crescendo with all the electricity I wanted. The whole combination of instruments was superb. It was even better than I could have imagined . . . so luscious. I didn't have to search anymore. I was fulfilled.

And when I was sequencing the tracks, I decided to start with this song. So it did become my opening number after all, but the performance was on a record rather than on a stage.

I actually had a great time doing this album, and it was the occasion for another treat . . . a lovely reunion with Stephen Sondheim. I wanted to sing "Everybody Says Don't" from *Anyone Can Whistle* because the lyric reflects what I've heard so often in my life! And I had a very distinct concept for the arrangement. I wanted that discordant sound and worked with the orchestrator Bill Ross, who's since become a wonderful friend and has conducted for me in the studio and on tour many times.

I like unexpected juxtapositions. "Everybody Says Don't" is a very fast song, and I thought it would be interesting to put high violins against the low syncopation of the basses. I couldn't name the precise notes I had in mind but could only sing him the angular string lines, which we incorporated into the final arrangement. Bill is amazing at bringing the sounds I hear in my head to life. He's also a master conductor, who always wants a camera in the booth, so he can watch me on a monitor as I sing. He needs to see me because he's so sensitive to the fact that I have to be in the moment, and I never do it the same way twice. I may take longer on a particular phrase or breathe in a different place. It all has to do with the images in my mind and how I'm responding to the music as I'm singing it. Bill can anticipate from one phrase to another, where I'm going and how I'm going to get there, because he can sense where I'm breathing. He's so in the moment with me that he, and consequently the orchestra, literally breathes with me.

The second Sondheim song on the album is "Children Will Listen," which I've adored ever since I saw *Into the Woods*. I thought it was one of the most compelling and perceptive songs I'd ever heard, because it was about the responsibility parents have toward their children, and how their words make an impression that stays with them for the rest of their lives. It really resonated with me. The only problem was that the song in the show was too short!

So I called Steve and asked if he had anything that was cut from the score that we might use to expand it. And it turned out he had these fabulous quatrains, and he adapted them to create a verse and a bridge. Once again I got to watch him take his own song apart and then put it back together again. I'm so grateful to him for his willingness to keep working on something that was already brilliant and reinvent it for me. (I think he just loved challenges.)

That reminds me of another story. I fell in love with another song Steve wrote called "I Remember" and wanted to include it on my *Christmas Memories* album in 2001. The only problem was it had nothing to do with Christmas (other than a mention of snow), so I called him up and said, "Steve, I love this song, but could you get the idea of Christmas in there?"

It was kind of a crazy thing to ask. The song, from a teleplay called *Evening Primrose*, was sung by a girl who had been living in a department store since she was a child (also crazy, as a premise).

But the lyrics were fascinating . . . so simple and poetic, almost like haiku:

I remember sky, it was blue as ink
Or at least I think, I remember sky . . .

And the music was delicate and wistful, and I wanted to sing it right away. That's me . . . instant gratification. I was too impatient to wait for another album.

And Steve came through again. A few days later he sent me a cassette of him singing a new opening verse:

I awake on a chilly Christmas morning, watch the choirs singing carols on TV
I gaze out through my window at a dozen other windows, then I plug in my artificial tree
And like a dream I begin to remember every Christmas I used to know
A thousand miles away, a million years ago

It's quirky and unusual, just like the rest of the song, and Bill Ross outdid himself on this arrangement. (It's one of my favorites.)

Back to *Back to Broadway.* I also wanted to sing Steve's glorious song "Move On," from *Sunday in the Park with George.* It sent chills up my spine when I first heard it on Broadway, because it so perfectly captured the truth that even in a relationship that fails, there is something of value. And the trick is to learn from it:

Stop worrying where you're going, move on
If you can know where you're going, you've gone
Just keep moving on . . .
I chose and my world was shaken, so what?
The choice may have been mistaken, the choosing was not
You have to move on

Another great song to act. And the melody is so beautiful. In the show, the song is performed as a duet, and I asked Steve if he could remake it into a solo piece for me. I suggested that perhaps he could incorporate some of another song from the show, "We Do Not Belong Together," and clearly we were on the same wavelength, because he told me that "Move On" was originally conceived as an extension of that song.

It was so exciting to watch this new version emerge, and I decided it was the ideal message to end the album.

Steve was so emotionally astute. He wrote so eloquently about love in all its manifestations, which is interesting to me because we both grew up with mothers who were withholding, who didn't express their love. I wonder if that's another reason why we always connected.

One more story about Steve. In 2016, for my *Encore* album, we worked together on five more of his songs, including another from *Evening Primrose* called "Take Me to the World." As always I was closely examining every line, and there were things I wanted to discuss with him. Some were minor adjustments, like changing "the world" to "a world" in one line. But there happened to be one line that really bothered me. The character wants the man to take her out into the world, and she says, "Let me be a world with you." When I first read it, I thought, *Huh?* It didn't even make sense. I thought it should be "Let *it* be a world with you."

I couldn't believe Steve had written it the other way. And guess what? He didn't.

I told him to look at the sheet music he sent me, and he said, "Oh my God. It's transcribed wrong." (That happens more than you might think.)

He said he had never noticed the mistake before. My thought about how it should read turned out to be what he had originally written!

Back to Broadway was a milestone in my career . . . my fiftieth album for Columbia, and the first to debut at number 1 on the charts when it was released in June 1993. That made the record company *really* happy.

And for me personally, there's a whole other layer of emotion I associate with this album, because there was another Steve in my life. As I wrote in my liner notes, "This album is dedicated to the memory of my dear friend Steve Ross . . . who will live in my heart forever."

Here's what most people might know about Steve. He was an incredibly successful businessman who took over Warner Bros. when the studio was in a slump and built it into the largest media and entertainment company in the world at the time. He was a visionary who anticipated the impact of cable TV and video games, a brilliant boss who hired talented people and encouraged them to take risks.

But that résumé barely begins to describe him. To me he was more than a friend. He was a father figure because he was everything I imagined my father would have been . . . kind, generous, and loving.

When Marty was negotiating for me to do *What's Up, Doc?* for Warner Bros., I said, "Maybe Warners could buy my New York town house as part of the deal." Remember, I had bought it on the rebound after being rejected by two co-op boards. The whole experience had made me feel so unwelcome in my own city that I decided to move to LA.

I really needed to get this house off my hands, and Steve Ross, as head of the company, apparently said, "I'll buy it" . . . solving my problem in one fell swoop. Later I heard Warners resold it at a profit. That's typical of Steve. He was a fabulous dealmaker.

I know I thanked him profusely when we met, and he made a great impression on me. Steve was very tall, with white hair, very distinguished looking, an elegant man with the sweetest smile. Super smart, but also very nice.

When I was producing *A Star Is Born* for Warners, most Hollywood executives tended to dismiss Jon Peters. But Steve took the time to meet with him privately . . . the two of them went for a long ride in Jon's red Ferrari . . . and he never said anything disparaging about Jon. Very classy. Perhaps Steve wasn't worried about him because he knew he could rely on me to be responsible for this movie, since I had final cut.

And I could rely on Warners to support my vision.

They once also rescued me from the vacation in hell. Jon and I, with our kids, along with friends and their kids, had rented houseboats on Lake Powell. And then everything that could possibly go wrong went wrong. Our friends' boat broke down, so suddenly we had eleven people on ours, with only one tiny bathroom. And then the rains came, and the water got rough. Winds were rocking the boat, and bats were swooping down at night. All I could think of was rabies, because Robert Redford had been bitten by a bat on Lake Powell just before we started filming *The Way We Were*, and had to undergo weeks of painful injections in his stomach. Just the thought of those shots made me feel sick. And then Jon drove the boat into a sandbar.

That was it. I called Warners and said, "Get me out of here!"

I should explain that Steve was very good to his friends. He allowed us to use the company plane, and it took me lots of places over the years. This time they had to send a little plane to fit a very short runway. When we saw it touch down, it was like the gods descending from heaven.

I did two more movies . . . *The Main Event* and *Nuts* . . . at Warners with Steve's colleagues Bob Daly and Terry Semel, and we all became friends. I also have fond memories of working with Rob Friedman and Joe Hyams on publicity. We were a close and loving team. I miss those days and those relationships.

Steve, his wife, Courtney, and I instantly bonded. She and I went to the Golden Door once . . . she was trying to gain weight, and I was trying to lose weight. But I ate all the cookies she left on her plate and ended up gaining five pounds.

Sometimes we'd go out to dinner with Quincy Jones (who was their dear friend, as well as mine) and laugh so much it hurt. We would vacation together, flying on the company plane down to the Warners' villa in Acapulco. Steve and I both loved a candy bar we used to eat as kids in Brooklyn . . . Goldenberg's Peanut Chews . . . and every Warners' plane was stocked with them. That was dangerous. Whenever I walked by the food, I would take one. Or he might fly us to the Bahamas in the winter, and we'd play backgammon in the sand. Steve was a champion player, as well as being an amazing card shark (so adept that he was banned from Las Vegas because of his talents, like dealing thirds and counting cards). He could even do magic tricks with cards and was kind enough to show me some (which of course I instantly forgot).

And he was the undisputed champion when it came to giving gifts. He took great joy in surprising people he loved with things that he knew would excite them.

I remember when I tried to buy an Art Deco sculpture by Boris Lovet-Lorski at auction. But I didn't bid high enough, so I lost it. Months later, when I got off the plane in New York from Europe after shooting *Yentl*, I wanted to visit some art galleries, and there was the same sculpture! Only now it was three times more expensive, and I thought, *No, I can't pay that price for it.* And then a couple of weeks later, Steve and Courtney gave a dinner party for me at their New York apartment. Pierre Trudeau was my escort, and as Steve was showing us around and we were admiring their dazzling art collection, we went up the staircase, where I spotted this same sculpture at the top, sitting on a gorgeous Josef Hoffmann pedestal.

I was so excited that I shouted, "Oh my God, you have that sculpture! I'm so glad it belongs to people I love."

I told Steve the story about losing it at auction, and he said, "Open the card."

What card? I hadn't even noticed it, tucked behind the statue. So I opened it and for a moment I couldn't quite comprehend what I was reading.

It said the sculpture was a gift to me for finishing *Yentl* . . . a movie that wasn't even for Warner Bros.!

I'll never forget that moment.

I tried so hard to give Courtney and Steve equally thoughtful gifts in return, but it was difficult to compete. After they invited me to join them on one of their boat trips (Steve introduced me to the concept of a private cruise, and always knew the best boats to rent), I found a nineteenth-century Noah's ark in perfect condition, with all the little pairs of animals, at a folk art auction. I was so happy when I saw it displayed in a special case in their East Hampton home.

At least I was able to rise to Steve's defense in 1984 when Rupert Murdoch was threatening a hostile takeover of Warner Bros. I wrote a letter to Steve in support that was circulated to the shareholders and said, in part, "Due to the present circumstances, I find it necessary to tell you if for any reason you are not with Warner Brothers, I would choose not to be there either." I hope it helped a bit. In any event, Steve survived the challenge and the company prospered.

I wanted him to know he could count on me, because I knew I could count on him. He was endlessly generous, and his generosity extended to the world. Steve was a true humanitarian, contributing to an array of worthy causes. He was also a major contributor to the building at Hebrew University named after my father, for which I will always be grateful.

Then, in 1985, I got a call from Courtney. She told me Steve had been operated on for prostate cancer, and the surgery was successful. But when we hung up, I started to cry, realizing how much he meant to me. In my journal I wrote, "He's such a good human being. Why does he have to get sick? Why does he have to be in pain . . . go through fear and anxiety. It's not fair."

Thank God he recovered, and we went on to share more good times. I've already written about the boat trip we took through the Greek islands in 1989, when I was preparing *The Prince of Tides.* Clearly his fellow businessmen knew Steve to be a good negotiator, but they should have seen him in Bodrum, Turkey, bargaining for seventy-eight pairs of pointed Turkish slippers to give to his friends . . . or on the streets of Corfu, bargaining with a vendor for beaded bracelets and caftans. In other words, he *loved* to negotiate. Typical of Steve, he wanted to share something in return, so he gave them paraphernalia from the Warners' movie *Batman*. Our boat was laden with huge duffel bags stuffed with *Batman* gear . . . T-shirts, caps, jackets, sweatshirts, watches, hats. And as we left every port, we would see all these vendors lined up and waving good-bye, in their full *Batman* regalia. It was quite a sight.

And then Steve, who considered himself a very lucky man, ran out of luck. In the fall of 1991, I was devastated when I learned that his cancer had returned, and he started another round of chemotherapy. When I had the first screenings of *The Prince of Tides*, he was too ill to come. Then, in October 1992, he underwent another radical surgery. I remember the moment when I got a call from Steve. He said, "Are you sitting down?" And then he told me that the cancer was gone.

I was ecstatic, so relieved and happy for him. That's when I decided to get him the most beautiful pocket watch I could find . . . platinum and black onyx Art Deco made by Cartier in 1925. It was technically for his birthday in April, but I couldn't wait and decided to give it to him early as a recovery gift. I had it engraved on the back: "Cherish the time . . . as I cherish you. Love, Barbra."

But it turned out that the cancer wasn't gone after all, and on December 20, 1992, Steve died. I flew out for the funeral on the Warners' plane, along with all the Warners' people he loved, like Bob, Terry, Quincy, and others. The ceremony was held at the Guild Hall in East Hampton, and more of his dear friends, like Steven Spielberg and Dustin Hoffman, were there. I could barely hold it together, but I did manage to get up and say a few words to Steve:

> *I'll always remember the times we spent together . . . the fun, the games, the trips. You taught me the true art of bargaining. You tried to teach me how to enjoy life every minute, and like you, to be very generous. Because in the long run, what matters is not how rich you are when you leave this earth, but how rich your life was . . . in dreams fulfilled, in friendships, in loving and being loved . . . for how many people carry you around in their hearts after you're gone.*
>
> *And we all know you're here in spades, Steve, with a list a mile long. We will carry you around forever.*
>
> *He wasn't my father, but I loved him . . . I love you, Steve, as if you were my father.*

This is for you . . . and especially your children, Mark, Toni, and for you, Nicole.

And then I *tried* to sing "Papa, Can You Hear Me," which wasn't easy since I was choking back tears . . . but it was the least I could do for the second father I lost.

FORTY-SEVEN

Politics

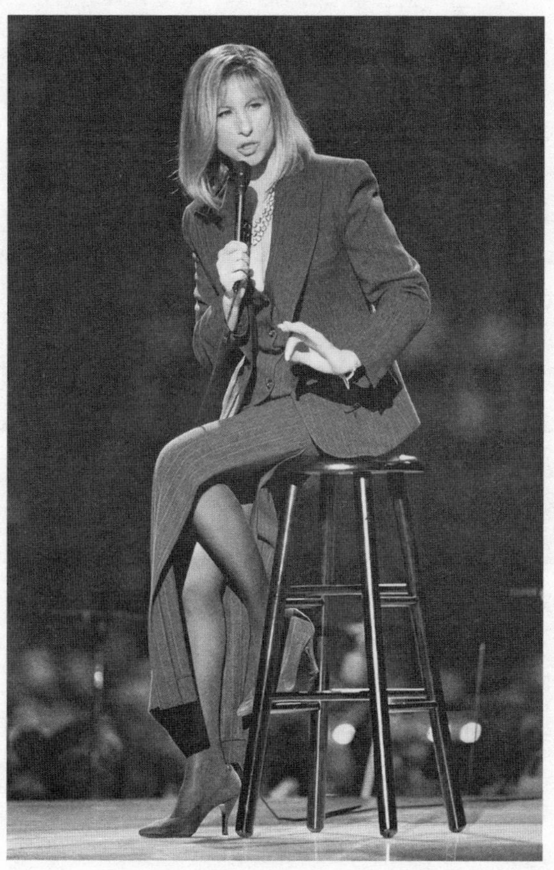

In 1992, after eight years of Ronald Reagan and four years of George H. W. Bush . . . with tax cuts for the rich, cuts in programs for the poor, corporations favored over people, and the savings and loan crisis . . . I wanted a Democrat in the White House. At first I was supporting Senator Tom Harkin of Iowa, and then my friend Mike Medavoy took me to hear another candidate . . . the young, largely unknown governor of Arkansas, Bill Clinton.

I listened to him speak and was blown away. He knew both his history and the current state of the country, which gave him complete command of the issues. Even more unusual, he could take a complicated subject and explain it in such simple terms that anyone could understand. To me the problems facing us were overwhelming . . . social injustice, gender inequality, nuclear proliferation, climate change. But Bill Clinton seemed to think that if there was a problem, there must also be a solution. And it felt as if he were enjoying the challenge! Everything he said made sense, and the policies he proposed were clear and detailed.

I thought to myself, *This guy could actually get elected.* He had it all . . . mind and heart, intellect and soul. He was smart *and* charismatic . . . a country boy who went on to become a Rhodes Scholar and a Yale Law School grad, yet he still retained that down-home common touch.

Mike was a friend of Bill's and introduced me to him, but it was a brief moment, in a hallway. We didn't talk that night. Still, he made a vivid impression. I was thrilled when he won the nomination and chose Al Gore, who shared my concern for the environment, as his vice president. I wanted to do whatever I could to help them get elected. So when the Hollywood Women's Political Committee was planning a fundraiser in September, I agreed to sing. And that's where I had my first real opportunity to talk to Bill and Hillary Clinton, as we sat together at a dinner table in the producer Ted Field's backyard.

They were the most appealing couple. She was just as sharp as he was, but seemed a bit shy in front of the crowd . . . something I recognized. But Bill was in his element, genuinely delighted to meet everyone who approached him. He seemed to be more engaged in life than anyone else around. And the kind of interest and attention he gave to each person was compelling. It drew people in and made them feel special.

As we were chatting he said, "You know, my favorite song of yours is 'Evergreen.'"

"Well, I'm not singing it tonight but I'll tell you what. If you become president, I'll sing it at your inauguration."

I couldn't believe I promised that (me, volunteering to sing in front of millions of people!), but I really wanted this man to get elected. One of the songs

I did sing that night was "It Had to Be You" with new lyrics, written by Marilyn and Alan:

The thought of a change gives me a thrill
Can't wait to call you President Bill
It has to be you
And Hillary too
It has to be you.

The songs and speeches that night were transmitted via closed-circuit television to multiple fundraisers around the country. That was smart, and I remember exactly what I said that night, because I still feel it very strongly. I told the audience that I'm proud to be the "L-word" . . . liberal. And I'm proud to be the "F-word" . . . feminist. And I'm equally proud to be a part of the Hollywood artistic community. Then I looked right at the camera and said, "So yes, I'm proud to be a liberal, feminist, American artist."

And then I went into my final song, "God Bless America." After I finished it, I invited Bill, Hillary, and my fellow artists to join me onstage for a reprise, and we all sang it together. The evening was over. I had already asked a few friends to join me at my house for dessert, and on the spur of the moment, I went up to Hillary and said, "I live just around the corner. I'd love for you and Bill to come over and see my house." And they came!

That was the beginning of our friendship.

Bill and I both grew up without fathers . . . his died three months before he was born. We talked about it when he called to thank me for singing.

I told him, "I never knew my father, and that kind of loss leaves an imprint on your soul."

He knew exactly what I meant.

Both of us were ambitious at a young age, and I wondered if he, too, felt the need to accomplish so much because his father's life was cut so short.

Both of us grew up with stepfathers, and his was also a used-car salesman, like mine. I thought that was an amazing coincidence, along with the fact that we both happened to meet President John F. Kennedy in the same year, 1963, when I sang for him at the White House Correspondents' Dinner, and sixteen-year-old Bill shook his hand in the Rose Garden.

So even though Bill was from Hope, Arkansas, and I was from Brooklyn, New York, it was easy to relate.

I remember jokingly telling him, "You stole my line!" I was referring to the "I feel your pain" moment from *The Prince of Tides*. Coincidentally Bill had said the same words, and the press turned it into a catchphrase of his campaign, because it captured something essential about his character. The fact is, he did have real empathy for people, and that became clear during the debates.

Before the first one, against George H. W. Bush and Ross Perot, I sent him a telegram and said: "Don't be afraid to let your passion and anger show. The best defense is a strong offense. We honor your convictions and integrity and we will be rooting for you." I was talking to him like a director.

Frankly, he didn't need my help. On November 3, Bill Clinton and Al Gore were elected.

That was exhilarating. It felt as if there were a new spirit in the air. I don't think there's ever been anything quite like their inauguration. Every entertainer you could think of wanted to participate. To start things off on Sunday, January 17, Quincy Jones produced a free concert at the Lincoln Memorial, featuring a fantastic lineup, from Diana Ross to opera singer Kathleen Battle. I stopped by to see Quincy, and we went out together afterward to celebrate.

I had agreed to sing at the Presidential Gala on Tuesday (the night before the inauguration), along with stars like Aretha Franklin, Michael Jackson, Judy Collins, Chuck Berry, and Fleetwood Mac.

That day, driving to Landover for the performance, the traffic was bad, and it was taking too long, even though we had a police escort. Jason, Richard Baskin, Donna Karan, and Stephan Weiss had come with me to Washington. (Donna had made Clinton's suit for the inauguration.) We were all in one car. And then my friend Ellen and her husband at the time, Bruce Gilbert, and their kids couldn't get a cab, so I asked if they could ride in the police car. Bruce happened to mention it would be fun to drive it . . . and the federal marshal tossed him the keys! They were in front of us, and as we kept getting slowed down, I remember thinking, *Put on the sirens!* And he did, so we could speed through a few intersections. The kids loved it.

Eventually we arrived in plenty of time. So that was it. No excuse. I had to sing. I was scared but excited. It was such an amazing thing to finally have a president whose values reflected mine.

I was the last to go on. Warren Beatty and his wife, Annette Bening, introduced me. I told the story about Bill and "Evergreen" and said, "This is a promise I'm delighted to keep." The atmosphere was electric. We were all so happy to be there. Bill was beaming.

Then I did "Children Will Listen," a Sondheim song I had chosen with Hillary in mind, because she has always been a forceful advocate for children. I was a little hoarse that night, and I apologized, saying, "Thank God the president-elect has made it fashionable." That got a laugh, and then I went on to something more serious. "I'm thankful for the blessings bestowed upon us . . . the richness and beauty of our land, the diversity of our people, and especially for the new leadership which will take us forward to a time of hope and healing." The audience applauded. I continued, "I'm thankful for our new vice president, because in your hands I know the planet will have a true and devoted caretaker." More applause. "And I am *so* grateful for our new president, who carries the burdens of our expectations in this unsettled world. The tasks are overwhelming, but you inspire in us a confidence and trust . . . a positive sense of the future that is new and wonderful. I pray for your health, your stamina, and your joy in the work that lies before you. We are all of us truly blessed."

That was the lead-in to my final song, "God Bless America." I found it incredibly moving to stand there and sing it for this man . . . with tears welling in my eyes . . . because we were all wishing the best for him, and for our beloved country.

And then I had the honor of introducing the forty-second president of the United States. Bill Clinton made his way up onto the stage, and we shared a long, heartfelt hug. The whole auditorium erupted in applause that just wouldn't stop. It was a glorious moment, and I was so proud to be part of it.

The next morning we all watched Bill and Al take the oath of office in the freezing cold. My fingers felt frostbitten, even though I was wearing gloves tucked inside a fur muff. With my long gray wool coat and a Russian fur hat, I looked like a Cossack (as Jule Styne used to say).

That night we got all dressed up for the Arkansas Ball and walked into a convention center that was standing room only, jammed with people. We were ushered into some sort of holding area. By this time I was starving, and looking around desperately for food. I didn't see any . . . maybe the Democrats were trying to save money! That's when I bumped into Hillary's mom, Dorothy Rodham.

We were talking, and then we heard someone shout, "They're here! The president's coming!" A man motioned for us to follow him, and suddenly Richard, Donna, Stephan, Bruce, Ellen, and I found ourselves up onstage, standing next to Bill's mother, Virginia Clinton, and Chelsea.

Bill introduced his family to the crowd and I thought, *How sweet* . . . and stayed off to the side, while he spoke for a few moments and thanked everyone. He and Hillary, who looked absolutely radiant, danced together. And then the great Ben E. King handed Bill his sax, and the president of the United States played "Your Mama Don't Dance" with the band, and the crowd went wild. We were all giddy with joy.

In the midst of the festivities, with all the attention focused on the new president, he still thought about his brother. Bill turned to his mother and said, "Roger's singing next door at the MTV Ball. You best get over there." And then he turned to me: "Barbra, why don't you go with Mother."

I looked at her and said, "Do you mind if I come with you?"

That was the night I met Virginia Clinton.

She took me by the hand and we walked off together. At that moment Richard took a photo of the two of us, from the back (I love pictures from the back, because they're revealing in a whole other way), and that photo is one of my most treasured possessions. It marks the beginning of a remarkable relationship. Virginia was such a warm, loving, and supportive woman. It was easy to see where Bill Clinton got those same qualities.

After the MTV Ball, I remember sitting down on some wide carpeted steps . . . my feet hurt and I had to take off my shoes. That's when Al Gore happened to walk by, and we had a great chat (while his aide kept saying, "Mr. Vice President, we have to go"). Ted Kennedy was giving an after-party, and my friends and I also went to that. (I had known him since we met at the *Funny Lady* premiere.)

This inauguration was a splendid moment in time. It felt as if the whole country was celebrating with us. CBS paid more than $8 million to televise the Presidential Gala, one reporter wrote, "only because Streisand had promised to sing" . . . and that money went toward the cost of the inauguration. It made me feel good that I might have helped in some little way.

So imagine my surprise a week later when someone showed me the front page of the *New York Post*, blazoned with the headline: SENATOR YENTL. They had twisted whatever I said at the inauguration into a story claiming that I was planning to run for the Senate . . . against Democrat Patrick Moynihan.

Usually I don't bother to respond to this kind of nonsense, but in this case I quickly issued a statement that I was *not* running for anything. I explained, "There should be no confusion between someone with political passion and someone with political ambition."

Trust me, the last thing I want is to wake up every morning and go to Congress. I already have acid reflux.

Then, the following day, I opened *The New York Times* and saw a caricature of me on the Op-Ed page, accompanying an article that was also criticizing me . . . not for anything substantive, but for what I *wore* at the Presidential Gala.

Really?

I suppose my outfit was a bit unconventional. I had seen a charcoal-gray pinstriped wool daytime suit with a short skirt in Donna's showroom, and it was exactly the sort of thing I liked and felt comfortable in. Then, in order to dress it up for evening, I asked her if she could make me a full-length skirt and a vest to go with the jacket, and that's what I had on that night. The long, slim skirt had a slit up the side, and I wore the vest instead of a blouse, with a three-strand nineteenth-century diamond necklace (which I had also worn during the dinner-party scene in *The Prince of Tides*). Again, I seem to be drawn to that masculine-feminine dichotomy . . . a menswear fabric on a woman.

So what was this writer (a woman, by the way) objecting to? Was it a crime to have worn a tailored suit rather than a fancy gown? Apparently so, because she critiqued it for being "a mixed metaphor—a woman letting us know that underneath her peekaboo power suit, underneath all her bravado and accomplishments, she is still an accessible femme fatale."

Yeah, that's right!

At first I took it as a compliment until I realized what she was actually implying. In other words, How dare I wear a suit that looked powerful as well as alluring? She denounced it as a "disturbing signal," and "a coy mixed message," but frankly, what's wrong with that mix? I believe women are many things. Was this writer so narrow minded that she would deny all our capabilities? Aren't women more complex than that?

Why can't women be accomplished *and* attractive, strong *and* sensitive, intelligent *and* sensual?

In other words, we're both. It's not either/or . . . like that age-old stereotype of the madonna and the whore. Society has been trying to put us into one box or the other for centuries. But looking at this outfit now (because I certainly didn't analyze it before I decided to wear it), I see that it represented a more multifaceted vision of women. It was a masculine-looking suit with a glimpse of leg, a hint of cleavage that accentuates the feminine. And why should femininity be fatal? That's another myth, like Circe or the Sirens. Okay, blame the women! Again, it's men not wanting to take responsibility for their own sexual impulses . . . and maybe also not allowing women to feel those impulses as well.

I was interested to see that several men came to my defense in the Letters to the Editor column . . . "Keep the peekaboo power suit, Barbra; you earned it." But the best response was from feminist scholar Camille Paglia, who wrote, "Barbra Streisand looked spectacular. Radiating molten sexuality and stunning artistic power, she nearly upstaged President Clinton. She was all man and all woman."

I loved that. She certainly got the message and had no problem with it.

Singing at the inauguration was an honor, and it really sparked my curiosity.

Now I became a political junkie. I subscribed to *The Nation* and *The Economist.* I had to be up on every issue, and things in Washington were happening fast. This president had already gotten the Family and Medical Leave Act passed, lifted the ban on fetal tissue research, and eliminated the gag rule on doctors at public health clinics. He was pushing the "Motor Voter" bill through Congress so people could vote more easily, and he was determined to tackle another major challenge . . . the soaring cost of health care, which I was concerned about too.

In March I was invited, along with Mike Medavoy, to attend a briefing by the health-care task force. We were part of a Hollywood contingent that was there to offer advice on communications and marketing . . . how to get the administration's message across to the public.

And most exciting of all, we got to stay at the White House . . . Mike and his wife in the Lincoln Bedroom and me in the Queens' Bedroom, where so many royal guests, including Queen Elizabeth, have slept.

The room was beautiful, with a mahogany four-poster bed topped with a canopy, and dusty-rose walls with white trim. An elegant butler, wearing gloves, helped me and the Medavoys get settled after we arrived on Friday evening. Then we went over to the West Wing and met Betty Currie, Bill Clinton's personal secretary, and Marsha Scott, who headed the personnel office (two lovely women who became my friends). Bill must have stepped out of the Oval Office for a moment to say hello, because I remember him telling us that he'd join us as soon as he could, and to get comfortable.

Once we were back upstairs, I took the president at his word and changed into my sneakers, with pants and a big sweater. Then Bill was knocking on our doors and asked if we would like a tour. I had never spent any time at the White House, and I had no idea how moving it would be to walk through those rooms where so much history had been made. Clinton had only been living there for two months, but he already knew the stories behind every painting . . . like the Gilbert Stuart portrait of George Washington, saved by Dolley Madison, who had it taken down and carried off in a wagon just before the White House was burned by the British during the War of 1812. If there was a battle scene, he knew the date and place of the battle and how it had turned out.

He led the way into the Blue Room with its gilded French Empire furniture. Then came the Red Room, where Jackie Kennedy chose American Empire furniture with neoclassical motifs. But the real revelation for me was the quiet beauty of the eighteenth-century American furniture in the Green Room. These chairs and tables did not rely on gilt to attract attention. Instead, all you had to focus on were the pure, graceful lines, the grain of the wood, the elegant carving, the impeccable joinery. It was simple and understated. You could see the touch of the hand in every detail. No wonder some of the makers signed their pieces.

Standing there I was so proud to be an American, and so inspired, that I began to collect eighteenth-century American furniture, and ended up redoing my New York apartment and filling it with the best examples I could find.

Eventually we worked our way down to the movie theater. A bunch of staffers were there, watching a basketball game. I picked up a bag of popcorn, but we ended up sitting and talking in another room with more of Bill's friends. I had brought him an early copy of my new album, *Back to Broadway*, and he wanted to play it for everyone, even though I could see he was tired.

Saturday morning was the health-care summit. This administration was ambitious enough to try to improve the system, even though they knew how hard it would be. Bill had appointed Hillary to head the task force, but she wasn't there for this meeting because her father had suffered a stroke back in Little Rock, and she was at the hospital with him. So I didn't hear her speak that day, but I still remember how articulate and well informed she was when she testified before Congress later in September, answering hundreds of questions. It was a dazzling performance. She was a woman ahead of her time, and she was punished for it.

Bill Clinton and Al Gore were scheduled to attend the annual Gridiron Club dinner that night, and somehow Mike, his wife, and I got to tag along. I didn't have a long dress . . . I didn't know we'd be going to anything fancy . . . but I had a black skirt and a black top that was long enough that I could pull the skirt down, so it looked a bit more formal. Virginia Clinton, who was also staying at the White House that weekend, told me about the White House hairdresser, and we went together that afternoon to have our hair done. We sat under the hairdryers, talking, and then every time we remembered where we were, we would start to giggle.

At the dinner that night, the president and vice president were roasted in silly skits and songs performed by otherwise serious journalists. Who knew they could be such hams? (Everybody wants to be in show business!)

When we got back to the White House, instead of going to bed, we stayed up and played hearts with the president late into the night. (He loves games just as much as I do. Needless to say, he won.) The four of us were up in the family's private quarters . . . just a small, comfortable room with a little kitchen where you could make yourself a peanut butter and jelly sandwich (the total opposite of the stately rooms downstairs).

On Sunday I flew back to Los Angeles, and less than twenty-four hours later I was onstage at the Oscars to present the award for Best Director.

The press had dubbed 1992 the "Year of the Woman." But in the November election, out of 434 people elected to the House of Representatives, only 47 were women, and out of 100 people elected to the Senate, only 4 were women (for a grand total of 6 women in the Senate).

Not exactly an earth-shattering showing.

Still, the Academy had picked up on the idea, and the theme that night was "Oscar celebrates women and the movies." Of course there were no women actually nominated as Best Director, once again. Someone suggested that they might have asked me to present this particular award because I was shut out of the category the year before, and the irony of that was not lost on me.

It's always hard to know what to say at moments like these. You want to make a point, but you don't want to be too confrontational. So I thought a lot about it, and in the end, when I walked onstage, I looked out at the audience and said: "Tonight the Academy honors women and the movies. That's very nice, but I look forward to the time when tributes like this will no longer be necessary . . . a time when there couldn't possibly be a year of the woman because there will be so many in prominent positions. This award is not for a woman director or a man director. This award is for the best director, and it is my privilege to present it tonight."

Clint Eastwood won, by the way, for *Unforgiven*, which was nice, because we knew each other. He once asked me to star with him in a movie called *The Gauntlet*, but it was violent, and the idea of playing a role that required being confined inside a bus for weeks was not tempting. Even before that I remember sitting with Clint and his wife at some event, when he touched my ear and said, "You have great ears." That was a very original compliment, I must say.

In May I returned to Washington for the White House Correspondents' Dinner. I wanted to go because the invitation meant something to me . . . thirty years earlier, I sang for President Kennedy at the same event. This time I was there as a guest of *Newsweek*, and Richard Baskin came with me.

I didn't know Washington, D.C., so I had blocked out a week to do all the touristy things I never had time for previously. The U.S. Capitol, the Supreme Court, the Lincoln Memorial . . . all those majestic landmarks were on my list. But what I really wanted to see was something much smaller . . . Monticello, the house Thomas Jefferson designed for himself.

I had read a bit about Jefferson and his many vocations . . . lawyer, linguist, architect, naturalist, inventor. There's that famous line, said by President John F. Kennedy at a dinner honoring Nobel Prize winners: "I think this is the most extraordinary collection of talent, of human knowledge, that has ever been gathered together at the White House, with the possible exception of when Thomas Jefferson dined alone."

I wanted to see how this brilliant man lived, to walk through his rooms. I thought the house he built was stunningly beautiful and also surprisingly modest. There was nothing grandiose. He understood the beauty of simplicity and believed in classical proportions . . . as well as practicality. Cabinets on either side of the dining-room fireplace hid dumbwaiters that brought up wine from the cellar below. A revolving door leading to a passage to the kitchen had rounded shelves on one side, where dishes could be placed and then the door could be spun around to the dining room. How clever!

Like a botanist, Jefferson kept diaries with detailed notes on how his various plants, vegetables, fruits, and flowers were doing. I was charmed by that and always wanted to do something similar for my own garden (but never got around to it).

The biggest discovery for me, though, was that Jefferson entered the competition to design the White House, anonymously . . . and lost. But no matter, as Bill Clinton once said, because he had already designed the architecture of the country, when he drafted the Declaration of Independence. His words still ring out, clear as a bell: "We hold these truths to be self-evident, that all men are created equal, that they are endowed by their Creator with certain unalienable Rights, that among these are Life, Liberty and the pursuit of Happiness."

And yet . . . standing in those rooms, I was haunted by the question: How could the man who denounced slavery as "an abominable crime" and a "moral depravity" continue to enslave people? Weren't they also entitled to life, liberty, and the pursuit of happiness? How could the same person be so judicious and compassionate in the abstract, and yet overlook the reality of the situation in his own home?

Jefferson did not live up to his own ideals. And as a country, we still haven't managed to live up to those words he wrote in the Declaration of Independence either.

After a special tour of the Library of Congress, I went to the National Archives. I was taken down into the basement vaults, where they gave me a pair of gloves so I could touch the old documents. I saw George Washington's first inaugural address, the Monroe Doctrine, and the Louisiana Purchase. And I got to hold the Emancipation Proclamation in my hands. It's surprising how faint the handwriting is. You can barely make out those words that changed the course of the war. I thought about all the bloodshed over that ideal of freedom, how many people died fighting for the words in my hands. It was humbling.

I made a trip to Mount Vernon, George Washington's home, where I asked if Washington had planted any cherry trees, to atone for chopping one down when he was a boy. The curator laughed and told me that famous story was a myth. Apparently it first appeared in a biography, written after Washington's death, by a minister who wanted to promote the president as a role model, so he had him contritely confessing to his father, "I cannot tell a lie." And then the story was reprinted in children's textbooks for over a hundred years.

There it is again . . . the power of the printed word.

I also visited the Smithsonian and spent hours at the Holocaust Memorial Museum watching films about the survivors, who never surrendered to cynicism. That touched me very deeply. One woman spoke of sharing her one piece of bread with somebody who she felt needed it more than she did, and that incredible kindness and selflessness under the most dire circumstances brought tears to my eyes. It reaffirmed my faith in humanity. These people weren't hardened. Despite everything, they still believed in the preciousness of life.

I was invited to lunch by Janet Reno, whom Bill Clinton had named attorney general. That was another milestone. She was the first woman to serve in that position. I liked her immediately. She was so direct and unassuming, and told me, "Every day I'm in the White House, I feel like pinching myself."

Honestly, that whole week in Washington I felt the same way.

And then it happened again. My remarkable trip, this profound learning experience, was completely misrepresented in the newspapers. On the front page of *The New York Times*, Maureen Dowd slammed the Clinton White House for being "star-struck" and simultaneously savaged all the Hollywood stars who had the audacity to take politics seriously. As far as she was concerned, we were taking *ourselves* too seriously.

The photograph they used to represent this was me at the Correspondents' Dinner, talking to General Colin Powell. According to her, I had been discussing "Bosnia and homosexuals in the military" with him. In fact, I knew nothing about Bosnia, and we didn't discuss the military that night because I had already discussed it with him earlier. (Of course I believe gays should be allowed to serve openly in the military. In my humble opinion, anybody who is willing to die for our country deserves complete and total respect.)

I had first met Colin the previous June at the American Academy of Achievement conference, where four hundred of the brightest high school students were invited to hear prominent people discuss the reasons for their success. I had to give a speech, along with the other honorees. That's where I also met Bill

Gates . . . opera singer Jessye Norman . . . and physicist Arno Penzias, who had won the Nobel Prize for his contribution to the Big Bang theory of the universe. (Imagine giving a speech in front of these people!) Also attending were the directors of both the CIA and the FBI (kind of stiff), and Colin's fellow general Norman Schwarzkopf (very warm). Both generals were easy to talk to and we ended up spending a lot of time together.

So when I saw Colin again at the Correspondents' Dinner, we just naturally gravitated to each other. We liked to kid around. He was a boy from the Bronx, and I was a girl from Brooklyn, so we bonded over our backgrounds. And would you believe he spoke Yiddish? (Better than I did, by the way . . . turns out he had worked for a Jewish store owner as a teenager.) I loved his down-to-earth manner, and I was interested in his perspective on the world.

Yet Maureen Dowd was insinuating that my conversation with him and my lunch with Janet Reno were somehow improper, as if I were stepping out of bounds. The criticism was all too familiar. I had already heard, How dare you direct?

Now it was, How dare you be interested in politics?

It felt as if the same people in the press who were going after Clinton were trying to embarrass Colin because of his fleeting association with me. Luckily he took it all in stride and sent me the most charming fax:

> ***Sorry this became a media feeding frenzy for you. I, however, have become the most envied man in the Pentagon. My wife loves the photo. My daughters mumble under their breath about Dad thinking "he's something hot." My son brags to his friends.***
>
> ***When can we do it again, huh, Barbra?***
>
> ***Cheers,***
>
> ***Colin***

In that same *New York Times* article, Maureen's pal Leon Wieseltier, the cultural editor of *The New Republic*, dismissed the whole entertainment industry in one fell quote: "The idea that these insulated and bubble-headed people should help make policy is ridiculous."

Well, first of all, we weren't making policy, and second, I wouldn't call Sid

Sheinberg, the president of Universal Studios, who was one of the attendees at the health-care briefing, "bubble-headed." (Is Robert Redford, who has been defending the environment for decades, a bubblehead? Is Elizabeth Taylor, who was one of the first to speak out for AIDS victims, a bubblehead?) It seemed to me that the president of Universal deserved to be treated with as much respect as any automobile executive. After all, Hollywood produced movies the whole world wanted to see, took in millions of dollars, created thousands of jobs, and generated huge tax revenue.

So why such a venomous attitude toward us . . . and toward Bill Clinton?

There was a joke currently making the rounds: The pope and President Clinton were having a meeting in a rowboat in the middle of a lake, for security reasons. A gust of wind came along and blew the pope's hat off. Clinton said, "No problem. I'll take care of it," and climbed out of the boat, walked across the water, and retrieved the hat. Next day the headline in the paper was not CLINTON WALKED ON WATER but CLINTON CAN'T SWIM.

I felt a certain kinship with him. Around this same time, someone told me a joke that was going around about me: A man was choking to death in a restaurant and Barbra Streisand was sitting at the next table. She rushed over and did the Heimlich maneuver and saved his life. Next day the headline read: BARBRA STREISAND TAKES THE FOOD RIGHT OUT OF A PERSON'S MOUTH.

You can't win.

People can take an ounce of truth and turn it into a gallon of lies. Sometimes I think the only people who enjoy freedom of the press are the people who own the presses.

But I want to make one thing very clear . . . I have great respect for the press and I admire serious journalists. I just don't have much affection for those who don't get their facts straight and have an axe to grind.

I did several interviews to try to clear up the misconceptions perpetrated by Dowd and others. I didn't like the fact that people were basically using Hollywood to discredit the president.

Frankly, I think some of the men who were particularly critical of Bill were jealous. Here was this guy who came out of nowhere and jumped ahead of them. He was president and they were not. And who knows? Maybe they also resented the fact that he had a great head of hair!

In any event, I was thrilled by what he was accomplishing and proud to be part of his huge circle of friends.

And yes, I have opinions. And it is my right to express them, just like any other citizen.

Actually, I think it's our responsibility. As Teddy Roosevelt said, it's "the first duty of an American citizen" to be involved with politics.

FORTY-EIGHT

Who Said I'd Never Sing Live Again?

Going to Washington and meeting so many intelligent, dedicated people who were now running our country gave me a new sense of optimism. I felt energized and inspired. I wanted to be more engaged with the world. When I talked to Marilyn, she said, "You're coming out of your cocoon."

I never thought of it that way, but it's interesting that other people did.

I wanted to be more open to other people, more present, more productive. I was even thinking about doing my first concert in twenty-seven years . . . but first I'd have to let go of the fear that was holding me back.

One Christmas Donna Karan had rented a house in Sun Valley and was throwing a party. Liza Minnelli came and brought Billy Stritch, her longtime accompanist. While the snow fell outside, we sat and talked in the living room, where there happened to be a grand piano, and as Donna says, "If you have a piano, Liza sings. I don't even have to ask." And sure enough, Billy sat down at the piano, and Liza walked over and began to sing.

I remember thinking, *Oh my God, how could she just get up and sing in front of all these people?* This was a brightly lit room, and she could see everyone's face. Wasn't that distracting?

I guess not for her.

But it would be impossible for me.

I need the darkness of a theater to go into my own private world like I do when I'm acting. If I can see individual faces, it throws me off because suddenly I'm watching them, and then I get worried about their reactions . . . especially if I think they don't seem very interested. In many ways, I'm still the girl who turned to face the wall in Cis's kitchen, because I didn't want to be watched while I sang.

Liza wasn't worried. She looked happy, and I remembered reading that her mother, Judy Garland, would also get up and sing at Hollywood parties. Maybe it's in the DNA. (No, maybe it's not, because my mother would sing at the drop of a hat.)

People were applauding for Liza, and so was I, but I can still feel myself in that chair, quietly trying to blend into the furniture because I was afraid that now someone was going to ask *me* to sing.

Then I thought, *This is ridiculous.* I've been singing professionally since I was eighteen. Why can't I get up like that?

A few months later my friend David Foster, the record producer, was giving a party for the Canadian prime minister, Brian Mulroney. (David is Canadian too.) He asked me in advance if I would sing, and I said, "No. I can't."

"Oh, come on, Barbra," he said. "One song . . ."

Well, David can be very persuasive, and besides, I wanted to challenge myself. I was determined to get over my fear. So I agreed to try.

The song we chose was "Some Enchanted Evening," and David was going to play the piano for me.

The night of the party arrived. I enjoyed talking to Brian and his wife, Mila. They were a delightful couple. He told me that President Clinton had said to say hello, and it was nice to think that these two leaders were friends.

I'm sure there was lovely food, which I ate because I eat when I'm nervous. (Well, I also eat when I'm *not* nervous.) But all I really remember is the fear. I was dreading the moment when I'd have to perform. I sat at my table, watching Natalie Cole get up and sing beautifully (while I was thinking, *Why don't you do a few more songs?*). Lionel Ritchie was great but then he was through (too soon for me). And I heard David call my name.

The moment had arrived.

I walked over to the microphone, feeling stuffed. (I knew I shouldn't have eaten right before I was supposed to sing. Because then there was a chance I'd burp, and then I'd have to rephrase around the burps!)

The music began . . . I started to sing . . . and then I froze. In front of all those people, I had to stop after a few bars and say, "I'm sorry. I just can't. I have to sit down."

My knees were shaking, my heart was pounding, I didn't like the sound of my voice. Nothing was right.

Besides, I could see people staring at me.

By the way, when I have to fill out some form where they ask for your profession, I'll often write down "performer," because it's short and it encompasses several aspects of my career.

So I'm *supposed* to be a performer, but how can I call myself one if I don't really like to perform?

It's kind of complex to explain. When I had something to prove to my mother and myself, I had a need to perform. I also had to make a living, so it was great to be paid to sing at the Bon Soir, and it actually became fun. I was thrilled to get a supporting part in a Broadway show and then the lead in *Funny Girl* . . . but I loved the rehearsal process more than the actual performances.

Once I had proved that I could get up onstage and be successful, I didn't want to do it anymore. But I love acting in movies or recording in the studio, because it's private.

Performing for a paying audience is a very different thing.

I've heard people speak about how they love to entertain and can't wait to get onstage. They gush about how wonderful the audience is, and after a number they'll often pause to milk the applause. (I'd rather go into the next number fast.) To me, it feels as if their need to be liked is so naked it's almost embarrassing.

Sometimes I wonder if I'm in the right profession. I don't live to be onstage. It doesn't feed my soul. I'm not looking for adulation . . . what attracts me has always been the excitement of the work.

Please don't get me wrong. I truly appreciate the applause. I've had many moments onstage when I can feel the love from the audience, and I'm very grateful. But it's not the kind of love that fulfills me.

I'd rather be loved by just one person, for my real self, than have all the applause in the world.

Besides, I don't like having to get all dressed up and strut around the stage as if I'm in some sort of beauty pageant. It doesn't come naturally to me. It's not who I am. And I can't stand high heels. They hurt my feet. Frankly, I just want to make my music . . . in the studio, with my headphones on, surrounded by other musicians, and afterward, often alone with just an engineer, late at night . . . where I'm not trying to impress anybody but myself.

And here's the truth. Deep down, I'm worried that I won't live up to the audience's expectations.

So for decades, ever since 1967 when I forgot the words in Central Park, I rarely sang in public. I've said in print that it was twenty-seven years between concerts, because I wasn't counting certain performances. I guess I didn't think of the shows I did early on in Las Vegas as concerts, and they went right out of my head. And I had to give the *One Voice* concert because stopping nuclear proliferation was more important than my nerves. And when we changed the composition of the Senate, it made me realize that if I had any sort of power, it was this, and I should use it.

So the few times I did sing live, in public, it was always for a cause. The money raised would be used to do good things, and that was very motivating. To contribute in some small way was rewarding to my soul. It reminds me of a Jewish tradition. When I was growing up, we had a *pushke* . . . a little charity box to save some coins for people who were poorer than we were.

The *One Voice* concert nudged me to dip my toe in, and then a few things happened to push me right into the water. In 1992 I was honored with the Grammy Legend Award, and what made it even more special was that it was presented by Stephen Sondheim. He was articulate, as always, and said, "She's the delight of every writer who hopes for a performance of his song better than what he heard in his head. She not only possesses one of the most exceptional voices in the world, but her musical instincts are unsurpassed, and that's a formidable combination."

I thought *he* was a formidable combination . . . a great composer *and* lyricist . . . and I was very moved that he would take the time to do this for me. I came out onstage, and we hugged, and he then went on to read the citation. When he came to the line "your relentless pursuit of perfection," we looked at each other (because he knew just how relentless I was), and he exclaimed, "I can't think of anybody who deserves it more. You're terrific!" We shared a laugh and a kiss on the cheek. I thanked Steve, but as I said to the audience when the applause finally died down, "In all honesty, I don't feel like a legend. I feel more like a work in progress."

This was an award for lifetime achievement, but I was in the middle of my life!

Still, it did make me look back on my recording career. I felt so grateful to this industry, and to the fans who had always supported me. They were incredibly loyal, they continued to buy my records, and I owed them a lot. The fact that I hadn't given them a concert in years made me feel guilty. (It's a Jewish thing.) People would come up to me and ask, "Are we ever going to see you live again?" and I didn't know quite what to say.

That night at the Grammys, to express my appreciation, I sang a few bars from the first song I ever recorded when I was thirteen years old . . . "You'll never know just how much I love you." Then I stopped, looked around, and said, "Who said I'd never sing live again?"

And then I walked off the stage.

Not too long after that Kirk Kerkorian called Marty. I had already opened one Las Vegas hotel for him back in 1969, and now he wanted me to open another . . . the MGM Grand . . . on New Year's Eve 1993. I said no. The thought of performing in such a huge arena . . . about fourteen thousand seats . . . absolutely terrified me. I didn't care how much money he was offering.

And then Kirk did something extraordinary. In addition to a lavish fee, he volunteered to give $3 million to the charities of my choice, if I would just consider the deal. And he would still give the money even if I ended up turning him down!

What a mind that man had . . . brilliant. No wonder Kirk was so successful. Not only was he smart, he was also extremely generous and very shy. It was such an unexpected quality, and it made me like him even more. I was shocked that he was willing to basically hand me such a large sum, and said, "Why would you do that?"

He said, "I like where you give your money."

How could I deprive a charity of so large a gift? I called Marge Tabankin, the director of my foundation, and asked her to put together a list of my recent donations as well as new possibilities. AIDS research, the environment, civil rights, women's rights, interfaith organizations, groups supporting children . . . there were so many worthy causes that I believed in!

And then I said yes, because I couldn't just take Kirk's money and give him nothing in return. I would feel even more guilty!

Besides, I thought it was time to push through the fear.

The stage fright started back during *Funny Girl* on Broadway, when Sydney Chaplin's behavior sent me straight into analysis. And the aftereffects of that fear were profound. I remember going to see Sondheim's *Follies*, and at one point the actor John McMartin started to do a song and dance but it quickly went wrong. He forgot his lines, the tune, the steps. I had a panic attack . . . I thought it was really happening to him, but it was actually part of the script. Still, I had to leave.

And then in my thirties I was plagued with more anxiety-related problems. As I wrote in my journal, "I wish my stomach was absolutely normal again. I wish I could accept my fears and think everything will turn out okay. I want to be more loving, even to myself. I want to learn how to redirect negative thoughts into positive ones."

I also wrote, "Fear is a big thing. It's fear of failure, fear of loving, fear of rejection, fear of humiliation." And as I learned from my work with certain therapists, I needed to accept that fear, rather than judge myself so critically.

That was a revelation. So I could turn my attitude around and actually use the fear. And it worked . . . my biggest triumphs have occurred when I acknowledged the fear but went forward in spite of it. As Brugh Joy used to say, "What is courage? Courage is to be frightened, but to go ahead anyway."

And that's what I resolved to do now . . .

The first person I told was Virginia Clinton. I'll never forget that conversation. It was May 1993.

I called her and said, "I think I'm going to go back and sing after all these years."

And she said, "Barbra, I'm going to be there!"

That wasn't a given. She was battling a recurrence of the breast cancer that had initially been diagnosed in 1990, and it was not easy for her to travel.

At that point the schedule wasn't set yet, but once I committed to two shows, one on New Year's Eve and the second on New Year's Day (*Great*, I thought. *We open one night and close the next . . . a short run!*), I called her again.

"I really want you to be part of it," I told her. "I hope you'll come as my guest to the show."

"Of course I'd like to come!" she said. "If I had my way, every place you sing I'd be there!"

"Which night would you like to come?"

"What do you mean? How many nights are you singing?"

"Two."

"Then I want to be there both nights!"

I honestly think one of the reasons I finally said yes to this concert was just because I wanted to sing for Virginia.

She was so loving toward me, and I could be completely honest with her. I said, "This is a challenge for me, because I don't like performing. I just don't. But I think I'm going into a new phase. It's about wanting to give back, but also to receive . . . to allow in that love, like I felt when I sang at the inauguration."

And then I let her in on a little secret.

"I hate New Year's Eve. I used to spend so many of them alone and unhappy. I never know what to do with myself, whether to stay in or go out, so this gives me a focus. It's something to do."

Now that I had committed to this concert, I had the daunting task of putting it together.

I didn't want to do what a lot of people do, which is just sing their greatest hits, one after another. Instead I wanted each song to emerge from a moment, some experience I'd had . . . maybe when I was younger and never had a date, or the first touch from a boy in my late teens. My idea was to pick songs that would tell the story of how I grew into the woman I am and express what I was feeling at pivotal moments.

Well, I already knew what I would be feeling when I first walked out onto that stage . . . sheer terror.

And then I knew exactly what song I should sing . . . Andrew Lloyd Webber's "As If We Never Said Goodbye" from his musical *Sunset Boulevard* . . . because it begins with the perfect lines:

I don't know why I'm frightened
I know my way around here.

I had already recorded it for my *Back to Broadway* album, and I could totally relate to it as an actress. But there was just one thing . . . the lyric was about a movie star returning to the studio where she had made her pictures, and I thought, *Maybe it could be rewritten to be about someone returning to the concert stage . . .*

So just as I had called Steve to ask if he could rewrite "Putting It Together," I called Andrew, and he put me in touch with the lyricists, Don Black and Christopher Hampton. They were very receptive. They came to my house, we talked about what needed to be changed, and they reworked it beautifully. Their original images like "the cardboard trees, the painted scenes" became "the band, the lights, familiar sights" . . . and they even managed to allude to my own personal journey:

I guess in every lifetime, you go through different stages
You grow, you learn, you try to turn new pages

Then I thought, *Okay, what do I do after I sing that song? What's the next moment?*

Well, if I hadn't dropped dead from nerves, I would be feeling, *Phew! I got through it . . . I can still do this.* And that instantly made me think of Sondheim's brilliant song "I'm Still Here." It was funny and self-deprecating and triumphant all at once. But there was just one problem . . . all the Depression-era references that worked for the character who sang it in *Follies* had nothing to do with me. And this time it wouldn't be simply a matter of changing a few words. It would mean rewriting the whole song.

Once again I called Steve. And once again he was incredible! Actually, I think we share a sense of self-doubt, the idea that something can always be better (it's a Jewish thing). And here we were again, two opinionated Jews, reexamining every word, analyzing every emotion. And he reimagined the whole lyric just for me. One line after another, each more and more clever:

One day you're hailed for blazing trails
Next day you're nailed for fingernails

Very apt, but Steve was just getting started. He went on:

Talent she's got, but those screeches—
Sounds like her throat's in a sling
And now they say, "Talent she's got, but those speeches—
Why can't she shut up and sing?"

I was hearing that a lot lately. And then he went on to a point I had made in speeches about the ways men and women are treated differently:

"Songwriting, acting, producing—
What makes her think that she can?
Or better yet, songwriting, acting, producing—
What does she think, she's a man?"

Exactly. But the best was yet to come:

I've kept my clothes and kept my space.
I've kept my nose to spite my face

God, how I love working with smart people!

Now I had to write the rest of the show. Marilyn and Alan said they'd love to work on it with me. And I thought, *Why not?* It would be more fun if I could do it with friends. I told them about various moments in my life that might lead into music.

How could I tell my story? What would be interesting? Unexpected?

And that's when it occurred to me . . . Where do I tell my stories? Who do I talk to?

Oh . . . my therapist! And I certainly had a lot of experience with therapy. That sparked an idea . . . what if I was talking to a therapist onstage, but you never actually saw him. All you would hear is his voice . . . since I love voice-overs. We eventually made it three therapists . . . one woman and two men, one older, one younger. I thought it would be funny to have a chair onstage to represent each therapist, but with nobody in it . . . just an overhead light on the chair and a disembodied voice. I'd hire actors to record the lines, and they could ask questions that would lead me in all sorts of directions. I could talk about moments that shaped my life as a girl, as a woman, as an actress. It would be kind of intimate and very personal.

Simultaneously we were also thinking about what songs I could sing. Sometimes the song came first and led to a story . . . and sometimes a story led to a song.

I brought Marvin Hamlisch into the discussion, because I knew he would be a huge help choosing the material. I really wanted him to conduct the concert for me and arrange the music, but I didn't think he could do it because he had so many other projects. But to my surprise he said yes! Now that's a true friend. He knew his mere presence onstage would reassure me.

There are so many parts to putting on a show, and since I was also the director I was involved in every one of them. When David George brought in his initial design for the set, it was very modern, which is not my style. I couldn't relate to it, and just seeing what felt wrong made me realize what would be right. We sat down, and I described my vision, and it was like nothing you'd normally see in Las Vegas. At first David was a bit stunned. As he explained, "Most artists are just looking for the biggest flash you can bring them," but my concept had no glitz, no glitter.

Instead, I was so inspired by my trip to Monticello that I wanted to recreate it. I loved the tearoom, with its big windows draped with sheer curtains in creamy ivory. I took out my book on Monticello and showed David pictures. But that tearoom was just a starting point, because we ended up taking various elements from the house . . . Doric columns, elegant moldings, the tall windows rounded at the top in the conservatory . . . and putting them together in our own way.

I thought it would be more dramatic if I could enter and then come down a staircase, with a beautiful mahogany banister, so David designed one for me. I've always loved rooms where you walk in and there's a round table in the center, with a vase of flowers, and I also wanted the floor of the stage to be on slightly different levels, so it could function almost as different rooms, and I could move from one to the other.

Instinctively I think I was imagining a set that would be more like a home, to make me feel more comfortable onstage. Besides, given how enormous the arena at the MGM Grand was, I wanted to warm it up.

And I know myself. I'm happier if I'm surrounded by beautiful things. And David did a wonderful job, especially on the curtains. They elegantly draped the walls and also floated above the tall windows, which gave the set more height. And I could see Marvin and the orchestra behind those windows, which made me feel more secure.

Then I chose several pieces of eighteenth-century-style furniture. I wanted them all upholstered in different ivory fabrics . . . very simple and monochromatic, which always appeals to me. I was so pleased with the finished set, I could have lived there.

Then I thought, *Why should the audience see the same exact set when they come back after intermission?* So I asked David if he could put down off-white carpeting for the second act, to change the look. And we flew out the windows to completely reveal the orchestra and took away most of the furniture, to give it more of a traditional concert atmosphere.

I even asked him to make sure all the flowers on the set were off-white, because they would take the light, and when the lights changed color, they would change along with it.

There's another component to the design of a concert that's invisible but crucial, and that's the sound. The acoustics in these huge arenas are not ideal, but my feeling is that the people who were paying to see me deserved the absolute best. I wanted my voice to sound like it does in the recording studio, and in order to achieve that, we hired the best audio engineer in the business, Bruce Jackson. When he recommended carpeting the entire arena, even under the seats, and hanging heavy drapes along the walls, I'm sure Marty blanched, but I didn't care how much it cost. And it worked, eliminating any bounce back. Bruce also designed special stage monitors for me, because I can't wear those in-ear monitors (known as earwigs) that other performers use so they can hear themselves sing. (I think my ear holes are too tiny.)

I know I could sound better if I used those things, because you can hear the mix of your voice with the orchestra, just as you would wearing headphones. I've tried to have an earwig custom-made for me. First they have to pour this liquid plastic into your ear to make a mold, and I was afraid it would go into my brain, so I made Marty do it first. And then after it was fabricated, it still didn't fit. The other problem is that you have to be wired up to a backpack, like I was in *Funny Girl*. I hate all these contraptions. Also, the earwig blocks out the sound of the audience, and if I'm going to perform live, I want to hear them.

This all goes back to the fact that you can't have everything.

And then there's one last aspect to the concert design . . . what was I going to wear? I wanted the set and my outfits to complement each other. For the first act I was envisioning something as elegant as the set. I've always liked the classic simplicity of black and white, and with that in mind I started sketching.

In order to sing I have to be able to breathe, so a dress can't be too tight around the diaphragm, and because I like to eat, an Empire-style gown works well for me. And then I show what I want to show . . . like my shoulders. As Donna says, "A woman never gains weight in her shoulders." So I sketched an off-the-shoulder neckline, with a V-shaped décolleté. I saw it in black velvet, and then I thought it would be more interesting if the skirt parted in front, starting at the base of the V and then gradually widening all the way down, to reveal an ivory satin insert. It would catch the light when I moved. Finally, for just a touch of sparkle, I added a line of tiny pearls and rhinestones along each edge of the black velvet, where it parted.

Serendipitously Donna had the perfect fabrics, new at the time . . . a *stretchy* black velvet and even a stretchy ivory satin, so I could sing without worrying about seams splitting! I thought I'd leave my throat bare . . . no necklace. Instead, just one antique pin made of diamonds and pearls, to accent the base of the V, and a pair of delicate diamond and pearl earrings.

Done.

For the second act, with all that off-white carpet, I wanted to wear an off-white wool suit in my favorite style . . . tailored jacket, vest, and a long, slim skirt with a slit so I could walk comfortably. It was trimmed with little rhinestones and pearls, and vertical lines of bugle beads created a subtle stripe effect on the vest.

And that was it. No frills. No dancers. No multiple costume changes. I was planning a very different kind of show than you typically see in Las Vegas, and that worried me a bit. But when tickets went on sale in November, there were more than a million calls, and Marty told me both concerts sold out in eighteen minutes.

What a relief! I always think nobody is going to show up.

Meanwhile, I was working every moment I could with Marilyn, Alan, and Marvin. It was such a delight to be in rehearsal again with Marvin after so many years. We always had a special rapport. From the very beginning, we recognized each other's talents, and without explaining how or why, we also understood each other's anxieties. We were both kind of hypochondriacs . . . always having allergy or sinus attacks.

"Sinus, that's a Jewish thing," Marvin would say, which would make me laugh.

I knew exactly what he meant and that phrase, "It's a Jewish thing," became a running joke between us. If we took a break during rehearsal to have lunch (we both love food), before we even finished our meal we'd be talking about where to go for the next . . . "It's a Jewish thing."

Back at the piano, when he'd play a new arrangement for me, he might hit a major chord and I'd say, "Wait, wait . . . can't that be a minor chord?"

He'd turn to the musicians and explain, "It's a Jewish thing."

They'd laugh. They loved him because he was Leonard Bernstein and Jack Benny rolled into one. He made the work fun.

And I'll never get over how he would listen to any suggestions I might make, quickly play me a few options, and if I asked for more substantial changes, Boom! By the next morning the new arrangement would be done, when other people would normally take days. Marvin was brilliant, charming, and hilarious . . . the perfect collaborator.

It was great to be working with my friends and tossing around ideas, dreaming up a show. I told Marilyn and Alan about falling in love with Marlon Brando when I was thirteen years old and saw *Guys and Dolls*. I was jealous of his costar,

Jean Simmons, who got to kiss him and have him fall in love with her. I wanted him to fall in love with me!

And I thought, *Wouldn't it be fun to show some footage from that film, but take out Jean's image and replace it with a photo of thirteen-year-old me?*

We decided to use the scene where Marlon sings "I'll Know" to her, because I've loved that song ever since I heard him sing it. And our video editor, Tom McQuade, figured out how to pull a frame from an old black-and-white home movie of me (dancing with my cousin Lowell at his bar mitzvah), color it, and insert it into the film. That was pure wish fulfillment on my part . . . finally my idol was singing to me, and I got to do a duet with him. And then, just as he's reaching out for an embrace, my image dissolves back into Jean Simmons on-screen, and the fantasy is over. He kisses her, not me! My first real heartbreak.

I was so wrapped up in preparing the show that I could almost ignore my nerves . . . until we arrived in Las Vegas. That's when reality hit, and I was terrified. It's one thing to vow that you're going to conquer your fears and another thing entirely to do it. Before the first performance I was upstairs in my suite trying to calm myself by listening to tapes from a woman named Darby Long, whom I had met through my dear friend Evelyn Ostin. One of the tapes was about having a positive attitude, and the other one, "Excellence," reminded me of something I had realized when I was fifteen . . . that there is no such thing as perfection. That's when I wrote in my journal "Perfection is imperfection."

That's because perfection is cold and a bit inhuman. It doesn't leave room for life or vulnerability. I still believe that, but the reality is that I want my work to be the best it can be. And I push and push to make it that way. I did feel, as I was getting older and, I hope, wiser, that I was letting go of the *need* for everything to be perfect.

It's hard. I still walk into a room, and if I see that two vases on a table are not equally distant from the center, I have to move them. Yet when I did my Deco house, it was interesting to explore asymmetry . . . but that's another book.

I know how imperfect I am, and I've spent my life trying to be a better person . . . a more loving wife, mother, and friend. I'd also like to be a better actress, director, and musician, but I can't always make the films I want to make, or hit every note with the purest tone, or even build a house without a mistake. It's impossible. And I think the journey for me is to really accept that nothing is ever going to be perfect.

The Navajos made the most beautiful blankets, but since they believed that only God was perfect, they would deliberately weave in a tiny flaw to show that they were not competing with God.

And what I took from the tape was that *striving* for excellence would be enough . . . and I knew I could do that.

It was time to go down to my dressing room backstage and get ready for the performance. Renata, as always, had everything arranged perfectly for me, so I could put on my makeup and not have to think twice about where anything was.

There's no way I could have done this concert (or much of anything else) without Renata. She organizes everything . . . food, clothing, jewelry, dogs, packing and unpacking, setting up the hotel room . . . and she runs the entire household when we're home and cooks the most amazing meals. She's like a mother, a sister, and the absolute greatest assistant because she can do anything. As she says, "Just tell me what you want, and I'll get it for you." She's been with me going on fifty years (and she doesn't even look forty!). We've been together so long that she often knows what I need before I do. For example, just at the moment when I notice my throat hurts a little, she's there with a cup of tea and honey, reading my mind. She has a rare sensitivity, the greatest taste, and she makes the best chicken soup (and she's not even Jewish!). In addition to that, she's brilliant, kind, utterly loyal, and the one person I can trust to handle things. It's unbelievable how much she does, and what's even more remarkable is that she does it all with so much love. I can only think that my father must have sent her to me. I am blessed to have Renata in my life, and as I've told her many times, I couldn't imagine life without her.

Back to that dressing room. I went through the motions of getting ready almost automatically. It's hard to focus on anything when you're overwhelmed with fear.

Richard Baskin came in and as soon as he saw how upset I was, he tried to comfort me. But nothing worked. My heart was pounding. I honestly didn't know if I'd be able to walk out onstage. When I get scared, my voice shakes, and that doesn't help my singing. I can't control it.

I was already imagining the worst. What if the concert was a disaster?

Joanne Segel was holding my hands and trying to get me to meditate and breathe deeply. Marge was right beside her, doing her best to reassure me. As she told me later, "When I saw how traumatized you were, I thought, Nobody should be in this kind of pain to be able to do what they do."

And then there was a knock on the door. It felt like that moment when they come to wheel you in for surgery.

It was Marty, come to escort me to the stage, as he has done for every performance (for over sixty years now). I pulled myself together, even though I was still feeling shaky. He held my arm and made sure I didn't trip over the tangle of cables backstage in the darkness. Renata was right behind us, holding up the back of my dress with one hand, balancing a thermos of tea in the other, and carrying a satchel over her shoulder filled with any last-minute fixes I might need . . . makeup, honey, hairbrush, water.

I could see Marvin in his place, conducting the sixty-four-piece orchestra as they played the overture and he glanced over at me . . . Ready?

Not really. But it was now or never.

I nodded.

Renata clasped my hands, infusing me with her love and her steadfast faith in me. I closed my eyes and took a deep breath . . . and then, as the final bars of "People" resounded through the arena, I started up the backstage staircase. A stagehand standing at the top pulled the curtain aside and I stepped out onto the balcony of the set and into the bright lights. Now I was grateful for that mahogany banister . . . I was trembling so much that I had to hold on to it for dear life, to steady myself.

I didn't know how the audience would react, but they instantly rose up from their seats, cheering and clapping. The applause was so long and so loud that it was almost like a physical wave rushing over me.

I looked out at the crowd. It's an extraordinary feeling . . . this outpouring of emotion was overwhelming. It brought a huge smile to my face, and I shook my head in amazement when they wouldn't stop applauding. I couldn't say a word. All I could do, in a spontaneous gesture, was put my hand over my pounding heart, because they had touched it so deeply.

Then the orchestra began to play, the house lights went down, and I began to sing . . . "I don't know why I'm frightened." The first notes were a little wobbly, but I willed myself to get control of my voice. And I could feel the audience was right there, rooting for me. When I came to the line "Why everything's as if we never said goodbye," there was another burst of applause. It was as if they always knew I could still do this!

And then I was walking down the staircase and out into the middle of the stage as the song builds to the climax:

I've been in the wings too long, all that's in the past
Now I'm standing center stage, I've come home at last!

That's when the music swells and the drums roll and my voice soars to full volume . . . and the crowd went wild. They stood up as one and cheered. And I knew I was home free. I glanced over to Marvin once I had finished the song, and we shared the moment.

This concert was very personal to me, and I was proud of what we had created. After several songs, when I leaned back in the chaise and said, "It's all crazy, you know, I just can't believe what's happening these days, Doctor," and the light went on over an empty chair, and a Viennese-accented male voice started to question me, the audience got it immediately. We didn't need to set up the therapist bits with any tedious explanation. The show worked more like a film, where you just cut from one scene to another.

I told the first therapist about being in high school and waiting for a boy before a blind date, which led into "Will He Like Me?" It was a way to continue the conversation in song. Then I walked over to the other end of the stage to sit on the neoclassical daybed and speak to a different therapist. That was a way to advance time, as I talked about another period in my life. I liked the fact that there was a logical reason for the move. Of course, you also want to give both sides of the arena a closer look.

It was fun casting voices for the therapists, and I wanted the second to be a woman, to cue a soft, gentle tone. She was asking about relationships, and I told her about the first time I felt attracted to someone, and sang "He Touched Me." It's such a tender song about a tender moment.

When the third therapist, another man, asked if I'd ever been in therapy before, I did a double take that got a big laugh. And that led into the remark, "With all the transference and countertransference, sometimes I don't know whether I'm the patient or the doctor," which segued seamlessly into a montage from my movies that I had worked on with Tom for many late nights. We spent hours taking various pieces of film from *Clear Day*, *Nuts*, and *The Prince of Tides* and editing them so it seemed as if all the characters I played were talking to one another. I loved that segment.

Since we had a big Jumbotron screen, I wanted to take advantage of it. The second act began with a montage of scenes from *Yentl*, *Funny Girl*, and finally the moment when I see Robert Redford asleep on a barstool at El Morocco and reach out to touch his hair. That was my cue to come back out onstage and sing "The Way We Were."

Later we showed images of Jason through the years while I sang another Sondheim song to him, which begins with the line "Nothing's gonna harm you, not while I'm around." The montage opened with a baby picture of him at twelve weeks old, with his hands clasped under his chin. He was like a little Buddha, so wise . . . and still is. I love the intelligence in his deep brown eyes. I have that picture on my dressing table to this day.

Near the end of the show, to accompany "Happy Days Are Here Again" and illustrate the new spirit sweeping the country, I wanted a video that felt more like a modern-day newsreel and highlighted all the progress that was being made by President Clinton on women's rights, civil rights, and the economy . . . inflation down, unemployment down, the deficit shrinking. It was important to me to make those points, and to do so in the most effective and appealing way.

So, a little politics, and other moments of pure pleasure . . . like singing "Someday My Prince Will Come" to my goddaughter Caleigh, because it was her favorite song. In so many of the songs I choose, love is the theme. As I said to the audience, "I believe that the most powerful source of energy is the human heart."

I was so happy when I got through the first performance! The second night was much easier, because I was more relaxed . . . so relaxed that when I forgot the words to the song I wrote, "Evergreen," I could make a joke about it. This was one I thought I knew, so I didn't bother looking at the teleprompter . . . which is not always in my eyeline, by the way. But one of the reasons I could do this concert in the first place was because I had the security of the teleprompter, even though I didn't watch it constantly. I just needed to know it was there.

And the audience was incredible. I lost count of the standing ovations, and at the end of the second night, they were even stomping their feet. I felt a huge sense of relief . . . thank God it was over! But I was also very gratified by the response.

So many friends and family had come to support me . . . Jason, as always . . . Elliott and his mother, Lucy; my sister, Rozzie; my brother, Shelly, and his wife, Judy; Marilyn and Alan; Cis and Harvey; Donna and Stephan; Steven Spielberg and Kate Capshaw; Quincy Jones; Michael Douglas; Sydney Pollack; Peter Bogdanovich; Gregory Peck and his wife, Veronique; Richard Gere and Cindy Crawford; Andre Agassi; Bella Abzug; David Foster; and Alec Baldwin and Kim Basinger. I was especially honored to have Coretta Scott King in the audience.

And when I looked out at the crowd on opening night, I could see Virginia Clinton sitting next to her husband, Dick Kelley, and they were both smiling up at me, lifting my spirits and making me feel special and secure.

But I didn't see my mother. I had flown her out, along with two friends, so she could attend the show. I had arranged everything in the hotel for her comfort, and had them provide a wheelchair so she wouldn't have to walk the long corridors (they also had one for Virginia). But my mom was not in her seat.

What could have happened to her?

Was she all right?

FORTY-NINE

My Mother

Where was my mother?

For a moment I was plunged back to the same feeling I had as a six-year-old, waking up from a tonsillectomy in a strange hospital room, and my mother wasn't there.

When I looked out at the audience on the opening night of *Funny Girl*, my mother wasn't there either. Her excuse, on both occasions, was that she was too nervous and had to get up and walk around.

And now, on this night when I could have used all the support I could get, once again she wasn't there.

It was only when I started writing this book that Joanne finally told me the full story. She and her husband, Gil, happened to be walking into the MGM Grand just as my mother was being wheeled out by a hotel aide, with her two friends. As Joanne described the scene to me, there were lines of people as far as the eye could see . . . people with tickets waiting to get into the concert and others who had been there since early morning, hoping that there might be a cancellation.

Joanne greeted Diana and said, "Isn't this exciting!"

Diana said, "We're going out."

Joanne stared at her and asked, "What do you mean? Aren't you going to see Barbra?"

"Well, it's New Year's Eve, and my friends and I really want to go out."

Joanne was dumbfounded. "See all these people in line?" she asked. "They've come from all over this country, and the world, to see your daughter. And look at all the people waiting, just on the chance a seat might turn up. They'd do anything to get in, and you're going *out*?"

Diana was unmoved. "We want to go out on the town and have fun." She looked up at her friends to indicate the conversation was over, and just as they began to push past Gil and Joanne, she offhandedly added, "Could you tell Barbra for me?"

Joanne didn't say anything to me that night or in all the years since, because she didn't want to hurt me.

That brought back another flash of memory, from that time when I was about seven and my mother was taking me to the movies. I was so excited . . . and then she changed her mind in the middle of the street, and we turned around and went home.

It's a moment I've remembered all my life. I couldn't trust that she would keep her word. She would say something and then not follow through, which left me feeling deeply disappointed and utterly helpless, because I had no control.

It's very unsettling, not to be able to count on your own mother.

When I called to let her know I was doing the Las Vegas concert, I told her about the generous fee Kirk Kerkorian had offered. I suppose I wanted her to feel proud of me and share my excitement, because I knew money was the one thing she understood. All she could say was, "Why would they pay *you* so much to sing?"

She could kill any pleasure I felt in an instant. So I was never thrilled when I knew she was coming to see me perform, because it just made me anxious. What was she going to say this time? What fault would she find?

I said, "Mom, do you want to come to the show?" And since I never expected her to come to more than one performance, I asked, "Which night?"

"I'll come the first night," she said.

And then she didn't keep her word again.

Why was I surprised? I had learned that it makes no sense to do the same thing over and over again and expect a different result. But even though I understood it intellectually, it's still hard to break the pattern.

The fact that she couldn't be bothered to be there on one of the most important nights of my life was like a slap in the face. It was as if she was sending me a message: Maybe other people think you're so great, but I don't.

But here's the funny thing. I never thought I was great. That's what she never understood.

I think the first time I truly understood that her behavior was not normal was Christmas Eve 1964. I was twenty-two years old, doing *Funny Girl* on Broadway, and Elliott and I had invited a few of our closest friends and my mother to our Central Park West apartment. I was looking forward to a nice, quiet dinner and the opportunity to exchange a few gifts.

I knew what my mother would like as a present. I remember her asking me once what Elliott had gotten me for my birthday. This was before we were married, and he had done something sweet and romantic . . . he gave me a rose and got us a hotel room. But I told her he had given me cash, because I knew she would approve of that. So I always gave her cash on special occasions, plus a gift. I had found a book of photos of 1940s movie stars that I thought she might like, and on the title page I wrote, "This could have been you, Mom! Love, Barbra and Elliott." I really believed she could have had a career, if she had ever really tried. She was pretty and had a beautiful voice.

As everyone was handing out presents, I gave the book to her. She unwrapped it and saw the inscription. Then she looked around at all the gifts that were being given to me and suddenly asked in a loud voice, "Where are *my* presents? Why are you giving presents to *her*? You should be giving presents to *me*! I'm the mother!"

And then she stood up and went into an absolute rage, screaming, "*I'm the mother! She's nothing without me!*" Her eyes were closed and tears began to stream down her cheeks.

The room went absolutely still. Elliott quickly took her by her forearms and had to practically drag her into the little room off the kitchen, to try to calm her down.

I was in shock. I had to go sit by myself in the den to try to process what I had just witnessed. I thought, *Is this possible?* Could it be that my own mother was jealous of me? That instead of being proud of me, she actually resented my success?

At that moment it hit me like a revelation. And it made sense. Of course it was possible. This was a woman who used to sing to a broomstick, pretending it was a microphone, as she told one reporter. She was eager to make a record (and took me with her, when I was thirteen), but she never did anything with it. I always told her how beautiful her voice was. Once I asked her, "Why didn't you try to be a singer?"

She said, "I was too shy."

Well, I'm shy, too, but that didn't stop me. She had a dream, but she never pursued it. She probably felt regretful, watching me do things she never had the courage to do.

Her quotes in old interviews are very telling. She takes credit for any musical talent in the family: "I sang around the house, and they copied me." (That's funny. I certainly never sang around the house.) According to one article in *The New York Times*, Diana "still hopes for a show business career." (She was sixty-one at the time.) But some of the things she says about me are difficult to read: "I never thought of her as an actress. I was against it. I thought she wasn't good-looking enough."

That hurts.

It must be nice to have a mother who tells you that you can do anything you put your mind to. My mother was not that mother. She never encouraged my dreams. She didn't even ask me what they were. I felt bad that her own dreams remained unfulfilled, and now I had to come to terms with the fact that she was jealous.

I think this is why I'm so sensitive to any hint of jealousy, even now. I don't want anyone to be envious of me. It really damages relationships. It's isolating, and I don't like that feeling.

When I was a kid, I didn't feel as if I belonged anywhere. My mother didn't understand me. I was so different from her. I remember saying, "Okay, Ma. Was I left on the doorstep or what?"

That reminds me of another conversation with her, after the filming of *Color Me Barbra.* I had already been working for something like twenty-four hours straight at the Philadelphia museum when Rex Reed came to interview me. I had to talk to him while I was doing my own makeup, gluing sequins under my eyebrows to go with the modern art segment. And then he went on TV and told a ridiculous story about how I had eaten a banana and thrown the peel on the floor. That would never have happened, as anyone who knows me knows, because one thing I am is obsessively neat. I was appalled that he would make this up. (I later found out that he was pissed off because he had been kept waiting.) When I was venting to my mother about this, she said, "*Did* you throw the peel on the floor?"

"What do you mean, did I? Mom, you've been to my apartment. You know I can't stand it if anything's out of place. Do you think that I would throw a banana peel on the floor?"

"Well," she said, "I don't know. It could've happened."

Great. So my own mother doesn't believe me.

When I told Marilyn Bergman about this conversation, she said, "That's it, in a nutshell." My mother's doubts brought back all my childhood frustration at not being seen or understood. I thought, *My mother doesn't know who I am.* She never did and she never will. And that's profoundly sad to me.

Marilyn could be very astute, and she went straight to the heart of the matter: "If you don't have a source of unconditional love as a child, if you don't for a period of time feel like you're the center of the universe, you will probably try to attain that for the rest of your life."

That was a brilliant analysis, very eye-opening. Since I never felt really cared for, I've never felt that sense of real security, deep down.

I once read a book that quoted some psychologist saying that there's no such thing as unconditional love. I don't buy it. I know I love my son unconditionally. Even if Jason were to tell me that he had done something really bad, I know I would find a way to understand why he had done it and support him . . . because I believe in his goodness. I know his heart, his mind, his soul.

But because I never felt that kind of love and support, I thought there must be something wrong with me.

That's always been my question. Will anyone ever love me unconditionally?

It took years to come to terms with that. And part of that involved accepting my mother for who she is. As a wise friend once told me, "Suffering is the resistance to what is."

I want to be very clear about one thing. I know my mother did the best she could. When my father died at thirty-five years old and left her with two children and no means of support, she must have been terrified. The world had betrayed her, and she was bitter and resentful. I think she just shut down inside.

I can understand that.

When I had ear noises and chest pains, she didn't want to hear about them . . . probably because it scared her. As she told me later, "I wouldn't know where to take you anyway."

It was as if I didn't have a mother.

I've tried to talk to her about this over the years, because I wanted to understand myself, through her. I even taped our conversation one day, because I wanted to know more about my upbringing and get some stories straight. When I think back to my childhood in the projects, she was so sour and grumpy. I felt as if she were always angry with me. So I asked her, "Was I such a terrible kid?"

She said, "You were not a child that you could easily get along with. You wanted certain things your way."

That's true. I've always had a strong will, and I must have been a handful. I know I do want things my own way. And when I look closely at myself, I have to admit I'm not the most friendly, outgoing person. And I think that's because my mother wasn't warm and affectionate with me, or anybody. I didn't invite friends over after school because I was embarrassed when she wouldn't even offer them a cookie (forget the milk).

Then I asked her, "How come you never put your arms around me, or hugged me?"

She said, "I didn't know you expected that."

What an odd response. And she went on to say, "If a parent has to cuddle a child and maul all over it all the time, there's something wrong . . . the child is sick. I don't believe in too much affection."

Well, that explains why I was always uncomfortable when people hugged me. Since I never experienced it as a child, I was suspicious of it. (I'm much better about that today.)

Later on in the tape I said, "I don't remember you saying anything constructive or pleasant about me. You never told me I looked good. You never told me I was smart."

She said, "I didn't know you expected compliments. I knew that you were good. Why do I have to go piling on you and make you feel bigheaded or whatever?"

But how would a child know, without being told? And even when I was grown up, my mother never understood how much a compliment from her would have meant to me.

I realize my mother did show love, in some ways. Love, to her, was giving me food. When I moved to Manhattan to study acting, she used to bring me things like half a cantaloupe, some chicken soup, and a couple stalks of celery.

But she didn't say the words. Even with my dogs, I see how much they love it when I tell them "You're so adorable. I love you!" I see how their tails wag and their heads tilt and their eyes light up.

Everyone needs to be told they are loved.

Recently I was shown some photographs from 1984, when I was given the Scopus Award by the American Friends of the Hebrew University of Jerusalem. The gala in LA was a benefit for the Emanuel Streisand Building for Jewish Studies, which I had endowed to honor my father and his commitment to education.

It was a glorious evening . . . my friend (and former laureate) Gregory Peck was there, Shirley MacLaine was the master of ceremonies, and Neil Diamond serenaded the crowd. As I told the audience, this is "like the bat mitzvah I never had."

I had a dress made for me, which was copied from the Gustav Klimt portrait of Adele Bloch-Bauer that I had loved for many years. The gold fabric was embroidered with sequins and beads, to mimic the dazzling patterns in the painting. I'm smiling in all the photos with Greg, Shirley, and Neil . . . and then this lovely event was ruined.

I had come with Richard Baskin, who pulled me aside to tell me that my mother was screaming in the ladies' room. And sure enough, when I rushed in I saw all these women in shock because my mother was yelling, "Why are they honoring *her*? Why aren't they honoring *me*? I'm the mother!" It was surreal, like a repeat of that Christmas Eve dinner. I finally had to shake her in order to get her to stop shouting.

Being with my mother was like walking through a minefield. I never knew when the next explosion was coming. One Yom Kippur, when I picked her up to go to the synagogue, she started an argument in the car. Then as we sat together in the pew, I silently prayed to God . . . *Please help me love her. Please help me forgive her.*

After making *The Prince of Tides*, I took the lesson of the film to heart . . . when my mother was having her heart fixed, literally . . . and tried to forgive her.

I *do* love her. But that doesn't mean I like her. (Although I'll always be grateful that she made love with my father at a particular moment on a particular night, and therefore I entered the world.)

She was just naturally negative. There were many times when gossip columnists would print some nasty article about me. Usually I don't see that kind of junk, but my mother would cut out the articles and send them to me. I called her up one day and said, "Mom, why do you send me these things? Do you *want* to make me feel bad?"

She tried to defend herself, saying, "Well, I thought you should know."

I could hardly speak. Tears came to my eyes. I just said quietly, "Mom, please don't send me these articles. I can't take you hurting me anymore."

After a long pause, and for the first time in my life, she said, "I'm sorry. I won't do that again."

That was unexpected, but nice to hear.

Back to New Year's Eve in Las Vegas 1993. My mother did come to the second show, the next night. I had her stand up so she could take a bow (and then I had to tell her to sit down, because she could have stayed there forever!). At the end of the performance, as she was taken away in her wheelchair, she was delighted to have the camera on her and she was blowing kisses to the crowd.

I wanted a picture with my mother and Virginia, and asked Firooz Zahedi, who was documenting the event, to take it for me backstage. It's a wonderful photo. I'm in the middle of these two women, who were both so important in my life, and as soon as I saw the finished print I noticed something that didn't even register at the time. Virginia and I are holding hands, but my mother and I were not.

FIFTY

Virginia

I think I finally had to accept the truth. I would never get what I needed from my mother.

Would I ever get it from anyone?

One day I got a call from my friend Evelyn, who wanted me to meet someone special who had been helpful to her in a spiritual way. So I invited this woman over, and we were talking when she said, "You've had an angel on your shoulder."

What? An angel . . . really?

She went on, "It's been a male."

Okay, I thought. *Probably my father, watching out for me. If so, he's done a good job.*

Then she said, "It's changing now, and a woman is going to come into your life."

Frankly, the whole idea sounded more like wishful thinking than reality.

My mind immediately went to the women I already knew. I've had a string of older female friends . . . first it was Muriel Choy, then Cis, and then Marilyn, Joanne, and Evelyn. All of these women had this amazing ability to love, and to show their love. They complimented people and said loving things . . . all those simple, instinctive gestures that always felt awkward to me.

Who could this new woman be?

Little did I know it would turn out to be Bill Clinton's mother, Virginia.

From the moment she took my hand at his inauguration and we walked off together, I felt an instant connection. It was one of those connections without words (almost like love at first sight). Who knows what that chemistry is? But when you first meet certain people, you know right away if you could ever be close to them.

Somehow our inner selves communicated. Hearts probably can touch without words.

I'll always remember the way she took my hand . . . usually I don't like to be touched by people I don't know, but this felt completely natural.

And then we spent that March weekend together at the White House. That was such fun . . . having our hair done, chatting like girlfriends. I was surprised by how close we were immediately, how freely and easily we could speak about meaningful things.

I once asked her how she managed to raise such an extraordinary child when she was a single mother, in those early years after her first husband's death.

"How do you account for Bill?"

"There's no accounting for him," she replied. "He's like you. He was born with this great, great ability. But it would not have happened if he hadn't cultivated it. Now he did it, and you've done it."

I wasn't so sure of my own skills, but Virginia saw something similar in her son and me and was pleased that we were friends.

I made a point of calling her every week. I knew she was ill and I wanted to check up on her. But she was more interested in hearing about me.

I was in the midst of preparing my concert and I told her how nervous I felt about performing onstage again. "Oh, Barbra," she said. "Anybody with your talent would be running up and down the street flaunting it! It's God's gift."

I never thought of it that way.

She spoke of God in such a familiar, easy way. Her faith was part of the bedrock of her life, and we talked about it one day. I said, "I believe in a universal spirituality that crosses over all religions . . . Christian, Jewish, Muslim, whatever . . . it doesn't matter because it all comes down to love."

As they say in most religions, Love thy neighbor as thyself.

"And now I'm wondering if there's a way to get this message across in my concert, without people thinking I'm hitting them over the head with any kind of religious preaching."

Virginia embodied that kind of spirituality to me. Her religion was kindness.

After every conversation with her, I felt enriched.

She was so excited about the concert. "This will really give me something to look forward to!"

I was worried about her health and told her, "I want you to be well and strong. Is there anything I can do for you?"

"Not a thing in the world. I'm going to be fine. I really am."

She always took the positive view, rather than the negative. And she never wanted to impose her problems on me. Instead, she was always upbeat, even as she went through another round of grueling chemotherapy. When she lost her hair, all she said was, "You oughta see my wig!"

"Does it look exactly like your hair?"

"It's thicker and more beautiful."

"Did they put in your white streak?"

"Oh yes!"

I sent her Norman Cousins's book about the healing power of laughter, videotapes of Marx Brothers movies, and CDs of music I thought she might like. And then I found out she didn't have a CD player, so I sent her one as well. She was so grateful, and asked, very politely, if it would be possible for me to send her CDs of *my* albums. In her thank-you note she wrote, "Do you know how wonderful it is, not to be able to sing myself but to hear your beautiful voice resounding through my house?"

It's funny . . . her voice, with its enchanting Southern lilt, was music to *my* ears.

I sent her a copy of the picture of the two of us at the inauguration ball and she told me, "I love this picture of our backs. You must know by now how many photographs I have, but no one will ever take this picture from me!"

She really appreciated our friendship, and said, "I need to write you a long letter and tell you my feelings, because if I tell you now I'm going to cry!"

Virginia didn't want to cry. She always chose happiness over sorrow. Even in the face of all her challenges, she was grateful for every day. (What a terrific role model! I'm still trying to follow her advice.)

She would end every conversation with affectionate words like "I sure love you, Barbra" or "Do you know how precious you are?"

It was so comforting to be wrapped in Virginia's warmth, and she embraced me as if I were part of her family. I'm looking at a note from her right now that begins "To my sweet wonderful daughter, my Barbra." There's even a lipstick print on the envelope, where she kissed it! That's Virginia. She wasn't afraid to express her love.

I was so touched that she thought of me as her daughter. I told her about my complicated relationship with my own mother, and she said, "Her loss is my gain."

I used to call Virginia my Southern mom, and she taught me something by her example . . . to love more openly, and to tell people that you love them. I had never been that effusive with endearments early on, but now I've certainly become better at sharing them.

In another letter she wrote, "I don't think many people know how hard you work . . . Please take care of yourself."

This was so typical . . . in the midst of her treatment, she was worried about me!

Bill told me the story of how Virginia and Dick spent Thanksgiving with them at Camp David, and when he asked if she was coming back for Christmas, she said, "Oh, I don't know."

"What do you mean, you don't know?"

"Well, I've got to go to Barbra's concert in Vegas, and I'm not sure you'll get me back in time."

So, as he said to me, "The White House at Christmastime was chopped liver compared to Barbra, and she only agreed to join her family after I promised faithfully to get her to you."

I was thrilled that she was coming, but what I didn't know . . . because she was always smiling and never complained . . . was that when I thought she was playing her beloved slot machines, she was actually getting two blood transfusions every day.

I can still see her on opening night in her black-and-gold-sequined jacket, with a leopard pictured on it . . . and that bold white streak in her black hair . . . and those long eyelashes. She told me, laughing, that every morning the first thing she did was wash her face and put on her eyelashes . . . she didn't go anywhere without them. That image always made me smile.

She was brave and funny and full of life, having her Scotch and soda in my suite before both shows. Normally I don't see people before I perform, but I made an exception for Virginia and Dick, who was such a doll. He treated Virginia with the care and respect she deserved.

Virginia loved the concert and was thrilled to come to the party afterward. I even asked if the casino could bring up a table, with a dealer, so she could play blackjack or whatever she wanted right there. And she couldn't wait to get back to those slot machines! She knew how to wring every morsel out of life, every moment of joy.

I noticed she wore the same jacket both nights, and wanted her to come back to Los Angeles with me so I could take her shopping and buy her some wonderful clothes. It would have given me so much pleasure. I hoped to take her to the Hollywood Park racetrack, too, so she could bet on the horses (and I wanted to bet on them myself, like I did when I was eighteen back in Detroit).

But sadly, she had to return home for more treatment.

And then I got an unexpected call from the president on January 5. He said, "Do you know where my mother is?"

I had to laugh, and told him, "This is so funny, because in a Jewish household it's always the mother looking for the son . . . 'you don't call, you don't write' (the guilt trip) . . . not the other way around."

Bill said he had tried to reach her in Las Vegas, but never could because obviously she was too busy going out and having a good time. And now he couldn't find her at home in Arkansas.

I finally got her on the phone late that night, around 9:00 p.m. her time. "Virginia," I told her, "your son is looking for you. You have to call him back!" We laughed about that, and I told her again that I couldn't wait for her to come to LA, and she invited me to come to Hot Springs, and we joked about who was coming to see who first. Before hanging up, I said, "I really love you, Virginia."

She said, "Barbra, I sure do love *you*."

And then everything changed.

My phone rang at 12:51 a.m., later that same night (I know the exact time, because I wrote it down in my journal). It was Roger Clinton, who told me that Virginia had passed away in her sleep.

No! No! It can't be. I had just spoken to her.

I was in a state of shock. Even though the president had told me that her prognosis was not good, I was hoping for a miracle. She was too good to die.

I flew to Arkansas for the funeral, which was held at the convention center . . . the only place large enough to accommodate all her friends. The reverend joked that they had considered holding it at the racetrack, where she had spent so many happy afternoons. Clearly he knew her well and loved her dearly. As he said very perceptively, Virginia "was like a rubber ball. The harder life put her down, the higher she bounced."

It was wonderful to listen to her friends reminisce, and to hear her favorite hymns, like "A Closer Walk with Thee," sung by a gospel choir. Bill told me a story about the soloist . . . at one point, she lost her voice, and prayed to God that if he would just give it back to her, she would devote the rest of her life to praising him. And then another woman sang a song I had never heard before. It was electrifying. The lyric spoke of how whenever we stand in the presence of God, we are "on holy ground." I was sitting behind Bill and tapped him on the shoulder . . . I was just so moved, and he turned around and nodded in agreement.

Once again I was struck by the power of music. Somehow it can be the connective tissue between souls. And on this occasion it seemed to unify all the people in the room, elevating our spirits with every note . . . almost like a direct link to God.

Afterward I asked the president, "Who is that woman, and what is that music? It's magnificent!" He told me that the singer was their friend Janice Sjostrand, and the song was called "On Holy Ground."

I knew then and there that I had to sing that song, and it became the impetus for an album I put together of inspirational songs about life and love and faith. I asked Marvin, Marilyn, and Alan to write a song especially for Virginia, and that became "Leading with Your Heart" (based on the title of her moving autobiography).

Another song written for the album was called "Higher Ground," by Steve Dorff. That became the title of the album, because that's the road I want to walk myself. I want to rise above petty thoughts and be more positive . . . and do good deeds and good work that means something to me.

And I dedicated the album to Virginia, who inspired it and set such a beautiful example, with her tenacity, optimism, and compassion . . . and her ability to love so profoundly.

After the funeral President Clinton kindly offered me (and Renata and Richard, who had accompanied me) a ride back to Washington on the smaller version of Air Force One. He could see how excited we were to be on that plane, and he was so dear, giving us boxes of M&Ms and playing cards emblazoned with the presidential seal as souvenirs. We talked about his mom, and he told me, "You kept her alive because there was no way she was going to miss your concert."

I told him, "You are so lucky to have had such a wonderful mother."

I was already in the process of establishing a fund to support breast cancer research at the University of Arkansas cancer center in her name, and I was happy to be the first of many contributors. In some small way I hoped it would be a tribute to her zest for life . . . such an incandescent spirit has to live on.

In 2016 Jim and I were at Bill Clinton's seventieth birthday, and he said something that touched me very deeply. It was so giving and loving, just like Virginia . . . he truly was his mother's child. This is how he introduced me: "When I met Barbra for the first time, I thought I had died and gone to heaven. I realized how shy she was but I loved talking to her, almost as much as hearing her sing. And then she became a friend of my mother's. Those two were joined at the hip, as if Barbra were another one of her kids. Barbra called my mother every single week for the rest of her life . . . And she owned me for life, because of the way she treated my mother."

It was so easy to love Virginia. She was like the mother I've always dreamed of, and I'm so grateful for the time we had together. I cherished her, and she opened her heart to me, giving me such love and support. She really helped me overcome my fears and get up on that MGM Grand stage, because I knew how much she wanted to hear me sing. It was such a motivating force . . . to sing for *her.*

My eyes are welling up as I write this. She was so ill, and yet no one would ever know it, because she was that strong . . . emotionally, mentally, spiritually. She would not waste one moment of her life complaining or being unhappy. That was a big lesson for me.

It's amazing how people come into your life when you really need them.

I can still see her smiling face and hear her laughter.

FIFTY-ONE

Some Guy Named Charles

Losing someone you love has a way of putting everything else into perspective. Most of my worries suddenly seemed inconsequential.

I kept thinking of my time with Virginia . . . how much she had enjoyed herself that last weekend in Las Vegas. And I hoped she knew how much she helped me get through those concerts. It's amazing how the support of someone you love can make all the difference. And I think that made me more open to the love pouring out from the rest of the audience.

I haven't looked at the DVD of this concert for twenty-five years, but I had to watch parts of it in order to write about it. And I can see from my smile that I was profoundly moved by those first bursts of applause . . . three standing ovations before I'd even finished the first song! I could tell that the audience was really glad to be there. And by the end of the second night, I had to admit that I kind of enjoyed myself too.

After I came home, I was still hearing from people who had been there. Gregory Peck, whom I adored, called and told me something so special that I wrote it down in my journal, because I didn't want to forget it. He said, "I've witnessed three great theatrical moments . . . Laurette Taylor in *The Glass Menagerie*, Marlon Brando in *A Streetcar Named Desire*, and you, the other night."

After the last performance, Marty was smiling from ear to ear. He'd been trying for decades to get me back on the concert stage. "You've got to tour!" he kept insisting, and he had already talked to me about taking this show on the road. But he understood when I told him I couldn't possibly commit to anything until I knew how it felt to be in front of an audience again.

And now I owed him an answer.

Of course it made sense to go on tour. After all, we had put so much work into this show and to abandon it after only two performances seemed like such a waste.

And I don't like to waste anything. That's the Brooklyn in me. I still use one tea bag for two cups of tea and turn out the lights whenever I leave a room. Years ago it was to save money. Now it's to save energy.

In many ways I'm still that child on Pulaski Street, and that's a problem and a gift . . . because I think the artist comes from that child. She plays, and that's where the imagination begins. Some kids create an imaginary friend. I created an imaginary doll from a hot-water bottle. If I hadn't felt that need to create my own reality, I might never have become an actress.

I never thought much about it until I started therapy, where I learned that being a whole person means bringing together all the various aspects of yourself . . . the child and the adult. And I had proved something to myself with these concerts. The child might have been frightened, but the adult took care of her.

I told Marty, "Let's do it."

But now that I was in the mood to tour, I couldn't.

As Marty explained, it takes three or four months to set up a tour . . . select the cities and arenas, pin down the dates, and do all the advertising to sell the tickets. I had this urge to go to London, a city I love, and Marty said, "Great, but that means we'll have to send the whole set by boat."

Thank God I had Marty to handle all those details. It made absolutely no sense to go all the way to Europe for just a few shows, but I guess he decided if that was the incentive I needed to do the tour, it was worth it.

Now I had to wait a few months . . . and just hope I didn't change my mind!

Meanwhile, I had work to do. We had filmed both nights of the concert, with my old pals Gary Smith and Dwight Hemion calling the shots. I had already begun looking at the footage. We had something like ten cameras on the floor, so there was a lot to go through. And now I was completely immersed in the editing process.

Marc Brickman had lit the show in the arena, and we used various colors to change the mood and complement each song. But we were limited in what we could achieve, because the palette you get with stage lights only goes so far, and it's basically primary colors, lots of blue, plus magenta. And then what you see in real life doesn't read exactly the same way to the TV cameras.

But now, sitting at the console in the editing room and watching the show on-screen, I discovered that just by moving the dials on the color panel I had access to an infinite range of hues. With a twist I could lighten the blue, or add a touch of gray, and suddenly I could get the kind of subtle shades I love . . . a delicate blue-gray, the palest lavender, a deep green. To get the perfect peach we had to mix a tiny bit of red into the yellow and then add a touch of white. I was mixing colors like an artist would mix dabs of paint on a palette. I had so much fun playing with those dials.

As I watched the footage over and over again, I saw other things that could be improved for the tour. I wanted to trim some of the therapists' dialogue. The Disney medley had begun as a special treat for my goddaughter, and now I decided to replace it with a medley from *Yentl.* We added a video montage of a couple of scenes from the movie, and while Yentl sings "A Piece of Sky" on-screen, I thought it would be interesting to harmonize with her onstage.

In the early days I'd often close my shows with "Happy Days Are Here Again," because it had a broader meaning that related to the mood of the country, and I performed it again in these shows. My interpretation was always changing . . . it could be happy or sad, depending on who was president at the time. And that kept it fresh for me. In Las Vegas I had done "My Man" and "For All We Know" as encores. But for the tour, I thought the final encore should also have a broader theme. So I added the song "Somewhere" because it had deep meaning for me. I chose it for all the disenfranchised people fighting to be seen and heard. And with that soaring melody, it just felt like a more uplifting note to end on.

The tour was scheduled to start in London on April 20, and then go to five American cities, which is fewer than most performers do. But even that seemed like a lot to me. I wasn't sure I could fill all these big arenas, but Marty had no doubt. Back in November, when the MGM Grand concert went on sale, he had actually gone to the office of the ticket service so he could watch all the calls come in. He saw how many thousands of people were shut out. And Marty always had a very clear idea of my own worth . . . I'm not sure I ever did.

Marty was convinced that the demand for the tour would be just as high, and he was right. When tickets went on sale on March 27, 1994, the phone lines were overwhelmed with more than five million calls in the first hour. People had to keep dialing and dialing, and many couldn't get through. All the performances were sold out in an hour, and in order to accommodate more of the requests, Marty persuaded me to add more shows to the schedule.

I arrived in London a few days early so I could get over my jet lag, eat more of those little tea sandwiches I could happily live on, and last but not least, fit in a few rehearsals. The sets and all the equipment had already been unloaded into Wembley Arena. Bruce Jackson and his team had hung his drapes and carpeted the whole auditorium, which they continued to do at each and every venue on the tour . . . 16,500 square feet of carpeting . . . just to make sure the audience would hear the best possible sound.

On the day before the first concert, I stepped out of rehearsal to meet the reporters who were gathered outside . . . but this press conference was not about me. It was to support a children's charity. The Boots chain of drugstores had donated one million pounds in my name to the Variety Club of Great Britain, which helps disadvantaged and disabled children. I was honored by their gift, which was a remarkable amount of money, and was happy to thank them publicly. And it seemed like serendipity, because I've always loved going into Boots and finding special creams with the prettiest Victorian packaging.

Their donation was the kind of gesture that made me feel like all the effort that went into these concerts was worth it. Besides being an opportunity to thank all the fans who had supported me, it was also a chance for me to give back in a more material way.

So we decided to build a charitable component into the tour. In each U.S. city, we gave money to schools for music and art programs that were being cut. I've always felt that if kids had a way to express themselves through art and music, they would have a healthy outlet for their emotions. Tickets were also set aside for local groups fighting poverty as well as national organizations like the Legal Aid Foundation and the National Resources Defense Council, and that generated over $10.25 million for charity, including $3 million to AIDS organizations.

I get a lot of satisfaction from giving. It enriches my soul, fills my heart, and makes me feel good. That's how I like to spend my money. I want to be of service. In fact, it's a responsibility, according to the Jewish concept of *tikkun olam*, which means "to repair the world."

I think we all want to change the world, even though that's an overwhelming task. But little by little, we can change ourselves . . . and those small changes will hopefully add up to a bigger change in the world.

On opening night in London, I was nervous all over again. It's interesting . . . I've read that the body responds the same way to excitement *and* fear. In both cases you feel a surge of adrenaline. Physiologically it's hard to tell the difference.

I just wish I could think of the pounding in my heart as excitement, rather than fear.

At least the audience was excited. The British have a reputation for being relatively restrained, but they stood up to applaud song after song. I felt so much warmth from them. This was the first time we did the *Yentl* medley in front of an audience. Later Tom told me how he pressed the button to start the *Yentl* video and then came out from backstage so he could watch how it played. "I could see the whole auditorium," he said, "and never in my life have I heard such thunderous applause. It was so loud and so long, it actually took my breath away."

We were originally planning to do just two shows in London, but we had to add two more to try to accommodate the demand. I was fine with that (more little sandwiches!).

On the second night Prince Charles came to the concert, and a portion of the ticket sales benefited his charity, The Prince's Trust. He arranged to come backstage before the show, since he couldn't come afterward, because the rules of royal protocol are that no one can leave the arena until he has departed. I was happy to see him again, and he was warm and friendly as ever.

I had put one of the Disney songs back into the program, because I thought it would be so much fun to sing "Someday My Prince Will Come" while a real prince was sitting in the Royal Box. Onstage I told the story of the first time we met in 1974, when I was recording songs for *Funny Lady* and we shared a cup of tea (as the news footage of that meeting played on the Jumbotron). And then I couldn't resist adding, "Who knows? If I had been nicer to him, I could have been the first *real* Jewish princess!"

That got a huge laugh. Luckily Prince Charles has a sense of humor.

The following day I walked out of my hotel suite and into the hall, where there was a table laden with all the flowers and gifts that had just arrived. One bouquet stood out because it didn't look like the usual sort of arrangement done by a florist. It was more loose and free, as if it were from someone's backyard. I asked Kim, "Who sent it?" And she said, "Oh, a fan. Some guy named Charles."

I said, "Let me see the card."

It *was* simply signed "Charles," but what Kim had failed to notice was the royal crest at the top. And the flowers were fresh from his garden! What a lovely gesture. And he wrote: "It was such a treat to attend your concert last night—You were *wonderful* and I adored every minute of it! Bless you for being so kind and generous to my trust—they *so* appreciated it."

Kim has never forgotten that moment and neither have I. Now we laugh about it, but back then she was mortified. And she's never missed a royal crest since!

I saw Prince Charles again later that year, when he was in Los Angeles and invited me to join him for tea at the Bel-Air Hotel. We're both interested in gardens and organic food and the health of the planet. Later he sent me some of the delicious organic oat biscuits he was making under his own brand, Duchy Originals. His idea was to build a cottage industry that would support small farmers, with all the profits going to charity.

Later I was told that Charles has said I was his "only pinup" (apparently he had a poster of me in his room at Cambridge), and he described me as "devastatingly attractive" with "great sex appeal."

Who knew?

Certainly not me, and it's probably better that I didn't when we met, because it would have made me self-conscious.

The next year, 1995, he invited me to come stay at his home, Highgrove, see his gardens, and attend a dinner to benefit a summer school for architecture students. Coincidentally, I was already planning to go to France for a friend's wedding, so I fit in a stop in London along the way. The prince is the most gracious host and made everything easy for me, even sending his car and chauffeur to the Dorchester hotel to pick me up, along with Renata, who accompanied me for the visit.

Highgrove is an elegant Georgian house, and the first thing I saw when we walked in was a huge table laden with flowers, beautiful objects, and books. It felt so inviting that I did the same thing in the entrance to the barn house I built later. I was very impressed with the decor, because it was English traditional in the best sense, artful as well as warm, with lots of charming chintz.

Before the dinner Prince Charles took all of us on a tour around his garden. It was a little challenging to walk in my long white gown, and my high heels kept sinking into the ground, but it was fun to recognize some of the same plants I was growing in LA. And then we went in to dinner, which was held in a splendid tent with antique furniture . . . all lit by candlelight. I was sitting next to Charles and couldn't help thinking, *I hope one of these candles doesn't fall over!*

Everything was perfect, and there was lots of interesting talk about art and architecture.

I slept in a beautiful bedroom with a big four-poster bed like the one I had in New York, which made me feel completely at home. The next morning I was sitting up in bed and Renata had just come in when there was a knock at the door, and a woman appeared with a lovely English breakfast on a tray. We were admiring the pretty dishes and the lace placemat when we suddenly noticed a little Jack Russell terrier peering up at me, with his front paws on the bed. He was very friendly, so Renata lifted him up and he cuddled in beside me, and I'll admit I shared a bit of egg with him.

After a while there was another knock at the door. This time it was Charles, who peeked in and said, "By any chance, is my dog inside?" Apparently he had been looking all over the house for Tigga, and when Renata pointed to the bed, he laughed and said, "Clearly you have another fan, because this dog never leaves my side!"

When I joined everyone for lunch, I met a couple who arranged luxury safaris in Africa. (Speaking of six degrees of separation, the man had just made a documentary with James Brolin in Kenya, but at this point I hadn't met Jim yet.)

It was so nice to have more time to talk with Charles. He walked me around the house and showed me paintings of his ancestors . . . names I knew only from history books, but they were all family to him.

What an extraordinary friendship! And it has lasted for decades. Recently, for my birthday, he sent me the loveliest card, with one of his own watercolors on the front. And on his birthday, I sent him four Barbra Streisand rosebushes for his garden, along with one of my drawings I thought he'd like, of flowers in a vase. And in 2022, when I had a big birthday, Kim surprised me with a wonderful video that started with Prime Minister Justin Trudeau, a friend for twenty years, who spoke of his father's friendship with me. And it closed with another friend of almost fifty years, Prince Charles, now King Charles III (I'm so happy for him, and I know he'll continue to fight for the environment).

Back to the tour. After London the next stop was Washington, D.C., where I was performing in the same arena where I sang for President Clinton on the night before his inauguration. I was happy to be back in the capital, because now I had friends in the government, and many came to the concert, including Congresswoman Nancy Pelosi and her husband, Paul; Betty Currie; Senator Barbara Boxer; Secretary of Labor Robert Reich; Secretary of Health and Human Services Donna Shalala; and Senator Barbara Mikulski . . . now in her second term, after the *One Voice* concert had helped elect her in 1986. (So we now had a grand total of seven women in the Senate.)

I was still consumed with politics, and loved talking to people who knew more about it than I did. When Bill Schneider, a political analyst on CNN, came backstage after the concert, the first thing I said to him was: "What the hell is Alan Greenspan doing raising the interest rates?"

In other words, I had no interest in talking about my show. I wanted to hear what he thought about the latest news.

On the second night, when President Clinton and the First Lady walked into the auditorium, the crowd burst into applause. Having them there was a thrill, and it was great to have a chance to talk backstage. Clinton was about to announce his second Supreme Court nominee, Stephen Breyer (the brilliant Ruth Bader Ginsburg was his first), and was accomplishing so much that I wanted to update the political montage in my show to include his latest achievements. So Tom McQuade would rent an editing room for a day in each city to make the changes.

I was constantly tweaking the show during this tour . . . rewriting the patter for each city, adding or subtracting songs. I would have been bored out of my mind if I had to do the exact same thing every night. And I varied my outfits as well. Donna had made me another black dress, made out of stretchy matte jersey, with a scoop neck and long, tight sleeves, and she sent it to me with two separate skirts . . . one was floor-length, made out of the same jersey, and the other was short, above the knee, and made out of georgette.

I called Donna up and told her I loved the dress.

She said, "Great! Which skirt did you choose?"

I said, "Both."

She laughed, but Donna knew me by now, and she listened while I explained my idea. I thought it would be more interesting if the dress had two layers . . . the long skirt, with a split in the middle, on top and then the short skirt underneath. That way, when I was standing still, the top layer would fall straight down and it would look like a long gown. But as soon as I moved, the fabric would part, and you'd see the shorter layer underneath, and show some leg.

I asked Donna if she could have the two skirts stitched together, and of course she knew exactly how to do it, and it worked perfectly.

Between rehearsals in D.C. I took time out to visit Frederick Douglass Junior High, the local school we had chosen for our donation. The music department had no money, but the teacher was very creative and was showing the kids how to make the most simple kinds of instruments, so at least they'd have something to play. I was so pleased when Sony decided to match our donation and buy enough real instruments for the whole class.

After D.C. the next stop was Auburn Hills, Michigan, a suburb of Detroit. I'll always have a soft spot for Detroit, because that was the first place I sang outside New York City, and everyone there was so kind to me. As I said to the audience that night, my friends there used to "take me into their homes and feed me. And I never forget people who feed me."

Bobby Sosnick, who had offered to help buy me out of my contract with my first manager all those years ago, was there. He was now one of the owners of the arena where I was playing. And I gave a big hug to Bernie Moray from

Robinson's Furniture, who gave me the couch fabric that I made into the dress I wore for my very first TV appearance on *The Jack Paar Show*. It brought back so many memories to see them again. (In 2016, at my last concert in Chicago, Bernie was there as well . . . ninety-seven years old, and looking fifteen years younger.)

That's the fun part of doing a tour . . . reconnecting with old friends . . . and working with dear friends like Marvin, who was always right behind me onstage, following my every breath (and also checking out the latest baseball scores). He also knew the best restaurants to order from in every city.

It's an unreal sort of life, being on tour. You're constantly moving, but all the tedious inconveniences of travel are gone. When it's time to check out of a hotel, you don't have to call down for a bellhop to help with the luggage, or worry about tipping everyone. Actually, you don't even have to bother to check out. It has already been done for you by the tour people, who will also pick up the luggage and deliver it to the next hotel. I would just get in the car and go wherever it took me.

The logistics of keeping a tour like this running smoothly are daunting. It took 19 trucks and 11 buses to transport the sets, the equipment, and the 155 people who were traveling with us . . . the crew, the musicians . . . and some also traveled by plane. It's like lugging a whole movie crew around. But I didn't have to worry about any of that. All I had to do was show up and sing.

But in Detroit I suddenly began to wonder how I was going to get through the rest of these concerts. I wasn't feeling so great. It's very exhausting to do so many shows, and my body and my voice have to be in pretty good shape. I try not to talk so much on my day off between shows (good luck with that), but I don't work out vocally. I don't practice, because it's boring.

And it was disturbing to watch the news every night and see reporters standing outside Jackie Onassis's apartment. She was very ill, and they were basically on a deathwatch. It made me profoundly sad that this extremely private person couldn't be left alone to leave this world in peace.

The last show in Detroit was on May 19, and as I came offstage at the end, someone told me that she had died. It was a blow, even though I knew it was coming. And I don't mean to suggest that we were close. I only *felt* as if I knew her, just like the rest of the world did, simply because she had been a public figure for so long.

And when I walked back onstage for the encore, I told them that Jackie was gone, and talked a bit about the time she had come to my house, and how lovely it was to have met her. She was such a remarkable woman, elegant and courageous. And way too young to die . . . only sixty-four. Another tragedy for that family.

I made it through that show . . . but be careful what you wish for. I didn't want to get up onstage again, and sure enough, I got sick. I was running a high fever, and the doctor's diagnosis was viral tracheolaryngitis, an inflammation of the vocal cords. I was ordered not to speak, or else I could permanently damage my voice.

I flew home to Los Angeles and was in bed for ten days, taking medications for my throat and for bronchitis. I had to postpone four shows in Anaheim and reschedule them for the end of the tour, which would obviously be a huge inconvenience for everyone who had already bought tickets. I felt terrible about that, and put out a statement to the press explaining my diagnosis and apologizing to the fans.

I wasn't completely well when I came back to do the June 2 show in Anaheim, but the last thing I wanted to do was cancel again. So I talked to a wonderful woman, Carolyn Conger, whom I had met through Brugh Joy, and said, "I don't know what to do. I'm still running a fever, but all these people are coming to the show, and I can't bear to disappoint them."

She said, "Think of the fever as a holy fire."

Ah ha! What an amazing image. She turned a negative into a positive. And that did it. I went on that night and even managed to joke with the audience, reading out a Top Ten list of reasons why I hadn't been able to perform. (David Letterman had already done his version, so I thought, *Why not do my own?*)

Mine included lines like "I was at home waiting for the cable guy," "There was a shoe sale at Nordstrom's," and "It took me three days to read Dan Quayle's new book—and four days to correct the spelling." That list got a lot of coverage in the papers and on TV. (I hadn't realized that the postponement had been such big news.)

And at the end of that show, I took my temperature and the fever was gone.

Ray Stark was there and said to Marty, "Who figured this show out?"

I guess he still couldn't believe that a woman could be that smart.

Ralph Fiennes was also in the audience that night and hitched a ride back to

LA with me in my motor home. I was happy to have more time with him because I was so impressed with his performance in *Schindler's List* and wanted to talk to him about *The Normal Heart.* (Even in the midst of the tour, I was still trying to push that project through.) I thought he would be brilliant in the role of Felix, the handsome man who captivates Ned. I wanted Ralph for the part because I knew he would be attractive to both men and women. Besides, he's a mesmerizing actor, with real charisma and soul.

For the next two concerts in San Jose, I was coughing a bit, and I had to drink a lot of tea between songs. Luckily I had a bit of a break before I had to sing in New York.

Ralph came to my house for dinner and a movie the night before I left for the East Coast. He brought me two books of poetry . . . the collected works of W. B. Yeats and T. S. Eliot's *Four Quartets.* I liked talking to Ralph, because he's interested in so many things, and by the time we went down to the screening room, I felt very comfortable. And then there was a subtle shift in the atmosphere. The look in his eyes as he gently touched my face and then my hair became almost too intimate, and I thought, *Oh no. This guy is so attractive.* But because I was hoping to direct him, I couldn't allow myself to succumb to his charms.

Believe me, it was tempting.

Instead, Ralph went home. The next morning I got on a plane. And he wrote me the loveliest note to thank me for the evening, which started with "Dear Barbra, I could have stayed all night!"

Little did he know . . .

Later I saw him play Hamlet in New York. He came to a party Donna Karan gave for me in London. And then a few years ago, my agent had a Christmas party in LA, and a man came up to me and said, "You don't recognize me." (He had shaved his head for a part.)

I said, "Oh my God . . . Rafe!" (That's the way it's pronounced, by the way.)

He said, "Do you remember sitting in your projection room at Carolwood? Do you remember . . . our bare feet were touching."

We just looked at each other. It was one of those moments when we were both thinking the same thing . . . and I finally told him why I couldn't respond that night. "I wanted to direct you, so I had to keep my objectivity."

We continued to talk, and I asked, "Why haven't you married again? Don't you want children?"

"I love too many women to get married," he said.

And more recently he turned up at my concert in Hyde Park in 2019.

I still wish we had been able to do *The Normal Heart* together.

Back to 1994. After my dinner with Ralph, I flew to Washington, D.C., and thank God I was finally better because I had an important engagement I didn't want to miss . . . President Clinton's first state dinner, for Emperor Akihito and Empress Michiko of Japan. I had invited Pierre Trudeau as my escort, but he couldn't join me because he was going to be in Europe. Then Marge Tabankin heard that Peter Jennings wanted to meet me and asked if she could give him my number. I thought, *Why not?* I was trying to get out of my shell and meet new people.

When Peter called, I realized I barely had any nights free, with the tour. So on a whim I asked if he wanted to go to the White House with me. And he did. The whole thing was kind of a fluke, but my attitude was, He's the anchorman on ABC. I can get my news firsthand!

I actually don't remember where we met the first time, but I do remember going to the state dinner with him. There's a ritual when you walk into the White House for one of these events. At a certain point in this long corridor, you stop for a photo, and the reporters ask you questions. I was a bit crushed when all they asked about was my dress. It was a beautiful pewter-gray outfit by Donna, and what was great about it was the way she mixed fabrics. The off-the-shoulder sweater-like top in cashmere was paired with a long, full taffeta skirt that trailed on the floor. So it was both casual and formal. But still . . . "That's what you want to know about . . . my dress?" (In 2011, when Jim and I arrived at another state dinner at the Obama White House, for the president of China, one woman reporter asked me, "Why do you think *you* were invited?" I thought that was rather rude, so I answered back, "Maybe because I worked in a Chinese restaurant!")

That first Clinton state dinner was held in a big white tent on the lawn. It was surprisingly relaxed for a formal occasion, and the food was delicious. The new chef had jettisoned all those fancy French dishes for simpler American fare. I still remember the lobster sausage with wild mushroom risotto. I had a fine time talking to everyone, and Peter was very attentive, but in the end I decided I'd rather get my news from the TV. Anyway, the evening was just what I needed . . . a distraction from my normal routine, which was focused on rewriting and refining the show for New York.

June 20 was opening night at Madison Square Garden, and my sweet Jule Styne and his wife, Maggie, were there. I introduced him to the audience before I sang his beautiful song "People" and couldn't help remembering that, if it hadn't been for his support, I might never have been cast in *Funny Girl.*

I will always be grateful to him.

Three months later he was gone. The cause was heart failure, which seems impossible, since he had the biggest heart. I'm so glad I got to give him one last hug that night. Jule believed in me from the very beginning and he will live in my heart forever.

Liza Minnelli was also at Madison Square Garden that night, and I dedicated "The Man That Got Away" to her mother, Judy Garland, who sang it so brilliantly in her version of *A Star Is Born.*

New York was like a homecoming for me, and choosing a school here was easy . . . the donation for the music department went to my alma mater, Erasmus Hall. I invited many people from my past to the concert . . . my childhood pals Barbara Sulman and Roslyn Arenstein . . . Muriel and Jimmy Choy . . . Irving Borookow . . . and lots of Streisands, including Shelly and his wife, Judy; his former wife, Ellen; my niece Rickie; and my cousins Lowell and Harvey. Of course Cis and Harvey were there, as always. And my beloved Gracie Davidson, who had been with me since *Funny Girl.* After she had a stroke, she went back to Brooklyn to live, and that's when I found out she had a whole other family . . . two older daughters besides the one I knew, Dorothy, who was my age. I sent a limo to get them, and when they came backstage, with Gracie in a wheelchair, they looked so beautiful, with all of them dressed in white.

I thought they might like a photo with Jesse Jackson, who was there, and he happily obliged. He was so sweet to Gracie, who could hardly talk at that point. (I remember one night at Carolwood, the phone rang while I was eating dinner, and Kim didn't want to interrupt me. As soon as I found out it was Gracie, I called her right back. Apparently one of my specials was on TV, and Gracie saw it and wanted to talk to me. Her daughter put her on, and in this halting, shaky voice, she said, "I . . . love . . . you." That made me cry, and I told her how much I loved her too.)

I have a copy of that picture of Gracie in my den, with Jesse leaning over her wheelchair and her daughters in the background. I didn't hear what he whispered in Gracie's ear, but I remember what he said to me, because I wrote it down in my journal: "You're extraordinary. You're a healer . . . touched by God."

I told him, "I feel very ordinary."

And he said, "That's good. Otherwise you'd have to put bricks in your pocket to keep your ass on the ground!"

Very funny! Jesse was always quick with a clever line.

The New York audiences were phenomenal. We had originally planned three shows, then we added two more, and still people were shut out. David Letterman made such a fuss for weeks on his TV show about how he couldn't get tickets, which gave Marty an idea. I didn't want to go on the show and sit down and chat, but Marty said, "Why don't you just walk in and drop two tickets on his desk?"

So that's what I did one night, unannounced, right while he was complaining. The audience went wild as I handed him the tickets, and as soon as they quieted down, I said, "I just wanted to tell you to stop kvetching already" . . . and walked off the stage.

By now Pierre Trudeau was back on this side of the Atlantic, and he flew in to see the show. He also accompanied me to a cocktail party where I was delighted to introduce my old friend to my new friend, Madeleine Albright. She was our hostess that evening and the U.S. ambassador to the United Nations, appointed by President Clinton. A few days earlier she had been my guest at the concert.

Madeleine and I first met in 1993 when she gave a talk at a meeting of the Hollywood Women's Political Committee in LA. She was already speaking, as she told me later, when she saw a woman walk in with a beret pulled down over her eyes, and thought to herself, "Oh my God, it's Barbra Streisand." After her speech, I went over to her table to apologize for being late, and before I could say a word, she said, "I've always admired you," and I said, "Not more than I admire *you*!" We laughed and talked, and she asked, "Do you ever come to New York?"

"Yes, I still have an apartment there."

"Great, because I want to invite you to one of the lunches I give in my official residence at the Waldorf Towers."

I said, "I'd love to come," because I knew she would have interesting people and I was curious to see the place because I had heard about their period rooms.

That lunch was the beginning of a very long friendship.

Madeleine was petite in size but a powerhouse of knowledge, and it was a privilege to talk politics with someone so deeply informed . . . and who spoke her mind in no uncertain terms. She was an unusual combination . . . a shrewd stateswoman who was somehow brilliant and adorable at the same time. We were both single in those days, and we had fun going to the theater, seeing movies in the Sony screening room, and shopping for antiques. We were girlfriends, who'd have dinner together and talk about everything from foreign policy to men.

Madeleine was born in Czechoslovakia. I felt a connection to that country after *Yentl*, and when she invited me to come to a Czech play and told me the title, *The Insect Comedy*, I said, "You won't believe this, but I played a butterfly in that play when I was eighteen!" Well, this latest version turned out to be some sort of musical or opera, and . . . put it this way . . . we wanted to leave after the first act (we spotted a mutual friend, Miloš Forman, on his way out as well). When Madeleine gave her security guard the signal, he told her that she had a call from the secretary-general (which was their prearranged excuse for leaving). But actually the call turned out to be true! So she had to take it, but when we found her driver and got in the car, we couldn't move because it had a flat tire. So we had to get out and find a cab. The whole night was a comedy of errors (much funnier than the play), but we eventually made it back to her residence, where we raided the refrigerator.

Madeleine had a warmth that went deeper than the niceties of diplomacy . . . no wonder so many leaders considered her a true friend. I remember going to her farm in Virginia for a picnic supper in honor of Václav Havel, the dissident playwright who became president of Czechoslovakia. He was inspiring, because instead of being resentful after his years as a political prisoner, he chose to focus on the good in people and move on, like Nelson Mandela.

Madeleine had the same kind of compassion, and when President Clinton named her as the first female secretary of state, she brought a new perspective to the job. Her family had been forced to flee tyranny, and she knew that freedom is fragile.

Madeleine was fifty-nine years old when she found out she was not Catholic as she had been raised, but Jewish. It was a lot to process at this stage of her life. (She also learned that more than two dozen relatives had died in the Holocaust.) My reaction was, Welcome to the tribe! Then I thought, *Oh my God, I wonder if this is part of why we bonded so instantly?*

But then Madeleine had the ability to connect with all kinds of people. She was loved and respected around the world. Havel even suggested she run for president of Czechoslovakia, but she said her heart was in America, where she had been welcomed as an eleven-year-old refugee. She was grateful for all the opportunities she had been given, and to open the doors for other women, she did something that no other secretary of state had done . . . she made women's rights central to foreign policy. She recognized something fundamental . . . that societies are healthier and more productive when women are politically and economically empowered.

So, going back to 1994 and these concerts, you can see why I was proud to have her at my show!

The demand for tickets was so great that at the last minute we actually added two *more* shows (so the final count for the tour was twenty-four . . . my lucky number). By this point we no longer had to set aside any tickets for CAA or Sony. All the freebies were gone. So everyone there was a real fan, and they were the best. And, as I wrote in my journal, "I sang my ass off" for them.

On the very last night Marty had arranged to have the last song, "Somewhere," broadcast live from Madison Square Garden to the Jumbotron in Times Square. (So in a way, I was back on Broadway!) I loved that thousands of people gathered to watch.

Now I had to go back to the Arrowhead Pond in Anaheim to do the shows that had been postponed. And that's when I decided to take advantage of this opportunity and film the concert again. By now I had relaxed into the show. I was definitely more comfortable onstage, and we decided to bring back the cameras and shoot the final performance on July 24. (That number always seems to work for me.)

The Anaheim shows were kind of fun to do, because I got to see so many of my friends from LA in one fell swoop: Irvin Kershner, Warren Beatty and Annette Bening, Sean Connery, Tom Hanks and Rita Wilson, Dustin Hoffman, Don Johnson, Bill Maher, Shirley MacLaine, Carol (and even Walter) Matthau, Kelly Preston and John Travolta, and Brenda Vaccaro. I couldn't believe Ralph Fiennes came again. And when Sidney and Joanna Poitier came backstage, Sidney told me, "I'm so glad I'm living while you are." (So sweet.) We had been partners in First Artists, and our friendship meant a lot to me.

And on that last night, at the end of the show, I told the audience, "This is a very special night for me, the closing night of my tour . . . I've learned a lot. I've conquered some of my fears . . . And I want you to know how grateful I am for the love and support that you've shown me, not only tonight but for all the years past. Thank you."

And then, even after three encores, the audience still wouldn't let me go. I had to come out again. I thanked them all for coming. And I thanked my mom, who was there . . . along with Jason, Elliott, and his mother, Lucy. And before I walked off the stage I looked directly at Roger Clinton and said: "For Virginia."

But the crowd wouldn't stop . . . they were still standing and applauding. So I had to come out one last time, and the show ended as it had started, back at the MGM Grand, with me at the top of the staircase with my hands on my heart, saying thank you once more to the audience, because I was so gratified by their response.

Now I had a whole other concert to edit in less than four weeks, because it was scheduled to run as a special on HBO on August 21. HBO didn't know which version they would be getting . . . the MGM Grand show or the Anaheim show . . . and neither did I!

Eventually I decided to go with the Anaheim show, and I was in the editing room every day, working with Dwight, Gary, and the editor, Bruce Motyer. After Dwight and Gary left for the night, I would stay on, working with Bruce until the early morning hours. And still we ran out of time. On that last night before the show was due to be broadcast, I never left the editing room. I was going over sound levels and final edits with Bruce. Then I would try to sleep briefly in a chair, while he made the changes. And then he would wake me up to show me what he had done.

HBO was getting more and more nervous, because we were still in the editing room and the show had to be on the air in a few hours. There were frantic discussions between Marty and the network about maybe getting a satellite truck over to us and doing a direct linkup from the editing room, without loading it into the HBO system first.

It was really down to the wire, but somehow we managed to get it over to the network with basically minutes to spare before the cutoff point.

So *Barbra: The Concert* went on as planned at 9:00 p.m. on August 21, and the executives at HBO announced that it was the highest-rated special in their history. In 1965 my first TV special, *My Name Is Barbra,* had won five Emmys, and thirty years later, this special was nominated for ten Emmys, and once again we won five (that was kind of magical), including Outstanding Variety, Music, or Comedy Special. Marvin won for Music Direction. Bruce Jackson was recognized for his amazing sound. And Marvin, Marilyn, and Alan won for the song they wrote specifically for the concert, "Ordinary Miracles." And I won for Outstanding Individual Performance.

But the one that meant the most to me was when Dwight and I won the DGA Award for Outstanding Directorial Achievement. And once again we were very honored when *Barbra: The Concert* received the prestigious Peabody Award, just as *My Name Is Barbra* had done earlier.

I was delighted . . . but I still liked the first version that I did at the MGM Grand as well. It had been hard to choose between them, and there was one other piece that was only in the MGM show . . . the Linda Richman skit. Mike Myers had played the character, a New York Jewish woman with big hair and long nails, on *Saturday Night Live* for years. The running joke was that Linda idolized me . . . as she famously said, my voice was "like buttah" . . . and Mike was so hilarious that the line became part of the culture. Just for fun I did a walk-on one night when he was doing the routine with Madonna and Roseanne Barr and completely surprised them.

And in Las Vegas, Mike aka Linda made a surprise appearance in the midst of the audience, and when I invited her to come up onstage, she said, "I'm starting to get a little *verklempt*," and then I said, "Now I'm getting *verklempt*. Talk amongst yourselves. I'll give you a topic . . . *The Prince of Tides* is neither about princes nor tides. Discuss."

It was so much fun, and Mike was a doll to do it. I really wanted more people to see it, which was another reason why I was thinking about releasing the MGM Grand version as well . . . after all, it was different! It took a few years, but it eventually came out on DVD in 2004.

What can I say? I like to keep all my options on the table till I'm forced to decide.

FIFTY-TWO

The Artist as Citizen

All during the period when I was putting the concert together, I still made time for politics. I campaigned for David Dinkins to be re-elected as mayor of New York, and was there with him when he lost. So I was depressed the next day, when suddenly the phone rang. It was Nelson Mandela.

We had met a few months earlier during his visit to LA, and now he wanted to thank me for a donation and invite me to come to South Africa: "I am waiting for you and will embrace you with open arms." He told me, "I still think of the moment when I met you in Los Angeles. Are you still looking as formidable as you did on that occasion?"

What a charmer . . . he had suffered so much, and yet he never let it break his spirit. He was so warmhearted that he made me feel there was hope for the world.

Meanwhile, I was also following what was going on in Washington. My favorite channel was C-SPAN, and I was getting a closer look into how our government worked. It was a remarkable experience to have a president and a First Lady who were actually my friends. I believed in what they were doing and felt personally invested in their success.

And as always, I had opinions.

Now, as anyone who has ever met Bill Clinton knows, he's very open and happy to talk, because he's genuinely interested in what other people think and feel. I suppose that's why I felt comfortable enough to ask him a few questions . . . actually, a lot of questions. I'm still that girl at the yeshiva who just couldn't accept things that didn't make sense to me. I always wanted to know *Why?*

Bill was ready to explain. "Send me a list of your questions," he told me, "and I'll answer them."

So I started jotting them down:

"How do we find the money to deal with America's rise in crime? I do believe we need more programs dedicated to our kids, rather than more prisons."

"Why can't more money come out of the defense budget? I'm told we don't need more than 180 billion, which would still be four times higher than Russia's defense budget or Japan's. This would give us 80 billion more for domestic needs."

As I'm rereading these now, I'm thinking, *Boy, I had a lot of nerve to pose those questions.* Clearly I was doing a lot of reading and taking notes. I don't remember much about my history courses in high school (I was so focused on becoming an actress), and I'm not sure we even had a Civics class. But now I was trying to make up for it. And I think this period, when I was paying more attention to what was going on in the world, was my real education.

I wrote to Clinton, "I hear you explaining your BTU tax on C-SPAN from New Hampshire, but it's too small an audience. Why not address the nation? Go on national TV and talk in simple terms so people can understand how that would affect their lives." (That's me, talking to him like a director again.)

Clinton's BTU tax was an early attempt to get people to conserve energy and encourage the use of non-fossil fuels, but the opposition was fierce, and many of the Democrats who voted for it lost their seats in the 1994 midterms. What a shame . . . if it had passed, we would be further ahead on tackling climate change.

I never understood the fast-buck mentality. Doesn't the oil and gas industry care about the survival of our planet?

I was very moved when I read about the Iroquois, who believed that before they made any decision, they had to consider how it would affect seven generations to come. That was incredibly farsighted and so wise.

As I'm now looking through all these scraps of paper with my notes, I'm betting I never sent most of them (just like the letters I used to write to Lee Strasberg on the subway). I really think they were more for me, to crystallize my own thinking.

I know I was surprised when President Clinton hired Dick Morris, the Republican strategist, and I told him so: "I'm a bit wary. How can anyone work for both sides? He has no moral center. I know you're trying to be bipartisan but his loyalty will not only be to you. I guess the polls are showing he's helping but how much faith can we put into polls?"

I remembered something that Shimon Peres had told me when I sat next to him at a dinner, and wanted to share it with Clinton. Shimon said, "A leader is like a bus driver. He must never turn around and look back at his passengers. It makes them nervous. They want him to keep his eyes straight on the road ahead."

In other words, do what *you* believe is right and don't pay too much attention to polls.

On another scrap of paper from 1996, I wrote, "I've been thinking lately about what makes a leader. What personality traits are common to people like you and FDR? A need for attention, a calling, a sense of civic duty? The need to be remembered?"

(Actually I think it's all of those.)

On the Academy Awards that year, a Holocaust survivor who was the subject of a winning documentary said something about those who died . . . they would never know "the magic of a boring evening at home."

That really struck me, so I quoted that to Clinton and added, "I must always remember to be grateful. P.S. Have you ever tried Ben & Jerry's Cherry Garcia low-fat yogurt?"

That note is a perfect example of how my mind works . . . it's all over the place, from leadership to low-fat yogurt.

Whenever President Clinton and I ran into each other at various fundraisers or other events, we would continue our conversations. That made me think back to my father, and his father, Isaac, who used to say, "Manny was so smart. He could talk to presidents."

And here I was, talking to this president, and being totally comfortable. The realization made me smile.

I may have been a little naïve and definitely earnest, wanting to share my thoughts, but I wasn't deluded. As I said in one note, "I know you're probably not interested in my opinions but I'm giving them to you anyway." Another ended with: "Looking forward to arguing with you about the positions I'd like you to take."

That was clearly a joke, because I don't remember any arguments, and if there had been, there's no question who would have won. I was operating on instinct . . . I thought I had a general feel for the zeitgeist . . . but he had command of the facts.

So I was lucky. He liked to teach, and I liked to learn.

Clinton was a quick-witted lawyer who thought several moves ahead. He could see the big picture and knew how to strategize in order to get what he wanted . . . a very useful skill for a leader. He sincerely believed in the government's ability to help people and came into office with an ambitious agenda, hoping to persuade others to go along. In that, he was an optimist, like his mother.

I'm so glad Bill Clinton was bold and thought big. Perhaps the most extraordinary moment of his first year as president occurred on September 13, 1993, when he stood between Yitzhak Rabin, the prime minister of Israel, and Yasser Arafat, the chairman of the Palestine Liberation Organization, on the White House lawn and gently nudged these two archenemies into a handshake. People in the audience gasped and then applauded.

The Oslo Accords, in which the PLO recognized Israel's right to exist, and Israel recognized the PLO as the legitimate representative of the Palestinian people, had just been signed. And Shimon Peres was the chief negotiator for the Israeli side.

I adored Shimon from the moment we met in 1984 after the Israeli premiere of *Yentl*, when he had been so proud of me . . . and now I was so proud of him for managing to do what so many people thought impossible. The Oslo Accords were a major breakthrough, a big step toward peace in the Middle East, and he, Rabin, and Arafat would later share the Nobel Peace Prize for their efforts.

But in September there was still a lot more work to be done in order to implement the agreement. Two months later Prime Minister Rabin was back at the White House, and I was pleased to be invited to a lunch in his honor. We met briefly in the receiving line, where he was polite but clearly preoccupied (he was saving the world, after all). A few days later I saw him and his wife, Leah, again at an Israel Policy Forum lunch in Los Angeles, and once again he seemed cool and contained . . . so different from Shimon, who was warm and engaging. I remember President Clinton telling me that he had grown very close to Rabin and even considered him a father figure. That felt familiar to me. I guess we were both searching for our lost fathers, in a sense, and my father figure was Shimon.

Looking back at this time, I can see how my political consciousness and my creative life were converging. I wanted to make films that dealt with meaningful subjects and issues that were important to me. A few months after I met Rabin, a script came to me that opened with a conversation among White House aides who were preparing for that pivotal meeting in the Rose Garden. Then it went back in time to cover fifty years of Middle Eastern history as told through the parallel stories of two boys . . . Rabin and Arafat . . . who became leaders of their rival factions. What I didn't know and what really interested me was that they were both born in Jerusalem and grew up only a few miles apart . . . and yet they were worlds apart in ideology. Their diametrically opposed beliefs were like a wall between them, and although their histories were intertwined, they had never met until that day at the White House.

The script was called *Two Hands That Shook the World*, and the underlying idea was to present a fair and balanced portrayal of the Arab-Israeli conflict. In fact, it was so evenhanded that we had gained the cooperation of both Rabin and Arafat, who had agreed to consult on the film, which was going to be made for Showtime.

And then on November 4, 1995, Rabin was assassinated by a right-wing fanatic, an Israeli who was opposed to his peace initiatives.

I wrote in my journal that day, as I was crying, "Why do good men have to be taken away from us?"

President Clinton flew to Israel to deliver one of the eulogies for his close friend, and took the opportunity to remind everyone of a basic truth: "Your prime minister was a martyr for peace, but he was a victim of hate. Surely, we must learn from his martyrdom that if people cannot let go of the hatred of their enemies, they risk sowing the seeds of hatred among themselves."

Two weeks later I went ahead with the announcement of our movie as planned and was proud to add a quote from Rabin's chief of staff to our press release: "The late prime minister was particularly enthusiastic about this project and, as his closest adviser, I hope and expect that it will be a fitting memorial to his personal quest for a lasting peace between all Arabs and Israelis, a mission he carried with him to his last hour."

And then the movie didn't get made, not because of anything significant. In fact, it was petty . . . the director wanted to be paid a million dollars, which would have set a new high for Showtime, so they refused (even though the producer who brought it to us, Cis, and I were all willing to make up the difference out of our own fees). So another worthy project died.

But I did manage to get a different TV movie made, which was considered even more controversial by some people. It was called *Serving in Silence: The Margarethe Cammermeyer Story*. It all started with an article I read in *The New York Times* in 1992. Colonel Cammermeyer's twenty-six-year career in the military as an army nurse was exemplary. She had been awarded the Bronze Star for her service in Vietnam. She had been named Nurse of the Year by the Veterans Administration. And then, when Grethe was up for a promotion to chief military nurse of the nation, she was asked a question during her security clearance: Are you a homosexual?

The answer had only recently become clear to her (after having been married for fifteen years and giving birth to four sons), and she answered truthfully: Yes.

As a result, she was discharged, and her career was over.

When I read this, it sent a shiver up my spine. Once again I was reminded of that line from Shaw's *Saint Joan*: "He who tells too much truth is sure to be hanged."

I remember thinking, *How dare they do this to a woman who has dedicated twenty-six years of her life to the Army?* Grethe had a spotless record. Obviously her dismissal had nothing to do with her performance. Instead, it was a blatant case of discrimination. And she had decided to challenge her dismissal in federal court.

I immediately called Cis and said, "We have to do something about this. We have to tell this story."

All this commotion around gays in the military had bothered me for some time. The official policy, which banned homosexuals from serving, just didn't make sense to me. You'd think that anyone who was willing to die for their country would be welcomed. Instead, gays were demonized. Just what were officials afraid of? That they would flirt in the foxholes?

Other countries, including Israel, Australia, Canada, Sweden, Norway, France, Belgium, Portugal, Spain, and South Korea, allowed homosexuals into the armed forces. Recruiters for our military were always encouraging every capable citizen to enlist. Grethe was clearly capable, which she had already proved over and over. It seemed absurd under the circumstances to worry about her sexual orientation.

One of the reasons I supported Bill Clinton was because he had campaigned on the promise to lift the ban. What I didn't fully realize was how much opposition he faced from the Joint Chiefs of Staff. Meanwhile, polls showed that the majority of the country did not support lifting the ban, and opposition was also solidifying in Congress. The House passed a resolution against ending it, and the Senate went along. And if Clinton persisted, they threatened to reverse his order with an amendment to the defense appropriations bill, which would be politically difficult for the president to veto. And even if he did, they had enough votes to overturn it.

So Clinton was stymied, and that's why he was forced to settle for the universally criticized "Don't ask, don't tell" policy . . . which basically meant that as long as a person didn't acknowledge being gay, the military would look the other way . . . but still had the right to dismiss anyone who was openly homosexual.

I was profoundly disappointed and didn't hesitate to tell President Clinton. (I'm sure he didn't need to hear this from me. He said he was disappointed himself.)

People are frightened of what they don't know, and that's why I wanted to make *Serving in Silence.* I thought if Americans got to know Grethe, they would identify with her. I believe we all have certain needs in common . . . we want to be happy, we want to be loved, we want to be respected, no matter what our sexual orientation. I believe we're basically more similar than different.

No one should have to live a lie.

But first I had to convince Grethe to allow me to tell her story. And I wanted to be very clear about what a project like this could mean for her. A TV movie can reach into the hearts and minds of millions of people in one night . . . that's the positive. But it also comes with a negative . . . her private life would be exposed, and I had to be sure she was willing to take that risk.

Our first meeting was at my house, and I was very direct. "Are you prepared to have your life displayed on television?"

And she said, "No."

That was a very sane reaction.

We talked, and I explained what I wanted to do with the film and how I thought it could help millions of people. It was only when I put it in this broader context that she could let go of herself, in a way. As Grethe said, "I had to be convinced that there was some redeeming reason for doing this." In the end she decided to do it not for herself, but for all of us who wanted a more tolerant society.

Like me, she believes that the truth does set you free.

So she gave up her privacy, and I promised to tell her story with grace, dignity, and truth.

It turns out that *Yentl* also helped. Grethe said, "I had seen Barbra in *Yentl,* and she had a nice voice, even though it wasn't country-western" (her favorite). And since I had played Yentl, she thought I would understand what it meant to be discriminated against and to live with a secret.

When I met Grethe and saw her blond Nordic coloring and strong bone structure, I immediately thought of Glenn Close. I felt that Glenn had the same kind of quiet authority as Grethe . . . a kind of cool reserve.

So I had some say in casting, and was thrilled when Judy Davis agreed to play the crucial role of Grethe's partner . . . but other than that, I left most of the details to Cis. She chose Alison Cross for the script (she had written the award-winning TV movie *Roe vs. Wade*).

From the beginning I saw *Serving in Silence* as a love story. Like *The Normal Heart*, it's about everyone's right to love.

I like doing stories about love. I think love is the single most important word in the human language.

I was busy with my concert tour, so I only had time to visit the set in Vancouver after I had finished editing *Barbra: The Concert* and it had aired on HBO.

I thought Jeff Bleckner did a beautiful job of directing Glenn and Judy. They were absolutely wonderful, and *Serving in Silence* attracted a huge audience when it was shown on NBC on February 6, 1995.

It's hard now to imagine just how controversial the subject was back then. One station in Alabama actually blacked out the screen when Glenn and Judy had their one kiss. But the response from viewers was gratifying, and the film was nominated for six Emmy awards, including Outstanding Made for Television Movie. It won three: Glenn Close for Outstanding Lead Actress, Judy Davis for Outstanding Supporting Actress, and Alison Cross for Outstanding Writing.

Coincidentally I was up for my own Emmys that night for *Barbra: The Concert*, but I think I was more excited about their awards than my own. I have a photograph of Glenn and me, both holding our trophies. And I was very proud when *Serving in Silence* also went on to win a Peabody Award, the LAMBDA Liberty Award, the GLAAD Media Award, and the National Education Association Award for the Advancement of Learning.

More important, Grethe also won her case and was reinstated into the National Guard. But fifteen more years had to pass before President Obama was finally able to abolish "Don't ask, don't tell" . . . and even in 2010 he faced pushback.

I'm glad the country finally caught up to the sentiments expressed in our movie, and I'm still grateful to Grethe for entrusting me with her story. *Serving in Silence* was a stress-free and joyful project . . . and for me, that's saying a lot.

It was the first of a group of films that Cis and I produced for TV on serious subjects. *Rescuers: Stories of Courage* was about Gentiles who risked their lives to rescue Jews during the Holocaust. *What Makes a Family* was about a lesbian couple who have a baby via artificial insemination. When the partner who carried the baby dies, her parents sue for custody of the child, and the other mother has to fight them in court. *The Long Island Incident* dealt with a mass shooting on a commuter train that motivated Carolyn McCarthy, whose husband was killed and son gravely injured, to become a congresswoman crusading for gun control. *Varian's War* tells the story of Varian Fry, who helped so many artists and writers escape the Nazis by smuggling them out of Vichy France. The list is extraordinary . . . names like Marc Chagall, Marcel Duchamp, Hannah Arendt, Max Ophuls, and Franz Werfel and his wife, Alma, who was Gustav Mahler's widow.

I didn't know until we did the research for that movie that Mahler had written the symphony I've always loved . . . Symphony no. 10 . . . in the midst of despair about his beloved wife's affair with another man. Suddenly I understood how he found those chords that expressed all those feelings of longing and loss . . . so deeply painful yet beautiful at the same time.

Another project was a documentary called *Reel Models: The First Women of Film*, about the forgotten women who helped shape the industry. Everyone thinks of D. W. Griffith as the father of film, but in 1896, nineteen years before he made *The Birth of a Nation*, a young French secretary named Alice Guy-Blaché was the first woman to direct a short film, and would eventually run her own studio. Twenty years later, Lois Weber was the highest-paid director at Universal Studios, where she boldly took on such taboo subjects as prostitution and anti-Semitism. In 1916 a dozen women were working regularly as directors in Hollywood.

One hundred years later, only four of the one hundred top-grossing films were directed by women. We were doing better in 1916!

It's funny . . . I found it very easy to speak out in my work, but it was different when I was asked to speak out in real life.

In 1994 I was approached by the Institute of Politics at Harvard's John F. Kennedy School of Government to be part of a program which over the years had brought in speakers ranging from Shinzo Abe, the prime minister of Japan, to Ted Turner, the founder of CNN.

I thought, *Oh my God* . . . I was intimidated, and yet it was hard to refuse, because they happened to catch me at just the right moment. I was so incensed at what was going on, and this was an opportunity to express my feelings about it.

People like Newt Gingrich were twisting the truth and making Clinton out to be some "tax and spend liberal." (What's new? And it's particularly ironic since Clinton turned out to be the only president in over seventy years to leave us with four consecutive budget surpluses.)

And in the midterms the Democrats took a beating (facing a double whammy from the oil lobby, which didn't like the gas tax, and the NRA, which didn't like the assault weapons ban). It was very depressing, and many people were urging Clinton to reverse course.

But I had a different take. I felt the wolves would pounce if they sensed weakness. Newt Gingrich and his crowd were spoiling for a fight. (I was appalled by Gingrich. Once, he was standing behind me at a state dinner for Tony Blair and said, "I'm your fan." I just couldn't help myself. I said, "I'm your enemy.")

As I wrote Clinton in a letter, "You can draw the contrast between your vision and his viciousness . . . and return to what you did so well in the campaign . . . putting a human face on the Republicans' cruel policies . . . Gingrich doesn't care a whit about poor mothers . . . he will paint you as a liberal who wants to give the hard-earned money of working people away to welfare mothers."

The Republicans were always inciting fear of the other, which usually meant anyone whose skin wasn't the same color as theirs.

I urged Clinton, "You must find ways of calming fear instead of inciting it."

This was a defining moment in his presidency, and that was another reason I agreed to speak at Harvard. I spent three months working on that speech, doing my research, talking to historians, theologians, political pundits. I didn't want to come off as anti-Republican. I thought of my speech more as pro-humanity.

I was so obsessed during this period that I probably drove my friends nuts. I had all these ideas ricocheting around my brain. I think I went through over fifty drafts. There was so much to say, and I couldn't fit everything in.

The pressure was starting to feel overwhelming, and I was tempted to just cancel the whole thing. During those last few weeks before I flew to Boston, I was so tense that I wasn't even hungry. That should tell you how anxious I was.

I arrived in Cambridge on Wednesday night, February 1, because Harvard had asked if I wanted to attend a class, and the one that interested me was Professor Laurence Tribe's on constitutional law, which took place the next morning. This was one of those times when I really wished I had gone to college. The lecture was fascinating, and I was scribbling down notes. There was a moment when he asked a question, and I raised my hand to answer it. I must have gotten it right, or at least right enough, because Larry and I became lasting friends.

After the class there was a lunch with some Harvard undergraduates and fellows from the Institute of Politics, hosted by John F. Kennedy, Jr. I thought he was a doll, just like his father. And he had that same twinkle in his eye, as I found out a year later when he asked me to be on the cover of his new magazine, *George*. His idea was to have me dress up in a slinky gown like Marilyn Monroe when she sang "Happy Birthday" to his father. I thought he was kidding at first, but he was serious. I told him I'd rather be a historical figure, so we settled on Betsy Ross sewing the flag.

On the day of the photo shoot, John wanted to be there, and he drove out to my house in Malibu with Ken Sunshine, my East Coast press rep. (Ken and I met when I was campaigning for Bella Abzug, and we've worked together on many political events.) Everyone was setting up the equipment in Grandma's house. (That's the little guesthouse on my property where I often work, recording music or editing films. My husband gave it that name because it looks like a house where a Grandma would feel at home.) Finally, the lights, the photographer, and I were all ready, but Ken and John were nowhere to be found. I went looking for them, and as I walked around the back of the main house, I saw two men splashing around in the pool. It was hot, and on a whim they had shucked off their clothes and jumped in.

I smiled and asked, "How's the water?"

Back to Harvard. After the lunch I was ushered off to be officially welcomed by Albert Carnesale, the dean of the Kennedy School of Government. Then our group was taken on a tour of the campus, and later there was a dinner with Dean Carnesale, Professor Tribe, Governor William Weld, Henry Louis Gates, Jr., Dr. Cornel West, Doris Kearns and Dick Goodwin, and Judge Leon Higgenbotham. Cis, Marge, and Marty were also there with me. I honestly didn't want that night to end . . . with such interesting people, the conversation was so rich . . . and besides, the next day meant the speech.

I really got spooked when I walked out and saw all the television lights, cameras, and reporters. I had assumed I would be facing a small audience of students and professors. Instead, more than seven hundred people were there, along with what seemed like the entire national press corps.

Dean Carnesale stood at the podium, and I sat down beside him while he gave the introduction, which was extremely complimentary but went on and on. Meanwhile, I was so scared, I wasn't sure I was going to survive long enough to give the speech! I actually gestured to him to speed it up and had to quickly get up from my seat to reach under the podium for a glass of water.

Finally it was my turn. My stomach hurt, my lips stuck together. If you watch the tape, you can see how nervous I was. I could hardly speak.

I had to acknowledge it, so I said: "I've stood up and performed in front of thousands of people, but let me tell you, this is much more frightening. Maybe it's because this is the John F. Kennedy School of Government at Harvard, and I'm neither a politician nor a professor." I paused, grasping the podium for dear life. "Perhaps some of my anxiety has to do with the fact that I've been told that a future president of the United States might very well be in this audience. And if that's true, I'm sure *she* will be the one to ask me the toughest questions."

That got cheers and a big round of applause. (Or maybe that was just my heart pounding.)

I told the audience my subject . . . the artist as citizen. What is the artist's political role? Why does it make so many people angry when artists speak out? It was something I'd been thinking about a lot since the backlash from my trip to D.C. Even though, as I admitted, "I guess I can call myself an artist, although after thirty years, the word still feels a bit pretentious. But I am, first and foremost, a citizen: a tax-paying, voting, concerned American citizen who happens to have opinions . . . a lot of them . . . which seems to bother some people."

I was still smarting from the way artists were derided not only by the Republicans, but also sometimes by the press. Newt Gingrich, even though he was apparently such a fan, was saying that we needed to balance the budget, and the first thing to go should be arts programs. But as I pointed out, "The government's contribution to the National Endowment for the Arts and PBS is actually quite meager. To put it in perspective, the entire budget for the NEA is equal to one F-22 fighter jet . . . and PBS costs each taxpayer less than one dollar a year . . .

"So maybe it's not about balancing the budget. Maybe it's about shutting the minds and mouths of artists who might have something thought-provoking to say."

That's because of the nature of our work. "We have to walk in other people's shoes and live in other people's skins. This does tend to make us more sympathetic to politics that are more tolerant. In our work, in our preparation, and in our research, we are continuously trying to educate ourselves. And with learning comes compassion. Education is the enemy of bigotry and hate. It's hard to hate someone you truly understand."

I deeply resented the notion that one political party owned the franchise on family values, personal responsibility, and religion. The Republicans were eager to invoke God, but was God really against gun control and food stamps for poor children? I found it very revealing that people who claimed to be pro-life did not believe in supporting children once they were born.

I was sick of the hypocrisy. If they were so concerned about law and order, why were they for putting more guns on the street?

President Kennedy once said he valued artists because they "knew the midnight as well as the high noon [and] understood the ordeal as well as the triumph of the human spirit." He was well aware that art can be controversial. As he said, the artist "must often sail against the currents of his time. This is not a popular role." (By the way, President Kennedy was the first to suggest creating the NEA.)

I have great respect for artists. Their work gives us a reflection of the times, and sometimes they challenge us to see what others would prefer to ignore. They can give voice to the voiceless, by speaking up when no one else will. And when that work is done well, it makes us think and feel . . . and stimulates change. Artists can be a country's conscience.

That's why art is the enemy of tyrants and dictators.

When politicians denounce artists and defund the arts, it's time to change the politicians.

I believe we all have not only the right, but the responsibility to be politically active and to question authority. As Teddy Roosevelt once said, "To announce that there must be no criticism of the president, or that we are to stand by the president, right or wrong, is not only unpatriotic and servile, but is morally treasonable to the American public."

I knew I was no expert, but along with every other American I did share one particular qualification. President Jimmy Carter put it very well, in his farewell address from the Oval Office: "In a few days I will lay down my official duties in this office, to take up once more the only title in our democracy superior to that of president, the title of citizen."

That sentiment really moved me, and I ended with these words: "So, until women are treated equally with men, until gays and minorities are not discriminated against, and until children have their full rights, artists must continue to speak out. I will be one of them. Sorry . . . but the artist as citizen is here to stay."

And then I basically collapsed with relief that the speech was over. I had to step offstage before the Q&A session, because I desperately needed a break.

They told me I could skip it, and I would have liked to, since speaking extemporaneously is one of my biggest fears. But I felt I had no choice. I had spent three months reading and learning as much as I could, and I didn't want to let the audience down. So I just went back and winged it.

One of the first questions was from a young woman. She started out, "You're an outstanding public speaker." I thanked her. Then she went on to add, "You're wealthy, you're intelligent, you're enormously popular . . ."

I broke in to ask, "You got a guy for me?"

That got a laugh. Finally I began to relax a bit.

But then she continued, "So would you please consider running for public office in ninety-six?" The audience applauded, but I said, "Oh no. No, no, no. I'm passionate about certain issues, but I think I can be much more effective doing what I do."

Making films is such a wonderful way to reach people . . . through a story. Sometimes you get emotionally blocked, and if you watch a movie, or listen to a particular song, it releases all that pent-up feeling. It frees you. And that can be more persuasive than some political stump speech.

Afterward I walked into the reception and cringed. There had to be at least a hundred guests. But everyone was so kind. Some people even said the Q&A was the best part of the evening, which made me feel good.

But then I began to feel terrible again . . . dizzy, a bit sick to my stomach . . . and I actually had to leave the dinner early. Suddenly, I needed to be alone. I just wanted to be done with this ordeal. And then guess what? There was a huge snowstorm that night, and the next morning, all the flights to and from Boston were canceled.

Well, that wasn't going to stop me from getting home. Kim called Amtrak, and the trains were running, so we all got tickets. It was amazing how many people found a reason to walk by our seats. I just kept my head down and played cards with Renata all the way to New York.

It was an eventful few days. The Harvard speech was on Friday, *Serving in Silence* aired on Monday, and to complete the trifecta, on Sunday night *The Prince of Tides* was shown for the first time on TV. As I was watching it, I noticed that every time a commercial came on, it was so loud that it was jarring. So I called up the network and asked if I could speak to the sound engineer.

I thought there might be something wrong with the movie's soundtrack . . .

was it too low? But I was naïve, because as the engineer explained to me, all commercials are automatically made louder. So then we talked about sound levels, and I politely asked if he could lower the volume two decibels for the commercials. He was very nice and he did it.

I guess this is what people mean when they call me a perfectionist.

FIFTY-THREE

The Mirror Has Two Faces

I just wanted to make a movie with a happy ending. Too many characters I've played . . . Fanny, Katie, Yentl, Lowenstein . . . wound up alone in the last reel. It was time for the girl to finally get the guy.

The Mirror Has Two Faces was a nice romantic comedy . . . although that label seems a little narrow. It's a comedy *and* a drama . . . life is funny and sad, and the most interesting comedies have something serious at their core. I thought it would be an easy project, and TriStar gave me the green light.

And I was giving myself a challenge as a director. I had worked on *Yentl* for fifteen years . . . five years intensively. *The Prince of Tides* absorbed about three and a half years of my life. I wanted to prove to myself that I could make a film more quickly, and figured a year and a half would be enough time for this one.

And we planned to shoot in New York, which came at just the right moment. I had recently bought a new house in Malibu and was having a few alterations made, as well as renovating the house next door, and I didn't want to be around for the construction.

So I thought, *I'm going to make this movie and I'm going to do it with only four and a half weeks of prep time.* It was the end of summer, and we needed to start shooting before the leaves fell from the trees.

And who knows? I might even have fun.

Richard LaGravenese and I had initially worked on the script back in 1992. He had been hired by TriStar to write a remake of a 1958 French film, but by the time his script got to me, little of the original movie remained except the title. Richard had dropped most of the convoluted plot and turned a dark melodrama into a romantic comedy, with deeper implications about two people disillusioned by love. Gregory Larkin is a mathematics professor who gets weak in the knees around beautiful women. When he's sexually attracted to someone, he loses control. He gets dizzy. He can't do his work, and he can't relate normally to a woman, so she inevitably leaves him. Since he wants to share his life with someone, he decides the only solution is to find a woman to whom he is not attracted, so that sex will not get in the way. He puts an ad in the paper and meets Rose Morgan, a lonely English professor who dresses in baggy clothes and pays little attention to her appearance. The two agree to enter into a sexless marriage, and then complications ensue.

I've always been fascinated by beauty. What is beauty, after all? What is beautiful to me might not be beautiful to you. So I guess you could say I'm interested in both the superficial aspect of appearance but also the more profound question of how a woman defines herself, based on how she thinks she looks.

And I wanted to explore how beauty affects men. What is attraction? Is it a physical perception or a soulful connection? Or both?

In the first script Richard wrote, the heroine had cosmetic surgery in order to try to make herself more attractive to her husband. I didn't see it that way. I thought the change should come from within.

So Richard came to my house, and we sat across from each other at my antique partners' desk and reworked the story. What I wanted to convey was that beauty is not only in the eye of the beholder but in the heart as well. You might be attracted to someone who's externally beautiful . . . but what is behind their eyes? If they don't have character, if they don't have soul, your impression of their beauty is going to fade quickly.

After Richard did another draft, I had a reading of the script with Gena Rowlands, Ray Liotta, George Segal, Teri Garr, Peter Bogdanovich, and Carrie Fisher. Quite a cast for a reading! Unfortunately it was clear to me that the script still needed a lot of work, and I set it aside to focus on developing *The Normal Heart*, preparing my concert at the MGM Grand, going on tour, and producing the Margarethe Cammermeyer story.

Richard also went on to other things, but we kept talking from time to time. And a year later when he sent me another draft, I saw new possibilities. I got excited about the story all over again and invited Richard back to discuss it.

Then Richard surprised me. When we first worked together, he had been a little aloof . . . almost arrogant. And now he wanted to explain why.

"You changed my life," he told me. "When I was nine years old, I saw *Funny Girl* and fell madly in love with you. I said to myself, That's what I want to do . . . be in movies. You were from Brooklyn, I was from Brooklyn, and you had this confidence and talent that knocked me out."

I was so touched, and told him so. And then he went on, "I was never so nervous about meeting anyone as I was with you. I was completely intimidated, and because I didn't want to seem like a fan, I was distant, and you probably thought I was rude."

He was right. But now I understood why. In the meantime, Richard had written a couple of successful movies, like *The Bridges of Madison County*, and he was much more confident. And we found new layers in the story. I wanted to expand the mother-daughter relationship, and thought it would be interesting to go deeper into that dynamic. Much of how a woman sees herself depends on how her parents perceived her. If you tell a little girl she's beautiful, that's what she'll always believe. And if you tell her she's not beautiful, she'll believe that.

And the story also gave us an opportunity to explore the many faces of love and delve deeper into the complexity of relationships . . . the fear of loving. Sex really does change things. It complicates relationships and makes each of us so vulnerable that we can be seriously hurt, or hurt our partner.

Richard brought up the idea of courtly love . . . the medieval notion of love between a knight and a noblewoman that was no less genuine even though it was never consummated. And we used it in Rose's lecture to her students about different types of love. As she says about these platonic relationships, "They took sex out of the equation, leaving them with a union of souls . . . Sex was always the fatal love potion . . . all consummation could lead to was madness, despair, or death."

You can see how Gregory, who has ducked into the lecture hall to check her out, can relate to that!

And then I added the bit about going to the movies, because I had been so profoundly affected by all those love scenes scored with beautiful music. Rose says, "Clinical experts, scholars, and my Aunt Esther are united in the belief that true love has spiritual dimensions, while romantic love is nothing but a lie . . . an illusion . . . a modern myth . . . a soulless manipulation. And speaking of manipulation, it's like going to the movies and we see the lovers on-screen kiss and the music swells and we buy it, right? So when my date takes me home and kisses me good night if I don't hear the Philharmonic in my head, I dump him."

It's hard for real life to live up to the movies.

The script was getting better, but we still didn't have an ending. Then I was in New York and feeling a little depressed one night, so I went to the opera at the Met. Decades earlier, when I was just nineteen, I told a newspaper reporter that I wanted to direct opera someday. And who knows, maybe I will. It's such a spectacular medium . . . theatricality on a grand scale with great music and great voices. But I'm not really an opera buff, so attending a performance was an unusual thing for me to do.

And once again, as Goethe said, the universe was presenting me with exactly what I needed.

The opera I saw was Franco Zeffirelli's dazzling production of Puccini's *Turandot*. Not only did it lift me out of my funk, but I heard that great aria "Nessun Dorma" and thought, *That's how I'm going to end this movie! With Puccini!*

Rose and Gregory should hear that glorious aria when they realize they're in love. And why do people want to fall in love, even though it can be painful? Rose answers that question in her lecture. She says, "Because that experience makes us feel completely alive, where every sense is heightened, every emotion is magnified, our everyday reality is shattered, and we are flung into the heavens . . . I read an article a while ago that said, 'When we fall in love, we hear Puccini in our heads.' I love that. I think it's because his music fully expresses our longing for passion in our lives and romantic love."

So that set the stage for my Puccini aria, but I still had to figure out how it would appear at the end.

We began filming in New York in October 1995, on sets we had built at the old Harlem Armory up on Fifth Avenue and 142nd Street, and on various locations like Tavern on the Green, the Monkey Bar, Bloomingdale's, and Columbia University. Rose and Gregory were both professors at Columbia, and that school had a special meaning for me, since my father had gone to Columbia Teachers College. It felt very right to me to be a teacher, just as he was. (After all, I had just lectured at Harvard! Then in May, Brandeis University presented me with an honorary doctorate. So I was on a roll, academically.)

And I was working with a brilliant cast, starting with the wonderful Jeff Bridges as Gregory. Jeff is a great actor who's also very good-looking, with a strong, masculine body. He exudes sexuality. You can just feel how much he appreciates women, which probably has something to do with the fact that he grew up with a great mom, Dorothy. She was a character . . . strong, opinionated, wonderful, warm, and funny. And she was so loving to me. One of the benefits of getting to know Jeff is that you also get to know his whole family, since they're so close. His father, Lloyd; his brother, Beau; his sister, Cindy; and his wife, Susan, all embraced me. I was included in their family gatherings, and Jeff brought Dorothy to my house for Mother's Day with my family. She was a hoot . . . making up dirty poems and reminiscing about how she taught the kids to act . . . "Okay, now give me an angry look! Sad! Happy!" As soon as I heard Jeff talk about his mother, I knew he would be easy to direct. (If you're going out with a man on a date, your first question should be, "What was your relationship with your mother like?")

To play Rose's mother I asked Gena Rowlands, who had been incredible at the reading, but she had another commitment. It was Cis who came up with the idea of the legendary Lauren Bacall. I had always admired her as a great beauty, but I became really fond of her when she and Jason Robards came to the opening night of *Funny Girl* on Broadway. She came to my apartment in New York to talk about the role, and I thought she was perfect, kind of flamboyant and tough, just as Hannah, the character, should be. And she was still a great beauty. The softness of her youthful face had been refined by age, so her marvelous bone structure was even more apparent. And she told me she was Jewish, which I didn't know. Her real name was Betty Joan Perske, and everybody called her Betty, which says a lot about how genuine she was.

For my sister I wanted a tall, very attractive woman as a contrast to my character, and she had to have a great figure to carry off Claire's skin-tight wardrobe (in contrast to what Rose wore). Mimi Rogers fit the bill perfectly. She was also delightful to work with and quite adept at comedy.

One day I was talking to Dick Guttman, my press rep, and said, "I'm looking for a very handsome guy . . . you know, someone like Pierce Brosnan . . . to play the man who marries my sister."

"How about Pierce Brosnan?" Dick said.

I said, "Are you kidding? He just played James Bond!"

Well, Dick happened to represent Pierce as well, and he mentioned the part to him, and we sent him the script. And Pierce called me and said, "I'll do it."

What made it even nicer is that Pierce is as charming in real life as he is on-screen. He's a very smart guy, yet he was able to play a very shallow character. I also like the woman who became his wife, Keely, who's a committed advocate for the environment. Austin Pendleton, whom I adored working with in *What's Up, Doc?*, played my previous boyfriend. I wanted a classic beauty for Gregory's ex and couldn't have found a better choice than the model Elle Macpherson. She was six feet of gorgeousness! And then George Segal, my old pal from *The Owl and the Pussycat*, took over the role of Gregory's best friend when Dudley Moore sadly couldn't continue because of health reasons. Brenda Vaccaro, whom I've known since the 1960s, played my best friend, which made our scenes easy. She's the sweetest girl, so funny, loving, and kind, and she has the best laugh.

This was the part that Donna Karan wanted. She begged, she pleaded, she even offered me $500,000 to let her play the role.

"Donna," I told her, "you know you'd have to do what I tell you. And you'd have to learn lines and say them again and again."

"Oh, I don't know if I could do that," she replied. "Can't I just talk to you like we do in real life?"

No . . .

I like improvisation but not when it's completely undisciplined. Time is money on a movie set, and you can't just fool around. I love Donna dearly, and she has many extraordinary talents, but I know her too well to think she would be capable of following direction. So her film debut is still on hold.

I've been looking through the journal I kept during the shoot, and the first weeks were definitely a challenge. It seemed as if there was one problem after another. We lost the sound when a generator failed. On our first night at Tavern on the Green, I took a look through the camera and as I was stepping away, I fell over a microphone box and hurt my back. Brenda's dress split. Betty's didn't fit. Every day there was some sort of disaster.

I had wanted Andrzej Bartkowiak to be the cinematographer, but he was busy on another film. So I hired Dante Spinotti because he had worked with Lina Wertmüller, and I figured he must get along with women directors.

The test shots he did outdoors were beautiful. I said, "This looks great." Then the next morning we went indoors to do some costume and makeup tests with interior lighting (which is a whole other ballgame) and did more that afternoon. When we saw the dailies, I said, "The afternoon tests look different. My eyes look a little blurry. What changed?"

"Nothing," he said. "It's exactly the same. You must have changed your eye makeup."

I said, "I've been wearing the same eye makeup for over thirty years!"

And then I found out from the focus puller that Dante had changed the filter. Why didn't he just tell me the truth?

I've had great rapport with so many wonderful cinematographers, and we worked together like partners. But after each take with Dante, there was no reaction.

I would have to ask, "Was it okay?"

And his response was, "I'll tell you when it's not okay."

I found that so unfriendly. Clearly Dante and I were having a hard time communicating with each other. Maybe it was the language barrier. Or sometimes two people just don't click.

Over Christmas we mutually decided that we should part ways, and by now luckily Andrzej was available. He started in January, and I wrote in my journal, "Wow! What a difference. Andrzej is so enthusiastic and kind. His operator is a pro." (It was the wonderful Dick Mingalone, who had worked for a few blissful days on *The Prince of Tides*.)

Now that I had Andrzej, the work became fun again.

I was getting great stuff from Jeff. We had an instant rapport . . . the kind of chemistry that adds sparks to a scene. We'd do a few takes and I'd say, "We've got it."

Sometimes he'd say, "Let's do it one more time. Let's just mess around. Just play."

Jeff had the confidence to be free . . . to explore . . . and it was fun to play with him. Like me he could access that part of himself that was still a child.

Betty was a different story. There was a moment in the script when Rose asks her mother, "How did it feel . . . being beautiful? . . . How did it feel, having people look at you with such admiration?" (I added that question about being beautiful, because I really wanted to know.)

This had to resonate with Lauren Bacall. She was a great beauty, and I had put photographs of her from the 1940s, in films like *To Have and Have Not*, around the set. All she needed to do was tell me the truth.

But I wasn't getting the reaction I wanted. The tone of her words was too breezy . . . too bright, too shallow. So I said to the crew, "Turn off the camera." (Secretly, I had already told them to ignore what I said and just keep rolling.)

Betty was so honest and direct in real life but she had a tendency to "act" when she thought the camera was on. And I wanted her to really think, rather than merely say the lines from the script.

So I asked her, "What was it like to be making your first film, working with Howard Hawks and falling in love with Humphrey Bogart?"

She thought for a long moment and then said, simply and quietly, with a wistful look on her face, "It was wonderful."

I said, "Print! We got it!"

She laughed when she realized she was being filmed.

The next evening, after shooting all day, I could see Betty was tired. But that was exactly what I needed for the scene we were scheduled to shoot the following morning . . . where she's supposed to have been up all night and she's sitting with Rose at the kitchen table. I knew if I let her go home to rest, she'd come in bright-eyed, with her hair done and her face freshly made up, and I wouldn't get what I wanted.

So I asked her to stay late, explaining that I wanted to do the scene now.

"I can't do it," she said. "I don't know the lines yet."

The fact is, I didn't want her to know the lines. I thought it would sound more real if she had to search for the words.

"That doesn't matter," I assured her. "Just put the script on the chair, and you can look at it if you need to."

Her hair was messy. She had a toothpick in her mouth, and she started to put it down. I told her, "Keep the toothpick."

This scene was a moment of truth between mother and daughter. Because Betty was unsure of her lines, her voice faltered, which made it even more poignant when she said: "You know that feeling that you have for Gregory. I don't think I ever felt that, not even for your father. It's not an easy thing for me to say, especially to you. It's an awful thing to look back on your life and realize that you've settled."

She's confessing something to her daughter that she's never dared admit, even to herself. And the scene is about the pain that's entwined with love . . . the mistakes parents make with their children . . . and the inevitable regret that comes with growing older.

But it wasn't quite there yet.

This was another case where the actress didn't have to "act." I just wanted her to be really simple.

So I asked how she felt about growing older. "Just tell me in your own words." (Meanwhile, I signaled to the cameraman to keep rolling.)

She had to think. Her eyes were cast downward. Many actors assume you have to look straight at the camera to make a moment register, but I think the most interesting moments happen when the actor is within himself . . . just look at some of Brando's performances and you'll see what I mean.

At that moment Betty wasn't trying to impress anyone, and wasn't conscious of how she looked . . . and that led to what's now on-screen. "The problem was that I always felt I had more time," she says. "Now, inside, I feel young, like a kid, that it's just the beginning and I have everything ahead of me. But I don't."

That was very moving. The mind stays young but the body grows old.

I loved hearing the truth in her voice. She was letting us into her own life. It was a golden moment, the kind I always look for on-screen. They reach out and touch you because they're so true.

Bravo, Betty!

Rose has come home to her mother's apartment because Gregory has rejected her romantic overture, and what happens next is the turning point of the movie. Her mother hands her a photograph of a two-year-old child, and Rose assumes it's her beautiful sister and says, "She was so pretty even then. Look at those eyes . . . those lips."

And her mother tells her, "That's not Claire. That's you."

Rose is astonished. "This was me? I . . . I was pretty?" (The photograph, by the way, is of my beautiful goddaughter Caleigh. I was still bald at two.)

"Your father adored you. He never felt that way about Claire. Only you." And for the first time in her life, Rose hears these words from her mother. "You were very pretty. Remember that."

This is where Rose's attitude about herself changes. She never thought of herself as pretty. That's not to say she wasn't . . . just that she was told that she wasn't. And now she has a different concept of herself. It boosts her self-confidence and unleashes a whole new set of possibilities. If she was beautiful once, she can be beautiful again, and her impulse is to reclaim that beauty. She's going to get her body in shape and, even more important, her mind. She's going to stop being so self-critical and let her true self be seen.

In the first three quarters of the movie, Rose never shows even an arm. Instead she covers herself up. She hides. But now she throws away her frumpy clothes, cuts and lightens her hair, puts on makeup. As we used to say in Brooklyn, she "got all *faputzed*."

It's as if Rose has been unveiled.

But the physical transformation is only the outward indication of the deeper changes inside. This is what I meant when I told Richard that the change has to come from within, and should have nothing to do with cosmetic surgery.

Her self-esteem has risen, along with her confidence. She finally recognizes her own worth. And along with this new attitude comes a new strength. Instead of feeling shy and insecure around Gregory, ducking her head and hiding her true feelings, she looks him straight in the eye and tells him that she doesn't want to continue their marriage. "I thought I could live with that. I thought it would be enough, but I lied. I lied to myself. I lied to you . . . I believe in love, and lust and sex and romance . . . I want mess and chaos . . . I want to feel passion and heat and sweat and madness!"

She leaves him. And when Alex, who dumped Rose once he met her sister, makes a play for her (he and Claire have since separated), Rose is tempted for a second. But then she's delighted to discover that any feelings she may have had for him are gone. As she tries to explain, "I never thought I was good enough for you."

He says, "Oh, but you are good enough for me, Rose. You are! You are!"

"I know, I know. But Alex, you're not good enough for me."

She sees him through new eyes (and I don't mean eyes that were surgically done), and *she* dumps *him*.

Our shoot happened to coincide with the worst winter in New York history. In January, Manhattan was brought to a halt by a record-breaking blizzard. I loved it. The snow muffled the city. It was so peaceful and quiet . . . everything was frosted in white. I had that same blissful feeling I had as a child, watching the snow fall from my first-floor window on Pulaski Street. And for months after that, the snow just kept falling, which wreaked havoc on our schedule. It's funny, because long before we started shooting, I had been asked to lend my two Edward Hopper paintings to an exhibition at the Whitney Museum, and I turned them down, because I didn't want to be away from them for so long. Little did I know that I was going to spend so much time in New York, making this movie . . . I could have visited them at the Whitney!

By the end of February basically all we had left to do was the last scene, with Rose and Gregory on the street in front of Rose's apartment building. But it was still freezing, and there was snow on the ground, which was a problem since the scene was supposed to take place in early fall. So we decided to shut down production and wait until May to film their big reconciliation scene (and even then we had to wire leaves onto the trees).

Meanwhile, that scene had evolved in the most serendipitous way . . .

When I'm directing, I always think of how I can use an actor's natural talents. One night back in January, Jeff invited me to a party for Terry Gilliam, and when he asked me to dance, I declined. I'm just too shy to get up and dance in front of people. But as I watched Jeff, I noticed he was a great dancer.

A few nights later, after we were done shooting for the day, he appeared at my dressing-room door with his favorite Van Morrison CDs and said, "Come on, dance with me!" It was unusual to have a dressing room big enough to dance in, but we had built the interior sets in the Armory's drill hall, which could hold an army regiment, so there was plenty of room. And I wasn't shy this time, because no one was watching. Dancing with Jeff was so easy . . . all I had to do was follow his lead as he turned me this way and that way and twirled me around. It was so much fun, and it became our little routine . . . practically every night after work, we would dance in my dressing room.

One night I played Jeff a song that Quincy Jones had produced and sent to me because he wanted me to hear this new young singer, Tamia. It was called "You Put a Move on My Heart," and it had a really good beat, so we danced to it a lot. All the tensions of filmmaking just fell away, and I could finally relax. It was the perfect way to end the day.

And then a light went on in my brain . . . this would be the perfect way to end the movie . . . and show off another aspect of Jeff's talent. We'll dance in the street!

I didn't want it to be choreographed or rehearsed. I wanted it to be just as free as we were in my dressing room.

It's the last shot of the film, and I told him, "We'll do it on the last night."

It's complicated to film on a real location, especially in Manhattan. We had to shut down several blocks of West End Avenue, bring in all our lights and equipment, and inform the residents that we would be disturbing their sleep. I always try to inconvenience people as little as possible, and we managed to do the whole sequence in one night. It starts when Gregory drives up in a taxi to Rose's apartment building, and since it's very late the doorman refuses to let him in. So he shouts up to Rose's window from the street, waking people up, and she comes down to talk to him. He's so emotional that he's stuttering, starting sentences and not finishing them.

Trying to calm him down, she says, "Gregory—what? I'm aging here. What is it you want to say?"

He's trying to explain how sorry he is for having hurt her, and that what she thought was a rejection wasn't a rejection at all. He was just scared.

"I wanted you so much, I couldn't see straight," he tells her and finally manages to get to the point. "Rose, I love you. And I want to be married to you."

Straight-faced, Rose replies, "Gregory, you *are* married to me."

He says, "That's right . . . that's right . . . right." They kiss, and he starts getting dizzy.

She tells him, "Oh no! It's all right. It'll pass. Just hold on to me."

"Rose, don't ever leave me again."

"I'm not leaving you. I love you."

In the film, one of the people who wakes up and leans out his window when Gregory is yelling is a big Italian guy, and now we see him smiling down at them and taking a record out of an album. (When I went to scout this location,

I looked up at the windows and that's when I realized how I could get that great aria by Puccini into this scene.)

Gregory says, "I don't care if you are pretty. I love you anyway."

She reassures him. "Listen, everything's going to drop as I get older, and I'm gaining weight as we speak."

As they kiss again, the lush, gorgeous voice of Luciano Pavarotti singing "Nessun Dorma" fills the air. Gregory and Rose look around in surprise. They don't see where the music is coming from. The heavens? You mean it's really true? This must be real love, because we hear music!

They look at each other and laugh. He pulls her into an embrace, and they kiss again as the glorious music swells to a climax. On the last note the frame freezes and then we hear the opening notes of the song "I Finally Found Someone," and Gregory and Rose begin to dance in the street.

There's a story behind that song. It began in the midst of a recording session. Suddenly I turned to the conductor and said, "Please stop for a moment. Don't anybody play anything. I have a melody in my head . . . just let me hum it and will someone in the booth please push the button so we can record it?"

When I asked Marvin if he would score *The Mirror Has Two Faces*, I played that tape for him and said, "What do you think of this, for the love theme?"

He said, "I think it's great!"

So my melody became the love theme, which Marvin used throughout the movie, and we developed it into a song for the end (Marvin added a wonderful bridge). I asked the Bergmans to write the lyrics, and you can hear that version, called "All of My Life" . . . but only on the soundtrack album.

It's a beautiful ballad, but it's not in the movie because it was too quiet and reflective. It didn't have that sexy beat that would make you want to dance, or a big enough build to convey the triumph of these two people finally getting together.

And then Jay Landers had an idea. "Since this song is about two people," he said, "maybe it should be a duet." He suggested Bryan Adams, who had just had another number 1 hit. I thought, *Terrific!* His sandpapery voice would be an interesting contrast to mine.

Unfortunately Bryan's record company was not so thrilled with the idea. They worried that singing with me would hurt his rock star image. But Bryan was enthusiastic after he heard the love theme and he wanted to take another shot at a song with his writing partner, "Mutt" Lange. Their first try wasn't quite right, but the second one was fabulous. They started with my theme and interwove it with a new countermelody, new lyrics, and a great beat that made the song more contemporary. I asked David Foster to produce the record, and he did a brilliant job.

It seemed fine to me to sing at the end of this movie, because it fit the characters and the moment. I could see the whole scene in my head. I told Andrzej, "Just give me a crane and a Steadicam, so one follows us from the top and the other's in the street. And the guy on the ground has to move with us, for full-length shots and close-ups."

And we had to do it fast, because we only had a small window of time before the sun came up.

Dancing with Jeff was so delicious. Not only is he a great leading man, but he could also lead me around and make me look more graceful than I am. At one point he even backed me into a parked car and did this incredibly sexy move, running his hand down my body and lifting my leg to his waist . . . like an erotic tango. And then I ran away and he reached out to me. We ran toward each other with our hands outstretched, and I fell into his arms. However I moved I could trust that he would catch me. And he had the most beatific smile on his face. I couldn't have asked for more as a director and an actress. And did I mention he's a great kisser? Lucky Susan.

It was so free and easy. We dipped and swayed, and sometimes in the middle of a move I'd gesture to Gregory Lundsgaard, the Steadicam operator, to come closer or move farther away. He was terrific . . . he was practically dancing with us!

I love that way of working. You sort of know what you're going to do, and yet you don't. Everybody's on their toes. Everybody's excited. We only had time for three takes, because the sun was rising and the light was getting too bright.

Before we started, I was standing in front of 505 West End Avenue when one of the residents came up to me and said, "I used to see you here all the time." It was only then that I realized this was the building where Peter Matz had lived, and where I came to rehearse when I was twenty years old and making my first album. (I changed the address from 505 to 404 for the movie, because most buildings don't want their real address used. And I like the number four better.)

More serendipity. And now here I was with a hundred people and an 85-foot crane, all working together to make my imagined dream come true. That's the thrill of directing.

And then there are always the challenges.

As we were getting ready to shoot the dance, I noticed that my pal David James, the still photographer (who also did *Yentl*), was nowhere in sight. I went over to the line producer, and asked, "Where's David?"

"Oh, he had to leave. He couldn't do the last night."

"And you didn't tell me? Why didn't you hire another photographer?" (Which would only have cost about five hundred dollars.) "This is the climax of the film. Didn't it occur to you that we might need pictures of this scene? Maybe for the ad campaign?"

And guess what? A photo from that last scene *did* end up being the poster for the film, and we were forced to pay thirty-five thousand dollars for a paparazzi shot. That's the kind of waste that drives me crazy.

I went back to Los Angeles and spent the summer in my newly renovated house, editing the film with my old friend Jeff Werner. Two months after we finished shooting, we had a print ready to show and did some test screenings. My heart was pounding before the first preview.

But the preview audiences were great. And when the film opened on November 15, 1996, the box office for the first weekend was bigger than any of my movies to date.

But then the reviews came in. Roger Ebert liked the movie and understood what I was trying to say. He even zeroed in on the Lauren Bacall scene, when I asked her how it felt to be beautiful. He said, "We get the eerie and magical sense that we are hearing Streisand and Bacall discussing this." Exactly right!

But other reviews were less than kind. That hurt. And it was amazing how some people managed to misinterpret the movie. A magazine editor in New York saw the picture and said, "I don't like the message of the movie. It means you have to be beautiful to be loved."

She completely missed the whole point! Rose just changed her attitude, not her face. And Gregory actually started falling in love with the old, unglamorous Rose. That frightened him, and that's why he ran away. Now he has to come to terms with her new self, and the irony is that Gregory loves her in spite of the fact that she's prettier now.

It's very complex . . . this thing called love.

I adored working with Jeff, and I was so happy when he told me he felt the same way: "You put a move on my heart." (That was particularly sweet, because it came from that song we danced to so often.)

I was thrilled when Lauren Bacall won the Screen Actors Guild Award for Best Supporting Actress, and was nominated for a BAFTA award. And I was so excited for her when she won the Golden Globe!

Coincidentally, Jeff Bridges happened to be the one to present Betty with the award. It was hard to believe that this was the *first* time she had been nominated for any screen performance during her entire career, and I was very touched by her speech. She said, "I must thank Barbra Streisand . . . Had it not been for her, this movie wouldn't have been made. Had it not been for her, I would not have been cast in this part. And had it not been for her, I wouldn't be standing here now . . . because of the way she directed this movie and my part in particular."

I called her afterward and said, "I'm so proud of you!" and thanked her for the kind words. I was nominated as an actress as well, but I can't stand the anxiety so I just stayed home and watched it on TV.

Marvin Hamlisch was also nominated for Best Original Score, and "I Finally Found Someone" was nominated for Best Original Song. None of us won, but the song was a huge hit, and was also nominated for an Academy Award. And so was Lauren Bacall. That was so special for her, and I was gratified that the Academy recognized her performance.

I decided to go to the Oscars, but I told the producers I couldn't sing the song. I knew I would be too nervous. So they asked Natalie Cole, who became ill at the last moment, and Celine Dion stepped in. (She was already scheduled to sing one of the other nominated songs.) I was sitting in the audience watching the show . . . delighted to see choreographer Michael Kidd, my friend from *Hello, Dolly!*, accept his honorary Oscar . . . when I suddenly started hemorrhaging. (I was having more problems with endometriosis.) I quickly got up and rushed to the bathroom. And by the time I could emerge, Celine had already sung the song. I didn't know that she was about to go on, and I was mortified to have missed her. But of course some of the papers tried to turn it into a scandal, as if I had deliberately dissed her.

Nothing could be further from the truth. Who wouldn't want to hear Celine sing a song that you cowrote? I found her afterward and apologized profusely. She completely understood. I told her, "We have to find a song to sing together."

And that led to "Tell Him," also produced by David Foster, which was nominated for a Grammy.

"I Finally Found Someone" didn't win an Oscar, and neither did Betty . . . which was even more of a disappointment.

I was already stressed by the whole experience, and it just reminded me of why I try to avoid these events. I was at a point in my life when I was thinking I'd had it with making movies. I had proved to myself that I could direct, but I was not sure I wanted to do it anymore.

And something else had occurred. I was not alone that night, because in a glorious case of life imitating art, I had met James Brolin.

Rose got the guy, and so did I!

FIFTY-FOUR

Jim

Jeff Werner and I were sitting at the editing console in Grandma's house when I suddenly remembered.

"What time is it?" I asked.

He looked at his watch. "Six thirty."

"Damn. I have to leave."

I did not want to go to this dinner party. When Christine Peters called to invite me two weeks earlier, I told her I was in the midst of editing *The Mirror Has Two Faces* and had no time for parties, but she insisted. There was someone she wanted me to meet . . . James Brolin.

I didn't know much about him, so she quickly filled me in. He had played the young, motorcycle-riding Dr. Steven Kiley in the TV series that made him famous, *Marcus Welby, M.D.,* but I had never seen it. More recently he had starred in another series, *Hotel.* That rang a bell . . . I had an image of a handsome man with dark, thick, wavy hair and a neatly trimmed beard. Christine said she had just met Jim at a party . . . he was very nice and he was *single*! She thought we might like each other, so she was arranging this dinner in order to get the two of us together on a blind date. (Well, only half blind, since we each knew what the other looked like.)

Reluctantly I said, "All right." But then I basically forgot about it, and now it was July 1, the night of the dinner, and too late to back out.

I had to go, even though the second shift of editors was already arriving. I got everyone started and ran out the door, saying, "I'll be back as soon as I can, probably around ten."

Renata drove me to Christine's house, because I haven't been behind the wheel of a car ever since the day I found myself going up a down ramp on the freeway. I was thinking about other things and got distracted, and that's when I decided it was safer to stay in the passenger seat.

When I walked into Christine's house, there were more people there than I expected. My shyness kicked in, so I decided to go downstairs to see Caleigh and Skye. (Christine's relationship with Jon didn't last, but ours did, and I was godmother to both her daughters.) On the way I caught a glimpse of a man leaning against the far wall, talking to someone, and I thought, *Is that him?* But where was the mountain man I was expecting, with the beard, the mustache, and the dark wavy hair? This guy was clean-shaven, with a buzz cut. At that moment he looked over to me and smiled in recognition. I weakly waved and just kept on walking.

And then I stayed downstairs, happily playing with the children, right through cocktails and hors d'oeuvres, until Christine called and said, "Dinner is being served. Get up here!"

There were three tables seating ten each out on the terrace, and only one chair wasn't taken. It was next to Jim, and now I got a closer look at his hair. It was odd, because it was white at the roots and sort of rust-colored at the tips. As I walked behind him to sit down, I did something unusual for me, because I don't normally touch a man's hair unless I'm working with him as an actor or a director. But now I lightly ran my fingers through Jim's buzz cut and asked, "Who fucked up your hair?"

Instead of being offended, Jim was impressed. As he told me later, his first thought was, I've met a lot of liars in Hollywood, but here's one person who tells the truth.

In fact, he had just had his hair buzzed, Marine-style, for a part, and was letting the dye for a previous role grow out. So his head did look a bit weird, kind of like a big bullet with stubble.

That was the start of a long conversation about everything from architecture to relationships. Neither of us talked to anyone else that night. A couple of hours later I remembered the editors and said, "I have to leave."

Jim said, "I'm taking you home."

"Thanks, but my assistant, Renata, is coming back with the car, and I have to work. I have two editors waiting for me."

"Tell 'em to go home."

Now it was my turn to be impressed . . . here was a man I barely knew, taking charge. And the amazing thing is that I went along with it. I called Renata and told her to go back to the house, turn on the lights for us, and tell the editors they were free to leave.

So Jim drove me home and then came in, and we continued our conversation. I even had Renata cancel my midnight massage (my big treat after working long hours) . . . the first time I had ever done that for a man. The two of us sat and talked in my living room until I finally looked at the clock and said, "I don't believe it. It's two a.m., and I have to be up early to work."

So we both stood up, and I said, "I'll walk you to the door."

That meant we had to pass through my large foyer, which is filled with American Federal furniture, including a table displaying candlesticks, a vase of flowers, and a brass tray with a decanter of port and several petite glasses.

It kind of looks like a stage set, and no one ever sits in the foyer.

But it was as if Jim and I didn't want to leave each other quite yet, because somehow we found ourselves sitting down again and talking for another hour. We even had a glass of port. (I used to drink it occasionally, before I got reflux.)

Finally we *really* had to part, and as we were saying good-bye, suddenly we both got kind of shy. It was a tense moment. Both of us were sensing that this could possibly have possibilities, and neither of us wanted to screw it up. Jim told me later that he didn't want to come on too strong, and I'm always self-conscious in these situations anyway.

When something has the potential to be serious, I think my natural tendency is to step back . . . because each step forward could be momentous. I become even more tentative, because new emotions are scary, and every little thing matters.

So I kept my distance at the door, but Jim was coming closer, and I thought, *I hope he doesn't try to kiss me . . .* because I wouldn't know how to react . . .

And then he just reached over and gave me a hug. It felt good.

I know I went to bed with a smile on my face because I wrote it down in my journal. I also noted that he was "very nice, attractive, manly" . . . and he had great teeth! Jim is blessed with an incredible bone structure . . . high cheekbones, a strong jawline, a patrician nose . . . and his face is so symmetrical that he looks terrific from both sides (unlike me). Actually, he reminded me of one of those heroic marble statues I saw in Washington, D.C. And I liked the fact that he was interested in more than just acting. He was a licensed pilot and had a passion for flying. He liked to build things with his hands. And he was older than me, thank God!

Thursday was the Fourth of July, and on Friday I was having some friends and their kids over, so I invited Jim to come and bring his eight-year-old daughter, Molly. I remember standing with her in the kitchen and offering her some ice cream.

I said, "I have four different flavors . . . chocolate, vanilla, strawberry, and coffee. Which would you like?"

She said, "I don't like ice cream."

What? I'd never met a kid who didn't like ice cream. She explained, "My mom says it isn't good for you." That was unusual, an eight-year-old who was so health conscious.

Meanwhile, every time I looked around for Jim, he was busy talking to someone else. I remember sitting with my friend Lynda Obst and saying, "I don't think this is going to work. Look at him. He doesn't seem interested in talking to me."

Actually, Jim explained later that he saw how everybody wanted time with me, and he didn't want to get in the way. And I was too reserved to go over to him, so it was awkward.

The next day I was planning to go to Skye's birthday party, and it turned out that Christine had invited Jim and Molly too. I was late because I knew he was coming and couldn't decide what to wear. It was a swimming party, and as soon as I got there, I knew I had made the wrong choice. Everyone was in shorts or a bathing suit, and I looked idiotic, completely out of place, dressed in a black top, black skirt, black tights, and black ballet slippers tied up with black satin ribbons . . . on a hot summer day. (What was I thinking?)

The kids were in the pool, and I spotted Jim across the lawn. He was wearing a Hawaiian shirt, and I don't like Hawaiian shirts. (They're too flamboyant and they distract from a person's face.)

And then it went downhill from there.

I happened to overhear Jim talking to a woman I knew, and he was telling her the same personal story he had told me that first night. Suddenly I felt less special, and I could feel myself withdraw. (I didn't realize then that they had been close neighbors in Montecito.)

For lunch there was a hot dog cart, and they smelled so good. I would have loved one, but I had woken up that morning motivated to diet for him. Besides, they're so messy to eat, and no doubt I would have spilled mustard on my top. So I resisted those, as well as the ice cream cones for dessert. I came over to the table with my iced tea, and Jim happened to be getting up just as I was sitting down.

I thought, *It's over.*

It's interesting how quickly I regressed from being charmed to "this will never work." I guess I was looking for the negative, and I found it. So I left, and Jim remembers that I didn't even say goodbye to him.

I went home so distressed that I asked Renata to make me a hot dog with mustard and relish. Fuck the diet. And then when I had finished it, I said, "I need another one." I ate them both in bed, with two coffee ice cream cones afterward (I can never have just one), while I read the latest issue of *The Economist.* I thought, *No more relationships. Back to politics.*

Jim called several times that night, but I wasn't ready to speak to him. I told Renata to say I was out.

Still, he didn't give up. He got my fax number and faxed me a note on Sunday morning: "Respond, or I will start faxing smut." That got my attention and made me laugh. He put in his telephone number, and then went on: "Tonight? Yes? No? Maybe? I am going to see my parents this a.m." (So he added his car phone number too.) "Love, Jim."

He wrote "Love." Can you imagine? Why would he write "love"? I never do that unless I truly love the person. How could he love me so soon?

After that fax (which I still have, framed on my desk), I had to call him back.

He asked, "When can I see you again?"

I liked that . . . right to the point! I said, "Well, you could take me to a movie, but I can't be gone long." So we went to a local theater, seven minutes away. I remember he sat on my left, and he kept turning his head and staring at me, instead of the screen. Finally I whispered, "Stop staring at me. You're making me self-conscious." (Actually, I secretly liked it.)

Our first dinner date was on July 10 at the Caffé Delfini, a small, unpretentious Italian restaurant where the main source of light was a little candle on each table. To me, that's horror lighting . . . no one looks good lit from below. So I took my empty wineglass and turned it over. Then I balanced the candle on the stem, which raised the light to a better position.

I can't help trying to fix the lighting wherever I go. I'll be in a friend's dining room and I'll say, "It's better to have taller candles, so the light will be at eye level." (Women will appreciate that.)

Jim and I had a lovely evening at the restaurant . . . relaxed, romantic. And he was so open with his emotions. He said he felt his heart flutter when we first met. (I was just reading this to Jim, who said, "Of course, I was born with a heart murmur." Did I mention he has a wicked sense of humor?)

The day after our dinner I was at the studio doing ADR (additional dialogue replacement or, in other words, rerecording some lines) with Jeff and Brenda. They had left, and I was about to do my own lines when Jim surprised me, looking very handsome in a black T-shirt. And I swear, his hair had even grown a little! He brought me a box of ginger tea and said, "It's good for the throat." I thought that was such a thoughtful choice, since I would be talking for hours.

Jim left to let me get on with my work, and then I got a call from James Newton Howard. I went into a little room with a sliding glass door, so I could speak to him privately. I hadn't seen him since he and his wife came to my concert in Anaheim, but now he was going on about how he had been thinking about me, and how much he missed me.

I said, "Since you called, I have something to tell you."

"What?"

"I think I met someone."

There was silence at the other end of the line. And then he said, "Go for it."

And I did.

For years, when I was busy acting in one film after another, I had no time for a truly committed relationship, and so it didn't happen. But now, when I had just directed this film and shaped the character of Rose . . . someone who *does* want romance in her life . . . it seemed as if, once again, imagination *does* create reality, because Jim appeared.

It's as if Rose knew more about my inner life than I did.

Deep down, I, too, wanted romance, but I had let my work take over. I tended to use work as a substitute for relationships.

Jim and I met at a point in my life when I had basically given up on finding someone. And frankly, I was all right with being on my own. I had my son, I had great friends to keep me company, my work was fulfilling, and I loved my new house in Malibu overlooking the ocean.

Maybe you have to be happy with yourself before you can be happy with someone else.

A little side story about that house I would eventually share with Jim. When I first saw it in 1984, I thought the location was spectacular. But Richard Baskin, my boyfriend at the time, said it was too close to the cliff, and there were many things I would have to change. For example, there was basically no entrance . . . the front door opened directly onto a narrow hallway with a crude staircase. And the main bedroom and bath were small. So that would mean another construction project, which was not appealing, since I had just spent five years building the Deco house. And then my business manager said, "You can't afford it anyway, until you sell the ranch."

So I walked away from the house . . . and then spent the next eleven years pining for it.

The couple who bought it spent three years remodeling. And since they'd heard I used to visit the construction site, they told their broker to bring me to see it. I walked in and thought, *Oh my God, this is unbelievable!* It was as if they had read my mind, because they did almost everything I would have done. They added an elegant entrance foyer with period moldings and columns and a beautiful curving staircase. It was exactly what I had imagined, and here it was in reality . . . what a gift!

As I was walking out of the main bedroom upstairs, I noticed a door I had missed. Was it a linen closet? A broom closet? I opened it and, oh my God, it was a whole other room, with another bath! I stood in that doorway and thought, *Now there's room for a man.* He could have a study here with a desk and a couch, his own closets, and his own bath. It would be perfect . . . if only I had the man.

It reminds me of that moment when I was a sixteen-year-old wannabe actress and stood in the bedroom doorway of my first New York apartment, looking at my unmade bed, and thought to myself, *I have to become famous just so I can get somebody else to make my bed.*

Amazingly enough, that thought did become reality.

But in 1987 reality hadn't yet caught up to my thoughts about the house. The broker said the owners were willing to sell it, and told me the price.

I could see charging double what they paid for it, or even triple, but quadruple? That felt as if they were completely taking advantage of me. I offered a bit less, but they wouldn't accept it. So it slipped out of my hands a second time.

But . . . third time lucky! Eventually the couple got divorced, the price came down, and in 1995 I finally bought the house I had wanted for so long.

And now that I had this room, perfect for a man, one had shown up . . . Jim.

Could it be the power of imagination working again?

I think so.

But then barely two weeks after we met, he had to leave for the Philippines to do a movie. We took a picture in my family room so we could remember our time together. Our smiles are so genuine. (Jim still keeps that photo on his bedside table.)

He called every day, and we were like teenagers . . . each call could last anywhere from two to five hours. Once I actually fell asleep on my dressing-room floor, with the phone in my hand. The poor guy spent practically his whole salary on those calls.

It can be easier to share very intimate things when the other person's in a faraway place. And we really got to know each other. I thought he was such an intriguing combination . . . tall, great-looking, and if we were in a plane and something happened to the pilot, he could take over! Jim was also a very good driver, from racing cars when he was younger. He was kindhearted and sensitive, and he made me feel safe. He told me, "I fell in love with you the first night we met, when you said, 'Who fucked up your hair?' I knew from that moment we would be together."

That made my heart skip a beat. And when he came home, as Jim says, "It was like a shampoo commercial. We just ran into each other's arms."

It was unusual for me to get this close to someone so quickly. But Jim wasn't intimidated by me. In fact, he was very supportive and said, "I want to empower you."

That stunned me, because so many men seem reluctant to grant a woman any power, and are resentful when she achieves it on her own. It was such an extraordinary thing to say, and very meaningful to me . . . not only because of the encouragement he was offering, but also because it showed he could see beyond my image to the vulnerability and insecurity underneath.

The cliché is that it's the woman who wants to pin down the man, but not in this case. Jim was actually overwhelming me a bit, with talk about the future. I was more wary. And I was still preoccupied with *The Mirror Has Two Faces,* completing the final cut.

The presidential election campaign was also heating up. In September I sang at a fundraiser for President Clinton, given by the Hollywood Women's Political Committee and held in Ted Field's backyard . . . so it was like déjà vu from 1992. Except this time I had Jim by my side, and I couldn't wait to introduce him to the president and First Lady.

They were so happy for us. "You deserve this," Bill told me, and Hillary said Jim was so handsome and invited us to come stay at the White House. Someone snapped a picture of me, flanked by the two men, and I remember Bill, with his big smile, saying, "She wants to be the cheese, and she's between her two biggest admirers in the world."

Everyone was full of love that night.

And once again I wrote to President Clinton about the upcoming debates. I told him to remember JFK, who barely looked at Nixon, and didn't do things like shaking his head at his responses. He didn't give his power away. So in my director mode, I told Bill, "Don't react to everything Dole says. Just look down and write your notes. It's more intriguing if the audience doesn't know what you're thinking until you say it."

On the day of the election, Renata and I flew to Little Rock at the invitation of the Clintons (Jim was in Ireland directing his first feature film, *My Brother's War*, and also acting in it). As soon as we got to the hotel, I called Jim as I'd promised, to let him know we'd arrived safely, and then I joined the rest of the group in the room where President Clinton and Vice President Gore were watching the results with their families. I ended up playing on the floor with Roger Clinton's two-year-old son, Tyler, who just emailed me the other day, by the way. He still calls me Auntie Barbra.

When Clinton was declared the winner at 9:00 p.m., everyone was elated, hugging and kissing. What a relief! The next morning we all had breakfast together. Bill ordered grits with cheese, and it looked so good that I asked him for a bite . . . and then I had to order a bowl for myself. Then I flew to New York and began a round of TV interviews to coincide with the premiere of *The Mirror Has Two Faces*, on November 10. Somehow Jim managed to arrange his schedule so he could fly in to escort me, and then flew right back to Ireland. He got a lot of points for making that effort.

I liked the fact that he was so attentive. While we were apart, he would send me sweet, funny faxes: "Do you miss me molesting you in the middle of the night?" And we had more marathon phone calls. One day we talked for seven and a half hours, in three installments. If only for the sake of the phone bill, it was good that I had already planned to spend Thanksgiving in Ireland with him.

Jim had rented a little cottage, and we found another for Renata close by. These were old, hand-built houses, and when I ran the water in the bathtub, it was brown. Jim said, "That's from the peat. It's good for you!"

Right.

All I can say is I must really have been in love, because I would get up when he had to get up, at 5:00 a.m., to make breakfast for him before he left for the set. I wanted to support him in his work, just as he had supported me. But as I've said, I can't cook. What Jim didn't know is that Renata would chop up the ingredients the night before, so all I had to do was put everything in the frying pan and turn on the flame. (I did put the bread into the toaster, *and* buttered it.)

That was a magical time. I had stepped away from my normal life of work,

work, work, and I felt free for a change, free to explore my nurturing instincts. I enjoyed doing things for this man.

We were in the west of Ireland, on the Connemara coast, but I got to see more of the country, because Jim is an adventurer. He likes to get in the car and go places, even if he's not sure exactly where he's going. He doesn't even want to make reservations. He'd rather discover a charming restaurant along the way.

I'm the opposite. I like to know exactly where I'm going and have everything planned out in advance. And I dread getting lost on some deserted country road with no phones, no GPS, and no one to help. So I'm always anticipating the worst, while he's ready for the best, assuming that the fates will take care of him . . . and they usually do.

Sometimes on weekends we'd take long drives through the Irish countryside, which gave a whole new meaning to the word "green." I've never seen so many different shades. Each landscape was like a pastoral painting, the hillsides dotted with sheep. And I've never experienced so many different kinds of weather in one day. It could go from a gray mist to sheets of rain to brilliant sunshine, and that was just in the morning.

I remember many moments from that trip. We spent a night at the thirteenth-century Ashford Castle, which had been turned into a luxurious hotel. We were given the John Wayne suite . . . apparently he, Maureen O'Hara, and director John Ford stayed at the castle when they were filming *The Quiet Man* in 1951. And no one could forget it because they seemed to have Wayne's movies playing around the clock.

On the ride back to our more humble cottage, I was hungry, as usual, so we stopped at a pub and had great Irish soda bread with the best tomato soup I've ever tasted (even better than Campbell's).

In one restaurant in Galway where we often went for dinner, I heard this hauntingly beautiful piece of music . . . an instrumental, with just a piano and a violin. I asked what it was and was told it was "Heartstrings," from an album called *Songs from a Secret Garden* (and since the restaurant only had three CDs, we got to know that album well). I thought it was very moving, and since Jim was looking for a piece of music for his film, I suggested that it might work at the end. He agreed and he used it.

I was trying to remember when he first asked me to marry him, so I just stopped writing for a moment to ask Jim, and he said, "It was almost from the very beginning. My knees were getting sore."

I probably didn't take him seriously.

He says, "You were gun-shy. I realized I had to let you get used to the idea. So I'd back off for a while, and let you think it over."

I do remember that he asked me again in Ireland.

It's hard for me to trust . . . and I guess I kept testing him unconsciously.

I remember a night when we were in New York. There was an opera I wanted to see at the Met, and I invited Cis and Harvey to join us. Our two seats were right in front of theirs, and I was hoping Jim would put his arm around me so they could see how much I meant to him. But he didn't do it . . . he didn't conform to this vision I had in my head. (Jim is not comfortable showing affection in public, but I didn't know that then.)

I was so upset that I got up and went into the bathroom to compose myself. When I tried to go back into the auditorium, the usher said I couldn't return to my seat until the end of the act. That made me feel even more distressed, and suddenly I felt so exposed, just standing there. My infantile hurt evolved into anger. So I turned around and walked out of the Met and asked the driver of the car we had come in to take me home to my apartment.

I left Jim sitting there, along with Cis and Harvey. (I still can't believe I did that.)

Eventually they realized something was wrong, got up, and found out what I had done. Jim called me from the Met and said, "I'm going straight to the airport and going home."

That shocked me right out of my anger, and we worked it out on the phone. Thank God he got in a cab and came back to my apartment that night. And I never did anything like that again.

As I wrote in my journal, "I still don't understand myself. Sometimes I make crazy decisions . . . I wish I could get less angry. I wish I could transcend certain feelings."

I realized my behavior at the Met was irrational, but in some ways I'm still that child, abandoned by her father. Maybe I wanted to abandon Jim before he abandoned me.

And then there were other moments when I felt so secure with him.

Of course there was the physical attraction (very important). I loved his presence, his easygoing nature, his smile. I never get tired of looking at him. And we were perfect as lovers. We fit.

He was so giving . . . a man who is delighted by and appreciates a woman.

I remember being in the pool with him early on. I would climb on his back, and he would carry me around in the water. My chin would be resting on his shoulder and I thought, *This must be how a child feels*, peering out at the world with no fear, because she was safe in her daddy's arms.

So I was that vulnerable little girl, as well as the satisfied woman and all the other versions of my personality. Jim says he never knows who he's going to get when he walks through the door, and yet he seems to accept all the different parts of me. As I wrote in my journal, "I'm like a box of See's Candies" . . . you can't tell if a piece is going to be sweet or salty, soft or crunchy. Will there be an almond or a kumquat inside?

I just read that paragraph to Jim, and he said, "That's why I never get bored with you."

I think the real reason our relationship has endured is that we're both willing to work at it. Jim and I are very different. As he's said to me, "You're an expert at looking for what's wrong, while I'm just happy to wake up in the morning." (He'll live much longer than me. He keeps saying he's going to live to be 100, and recently upped it to 110. He probably will, with that attitude.)

Like any other couple, we've had our issues, but I really felt it was important to try to work on them. And during our early years together, at times we needed a referee. So I would book a joint session with my former therapist, who taught us how to negotiate our differences. As Jim says, "We could be so angry, but after one of those sessions, it was as if somebody put a pin in a balloon. We always felt closer."

One thing we learned was very simple . . . how to really listen to each other, without interrupting.

And I noticed something. Jim was the first one to get tears in his eyes when he was talking about his feelings. He's a very masculine man, yet he's not afraid of his feminine side, thank God. And I love the way Jim makes me feel more feminine, but he's also secure enough in his own masculinity to accept the masculine part of me.

I find now that my anger, when it comes, is usually a cover-up for feeling hurt. I used to say everything I felt. I just blurted it out. When I was reading this to Jim, he said, "I always loved your honesty . . . till it pissed me off."

Elliott once told me that I used truth as a weapon, and that really struck home.

I don't do that anymore, and what helped me to change was reading a book by the Dalai Lama. What I took from it is that one should tell the truth, but with compassion.

Something may be true, but saying it out loud can also hurt someone so deeply that it can never be rectified. I've learned more over the years about choosing my battles and when to back off, because I want to be a partner, not an adversary.

And Jim is so accommodating. If I say, "Should we go for a swim?" he says, "Whatever you want to do." If I say, "Let's go out to eat," he'll say, "Where would you like to go?" If I say, "I'm going to work on my music in Grandma's house," he'll say, "I'll come with you." That really makes me feel loved.

And then he said something one night that I'll never forget. We were lying in bed, spooning. He was holding me, and just as I was about to fall asleep, he whispered in my ear, "I don't want to fall asleep."

Drowsily, I asked, "Why not?"

"'Cause I'll miss you."

What a beautiful, poetic thing to say. And it captured a moment of complete bliss . . . physical, emotional, spiritual.

I told that story when Jim and I appeared on *20/20* with Barbara Walters in 1997, and the songwriter Diane Warren happened to be watching that night. She was so taken with Jim's words and thought the idea was so original that she was inspired to write a song and use it in the lyric:

I don't want to close my eyes
I don't want to fall asleep
'Cause I'd miss you, babe
And I don't want to miss a thing.

Performed by Aerosmith, "I Don't Want to Miss a Thing" debuted at number 1 and became their biggest hit, selling millions of copies around the world. It was so gratifying to see so many people responding to Jim's words.

Well, no wonder . . . so did I!

I guess everybody wants romance, and now I had it in my real life, rather than just in a movie. It was such a switch . . . I no longer had to rely on work for satisfaction and was happy to set it aside so I could spend more time with Jim. When he was shooting a TV series called *Pensacola* in San Diego and only able to come home on weekends, Renata would drive me back and forth so I could stay with him during the week. While he worked, I would explore all the charming little flower and antique shops in La Jolla, and then he'd come back for dinner, and we'd have the night to ourselves. My life revolved around him, for a change, and that was lovely.

I had always thought if I got married again, it would have to be to someone more like my father . . . a professor or a doctor or a lawyer.

Jim is none of those things, but then neither am I.

I got tired of looking for perfection . . . it doesn't exist.

So when he asked me to marry him again, I finally said yes.

In June 1998, we had been living together for two years and were up in Big Sur on a mini-vacation when we started thinking about dates. Should it be a fall wedding, or maybe around New Year's Eve? I'd watched friends of mine plan their weddings, and it usually took six to eight months.

But then I thought, *Wait a minute. I don't want to have two dates to deal with.* Which do you celebrate, the day we got married or the day we met?

I told Jim, "Let's get married on July first, because that's our real anniversary."

That meant I had two and a half weeks to plan a wedding.

Yikes.

But then I figured, Well, I did *The Mirror Has Two Faces* with only four and a half weeks of preproduction. So this was just another challenge.

My first thought was the dress. Elliott and I had gotten married on the fly, and all I had to wear was my cotton seersucker suit, but this time I wanted a traditional wedding dress . . . and a *real* wedding, with friends and music and a cake.

Jim started looking for wedding dresses online (he was always way ahead of me in dealing with computers). Meanwhile, I remembered an antique lace dress from 1910 in my closet . . . that would be great, no fittings! And I had just the right rose for the bouquet. Tom Carruth, who bred my namesake rose, had given me a new hybrid to plant, and it was the most beautiful beigey color . . . like English tea with milk. (I suggested naming it Tea Time, but that was already taken, so Tom dubbed it Koko Loco.) That rose matched the old lace perfectly.

But when I called Donna Karan to tell her we had finally picked a date, she said, "I'm making your dress! This is so exciting . . . it will be my present to you!"

What a lovely gesture! I started to do some sketches of what I was envisioning . . . off the shoulder, an Empire waist with a long, flowing skirt . . . and sent them to her. She showed me samples of various fabrics, including an off-white lacy tulle embroidered with tiny crystal beads (accenting the design of the lace) that was absolutely incredible. Then there was a simpler off-white tulle, dotted with specks of silver, that would be pretty for the veil.

But once Donna ordered the lacy tulle, it would have to be hand-beaded in India. Could it be done in time? And she had her own ideas of how the dress should look . . . something that was closer to the body. She didn't want to show me a sketch and said, "I have to drape it on you." So she and her patternmaker, Nelly, flew to Los Angeles with some plain white chiffon and started shaping and gathering, pinning and tucking it on me. The result looked rather odd, but Donna kept saying, "It'll hang differently in the beaded fabric." I had my doubts, but I decided to put my faith in my friend.

Meanwhile, I think I called the caterer first, even before I called my family, because the caterer had to reserve the date! And we couldn't have a wedding without all our favorite foods. For the hors d'oeuvres, I definitely wanted smoked salmon with leek crème fraîche, baby blintzes, wonton pillows stuffed with vegetables, sushi, coconut shrimp, and pizza. (Everyone loves pizza.) The main course had to include soft-shell crabs, wild mushroom ravioli, grilled vegetables, and potatoes au gratin, among other things. I had a long list of desserts and was trying to narrow it down, choosing between brownies with walnuts (and some without), warm chocolate lava cake, fresh berry tarts, profiteroles filled with vanilla ice cream, and little cones filled with coffee ice cream. Jim wanted lemon meringue tarts and chocolate bread pudding. And then I thought, *We'll just have them all . . . why not?*

The other call I made right away was to Marvin Hamlisch, because I knew that if he was in charge of the music, it would be done properly, and that would mean one less thing to worry about. He's such a doll . . . here he was, the winner of Oscars, Emmys, Grammys, and the Pulitzer Prize, and he's back to playing weddings!

I had decided the best place to get married was in our own house (more private, and no traveling). Our guests would be seated in the living room for the ceremony, and I could walk down the aisle to join Jim and the rabbi in the windowed alcove I had built. I was thinking a chamber music ensemble might be nice at the ceremony. We could take all the furniture out of the dining room and put the musicians in there.

Jim and I went to meet with the rabbi to talk about the kind of service we wanted, which took longer than expected, so we were late for a dinner at John Travolta and Kelly Preston's house. Marlon Brando, Tom Hanks, and Rita Wilson were also there, and we were so full of excitement that we had to tell them our big news and invite them to the wedding (first swearing them to secrecy).

The guest list was deliberately small . . . only our closest friends and family. And it was important to me that each couple we invited was happily married . . . like Marilyn and Alan Bergman, Gil and Joanne Segal, Evelyn and Mo Ostin . . . because that was the kind of energy I wanted to surround us on this day. We didn't send out formal invitations . . . instead Kim discreetly made calls asking people to save the date for "a special celebration." I really didn't want the whole world alerted to what was going to happen.

On Monday, two days before the wedding, the ivory tent was raised, and the tables were being set with Sèvres porcelain plates and French flatware that I had chosen. In the garden, every rosebush was deadheaded and every flowerbed was tidied up. It had never looked more glorious.

And if I couldn't actually get married in the garden (too exposed), at least we could bring the garden inside. On each table in the tent were bouquets of sweet peas, roses, and hydrangeas in shades of lavender, burgundy, pink, and ivory to match the china. In the living room, the flowers were chosen to match the apple-green drapes and the shades of burgundy, pink, and ivory in the rug. Garlands of smilax, with lilies, roses, stephanotis . . . and the most unusual amaranthus, which dangled like raspberry icicles . . . adorned the windows in the alcove. Gardenias, lilies of the valley, lupine, and more roses scented the air.

That night, Donna and Stephan arrived from New York, along with Nelly and another seamstress, Anna . . . and the dress. Actually, she had made two dresses. One followed the lines of my original sketch . . . just in case I decided I still liked that best. (I was so touched that she had gone to double the trouble, just to make sure I was happy.) I tried that one on first. It was more like what I've always worn.

But then I put on the dress she had draped on me, and I heard Renata gasp. It truly was dazzling, and the shape was new for me. The lacy tulle was gathered under the bust and then fell closely around my hips and legs, to end in a swirl on the floor at my feet . . . actually, the silhouette reminded me of one of those Art Nouveau vases of the dancer Loie Fuller that I used to collect. And what was even more extraordinary was the way the delicate crystal beads caught the light. "You look as if you were sprayed with a thousand sparkling stars," said Donna, with a big smile. There was no question which to choose . . . my brilliant friend was right.

On the morning of the wedding, I was in constant motion, checking on every detail. In my robe and slippers I was switching place cards around on the tables . . . to make sure everybody was sitting next to someone they liked . . . and rearranging flowers. The dark ivy and rose garland on the staircase banister needed something to brighten it a bit. We fixed that by weaving in an ivory lace ribbon.

I wanted to give Jim a gift, but I had already given him a rare antique Rolex Daytona watch a few months before. So what could I do that would be very special? At first I tried to write him a note that expressed all the sentiments I wanted to share with him, and that's when I had an idea . . . I could say it better in song. Jim loved the melody called "Heartstrings" from that Irish album, so I asked Jay Landers to get Ann Hampton Calloway (a very good songwriter, and I thought she was Irish) to write lyrics to it so I could sing it to him.

Yes, me, the woman who hates performing in front of people, and who had never sung at anyone else's wedding, was actually going to sing at my own, only because I knew it would be meaningful to Jim.

And now I was calling Jay in a panic, because in order to sing I needed an instrumental track in my key, and it still hadn't arrived.

More stress . . . my dress was gorgeous, but it wasn't quite finished yet. It still needed to be hemmed, and Nelly and Anna were busy doing that, along with adding a few final touches. And to top it all off, on the day before, there had been a fire near the 405 freeway, and a landslide had closed part of the Pacific Coast Highway. My mind immediately went to the worst-case scenario.

How ironic if after all this work, no one would be able to get here!

I was having an anxiety attack. But there was no more time . . . I had to start getting ready. My heart was beating a mile a minute when I stepped into the shower. (I'm getting tense just writing this. It's a moment I'll never forget.) But finally I stood still, leaning against the tiles. I closed my eyes and said to myself, *There is nothing more I can do. This is my wedding day and these are our friends. They don't care about the dress or the flowers or the song. They just want us to be happy. So let go and let God.* And I pictured all my tensions flowing down the drain with the water.

And somehow it all came together. The caterer and her staff arrived in plenty of time with the food, and all of our guests made it to Malibu as well, even though there was one last obstacle . . . the crowd of paparazzi and TV cameras at the end of our street. Once there, old friends and colleagues like Irvin Kershner, Sydney Pollack, and Quincy Jones were picked up and driven to the gate of Grandma's house. Then they walked into the garden, where music from *Songs from a Secret Garden* was playing out of hidden speakers and waiters were passing trays of drinks and hors d'oeuvres. (I had to add little potatoes topped with caviar at the last minute.) It was a blissfully bucolic scene . . . except for the whirr of one helicopter.

The previous day, after helicopters had hovered filming all the preparations, I had called the major news networks and said, "Please don't ruin my wedding tomorrow by flying helicopters over my house. The noise will be horrible." And they graciously complied. But there was one paparazzi helicopter that kept buzzing over the guests in the garden and then the house, even during the ceremony.

Nothing is sacred to these people when there's a chance of getting a photograph they can sell.

Just before 8:00 p.m. our guests were directed toward the house, where the flagstone path that leads to the front door was lined with ten violinists, five on each side, and an upright bass, playing love songs. (I specifically asked them not to play any of my songs.)

Donna, Renata, Nelly, and Anna had helped me into the dress, but I hadn't had time to figure out my hair. Finally I said to Soonie, "Just put it up." And the vintage bridal wreath of wax flowers, which Renata had found for me to hold the tulle veil, was placed on my head. Something about that look felt vaguely familiar, but it was only when I saw the photos later that I realized what it was . . . my hairdo was like the one I had as the pregnant bride in *Funny Girl.* Oy!

Once all the guests were seated, Jim's brother, Brian, my brother, Shelly, Richard Baskin, and the ever-faithful Marty took their places on either side of the rabbi as the bridal procession began. The music was the melody to "Just One Lifetime," a song I was considering for an album of love songs inspired by my relationship with Jim. (Marvin had arranged it for the sixteen-piece chamber music ensemble.) Jim escorted his mother, Helen, down the aisle and sat her in the front row on the left, next to his father, and then stood in front of the rabbi. (My mother, too frail to walk, was already in her seat on the right.) Then Jim's son Josh, who was his best man, walked down and stood beside his father. Next Rozzie, my maid of honor, took her place beside Shelly, and then came the children . . . Molly and Trevor, Josh's son, were the ring bearers, and Josh's daughter Eden and my niece Haley were flower girls.

I had told Marvin that I didn't like the melody to "Here Comes the Bride," so he wrote an atonal version of it and we only used the first few bars as I appeared in the doorway.

And then I started down the aisle, escorted by my dear and beautiful son, Jason, as Caleigh and Skye carefully held the end of my fifteen-foot veil.

That's when the glorious music began. This was a piece I had fallen in love with, written by André Previn for the movie *The Four Horsemen of the Apocalypse.* I first heard it on an album of movie themes that John Williams put together and sent to me, because it included "Papa, Can You Hear Me?" I remember thinking, *I want to walk down the aisle to this* . . . it was so lush and romantic. (Sometime later I asked Marilyn and Alan to write lyrics to it, and it became "More in Love with You," which I sang on *The Movie Album.*)

I could see Jim waiting for me, with a big smile on his face. He looked so handsome in his tux. When I reached the front row, I spontaneously bent down and kissed my mother, and then turned to kiss Jim's mother as well . . . as if to say thank you for bringing us to this moment. (Without you two girls, we wouldn't be here!)

And then I took my place beside Jim. The rabbi started to speak to us. Of course we couldn't hear him very well because of the helicopter hovering outside, which was disobeying the rules! They're not supposed to fly below five hundred feet, but it was practically alongside the house.

After we both promised to love, honor, and cherish each other . . . "I do" . . . we crushed the ceremonial glass, according to Jewish tradition, and then we kissed. Our guests cheered. Then everyone moved to the tent for dinner, and after they had a chance to devour all that delicious food, Richard Baskin stood up and gave the first toast. He turned to me and said, "I have to say that in fifteen years, I have never seen you more radiant, more beautiful, or happier than you are tonight . . . You are a singular, nonrecurring event in the universe, and as I got to know Jim, it was very clear to me that he was a good man, an honest man, and that he was obviously completely, totally, and wildly in love. And I realized that this once-in-a-lifetime person had found her once-in-a-lifetime man." He went on to say that the most important thing was to be kind to each other, which really resonated with me.

Then Marty got up and said, "I've had the pride and pleasure of being involved in Barbra's life for thirty-eight years now" . . . I chimed in, "I was only four!" . . . and then he went on to wish us all the best. Renata stood up and said, "Twenty-four years ago I came to work for Barbra, thinking I'll probably stay six months, save some money, go to Disneyland. Now a quarter century later, I still haven't seen Disneyland, but I have had more thrills than any roller coaster or any amusement park or any merry-go-round." I called out, "We're taking you to Disneyland!"

She wished us "boundless joy and happiness," and I was very moved when she said, "Jim, you have the rarest flower in the world, and I know you'll take care of her accordingly."

Then Josh read a poem he had written for us, and I especially loved these lines:

My father and
His bride
Look at how they watch each other
Those silhouetted moments
When all is stripped away
And eyes are the only life

And touch is every moment remembered
I want to learn
What feeling is
Without thinking.

Even though I knew he wrote poetry, I was so struck by his sensitivity. The observations were utterly beautiful. And Marvin was funny and charming, entertaining everyone as he played around on the piano and improvised a song for us. And then it was my turn to get up on the little stage and sing to Jim, who had no idea what was coming next but sweetly sat down on the steps at my feet.

It was such a last-minute thing . . . the track had just arrived . . . and there was no time to rehearse. So I was already apologizing, even before I began: "I haven't really sung for a year, since I did my last album . . . hopefully it'll be the right track in the right key, or whatever." Everyone laughed, and somebody shouted, "Just sing it, baby."

I said, "Okay," and told them to put on the track. The music started, but then I interrupted. "I just want to tell you something." Everyone laughed again, but I had to explain what the music meant to us. I was holding the sheet of lyrics in my hand and clearly anxious about this whole thing because I kept stalling. "I hope I come in at the right time and all that, but forgive me." It was ridiculously awkward. I had to put on my glasses so I could see, and Jim offered to reach up and hold the lyrics for me.

Finally I sang, and thank God the words were more articulate than I was:

I've dreamed of you, always feeling you were there
And all my life I have searched for you everywhere . . .

And just when I thought love had passed me by we met
That first look in your eyes I can't forget . . .

Come dream with me as I've dreamed of you all my life

And then it was time to cut the cake. That's when Jim spoke. He said, "You expect me to follow that? I don't think so. I'll only screw it up." But then he went on, "I can't tell you how lucky I am that this would happen to me so late in life. Every day, every night, every morning is a new adventure. Sleeping is a waste of time. I can't wait to see her again in the morning."

A wedding is such a miraculous event . . . that two people would even find each other is a blessing in the first place. We had made this commitment . . . we were husband and wife . . . and it felt very good and right. It was so nice to say "my husband," and I could feel a shift in Jim as well, as if he had a new sense of possession and responsibility. We were both so happy, and so were our friends. Everyone ate and talked and danced, but I never had a chance to sample any of the food I had chosen. I was too busy going from table to table, hugging and talking to everybody. By the end of the evening I could barely stand up straight (that ethereal dress weighed a ton), and it was only after the last guest had left that I could finally take it off and sit down. That's when I realized I was starving. Jim found some leftover ravioli, and we ate it cold.

We waited till 4:00 a.m. to leave the house, in order to avoid the paparazzi, and drove straight to the marina. We love boats, and for our honeymoon we had decided to rent a boat and cruise around Catalina and the Channel Islands, just off the coast. (The honeymoon had to be short, because Jim was still shooting *Pensacola.*) Donna and Stephan rented their own boat and followed us along. And there was room for a masseuse on their boat, so we could all have massages (now I'd have time for one!).

When Jim and I were finally settled on our boat, I looked at him and thought, *We did it!* We managed to pull off a wedding in two and a half weeks and maintain our privacy (almost). Our friend Deborah Wald, a really good photographer, offered to take pictures to capture the event, and some were released to the press, after she got our approval. (We also have some very amateur videos that have never been edited. Maybe we'll have it done for our twenty-fifth anniversary.)

It had been such a long, exhausting day, and I was just starting to relax when all of a sudden I saw this huge black spot in one eye. I got scared and called my eye doctor. He explained that it was a floater (probably a result of all that stress), and said it would gradually dissolve. Until then he advised putting a patch over the eye. So I had to improvise one, and that's what I was doing on my wedding night. I looked like a pirate. (Luckily many nights over the two years we had been together were like wedding nights.) And then the sea got rough, and of course there was a boat filled with more paparazzi trying to follow us, but we went so fast that we managed to shake them off.

And you know what? I decided not to worry about them or anything else . . . because I was with my husband, and that was all that mattered. We got off the boat to see a few sights, and when my legs started to hurt as we were walking up a hill on one of those islands, my husband put me on his back and carried me up the rest of the way.

What more could you want?

FIFTY-FIVE

Timeless

For me, 1998 will always be the year Jim and I got married. But it was also the year when I was shocked to see how far the right wing would go to try to take down President Clinton, who threatened their grip on power because he was doing his job so well. The economy was booming, crime was down, and the minimum wage was up. He was making government work for the people rather than for the corporations, and that's what the Republicans really couldn't stand. If it was up to them, they would take away a woman's right to choose, repeal environmental protections, and raid Social Security to give tax cuts to the rich. They would protect the NRA, deny civil rights, block campaign finance laws, and kill health-care reform.

But their agenda wasn't very popular, so they had to distract people from the fact that they had no solutions to the serious issues facing the country. And what better distraction than a scandal about the president's private life?

In my humble opinion what Bill Clinton did behind closed doors was none of our business. The American people elected him, twice, to be president . . . not pope!

And then there's the fact that at least twenty of the Republicans who were so eager to condemn Clinton turned out to have problematic private lives of their own, including ongoing affairs . . . some of which produced children. Newt Gingrich divorced his wife while she was dying of cancer to marry a younger woman with whom he was having an affair, and then divorced that woman after she was diagnosed with multiple sclerosis to marry someone even younger. When he resigned as Speaker of the House (due not to ethics, but to the party's poor performance in the midterms), his successor, Robert Livingston, had to resign as well when his own multiple affairs came to light. And then his replacement, Dennis Hastert, admitted many years later that he had sexually abused boys when he was a wrestling coach. I could go on, but you get the picture.

The hypocrisy was mind-boggling. You'd think that people who made such a show of their religious faith would have been more familiar with the biblical warning "Let he who is without sin cast the first stone."

I watched Clinton speak to the nation right after he testified to the grand jury. He admitted that what he had done was wrong and took full responsibility. And yet, looking at it as a director, I felt there was a disconnect between his words and the feelings he was trying to express.

So you know me . . . I had to tell him, because he was my friend, and I knew how painful this must be. When I eventually reached him by phone, I said that I thought he sounded too angry, which undercut his apology. (I've learned that it's never a good idea to react out of anger.) I was hesitant to even seem to be criticizing him, because that's the last thing he needed. But he agreed with me. He wished he had come off as contrite as he felt.

My sense was that the American people would respond if he asked for understanding and forgiveness. They would understand the difference between a lie about a private affair versus a lie about the affairs of state. And they did. They continued to support him even after the House of Representatives went ahead and impeached him in December. In February 1999 he was acquitted in the Senate . . . and his approval rating rose to an all-time high of 73 percent. Clearly a huge majority recognized that this was a politically motivated hit job. Common sense told them that Bill Clinton's offense did not rise to the level of "high crimes and misdemeanors," as specified in the Constitution.

I believe Bill Clinton was a great president, and I think history will agree. He put the country on the path to prosperity with record economic growth . . . 22 million jobs were created during his administration. He advanced the cause of women. He enacted gun control legislation and banned assault weapons. He passed the Family and Medical Leave Act and almost doubled the funding for medical research at the National Institutes of Health. He left us with cleaner water and air. He brokered a peace agreement in Bosnia and a cease-fire in Northern Ireland, and even brought us breathtakingly close to an Israeli-Palestinian accord.

That was his gift . . . to bring people together and find common ground. He was a uniter, not a divider.

After that intense year, I was ready to refocus on my own work. Once again I was asked to do a concert at the MGM Grand in Las Vegas on New Year's Eve, this time to usher in the new millennium. That struck me as a significant milestone, and the offer was so generous I could hardly refuse. We started to put together a show called *Timeless* (which I codirected with the delightful Kenny Ortega). One performance turned into two, and then Marty proposed taking the show to Australia. That was tempting, because Jim loves to travel, and I could combine work with pleasure. Besides, I was having my own issues with privacy. Every time my husband and I took a walk on the beach or even drove to a lot to look at cars, some photographer would pop up out of nowhere. So I was eager to get out of town, and Australia seemed about as far as you could get!

It would also be an opportunity for the two of us to take some time for ourselves and visit New Zealand, Bali, and China while we were on that side of the world. After my marriage, my priorities shifted. I wanted to spend more time with my husband, to slow down and just enjoy life.

In a way, I was responding to a message from my father.

One evening, after a visit with Evelyn and Joanne, who were talking about the wonderful relationships they had with their fathers . . . which made me feel so bereft . . . I went up to my office, and there on the table was a letter that had just come in the mail. I opened it and inside was a three-page poem, written by my father when he was nineteen, for a girl he was seeing. She had kept it all these years and then passed it along to my cousin Mel Streisand to give to me, after she met him at a synagogue in Brooklyn and asked if we were related.

What an amazing gift! I was stunned. And it felt almost mystical to receive it on this particular night, when I was missing him so much. And now here were his words . . . as if he were somehow speaking to me.

He wrote in an almost Shakespearean style, about the wonders and woes of life and how love makes it meaningful. It was passionate and soulful and sincere.

His mind was so interesting. At the top of the first page (the entire poem is now framed on a table outside my bedroom), he wrote, "Dedicated to 4 words which with careful search, may be found in this poem."

Initially no one could figure it out, but then we solved the puzzle. If you took the first letter of the first word in the first line of each stanza, it spelled out a hidden message: "I love thee Dorothy."

I shared the poem with the audience at my concert and explained why I found it so moving. The lesson was that the only thing that really matters in life is love.

Wise advice, and I took it to heart. I was not going to let my career rule my life. That's why I had announced that these would be my last concerts . . . just two dates in Las Vegas, four in Australia, and two each in Los Angeles and New York, so I could finish in the place where I started.

My first show in Australia, at a football stadium in Sydney, had to be canceled because it was raining so hard. It was rescheduled for the next night, and luckily the skies cleared up. But for the second performance, it was raining again, and this time we had no leeway. The show had to go on, so I quipped, "Welcome to the *Wet* album . . . live!" I was concerned for the audience and kept asking if they were all right, sitting in chairs on the field in their clear plastic raincoats with clear plastic umbrellas. I got wet, too, whenever I walked downstage. I had been warned that it was dangerous to sing in the rain, with all the electronic wires around, but I decided to take a chance. It was kind of exciting, but then the downpour got worse. The stagehands spent the whole intermission mopping the stage, and I thought, *Great. Forget about getting into my white gown for act two.* Instead I changed into a simple top, stretchy pants, and sneakers, and put on a traditional made-in-Australia oilskin raincoat and an outback-style cowboy hat . . . and sang "Come Rain or Come Shine" as an extra encore.

In New York, my father's former girlfriend attended my second-to-last concert at Madison Square Garden. I had called to thank her for giving me the poem and invited her to come. I even introduced her to the audience, and we talked backstage. I was eager to hear anything she could remember about my father. (It was a while ago . . . she was ninety-two years old!) "He always dressed nice and was very polite," she told me.

When it came to the final song in the final concert, I introduced it this way: "There's a song that's been there for me since the beginning. I've sung it for over thirty-five years":

People, people who need people
Are the luckiest people in the world . . .

And then I left the stage with the words "Be good to each other. Good night."

At the time I firmly believed that I would never do a concert tour again. I was determined to say goodbye to all that and put my energy into new endeavors . . . like campaigning for Al Gore. After he accepted the Democratic nomination on the final night of the convention, there was a gala, and I closed the evening with four songs. I also gave a brief speech, because it was crucial to me that everybody in America understand just how important this election was. After running through a list of the Democrats' accomplishments, and commending Gore for his stance on the environment, I tried to sum up the stakes in one sentence: "The first three reasons to vote for Al Gore are . . . the Supreme Court . . . the Supreme Court . . . and the Supreme Court!"

After the 2000 election, the power of the Supreme Court was made chillingly clear when it stopped the recount in Florida and handed the presidency to George W. Bush. Gore had won the national popular vote by over half a million . . . 543,895 votes, to be exact . . . and yet he lost Florida, and therefore the Electoral College, by the slimmest of margins . . . 537 votes.

My nightmare had come true.

A week later I was still reeling from the news when I flew to Washington to accept the National Medal of Arts. I was honored to be in such amazing company . . . Maya Angelou, Itzhak Perlman, Mikhail Baryshnikov . . . and especially proud to receive it from my friend President Clinton. He was eloquent as always, and I think I was blushing by the end of his speech, when he said, "She has a great mind and enormous creative capacity, a huge heart, and the voice of a generation. I'm glad we have this one honor left to give her, and I thank her for all she has given to us." That really touched me. Then he placed the medal around my neck and gave me a huge hug.

There was a black-tie dinner that night at the White House for all the recipients, and on our way there, Jim and I stopped to spend some time with Al and Tipper Gore at their house.

Now, I think if any of us had just been cheated out of the presidency, we would probably be apoplectic. I know I didn't want him to concede. But Gore is a man of honor, and it was a matter of principle to him to behave honorably. He was not going to challenge the unprecedented Supreme Court decision and put the country through another crisis.

Just think how different our world would be if Gore had become president. There would have been no Iraq War, and he would have mobilized the government to tackle climate change.

Such a tragic loss . . .

And I thought some Democrats were compounding the tragedy by their passivity. I couldn't just sit and stew. So in March 2001, I wrote a letter titled "Nice Guys Finish Last" and sent it to key Democrats in Congress. I didn't hold back: "What has happened to the Democrats since the November election? Some of you seem paralyzed, demoralized, and depressed. I hope you're through arguing among yourselves and distancing yourselves from President Clinton. Let's not let them divert attention from the success of his administration over the past eight years."

I've noticed that Republicans, whether they agree or not, stick together. They follow the leader. They understand the power of unity. Democrats believe in individualism. It's great to have diverse points of view, but you have to come together in order to win an election. After that, you can argue over your individual opinions, and then to pass legislation you have to present a united front.

I went on to say,

> *The public responds to strength. You don't have to be ruthless like the Republicans, just be strong . . . This is a key moment in our history. We cannot let the right wing roll back thirty years of social progress . . . We have a Congress passing laws that benefit corporations and the privileged few at the expense of the working men and women of this country . . . By usurping Congress's power to make laws, the right wing of the Supreme Court is substituting its judgment for the will of the people . . .*
>
> *Despite the problems we face, Democrats are the party of, by, and for the people, while Republicans are the party of, by, and for the corporation. Keep reminding people of that! Our leaders and policymakers have to fight for the concepts and ideals that have shaped the Democratic Party for generations . . . Just being nice doesn't work. Let's act now and fight before it's too late! I know you can do it.*

While I was consumed with the state of the country, I had also developed another absorbing interest. As I wrote in my journal, "I'm addicted to the stock market . . . the risk and the reward. It gives me the drama I need for the day." From about 1998 to 2000, I was trading Monday through Friday, from 6:30 a.m. to 1:00 p.m. (which proves my level of commitment, because I'm *not* a morning person). But somehow the siren song of the stock market penetrated my sleep. At 6:25 my eyes would open wide, without an alarm. I'd get up, throw on my bathrobe, sit down at my new desk with a cup of hot chocolate, and start trading.

That was a whole new learning experience. Playing the stock market is like gambling, and I like gambling. Whenever I sang in Las Vegas, I would play blackjack, where you really have to follow the cards and calculate the odds. That interests me because it's about mathematics, as well as instinct. And now I had to follow the news and pick stocks. I read about this new drug for men called Viagra and thought, *That's going to be very popular!* It was made by Pfizer, so I immediately bought some shares. I chose Apple because I liked their products. Renata loves Starbucks coffee, so I bought Starbucks. One time I picked a stock because it had my initials. (I don't pretend to be any smarter than a monkey throwing darts, as they say.)

It was fun. I was riding the momentum of the market like a roller coaster, and it was scary and thrilling at the same time. The main reason I loved it was because it was private. I didn't have to act or sing. Nobody was looking at me. I could do all my transactions over the phone, in my nightgown.

So this was my kind of job, and I treated it seriously, keeping a record of every trade I made in a notebook. It was kind of like going to work at Michael Press, except I was making a lot more than forty-five dollars a week. In fact, I was doing so well that the head of the company that handles the bulk of my investments offered me a desk in his office. I laughed, but he wasn't kidding.

One month, I made six figures buying and selling eBay, Amazon, AOL, and Apple, and that's what got Donna Karan interested. She wanted to give me a million dollars to invest for her. At first I said no. I wasn't happy when I lost my own money (which also happened, by the way), but I would be absolutely horrified to lose my friend's money.

I asked her, "Are you willing to lose it all? One million dollars?" And she said, "Yes!" (I think that's because her husband, Stephan, who was not only an artist but also a smart businessman, had just made a fantastic deal for her to sell her company.) And if we had profits, we both agreed to spend it on renting boats, which was our favorite kind of vacation.

So I relented, and was sorry I did. The first day, I bought eBay and Amazon, and then they dropped about twenty points each. Neither of these were blue-chip stocks in the Dow at this point. Instead they were known as "FANGs," and some money managers wouldn't touch them. But I thought they were the most potentially valuable, and they could perform better more quickly because of the volatility.

But it was so stressful to have this new responsibility hanging over my head. It took all the fun out of trading. When I didn't have a winning week, I couldn't even call Donna just to talk, as we normally did, because I was so upset. She must have sensed my withdrawal. Somehow, thank God, I managed to nearly double her money to $1.8 million in five months.

That was the last time I ever traded for somebody else.

I still trade for myself, just not as regularly as I used to. And I'm no longer playing with such big sums. After being burned several times (I lost my shirt, my dress, and my nerve in the 2008 financial meltdown), I decided to stick to bonds. I couldn't even think about the market.

But it still holds an allure. Sometimes before I go to bed, I'll look at the futures, to get a preview of what the Dow and the Nasdaq might do. Jim plays the market as well, but he's much bolder than I am. When I see an opportunity now, I might buy fifty to one hundred shares. He'll buy a thousand or more. It's a fascinating game, which we both enjoy. Then we'll compare notes after the closing bell sounds and see who did better. It's a friendly competition, and I think I'm actually happier when he wins!

No wonder I had less and less interest in acting again. I was too busy!

But I did have to get out of my bathrobe and leave my cozy room when I was given the Cecil B. DeMille Lifetime Achievement Award at the Golden Globes in 2000. My friend Shirley MacLaine did a commentary as clips from my films were shown, then called me up to the stage. After watching myself go from twenty-five to fifty-four, I said, "What a great business. You get to age publicly."

I feel very grateful to have had my career. And that night, looking back, I was reminded just how lucky I was, especially to have had William Wyler start me off on-screen. But I also wanted to be very clear about the obstacles, because an actor's life is so difficult . . . you're constantly facing rejection . . . and success depends on so much that's beyond your control. "Someone asked me recently if they should be an actor, and I said, 'If you have to ask, then the answer is no.'" I think the only reason to subject yourself to this is because you're so passionate about it that you have no other choice.

And then I felt honored all over again when the American Film Institute chose me to receive their Lifetime Achievement Award in 2001 . . . even though the prospect of a whole event devoted to my work was a little daunting. I couldn't help thinking of drowning, when your whole life supposedly passes before your eyes.

But it turned out to be a wonderful, heartwarming evening. Gary Smith produced it beautifully, and his wife, Maxine, who knows me so well, decorated the set with the kind of Art Nouveau pieces I love. She and I became friends back in 1973 when Gary was doing my TV special in London. We realized we had so much in common . . . even the same Jewish summer camp!

I didn't have to give them any ideas. All I had to do was sit back and watch. Marvin and the Bergmans wrote a special song to open the show, and so many friends and colleagues came to share their stories about me. Elizabeth Taylor walked onstage and said, "I have been so overwhelmed by your talent that for years I have been terrified of you. You are just too big, too perfect, too wonderful."

Elizabeth Taylor is one of the biggest movie stars in history! When I was a teenager reading movie magazines, I used to be so impressed by her exciting life. Now she's saying that she was intimidated by *me*?

Warren Beatty described meeting me when I had just turned sixteen. "Even then you had that one-of-a-kind mix of intelligence, critical skepticism, and eroticism that we all know and love so well."

Eroticism? Hmmm . . . interesting choice of word, and it may have said more about Warren than me! He can be very astute, and also funny, which is part of what makes him so charming. He went on, "Speaking as someone who knows you well enough to remember your cholesterol levels, I'm proud to be your friend, not only because of your integrity as an artist but your integrity as a citizen, and your willingness to risk speaking up for what you think is right, no matter what it costs you."

That meant a lot, coming from him, because he, too, never shied away from politics.

It was quite an experience, to sit there and listen to all these remarkable people who had been part of my life, like Phyllis Diller and Dustin Hoffman. Dustin told a funny story about hearing me sing for the first time on *PM East* when we were both kids in the same acting class: "My jaw dropped, and the hair rose on my arms and the back of my neck . . . It was the first time that I had ever seen that kind of talent from somebody I knew. The talent was so big that I vowed never to speak to her again!"

Then there was Irvin Kershner, Ryan O'Neal, Robert Redford, Sydney Pollack, Kris Kristofferson, Quincy Jones, Nehemiah Persoff, Amy Irving, Nick Nolte, Jeff Bridges, Lauren Bacall. My heart was expanding to take in the love I was feeling. I was especially moved when Anjelica Huston said, "It's no secret that my father was drawn to storytellers, mavericks, innovators. And he admired you so, Barbra. You carry the flag for women directors." (He once said I should have played Cleopatra. Little did he know how much I wanted to do exactly that.)

And there was President Clinton on tape, observing, "I'm sure I'm not the only one of your friends who's noticed that you tend to try and direct things not only on-screen, but off as well. I don't know how many times over the last eight years when I'd get a fax or a call from you trying to help direct me to make America and the world better for our children and our future." (Wait till he reads all the notes I *didn't* send!)

Then Sidney Poitier, my old friend, introduced me. I was totally overwhelmed when I made my way to the stage so he could present me with the award. Finally, I could thank everyone who spoke that night, including those who were there from the beginning, like Cis, the Bergmans, Marty, and Marvin, who was at the piano once again.

I always thought of myself as an outsider, but now I really felt like part of this community. And what a special group . . . people who had devoted their lives to the craft of making films. I said, "Jim and I go out to the movies a lot, and I realize the true power of the movies when I'm part of the audience. United in the dark, we're really more alike than not alike, caring about the same things . . . love, peace, hope, family."

Looking back on that night, I think the person who truly surprised me most was Jason. One moment he was sitting beside me and then suddenly he was up onstage. I had no idea he was planning to speak because he never wants to be the center of attention at these events. Tears came to my eyes as he told the audience how much he wanted the part in *The Prince of Tides*: "I want to thank you, Mom, for letting me work with you . . . The experience really deepened and expanded our relationship on a personal level. So thank you. I'm glad I got to play your son in a film about mothers and sons, and I'm glad to be here as your son to tell you I love you."

His words went straight to my heart. It was so wonderful to have him nearby while I was making that film. Casting him was an important decision, and I was so proud of his work, and of him . . . his honesty, his talent, his intelligence, his kindness.

Jason is an old soul. He always had a very strong sense of self, and today he expresses it through his music, his pottery, and his art. One day when we were painting together in Grandma's house, I said, "Let's paint those Shaker boxes." My version looked kind of predictable compared to his. He always had his own way of seeing things. Jason is innately creative, but he never wanted to be in the spotlight (as opposed to me at fourteen). He simply pursued whatever interested him and followed his own path.

Our conversations these days range from politics to plants. Recently he designed and built a beautiful house on a hill in Northern California, with a low stone wall flanking the driveway and fruit trees all the way up. Then he planted a garden and added a small greenhouse.

I could talk about plants for hours (and I do). Back when I was planning the garden for the ranch, I actually spent three months visiting nurseries and choosing each plant. I was so obsessed that I used to murmur the Latin names in my sleep . . . *Pittosporum undulatum.* And now there's an old, beautiful olive tree on my property that I love. But the leaves on one branch turned brown, and I was so pained looking at that every day. So I asked my gardener if he could go up there on a ladder and paint the leaves green. (Don't worry, we made sure it wouldn't hurt the tree.)

Jason loves flowers as much as I do, and recently, on one of our phone calls, he asked, "Have you ever seen a light-blue delphinium?"

Well, that launched us into a discussion about all their colors, and whether they're annual or perennial. We both love delphiniums because they're tall and majestic, yet delicate at the same time.

Inside his house there's a lovely guest room, which I know is always ready for Jim and me if we want to escape. And everywhere I look there's some intriguing object he's collected. When I ask where he found it, the answer is usually eBay, rather than some high-end antique store. Jason is someone who understands my search for beauty, because he shares that same gene.

CHAPTER FIFTY-SIX

Giving Back

THE BARBRA STREISAND
WOMEN'S CARDIOVASC
RESEARCH AND EDUCATIO
CS

Family, friends, and dogs who love you . . . that's what really matters, and I was reminded of that on September 11, 2001. That morning, Jim and I were asleep in bed when Renata called, woke us up, and told us to turn on the TV. It was horrific.

I was shocked and heartbroken, like the rest of the country. The Emmys had been scheduled for a few days later, but I couldn't imagine how they could hold them, and was relieved when the ceremony was postponed. Then when it was rescheduled for November, Gary Smith, who was the producer, asked if I would close the show with the song "You'll Never Walk Alone" in memory of those who perished.

I was torn. To even hold an awards show in the aftermath of tragedy seemed trivial, and I was afraid that a big televised Hollywood event like this would present another target for the terrorists. But then I thought, *I have to do it, if only to show that we're not intimidated.* And if there was even the slightest chance that the song would comfort someone in some small way, then it would be worth it.

And if something did happen . . . Well, I'll go out singing.

At the last Emmys I attended, my heart was pounding so fast that I vowed never to put myself through that again. So this time I deliberately arrived just before I had to sing. Marty greeted me at the car with the words "You just won the Emmy and you weren't here." It was great to be recognized for my performance in *Timeless*, but honestly, any award seemed inconsequential in the face of what our country was going through.

My appearance had not been announced, and I walked out onto a dark stage and looked at the names of the victims projected on the screen behind me, above candles and flowers heaped on the floor. I sang the first lines of the song in shadow and then turned to the audience as the light hit me. I was nervous, of course, but those feelings were overwhelmed by a sense of purpose.

In the pressroom afterward I was asked how I felt, and I said, "I'm just grateful we live in a country where we're allowed to sing, and to have music, and express ourselves and our emotions. It's a very sad time in our history, a frightening time. And I wanted to give something back" in whatever way I could. The song was for those who died and the survivors who had to go on . . . as we all have to go on through our fears . . . but I hoped somehow that this experience would actually make us into better people, who are kinder to one another. "Every day is a blessing now, and I think it makes us very grateful for what we have . . . The power of love is stronger than death."

In March 2002, I was at my mother's bedside when she died. For the past six years she had been suffering from Alzheimer's disease. Thank God for Prozac . . . when she started to get very agitated, her doctor prescribed it and that was incredible . . . she forgot to be angry.

But it was impossible to have a conversation with her. And then I thought, *I wonder if she would remember the songs she used to sing?* One day when I was visiting, I started to sing "One Kiss," which she had recorded when we went to that

Manhattan studio a lifetime ago . . . and my mother joined in! She couldn't remember the words (and I only knew the words to the first line), but she could still sing the melody with me. It just shows you the power of music. It burrows deep into your brain, and even deeper into your soul.

During her final months, it was painful to watch her drastic decline. And when she took her last breath, I thought, *At least she's at rest*, and cut off a lock of her hair in an impulse to just keep something of hers. But I couldn't cry. I felt bad about that, but it was as if I had no emotion left.

That night, after I came back from the hospital, Jim took me to Palm Springs, where our friend Todd Morgan lent us his house for a few days, and my husband had flowers delivered for me. The next morning I was bringing some of the bouquet into the bedroom when the phone rang. It was Bill Clinton, who said, "I just heard about your mother."

"How did you find me?" I asked.

He laughed and replied, "I may have lost my power, but I haven't lost my initiative."

We talked about our mothers for a while. Just as I had called him when Virginia died, he wanted to check on me. And then he asked if I had read *The Four Agreements*, a book by Don Miguel Ruiz.

"You're not going to believe this," I told him. "I'm sitting on my friend's bed, and right next to me, on the bedside table, is that book."

It was as if the universe was conspiring to lead me to it, which makes sense, since it turned out to be so meaningful to me. I don't remember all the lessons in the book, but I do remember the Four Agreements: "Be impeccable with your word" (if you say you're going to do something, do it!) and "Don't make assumptions" (I've learned the hard way about that one). Wait, what were the other two? Jim just looked it up for me: "Don't take anything personally" (I'm still working on that) and "Always do your best" (I think that's in my nature).

After my friend Joanne later introduced me to Don Miguel Ruiz, I invited him to come see my house. I offered him an ice cream cone, and we sat on the patio outside Grandma's house, looking at the ocean. It felt blissful, being with this wise and gentle man, appreciating life, and nature.

He reminded me of the Dalai Lama in the way he smiled and simply enjoyed being in the moment. Ruiz was not that old, and I was surprised to hear he had had a near-fatal heart attack (and he eventually had a heart transplant), but the way he talked about death was very reassuring. He considered it part of the natural progression of life . . . and I was glad to know he recovered beautifully and went on to write more books!

Hearing about his experience, and thinking about my mother, made me want to push all my daily distractions aside. I wanted to focus on what was genuinely important. The next time I sang in public, after the Emmys, was to raise money for Democratic congressional candidates in 2002. And I sang for John Kerry in 2004. That campaign was another shock. I was sickened to watch how the Republicans managed to take a decorated war hero and twist the facts to smear him, dismissing his combat medals and questioning his patriotism. They knew that Kerry's war record made Bush, who had avoided serving in Vietnam, look bad in comparison. So they shamelessly lied. As I said in a speech when I was given an award that year by the Human Rights Campaign, "I've never seen anything as ruthless or as relentless as this. They can take a slur hatched at the Republican National Committee or a lie huckstered by the Heritage Foundation, repeat it on Fox, hit it on Limbaugh, print it in *The Wall Street Journal*, until it's coming out of every media outlet imaginable. Repeating lies over and over doesn't make them any more true. But it does make people believe the lies a little more until finally they stop demanding the truth."

About two weeks after the election . . . and the disappointment of Kerry's loss . . . Jim and I flew down to Little Rock for the dedication of Bill Clinton's presidential library. It was pouring rain that day, and the ceremony took place outside, where thousands of guests were seated on folding chairs, huddling under umbrellas. It was comforting to see Bill and Hillary again and so many friends, like Shimon Peres. But even more inspiring was the vision of bipartisanship this event represented, since every living president except Gerald Ford (who was ill) was there . . . both Democrats and Republicans . . . including the newly reelected Bush, as well as John Kerry and Al Gore.

And then it was back to my other life. In December *Meet the Fockers* was released. I had turned that movie down at first, but then Jay Roach, the director, called. I liked him, and it always feels good when a director really wants you for a part. Roz Focker was a sex therapist, so that had possibilities, and Jay was wonderfully open to all my ideas about the character. But I was still hesitating when Ben Stiller called and said I absolutely had to play his mother. Dustin

Hoffman would be playing his father, so that was another incentive. Finally, we would get to work together.

I thought, *What the hell?* It was eight years since I had done a movie, so it was time to put my toe back in the water. And it would be nice to do a comedy again.

Dustin and I had so much fun. We treated the script as a starting point and then improvised a lot, just like we used to do in acting class. We knew each other when we were hardly "star material" . . . he was a janitor and I was a babysitter. Strange to think that was more than forty years ago, since it felt like yesterday. Dustin is five years older than me, but coincidentally our film careers took off at the same time . . . he was making *The Graduate* while I was shooting *Funny Girl*.

I also knew Robert De Niro, who was playing the bride-to-be's father, through Cis, who had cast him in *The Deer Hunter.* When I first read the script, our characters didn't have much to do with each other, but I thought it would be funny to be more hands on with Bob. Since I was playing a sex therapist, I suggested giving him a massage. I once had a masseuse who sat on my back, so why not try that? Bob really got into it and kept saying, "Press harder. Harder!" To this day my left thumb joint has never recovered . . . and every year, Bob sends me flowers on my birthday (not sure if that's guilt or affection!).

On a side note, this was the first time I felt the effect of Hollywood's unequal pay scale for men and women. I didn't ask what the other actors were making, but I was definitely hurt when I found out that Dustin was getting three times as much as me, plus a tiny percentage, which is significant on a movie that made $520 million. I was given some excuse about how I had been the last to sign, but the only thing that made me feel better was when my dear friend Ron Meyer, who was the head of Universal, gave me a bonus . . . the first and only time I ever got one. I guess he, too, thought it was unfair.

Anyway, I'd rather remember the good times on that movie. It was lovely to work with Blythe Danner again, and we all laughed a lot. The only thing I had to do was learn lines, rather than direct, so it was easy . . . but dull!

All I ever wanted to be was an actress, but when I think back, I suppose something changed in my attitude toward acting over the years. People used to call me ambitious, but if I was so ambitious, why had I turned down so many movies? I remember being offered *The War of the Roses* (to act in and direct) and thinking, *You have to give this woman a reason for doing all these crazy things to her husband . . . make him a cheater. Give her some flaw as well so he's equally motivated.* I thought it needed more truth behind the gags, but nobody went for that.

I was sitting by my pool at Carolwood when I read *Shadowlands*, sent to me by Sydney Pollack, who had decided not to direct and thought I might want to. I loved the script . . . I could envision every scene. It was exciting to think I could film at Oxford University in England. And I really responded to the characters. Of course I should play this Jewish woman from the Bronx who falls in love with C. S. Lewis (a true story, and Anthony Hopkins would be brilliant). It was perfect for me. But I had just come off *The Prince of Tides* and was enjoying my summer.

So I turned it down, even though it was tempting. I really am a mass of contradictions. For every reason to say yes, I can find two to say no.

I guess this is why I haven't been in that many movies . . . only nineteen . . . while other actresses who came up at the same time have done fifty or more. But the fact is, I was becoming less ambitious. When I felt fulfilled in my personal life, I had no desire to act. Besides, I needed to feel passionate about a film, but sometimes even when I did, I could be lazy. And both qualities . . . the passion and the laziness . . . are equally present in me.

Before *Meet the Fockers* I had only made three movies in twenty years. The reality is, I got very frustrated when I couldn't make the movies I had spent years developing, like *The Normal Heart* or *Skinny and Cat.* That deeply discouraged me.

And then Cis, my partner in Barwood Films and one of my first surrogate mothers, slowly succumbed to dementia. It was heartbreaking to watch. I lost the person I had trusted most since I was sixteen. She was the one who knew how to find writers and get projects off the ground. That wasn't my strong suit, and without her to push me, and everyone else, projects stalled. And I never wanted to replace her.

It might still be satisfying to act, if I could work with a good director on an interesting movie. But as several producers have told me, they would have hired me but thought the part, or the salary, was too small . . . and never asked.

It's ironic . . . you can get to a point where you're elevated into oblivion.

Looking back, I feel as if I didn't fulfill my potential. And now it's too late . . . although Sarah Bernhardt dared to play Juliet when she was seventy-four! And

Sarah had just taken on the title role in a motion picture, the new medium, when she died at the age of seventy-nine (still attracting lovers till the end).

I admire her spirit, and still sometimes think about playing her, and the story I would want to tell. One idea came to me when I was sitting at my dressing table, looking at myself in a magnifying mirror, trying to put on my eyeliner. I used to be able to draw a perfectly straight line, but now my hand isn't as steady. And I thought, *This would be a good opening* . . . for Sarah in her later years, backstage at the theater, staring into her dressing-room mirror as she's putting on her makeup with a shaking hand. Still, when there's a knock on the door, she's ready. And once she's on stage, inhabiting a character, the audience will believe every word she says.

I wish I had played Sarah. But I couldn't make it happen. So I took my creative energy and put it into building a house . . . an elegant barn . . . something I had been thinking about for years. I wrote about that process in my first book, *My Passion for Design*, and included plenty of photographs of my house . . . which reminds me of something.

I'd like to set the record straight about the so-called "Streisand effect." When I first heard the term, I naïvely thought, *Is that about the effect of my music?* Little did I know. Then my assistant showed me all the references to it on the internet, and I was appalled.

Let me say this loud and clear. Contrary to the explanation on Wikipedia, I did not attempt to "suppress" a photograph of my house. My issue was never with the photo . . . it was only about the use of my name attached to the photo.

To cut a long story short, when a wealthy businessman took it upon himself to photograph thousands of homes along the California coast and create a website in 2002, all the homes were identified only by longitude and latitude and not by the owners' names . . . except for five celebrities, including me. Suddenly there was a photo on the internet with my house, my name, and the exact coordinates where I lived. That put the safety of my family and myself at risk. We had already experienced several incidents with intruders over the years. So I hope you can understand my concern.

And this is what every description of the "Streisand effect" gets wrong. I wasn't trying to remove the photo. All I asked was that this man please just treat me like everyone else and remove my name, for security reasons. But he refused.

Interesting . . . if his aim was to document coastal erosion, as he insisted, the use of my name served no environmental purpose. Could there possibly have been another motive? Did he want to draw more attention to his site by using my name?

I turned to the only recourse I had . . . a lawsuit.

The great Supreme Court justice Louis Brandeis believed in everyone's right "to have their privacy and safety protected." But as my friend, the brilliant constitutional scholar Laurence Tribe, told me later, "I wish you would've called me, because I would have told you that you couldn't win . . . with the internet, we've *all* lost our privacy."

I felt I was standing up for a principle, but in retrospect, it was a mistake. I also assumed that my lawyer had done exactly as I wished and simply asked to take my name off the photo . . . but the lesson I had to learn again was, Never assume. (It's also my fault. I should have taken the time to read all the legal documents.)

Acting on principle proved to be very costly, not only financially but also emotionally, since it pains me to see my name used in such a negative way, as if I had tried to suppress the press, when that was never my intention. As a lifelong Democrat, I support a free press.

Recently I tried to correct the Wikipedia entry to reflect the actual facts, but we were told that would be impossible.

Why? Isn't the truth enough?

It's ironic. Today we have instant access to more information than ever on the internet, but we're actually less informed because it's too easy for anyone to spread lies with no accountability.

The other irony of the situation is that if I had won the lawsuit (which I didn't), any proceeds, as I stated, would be donated to organizations that protect the environment (which was supposed to be the photo's purpose in the first place). That's a cause I have supported for decades. And I would rather focus my energies there.

In 2006 I found a new way to do that when the Clinton Climate Initiative caught my attention. I was so impressed with the practicality of its approach . . . like retrofitting existing buildings to reduce the energy they consume by one third. It started with the Empire State Building, and then brought mayors together from cities around the world so they could jointly order energy-efficient materials for buildings, traffic lights, street lights, buses . . . and therefore make the cost more affordable.

When President Clinton called me up to the stage at a conference in New York to thank me for my one-million-dollar pledge (the biggest donation my foundation had ever made at that point, because I was so concerned about climate change), Rupert Murdoch was in the audience. And I said exactly what I was thinking: "Mr. Murdoch, you're a billionaire and you only gave half a million dollars. Don't you think you should write another check?"

Everybody laughed. (Maybe not Murdoch. I wonder if he ever matched my donation.)

In order to continue to be able to make gifts like that, I needed to replenish my coffers, which is why I changed my mind and decided to do another concert tour. Since I had said that my previous tour was going to be my last, I felt I owed the public an explanation. So I wrote in the concert program, "My motivation for returning to the concert stage is to raise funds for causes that are important to us all. It can easily be summed up in the words of the immortal Dolly Levi: 'Money is like manure. It's not worth a thing unless it's spread around, encouraging young things to grow.'" There were so many worthy organizations I wanted to support through the Streisand Foundation.

By the way, none of my subsequent concerts was ever billed as a farewell tour. I had learned my lesson: Never say never! Or as I said in one of my most recent concerts, "It's not over until the fat lady sings, and I'm not *that* fat!"

So we put together a new show and took it to twelve American cities and two in Canada. I thought of it as a challenge to myself. Was I still up to the game?

Thankfully the audience response was incredible, and I could feel the love. And it turns out a tour is one way to catch up with friends who came to see me . . . Bill and Hillary Clinton in New York, Madeleine Albright in D.C., Oprah in Chicago, Nancy Pelosi in Los Angeles, and many more. Oprah came to visit me at the hotel where I was staying. Over a glass of champagne, she asked what I thought about her backing a presidential candidate, which she'd never done before. "Absolutely," I told her. "If you believe in someone, you should tell people, because your voice is powerful." It turned out to be Barack Obama, whom I first met in 2004 when he was running for the Senate. He was one of those charismatic people who just stop you in your tracks. I was impressed by his sincerity, his grace, and his intelligence, not to mention his beautiful teeth.

In Phoenix, Kris Kristofferson happened to be playing across town the same night as my concert. I had just finished my encore and left the stage when I returned with a surprise guest, Kris, to the delight of the audience. We shared a long hug, and the crowd went wild. He still had that same shy, sweet smile, and it was wonderful to see him again.

The tour went so well that I let Marty persuade me to take it to seven cities in Europe in the summer of 2007, but only if I could have several days off in between shows, so I could go to museums, eat in great restaurants . . . and go antique shopping. That was definitely not cost-effective, because between the crew and the musicians there were 158 people in the company who had to be paid whether they were working or not. But that was the only way I would agree to do it. I needed those days to recharge. And to make it even more fun, I invited Maxine and Gary Smith to come along. That meant Jim would have a pal to hang around with while Maxine and I went antiquing. Kim had given me a guide to the major flea markets, and I basically built the tour schedule around them. After all, I needed to furnish the barn!

One Sunday in the Loire Valley in France, I decided on the spur of the moment to go to Brussels, because the first buildings in the Art Nouveau style are there. I wanted to see the architect Victor Horta's house, which is now a museum, because I was planning an Art Nouveau room on the lower level of the barn. So we got into a car for the five-hour trip (the cook at the little hotel packed the most delicious apple tart I've ever had) and saw a city I would have missed otherwise.

Somehow, in between all this, I managed to give a few concerts. Zurich was first and then Vienna, where for once my favorite dessert, Kaiserschmarrn (fluffy bits of caramelized pancake), took second place to the art. This was the city where Klimt and Schiele had lived, and I wanted to see as much of their work as I could. At the Albertina I was mesmerized by the magnificent Klimt portraits, especially the *Portrait of Fritza Riedler* in her ethereal white dress and pearl choker. At the Belvedere I was shown into the director's office, where I was surprised to see two photographs of me on his desk. One was the photo taken in London in 1969, alongside the Klimt and two Schieles I had just bought. The other was of me in the gold gown I loved and tried to copy from Klimt's *Portrait of Adele Bloch-Bauer.* The Belvedere has more Klimts than anywhere else in the world, and it was so exciting to finally get to see his most iconic work, *The Kiss*. I think I stood in front of it for thirty minutes.

The next day I spent two hours at the Leopold Museum, which has the largest collection of Schiele's work. Elizabeth Leopold, who founded the museum with her husband, came to meet me, and as we were walking through the galleries, she led me to one wall and said, "I thought you might be interested in this." And there was *my* Schiele, the *Nude with Mauve Stockings*, which I had bought in 1969. I could have kicked myself all over again for selling it, but at least there was some small satisfaction in knowing that they, too, had appreciated it, and it now belonged to the museum.

Oh, and then there was the concert, which took place on a stage erected in front of the Schönbrunn Palace, the summer home of the Habsburg emperors. I don't think I've ever sung in a more regal setting. You can't help but be awed by the history, not to mention the wallpapers!

In Paris, Charles Aznavour, Alain Delon, and Jean-Paul Belmondo were in the audience, along with Michel Legrand . . . I sang his beautiful song "The Summer Knows," just for him. Belmondo was leaning on a cane when he knocked on my dressing-room door, and he was as compelling as ever, with that tough face combined with vulnerability underneath. Charles, Alain, and Michel were also at the Élysée Palace when President Nicolas Sarkozy presented me with the Légion d'honneur, France's highest accolade. That was a thrilling moment, and I was so glad that Jason could be there with me, along with Jim, Marty, Renata, and my beloved dog, Sammie.

The next stop was Berlin. When I was much younger, I felt I could never sing in Germany, because several family members lost their lives during World War II. But now I thought, *Why should contemporary Germans be blamed for the sins of their fathers or their grandfathers?*

And yet the past still cast a shadow on the present, especially since the amphitheater where I sang was built to Hitler's specifications for the 1936 Olympics. I walked with Marty through these zigzag tunnels to reach the stage . . . the same tunnels Hitler had walked down, we were told, and all the sharp turns had been designed to prevent anyone from taking a shot at him. That sent a chill up my spine.

I'd been a little wary about what kind of response I'd get in Germany . . . it was well-known that for years I had turned down many requests to sing there. And yet the audience erupted into huge applause as soon as they saw me. Since it was still light outside when the concert started, I could see every face, with so many smiles from ear to ear. I didn't expect such enthusiasm.

Jim was there, as always. He never misses a show. (I once asked him, "Don't you ever get bored watching me?" And he said, "No. It's always different.") That night, during the Q&A with the audience, I picked up a card and instead of the usual question, it said, "Hand the mic to Bill Ross," who was conducting.

"Is this a joke?" I asked.

Then Bill announced that the next day was Jim and my anniversary, and that he was speaking for the whole crew as he congratulated us. And the orchestra broke into the music we played at our wedding, the love theme from *The Four Horsemen of the Apocalypse*. That was a complete surprise, and then Jim surprised me as well by coming out onstage, bearing a huge cake with bittersweet chocolate icing. And my undemonstrative husband actually kissed me in public!

It was an enchanting night, and I was a bit overwhelmed by all the standing ovations. As I said at the end of the show, "Thank you for coming. Thank you for waiting for me. Thank you for being a fantastic audience! I'll never forget you."

It's great to go on tour and have your work be appreciated, but what was even more gratifying was what it meant for my foundation.

And I had a new cause.

In 2007 I read an article in *The New York Times* and was shocked to learn that heart disease kills more women than men. In fact, it kills more women than all cancers combined. But in the last fifty years, almost all research on the subject had been done on men.

That made no sense to me. How can you treat a woman for a life-threatening disease based on diagnostics and technologies created for men? Women have a very different physiology . . . different plumbing, different-sized hearts, smaller valves, smaller arteries. That's why a heart attack can present differently in a woman.

Years before, Dr. Bernadine Healy, the first female director of the National Institutes of Health, had identified what she called "the Yentl Syndrome" to describe what happens when a woman goes to the emergency room with symptoms that don't conform to those of the classic male heart attack. Often she's not taken seriously, misdiagnosed, and undertreated. Maybe she's told she's having a panic attack and is sent home with an antacid. Sometimes she takes the pill, goes to bed, and never wakes up.

This is why one in three women were dying from heart disease.

I've always been outspoken on issues of inequality, whether it's about civil rights, gay rights, or gender discrimination. And it turns out that gender does matter when it comes to medical science, especially in clinical research. The inequality even extends to mice in the labs. They're all male! When I asked why, the answer I got was that female mice have hormones, so they're more complex. Well, so are women!

I wanted to find someone who was working to right this imbalance, and that led me to Dr. Noel Bairey Merz, a world-renowned cardiologist specializing in both the research and treatment of female-pattern heart disease at the Cedars-Sinai Women's Heart Center. At first I endowed a research and education program, and was fascinated to learn that one of her colleagues, Dr. Doris Taylor, had actually grown the first human heart from stem cells. She had a breakthrough when she discovered that using only female stem cells was the solution, because male stem cells didn't work. They got totally lost. (Like men, I guess male stem cells won't ask for directions!)

I was so impassioned about this cause that I went to Washington, D.C., several times to lobby Congress for more money for research on women. I gave speeches and appeared on television to raise awareness among women, *before* they found themselves in the hospital. And the public speaking was worth it, because our partnership with all these brilliant scientists worked. Now the NIH has put more money into women's heart disease . . . more women are included in clinical trials . . . and there are even female mice in the labs!

As a result, the number of women dying from heart disease is down to one in four.

This is how change happens . . . when women work together and speak up.

FIFTY-SEVEN

How Much Do I Love You?

Philanthropy . . . and politics. Those were my passions now.

When Hillary Clinton decided to run for president in 2007, I endorsed her because I thought she was brilliant and would do a great job for the country. Besides, I felt it was about time that we had a female head of state. Other nations had already chosen Indira Gandhi, Golda Meir, and Angela Merkel. Why were we so far behind?

But the momentum was with another candidate, Barack Obama, and after Hillary ceded the nomination to him, I, too, gave him my support. When I was asked to sing at a fundraiser, I gladly said yes. And I was jubilant when this extraordinary man was elected in November 2008.

In December I was at the White House for a reception with outgoing President Bush, invited along with the other recipients of the Kennedy Center Honors. (Apparently Bush had called Bill Clinton beforehand to ask whether I was likely to say something embarrassing, since I had been very vocal about my objections to his policies for eight years. I told Bill to tell Bush not to worry. I would never embarrass him on an occasion like this.)

This was the first time I had met President Bush, so I extended my hand and was surprised when he said, "Aw c'mon, gimme a hug and a kiss." I must say I was taken aback by his warmth and found him completely disarming (even though he was probably kissing me hello while I was kissing him goodbye).

During the White House ceremony, he listed my achievements and then said, "Barbra's also a person of passionate convictions and opinions that she is not afraid to share." I cupped my hands over my mouth in mock contrition as the guests laughed. Bush laughed, too, and added, "I don't know. At least that's what they tell me. You know, it kind of makes me think of another Barbara who's not afraid to speak her mind." (Ah yes . . . men and their mothers!)

It helps to have a sense of humor if you're a politician.

On my way into the theater for the gala that night, I was bombarded with questions from the press about our meeting . . . apparently that kiss created quite a stir. I simply said, "On an evening like this, art transcends politics," and took my seat with the other honorees alongside the president and First Lady. I won't go into all the wonderful artists who performed during the part of the program that was a tribute to me, but I was particularly touched by the words of two extraordinary women.

Queen Latifah spoke of watching me as a young girl and being inspired to leap over barriers: "Barbra threw out the rule book when it came to a standardized idea of what a movie star was . . . We don't just do what the boys want us to do. We can do it all. We can sing, we can act, we can produce, and we can lead, not just the people who are working with us, but all the girls who have dreams like you did. You just have to have the courage, like Miss Streisand, to reach for them." I blew her a kiss, and then she ended with the words "An original doesn't conform to our expectations, she changes them . . . forever."

And when Beyoncé came out to sing "The Way We Were," I was thrilled. After her last note, in the midst of the applause, she looked up at me and said, "It's an honor to sing for you, Miss Streisand." At the party afterward, she was so charming and complimentary, and I told her I felt the same way about her. She's done such imaginative work in her music and her videos . . . she just knocks me out.

And it happens that we have something else in common. It turned out she was unhappy with her performance and had already done another take (for the version to be shown on TV later). I totally identified with that! And she was outstanding at the inaugural ball a few weeks later.

I was feeling so happy and hopeful about the future of our country. And I think that came out in my music. That year I released *Love Is the Answer.* It was Marty's idea to promote the album by having a contest where fans could win a ticket to a "one-night-only" performance (my kind of run!) in a little Greenwich Village nightclub . . . going back to my roots. Ironically, the only club from that era still standing was the Village Vanguard, where the owner, Max Gordon, had turned me down when I was eighteen.

On the night of the show, my old friend Rick Edelstein, who had arranged that audition, stood up to tell that story. We packed 123 people into that minuscule room. I had to squeeze through the crowd to get to the tiny stage, and I said, "Oh my God, this is hysterical. I mean, are we a box of sardines here or what?" Crammed in with the contest winners were a few more recognizable faces, like Bill and Hillary Clinton, Nicole Kidman, and Sarah Jessica Parker, as well as old friends like Marilyn and Alan, Jule Styne's widow, Maggie . . . and Jim, who was right in front. (Most of my guests were watching from a more spacious room at the Waldorf, where we had arranged food, drink, and a live feed.)

At least there was one less thing to worry about. As I joked, "It's hard to have stage fright with practically no stage!"

I was singing old standards from the album like "In the Wee Small Hours of the Morning" and "Make Someone Happy," accompanied by only a quartet of musicians, just like the old days, and it was all very cozy and relaxed.

And Marty was right. It got *Love Is the Answer* off to a great start . . . it debuted at the top of the charts and became my ninth number 1 album.

The next time I sang live was in 2011 when I was honored by MusiCares, a wonderful organization that helps musicians in need (and they raised $4 million that night!). I love Bill Maher, who was the host, and Prince introduced me, which was a lovely surprise, because I had never met him and always found him so interesting. But he seemed kind of stiff and awkward, and it was only years later that I got the full story from my assistant Grace Handy, who happened to have a connection to Prince. As an associate of his told her, "Barbra is one of the only people in the world Prince really admired and looked up to. He was a bit awestruck that night."

Since I was a fan of his, it was intriguing to find out he was a fan of mine. Grace told me such wonderful stories about him . . . as an eighteen-year-old in December 1976, he loved *A Star Is Born* so much that he saw it six times. The poster was the only thing he had hanging on his bedroom wall. He even recorded a demo of "Evergreen." Then, after he saw *Yentl*, he had his assistants watch and study the film, saying "She did it all!" And in March 2016, just a few weeks before he died, he was performing in Toronto and asked the audience, "Did anybody see *The Way We Were*? Do you remember the part where Robert Redford broke up with Barbra Streisand? The only person that she could call . . . was him." (I love that part too!)

I was so moved that Prince thought so highly of my work. I wish he had come backstage that night to talk, but apparently he was too shy, which I understand completely. I think part of that is the fear of being rejected, which is common to a lot of talented people, as I've discovered. And that vulnerability comes through in the work, no matter how confident you pretend to be. I actually think that's what touches people who are watching or listening.

If I had known how Prince felt, I would have made an effort to reach out to him and tell him how much I admired *his* work . . . his originality, his style, his enormous talent. Who knows? Maybe we could've even done a duet together.

And then he was gone, at such a young age. What a loss.

I remember not being too scared that night at MusiCares. I don't think my voice was trembling even on the first verse of "The Windmills of Your Mind," which I did a cappella. It probably helped that I wasn't singing for myself but for a good cause.

But two nights later my fear returned when I sang "Evergreen" at the Grammys . . . twenty-five years after it had won Song of the Year. I knew it would be lovely to have Kris Kristofferson introduce me, and I was proud of the music I wrote, so how could I say no?

But when I looked out at the audience . . . a much younger group, with the latest hip-hop and rap stars dressed in wild outfits . . . it was like that moment when I came out to sing in the midst of the rock concert we put on for *A Star Is Born.* I was afraid that the younger generation wouldn't appreciate "Evergreen" then, and I felt that same pang of fear now.

I was trembling so much that I had to clutch the microphone stand and hope I wouldn't fall over. Boy, was I glad to get to the end of the song. And, like always, I didn't know quite what to do when the audience stood up and cheered. You'd think I'd be more sure of myself by now, but no, I just stood there like a deer in the headlights and glanced around, looking for which way I was supposed to get off. And now that it was over I was suddenly starving. I quickly got out of my gown and skipped the fancy after-parties to go to a Chinese restaurant!

Oh, I see I passed right over *Little Fockers*, which I can't say much about because I barely remember it, except for one moment. We actors were sitting with a different director this time, going over a scene that involved all six of us. He said he had planned three days to shoot it and I thought to myself, *Why?* He could do it in half the time if he used two cameras and kept them moving to accommodate the actors, and he'd get more interesting shots.

It just reminded me how much I missed directing. And if I wanted to make movies, maybe it was time to stop turning so many things down.

There was a director, Anne Fletcher, who had been pursuing me for a year to play a Jewish mother in *The Guilt Trip.* And she wouldn't take no for an answer. I liked her and the man who wrote it, Dan Fogelman. Plus it was a leading role, which I hadn't done for a long time.

And as a friend reminded me, "You're an actress. So why don't you act?"

So I took the role. Seth Rogen, who played my son, is as funny off-screen as on, and I liked the way he could insert something a little unexpected into a comic tirade. But the scene I liked best was a quiet moment, where I tell him about this one man I loved and lost, while we're eating ice cream at the kitchen table. And if I was going to eat ice cream take after take, I wanted it to be my favorite, Brazilian Coffee, made by McConnell's in Santa Barbara. So I called them up and said, "Could you send me some for the scene?"

And you know what arrived? Three huge tubs, with almost three gallons in each one! I was in heaven! Every day on the set I'd have two scoops on a sugar cone, and of course I'd make one for Seth, and after the scene was shot we still had enough to feed the whole crew for a week. They loved that.

One evening we were on location in a parking lot and losing the light, so Anne said we would have to do the rest another day at the studio. But I saw a way to speed up the shoot so we could finish it then. Since I was also an executive producer and had intervened to make sure she got the English cinematographer she wanted, even though it would cost more, I felt I could go over to him and describe a shot with a Steadicam that could capture both Seth and me simultaneously. He thought it would work, so I suggested it to Anne. It was a little tricky but it was such fun to do, and we finished on schedule!

Now I really wanted a movie of my own to direct. But since I didn't have one, I had to put my energy into other things. In 2012 I held a benefit at my house for the Women's Heart Center, where I reiterated my plea for gender equality in medical research. Bill Clinton, who had increased funding for women's health while he was president, was kind enough to come and lend his support. And he was very funny: "If she were a member of Congress and I were still president, she would be on what I called our Just Say Yes list. We had a very small list of congressmen—literally fewer than ten people—that when they call you for something, just go and tell them yes, because you're gonna do it sooner or later . . . So she called and started, you know, laying down the law to me about all the facts here. And so I just finally said, 'Stop! What do you want me to do?'"

Everyone laughed. (I did try to make the trip to LA worth his while . . . I showed him how to download Rummikub on his laptop, so he could play when he was alone.)

At the dinner that night, the director of the Cedars-Sinai Heart Institute announced that they had chosen to rename the center in my honor. As a teenager, I wanted nothing more than to see my name in lights on a theater marquee. I couldn't have guessed how much more satisfying it would be to see my name in stainless steel on the Barbra Streisand Women's Heart Center.

Later that summer I was working with Jay Landers, Bill Ross, and Richard Jay-Alexander (my fantastic codirector) in Grandma's house, putting together a new show, *Back to Brooklyn.* It was a celebration of music I loved, written by people I loved, and one of those people was Marvin Hamlisch. I'm always looking for new songs, and I had just heard a demo tape of a virtually unknown song Marvin had written called "Any Moment Now," from a show that flopped on Broadway. I immediately responded to it because it was so actable . . . a duet between a husband and wife that told you a lot about their relationship . . . but it really didn't fit into the concept of this concert. (Still, it sparked the idea of doing an album of Broadway songs that would combine music and dialogue, which percolated for a few more years until it became *Encore*, released in 2016.)

We were trying to come up with new ways to do the old hits I've sung a million times. Often I'll go back to the original version, and that's what we decided to do with "The Way We Were" . . . to use Marvin's original orchestration from the movie, which I've always loved. I wanted to give Marvin that news, and tell him how much I liked "Any Moment Now," so I wrote myself a note to call him. Then Bill mentioned that he'd been asked to do some additional scoring on a movie Marvin was working on, and I thought, *Uh-oh. That's not good news.* So I was worried.

When we finished rehearsing around 11:00 p.m., I called Marvin, but couldn't reach him. Then I called the Bergmans to see if they knew where he was, but they hadn't been able to get ahold of him either.

The next morning . . . I find it hard even to write this now, because I've blotted out any memory of how I found out he had died. I can't convey my shock. He was only sixty-eight. And I was devastated that I never got to tell him how much I loved him, one last time.

I had known Marvin for almost fifty years. He was there at the piano for *Funny Girl*, and he was there for my concert tours, and he even played at my wedding. Success never spoiled Marvin . . . it just made him more of what he was . . . gifted, adorable, funny, generous, kind, thoughtful. He never forgot my birthday and always sent me exactly the kind of flowers I like . . . several small and fragrant arrangements, so I could place them in different rooms.

Among the many scores he wrote was *A Chorus Line*, and . . . borrowing the words of one lyric . . . he was a "singular sensation." An extraordinary musical talent, and a beautiful human being. He had the wisdom of an adult and the enthusiasm of a child.

When I flew to New York to sing at his memorial in September, I walked out onstage and simply said his name, in a broad New York accent . . . "Maah-vin" . . .

and the audience laughed. The name itself just makes me smile, because it reminds me of Brooklyn. I could imagine his mother leaning out the window, calling "Maahvin! Maahvin!"

If you believe in the spirit living on, which I do, then I'm almost certain that Marvin was with us in some way, listening and getting a kick out of this celebration of his wonderful life. Each of us was there because we loved him, and I know all that love had to reach him . . . any moment now.

A week later *Release Me* came out . . . an album of songs from my vault that hadn't made it onto other albums, for one reason or another. I dedicated it to Marvin.

And when I was asked to sing "The Way We Were" at the Oscars in tribute to him, there was no question. When I walked out onstage at the end of the In Memoriam segment, humming the first bars of the song, I felt wobbly in my high heels. I made my way to the front, spoke a few words about my dear friend, and started to sing. Suddenly my right leg was shaking so much that I was afraid the audience would see it, even under my long gown. But thank God I got through the performance, because I told myself this is not about me. This is about Marvin.

Back to *Back to Brooklyn*. This particular concert turned out to be very meaningful for me, because I got to sing with my son.

That was completely unexpected.

I remember singing with him when he was very young, two or three years old, but knowing all the words to "Itsy Bitsy Spider" didn't necessarily suggest that he'd have a future in music. And once, when he was fifteen, I happened to walk by the closed door to his room and heard this beautiful humming sound. I knocked and said, "Jason, is that you?"

"Mom, go away" was the response.

And that was the only response, until decades later when he told me, "You know, I've started to sing and I'm working on some music."

"Really?" I was so surprised, because I could only imagine how tough that was, being *my* son. Still, I was very pleased and didn't want to say too much. He was obviously going about this in his own way, exploring it all by himself. Then he sent me a recording that he'd made of the song "How Deep Is the Ocean," written back in the 1930s by Irving Berlin. I was sitting in the family room when I listened to it and I nearly fell off the couch. First of all, his voice was so gorgeous! It had overtones, as if he were singing all the notes in a chord at the same time . . . almost as if he had a little chamber music quartet right there in his throat. My heart was swelling, and I was so happy for my son. I thought, *Holy mackerel, not only can he sing, but he can also envision how the whole song should sound* . . . the arrangement he had worked out with his collaborator, Stephan Oberhoff, was so inventive. I couldn't say enough good things to him.

Then in April 2012 Donna Karan and Richard Baskin gave me a seventieth birthday party at a small local restaurant. This is where Johnny Mathis surprised me with that marvelous serenade. And the other highlight of the evening was a film Jason made of photos of the two of us, and the soundtrack was this haunting arrangement of a 1940s standard, "Nature Boy," sung in such a beautiful and soulful way that the room went really quiet. Afterward I could hear people whispering, "Who is that singing?"

I said proudly, "It's Jason!"

He just blew me away with this film. He had chosen the perfect song, and the sweetness of his voice, combined with the originality of the arrangement, was exquisite!

I knew my son was smart, kind, and gentle, creative and artistic, but I didn't know he had such an amazing voice. He had kept it to himself for so long, and then he went with his instinct, finally believing in his own talent, and had the courage to let it emerge.

I was so moved and impressed. And so was everyone else. Jason was showered with compliments. Quincy Jones came up to him and announced, "We're going to make an album together."

Jason said, "We are?" He was stunned.

I said, "Jason, I have to sing with you." I was already thinking about another duets album (which eventually became *Partners* in 2014, my tenth number 1 album), and now he had inadvertently presented me with the perfect duet for a mother and son. The lyric to "How Deep Is the Ocean" expressed exactly how I felt:

How much do I love you?
I'll tell you no lie
How deep is the ocean?
How high is the sky?

And I had another idea. I said, "Honey, you have to be part of the *Back to Brooklyn* concert so we can sing this together onstage. I want you to come on tour with me."

I mean, what mother wouldn't like to spend more time with her son?

But Jason was wary. He had done everything up to now on his own, and he didn't want anyone to think he was riding on my coattails. So I asked him to come and meet with Jay, Richard Jay-Alexander, Bill Ross, and me, just to discuss the possibilities . . . how the duet might work, who would sing which lines. Then we started to play around with the harmonies, and that's when Bill said, "This is terrific!" and I could see Jason becoming more engaged and more confident. Still, it took all of us to convince him to say yes.

And then my son, who had barely sung in front of anyone, was suddenly onstage in these huge arenas, performing for twenty thousand people. And it was as if he had been doing this all his life.

I remember the first time Jason and I did our duet in front of an audience. Before I brought him out, I showed the film he had made for my birthday, and then I said, "I'd like to introduce you to the filmmaker *and* the singer. Please welcome my pride and joy, my son, Jason Emanuel Gould." We sat down on stools (it was the second act, so I deserved to sit!) and talked a bit. I explained how he would visit the sets of my movies, whether it was *Funny Girl* or *Hello, Dolly!*, and before long he knew the words to some of my songs. And we would sing them together.

With impeccable timing Jason asked, "Did we ever sing anything from anything that you weren't in?"

That got a big laugh. I spoke about hearing his record (and told the audience it was for sale in the lobby, like any supportive mother!). Then Jason started the song. He had just gotten through the first two lines . . . "How much do I love you? I'll tell you no lie" . . . when there was a spontaneous burst of applause. That's the kind of reaction you can't manufacture. I could feel that genuine ripple of delight that comes from an audience when they like someone. Then on the fourth line, when he improvised a vocal riff on "How hiiigh is the sky," there was more applause. And when he finished his solo portion of the song, they applauded for a third time!

I just leaned back on my stool and swooned.

After our duet I stepped out of the spotlight and watched him sing "This Masquerade," walking around the stage with complete command.

I was kvelling. For someone so shy, it was extraordinary.

That worked so well that I thought, *Why not make it a family affair?* So I asked my sister, Rozzie, to join us on the tour later. She has a very pretty voice, and she's totally unlike me. She loves to perform.

The North American tour, twelve performances in ten cities, finished in November. Then in April 2013 the Film Society of Lincoln Center chose me to receive their Chaplin Award, named for the great Charlie Chaplin. I'm always touched when people I've worked with take the time to come and speak.

> *"I found her totally engaging to act with. I found her to be beautiful. I still think she's beautiful. And that beauty is thorough and she is skilled. And I benefited from all of that. So I guess you can say I'm just a lucky guy."*
>
> —Robert Redford

> *"Barbra Streisand is somebody that I shall never forget in my life . . . I don't think I will ever love anyone more than Barbra Streisand, in the film business."*
>
> —Omar Sharif

> *"I am grateful that she made those three magnificent movies that she produced, directed, and starred in. I'm grateful that she was a magnificent* Funny Girl. *I am grateful that I still get choked up when I watch* The Way We Were."
>
> —Bill Clinton

The award was even more special because Bill Clinton was the one to hand it to me. And it was a delight to see Hillary too.

The ceremony was very moving, but I couldn't help being struck by the irony of the situation. This award was honoring my achievements in film, but I couldn't get the go-ahead on any of the films I wanted to make.

Since 1984 I had been developing a script about Margaret Bourke-White, a woman ahead of her time. She was the first female photojournalist for *Life* magazine, a trailblazer who talked her way into steel mills and sharecroppers' shacks to photograph the beauty she saw there. Her passion for her work was just as strong as her passion for a man, the writer Erskine Caldwell. But when she went off to cover World War II, he divorced her. He wanted a wife who would stay home and serve him dinner, while she wanted to report the news and serve her country.

Originally I was going to play Margaret, direct, and coproduce, but the project stalled when another version came out on TV. Still, I never lost my passion for this story, and in 2012 I managed to resurrect it. I was excited to get commitments from Cate Blanchett and Colin Firth to star (right after his Oscar for *The King's Speech*), with me to direct. Then, while I was away on the *Back to Brooklyn* tour, my coproducer signed a deal with another company, shutting me out. All the work I had done on the script apparently belonged to someone else, everything I had so carefully put together collapsed, and the result was that the movie never got made.

And then there was my other project.

I had a dream . . . I wanted to play Momma Rose in *Gypsy*.

I started my movie career in a great musical and I wanted to end it with another, and many people consider *Gypsy* the greatest Broadway musical of all time. Based on the famous stripper Gypsy Rose Lee's memoir of life with the ultimate stage mother, Rose, it was written by Arthur Laurents, with music by Jule Styne and lyrics by Stephen Sondheim. I thought it would be the perfect bookend to *Funny Girl* (which also had music by Jule).

This dream has been part of my life, in one way or another, for a long time. Arthur first asked me to do it onstage in 1974, but I turned him down because I thought I was too young . . . only thirty-one . . . for the role. Still, his instinct was right. And when Jule Styne wanted me to make a new movie version in 1982, he was operating on the same instinct. He sent me a telegram in which he wrote: "I feel your doing this powerful story and playing Momma Rose would be history, especially to have you sing the score." I was forty by then, so that would work, but I was in the midst of making *Yentl* and couldn't think of anything else. Then in 1989, I had Marty and my agents put together a proposal, but was told that Steve and Arthur didn't want another movie made. (Neither was fond of the 1962 film. I didn't like it either.) And I was still hoping to do it someday, because I had a vision of what it should be, and listed it in my journal as the project I most wanted to make.

In 2007, I asked Marty to look into getting the rights again, but he was unsuccessful. Then in 2010, I was at a party, and a producer came up to me and asked, "What role do you want to play next?"

The answer was easy: "Momma Rose in *Gypsy*."

I told him that I had been trying to get the rights for years, and he said, "I'll get them for you."

"If you can get the rights," I said, "you can coproduce it with me."

Rose is a woman who never achieved her own dreams and then has to watch her daughter become a star. It's a role I understood completely, because of my experience with my own mother. The truth at the heart of the play is that Rose spent years trying to make her daughters famous when she really wanted to be famous herself. My mother also had dreams of being a singer, but unlike Rose, who pushed her daughters into show business, my mother discouraged me. Just as Rose never thought Louise had much talent (and favored her prettier sister, June), my mother never thought I could make it as an actress. And that made me even more determined, just like Louise, to prove to her, and to the world, that I was more than she thought I could be. And when I succeeded against all odds, my mother was jealous of my success . . . just like Rose.

So I knew both these characters, and I think that's what made this play particularly resonant for me. I, too, had a dream. And like Momma Rose, I wouldn't take no for an answer. I was blunt. I was defiant. I thought I could play her in all her fierceness and flaws . . . with all her humor, toughness, and vulnerability.

At the end of the play everyone she's close to has walked out on her, and she's left alone with her unfulfilled dreams. That's when she sings the great 11-o'clock number, "Rose's Turn." It's the musical theater equivalent of King Lear raging on the heath, and it should be frightening . . . and heartbreaking.

I knew exactly how I would do it, and I understood why, once I started writing this book and thinking about my mother. I felt more sympathy for her when I realized how painful it must have been to watch me become what she could have become, with her beautiful voice and pretty face. So underneath Rose's anger is the pain of the little girl inside who wanted to be recognized and applauded.

And as always, Sondheim embeds clues to a character's emotional trajectory in the lyric. Rose stops the song cold a couple of times on the word "Momma." What did that mean? I knew from my research that her mother used to leave her for months at a time to go off and sell corsets to prostitutes in mining towns. I thought it would be interesting to reveal some of that backstory, and I had an idea about how to do it.

So I wrote down my concept for the opening of the film, which I envisioned as flashbacks that would play along with the overture. In one, you'd see the mother walking out the door with her suitcases and Rose as a little girl running after her, tugging at her coat and crying that same "Momma! Momma!" while her father pulls her back.

I could visualize the whole movie in my head, so of course I wanted to direct, and I knew I could sing the hell out of that score.

In January 2011 it looked as if the producer was going to get the rights from Warner Bros., the studio that made the original movie. In February Arthur jumped the gun and told the press that a new version was in the works, with me as Momma Rose. Since he hated the Rosalind Russell movie, he said, "I would be very pleased if we had a different film version for the historical record."

And the reaction from the public was extremely encouraging, except for some grumbling that I was too old for the role.

I'm always the wrong age for my films. I was too young to play the mature Fanny Brice in *Funny Girl*. Too young for *Hello, Dolly!* Too old for *Yentl*. So why should I let age stop me now?

And as Arthur told me, "First, nobody who's ever played the role is the right age. Second, does it really matter?"

Then in March, Arthur did another interview and announced that he had changed his mind and didn't want a new movie after all. There were headlines in the papers reporting that the movie was canceled, with lines like "Arthur Laurents put the kibosh on it, as gays of a certain age throw themselves out their windows by the thousand."

I got on the phone with Arthur and told him how much I admired his book for the musical, and invited him to come to LA to work on the screenplay with me. I managed to resurrect the film, and my friend Ron Meyer was instrumental in giving it a new home at Universal. But that turned out to be my last conversation with Arthur. In May, he died at the age of ninety-three, with the deal still uncertain.

I was determined to make this movie. I even decided to give people a little preview in the *Back to Brooklyn* concert. The first act finished with a Jule Styne medley that featured two songs from *Gypsy*, including a bit of "Rose's Turn." After all the publicity about whether the movie was on or off, it was like a declaration . . . I was going to play this role no matter what!

But there was one more obstacle. All the original authors had to give their approval, and Sondheim had one condition. As he told me, "You can act or direct. I just don't think you should do both jobs."

"Is it that you didn't like *Yentl*?" I asked him.

"No, no," he replied, "I liked *Yentl*. I just think in this case it would be too hard."

He wouldn't believe me when I said it would actually be easier.

He explained, "I don't want you to split your energies."

And he was adamant. So now I had to search for another director. As much as I admired and loved working with Steve on every song I sang of his, because we shared the same passion to probe every underlying nuance, it's hard to forgive his stopping the momentum when Universal had given me the go-ahead to act and direct. Underneath it all, I think he really thought *Gypsy* should remain a play, not a movie.

And since the movie was not happening anytime soon, I agreed to Marty's plan to take the concert to Europe in June 2013. We started in London and then went to Amsterdam, where we had to add a second show, which was great since that gave me more days for the museums! When I was last there, it was to study the Rembrandts at the Rijksmuseum before I made *Yentl*, but now I wanted to spend more time at the Van Gogh Museum. I had been swept away by van Gogh's work early on. It's so visceral, with those thick, swirling brushstrokes that can barely contain the artist's emotions. And there, in a glass case, were his worn-out brushes and tubes of paint, which were so touching to see.

I also went back to the Rijksmuseum, where Jeroen Krabbé, the Dutch actor who played my husband in *The Prince of Tides*, joined us. It was such a pleasure to see Jeroen again. He looked fit and happy . . . he biked back and forth to the hotel! And he had planned a very special day for the whole crew. First, there was a boat trip through the canals with dinner on board, and then the boat dropped us off by the Anne Frank House, where he had arranged a late-night visit.

Remember, the first play I ever saw on Broadway was *The Diary of Anne Frank*, and from that moment on I've felt connected to her. In her diary she writes with almost painful truth about her feelings. She was so young, only fourteen, and you're plunged right back into those first stirrings of romantic love as she describes, with incredible sensitivity, her relationship with Peter, the boy who's in hiding with her.

I had been to the house on my first trip to Amsterdam. But this time the director took us up the steep ladder that leads to the attic, where most people are not allowed to go because of liability issues. We sat by the window in the dark, as she and Peter did, so no one would see them from the street. As she explained, it was easier for the two of them to talk simply and honestly in the darkness. I watched the moon rise and remembered how eager she was to catch a glimpse of it, how thrilled she was to sit by the open window and smell the rain and feel the wind on her cheek and watch the clouds racing by. Looking out a window was taking a risk, but when she could see the sky and the chestnut tree, it calmed her.

It was chilling to sit in that attic in the dark, imagining how she must have felt . . . at any moment there could be a pounding on the door that meant the Gestapo had come for them. I so admire Anne's courage and her strength and her irrepressible spirit. She was determined to make something meaningful of her life. She also wanted to be remembered after death, and I could identify with that.

Yet how can I even presume to identify with her . . . she was locked in a room, just because she was Jewish!

But I feel as if I know her, because she put all her innermost thoughts down in her diary. She had opinions and she had goals. She wanted to be a writer, and you can see her exploring all sorts of ideas. She was disturbed by the way women were considered inferior to men. She was horrified by the waste and futility of war, but she didn't do the obvious and blame it on someone else. She felt that there was a destructive urge in everyone, and said that we all have to change.

And somehow, even forced to live in hiding, with constant fear, she held on to her fundamental optimism. In spite of everything, as she writes in one of the last passages in her diary, she still believed that people are basically good at heart.

I look at the world today, and it's hard to have that kind of hope. I'm worried about global warming and the bees disappearing. I'm heartbroken by the senseless violence that headlines almost every news report. I'm appalled by the endless evidence of man's inhumanity to man.

Anne Frank represents the opposite. I wish everyone would read her diary and be inspired. She was constantly striving to be her best self, and so should we.

After Amsterdam it was on to Germany, which still feels haunted by that history to me. And I had the most extraordinary reception in Cologne, where I sang twenty-two songs and received twenty-two standing ovations. I've never had a reaction quite like that before. In Berlin the welcome was overwhelming when I came out, wearing an unusual outfit for me because it was so sparkly . . . Donna had designed an evening jacket, a low-cut top, and a long form-fitting skirt that flared out at the bottom, all covered in gold sequins that shimmered in the light. Thank God it was made of stretchy material, because I was lucky to fit into it after I had eaten so much bratwurst and pastries.

For a segment of the show, I was joined by the fabulous musician Chris Botti, who came along for the entire tour. I had fun singing duets with him and his trumpet. Chris is a doll, but I couldn't believe his lifestyle . . . he spends most of his time on tour. When we were onstage in Brooklyn, he told me that he'll often do two hundred fifty to three hundred dates a year. Then he asked, "How many do you do?"

I knew, because Marty and I had counted them up. "I've done eighty-four, including tonight."

He said, "Eighty-four shows a year? That's pretty great."

I said, "No, eighty-four shows since I started, in 1963!" He couldn't believe it.

The last stop on the tour was Israel, where I had never given a concert before. But it seemed as if now was the time, because Shimon Peres, the president of Israel (and the world's oldest head of state), had asked me to sing at his ninetieth birthday celebration, and I wanted to be there for him. So if I was coming for that, it made sense to schedule two shows as well. In fact, we had to block out a whole week to accommodate all the events.

After our plane landed on Sunday, the first place I wanted to visit was the

Western Wall, a sacred place of prayer in the Old City of Jerusalem. I slipped a note between the stone slabs, but I'm not telling you what I wrote because then it won't come true!

On Monday thoughts of my father filled my head as I was given an honorary Doctorate in Philosophy from the Hebrew University. It was my first visit since 1984, when I dedicated the Emanuel Streisand Building for Jewish Studies to honor my father, who had devoted his life to education. So in a sense, for me, this degree belonged to him as well, because he had a thirst for knowledge and would have thrived in a place like this. As I said in my acceptance speech, "One of the things I've always admired about this university is the fact that here . . . women and men, Jews and Arabs, Christians and Muslims, native-born and immigrants . . . sit together in classes, share the same cafeterias, learn from the same professors, and dream together of a good and meaningful life. I wish the world were more like the hallways of the Hebrew University."

And then, because I'm still that girl who asks questions, even though that's gotten me into trouble sometimes, I brought up some uncomfortable truths about gender inequality. "It's distressing . . . to read about women in Israel being forced to sit in the back of a bus . . . or when we hear about the 'Women of the Wall' having metal chairs hurled at them while they attempt to peacefully and legally pray . . . or women being banned from singing in public ceremonies." Those were the reactions of the ultra-Orthodox, who wouldn't acknowledge those with more liberal attitudes, and as I said, "I don't pretend to know all the historical, legal, or cultural details . . . but to remain silent about these things is tantamount to accepting them. So I continue to ask, Why?"

That speech got a lot of attention in the Israeli press . . . not uniformly positive . . . so it was very reassuring later that evening when Shimon Peres complimented me on it. He had invited me to join him at the President's House for a meeting with kids from the Make-A-Wish Foundation. These children were battling life-threatening diseases, and yet they were so positive . . . and full of questions. I loved talking to them, and noticed something, which I later asked him about.

"It's so interesting . . . the kids call you Shimon, right?"

"That's my name."

"They don't call you President Peres?"

"I don't want them to. President is a title. Shimon is a person."

"Ah, that's wonderful!"

"And I prefer to be a person than a title."

That says so much about this man.

Tuesday was the birthday celebration, planned to coincide with the Israeli Presidential Conference, which drew leaders from all over the world. Before the festivities began, Jim and I were invited to join Shimon, Bill Clinton, Tony Blair, and Prime Minister Benjamin Netanyahu in Shimon's private chambers. Once again I was reminded of those words about my father: "Manny was so smart. He could talk to presidents."

I was very preoccupied that night. I had just gotten off the phone with my friend Howard, who's an art dealer, trying to decide how much to bid for a Modigliani painting. I've loved his work ever since I saw that nude in the window of Klaus Perls's gallery when I was twenty-one.

It's hard to explain what draws you to a particular artist. You look at a painting and it grabs you or it doesn't.

I'm not a fan of abstract art. I don't understand it. I don't see any emotion in it, and therefore I don't feel anything when I look at it.

But Modigliani really moves me. I think he paints from his soul, like van Gogh. And when I began to read more about him, I found out he was Jewish, born in Italy. (Is that why I felt such a strong connection to him?) He never had much recognition during his lifetime. He was poor, and the people who posed for him were his friends and lovers, so there's an emotional component that somehow mixes in with the paint.

And that night in Israel, the painting I wanted was being auctioned at exactly the same time I would be onstage singing.

Why does everything happen at once? Just a month earlier I was in the middle of a dentist appointment when a Modigliani painting I really wanted, *The Jewess*, came up for auction. The bib was around my neck and they had already given me Novocain when I said to the dentist, "Wait a minute! You can't start yet!" I took out my phone and said, "I need to bid on a painting!"

The Jewess is a portrait of Maud Abrantes, an American woman who was Modigliani's lover, and she even had a bump on her nose, like me. (He seemed to appreciate women with unconventional looks, and long noses. If I had lived during that time, perhaps I could have been one of his models, and then become one of his lovers . . . Dream on, Barbra!) Maud's gaze is direct . . . what she's thinking remains a mystery . . . and I was fascinated with her. The bidding began, and Howard, who was in the room, said one man put up his paddle and just held it there, never putting it down, even as the price went higher and higher. He felt this man was determined to buy it, no matter what, so I stopped bidding. Later I was so upset with myself. Why did I stop? Maybe I shouldn't have given up. And that loss haunts me to this day.

So this time I was prepared to go higher, but the stress of the auction, not to mention the pressure of singing in front of all these dignitaries, had turned me into a nervous wreck. I was sitting in the front row for the program, with Bill and Shimon on one side and President Paul Nagame of Rwanda and Tony Blair on the other. When I got up onstage, I spoke about how I admired Shimon "for his courage, for always being willing to challenge the status quo and to never accept that something is impossible."

And then I sang the song he had requested, "Avinu Malkeinu," a prayer to God to have compassion for us and our children. Shimon and Bill were the first to stand up and applaud. I closed with "People," and then Shimon got up to speak and said it was "worth waiting ninety years to hear such a heavenly voice," which touched my heart.

When the program was over and we were all being led out by security, I heard Renata yelling, way behind me, "You got it! You got it!"

"Got what?" I had totally forgotten about the painting.

I was so happy. And after all that tension, the concerts went like a dream.

But what I treasure most from that trip is the call I received from Shimon on the morning of the last concert. He said, "Hi, Bar . . . ba . . . raaa," in his Hebrew accent. "I want to tell you, what you did in three days, nobody could have done."

I wasn't sure what he meant, and he went on to explain. "You promoted the heart of our people . . . it was a new spirit, a new mood, a new hope."

"Thank you, Shimon. That's so lovely."

"I don't know if you read all the reactions in the papers."

"No, we couldn't translate it, so I don't know what it says."

"I am translating it for you, believe me, you don't need to read more. You have simply changed the mood of a nation."

"Oh my God." Did I really do that?

"You brought to them the whole beauty and depth of the Jewish soul."

"Thank you for telling me that, Shimon. I'm deeply honored."

And then he continued, "Wherever I go, I am so proud. So thankful . . . Your voice is unique, so are your emotions, and they went together. People felt it. You came not just to sing. You came really to deliver a message, 'Don't let your heart fall down.'"

I interpreted that to mean, as I told him, "Yes, keep up your spirit. Keep up the hope. And I thank *you*, Shimon, for what *you* are doing for the world, your country, and the people, because *you* fill them with the spirit of the heart and love."

I had the pleasure of seeing Shimon a few more times in Los Angeles, and then I got the call that he had only a few more hours to live. He left this world on September 28, 2016, and I issued this statement:

> *My heart is bleeding . . . my tears are falling . . . because Shimon Peres is no longer in this world. He was a father figure not only to his beloved country of Israel, but also to me, because he was what I imagined my father would have been like.*
>
> *Shimon's mind was expansive, and his heart was compassionate. He was a brilliant statesman, gifted with the ability to listen to others who did not share his views and yet determined to find a path forward.*
>
> *He was a voice of reason who also happened to have the sensibility of a poet . . . thoughtful and soft-spoken, but his words echoed loudly around the world.*
>
> *I adored Shimon . . . and I'm so grateful that I was able to spend some time with him over the years, and sing for him at his 90th birthday celebration in Israel.*
>
> *Thank God his spirit, his wisdom, and his ideals will live forever.*
>
> *May he rest in peace.*

FIFTY-EIGHT

Old Friends

Even though I turn down most awards these days, I had to accept the Board of Governors Award from the American Society of Cinematographers in 2015 because it was a chance to publicly thank all the great cinematographers I've had the pleasure of working with.

But I almost didn't make it to the ballroom that night. When I stopped to take off my boots and change into my heels, I couldn't get them on. Suddenly they were too tight. A friend from New York was with me, and I looked at her heels, which just happened to be the right color, and asked, "What size are you?"

"Eight and a half," she said, and slipped them off.

Thank God they fit, and nobody noticed that one of us was barefoot as we walked to our table with Jim. And I could walk up onstage when Andrzej Bartkowiak presented me with the award. As I said that night, "I was so lucky! I got to work with some of the best cinematographers in the world!" (And if you've gotten this far, you've read all about them, beginning with my dear Harry Stradling.) I have such respect for their craft, and I learned so much from each of these men. Every director needs a partner, someone to support their vision, and I'm so grateful to all my cinematographers for always making me and my work look good. It was a wonderful evening, and so great to see Andrzej.

That's actually the best reason to go to awards shows . . . because you get to catch up with old friends. Like Robert Redford . . . Bob and I keep introducing each other at various events. I presented him with an honorary Oscar for lifetime achievement in 2002. He surprised me by joining me on *Oprah* in 2010. And in 2015, I was back at Lincoln Center to present him with the Chaplin Award. I had written a speech, and it was on the teleprompter, but when I walked out to the podium, I couldn't see the words clearly. (I should have taken the time to check beforehand.) So I had to yell for Renata (who I knew was watching from the wings, as usual) to bring me my glasses.

After the ceremony Bob and I were backstage, signing posters for the Film Society, when his wife, Sibylle Szaggars, came by to say hello. She's a painter, and I knew Bob started out as one, because he had told me about going to Paris in his twenties to paint. So I mentioned that I had started to paint as well.

"You see, there was this painting by Modigliani called *The Jewess* that I desperately wanted—"

"Modigliani?" Bob interrupted. "He's my favorite artist of all time."

"Really?"

"Oh God, yes. I didn't want to be an actor. I wanted to be Modigliani."

I said, "That's so interesting, because I really respond to him as well. And when I lost that painting at auction, I couldn't bear it . . . so I painted it myself."

Bob said, "You did *what*?"

"I painted my own version. It was the first thing I ever painted. Of course I didn't sign it Modigliani. I signed it Barbra."

He couldn't help laughing.

Well, a few months later it was his turn to present me with a Leadership Award at a Women in Entertainment breakfast. After he gave me a lovely introduction, the first words I spoke were, "We have to stop meeting like this! It was wonderful being married to you for a while, but our relationship is over!" That got a big laugh.

Afterward he came to my house for lunch. I had lured him with the prospect of seeing my real Modigliani, but I have a one-track mind, and what I really wanted to discuss was the sequel to *The Way We Were.* I don't think he had ever seen the treatment I started writing back in the 1980s, and I wanted to remind him of what it could be. I knew these characters so well, and I always thought they had more to say to each other. In the first movie, principle won out over passion . . . Katie let Hubbell go, which was the rational thing to do under the circumstances. But in the sequel, passion wins out.

I may have rushed through the tour of my art because I could hardly wait to describe my ideas to him, which I finally got to over lunch. I outlined the story, which takes place at another pivotal time in our nation's history. Katie and Hubbell meet again in 1968 when their daughter, Rachel, now in college at Berkeley, gets arrested as she's leading a student protest against the Vietnam War (obviously Katie's daughter!). Hubbell, who's now a TV journalist, is covering the ensuing riot, and just as he recognizes the daughter he's only seen in photos, the police haul her away. He calls Katie in New York to tell her that he's bailed Rachel out of jail. Katie flies out immediately, and they're brought together again by their concern for their daughter.

Without going into the whole plot, let me just say that the attraction between Katie and Hubbell is still there. But what's interesting is the way they've both changed. He's become more political while Katie, who's now a book editor with a husband and a teenage son, has become less active, although her political convictions remain strong. So it's easier now for them to meet in the middle, so to speak. And then Rachel, who's angry with her father for being absent all her life and yet enchanted with him as well, suddenly finds herself in competition with her mother. The emotional dynamic of this triangle becomes very complex . . . kind of a three-way love story. Finally, everything comes to a climax when they're at the Democratic National Convention in Chicago, where all hell breaks loose with riots in the street.

For twenty years Sydney and I tried to make progress on the sequel. Various scripts were commissioned, but none completely worked. Arthur Laurents had some good ideas, but his started by replaying the last scene from the original movie and ended with what also felt like a retread. I envisioned a whole other way into the story . . . you'd see Katie, disheveled as she runs through a hospital . . . and it's not until the end of the movie that you know who she's looking for. David Rayfiel had a wonderful scene in a restaurant, where you sense the undercurrents between father, mother, and daughter.

But the sequel that was shaping itself in my mind was more complex than anything I had read. And it ended in the only way I felt it could, to be true to the characters.

Eventually I took a stab at writing it myself and put together a treatment. But we were fighting a losing battle, because Bob isn't a fan of sequels.

Still, as he and I talked this time, there was a moment of "Could this really happen?" And Bob said something like, "If we do this, I'd love to write my own part." (He may have been kidding.) Anyway, I gave him a copy of my treatment so he could read it at home. And then I never heard back from him.

I didn't want to pressure Bob, so I never called him either. Frankly, I think age was a big concern for him. It didn't bother me as much. After all, we were both too old to be in college in the original. When the acting is good, I think the audience suspends disbelief.

But I had to face the fact that the moment had passed, and the sequel will live only in my mind.

More recently, we were on the phone and got into a discussion about art. He told me that he's gone back to sketching again.

I was curious about his work, so I asked him to send me some of his early drawings. "If you show me yours, I'll show you mine."

He laughed and said, "Absolutely!"

So I sent him the first sketch I ever did, when my art teacher said, "Draw me," and also included a pencil sketch of apples, because it seems like all the Impressionists drew apples.

And Bob sent me some of his early sketches of people, which were very powerful because of the bold strokes and thick black lines . . . very expressionistic, which made sense because he had told me that when he looked at people, he would see the face that they wanted to present to the world. And then he would sketch what he thought they really were underneath.

It's that kind of perception that makes him such a good actor.

Back to 2015. It was nice to find myself seated next to two other old friends, Stephen Sondheim and Steven Spielberg, when we were all at the White House in November. We were about to receive what they call the nation's highest civilian award, the Presidential Medal of Freedom, from President Obama. He was very engaging that day, warming up a formal occasion with funny ad-libs. For example, when he started to read the description of me: "Born in Brooklyn to a middle-class Jewish family," he stopped, turned to me, and said, "I didn't know you were Jewish, Barbra." That got a huge laugh. He mentioned what he called my chutzpah (pronouncing it perfectly), then continued, "And it helps when you've got amazing talent, all of which made her a global sensation—one whose voice has been described as 'liquid diamonds' . . . Off the stage, she has been a passionate advocate for issues like heart disease and women's equality. I'm getting all *verklempt* just thinking about it."

He was so relaxed and charming, chatting with all of us, that it was hard to believe he had just come from a joint press conference with President François Hollande of France, where he had expressed his condolences after the terrorist attacks in Paris and vowed to work together to defeat ISIS. Clearly, a successful president has to be able to compartmentalize in order to get anything done, but I was still very impressed by his ability to turn on a dime so gracefully.

And I only found out later that he had faced yet another security crisis that day. Ken Sunshine, who was also there for the ceremony, told me that a Secret Service agent had come to the Oval Office and informed the president that Barbra Streisand was bringing a dog into the White House and asked what they should do.

Apparently no one brings a dog to the White House, but I didn't know that. Sammie goes everywhere with me . . . even to the ballet or the theater, because she's such a good little girl. She never barks. She's just happy to be with us. And Renata had her tucked in her carrier bag, slung over her shoulder, when we arrived. We had no idea that we were breaking the rules, and I still wouldn't know if Kenny hadn't told me, because everyone was impeccably polite.

And President Obama, as always, remained cool in the crisis. As Kenny said, he looked the Secret Service agent in the eye and made his decision: "Whatever Barbra wants, Barbra gets."

If only that were true . . . but 2016 shattered any such illusions.

The year started off just fine. I was recording the *Encore* album (the idea planted years ago when I heard Marvin's song "Any Moment Now" was finally coming to fruition). This would be another album of Broadway songs, but what made it different was that I also wanted to add a bit of the scene that each song grew out of. This was an iffy idea, and I doubt anyone at the record company considered it commercial, but I was intrigued with the concept of integrating music with dialogue. And this time, instead of duets with other singers as usual, I wanted to sing with actors. And the best part for me was that I would get to direct them!

So I needed actors who could sing, and the first person I called was Hugh Jackman. I went to see him in Jez Butterworth's play *The River* in New York, met with him backstage to congratulate him on his brilliant performance, and played Marvin's song for him. He said yes immediately, and then everyone else I asked also said yes, and I had the best time working with all these superb actors! Hugh is an accomplished singer, but others, like Melissa McCarthy, had never been in a recording studio before. She warned me, "I can't sing!" I told her not to worry . . . the lyrics of "Anything You Can Do (I Can Do Better)" had been rewritten to suit us, and the lines were so funny that her voice didn't matter. She's such a fine comedian, and her delivery was more important.

Very gently I did manage to coax the right notes out of her, and we ended up laughing a lot, as you can see if you watch the YouTube video of the two of us in the studio. There's a moment when she sings a phrase and I put my hand on her arm and say, "Wooo! Good!" She looks at me, stunned . . . "Yeah?" . . . and then puts her hand on my hand and says solemnly, "Let me just have this moment."

Jamie Foxx was a complete natural in the recording booth, just as he is on-screen, and he wanted it to be exactly right. Just like Bradley Cooper, who only had a speaking part in "At the Ballet" from *A Chorus Line* and recorded it for us on his iPhone, which worked perfectly since he was portraying a director talking over a microphone to the women auditioning . . . Daisy Ridley, Anne

Hathaway, and me. And then he called and asked, "Should I change that reading?" He was so eager to give me more options, so willing to find new ways to deliver the same lines. I love actors like that, who think it can always be better.

And I have to give a quick shout-out to Alec Baldwin, Antonio Banderas, Seth MacFarlane, Chris Pine, and Patrick Wilson, my other collaborators, because it was such a treat to work with them as well! (Watch the official videos on YouTube to see how much fun we had working on this album.)

Then one afternoon, during a break at the studio, Marty made a pitch. He laid out his proposal for a new concert tour, reminding me that with the release of *Partners* in 2014, I became, as he said, "the only artist in history to have a number one album in six consecutive decades." (Am I that old? Yup, I sure am.) Marty thought that was something to celebrate and suggested doing songs from each of those ten number 1 albums, along with a few from the album we were just finishing up.

I have to admit I had absolutely no interest in going back on tour . . . but there was another painting by Modigliani coming up for auction that was very tempting, and also it would be nice to support more worthwhile causes through my foundation . . .

So I said yes.

In June, before rehearsals began, I was delighted to present the Tony Award for Best Musical to Lin-Manuel Miranda for *Hamilton*, which Jim and I had seen and loved. It was so inventive, and Lin-Manuel was so dear, introducing me to his whole family at the party afterward. And then in August I was back on the road with *Barbra: The Music, the Mem'ries, the Magic*, and when *Encore* was released at the end of the month, it became my eleventh number 1 album.

Meanwhile, the election campaign was consuming more and more of my attention. Hillary Clinton was running for president, and as a former First Lady, senator, and secretary of state, there was no one more qualified for the job. And then there was Donald Trump, the reality-TV-show real estate developer who insulted women, immigrants, and the disabled, stiffed his contractors, and had gone bankrupt six times.

Guess who I was supporting?

In September, I sang at an LGBTQ+ fundraiser for Hillary and sat next to her at dinner that night. She was a bit hoarse (not unusual for someone in the midst of a campaign), and I was worried she wasn't taking care of herself. "Where's your tea?" I asked and then said, "Here, take mine." Two days later she was diagnosed with walking pneumonia . . . but she barely let that stop her. I already knew she had incredible stamina. After all, she had endured an eleven-hour grilling about Benghazi by Republicans who were determined to take her down, but didn't succeed because she parried every attack with facts and never lost her composure (a perfect quality for a would-be president).

I was struck by the attitude on display that day. There was something gleeful in the way the Republicans went after this accomplished woman. It was as if the more she had achieved, the more she had to be punished.

And that goes back to something I've felt for many years . . . strong, powerful women are often regarded with disdain in our culture. Some men are threatened by them, and some women are jealous of them.

Hillary had a long record of public service, while Trump had never done anything to help others. He only cared about serving himself. Hillary had negotiated with leaders around the world to keep us safe from various threats, while Trump said, "If we have nuclear weapons, why can't we use them?"

His ignorance was astounding. He called climate change "a hoax" and appealed to the basest instincts of the crowd, encouraging them to "knock the crap" out of protesters and reporters, as he railed against the press as "the enemy of the people." He smeared Hillary as "crooked" and "corrupt" and led chants to "Lock her up!" But when he was throwing those words at Hillary, he was unconsciously describing himself. He's crooked, so he calls her crooked. Trump is a classic example of what some psychologists call "the disowned self" . . . a person who projects his own flaws onto others while refusing to recognize them in himself. As one headline in *The Washington Post* read: TRUMP'S HISTORY OF CORRUPTION IS MIND-BOGGLING.

He lies as easily as he breathes. And as history has shown, if you repeat a lie long enough and loud enough, people will believe it.

I was shocked that Trump had gotten this far. You wouldn't go to a doctor who has no qualifications or experience in treating your disease. Why on earth would people want to entrust our country to a narcissist whose lack of experience, recklessness, and blatant disregard for the truth made him completely unfit to be president?

On election night I was sitting next to Marilyn and Alan in Senator Barbara Boxer's hotel suite in Beverly Hills, very nervous. The polls projected Hillary as the winner, but as we watched the numbers come in, my heart sank, and I felt as if my soul had left my body. How could this be happening?

Later, it was all too clear. Due to voter suppression, gerrymandering, James Comey, the antiquated Electoral College, and Russian interference (amplified by Facebook), we got Donald Trump instead.

How could Hillary get almost three million more votes and not be sitting in the Oval Office? Isn't it time we actually allowed the people to pick the president? What happened to "one person, one vote"?

But the Republicans can't let that happen. As I'm writing this book, only *one* Republican has won the popular vote in *eight* presidential elections . . . which indicates their policies aren't actually that popular, so they've become very good at fighting dirty in order to win. Trump fanned the flames of fear and resentment, and he didn't care if he tore the country apart in the process.

I was sick of all the hate and division Trump was provoking, especially toward immigrants. Back in 2012, when Bill Clinton spoke at my house to raise money to fight heart disease, he said something that stayed with me. A recent study had shown that no matter the color of your skin or where you were born . . . Cuba or China, Malaysia or Madagascar . . . your genetic makeup is 99.9 percent identical to that of every person on the face of the earth. I thought that was fascinating and shared it with the audience at my concert.

And when I resumed the tour in Houston in late November, I invited former president George H. W. Bush and his wife, Barbara, to be my guests . . . on the principle that reasonable people, whether they're Republican or Democrat, should be able to talk to one another. We met backstage before the show, and I gave him some socks, because I knew he collected them, and gave her my first book, because I heard she liked decorating too. Barbara gave me a scarf. We shared some laughs as we talked about our dogs as well as the state of the union. And during the concert, when I introduced them to the audience, they got a standing ovation. A lot of people from NASA and the military were there, and it was a wonderful night.

I believe that what brings us together is stronger than what drives us apart. But even at his inauguration, Trump was incapable of rising to the occasion and bringing a sense of unity to the nation. Instead he painted a dark apocalyptic picture of "American carnage" that had people wrinkling their brows and wondering, "What is he talking about?" It had little to do with reality but said a lot about his mental state.

The day after, at the LA branch of the Women's March . . . the largest single-day protest in U.S. history . . . I began my speech with a quote from H. L. Mencken, who said in 1920: "On some great and glorious day the plain folks of the land will reach their heart's desire at last and the White House will be adorned by a downright moron."

Anyone with actual knowledge was a threat to Trump, so he tried to devalue it. Meanwhile, he was trampling on basic common decency, and his rude behavior gave his followers the license to be equally mean. What worried me was that the younger generation would emulate this man, who showed no kindness or empathy for other human beings.

My tour ended with a final performance in Brooklyn in May 2017, and just before the lights dimmed Bill and Hillary Clinton took their seats. I could hear the commotion from where I was standing backstage . . . practically the whole auditorium rose to their feet to applaud Hillary. It was a spontaneous tribute, and when I came out I acknowledged them from the stage. It was incredibly moving, and I felt this immense sense of loss, thinking of what could have been.

The year brought another huge loss . . . my beloved companion, Sammie, left this world. It was my husband who gave her to me in 2003 as an anniversary present. Jim picked Sammie out because she was the only one of the litter who engaged with him (maybe because he's so handsome, or because they both had pure white hair!). Sammie was different than the other puppies. Her hair was curly, not straight like most Cotons de Tulear. She was the odd one out, just like I felt as a little girl. And Sammie was *my* little girl.

Have you ever heard of a dog that talks? When I asked her a question, she would make certain sounds to answer me, or wiggle her backside if she was very excited by the proposition. She could sense my moods and react to them, tilting her head and looking quizzically at me, as if to ask, "What's going on?" And it was a relief to escape whatever was worrying me and throw one of her stuffed toys, then chase her as she ran after it. Eventually she'd dash up her little stairs at the foot of my bed to get up by the pillows, where she knew she was safe.

Sammie was still a puppy when I brought her to work with me on *Meet the Fockers*, and the crew was so nice . . . they even made a little chair especially for her. On those early morning drives in my motor home to the studio, we'd both fall asleep with me holding her as she lay across my chest, like a real baby. At home she often liked to sleep on my pillow, right on top of my head. Then as she got older, she would follow Renata into her room at night, since Jim and I stayed up too late for her. Renata took care of Sammie with the same kind of loving attention that she gave to me, and she was just as devoted to her as I was.

Sammie was a great traveler who came with us on every trip, and to every concert. She never missed a rehearsal and would lie on the piano, keeping an eye on me. Just like Sadie, my first dog, she knew all the musical cues. Then, while I was onstage during the actual show, she might take a nap on top of my shoes in the dressing room. But she could tell by the music on the speaker when to open her eyes, and she'd be standing by the door to greet me at intermission . . . a warm, fluffy bundle of love and support. And at the end of the concert, Renata would often bring her out to join me for the last curtain call. But I think she had stage fright like me, because she would run offstage as fast as she could.

When I was going through all the film from *Barbra: The Music, the Mem'ries, the Magic* for a Netflix special, Sammie was right beside me and the editor as we worked in Grandma's house. If Renata came to fetch her, she'd hide under the editing table . . . unless it was time for a meal, of course. She was just like me. She loved to eat.

I knew Sammie was sick when she began to ignore her food. After we found out there was a tumor in her lungs, we took her to various specialists, and I called experts at two universities who were doing research on cancer in dogs to make sure we were doing everything we could for her. It was decided that the tumor should be removed, and on the day of the operation, the doctor came out to tell me that the anesthesia was making Sammie's heart slow down.

She asked, "What do you want to do?"

"Stop," I said. "Just get her off the table. I'm bringing her home."

Sammie managed to hold on for quite a while, but toward the end we were taking her to the hospital every day to get the fluid in her lungs drained. It was painful to see her suffer, and then the last day was horrific. We were in the car going home and found ourselves stuck in a traffic jam at 5:00 p.m., when Sammie suddenly made a sound I'll never forget, a terrible high-pitched cry that went on and on. We felt so helpless, and couldn't move to get back to the hospital. I was holding Sammie and trying to comfort her while Renata dialed the veterinarian who had treated her since she was a baby. "It sounds like she's having a seizure," he said, "but I want you to know she's not in pain." (I hope that's true. I still cringe every time we drive past that place on the road.) He told us to bring her in and he'd wait for us.

I knew we had to put her out of her misery, but I couldn't stand the thought of losing her forever. The only thing that made it bearable was the hope that I could keep some part of her alive. A friend of mine had cloned his dog, and we were prepared to do the same thing. Sammie's doctor had the test tubes ready and scraped some cells from the inside of her cheek and the skin on her tummy to send off to the lab. Then he put her to sleep as I was petting her . . . and in seconds our little girl was gone.

It has been said that grief is the measure of the depth of the love we have shared. As I'm writing this, the tears are running down my cheeks again. Sammie and I had such a close connection for fourteen years, and without her, the house felt so empty. Jim was across the world in Romania, directing a movie.

And then two days after Sammie died, the most extraordinary thing happened. On a clear day with not a cloud in the sky, I was just standing in my pool, thinking about her and missing her desperately, when all of a sudden I heard a popping sound. I looked up into the sky and there was this white puff. I thought, *Sammie?* I got out of the pool, and by the time I grabbed my phone to take a picture, the puff of white had transformed into the image of a dog from the back, with a tail, two hind legs, and two ears sticking out. It looked like Sammie running. I yelled for Renata to come out, and thank God she had her phone because she captured what happened next. Across the ocean and above the horizon, a dark cloud appeared, with this white puff on top that looked like the head of a dog. Then it quickly morphed into the whole figure of a white dog, standing on four legs on top of a gray cloud.

How was this possible? It was a phenomenon, and people might roll their eyes if they didn't see these photos. But if you believe in the mystical side of life, as I do, it's not hard to explain . . . this was Sammie telling me that she was okay, riding high on a cloud up in heaven.

Jim called, and I told him about Sammie, but he was so far away, and I felt so alone. Then another crazy thing happened. The next day I was sitting in bed, trying to write, when I looked up and saw a man in the doorway holding a bouquet of flowers. My first thought was, *Why is the delivery man coming into my bedroom?* For a moment, I didn't even realize it was my husband, because as far as I knew he was still in Romania. But as soon as Jim heard the news, he put everything on hold and flew home. I was so happy that he came to be with me.

We buried Sammie in a special garden I created around her tombstone, which has her picture on it in porcelain (like they do in Europe). And there's a bench where Renata and I often sit when we want to remember all the good times we had with her.

I was bereft without Sammie, but had mixed feelings about getting another dog. I knew I could never replace her, just as I could never replace Sadie. But months later I got a call from Sammie's breeder. "I have this little puppy," she told me, "the only one in the litter. She's not curly, but her mother's name is Funny Girl." How could I turn her down? She must have been so lonely, with no siblings to play with. So I took her and named her Fanny.

Two months later I got a call from the cloning lab. They had warned us from the beginning that the cells might not take, but it turned out that not only did the process work, but it produced more dogs than I anticipated.

So now I have three dogs . . . Fanny, the eldest, who often looks at Violet and Scarlet as if she can't believe what has happened. She was the only child, and now she has to share her home with two rambunctious invaders. They're both curly-haired like Sammie and look so much alike that I had to put lavender and red silk flowers on their collars to identify them. And when I trim the hair around their faces, I do the two a bit differently (one has a shorter cut). But now that their personalities have emerged, it's easier to tell them apart. Scarlet is wild, and my husband plays with her more roughly, as if she were one of the big dogs he used to have. She's the alpha dog, and gravitates to Jim. My little Violet is shyer and quieter. She sticks close to me and wants to be picked up and held, but if I'm busy with something else, like eating lunch in the kitchen, she'll settle for the chair next to me.

It's fascinating to see certain traits that remind me of Sammie, yet each of these beloved creatures is a unique being. You can clone the look of a dog but you can't clone the soul.

Still, every time I look at their faces, I think of my Samantha.

FIFTY-NINE

A Reason to Sing

As Trump lurched through his presidency, leaving chaos in his wake, I would lie in bed at night with his latest outrage running through my mind. It was shocking to watch him trash fundamental democratic principles like freedom of speech and freedom of the press. He demolished our standing in the world and put the security of our country, and our planet, at risk by abandoning the Paris climate accords and the Iran nuclear deal. He was a one-man weapon of mass destruction.

In the morning I'd wake up and hold my breath as I turned on my phone to check the news, thinking, *It can't be worse than yesterday.* Then I'd read the latest headlines and realize, *Ohhhhhh yes . . . it is worse!*

I was exploding with anger, so I dashed off tweets and drafted dozens of articles for *The Huffington Post.* I was trying to get rid of all the negative energy

I felt. Meanwhile, it was time to do another album, but that seemed so irrelevant until I thought, *Why not make an album about what's on my mind?*

Thank God for music. I could use it to express my feelings, and that was a great release. It gave me a reason to sing.

I was looking forward to a dinner with the Bergmans, because it would be a chance to discuss the new album, politics, and many other subjects. But during this period, I had noticed that Marilyn was becoming less and less present. I was losing my dear friend to the same dementia that had afflicted her mother, and that had been Marilyn's own greatest fear. I could see the confusion in her eyes when she gripped my hand, as if to say, I'm still here . . . inside. Then came the moment at her ninetieth birthday party when she didn't even know who I was . . . that was agonizing. This woman who was so smart and articulate was betrayed by her own brain. So, three pivotal women in my life . . . my mother, Cis, and Marilyn . . . were all stricken with the same disease.

Alan took the most tender care of Marilyn all through her decline. For me, they were such a role model of what a great marriage could be . . . always kind and loving to each other in a perfect partnership, as they lived and worked together for over sixty years.

Over dinner that night, I told them about my concept for the album, but it was only Alan who could respond. I talked about the fact that with so many challenges facing our country, all Trump could think about was building a wall that cost billions and wouldn't solve anything. A few days later Alan sent me a lyric called "Walls." I was immediately struck by the title, because it was the perfect symbol for the deep divisions unsettling our country and the world. "This is great!" I told him on the phone. "And *Walls* could be the title of the album. I can just see the cover!" (And knew exactly where I could shoot it, against the stone wall leading into Jim's workshop. I wouldn't even have to leave my property!)

Here's the original lyric:

Walls, high and low, thick and thin
They keep you out, they keep you in
Walls, narrow and wide, round or square
With warning signs, "Watch out, beware!"

Brick by brick they build them, but it seems to me
Brick by brick they build them where they shouldn't be

Walls, here and there, ev'rywhere
In ev'ry city, ev'ry town
We would have that better day
If all the walls came tumbling down.

It was so unusual for Alan to write a lyric before he had any music, so that was exciting. Now all we needed was a composer . . . and I happened to be working with Walter Afanasieff, a terrific producer who had also written wonderful melodies. Jay put him together with Alan, and everything fell into place. I vividly remember the day in March 2018 when Walter sat down at the piano in Grandma's house and played what they had come up with for Jay and me.

I immediately called Alan and told him how much I loved the song. "But . . . I have one other thought. I'd like to broaden the idea so that it's not just about physical walls but also about the emotional walls that can build up between people . . . friends, lovers, husbands, and wives." Alan really liked my suggestion.

Walter was sitting right there at the piano and without missing a beat started to improvise something that could work musically for the new concept (which is something like a second bridge). I looked at him and screamed with delight, "Yes! That's *really* good! It even lifts the melody." I started to sing along with his chords, and Alan, on speakerphone, got excited and said, "Keep going! Keep going!" And then Walter said he had to get home as quickly as possible to record a demo while the music was fresh in his mind. The next day he came back to play the complete song for me. It was perfect. I was so excited to sing it. And it was all so easy because it felt inevitable . . . it was the right idea musically and lyrically. And Alan wrote these new lines that totally captured what I had in mind:

Brick by brick, at times they're of a diff'rent kind
Brick by brick, they're built around the heart and mind
Sometimes lasting longer than the ones that are made of stone

Keeping us apart and alone

These are walls that we don't see,
That we build between the you and me
Made of broken dreams and wounded feelings that go on
Like walls we wish to go away, could we have ourselves that better day
If we took the chance to simply say that we forgive
And then we'd forget . . . they'd be gone

Then the song went back to the original melody. I called Alan and said, "Thank you. This is beautiful . . . but I have *one* more tiny thought. Shouldn't we be building bridges rather than walls? Could you try to get in a line about that?"

And he did it wonderfully, adding:

We should be building bridges to a better day
Where no walls would stand in the way

That was just right.

I remember the genesis of another song. I was with Jim in the truck (his beloved Raptor), and we had the radio on, listening to the news and hearing Trump with his lies again. It was making my head spin. As I've said before, I can't stand being lied to, and I don't think the country should be lied to either. And I just couldn't comprehend how he could tell all these lies with absolutely no guilt (clearly he's not Jewish).

And I thought, *I'd like to write a song about this.* So I started jotting down notes on a piece of paper . . . "lies lies lies" . . . "how do you sleep at night?" And that evolved into "Don't Lie to Me," which became the first single and a music video I directed. At first I wanted to keep the song a bit ambiguous. After all, I could be singing "Don't lie to me" to a lover. But then I thought, *Who am I kidding?* . . . and just let it rip. Although Trump is not mentioned by name, the song is clearly about him.

After all the angst, this turned out to be a very creative time. I was going back and forth from one room and one project to another . . . mixing the album with my lightning-fast engineer, Jochem van der Saag, in his music editing room and then, while he made my latest changes, stepping out into his living room to look at my computer and review the latest changes I had made on *A Star Is Born* for the new Netflix release.

Walls came out on November 2. I did Bill Maher's show that night, my granddaughter Westlyn was born on November 3 . . . and five days later the burning world was at my doorstep. The Woolsey fire ignited on November 8 and spread overnight. Renata woke us up with a call at 7:00 a.m. and told us a mandatory evacuation had been announced. Jim and I took a quick look from our little balcony and could see actual flames up the coastline. It was so scary. I could feel my heart pounding and my throat closing up.

It just shows you how life can change in an instant. The night before, I was on a high after lingering over my dining table with some of the greatest filmmakers in the world . . . Alejandro Iñárritu, Guillermo del Toro, and Damien Chazelle, all Oscar winners. And we were joined by Leonardo DiCaprio, who won his own Oscar as the star of Alejandro's *The Revenant.* Alejandro had never seen my barn, so he came early for a tour, and was so engrossed by the objects, wanting to hear every detail, that it made me appreciate my things anew, through his eyes.

And now the barn and everything else we had built was being threatened, and I was rushing out the door with Fanny in my arms, still in my nightgown with just a bathrobe thrown over it as I stepped into my closest pair of boots and got into the car with Jim. Renata was going to follow us in her car with the other two doggies, and I was worried about her because traffic was bumper to bumper on the coast highway, and she didn't have much gas. I was berating myself for being totally unprepared . . . I forgot my prescription pills and didn't have a leash for Fanny, which I only discovered when we stopped in a parking lot to walk her (where I asked a stranger to borrow his leash). What a relief when we all finally made it to my friend Ellen's house. We were planning to go to a hotel, but she insisted we stay with her and her husband, and our sleepover ended up lasting two weeks, with five people and seven dogs all together, and all getting along fine.

It's hard to look back on that terrible time . . . there's nothing quite like watching your neighborhood go up in flames on TV. It was apocalyptic. Thank God for the wonderfully dedicated men who take care of my property and have been with me for many years. They refused to leave and did everything they could to protect our little compound. I was terrified for them, but my head manager, Vicente, reassured me that if the fire got too close, they could escape down the cliff and jump into the small boat he had rented. I was very moved by their loyalty and bravery.

We actually have a fire station near our road, but its trucks had gone to Pepperdine University, where the fire was endangering the students. Our insurance company was supposed to have its own fire truck, but it never showed up. We couldn't count on water from the hydrants to hose down the houses, so my assistant Pam Lyster followed up on a tip I heard from a friend and got a private truck filled with water to the property, in case my guys ran out of pool water. She also arranged with a woman in the neighborhood to deliver food for them.

Tragically, three houses on our street burned down, along with many more in the vicinity. But in a quirk of fate, I had given my daughter-in-law, Kathryn, a baby shower a few weeks earlier and rented a lot down the street for all of her friends to park their cars. Vicente had gone over there to clear all the brush, and I truly believe that saved our house. Otherwise the fire would have just kept moving up our road.

We were extremely lucky, but my heart breaks for those who lost so much.

At least we still had a house, although when we came home it was unlivable. Everything reeked of smoke and was dusted with soot, which required an industrial cleaning, so we went to a hotel in Santa Monica for another week and then spent a weekend at another friend's house up in Ojai. We were like vagabonds, wandering around with our bags.

It was profoundly unsettling, as if everything I relied on . . . from my house to our democracy . . . was suddenly insecure. And as if that weren't enough, in February 2019 I read the news online that the producer who was supposedly my partner had taken the rights to *Gypsy* and sold them to another production company without my knowledge.

I was stunned. I know this might seem relatively inconsequential, but in combination with everything else, it was a crushing blow. Suddenly I was cut out of a project that I had initiated and spent years trying to bring to the screen.

I had poured so much of myself into rewriting the script. The first writer, in 2012, had not been a good match for this material. I thought the original play was brilliant and wanted to restore more of Arthur's dialogue (interesting, just like in *The Way We Were*). Since I could visualize how the story should unfold, I worked with another writer to get it down on paper . . . which lines to use from the play, where I might add some new scenes to open it up, and how I imagined the musical numbers for the screen.

For example, there might be a scene where Herbie, Rose, and the girls are walking back to their hotel, which is next to an ice cream parlor, and he gives the girls some change to buy themselves a cone. (Of course I imagined an ice cream scene.) When they come out, Rose is leaning against a parked car, deep in conversation with Herbie, who's feeling her out about a possible future as a family. And the girls rush past them into the hotel to go upstairs and sit on the fire escape, because they sense something's going on and they want to eavesdrop. So the camera would alternate between various shots of the two adults and the two girls, giggling and licking their cones as they sing "If Momma Was Married." On one of my phone calls with Sondheim, I happened to mention this idea, and he said, "As a matter of fact, that's the way I would have liked it to be staged in the show, using the second floor of the set. But we couldn't do it, because the girl who played June was afraid of heights."

Can you imagine that? It felt like old times, when Steve and I would explore all the possibilities in a song and be so in sync.

I was really excited by the potential. And before all my ideas were typed up by another writer, I told this producer that since I was shaping the film and collaborating on the script, this time I'd like to share the credit.

I never paid much attention to credits (only to learn later that I should have) and often gave them away, because the work was the only thing that really mattered to me.

Meanwhile, something had changed in the industry. In the past, a director like Sydney Pollack would work closely on a script . . . just as I did on every film I directed and those I produced, like *A Star Is Born* and *Nuts*. But it wouldn't have occurred to me to ask for a writing credit on those projects. I thought that was just part of what a director or producer did. But now more actors were directing and had no qualms about taking a writing credit as well.

I look back at my own behavior and wonder why women are so often embarrassed to ask for what they are due. When I returned to the concert stage in 1993, I wrote the script with the Bergmans, based on moments from my own life. But since they were trying to establish themselves as writers of more than just lyrics, I let them have the sole credit. Their friendship was more important to me.

And in 1986, when I produced and directed the TV special about the making of *The Broadway Album*, here again I didn't take the credit. I didn't want to risk getting attacked again for doing more than just acting or singing.

Why did I keep doing this, when I've always believed women should take credit for their own work?

If I could change one thing about myself (actually, there are many), I wish I would have been stronger in these situations, but it's that insecure part of me that inevitably reappears. Even when I believe my work is good, I always think it could be better. So I can be too ready to devalue it.

With that in mind, going back to *Gypsy* . . . my coproducer had assured me that since I was working line by line on the script, the credit would be shared.

But then *that* didn't happen either.

It still shocks me when people don't keep their word (another lesson from *The Four Agreements*: Be true to your word). Marty and I have worked together for sixty years and we've never had a contract, just a handshake. But those days are gone, I guess.

I was very upset, and yet I did what women often do. I kept my feelings inside. I told myself that getting the movie made was more important. And I didn't want to rock the boat, because from one month to the next it was unclear whether the movie was on or off, as various studios and directors came in and then fell out.

A lot of time was wasted, because I wasn't trusted to both act and direct, as I'd already done on three different movies. But I just kept pushing . . . until the dream came crashing down.

The loss of *Gypsy* will always be a huge disappointment to me. I wanted to make it not only for myself, but for Jule Styne . . . and Jerry Robbins (who had directed the original production) . . . and Arthur Laurents . . . and Stephen Sondheim. And as I write this, all of these brilliant men are no longer with us.

After *Gypsy*, I thought, *I can't do this anymore . . .* invest so much time and effort only to watch yet another film fall apart. It felt as if my creative life was coming to an end, and that was depressing. But then once again music came to my rescue.

The producers of an annual summer music festival in Hyde Park asked Marty if I would give a concert in July 2019. It would only be one night, I love London, and the offer was too generous to refuse. And it seemed like serendipity, because Jim and I were already planning to be in Europe at that time, to meet up with some friends who had a house in France.

So I said yes and planned the show with my team. When we were ready to go, I had to take a friend's plane so I could bring my three dogs and moderate the air pressure so my ears wouldn't be clogged for days. It's a very long flight from LA to London, and I'm claustrophobic, so I decided to break it up with a stopover in New York. That meant we all could get off the plane for a few hours. But I also had an ulterior motive. I really wanted to see *The Ferryman* (also by Jez Butterworth), which had won the Tony Award for Best Play and was directed by Sam Mendes. I think he's a fabulous director, and this was my only chance to see it, because it was closing that weekend.

Even though this one stop would be very costly (those extra hours meant the plane had to change crews), I thought, *Do it! Go see the play!*

I'm still that sixteen-year-old who loves the theater.

As we were getting closer to New York, I glanced at the on-screen map that shows you where the plane is, and was surprised to see that instead of taking the normal route, we were heading south. What? Time was tight already. Why were we going in the wrong direction?

I asked, and was told that the airspace was closed due to Trump's upcoming Fourth of July military parade. (He seems to have confused America with North Korea. Thank God they wouldn't let him tear up Pennsylvania Avenue with his tanks.) As a result, we had to detour way down south and then come up the Eastern Seaboard. I was frantic. Now we would be so late getting in that we were in danger of missing the play entirely!

Thank God another friend saved the day by sending his helicopter to pick us up on the tarmac at Teterboro and then fly us directly into the city, which took exactly six minutes. His car was waiting in Manhattan, but it was taking longer to drive the few blocks to the theater than it took to fly from New Jersey, so Jim and I had to abandon the car and run the rest of the way through the streets. The manager had held the curtain as long as she could and was now waiting at the door for us . . . luckily we only missed the first scene. And the play was terrific, so all that effort was worth it!

Then after seeing *The Ferryman* in New York on Tuesday we saw *The Lehman Trilogy* in London on Thursday, also directed by Sam Mendes, on my only free night before the concert. I tweeted about both plays and received a lovely note from Sam in return.

On Saturday morning I had just a couple of hours onstage with the musicians for the sound check before that day's performers arrived. I looked out at the vast empty field and still had that old fear: *What if hardly anyone shows up for me?*

But on Sunday night when I walked out onstage, the field was completely packed, and I was greeted with waves of applause from the huge crowd. I had a moment of déjà vu, thinking back to my concert in Central Park on a similar summer night in 1967, and felt a rush of gratitude to see that my audience was still there, after all these years.

In fact, it was a complete sellout, and they even managed to squeeze more people in, for a beyond-capacity total of seventy thousand . . . another memory, because that's the same size as the crowd we had at Sun Devil Stadium for the big outdoor concert scene in *A Star Is Born.* Here again I could see all these young people in the audience as I started to sing "Evergreen" . . . and guess what? They knew all the words and were singing along! Then when my costar from that film, Kris Kristofferson, walked out, he was greeted with a big burst of applause, and we did a duet on "Lost Inside of You." Lionel Richie and Ramin Karimloo also joined me for a couple of songs, but we didn't have much time to rehearse, so it was a bit like walking a tightrope without a net. (And there were no standing ovations to reassure me, since everyone was already standing, because there were no seats!)

There's something magical about sharing music under the stars, and that's why it felt right to sing "Silent Night," just as I had done in Central Park. In between songs I reminisced about my visits to London, but also used the opportunity to talk about something more serious . . . the state of the world. I wanted to remind people that we have the power to change things, but we have to speak up. As I said, "In my humble opinion, there are some things I hope we can all agree upon: the antidote to lies is truth . . . the remedy to war is peace . . . and the solution to hate is love." That led me into the first lines, sung a cappella, of another song: "What the world needs now is love, sweet love . . ." And the whole audience joined in, which was especially moving.

At the end of the show, as I said goodbye Renata brought out all three doggies, who were completely unfazed by their theatrical debut. Back at my trailer there was a parade of guests . . . including friends like Ralph Fiennes, Antonio

Banderas, Leslie Bricusse, Helen Mirren and Taylor Hackford, Daisy Ridley, Valentino, Richard E. Grant, Donna Karan, and Maxine Smith. I would have liked to say hello to Tilda Swinton, Kate Moss, and my dear Peter MacDonald, who somehow didn't make it backstage. At least I got to hug Mila Radova, my interpreter from *Yentl*, who had come all the way from Czechoslovakia!

I was so busy talking that I never had a chance to eat, and when we finally got back to my suite at the Savoy, I was starving. So at 3:00 a.m. we called room service and ordered lots of club sandwiches for my team . . . with extra French fries for Renata (which she never got to eat, because she was too busy packing). Meanwhile, Jim was looking at Twitter and YouTube on his phone and showed me what people were posting as they headed home from the show . . . like a video taken in the tube station, where the crowd continued the concert by breaking into their own rendition of "The Way We Were." That really warmed my heart.

And then Marty convinced me that since we had put this concert together, we might as well do it two more times. So after Jim and I took our vacation in France, I basically worked my way back home to the West Coast, stopping first in New York and then Chicago . . . changing the show in the meantime, and my costume. In the second act, I went from black to white (more specifically, ivory), with a delicate, antique-looking coat I found in Donna's closet, and then she whipped up a satiny gown to go under it in two days.

In Chicago, I had a surprise for the audience. I sang the first line of "Enough Is Enough," and then Ariana Grande walked out singing the second. Excitement swept the auditorium. Suddenly everyone was on their feet, dancing to that disco beat. Ariana was a joy to sing with.

Luckily my voice was still there for me, which is kind of miraculous, since I've never taken care of it. If I do any vocal exercises at all, it's usually last minute, on the way to the recording studio (or the arena) in the car.

Singing was something I took for granted.

Not anymore . . . I'm very thankful that God gave me this instrument. It's the gift that started my career.

Decades of recording tracks, concert videos, film reels, letters, and photographs are now stored in my archives. When I was considering what to do with all this (I think they'll go to the Library of Congress), I read an article about some of the items in Bob Dylan's archives and was touched to find out he had saved a note from me. As I recall, back in the 1970s he sent me flowers and a charming note, written in colored pencil with childlike letters, asking me if I would like to sing with him. In return I sent him the note that's in his archives, thanking him for the flowers and the invitation. But for whatever reason, it didn't happen.

Years later, when *Yentl* was about to come out, he sent me his latest album along with another letter. In it he wrote, "There are some songs on this album which I'm sure you would love to do." He adds, "I'm looking forward to seeing your movie. Maybe you can direct me in one of mine." And then he goes on to say, "You are my favorite star. Your self-determination, wit and temperament and sense of justice have always appealed to me."

That feeling goes both ways, because I have such respect for his talent. We started out at the same time . . . Bob Dylan, the Beatles, and me.

Then in 2020, a transcript of an unpublished interview he did in 1971 was all over the news because when he was asked about "Lay Lady Lay," he said, "Actually, it was written for Barbra Streisand."

Really? I asked Jay to check it out, so he got on the phone to one of Dylan's colleagues, and Bob confirmed that yes, he had me in mind when he wrote it. Needless to say, I was very flattered.

I should have called him and said, "So Bob, what song were you thinking we could sing together? And let's do it now, because we're not getting any younger!"

These days, I'm constantly reminded of the fragility of life.

Marilyn Bergman is gone, at ninety-three . . . the same age as my mother when she died. I was only twenty when we met, and she and Alan became my family. Our children . . . their daughter, Julie, and my son, Jason . . . grew up together. Her husband, Alan, is still writing every day at ninety-seven . . . God love him.

You hope certain people will be with you forever, but then reality strikes. I've lost too many friends recently . . . Peter Bogdanovich, Sidney Poitier, Colin Powell, and my brilliant friend Madeleine Albright, who was such an inspiration to me.

What she wrote about in her 2018 book *Fascism: A Warning* has come to pass, as authoritarians take charge in more and more countries. And one of their first targets is women. History has shown that a crackdown on women's rights is one of the initial signs of a crackdown on democracy. And we're seeing it right now in America with the Supreme Court overturning *Roe v. Wade.* For almost fifty years, women had the right to choose whether or not to have a child, which is a no-brainer. That decision should not belong to the state.

Have women become too successful, rising to prominent positions in boardrooms, courthouses, and the halls of government? Are some men so desperate to limit a woman's autonomy?

Because this sure sounds as if they're saying, *Go back to the kitchen, babe.*

And Clarence Thomas, in his concurring opinion, has given us a preview of what's next. He clearly believes that the right to contraception and the right to same-sex marriage should be overturned as well.

It doesn't matter that a majority of Americans support those rights, because thanks to Republican shenanigans that enshrined their minority rule, Thomas and his cohorts are now in charge.

A majority of Americans also support gun safety legislation. Yet in a nation reeling from gun violence, the court has now made it more difficult for states to enact laws to protect their own citizens . . . and to top it off, they're trying to cripple the Environmental Protection Agency as well. Have they been bought by the corporations that are reaping profits from selling guns, polluting our water, and promoting fossil fuels? Meanwhile, temperatures are soaring, glaciers are melting, seas are rising, fires are raging. We have disrupted the exquisite balance of nature in our reckless pursuit of the blessed buck, with no concern for future generations or the life of the planet itself.

I can't comprehend this. How can anyone deny the overwhelming evidence of climate change? The facts are indisputable. Yet again, is the truth not enough?

And what's even more chilling is that many people no longer seem able to distinguish between truth and lies . . . or even care about the difference.

I believe in the power of the truth. It's always worked for me as an actress and a singer and a filmmaker. I've seen how strongly people are moved by the truth when they recognize it in a performance. There's no place for lies in art.

And as I come to the end of this book, I've been thinking about what kind of legacy I will leave. The albums, the TV specials, the concert films, the movies are part of the record and out in the world.

But there's another aspect of my work that means just as much to me, and that's philanthropy. My concern about the environmental crisis and nuclear proliferation led me to create the Streisand Foundation in 1986, and one of my first big grants established a chair at the Environmental Defense Fund, initially held by Michael Oppenheimer, who's still doing groundbreaking research today.

Since then, the foundation has awarded thousands of grants to organizations that work to strengthen our democracy and advance voting rights, women's rights, civil rights, and human rights. Now I want to do even more. That's why I've endowed the Barbra Streisand Institute at UCLA, which will include four research centers:

The Center for Truth in the Public Sphere
The Center for the Impact of Climate Change
The Center for the Dynamics of Intimacy and Power Between Women and Men
The Center for the Impact of Art on the Culture

The institute will be a living legacy, where scholars can explore ideas and seek solutions to the vital issues that affect us all.

I've received so much from the public, and that's why it's so important to me to give back and do whatever I can to promote a more promising future. And the Center for Truth in the Public Sphere is at the top of my list. I want to find out what drives some people to prefer lies over truth and to vote against their own interests. I want to find a way to heal our divisions and stop this internal war that's tearing our country apart.

Thank God for the younger generation, who are gender-blind and color-blind, and who care deeply about the environment. They are our best hope, and we owe them a livable planet.

I care about the future, and we're all in this together. You may not think anything you do could make a difference, but that's not true. So I'm going to say this again, because it feels as if we're at a make-or-break moment for our democracy. We each have something very powerful . . . a voice . . . and a vote . . . and I implore you to use both. Each and every one of us counts, and if we raise our voices and work together, we could make this a more fair, just, and compassionate world.

Epilogue

Nothing's impossible.

I became a movie star, even though I didn't fit the conventional image . . . me with my asymmetrical face, my notable nose . . . and my big mouth. I had a dream, and I didn't listen to the people who tried to stop me. I just kept forging ahead, and who knows? Maybe I did will my vision into reality.

To do that, I had to focus on my work. And I think I got that from my father. After he and my mother had been dating for a few months, he told her he couldn't see her for a year because he had to study for his master's degree. That's how devoted he was to his work. My mother didn't understand that, and after a year went by, she told her sister Anna, "If he ever calls again, tell him I'm out." And then one day she was going somewhere on the trolley and lo and behold, my father stepped into the same car on the same trolley! And they reconnected.

This is why I believe in destiny. Certain things are just meant to be . . . otherwise I wouldn't even exist to be writing this book! I was meant to live the life I've led. It was *bashert*.

And like my father, I want to keep learning and growing. I do think I've become less judgmental and more loving . . . although I'm still impatient. When I call someone and they say hello, half the time I don't bother to say hello back. I just go right into what I want to tell them, which reminds me of a conversation I had with Jason when he was two and a half years old. (I used to tape him regularly, ever since he was a baby, because I wanted to remember the sound of his voice as he grew up.) I never believed in talking down to a child, and I was trying to explain that he should be polite and say hello and goodbye to the doorman when he comes in and out of our New York apartment building.

But Jason had his own theory: "Well, you *thee* (he had the cutest lisp), if I go to people's houses I can't say hellos and goodbyes."

"Why not?"

"Because I used them all up."

"But honey, we have unlimited hellos and goodbyes. Do you know how happy it makes people when you say hello to them? Then they know that you see them, and it's just a feeling of love, a feeling of niceness."

By now he was getting a little frustrated and said, "Well you *thee*, in MY *dif-ferenth*, in my kind of world is saying NO hellos and goodbyes. Your world IS saying hellos and goodbyes. You *thee*?"

Jason is very logical, like my father, and me. But I admit I don't always follow my own advice. I'm not good at hellos, and now I'm realizing I'm not so good at goodbyes either . . .

I've always had a project. Writing this book was the latest, but putting it together has taken much longer than I anticipated because it's not in my nature to live in the past. And now that I've shared all these memories, some painful but many sweet, I can see the full scope of my career. I've done what I wanted to do . . . although I feel I still could have done more. But at this point in my life, I want to step out of the spotlight, at least for a while.

Looking back, it was much more fun to dream of being famous than to actually *be* famous.

It made me nervous to be put on a pedestal, as if I were no longer human. I didn't like all the ridiculous stories they made up, or the envy my success provoked.

Fame is a hollow trophy.

No matter who you are, you can only eat one pastrami sandwich at a time.

I said in the prologue that I don't think success really changes you. It just makes you more of who you already are. And I'm still that girl who was always speaking up, trusting my instincts about how a song should sound or a character should behave or a movie should unfold.

And now it feels as if I'm coming full circle again, back to the beginning of my career. My latest album was taken from the tapes that were initially planned to be my first album, recorded live at the Bon Soir in 1962, when I was twenty years old. We had to abandon it back then because I didn't like the overall sound, and neither did the record company . . . the acoustics at the club were the problem. But now, thanks to new technology and the skills of Jochem, my engineer . . . along with Jay, who oversaw the project . . . the album has finally made its debut after sixty years.

One night I was in Jochem's studio for five hours, listening to the original tapes along with Marty, who was there when they were recorded. Marty is ninety-three now and still sharp, thank God, because I don't know what I'd do without his support. He's been a constant in my life since I was nineteen, someone I've always relied on to manage my career with wisdom and integrity. (And for decades, he has sent me three gardenias every week, because he knows I love the scent.)

Settled into another chair was Jay, who's now been my A&R man for three decades. I respect his opinion, and I enjoy working with him because he's smart, dedicated, calm, and fun to be around. (We laugh a lot, and he remembers more about my recording career than I do, because he takes notes at every session.)

And Jim was with me, because he enjoys listening to my music and can somehow do his own work at the same time.

As I sat down on the sofa, Jochem asked, "Don't you want to sit closer to the speakers, like you usually do?"

"No, no," I told him, "I'm fine here."

That's because I had the coffee table with all the food right in front of me. His wife, Annie, had set out fruit and cheese, breads and dips, olives and chocolates, and my favorite bite-size sesame crackers (that she brought all the way from Taiwan). And it was all presented so beautifully . . . what I first thought was a rose turned out to be carefully molded slices of salami. Very artistic.

I was so busy eating that I could hardly focus on the tapes.

My voice was higher back then . . . I kind of sounded like a bird.

"Listen to that," Jay said. "How pure."

"Yeah, right," I said, and reached for another cheese twist. But as we listened, I had to admit, "That girl isn't half bad."

Marty and Jay laughed.

Jochem had done wonders with the mix, subtly rebalancing the three original tracks so you can hear each song as it was meant to sound. He even got rid of the hiss. But he didn't touch my voice, because whatever fascination this album might have is rooted in the fact that, as Jay says, it's a historical document, a record of a particular moment when I was just starting out.

I sang twenty-four songs over the three nights we recorded in the club, changing them around for each show just to keep it interesting for myself. I'll always look back on the Bon Soir with fondness. It was where all the buzz about this new girl named Barbra (without an *a*) Streisand began.

Finishing this album reminded me of an idea I had for another one. I could do songs I forgot to sing . . . recently I came across the lists I made when I was eighteen and just starting to get booked into little clubs. I'm looking forward to going back into the studio, where I don't have to dress up, put on makeup, watch my posture, and hold in my stomach. In other words, I don't have to live up to anyone's expectations but my own. When I'm in the recording booth, it's just me and the music.

I feel grateful to be able to keep recording. I really appreciate the love and support of the public. And I'm so fortunate to have met my husband, after being alone for so many years. As I'm finishing this book, we've been married twenty-four years (that number again), which just proves that love is ageless and evergreen. It's wonderful to look up and see Jim beside me on the couch as we sit by the fire in the evening. The dogs are curled up between us, and Renata is making dinner while I'm going through the day's notes and Jim's working on his laptop. We don't have to say anything . . . the mere presence of each other is comforting. Every day is a blessing, and I want to appreciate every moment.

You never know what will happen next. On my last birthday, I received an extraordinary gift . . . from my mother, no less. It was an unfinished painting of me as an adult, with a sketch of my father above me, which my mother commissioned in the 1980s but never picked up. An old friend of hers sent it to me, along with a letter, because she wanted to tell me what Diana had confided to her over the years. For the first time, I heard my mother's stories about how my father would come home and pick me up even before he took off his coat . . . about how he liked to show me off, carrying me facing forward on the street, because, as he said, "I want her to always see where she's headed" . . . about how he loved my "sweet baby smell." And he would kiss me on the side of my neck, "like he had once kissed me," as my mother told her friend.

Then this friend described how she asked my mother if she was jealous of my father's attention to me, and Diana just looked down at the floor and, after a long pause, whispered, "Yes." My mother said that as I got older, I was "too much" for her. And when she saw me turn to other women for advice, it just confirmed her notion that she wasn't "good enough or smart enough" for me. I could feel the pain in my mother's words. And when I read that she was sorry she never told me how proud she was of me, and that she loved me, it brought tears to my eyes. I felt as if she was finally saying it to me. It was a message I had always longed to hear . . . just like those words from my father, enclosed in that other unexpected letter all those years ago.

And I understood that my mother did love me, in her way. That was the real gift, along with her stories of my father's love for me. I never had a photo with him, but now I will always have these wonderful images in my head, and in my heart.

So my mother filled in a very important part of the past for me. And now I can move on and look to the future. My husband, Jim, has given me the ultimate gift . . . a family, and we have all these little grandchildren to spoil. I wrote this book because I wanted to tell the truth about my life, and perhaps someday they'll read it. I'd like them to know who I am, who I was, and what I believe in. Right now I'm just "Gamma," and no other title has given me more pleasure. I cherish every moment I spend with Westlyn and her little sister, Chapel, and now Jim's daughter, Molly, just gave us a grandson named Sol. It's so interesting to watch them discover the world.

And I'm looking forward to seeing another piece of sky. Jim's favorite kind of travel is to get in his pickup truck and just go, like we did on one of our first trips. He wanted to show me some of the Native American sites in the Southwest, so I packed a cooler with my nonfat yogurt and cottage cheese. (What if our truck broke down and we had to survive in the desert?) We spent the first night in Las Vegas, where a friend had given us a fancy hotel suite, but the refrigerator was broken, so I had no place to put my food. Then late the next night we ended up at the only motel in Moab that still had a vacancy (my husband doesn't like to book ahead). He was worried because the room smelled of cigarettes, but I thought it was great to just pull up to the door (no lobby to walk through). I made a beeline for the little refrigerator, which worked! And I couldn't believe all the great stuff you can get in truck stops . . . roasted almonds, hot dogs, ice cream, and even the best rice pudding! We'd buy the fixings for sandwiches and I'd make them on my lap as Jim drove. It was lovely to just sit close together on the truck's bench seat.

Life is a miracle, and I'm ready to relax and enjoy it, maybe get back in the truck on a clear day. I want to go where the wind takes me. I'm not sure where that is, but I want to be light enough to let it bring me where I should go.

So, here's to life, to dreamers and their dreams . . . I wish you love, and many, many happy days.

I think I truly am one of the luckiest people in the world.

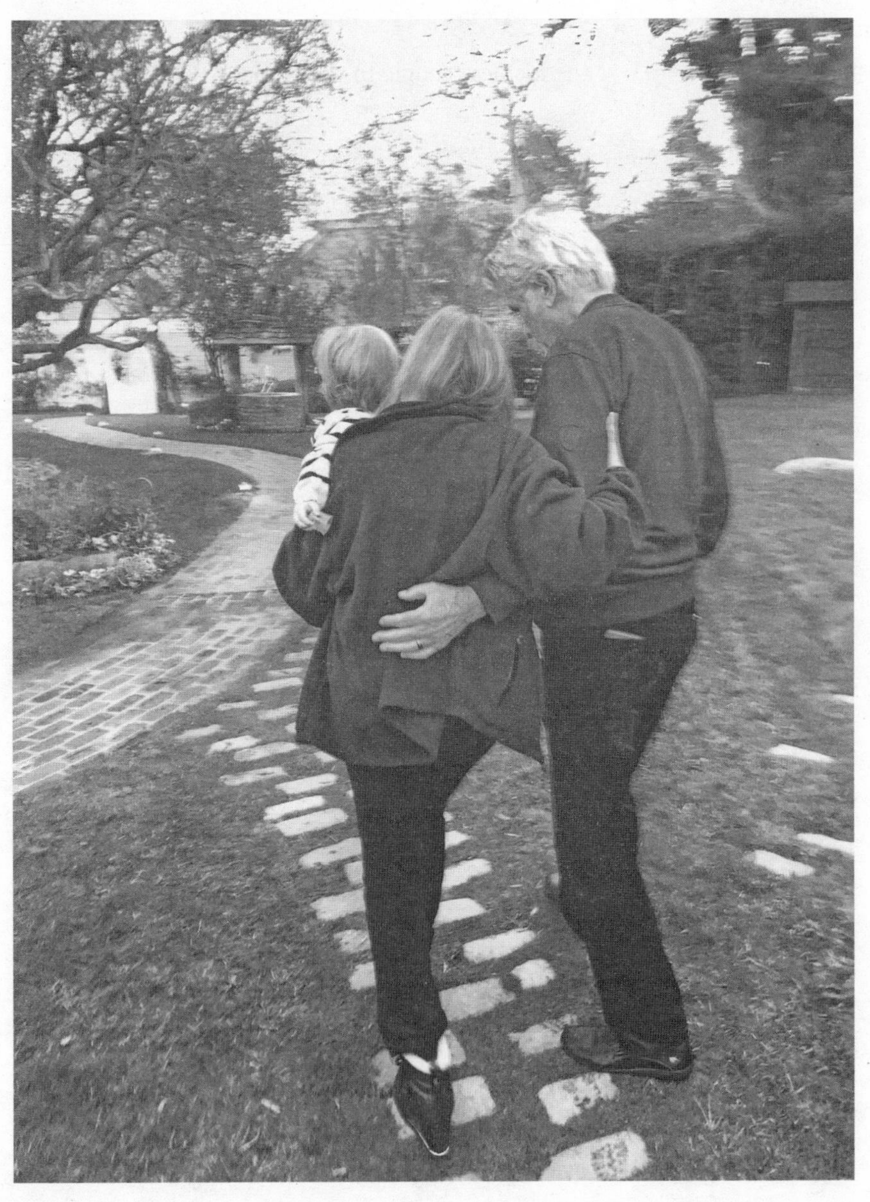

Acknowledgments

Finally, this book is done. (Although the people at Viking did have to rip it out of my hands.) I thought writing a book would be easier than making a movie, but boy, was I wrong. To share so much about my life doesn't come naturally to me, but I want to thank the people who were by my side on this journey.

First of all, my amazing editor, Christine Pittel, who has become one of my closest friends, and my latest "mom" (even though she's younger than me). Whenever I wanted to chuck the whole thing, she understood because she could see how difficult it was for me to open up about my most intimate thoughts. But as she kept reminding me, "There's no point in writing unless you leave some blood on the page." She was always pushing me to go deeper.

My dear husband, Jim, who takes me wherever I want to go, and sits next to me in bed as we both work. When I would read passages over the phone to Christine, he was very encouraging, saying things like, "That sounded so good." And he never complained, even when we worked late into the night and he had to fall asleep to the sound of my voice, still talking.

My beautiful son, Jason Emanuel, who has always supported me unconditionally, in my work and my causes. He's given me so much pleasure watching him grow and express his extraordinary talents. But I think what I admire most about him is that he's such a *mensch* . . . a good person, smart, thoughtful, kind, and honest. And he's found a way to be happy (it's taken me much longer). I can talk to him about anything and there's no conversation that doesn't end with "I love you."

And then there's the unique and irreplaceable Renata Buser, who I'm nominating for sainthood! She's been with me for fifty years and is so loving and generous to me, my family, and our adorable doggies. This is a woman who can do anything and everything and make it all look easy. She even does the most exquisite flower arrangements.

I didn't realize that writing this book would take so long (ten years!) and I'd like to thank my patient executive editor at Viking, Rick Kot, and the president and publisher of Viking Penguin, Brian Tart, for giving me the time I needed to get it right. I also want to send my appreciation to all the people at Viking who worked on the book in any way. And I'm much obliged to my attorney Robert Barnett and my manager, Marty Erlichman, for setting it all up, and to Ken Sunshine for handling the press.

A big thank you to Kim Skalecki, who kept copious notes of my schedule for forty-five years and organizes my archives today. She could produce photographs and anything else I asked for at a moment's notice . . . and I want to thank all the great photographers who generously gave me their pictures. I could always count on Jay Landers to answer any questions about my recordings. He's been a tremendous support on so many projects. And my deepest gratitude to Isabella Giovannini, the first person outside the process who I trusted to read the manuscript. Her comments were so intelligent, insightful, and loving . . . and her help during the final stretch was invaluable.

I'd also like to thank my devoted assistants who ran my office during this period . . . Pamela Lyster, Grace Handy, and the youngest, Grace Steele, who could execute my designs for the book on the computer. And whenever there was a question about a date or a detail, we were all grateful to Matt Howe, who has gathered so much information on his website Barbra-Archives.info, and was always generous and responsive. And my thanks to the delightful Craig Hall, who lives halfway around the world and keeps up my website and social media.

Certain people have been part of my life for many years, and I want to thank them . . . Marge Tabankin, who was the director of the Barbra Streisand Foundation from its start in 1986 and is still an advisor and dear friend. Now Frank Smith and Jesse Brown have taken over, to help me fund progressive organizations committed to a better world.

The wonderful Soonie Paik, who's been doing my hair since *A Star Is Born*. And the only reason I exercise is because I love my trainer Gaylene Ray, who's been working me out for forty-four years, always with a smile and the latest political news.

I truly appreciate my longtime friends, like Donna Karan. We vacation together, we design together, we argue together. And I'm blessed to have several other loyal friends I can confide in . . . you know who you are.

My heart is full of gratitude . . . and I cherish you all.

Love, Barbra

Image Credits

All photos Courtesy of Barbra Streisand Archives unless otherwise noted.

CHAPTER OPENING PHOTOS

Frontispiece, Chapters 23, 31: Steve Schapiro, Compliments of Steve Schapiro Estate

Chapters 4, 7: Don Hunstein © Sony Music Entertainment

Chapters 6, 11: Courtesy of Sony Music Archives

Chapter 9: Don Bronstein/Courtesy of Sony Music Archives

Chapter 12: Courtesy of Barbra Streisand Archives/Bill Eppridge

Chapter 13: Courtesy of Barbra Streisand Archives/Joe Covello/Black Star

Chapters 14, 15: FUNNY GIRL © 1968, renewed 1996 Columbia Pictures Industries, Inc. All rights reserved. Courtesy of Columbia Pictures

Chapter 17: "Hello, Dolly!" © 1969 20th Century Studios, Inc.

Chapter 18: Getty Images

Chapter 19: Copyright ©1969, Photo by Lawrence Schiller, All rights reserved.

Chapter 20: THE OWL AND THE PUSSYCAT ©1970, renewed 1998 Columbia Pictures Industries, Inc. All rights reserved. Courtesy of Columbia Pictures

Chapters 22, 30, 32, 41: Licensed by Warner Bros. Entertainment Inc. All rights reserved.

Chapter 24: THE WAY WE WERE ©1973, renewed 2001 Columbia Pictures Industries, Inc. All rights reserved. Courtesy of Columbia Pictures

Chapter 25: Courtesy of Barbra Streisand Archives/Baron Wollman

Chapter 26: FOR PETE'S SAKE © 1974, renewed 2002 Columbia Pictures Industries, Inc. All rights reserved. Courtesy of Columbia Pictures

Chapter 27: FUNNY LADY © 1974, renewed 2002 Columbia Pictures Industries, Inc. All rights reserved. Courtesy of Columbia Pictures

Chapter 28: Courtesy of Sony Music/Sam Emerson

Chapters 29, 33: © International Center of Photography and Francesco Scavullo Trust Beneficiaries

Chapter 34: Mario Casilli/mptvimages.com

Chapters 35, 36: YENTL © 1983 Ladbroke Entertainments Limited. All rights reserved. Courtesy of MGM Media Licensing

Chapter 38: Courtesy of Sony Music/Mark Sennet

Chapter 39: Photo © 1986 by Spike Nannarello

Chapters 40, 47, 59: Kevin Mazur/Getty Images

Chapter 42: Randee St. Nicholas

Chapters 43, 51: Ron Galella/Getty Images

Chapters 44, 45: THE PRINCE OF TIDES © 1991 Columbia Pictures Industries, Inc. All rights reserved. Courtesy of Columbia Pictures

Chapter 46: Courtesy of Sony Music/Dan Zaitz

Chapter 48: Courtesy of Barbra Streisand Archives/Firooz Zahedi

Chapter 49: Courtesy of Barbra Streisand Archives/Annie Leibovitz

Chapter 50: Courtesy of Barbra Streisand Archives/Firooz Zahedi

Chapter 53: THE MIRROR HAS TWO FACES © 1996 TriStar Pictures, Inc. All rights reserved. Courtesy of TriStar Pictures

Chapter 54: Deborah Wald

Chapter 55: Kevin Mazur/Getty Images

Chapter 56: Photo by Thomas Neerken

Chapters 57, 58: Russell James

FIRST PHOTO INSERT

Page 1: (lower right) Sheldon Streisand

Page 2: (top right) Sheldon Streisand

Page 3: (top left) Avery Willard/Billy Rose Collection/NY Public Library; (center right) Bob Schulenberg

Page 5: (top left) Milton Rosenstock—Courtesy of Barbra Streisand Archives; (top right) Bob Willoughby/mptvimages.com; (center right) Bill Eppridge; (bottom) FUNNY GIRL © 1968, renewed 1996 Columbia Pictures Industries, Inc. All rights reserved. Courtesy of Columbia Pictures

Page 6: (bottom) Courtesy of Barbra Streisand Archives/Bill Eppridge

Page 7: (center) Courtesy of Barbra Streisand Archives/Bill Eppridge

Page 8: (top right) Courtesy of Barbra Streisand Archives/Joe Covello/Black Star; (center and bottom) FUNNY GIRL © 1968, renewed 1996 Columbia Pictures Industries, Inc. All rights reserved. Courtesy of Columbia Pictures

Page 9: (top) Courtesy of Barbra Streisand Archives/Elliott Gould; (bottom) FUNNY GIRL © 1968, renewed 1996 Columbia Pictures Industries, Inc. All rights reserved. Courtesy of Columbia Pictures

Page 10: (top left) Steve Schapiro, Compliments of Steve Schapiro Estate; (center) Copyright ©1969, Photo by Lawrence Schiller, All rights reserved.
Page 11: (top left and center left) "Hello, Dolly!" © 1969 20th Century Studios, Inc. Courtesy of 20th Century Fox Studios, Inc.; (top right and bottom left) Copyright ©1969, Photo by Lawrence Schiller, All rights reserved; (bottom right) Courtesy of Columbia Pictures and the Academy of Motion Picture Arts and Sciences. Oscar statuette © A.M.P.A.S. ®
Page 12: (top) THE OWL AND THE PUSSYCAT ©1970, renewed 1998 Columbia Pictures Industries, Inc. All rights reserved; (center left) Courtesy of Barbra Streisand Archives/Bo-Erick Gyberg; (center right) Courtesy of Barbra Streisand Archives/Michael J. Nordstom
Page 13: (top and center) THE WAY WE WERE ©1973, renewed 2001 Columbia Pictures Industries, Inc. All rights reserved. Courtesy of Columbia Pictures; (bottom) Licensed by Warner Bros. Entertainment Inc. All rights reserved.
Page 14: (top left) Tom Wargacki/Wire Image; (top right) FOR PETE'S SAKE © 1974, renewed 2002 Columbia Pictures Industries, Inc. All rights reserved. Courtesy of Columbia Pictures; (center left) FUNNY LADY © 1974, renewed 2002 Columbia Pictures Industries, Inc. All rights reserved. Courtesy of Columbia Pictures; (center right) Courtesy of Barbra Streisand Archives/Mark Sennet; (bottom) FUNNY LADY © 1974, renewed 2002 Columbia Pictures Industries, Inc. All rights reserved. Courtesy of Columbia Pictures
Page 15: (top left) Licensed by Warner Bros. Entertainment Inc. All rights reserved; (center top) Gary Lewis/mptvimages.com/Courtesy of the Academy of Motion Picture Arts and Sciences, Oscar statuette © A.M.P.A.S. ®; (top right) Licensed by Warner Bros. Entertainment Inc. All rights reserved; (center left) Warner Bros. Entertainment Inc. All rights reserved; (center right) Warner Bros. Entertainment Inc. All rights reserved.
Page 16: (top) Mario Casilli/mptvimages.com; (center) Licensed by Warner Bros. Entertainment Inc. All rights reserved; (bottom) Licensed by Warner Bros. Entertainment Inc. All rights reserved.

Second Photo Insert

Page 2: All photos courtesy of MGM Media Licensing YENTL © 1983 Ladbroke Entertainments Limited. All rights reserved.
Page 3: (top left) Courtesy of Barbra Streisand Archives/Umberto Pizzi; (center) Javier Mendoza/Herald Examiner Collection; (bottom) Courtesy of Barbra Streisand Archives/Alan Berliner
Page 4: (bottom) Courtesy of Barbra Streisand Archives
Page 5: All photos THE PRINCE OF TIDES © 1991 Columbia Pictures Industries, Inc. All rights reserved. Courtesy of Columbia Pictures
Page 6: (top left) Mark Sennet; (center) Ebet Roberts; (bottom) Ron Galella/Getty Images
Page 7: (top, center, and bottom left) THE MIRROR HAS TWO FACES © 1996 TriStar Pictures, Inc. All rights reserved. Courtesy of TriStar Pictures
Page 8: All photos Firooz Zahedi
Page 9: (top) Kevin Mazur/Getty Images
Page 10: (top) © 1992 photo by Spike Nannarello; (bottom left and right) Alex J. Berliner/ABImages
Page 11: (bottom) Kevin Mazur/Getty Images
Page 12: (bottom) Deborah Wald
Page 13: (top and bottom left) Russell James; (bottom right) Eric Charbonneau
Page 14: Russell James
Page 15: (top) Kevin Mazur/Getty Images; (bottom) Photo of Barbra Streisand on stage, Hyde Park UK (2019) Courtesy of Cheche Alara
Page 16: (top left) Russell James; (bottom left) Joseph Marzullo/MediaPunch
Page 17: (top) Walter McBride
Page 18: (bottom) Russell James
Page 19: (top right, middle row, and bottom right) Deborah Wald; (bottom left) Alex J. Berliner/ABImages
Page 20: (top left) Wood Kuzoumi; (top center) Photo by Philippe Halsman © Philippe Halsman Estate 2023; (top right) Licensed by Warner Bros. Entertainment Inc. All rights reserved; (center left) Photo by Greg Gorman; (center) FOR PETE'S SAKE © 1974, renewed 2002 Columbia Pictures Industries, Inc. All rights reserved. Courtesy of Columbia Pictures; (center right) Randee St. Nicholas; (bottom left) Firooz Zahedi; (bottom center) Jason Merritt/Getty Images Entertainment; (bottom right) Russell James
Page 21: (second row, third photo) Deborah Wald; (third row, second photo) Russell James; (third row, third photo) Eric Charbonneau
Page 22: (first row, left) National Archives; (third row, center) © 1992 Michael J. Jacobs/MJP; (fourth row, left) © 1992 Michael J. Jacobs/MJP; (fourth row, right) Kevin Mazur/Getty Images; (fifth row, center) Kevin Mazur/Getty Images
Page 23: (first row, right) Steve Schapiro, Compliments of Steve Schapiro Estate; (second row, center) Shutterstock; (fourth row, second from left) Bob Levey/WireImage via Getty Images; (fourth row, third from left) Kevin Mazur/Getty Images
Page 24: Courtesy of Sony Music Archives

GOOD FRIENDS
(PAGE 21)

Top row: Evelyn Ostin, Joanne and Gil Segel; Richard Baskin, Ellen Gilbert, Renata Buser; Quincy Jones, Alan and Marilyn Bergman
Second row: Donna Karan; Ron Meyer; Kelly Preston and John Travolta; Mike and Irena Medavoy
Third row: Maxine Smith; Russell James; Norman Lear; Cis Corman and Marilyn Bergman
Fourth row: Todd Morgan; Steven Spielberg; Marge Tabankin; David Foster and Andre Agassi

SOME EXTRAORDINARY PEOPLE I'VE MET OVER THE YEARS!
(PAGE 22)

Top row: President John F. Kennedy; Daniel Ellsberg, John Lennon, Yoko Ono, and Ringo Starr
Second row: Bella Abzug; General Colin Powell; President William Jefferson and First Lady Hillary Clinton, Caleigh and Skye Peters

Third row: Secretary of State Madeleine Albright; Governor Bill Clinton; Speaker Nancy Pelosi
Fourth row: Whoopi Goldberg and Hillary Clinton; President Shimon Peres; President and Secretary Clinton
Fifth row: President Barack Obama; Performing at President Clinton's Inauguration; Diana, Princess of Wales and Nick Nolte

(PAGE 23)

Top row: President Lyndon Johnson; George McGovern and Quincy Jones
Second row: Senator Ted Kennedy; Nelson Mandela; Anita Hill and Senator Barbara Boxer
Third row: Maya Angelou; HRH Prince Charles; James Caan and President Gerald Ford
Fourth row: Senator John McCain; President George H. W. Bush; President William Jefferson and First Lady Hillary Clinton; Gerry Adams
Fifth row: Jim, Sophie Trudeau, Prime Minister Justin Trudeau; Vice President Al Gore and Caleigh; King Hussein of Jordan

Text Credits

LETTERS

Grateful acknowledgment is made for permission to use the following materials:

Excerpts from Larry Kramer's unpublished letters to Barbra Streisand. Used by permission of Will Schwalbe on behalf of David Webster.

Excerpts from Arthur Laurents's unpublished letter to Barbra Streisand. Used by permission of Jonathan Lomma on behalf of the Estate of Arthur Laurents.

Excerpts from an unpublished telegram from Jerome Robbins to Isobel Lennart. Used by permission of Luke Janklow and Chris Pennington on behalf of the Robbins Archive.

Excerpts from Omar Sharif's unpublished letters. Used by permission of Tarek Sharif on behalf of the Estate of Omar Sharif.

Excerpt from George Balanchine's unpublished letter to Barbra Streisand. BALANCHINE is a trademark of The George Balanchine Trust. Used by permission of The George Balanchine Trust.

Excerpts from unpublished writings of Pat Conroy, including letters and inscriptions. Used by permission of the Pat Conroy Literary Center and Cassandra King Conroy on behalf of the Estate of Pat Conroy.

Excerpt from Henry Fonda's unpublished letter to Barbra Streisand. Used by permission of Jane Fonda.

Excerpts from Stephen Sondheim's unpublished note to Barbra Streisand © The Estate of Stephen Sondheim. Used by permission.

Excerpts from Anthony Newley's unpublished letters to Barbra Streisand. Used by permission of Lisa Alter and the Anthony Newley Estate.

Excerpts from Harry Stradling Sr.'s unpublished letter to Barbra Streisand. Used by permission of the Stradling Family.

ESSAY

Grateful acknowledgment is made for permission to use the following material:

The Jerome Robbins essay from Roddy McDowall's *Double Exposure* originally published by Delacorte, an imprint of Penguin Random House and reprinted by courtesy of the Robbins Right Trust.

MUSIC LYRICS

Grateful acknowledgment is made for permission to use the following lyric excerpts:

Answer Me (Barbra Streisand/Paul Williams/Kenneth Ascher) BJS Music Corp./Sunset Squid Music c/o WC Music Corp.

As If We Never Said Goodbye (Andrew Lloyd Webber/Don Black/Christopher Hampton) The Really Useful Group Ltd. c/o Universal Music Publishing

By the Way (Barbra Streisand/Rupert Holmes) BJS Music Corp./Widescreen Music

Cry Me a River (Arthur Hamilton) Chappell & Co./Harmony Grace Publishing

Don't Rain on My Parade (Jule Styne/Bob Merrill) Broadway Tunes LLC DBA Sons of Funny Girl/ Chappell & Co.

Gotta Move (Peter Matz) Alley Music Corp. co Round Hill Music/Trio Music Company c/o BMG Bumblebee

How Deep Is the Ocean (Irving Berlin) Irving Berlin Music c/o Universal Music Publishing

I Don't Want to Miss a Thing (Diane Warren) Realsongs

I Hate Music (Leonard Bernstein) Warner Bros., Inc. c/o Warner Chappell Music

I'm Still Here (Stephen Sondheim) Herald Square Music, Inc. c/o Carlin America, Inc./Round Hill Music

I've Dreamed of You (Rolf Lovland/Ann Callaway) Emanuel Music/Halaron Music/Works of Heart/ Warner Chappell Music

If I Loved You (Richard Rodgers & Oscar Hammerstein II) Williamson Music c/o Concord Music

Let Me Go (Randy Newman) Screen Gems EMI Music

Ma Première Chanson (Barbra Streisand/Eddy Marnay) BJS Music Corp.

Miss Marmelstein (Harold Rome) Chappell & Co.

Move On (Stephen Sondheim) Revelation Music/ Rilting Music/Warner Chappell Music

Much More (Harvey Schmidt/Tom Jones) Chappell & Co.

No Wonder (Michel Legrand/Alan & Marilyn Bergman) Emanuel Music/EMI April Music Inc./F Sharp Productions, Ltd/Spirit Two Music Crescendo

People (Jule Styne/Bob Merrill) Broadway Tunes LLC DBA Sons of Funny Girl/Chappell & Co.

Putting It Together (Stephen Sondheim) Revelation Music/Rilting Music/Warner Chappell Music

Send in the Clowns (Stephen Sondheim) Revelation Music/Rilting Music/Warner Chappell Music

So Pretty (Leonard Bernstein/Betty Comden/ Adolph Green) Leonard Bernstein Music c/o Universal Music Publishing

Some Enchanted Evening (Richard Rodgers & Oscar Hammerstein II) Williamson Music c/o Concord Music Publishing

Somewhere (Leonard Bernstein/Stephen Sondheim) Leonard Bernstein Music/Chappell & Co.

Stoney End (Laura Nyro) EMI Blackwood Music

Too Much Woman (Anthony Newley) Downtown Music

Value (Jeff Harris) Frank Music c/o MPL Music Publishing

The Way We Were (Marvin Hamlisch/Alan & Marilyn Bergman) Colgems EMI

Who Can I Turn To (When Nobody Needs Me)? (Anthony Newley/Leslie Bricusse) Downtown Music/ TRO Essex Music Group

Walls (Walter Afanasieff/Alan & Marilyn Bergman) Wally World Music co Kobalt Songs/Alamar Music Co. c/o Spirit Two Music Crescendo